2014 Index of Economic Freedom

CONTRIBUTORS

Ambassador Terry Miller is Director of the Center for International Trade and Economics and Mark A. Kolokotrones Fellow in Economic Freedom at The Heritage Foundation.

Anthony B. Kim is Senior Policy Analyst in the Center for International Trade and Economics at The Heritage Foundation.

Kim R. Holmes, PhD, is a Distinguished Fellow at The Heritage Foundation.

Senator Jim DeMint is President of The Heritage Foundation.

Edwin J. Feulner, PhD, is Founder of The Heritage Foundation.

James M. Roberts is Research Fellow for Economic Freedom and Growth in the Center for International Trade and Economics at The Heritage Foundation.

Bryan Riley is Jay Van Andel Senior Analyst in Trade Policy in the Center for International Trade and Economics at The Heritage Foundation.

Ryan Olson is a Research Assistant in the Center for International Trade and Economics at The Heritage Foundation.

Paul A. Gigot is Editor of *The Wall Street Journal* Editorial Page.

Sergio Daga, Contributing Editor for Latin America, is Research Director in the Políticas Públicas para la Libertad (Populi), a Bolivian think tank.

John Tomasi, PhD, is Professor of Political Science and Director of the Political Theory Project at Brown University.

2014 Index of Economic Freedom

Ambassador Terry Miller

Anthony B. Kim

Kim R. Holmes, PhD

with James M. Roberts, Bryan Riley, and Ryan Olson

The Heritage Foundation
LEADERSHIP FOR AMERICA

THE WALL STREET JOURNAL.

The Heritage Foundation
214 Massachusetts Avenue, NE
Washington, DC 20002
(202) 546-4400
heritage.org

The Wall Street Journal
Dow Jones & Company, Inc.
200 Liberty Street
New York, NY 10281
(212) 416-2000
www.wsj.com

ISBN: 978-0-89195-285-5
ISSN: 1095-7308

Contents

Foreword

A benefit of watching the ebb and flow of economic freedom over a long career in journalism is that you earn some standing to draw conclusions. One lesson I've learned is that prosperity is not a national birthright. It must be earned by each new generation in every country on Earth, even those that have long been prosperous. Another lesson is that the right policy choices are not self-replicating but must be relearned and fought for again and again. There are no permanent victories in the war of ideas, but the saving grace is that there are also no permanent defeats.

Those lessons shine brightly through the 2014 *Index of Economic Freedom,* perhaps even more now than in any previous year since *The Wall Street Journal* embarked with The Heritage Foundation on this scorecard of economic liberty. Some of the biggest gainers this year, as in recent years, were thought to be hopeless cases a generation ago.

One such group is the former nations of the Soviet Union, which had only recently broken apart in 1995, the *Index's* first year. The Baltic States have tried to follow the Hong Kong and Singapore example of small nations opening themselves to capital and competition, and they have largely prospered because of it. Estonia now ranks 11th in the *Index,* one spot ahead of the United States. Lithuania is 21st and Latvia is 42nd, despite having endured brutal recessions in the past decade. They reformed their economies, shrank the size of their governments, and let the talents of their people emerge. The French and Italians could learn from their examples.

Chile, which was once close to following the lawless statism of Argentina, now ranks 7th. It is on the cusp of being considered a developed country, which is a just reward for good policy but carries the risk that its people may forget what made them prosperous. In its recent presidential election, Chile's electorate rejected its center-right ruling party and tilted to the populist left. Next year's policy trend in Santiago will be worth watching.

The electorate in Malaysia, meanwhile, rewarded its ruling party with another term after it made a priority of easing some political and economic controls and inviting foreign investment. The reforms arguably helped the UMNO coalition beat back a strong challenge from a rising middle class that also wants more freedom to express itself politically. Malaysia ranks 37th in the *Index* compared to 87th in 2004, and it too is reaching toward developed-country status.

On the other hand, countries can quickly descend in the ranks, even nations with a proud history of free markets. The U.S. is the most dispiriting example, given its history and its continued importance to global growth. America's freedom score has declined for seven years in a row and now ranks 12th, just ahead of Bahrain and four spots behind Mauritius.

The U.S. is the classic case of having forgotten the hard-earned lessons of the recent past. America pulled itself out of the despond of the 1970s with policies of lower taxes, less regulation, steady monetary policy, and spending restraint. A two-decade boom followed with little interruption. Then a kind of collective amnesia set in during the 2000s that led to major policy errors and a credit mania, followed by a panic and crash that created a new political opening for those who wanted to expand state control of finance, health care, and energy markets. The last two years of the Bush presidency and first two Obama years marked the largest expansion of state power in the U.S. since the 1930s.

A political reaction in 2010 slowed government's rise, but the economic damage has been extensive and continues to be felt in subpar growth, mediocre business investment, and fewer job prospects for the poor and less skilled. This dismal record, combined with the failed launch of Obamacare, may create a new opening for the forces of freedom. That will also require a new political champion who can make the arguments for liberty that a younger generation has never learned and hasn't heard from a Republican presidential nominee since Reagan.

Though it pains this American a little to write it, another lesson of 20 years of this *Index* is that the spread of good economic ideas doesn't depend as much as it once did on America. The diffusion of ideas and experience through modern communication and the Internet means that there are followers of Hayek in Shanghai and admirers of Milton Friedman in Mexico. Perhaps other nations will now take the global lead in showing the way toward rising incomes for all, especially the poor, as America tries to find its way back to the principles of liberty that made it great.

Paul A. Gigot
Editorial Page Editor
The Wall Street Journal
November 2013

Preface

In 1995, former U.S. Treasury Secretary William Simon described the *Index of Economic Freedom* as "the most important study The Heritage Foundation has ever published." As the *Index* celebrates its 20th anniversary in 2014, we have the opportunity to look back and see whether the publication has lived up to its promise, in Simon's words, to "revolutionize the debate over ... global economic development."

In a special essay that leads off the book this year, founding editor Kim R. Holmes traces the development of the *Index* over the past two decades, from its birth as the brainchild of a small group of free-market economists inspired by the renowned Milton Friedman through its development into what has been described as "an essential guide to growth for those who want to understand why some countries prosper and others lag behind."

New *Index* co-editor Anthony B. Kim looks at the issue from a different direction, charting the progress over the 20 years of the *Index*'s history of those countries that have most vigorously pursued principles of economic freedom. His conclusion is not surprising: Countries that have sustained higher levels of economic freedom have achieved levels of prosperity unheard of in the history of humankind.

It is no coincidence that the explosion of economic liberty has coincided with a massive reduction in worldwide poverty, disease, and hunger. The acceptance of the free-market system as the fundamental basis for economic development in almost every country has provided a foundation for economic growth and human progress throughout the world.

A successful life, of course, is not just about economic prosperity. Freedom itself, whether political or economic, physical or spiritual, may be among the highest attainments of civilization. Amartya Sen, a Nobel Prize winner in economics, has written that "[t]he success of a society is to be evaluated ... primarily by the substantive freedoms that the members of that society enjoy." In the 2014 *Index*, Professor John Tomasi of Brown University expands on this theme, arguing that economic freedom not only produces massive economic and social benefits, but also is the most moral of societal arrangements and a societal good in its own right.

The 20-year database that now supports the analysis in the *Index of Economic Freedom* has proven to be an invaluable tool for policymakers, researchers, and academics. Yet I think that it may be even more important for those who continue the struggle to advance freedom, and especially economic freedom, around the world.

People will not fight for freedom unless they understand it, value it, and believe it is at risk. For champions of freedom, the *Index* provides an objective measure of their country's progress, or lack thereof, in fostering an environment that unleashes the ingenuity and energy of individuals who, through the "invisible hand" of the free market, promote the good of all through the pursuit of their own personally defined goals.

For Americans like me, who have benefitted from the legacy of a society justly called the "land of the free," the 2014 *Index* paints a disturbing picture. The overall world progress in advancing economic freedom is a source of both satisfaction and pride, given the historical record of the United States in promoting and defending freedom. And yet the recent record of the United States in the *Index*—seven consecutive years of declining economic freedom—is a serious cause for alarm. Families, businesses, and community organizations across America, what the 18th century philosopher Edmund Burke dubbed the "little platoons" of society, are being squeezed by the government's assault on our economic freedom. As a result, we have fewer pathways to individual and collective success.

As my predecessor as President of The Heritage Foundation, Ed Feulner, is wont to say, "There are no permanent victories." Indeed, the struggle for freedom is one that must be renewed by every generation. As the *Index of Economic Freedom* reaches its 20th year, it is time for a new generation of Americans, and freedom-loving people around the world, to join in the struggle for economic freedom. As President Ronald Reagan once reminded us:

> You and I are told we must choose between a left or right, but I suggest there is no such thing as a left or right. There is only an up or down. Up to man's age-old dream—the maximum of individual freedom consistent with order—or down to the ant heap of totalitarianism.

The *Index of Economic Freedom* provides ample examples of successful policies proven in action. It is up to the people to provide the political will to implement them.

Jim DeMint, President
The Heritage Foundation
November 2013

Acknowledgments

This year marks the 20th anniversary of the *Index of Economic Freedom*. Countless individuals and organizations have contributed to the *Index* since 1995, and this year's edition is yet another product of collaborative effort and ever-growing support from people and organizations around the world.

While it is impossible to mention all who contribute to our success, we wish to express our profound gratitude to the myriad individuals serving with various international organizations, accounting firms, businesses, research institutions, U.S. government agencies, foreign embassies, and other organizations who provide data used in the *Index*. Their assistance is vital and appreciated each year. Very special thanks go to Paul Gigot and Mary Anastasia O'Grady at *The Wall Street Journal,* whose partnership and support we truly cherish.

The Heritage Foundation's Center for International Trade and Economics (CITE) produces the *Index*. The CITE team of James Roberts, Bryan Riley, and Ryan Olson shared responsibility for grading the 10 components of economic freedom, analyzing the results, and producing the country reports included in this edition. CITE interns Alex Bezahler, Petra Niedermayerova, Stevan Novakovich, Sally Platt, Drew Ringley, Bethany Rudibaugh, Ashlee Smith, and Phillip Shattan contributed substantial research. Visiting Fellow Sergio Daga contributed a special chapter and has joined the team as Contributing Editor for Latin America.

The new President of The Heritage Foundation, Senator Jim DeMint, has enthusiastically endorsed the *Index* and has provided generous support and encouragement during his first year. Likewise, Dr. James Carafano, the new Vice President for Foreign and Defense Policy Studies, has provided innovative advice and guidance on all aspects of *Index* production and marketing and has been tireless in his efforts to ensure that we had adequate resources for the project. The continuing support from Phil Truluck, Executive Vice President of The Heritage Foundation; Group Vice Presidents David Addington, Ed Corrigan, John Fogarty, and Geoff Lysaught; Vice Presidents Becky Norton Dunlop, Mike Gonzalez, John Von Kannon, Derrick Morgan, and Genevieve Wood; and Chief of Staff Bret Bernhardt is sincerely appreciated.

Others at The Heritage Foundation also made valuable contributions to this year's *Index*. In the Kathryn and Shelby Cullom Davis Institute for International Studies, a great debt is owed to the policy experts who wrote country backgrounds informed by their regional expertise. This year's contributors were Ariel Cohen, James Phillips,

Jessica Zuckerman, and Charlotte Florance of the Douglas and Sarah Allison Center for Foreign Policy Studies, who were assisted by interns Stefan Gochev, Noelle Suarez-Murias, and Andrew Scarpitta; Lisa Curtis, Bruce Klingner, Derek Scissors, and Director Walter Lohman of the Asian Studies Center; and Luke Coffey and Daniel Kochis of the Margaret Thatcher Center for Freedom.

The *Index of Economic Freedom* is a substantial publication brought to print each year by the incredibly talented team in Creative. Director Melissa Bluey, Elizabeth Brewer, Doug Sampson, and Casi Long were responsible for all aspects of the production process.

The *Index* stands on its commitment to accuracy, and we wish to express our deepest appreciation to Senior Editor Richard Odermatt and Deputy Director of Research Editing Therese Pennefather, who are responsible for final review of the completed text, and Senior Copy Editor William T. Poole, who bears the primary responsibility for perfecting the language of the entire book. We are likewise grateful to Senior Data Graphics Editor John Fleming, who produced an automated system for generating some of our charts and carefully reviewed all graphics included in the book.

The availability of the entire *Index* and related raw data online at www.heritage.org/index has greatly expanded the publication's reach and accessibility. The transposition to the Web each year would not be possible without the expertise of Director of Marketing Technology Tim McGovern and his team, including Roger Spurzem, Jim Lawruk, and Maria Sousa. We are also grateful to Chief Executive Officer Mike Needham and his team at Heritage Action for America for their help in spreading the word about the benefits of economic freedom.

We also wish to acknowledge our enduring debt to Chairman Thomas A. Saunders III and the Heritage Board of Trustees, and particularly to Ambassador J. William Middendorf II, who originally encouraged us to undertake such a study of global economic freedom.

Finally, we would be remiss if we did not, in this 20th anniversary edition of the *Index of Economic Freedom,* acknowledge the contribution of an extraordinary individual to the success of this publication over the years. Dr. Edwin J. Feulner, Founder and former President of The Heritage Foundation, provided inspiration, guidance, and support without which the project could never have become a reality.

Ambassador Terry Miller
Anthony B. Kim
Kim R. Holmes, PhD
November 2013

The *Index* at 20: Executive Highlights

The 2014 *Index of Economic Freedom* is the 20th anniversary edition. For two decades, the *Index,* a joint publication of The Heritage Foundation and *The Wall Street Journal,* has tracked the progress of economic freedom around the globe, evolving into a data-driven practical policy guidebook that covers 186 countries encompassing 99 percent of the world's population.

- The 20th edition of the *Index* shows economic freedom once again on the rise. Much of the momentum lost during the past five years has been regained. The global average economic freedom score in the 2014 *Index* is 60.3, the highest average in the 20-year history of the *Index*. The average is 0.7 point higher than last year and a 2.7 point improvement from 1995.
- In measuring economic freedom, the *Index* analyzes countries' commitment to the rule of law, principles of limited government, regulatory efficiency, and open markets. Judged by these standards, the global economy as a whole has become "moderately free." Scores improved in eight of the 10 economic freedoms, with investment freedom gaining an impressive 3.3 points on average. Labor freedom and government spending scores were higher by an average of about 1 point or more. Average scores declined only in the area of rule of law, with property rights and freedom from corruption losing 0.3 point each.
- 114 countries, the majority of which are less developed, contributed to the growth in economic freedom over the past year; 43 countries, including Singapore, Sweden, Colombia, Poland, Cape Verde, and Turkey, achieved their highest economic freedom scores ever in the 2014 *Index*.
- While four countries recorded no score change, declines in economic freedom were registered in 59 countries, including nine advanced economies.
- The United States continues to lose ground to its competitors in the global race to advance economic freedom and prosperity. Registering a decline in economic freedom for the seventh year in a row, the U.S. tumbled from the ranks of the top 10 freest economies, falling two spots in the rankings to 12th place. The U.S. score has declined almost 6 points since 2007, placing the U.S. among those countries

considered to be only "mostly free." In the 2014 *Index*, the U.S. recorded notable declines in fiscal freedom, business freedom, and property rights.

- Average levels of economic freedom improved in all regions of the world except North America and the Middle East/North Africa. The Asia–Pacific region, led by Burma, Malaysia, and Samoa, showed the greatest gains, with an average increase exceeding 1 point. Sub-Saharan Africa did almost as well, with countries gaining 0.9 point on average. Europe and the South and Central America/Caribbean region recorded average score improvements of 0.5 point and 0.3 point, respectively.
- Despite the global progress over the past two decades, the number of people living in economically "unfree" countries remains very high: 4.5 billion, or about 65 percent of the world's population. More than half of these people live in just two countries, China and India, where advancement toward greater economic freedom has been patchy at best.
- The 20 years of *Index* data attest unequivocally that economies achieving or sustaining higher levels of economic freedom measurably outperform others in achieving dynamic economic growth, long-term prosperity, and greater progress in many dimensions of social and human development.

Commemorating the 20 years of the *Index*, the 2014 edition features four notable chapters that show why, now more than ever, it is imperative that economic freedom be defended and advanced.

- Dr. Kim R. Holmes, a founding editor of the *Index*, looks back over its 20-year history and highlights key milestones of the *Index* in the context of its development, its impact, and the overall policy lessons that have been learned. His key finding: More than any other political or policy approach, economic freedom generates more opportunities and greater well-being for more people. The *Index* has clearly demonstrated the power of free-market, limited-government, rules-based capitalism to help people prosper.
- Anthony B. Kim analyzes long-term trends in the 20-year *Index* database and documents the measurable benefits of policies that improve economic freedom. For the past two decades, countries that have accepted the challenge of enhancing economic freedom have reaped great rewards and have set a powerful example for others to follow. Advancing economic freedom is the proven path to greater prosperity and progress.
- Dr. John Tomasi of Brown University develops a strong moral case for economic freedom, laying out both the institutional and the individual cases for economic freedom. Economic liberty must be defended not only because it has a proven record of securing political and material benefits, but also because it ensures that ordinary people can make their own choices and actions in pursuit of their dreams.
- Sergio Daga, Research Director of Populi, a Bolivian think tank, examines the effectiveness of government conditional cash transfer programs that have become the most common social assistance intervention by governments in many less developed economies. As Daga concludes, countries that embrace government-led money transfer programs would achieve better results in poverty reduction by removing barriers to economic freedom and reducing dependence on the state.

THE GLOBAL ECONOMIC FREEDOM RANKINGS

- Competition for the top spot in the *Index* rankings has intensified. Hong Kong maintained its status as the world's freest economy, a remarkable distinction that it has achieved for 20 consecutive years. Singapore, the second-freest economy, has closed the gap between itself and Hong Kong to only 0.7 point, the second narrowest difference in *Index* history.
- Along with Hong Kong, Singapore, Australia, Switzerland, New Zealand, and Canada are the only economies considered "free" with economic freedom scores above 80 on the 0-to-

100 *Index* grading scale. Australia continues in third place, a position it has held since 2009, while Switzerland has overtaken New Zealand and is now in fourth place, its highest ranking ever. Canada remains the world's sixth-freest economy for the fourth year in a row.

- Chile (seventh) and Mauritius (eighth), two small but reform-minded economies, are the highest-ranking developing countries in the *Index*. Their relative economic strength is no fluke. Both have demonstrated persistent commitment to the rule of law, limited government, regulatory efficiency, and open markets through good times and bad.
- Ireland (ninth) has moved up by two slots, overtaking the U.S., and Denmark, which moves down to 10th place.
- A notable realignment of European countries continues to be underway in terms of advancing economic freedom. Eighteen, including Germany, Sweden, Lithuania, Georgia, Austria, the Czech Republic, Norway, Macedonia, Latvia, Poland, Bulgaria, and Romania, recorded their highest economic freedom scores ever in the 2014 *Index*. By contrast, five others (Greece, Italy, France, Cyprus, and the United Kingdom) registered scores lower than those they first received nearly two decades ago when the *Index* began recording economic freedom.
- Progress among the so-called BRIC nations has stalled. Brazil plunged 14 places in the rankings to 114th and is now judged "mostly unfree" in the *Index*. The rankings of the other BRIC countries—Russia, India, and China—declined slightly to 140th, 120th, and 137th, respectively.
- Liberia and Sierra Leone, two post-conflict countries, have moved up and are no longer considered "repressed" economies. Notably, six of the 11 countries that recorded ranking improvements of 10 places or more are from the Sub-Saharan Africa region.

2014 *Index of Economic Freedom* World Rankings

World Rank	Country	Overall Score	Change from 2013	Property Rights	Freedom from Corruption	Fiscal Freedom	Government Spending	Business Freedom	Labor Freedom	Monetary Freedom	Trade Freedom	Investment Freedom	Financial Freedom
1	Hong Kong	90.1	0.8	90	82.3	93.0	89.7	98.9	95.5	82.0	90.0	90	90
2	Singapore	89.4	1.4	90	91.9	91.2	91.2	96.8	96.5	81.5	90.0	85	80
3	Australia	82.0	-0.6	90	87.7	64.2	62.6	94.6	79.2	80.5	86.4	85	90
4	Switzerland	81.6	0.6	90	88.1	68.9	65.7	75.4	87.4	85.2	90.0	85	80
5	New Zealand	81.2	-0.2	95	94.0	71.2	32.3	96.1	90.2	86.3	86.8	80	80
6	Canada	80.2	0.8	90	87.7	79.7	47.3	89.3	83.1	76.3	88.3	80	80
7	Chile	78.7	-0.3	90	72.3	76.5	83.8	69.3	69.3	84.1	82.0	90	70
8	Mauritius	76.5	-0.4	65	53.4	92.2	81.8	74.4	78.0	76.7	88.6	85	70
9	Ireland	76.2	0.5	90	74.8	74.0	30.6	83.4	79.5	81.7	87.8	90	70
10	Denmark	76.1	0.0	90	93.7	39.3	0.5	98.1	91.2	80.0	87.8	90	90
11	Estonia	75.9	0.6	90	64.2	80.4	56.0	77.6	55.9	76.9	87.8	90	80
12	United States	75.5	-0.5	80	72.0	65.8	48.1	89.2	97.2	75.4	86.8	70	70
13	Bahrain	75.1	-0.4	60	49.4	99.9	71.4	76.3	82.0	78.4	78.6	75	80
14	United Kingdom	74.9	0.1	90	76.4	56.6	29.5	92.0	73.1	73.5	87.8	90	80
15	The Netherlands	74.2	0.7	90	88.0	51.7	25.6	89.7	59.6	79.9	87.8	90	80
16	Luxembourg	74.2	0.0	90	84.1	62.8	47.6	72.6	43.1	78.9	87.8	95	80
17	Taiwan	73.9	1.2	70	59.7	80.3	84.7	93.9	53.1	81.7	85.8	70	60
18	Germany	73.4	0.6	90	80.1	61.2	38.2	89.9	46.4	80.8	87.8	90	70
19	Finland	73.4	-0.6	90	93.4	65.1	8.9	93.6	46.5	78.9	87.8	90	80
20	Sweden	73.1	0.2	90	92.3	42.9	21.4	91.1	52.9	82.5	87.8	90	80
21	Lithuania	73.0	0.9	60	49.9	92.9	55.9	85.7	59.0	78.6	87.8	80	80
22	Georgia	72.6	0.4	40	42.8	87.3	69.7	87.8	91.2	78.4	88.6	80	60
23	Iceland	72.4	0.3	90	84.2	72.9	32.9	91.2	59.1	76.0	87.9	70	60
24	Austria	72.4	0.6	90	75.5	51.0	23.5	76.3	80.5	79.5	87.8	90	70
25	Japan	72.4	0.6	80	77.8	69.2	47.1	80.0	79.8	87.5	82.4	70	50
26	Czech Republic	72.2	1.3	70	45.3	81.7	43.8	70.1	84.0	79.4	87.8	80	80
27	Botswana	72.0	1.4	70	61.2	81.0	69.8	68.5	69.7	72.4	82.7	75	70
28	United Arab Emirates	71.4	0.3	55	66.4	99.6	83.1	74.4	82.9	84.6	82.5	35	50
29	Macau	71.3	-0.4	60	49.7	71.4	91.7	60.0	55.0	79.8	90.0	85	70
30	Qatar	71.2	-0.1	70	72.4	99.9	72.1	71.7	70.0	81.2	79.8	45	50
31	South Korea	71.2	0.9	70	54.0	72.6	72.6	92.8	47.8	79.6	72.6	70	80
32	Norway	70.9	0.4	90	88.1	50.6	42.2	90.9	44.6	78.7	89.1	75	60
33	Saint Lucia	70.7	0.3	70	70.6	75.7	63.6	83.1	84.5	82.7	71.9	65	40
34	Colombia	70.7	1.1	50	33.2	80.6	74.9	85.2	80.5	78.8	78.8	75	70
35	Belgium	69.9	0.7	80	74.2	44.8	14.8	89.9	72.7	79.5	87.8	85	70
36	The Bahamas	69.8	-0.3	70	66.6	97.3	84.1	70.7	81.5	75.1	52.2	30	70

2014 *Index of Economic Freedom* World Rankings

World Rank	Country	Overall Score	Change from 2013	Property Rights	Freedom from Corruption	Fiscal Freedom	Government Spending	Business Freedom	Labor Freedom	Monetary Freedom	Trade Freedom	Investment Freedom	Financial Freedom
37	Malaysia	69.6	3.5	55	44.3	84.6	75.6	85.6	78.5	81.0	76.4	55	60
38	Uruguay	69.3	-0.4	70	70.6	77.4	68.0	74.5	68.1	72.1	82.5	80	30
39	Jordan	69.2	-1.2	60	45.6	94.0	66.9	62.0	72.9	81.3	79.6	70	60
40	Brunei	69.0	N/A	40	53.3	90.2	66.1	68.2	96.5	74.2	81.8	70	50
41	Armenia	68.9	-0.5	30	26.7	86.5	81.3	83.1	78.5	77.0	85.5	70	70
42	Latvia	68.7	2.2	50	43.6	84.6	54.9	82.5	68.5	79.7	87.8	85	50
43	Macedonia	68.6	0.4	35	39.6	91.4	70.7	81.0	78.8	83.5	85.9	60	60
44	Israel	68.4	1.5	75	59.3	60.1	40.3	73.2	63.0	80.6	82.9	80	70
45	Barbados	68.3	-1.0	80	77.9	74.0	49.8	72.8	78.4	74.6	60.6	55	60
46	Cyprus	67.6	-1.4	70	64.0	79.7	36.2	79.7	70.2	78.8	82.8	65	50
47	Peru	67.4	-0.8	40	34.0	79.1	89.1	70.6	61.4	83.3	87.0	70	60
48	Oman	67.4	-0.7	50	48.2	98.5	56.0	68.3	75.5	73.6	78.7	65	60
49	Spain	67.2	-0.8	70	62.6	54.0	38.7	77.3	52.2	79.9	87.8	80	70
50	Poland	67.0	1.0	60	54.8	76.1	43.2	70.1	60.4	77.8	87.8	70	70
51	Hungary	67.0	-0.3	60	48.6	81.1	26.8	79.3	65.7	75.6	87.8	75	70
52	Saint Vincent and the Grenadines	67.0	0.3	70	61.1	73.7	72.4	76.3	78.7	79.8	67.6	50	40
53	Costa Rica	66.9	-0.1	50	50.9	80.0	90.0	64.9	53.3	76.3	83.8	70	50
54	Albania	66.9	1.7	30	30.4	92.7	75.6	78.1	49.7	80.0	87.5	75	70
55	Mexico	66.8	-0.2	50	29.7	80.9	78.9	76.8	58.3	77.4	85.6	70	60
56	Jamaica	66.7	-0.1	40	33.0	77.2	69.4	84.6	75.6	77.3	75.1	85	50
57	Slovak Republic	66.4	-2.3	50	41.8	80.2	56.0	67.0	53.6	78.1	87.8	80	70
58	Malta	66.4	-1.1	75	55.8	63.7	47.2	62.4	53.2	79.1	87.8	80	60
59	El Salvador	66.2	-0.5	40	34.3	79.6	85.8	59.6	63.3	80.0	79.0	70	70
60	Cape Verde	66.1	2.4	70	54.9	77.4	68.6	63.8	48.0	79.1	69.6	70	60
61	Bulgaria	65.7	0.7	30	35.2	91.2	64.5	73.5	80.2	79.6	87.8	55	60
62	Romania	65.5	0.4	40	37.7	87.0	59.2	71.0	65.2	77.1	87.8	80	50
63	Dominica	65.2	1.3	60	53.5	72.9	61.7	75.0	70.7	85.8	72.7	70	30
64	Turkey	64.9	2.0	50	44.0	77.5	63.5	67.6	59.7	71.8	84.5	70	60
65	Rwanda	64.7	0.6	30	46.9	80.3	78.2	69.6	84.1	74.8	77.7	65	40
66	Ghana	64.2	2.9	50	40.4	85.4	83.3	62.6	60.2	65.8	64.8	70	60
67	Kazakhstan	63.7	0.7	30	25.7	92.9	85.0	74.4	86.7	74.4	78.2	40	50
68	Montenegro	63.6	1.0	40	37.8	92.5	42.6	77.6	68.6	78.6	83.1	65	50
69	Portugal	63.5	0.4	70	61.1	60.1	26.8	84.9	34.6	79.3	87.8	70	60
70	France	63.5	-0.6	80	69.9	48.4	5.6	79.9	51.8	76.1	82.8	70	70
71	Panama	63.4	0.9	30	34.0	84.3	78.7	73.0	39.4	75.1	74.2	75	70

2014 *Index of Economic Freedom* World Rankings

World Rank	Country	Overall Score	Change from 2013	Property Rights	Freedom from Corruption	Fiscal Freedom	Government Spending	Business Freedom	Labor Freedom	Monetary Freedom	Trade Freedom	Investment Freedom	Financial Freedom
72	Thailand	63.3	-0.8	45	33.6	79.7	83.6	71.4	61.6	68.6	75.0	45	70
73	Trinidad and Tobago	62.7	0.4	50	34.0	84.8	62.5	59.4	76.4	71.7	78.6	60	50
74	Slovenia	62.7	1.0	60	61.0	58.9	22.6	85.4	51.0	80.3	87.8	70	50
75	South Africa	62.5	0.7	50	41.6	68.7	69.1	74.5	54.4	75.3	76.1	55	60
76	Kuwait	62.3	-0.8	50	43.7	97.7	55.6	57.7	63.6	73.2	76.7	55	50
77	Saudi Arabia	62.2	1.6	40	43.7	99.7	63.1	67.3	75.8	68.7	74.0	40	50
78	Paraguay	62.0	0.9	30	20.5	96.2	89.0	58.0	28.9	80.9	81.1	75	60
79	Madagascar	61.7	-0.3	40	27.3	90.8	92.3	62.8	43.9	77.6	77.8	55	50
80	Dominican Republic	61.3	1.6	30	27.3	83.7	92.3	56.1	55.2	75.7	77.8	75	40
81	Azerbaijan	61.3	1.6	20	22.7	88.1	64.8	73.5	77.9	78.8	77.2	60	50
82	Swaziland	61.2	4.0	40	31.6	74.7	70.9	64.2	71.7	72.3	81.5	65	40
83	Guatemala	61.2	1.2	25	28.7	79.6	93.6	58.4	49.3	76.7	85.4	65	50
84	Samoa	61.1	4.0	60	38.0	79.9	42.2	73.7	80.3	76.1	75.8	55	30
85	Kyrgyz Republic	61.1	1.5	20	19.2	94.6	60.2	74.2	83.8	73.7	75.2	60	50
86	Italy	60.9	0.3	50	38.5	55.5	25.6	75.5	52.5	78.9	87.8	85	60
87	Croatia	60.4	-0.9	40	41.1	69.4	45.8	61.4	39.4	79.2	87.4	80	60
88	Zambia	60.4	1.7	30	31.3	71.8	82.9	74.9	50.1	68.0	84.6	60	50
89	The Philippines	60.1	1.9	30	26.1	79.2	92.3	59.9	49.7	78.0	75.5	60	50
90	Sri Lanka	60.0	-0.7	40	33.4	84.9	86.3	74.4	59.2	68.0	73.6	40	40
91	Uganda	59.9	-1.2	30	23.8	79.1	87.3	45.1	87.4	71.0	75.4	60	40
92	The Gambia	59.5	0.7	30	31.7	79.0	79.8	57.4	65.8	71.3	65.0	65	50
93	Vanuatu	59.5	2.9	40	33.5	97.3	81.7	54.8	56.8	82.7	48.0	60	40
94	Namibia	59.4	-0.9	30	44.2	66.9	58.8	64.4	81.9	75.0	82.9	50	40
95	Serbia	59.4	0.8	40	34.0	83.1	38.6	59.3	70.1	66.9	77.0	75	50
96	Lebanon	59.4	-0.1	20	24.5	90.9	73.7	55.6	58.7	74.5	75.8	60	60
97	Mongolia	58.9	-2.8	30	28.2	81.8	39.1	71.8	81.1	72.4	74.7	50	60
98	Burkina Faso	58.9	-1.0	30	31.3	83.0	82.3	60.7	55.0	78.8	67.8	60	40
99	Fiji	58.7	1.5	25	20.0	82.3	76.2	64.9	73.1	75.2	70.2	50	50
100	Indonesia	58.5	1.6	30	28.0	83.4	89.8	54.8	47.8	76.4	74.8	40	60
101	Bosnia and Herzegovina	58.4	1.1	20	33.9	82.9	27.4	55.5	62.4	80.1	86.9	75	60
102	Nicaragua	58.4	1.8	15	24.1	78.6	80.0	52.6	60.3	72.8	85.4	65	50
103	Morocco	58.3	-1.3	40	33.3	71.3	64.1	76.2	31.5	78.1	58.8	70	60
104	Tonga	58.2	2.2	20	28.6	86.7	74.8	74.6	91.2	71.3	79.5	35	20
105	Gabon	57.8	0.0	40	29.1	74.5	81.7	58.9	63.0	75.1	61.0	55	40
106	Tanzania	57.8	-0.1	30	28.8	79.7	78.3	47.0	61.1	66.0	76.8	60	50
107	Côte d'Ivoire	57.7	3.6	30	22.1	79.1	79.8	55.1	59.0	80.6	71.4	50	50

2014 *Index of Economic Freedom* World Rankings

World Rank	Country	Overall Score	Change from 2013	Property Rights	Freedom from Corruption	Fiscal Freedom	Government Spending	Business Freedom	Labor Freedom	Monetary Freedom	Trade Freedom	Investment Freedom	Financial Freedom
108	Cambodia	57.4	-1.1	30	18.7	90.8	88.4	36.6	50.2	77.9	71.0	60	50
109	Tunisia	57.3	0.3	40	39.2	74.3	63.8	80.7	72.6	75.9	61.8	35	30
110	Moldova	57.3	1.8	40	29.5	85.8	54.4	70.1	37.9	75.0	80.1	50	50
111	Kenya	57.1	1.2	30	21.0	78.0	74.6	55.8	64.0	74.9	72.8	50	50
112	Honduras	57.1	-1.3	30	23.7	84.9	79.8	55.4	26.5	75.1	75.4	60	60
113	Benin	57.1	-0.5	30	29.5	68.3	86.1	51.0	50.5	75.4	60.0	70	50
114	Brazil	56.9	-0.8	50	37.9	68.8	54.1	53.8	49.8	69.9	69.3	55	60
115	Belize	56.7	-0.6	30	6.7	82.1	74.2	71.6	67.2	77.6	67.8	40	50
116	Bhutan	56.7	1.7	60	58.8	82.9	57.2	59.4	83.6	65.8	49.4	20	30
117	Seychelles	56.2	1.3	50	48.5	76.8	61.8	67.6	68.5	75.1	33.4	50	30
118	Djibouti	55.9	2.0	30	30.9	80.6	62.8	42.7	65.1	77.2	54.8	65	50
119	Greece	55.7	0.3	40	33.2	65.9	19.2	75.8	53.9	76.3	82.8	60	50
120	India	55.7	0.5	50	31.5	79.4	77.8	37.7	74.0	65.5	65.6	35	40
121	Guyana	55.7	1.9	30	24.4	68.4	71.8	64.3	72.6	78.1	72.0	45	30
122	Mali	55.5	-0.9	20	27.7	69.8	81.7	48.0	63.2	76.7	73.2	55	40
123	Yemen	55.5	-0.4	30	19.4	91.7	74.9	59.2	54.9	62.1	82.4	50	30
124	Malawi	55.4	0.1	45	31.9	78.0	63.0	38.9	60.3	64.1	72.7	50	50
125	Senegal	55.4	-0.1	40	29.5	65.1	75.4	47.5	41.5	81.8	73.2	60	40
126	Pakistan	55.2	0.1	30	22.7	80.6	88.3	69.4	47.3	68.5	64.8	40	40
127	Niger	55.1	1.2	30	26.0	76.8	88.4	35.2	45.4	88.3	65.6	55	40
128	Mozambique	55.0	0.0	30	26.2	75.7	64.6	65.2	36.7	80.8	75.5	45	50
129	Nigeria	54.3	-0.8	30	22.7	85.0	74.5	48.0	66.4	73.1	63.8	40	40
130	Suriname	54.2	2.2	40	32.9	69.0	78.3	41.8	81.8	71.8	66.2	30	30
131	Bangladesh	54.1	1.5	20	23.3	72.5	92.3	70.8	51.9	65.9	59.0	55	30
132	Papua New Guinea	53.9	0.3	20	20.2	66.7	75.4	57.0	73.7	75.5	85.1	35	30
133	Guinea	53.5	2.3	20	19.2	69.3	86.2	51.8	73.4	64.1	61.2	50	40
134	Mauritania	53.2	0.9	25	23.9	81.7	75.8	38.0	53.1	75.5	69.0	50	40
135	Egypt	52.9	-1.9	20	28.6	85.6	69.6	62.7	45.7	60.5	71.4	45	40
136	Cameroon	52.6	0.3	30	21.9	71.7	86.0	45.0	56.1	69.4	61.2	35	50
137	China	52.5	0.6	20	35.0	69.9	82.9	49.7	61.9	73.3	71.8	30	30
138	Liberia	52.4	3.1	30	33.8	83.6	70.5	62.3	47.0	72.9	64.1	40	20
139	Tajikistan	52.0	-1.4	20	19.4	92.3	78.1	58.4	45.5	67.7	73.2	25	40
140	Russia	51.9	0.8	25	22.1	85.6	61.5	70.0	55.8	69.4	74.6	25	30
141	Burundi	51.4	2.4	20	15.9	73.5	51.9	59.8	63.1	68.2	71.8	60	30
142	Comoros	51.4	3.9	30	22.1	64.5	85.3	49.4	50.1	74.5	72.7	35	30
143	Guinea-Bissau	51.3	0.2	20	20.2	89.0	86.6	40.5	61.4	74.4	61.4	30	30

2014 *Index of Economic Freedom* World Rankings

World Rank	Country	Overall Score	Change from 2013	Property Rights	Freedom from Corruption	Fiscal Freedom	Government Spending	Business Freedom	Labor Freedom	Monetary Freedom	Trade Freedom	Investment Freedom	Financial Freedom
144	Laos	51.2	1.1	15	18.6	86.6	86.7	60.7	54.9	75.5	58.6	35	20
145	Maldives	51.0	2.0	20	21.9	97.4	43.8	87.4	71.7	69.4	43.8	25	30
146	Algeria	50.8	1.2	30	28.7	80.5	51.0	66.3	48.3	67.8	60.8	45	30
147	Vietnam	50.8	-0.2	15	26.9	77.0	71.4	62.0	68.3	63.6	78.7	15	30
148	Sierra Leone	50.5	2.2	15	24.6	80.7	85.7	55.3	28.7	70.2	70.2	55	20
149	Nepal	50.1	-0.3	30	21.3	85.9	89.6	58.5	43.8	76.3	61.0	5	30
150	Belarus	50.1	2.1	20	24.6	89.2	61.2	73.4	77.7	33.9	81.4	30	10
151	Ethiopia	50.0	0.6	30	27.0	77.5	89.9	57.8	54.7	59.0	64.2	20	20
152	Togo	49.9	1.1	30	23.8	69.7	82.4	43.3	42.8	79.3	62.8	35	30
153	Micronesia	49.8	-0.3	30	30.0	97.5	0.0	51.7	77.9	75.2	81.0	25	30
154	Lesotho	49.5	1.6	40	37.1	67.4	0.0	54.0	62.4	75.5	68.6	50	40
155	Ukraine	49.3	3.0	30	21.9	79.1	37.5	59.8	49.8	78.7	86.2	20	30
156	Haiti	48.9	0.8	10	16.9	80.3	66.3	33.3	68.5	73.6	70.4	40	30
157	São Tomé and Príncipe	48.8	0.8	20	32.5	86.9	27.9	52.6	44.7	68.3	75.3	50	30
158	Bolivia	48.4	0.5	10	28.1	87.1	62.5	53.4	29.9	70.0	77.6	15	50
159	Ecuador	48.0	1.1	20	26.0	79.8	41.8	52.8	52.0	66.1	71.8	30	40
160	Angola	47.7	0.4	15	17.7	87.7	55.3	47.5	40.1	63.6	70.1	40	40
161	Central African Republic	46.7	-3.7	10	20.6	65.1	92.6	33.9	40.4	72.5	51.8	50	30
162	Burma	46.5	7.3	10	11.6	86.9	89.2	28.3	75.7	64.8	73.6	15	10
163	Uzbekistan	46.5	0.5	15	13.4	90.3	70.4	75.7	60.8	63.1	66.1	0	10
164	Kiribati	46.3	0.4	30	29.2	71.4	0.0	57.0	83.6	81.3	55.4	25	30
165	Solomon Islands	46.2	1.2	30	25.0	61.4	21.3	65.2	65.2	75.4	73.0	15	30
166	Argentina	44.6	-2.1	15	29.5	63.5	49.9	53.9	44.9	60.0	68.9	30	30
167	Chad	44.5	-0.7	20	15.9	46.2	80.0	24.9	43.3	69.8	55.2	50	40
168	Equatorial Guinea	44.4	2.1	10	16.6	75.5	62.6	43.4	41.5	75.4	53.8	35	30
169	Congo, Rep. of	43.7	0.2	10	20.6	67.5	79.6	35.1	47.0	72.0	55.6	20	30
170	Timor-Leste	43.2	-0.5	20	25.4	64.7	0.0	45.4	79.2	68.3	64.4	45	20
171	Turkmenistan	42.2	-0.4	5	13.4	95.2	93.0	30.0	30.0	65.9	79.2	0	10
172	Congo, Dem. Rep. of	40.6	1.0	10	17.6	69.4	74.6	30.0	38.5	63.0	63.0	20	20
173	Iran	40.3	-2.9	10	23.4	80.6	85.9	62.3	41.7	47.3	41.4	0	10
174	Eritrea	38.5	2.2	10	22.9	57.0	66.1	18.6	63.6	57.6	69.1	0	20
175	Venezuela	36.3	0.2	5	16.5	75.3	51.8	43.4	33.7	49.7	62.7	5	20
176	Zimbabwe	35.5	6.9	10	19.3	63.3	64.0	34.5	22.2	73.0	54.2	5	10
177	Cuba	28.7	0.2	10	41.2	60.0	0.0	20.0	20.0	65.8	60.0	0	10
178	North Korea	1.0	-0.5	5	5.0	0.0	0.0	0.0	0.0	0.0	0.0	0	0
N/A	Afghanistan	N/A	N/A	N/A	10.0	91.2	84.2	63.1	75.0	74.3	N/A	65	N/A

2014 *Index of Economic Freedom* World Rankings

World Rank	Country	Overall Score	Change from 2013	Property Rights	Freedom from Corruption	Fiscal Freedom	Government Spending	Business Freedom	Labor Freedom	Monetary Freedom	Trade Freedom	Investment Freedom	Financial Freedom
N/A	Iraq	N/A	N/A	N/A	13.7	95.5	40.3	56.9	73.4	70.0	N/A	N/A	N/A
N/A	Kosovo	N/A	N/A	30	28.6	92.7	73.0	58.1	71.3	72.7	N/A	65	N/A
N/A	Libya	N/A	N/A	10	18.3	95.0	0.0	50.1	77.9	66.9	N/A	5	20
N/A	Liechtenstein	N/A	N/A	N/A	N/A	N/A	N/A	N/A	N/A	N/A	90.0	85	80
N/A	Somalia	N/A	N/A	N/A	5.0	N/A	N/A	N/A	N/A	N/A	N/A	N/A	N/A
N/A	Sudan	N/A	N/A	N/A	9.8	85.1	90.3	54.5	49.1	55.8	55.6	15	N/A
N/A	Syria	N/A	N/A	10	23.3	N/A	N/A	60.4	55.1	N/A	N/A	0	20

Two Decades of Measuring Economic Freedom: A Look Back at the *Index*

Kim R. Holmes, PhD

Welcome to the 20th anniversary edition of the *Index of Economic Freedom*. What began as the brainchild of free-market economists in the 1980s is today a world-renowned landmark measuring economic progress in over 180 countries.

Each year, government officials from around the world tell us they pay close attention to their *Index* scores, using them as a guide for key policy decisions. Companies use the *Index* to guide investments and manage risk, and universities work it into their curricula. Its growing popularity is evident in the fact that the number of visits to its website, launched in 2001, has risen from nearly 700,000 in 2008 to almost 1.9 million in 2012 and is on track to surpass 2.4 million in 2013.

Why such success? The main reason is that the message of the *Index* rings true: More than any other political or policy approach, economic freedom generates more opportunities and greater well-being for more people, no matter where they live. Over the past two decades, the *Index of Economic Freedom* has documented the critical link between economic opportunity and prosperity. It has also demonstrated the power of free-market, limited-government, rules-based capitalism in helping people to prosper.

CREATING AN INDEX OF ECONOMIC FREEDOM

The idea of creating an index to measure the impact of economic freedom in the world began percolating in the 1980s. Nobel laureate Milton Friedman talked of producing one, and it was discussed periodically at meetings of free-market economists during that decade.

In the late 1980s, one of the biggest policy interests in Washington was measuring the efficacy of foreign aid. In 1989, U.S. Agency for International Development (USAID) Administrator Alan Woods proposed an "Economic Opportunity Index" to evaluate the U.S. government's foreign aid programs.[1] That same year, Heritage analyst Ed Hudgins analyzed the "Woods Report" in a *Backgrounder* and called on Congress to consider using such an index to rewrite the decades-old Foreign Assistance Act so as to improve the allocation of U.S. aid to developing countries.[2]

A few years later, in 1992, the chairman of the President's Commission on the Management of AID Programs, George M. Ferris, and commission member Jack Kemp urged USAID to adopt a quantitative measure of economic freedom to help decide the allocation of U.S. foreign aid.[3]

Several members of Heritage's Board of Trustees had expressed early interest in the notion of measuring economic freedom around the world. William E. Simon, former Secretary of the Treasury, and Ambassador J. William Middendorf II both had talked about quantitative measures that would permit comparative analysis on a national basis. The subject was debated in detail at Heritage Board Meetings and Ed Feulner, Heritage's President, was encouraged to move ahead with the concept to see if it could develop into a usable product

The decision to launch a formal Heritage project to produce the *Index* was made in 1993 after a conversation that I, as Vice President for Foreign and Defense Policy Studies, had with then-Heritage President Ed Feulner. We were discussing our plans for the upcoming year when he asked whether I thought an index on economic freedom could be produced. I replied that many economists had talked a great deal about it but so far had been unable to agree on how to go about it.

I took Feulner's question as a mandate to decide whether Heritage could succeed where others had failed. I went back and discussed the matter with my staff, particularly Jay Kingham Fellow in Regulatory Affairs Thomas Sheehy and a young analyst, Bryan T. Johnson. Then I recommended going forward.

In early 1994, Heritage experts were invited to testify before Congress on the idea of an index of economic freedom. I testified before the House Foreign Affairs Committee, Johnson appeared before the Senate Foreign Relations Committee, and Sheehy testified before the Senate Foreign Relations Committee on foreign aid. In his testimony, Sheehy discussed the need for creating an index of economic freedom to help the U.S. government determine the best candidates for U.S. aid. A few months later, he went into more detail in a Heritage *Backgrounder*.[4]

The main question was how to create a methodology for an index. Throughout the early 1990s, the Fraser Institute, a Canadian-based think tank led by Michael Walker, had held a series of workshops to discuss the prospects for a world economic freedom index. Sometimes attended by Milton Friedman, who later chaired Fraser's economic freedom project, the sessions examined the question of a methodology. Ed Hudgins, who led Heritage's international economics center at that time, had attended them and shared the concerns raised and conclusions drawn with his Heritage colleagues. When we made the decision to develop a methodology, the task fell to Johnson. He conferred with Hudgins, who by that time had moved to the Cato Institute, and then devised the 10 factors we ultimately used for the first *Index*.

The aim from the outset was to make the methodology transparent and simple enough that non-economists, including Members of Congress and their staffs, would find it user-friendly. In practice, this meant using data that were readily available, reliable, and consistent. The Heritage methodology may not have captured all of the theoretical nuances of economic theory, but it did reflect the main economic and institutional factors involved in economic freedom and growth. The methodology was largely an in-house affair, operationalized by Johnson, who with Sheehy undertook the time-consuming task of grading over a hundred countries. By the second half of 1994, they were ready to go.

So, late in 1994, we launched our first *Index of Economic Freedom*[5] in New York City. Feulner, co-authors Johnson and Sheehy, and I, as supervising editor, were there. Also present were former Treasury Secretary William Simon; *National Review* editor William F. Buckley; and *Forbes* magazine president and editor in chief Steve Forbes. At a private meeting with some of America's most important CEOs, such as the president of American Express, the Heritage crew explained how the *Index* worked and, using a graph called "The Curve of Economic Freedom," how it showed a statistically significant relationship between economic freedom and long-term growth.

That first *Index* was an instant success. According to Ed Feulner, "Former Treasury Secretary William Simon told me after reviewing a draft copy of *The Index of Economic Freedom* that it may well be the single most important publication ever published by The Heritage Foundation...."[6] Milton Friedman told Johnson and me that he was "glad someone finally ended up doing this." When we traveled to Hong Kong in early 1995 to release it overseas, our press conference attracted a huge number of media, kicking off that city's long-running interest in keeping its *Index* ranking as the freest economy in the world. The *Index* was attracting national and global attention, even in its first edition, not only because of its compelling message on economic freedom, but also because it gave countries an easy way to measure and compare themselves on the world economic stage.

By 1997, the *Index* was so well known that William Simon advised the Air Force Academy to start a program on economic freedom. Ed Feulner was invited to present the concept to the Academy. That same year, at the request of Dow Jones CEO Peter Kann, the Editorial Page of *The Wall Street Journal* joined Heritage as the *Index*'s co-publisher; Melanie Kirkpatrick became a co-editor and, along with editorial page editor Robert Bartley, forged an exciting and constructive partnership with Heritage that lasts to this day.

In Asia, the *Index* had become so widely known that even average people had heard of it. Upon checking into a hotel in Singapore on one of the promotional tours in those early years, I was greeted by a clerk proclaiming, "We're number two," referring to Singapore's *Index* score and revealing how much of a household name it had become there. In Croatia, popular evening TV quiz shows like our *Jeopardy* featured a question about that country's *Index* score in 2007; two contestants actually cited *Index* statistics from memory.[7]

Naturally, with so much attention, the *Index* also came under heavy scrutiny. Some developmental economists objected to its criticism of government-to-government foreign aid programs. Liberal economists were hostile to the message on economic freedom. Some economists objected to our refusal to weight economic factors. But when the Fraser Institute's first *Economic Freedom in the World* report[8] appeared nearly two years after the first *Index*, its findings were not all that different from those of the Heritage *Index* even though it employed a more complicated methodology that weighted the relative importance of various factors. A 1997 Cato Institute study that compared the results of the Heritage and Fraser indexes concluded that, "[d]espite underlying differences in purpose, methodology, and philosophy, the various surveys produce rankings that have much in common."[9]

One of the reasons the *Index* has fared so well is that its findings conform to economic reality and thus are not merely about theory. In his autobiography, published after he retired as chairman of the Federal Reserve Board, Alan Greenspan summed up this point succinctly:

> The ultimate test of the usefulness of such a scoring process [for example, the *Index*] is whether it correlates with economic performance. And it does. The correlation coefficient of 157 countries between their "Economic Freedom Score" and the log of their per capita incomes is 0.65, impressive for such a motley body of data.[10]

IMPACT OF THE *INDEX*

Over the years, the impact of the *Index* has fallen into distinct categories. The most important is its influence on government policies in countries in every region of the world. Topping the list is Hong Kong. Its government adopted the first *Index* as a key barometer in measuring its economic success. This interest persisted even after the handover of Hong Kong from the British to the People's Republic of China on July 1, 1997. The government took out full-page advertisements in the press whenever it scored "number one" on the *Index*. Press conferences there with Heritage analysts are always jam-packed, treated as high-profile and almost official affairs. Indeed, press coverage of the *Index* release sometimes amounts to hundreds of articles in local and Asian papers.

The story that best demonstrates the impact of the *Index* on Hong Kong is the reaction to the 1999 edition, known as the "year of the asterisk."[11] Hong Kong had responded to the Asian economic crisis by purchasing large amounts of securities on the stock market. Since it occurred after the June 30 cutoff date for data for the 1999 edition, this action did not affect Hong Kong's score that year. However, as the editors of the *Index* explained in an asterisk attached to its still–number one ranking, if this action were not reversed, Hong Kong would lose its number one ranking in the next edition. In a tense meeting between the Heritage delegation, led by Ed Feulner, and then-Hong Kong Financial Secretary Donald Tsang, it was clear that something would have to give for Hong Kong to retain its coveted position.

And something did give. Before the data deadline for the 2000 edition, Hong Kong sold off the securities. As a result, it retained its position as the world's "freest economy" in the *2000 Index*,[12] and the asterisk was dropped. It was clear to all that the *Index* had been the key factor in driving the decision (Hong Kong officials admitted as much to Feulner and other Heritage personnel). Most important, however, was how the rest of the world took note. Seeing the impact on Hong Kong, droves of embassy and foreign government officials began visiting Heritage to provide input, hoping to influence their country's scores. One government went so far as to present me with a scoring of itself, complete with a perfectly formatted country page that matched the formatting style of the book.

Other areas of impact have involved U.S. law and policy. Following the release of the first edition, Representative Bob Livingston, chairman of the House Appropriations Committee, used findings from the *Index* to reduce foreign aid by some 40 percent by fiscal year 1996.[13] Other legislation was proposed in the 1990s, but none made its way into law because the Clinton Administration and Democrats in Congress opposed placing conditions on foreign aid. Eventually, however, in 2004, with George W. Bush in the White House, the impact of the *Index* on the way foreign aid would be distributed was recognizable in the work of a newly established U.S. government agency, the Millennium Challenge Corporation. Each year, the MCC requests our annual trade freedom score before the *Index*'s official release date to help it determine which countries will qualify for performance-based aid compacts.

Recognizing the importance of economic freedom and the usefulness of the *Index* as a policy tool, other international organizations such as the World Bank[14] and the Organisation for Economic Co-operation and Development[15] have featured *Index* results in their database and use our analysis and scoring in their studies on the effectiveness of development assistance. Notably, for the *2012 Index*, the World Bank's vice president for Africa contributed an essay highlighting the urgency of increasing economic freedom to improve development prospects.[16] *Index* findings also have been used in other international indexes, such as the Bertelsmann Stiftung's *Transformation Index*[17] and the Legatum Institute's first *Prosperity Index* (published in 2009).[18]

Another target of influence for the *Index* is American corporations. After its release, *Washington Post* investment columnist James Glassman spoke favorably of that first *Index* in his Sunday column.[19] In 2004, Steve Forbes called the *Index* "a superb source for business conditions in countless countries."[20] Robert Ulrich, Chairman and CEO of Target Corporations and Target Stores, reiterated that point in 2005, calling the *Index* an "important reference book for any business that invests overseas and is engaged in today's global marketplace."[21] In 1996, executives at General Motors invited Tom Sheehy to Michigan to brief them on how the *Index* could be used to direct overseas investments.[22] Bryan Johnson recalls Procter and Gamble integrating *Index* findings into its long-range investment plans and Franklin Templeton Investments using material from the *Index* in marketing its own products.[23] Samson Capital Advisors has including *Index* findings in its analysis of currency returns, and in 2013, UBS Investment Research included information on *Index* country scores in its report to subscribers on global emerging markets.[24] There has even been interest in creating a marketable fund based directly on the *Index* as a portfolio investment tool.

One of the most surprising uses of the *Index* is as an educational tool. It has become quite popular as a textbook and research source for high-school teachers and university professors. For example, Mark C. Green, Professor of Marketing at Simpson College, included a chart from the *Index* in his college textbook *Global Marketing*, which is used in courses at over 200 colleges and universities. Three widely used textbooks on economics published by McGraw-Hill drew on source materials from the *Index*. It was often used as well by scholars for their primary research work. Not only the raw data of scores, but the analyses provided in each year's editions were often cited by scholars both here and abroad.[25] Several Federal Reserve Banks (such as St. Louis, New York, Dallas, and Atlanta) have used *Index* materials in their educational outreach programs. The bank in St. Louis, for example, made the *Index* a centerpiece in its online education course called "Which Came First—Democracy or Growth?"[26]

The culmination of the *Index*'s history in American education, however, came under the tutelage of the current lead editor, Terry Miller. A former senior State Department diplomat who specialized in international economics, Miller undertook a major effort to highlight the *Index* as an educational tool. It is no surprise that the most enthusiastic response has come from graduate schools of international business, with *Index* data featured increasingly in scholarly research and exhibited annually at the Academy of International Business. Economic freedom is, after all, the foundation for economic and commercial success. Even more interesting, perhaps, has been the positive reception on undergraduate campuses for the *Index*'s message of revolutionary economic change and rapid development through individual empowerment.

Over the years, Heritage has partnered with a number of international think tanks and institutes in producing the *Index* and promoting the cause of economic freedom. Fourteen current partners are listed in the back of this volume. This year, the *Index* has its first international contributing editor, Sergio Daga of the Fundación Políticas Publicas para la Libertad–POPULI in Bolivia. The *Index* or its major sections are now translated regularly into Spanish and Portuguese, and excerpts have appeared in French, Italian, Polish, and Bulgarian, among other languages.

POLICY LESSONS

Equally important to the *Index*'s legacy are its policy lessons. Looking back on its 20 years of tracking economic freedom, certain of these lessons stand out. The *Index* has documented the linkage between economic freedom and long-term prosperity that had been suspected for some time, but as our editors and analysts have drilled further down into the rich accumulation of data and findings over these two decades, they have discovered other connections as well. We should pause and take a look at them.

The most prominent of these connections is the link between economic freedom and per capita GDP. As noted, the first edition of the *Index* included a chart called "The Curve of Economic Freedom."[27] Most of the statistical work for it was done by Heritage economist Bill Beach with the support of Bryan Johnson. Charting their findings showed a sweeping upward curve of economic freedom scores compared with per capita GDP, establishing with statistical certainty the connection between economic freedom and prosperity. In plain language, the more economically free a country is, the wealthier its people are. The linkage is unmistakable, and the data each year confirm it. Economists may argue about whether other factors such as education, roads, and natural resources lead to economic prosperity, but none could dispute that economic freedom is a key ingredient.

The link between prosperity (wealth measured by per capita GDP or income) and freedom was clear, but this did not answer the larger question of whether there was a link between economic freedom and economic growth. Drawing on strides in economic growth theory, Heritage economists Beach and Gareth Davis tackled this question in the 1997 edition. Using data developed by Harvard economists Robert Barro and

Jong-Wha-Lee, they argued that "institutional settings strongly influence the rate of economic growth."[28] Their analysis showed a "statistically significant relationship," at a 99 percent confidence level, between economic freedom and economic growth. For the 2000 edition, Barro himself contributed a chapter that extrapolated on this theme, concluding that property rights and the rule of law (but not democratic elections) were key determinants of economic growth.[29] Barro revisited the issue in the 2013 edition of the *Index*, confirming his results with an updated data set.[30]

The relationship between economic freedom and democracy or political freedom is a long-standing issue. The year before Barro first tackled it, Bryan Johnson had looked at the relationship between economic freedom and political freedom. Conducting a regression analysis of data derived from the *Index* and Freedom House's annual survey of political freedom, he concluded that "those countries that are more economically free also are more politically free and have higher levels of civil liberties than those countries with less economic freedom."[31] This confirmed what many had already expected: Advanced economies tend to be more democratic, while undeveloped ones are more often poor and undemocratic.

One of the most lasting lessons from the *Index* findings over these two decades is the importance of international trade for economic growth. This was a theme in the 2001 edition, which contained an essay by *The Wall Street Journal*'s Mary O'Grady titled "First, Open Markets."[32] O'Grady focused mainly on the benefits of free trade to Latin America, but she and others argued that the general effect of free trade was to encourage liberalization of all areas of the economy. Free trade, for example, makes it easier to protect property rights. Free trade agreements institutionalize market openings and encourage others to follow suit.

Because of the importance of this issue, I directed our *Index* analysts to pen a chapter for the 2001 edition on the arguments for creating a global free trade area.[33] The idea was to bring together not only existing free trader nations, but also aspiring ones, creating global momentum in favor of open trade (particularly in the wake of the Asian economic crisis and the recent lack of progress in free trade talks). Variations of this idea were later picked up by presidential candidates such as Rudy Giuliani and Mitt Romney.

When Terry Miller took over as lead editor for the 2009 edition, he began to explore the larger universe of economic freedom. He wanted to understand better the broader benefits and how economic freedom related to other aspects of human development.

In the 2010 edition, for example, Miller compared data from the United Nations Human Development Reports' "Human Poverty Index" with our economic freedom scores.[34] He found that poverty rates dropped faster in economically free countries than in those that were losing economic freedom. He performed a similar comparative analysis of data on social instability and discovered that there was considerably more social unrest in countries that were economically repressed. The social benefits of economic freedom are widespread and palpable. As Miller concluded, "The prosperity that flows from economic freedom results in greater access to education, reduced illiteracy, increased access to higher quality health care and food supplies, and longer life expectancy."[35] The data from a broad spectrum of global sources made clear that the freer a country was, the greater would be the well-being of its people across the board.

In the 2011 edition, this comparative approach was taken to even higher levels. Using data from the Yale Center for Environmental Law and Policy and other groups, former Heritage Foundation Senior Fellow Ben Lieberman compared the environmental performance of 163 nations with *Index* scores on economic freedom.[36] He discovered that a nation's wealth "correlates highly" with the "Environmental Performance Index." Since the wealthiest nations also happen to be the most economically free, he concluded that free economies do the best job of protecting the environment. The reason is straightforward: "One can think of environmental protection as a good that only prosperous societies can afford."[37]

People struggling for economic survival do not have the luxury of worrying about or paying for cleaner water or air. The policy implication is obvious: If an environmentalist wants to protect the environment, he or she should advocate policies that promote economic freedom rather than more state-controlled environmental restrictions on the world's poor and economically repressed countries.

Over the past few years, under the leadership of Miller and his assistant Anthony Kim, the *Index* has also played an important role in documenting the decline of economic freedom in the United States. The election of President Barack Obama in 2008 ushered in an era of high government spending, regulation, and new taxes. It was not long before these policies began to affect America's ranking as one of the world's freest economies. The U.S. dropped out of the top ranks of the freest economies in 2010. Its score dropped another spot in 2011 and ended up in 10th place in both editions preceding this one—and well below the other freest economies. Even Canada, with socialized medicine, scored higher. For over five years, as the *Index* documents, our nation's economic freedom has been unambiguously eroded by excessive government spending and growth-stifling regulations, an unreformed tax system, and creeping cronyism that undermines the rule of law.

The last big change under Miller's leadership has been the push to achieve truly universal coverage of countries around the world. The number of countries included in the *Index* has grown from 157 in 2007 to 186 in this year's edition, making the *Index* by far the most comprehensive study of its type.

20 YEARS OF MAKING A DIFFERENCE

Looking back on the 20 years of research in the *Index of Economic Freedom*, former Heritage President Ed Feulner explained to me the keys to its success:

> It was its timeliness, continuity, and transparency that made the difference. It came out every year at the same time, so people could depend on using it to measure the progress of economic freedom. It built up a huge base of data that policymakers and scholars could use to make comparisons and draw broader conclusions. And it was easy to understand and simple to use.

As one of the founders of the *Index*, I would add that the research quality and dedication of the Heritage people involved, including all of the country and regional experts, has made a huge difference. Our partnership with *The Wall Street Journal*, particularly in the early days with Melanie Kirkpatrick and later with Mary O'Grady, obviously has been a key to its success. It helped to bring wider recognition, and input from their editors has contributed to making the *Index* a world-class product. I have been privileged to work with them and others, both in and outside of Heritage, who are among the best minds in the business. I will always be thankful for the opportunity to have been part of this wonderful enterprise.

Endnotes

1 Alan Woods, *Development and the National Interest: U.S. Economic Assistance into the 21st Century* (Washington: U.S. Agency for International Development, 1989).

2 Edward L. Hudgins, "The Woods Report: Foreign Aid and Economic Growth," Heritage Foundation *Backgrounder* No. 708, May 18, 1989, http://s3.amazonaws.com/thf_media/1989/pdf/bg708.pdf.708.

3 President's Commission on the Management of AID Programs, *Report to the President—An Action Plan*, April 16, 1992, p. 20, http://pdf.usaid.gov/pdf_docs/PCAAA222.pdf.

4 See Thomas P. Sheehy, "Rethinking Foreign Aid: The Index of Economic Freedom," testimony before the Senate Foreign Relations Committee, March 1, 1994, as published in Heritage Foundation *Lecture* No. 485, March 25, 1994, http://www.heritage.org/research/lecture/rethinking-foreign-aid-the-index-of-economic-freedom; see also Thomas P. Sheehy, "The Index of Economic Freedom: A Tool for Real Reform of Foreign Aid," Heritage Foundation *Backgrounder* No. 986, May 6, 1994, http://www.heritage.org/research/reports/1994/05/the-index-of-economic-freedom-a-tool-for-real-reform-of-foreign-aid.

5 Bryan T. Johnson and Thomas P. Sheehy, *The Index of Economic Freedom* (Washington: The Heritage Foundation, 1995).

6 Edwin J. Feulner, Jr., "Foreword," in ibid., p. v.

7 From discussions with Joel Anand-Samy of the Adriatic Institute, with permission to cite.

8 James Gwartney, Robert Lawson, and Walter Block, *Economic Freedom of the World: 1975–1995* (Vancouver, B.C.: Fraser Institute, 1996).

9 Steve H. Hanke and Stephen J. K. Walters, "Economic Freedom, Prosperity, and Equality: A Survey," *Cato Journal*, Vol. 17, No. 2 (Fall 1997), p. 134. Hanke of Johns Hopkins University and Walters of Loyola College in Maryland found a relationship in the 99 percent statistically significant range between the Heritage and Fraser rankings.

10 Alan Greenspan, *The Age of Turbulence: Adventures in a New World* (New York: Penguin Group, 2007), p. 277.

11 Bryan T. Johnson, Kim R. Holmes, and Melanie Kirkpatrick, *1999 Index of Economic Freedom* (Washington: The Heritage Foundation and Dow Jones & Company, Inc., 1999), http://www.heritage.org/index/.

12 Gerald P. O'Driscoll, Jr., Kim R. Holmes, and Melanie Kirkpatrick, *2000 Index of Economic Freedom* (Washington: The Heritage Foundation and Dow Jones & Company, Inc., 2000).

13 Lee Edwards, *The Power of Ideas: The Heritage Foundation at 25 Years* (Ottawa, Ill. Jameson Books, 1997), p. 154.

14 See, for example, analysis of "Banking Freedom" using *Index* scores in Thorsten Beck, Asli Demirguc-Kunt, and Ross Levine, "Bank Concentration and Crises," *Journal of Banking and Finance,* Vol. 27 (2003), http://econ.worldbank.org/wbsite/external/extdec/extresearch/0,,contentMDK:20699045~pagePK:64214825~piPK:64214943~theSitePK:469382,00.html.

15 See, for example, Organisation for Economic Co-operation and Development, *Studies on SMEs and Entrepreneurship, Thailand: Key Issues and Policies*, 2011, p. 74.

16 The Honorable Obiageli Ezekwesili, "Fighting Poverty Through Economic Freedom," Chapter 5 in Ambassador Terry Miller, Kim R. Holmes, and Edwin J. Feulner, *2012 Index of Economic Freedom* (Washington: The Heritage Foundation and Dow Jones & Company, Inc., 2012), pp. 69–73.

17 See Bertelsmann Stiftung, *Transformation Index BTI*, http://www.bertelsmann-stiftung.de/cps/rde/xchg/SID-7416E337-45920379/bst_engl/hs.xsl/307.htm.

18 See Legatum Institute, *2009 Legatum Prosperity Index Report*, October 1, 2009, http://www.li.com/publications/the-2009-legatum-prosperity-index-report.

19 Edwards, *The Power of Ideas*, p. 154.

20 Marc A. Miles, Edwin J. Feulner, Jr., and Mary Anastasia O'Grady, *2004 Index of Economic Freedom* (Washington: The Heritage Foundation and Dow Jones & Company, Inc., 2004), back cover.

21 Marc A. Miles, Edwin J. Feulner, and Mary Anastasia O'Grady, *2005 Index of Economic Freedom* (Washington: The Heritage Foundation and Dow Jones & Company, Inc., 2005), back cover.

22 Information provided in e-mail correspondence with author, with permission to cite.

23 Information provided in e-mail correspondence with author, with permission to cite.

24 Information provided in e-mail correspondence with current *Index* staff, with permission to cite.

25 For example, see Professor Lutz-Christian Wolff, *The Law of Cross-Border Business Transactions: Principles, Concepts, Skills* (The Netherlands: Wolters Kluwer Law & Business, June 2013). Wolff is a professor at the Chinese University of Hong Kong.

26 Federal Reserve Bank of St. Louis, "Which Came First—Democracy or Growth?" Spring 2009 *Inside the Vault* Lesson Plan, http://www.stlouisfed.org/education_resources/assets/lesson_plans/09ITV_DemocracyGrowth.pdf.

27 Chart, "The Curve of Economic Freedom," in Johnson and Sheehy, 1995 *Index of Economic Freedom*, p. xi.

28 William W. Beach and Gareth Davis, "The Index of Economic Freedom and Economic Growth," Chapter 1 in Kim R. Holmes, Bryan T. Johnson, and Melanie Kirkpatrick, *1997 Index of Economic Freedom* (Washington: The Heritage Foundation and Dow Jones & Company, Inc., 1997), p. 3.

29 Robert J. Barro, "Rule of Law, Democracy, and Economic Performance," Chapter 2 in O'Driscoll, Holmes, and Kirkpatrick, *2000 Index of Economic Freedom*, p. 47.

30 Robert J. Barro, "Democracy, Law and Order, and Economic Growth," Chapter 3 in Ambassador Terry Miller, Kim R. Holmes, and Edwin J. Feulner, *2013 Index of Economic Freedom* (Washington: The Heritage Foundation and Dow Jones & Company, Inc., 2013), p. 41.

31 Bryan T. Johnson, "Comparing Economic Freedom and Political Freedom," in Johnson, Holmes, and Kirkpatrick, *1999 Index of Economic Freedom*, p. 34. A 1997 Cato Institute study reported similar observations; its authors called results of their regression analyses "quite remarkable" because they showed that, "while both economic freedom and political/civil liberty contribute significantly to prosperity, gains in economic freedom have a 'prosperity dividend' that is three to six times greater than that which would be obtained from comparable gains in political/civil liberty." Hanke and Walters, "Economic Freedom, Prosperity, and Equality: A Survey," p. 139.

32 Mary Anastasia O'Grady, "First, Open Markets," Chapter 2 in Gerald P. O'Driscoll, Jr., Kim R. Holmes, and Melanie Kirkpatrick, *2001 Index of Economic Freedom* (Washington, D.C.: The Heritage Foundation and Dow Jones & Company, Inc., 2001), pp. 25–32.

33 John C. Hulsman, Gerald P. O'Driscoll, Jr., and Denise H. Froning, "The Free Trade Association: A Trade Agenda for the New Global Economy," Chapter 3 in ibid., pp. 33–41.

34 Ambassador Terry Miller, "Economic Freedom in Uncertain Times," Chapter 1 in Ambassador Terry Miller and Kim R. Holmes, *2010 Index of Economic Freedom* (Washington: The Heritage Foundation and Dow Jones & Company, Inc., 2010), pp. 9–20.

35 Ibid., p. 18.

36 Ben Lieberman, "A Free Economy Is a Clean Economy: How Free Markets Improve the Environment," Chapter 4 in Ambassador Terry Miller and Kim R. Holmes, *2011 Index of Economic Freedom* (Washington: The Heritage Foundation and Dow Jones & Company, Inc., 2011), pp. 53–60.

37 Ibid., p. 55.

Chapter 1

Economic Freedom: Global and Regional Patterns

Ambassador Terry Miller and Anthony B. Kim

The 2014 *Index of Economic Freedom*, covering 186 countries in six regions, finds economic freedom advancing worldwide despite challenging economic and political environments. The global average economic freedom score has reached 60.3, the highest ever recorded in the 20-year history of the *Index*. World economic freedom has improved by 0.7 point from last year and 2.7 points from 1995. Much of the momentum toward greater freedom that had been lost during the past five years has been regained.

Of the 178 economies numerically graded in the 2014 *Index*, six have earned the designation of "free" with scores above 80. The next 28 countries, with scores between 70 and 80, are considered "mostly free." These 34 economies sustain and provide institutional environments in which individuals and private enterprises enjoy a substantial degree of economic freedom in the pursuit of greater opportunity and prosperity.

The largest portion of the countries graded—117 economies—have freedom scores between 50 and 70. Of those, 56 economies are considered "moderately free" (scores of 60–70), and 61 are "mostly unfree" (scores of 50–60). Twenty-seven countries have "repressed" economies with scores below 50.

Despite the global progress over the past two decades, which occurred most dramatically in the 10 years from 1998 to 2007, the number of people living in economically "unfree" countries remains very high: 4.5 billion, or about 65 percent of the world's population. The path to prosperity for these individuals is very difficult indeed. More than half of these people live in just two countries, China and India, where advancement toward greater economic freedom has been patchy at best.

DIVERGING PATHS OF ECONOMIC FREEDOM

The advancement of global economic freedom to its highest level in the 2014 *Index* is particularly welcome given that the notable upsurge has been driven by developing and emerging economies around the world.

- 114 countries, the majority of which are less developed, contributed to the growth in eco-

Global Average Economic Freedom

Average Score in the *Index of Economic Freedom* Since 1995

Source: Terry Miller, Anthony B. Kim, and Kim R. Holmes, *2014 Index of Economic Freedom* (Washington, D.C.: The Heritage Foundation and Dow Jones & Company, Inc., 2014), http://www.heritage.org/index.

Chart 1 heritage.org

nomic freedom over the past year; 43 countries, including Singapore, Sweden, Colombia, Poland, Cape Verde, and Turkey, achieved their highest economic freedom scores ever in the 2014 *Index*.

- Score improvements in 17 countries, 16 of which are less developed, were significant enough to merit upgrades in the countries' economic freedom status in the *Index*. Notably, Colombia became a "mostly free" economy for the first time. Seven developing countries, including the Philippines and Zambia, have advanced into the ranks of the "moderately free," and eight countries have moved out of the status of economically "repressed."
- Declining economic freedom was reported in 59 countries, including nine advanced economies such as the United States, France, Spain, and Cyprus. Four countries recorded no score change.
- Progress among the so-called BRIC nations has stalled. Brazil plunged 14 places in the rankings to 114th and is now rated "mostly unfree" in the *Index*. The rankings of the other BRIC countries—Russia, India, and China—declined slightly to 140th, 120th, and 137th, respectively.
- Liberia and Sierra Leone, two post-conflict countries, have moved up and are no longer considered "repressed" economies. Notably,

six of the 11 countries that recorded ranking improvements of 10 places or more are from the Sub-Saharan Africa region.

- Four emerging economies have achieved notable score gains over the past five years: Colombia, Poland, the United Arab Emirates, and Indonesia. With a five-year cumulative score increase of over five points, each of these countries has recorded five years of sustained growth in economic freedom, successfully navigating the global economic uncertainty and turning what could have been a setback into an opportunity to upgrade its economic system.
- By sharp contrast, the United States has been on the opposite path as the only country to have recorded a loss of economic freedom for seven straight years.

COMPOSITION OF THE WORLD'S TOP 10 FREEST ECONOMIES

The top 10 freest economies make up a high-performing group that has demonstrated persistent commitment to the rule of law, limited government, regulatory efficiency, and open markets through good times and bad. The 2014 *Index* has recorded noticeable achievements and a few realignments within this highly ranked group.

- Competition for the top spot in the *Index* rankings has intensified. Hong Kong maintained its status as the world's freest economy, a remarkable distinction that it has achieved for 20 consecutive years. Singapore, the second freest economy, has closed the gap between itself and Hong Kong to only 0.7 point, the second narrowest difference in *Index* history.
- Australia, Switzerland, New Zealand, and Canada join Hong Kong and Singapore as the only economies considered "free" with economic freedom scores above 80 on the 0-to-100 *Index* grading scale. Australia took third place, a position it has held since 2009, while Switzerland has overtaken New Zealand and is now in fourth place, its highest ranking ever. Canada remains the world's sixth freest economy for the fourth year in a row.
- Chile (seventh) and Mauritius (eighth), two small but reform-minded economies, are the highest ranking developing countries in the *Index*.
- In addition to Switzerland, two other European countries are listed in the top 10. Ireland recorded a small score improvement, ending a half-decade of declining economic freedom, and returned to the top 10 after a year's absence. Denmark earned designation as the world's 10th freest economy.
- With its economic freedom continuing to decline, the United States is no longer one of the world's 10 freest economies Its score plummeted sharply to 75.5, the second lowest rating the country has ever recorded in the 20-year history of the *Index*. With score declines each year from 2008 until 2014, the U.S. has dropped to 12th place, tying its lowest ranking since the inception of the *Index* two decades ago. Now considered only a "mostly free" economy, the U.S. has earned the dubious distinction of having recorded one of the longest sustained declines in economic freedom, second only to Argentina, of any country in the history of the *Index*.

DETERIORATION OF THE RULE OF LAW

In measuring economic freedom, the *Index* analyzes countries' commitment to the rule of law, principles of limited government, regulatory efficiency, and open markets. Judged by these standards, the global economy as a whole has become "moderately free." Scores improved in eight of the 10 economic freedoms as summarized in "The 10 Economic Freedoms: A Global Look" on the next page. Investment freedom has gained an impressive 3.3 points on average, while labor freedom and government spending scores were higher by an average of one point or more. Average scores declined only in the area of rule of law, with property rights and freedom from corruption losing 0.3 point each.

WHY ECONOMIC FREEDOM MATTERS: GLOBAL SNAPSHOTS

The *Index* results, when compared with data measuring economic and social conditions in countries around the world, provide strong

The Ten Economic Freedoms: A Global Look

Score Changes

RULE OF LAW		GOVERNMENT SIZE		REGULATORY EFFICIENCY		OPEN MARKETS	
Property Rights	**-0.3**	Fiscal Freedom	**+0.1**	Business Freedom	**+0.3**	Trade Freedom	**+0.3**
Freedom from Corruption	**-0.3**	Government Spending	**+1.6**	Labor Freedom	**+1.0**	Investment Freedom	**+3.3**
				Monetary Freedom	**+0.5**	Financial Freedom	**+0.1**

RULE OF LAW

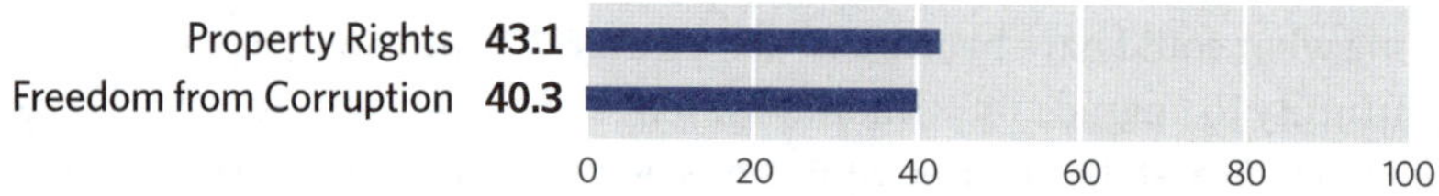

Twelve countries' property rights scores have declined, and some governments have sought to justify expropriations and nationalizations on the basis of the ongoing economic turmoil. The global average score for freedom from corruption continues to lag behind scores for other components of economic freedom. Populations in some countries have responded to repressive government economic policies with demonstrations that have sometimes turned violent.

GOVERNMENT SIZE

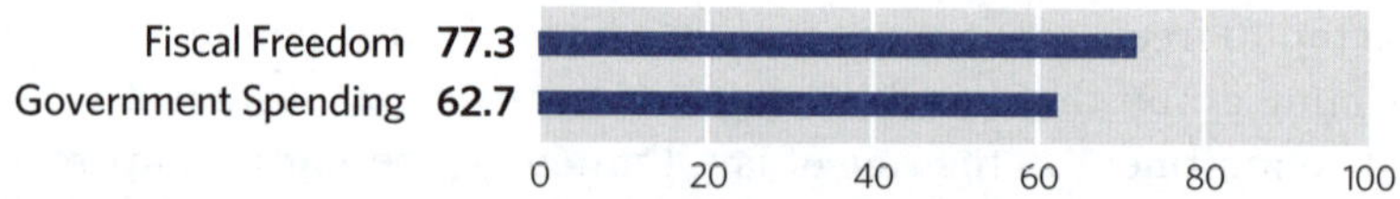

The average top individual income tax rate for all countries is 28 percent, and the average top corporate tax rate is 24.1 percent. The average overall tax burden as a percentage of GDP is 22.3 percent. The average level of government spending as a percentage of GDP is 34.2 percent. The average level of gross public debt as a percentage of GDP in advanced economies has reached over 70 percent.

REGULATORY EFFICIENCY

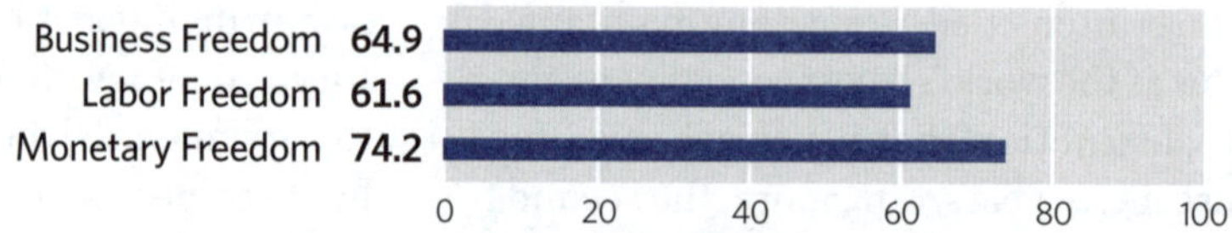

Many economies have continued to streamline and modernize their business frameworks. Globally, starting a business takes seven procedures and 25 days, while completing licensing requirements takes an average of 175 days. For the world as a whole, labor market reform has progressed. The 2014 *Index* registered a continued improvement in monetary freedom as a result of reduced inflationary pressures.

OPEN MARKETS

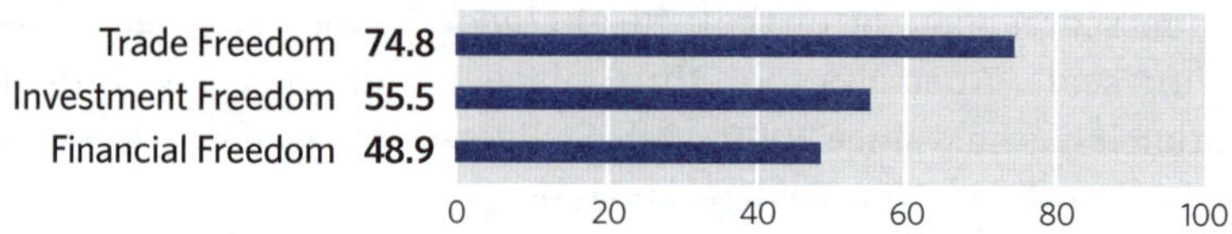

Global trade freedom is stuck in neutral. Although progress was uneven, investment freedom advanced in the 2014 *Index*. Overall, the average financial freedom score remained essentially unchanged from the previous year. Despite some progress toward stability, the global financial system has been under continuing strain and uncertainty, in large part because of the ongoing European sovereign debt turmoil.

Economic Freedom and Prosperity

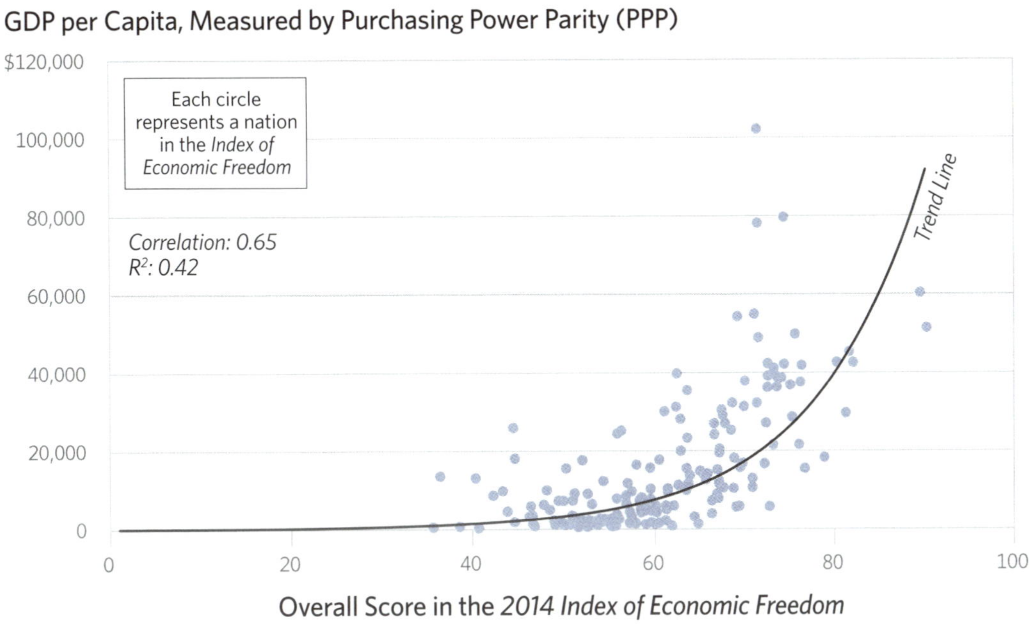

Sources: Terry Miller, Anthony B. Kim, and Kim R. Holmes, *2014 Index of Economic Freedom* (Washington, D.C.: The Heritage Foundation and Dow Jones & Company, Inc., 2014), http://www.heritage.org/index; and International Monetary Fund, World Economic Outlook Databases, http://www.imf.org/external/ns/cs.aspx?id=28 (accessed November 13, 2013).

Chart 2 heritage.org

evidence of the free-market system's success in promoting prosperity, human development, and democratic governance. Key features of that system, including private property rights, openness, and flexibility, are virtually uncontested as desirable features of economic policy.

Improving Lives Around the Globe. There are clear relationships between economic freedom and numerous positive economic and social indicators, the most prominent being the strong relationship between the level of economic freedom and the level of prosperity in a given country.

Economies rated "free" or "mostly free" in the 2014 *Index* enjoy incomes that are more than three times higher than average incomes in all other countries and more than 10 times higher than the incomes of "repressed" economies. Economic freedom is key to enhancing overall well-being, taking into account other factors such as health, education, security, and political governance.

Greater economic freedom is strongly correlated with overall human development as measured by the United Nations Human Development Index, which measures life expectancy, literacy, education, and the standard of living in countries worldwide. The prosperity that flows from economic freedom results in greater access to education, reduced illiteracy, increased access to higher-quality health care and food supplies, and longer life expectancy. (See Chart 3.)

Debate over the complex interplay between economic freedom and democracy or political freedom has been renewed and intensified over the past three years, particularly as the Middle East and North Africa region has undergone a challenging period, but the positive relationship between the two is undeniable. By empowering people to exercise greater control of their daily

Economic Freedom and Human Development

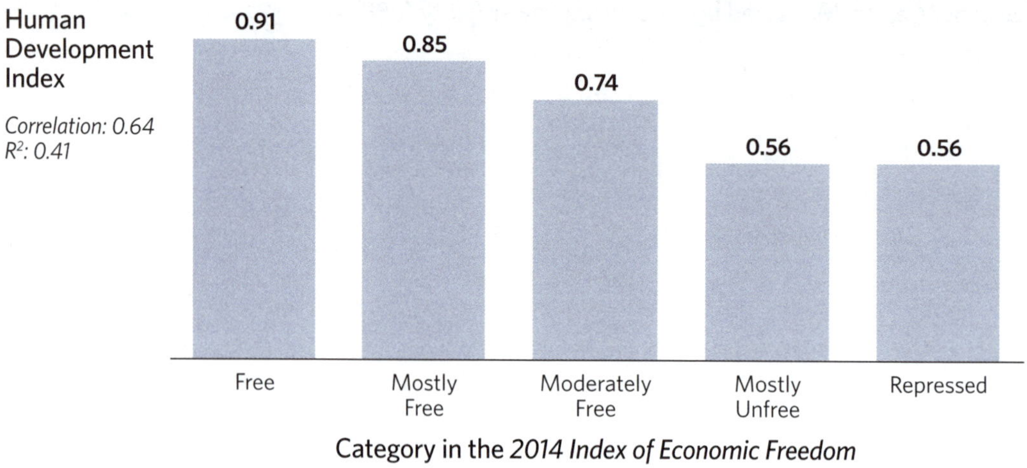

Sources: Terry Miller, Anthony B. Kim, and Kim R. Holmes, *2014 Index of Economic Freedom* (Washington, D.C.: The Heritage Foundation and Dow Jones & Company, Inc., 2014), http://www.heritage.org/index; and United Nations, Human Development Programme, "Human Development Report 2013," http://hdr.undp.org/en/reports/global/hdr2013/ (accessed November 13, 2013).

Chart 3 heritage.org

Economic Freedom and Democratic Governance

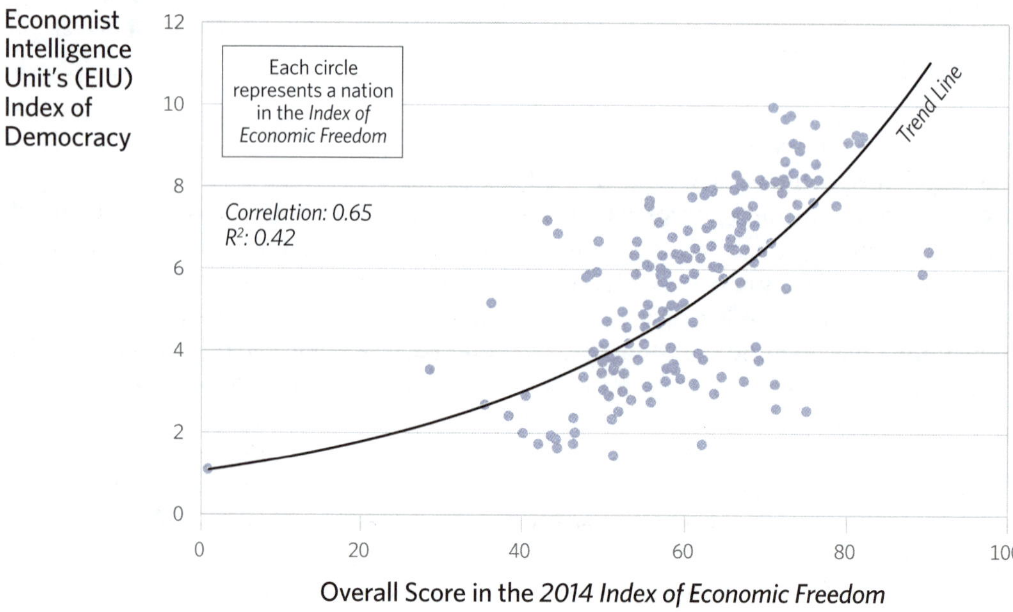

Sources: Terry Miller, Anthony B. Kim, and Kim R. Holmes, *2014 Index of Economic Freedom* (Washington, D.C.: The Heritage Foundation and Dow Jones & Company, Inc., 2014), http://www.heritage.org/index; and Economist Intelligence Unit, "Democracy Index 2012: Democracy at a Standstill," https://portoncv.gov.cv/dhub/porton.por_global.open_file?p_doc_id=1034 (accessed November 13, 2013).

Chart 4 heritage.org

lives, economic freedom ultimately nurtures political reform as well by making it possible for individuals to gain the economic resources necessary to challenge entrenched interests or compete for political power, thereby encouraging the creation of more pluralistic societies (Chart 4).

Pursuit of greater economic freedom is thus an important stepping stone to democracy. It empowers the poor and builds the middle class. It is a philosophy that encourages entrepreneurship and disperses economic power and decision-making throughout an economy.

Promoting Innovation and Environmental Sustainability. Also notably, in countries around the world, economic freedom has been shown to increase countries' capacity for innovation and to improve overall environmental performance as well. The positive link between economic freedom and higher levels of innovation ensures greater economic dynamism in coping with various developmental challenges, and the most remarkable improvements in clean energy use and energy efficiency over the past decades have occurred not as a result of government regulation, but rather because of advances in economic freedom and freer trade that have unleashed greater economic opportunity and generated a virtuous cycle of investment, innovation (including in greener technologies), and dynamic economic growth (Charts 5 and 6).

REGIONAL RESULTS

Each of the six *Index* regions continues to be represented by at least one country that ranks among the top 20 freest economies in the 2014 *Index*. Half of the leading economies are from Europe, led by Switzerland and Ireland. Five of the top 20 performers are in the Asia–Pacific region, with Taiwan further advancing within the ranks of the economically "mostly free." Canada and the U.S. represent North America among the top 20. The other regions are represented by one country each among the 20 freest economies: Chile (South and Central America/Caribbean); Mauritius (Sub-Saharan Africa); and Bahrain (Middle East and North Africa).

While these countries differ greatly in their histories, political systems, and economic pro-

Comparing Regional Average Scores to the Global Average

Above or Equal to Global Average | Below Global Average

	North America	Europe	Middle East/ North Africa	South and Central America/ Caribbean	Asia-Pacific	Sub-Saharan Africa	GLOBAL AVERAGE
Overall	74.1	67.1	61.5	59.7	58.5	54.6	**60.3**
Property Rights	73.3	61.0	43.3	40.0	38.2	30.5	**43.1**
Freedom from Corruption	63.2	55.5	41.7	38.3	35.8	29.3	**40.3**
Fiscal Freedom	75.5	71.8	88.3	78.3	80.2	75.3	**77.3**
Government Spending	58.1	41.7	66.1	69.6	66.6	73.5	**62.7**
Business Freedom	85.1	78.1	67.6	61.6	65.5	51.8	**64.9**
Labor Freedom	79.5	62.1	62.6	59.4	67.2	55.9	**61.6**
Monetary Freedom	76.4	77.2	72.5	74.5	72.6	72.7	**74.2**
Trade Freedom	86.9	86.3	72.4	73.7	71.3	67.9	**74.8**
Investment Freedom	73.3	74.0	51.3	54.3	44.3	49.3	**55.5**
Financial Freedom	70.0	63.0	48.7	47.2	43.3	40.2	**48.9**

Sources: Terry Miller, Anthony B. Kim, and Kim R. Holmes, *2014 Index of Economic Freedom* (Washington, D.C.: The Heritage Foundation and Dow Jones & Company, Inc., 2014), http://www.heritage.org/index.

Table 1 heritage.org

Economic Freedom and Innovation

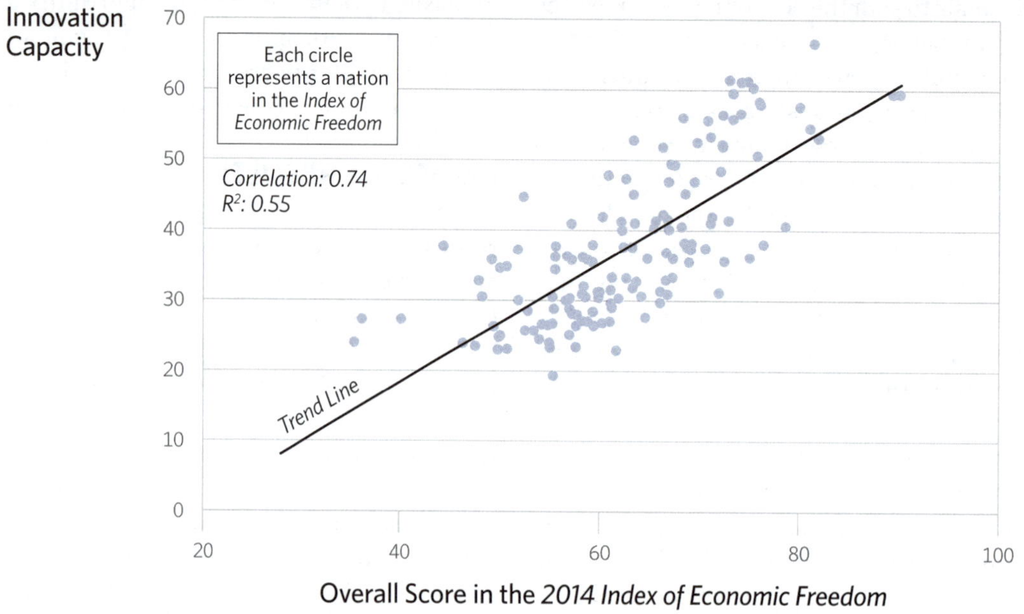

Sources: Terry Miller, Anthony B. Kim, and Kim R. Holmes, *2014 Index of Economic Freedom* (Washington, D.C.: The Heritage Foundation and Dow Jones & Company, Inc., 2014), http://www.heritage.org/index; and *The Global Innovation Index 2013: The Local Dynamics of Innovation* (Geneva, Ithaca, and Fontainebleau: Cornell University, INSEAD, and WIPO, 2013), http://www.globalinnovationindex.org/content.aspx?page=gii-full-report-2013 (accessed November 13, 2013).

Chart 5 heritage.org

Economic Freedom and the Environment

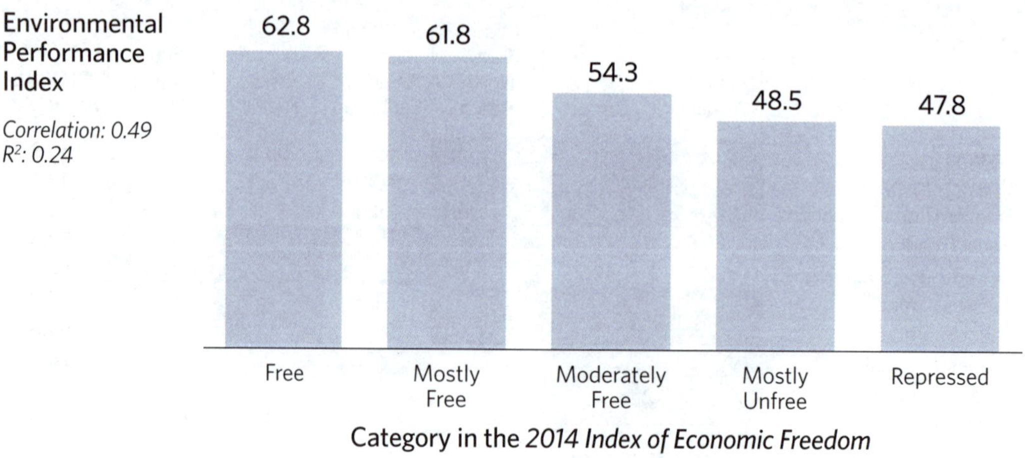

Sources: Terry Miller, Anthony B. Kim, and Kim R. Holmes, *2014 Index of Economic Freedom* (Washington, D.C.: The Heritage Foundation and Dow Jones & Company, Inc., 2014), http://www.heritage.org/index; and Yale University, "2012 Environmental Performance Index," http://epi.yale.edu/downloads (accessed November 13, 2013)

Chart 6 heritage.org

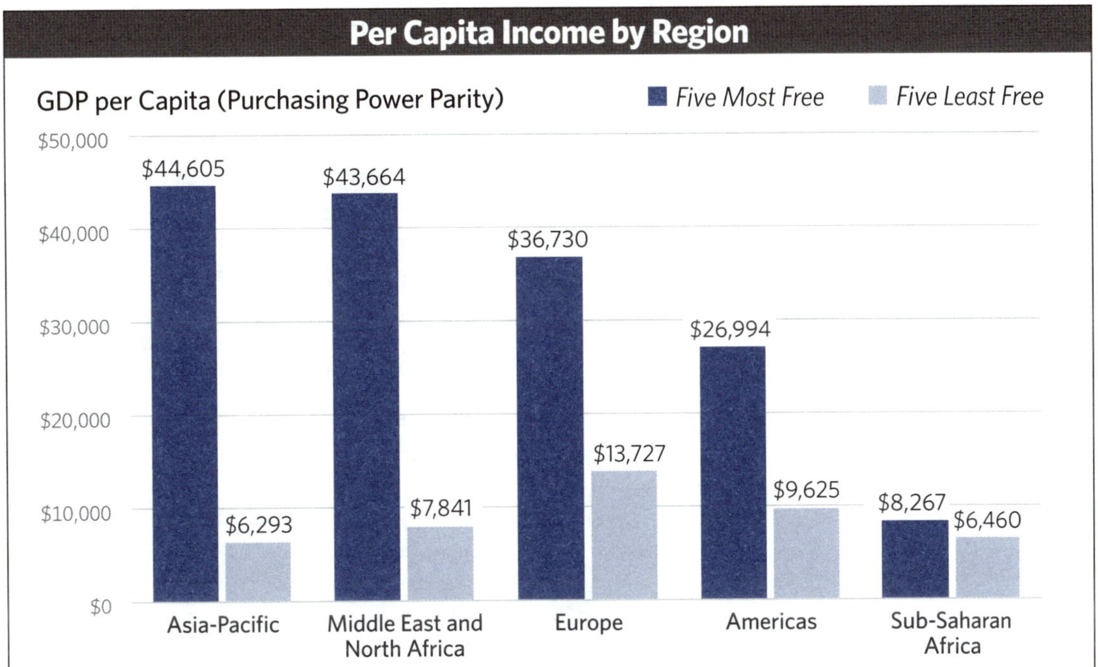

Sources: Terry Miller, Anthony B. Kim, and Kim R. Holmes, *2014 Index of Economic Freedom* (Washington, D.C.: The Heritage Foundation and Dow Jones & Company, Inc., 2014), http://www.heritage.org/index, and International Monetary Fund, World Economic Outlook Databases, http://www.imf.org/external/ns/cs.aspx?id=28 (accessed November 13, 2013).

Chart 7 heritage.org

files, they share key characteristics. These top-performing economies in the *Index* are not necessarily geographically large or richly blessed with natural resources. Many economies have managed to expand opportunities for their citizens by enhancing their economic dynamism and vitality with high levels of economic freedom.

While the global average score for the 2014 *Index* has advanced notably, progress has not been uniform across the regions. On average, economic freedom made no progress in North America and actually declined in the Middle East/North Africa region. In the other four regions, economic freedom advanced. The Asia–Pacific region achieved the largest score improvement, with countries gaining slightly over one point on average. Sub-Saharan Africa gained the second most economic freedom on average: 0.9 point. Europe and the South and Central America/Caribbean region also recorded average score improvements of 0.5 point and 0.3 point, respectively.

Average levels of economic freedom vary widely among the regions. North America and Europe continue to record the highest average economic freedom scores among the six regions: 74.1 and 67.1, respectively. Despite the ongoing economic and political turmoil in some countries in the Middle East and North Africa, the region as a whole still achieved an average economic freedom score above 60 due to high levels of economic freedom in Bahrain, Qatar, and the United Arab Emirates. Average economic freedom scores in the South and Central America/Caribbean region, the Asia–Pacific region, and Sub-Saharan Africa continue to be below 60.

Although levels of economic freedom vary across the regions, the strongly positive relationship between economic freedom and prosperity is apparent throughout the world: In every region, per capita incomes are much higher in countries that are economically free. (See Chart 7.)

Economic Freedom: Regional Variations (Regional Average)

Regional Ranking	North America (74.1)	Middle East / North Africa (61.5)	South and Central America/ Caribbean (59.7)	Asia-Pacific (58.5)	Europe (67.1)	Sub-Saharan Africa (54.6)
1	Canada	Bahrain	Chile	Hong Kong	Switzerland	Mauritius
2	United States	United Arab Emirates	Saint Lucia	Singapore	Ireland	Botswana
3	Mexico	Qatar	Colombia	Australia	Denmark	Cape Verde
4		Jordan	The Bahamas	New Zealand	Estonia	Rwanda
5		Israel	Uruguay	Taiwan	United Kingdom	Ghana
6		Oman	Barbados	Japan	The Netherlands	South Africa
7		Kuwait	Peru	Macau	Luxembourg	Madagascar
8		Saudi Arabia	Saint Vincent and the Grenadines	South Korea	Germany	Swaziland
9		Lebanon	Costa Rica	Malaysia	Finland	Zambia
10		Morocco	Jamaica	Brunei	Sweden	Uganda
11		Tunisia	El Salvador	Kazakhstan	Lithuania	The Gambia
12		Yemen	Dominica	Thailand	Georgia	Namibia
13		Egypt	Panama	Azerbaijan	Iceland	Burkina Faso
14		Algeria	Trinidad and Tobago	Samoa	Austria	Gabon
15		Iran	Paraguay	Kyrgyz Republic	Czech Republic	Tanzania
16			Dominican Republic	The Philippines	Norway	Côte d'Ivoire
17			Guatemala	Sri Lanka	Belgium	Kenya
18			Nicaragua	Vanuatu	Armenia	Benin
19			Honduras	Mongolia	Latvia	Seychelles
20			Brazil	Fiji	Macedonia	Djibouti
21			Belize	Indonesia	Cyprus	Mali
22			Guyana	Tonga	Spain	Malawi
23			Suriname	Cambodia	Poland	Senegal
24			Haiti	Bhutan	Hungary	Niger
25			Bolivia	India	Albania	Mozambique
26			Ecuador	Pakistan	Slovak Republic	Nigeria
27			Argentina	Bangladesh	Malta	Guinea
28			Venezuela	Papua New Guinea	Bulgaria	Mauritania
29			Cuba	China	Romania	Cameroon
30				Tajikistan	Turkey	Liberia
31				Laos	Montenegro	Burundi
32				Maldives	Portugal	Comoros
33				Vietnam	France	Guinea-Bissau
34				Nepal	Slovenia	Sierra Leone
35				Micronesia	Italy	Ethiopia
36				Burma	Croatia	Togo
37				Uzbekistan	Serbia	Lesotho
38				Kiribati	Bosnia and Herzegovina	São Tomé and Príncipe
39				Solomon Islands	Moldova	Angola
40				Timor-Leste	Greece	Central African Republic
41				Turkmenistan	Russia	Chad
42				North Korea	Belarus	Equatorial Guinea
43					Ukraine	Congo, Rep. of
44						Congo, Dem. Rep. of
45						Eritrea
46						Zimbabwe

Economic Freedom Scores

- 80–100 Free
- 70–79.9 Mostly Free
- 60–69.9 Moderately Free
- 50–59.9 Mostly Unfree
- 0–49.9 Repressed
- Not Ranked

North America

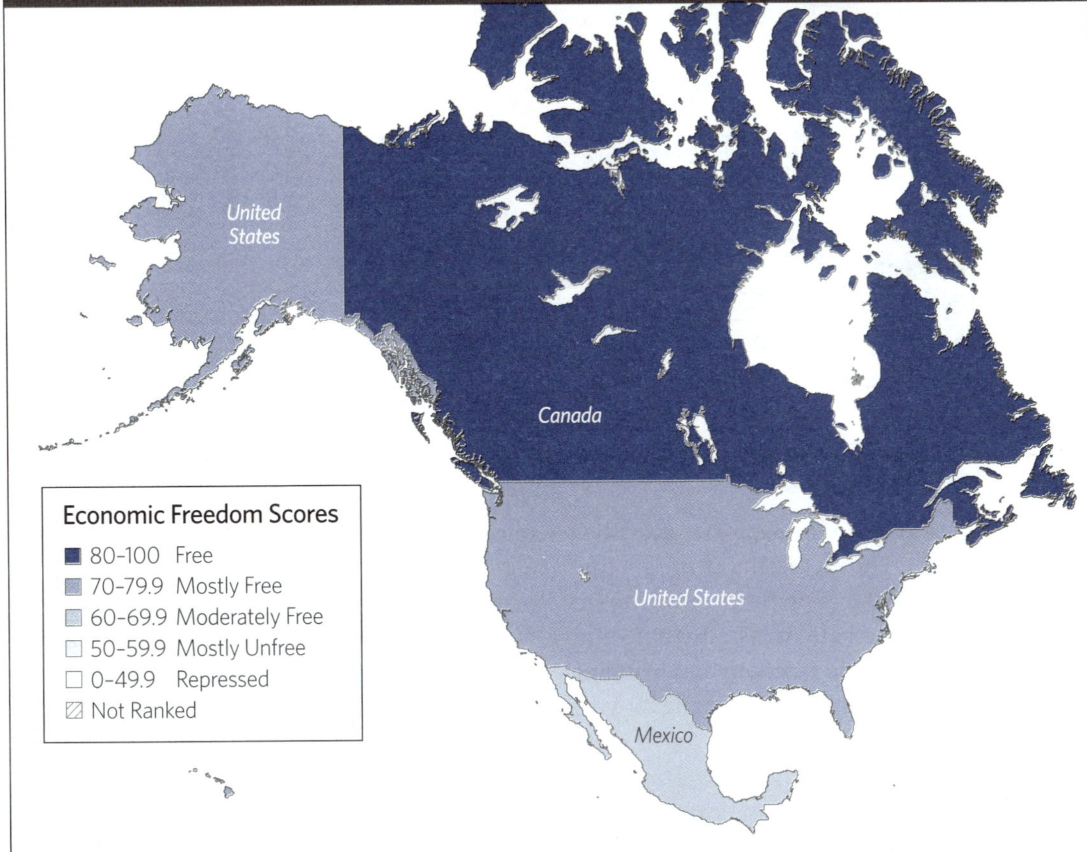

Source: Terry Miller, Anthony B. Kim, and Kim R. Holmes, *2014 Index of Economic Freedom* (Washington, D.C.: The Heritage Foundation and Dow Jones & Company, Inc., 2014), http://www.heritage.org/index.

Map 1 heritage.org

NORTH AMERICA: AMERICA'S STARTLING DECLINE

North America's three countries have been linked by a regional trade agreement, the North American Free Trade Agreement (NAFTA), since 1994. Over the past 20 years, NAFTA has been a positive force, connecting more than 400 million people in an economic area with about one-third of the world's total GDP. The region has long benefited from its openness to international trade and investment. Although it enjoys the highest degree of economic freedom among the six regions, it has undergone a notable reordering in recent years: While Canada has solidified its status as a "free" economy, the U.S. and Mexico are seemingly stuck in the "mostly free" and "moderately free" categories, respectively.

The overall economic policy direction of the United States in recent years has involved substantial growth in the size and scope of government, accelerating the erosion of economic freedom and contributing directly to America's fall from the top 10 freest economies. Specific policies that have curtailed economic freedom in the U.S. have entailed intrusive and costly regulations in areas like finance, health care, and the environment. These have injected uncertainty into business decision-making that has slowed job creation and hiring and hurt economic recovery and growth. The absence of meaningful fiscal reform has weakened the government's

Economic Freedom in North American Countries

World Rank	Region Rank	Country	Overall Score	Change from 2013	Property Rights	Freedom from Corruption	Fiscal Freedom	Government Spending	Business Freedom	Labor Freedom	Monetary Freedom	Trade Freedom	Investment Freedom	Financial Freedom
6	1	Canada	80.2	0.8	90	87.7	79.7	47.3	89.3	83.1	76.3	88.3	80	80
12	2	United States	75.5	-0.5	80	72.0	65.8	48.1	89.2	97.2	75.4	86.8	70	70
55	3	Mexico	66.8	-0.2	50	29.7	80.9	78.9	76.8	58.3	77.4	85.6	70	60

Table 2 heritage.org

balance sheet and led to the explosive growth of government debt. The increasing cronyism that has accompanied the growth of government has undermined the rule of law, further eroding America's economic freedom and bringing it down to its second lowest level in the 20-year history of the *Index*.

EUROPE: CHANGING OF THE GUARD

In Europe, long-established free-market institutions in many countries allow the region to score above the world averages in most categories of economic freedom. Taken as a whole, however, the region has been undergoing tumultuous and uncertain times epitomized by the ongoing sovereign debt crisis affecting the eurozone. Europe's overall economic freedom rating remains undermined by weak scores in the management of public spending, reflecting the cost of expanding government services and transfer payments that plainly hinder both productivity growth and dynamic job creation. Stagnant growth has also exacerbated debt levels, leaving many European countries with no choice but to cut spending to reduce unsustainable fiscal deficits.

Still, 10 of the world's 20 freest countries, led by Switzerland, are in Europe. A notable realignment of European countries continues to be underway in terms of advancing economic freedom. Eighteen, including Germany, Sweden, Lithuania, Georgia, Austria, the Czech Republic, Norway, Macedonia, Latvia, Poland, Bulgaria, and Romania, recorded their highest economic freedom scores ever in the 2014 *Index*. By contrast, five others (Greece, Italy, France, Cyprus, and the United Kingdom) registered scores lower than those they first received nearly two decades ago when the *Index* began to record economic freedom.

One-Year Freedom Score Change

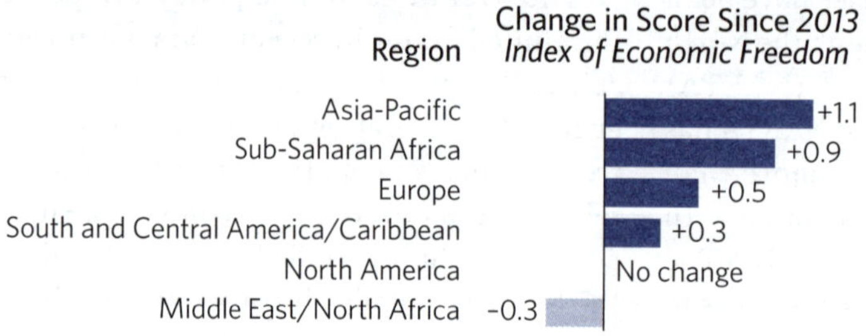

Source: Terry Miller, Anthony B. Kim, and Kim R. Holmes, *2014 Index of Economic Freedom* (Washington, D.C.: The Heritage Foundation and Dow Jones & Company, Inc., 2014), http://www.heritage.org/index.

Chart 8 heritage.org

Europe

Source: Terry Miller, Anthony B. Kim, and Kim R. Holmes, *2014 Index of Economic Freedom* (Washington, D.C.: The Heritage Foundation and Dow Jones & Company, Inc., 2014), http://www.heritage.org/index.

Map 2 heritage.org

Economic Freedom in European Countries

World Rank	Region Rank	Country	Overall Score	Change from 2013	Property Rights	Freedom from Corruption	Fiscal Freedom	Government Spending	Business Freedom	Labor Freedom	Monetary Freedom	Trade Freedom	Investment Freedom	Financial Freedom
4	1	Switzerland	81.6	0.6	90	88.1	68.9	65.7	75.4	87.4	85.2	90.0	85	80
9	2	Ireland	76.2	0.5	90	74.8	74.0	30.6	83.4	79.5	81.7	87.8	90	70
10	3	Denmark	76.1	0.0	90	93.7	39.3	0.5	98.1	91.2	80.0	87.8	90	90
11	4	Estonia	75.9	0.6	90	64.2	80.4	56.0	77.6	55.9	76.9	87.8	90	80
14	5	United Kingdom	74.9	0.1	90	76.4	56.6	29.5	92.0	73.1	73.5	87.8	90	80
15	6	The Netherlands	74.2	0.7	90	88.0	51.7	25.6	89.7	59.6	79.9	87.8	90	80
16	7	Luxembourg	74.2	0.0	90	84.1	62.8	47.6	72.6	43.1	78.9	87.8	95	80
18	8	Germany	73.4	0.6	90	80.1	61.2	38.2	89.9	46.4	80.8	87.8	90	70
19	9	Finland	73.4	-0.6	90	93.4	65.1	8.9	93.6	46.5	78.9	87.8	90	80
20	10	Sweden	73.1	0.2	90	92.3	42.9	21.4	91.1	52.9	82.5	87.8	90	80
21	11	Lithuania	73.0	0.9	60	49.9	92.9	55.9	85.7	59.0	78.6	87.8	80	80
22	12	Georgia	72.6	0.4	40	42.8	87.3	69.7	87.8	91.2	78.4	88.6	80	60
23	13	Iceland	72.4	0.3	90	84.2	72.9	32.9	91.2	59.1	76.0	87.9	70	60
24	14	Austria	72.4	0.6	90	75.5	51.0	23.5	76.3	80.5	79.5	87.8	90	70
26	15	Czech Republic	72.2	1.3	70	45.3	81.7	43.8	70.1	84.0	79.4	87.8	80	80
32	16	Norway	70.9	0.4	90	88.1	50.6	42.2	90.9	44.6	78.7	89.1	75	60
35	17	Belgium	69.9	0.7	80	74.2	44.8	14.8	89.9	72.7	79.5	87.8	85	70
41	18	Armenia	68.9	-0.5	30	26.7	86.5	81.3	83.1	78.5	77.0	85.5	70	70
42	19	Latvia	68.7	2.2	50	43.6	84.6	54.9	82.5	68.5	79.7	87.8	85	50
43	20	Macedonia	68.6	0.4	35	39.6	91.4	70.7	81.0	78.8	83.5	85.9	60	60
46	21	Cyprus	67.6	-1.4	70	64.0	79.7	36.2	79.7	70.2	78.8	82.8	65	50
49	22	Spain	67.2	-0.8	70	62.6	54.0	38.7	77.3	52.2	79.9	87.8	80	70
50	23	Poland	67.0	1.0	60	54.8	76.1	43.2	70.1	60.4	77.8	87.8	70	70
51	24	Hungary	67.0	-0.3	60	48.6	81.1	26.8	79.3	65.7	75.6	87.8	75	70
54	25	Albania	66.9	1.7	30	30.4	92.7	75.6	78.1	49.7	80.0	87.5	75	70
57	26	Slovak Republic	66.4	-2.3	50	41.8	80.2	56.0	67.0	53.6	78.1	87.8	80	70
58	27	Malta	66.4	-1.1	75	55.8	63.7	47.2	62.4	53.2	79.1	87.8	80	60
61	28	Bulgaria	65.7	0.7	30	35.2	91.2	64.5	73.5	80.2	79.6	87.8	55	60
62	29	Romania	65.5	0.4	40	37.7	87.0	59.2	71.0	65.2	77.1	87.8	80	50
64	30	Turkey	64.9	2.0	50	44.0	77.5	63.5	67.6	59.7	71.8	84.5	70	60

(continued on next page)

Table 3 heritage.org

Economic Freedom in European Countries (continued)

World Rank	Region Rank	Country	Overall Score	Change from 2013	Property Rights	Freedom from Corruption	Fiscal Freedom	Government Spending	Business Freedom	Labor Freedom	Monetary Freedom	Trade Freedom	Investment Freedom	Financial Freedom
68	31	Montenegro	63.6	1.0	40	37.8	92.5	42.6	77.6	68.6	78.6	83.1	65	50
69	32	Portugal	63.5	0.4	70	61.1	60.1	26.8	84.9	34.6	79.3	87.8	70	60
70	33	France	63.5	-0.6	80	69.9	48.4	5.6	79.9	51.8	76.1	82.8	70	70
74	34	Slovenia	62.7	1.0	60	61.0	58.9	22.6	85.4	51.0	80.3	87.8	70	50
86	35	Italy	60.9	0.3	50	38.5	55.5	25.6	75.5	52.5	78.9	87.8	85	60
87	36	Croatia	60.4	-0.9	40	41.1	69.4	45.8	61.4	39.4	79.2	87.4	80	60
95	37	Serbia	59.4	0.8	40	34.0	83.1	38.6	59.3	70.1	66.9	77.0	75	50
101	38	Bosnia and Herzegovina	58.4	1.1	20	33.9	82.9	27.4	55.5	62.4	80.1	86.9	75	60
110	39	Moldova	57.3	1.8	40	29.5	85.8	54.4	70.1	37.9	75.0	80.1	50	50
119	40	Greece	55.7	0.3	40	33.2	65.9	19.2	75.8	53.9	76.3	82.8	60	50
140	41	Russia	51.9	0.8	25	22.1	85.6	61.5	70.0	55.8	69.4	74.6	25	30
150	42	Belarus	50.1	2.1	20	24.6	89.2	61.2	73.4	77.7	33.9	81.4	30	10
155	43	Ukraine	49.3	3.0	30	21.9	79.1	37.5	59.8	49.8	78.7	86.2	20	30
N/A	N/A	Kosovo	N/A	N/A	30	28.6	92.7	73.0	58.1	71.3	72.7	N/A	65	N/A
N/A	N/A	Liechtenstein	N/A	N/A	N/A	N/A	N/A	N/A	N/A	N/A	N/A	90.0	85	80

Table 3 heritage.org

Sweden is a particularly interesting case, rising to 20th place in the *Index* despite extraordinarily high levels of per capita government spending. Unlike the troubled welfare states of Greece, Italy, and Portugal, the Swedish economy boasts highly efficient regulatory and legal regimes in addition to a high level of transparency and low corruption. These institutional assets strongly sustain productivity growth and promote resilience. In the 2014 *Index*, Sweden has recorded its highest economic freedom score ever.

Three Baltic nations—Estonia, Latvia, and Lithuania—continue to advance. All three countries have recorded consecutive years of score improvements, demonstrating high levels of economic resilience. Both Lithuania and Latvia have recorded their highest economic freedom scores ever in the 2014 *Index*.

SOUTH AND CENTRAL AMERICA/ CARIBBEAN: MIXED PROGRESS

The South and Central America/Caribbean region, which consists of 29 economies, is one of the world's most diverse, economically as well as politically.

Progress toward greater economic freedom has been made in more than half of the countries in the region. Seventeen countries recorded gains in economic freedom, while 12 had declines. The countries in the South and Central America/Caribbean region perform better than the world averages in four of the 10 components of economic freedom, including fiscal freedom and investment freedom. Corruption and a lack of protection for property rights are the major problem areas, reflecting long-standing issues of poor governance and weak rule of law.

South and Central America/Caribbean

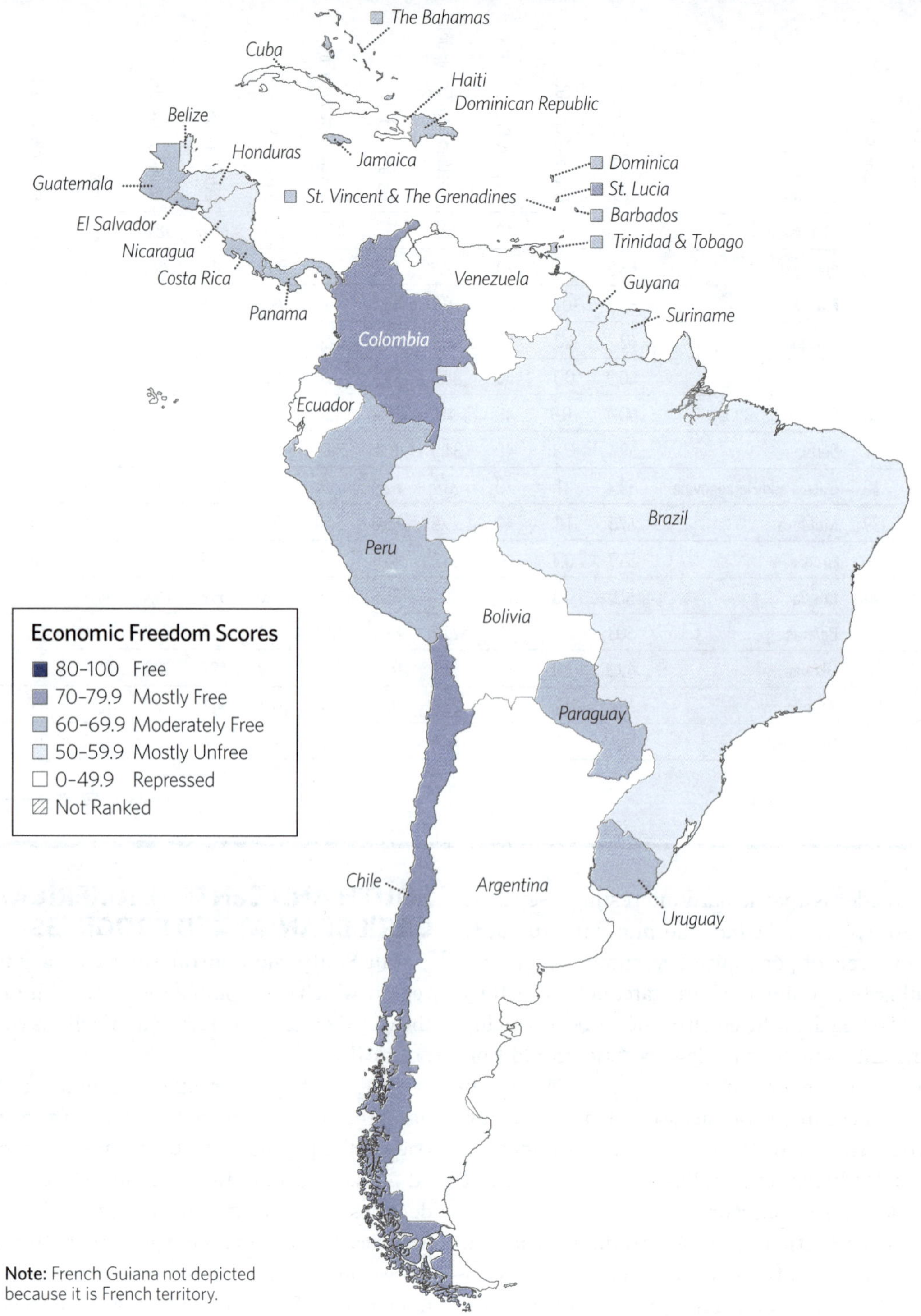

Note: French Guiana not depicted because it is French territory.

Source: Terry Miller, Anthony B. Kim, and Kim R. Holmes, *2014 Index of Economic Freedom* (Washington, D.C.: The Heritage Foundation and Dow Jones & Company, Inc., 2014), http://www.heritage.org/index.

Map 3 heritage.org

Economic Freedom in South and Central America/ Caribbean Countries

World Rank	Region Rank	Country	Overall Score	Change from 2013	Property Rights	Freedom from Corruption	Fiscal Freedom	Government Spending	Business Freedom	Labor Freedom	Monetary Freedom	Trade Freedom	Investment Freedom	Financial Freedom
7	1	Chile	78.7	-0.3	90	72.3	76.5	83.8	69.3	69.3	84.1	82.0	90	70
33	2	Saint Lucia	70.7	0.3	70	70.6	75.7	63.6	83.1	84.5	82.7	71.9	65	40
34	3	Colombia	70.7	1.1	50	33.2	80.6	74.9	85.2	80.5	78.8	78.8	75	70
36	4	The Bahamas	69.8	-0.3	70	66.6	97.3	84.1	70.7	81.5	75.1	52.2	30	70
38	5	Uruguay	69.3	-0.4	70	70.6	77.4	68.0	74.5	68.1	72.1	82.5	80	30
45	6	Barbados	68.3	-1.0	80	77.9	74.0	49.8	72.8	78.4	74.6	60.6	55	60
47	7	Peru	67.4	-0.8	40	34.0	79.1	89.1	70.6	61.4	83.3	87.0	70	60
52	8	Saint Vincent and the Grenadines	67.0	0.3	70	61.1	73.7	72.4	76.3	78.7	79.8	67.6	50	40
53	9	Costa Rica	66.9	-0.1	50	50.9	80.0	90.0	64.9	53.3	76.3	83.8	70	50
56	10	Jamaica	66.7	-0.1	40	33.0	77.2	69.4	84.6	75.6	77.3	75.1	85	50
59	11	El Salvador	66.2	-0.5	40	34.3	79.6	85.8	59.6	63.3	80.0	79.0	70	70
63	12	Dominica	65.2	1.3	60	53.5	72.9	61.7	75.0	70.7	85.8	72.7	70	30
71	13	Panama	63.4	0.9	30	34.0	84.3	78.7	73.0	39.4	75.1	74.2	75	70
73	14	Trinidad and Tobago	62.7	0.4	50	34.0	84.8	62.5	59.4	76.4	71.7	78.6	60	50
78	15	Paraguay	62.0	0.9	30	20.5	96.2	89.0	58.0	28.9	80.9	81.1	75	60
80	16	Dominican Republic	61.3	1.6	30	27.3	83.7	92.3	56.1	55.2	75.7	77.8	75	40
83	17	Guatemala	61.2	1.2	25	28.7	79.6	93.6	58.4	49.3	76.7	85.4	65	50
102	18	Nicaragua	58.4	1.8	15	24.1	78.6	80.0	52.6	60.3	72.8	85.4	65	50
112	19	Honduras	57.1	-1.3	30	23.7	84.9	79.8	55.4	26.5	75.1	75.4	60	60
114	20	Brazil	56.9	-0.8	50	37.9	68.8	54.1	53.8	49.8	69.9	69.3	55	60
115	21	Belize	56.7	-0.6	30	6.7	82.1	74.2	71.6	67.2	77.6	67.8	40	50
121	22	Guyana	55.7	1.9	30	24.4	68.4	71.8	64.3	72.6	78.1	72.0	45	30
130	23	Suriname	54.2	2.2	40	32.9	69.0	78.3	41.8	81.8	71.8	66.2	30	30
156	24	Haiti	48.9	0.8	10	16.9	80.3	66.3	33.3	68.5	73.6	70.4	40	30
158	25	Bolivia	48.4	0.5	10	28.1	87.1	62.5	53.4	29.9	70.0	77.6	15	50
159	26	Ecuador	48.0	1.1	20	26.0	79.8	41.8	52.8	52.0	66.1	71.8	30	40
166	27	Argentina	44.6	-2.1	15	29.5	63.5	49.9	53.9	44.9	60.0	68.9	30	30
175	28	Venezuela	36.3	0.2	5	16.5	75.3	51.8	43.4	33.7	49.7	62.7	5	20
177	29	Cuba	28.7	0.2	10	41.2	60.0	0.0	20.0	20.0	65.8	60.0	0	10

Table 4 heritage.org

Middle East/North Africa

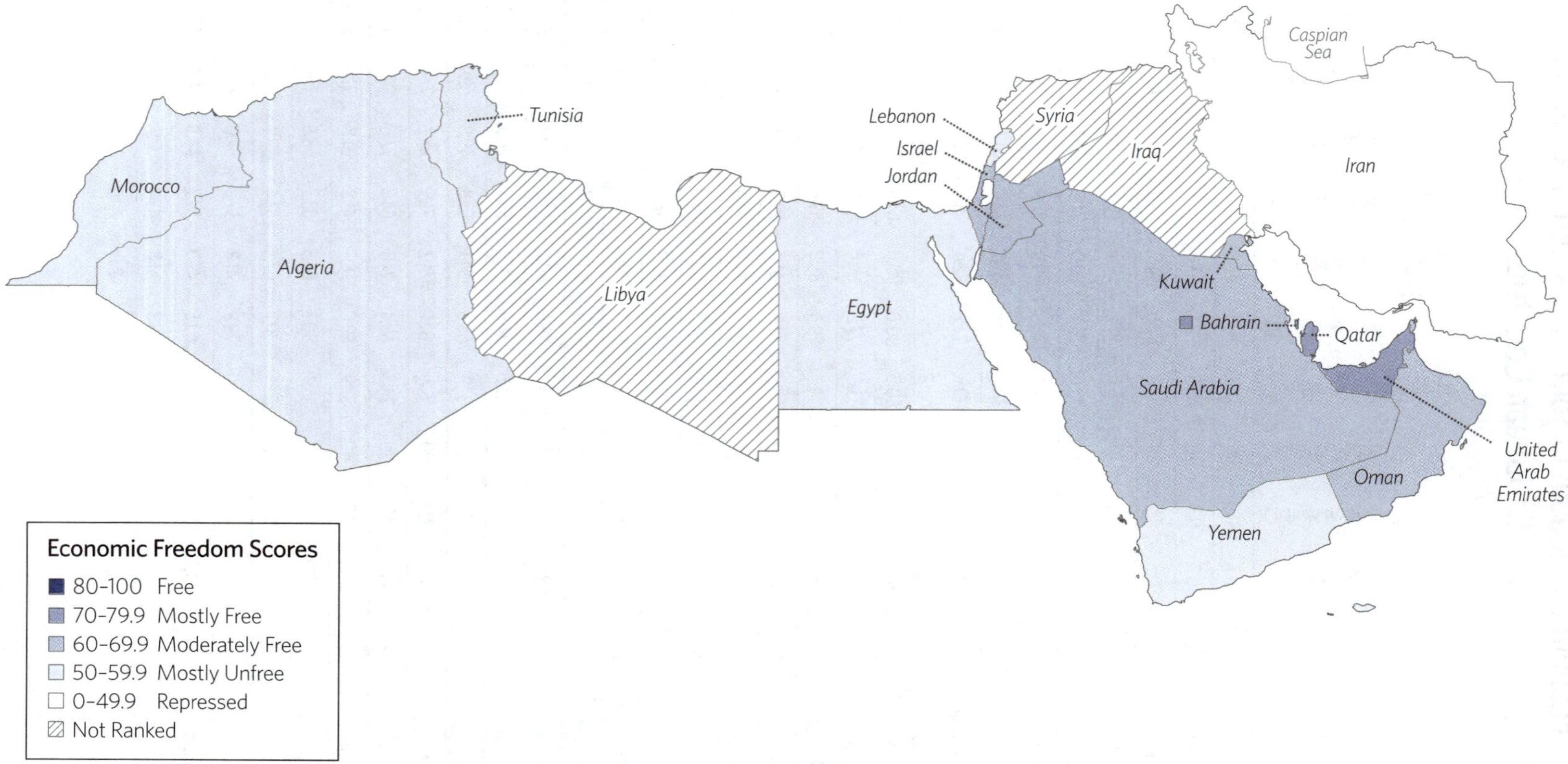

Source: Terry Miller, Anthony B. Kim, and Kim R. Holmes, *2014 Index of Economic Freedom* (Washington, D.C.: The Heritage Foundation and Dow Jones & Company, Inc., 2014), http://www.heritage.org/index.

Map 4 **heritage.org**

Economic Freedom in Middle East/North African Countries

World Rank	Region Rank	Country	Overall Score	Change from 2013	Property Rights	Freedom from Corruption	Fiscal Freedom	Government Spending	Business Freedom	Labor Freedom	Monetary Freedom	Trade Freedom	Investment Freedom	Financial Freedom
13	1	Bahrain	75.1	-0.4	60	49.4	99.9	71.4	76.3	82.0	78.4	78.6	75	80
28	2	United Arab Emirates	71.4	0.3	55	66.4	99.6	83.1	74.4	82.9	84.6	82.5	35	50
30	3	Qatar	71.2	-0.1	70	72.4	99.9	72.1	71.7	70.0	81.2	79.8	45	50
39	4	Jordan	69.2	-1.2	60	45.6	94.0	66.9	62.0	72.9	81.3	79.6	70	60
44	5	Israel	68.4	1.5	75	59.3	60.1	40.3	73.2	63.0	80.6	82.9	80	70
48	6	Oman	67.4	-0.7	50	48.2	98.5	56.0	68.3	75.5	73.6	78.7	65	60
76	7	Kuwait	62.3	-0.8	50	43.7	97.7	55.6	57.7	63.6	73.2	76.7	55	50
77	8	Saudi Arabia	62.2	1.6	40	43.7	99.7	63.1	67.3	75.8	68.7	74.0	40	50
96	9	Lebanon	59.4	-0.1	20	24.5	90.9	73.7	55.6	58.7	74.5	75.8	60	60
103	10	Morocco	58.3	-1.3	40	33.3	71.3	64.1	76.2	31.5	78.1	58.8	70	60
109	11	Tunisia	57.3	0.3	40	39.2	74.3	63.8	80.7	72.6	75.9	61.8	35	30
123	12	Yemen	55.5	-0.4	30	19.4	91.7	74.9	59.2	54.9	62.1	82.4	50	30
135	13	Egypt	52.9	-1.9	20	28.6	85.6	69.6	62.7	45.7	60.5	71.4	45	40
146	14	Algeria	50.8	1.2	30	28.7	80.5	51.0	66.3	48.3	67.8	60.8	45	30
173	15	Iran	40.3	-2.9	10	23.4	80.6	85.9	62.3	41.7	47.3	41.4	0	10
N/A	N/A	Iraq	N/A	N/A	N/A	13.7	95.5	40.3	56.9	73.4	70.0	N/A	N/A	N/A
N/A	N/A	Libya	N/A	N/A	10	18.3	95.0	0.0	50.1	77.9	66.9	N/A	5	20
N/A	N/A	Syria	N/A	N/A	10	23.3	N/A	N/A	60.4	55.1	N/A	N/A	0	20

Table 5 heritage.org

Chile has been rated consistently as one of the "mostly free" economies with economic freedom scores above 70. Achieving its highest economic freedom score ever in the 2014 *Index*, Colombia has become a "mostly free" economy for the first time. By sharp contrast, Cuba remains the least free economy in the region, and Argentina has plunged further to the ranks of the economically "mostly unfree."

MIDDLE EAST/NORTH AFRICA: AT A CRITICAL CROSSROADS

The Middle East/North Africa region, which consists of 18 countries, continues to undergo widespread turmoil, and many of its economies remain only "moderately free" or "mostly unfree."

Structural and institutional problems abound, and the regional unemployment rate, which averages more than 10 percent, is among the highest in the world and is most pronounced among younger members of the labor force. The region's troubles are complex, rooted in decades of authoritarianism that has kept power and resources monopolized in the hands of a few. The problems will not be solved simply by holding elections with more political parties or allowing freedom of expression. Hard institutional reforms that reduce the state's role in the economy and in people's lives are required. Leaders

Asia and the Pacific

Source: Terry Miller, Anthony B. Kim, and Kim R. Holmes, *2014 Index of Economic Freedom* (Washington, D.C.: The Heritage Foundation and Dow Jones & Company, Inc., 2014), http://www.heritage.org/index.

Map 5 heritage.org

Economic Freedom in Asia-Pacific Countries

World Rank	Region Rank	Country	Overall Score	Change from 2013	Property Rights	Freedom from Corruption	Fiscal Freedom	Government Spending	Business Freedom	Labor Freedom	Monetary Freedom	Trade Freedom	Investment Freedom	Financial Freedom
1	1	Hong Kong	90.1	0.8	90	82.3	93.0	89.7	98.9	95.5	82.0	90.0	90	90
2	2	Singapore	89.4	1.4	90	91.9	91.2	91.2	96.8	96.5	81.5	90.0	85	80
3	3	Australia	82.0	-0.6	90	87.7	64.2	62.6	94.6	79.2	80.5	86.4	85	90
5	4	New Zealand	81.2	-0.2	95	94.0	71.2	32.3	96.1	90.2	86.3	86.8	80	80
17	5	Taiwan	73.9	1.2	70	59.7	80.3	84.7	93.9	53.1	81.7	85.8	70	60
25	6	Japan	72.4	0.6	80	77.8	69.2	47.1	80.0	79.8	87.5	82.4	70	50
29	7	Macau	71.3	-0.4	60	49.7	71.4	91.7	60.0	55.0	79.8	90.0	85	70
31	8	South Korea	71.2	0.9	70	54.0	72.6	72.6	92.8	47.8	79.6	72.6	70	80
37	9	Malaysia	69.6	3.5	55	44.3	84.6	75.6	85.6	78.5	81.0	76.4	55	60
40	10	Brunei	69.0	N/A	40	53.3	90.2	66.1	68.2	96.5	74.2	81.8	70	50
67	11	Kazakhstan	63.7	0.7	30	25.7	92.9	85.0	74.4	86.7	74.4	78.2	40	50
72	12	Thailand	63.3	-0.8	45	33.6	79.7	83.6	71.4	61.6	68.6	75.0	45	70
81	13	Azerbaijan	61.3	1.6	20	22.7	88.1	64.8	73.5	77.9	78.8	77.2	60	50
84	14	Samoa	61.1	4.0	60	38.0	79.9	42.2	73.7	80.3	76.1	75.8	55	30
85	15	Kyrgyz Republic	61.1	1.5	20	19.2	94.6	60.2	74.2	83.8	73.7	75.2	60	50
89	16	The Philippines	60.1	1.9	30	26.1	79.2	92.3	59.9	49.7	78.0	75.5	60	50
90	17	Sri Lanka	60.0	-0.7	40	33.4	84.9	86.3	74.4	59.2	68.0	73.6	40	40
93	18	Vanuatu	59.5	2.9	40	33.5	97.3	81.7	54.8	56.8	82.7	48.0	60	40
97	19	Mongolia	58.9	-2.8	30	28.2	81.8	39.1	71.8	81.1	72.4	74.7	50	60
99	20	Fiji	58.7	1.5	25	20.0	82.3	76.2	64.9	73.1	75.2	70.2	50	50
100	21	Indonesia	58.5	1.6	30	28.0	83.4	89.8	54.8	47.8	76.4	74.8	40	60
104	22	Tonga	58.2	2.2	20	28.6	86.7	74.8	74.6	91.2	71.3	79.5	35	20
108	23	Cambodia	57.4	-1.1	30	18.7	90.8	88.4	36.6	50.2	77.9	71.0	60	50
116	24	Bhutan	56.7	1.7	60	58.8	82.9	57.2	59.4	83.6	65.8	49.4	20	30
120	25	India	55.7	0.5	50	31.5	79.4	77.8	37.7	74.0	65.5	65.6	35	40
126	26	Pakistan	55.2	0.1	30	22.7	80.6	88.3	69.4	47.3	68.5	64.8	40	40
131	27	Bangladesh	54.1	1.5	20	23.3	72.5	92.3	70.8	51.9	65.9	59.0	55	30
132	28	Papua New Guinea	53.9	0.3	20	20.2	66.7	75.4	57.0	73.7	75.5	85.1	35	30
137	29	China	52.5	0.6	20	35.0	69.9	82.9	49.7	61.9	73.3	71.8	30	30
139	30	Tajikistan	52.0	-1.4	20	19.4	92.3	78.1	58.4	45.5	67.7	73.2	25	40

(continued on next page)

Table 6 heritage.org

Economic Freedom in Asia-Pacific Countries (continued)

World Rank	Region Rank	Country	Overall Score	Change from 2013	Property Rights	Freedom from Corruption	Fiscal Freedom	Government Spending	Business Freedom	Labor Freedom	Monetary Freedom	Trade Freedom	Investment Freedom	Financial Freedom
144	31	Laos	51.2	1.1	15	18.6	86.6	86.7	60.7	54.9	75.5	58.6	35	20
145	32	Maldives	51.0	2.0	20	21.9	97.4	43.8	87.4	71.7	69.4	43.8	25	30
147	33	Vietnam	50.8	-0.2	15	26.9	77.0	71.4	62.0	68.3	63.6	78.7	15	30
149	34	Nepal	50.1	-0.3	30	21.3	85.9	89.6	58.5	43.8	76.3	61.0	5	30
153	35	Micronesia	49.8	-0.3	30	30.0	97.5	0.0	51.7	77.9	75.2	81.0	25	30
162	36	Burma	46.5	7.3	10	11.6	86.9	89.2	28.3	75.7	64.8	73.6	15	10
163	37	Uzbekistan	46.5	0.5	15	13.4	90.3	70.4	75.7	60.8	63.1	66.1	0	10
164	38	Kiribati	46.3	0.4	30	29.2	71.4	0.0	57.0	83.6	81.3	55.4	25	30
165	39	Solomon Islands	46.2	1.2	30	25.0	61.4	21.3	65.2	65.2	75.4	73.0	15	30
170	40	Timor-Leste	43.2	-0.5	20	25.4	64.7	0.0	45.4	79.2	68.3	64.4	45	20
171	41	Turkmenistan	42.2	-0.4	5	13.4	95.2	93.0	30.0	30.0	65.9	79.2	0	10
178	42	North Korea	1.0	-0.5	5	5.0	0.0	0.0	0.0	0.0	0.0	0.0	0	0
N/A	N/A	Afghanistan	N/A	N/A	N/A	10.0	91.2	84.2	63.1	75.0	74.3	N/A	65	N/A

Table 6 heritage.org

have already fallen, yet regimes and institutions remain and craftily guard their power.

Scores for most of the countries in the region are concentrated between 50 and 70. Saudi Arabia and Israel have recorded two of the largest score gains. Progress made in those two countries has been underpinned by efforts to strengthen the business climate, boost investment, and foster the emergence of a more vibrant private sector. The United Arab Emirates has advanced its economic freedom for five consecutive years. In the 2014 *Index*, the UAE has advanced steadily into the ranks of the "mostly free" economies, with progress due in large part to the government's consistent commitment to economic reforms that have encouraged a dynamically evolving private sector.

Bahrain, ranked 13th globally with an economic freedom score of 75.1, is the only Middle Eastern country among the world's 20 freest economies. It has been undertaking a challenging transition to greater openness and transparency, more visibly since early 2011. Enhancing the foundations of economic freedom through improvements in property rights and corruption will be critical to ensuring success.

Qatar continues as the other "mostly free" economy in the region. While very different politically, five "moderately free" economies, including Jordan, Israel, Oman, Kuwait, and Saudi Arabia, share a common commitment to economic freedom that is significantly greater than that of the remaining countries in the region.

ASIA–PACIFIC: THE MOST IMPROVED REGION

The Asia–Pacific region contains over half of the world's population: one-third in China and nearly another third in India.

Sub-Saharan Africa

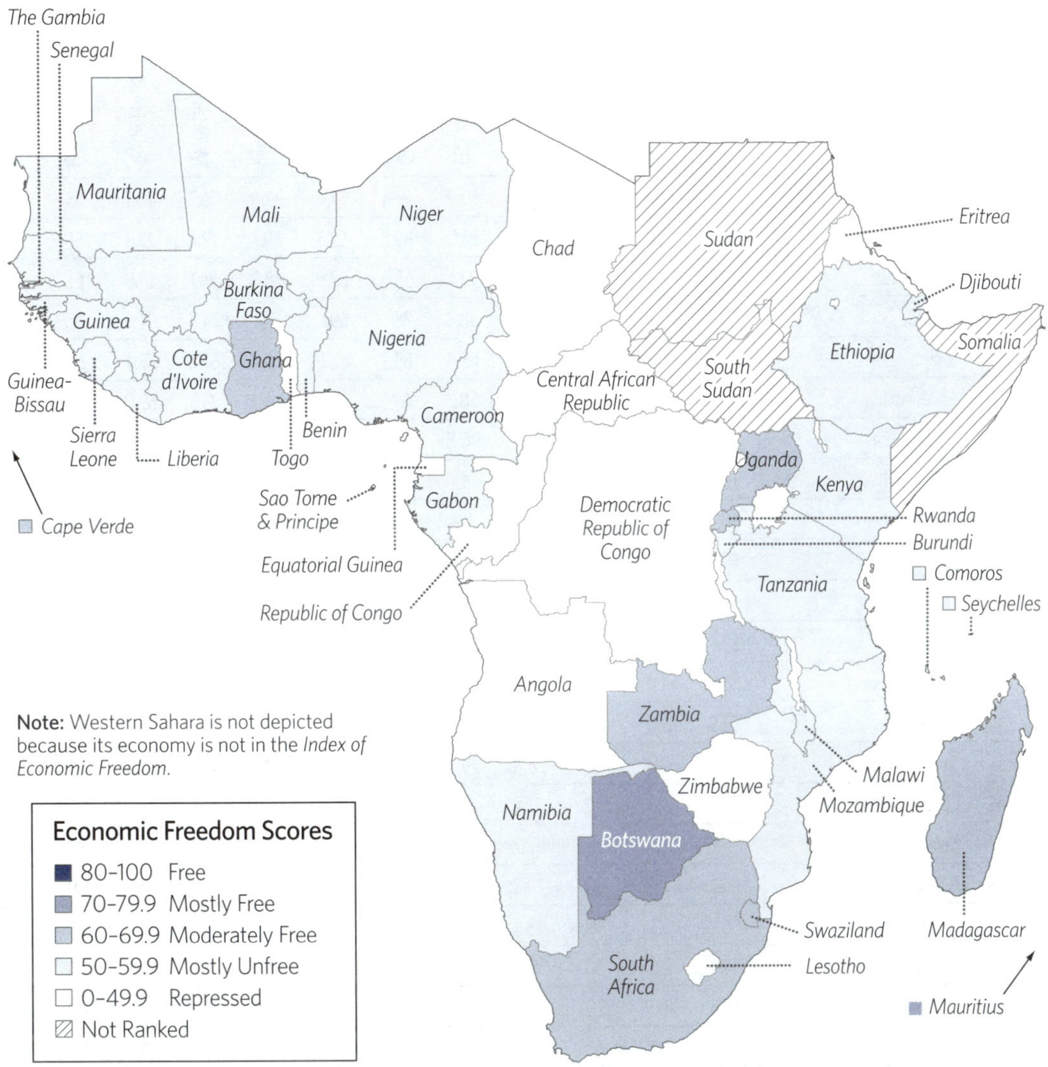

Note: Western Sahara is not depicted because its economy is not in the *Index of Economic Freedom*.

Source: Terry Miller, Anthony B. Kim, and Kim R. Holmes, *2014 Index of Economic Freedom* (Washington, D.C.: The Heritage Foundation and Dow Jones & Company, Inc., 2014), http://www.heritage.org/index.

Map 6 heritage.org

The Asia–Pacific region is distinguished by the extraordinary disparity in levels of economic freedom among its economies. Four of the world's 10 freest economies—Hong Kong, Singapore, Australia, and New Zealand—are in this region, yet most of the other countries remain "mostly unfree." Countries such as Turkmenistan and Burma have economies that are "repressed." North Korea, which continues to reject any form of free-market activity, remains the least free economy in both the region and the world.

Leading the world in three of the 10 economic freedoms, Hong Kong once again is the freest economy overall in the 2014 *Index*. With the emergence of a more dynamic and competitive financial sector, Singapore continues to boost its productivity through its openness to global trade and investment and has maintained its hold on

Economic Freedom in Sub-Saharan Africa Countries

World Rank	Region Rank	Country	Overall Score	Change from 2013	Property Rights	Freedom from Corruption	Fiscal Freedom	Government Spending	Business Freedom	Labor Freedom	Monetary Freedom	Trade Freedom	Investment Freedom	Financial Freedom
8	1	Mauritius	76.5	-0.4	65	53.4	92.2	81.8	74.4	78.0	76.7	76.1	55	60
27	2	Botswana	72.0	1.4	70	61.2	81.0	69.8	68.5	69.7	72.4	77.8	55	50
60	3	Cape Verde	66.1	2.4	70	54.9	77.4	68.6	63.8	48.0	79.1	81.5	65	40
65	4	Rwanda	64.7	0.6	30	46.9	80.3	78.2	69.6	84.1	74.8	84.6	60	50
66	5	Ghana	64.2	2.9	50	40.4	85.4	83.3	62.6	60.2	65.8	75.4	60	40
75	6	South Africa	62.5	0.7	50	41.6	68.7	69.1	74.5	54.4	75.3	65.0	65	50
79	7	Madagascar	61.7	-0.3	40	27.3	90.8	92.3	62.8	43.9	77.6	82.9	50	40
82	8	Swaziland	61.2	4.0	40	31.6	74.7	70.9	64.2	71.7	72.3	67.8	60	40
88	9	Zambia	60.4	1.7	30	31.3	71.8	82.9	74.9	50.1	68.0	61.0	55	40
91	10	Uganda	59.9	-1.2	30	23.8	79.1	87.3	45.1	87.4	71.0	76.8	60	50
92	11	The Gambia	59.5	0.7	30	31.7	79.0	79.8	57.4	65.8	71.3	71.4	50	50
94	12	Namibia	59.4	-0.9	30	44.2	66.9	58.8	64.4	81.9	75.0	72.8	50	50
98	13	Burkina Faso	58.9	-1.0	30	31.3	83.0	82.3	60.7	55.0	78.8	60.0	70	50
105	14	Gabon	57.8	0.0	40	29.1	74.5	81.7	58.9	63.0	75.1	33.4	50	30
106	15	Tanzania	57.8	-0.1	30	28.8	79.7	78.3	47.0	61.1	66.0	54.8	65	50
107	16	Côte d'Ivoire	57.7	3.6	30	22.1	79.1	79.8	55.1	59.0	80.6	73.2	55	40
111	17	Kenya	57.1	1.2	30	21.0	78.0	74.6	55.8	64.0	74.9	72.7	50	50
113	18	Benin	57.1	-0.5	30	29.5	68.3	86.1	51.0	50.5	75.4	73.2	60	40
117	19	Seychelles	56.2	1.3	50	48.5	76.8	61.8	67.6	68.5	75.1	65.6	55	40
118	20	Djibouti	55.9	2.0	30	30.9	80.6	62.8	42.7	65.1	77.2	75.5	45	50
122	21	Mali	55.5	-0.9	20	27.7	69.8	81.7	48.0	63.2	76.7	63.8	40	40
124	22	Malawi	55.4	0.1	45	31.9	78.0	63.0	38.9	60.3	64.1	61.2	50	40
125	23	Senegal	55.4	-0.1	40	29.5	65.1	75.4	47.5	41.5	81.8	69.0	50	40
127	24	Niger	55.1	1.2	30	26.0	76.8	88.4	35.2	45.4	88.3	61.2	35	50
128	25	Mozambique	55.0	0.0	30	26.2	75.7	64.6	65.2	36.7	80.8	64.1	40	20

(continued on next page)

second place in the rankings, narrowing the gap slightly with Hong Kong. Australia and New Zealand continue to set the standard for clean, corruption-free government and benefit significantly from their transparent and efficient business environments and open-market policies.

India and China remain "mostly unfree." These two countries' high economic growth has not been deeply rooted in policies that promote economic freedom. The foundations for long-term economic development continue to be fragile in the absence of effectively functioning legal frameworks. Progress with market-oriented reforms has been uneven and has often backtracked at the urging of those with a political interest in maintaining the status quo.

Economic Freedom in Sub-Saharan Africa Countries (continued)

World Rank	Region Rank	Country	Overall Score	Change from 2013	Property Rights	Freedom from Corruption	Fiscal Freedom	Government Spending	Business Freedom	Labor Freedom	Monetary Freedom	Trade Freedom	Investment Freedom	Financial Freedom
129	26	Nigeria	54.3	-0.8	30	22.7	85.0	74.5	48.0	66.4	73.1	71.8	60	30
133	27	Guinea	53.5	2.3	20	19.2	69.3	86.2	51.8	73.4	64.1	72.7	35	30
134	28	Mauritania	53.2	0.9	25	23.9	81.7	75.8	38.0	53.1	75.5	61.4	30	30
136	29	Cameroon	52.6	0.3	30	21.9	71.7	86.0	45.0	56.1	69.4	70.2	55	20
138	30	Liberia	52.4	3.1	30	33.8	83.6	70.5	62.3	47.0	72.9	64.2	20	20
141	31	Burundi	51.4	2.4	20	15.9	73.5	51.9	59.8	63.1	68.2	62.8	35	30
142	32	Comoros	51.4	3.9	30	22.1	64.5	85.3	49.4	50.1	74.5	68.6	50	40
143	33	Guinea-Bissau	51.3	0.2	20	20.2	89.0	86.6	40.5	61.4	74.4	75.3	50	30
148	34	Sierra Leone	50.5	2.2	15	24.6	80.7	85.7	55.3	28.7	70.2	70.1	40	40
151	35	Ethiopia	50.0	0.6	30	27.0	77.5	89.9	57.8	54.7	59.0	51.8	50	30
152	36	Togo	49.9	1.1	30	23.8	69.7	82.4	43.3	42.8	79.3	55.2	50	40
154	37	Lesotho	49.5	1.6	40	37.1	67.4	0.0	54.0	62.4	75.5	53.8	35	30
157	38	São Tomé and Príncipe	48.8	0.8	20	32.5	86.9	27.9	52.6	44.7	68.3	55.6	20	30
160	39	Angola	47.7	0.4	15	17.7	87.7	55.3	47.5	40.1	63.6	63.0	20	20
161	40	Central African Republic	46.7	-3.7	10	20.6	65.1	92.6	33.9	40.4	72.5	69.1	0	20
167	41	Chad	44.5	-0.7	20	15.9	46.2	80.0	24.9	43.3	69.8	54.2	5	10
168	42	Equatorial Guinea	44.4	2.1	10	16.6	75.5	62.6	43.4	41.5	75.4	N/A	N/A	N/A
169	43	Congo, Rep. of	43.7	0.2	10	20.6	67.5	79.6	35.1	47.0	72.0	55.6	15	N/A
172	44	Congo, Dem. Rep. of	40.6	1.0	10	17.6	69.4	74.6	30.0	38.5	63.0	63.0	20	20
174	45	Eritrea	38.5	2.2	10	22.9	57.0	66.1	18.6	63.6	57.6	69.1	0	20
176	46	Zimbabwe	35.5	6.9	10	19.3	63.3	64.0	34.5	22.2	73.0	54.2	5	10
N/A	N/A	Somalia	N/A	N/A	N/A	5.0	N/A	N/A	N/A	N/A	N/A	N/A	N/A	N/A
N/A	N/A	Sudan	N/A	N/A	N/A	9.8	85.1	90.3	54.5	49.1	55.8	55.6	15	N/A

Table 7 heritage.org

SUB-SAHARAN AFRICA: SLOW BUT CONTINUING PROGRESS

Africa's overall level of economic freedom is weaker than that of any other region. However, the 2014 *Index* has identified encouraging developments. No other region has made greater strides in economic freedom than Sub-Saharan Africa over the past two years. With an average score gain of 0.9 point that reflects a net gain of economic freedom in 20 countries, the Sub-Saharan Africa region is the second most improved region in the 2014 *Index*.

Following Mauritius, which continues to be one of the top 10 freest economies, Botswana remains the region's second freest economy, followed by Cape Verde and Rwanda. Securing its status as one of the world's "moderately free" economies, Cape Verde, a small island nation, has registered an impressive score gain of more than two points over the past year. Reforms in these countries have supported economic expansion and a gradual reduction in poverty. The positive economic results achieved through advancing economic freedom have created valuable momentum for additional institutional reforms that are needed to ensure long-term economic development. Regrettably, economic freedom in the region's largest economy, South Africa, has declined over the past decade, dimming hopes for a more prosperous and stable future on the African continent's southern tip.

Overall, Africa's competitiveness has improved in specific areas, with many countries ensuring more sustainable fiscal policies, better-managed inflation, and more efficient markets. However, many African countries are low in the rankings: Of the 20 lowest-ranked economies, 13 are from Africa. Looking forward, African economies must continue to develop economic environments that are based on productivity enhancements. This means keeping a clear focus on strengthening the institutional, physical, and human capital prerequisites for a strong and competitive private sector.

THE *INDEX* AT 20: RENEWED COMMITMENT TO ADVANCING FREEDOM

As documented in this chapter, every region includes positive examples of countries that have chosen freedom and reaped the rewards for their citizens. As shown in the *Index* over the past 20 years, economic freedom is the indispensable link between economic potential and prosperous outcomes. No other system comes close in terms of providing for broad-based economic growth and progress. Those who are looking for solutions rather than excuses will find in this *Index* the economic policies and concrete examples that can promote entrepreneurship and long-term economic growth irrespective of history, resources, or level of development.

A recurring theme of human history has been resilience and revival. As Friedrich A. Hayek once observed, "If old truths are to retain their hold on men's minds, they must be restated in the language and concepts of successive generations." As we celebrate the 20th edition of the *Index of Economic Freedom*, it is time to renew our commitment to measuring, explaining, and fostering economic freedom with even greater clarity and conviction so that new generations can understand and benefit from its proven principles.

Chapter 2

Advancing Freedom: The Path to Greater Development and Progress

Anthony B. Kim

The 20th edition of the *Index of Economic Freedom* shows economic freedom once again on the rise, reaching the highest point in the *Index*'s 20-year history. Behind this record are stories of human progress and the achievements of countries and their citizens—literally billions of people around the world whose lives have measurably improved. There are also stories of backsliding, regression, and even failure.

As previous editions of the *Index* have documented, the link between economic freedom and long-term development is clear and strong. Countries that allow their citizens more economic freedom reach higher incomes and better standards of life. People in economically free societies live longer. They have better health. They are able to be better stewards of the environment, and they push forward the frontiers of human achievement in science and technology through greater innovation.

With the perspective of 20 years, it is apparent that despite ups and downs, the principles and lessons of economic freedom have been widely understood, accepted, and implemented in practice by a significant number of countries around the globe. Their progress is seen in the score changes. The poorer performing countries, by contrast, have tried only some of the ideas, adulterated others, or even, in a few cases, rejected them outright.

The negative consequences are readily apparent in countries falling in the rankings. The *Index* provides compelling evidence that economic prosperity and economic freedom go hand in hand. Lasting prosperity cannot exist in the absence of economic freedom.

To be sure, there have been setbacks for economic freedom over the past two decades. (See Chart 1.) Some of them were quite severe as in the aftermaths of the 1997 Asian financial crisis and the 2008 global financial turmoil.

Looking back, however, the crises have served as critical tests of countries' commitments to preserving and advancing economic freedom. The political and policy choices that emerged from the crises and in subsequent years have led

Improving or Declining Economic Freedom

Share of Countries in the *Index of Economic Freedom* Whose Scores Improved or Declined

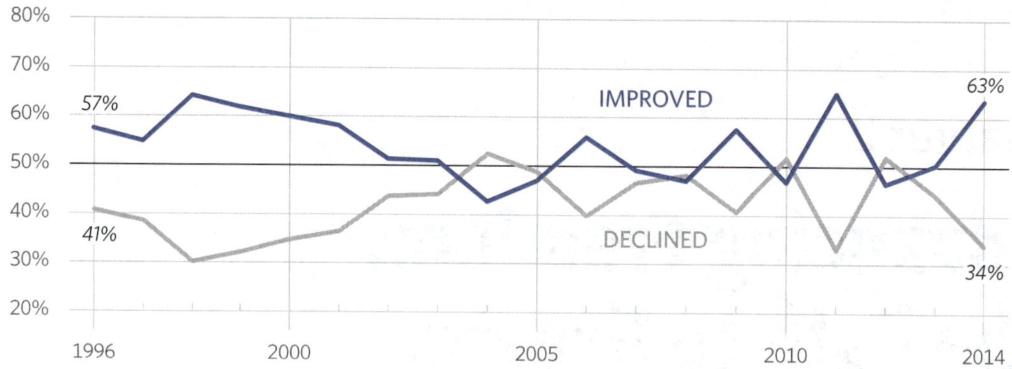

Source: Terry Miller, Anthony B. Kim, and Kim R. Holmes, *2014 Index of Economic Freedom* (Washington, D.C.: The Heritage Foundation and Dow Jones & Company, Inc., 2014), http://www.heritage.org/index.

Chart 1 heritage.org

to diverging trends of economic freedom with far-reaching economic consequences for those who have chosen different paths. Countries that have acknowledged the limits of government and continued their commitment to sustaining economic freedom have reaped tangible rewards of swift economic rebound and renewed dynamism. By contrast, those that have relinquished economic freedom with short-sighted interventionist and populist policies have prolonged the crises and fallen into the trap of economic stagnation and greater uncertainty.

These real examples of the consequences of the rise and fall of economic freedom in countries around the globe demonstrate unmistakably that economic prosperity is not a national birthright: Rich economies can fall into self-inflicted stagnation all too quickly, while long-suffering underdeveloped nations can ascend from poverty to economic dynamism in a matter of years.

As the *Index* has documented over the past two decades, the most critical variable in sustaining the wealth of nations and the most effective means to eliminating poverty is economic freedom.

The findings of the 2014 *Index* once again evince the strongly positive link between advancing economic freedom and achieving greater prosperity. Chart 2 shows the most basic benefit of economic freedom, confirmed now with data covering 20 years: the strong relationship between economic freedom and levels of per capita income. For countries that achieve scores that reflect even moderate levels of economic freedom (60 or above), the relationship between economic freedom and per capita GDP is highly significant.

Greater levels of economic freedom have had a major positive impact on poverty levels over the past decade. Poverty intensity, as measured by the United Nations Development Programme (UNDP) Multidimensional Poverty Index that assesses the nature and intensity of deprivation at the individual level in education, health, and standard of living, is much lower on average in countries with higher levels of economic freedom. The intensity of poverty in countries whose economies are considered mostly free or moderately free is only about one-fourth the level in countries that are rated less free.

TWENTY YEARS OF ADVANCING ECONOMIC FREEDOM

By a great many measures, the past 20 years during which the *Index* has been charting the advance of economic freedom have been the

Economic Freedom, Standard of Living, and Poverty

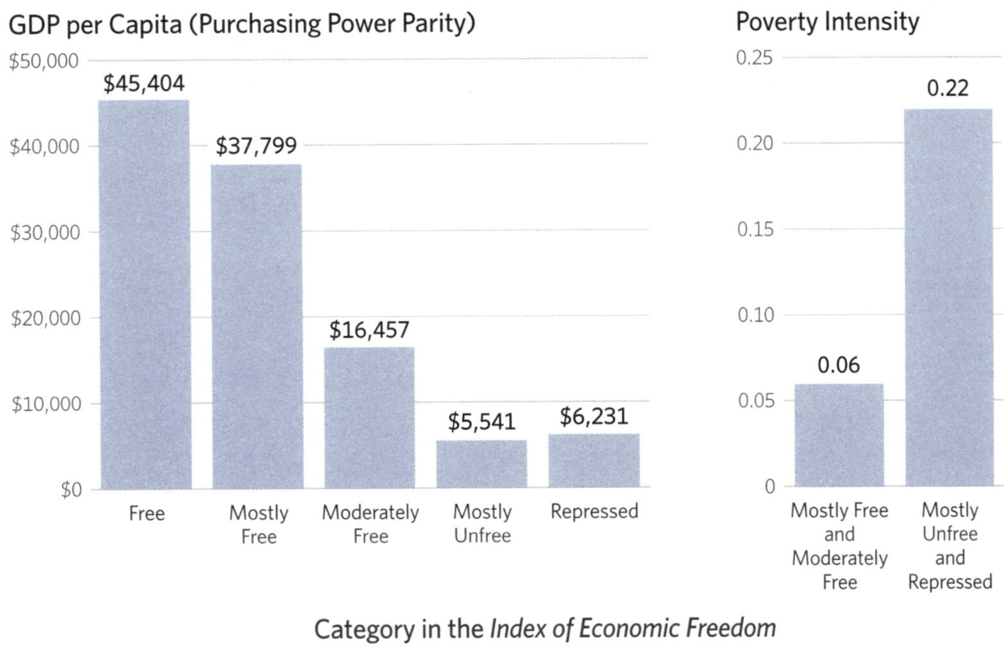

Sources: Terry Miller, Anthony B. Kim, and Kim R. Holmes, *2014 Index of Economic Freedom* (Washington, D.C.: The Heritage Foundation and Dow Jones & Company, Inc., 2014), http://www.heritage.org/index; International Monetary Fund, World Economic Outlook Databases, http://www.imf.org/external/ns/cs.aspx?id=28 (accessed November 13, 2013); and United Nations, Human Development Programme, "Human Development Report 2013," http://hdr.undp.org/en/reports/global/hdr2013/ (accessed November 13, 2013).

Chart 2 heritage.org

most prosperous in the history of humankind. More people are living better lives than ever before. Some, unfortunately, are not. As *Index* editor Terry Miller pointed out in these pages in 2009, it is a human tragedy—an appalling, avoidable human tragedy—that not all of the world's people have participated in our era's explosion of prosperity.[1]

Since 1995, when the *Index* started documenting economic policies that promote broader economic growth and greater well-being, we have learned that:[2]

- Those countries that practice some version of free-market capitalism, with economies open to global trade and investment, do better than those that are protectionist or that shun economic linkages with others.
- Competition promotes greater productivity and a more efficient allocation of resources than central planning.
- Private ownership and the protection of individuals and enterprises by the rule of law encourage effort and initiative more than do collectivism and socialism.
- Governments that dominate their countries' economies impoverish their citizens through economic stagnation.

The free-market system that is rooted in economic freedom has fueled unprecedented economic growth around the world. As Chart 3 illustrates, over the past two decades in which the global economy has moved toward greater economic freedom, becoming "moderately free" overall, the world economy achieved real GDP expansion by around 70 percent, lifting hundreds of millions of people out of poverty.

As Economic Freedom Rises, Global Economy Expands and Poverty Declines

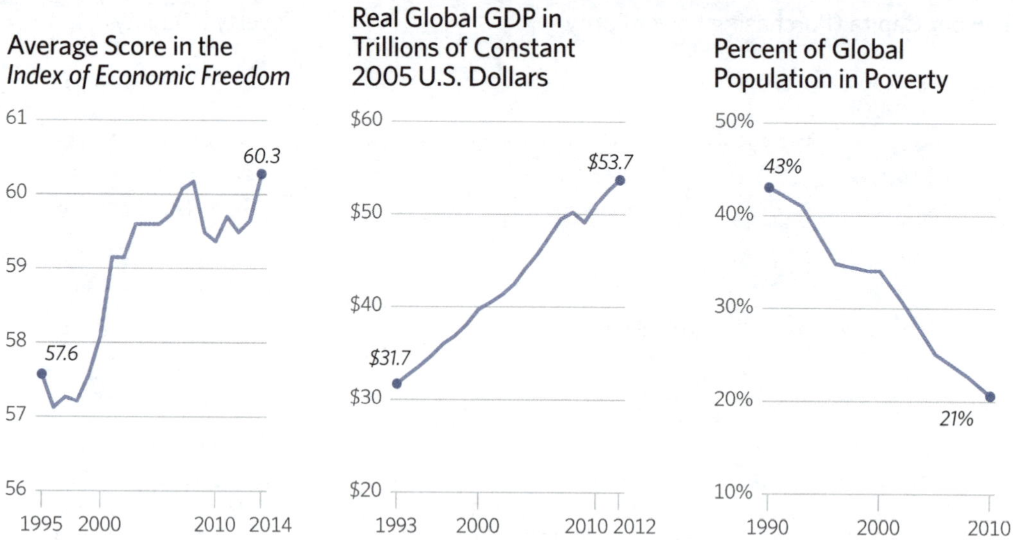

Sources: Terry Miller, Anthony B. Kim, and Kim R. Holmes, *2014 Index of Economic Freedom* (Washington, D.C.: The Heritage Foundation and Dow Jones & Company, Inc., 2014), http://www.heritage.org/index; The World Bank, World Development Indicators Online, http://databank.worldbank.org/data/views/variableSelection/selectvariables.aspx?source=world-development-indicators (accessed November 13, 2013); and The World Bank, PovcalNet, http://iresearch.worldbank.org/PovcalNet/index.htm?1 (accessed November 13, 2013). Some figures have been interpolated.

Chart 3 heritage.org

With global economic freedom rising over the past two decades, the world has recorded significant economic growth, and the global poverty rate has been cut in half. Opening the gates of prosperity to ever more people around the world, economic freedom has made the world a profoundly better place.

THE IMPORTANCE OF GROWING ECONOMIC FREEDOM

Any discussion about advancing economic freedom is essentially a story of the empowerment of people. Strengthening and expanding freedom improves each individual's chance to achieve his or her goals and own and enjoy the value of what he or she creates. Amartya Sen, a Nobel laureate economist who has made considerable contributions to development economics, once noted that "[d]evelopment consists of the removal of various types of unfreedoms that leave people with little choice and little opportunity for exercising their reasoned agency."[3] People crave liberation from poverty, and they hunger for the dignity of free will. By reducing barriers to these fundamentals, the forces of economic freedom create a framework in which people can fulfill their dreams of success.

In this vein, one of the most important goals of economic policy in almost every country in the world is to increase the rate of economic growth. Since the *Index of Economic Freedom* is primarily a measure of the economic policy environment in various countries, the 20-year history of the *Index* and its database have a lot to say about what really drives economic growth and related human progress in different aspects. There is strong support within the global database for the idea that improvements in economic freedom are an important determinant of rates of growth. Key drivers of this economic growth and poverty reduction are the high levels of flexibility and resilience that come with economic freedom.

More specifically, as documented in the previous editions of the *Index* and supported by

Advancing Economic Freedom Leads to Higher Economic Growth

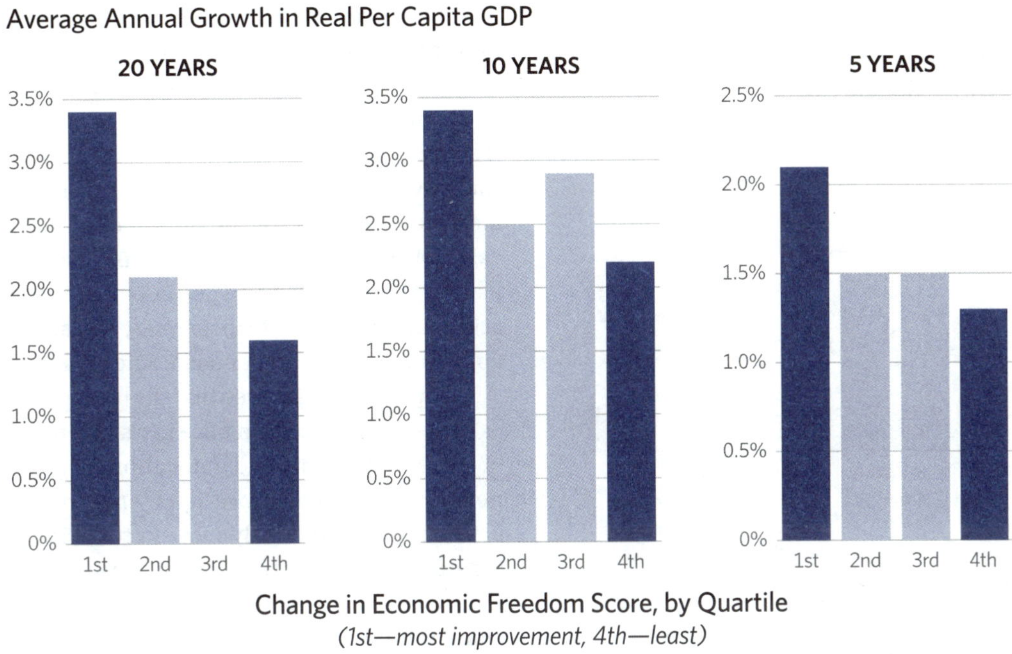

Sources: Terry Miller, Anthony B. Kim, and Kim R. Holmes, *2014 Index of Economic Freedom* (Washington, D.C.: The Heritage Foundation and Dow Jones & Company, Inc., 2014), http://www.heritage.org/index; and The World Bank, World Development Indicators Online, http://databank.worldbank.org/data/views/variableSelection/selectvariables.aspx?source=world-development-indicators (accessed November 13, 2013). Changes in economic freedom score have been calculated as the annual compound growth rate.

Chart 4 heritage.org

volumes of academic research, vibrant and lasting economic growth results when governments implement policies that enhance economic freedom and empower individuals with greater choice and more opportunities. In fact, the advancement of economic freedom is the most straightforward path to dynamic growth and true progress for the greatest number of people.

As Chart 4 demonstrates, there is a robust relationship between improving economic freedom and achieving higher per capita economic growth. Whether long-term (20 years), medium-term (10 years), or short-term (5 years), the relationship between changes in economic freedom and changes in economic growth is consistently positive.

Undeniably, countries moving toward greater economic freedom tend to achieve higher rates of growth in per capita GDP over time. In all of the three specific periods examined in this 20-year *Index* database, the average annual per capita economic growth rates of countries that have grown economic freedom most are at least 50 percent higher than those of countries where freedom has stagnated or eroded.

Even better, advancing economic freedom produces dynamic and inclusive growth for ordinary people in a society. Economic freedom, cultivated by the rule of law, limited government, regulatory efficiency, and open markets, has proven to be critical to generating the broader-based economic growth that creates opportunities in all sectors of society.

ECONOMIC FREEDOM: THE REAL AGENT OF REVOLUTION

As emphasized in the *Index* and confirmed by its findings, sustaining vibrant growth and broader-based economic expansion requires that countries be committed to putting into practice three fundamental principles of economic freedom: empowerment of the individual, non-discrimination, and open competition.

In pursuing these principles of economic freedom and the policies necessary to realize them over the past 20 years, many governments have facilitated the free flow of goods and services, improved the ease of doing business, established monetary stability, and cut taxes, all while accentuating greater transparency and accountability under more dependable rule of law.

It is encouraging to see that the powerful forces of economic freedom have fostered the spirit of entrepreneurship and innovation that creates new products and more jobs, spreading the benefits of economic dynamism to an increasing number of countries around the globe over the past 20 years. As Chart 5 summarizes, more countries are classified as at least "moderately free," with scores of above 60, today than in the 1995 *Index*.

The advancement of global economic freedom to its highest level ever in the 2014 *Index*,

Share of Countries Scoring 60 or Higher in the *Index*

Countries Categorized as Free, Mostly Free, or Moderately Free

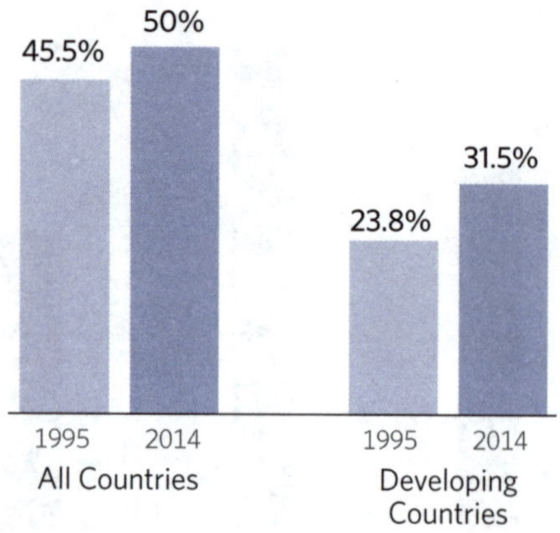

Source: Terry Miller, Anthony B. Kim, and Kim R. Holmes, *2014 Index of Economic Freedom* (Washington, D.C.: The Heritage Foundation and Dow Jones & Company, Inc., 2014), http://www.heritage.org/index.

Chart 5 heritage.org

Countries with Major Category Changes

	Score in First Year in *Index*		Score in *2014 Index*		Change
Azerbaijan	30.0	Repressed	61.3	Moderately Free	+31.3
Georgia	44.1	Repressed	72.6	Mostly Free	+28.5
Armenia	42.2	Repressed	68.9	Moderately Free	+26.7
Rwanda	38.3	Repressed	64.7	Moderately Free	+26.4
Lithuania	49.7	Repressed	73.0	Mostly Free	+23.3
Romania	42.9	Repressed	65.5	Moderately Free	+22.6
Kazakhstan	41.7	Repressed	63.7	Moderately Free	+22.0
Albania	49.7	Repressed	66.9	Moderately Free	+17.2
Cape Verde	49.7	Repressed	66.1	Moderately Free	+16.4
Croatia	48.0	Repressed	60.4	Moderately Free	+12.4
Ecuador	57.7	Mostly Unfree	48.0	Repressed	-9.7
Argentina	68.0	Moderately Free	44.6	Repressed	-23.4
Venzuela	59.8	Mostly Unfree	36.3	Repressed	-23.5

Source: Terry Miller, Anthony B. Kim, and Kim R. Holmes, *2014 Index of Economic Freedom* (Washington, D.C.: The Heritage Foundation and Dow Jones & Company, Inc., 2014), http://www.heritage.org/index.

Chart 6 heritage.org

with a greater number of countries rated at least "moderately free," is particularly welcome given that the notable upsurge has been driven mainly by developing and emerging economies around the world, which now account for the first time in the modern era for about half of the global economy's output.[4]

Globally, 124 countries have improved their economic freedom scores relative to the first year in which they were rated in the *Index*, while 52 countries have recorded score declines.

Most notably, 10 developing countries across the globe that were rated as "repressed" economies in the first years they were graded in the *Index* almost 20 years ago have successfully leaped forward into the ranks of the "moderately free" or "mostly free." (See Chart 6.)

This is quite a geographically and economically diverse group, encompassing African countries, Eastern European countries, and members of the former Soviet Union. Over the past two decades, these 10 developing economies as a group have recorded an average annual economic growth rate of 5 percent, which is 1.2 percentage points higher than the average of all other countries.

On the other end of the scale, three countries—Argentina, Ecuador, and Venezuela—have dropped into the ranks of the "repressed" over the past two decades. (See Chart 6.) These economies were rated more highly in the first years they were graded in the *Index* but since then have steadily lost economic freedom. These three have recorded growth rates that, on average, lag almost two percentage points behind those that have graduated from "repressed" status.

Improving Economic Freedom Means Greater Human Development

Average Annual Growth in Human Development Index, 2000–2012

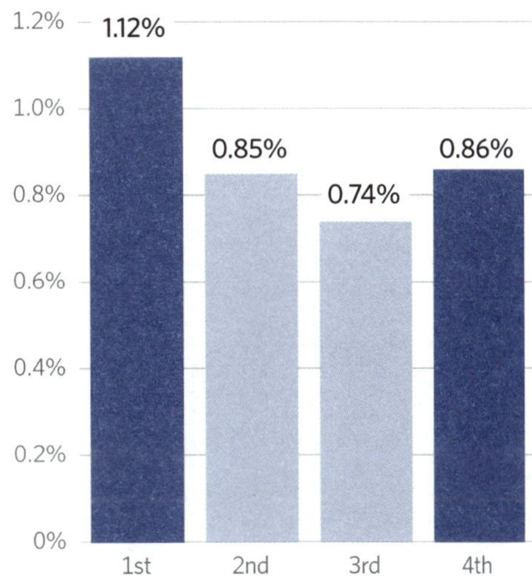

Change in Economic Freedom Score, by Quartile

(1st—most improvement, 4th—least)

Sources: Terry Miller, Anthony B. Kim, and Kim R. Holmes, *2014 Index of Economic Freedom* (Washington, D.C.: The Heritage Foundation and Dow Jones & Company, Inc., 2014), http://www.heritage.org/index; and United Nations, Human Development Programme, International Human Development Indicators, http://hdr.undp.org/en/statistics/ (accessed November 13, 2013).

Chart 7 heritage.org

ECONOMIC FREEDOM: A VITAL MEANS FOR CHARTING GREATER PROGRESS

Growing economic freedom is unequivocally about achieving greater overall prosperity that goes beyond materialistic and monetary dimensions of well-being. Improvements in economic freedom enhance economic dynamism and, thus, overall human developmental progress.

Advancing economic freedom is strongly related to the enhancement of overall human development as measured by the UNDP Human Development Index, a composite assessment of health, education, and standard of living. As Chart 7 shows, since the beginning of this century, countries that have improved their economic freedom to greater degrees have also achieved much greater enhancement of human development.

Governments that choose policies that increase economic freedom are placing their societies on the pathway to more education opportunities, better health care, and greater standards of living for their citizens. Those governments in the first quartile that have embraced

Moving Ahead or Falling Behind?

Rank According to Long-Term Score Change

Rank	Country	Score Change
1	Azerbaijan	31.3
2	Bosnia and Herzegovina	29.0
3	Georgia	28.5
4	Armenia	26.7
5	Rwanda	26.4
6	Moldova	24.3
7	Lithuania	23.3
8	Romania	22.6
9	Kazakhstan	22.0
10	Angola	20.3
11	Guinea-Bissau	17.8
12	Suriname	17.5
13	Albania	17.2
14	Cape Verde	16.4
15	Poland	16.3
16	Nicaragua	15.9
17	Bulgaria	15.7
18	Botswana	15.2
19	Uzbekistan	15.0
20	Latvia	13.7
21	Samoa	13.5
22	Bangladesh	13.2
23	Laos	12.7
24	Croatia	12.4
25	Slovenia	12.3
26	Hungary	11.8
27	Sweden	11.7
28	Mongolia	11.1
29	Tajikistan	10.9
30	Canada	10.8
31	Estonia	10.7
32	India	10.6
33	Macedonia	10.6
34	Peru	10.5
35	Madagascar	10.1
36	Malta	10.1
37	Guyana	10.0
38	Belarus	9.7
39	Finland	9.7
40	Burkina Faso	9.5
41	Mozambique	9.5
42	Ukraine	9.4
43	Kyrgyz Republic	9.3
44	Niger	9.3
45	Qatar	9.2
46	Vietnam	9.1
47	Denmark	8.8
48	Ghana	8.6
49	Seychelles	8.4
50	Comoros	8.1
51	Mauritius	8.0
52	Australia	7.9
53	Ireland	7.7
54	Mauritania	7.7
55	Chile	7.5
56	Ethiopia	7.4
57	Egypt	7.2
58	Turkmenistan	7.2
59	Nigeria	7.0
60	Israel	6.9
61	Uruguay	6.8
62	The Gambia	6.6
63	Jordan	6.5
64	Turkey	6.5
65	Colombia	6.2
66	Barbados	6.0
67	Burundi	6.0
68	Slovak Republic	6.0
69	Haiti	5.9
70	Yemen	5.7
71	Brazil	5.5
72	Dominican Republic	5.5
73	Norway	5.5
74	Montenegro	5.4
75	Zambia	5.3
76	The Philippines	5.1
77	São Tomé and Príncipe	5.0
78	Switzerland	4.8
79	Cambodia	4.6
80	The Netherlands	4.5
81	Czech Republic	4.4
82	Spain	4.4
83	Côte d'Ivoire	4.3
84	Liberia	4.3
85	Iran	4.2
86	Tonga	4.1
87	Fiji	4.0
88	Belgium	3.9
89	Mexico	3.7
90	Germany	3.6
91	Indonesia	3.6
92	Congo, Rep. of	3.4
93	Mali	3.1
94	New Zealand	3.1
95	Singapore	3.1
96	Serbia	2.8
97	Saint Vincent and the Grenadines	2.7
98	Benin	2.6
99	Dominica	2.6
100	Kenya	2.6
101	Lesotho	2.5
102	Austria	2.4
103	Jamaica	2.3
104	Iceland	1.9
105	Saint Lucia	1.9
106	South Africa	1.8
107	Luxembourg	1.7
108	Togo	1.7
109	Hong Kong	1.5
110	Burma	1.4
111	Djibouti	1.4
112	Cameroon	1.3
113	Portugal	1.1
114	Vanuatu	1.1
115	Cuba	0.9
116	Russia	0.8
117	Malawi	0.7
118	Sierra Leone	0.7
119	Kiribati	0.6
120	China	0.5
121	Tanzania	0.5
122	Gabon	0.3
123	Solomon Islands	0.2
124	Honduras	0.1
125	Eritrea	0.0
126	Cyprus	-0.1
127	Nepal	-0.2
128	United Arab Emirates	-0.2
129	Italy	-0.3
130	Maldives	-0.3
131	Taiwan	-0.3
132	Chad	-0.6
133	Sri Lanka	-0.6
134	Equatorial Guinea	-0.7
135	Macau	-0.7
136	Congo, Dem. Rep. of	-0.8
137	Guatemala	-0.8
138	South Korea	-0.8
139	France	-0.9
140	Bhutan	-1.0
141	Bahrain	-1.1
142	Costa Rica	-1.1
143	United States	-1.2
144	Micronesia	-1.9
145	The Bahamas	-2.0
146	Swaziland	-2.1
147	Namibia	-2.2
148	Malaysia	-2.3
149	Pakistan	-2.4
150	Japan	-2.6
151	Oman	-2.8
152	Senegal	-2.8
153	El Salvador	-2.9
154	Uganda	-3.0
155	United Kingdom	-3.0
156	Kuwait	-3.8
157	Lebanon	-3.8
158	Paraguay	-3.9
159	Morocco	-4.5
160	Papua New Guinea	-4.7
161	Algeria	-4.9
162	Greece	-5.5
163	Guinea	-5.9
164	Saudi Arabia	-6.1
165	Tunisia	-6.1
166	Belize	-6.2
167	Trinidad and Tobago	-6.5
168	Timor-Leste	-7.3
169	North Korea	-7.9
170	Thailand	-8.0
171	Panama	-8.2
172	Bolivia	-8.4
173	Ecuador	-9.7
174	Zimbabwe	-13.0
175	Central African Republic	-13.1
176	Argentina	-23.4
177	Venezuela	-23.5
N/A	Brunei	N/A

Score change over the country's history in the *Index*. For more information, see Appendix, *Index of Economic Freedom* Scores, 1995–2014.

Economic Freedom and Political Freedom Advance in Tandem

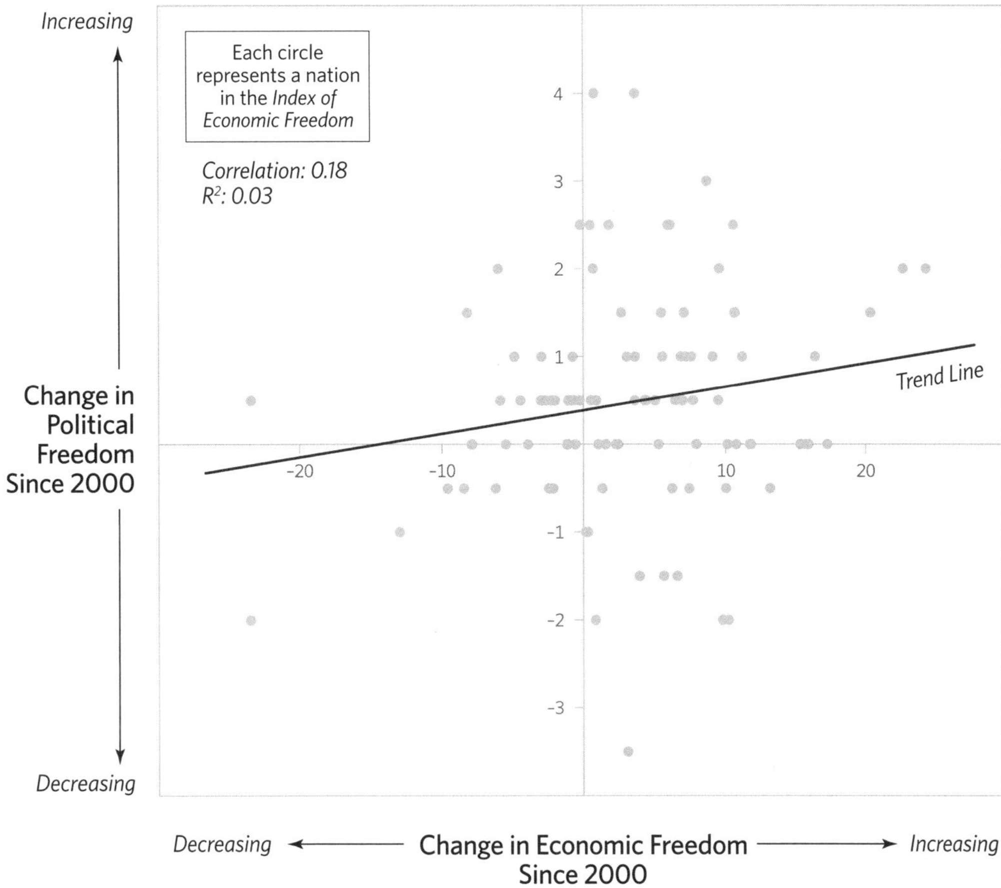

Sources: Terry Miller, Anthony B. Kim, and Kim R. Holmes, *2014 Index of Economic Freedom* (Washington, D.C.: The Heritage Foundation and Dow Jones & Company, Inc., 2014), http://www.heritage.org/index; and Freedom House, "2013 Freedom in the World," Comparative and Historical Data, http://www.freedomhouse.org/report-types/freedom-world (accessed November 13, 2013).

Chart 8 heritage.org

policies that enhance economic freedom have recorded at least a 30 percent higher average annual growth rate of overall human development since 2000 in comparison to the others.

Greater economic freedom can also provide more fertile ground for effective and democratic governance. Advancing economic freedom is about empowering more people to exercise greater control of their daily decision-making processes. In doing so, economic freedom ultimately nurtures political reform as well. Economic freedom encourages a pluralistic society and makes it possible for independent sources of ideas and resources to counterbalance entrenched political power.

Debate about the direction of causality between economic freedom and democracy has become more controversial in recent years due to the multifaceted interaction between the two. However, the positive relationship that exists between economic freedom and political freedom is undeniable. Chart 8 demonstrates that there is a positive linkage between advancing economic freedom and greater political freedom as measured by Freedom House. Although the relationship is not as robust as one might hope to see, over the past two decades, countries that have advanced their economic freedom have tended to achieve greater enhancement of political freedom in general.

Undoubtedly, achieving greater political freedom and well-functioning democracy is a messy and often excruciating process. However, the complex interplay between improving economic freedom and advancing political freedom is something positive and merits further examination.

THE *INDEX* BEYOND 20

Improving and maintaining economic freedom is the proven way to generate positive cycles of economic growth and lasting prosperity. Economies that have advanced economic freedom have achieved overall levels of growth higher than those achieved by countries where economic freedoms have been curtailed by the heavy hand of government. No other systems that have been tried have come close in terms of providing broad-based prosperity. Countries that have not joined the march of freedom have left their citizens lagging behind and even, in the worst cases, stuck in poverty or destitution.

Such failures are inexcusable. Most important, they are preventable. It is too soon to know how coming years will play out as the *Index of Economic Freedom* enters its third decade. Nonetheless, it is both heartening to know that economic freedom is again on the march and safe to predict that countries that find the political will and wisdom to advance economic freedom will see their citizens prosper in the years ahead.

Endnotes

1 Ambassador Terry Miller and Anthony B. Kim, "Fifteen Years of Advancing Freedom," chapter 2 in Terry Miller and Kim R. Holmes, *2009 Index of Economic Freedom* (Washington: The Heritage Foundation and Dow Jones & Company, Inc., 2009), p. 17.

2 Ibid.

3 Amartya Sen, *Development as Freedom* (New York: Anchor Books, 1999), p. xii.

4 International Monetary Fund, World Economic Outlook Databases, October 2013, http://www.imf.org/external/pubs/ft/weo/2013/02/weodata/index.aspx.

Chapter 3

The Moral Case for Economic Liberty

John Tomasi, PhD

Readers of the *Index of Economic Freedom* are familiar with the political and material case for economic liberty. There is a robust positive correlation between the protection of economic freedom and the achievement of such important goals as material prosperity and political liberty. As the authors of the 2013 *Index* summarized that year's findings, "Countries with higher levels of economic freedom substantially outperform others in economic growth, per capita incomes, health care, education, protection of the environment, and reduction of poverty...."[1] This can be called the institutional case for economic freedom.

However, if we believe it is important that people everywhere enjoy goods such as decent health care, a clean environment, and rising per capita wages, then, in drawing attention to the link between economic freedom and the production of these political and material values—that is, in making the institutional case for economic liberty—we are, *ipso facto*, also making a moral case for economic freedom. We should defend economic liberty not only because such liberties have a proven record of securing political and material benefits, vitally important as those goods may be. By protecting economic liberty, there is also a sense in which we respect other people as our moral equals. In particular, when we insist that governments protect private economic liberty, we insist that those governments respect their citizens as responsible authors of their own lives.

When people are free, they think of themselves as in some sense the central causes of the particular lives they are leading. It is not just captains of industry or heroes of Ayn Rand novels who define themselves through their accomplishments in the economic realm. Many ordinary people—middle-class parents, single mothers, entry-level workers, small-scale entrepreneurs in the developing world—become who they are and express who they hope to be by the personal choices they make regarding work, saving, and spending. These are areas in which people earn esteem from others and feel a proper pride for things they themselves do.

To fully understand the moral importance of economic liberty, we may need to widen the lens through which we view the world. In economic affairs, after all, it is not only the outcome that matters: The process must be considered too. Possessing some particular bundle of material goods, from this perspective, becomes more meaningful if one possesses that bundle because of one's own actions and choices. Diminishing personal agency in economic affairs—no matter how lofty the social goal—may drain vital blood from a person's life. When private economic freedoms are curtailed, people become in some important sense less free.

MAKING THE PERSONAL CASE FOR ECONOMIC LIBERTY

None of this is to diminish the importance of the institutional case for economic freedom: Economic liberties are linked to other basic rights and liberties, promote the creation of social wealth, reduce government corruption, and mitigate the dangers of concentrated political power. But in addition to this, individuals everywhere have a moral right to be respected as causes—or, as I prefer, as responsible authors—of their own lives. Thus, the personal case for private economic liberty is worth making too.

The *Index of Economic Freedom* sets out and measures 10 separate areas of economic freedom, a comprehensive scheme that attends to important institutional dimensions of economic liberty. To make the personal case for economic liberty, we need to cut up the conceptual space a bit differently by focusing on the first-person aspects of economic freedom.

James Nickel, a prominent philosopher of human rights, distinguishes four (partially overlapping) categories of economic liberty, all of which protect autonomy of action in economic affairs. Nickel's four categories are liberties of labor, transacting, holding, and using.[2]

- Regarding the economic liberty of labor, Nickel says: "This is the liberty to employ one's body and time in productive activity that one has chosen or accepted, and under arrangements that one has chosen or accepted."
- The liberty of transacting allows individuals to engage in free economic activity. "This is the freedom to manage one's economic affairs at the individual and household levels and on larger scales as well." Transacting involves the liberty to trade in the marketplace, to create things for sale, and to save and invest. It also covers the freedom of individuals and groups to start, run, and close down businesses such as factories, shops, farms, and commercial enterprises of many sorts.
- The economic liberty of holding concerns freedom in the realm of private property. "This category covers legitimate ways of acquiring and holding productive property, using and developing property for commercial and productive purposes, and property transactions such as investing, buying, selling, trading and giving."
- Finally, there is a range of liberties concerning using. "This is the liberty to make use of legitimately acquired resources for consumption and production." The liberty of using protects the freedom of citizens to buy, use, and consume natural resources, consumer goods, and services. On the commercial level, this liberty protects production-related consumption (such as deciding which parts to use or which power sources to purchase). On the domestic level, it protects a range of personal economic decision making, including questions about what to eat and drink, what to wear, what type of housing to have, and a wide range of services one might choose to purchase.

To simplify, I will refer to these first-person economic liberties as the liberties of working and owning.

Most legal systems include some degree of protection for each of these categories of economic liberty. However, systems differ dramatically in the way they specify the activities that are to be protected in each category. Significantly, systems also differ with respect to the degree of importance they assign to such protections when they conflict with other social goals and values.[3]

THE CLASSICAL LIBERAL FRAMEWORK

I will be setting out the personal case for economic liberty within a classical liberal framework. This is the framework pioneered by radical

English thinkers such as John Lilburne and John Locke, developed in the American context by Founders such as James Madison, and defended in our day by legal scholars such as Richard Epstein.

Classical liberals affirm what we might call a thick conception of economic liberty. They tend to interpret each category of private economic liberty as having a wide scope. Regarding the liberties of holding (or "owning"), for example, classical liberals affirm not only the right to ownership of personal property (as guaranteed even by most socialist systems), but rights to the private ownership of productive property as well. People should be free to start small businesses, to join in large capital ventures with others, and generally to establish economic entities of a great variety of kinds (including, if they wish, worker-directed cooperatives).

Closely connected, classical liberals typically interpret the economic liberty of labor to include a wide freedom of individuals to negotiate personally the terms of their employment (including both wage rates and number of hours to be worked). Classical liberals interpret the economic liberty of transacting to include the right of individuals to decide for themselves how much to save for retirement, to decide how much to invest in health care, and to make decisions about many other issues of long-term financial planning.

Further, classical liberals see these wide-ranging economic liberties as being especially weighty compared to other social values. They see economic liberties as having a political status comparable to that of the other traditional liberal rights and liberties, such as liberties of speech and association. But classical liberals do not treat economic liberties as moral absolutes or as in any way more basic than the other fundamental rights and liberties. While important, such liberties do not trump every other social concern.

This last feature distinguishes classical liberalism from a closely related but importantly distinct tradition that we might call libertarianism. By libertarians, I am thinking of historical figures such as Lysander Spooner and more recent writers such as Murray Rothbard, Robert Nozick, and Ayn Rand.[4] Classical liberals and libertarians share an appreciation for the great institutional and personal importance of private economic liberty, but while classical liberals see economic liberties as being among the weightiest rights, libertarians tend to see property rights as the weightiest rights of all and even as moral absolutes.

Thus, unlike the libertarians, classical liberals accept that even the weightiest economic liberties can sometimes be curtailed or regulated to preserve other foundational liberties and sometimes to allow the pursuit of other important social purposes as well. For example, classical liberals would not think the state should enforce contracts that alienate citizens from their other basic rights and liberties (for example, an economic contract that required a person to engage in some form of religious devotion or to enter into slavery). Second, classical liberals traditionally grant that governments have some (albeit carefully limited) powers of eminent domain. They also recognize that governments have the power to act to maintain free and competitive markets (for example, by regulating or breaking up monopolies of scarce resources or by forbidding various forms of collusion and price fixing).

My thesis is that liberties of working and owning, interpreted within a wider classical liberal framework, have great personal moral value. While this might not surprise regular readers of the *Index of Economic Freedom*, it is of the utmost importance to understand how controversial this idea is and that it is controversial not just within moribund pockets of Marxists and socialists, but also across wide swaths of people living in (and voting in) the contemporary liberal democracies of the West.

Far from being a lofty ideal, the idea of living in a world in which there exist big and growing businesses, where workers typically negotiate the terms of their own employment, and where individuals are largely responsible for saving for their own retirement or for making their own arrangements for medical care is seen by many people as living in a world of injustice, exploitation, and vulnerability that can be corrected only by an extensive system of governmental regulations and the erection of expansive tax-funded social service programs. Thus, many people reject the personal case for economic liberty.

Further, many of our fellow citizens also reject the personal case for economic liberty on what they believe to be moral grounds. If a world of personal economic liberty is said to be unjust and exploitative, then many people will rally against those liberties when they hear the moral call. To understand this perspective and how powerfully it shapes the view of many people within Western democracies, it is important to examine its historical roots.

CRITICS OF ECONOMIC LIBERTY: MILL, KEYNES, AND RAWLS

John Stuart Mill, writing in the mid-1800s, was one of the first thinkers in the liberal tradition to raise doubts about the moral importance of economic liberty. Earlier classical liberals, such as James Madison and Benjamin Constant, had seen economic liberty as fully on a par with the civil and political rights of individuals: the right to a fair trial, freedom of expression, political participation, personal autonomy, and so on. But when Mill surveyed the traditional list of liberal liberties, he singled out the economic liberties for relegation to a distinctly secondary place.

Mill's official argument for treating the economic liberties in this exceptional way is based on his distinction between two spheres of human activity. In the sphere of liberty are activities that primarily concern only the individual or, if they involve other people, do so only with their free consent and participation. Mill saw this as the sphere of individual liberty.[5]

The other sphere, that of coercion, concerns activities that directly affect other people. Because society has a direct interest in the activities within this sphere, the state may properly exercise coercion there to promote the common good. While Mill sees freedoms of speech and assembly, conscience and religion, and other activities that are central to becoming the author of one's own life as self-regarding activities (that is, as aspects of liberty), he insists that economic activities—seeking a job, deciding whether to save or spend the income one earns—are other-regarding and thus not aspects of liberty properly understood. In Mill's succinct formulation, "trade is a social act."[6] Thus, trade is a domain subject to social control and regulation rather than being a domain of protected liberty.

This is a surprisingly weak argument from a philosopher of Mill's caliber. After all, speech and assembly are acts that affect others, and in that sense, they appear to be just as "social" as trade.[7] So it seems we must look deeper to understand why Mill denigrates the personal importance of economic liberty in this way.

Mill's moral and political philosophy rests ultimately on a perfectionist ideal of the person. Mill sees individuality as capturing something close to the moral essence of personhood. While a self-proclaimed utilitarian, Mill emphasizes that he means "utility in the largest sense, grounded on the permanent interests of man as a progressive being."[8] Chief among those interests is that of developing a life plan to suit one's character. By creating such a plan, people express their distinctive sense of what is valuable and worth doing in life. By developing and pursuing such a plan, people develop their higher capacities of reasoning, develop intimate connections with others, and enhance their moral sensitivities. Mill saw intellectual pursuits as central to a well-lived life, but he famously claimed to be open to experimentation and readily acknowledged that there might be a wide range of activities and life plans that people can use to develop themselves as individuals.

However, perhaps surveying the scene from his position of social privilege, Mill did not see how activities in the economic sphere could contribute to individuality in his sense. Freedoms of thought and association are important to forming and carrying out a life worthy of a progressive being, but Mill does not see economic liberties—the freedom to hold productive property or to enter into economic contracts—as playing any central role in this process. Starting a business, holding a job, seeking a promotion, being a breadwinner for one's family, saving for the future—these are roles that economic necessity may require people to play from time to time, but none of these activities is constitutive of liberty.

Economic life provides barren soil for the development of individuality. Progressive beings do not need economic liberty to "pursue their own good their own way." For Mill, economic liberties are instrumentally valuable: "property is only a means to an end, not itself the end."[9]

Mill is not the only hero of the Left to argue against the personal importance of economic liberty. In 1930, John Maynard Keynes wrote a remarkable essay, "Economic Possibilities for Our Grandchildren."[10] Writing at a time of economic despair, Keynes expressed long-term optimism: Within one hundred years, during the lifetimes of his own grandchildren, the economies of Western democracies such as the United States and the United Kingdom would have grown approximately tenfold. At that point, roughly in 2030, Western economies would have grown enough. The economic problem, the problem of scarcity that has bedeviled mankind since our appearance on this planet, would at last have been solved. That is, we would have reached a point of sufficient wealth so that increases in capital accumulation could—and Keynes says should—cease. When this not-too-distant day of prosperity dawned, Keynes suggested, a great moral change could at last be welcomed across our social world.

What would change when the economic problem is solved? Keynes says that, finally, the busy, industrious, purposive, economic "bourgeois virtues"—taking risks and toiling, scrimping today in order to save for tomorrow, striving and sacrificing so that the lives of one's children might be better than one's own—might at last be recognized as the ugly vices that they have always been. We needed those deluded "virtues" to get us to the stage of sufficient wealth, but once wealth arrives, the central human problem will not be how to work better. Rather, our great problem will be how best to spend the leisure time that the toils of our parents, grandparents, and great-great-grandparents have bought us.

Keynes suggests that, for the first time in human history, life will not center on economic problems at all. Instead, life will center at last on the only properly human question: how, amid the abundance of wealth, "to live, wisely, agreeably, and well." And what about those who continue to show personal concern for economic questions, clinging to the traditional values of hard work and industry, self-reliance and personal responsibility? In these new conditions, Keynes says that such attitudes are not virtues but "morbid neuroses." People who exhibit them, Keynes suggests (perhaps jokingly?), should be confined to mental institutions.

Similarly, though less colorfully, John Rawls, writing in 1971, produced a great manifesto of social justice. Rawls offers a machinery that is designed to identify a strong set of distributive principles of justice, constrained only by a short list of basic rights and liberties that limit the reach and power of government. Rawls's spare list of basic rights includes protections in such familiar areas of human freedom as association and speech. However, following in the tradition of Mill and Keynes, Rawls makes no special place for the economic liberties of capitalism. Indeed, on his account, the requirements of liberal justice could be satisfied in what he calls a "democratic socialist" regime: that is, a regime that limited economic liberty even to the point of denying the private ownership of productive property.

WHAT WE VALUE AND WHO WE ARE

With all respect, I disagree with this tradition of thinking. Economic liberties are valuable not only because of their well-documented institutional and material advantages (for example, because the protection of economic liberty is positively correlated with lower levels of corruption and with increases in per capita income). Though Lord Keynes may have looked down his long nose on the familiar work-a-day virtues associated with the economic liberties, for many ordinary working people, the development and exercise of these virtues in support of one's own dreams and the dreams one has for loved ones comes close to the core of life.

When we make decisions about how much we are willing to work, at what wages, and in which business sector or profession, just as when we make decisions about whether to spend now or save for later, we are not engaged in activities that are morally trivial. Instead, through our activities in these economic aspects of our lives, each of us says something important about what we value and, indeed, about who we are. Decisions about saving and spending, for example, are among the most common of economic quandaries, and these questions regularly confront people in free societies regardless of their income level. Those questions, distinctively, require that each of us think carefully about the relationship between the person we are now and the person we will become in the future.

Temporal thinking of that sort is closely connected to the process of becoming an adult. Such decisions are among the most distinctive forms of taking responsibility for one's own life and doing so in light of one's own dreams, values, and character. Economic choices about spending and saving, as with other economic decisions, such as setting oneself on one course of study or on one career path rather than another, constitute a kind of passageway from childhood or late adolescence toward full adulthood. Citizens who are denied the chance to make such choices for themselves or whose range of decision-making in these areas is truncated by others (no matter how well meaning) will live comparatively stunted lives, lives that are in some sense less fully adult.

Intriguingly, a similar assertion about the personal importance of economic liberty was made by leaders of the feminist movement during the 19th century. Early feminist leaders such as Voltairine De Cleyre argued against patriarchy in a way that put the personal importance of economic liberty front and center. No matter how "gilded" the social cage that men of that era had constructed for women, no matter how abundant the material goods made available within that cage or how tender the treatment, feminist leaders of that era, denied their economic liberties, denied the chance to have some role in the creation and selection of whatever goods they were to enjoy, insisted that a great moral wrong was being done to them.[11]

By denying women their economic liberties, men had prevented them from fully developing as free and independent adults—as moral equals, each one in charge of her own life. No amount of pointing to the comforts that they were being provided by their male protectors could make up for this fact. Denied full economic liberty, women of the era had been fundamentally disrespected: Their moral agency, their capacity for responsible self-authorship, had been stunted and denied.

That early feminist defense of economic liberty might well be turned against the material ambitions of some contemporary social democracies. Here again, no matter how gilded the cage of a social democracy may seem, no matter how comfortable and plentiful the social guarantees, if the cost of receiving those benefits is the violation or truncation of personal economic liberty, then there is something objectionable about this scheme. This is a world, whatever its material bounty, with great moral loss. That loss is what I mean by the personal value of economic liberty.

BREAKING FREE OF OLD DICHOTOMIES

Perhaps the most alarming finding in recent editions of the *Index of Economic Freedom* has been the sharp decline in economic liberty in the United States, once a beacon of economic liberty. I believe that the personal case for economic liberty has been presented too weakly in recent years. That moral ideal has dimmed and no longer burns brightly in the mind of every citizen. Part of the reason may be that in some countries, citizens recently have become willing to heed the siren call of politicians offering ever more government services and goods in exchange for citizens giving up ever more personal economic liberty. Often, those offers of governmental services are presented as required by morality itself—say, under the banner of fairness or social justice. Thus, within contemporary political discourse, we find the personal case for economic liberty pitted against another set of powerful moral ideas: the idea of material justice.

And so citizens today face a set of political choices that are equally stark and unhappy:

democracy *or* capitalism, economic liberty *or* material justice, free markets *or* fairness. One side or the other, everyone has to choose. No wonder our societies have become so divided and the political rhetoric so extreme.

Thankfully, one of the most exciting developments in recent political and economic thinking has been an attempt to break free from those old dichotomies.[12] And here again, the *Index of Economic Freedom* has an important role to play.

One way to break the ideological deadlock might be to hold tight to both the personal and institutional cases for economic liberty but to present the institutional case in a way that emphasizes economic liberty's benefits for all classes of citizens and most especially for ordinary working people, including workers at the very bottom of the existing pay scale. If we consistently find a positive correlation between economic liberty and important social goods such as economic growth and rising per capita income, the program of economic liberty might itself be defended on grounds of material justice and fairness too. If that message can be communicated to our fellow citizens, then a democratic case for economic liberty might be forged once again, thus better securing those liberties about which in recent years there has been so much doubt.

If we attend to the full index of economic liberties, their personal value as well as their capacity to create wealth that might be enjoyed by all, we may find ourselves living in a world of both social abundance and personal freedom: democracy *and* capitalism, economic liberty *and* material justice, free markets *and* fairness. By making this fuller case for economic liberty, perhaps people do not have to choose after all.

Endnotes

1 "Executive Highlights," in Terry Miller, Kim R. Holmes, and Edwin J. Feulner, *2013 Index of Economic Freedom* (Washington: The Heritage Foundation and Dow Jones & Company, Inc., 2013), p. 1.

2 James Nickel, "Economic Liberties," in *The Idea of a Political Liberalism: Essays on Rawls* (Lanham, Md.: Rowman & Littlefield, 2000, pp. 155–176. See also Lawrence C. Becker, *Property Rights: Philosophical Foundations* (London: Routledge & Kegan Paul, 1981), pp. 11–21.

3 A classic discussion is Anthony Honoré, "Ownership," in *Oxford Essays in Jurisprudence: Fourth Series*, ed. Jeremy Horder (New York: Oxford University Press, 2000), pp. 107–147, at 108.

4 Lysander Spooner, *No Treason* (Boston: Kessinger Publishing, 2004); Murray Newton Rothbard, *For a New Liberty: The Libertarian Manifesto* (Auburn, Ala.: Ludwig von Mises Institute, 1985); Ayn Rand, *Atlas Shrugged* (New York: Ashgate Publishing Ltd., 2012); Robert Nozick, *Anarchy, State, and Utopia* (New York: Basic Books, 1974).

5 John Stuart Mill, *On Liberty* (London: Longman, Roberts & Green, 1869), esp. chap. I, sect. 12.

6 Ibid., p. 94.

7 Daniel Jacobson, "Mill on Liberty, Speech, and the Free Society," *Philosophy & Public Affairs*, Vol. 29, No. 3 (Summer 2000), pp. 276–309, at 293–295.

8 Mill, *On Liberty*, chap. 1, sect. 11, p. 15.

9 John Stuart Mill, *Principles of Political Economy with Some of Their Applications to Social Philosophy* (London: Longmans, Green, 1909), Book II, chap. II, sect. 4.

10 John Maynard Keynes, "Economic Possibilities of Our Grandchildren," in John Maynard Keynes, *Essays in Persuasion* (New York: W.W. Norton & Co., 1963), pp. 358–373.

11 Voltairine de Cleyre, *Exquisite Rebel: The Essays of Voltairine de Cleyre—Anarchist, Feminist, Genius*, ed. Sharon Presley and Crispin Sartwell (New York: State University of New York Press, 2005).

12 See, for example, Arthur C. Brooks, *The Road to Freedom: How to Win the Fight for Free Enterprise* (New York: Basic Books, 2012), and Stephen Moore, *Who's the Fairest of Them All? The Truth About Opportunity, Taxes, and Wealth in America* (New York: Encounter Books, 2012). I offer a philosophical defense of this idea in *Free Market Fairness* (Princeton, N.J.: Princeton University Press, 2012). I am grateful to the Princeton University Press for allowing me to draw on material from *Free Market Fairness* for this essay.

Chapter 4

Antidote to Poverty: Economic Freedom, Not Government Dependency

Sergio Daga

In 1979, Nobel Laureate Milton Friedman stated, "no economic system in history has been as successful at lifting people out of poverty as that of capitalism and free trade, based on principles of economic freedom." He also remarked, "there is no alternative way so far discovered of improving the lots of ordinary people that can hold a candle to the productive activities that are unleashed by a free enterprise system."[1]

Economic freedom has done more for the poor throughout the world than any taxpayer-funded social program or welfare check ever could. This system based on individual freedom, private property, limited government, and limited regulation has improved the lives of millions of people worldwide. Every year, the results of The Heritage Foundation's *Index of Economic Freedom* reinforce the conclusion that the world's freest economies have less human poverty and higher living standards.

Notwithstanding the overwhelming evidence of success over the past two centuries, however, critics continue to insist that economic freedom has been a failure. A frequent charge is that governments that prioritize policies such as low tax rates, impartial rule of law, strong private property rights, and unfettered access to markets generally fail to provide citizens with adequate social benefits such as health care and education—key components of the multidimensional measures of poverty. The results of the *Index of Economic Freedom* tell a quite different story. In fact, greater economic freedom correlates with better outcomes in education and health.[2]

Attempts to improve people's quality of life have been particularly important in emerging and less developed economies because of their relatively higher poverty rates. In fact, while the poverty headcount rate in most developed countries is close to zero according to the international measure of $2 a day (in PPP),[3] in the rest of the world, poverty affects the lives of billions.[4] It is logical and understandable that governments in these economies and the international aid community worry about this problem and occasionally make new plans and programs to eradicate poverty. The Millennium Development Goals, promising to cut poverty in half by 2015, are one example.[5]

The idea of cash transfers to the poor, a form of social assistance programs that emerged in the mid-1990s, has recently captured increased attention from policymakers and scholars due to the increasing number of countries that have been adopting such programs.[6] Today, these types of programs are the most common social assistance interventions in many emerging and less-developed economies, especially in Latin America, and more recently in Africa and Asia.

Cash transfers are increasingly popular both within the donor community and among policymakers in developing countries that are seeking more innovative ways to improve welfare. The idea behind cash transfer programs is that distributing cash to the poor seems more efficient than public-sector spending.

There are different variations of cash transfers, but they can be grouped into two types: conditional or unconditional. Although unconditional cash transfers, such as pensions to the elderly, are still in force and represent a significant amount of money in public budgets, the introduction of conditionality on cash transfers has become more popular among governments because of the political benefits that can accrue to the ruling party or the central government. Adding requirements that the poor "do something" might be necessary in helping to make cash transfers politically acceptable even while having little to do with the eventual success or failure of the program in meeting its goals.[7]

Moreover, studies of cash transfers in developing countries have concluded that the determining factor for beneficiaries in executing the pre-specified actions was the increase in income, not the conditionality, which had no discernable impact. Thus, the conditions attached to such programs and the additional cost of enforcing them may be less valuable than the cash itself.[8]

Conditional cash transfer (CCT) programs aim to break the intergenerational transmission of poverty by conditioning payments on compliance with co-responsibilities intended to develop children's human capital. By introducing these programs, proponents expect that conditions would allow the accumulation of sufficient human capital to drive the next generation out of poverty so that social assistance would no longer be needed in the future.[9]

All of the above seem noble intentions, but there is little evidence that such programs have resulted in improvements in the quality of life of poor families. Public services in most of the developing world still lack quality, mainly because governments generally insist on maintaining a monopoly on the service in question and are reluctant to accept private competition. Additionally, these types of programs have not helped the poor to get permanent jobs because their labor skills and productivity remain unchanged. Moreover, year after year, the coverage of these programs increases along with the amount of money needed to keep them running, and there is strong evidence that due to poor monitoring and control mechanisms, these programs are creating clientelistic behavior on the part of politicians.

Sadly, many of the countries that have introduced cash transfer programs have not made any improvements in advancing economic freedom. Structural policy changes that foster rule of law, limited government, regulatory efficiency, and open markets—key elements of economic freedom—are needed to break the intergenerational transmission of poverty. Delays in the implementation of such policies are typically the main reason why some countries fail to eradicate poverty or provide higher living standards for their inhabitants.

CONDITIONAL CASH TRANSFER PROGRAMS

One of the main arguments by the proponents of cash transfer programs is advanced by Ariel Fiszbein and Norbert Schady:

> Although market-driven economic growth is likely to be the main driver of poverty reduction in most countries, markets cannot do it alone. Public policy plays a central role in providing the institutional foundations within which markets operate, in providing public goods, and in correcting market failures.

In addition to laying the foundations for economic growth, policy can supplement the effects of growth on poverty reduction, and one of the instruments that governments can use to that end is direct redistribution of resources to poor households.[10]

Under this premise, CCT programs have received significant and increasing attention. Many countries in the developing world have created programs that make regular payments to poor households on the condition that those households undertake pre-specified actions such as periodic health and nutrition checkups, growth monitoring, and vaccinations for children younger than five years of age. Education conditions usually include school enrollment and attendance on 80 percent–85 percent of school days, but in many cases, there are no measures of performance.

By 2011, at least 18 countries in Latin America had implemented such programs. Elsewhere, there are large-scale programs in Bangladesh, Indonesia, and Turkey and pilot programs in Cambodia, Malawi, Morocco, Pakistan, and South Africa, among others. Just in Latin America, the number of beneficiaries grew from 38 million in 2001 to 135 million in 2010.[11]

The largest programs in terms of absolute coverage are located in Mexico and Brazil. In Mexico, the program is called *Oportunidades*. It started in 1997 with 300,000 beneficiary households and now covers almost 6 million households. In Brazil, *Bolsa Familia* started in the municipalities of Brasilia and Campinas and now serves 11 million families (58 million people) countrywide. The smallest program in terms of coverage is located in Chile, serving 215,000 households. In terms of relative coverage, programs range from approximately 40 percent of the population (Ecuador) to about 20 percent (Brazil and Mexico) to 1 percent (Cambodia). Santiago Levy and Norbert Schady show that for 16 countries in Latin America, average coverage is one out of every four households.[12]

In terms of budget, the costs range from about 0.50 percent of gross domestic product (GDP) in such countries as Brazil, Ecuador, and Mexico to 0.08 percent of GDP (Chile). The generosity of benefits ranges from 20 percent of mean household consumption in Mexico to 4 percent in Honduras and even less for programs in Bangladesh, Cambodia, and Pakistan.

IMPACT OF CONDITIONAL CASH TRANSFER PROGRAMS

The impact of CCT programs individually is difficult to evaluate. Programs vary widely, both in the quality of their evaluation methods and in the extent of control and monitoring schemes. Governments that have adopted strict operational rules show more positive plausible results than those that have implemented more flexible designs or looser rules.

The ultimate goal of CCT programs is to alleviate and break the intergenerational transmission of poverty by inducing parents to use public health and education services for their children. In almost 15 years, these programs, both in Latin America and in the rest of world, have yielded mixed results. Following are case studies of *Oportunidades* in Mexico and *Bono Juancito Pinto* (BJP) in Bolivia.

Oportunidades[13]

Mexico's *Oportunidades* program has its roots in a predecessor program, *Progresa*, initiated under President Ernesto Zedillo and the Partido Revolucionario Institucional (PRI) in 1997. *Progresa*, the first large-scale CCT, focused on promoting education, health, and nutrition among the poor in rural Mexico. The program was submitted to evaluation after its first year, and studies demonstrated that it positively affected school attendance and the frequency of health clinic visits among its beneficiaries, in addition to reducing the number of families living in extreme poverty by nearly 3 percent during its first five years of operation.

Thus, despite initial skepticism, President Vicente Fox and the Partido Acción Nacional (PAN) decided to maintain the program upon coming to power in 2000. In 2002, Fox put his own stamp on the program, changing its name to *Oportunidades*, emphasizing the importance of co-responsibility between the government and the poor, and extending the program's reach both to involve a greater proportion of the rural poor and to include the urban and semi-urban poor. The monthly cash transfer under *Oportunidades* is $20 per family per month.

Since its beginning, *Oportunidades* has been subject to randomized evaluations, and results show that school enrollment and preventive health care utilization have increased. The program helped to increase enrollment in secondary school by 6 percentage points for boys and 9 percentage points for girls. For girls, who often drop out before secondary school, the number of those making the transition to secondary school increased by 15 percentage points. Children in the program also entered school at an earlier age and repeated fewer grades. *Oportunidades* had relatively little impact, however, on school attendance rates, on achievement on standardized tests, or in bringing dropouts back to school.

Health visits increased by 18 percent in *Oportunidades* localities, and illnesses among *Oportunidades* children up to five years old were reduced by 12 percent. Stunting was reduced in *Oportunidades* children by 10 points. Although the exact mechanism that triggers improvement is not known with certainty, it may result from one or several program characteristics, such as the provision of higher incomes that permit increased expenditure on food, growth monitoring and information about nutrition and child care, or nutritional supplements.

Bono Juancito Pinto

Bolivia's *Bono Juancito Pinto* program was implemented in 2006 by President Evo Morales to encourage parents to send their children to school. If a child attends school at least 80 percent of the time, parents receive approximately $30 at the end of the academic year. This program is funded mainly by natural resource revenues from the state-owned oil and mining companies.

At the beginning, the bonus was supposed to be given only to students in public school between first and fifth grade. However, the government has relaxed the requirements each year, and since 2013, students in public school from first to tenth grade have received the bonus. The total amount spent in the program has increased from $27 million in 2006 to $60 million in 2013, which represents 0.25 percent of Bolivia's nominal GDP. Student coverage has increased from 1 million to nearly 2 million. These numbers merit some skepticism. A comparison of numbers from the Minister of Economy, in charge of giving the bonus, and the Minister of Education shows that the number of students receiving the bonus every year is greater than the number of students enrolled in school each year.[14]

To date, no official evaluation document has been issued by the Bolivian government. However, a few attempts have been made recently to evaluate the program's impact according to its objective. Using micro simulation techniques, Ernesto Yañez Aguilar finds that the BJP has had a positive impact on reducing school absenteeism in primary schools, has helped to reduce the extreme poverty rate, and has improved income distribution, especially in the rural sector.[15] Flavia Marco Navarro shows that the program has had a positive impact on school attendance and a slight impact on the dropout rate, while the effect on enrollment is less clear.[16]

On the other hand, Sergio Daga and Roberto Orihuela find that the net enrollment rate for beneficiaries of the bonus (students from first to eighth grade) has not increased; actually, it decreased from 94 percent in 2006 to 82 percent in 2011.[17] The drop is especially surprising given that the net enrollment rate for students that do not benefit from the bonus increased from 60 percent in 2005 to 70 percent in 2011. Additionally, the study shows that dropout rates among beneficiaries have decreased, so any possible impact of the bonus is unclear.

Most shocking is that the failure rate among beneficiaries of the bonus increased sharply from less than 1 percent in 2005 to 6.1 percent in 2011, while the failure rate among those who do not benefit from the bonus decreased from 7.4 percent in 2006 to 5.7 percent in 2011.

CONCERNS ABOUT CONDITIONAL CASH TRANSFER PROGRAMS

According to Santiago Levy and Norbert Schady, careful randomized evaluations of some CCT programs in Latin America have shown that, on average, they have increased school enrollment and attendance and the utilization of preventive health services.[18] However, despite these apparently positive results, there are at least four main concerns.

Poor Quality of Public Services

While cash transfer programs have increased school enrollment, the evidence on whether the additional schooling results in better learning outcomes for children who were brought into school by these programs is mixed. Tania Barham, Karen Macours, and John Maluccio find that in Nicaragua, boys (but not girls) whose families received transfers from the *Red de Protección Social* program when they were between nine and 11 years of age have test scores that are approximately 0.2 standard deviations higher 10 years later.[19]

On the other hand, Jere Behrman, Susan Parker, and Petra Todd find that children in Mexico who received *Progresa* transfers do not have higher test scores than comparable children who did not receive them.[20] Although the reasons for this finding are unclear, the poor quality of education and the fact that many of the children who were brought into school are drawn from the lower end of the distribution of ability are probably part of the explanation.

More generally, while conditional cash transfers have increased the utilization of health and educational services, impacts on final human capital outcomes have been more limited. As a result, the effect that conditional cash transfers have on reducing the intergenerational transmission of poverty—a key objective of these programs—may be limited.[21]

Reduced Incentives to Work

In some cases, the transfers may be so large that they can have a negative effect on incentives to work.[22] In Ecuador and Mexico, transfers have increased substantially in magnitude. In Mexico's *Progresa* (since renamed *Oportunidades*), transfers are now equivalent to over 40 percent of household pre-transfer income in the lowest quintile of the distribution. Transfer income also represents a sizeable share of total income in Ecuador, where the program is also very large in scope, covering almost 40 percent of the population. If leisure is a normal good, we might expect that the income effect of transfers of this magnitude would reduce labor supply.

Moreover, many of the cash transfer programs periodically "recertify" beneficiaries to ensure that they are still poor enough to qualify for continued eligibility. This obviously introduces an incentive for households to continue to be (or at least appear to be) poor. Adriana Camacho and Emily Conover show that once the exact formula used to calculate the proxy means test that determined eligibility for Colombia's *Familas en Acción* program was made public, there was substantial heaping of households just below the cutoff value.[23]

In Chile (and in some other countries), having a household member with a physical or mental disability increases the value of the subsidy. Rodrigo Herrera, Osvaldo Larrañaga, and Amanda Telias show that among the poorest households, almost 80 percent report having a household member with a disability on the *Ficha de Protección Social*, the survey that is used to determine assistance levels. In comparison, on the national CASEN household survey, which does not determine eligibility for transfers, only 20 percent of the poorest households report having a member with a disability.[24]

Formal vs. Informal Employment

Conditional cash transfers can also favor informal over formal employment. The Uruguayan PANES program explicitly disqualified recipients if their formal sector earnings increased above a predetermined value. Verónica Amarante, Marco Manacorda, Andrea Vigorito, and Mariana Zerpa show that PANES substantially reduced formal employment among men and that these effects persisted at least two years after the program ended.[25]

Political Clientelism

The political clientelism that CCT programs may create is a derivative effect that has yet to be fully investigated. Emerging and less developed economies have suffered from political clientelism, especially regarding social assistance programs, for a long time. As World Bank CCT scholar Laura Rawlings points out, traditionally, "there has been criticism of paternalism, clientelism and corruption in social assistance programs, many of which are perceived as vehicles for political patronage."[26] CCT programs seem to follow the same pattern.

Since CCT programs are generally administered by the central government, they invariably affect the relationship between program beneficiaries and the executive in the central government. Given this connection, certain features of CCT programs indicate that the executive is focused more on using the program for short-term political gains (earning political capital) than on attaining its long-term goals (building human capital to break the cycle of intergenerational poverty). The most salient features in this respect include the process of targeting beneficiaries, the degree of the central government's involvement in program operations, the method of oversight, and the investment in the supply side of the program.

For example, the largest CCT program, *Bolsa Familia* in Brazil, has been very successful in targeting the poorest members of Brazilian society, but it has also done so in a way that inculcates significant allegiance to the central government among program beneficiaries. The combination of strong central government involvement in program operations, weak oversight of compliance with program conditions, and a lack of supply-side investment indicates that *Bolsa Familia* is more focused on short-term political goals than it is on long-term structural reform.

ECONOMIC FREEDOM AND POVERTY ALLEVIATION

The Honorable Obiageli Ezekwesili, a Nigerian citizen and then Vice President of the World Bank for Africa, highlighted the importance of economic freedom in fighting poverty in a lecture at The Heritage Foundation in October 2011.[27] She stressed, based on a research paper published by Jean-Pierre Chauffour,[28] that economic freedom and civil and political liberties are at the root of the reasons why some countries achieve and sustain better economic outcomes while others do not. The expansion of the conditions of freedom—whether economic, civil or political—over time positively influences long-run economic growth and therefore promotes higher income levels and lower poverty rates.

She also mentioned that the *Index of Economic Freedom* underlines the positive role that economic freedom plays in enabling prosperity, raising living standards, curbing poverty, and improving economic growth and social well-being. She quoted Nelson Mandela: "Money won't create success; the freedom to make it will."

Ms. Ezekwesili said that prioritizing economic freedom over social entitlements could be an effective way to reform the welfare state in many developing countries, especially if they want to make their economies more sustainable in the long run. In other words, deregulation, lower taxes, and less interference in the market would make these countries much more prosperous, not less, and ultimately eliminate the need for the state to engage in huge social spending that creates only more dependence and marginalization.

As noted, one of the strongest results of The Heritage Foundation's *Index of Economic Freedom* is that countries that prioritize economic freedom tend to be richer, tend to grow faster, and tend to reduce poverty faster, and their people tend to live longer and to be more educated. They tend to be less corrupt, to respect human rights more, to promote gender equity, and to have more of their people employed.

Looking at the level of economic freedom in the countries that have implemented conditional cash transfer programs in recent years, it should not be surprising to see that the vast majority of them are considered either mostly unfree or just moderately free economies based on their average score in the *Index of Economic Freedom* in the past

Countries in the World with CCT Programs, by Region and Economic Freedom

Region	Country	Score in the *Index of Economic Freedom,* 2009–2014	*Index* Category
Sub-Saharan Africa	Burkina Faso	59.8	Mostly Unfree
	Kenya	57.3	Mostly Unfree
	Nigeria	55.7	Mostly Unfree
East Asia and Pacific	The Philippines	57.4	Mostly Unfree
	Cambodia	57.4	Mostly Unfree
	Indonesia	56.1	Mostly Unfree
Europe and Central Asia	Turkey	63.3	Moderately Free
Latin America and Caribbean	Chile	78.2	Mostly Free
	El Salvador	68.3	Moderately Free
	Peru	67.5	Moderately Free
	Colombia	67.4	Moderately Free
	Mexico	66.8	Moderately Free
	Jamaica	65.8	Moderately Free
	Panama	64.2	Moderately Free
	Paraguay	61.6	Moderately Free
	Guatemala	60.7	Moderately Free
	Dominican Republic	60.1	Moderately Free
	Honduras	58.3	Mostly Unfree
	Nicaragua	58.3	Mostly Unfree
	Brazil	56.8	Mostly Unfree
	Bolivia	49.9	Repressed
	Argentina	49.1	Repressed
	Ecuador	48.7	Repressed
Middle East and North Africa	Yemen	55.4	Mostly Unfree
South Asia	Pakistan	55.4	Mostly Unfree
	India	54.7	Mostly Unfree
	Bangladesh	51.9	Mostly Unfree

Sources: Terry Miller, Anthony B. Kim, and Kim R. Holmes, *2014 Index of Economic Freedom* (Washington, D.C.: The Heritage Foundation and Dow Jones & Company, Inc., 2014), http://www.heritage.org/index; and Ariel Fiszbein and Norbert Schady, "Conditional Cash Transfers: Reducing Present and Future Poverty," World Bank *Policy Research Report* No. 47603, February 9, 2009, http://documents.worldbank.org/curated/en/2009/01/10298306/conditional-cash-transfers-reducing-present-future-poverty (accessed November 6, 2013).

Table 1 heritage.org

six years. (See Table 1.) Ecuador is an especially vivid case. This country is considered a repressed economy, and its CCT program has the highest relative coverage in terms of its total population, reaching more than 40 percent. (See Table 2.)

The countries that have implemented CCT programs have common features: They lack property rights, suffer from corruption, have rigid labor market laws, and restrict capital mobility. Investors' perception is that governments in these countries do not provide adequate protection for their investments.

Under these circumstances, the ability of individuals in these countries to create and

Number of CCT Program Beneficiaries in Selected Latin American and Caribbean Countries in 2010

Country	Beneficiaries (millions of people)	Population (millions of people)	Beneficiaries as Share of Total Population
Argentina	11.8	40.4	29%
Bolivia	2.1	10.1	20%
Brazil	52.4	194.9	27%
Chile	1.2	17.1	7%
Colombia	17.8	46.3	38%
Costa Rica	0.19	4.6	4%
Dominican Republic	3.0	9.9	30%
Ecuador	6.2	14.5	42%
El Salvador	0.5	6.2	8%
Guatemala	3.3	14.4	23%
Honduras	1.1	7.6	14%
Mexico	27.3	113.4	24%
Panama	0.4	3.5	10%
Paraguay	0.5	6.5	9%
Peru	2.6	29.1	9%
Uruguay	0.8	3.4	23%

Source: Marco Stampini and Leopoldo Tornarolli, "The Growth of Conditional Cash Transfers in Latin America and the Caribbean: Did They Go Too Far?" Institute for the Study of Labor *Policy Paper* No. 49, November 2012, http://ftp.iza.org/pp49.pdf (accessed November 6, 2013).

Table 2 heritage.org

accumulate wealth, engage in entrepreneurial activities, and make long-term investment plans is constrained. Alleviating poverty in a sustainable way will be impossible in these countries until their governments remove the real obstacles that restrict economic freedom.

CONCLUSION

The latest attempt to fight poverty is the idea of conditional cash transfers to the poor, a form of social assistance program that has become very popular in Latin America and more recently in Asia and Africa. Typically, such programs transfer money to the poor conditioned on the utilization of health and education public services. The main goal, according to proponents, is to break the intergenerational transmission of poverty by the accumulation of sufficient human capital so that social assistance would no longer be needed in the future.

In countries where this was possible, careful randomized evaluations of some CCT programs have shown that, on average, they have increased school enrollment and attendance and the utilization of preventive health services. In others, where CCT programs were implemented under more flexible designs or looser rules, the positive impacts are less clear.

There are at least four main concerns that are likely to undercut the effectiveness of these programs.

- Public services in most of the developing world still lack quality;
- In some cases, transfers may be so large that they can have a negative effect on incentives to work;
- There is evidence in some countries that cash transfers could favor informal over formal employment; and
- CCT programs affect the relationship between program beneficiaries and the government,

with certain features of CCT programs designed apparently more to achieve short-term political gains than to attain their long-term stated development goals.

Every year, the results of The Heritage Foundation's *Index of Economic Freedom* reinforce the conclusion that the world's freest economies have less human poverty and higher living standards. The countries that have made significant achievements in poverty reduction in a sustainable way have done it by implementing policies that prioritize rule of law, limited government interventions, regulatory efficiency, and open markets.

With a few exceptions, countries that have implemented conditional cash transfer programs lack property rights, suffer from corruption, have rigid labor market laws, restrict capital mobility, and offer few protections for investment. They would achieve better results if they focused more on removing barriers to economic freedom and less on actions that encourage more dependence on the state.

Endnotes

1 Anthony B. Kim and Ambassador Terry Miller, "Commemorating Milton Friedman's 100th Birthday with the *Index of Economic Freedom*," Heritage Foundation *Special Report* No. 114, July 31, 2012, http://thf_media.s3.amazonaws.com/2012/pdf/sr114.pdf (accessed July 15, 2013).

2 James M. Roberts and Ryan Olson, "How Economic Freedom Promotes Better Health Care, Education, and Environmental Quality," Heritage Foundation *Special Report* No. 139, September 11, 2013, http://thf_media.s3.amazonaws.com/2013/pdf/SR139.pdf (accessed September 17, 2013).

3 The purchasing power parity (PPP) conversion factor shows how much of a country's currency is needed in that country to buy what $1 would buy in the United States. By using the PPP conversion factor instead of the currency exchange rate, it is possible to convert a country's GNP per capita calculated in national currency units into GNP per capita in U.S. dollars while taking into account the difference in domestic prices for the same goods. Thus, PPP helps to compare GNPs of different countries more accurately.

4 According to the *World Development Indicators* published by the World Bank in 2013, the poverty headcount ratio at $2 a day (PPP) in low- and middle-income countries is 40.7 percent, which accounts for 2.3 billion people.

5 United Nations, *The Millennium Development Goals Report 2013*, http://www.un.org/millenniumgoals/pdf/report-2013/mdg-report-2013-english.pdf (accessed October 2, 2013).

6 Ariel Fiszbein and Norbert Schady, *Conditional Cash Transfers: Reducing Present and Future Poverty*, World Bank *Policy Research Report* No. 47603, February 9, 2009, http://documents.worldbank.org/curated/en/2009/01/10298306/conditional-cash-transfers-reducing-present-future-poverty (accessed February 14, 2013).

7 Samuel Morley and David Coady, *From Social Assistance to Social Development: Targeted Education Subsidies in Developing Countries*, Center for Global Development and International Food Policy Research Institute, 2003, http://international.cgdev.org/sites/default/files/Morley_Coady_Main_Text.pdf (accessed September 17, 2013).

8 Sarah Baird, Craig McIntosh, and Berk Ozler, "Cash or Condition? Evidence from a Randomized Cash Transfer Program," World Bank *Policy Research Working Paper* No. 5259, March 2010, http://elibrary.worldbank.org/content/workingpaper/10.1596/1813-9450-5259 (accessed September 17, 2013).

9 Marco Stampini and Leopoldo Tornarolli, "The Growth of Conditional Cash Transfers in Latin America and the Caribbean: Did They Go Too Far?" Institute for the Study of Labor *Policy Paper* No. 49, November 2012, http://ftp.iza.org/pp49.pdf (accessed August 6, 2013).

10 Fiszbein and Schady, *Conditional Cash Transfers: Reducing Present and Future Poverty*, p. 8.

11 Stampini and Tornarolli, "The Growth of Conditional Cash Transfers in Latin America and the Caribbean," p. 2.

12 Santiago Levy and Norbert Schady, "Latin America's Social Policy Challenge: Education, Social Insurance, Redistribution," *Journal of Economic Perspectives*, Vol. 27, No. 2 (Spring 2013), pp. 193–218, http://pubs.aeaweb.org/doi/pdfplus/10.1257/jep.27.2.193 (accessed September 10, 2013).

13 Renee Gardner Sewall, "Conditional Cash Transfer Programs in Latin America," *SAIS Review of International Affairs*, Vol. 28, No. 2 (Summer–Fall 2008), pp. 175–187, http://muse.jhu.edu/journals/sais/summary/v028/28.2.sewall.html (accessed February 5, 2013).

14 Sergio Daga and Roberto Orihuela, "Transferencias Monetarias Condicionadas en Bolivia: el Bono Juancito Pinto," in *Desarrollo económico y pobreza en América Latina: El rol de los Planes Sociales*, Atlas Network and Asociación de Iberoamericanos por la Libertad, 2012, http://www.asociacionail.com/publicaciones/159-desarrollo-economico-y-pobreza-en-america-latina (accessed August 27, 2013).

15 Ernesto Yáñez Aguilar, "El Impacto del Bono Juancito Pinto: Un Análisis de Micro Simulaciones," Instituto de Investigaciones Socio Económicas *Working Paper* No. 06/12, June 2012, http://www.iisec.ucb.edu.bo/papers/2011-2015/iisec-dt-2012-06.pdf (accessed February 14, 2013).

16 Flavia Marco Navarro, "El Bono Juancito Pinto del Estado Plurinacional de Bolivia," United Nations, Comision Económica para América Latina y el Caribe (CEPAL), 2012, http://www.eclac.org/publicaciones/xml/1/48161/ElbonoJuancitoPinto.pdf (accessed February 14, 2013).

17 Daga and Orihuela, "Transferencias Monetarias Condicionadas en Bolivia: el Bono Juancito Pinto."

18 Levy and Schady, "Latin America's Social Policy Challenge."

19 Tania Barham, Karen Macours, John A. Maluccio, "More Schooling *and* More Learning? Effects of a 3-Year Conditional Cash Transfer Program in Nicaragua After 10 Years," October 21, 2012, http://www.dartmouth.edu/~neudc2012/docs/paper_304.pdf (accessed September 28, 2013).

20 Jere R. Behrman, Susan W. Parker, and Petra E. Todd, "Medium-Term Impacts of the *Oportunidades* Conditional Cash Transfer Program on Rural Youth in Mexico," Chapter 7 in Stephan Klasen and Felicitas Nowak-Lehmann, eds., *Poverty, Inequality, and Policy in Latin America* (Cambridge, Mass.: MIT Press, 2009), pp. 219–270, http://athena.sas.upenn.edu/petra/papers/mitpressbook.pdf (accessed September 28, 2013).

21 Santiago Levy, "Progress Against Poverty: Sustaining Mexico's Progresa-Oportunidades Program," Brookings Institution, January 8, 2007, http://www.brookings.edu/~/media/events/2007/1/08poverty/20070108.pdf (accessed September 28, 2013).

22 Levy and Schady, "Latin America's Social Policy Challenge," p. 208.

23 Adriana Camacho and Emily Conover, "Manipulation of Social Program Eligibility," *American Economic Journal: Economic Policy*, Vol. 3, Issue 2 (May 2011), Web Appendix, http://www.aeaweb.org/aej/pol/app/2010-0061_app.pdf (accessed September 30, 2013).

24 Rodrigo Herrera, Osvaldo Larrañaga, and Amanda Telias, "La Ficha de Protección Social," Programa de las Naciones Unidas para el Desarrollo *Working Paper* No. 3, 2010, http://www.pnud.cl/areas/ReduccionPobreza/2012/2010_3.pdf (accessed September 30, 2013).

25 Verónica Amarante, Marco Manacorda, Andrea Vigorito, and Mariana Zerpa, "Social Assistance and Labor Market Outcomes: Evidence from the Uruguayan PANES," Inter-American Development Bank, September 2011, http://www.iadb.org/en/publications/publication-detail,7101.html?id=68009#.Uk2_ztJWyM4 (accessed September 30, 2013).

26 Quoted in Sewall, "Conditional Cash Transfer Programs in Latin America," p. 178.

27 Published as Chapter 5, "Fighting Poverty Through Economic Freedom," in Terry Miller, Kim R. Holmes, and Edwin J. Feulner, *2012 Index of Economic Freedom* (Washington: The Heritage Foundation and Dow Jones & Company, Inc., 2012), pp. 69–73, http://www.heritage.org/index/download.

28 Jean-Pierre Chauffour, "On the Relevance of Freedom and Entitlement in Development: New Empirical Evidence (1975–2007)," World Bank *Policy Research Working Paper* No. 5660, May 2011, http://econ.worldbank.org/external/default/main?pagePK=64165259&piPK=64165421&theSitePK=469372&menuPK=64166093&entityID=000158349_20110516090121 (accessed October 4, 2013).

Chapter 5

Defining Economic Freedom

Ambassador Terry Miller and Anthony B. Kim

> A major source of objection to a free economy is precisely that it ... gives people what they want instead of what a particular group thinks they ought to want. Underlying most arguments against the free market is a lack of belief in freedom itself.
>
> —Milton Friedman[1]

Economic freedom is the condition in which individuals can act with maximum autonomy and minimum obstruction in the pursuit of their economic livelihood and greater prosperity. Any discussion of economic freedom has at its heart reflection on the critical relationship between individuals and the government.

As Friedrich Hayek once observed, "To be controlled in our economic pursuits means to be controlled in everything."[2] Hayek's keen insights on economic freedom are based on the moral truth that each person is, as a matter of natural right, a free and responsible being with inalienable dignity and fundamental liberties that righteous and effective political systems should regard as unassailable.

GUIDING PRINCIPLES OF ECONOMIC FREEDOM

In an economically free society, each person controls the fruits of his or her own labor and initiative. Individuals are empowered—indeed, entitled—to pursue their dreams by means of their own free choice.

In an economically free society, individuals succeed or fail based on their individual effort and ability. The institutions of a free and open market society do not discriminate either against or in favor of individuals based on their race, ethnic background, gender, class, family connections, or any other factor unrelated to individual merit. Government decision-making is characterized by openness and transparency, which illuminates the shadows where discrimination might flourish and promotes equal opportunity for all.

In an economically free society, the power of economic decision-making is widely dispersed, and the allocation of resources for production and consumption is on the basis of open competition so that every individual or firm gets a fair chance to succeed.

These three fundamental principles of economic freedom—empowerment of the individual, non-discrimination, and open competition—underpin every measurement and policy idea presented in the *Index of Economic Freedom*.

ECONOMIC FREEDOM: AUTONOMY, NOT ANARCHY

In general, state action or government control that interferes with individual autonomy limits economic freedom. The *Index of Economic Freedom* is not, however, a call for anarchy. The goal of economic freedom is not simply an absence of government coercion or constraint, but the creation and maintenance of a mutual sense of liberty for all. As individuals enjoy the blessings of economic freedom, they in turn have a responsibility to respect the economic rights and freedoms of others within the rule of law. Governments are instituted to ensure basic protections against the ravages of nature or the predations of one citizen over another. Positive economic rights such as property and contracts are given societal as well as individual defense against the destructive tendencies of others.

A comprehensive view of economic freedom encompasses all liberties and rights of production, distribution, or consumption of goods and services. The highest forms of economic freedom should provide an absolute right of property ownership; full freedom of movement for labor, capital, and goods; and an absolute absence of coercion or constraint of economic activity beyond that which is necessary for the protection and maintenance of liberty itself. An economically free society encourages handling of economic decisions in a decentralized fashion. Individuals are free to work, produce, consume, and invest in any way they choose under the even-handed application of laws, with their economic freedoms at once both protected and respected by the state.

However, some government action is necessary for the citizens of a nation to defend themselves, promote the peaceful evolution of civil society, and enjoy the fruits of their labor. For example, citizens are taxed to provide revenue for public safety, the protection of property, and the common defense. There can also be other goods—what economists call "public goods"—that may be supplied more efficiently by government than through private means. Some public goods, such as the maintenance of a police force to protect property rights, a monetary authority to maintain a sound currency, and an impartial judiciary to enforce contracts among parties, are themselves vital ingredients of an economically free society. When government action rises beyond the minimal necessary level, however, it leads inevitably and quickly to the loss of freedom—and the first freedom affected is often economic freedom.[3]

Throughout history, governments have imposed a wide array of constraints on economic activity. Such constraints, though sometimes imposed in the name of equality or some other noble societal purpose, are in reality imposed most often for the benefit of societal elites or special interests, and they come with a high cost to society as a whole. By substituting political judgments for those of the marketplace, government diverts entrepreneurial resources and energy from productive activities to rent-seeking, the quest for economically unearned benefits. The result is lower productivity, economic stagnation, and declining prosperity.

Government provision of goods and services beyond those that are clearly considered public goods imposes a separate constraint on economic activity as well, crowding out private-sector activity and usurping resources that might otherwise have been available for private investment or consumption. Constraining economic choice distorts and diminishes the production, distribution, and consumption of goods and services (including, of course, labor services). The wealth of a nation inevitably declines as a result.

MEASURING ECONOMIC FREEDOM

Assessing economic freedom in countries as diverse as Hong Kong and Venezuela, Zimbabwe and Singapore, or Switzerland and Cuba is not an easy task. As the number and variety of countries included in the *Index* have increased, it has become ever more difficult to find consistent and reliable data covering them all. We are indebted to various governmental and non-governmental international organizations that have undertaken the arduous task of data collection in their various areas of focus and have shared their data with us.

The *Index of Economic Freedom* takes a broad and comprehensive view of country performance, measuring 10 separate areas of economic freedom. Some of the aspects of economic freedom that are evaluated are concerned with a country's interactions with the rest of the world—for example, the extent of an economy's openness to global investment or trade. Most, however, focus on policies within a country, assessing the liberty of individuals to use their labor or finances without undue restraint and government interference.

Each of the economic freedoms plays a vital role in developing and sustaining personal and national prosperity. All are complementary in their impact, however, and progress in one area is often likely to reinforce or even inspire progress in another. Similarly, repressed economic freedom in one area—respect for property rights, for example—may make it much more difficult to achieve high levels of freedom in other categories.

Each economic freedom is individually scored on a scale of 0 to 100. A country's overall economic freedom score is a simple average of its scores on the 10 individual freedoms. Information about the methodology used to compute each component score is detailed in the appendix.

For presentational clarity, the 10 economic freedoms are grouped into four broad categories:

- **Rule of law** (property rights, freedom from corruption);
- **Government size** (fiscal freedom, government spending);
- **Regulatory efficiency** (business freedom, labor freedom, monetary freedom); and
- **Market openness** (trade freedom, investment freedom, financial freedom).

RULE OF LAW

Property Rights. The ability to accumulate private property and wealth is understood to be a central motivating force for workers and investors in a market economy. The recognition of private property rights and an effective rule of law to protect them are vital features of a fully functioning market economy. Secure property rights give citizens the confidence to undertake entrepreneurial activity, save their income, and make long-term plans because they know that their income, savings, and property (both real and intellectual) are safe from unfair expropriation or theft.

The protection of private property requires an autonomous and accountable judicial system that is available to all equally and without discrimination. The independence, transparency, and effectiveness of the judicial system have proven to be key determinants of a country's prospects for long-term economic growth. Such a system is also vital to the maintenance of peace and security and the protection of human rights.

A key aspect of property rights protection is the enforcement of contracts. The voluntary undertaking of contractual obligations is the foundation of the market system and the basis for economic specialization, gains from commercial exchange, and trade among nations. Even-handed government enforcement of private contracts is essential to ensuring equity and integrity in the marketplace.

Freedom from Corruption. In the context of economic freedom, corruption can best be understood as the failure of integrity in the economic system, a distortion by which individuals or special-interest groups are able to gain at the expense of the whole. Often a direct result of the government's concentration of economic or political power, corruption manifests itself in many forms such as bribery, extortion, nepotism, cronyism, patronage, embezzlement, and graft.

Corruption can infect all parts of an economy in systematic ways. There is a direct relationship between the extent of government intervention in economic activity and the amount of corruption. In particular, excessive and redundant government regulations provide opportunities for bribery or graft. In addition, government regulations or restrictions in one area may create informal markets in another. For example, a country that imposes numerous burdensome barriers on conducting business, including regulatory red tape and high transaction costs, can incentivize bribery and encourage illegitimate market interactions.

Ensuring transparency is key to dealing effectively with corruption. Openness in regulatory procedures and processes can promote equitable treatment and greater efficiency.

GOVERNMENT SIZE

Fiscal Freedom. Fiscal freedom is a direct measure of the extent to which government permits individuals and businesses to keep and manage their income and wealth for their own benefit and use. A government can impose fiscal burdens on economic activity through taxation, but it also does so when it incurs public debt that ultimately must be paid off through taxation.

The marginal tax rate confronting an individual is, in effect, the government's cut of the profit from his or her next unit of work or engagement in a new entrepreneurial venture; whatever remains after the tax is the individual's actual reward for the effort. Therefore, the higher the government's cut, the lower the individual's reward—and the lower the incentive to undertake the work at all. Higher tax rates interfere with the ability of individuals and firms to pursue their goals in the marketplace and thereby reduce overall private-sector activity.

While individual and corporate income tax rates are important to economic freedom, they are not a comprehensive measure of the tax burden. Governments impose many other indirect taxes, including payroll, sales, and excise taxes, as well as tariffs and the value-added tax (VAT). In the *Index of Economic Freedom*, the burden of these taxes is captured by measuring the overall tax burden from all forms of taxation as a percentage of total GDP.

Government Spending. The cost of excessive government is a central issue in economic freedom, both in terms of generating revenue (see fiscal freedom) and in terms of spending. Government spending comes in many forms. Some government spending—for example, to provide infrastructure, fund research, or improve human capital—may be considered investment. Government also spends on public goods, the benefits of which accrue broadly to society in ways that markets cannot price appropriately.

All government spending that must eventually be financed by higher taxation, however, entails an opportunity cost. This cost is the value of the private consumption or investment that would have occurred had the resources involved been left in the private sector.

Excessive government spending runs a great risk of crowding out private economic activity. Even if an economy achieves faster growth through more government spending, such economic expansion tends to be only temporary, distorting the market allocation of resources and private investment incentives. Even worse, a government's insulation from market discipline often leads to bureaucracy, lower productivity, inefficiency, and mounting public debt that imposes an even greater burden on future generations.

As many economies have experienced in recent years, high levels of public debt accumulated through irresponsible government spending undermine economic freedom and prevent dynamic entrepreneurial growth.

REGULATORY EFFICIENCY

Business Freedom. Business freedom is about an individual's right to establish and run an enterprise without undue interference from the state. Burdensome and redundant regulations are the most common barriers to the free conduct of entrepreneurial activity.

By increasing the costs of production, regulations can make it difficult for entrepreneurs to succeed in the marketplace. Although many regulations hinder business productivity and profitability, the most inhibiting to entrepreneurship are those that are associated with licensing new businesses.

In some countries, as well as many states in the United States, the procedure for obtaining a business license can be as simple as mailing in a registration form with a minimal fee. In Hong Kong, for example, obtaining a business license requires filling out a single form, and the process can be completed in a few hours. In other economies, such as India and parts of South America, the process of obtaining a business license can take much longer, involving endless trips to government offices and repeated encounters with officious and sometimes corrupt bureaucrats.

Once a business is open, government regulation may interfere with the normal decision-making or price-setting process. Interestingly, two countries with the same set of regulations can impose different regulatory burdens. If one country applies its regulations evenly and transparently, this can lower the regulatory burden by facilitating long-term business planning. If the other applies regulations inconsistently, it raises the regulatory burden by creating an unpredictable business environment. Rigid and onerous bankruptcy procedures are also distortionary, providing a disincentive for entrepreneurs to start businesses in the first place.

Labor Freedom. The ability of individuals to work as much as they want and wherever they want is a key component of economic freedom. By the same token, the ability of businesses to contract freely for labor and dismiss redundant workers when they are no longer needed is a vital mechanism for enhancing productivity and sustaining overall economic growth. The core principle of any market is free, voluntary exchange. That is as true in the labor market as it is in the market for goods.

State intervention generates the same problems in the labor market that it produces in any other market. Government regulations take a variety of forms, including wage controls, restrictions on hiring and firing, and other constraints. In many countries, unions play an important role in regulating labor freedom and, depending on the nature of their activity, may be either a force for greater freedom or an impediment to the efficient functioning of labor markets.

Onerous labor laws penalize businesses and workers alike. Rigid labor regulations prevent employers and employees from freely negotiating changes in terms and conditions of work, resulting often in a chronic mismatch of labor supply and demand. In general, the greater the degree of labor freedom, the lower the rate of unemployment in an economy.

Monetary Freedom. Monetary freedom requires a stable currency and market-determined prices. Whether acting as entrepreneurs or as consumers, free people need a steady and reliable currency as a medium of exchange, unit of account, and store of value. Without monetary freedom, it is difficult to create long-term value or amass capital.

The value of a country's currency can be influenced significantly by the monetary policy of its government. With a monetary policy that endeavors to fight inflation, maintain price stability, and preserve the nation's wealth, people can rely on market prices for the foreseeable future. Investments, savings, and other longer-term plans can be made more confidently. An inflationary policy, by contrast, confiscates wealth like an invisible tax and also distorts prices, misallocates resources, and raises the cost of doing business.

There is no single accepted theory of the right monetary policy for a free society. At one time, the gold standard enjoyed widespread support. What characterizes almost all monetary theories today, however, is support for low inflation and an independent central bank. There is also widespread recognition that price controls corrupt market efficiency and lead to shortages or surpluses.

MARKET OPENNESS

Trade Freedom. Trade freedom reflects an economy's openness to the flow of goods and services from around the world and the citizen's ability to interact freely as buyer or seller in the international marketplace. Trade restrictions can manifest themselves in the form of tariffs, export taxes, trade quotas, or outright trade bans. However, trade restrictions also appear in more subtle ways, particularly in the form of regulatory barriers.

The degree to which government hinders the free flow of foreign commerce has a direct bearing on the ability of individuals to pursue their economic goals and maximize their productivity and well-being. Tariffs, for example, directly increase the prices that local consumers pay for foreign imports, but they also distort production incentives for local producers, causing them to produce either a good for which they lack a comparative advantage or more of a protected good than is economically efficient. This impedes overall economic efficiency and growth.

In many cases, trade limitations also put advanced-technology products and services beyond the reach of local entrepreneurs, limiting their own productive development.

Investment Freedom. A free and open investment environment provides maximum entrepreneurial opportunities and incentives for expanded economic activity, greater productivity, and job creation. The benefits of such an environment flow not only to the individual companies that take the entrepreneurial risk in expectation of greater return, but also to society as a whole. An effective investment framework will be characterized by transparency and equity, supporting all types of firms rather than just large or strategically important companies, and will encourage rather than discourage innovation and competition.

Restrictions on the movement of capital, both domestic and international, undermine the efficient allocation of resources and reduce productivity, distorting economic decision-making. Restrictions on cross-border investment can limit both inflows and outflows of capital, thereby shrinking markets and reducing opportunities for growth.

In an environment in which individuals and companies are free to choose where and how to invest, capital will flow to its best use: to the sectors and activities where it is most needed and the returns are greatest. State action to redirect the flow of capital and limit choice is an imposition on the freedom of both the investor and the person seeking capital. The more restrictions a country imposes on investment, the lower its level of entrepreneurial activity.

Financial Freedom. An accessible and well-functioning formal financial system ensures the availability of diversified savings, credit, payment, and investment services to individuals. By expanding financing opportunities and promoting entrepreneurship, an open banking environment encourages competition in order to provide the most efficient financial intermediation between households and firms as well as between investors and entrepreneurs.

Through a process driven by supply and demand, markets provide real-time information on prices and immediate discipline for those who have made bad decisions. This process depends on transparency in the market and the integrity of the information being made available. A prudent and effective regulatory system, through disclosure requirements and independent auditing, ensures both.

Increasingly, the central role played by banks is being complemented by other financial services that offer alternative means for raising capital or diversifying risk. As with the banking system, the useful role for government in regulating these institutions lies in ensuring transparency; promoting disclosure of assets, liabilities, and risks; and ensuring integrity.

Banking and financial regulation by the state that goes beyond the assurance of transparency and honesty in financial markets can impede efficiency, increase the costs of financing entrepreneurial activity, and limit competition. If the government intervenes in the stock market, for instance, it contravenes the choices of millions of individuals by interfering with the pricing of capital—the most critical function of a market economy. Equity markets measure, on a continual basis, the expected profits and losses in publicly held companies. This measurement is essential in allocating capital resources to their highest-valued uses and thereby satisfying consumers' most urgent requirements.

ECONOMIC FREEDOM: AN END IN ITSELF, A MEANS FOR PROGRESS

Economic freedom, enhanced and secured by the rule of law, government size, regulatory efficiency, and market openness, is a vital element of human dignity, enabling individuals to plan and direct their lives in ways that maximize their happiness as they see fit. In addition, economic freedom is the key to achieving the broad-based economic dynamism that ensures lasting growth and increased prosperity for society as a whole.

In other words, economic freedom is valuable as an end itself. But just as important is that, with its 10 freedoms interacting with and complementing each other, economic freedom is also about a multidimensional process of achieving economic progress. As Hayek foresaw decades ago, "the guiding principle in any attempt to create a world of free men must be this: a policy of freedom for the individual is the only truly progressive policy."[4]

The link between freedom and human progress has never been clearer. Twenty years of data in the *Index of Economic Freedom* have documented the clear association between higher levels of economic freedom and greater levels of overall well-being. Equally important, improvements in economic freedom, from whatever level, have been shown to enhance economic dynamism and measurable human development that entails better health, longer lives, greater education, and cleaner environments.

As indicated by the findings of the *Index* over the past 20 years, sustaining dynamic and inclusive economic expansion is in fact about putting into practice three fundamental principles of economic freedom: empowerment of the individual, non-discrimination, and open competition. Governments that choose policies that enhance economic freedom are placing their societies on the path to generating the broader-based economic dynamism that brings more opportunities for people to work, produce, and save.

Endnotes

1. Milton Friedman, *Capitalism and Freedom* (Chicago: University of Chicago Press, 1962).
2. Friedrich A. Hayek, *The Road to Serfdom* (Chicago: University of Chicago Press, 1944).
3. "The property which every man has in his own labor, as it is the original foundation of all other property, so it is the most sacred and inviolable." Adam Smith, *An Inquiry into the Nature and Causes of the Wealth of Nations* (New York: The Modern Library, 1937), pp. 121–122; first published in 1776.
4. Hayek, *The Road to Serfdom.*

Chapter 6

The Countries

This chapter reports data on economic freedom for each of the countries included in the 2014 *Index of Economic Freedom*, the 20th anniversary edition. This year, Brunei is graded in the *Index* for the first time. Of the 186 countries included in the 2014 *Index*, 178 are fully scored and ranked. Because of insufficient data, Afghanistan, Iraq, Kosovo, Libya, Somalia, Sudan, Syria, and Liechtenstein are covered without numerical grading.

For analytical understanding and presentational clarity, the 10 economic freedoms are grouped into four broad categories of economic freedom:

- **Rule of law** (property rights, freedom from corruption);
- **Government size** (fiscal freedom, government spending);
- **Regulatory efficiency** (business freedom, labor freedom, monetary freedom); and
- **Market openness** (trade freedom, investment freedom, financial freedom).

Ranked countries are given a score ranging from 0 to 100 on each of the 10 components of economic freedom, and these scores are then averaged (using equal weights) to compute the country's final economic freedom score. In addition to the scores, the country pages include in each case a brief introduction describing the economic strengths and weaknesses and the political and economic background influencing a country's performance, as well as a statistical profile documenting the country's main economic indicators.

To assure objectivity and reliability within each of the 10 components on which the countries are graded, every effort has been made to use the same data source consistently for all countries; when data are unavailable from the primary source, secondary sources are used. (For details, see Appendix, "Methodology.")

DEFINING THE "QUICK FACTS"

Each country page includes "Quick Facts" with nine different categories of information. Unless otherwise indicated, the data in each country's profile are for 2012 (the year for which the most recent data are widely available) and in current 2012 U.S. dollars (also the most recent available). The few cases in which no reliable statistical data were available are indicated by "n/a." Definitions and sources for each category of information are as follows.

Population: 2012 data from World Bank, *World Development Indicators Online 2013*. For some countries, another source is the country's statistical agency and/or central bank.

GDP: Gross domestic product—total production of goods and services—adjusted to reflect purchasing power parity (PPP). The primary source for GDP data is World Bank, *World Development Indicators Online 2013*. The major secondary source is International Monetary Fund, *World Economic Outlook Database, 2013*. Other sources include a country's statistical agency and/or central bank.

GDP growth rate: The annual percentage growth rate of real GDP derived from constant national currency units. Annual percent changes are year-on-year. The primary source is International Monetary Fund, *World Economic Outlook Database, 2013*. Secondary sources include World Bank, *World Development Indicators Online 2013*; Economist Intelligence Unit, *Data Tool*; Asian Development Bank, *Asian Development Outlook 2013*; and a country's statistical agency and/or central bank.

GDP five-year compound annual growth: The compound average growth rate measured over a specified period of time. The compound annual growth rate is measured using data from 2007 to 2012, based on real GDP expressed in constant national currency units. It is calculated by taking the *n*th root of the total percentage growth rate, where *n* is the number of years in the period being considered. The primary source is International Monetary Fund, *World Economic Outlook Database, 2013*. Secondary sources are World Bank, *World Development Indicators Online 2013*, and Asian Development Bank, *Asian Development Outlook 2013*.

GDP per capita: Gross domestic product (adjusted for PPP) divided by total population. The sources for these data are World Bank, *World Development Indicators Online 2013*; International Monetary Fund, *World Economic Outlook Database, 2013*; U.S. Central Intelligence Agency, *The World Factbook 2013*; and a country's statistical agency and/or central bank.

Unemployment rate: A measure of the portion of the workforce that is not employed but is actively seeking work. The primary sources are U.S. Central Intelligence Agency, *The World Factbook 2013*; Economist Intelligence Unit, *Data Tool*; Organisation for Economic Co-operation and Development, *OECD. Stat Extracts*; International Monetary Fund, *Article IV Staff Reports, 2010–2013*; and a country's statistical agency.

Inflation: The annual percent change in consumer prices as measured for 2012 (or the most recent available year). The primary source for 2012 data is International Monetary Fund, *World Economic Outlook Database, 2013*. Secondary sources are Economist Intelligence Unit, *Data Tool*; Asian Development Bank, *Asian Development Outlook 2013*; and a country's statistical agency and/or central bank.

Foreign direct investment (FDI) inward flow: This indicates the total annual inward flow of FDI. Data are in current 2012 U.S. dollars, reported in millions. FDI flows are defined as investments that acquire a lasting management interest (10 percent or more of voting stock) in a local enterprise by an investor operating in another country. Such investment is the sum of equity capital, reinvestment of earnings, other long-term capital, and short-term capital as shown in the balance of payments and both short-term and long-term international loans. Data are from United Nations Conference on Trade and Development, *World Investment Report 2013*.

Public debt: Gross government debt as a percentage of GDP, which indicates the cumulative total of all government borrowings less repayments that are denominated in a country's currency. Public debt is different from external debt, which reflects the foreign currency liabilities of both the private and public sectors and must be financed out of foreign exchange earnings. The primary sources for 2012 data are International Monetary Fund, *World Economic Outlook Database, 2013*; International Monetary Fund, *Article IV Staff Reports*, 2010–2013; and a country's statistical agency. The data source for U.S. public debt is United States Office of Management and Budget. Concerning the U.S. data, gross debt includes both publicly held debt (bonds and Treasury bills held by foreigners, corporations, individual citizens, investment vehicles, etc.) and intra-governmental debt such as Social Security trust funds.

COMMONLY USED ACRONYMS

CARICOM: Caribbean Community and Common Market, composed of Antigua and Barbuda, the Bahamas, Barbados, Belize, Dominica, Grenada, Guyana, Haiti, Jamaica, Montserrat, Saint Lucia, Saint Kitts and Nevis, Saint Vincent and the Grenadines, Suriname, and Trinidad and Tobago.

CEMAC: Central African Economic and Monetary Community, which includes Cameroon, the Central African Republic, Chad, the Republic of Congo, Equatorial Guinea, and Gabon.

EU: European Union, consisting of Austria, Belgium, Bulgaria, Cyprus, the Czech Republic, Denmark, Estonia, Finland, France, Germany, Greece, Hungary, Ireland, Italy, Latvia, Lithuania, Luxembourg, Malta, the Netherlands, Poland, Portugal, Romania, Slovakia, Slovenia, Spain, Sweden, and the United Kingdom.

IMF: International Monetary Fund, established in 1945 to help stabilize countries during crises; now includes 188 member countries.

OECD: Organisation for Economic Co-operation and Development, an international organization of developed countries, founded in 1948; now includes 34 member countries.

SACU: Southern African Customs Union, consisting of Botswana, Lesotho, Namibia, South Africa, and Swaziland.

WTO: World Trade Organization, founded in 1995 as the central organization dealing with the rules of trade between nations and based on signed agreements among member countries. As of August 2013, there were 159 member economies.

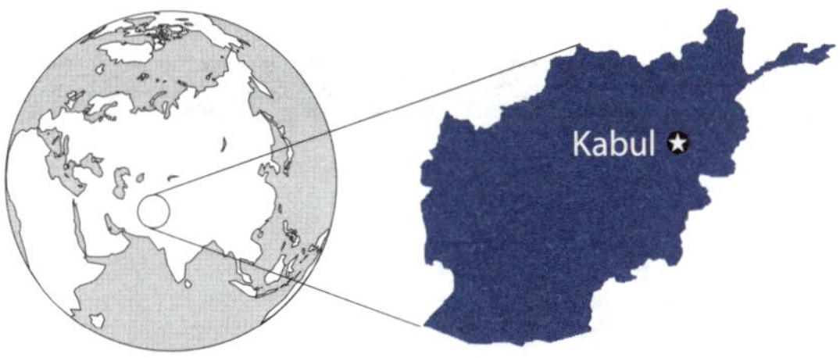

AFGHANISTAN

Economic Freedom Score

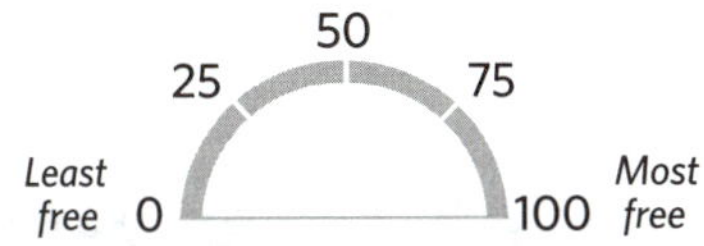

This economy is not graded

World Rank: Not Ranked | **Regional Rank: Not Ranked**

Afghanistan's economic freedom could not be graded because of a lack of reliable comparable data. The government's compilations of official economic data are not comprehensive, and many of the international sources relied upon for *Index* grading contain incomplete data on Afghanistan. This assessment is based on the limited data available from government and international sources.

Over the past 10 years, Afghanistan has undergone a challenging economic transition requiring significant institutional development. Growth rates have been high but volatile. Real GDP growth, driven mainly by agriculture and construction, has averaged almost 10 percent over the past five years. Large volumes of foreign aid have yielded some improvements in such areas as health and education.

Operating under difficult developmental circumstances, Afghanistan remains severely burdened by numerous systemic shortcomings worsened by ongoing security challenges. The government's weakness, exacerbated by vested interests and corruption, has hindered politically difficult policy reforms and eroded trust. Previously implemented reform measures have not been sustained, with political uncertainties further undermining progress in economic reconstruction.

BACKGROUND: President Hamid Karzai is constitutionally required to hand power to a successor following elections scheduled for April 2014. The U.S. and NATO have committed to withdrawing all combat forces by the end of 2014 but will continue to fund and train the Afghan National Army and provide development aid. A bilateral security agreement will determine the levels and conditions of a post-2014 U.S. troop presence. The U.S. is seeking peace talks with the Taliban, but insurgents continue to battle coalition and Afghan forces. Afghanistan is one of the world's poorest countries. GDP is growing, but the economy remains hobbled by poor infrastructure, insurgency, and corruption. The agricultural sector depends heavily on cultivation of the opium poppy, and illegal drug trafficking fuels violence and instability.

Freedom Trend

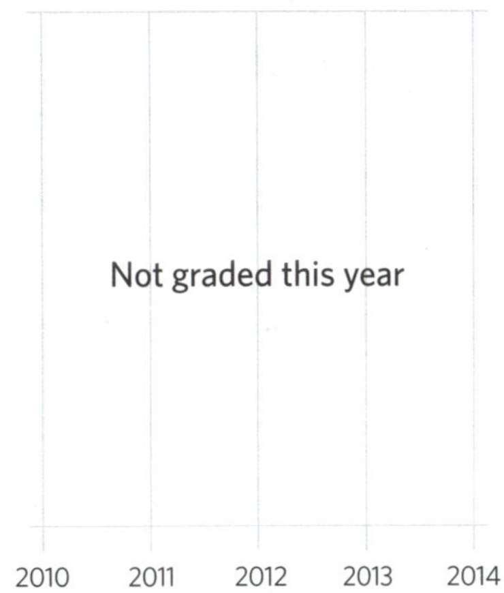

Country Comparisons

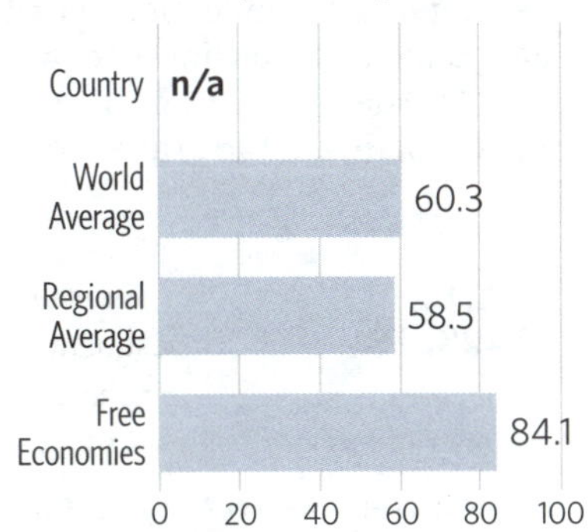

Quick Facts

Population: 32.0 million
GDP (PPP): $33.7 billion
10.2% growth in 2012
5-year compound annual growth 9.9%
$1,054 per capita
Unemployment: 35.0%
Inflation (CPI): 4.4%
FDI Inflow: $93.8 million
Public Debt: 12.1% of GDP

2012 data unless otherwise noted.
Data compiled as of September 2013.

How Do We Measure Economic Freedom?
See page 471 for an explanation of the methodology or visit the *Index* Web site at *heritage.org/index.*

AFGHANISTAN (continued)

THE TEN ECONOMIC FREEDOMS

Score ▬ Country | World Average

RULE OF LAW

	Score	Rank	1-Year Change
Property Rights	n/a	—	n/a
Freedom from Corruption	10.0	181st	-5.0

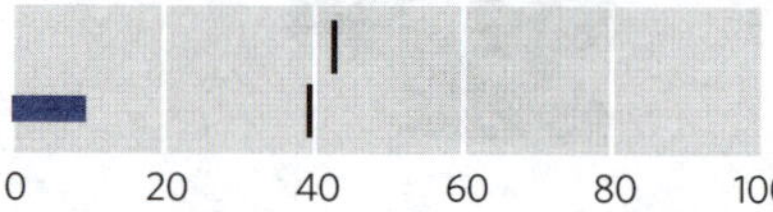

Fueled by proceeds from opium trafficking and unimpeded by weak state institutions, corruption permeates Afghanistan from the presidency down to the lowest levels of government. The judicial system is severely underdeveloped. Weak protection of property rights due to a lack of property registries or a land titling database leads to land title disputes. An estimated 80 percent of land is held and transferred informally.

GOVERNMENT SIZE

	Score	Rank	1-Year Change
Fiscal Freedom	91.2	27th	n/a
Government Spending	84.2	35th	+1.0

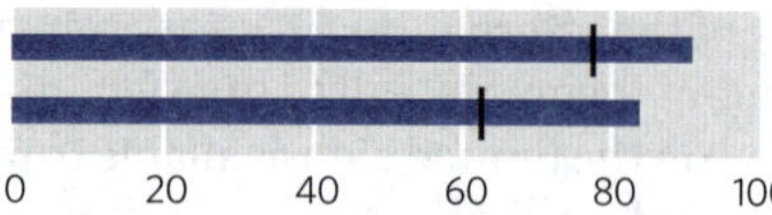

The top individual income and corporate tax rates are 20 percent. Other taxes include sales taxes. Tax revenue remains relatively low at 8.7 percent of GDP. The government still remains heavily reliant on foreign assistance to cover budget shortfalls and has missed established budget goals. Expenditures have risen to 23 percent of gross domestic product.

REGULATORY EFFICIENCY

	Score	Rank	1-Year Change
Business Freedom	63.1	98th	+3.4
Labor Freedom	75.0	48th	-0.8
Monetary Freedom	74.3	114th	+4.8

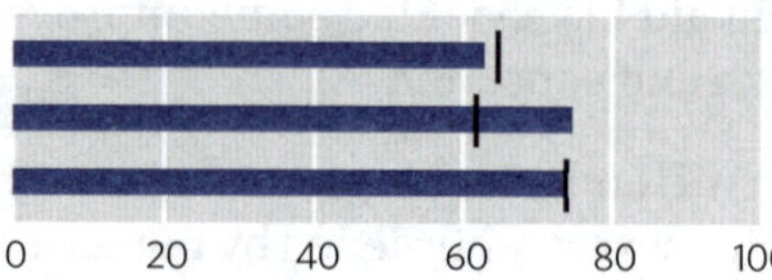

Despite recent reforms, the inefficient business environment still impedes broader economic development. Application of regulations has been inconsistent and non-transparent. On average, launching a business requires four procedures, but obtaining necessary permits can take over 300 days. In the absence of a well-functioning labor market, informal labor activity persists in many sectors. Inflation has decreased to below 5 percent.

OPEN MARKETS

	Score	Rank	1-Year Change
Trade Freedom	n/a	—	n/a
Investment Freedom	65.0	68th	0
Financial Freedom	n/a	—	n/a

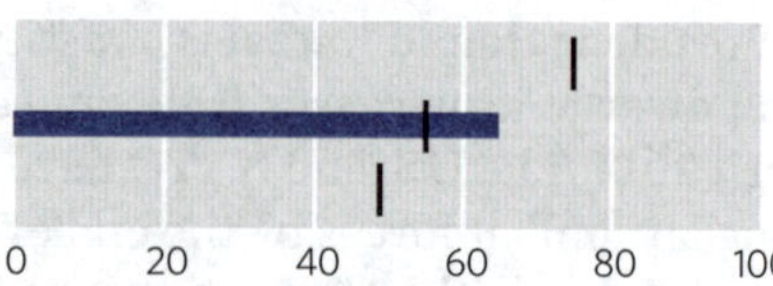

Afghanistan has a 6.4 percent average tariff rate, and non-tariff barriers that include customs delays deter imports. Foreign ownership of land is prohibited, and the government regulates investment in some sectors, including insurance and telecommunications. The underdeveloped financial system has only a limited role in the economy, hampering private entrepreneurial growth. The banking sector, whose laws are often bent, remains fragile.

Long-Term Score Change: n/a

RULE OF LAW		GOVERNMENT SIZE		REGULATORY EFFICIENCY		OPEN MARKETS	
Property Rights	n/a	Fiscal Freedom	n/a	Business Freedom	n/a	Trade Freedom	n/a
Freedom from Corruption	n/a	Government Spending	n/a	Labor Freedom	n/a	Investment Freedom	n/a
				Monetary Freedom	n/a	Financial Freedom	n/a

ALBANIA

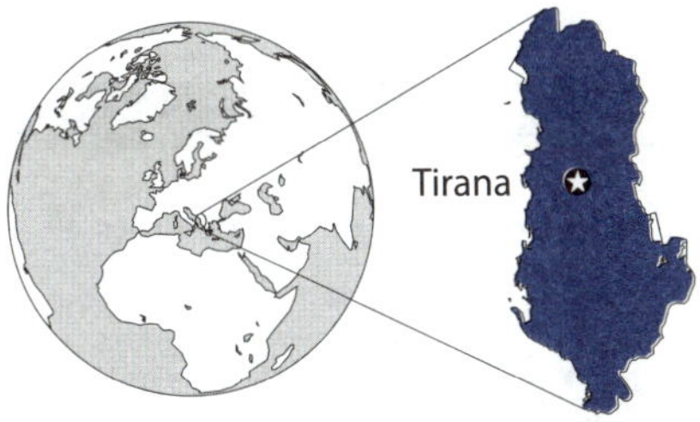

World Rank: **54** Regional Rank: **25**

Economic Freedom Score

Albania's economic freedom score is 66.9, making its economy the 54th freest in the 2014 *Index*. Its overall score has increased by 1.7 points, with notable improvements in investment freedom and trade freedom. Albania is ranked 25th among the 43 countries in the Europe region, and its overall score is above the world average.

Over the 20-year history of the *Index,* Albania has advanced its economic freedom score by about 17 points, a top 20 improvement. With score increases in nine of the 10 economic freedoms, Albania has risen gradually into the "moderately free" category. Notable structural reforms have included trade liberalization, privatization, implementation of competitive flat tax rates, and modernization of the regulatory environment. Along with the effective maintenance of low inflation, greater monetary stability has also been achieved.

The judiciary remains subject to political interference, and deeper institutional reforms to eradicate lingering corruption and increase judicial independence are critical to ensuring greater economic freedom in Albania. Rising fiscal deficits in recent years have increased public debt to above 60 percent of GDP, the legal limit set in 2008.

BACKGROUND: Communist rule in Albania ended in 1992. Socialist Edi Rama was elected prime minister in June 2013, defeating conservative incumbent Sali Berisha, who had been prime minister since 2005. Rama campaigned on a promise to secure European Union candidacy status within a year. Albania achieved full membership in NATO in April 2009 and continues to make a small contribution to the NATO-led mission in Afghanistan. Despite some reforms, Albania is one of Europe's poorest countries. Transportation and energy infrastructure are poor by European standards. The economy is dominated by agriculture and services, including tourism.

How Do We Measure Economic Freedom?
See page 471 for an explanation of the methodology or visit the *Index* Web site at *heritage.org/index.*

Freedom Trend

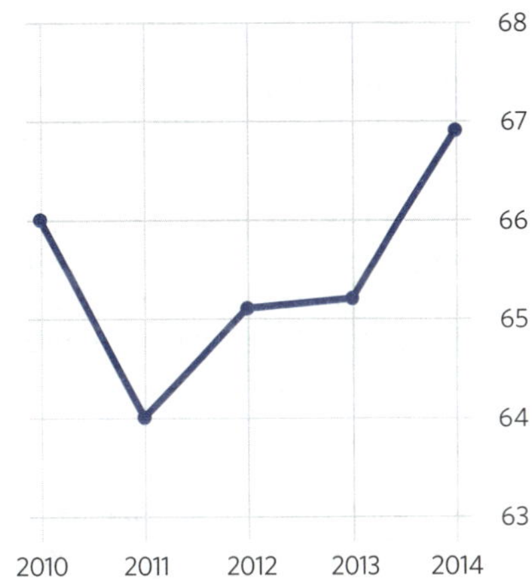

Country Comparisons

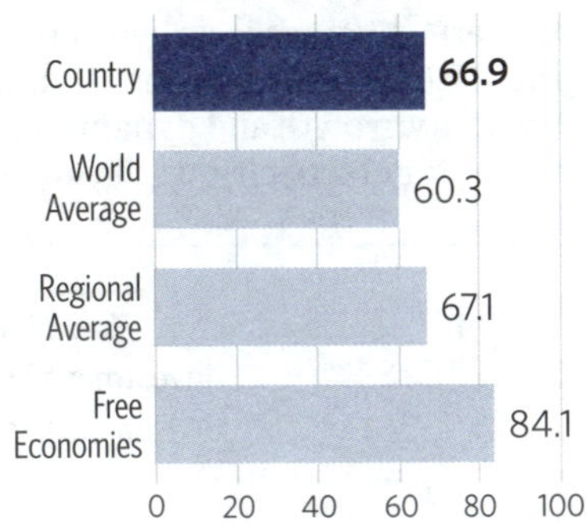

Quick Facts

Population: 3.2 million
GDP (PPP): $26.1 billion
1.3% growth in 2012
5-year compound annual growth 3.7%
$8,052 per capita
Unemployment: 15.0% (2008)
Inflation (CPI): 2.0%
FDI Inflow: $957.0 million
Public Debt: 60.6% of GDP

2012 data unless otherwise noted.
Data compiled as of September 2013.

THE TEN ECONOMIC FREEDOMS

Score ■ Country | World Average

RULE OF LAW

	Score	Rank	1-Year Change
Property Rights	30.0	93rd	0
Freedom from Corruption	30.4	101st	-0.6

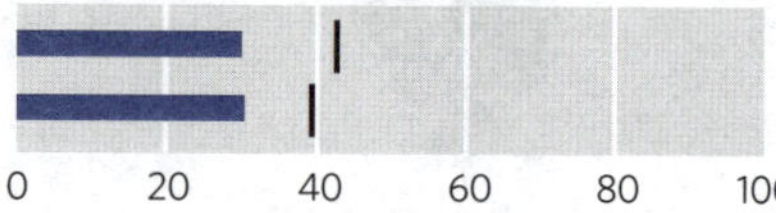

A weak regulatory environment, opaque government procurement rules, a culture of impunity, and political interference make it difficult for the judiciary to deal with high-level and deeply rooted corruption in Albania, a major transit country for human trafficking and illegal arms and narcotics. Protection of intellectual property rights is weak, and Albania still lacks a clear property rights system, particularly for land tenure.

GOVERNMENT SIZE

	Score	Rank	1-Year Change
Fiscal Freedom	92.7	20th	+0.1
Government Spending	75.6	65th	+0.5

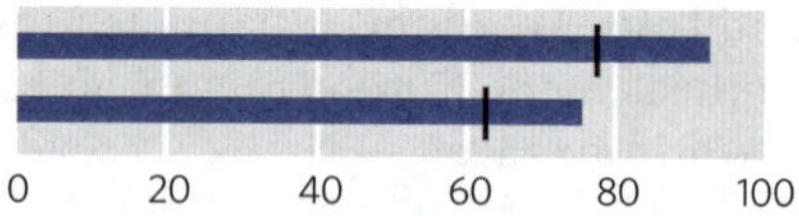

The top individual income and corporate tax rates are 10 percent. Other taxes include a value-added tax (VAT) and an inheritance tax. The overall tax burden has fallen slightly to 23 percent of total domestic income. Government expenditures stand at 28.5 percent of GDP. The slowing domestic economy has put internal pressures on public finances, pushing up public debt to 61 percent of GDP.

REGULATORY EFFICIENCY

	Score	Rank	1-Year Change
Business Freedom	78.1	36th	-2.9
Labor Freedom	49.7	140th	+0.7
Monetary Freedom	80.0	31st	+1.6

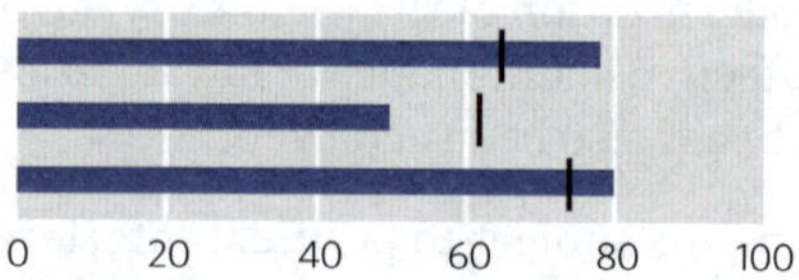

The efficient regulatory framework supports business formation. The number of days needed to start a business has been cut to four, with no minimum capital required. Despite efforts to increase flexibility in the labor market, relatively rigid employment regulations hinder productivity growth and dynamic job creation. Price controls and state subsidies distort domestic prices for electricity, water, and railroad transportation.

OPEN MARKETS

	Score	Rank	1-Year Change
Trade Freedom	87.5	35th	+7.7
Investment Freedom	75.0	35th	+10.0
Financial Freedom	70.0	19th	0

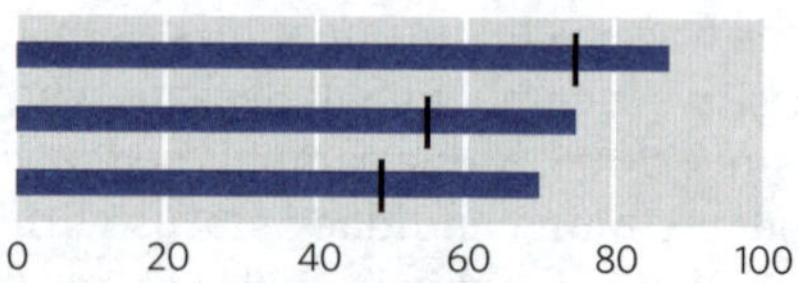

Albania's average tariff rate has improved significantly from 5.1 percent to a relatively low 1.3 percent. The country officially welcomes foreign investment, but red tape and insufficient protection of property rights discourage investment. The financial system remains relatively well-developed and stable despite the challenging external environment. The banking sector is well-provisioned, but the share of non-performing loans has been rising.

Long-Term Score Change (since 1995)

RULE OF LAW		GOVERNMENT SIZE		REGULATORY EFFICIENCY		OPEN MARKETS	
Property Rights	**-20.0**	Fiscal Freedom	**+11.0**	Business Freedom	**+8.1**	Trade Freedom	**+28.5**
Freedom from Corruption	**+20.4**	Government Spending	**+41.3**	Labor Freedom	**+0.8**	Investment Freedom	**+5.0**
				Monetary Freedom	**+57.9**	Financial Freedom	**+20.0**

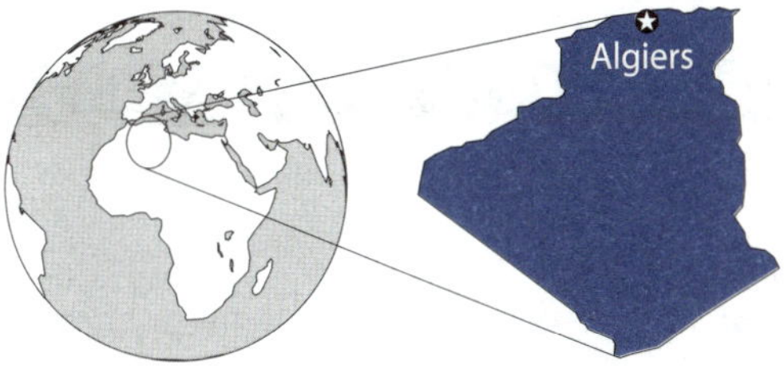

ALGERIA

World Rank: 146 **Regional Rank: 14**

Economic Freedom Score

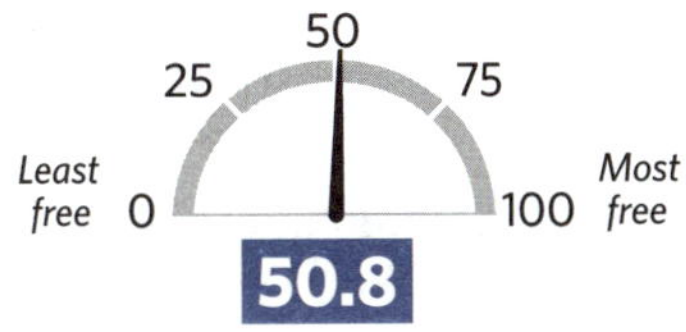

Algeria's economic freedom score is 50.8, making its economy the 146th freest in the 2014 *Index*. Its overall score is 1.2 points better than last year due to notable score improvements in investment freedom and the management of government spending. Algeria is ranked 14th among the 15 countries in the Middle East and North Africa region, and its score remains lower than both the regional and world averages.

Over the 20-year history of the *Index*, Algeria's economic freedom score has declined by almost 5 points, one of the 20 worst losses of economic freedom. Seven of the 10 economic freedoms, notably property rights, freedom from corruption, the management of government spending, and financial freedom, have declined. The Algerian economy remains just at the bottom of the category of "mostly unfree" states.

As policies to sustain reform measures have been neglected or even reversed, Algeria has become more dependent on the hydrocarbon sector. In light of increasing social discontent, the government in recent years has adopted expansionary public spending programs, making little progress in improving fiscal governance.

BACKGROUND: President Abdelaziz Bouteflika won a third term in 2009 in an election that was boycotted by some political parties. After the "Arab Spring" protests swept neighboring Tunisia and Libya, the government introduced some political reforms, including an end to state-of-emergency restrictions that had lasted almost two decades. The socialist model adopted after Algeria gained its independence from France in 1962 has hampered development. Formal-sector unemployment remains persistently high, and there is a housing shortage. Algeria is the world's sixth-largest exporter of natural gas and has the world's 10th-largest natural gas reserves and 16th-largest oil reserves. The government began a five-year, $286 billion program to modernize infrastructure in 2010 and appears to be trying to attract foreign and domestic private investment and to diversify the economy.

Freedom Trend

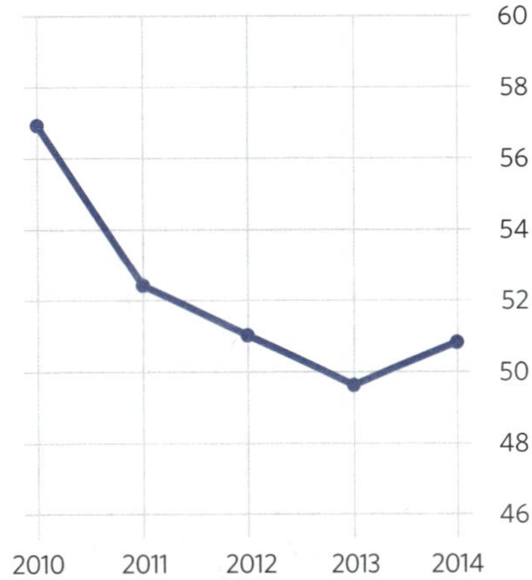

Country Comparisons

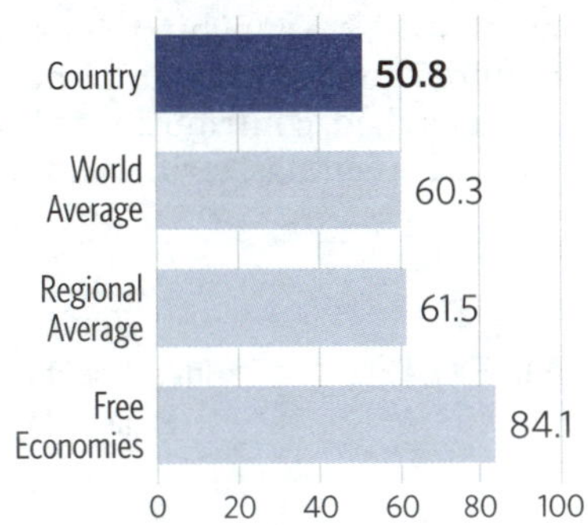

Quick Facts

Population: 36.5 million
GDP (PPP): $272.9 billion
2.5% growth in 2012
5-year compound annual growth 2.4%
$7,477 per capita
Unemployment: 9.7%
Inflation (CPI): 8.9%
FDI Inflow: $1.5 billion
Public Debt: 9.9% of GDP

2012 data unless otherwise noted.
Data compiled as of September 2013.

How Do We Measure Economic Freedom?
See page 471 for an explanation of the methodology or visit the *Index* Web site at *heritage.org/index*.

THE TEN ECONOMIC FREEDOMS

Legend: Country | World Average

RULE OF LAW

	Score	Rank	1-Year Change
Property Rights	30.0	93rd	0
Freedom from Corruption	28.7	111th	-0.3

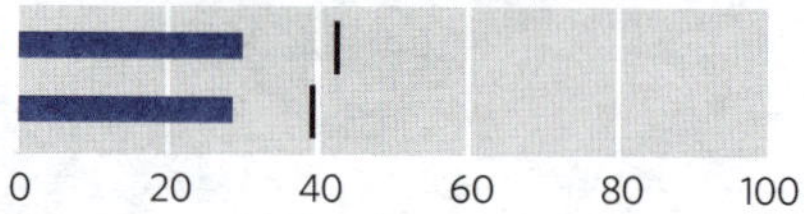

An estimated one-half of all economic transactions occur in the informal sector, beyond the reach of Algeria's generally weak, slow, and opaque judiciary system. An investigation into the state oil and gas company (Sonatrach) was launched in 2013 after the interior minister reported that up to one-quarter of the domestic production of petroleum products is smuggled out of the country. Most real property remains in government hands.

GOVERNMENT SIZE

	Score	Rank	1-Year Change
Fiscal Freedom	80.5	80th	+0.1
Government Spending	51.0	134th	+6.9

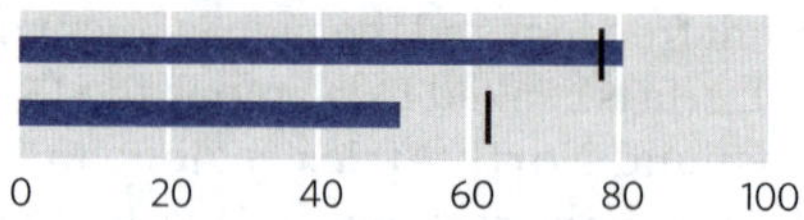

The top individual income tax rate is 35 percent. The corporate tax rate is two-tiered: 25 percent for the non-tourism services sector and 19 percent for the tourism and production sectors. Other taxes include a value-added tax (VAT). The overall tax burden is 10 percent of GDP, and public debt is about 10 percent of the economy. Government spending is slightly over 40 percent of GDP. The hydrocarbon sector continues to boost public finances.

REGULATORY EFFICIENCY

	Score	Rank	1-Year Change
Business Freedom	66.3	89th	+1.1
Labor Freedom	48.3	144th	-4.3
Monetary Freedom	67.8	155th	-8.8

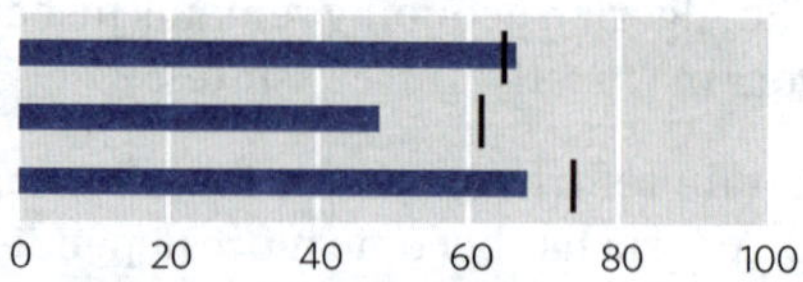

Significant bureaucratic impediments to entrepreneurial activity and economic development persist. Launching a business requires over 10 procedures, there are minimum capital requirements, and obtaining necessary permits can take more than 200 days. The labor market remains rigid, contributing to high youth unemployment of over 20 percent. The government uses price ceilings, tariffs, and redistribution schemes to control prices.

OPEN MARKETS

	Score	Rank	1-Year Change
Trade Freedom	60.8	159th	-7.0
Investment Freedom	45.0	125th	+25.0
Financial Freedom	30.0	132nd	0

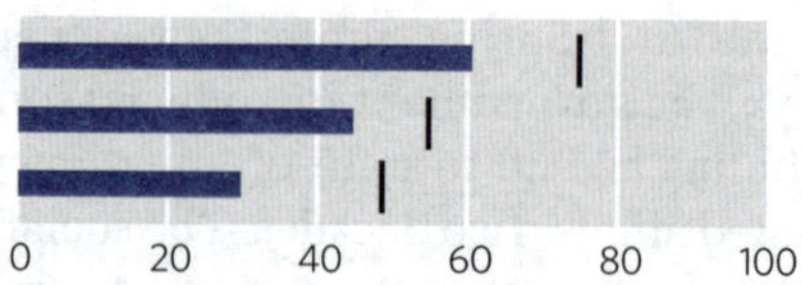

Algeria has a 12.1 percent average tariff rate. The government restricts imports of medicine, medical products, and used earth-moving equipment. It also screens foreign investment, and foreign participation in new investments may not exceed 49 percent. Reflecting the difficult access to financing, credits to the private sector remain low. The equity market is underdeveloped, with a capitalization of less than 1 percent of GDP.

Long-Term Score Change (since 1995)

RULE OF LAW		GOVERNMENT SIZE		REGULATORY EFFICIENCY		OPEN MARKETS	
Property Rights	**-20.0**	Fiscal Freedom	**+31.7**	Business Freedom	**-3.7**	Trade Freedom	**+6.6**
Freedom from Corruption	**-21.3**	Government Spending	**-18.5**	Labor Freedom	**-7.6**	Investment Freedom	**-5.0**
				Monetary Freedom	**+8.6**	Financial Freedom	**-20.0**

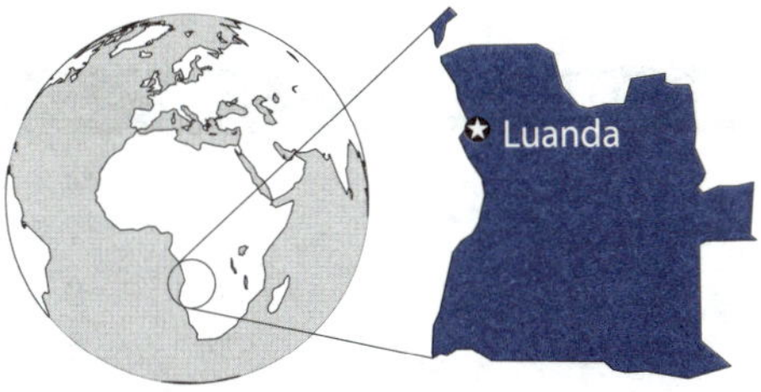

ANGOLA

World Rank: **160** Regional Rank: **39**

Economic Freedom Score

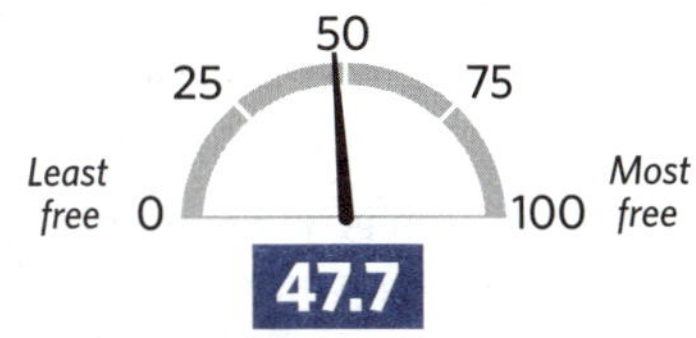

Angola's economic freedom score is 47.7, making its economy the 160th freest in the 2014 *Index*. Its overall score has improved by 0.4 point due to improved scores in fiscal freedom, investment freedom, and business freedom. Angola is ranked 39th out of 46 countries in the Sub-Saharan Africa region, and its score remains far below world and regional averages.

Over the 20-year history of the *Index,* Angola has advanced its economic freedom by 20.3 points, one of the 10 best improvements. Angolans enjoy enhanced freedom in seven of the 10 economic freedom categories, including monetary freedom and trade freedom. Grading of Angola had been temporarily suspended from 2001 to 2005, and much of its notable progress over the history of the *Index* has occurred since 2006 when the *Index* resumed assessing Angola's economic freedom.

However, the lack of capable public institutions and weak rule of law continue to undermine the successful implementation of other critical reforms. Tariff and non-tariff barriers, coupled with burdensome investment regulations, continue to hamper development of a more dynamic private sector and interfere with diversification of the country's economic base.

BACKGROUND: José Eduardo dos Santos has been president of Angola for more than three decades. His Popular Movement for the Liberation of Angola (MPLA) won parliamentary elections in August 2012, only the second such elections since the end of the 27-year civil war in 2002. Angola is Africa's second-largest oil producer, with many of its proven reserves concentrated in Cabinda province, a region plagued by a long-standing separatist conflict. The country also has natural gas, diamonds, good hydroelectric potential, and rich agricultural land. Nonetheless, Angolans largely remain poor and dependent on subsistence agriculture. Corruption and public-sector mismanagement are endemic, particularly in the oil sector, which accounts for approximately 85 percent of GDP and 80 percent of government revenue.

Freedom Trend

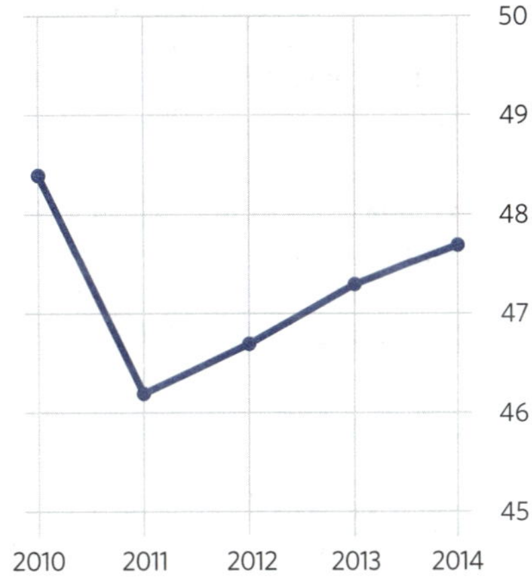

Country Comparisons

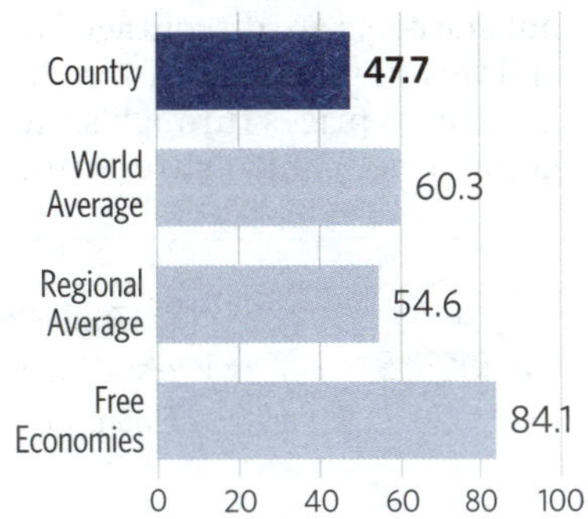

Quick Facts

Population: 20.2 million
GDP (PPP): $128.3 billion
8.4% growth in 2012
5-year compound annual growth 6.3%
$6,347 per capita
Unemployment: n/a
Inflation (CPI): 10.3%
FDI Inflow: –$6.9 billion
Public Debt: 29.3% of GDP

2012 data unless otherwise noted.
Data compiled as of September 2013.

How Do We Measure Economic Freedom?
See page 471 for an explanation of the methodology or visit the *Index* Web site at *heritage.org/index.*

THE TEN ECONOMIC FREEDOMS

Score ■ Country | World Average

RULE OF LAW

	Score	Rank	1-Year Change
Property Rights	15.0	*159th*	0
Freedom from Corruption	17.7	*170th*	-2.3

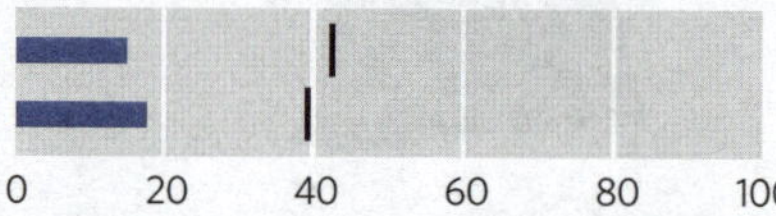

Corruption is widespread among government officials at all levels. Investigations and prosecutions of government officials are practically nonexistent. Recourse to the judicial system is discouraged by time-consuming procedures and the appearance of extensive executive influence on outcomes. Legal fees and property registration can be prohibitively expensive, and the overall protection of property rights is weak.

GOVERNMENT SIZE

	Score	Rank	1-Year Change
Fiscal Freedom	87.7	*38th*	+5.1
Government Spending	55.3	*128th*	-5.3

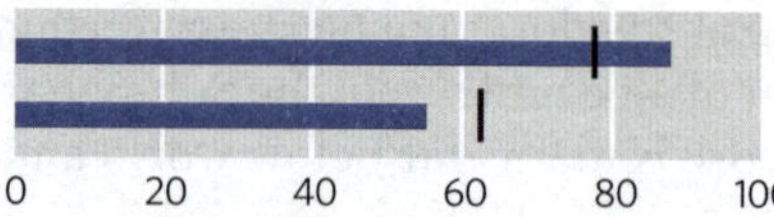

Angola's top individual income tax rate is 17 percent, and the top corporate tax rate is 30 percent. Taxes on petroleum industry income can reach as high as 68 percent. Other levies include fuel and consumption taxes. The overall tax burden equals 6.1 percent of total domestic income. Public spending is 38.6 percent of GDP, and public debt remains below 30 percent of GDP.

REGULATORY EFFICIENCY

	Score	Rank	1-Year Change
Business Freedom	47.5	*157th*	+4.4
Labor Freedom	40.1	*168th*	-4.7
Monetary Freedom	63.6	*170th*	+2.1

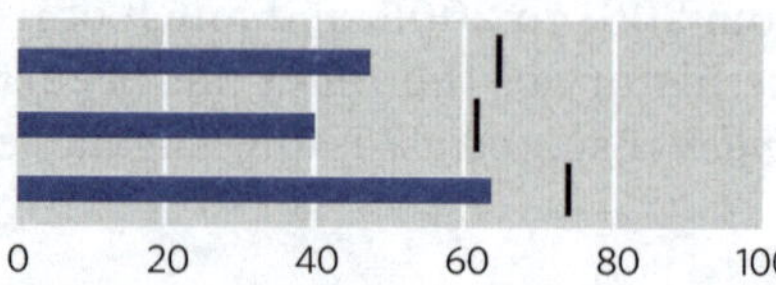

Reform measures in recent years have streamlined the procedures for establishing a business, but start-ups are discouraged by other institutional deficiencies such as pervasive corruption and very limited access to credit. The labor market remains underdeveloped. The government influences prices through state-owned enterprises, subsidies, and agriculture-support programs. Price controls are pervasive in many sectors, including fuel and electricity.

OPEN MARKETS

	Score	Rank	1-Year Change
Trade Freedom	70.1	*129th*	-0.1
Investment Freedom	40.0	*132nd*	+5.0
Financial Freedom	40.0	*107th*	0

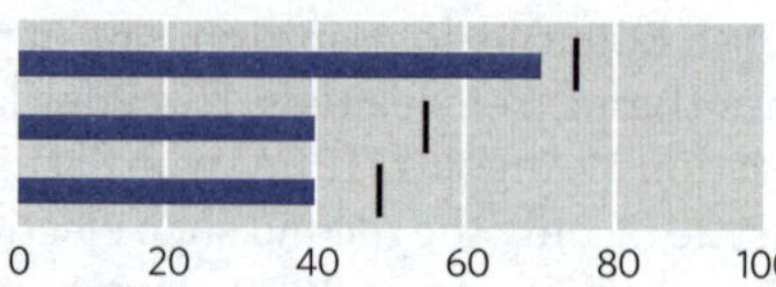

Angola has a 7.4 percent average tariff rate. There are some restrictions on agricultural imports, and government procurement policies favor domestic industries. Foreign investors face bureaucratic and legal obstacles. Public utilization of banking services remains low, and only about 10 percent of the population maintains a bank account. The capital market is underdeveloped.

Long-Term Score Change (since 1995)

RULE OF LAW		GOVERNMENT SIZE		REGULATORY EFFICIENCY		OPEN MARKETS	
Property Rights	**–15.0**	Fiscal Freedom	**+26.1**	Business Freedom	**+7.5**	Trade Freedom	**+45.1**
Freedom from Corruption	**–12.3**	Government Spending	**+55.3**	Labor Freedom	**–4.8**	Investment Freedom	**+10.0**
				Monetary Freedom	**+63.6**	Financial Freedom	**+10.0**

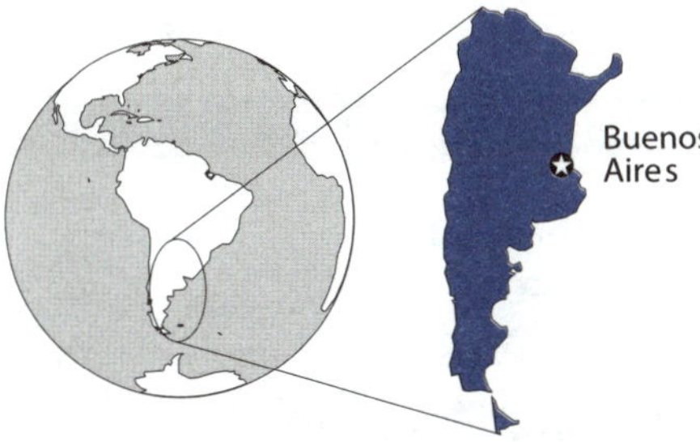

ARGENTINA

World Rank: **166** Regional Rank: **27**

Economic Freedom Score

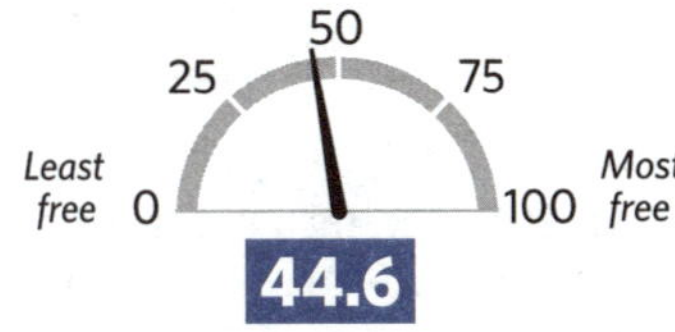

Argentina's economic freedom score is 44.6, making its economy the 166th freest in the 2014 *Index*. Its overall score has decreased by 2.1 points, reflecting substantial declines in investment freedom, business freedom, labor freedom, and the management of government spending. Argentina ranks 27th out of 29 countries in the South and Central America/Caribbean region, and its overall score is far below the regional and world averages.

Over the 20-year history of the *Index*, Argentina's economic freedom has plunged to "repressed" status. With its overall score dropping by 23.4 points, the once "mostly free" economy has registered the second most severe score decline since the *Index* began measuring economic freedom. Eight of the 10 economic freedoms have deteriorated because of policies that include harsh capital controls, price fixing, restrictions on imports, and a series of nationalizations.

The state's interference in the Argentine economy has grown substantially since 2003, accelerating the erosion of economic freedom. Institutional shortcomings continue to undermine the foundations for lasting economic development. The judicial system has become more vulnerable to political interference, and corruption is prevalent. Regulatory pressure on the private sector has continued to rise, with populist spending measures and price controls further distorting markets.

BACKGROUND: Under President Cristina Fernández de Kirchner, Argentina has strengthened ties to governments in the region that are hostile to liberty and has threatened the Falkland Islands' right of self-determination. The judiciary has been politicized, and the central bank is no longer independent. The government's seizure of nearly $30 billion in private pension funds in 2008, failure to settle with creditors since the 2002 default, and expropriation of Spanish oil company Repsol's YPF subsidiary in 2012 have severely damaged Argentina's investment profile. Although the economy has benefited from booming commodity prices, expansionary fiscal and monetary policies have fueled already high inflation that is underreported in official statistics. Foreign currency controls have created a black market for dollars.

How Do We Measure Economic Freedom?
See page 471 for an explanation of the methodology or visit the *Index* Web site at *heritage.org/index*.

Freedom Trend

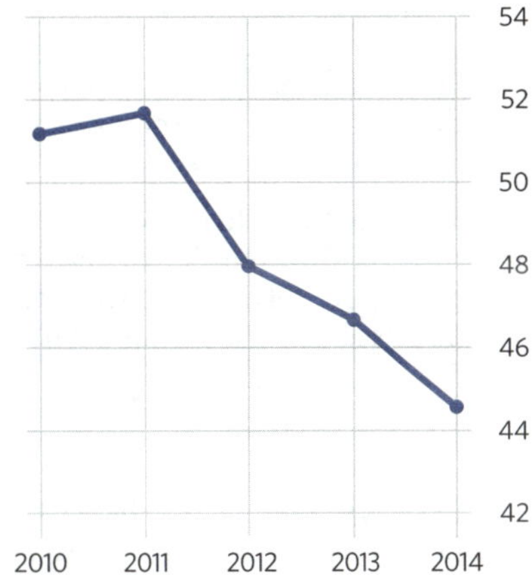

Country Comparisons

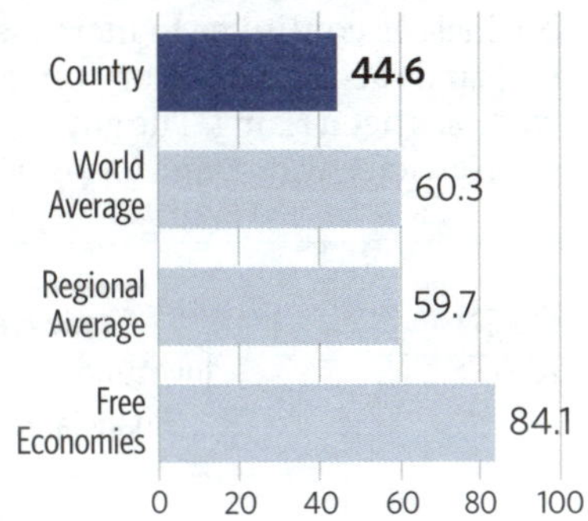

Quick Facts

Population: 41.0 million
GDP (PPP): $743.1 billion
1.9% growth in 2012
5-year compound annual growth 5.4%
$18,112 per capita
Unemployment: 7.2%
Inflation (CPI): 10.0%
FDI Inflow: $12.6 billion
Public Debt: 44.9% of GDP

2012 data unless otherwise noted.
Data compiled as of September 2013.

ARGENTINA (continued)

THE TEN ECONOMIC FREEDOMS

RULE OF LAW

	Score	Rank	1-Year Change
Property Rights	15.0	159th	0
Freedom from Corruption	29.5	107th	-0.5

In 2013, facing a deteriorating balance of payments, the government imposed draconian bans on foreign-currency transactions to protect dwindling dollar reserves. It also passed a law attempting to weaken the judiciary, already vulnerable to corruption. Protection of copyrights and patents is problematic. The government has seized private property and manipulates official inflation statistics to reduce interest paid to bondholders.

GOVERNMENT SIZE

	Score	Rank	1-Year Change
Fiscal Freedom	63.5	162nd	-0.8
Government Spending	49.9	135th	-2.2

The top individual and corporate tax rates are 35 percent. Other taxes include a value-added tax (VAT), a wealth tax, and a tax on financial transactions. Government revenue equals 34.6 percent of GDP, and government spending is 40.9 percent of total domestic income. Public debt is about 45 percent of GDP. Legal issues from previous debt defaults have increased public financial uncertainty.

REGULATORY EFFICIENCY

	Score	Rank	1-Year Change
Business Freedom	53.9	143rd	-6.2
Labor Freedom	44.9	156th	-2.5
Monetary Freedom	60.0	176th	-0.4

It takes 14 procedures and 26 days to open a business. Regulatory encroachment on private businesses continues to increase, with government interference discouraging entrepreneurship and raising regulatory uncertainty. The labor market lacks flexibility, and the minimum wage has been rising. The government manipulates official inflation statistics; regulates prices of electricity, water, and gasoline; and pressures companies to fix prices and wages.

OPEN MARKETS

	Score	Rank	1-Year Change
Trade Freedom	68.9	134th	+1.3
Investment Freedom	30.0	152nd	-10.0
Financial Freedom	30.0	132nd	0

Argentina has a 5.6 percent tariff rate. The government's policy of "import substitution" is one of many non-tariff barriers to trade. Investment rights are poorly protected. The financial sector remains subject to government interference. Twelve state-owned banks account for over 40 percent of total bank assets, and the presence of foreign banks has fallen in recent years.

Long-Term Score Change (since 1995)

RULE OF LAW		GOVERNMENT SIZE		REGULATORY EFFICIENCY		OPEN MARKETS	
Property Rights	-55.0	Fiscal Freedom	-17.2	Business Freedom	-31.1	Trade Freedom	+10.5
Freedom from Corruption	-20.5	Government Spending	-36.7	Labor Freedom	+1.0	Investment Freedom	-40.0
				Monetary Freedom	-1.2	Financial Freedom	-20.0

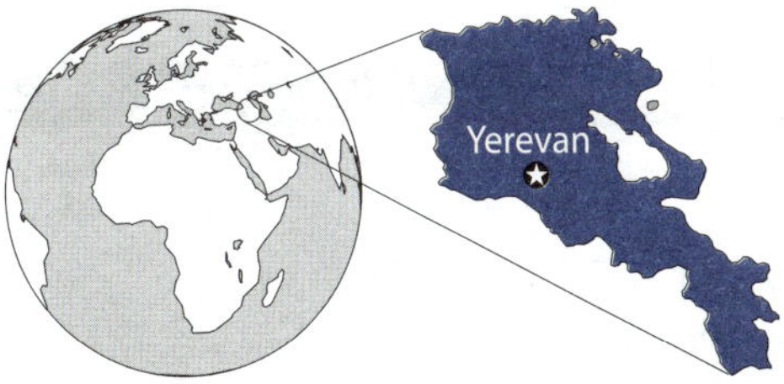

ARMENIA

Economic Freedom Score

World Rank: 41 **Regional Rank: 18**

Armenia's economic freedom score is 68.9, making its economy the 41st freest in the 2014 *Index*. Its overall score has declined by 0.5 point from last year, primarily due to combined deteriorations in investment freedom, business freedom, and fiscal freedom. Armenia is ranked 18th among the 43 countries in the Europe region, and its score is above the world and regional averages.

Over the 20-year history of the *Index,* Armenia has improved its economic freedom score by 26.7 points, the fourth largest score increase. Recording score improvements in eight of the 10 economic freedoms, including monetary freedom, management of public finance, trade freedom, and financial freedom, Armenia has advanced from economic repression 20 years ago to economically "moderately free" today. Facilitated by the broad advancement of economic freedom, diversification of the economic base has enhanced Armenia's economic dynamism and reduced poverty.

Nonetheless, substantial challenges remain, particularly in implementing deeper institutional and systemic reforms that are critical to strengthening the foundations of economic freedom. Both the protection of property rights and freedom from corruption are far below world standards, and the legal framework continues to be weak.

BACKGROUND: Armenia achieved independence from the Soviet Union in 1991. A cease-fire in its 24-year dispute with Azerbaijan over the Nagorno–Karabakh region has been in effect since 1994, but minor hostilities continue, and Armenia's borders with Azerbaijan and Turkey remain closed. President Serzh Sargsyan of the center-right Republican Party won re-election to a second five-year term in 2013. The economy relies on manufacturing, services, remittances, and agriculture. After a brief downturn in 2009, GDP growth resumed in 2010. The eurozone financial crisis remains a drag on the economy. The government, which relies heavily on loans from the World Bank, the International Monetary Fund, the Asian Development Bank, and Russia, as well as remittances from the diaspora, is running a modest budget deficit.

How Do We Measure Economic Freedom?
See page 471 for an explanation of the methodology or visit the *Index* Web site at *heritage.org/index.*

Freedom Trend

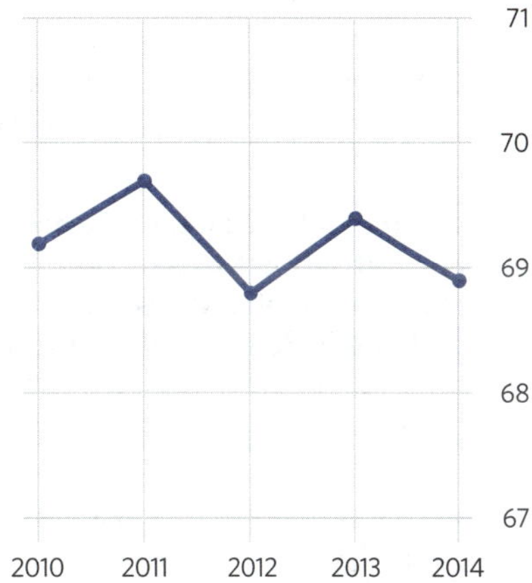

Country Comparisons

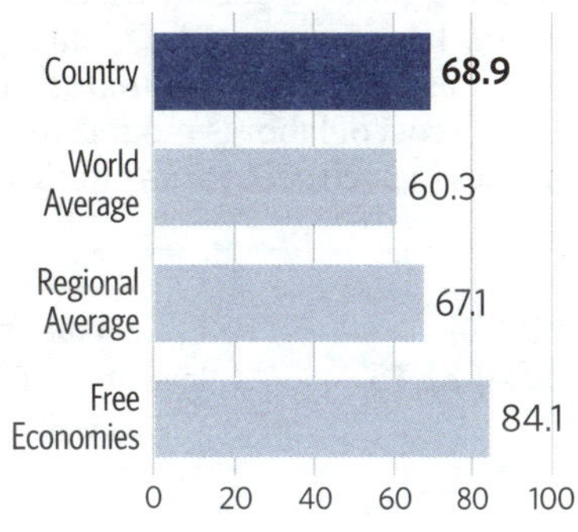

Quick Facts

Population: 3.4 million
GDP (PPP): $19.6 billion
7.2% growth in 2012
5-year compound annual growth 1.0%
$5,838 per capita
Unemployment: 19.0%
Inflation (CPI): 2.5%
FDI Inflow: $489.1 million
Public Debt: 39.5% of GDP

2012 data unless otherwise noted.
Data compiled as of September 2013.

THE TEN ECONOMIC FREEDOMS

RULE OF LAW

	Score	Rank	1-Year Change
Property Rights	30.0	93rd	0
Freedom from Corruption	26.7	124th	+0.7

Corruption plagues such critical areas as tax and customs operations, health, education, and law enforcement. Petty corruption is widespread throughout society, and anti-corruption measures have not been enforced effectively. The judicial system, hobbled by corruption and Soviet-era underdevelopment, impedes the enforcement of contracts. Protection of intellectual property rights is poor, and scores for rule of law are below average overall.

GOVERNMENT SIZE

	Score	Rank	1-Year Change
Fiscal Freedom	86.5	46th	-1.5
Government Spending	81.3	49th	-0.8

The top individual tax rate has risen to 26 percent, and the top corporate tax rate remains at 20 percent. Other taxes include a value-added tax (VAT) and an excise tax. The overall tax burden is 16.7 percent of domestic income. Government spending is 25 percent of domestic income, and public debt is equivalent to about 40 percent of the domestic economy. The government hopes to narrow the deficit with a large increase in tax revenue.

REGULATORY EFFICIENCY

	Score	Rank	1-Year Change
Business Freedom	83.1	27th	-4.5
Labor Freedom	78.5	35th	+1.4
Monetary Freedom	77.0	73rd	+4.0

The regulatory framework is relatively efficient, and a broad simplification of business procedures has encouraged regulatory efficiency. The minimum capital requirement for starting a business has been eliminated, and bankruptcy procedures have been modernized. The non-salary cost of labor is moderate, but the informal labor market is sizable. State subsidies distort prices in such sectors as public transportation, electricity, and gas.

OPEN MARKETS

	Score	Rank	1-Year Change
Trade Freedom	85.5	46th	+0.1
Investment Freedom	70.0	46th	-5.0
Financial Freedom	70.0	19th	0

Armenia has a 2.3 percent average tariff rate, and non-tariff barriers are relatively low. Bureaucratic barriers and non-transparent regulations deter foreign investment. The financial sector, dominated by banks, continues to evolve. The state no longer has a stake in any bank. The banking sector, although relatively small and fragmented, has been relatively well-capitalized and is open to foreign competition.

Long-Term Score Change (since 1996)

RULE OF LAW		GOVERNMENT SIZE		REGULATORY EFFICIENCY		OPEN MARKETS	
Property Rights	**-20.0**	Fiscal Freedom	**+10.7**	Business Freedom	**+28.1**	Trade Freedom	**+16.5**
Freedom from Corruption	**-23.3**	Government Spending	**+81.3**	Labor Freedom	**+16.4**	Investment Freedom	**+40.0**
				Monetary Freedom	**+77.0**	Financial Freedom	**+20.0**

AUSTRALIA

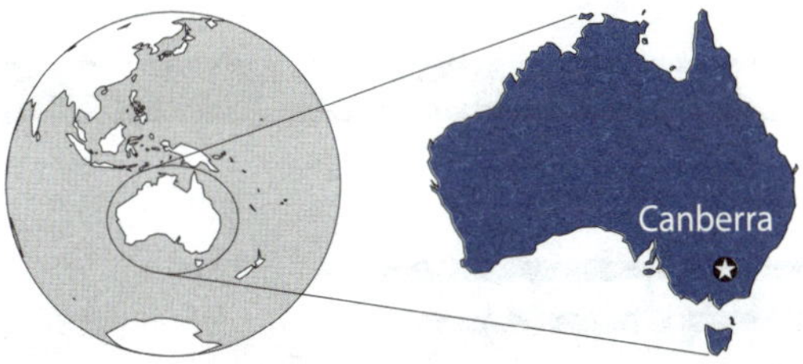

World Rank: **3** Regional Rank: **3**

Economic Freedom Score

Australia's economic freedom score is 82, making its economy the 3rd freest in the 2014 *Index*. Its overall score is 0.6 point lower than last year, with a gain in investment freedom outweighed by declines in monetary freedom and labor freedom. Australia is ranked 3rd out of 42 countries in the Asia–Pacific region.

Over the 20-year history of the *Index*, Australia has advanced its economic freedom score by 7.9 points, one of the 10 biggest improvements among developed economies. Substantial score increases in six of the 10 economic freedoms, including business freedom, investment freedom, and freedom from corruption, have enabled Australia to achieve and sustain its economically "free" status in the *Index*.

With an economy that benefits from sound fundamentals including monetary stability, low public debt, and a vibrant employment market, Australia has weathered the global economic uncertainty well. Openness to global trade and investment is firmly institutionalized, supported by a relatively efficient entrepreneurial framework and a well-functioning independent judiciary. Australia has a strong tradition of reliable property rights protection, and the legal system is transparent and evenly applied. Effective anti-corruption measures are in force.

BACKGROUND: Since the early 1980s, successive governments have deregulated financial and labor markets and reduced trade barriers. In September 2013, Liberal Party leader Tony Abbott became prime minister following his coalition's victory in national elections. Australia is one of the Asia–Pacific's richest countries and has enjoyed economic expansion for over two decades. It came through the global recession relatively unscathed, but stimulus spending by the previous Labor government generated a deficit. Australia is internationally competitive in services, technologies, and high-value-added manufactured goods. Mining and agriculture are important exports.

How Do We Measure Economic Freedom?
See page 471 for an explanation of the methodology or visit the *Index* Web site at *heritage.org/index*.

Freedom Trend

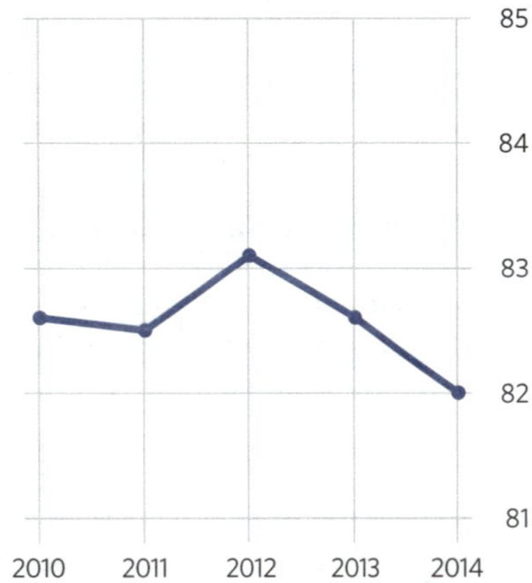

Country Comparisons

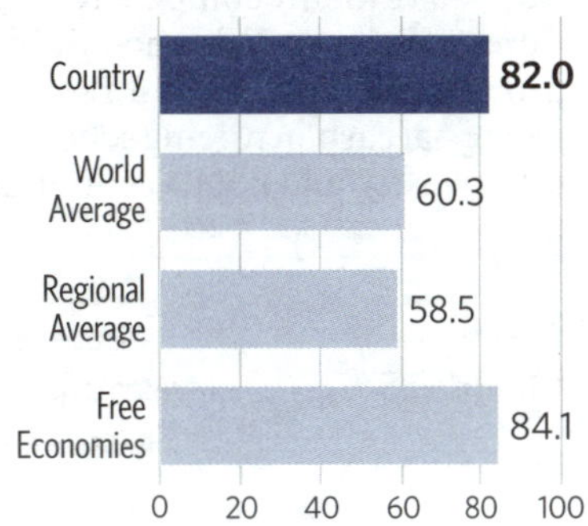

Quick Facts

Population: 22.8 million
GDP (PPP): $970.8 billion
3.6% growth in 2012
5-year compound annual growth 2.5%
$42,640 per capita
Unemployment: 5.2%
Inflation (CPI): 1.8%
FDI Inflow: $57.0 billion
Public Debt: 27.2% of GDP

2012 data unless otherwise noted.
Data compiled as of September 2013.

AUSTRALIA (continued)

THE TEN ECONOMIC FREEDOMS

		Score	Rank	1-Year Change
RULE OF LAW	Property Rights	90.0	2nd	0
	Freedom from Corruption	87.7	9th	-0.3

Anti-corruption measures generally discourage bribery of public officials. In 2013, however, a special Independent Commission Against Corruption investigated two former state ministers in New South Wales on allegations of a conspiracy to profit from mining leases. Australia's judicial system operates independently and impartially. Property rights are secure, and enforcement of contracts is reliable. Expropriation is highly unusual.

		Score	Rank	1-Year Change
GOVERNMENT SIZE	Fiscal Freedom	64.2	160th	-2.2
	Government Spending	62.6	111th	-0.2

Australia's top individual tax rate is 45 percent, and the top corporate tax rate is 30 percent. Other taxes include a value-added-tax (VAT) and a capital gains tax. The carbon tax has been abandoned for a cap-and-trade system. The overall tax burden has fallen to 25.6 percent of GDP. Government spending amounts to 35.3 percent of total domestic output, and public debt remains at 27.6 percent of GDP.

		Score	Rank	1-Year Change
REGULATORY EFFICIENCY	Business Freedom	94.6	5th	-0.9
	Labor Freedom	79.2	32nd	-4.3
	Monetary Freedom	80.5	27th	-3.3

Australia's highly competitive regulatory framework promotes business formation and operational efficiency. With no minimum capital standards, starting a company requires only one procedure. Flexible labor regulations enhance employment and productivity growth. A controversial carbon pricing scheme encourages consumers to use alternative energy sources that otherwise would not be economically viable.

		Score	Rank	1-Year Change
OPEN MARKETS	Trade Freedom	86.4	41st	+0.2
	Investment Freedom	85.0	13th	+5.0
	Financial Freedom	90.0	1st	0

Australia has a 1.8 percent average tariff rate. The government has reduced tariff and non-tariff barriers both unilaterally and through negotiated trade agreements. Foreign investment in a few "sensitive sectors" is limited. The open financial sector is highly competitive and well-developed. All banks are privately owned, and prudent regulations have allowed them to withstand the global financial turmoil with little disruption.

Long-Term Score Change (since 1995)

RULE OF LAW		GOVERNMENT SIZE		REGULATORY EFFICIENCY		OPEN MARKETS	
Property Rights	0	Fiscal Freedom	+4.6	Business Freedom	+24.6	Trade Freedom	+9.4
Freedom from Corruption	+17.7	Government Spending	+8.7	Labor Freedom	-6.6	Investment Freedom	+15.0
				Monetary Freedom	-6.2	Financial Freedom	0

AUSTRIA

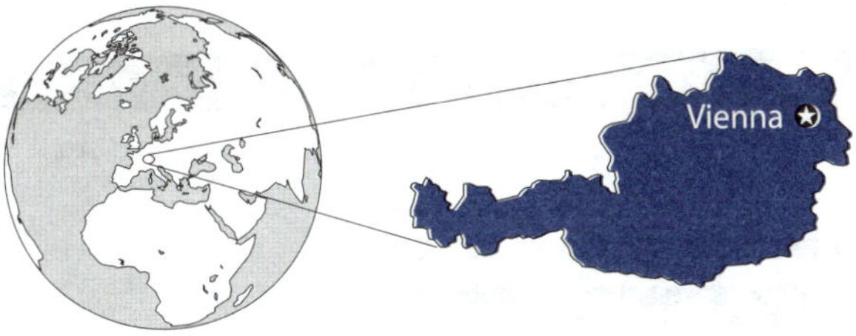

World Rank: **24** Regional Rank: **14**

Economic Freedom Score

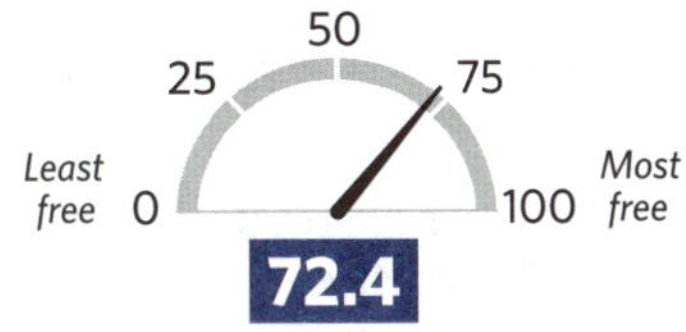

Austria's economic freedom score is 72.4, making its economy the 24th freest in the 2014 *Index*. Its score is 0.6 point better than last year due to improved scores for investment freedom, business freedom, and trade freedom. Austria is ranked 14th out of 43 countries in the Europe region, and its overall score is well above the regional and world averages.

Over the 20-year history of the *Index*, Austria has advanced its economic freedom score by 2.4 points. Recording score improvements of 10 points or more in six of the 10 economic freedoms, including business freedom, investment freedom, and the management of government spending, Austria has gradually become a "mostly free" economy. It has achieved its highest economic freedom score ever in the 2014 *Index*.

Continuing to sustain Austria's strong tradition of effective property protection, the legal system is transparent and efficiently maintained. The country's international orientation and vibrant banking sector have been the backbone of economic expansion. The corporate tax rate is comparatively low, but individuals still face an income tax rate of 50 percent and various other indirect taxes.

BACKGROUND: After the 2008 parliamentary elections, the center-left Social Democrats formed a governing coalition with the center-right Austrian People's Party. Social Democrat Werner Faymann is chancellor. GDP growth has slowed as a result of the eurozone crisis, yet Austria's economy is still stronger than those of many other EU nations, and unemployment is comparatively low. The government has gradually relinquished control of formerly nationalized oil, gas, steel, and engineering companies and has deregulated telecommunications and electricity. There are large service and industrial sectors and a small, highly developed agricultural industry. The economic impact of record flooding in the past year is expected to be limited and temporary. In 1995, Austria joined the European Union, which is the destination for 70 percent of its exports.

Freedom Trend

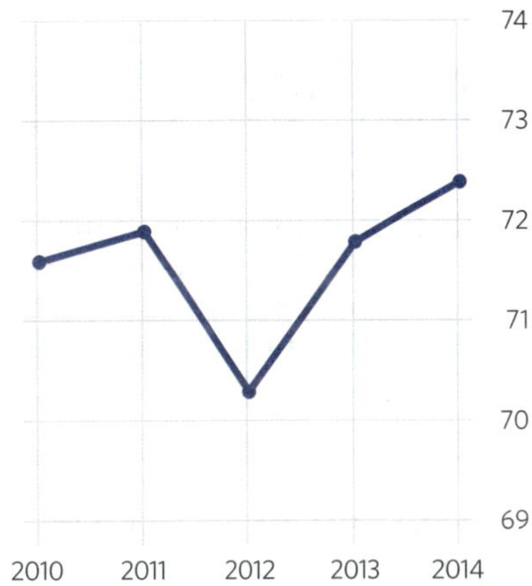

Country Comparisons

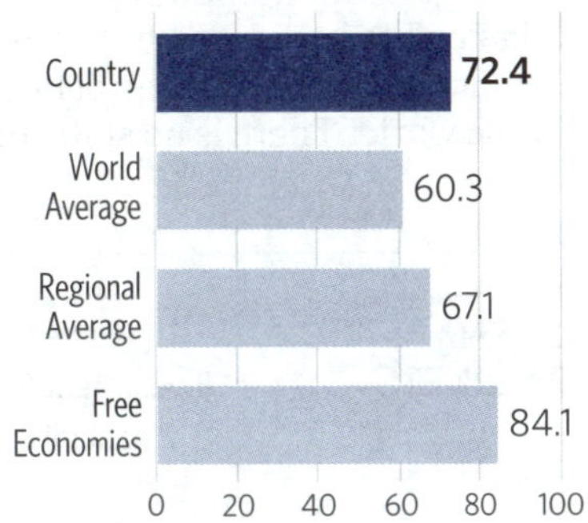

Quick Facts

Population: 8.5 million
GDP (PPP): $359.0 billion
0.8% growth in 2012
5-year compound annual growth 0.6%
$42,409 per capita
Unemployment: 4.4%
Inflation (CPI): 2.6%
FDI Inflow: $6.3 billion
Public Debt: 73.7% of GDP

2012 data unless otherwise noted.
Data compiled as of September 2013.

How Do We Measure Economic Freedom?
See page 471 for an explanation of the methodology or visit the *Index* Web site at *heritage.org/index*.

THE TEN ECONOMIC FREEDOMS

RULE OF LAW

	Score	Rank	1-Year Change
Property Rights	90.0	2nd	0
Freedom from Corruption	75.5	18th	-2.5

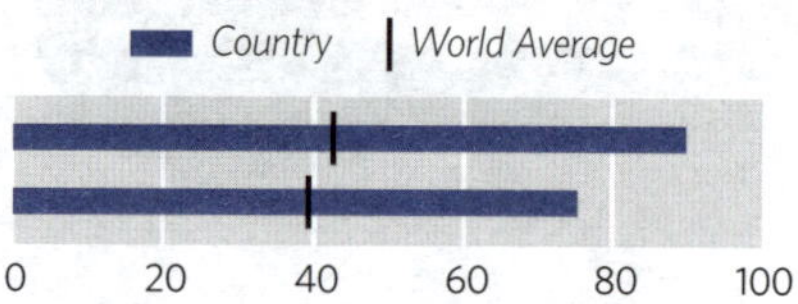

Instances of corruption are rare, although several prominent new cases involving government and business corruption were made public and investigated in the past year. The rule of law is respected, and the judiciary is independent. Contractual agreements are enforced effectively, and the protection of intellectual property is strong. The land registry was overhauled in 2012 to speed up registration procedures and reduce costs.

GOVERNMENT SIZE

	Score	Rank	1-Year Change
Fiscal Freedom	51.0	176th	-0.1
Government Spending	23.5	168th	0

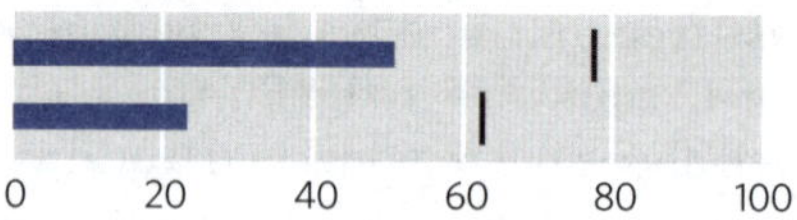

The top individual tax rate is 50 percent, and the top corporate tax rate is 25 percent. Other taxes include a value-added tax (VAT) and a tax on real estate transfers. The overall tax burden is 42.1 percent of total domestic income. Total government spending accounts for just over half of the size of the domestic economy, and public debt is equivalent to about 74 percent of GDP. Bank bailouts put unexpected pressure on the 2012 budget balance.

REGULATORY EFFICIENCY

	Score	Rank	1-Year Change
Business Freedom	76.3	41st	+2.7
Labor Freedom	80.5	26th	+0.1
Monetary Freedom	79.5	40th	+0.2

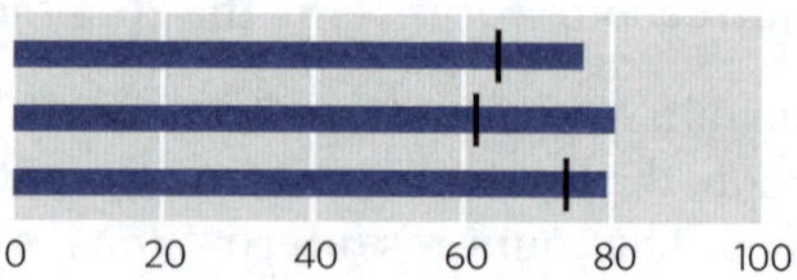

The regulatory framework generally facilitates entrepreneurial activity. Launching a business takes eight procedures, but obtaining necessary permits remains time-consuming. Hiring and dismissal regulations are not burdensome, but generous fringe benefits are among the costliest in the world. There is no statutory minimum wage.

OPEN MARKETS

	Score	Rank	1-Year Change
Trade Freedom	87.8	11th	+1.0
Investment Freedom	90.0	2nd	+5.0
Financial Freedom	70.0	19th	0

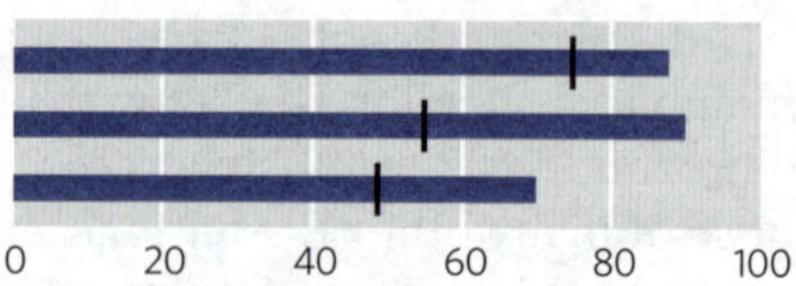

EU members have a low 1.1 percent average tariff rate and, in general, few non-tariff barriers to trade. Foreign investment in certain industries, including education and telecommunications, may be screened by the government. Offering a wide range of financial services, the banking sector continues to be competitive and is relatively well-capitalized. The country's five largest banking groups account for over 50 percent of total assets.

Long-Term Score Change (since 1995)

RULE OF LAW		GOVERNMENT SIZE		REGULATORY EFFICIENCY		OPEN MARKETS	
Property Rights	0	Fiscal Freedom	+4.7	Business Freedom	+6.3	Trade Freedom	+6.8
Freedom from Corruption	-14.5	Government Spending	+13.9	Labor Freedom	+6.8	Investment Freedom	+20.0
				Monetary Freedom	-3.3	Financial Freedom	-20.0

AZERBAIJAN

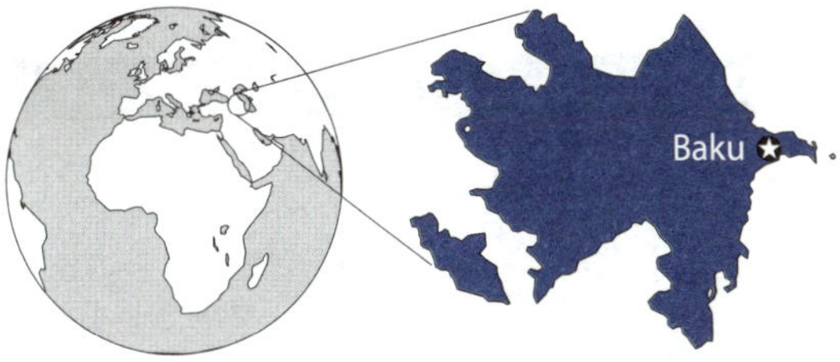

World Rank: **81** Regional Rank: **13**

Economic Freedom Score

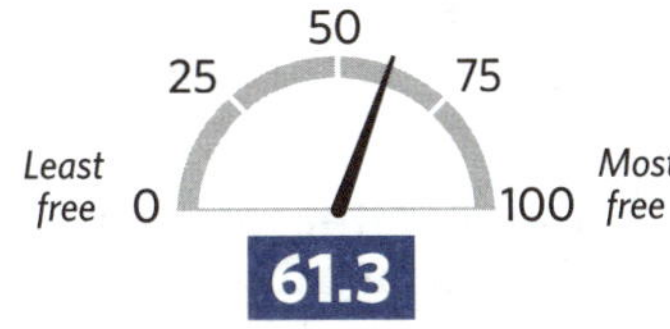

Azerbaijan's economic freedom score is 61.3, making its economy the 81st freest in the 2014 *Index*. Its overall score is 1.6 points higher than last year, reflecting improved scores in the management of public finance and property rights. Azerbaijan is ranked 13th out of 42 countries in the Asia–Pacific region, and its overall score is above the regional and global averages.

Over the 20-year history of the *Index*, Azerbaijan has advanced economic freedom significantly to become a "moderately free" economy for the first time in the 2014 *Index*. A series of major reform measures has enabled the country to rise from the status of economically "repressed." Score improvements of 10 points or more have been achieved in nine of the 10 economic freedoms, and Azerbaijan's overall improvement of 31.3 points is the biggest gain of any country.

By sharp contrast, Azerbaijan's rule of law has deteriorated over the past two decades and remains fragile, and the level of corruption continues to be substantial. Deeper systemic reforms to strengthen the independence of the judiciary and the protection of property rights are critically needed to ensure the country's continuing progress toward greater economic freedom.

BACKGROUND: Azerbaijan's dispute with Armenia over the Nagorno–Karabakh region has cost tens of thousands of lives and the loss of about a fifth of Azerbaijan's territory. A 2009 constitutional amendment abolishing presidential term limits allowed President Ilham Aliyev to be re-elected for a third term in October 2013. Oil and gas production, construction, and private investment are increasing, and exports of gas to Russia have also risen. In June 2012, Turkey and Azerbaijan agreed to build the Trans-Anatolian Natural Gas Pipeline, which will ease Europe's dependence on Russian gas. Negotiations on accession to the World Trade Organization continue.

Freedom Trend

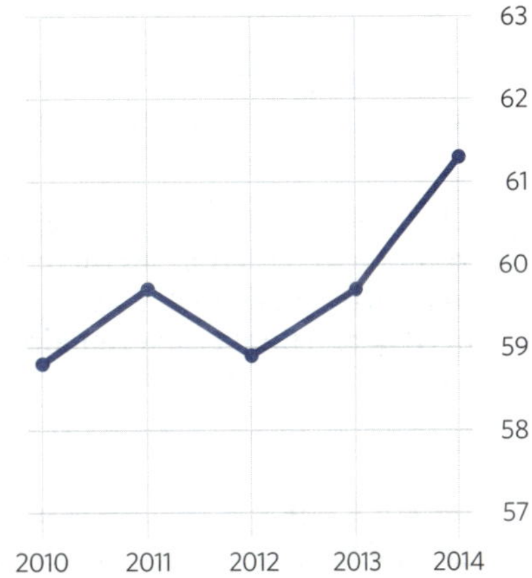

Country Comparisons

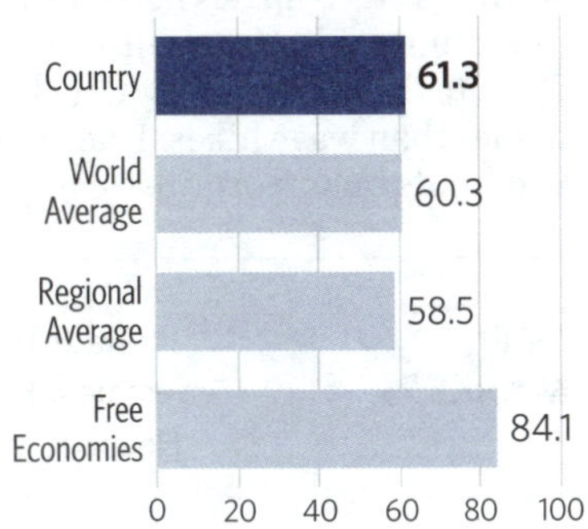

Quick Facts

Population: 9.2 million
GDP (PPP): $96.8 billion
2.2% growth in 2012
5-year compound annual growth 5.4%
$10,478 per capita
Unemployment: 6.0%
Inflation (CPI): 1.1%
FDI Inflow: $2.0 billion
Public Debt: 11.6% of GDP

2012 data unless otherwise noted.
Data compiled as of September 2013.

How Do We Measure Economic Freedom?
See page 471 for an explanation of the methodology or visit the *Index* Web site at *heritage.org/index.*

THE TEN ECONOMIC FREEDOMS

RULE OF LAW

	Score	Rank	1-Year Change
Property Rights	20.0	139th	-5.0
Freedom from Corruption	22.7	145th	-1.3

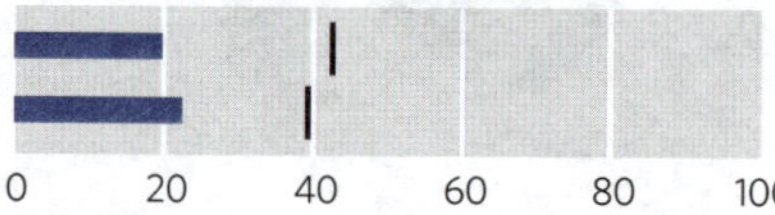

Although anti-corruption laws are in place, corrupt practices permeate all spheres of public life in Azerbaijan. About half of all citizens report having to pay bribes for such services as customs, education, land-related services, medical services, the police, registry and permit services, and utilities. The judiciary is burdened by non-transparent regulations and interference from the executive. Contract enforcement can be lax.

GOVERNMENT SIZE

	Score	Rank	1-Year Change
Fiscal Freedom	88.1	37th	+2.6
Government Spending	64.8	100th	-3.0

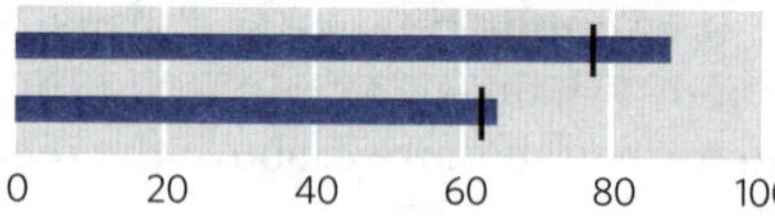

The top individual tax rate has fallen to 25 percent, and the top corporate tax rate remains at 20 percent. Other taxes include a value-added tax (VAT) and a property tax. The overall tax burden has risen to 12.8 percent of the domestic economy. Government spending is 34 percent of GDP, and public debt remains low. Withdrawals from the state oil fund have been increasing, cushioning public finances.

REGULATORY EFFICIENCY

	Score	Rank	1-Year Change
Business Freedom	73.5	60th	+4.3
Labor Freedom	77.9	40th	-1.5
Monetary Freedom	78.8	54th	+5.3

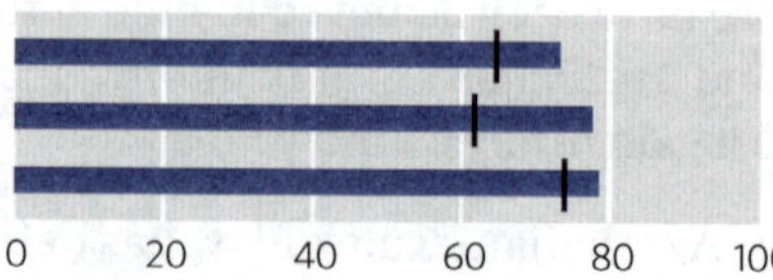

Business start-up has become simpler. Required procedures have been reduced to six, and no minimum capital is required. However, obtaining necessary permits takes more than 150 days. Despite the lack of a fully developed labor market, labor productivity growth has been slightly higher than wage hikes. Price controls are in place for most energy products, and monopolies and limits on imports also cause distortions in domestic prices.

OPEN MARKETS

	Score	Rank	1-Year Change
Trade Freedom	77.2	86th	0
Investment Freedom	60.0	80th	+5.0
Financial Freedom	50.0	69th	+10.0

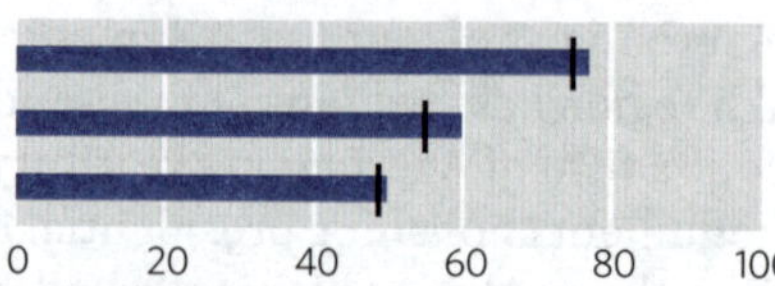

Azerbaijan's tariff rate is 3.9 percent. Weak legal institutions and non-transparent regulations act as barriers to trade and investment. The financial sector, dominated by banks, remains stable and relatively well-capitalized. The government has injected new capital into the majority state-owned International Bank of Azerbaijan, raising the state's share in the bank to slightly over 50 percent.

Long-Term Score Change (since 1996)

RULE OF LAW		GOVERNMENT SIZE		REGULATORY EFFICIENCY		OPEN MARKETS	
Property Rights	-10.0	Fiscal Freedom	+41.8	Business Freedom	+33.5	Trade Freedom	+22.2
Freedom from Corruption	+12.7	Government Spending	+16.0	Labor Freedom	+13.2	Investment Freedom	+50.0
				Monetary Freedom	+78.8	Financial Freedom	+20.0

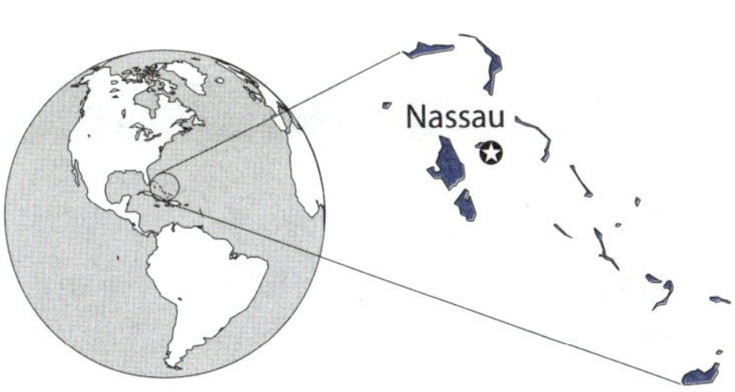

THE BAHAMAS

World Rank: 36 **Regional Rank: 4**

Economic Freedom Score

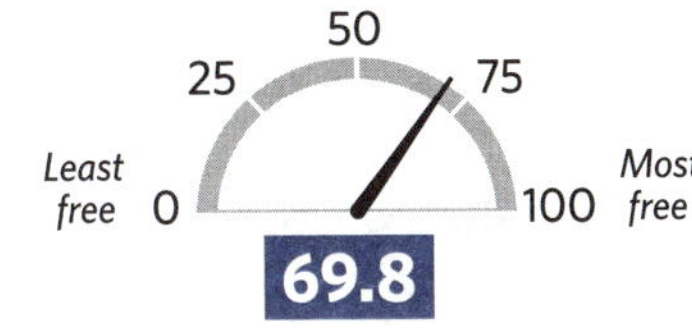

The Bahamas' economic freedom score is 69.8, making its economy the 36th freest in the 2014 *Index*. Its overall score has decreased by 0.3 point, with a notable decline in freedom from corruption outweighing a gain in trade freedom. The Bahamas is the 4th freest out of 29 countries in the South and Central America/Caribbean region, and its overall score remains higher than the regional and world averages.

Over the 20-year history of the *Index*, The Bahamas' economic freedom has deteriorated by 2 points. Although the score for trade freedom has improved by over 30 points, declines have occurred in six of the 10 economic freedoms, notably property rights and business freedom, which plummeted 20 points or more. The Bahamas had been a "mostly free" economy during the first 15 years but has been on a declining path of economic freedom since 2009 and has dropped into the ranks of the "moderately free" in the 2014 *Index*.

The island economy is equipped with a dynamic financial sector and has a competitive tax regime. There are no personal income or corporate taxes. However, a poor investment framework, characterized by government interference and lingering corruption, continues to undermine the Bahamas' overall economic freedom and long-term prospects for broader-based economic expansion.

BACKGROUND: The Bahamas is a member of the British Commonwealth and is governed as a constitutional parliamentary democracy. In May 2012, former Prime Minister Perry Christie led the Progressive Liberal Party back to power by defeating Prime Minister Hubert Ingraham's Free National Movement. The Bahamas is one of the Caribbean's most prosperous nations. Tourism generates about half of all jobs and accounts for more than 60 percent of GDP. Financial and business services account for more than one-third of GDP. Due to its geographic location, the Bahamas often serves as a major transshipment point for drug smugglers and illegal aliens seeking to enter the United States.

Freedom Trend

Country Comparisons

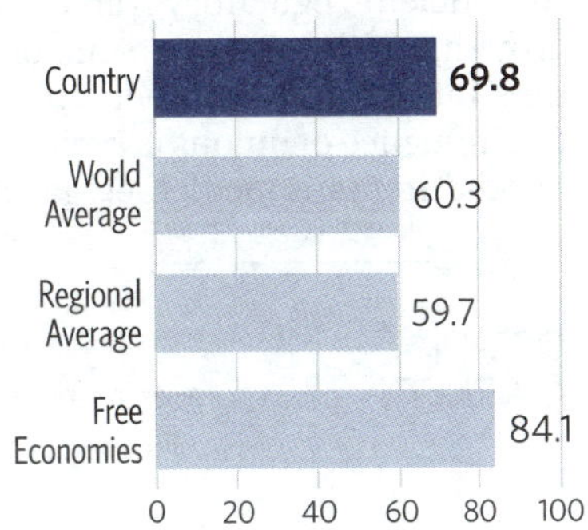

Quick Facts

Population: 0.4 million
GDP (PPP): $11.1 billion
2.5% growth in 2012
5-year compound annual growth −0.6%
$31,382 per capita
Unemployment: 11.0%
Inflation (CPI): 2.3%
FDI Inflow: $1.1 billion
Public Debt: 51.9% of GDP

2012 data unless otherwise noted.
Data compiled as of September 2013.

How Do We Measure Economic Freedom?
See page 471 for an explanation of the methodology or visit the *Index* Web site at *heritage.org/index*.

THE TEN ECONOMIC FREEDOMS

RULE OF LAW

	Score	Rank	1-Year Change
Property Rights	70.0	27th	0
Freedom from Corruption	66.6	27th	-6.4

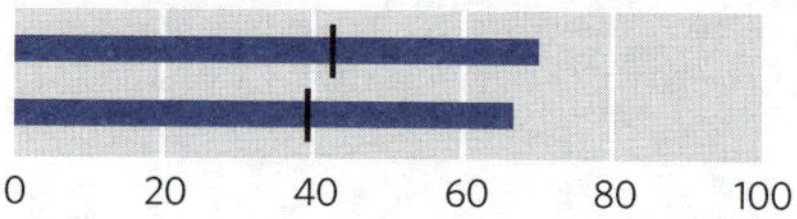

Corruption remains a problem at all levels of government. Top officials frequently face allegations of administrative graft, domestically and from abroad. The largely well-functioning judicial system, headed by the Supreme Court and a court of appeals, is independent and based on British common law. However, the judicial process tends to be very slow. Violent crime, often drug-related, continued to escalate in 2012.

GOVERNMENT SIZE

	Score	Rank	1-Year Change
Fiscal Freedom	97.3	9th	+0.3
Government Spending	84.1	36th	-0.8

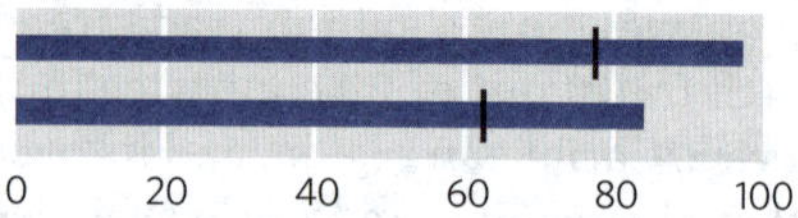

The Bahamas has some of the world's lowest tax rates, with no individual or corporate income taxes or value-added taxes (VATs). Instead, the government imposes national insurance taxes, property taxes, tariffs, and a stamp tax. The overall tax burden is 16.4 percent of gross domestic output. Government spending is 23 percent of the total economy, and public debt amounts to about 50 percent of GDP.

REGULATORY EFFICIENCY

	Score	Rank	1-Year Change
Business Freedom	70.7	73rd	-0.6
Labor Freedom	81.5	23rd	-0.1
Monetary Freedom	75.1	101st	-0.7

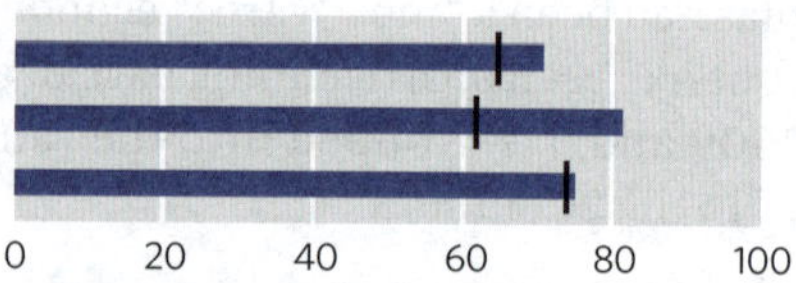

An efficient regulatory framework generally facilitates business formation and productivity growth, but the absence of major regulatory reforms in recent years has undermined the Bahamas' international competitiveness. Hiring and dismissal regulations are not burdensome, and the influence of unions is limited. The government influences domestic prices for such "breadbasket" items as medicines, gasoline, and petroleum gas.

OPEN MARKETS

	Score	Rank	1-Year Change
Trade Freedom	52.2	173rd	+5.2
Investment Freedom	30.0	152nd	0
Financial Freedom	70.0	19th	0

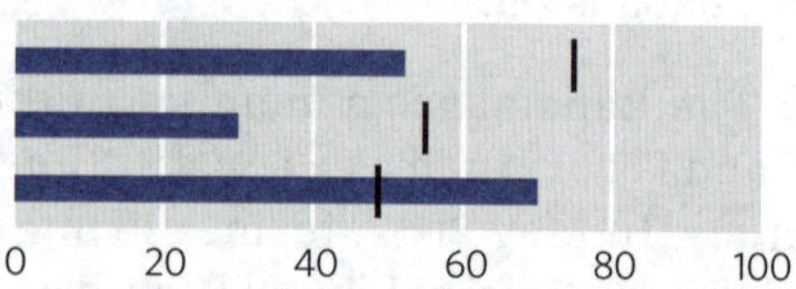

The average tariff rate of 18.9 percent is quite high due to the country's reliance on tariffs to finance the government. New foreign investment is subject to screening, and the current government has suggested nationalization of the Bahamas Telecommunications Company. The diversified banking sector remains stable, although the number of non-performing loans has increased.

Long-Term Score Change (since 1995)

RULE OF LAW		GOVERNMENT SIZE		REGULATORY EFFICIENCY		OPEN MARKETS	
Property Rights	-20.0	Fiscal Freedom	-0.3	Business Freedom	-29.3	Trade Freedom	+33.2
Freedom from Corruption	-3.4	Government Spending	-2.8	Labor Freedom	+1.5	Investment Freedom	0
				Monetary Freedom	-7.5	Financial Freedom	0

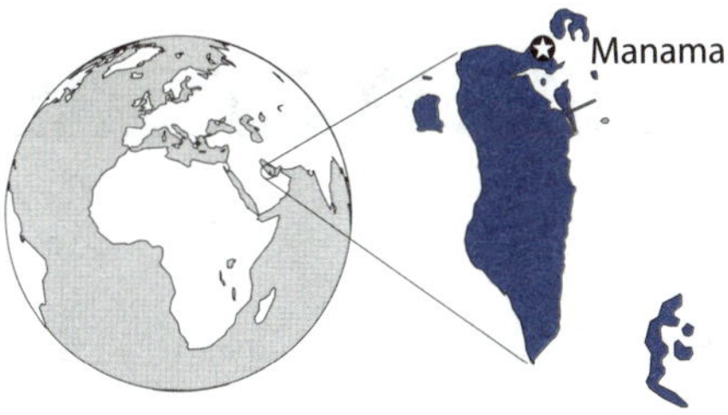

BAHRAIN

Economic Freedom Score

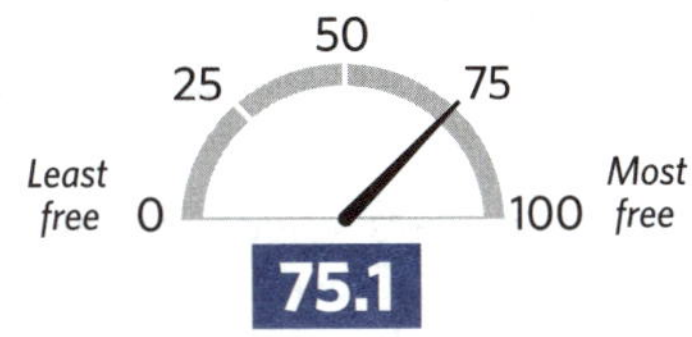

World Rank: **13**	Regional Rank: **1**

Bahrain's economic freedom score is 75.1, making its economy the 13th freest in the 2014 *Index*. Its overall score has decreased by 0.4 point due to slight deteriorations in labor freedom, trade freedom, and freedom from corruption. Bahrain continues to be the freest economy in the Middle East/North Africa region, and its economic freedom score is well above the world average.

Over the 20-year history of the *Index*, Bahrain has been consistently rated one of the "mostly free" economies achieving economic freedom scores above 70. Three of the country's 10 economic freedoms—financial freedom, investment freedom, and labor freedom—have recorded score gains of 10 or more points since *Index* grading began. Despite challenging external and internal political environments, Bahrain continues to be a financial hub for dynamic economic activity, with high levels of trade and investment bolstered by a competitive and efficient regulatory environment.

Bahrain's challenging transition to greater openness and diversification is based on foundations of economic freedom. Firmly institutionalizing the rule of law by enhancing judicial independence and transparency will be critical to stamping out lingering corruption and ensuring success in the country's ongoing evolution.

BACKGROUND: Bahrain gained its independence in 1971 and became a constitutional monarchy in 2002. In 2011, Shia opposition activists launched a protest campaign, demanding a new constitution and greater political power. After modest concessions and efforts at dialogue failed to stem the demonstrations, King Hamad declared an emergency and authorized a crackdown supported by Gulf Cooperation Council security forces. The government has sought to ease tensions through a national dialogue led by the crown prince. Efforts have been made to reduce dependence on declining oil reserves through policies that encourage investment in non-energy sectors. Home to many multinational firms that do business in the region, Bahrain has a modern communications and transportation infrastructure, a cosmopolitan outlook, and a free trade agreement with the U.S.

How Do We Measure Economic Freedom?
See page 471 for an explanation of the methodology or visit the *Index* Web site at *heritage.org/index*.

Freedom Trend

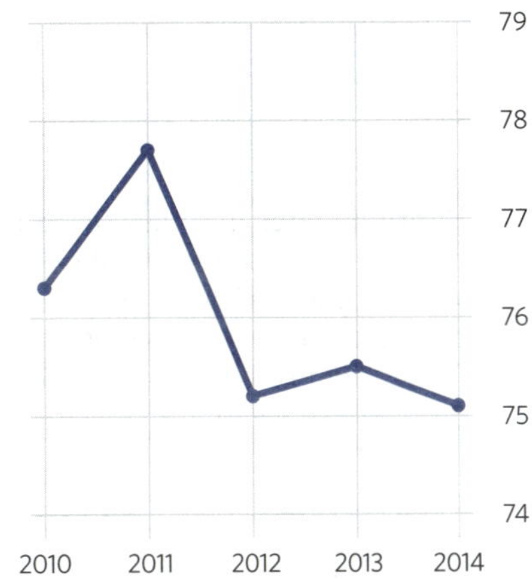

Country Comparisons

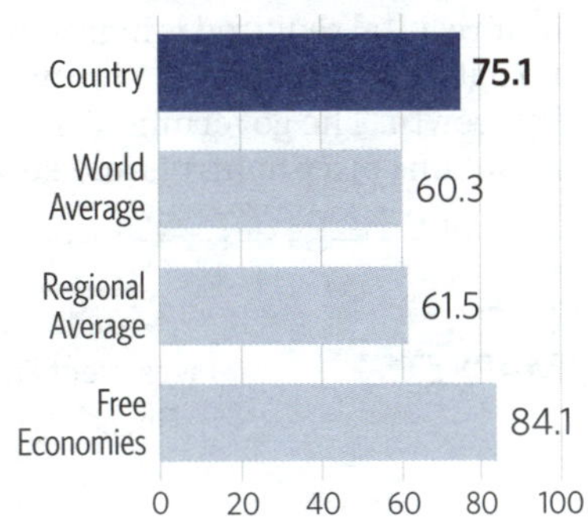

Quick Facts

Population: 1.2 million
GDP (PPP): $33.1 billion
3.9% growth in 2012
5-year compound annual growth 4.0%
$28,744 per capita
Unemployment: 3.4%
Inflation (CPI): 1.2%
FDI Inflow: $891.2 million
Public Debt: 33.7% of GDP

2012 data unless otherwise noted.
Data compiled as of September 2013.

THE TEN ECONOMIC FREEDOMS

Score ▬ Country | World Average

RULE OF LAW

	Score	Rank	1-Year Change
Property Rights	60.0	41st	+5.0
Freedom from Corruption	49.4	49th	-1.6

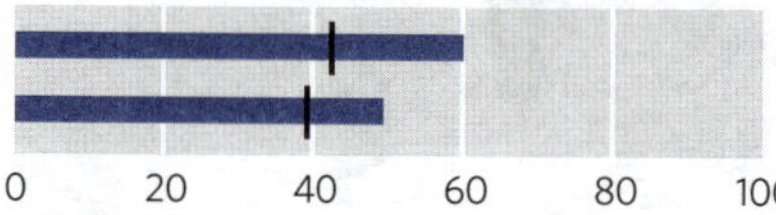

In the years since martial law was imposed after social unrest in 2011, the government has pursued a reformist domestic political agenda, although progress on further economic reforms appears to be on hold. The king holds some decision-making authority within the British-legacy legal system, but the judiciary is generally well regarded and unbiased. Expropriation, especially without compensation, is infrequent, and private property is secure.

GOVERNMENT SIZE

	Score	Rank	1-Year Change
Fiscal Freedom	99.9	2nd	0
Government Spending	71.4	83rd	-1.0

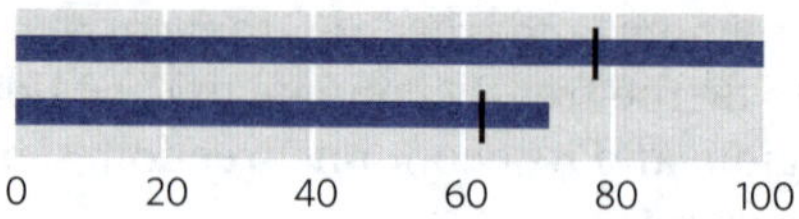

Bahrain levies no taxes on individual income. Oil companies must pay a 46 percent corporate income tax, but most other businesses are exempt from taxation. Other taxes include a stamp tax and a tax on property purchases. Government revenue equals 3.1 percent of GDP, and expenditures have climbed to 30.9 percent of domestic income, cushioned by energy exports. Public debt remains below 35 percent of GDP.

REGULATORY EFFICIENCY

	Score	Rank	1-Year Change
Business Freedom	76.3	41st	+0.5
Labor Freedom	82.0	20th	-8.4
Monetary Freedom	78.4	59th	+5.9

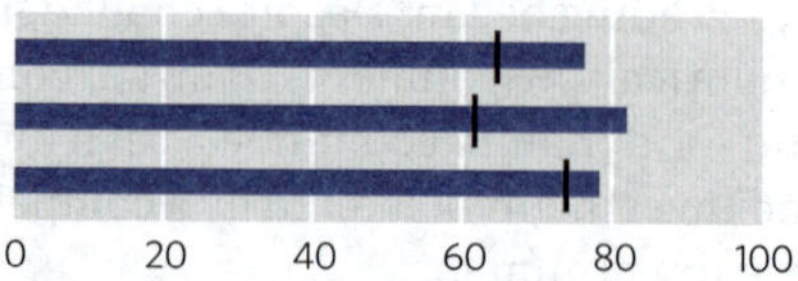

Starting a business costs less than 1 percent of the level of average annual income, but the minimum capital required is high. Obtaining needed permits is relatively time-consuming. There is no nationally mandated minimum wage, but wage increases have exceeded overall productivity growth. The government scaled back natural gas subsidies for industrial users in 2013 but maintains price controls and subsidies on food items, water, and electricity.

OPEN MARKETS

	Score	Rank	1-Year Change
Trade Freedom	78.6	79th	-4.2
Investment Freedom	75.0	35th	0
Financial Freedom	80.0	4th	0

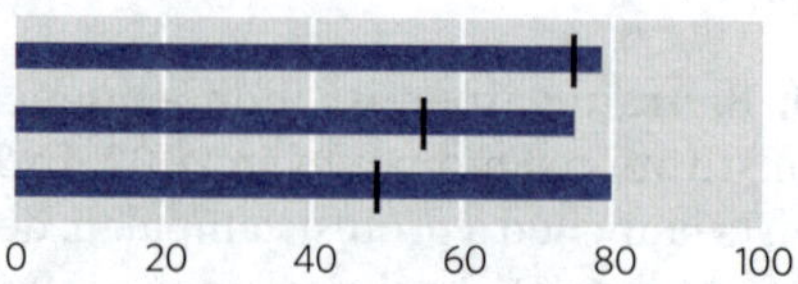

Bahrain has a 5.7 percent average tariff rate along with relatively few non-tariff barriers to trade. Several state-owned enterprises have yet to be privatized. As a regional financial hub, Bahrain's diverse and competitive financial institutions account for over 25 percent of GDP. Foreign and domestic investors have access to modern financial services on market terms.

Long-Term Score Change (since 1995)

RULE OF LAW		GOVERNMENT SIZE		REGULATORY EFFICIENCY		OPEN MARKETS	
Property Rights	0	Fiscal Freedom	+0.5	Business Freedom	-23.7	Trade Freedom	+0.2
Freedom from Corruption	-20.6	Government Spending	-0.3	Labor Freedom	+42.0	Investment Freedom	+25.0
				Monetary Freedom	-8.2	Financial Freedom	+10.0

BANGLADESH

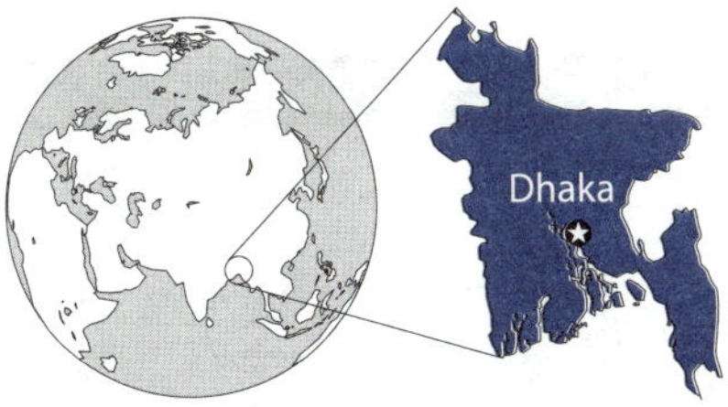

World Rank: **131** Regional Rank: **27**

Economic Freedom Score

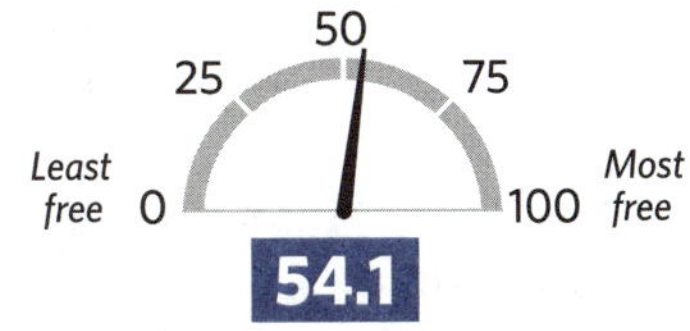

Bangladesh's economic freedom score is 54.1, making its economy the 131st freest in the 2014 *Index*. Its overall score has increased by 1.5 points since last year, reflecting improvements in trade freedom and business freedom that offset a notable decline in freedom from corruption. Bangladesh is ranked 27th out of 42 countries in the Asia–Pacific region.

Over the 20-year history of the *Index*, Bangladesh has advanced its economic freedom score by over 10 points. The overall score increase has been relatively broad-based in six of the 10 economic freedoms including trade freedom, business freedom, and fiscal freedom, the score for which has improved by more than 20 points.

Nonetheless, Bangladesh continues to be considered "mostly unfree" due to a serious lack of progress in other critical areas of economic freedom. The country has lagged in promoting the effective rule of law. The judicial system remains vulnerable to political interference, and property rights are not strongly protected. Lingering corruption further undermines enforcement of the rule of law and hampers the emergence of more vibrant economic activity.

BACKGROUND: The political landscape was marred by violence in early 2013 when a war crimes tribunal set up by the government of Prime Minister Sheikh Hasina Wajed to investigate and punish human rights violations during the war for independence in 1971 handed down its verdicts. The political volatility comes, however, in the context of overall economic and social gains of the past decade. Life expectancy has increased by 10 years, infant mortality has declined by nearly two-thirds, female literacy has doubled, and economic growth has averaged over 5 percent annually. Yet Bangladesh remains one of the world's poorest nations. The majority of its people work in agriculture, and garment manufacturing accounts for over 90 percent of export earnings. On April 24, 2013, a garment factory collapsed, killing over 1,100 workers and spurring calls for tighter regulations.

Freedom Trend

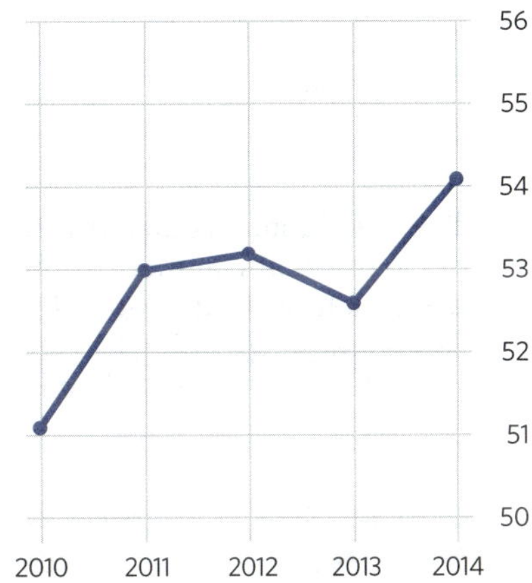

Country Comparisons

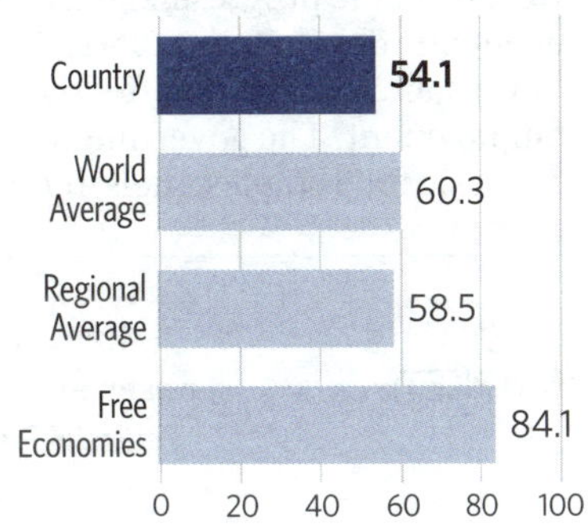

Quick Facts

Population: 150.0 million
GDP (PPP): $306.0 billion
6.1% growth in 2012
5-year compound annual growth 6.2%
$2,039 per capita
Unemployment: 5.0%
Inflation (CPI): 8.7%
FDI Inflow: $990.0 million
Public Debt: 31.7% of GDP

2012 data unless otherwise noted.
Data compiled as of September 2013.

How Do We Measure Economic Freedom?
See page 471 for an explanation of the methodology or visit the *Index* Web site at *heritage.org/index*.

THE TEN ECONOMIC FREEDOMS

RULE OF LAW

	Score	Rank	1-Year Change
Property Rights	20.0	139th	0
Freedom from Corruption	23.3	142nd	-3.7

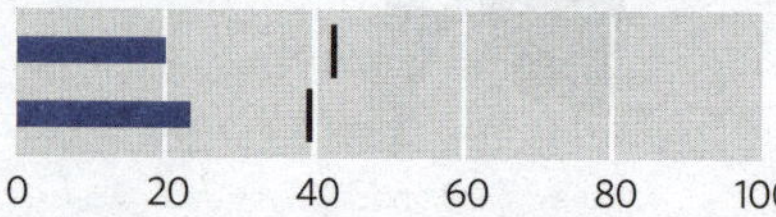

Corruption is a serious impediment to investment and economic growth in Bangladesh. By some estimates, bribes and other off-the-record payments paid by firms related to public procurement, tax and customs collection, and other regulatory authorities may reduce annual GDP by 3 percent. The British-legacy legal system provides for an independent judiciary, but contract enforcement and dispute settlement are inefficient.

GOVERNMENT SIZE

	Score	Rank	1-Year Change
Fiscal Freedom	72.5	129th	-0.2
Government Spending	92.3	6th	+0.2

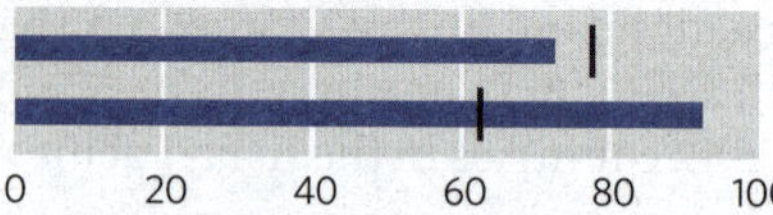

The individual income tax rate remains at 25 percent, and the corporate income tax rate is 45 percent. Financial institutions and mobile phone operators are taxed at higher rates. Other taxes include a value-added tax (VAT). Overall tax revenue has risen to 9.9 percent of GDP. Government spending has fallen slightly to 16 percent of the economy. The government has raised taxes on mobile phones to cover food subsidies.

REGULATORY EFFICIENCY

	Score	Rank	1-Year Change
Business Freedom	70.8	72nd	+2.8
Labor Freedom	51.9	131st	0
Monetary Freedom	65.9	162nd	+0.5

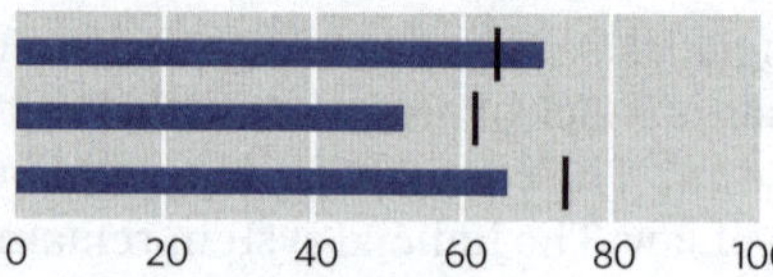

Despite some progress, significant bureaucratic impediments to entrepreneurial activity and economic development persist. The labor market remains underdeveloped, and enforcement of the labor codes is ineffective. The informal sector continues to be an important source of employment. The government maintains an extensive system of price controls and subsidies for basic food staples, fuels, fertilizers, and electricity.

OPEN MARKETS

	Score	Rank	1-Year Change
Trade Freedom	59.0	163rd	+5.0
Investment Freedom	55.0	96th	0
Financial Freedom	30.0	132nd	+10.0

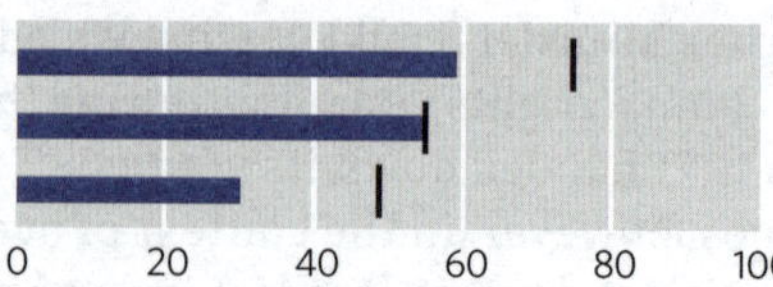

Bangladesh has a relatively high 13 percent average tariff rate due to its reliance on tariff revenue to finance the government. Regulations affecting investors can be non-transparent and burdensome. Amendments to the Bank Companies Act, intended to strengthen the independence of the central bank and reduce special treatment of the state-owned commercial banks, were passed in 2013.

Long-Term Score Change (since 1995)

RULE OF LAW		GOVERNMENT SIZE		REGULATORY EFFICIENCY		OPEN MARKETS	
Property Rights	**-10.0**	Fiscal Freedom	**+28.6**	Business Freedom	**+30.8**	Trade Freedom	**+59.0**
Freedom from Corruption	**+13.3**	Government Spending	**+0.8**	Labor Freedom	**-12.3**	Investment Freedom	**+5.0**
				Monetary Freedom	**-7.1**	Financial Freedom	**0**

BARBADOS

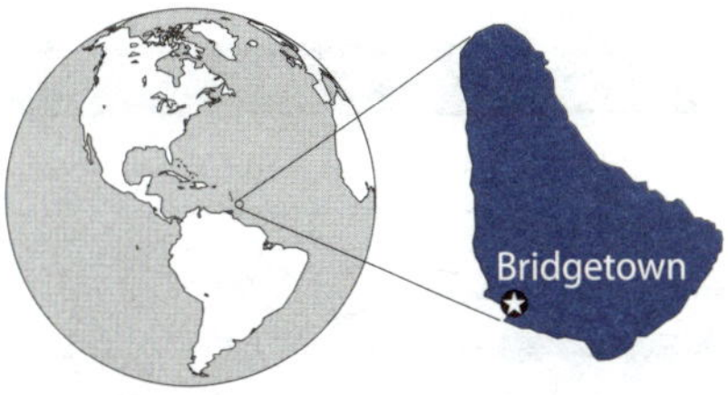

World Rank: 45 **Regional Rank: 6**

Economic Freedom Score

Freedom Trend

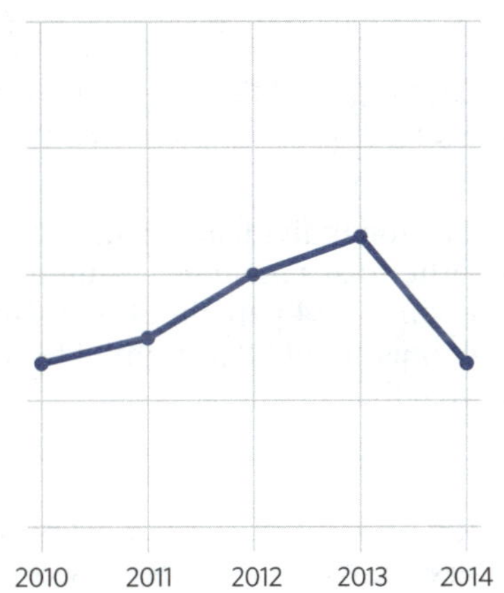

Country Comparisons

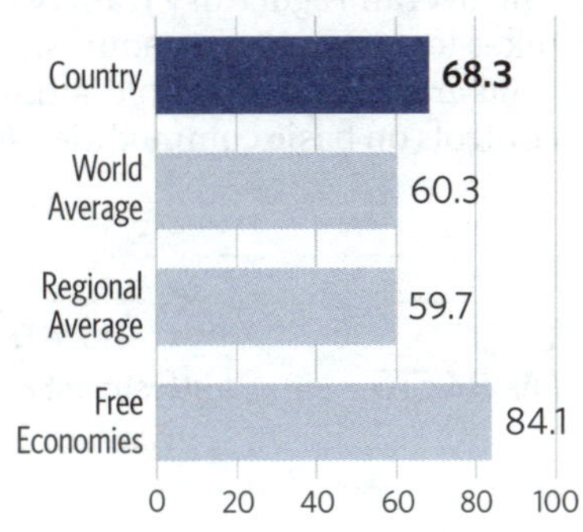

Barbados's economic freedom score is 68.3, making its economy the 45th freest in the 2014 *Index*. Its score is 1 point worse than last year due to deterioration in government spending, labor freedom, and business freedom. Barbados continues to be ranked 6th out of 29 countries in the South and Central America/Caribbean region, and its overall score remains well above the global and regional averages.

Over the 20-year history of the *Index*, Barbados has advanced its economic freedom score by 6 points. This modest overall gain has been driven by advancements in half of the 10 economic freedoms including trade freedom, fiscal freedom, freedom from corruption, and property rights. A high degree of regulatory efficiency has facilitated private-sector activity, and offshore finance and tourism continue to be important sources of economic growth.

However, in other critical areas of economic freedom such as investment freedom, financial freedom, and monetary freedom, Barbados has lost ground over the history of the *Index*. In particular, significantly increased public spending in recent years has led to chronic fiscal deficits. Expansionary government stimulus spending has had little impact on high unemployment, and inflation has increased.

BACKGROUND: Barbados is a parliamentary democracy and member of the British Commonwealth. Political stability is expected to continue under Prime Minister Freundel Stuart, whose Democratic Labour Party holds a very narrow parliamentary majority following elections in February 2012. Barbados has been transformed in recent decades from a low-income, agricultural economy producing mainly sugar and rum into a middle-income economy built on tourism and offshore banking that generates one of the highest per capita incomes in Latin America. However, tourist arrivals have declined in recent years. The financial services and construction industries were also hit hard during the 2008 global economic crisis, causing economic growth to remain below 1 percent.

How Do We Measure Economic Freedom?
See page 471 for an explanation of the methodology or visit the *Index* Web site at *heritage.org/index*.

Quick Facts

Population: 0.3 million
GDP (PPP): $7.1 billion
0.2% growth in 2012
5-year compound annual growth -0.6%
$25,373 per capita
Unemployment: 11.0%
Inflation (CPI): 4.6%
FDI Inflow: $356.4 million
Public Debt: 72.6% of GDP

2012 data unless otherwise noted.
Data compiled as of September 2013.

THE TEN ECONOMIC FREEDOMS

RULE OF LAW

	Score	Rank	1-Year Change
Property Rights	**80.0**	20th	0
Freedom from Corruption	**77.9**	15th	-0.1

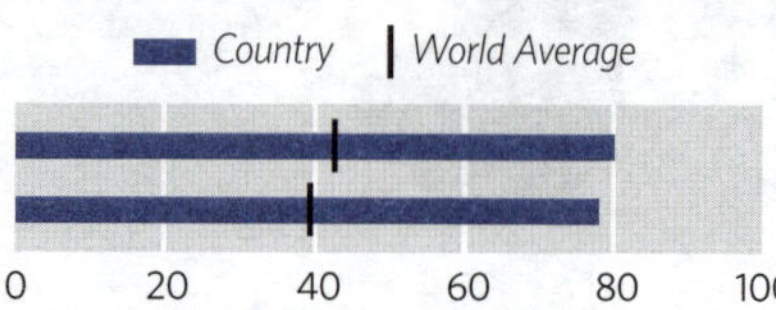

In 2013, the central bank issued new guidelines to increase transparency for financial institutions licensed to operate in Barbados. The court system is based on British common law and is generally unbiased and efficient. There are criminal penalties for official corruption, and enforcement of anti-corruption measures is generally effective. The protection of property rights is strong, and the rule of law is respected.

GOVERNMENT SIZE

	Score	Rank	1-Year Change
Fiscal Freedom	**74.0**	123rd	-0.5
Government Spending	**49.8**	136th	-4.4

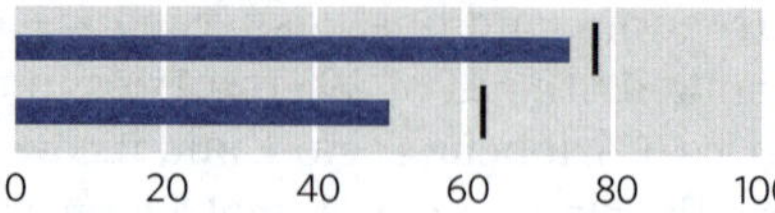

The top individual income tax rate is 35 percent, and the top corporate tax rate is 25 percent. Other taxes include a value-added tax (VAT) and a property tax. The overall tax burden has risen to 27.4 percent of GDP. Government spending is 41 percent of the economy, and public debt is about 73 percent of GDP. Slow growth and a sustained debt level are putting pressure on public finances.

REGULATORY EFFICIENCY

	Score	Rank	1-Year Change
Business Freedom	**72.8**	65th	-2.0
Labor Freedom	**78.4**	37th	-6.0
Monetary Freedom	**74.6**	109th	+2.5

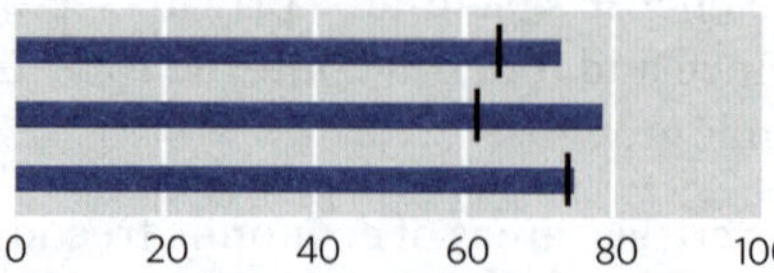

The overall regulatory framework supports entrepreneurial activity. Launching a business takes less than 10 procedures, and there is no minimum capital requirement. Labor regulations are relatively flexible, although enforcement can be lax. The government maintains price controls on basic commodities such as rice and flour, transportation, and fuel.

OPEN MARKETS

	Score	Rank	1-Year Change
Trade Freedom	**60.6**	160th	+0.1
Investment Freedom	**55.0**	96th	0
Financial Freedom	**60.0**	41st	0

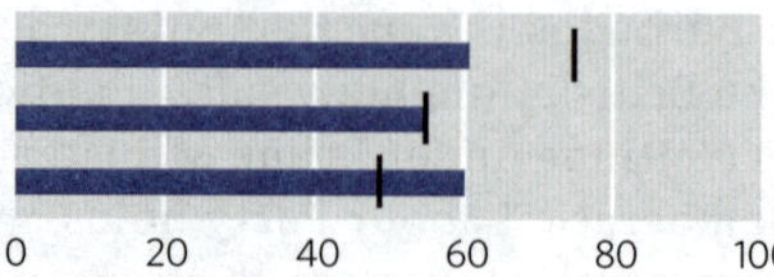

Barbados has a relatively high 14.7 percent average tariff due to its reliance on tariff revenue to finance the government. Foreign exchange is regulated by the government. In general, foreign and domestic investors are treated equally under the law. The banking sector provides a wide range of services for domestic and foreign investors, although securities markets are relatively illiquid.

Long-Term Score Change (since 1996)

RULE OF LAW		GOVERNMENT SIZE		REGULATORY EFFICIENCY		OPEN MARKETS	
Property Rights	**+30.0**	Fiscal Freedom	**+13.2**	Business Freedom	**+2.8**	Trade Freedom	**+11.6**
Freedom from Corruption	**+47.9**	Government Spending	**-21.7**	Labor Freedom	**-1.6**	Investment Freedom	**-15.0**
				Monetary Freedom	**-14.4**	Financial Freedom	**-10.0**

BELARUS

World Rank: 150 **Regional Rank: 42**

Economic Freedom Score

Belarus's economic freedom score is 50.1, making its economy the 150th freest in the 2014 *Index*. Its overall score is 2.1 points better than last year, mainly due to notable improvements in investment freedom and government spending. Belarus is ranked 42nd among the 43 countries in the Europe region.

Over the 20-year history of the *Index*, Belarus has improved its economic freedom score by 9.7 points, driven by gains in seven of the 10 economic freedoms including fiscal freedom, monetary freedom, and trade freedom. Offsetting much of the overall score gain, three other critical areas of economic freedom—property rights, investment freedom, and financial freedom—have recorded losses of 20 points or more over the same period.

In the 2014 *Index*, Belarus has moved up from the economic freedom status of "repressed" for the first time. Nonetheless, pervasive state controls persist in many areas of the economy, and widespread state investment and redistribution activities have stifled progress in the development of a modern diversified economy.

BACKGROUND: President Alexander Lukashenko, in power since 1994, rules all branches of government. The U.N. Human Rights Council has appointed a human rights investigator for Belarus. The European Union imposed targeted sanctions following beatings and arrests of opposition figures after Lukashenko falsified the December 2010 election results. Belarus's industry and state-controlled agriculture are not competitive. Russia maintains huge political influence in the government and economy. A significant portion of Russian oil and gas exports passes through the country. Efforts to promote greater economic union with Russia and Kazakhstan through a customs union and the projected Eurasian Union continue. Ties with Iran, Venezuela, and China are strengthening.

Freedom Trend

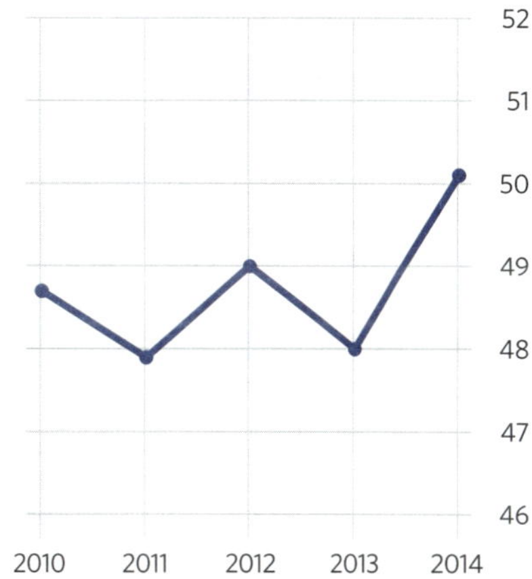

Country Comparisons

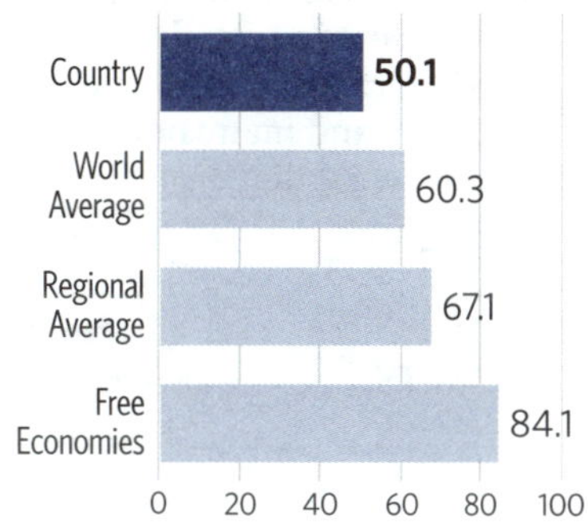

Quick Facts

Population: 9.4 million
GDP (PPP): $146.7 billion
1.5% growth in 2012
5-year compound annual growth 5.0%
$15,634 per capita
Unemployment: 0.6%
Inflation (CPI): 59.2%
FDI Inflow: $1.4 billion
Public Debt: 36.9% of GDP

2012 data unless otherwise noted.
Data compiled as of September 2013.

How Do We Measure Economic Freedom?
See page 471 for an explanation of the methodology or visit the *Index* Web site at *heritage.org/index.*

THE TEN ECONOMIC FREEDOMS

RULE OF LAW

	Score	Rank	1-Year Change
Property Rights	20.0	139th	0
Freedom from Corruption	24.6	132nd	+0.6

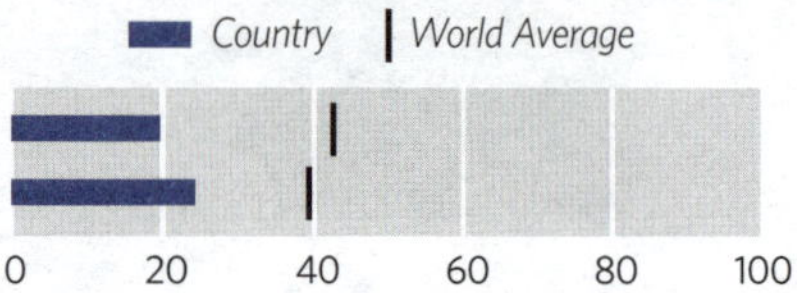

Since his election 20 years ago as the first (and to date the only) president of Belarus, Alexander Lukashenko has consolidated authoritarian power, destroying checks and balances and dominating all branches of government. Corruption is pervasive in both the private and public sectors, from the executive and judiciary to the police. Soviet-era state ownership of land and government-controlled collective farms continues.

GOVERNMENT SIZE

	Score	Rank	1-Year Change
Fiscal Freedom	89.2	35th	+0.4
Government Spending	61.2	118th	+17.7

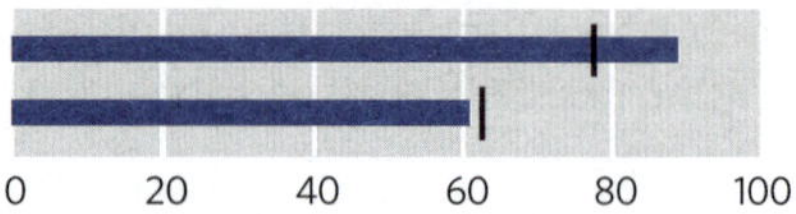

The top individual income tax rate is a flat 12 percent, and the top corporate tax rate is 18 percent. Other taxes include a value-added tax (VAT) and excise taxes. Overall tax revenue has fallen to 24.7 percent of GDP. Government spending is 36 percent of total domestic output, and public debt remains below 40 percent of GDP. A shakeup in the potash market could be a major threat to government finances.

REGULATORY EFFICIENCY

	Score	Rank	1-Year Change
Business Freedom	73.4	62nd	-1.8
Labor Freedom	77.7	42nd	+0.8
Monetary Freedom	33.9	182nd	-6.8

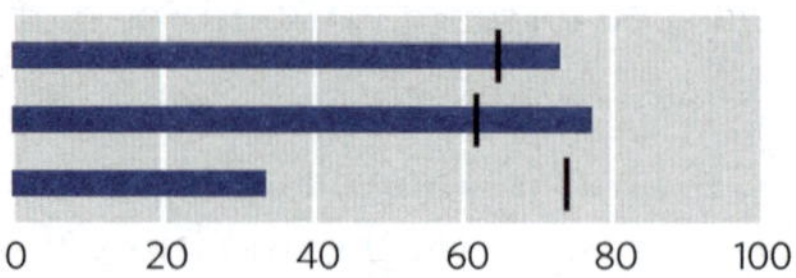

Starting a business takes five procedures, and no minimum capital is required. However, completing licensing requirements still takes over 100 days. The labor market remains stagnant. A large portion of the workforce is in the informal sector. The government subsidizes prices for energy and many household goods and fixes artificially low prices for products made by state-owned enterprises.

OPEN MARKETS

	Score	Rank	1-Year Change
Trade Freedom	81.4	67th	+0.6
Investment Freedom	30.0	152nd	+10.0
Financial Freedom	10.0	174th	0

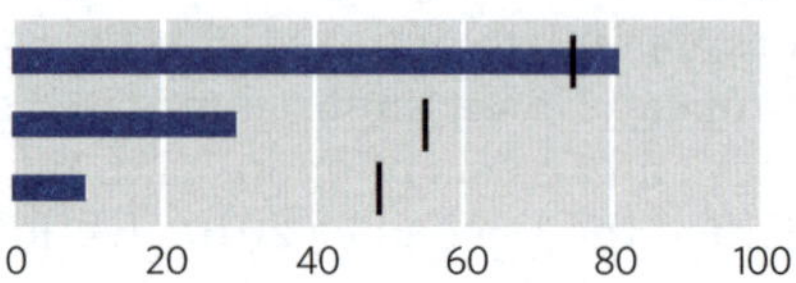

Belarus has a relatively low 1.8 percent average tariff rate, but importers may face long delays. New foreign investment is screened by the government. In general, investment and financial activity are severely limited by state interference and controls. Development of the financial sector has progressed slowly. Large state banks continue to dominate the banking system.

Long-Term Score Change (since 1995)

RULE OF LAW		GOVERNMENT SIZE		REGULATORY EFFICIENCY		OPEN MARKETS	
Property Rights	**-30.0**	Fiscal Freedom	**+47.2**	Business Freedom	**+3.4**	Trade Freedom	**+21.4**
Freedom from Corruption	**+14.6**	Government Spending	**+29.7**	Labor Freedom	**+5.7**	Investment Freedom	**-20.0**
				Monetary Freedom	**+33.9**	Financial Freedom	**-40.0**

BELGIUM

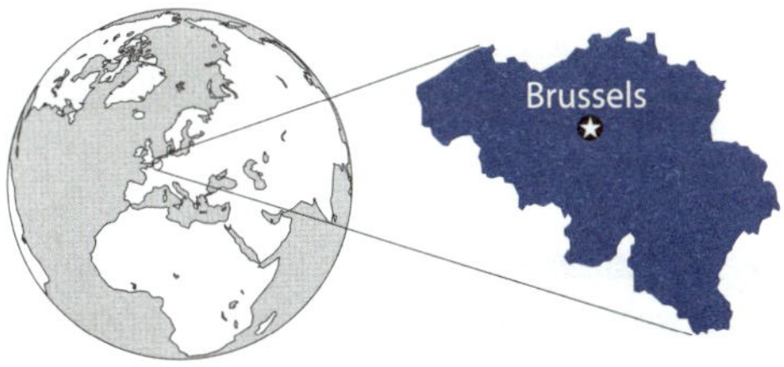

Economic Freedom Score

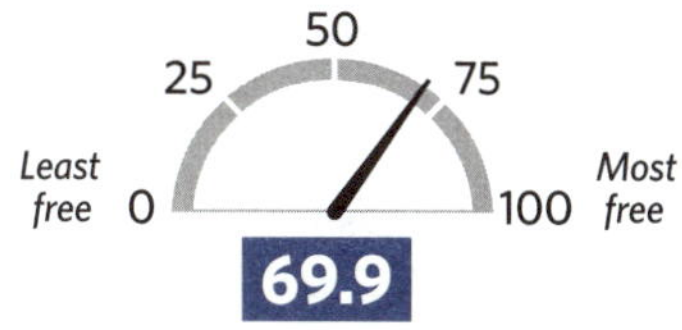

World Rank: 35 **Regional Rank: 17**

Belgium's economic freedom score is 69.9, making its economy the 35th freest in the 2014 *Index*. Its overall score has increased by 0.7 point from last year, primarily reflecting notable improvements in investment freedom and labor freedom that counterbalance declines in freedom from corruption and business freedom. Belgium is ranked 17th among the 43 countries in the Europe region, and its overall score is above the regional and global averages.

Over the 20-year history of the *Index*, Belgium's economic freedom has been largely stagnant. Despite notable score improvements in the areas of government size, regulatory efficiency, and open markets, the overall gain has been largely offset by combined declines in property rights and freedom from corruption. Belgium had risen to the status of economically "mostly free" during the second half of the 2000s but since 2011 has fallen back to the rank of "moderately free."

The economic recovery that began in mid-2009 has been uneven, and structural weaknesses that include a rigid labor market and high taxation continue to hinder international competitiveness. Expansionary public spending has generated significant budgetary pressure. With government debt nearing 100 percent of the size of the economy, reducing the chronic budget deficit needs to be a high priority.

BACKGROUND: Belgium is a federal state with three culturally different regions: Flanders, Wallonia, and the capital city of Brussels, which is home to NATO and the European Union. In April 2010, an electoral dispute between the Francophone and Flemish parties led to the collapse of the coalition government. New elections in June 2010 did not produce a government. Negotiations to form a new government were finally completed in December 2011, and Socialist Party member Elio Di Rupo was sworn in as prime minister. In October 2012, the Flemish Nationalist Party made significant gains in local elections, calling for greater autonomy for Belgium's Flemish-speaking regions. Services account for 75 percent of economic activity. Leading exports are electrical equipment, vehicles, diamonds, and chemicals.

How Do We Measure Economic Freedom?
See page 471 for an explanation of the methodology or visit the *Index* Web site at *heritage.org/index*.

Freedom Trend

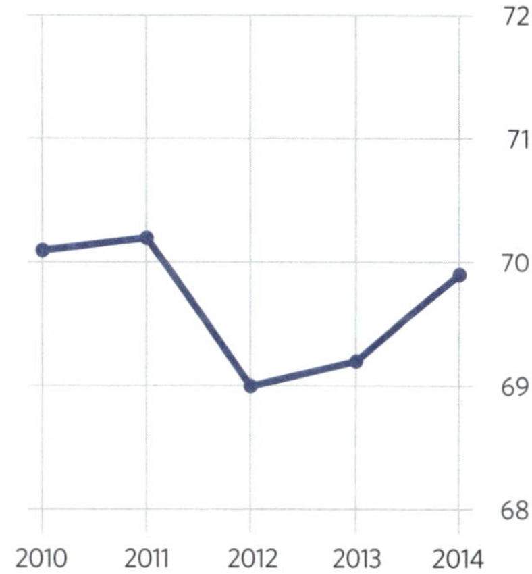

Country Comparisons

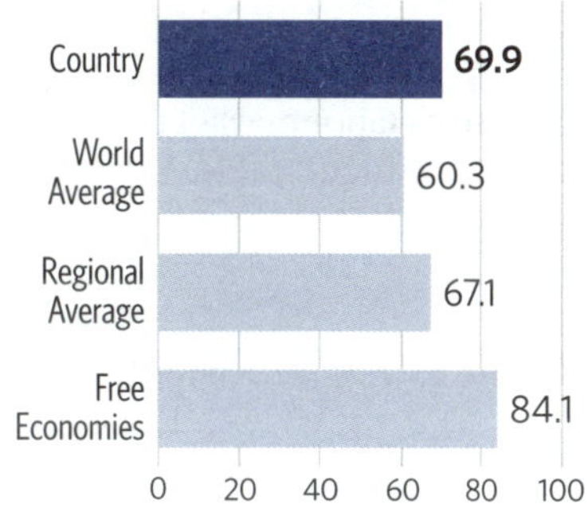

Quick Facts

Population: 11.1 million
GDP (PPP): $420.3 billion
-0.2% growth in 2012
5-year compound annual growth 0.4%
$37,883 per capita
Unemployment: 7.3%
Inflation (CPI): 2.6%
FDI Inflow: -$1.6 billion
Public Debt: 99.6% of GDP

2012 data unless otherwise noted.
Data compiled as of September 2013.

THE TEN ECONOMIC FREEDOMS

Legend: Country | World Average

		Score	Rank	1-Year Change
RULE OF LAW	Property Rights	80.0	20th	0
	Freedom from Corruption	74.2	20th	-0.8

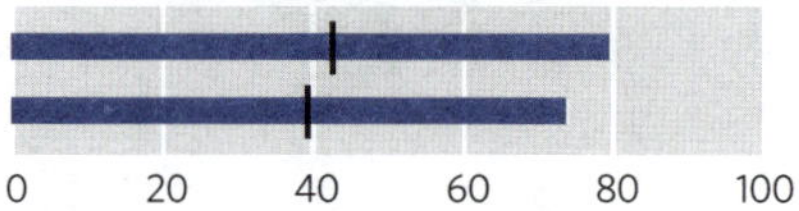

Corruption is minimal in Belgium and did not increase even during the 19-month political crisis of 2010–2011. The government prohibits and punishes all forms of bribery. Property rights are well protected by law. Laws are well codified, and the judicial system is generally respected, but the courts can be slow in practice. Enforcement actions to protect intellectual property rights can be especially protracted.

		Score	Rank	1-Year Change
GOVERNMENT SIZE	Fiscal Freedom	44.8	180th	-0.3
	Government Spending	14.8	173rd	+0.3

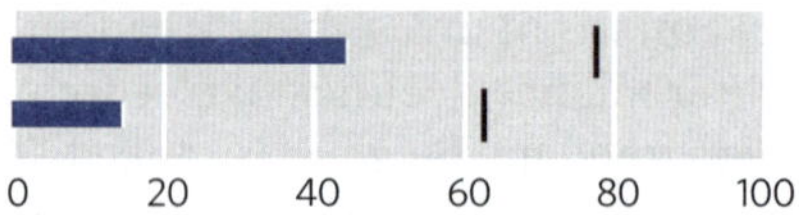

The top individual income tax rate is 50 percent, and the top corporate tax rate is 33 percent. Other taxes include a value-added tax (VAT) and an estate tax. Tax revenue equals 44 percent of GDP, and government expenditures equal 53 percent of the economy. Additional measures have been undertaken to raise revenue to cover chronic deficits that have pushed public debt to over 90 percent of GDP.

		Score	Rank	1-Year Change
REGULATORY EFFICIENCY	Business Freedom	89.9	13th	-1.7
	Labor Freedom	72.7	56th	+2.9
	Monetary Freedom	79.5	41st	+0.2

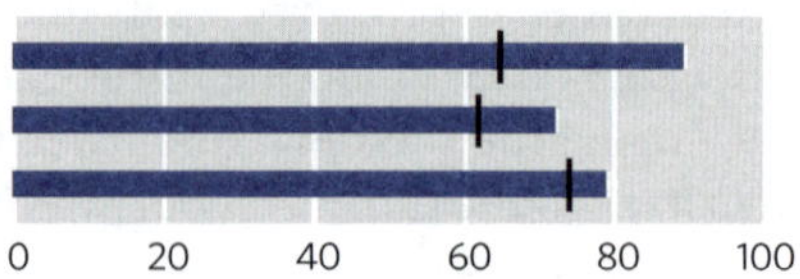

Starting a business takes less than five days on average and costs about 5 percent of the level of average annual income. Bankruptcy proceedings are relatively easy. Despite efforts to ease the rigidity of employment regulations, factors that include high sectoral minimum wages still hold back labor market flexibility. The state imposes price controls on a wide range of fuels and other products and services.

		Score	Rank	1-Year Change
OPEN MARKETS	Trade Freedom	87.8	11th	+1.0
	Investment Freedom	85.0	13th	+5.0
	Financial Freedom	70.0	19th	0

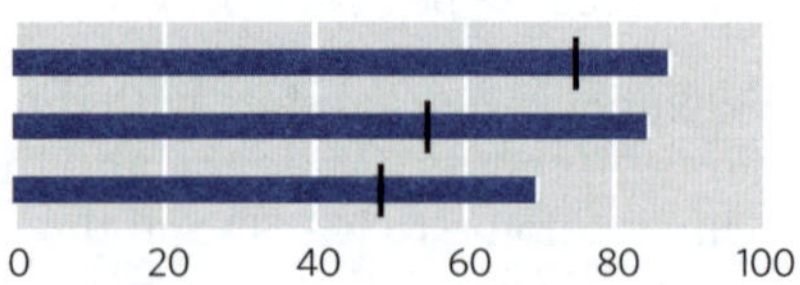

EU members have a low 1.1 percent average tariff rate and, in general, few non-tariff barriers to trade. Investment in some sectors of the economy may be screened by the government. The financial system remains relatively stable, but the banking sector has undergone restructuring and become smaller. Government bailouts in recent years have increased state ownership of banks to over 15 percent of total assets.

Long-Term Score Change (since 1996)

RULE OF LAW		GOVERNMENT SIZE		REGULATORY EFFICIENCY		OPEN MARKETS	
Property Rights	**-10.0**	Fiscal Freedom	**+10.8**	Business Freedom	**+19.9**	Trade Freedom	**+10.0**
Freedom from Corruption	**-15.8**	Government Spending	**+7.5**	Labor Freedom	**+4.7**	Investment Freedom	**+15.0**
				Monetary Freedom	**-5.5**	Financial Freedom	**0**

BELIZE

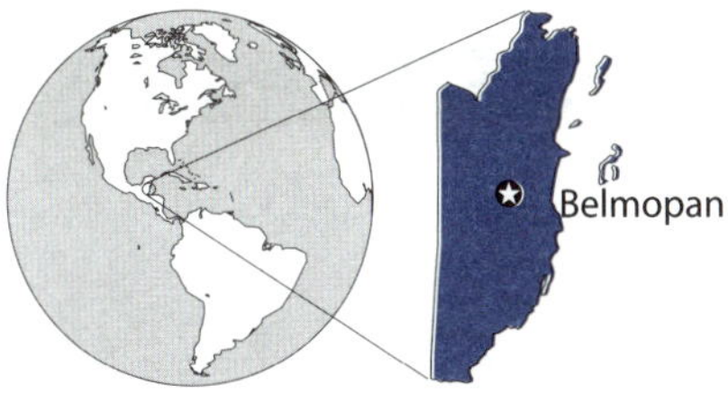

World Rank: **115** Regional Rank: **21**

Economic Freedom Score

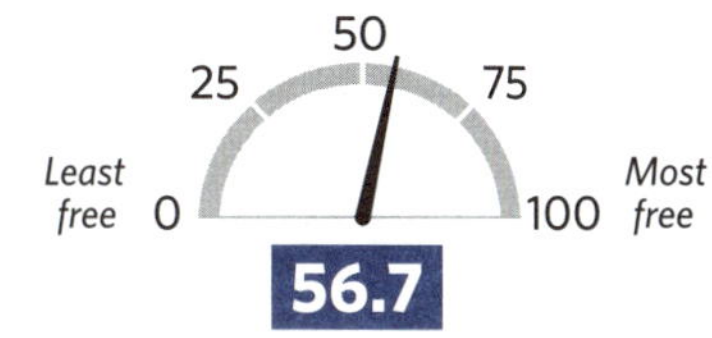

Belize's economic freedom score is 56.7, making its economy the 115th freest in the 2014 *Index*. Its overall score is 0.6 point worse than last year due to significant score reductions in trade freedom and labor freedom that offset a notable improvement in freedom from corruption. Belize is ranked 21st out of 29 countries in the South and Central America/Caribbean region.

Over the 20-year history of the *Index*, Belize's economic freedom score has declined by 6.2 points, the 12th largest rating deterioration. The gains achieved in trade freedom and the area of government size that measures fiscal freedom and government spending have been outweighed by substantial declines in investment freedom, property rights, and freedom from corruption, all of which deteriorated by at least 30 points over the same period.

Registering its lowest score ever in the 2014 *Index*, Belize's economic freedom status remains "mostly unfree." Economic dynamism is constrained by institutional weaknesses that undermine prospects for long-term broad-based economic development. In particular, the judicial system remains inefficient and vulnerable to political interference. Corruption, perceived as widespread, severely undermines entrepreneurial dynamism.

BACKGROUND: Belize is a parliamentary democracy and member of the British Commonwealth. Prime Minister Dean Barrow of the ruling United Democratic Party won re-election for a five-year term in March 2012, more than a year earlier than constitutionally mandated. Since taking office in 2008, Barrow's government has undermined foreign direct investment by expropriating Belize's commercial "crown jewels," the leading private telecommunications and electricity companies, owned by U.K. and Canadian investors, and the water company. He has also established close relations with the authoritarian Venezuelan government. Public-sector debt is above 70 percent of GDP and leaves little fiscal room for the government to maneuver, particularly as oil reserves continue to decline. Belize is plagued by high crime rates, the prevalence of HIV/AIDS, and rising unemployment.

How Do We Measure Economic Freedom?
See page 471 for an explanation of the methodology or visit the *Index* Web site at *heritage.org/index.*

Freedom Trend

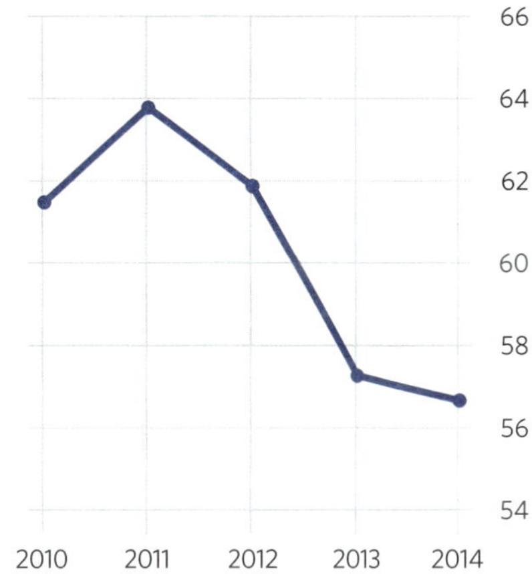

Country Comparisons

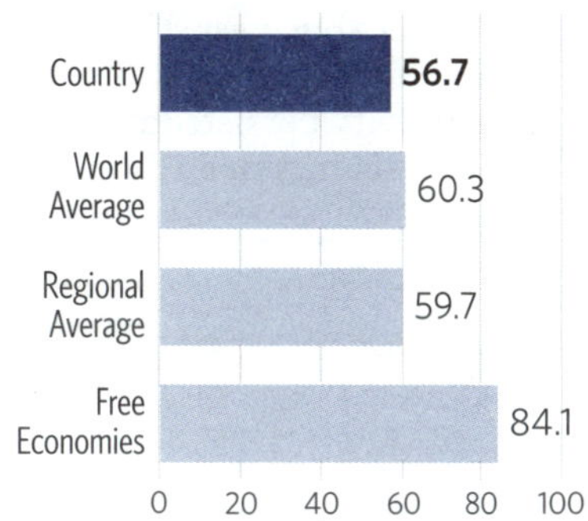

Quick Facts

Population: 0.3 million
GDP (PPP): $3.0 billion
5.3% growth in 2012
5-year compound annual growth 2.7%
$8,754 per capita
Unemployment: 16.1%
Inflation (CPI): 1.4%
FDI Inflow: $197.9 million
Public Debt: 78.1% of GDP

2012 data unless otherwise noted.
Data compiled as of September 2013.

THE TEN ECONOMIC FREEDOMS

		Score	Rank	1-Year Change
RULE OF LAW	Property Rights	30.0	93rd	0
	Freedom from Corruption	6.7	183rd	+6.7

Corruption is seen as widespread. Business owners complain that government officials, including police and others, often solicit bribes or show favoritism. The court system, although constitutionally independent, is often influenced by the executive. Expropriation of personal property is relatively rare, but the current government has expropriated major private foreign-owned electricity and telecommunications companies.

		Score	Rank	1-Year Change
GOVERNMENT SIZE	Fiscal Freedom	82.1	68th	-0.1
	Government Spending	74.2	75th	+1.6

The top individual income and corporate tax rates are 25 percent. Other taxes include a goods and services tax and a stamp duty. The overall tax burden amounts to 23.3 percent of gross domestic income. Government spending has fallen slightly to 29.3 percent of the total economy. Public debt is around 80 percent of GDP.

		Score	Rank	1-Year Change
REGULATORY EFFICIENCY	Business Freedom	71.6	69th	-1.0
	Labor Freedom	67.2	74th	-4.2
	Monetary Freedom	77.6	68th	+0.3

The inefficient business environment continues to impede broader economic development. Launching a business still costs about half the level of average annual income, although there is no minimum capital requirement. In the absence of a well-functioning labor market, informal labor activity persists in many sectors. The government maintains price controls on various products such as rice, sugar, and flour and subsidizes the cost of electricity.

		Score	Rank	1-Year Change
OPEN MARKETS	Trade Freedom	67.8	136th	-9.4
	Investment Freedom	40.0	132nd	0
	Financial Freedom	50.0	69th	0

Belize has an 11.1 percent average tariff rate, and tariffs are a significant source of government revenue. Expropriation of private property is a deterrent to new investment. The revised Domestic Banking and Financial Institutions Act came into force in January 2013, significantly expanding the role of the central bank. Credit allocation is influenced by the government.

Long-Term Score Change (since 1995)

RULE OF LAW		GOVERNMENT SIZE		REGULATORY EFFICIENCY		OPEN MARKETS	
Property Rights	-40.0	Fiscal Freedom	+18.9	Business Freedom	+1.6	Trade Freedom	+25.8
Freedom from Corruption	-43.3	Government Spending	+9.5	Labor Freedom	-16.1	Investment Freedom	-30.0
				Monetary Freedom	-9.0	Financial Freedom	0

BENIN

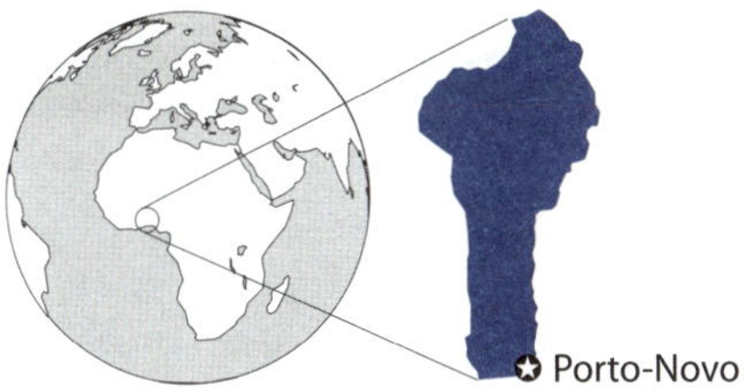

World Rank: **113** Regional Rank: **18**

Economic Freedom Score

Benin's economic freedom score is 57.1, making its economy the 113th freest in the 2014 *Index*. Its overall score is 0.5 point worse than last year due to score declines in monetary freedom and fiscal freedom that outweigh a combined gain from business freedom, trade freedom, and labor freedom. Benin is ranked 18th out of 46 countries in the Sub-Saharan Africa region, and its overall score is higher than the regional average.

Over the 20-year history of the *Index*, Benin's progress toward greater economic freedom has been patchy and modest. The overall score improvement has been merely 2.6 points, with hard-won gains in trade freedom, investment freedom, and monetary freedom offset by deteriorations in seven of the 10 economic freedoms including property rights, freedom from corruption, and business freedom. Benin had advanced to the status of "moderately free" during the late 1990s but since 2001 has fallen back to the ranks of the "mostly unfree."

The lack of progress in advancing economic freedom weakens Benin's prospects for lasting economic development. In the absence of a dynamic private sector, economic expansion remains fragile, and the poor quality of physical and legal infrastructure, impaired by the government's inefficiency in delivering public goods, exacerbates the problems.

BACKGROUND: President Mathieu Kérékou, who ruled for almost 20 years after a military coup, stepped down following a democratic transition in the early 1990s and later served two five-year elected terms. Current President Thomas Boni Yayi was elected in 2006 and re-elected for another five-year term in 2011. Police foiled a coup against Yayi in March 2013, arresting a cabinet member involved in the plot. In January 2012, Yayi was elected chairman of the African Union. Benin remains underdeveloped and dependent on subsistence agriculture. Cotton accounts for over 40 percent of foreign exchange earnings, 17 percent of exports, and about 7 percent of GDP. Piracy has increased off the coast, with reports of 20 incidents of oil tanker hijacking in 2011.

How Do We Measure Economic Freedom?
See page 471 for an explanation of the methodology or visit the *Index* Web site at *heritage.org/index*.

Freedom Trend

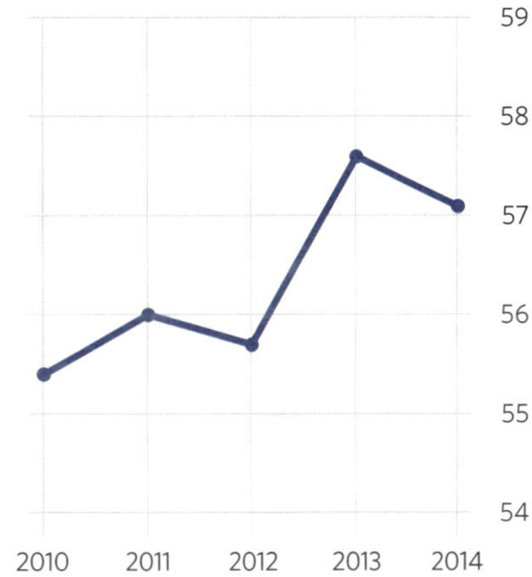

Country Comparisons

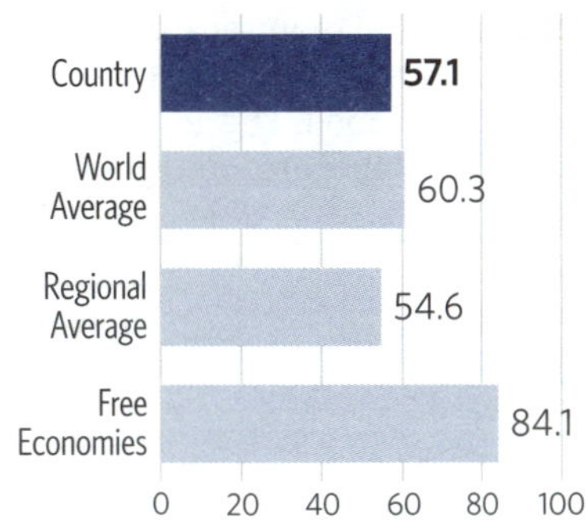

Quick Facts

Population: 9.4 million
GDP (PPP): $15.6 billion
3.8% growth in 2012
5-year compound annual growth 3.5%
$1,667 per capita
Unemployment: n/a
Inflation (CPI): 6.7%
FDI Inflow: $158.6 million
Public Debt: 32.5% of GDP

2012 data unless otherwise noted.
Data compiled as of September 2013.

THE TEN ECONOMIC FREEDOMS

Country | World Average

RULE OF LAW

	Score	Rank	1-Year Change
Property Rights	30.0	93rd	0
Freedom from Corruption	29.5	104th	-0.5

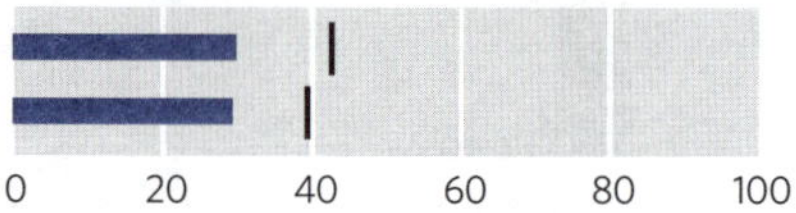

The government passed an anti-corruption law in 2011, but corruption remains a problem in the customs service, government procurement, and the judicial system. There is extensive smuggling of subsidized and adulterated gasoline from neighboring Nigeria. There are no separate commercial courts, and backlogs of civil cases cause long delays. In 2013, a law was passed to facilitate land investment for development.

GOVERNMENT SIZE

	Score	Rank	1-Year Change
Fiscal Freedom	68.3	148th	-7.8
Government Spending	86.1	27th	0

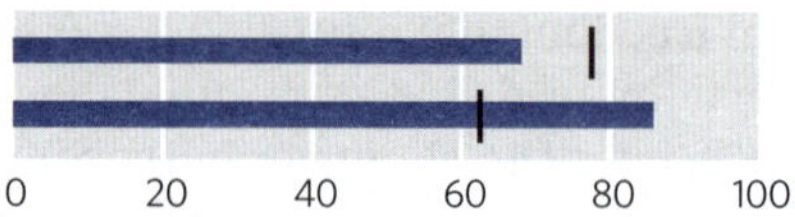

Benin's top individual income tax rate has risen to 45 percent. The top corporate tax rate is 30 percent (up to 45 percent for oil companies). The overall tax burden has fallen to 15.5 percent. A narrow tax base and large public wages continue to put pressure on public finances. Public expenditures are 21.5 percent of domestic output, and public debt hovers around 32 percent of GDP.

REGULATORY EFFICIENCY

	Score	Rank	1-Year Change
Business Freedom	51.0	151st	+5.6
Labor Freedom	50.5	134th	+0.8
Monetary Freedom	75.4	96th	-4.5

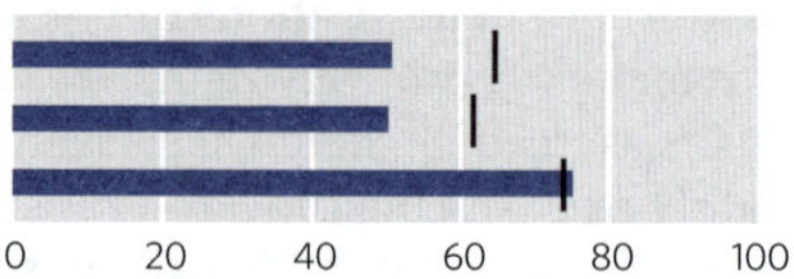

Launching a business still costs more than the level of average annual income, and the minimum capital required exceeds twice the income level. Getting all of the necessary permits takes more than 200 days. Despite flexible employment regulations, a formal labor market has not fully developed. The government subsidizes the production of cotton, and subsidized gasoline and diesel fuel are smuggled illegally from Nigeria.

OPEN MARKETS

	Score	Rank	1-Year Change
Trade Freedom	60.0	162nd	+0.7
Investment Freedom	70.0	46th	0
Financial Freedom	50.0	69th	0

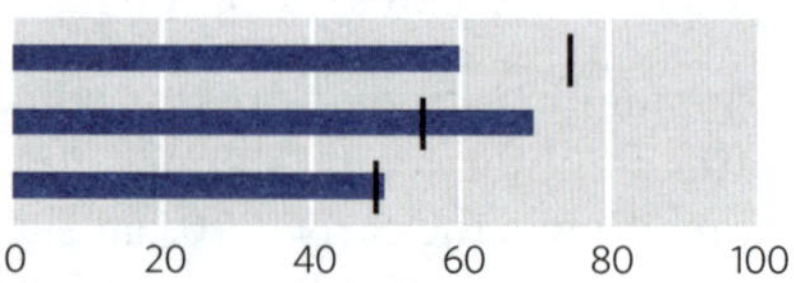

Benin has a 15 percent average tariff rate. The legal and regulatory systems can hinder international trade and investment. The financial system remains underdeveloped. Banks have continued to increase their domestic assets, and there are many microfinance institutions. Nonetheless, overall access to credit remains limited.

Long-Term Score Change (since 1996)

RULE OF LAW		GOVERNMENT SIZE		REGULATORY EFFICIENCY		OPEN MARKETS	
Property Rights	**-20.0**	Fiscal Freedom	**-3.7**	Business Freedom	**-19.0**	Trade Freedom	**+60.0**
Freedom from Corruption	**-20.5**	Government Spending	**-4.4**	Labor Freedom	**-2.1**	Investment Freedom	**+20.0**
				Monetary Freedom	**+17.4**	Financial Freedom	**0**

BHUTAN

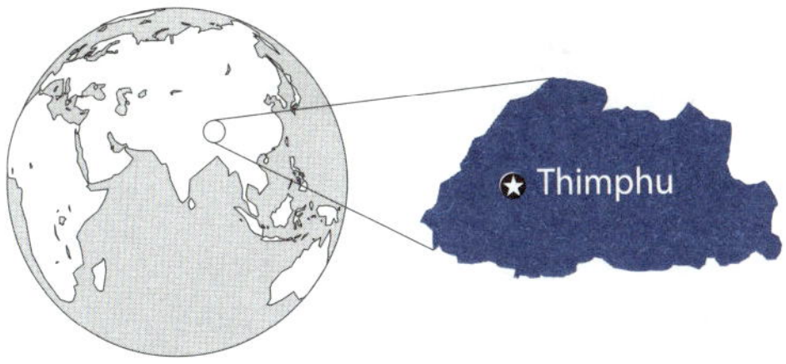

World Rank: **116** Regional Rank: **24**

Economic Freedom Score

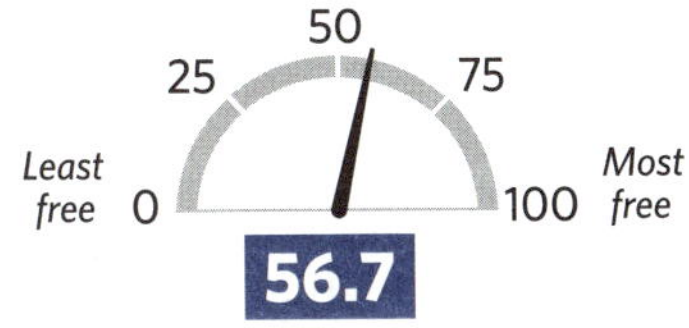

Freedom Trend

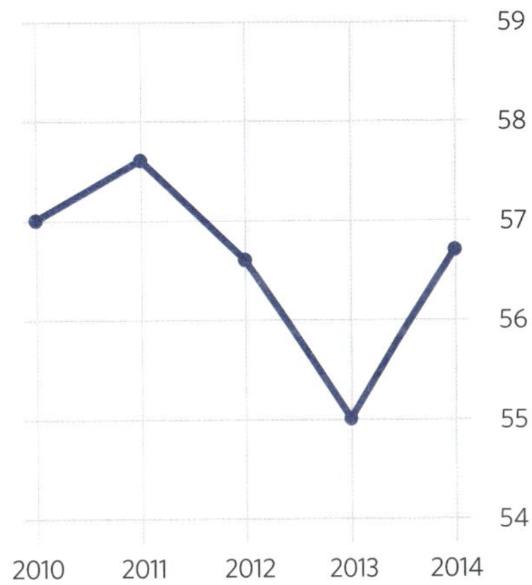

Country Comparisons

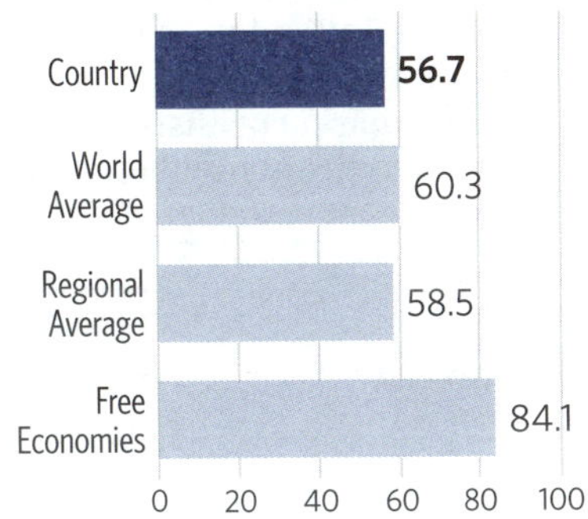

Bhutan's economic freedom score is 56.7, making its economy the 116th freest in the 2014 *Index*. Its score has increased 1.7 points from last year, primarily due to improved scores in government spending and freedom from corruption. Bhutan is ranked 24th out of 42 countries in the Asia–Pacific region, and its overall score is below the global and regional averages.

Since Bhutan's economic freedom was first assessed in the 2009 *Index*, its progress in implementing more targeted reforms to advance economic freedom has been stagnant at best. Although Bhutan has taken steps to modernize its economic structure and reduce poverty, only two of the 10 economic freedoms—trade freedom and freedom from corruption—have recorded score improvements. Declines of about 10 points in both investment freedom and monetary freedom have helped to keep the country within the status of "mostly unfree" in the *Index*.

A higher priority has been placed on measures to diversify the economy. The public sector, especially hydropower, which has driven strong economic growth over the past five years, has long been the main source of economic expansion. However, with the poverty rate still high, the government has recognized that broad-based development is crucial. Taxation of personal and corporate income is moderate, and relatively flexible employment regulations are a potential advantage for private-sector development.

BACKGROUND: Bhutan, a small Himalayan constitutional monarchy that made the transition from absolute monarchy to parliamentary democracy in March 2008, has one of the world's smallest and least-developed economies. Until a few decades ago, the country was still largely agrarian, with few roads, little electricity, and no modern hospitals. Rugged terrain makes the development of infrastructure difficult. Recent interregional economic cooperation, particularly involving trade with Bangladesh and India, is helping to encourage economic growth. Connections to global markets are limited and dominated significantly by India.

How Do We Measure Economic Freedom?
See page 471 for an explanation of the methodology or visit the *Index* Web site at *heritage.org/index*.

Quick Facts

Population: 0.7 million
GDP (PPP): $5.0 billion
9.7% growth in 2012
5-year compound annual growth 8.2%
$6,665 per capita
Unemployment: 3.2%
Inflation (CPI): 9.7%
FDI Inflow: $15.9 million
Public Debt: 72.1% of GDP

2012 data unless otherwise noted.
Data compiled as of September 2013.

THE TEN ECONOMIC FREEDOMS

RULE OF LAW

	Score	Rank	1-Year Change
Property Rights	60.0	41st	0
Freedom from Corruption	58.8	38th	+1.8

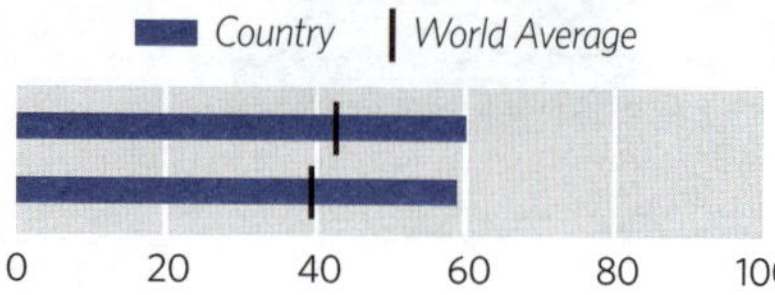

The government operates with limited transparency and accountability, but steps have been taken in recent years to improve both. The Anti-Corruption Commission has identified misuse of resources, bribery, collusion, and nepotism as major problems. Bhutan's civil and criminal codes include many modern provisions based on English common law. Property rights are generally better protected than in other South Asian countries.

GOVERNMENT SIZE

	Score	Rank	1-Year Change
Fiscal Freedom	82.9	65th	+0.2
Government Spending	57.2	122nd	+18.4

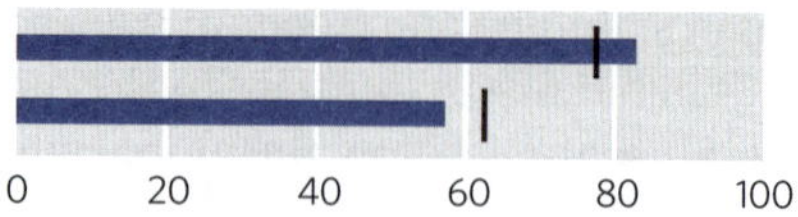

The top individual income tax rate is 25 percent, and the top corporate tax rate is 30 percent. Other taxes include a property tax and an excise tax. Overall tax revenue is 13.5 percent of GDP. Government expenditures amount to 37.8 percent of GDP, and public debt has risen to over 70 percent of the economy as the government has borrowed to finance the opening of new hydroelectric projects.

REGULATORY EFFICIENCY

	Score	Rank	1-Year Change
Business Freedom	59.4	116th	-1.1
Labor Freedom	83.6	16th	-0.8
Monetary Freedom	65.8	165th	-1.5

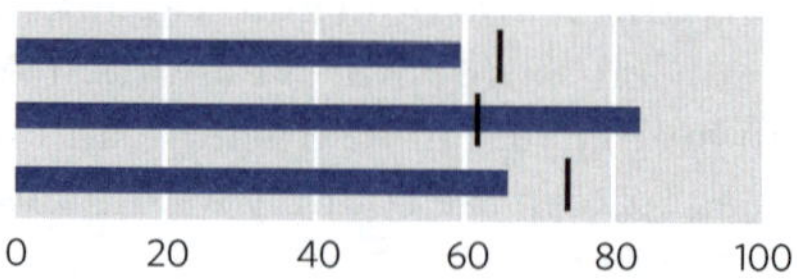

Starting a business is relatively straightforward, costing about 5 percent of the average annual income, but obtaining necessary licenses is time-consuming and costly. The labor market remains underdeveloped. Despite some improvement, the supply-and-demand imbalance in the labor market persists. Bhutan receives subsidized LPG and kerosene from India and maintains a significant number of financial and commercial controls.

OPEN MARKETS

	Score	Rank	1-Year Change
Trade Freedom	49.4	175th	-0.1
Investment Freedom	20.0	164th	0
Financial Freedom	30.0	132nd	0

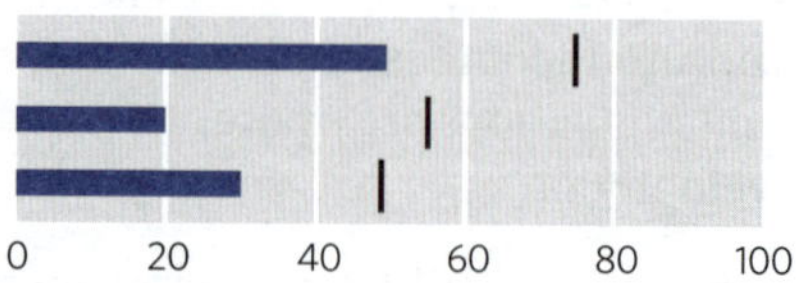

As of 2007, Bhutan had a 17.8 percent tariff rate. Importing is a slow and costly process. New foreign investments may be screened by the government. Despite some progress in improving efficiency, the government-controlled financial sector does not meet private-sector credit needs sufficiently. The banking sector remains burdened with non-performing loans.

Long-Term Score Change (since 2009)

RULE OF LAW		GOVERNMENT SIZE		REGULATORY EFFICIENCY		OPEN MARKETS	
Property Rights	0	Fiscal Freedom	-0.7	Business Freedom	-2.3	Trade Freedom	+7.4
Freedom from Corruption	+8.8	Government Spending	-1.0	Labor Freedom	-2.2	Investment Freedom	-10.0
				Monetary Freedom	-10.1	Financial Freedom	0

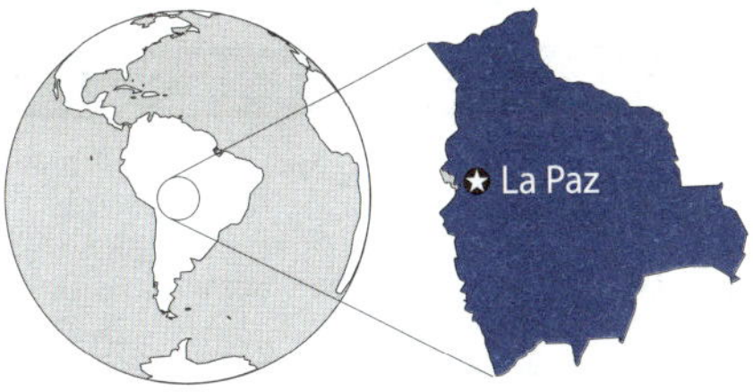

BOLIVIA

World Rank: **158** Regional Rank: **25**

Economic Freedom Score

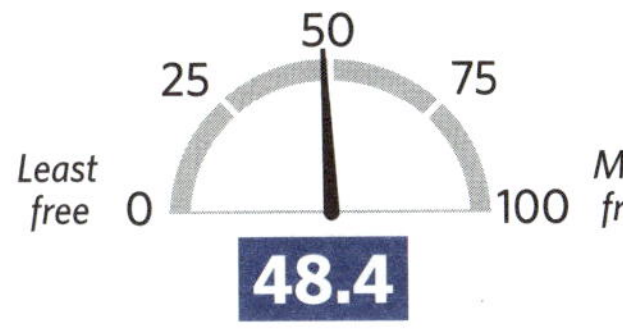

Freedom Trend

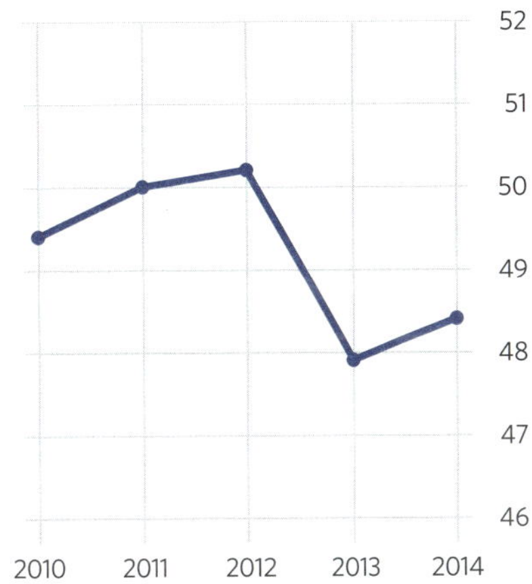

Country Comparisons

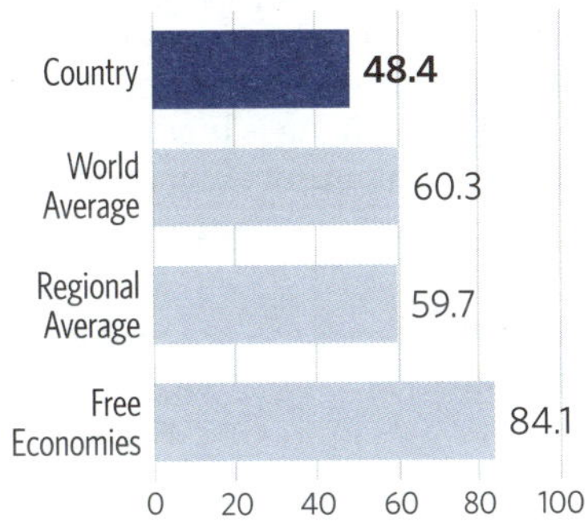

Bolivia's economic freedom score is 48.4, making its economy the 158th freest in the 2014 *Index*. Its overall score is 0.5 point better than last year, with notable improvements in investment freedom and trade freedom offsetting declines in business freedom, fiscal freedom, and government spending. Bolivia is ranked 25th out of 29 countries in the South and Central America/Caribbean region, and its overall score is far below the world and regional averages.

Over the 20-year history of the *Index*, Bolivia's economic freedom has deteriorated by 8.5 points, the sixth worst score drop. Significant declines have occurred in six of the 10 economic freedoms, notably property rights and investment freedom, whose scores plummeted 40 and 55 points, respectively. Regulatory efficiency, measured through business freedom, labor freedom, and monetary stability, also has greatly diminished as state interference in the economy has grown.

Bolivia was a "moderately free" economy during the first 10 years of the *Index* but has been on a downward spiral of economic freedom since 2005. With the economy plunging into the ranks of the "repressed" over the past two years, Bolivians are suffering in a climate of increasing economic subjugation. High commodity prices have driven recent strong economic growth, but long-term economic development remains constrained by institutional shortcomings.

BACKGROUND: Since taking office in 2005, President Evo Morales has used property confiscation and nationalization to redistribute wealth. A new constitution has expanded executive power and given the state greater control of key natural resources and industries, including gas and electricity. Re-elected in 2009 with 64 percent of the vote, Morales promised to move Bolivia toward "communitarian socialism." In Bolivia, the president can be re-elected only once, but Morales has announced that he will run for a third term in 2014. Under Morales, Bolivia associates closely with Cuba and Venezuela and has strengthened relations with Iran. Both foreign and local private investment have dropped, and approximately half of Bolivia's people still live in poverty. Nearly 60 percent of working arrangements are informal, and drug trafficking has increased.

Quick Facts

Population: 10.8 million
GDP (PPP): $55.2 billion
5.2% growth in 2012
5-year compound annual growth 4.8%
$5,099 per capita
Unemployment: 5.4%
Inflation (CPI): 4.5%
FDI Inflow: $1.1 billion
Public Debt: 33.1% of GDP

2012 data unless otherwise noted.
Data compiled as of September 2013.

How Do We Measure Economic Freedom?
See page 471 for an explanation of the methodology or visit the *Index* Web site at *heritage.org/index*.

THE TEN ECONOMIC FREEDOMS

RULE OF LAW

	Score	Rank	1-Year Change
Property Rights	10.0	166th	0
Freedom from Corruption	28.1	117th	+0.1

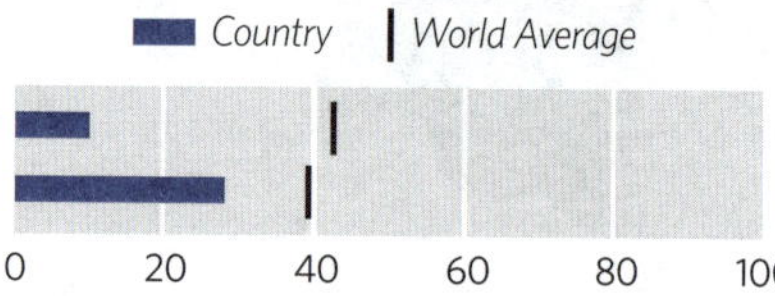

There have been numerous high-profile cases of government mismanagement, corruption, and abuse of political influence in the past year. The "Mother Earth Integral Development Law to Live Well," passed in October 2012, imposes unique intellectual property concepts and specifies that the state controls access to natural resources, especially vis-à-vis foreign investors. Expropriation is a problem, as is illegal squatting on rural private property.

GOVERNMENT SIZE

	Score	Rank	1-Year Change
Fiscal Freedom	87.1	40th	-1.7
Government Spending	62.5	114th	-1.6

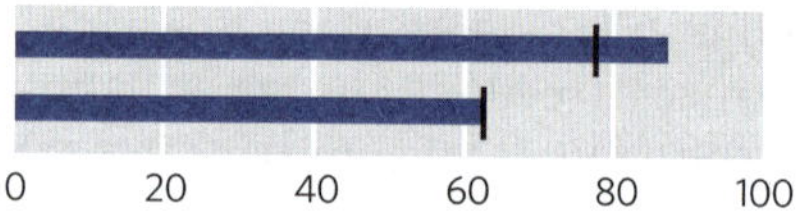

The top individual income tax rate is 13 percent, and the top corporate tax rate is 25 percent. Other taxes include a value-added tax (VAT) and a transactions tax. The overall tax burden is 22.2 percent of GDP. Government spending amounts to 35.4 percent of GDP and has been financed by gas and mining receipts. Public debt is around 33 percent of gross domestic output.

REGULATORY EFFICIENCY

	Score	Rank	1-Year Change
Business Freedom	53.4	145th	-2.4
Labor Freedom	29.9	178th	-0.9
Monetary Freedom	70.0	141st	+2.6

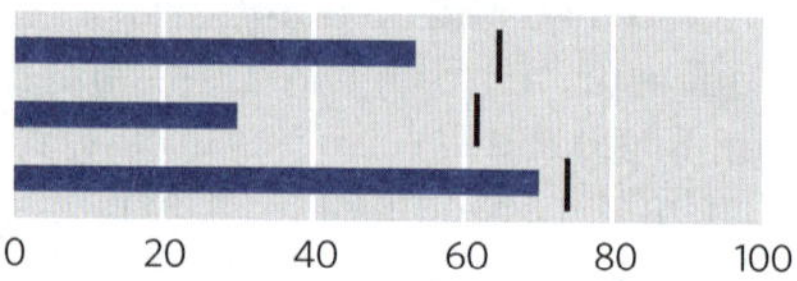

Despite some steps to reform the cumbersome regulatory framework, lingering bureaucracy and lack of transparency often make the formation and operation of private enterprises costly and burdensome. The non-salary cost of employing a worker is moderate, but overall rigidity in hiring and firing is high. Fuel prices, subsidized and controlled by the government, are frozen for years at a time. Electricity is also subsidized.

OPEN MARKETS

	Score	Rank	1-Year Change
Trade Freedom	77.6	85th	+3.3
Investment Freedom	15.0	169th	+5.0
Financial Freedom	50.0	69th	0

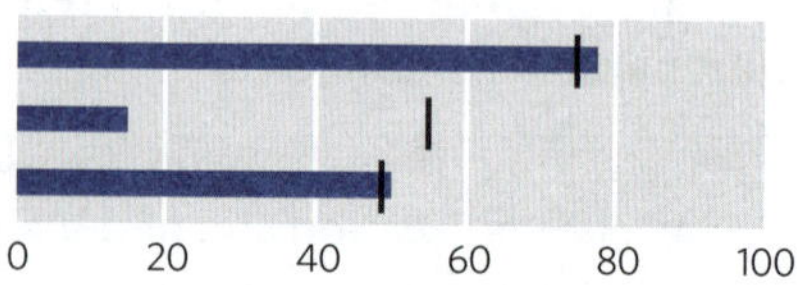

Bolivia has a 3.7 percent average tariff rate. Piracy and counterfeiting are not uncommon. The government screens new foreign investment, and the legal and regulatory systems may be difficult to navigate. The financial sector remains vulnerable to state interference, with credit to the private sector expanding slowly. Capital markets are focused on trading in government bonds.

Long-Term Score Change (since 1995)

RULE OF LAW		GOVERNMENT SIZE		REGULATORY EFFICIENCY		OPEN MARKETS	
Property Rights	**-40.0**	Fiscal Freedom	**-3.9**	Business Freedom	**-1.6**	Trade Freedom	**+12.2**
Freedom from Corruption	**+18.1**	Government Spending	**+1.8**	Labor Freedom	**-17.8**	Investment Freedom	**-55.0**
				Monetary Freedom	**-9.5**	Financial Freedom	**+20.0**

BOSNIA AND HERZEGOVINA

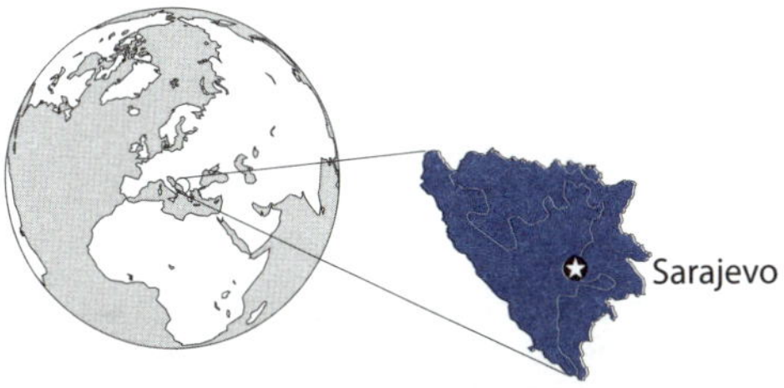

World Rank: 101 | **Regional Rank: 38**

Economic Freedom Score

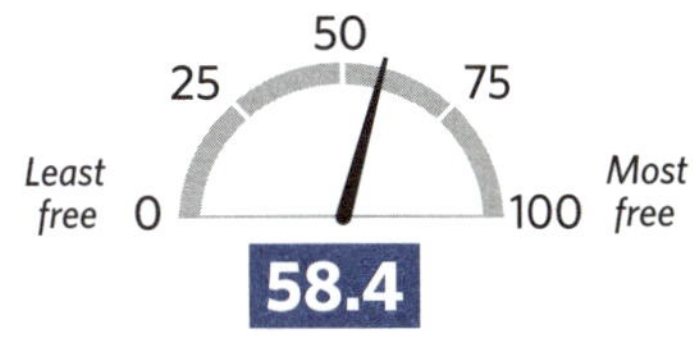

Freedom Trend

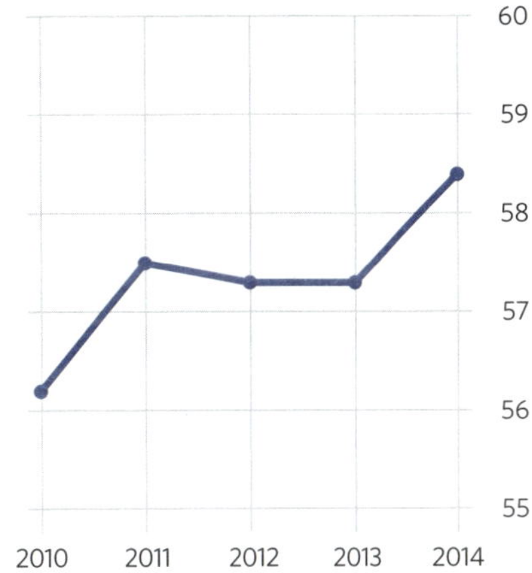

Country Comparisons

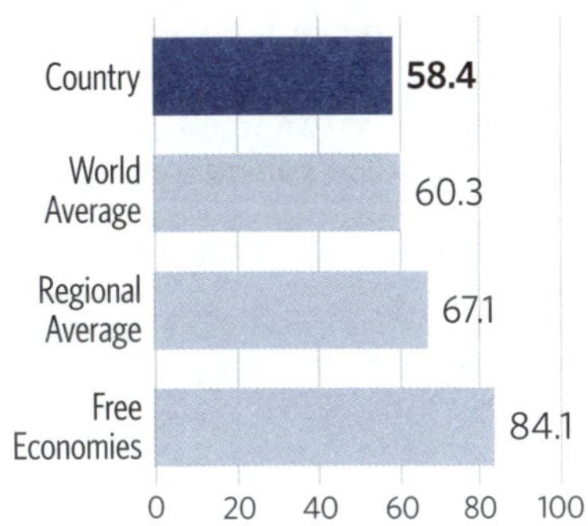

Bosnia and Herzegovina's economic freedom score is 58.4, making its economy the 101st freest in the 2014 *Index*. Its overall score has increased by 1.1 points, reflecting improvements in investment freedom, business freedom, and freedom from corruption. Bosnia and Herzegovina is ranked 38th out of 43 countries in the Europe region, and its score is below the global and regional averages.

Bosnia and Herzegovina was first ranked in the *Index* in 1998. Over the 17 years since then, its economic freedom score has advanced by about 29 points, the second best improvement of any country. With scores increasing in all 10 economic freedoms, Bosnia and Herzegovina has made tremendous strides in eliminating economically repressive policies. Implementation of gradual structural reforms to enhance regulatory efficiency and market openness has moved it into the mid-ranks of the *Index*. Greater monetary stability has also been achieved.

Nonetheless, Bosnia and Herzegovina's economy is still considered "mostly unfree." Deeper institutional reforms, particularly related to eradicating corruption and ensuring judicial independence, remain critical to further advancement of economic freedom and improvement of economic growth.

BACKGROUND: The 1995 Dayton Agreement ended three years of war in the former Yugoslavia and finalized Bosnia and Herzegovina's independence. The presidency rotates among three elected members every eight months inside a four-year term. Under a loose central government, two separate entities exist: the Republika Srpska (Serbian) and the Federation of Bosnia and Herzegovina (Muslim/Croat). The European Union signed a Stabilization and Association Agreement with Bosnia and Herzegovina in 2008. Bosnia also received a NATO Membership Action Plan in 2010 and is one of four official candidates to join NATO. The country is one of Europe's poorest. Agriculture is inefficient. There has been some privatization, but much of the industrial sector is also inefficient. Corruption is widespread. An institutionally weak central government has made implementation of economic reforms difficult.

How Do We Measure Economic Freedom?
See page 471 for an explanation of the methodology or visit the *Index* Web site at *heritage.org/index*.

Quick Facts

Population: 3.9 million
GDP (PPP): $31.9 billion
-0.7% growth in 2012
5-year compound annual growth 0.8%
$8,216 per capita
Unemployment: 28.0%
Inflation (CPI): 2.0%
FDI Inflow: $632.9 million
Public Debt: 44.3% of GDP

2012 data unless otherwise noted.
Data compiled as of September 2013.

THE TEN ECONOMIC FREEDOMS

Score ■ Country | World Average

RULE OF LAW

	Score	Rank	1-Year Change
Property Rights	20.0	139th	0
Freedom from Corruption	33.9	83rd	+1.9

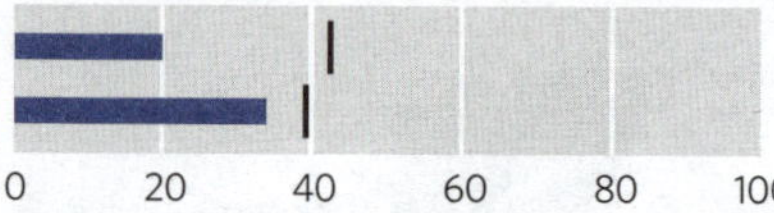

In the most high-profile corruption case since independence in 1992, the president of the Bosnian Federation and 18 other officials were arrested in April 2013 and charged with taking bribes in return for granting clemency to convicted criminals. The complex system of government lends itself to deadlock and prevents reform. Property registries are largely unreliable, leaving transfers open to dispute.

GOVERNMENT SIZE

	Score	Rank	1-Year Change
Fiscal Freedom	82.9	66th	-0.3
Government Spending	27.4	163rd	+0.5

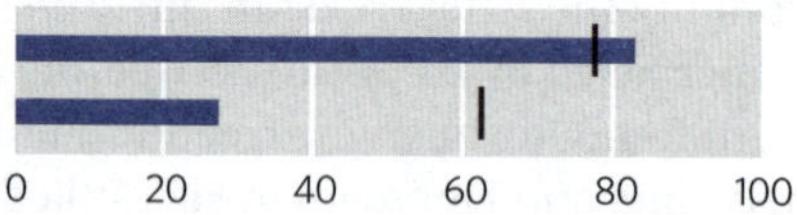

Tax policies in Bosnia and Herzegovina vary across governing entities. The top individual income and corporate tax rates are 10 percent. Other taxes include a value-added tax (VAT) and a property tax. Overall tax revenue is 38.9 percent of GDP. Government expenditures have fallen steadily to 49.2 percent of the domestic economy, and public debt remains below 45 percent of GDP.

REGULATORY EFFICIENCY

	Score	Rank	1-Year Change
Business Freedom	55.5	135th	+1.2
Labor Freedom	62.4	90th	+1.2
Monetary Freedom	80.1	29th	+1.1

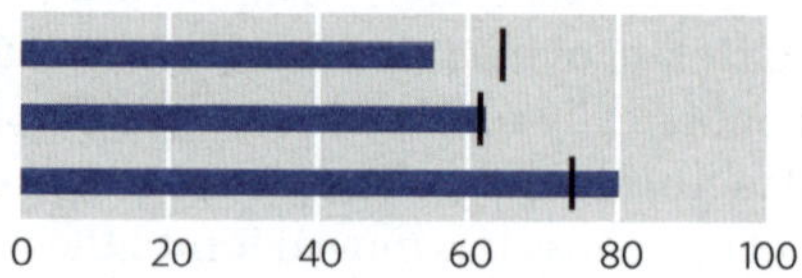

It takes 11 procedures and almost 40 days to incorporate a company. The process for obtaining necessary permits costs more than 10 times the level of average annual income and takes over 100 days. The labor market remains inefficient, with employment regulations not conducive to productivity and job growth. Energy-related subsidies amount to nearly 10 percent of GDP. The state also subsidizes agricultural production.

OPEN MARKETS

	Score	Rank	1-Year Change
Trade Freedom	86.9	38th	+0.5
Investment Freedom	75.0	35th	+5.0
Financial Freedom	60.0	41st	0

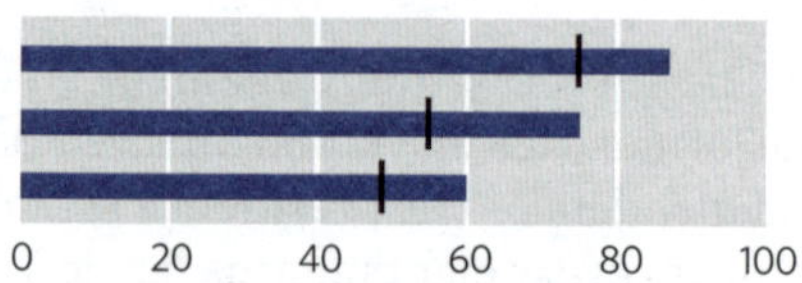

The country's 1.5 percent average tariff is relatively low. Its legal and regulatory systems may be difficult for foreign investors to navigate. The banking sector remains well-capitalized, but the level of non-performing loans has increased. Of the 29 banks that operate in the country, the 19 that are foreign owned account for over 85 percent of total assets in the sector.

Long-Term Score Change (since 1998)

RULE OF LAW		GOVERNMENT SIZE		REGULATORY EFFICIENCY		OPEN MARKETS	
Property Rights	**+10.0**	Fiscal Freedom	**+4.1**	Business Freedom	**+15.5**	Trade Freedom	**+17.5**
Freedom from Corruption	**+23.9**	Government Spending	**+10.8**	Labor Freedom	**+7.6**	Investment Freedom	**+45.0**
				Monetary Freedom	**+80.1**	Financial Freedom	**+50.0**

BOTSWANA

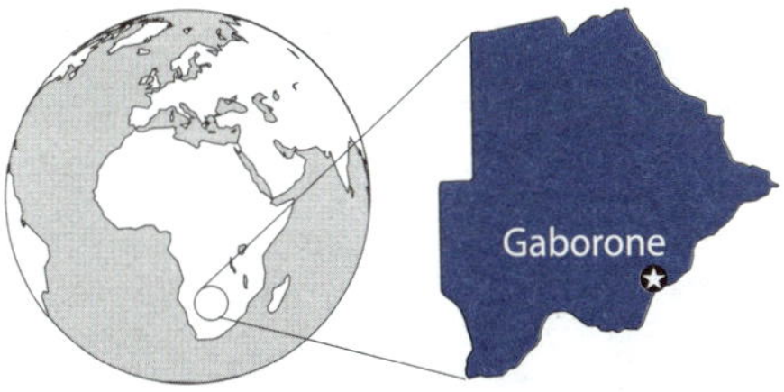

World Rank: **27** Regional Rank: **2**

Economic Freedom Score

Botswana's economic freedom score is 72, making its economy the 27th freest in the 2014 *Index*. Its overall score is 1.4 points better than last year, due primarily to improvements in investment freedom, trade freedom, and the management of public finance. Botswana continues to be ranked the 2nd freest economy in the Sub-Saharan Africa region, and its overall score is well above the regional and world averages.

Over the 20-year history of the *Index*, Botswana has improved its economic freedom by 15.3 points, the 18th biggest score improvement. A series of committed reform measures has enabled the country to rise from economically "mostly unfree" to "mostly free." Score improvements have been achieved in eight of the 10 economic freedoms, notably trade freedom, fiscal freedom, investment freedom, and freedom from corruption.

With overall competitiveness sustained by a relatively high degree of regulatory efficiency and market openness, Botswana's economic freedom has consistently been among the highest in the Sub-Saharan African region. Its economy has been increasingly diversified, in large part due to dynamic investment attracted by low taxes, political stability, and an educated workforce. Botswana continues to set an example in the management of large endowments of natural resources.

BACKGROUND: The Botswana Democratic Party has governed this multi-party democracy since independence in 1966. Ian Khama assumed the presidency in 2008 upon his predecessor's resignation and won a new five-year term in 2009. With significant natural resources and a market-oriented economy, Botswana has Africa's highest sovereign credit rating. Minerals (principally diamonds) account for three-fourths of exports and over 40 percent of GDP. Growth fell below 4 percent of GDP in 2012 partly because of a slowdown in the mining sector. In an attempt to diversify the economy through tourism, Botswana has focused on increasing conservation and creating extensive nature preserves. Botswana has one of the world's highest HIV/AIDS infection rates but is also among Africa's leaders in combating the disease.

How Do We Measure Economic Freedom?
See page 471 for an explanation of the methodology or visit the *Index* Web site at *heritage.org/index*.

Freedom Trend

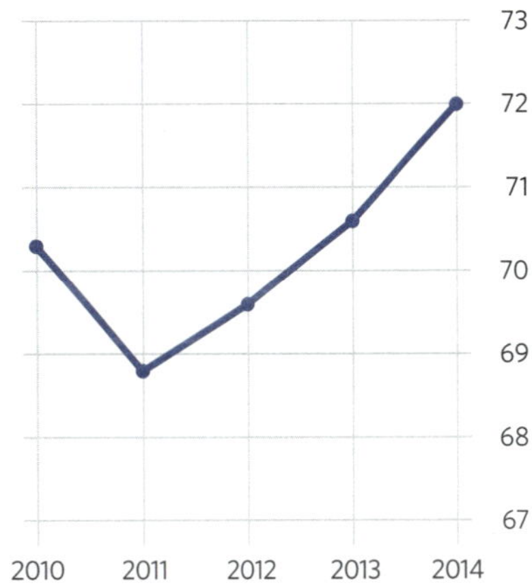

Country Comparisons

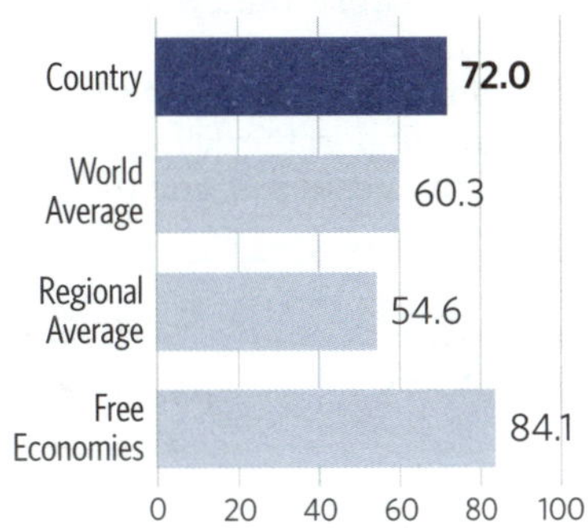

Quick Facts

Population: 1.9 million
GDP (PPP): $31.5 billion
3.8% growth in 2012
5-year compound annual growth 2.7%
$16,820 per capita
Unemployment: 17.8% (2009)
Inflation (CPI): 7.5%
FDI Inflow: $292.5 million
Public Debt: 14.9% of GDP

2012 data unless otherwise noted.
Data compiled as of September 2013.

THE TEN ECONOMIC FREEDOMS

RULE OF LAW

	Score	Rank	1-Year Change
Property Rights	70.0	27th	0
Freedom from Corruption	61.2	32nd	+0.2

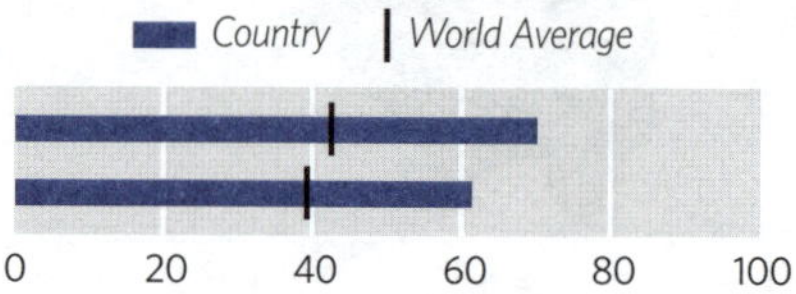

Botswana, the least corrupt country on the African continent, continues to perform strongly in international measures of corruption and takes a tough approach to crime. The legal system is sufficient to enforce secure commercial dealings. A landmark High Court ruling in October 2012 held that customary law could no longer be used to deny a woman's right to inheritance, setting a critical legal precedent.

GOVERNMENT SIZE

	Score	Rank	1-Year Change
Fiscal Freedom	81.0	73rd	+1.5
Government Spending	69.8	88th	+4.7

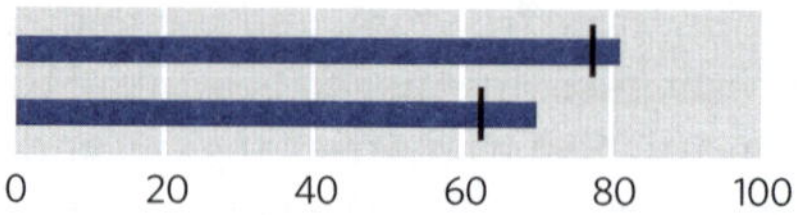

The top individual income tax rate is 25 percent, and the top corporate tax rate is 22 percent. Other taxes include a sales tax, a value-added tax (VAT), and a property tax. The overall tax burden has fallen to 28.1 percent of GDP. The government has attempted to curb spending to reduce the burdens of slower growth. Spending has fallen to 31.8 percent of GDP, and public debt has fallen to 15 percent of the domestic economy.

REGULATORY EFFICIENCY

	Score	Rank	1-Year Change
Business Freedom	68.5	82nd	-0.5
Labor Freedom	69.7	66th	-0.1
Monetary Freedom	72.4	128th	+0.4

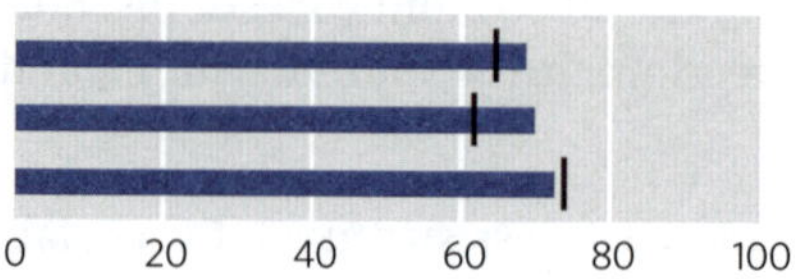

The regulatory framework generally facilitates entrepreneurial activity. With no minimum capital required, launching a business costs less than 2 percent of the level of average annual income. Obtaining necessary permits remains time-consuming and costly. Relatively flexible labor regulations support the development of an efficient labor market. The inefficient agricultural sector is highly subsidized, and the government influences prices through state-owned enterprises.

OPEN MARKETS

	Score	Rank	1-Year Change
Trade Freedom	82.7	59th	+3.0
Investment Freedom	75.0	35th	+5.0
Financial Freedom	70.0	19th	0

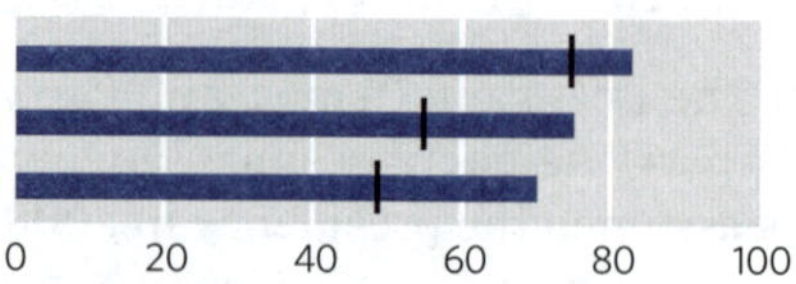

Botswana's average tariff rate is 3.6 percent. The importation of containers remains costly and time-consuming. New foreign investments may require licensing from the government. The small but vibrant financial sector has contributed to dynamic economic growth and economic diversification. The private sector's access to credit is maintained effectively by the banking sector and well-functioning capital markets.

Long-Term Score Change (since 1995)

RULE OF LAW		GOVERNMENT SIZE		REGULATORY EFFICIENCY		OPEN MARKETS	
Property Rights	**0**	Fiscal Freedom	**+27.3**	Business Freedom	**-1.5**	Trade Freedom	**+36.5**
Freedom from Corruption	**+11.2**	Government Spending	**+14.7**	Labor Freedom	**+3.1**	Investment Freedom	**+25.0**
				Monetary Freedom	**+6.6**	Financial Freedom	**+20.0**

BRAZIL

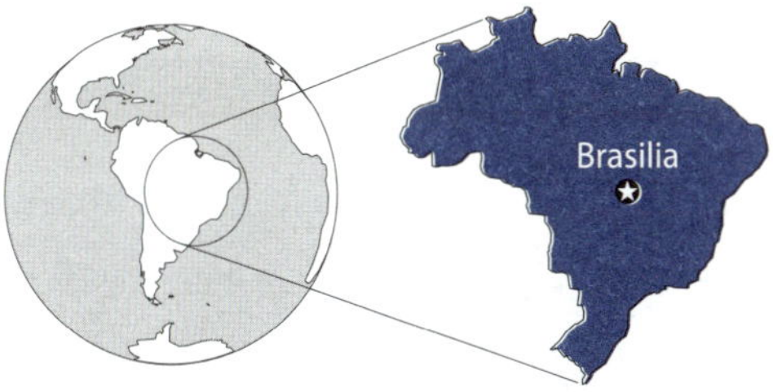

World Rank: **114** Regional Rank: **20**

Economic Freedom Score

Brazil's economic freedom score is 56.9, making its economy the 114th freest in the 2014 *Index*. Its score is 0.8 point worse than last year, with declines in labor freedom, monetary freedom, fiscal freedom, and trade freedom. Brazil is ranked 20th out of 29 countries in the South and Central America/Caribbean region, and its overall score is below the world average.

Over the 20-year history of the *Index*, Brazil's economic freedom score has improved by only 5.5 points. The combined improvement achieved in five of the 10 economic freedoms, including trade freedom, monetary freedom, and investment freedom, has been offset by deteriorations in the area of government size that measures the tax burden and government spending.

Brazil had advanced into the ranks of the "moderately free" economies in the *Index* during the first half of the 2000s, but since 2007, the economy has fallen back to the status of "mostly unfree." The lack of progress toward greater economic freedom has discouraged private-sector growth and continues to undermine realization of the economy's full potential.

BACKGROUND: Brazil is the world's seventh-largest economy, and its population of almost 200 million is heavily concentrated on the Atlantic coast. President Dilma Rousseff, former President Luiz Inacio "Lula" da Silva's hand-picked successor, became Brazil's first female president in 2011 and until mid-2013 enjoyed a high popularity rating. Increases in public transportation fares in 2013 provided an excuse for hard-left militants to vandalize property and block roads, but the events also heightened popular grievances against the corrupt political system and slowing economic growth. Brazil has benefited from surging prices for commodity exports. The middle class is growing, and millions have been lifted out of poverty, but heavy government intervention in the economy continues to cause the misallocation of capital, limit mobility, and fuel a sense of injustice. Ensuring security and adequate infrastructure for the 2014 World Cup and 2016 Rio Olympic games will challenge the government's administrative capacity.

How Do We Measure Economic Freedom?
See page 471 for an explanation of the methodology or visit the *Index* Web site at *heritage.org/index*.

Freedom Trend

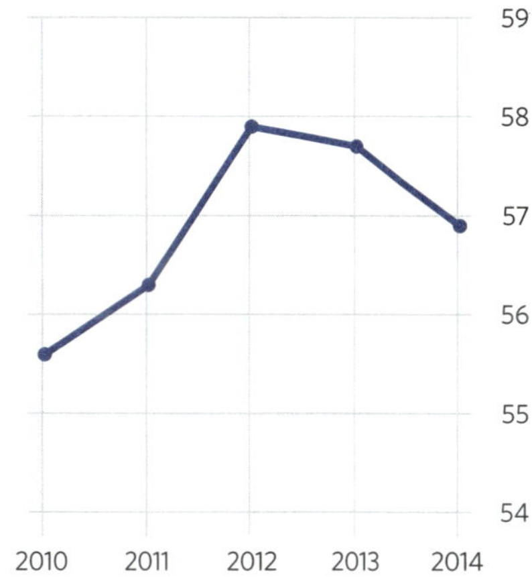

Country Comparisons

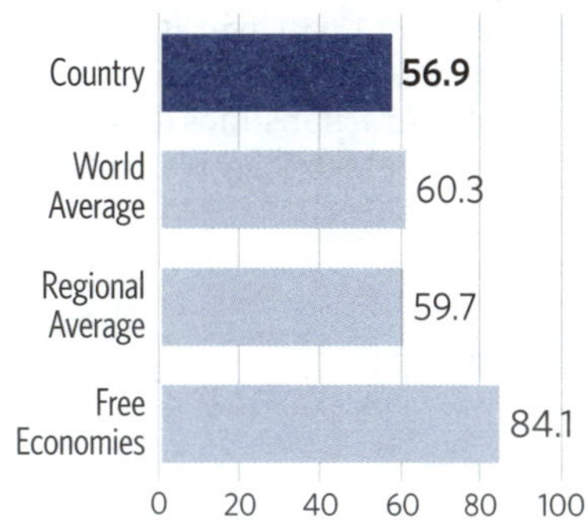

Quick Facts

Population: 198.4 million
GDP (PPP): $2.4 trillion
0.9% growth in 2012
5-year compound annual growth 3.2%
$11,875 per capita
Unemployment: 5.5%
Inflation (CPI): 5.4%
FDI Inflow: $65.3 billion
Public Debt: 68.5% of GDP

2012 data unless otherwise noted.
Data compiled as of September 2013.

THE TEN ECONOMIC FREEDOMS

RULE OF LAW

	Score	Rank	1-Year Change
Property Rights	50.0	53rd	0
Freedom from Corruption	37.9	72nd	-0.1

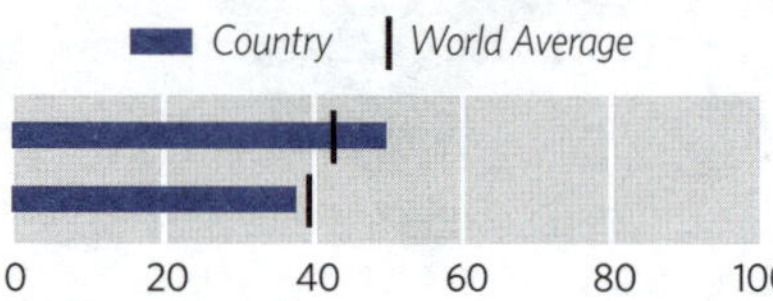

Corruption undermines economic freedom and sparked massive nationwide protests in 2013 over poor public services and the low level of political and institutional effectiveness. In the "Mensalão" case in 2012, some members of the Brazilian Congress were found guilty of participating in a pay-for-votes scheme. Contracts are generally considered secure, but the judiciary is inefficient and subject to political and economic influence.

GOVERNMENT SIZE

	Score	Rank	1-Year Change
Fiscal Freedom	68.8	145th	-1.5
Government Spending	54.1	131st	-0.7

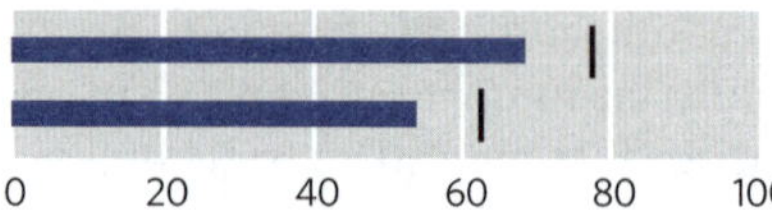

The top individual income tax rate is 27.5 percent. The top effective corporate tax rate is 34 percent, which includes a 15 percent corporate tax, a corporate surtax, and a 9 percent social contributions tax on net profits. Overall tax revenue is 34.8 percent of GDP. The government has vowed to boost spending to placate protesters, but expenditures remain steady at 39.1 percent of the domestic economy. Public debt is about 69 percent of GDP.

REGULATORY EFFICIENCY

	Score	Rank	1-Year Change
Business Freedom	53.8	144th	+0.8
Labor Freedom	49.8	138th	-7.4
Monetary Freedom	69.9	142nd	-4.5

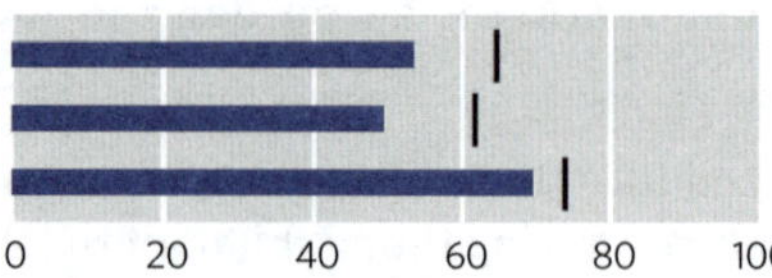

Regulatory efficiency remains poor, and the application of regulations is inconsistent and non-transparent. On average, it requires over 100 days to incorporate a company, and obtaining necessary permits takes 400 days. The labor market lacks flexibility and hinders job growth. Agricultural subsidies doubled from 2011 to 2013 and now total about $10 billion. In 2013, subsidies for electricity were also increased.

OPEN MARKETS

	Score	Rank	1-Year Change
Trade Freedom	69.3	131st	-0.4
Investment Freedom	55.0	96th	+5.0
Financial Freedom	60.0	41st	0

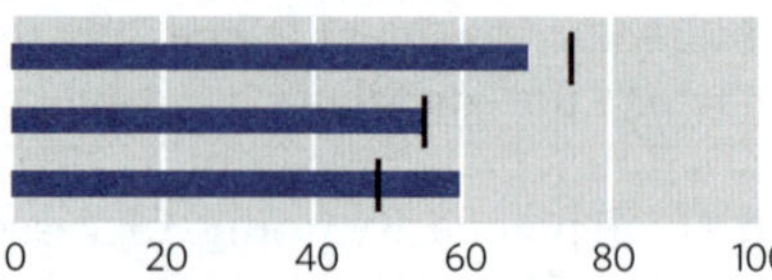

Brazil's average tariff rate is 7.9 percent. Brazilians are not allowed to import used clothing or cars. Foreign investment in several sectors of the economy is limited by the government. Banking and capital markets are increasingly diversified and growing. However, the role of the state in credit markets has also steadily expanded, and public banks now account for 50 percent of total loans to the private sector.

Long-Term Score Change (since 1995)

RULE OF LAW		GOVERNMENT SIZE		REGULATORY EFFICIENCY		OPEN MARKETS	
Property Rights	0	Fiscal Freedom	-7.9	Business Freedom	-1.2	Trade Freedom	+12.9
Freedom from Corruption	-12.1	Government Spending	-20.3	Labor Freedom	-14.8	Investment Freedom	+5.0
				Monetary Freedom	+69.9	Financial Freedom	+10.0

BRUNEI

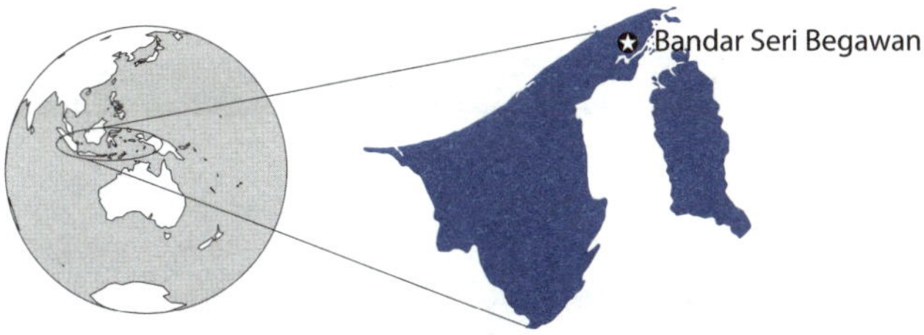

World Rank: **40** Regional Rank: **10**

Brunei's economic freedom has been assessed for the first time in the 2014 *Index*. The country's economic freedom score is 69, making its economy the 40th freest in the *Index*. Brunei is ranked 10th out of 42 countries in the Asia–Pacific region, and its overall score is much higher than the regional and world averages.

Brunei's economy performs quite competitively in most aspects of economic freedom. The economic system is characterized by a relatively high level of market openness that facilitates the country's engagement with the world through trade and investment, by a legal system that generally secures private property, and by macroeconomic stability.

The investment environment is generally efficient and transparent, although the regulatory framework needs to be more streamlined to enhance Brunei's overall economic freedom and competitiveness. The small financial sector, dominated by banks, has not suffered any serious impact from the global financial turmoil. In generating more broad-based private-sector development and diversifying the economy beyond the oil and gas industry, improving access to financing remains critical.

BACKGROUND: Brunei, which consists of two disconnected enclaves surrounded by the Malaysian state of Sarawak, lies on the northern coast of Borneo. The sultan serves as his own prime minister, minister of defense, and minister of finance. He is advised by several councils, including a Legislative Council and Privy Council, which he appoints. The oil and gas industry accounts for over half of GDP and 90 percent of government revenues. However, it provides for only a small fraction of employment, and most of the population works directly for the government. Brunei has extremely low manufacturing capacity and imports most of its manufactured goods and food. It is among the world's most prosperous countries due to its oil revenue, but long-standing efforts at economic diversification have met with only limited success.

How Do We Measure Economic Freedom?
See page 471 for an explanation of the methodology or visit the *Index* Web site at *heritage.org/index*.

Economic Freedom Score

Freedom Trend

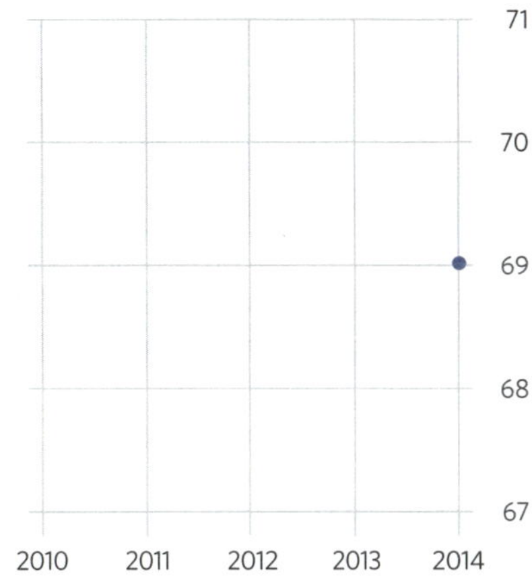

Country Comparisons

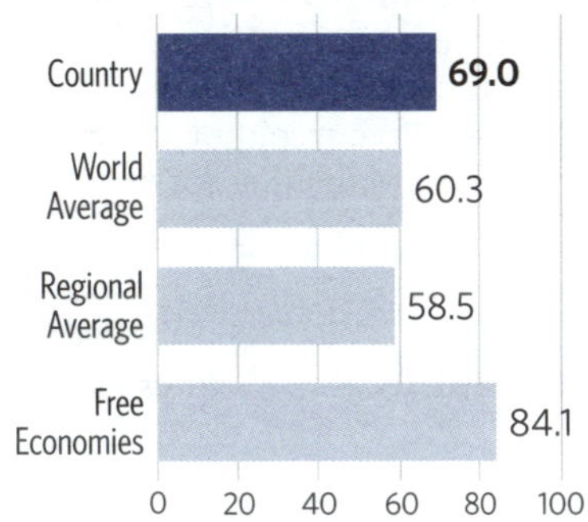

Quick Facts

Population: 0.4 million
GDP (PPP): $21.7 billion
1.3% growth in 2012
5-year compound annual growth 0.5%
$54,389 per capita
Unemployment: 2.7%
Inflation (CPI): 0.5%
FDI Inflow: $850.0 million
Public Debt: 2.4% of GDP

2012 data unless otherwise noted.
Data compiled as of September 2013.

THE TEN ECONOMIC FREEDOMS

RULE OF LAW

	Score	Rank	1-Year Change
Property Rights	40.0	70th	n/a
Freedom from Corruption	53.3	45th	n/a

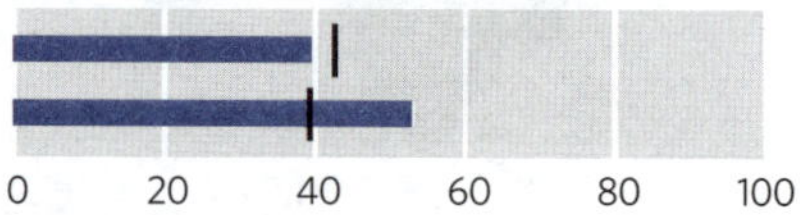

Somewhat robust anti-corruption efforts are offset by a relatively weak property rights regime. Only Brunei citizens are allowed to purchase land; foreign firms need a local partner. The constitution does not provide for an independent judiciary. Brunei is not an electoral democracy. The sultan continues to wield broad powers under a long-standing state of emergency, and no direct legislative elections have been held since 1962.

GOVERNMENT SIZE

	Score	Rank	1-Year Change
Fiscal Freedom	90.2	34th	n/a
Government Spending	66.1	98th	n/a

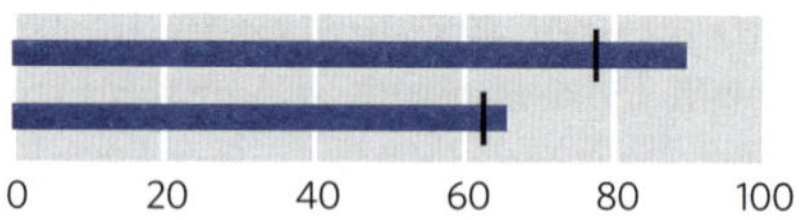

Brunei has no individual income tax, and its top corporate tax rate is 20 percent for most companies. The corporate tax rate for oil and gas companies is 55 percent. Other taxes include a social security tax. The overall tax burden is 24 percent of gross domestic output. Government spending is around one-third of the size of the domestic economy, and public debt is below 3 percent of GDP.

REGULATORY EFFICIENCY

	Score	Rank	1-Year Change
Business Freedom	68.2	84th	n/a
Labor Freedom	96.5	2nd	n/a
Monetary Freedom	74.2	115th	n/a

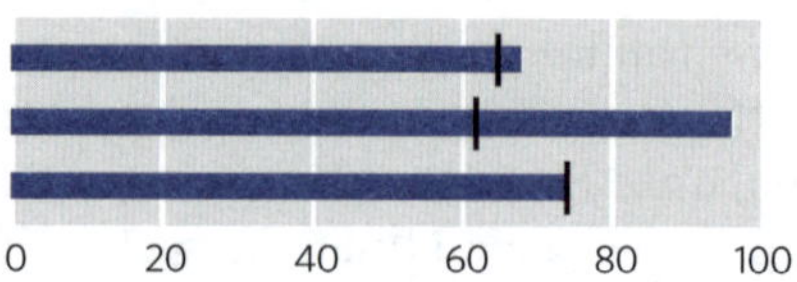

Despite some progress, procedures for establishing and registering a private enterprise remain time-consuming. There are no minimum capital requirements, but incorporating a business still takes about 100 days. The labor market is relatively flexible, and foreign workers account for over 70 percent of all private-sector employment. The state provides generous but price-distorting subsidies for nearly everything the average citizen needs.

OPEN MARKETS

	Score	Rank	1-Year Change
Trade Freedom	81.8	65th	n/a
Investment Freedom	70.0	46th	n/a
Financial Freedom	50.0	69th	n/a

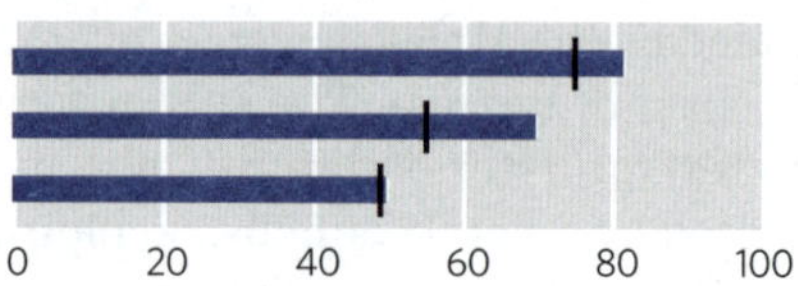

Brunei's average tariff rate is 4.1 percent, and there are few non-tariff barriers to trade. Foreign investment levels in some sectors of the economy are capped by the government, and foreigners may not own land. The small financial sector remains dominated by banking. The banking sector is well-capitalized and open to foreign competition. Islamic financial services have grown considerably in recent years.

Long-Term Score Change: n/a

RULE OF LAW		GOVERNMENT SIZE		REGULATORY EFFICIENCY		OPEN MARKETS	
Property Rights	**n/a**	Fiscal Freedom	**n/a**	Business Freedom	**n/a**	Trade Freedom	**n/a**
Freedom from Corruption	**n/a**	Government Spending	**n/a**	Labor Freedom	**n/a**	Investment Freedom	**n/a**
				Monetary Freedom	**n/a**	Financial Freedom	**n/a**

BULGARIA

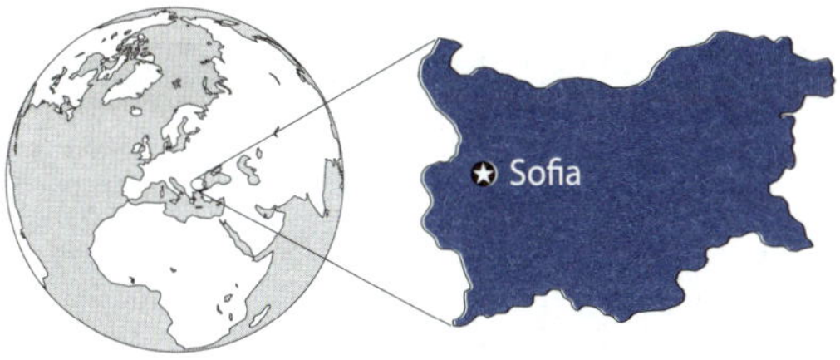

World Rank: **61** Regional Rank: **28**

Economic Freedom Score

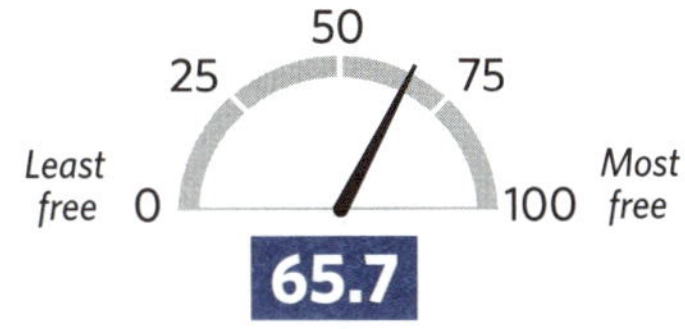

Freedom Trend

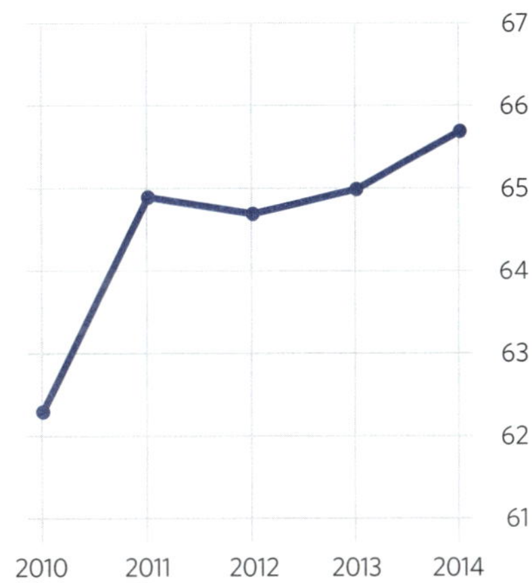

Country Comparisons

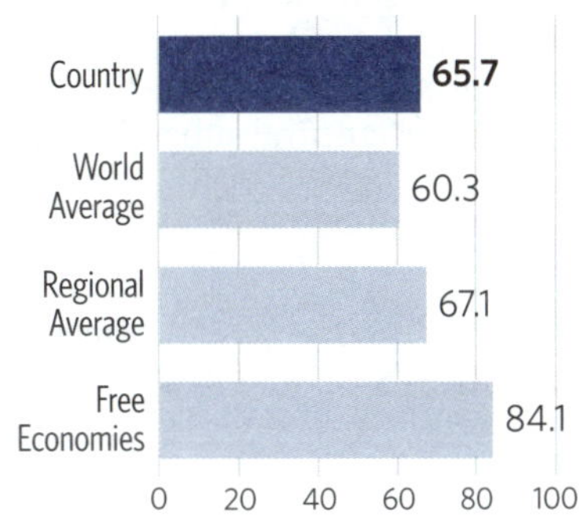

Bulgaria's economic freedom score is 65.7, making its economy the 61st freest in the 2014 *Index*. Its overall score is up by 0.7 point, reflecting improvements in labor freedom, freedom from corruption, trade freedom, and monetary freedom. Bulgaria is ranked 28th out of 43 countries in the Europe region, and its overall score is above the world average but below the regional average.

Over the 20-year history of the *Index*, Bulgaria has advanced its economic freedom score by about 16 points, a top 20 improvement. With score increases in seven of the 10 economic freedoms, Bulgaria has risen gradually to the ranks of the "moderately free." Notable structural reforms have included trade liberalization, privatization, implementation of competitive flat tax rates, and modernization of the regulatory environment. Along with the effective maintenance of low inflation, greater monetary stability has also been achieved.

In more recent years, Bulgaria has taken steps to restore fiscal discipline despite a challenging economic environment. Public debt and budget deficits remain among the lowest in the region. Continued reform efforts, particularly in strengthening the independence of the judiciary and eradicating corruption, are needed to solidify the foundations of economic freedom and ensure progress toward greater prosperity.

BACKGROUND: Bulgaria joined the European Union in January 2007. Prime Minister Boyko Borisov and his cabinet resigned in February 2013 after nationwide protests over low standards of living, high energy costs, and corruption. Former Finance Minister Plamen Oresharski became prime minister in May at the head of a Socialist Party–led coalition, but protests continued. Tourism, information technology and telecommunications, agriculture, pharmaceuticals, and textiles are the leading industries. Bulgaria is involved in two rival gas-pipeline projects: Russia's South Stream pipeline and the Azerbaijan/Turkey-backed Trans-Anatolian Natural Gas pipeline. Economic growth is stagnant, largely as a result of the EU economic crisis and internal instability. Bulgaria remains the EU's poorest country. Prospects for adoption of the euro in the near future have declined.

How Do We Measure Economic Freedom?
See page 471 for an explanation of the methodology or visit the *Index* Web site at *heritage.org/index.*

Quick Facts

Population: 7.3 million
GDP (PPP): $103.8 billion
0.8% growth in 2012
5-year compound annual growth 0.7%
$14,312 per capita
Unemployment: 12.4%
Inflation (CPI): 2.4%
FDI Inflow: $1.9 billion
Public Debt: 18.5% of GDP

2012 data unless otherwise noted.
Data compiled as of September 2013.

THE TEN ECONOMIC FREEDOMS

		Score	Rank	1-Year Change
RULE OF LAW	Property Rights	30.0	93rd	0
	Freedom from Corruption	35.2	76th	+2.2

Bulgaria's democracy is undercut by lack of transparent decision making and widespread corruption. The election of a controversial parliamentarian allegedly connected to organized crime as the new chairman of the State Agency for National Security sparked anti-government protests in June 2013. The judicial system does not enforce property rights effectively, and inconsistencies in regulation discourage private investment.

		Score	Rank	1-Year Change
GOVERNMENT SIZE	Fiscal Freedom	91.2	29th	-2.8
	Government Spending	64.5	102nd	+0.3

Bulgaria's top individual and corporate income tax rates are 10 percent. Other taxes include a value-added tax (VAT) and an estate tax. The overall tax burden is about 26 percent of total domestic income. The government budget has been tight as the country tries to maintain its peg to the euro. Expenditures are 34 percent of GDP, and public debt remains at around 18 percent of domestic income.

		Score	Rank	1-Year Change
REGULATORY EFFICIENCY	Business Freedom	73.5	60th	-0.1
	Labor Freedom	80.2	28th	+5.4
	Monetary Freedom	79.6	38th	+1.0

Business start-up procedures have been streamlined, and enforcement of commercial regulations is relatively consistent. Labor regulations are relatively flexible, although the non-salary cost of employees can be burdensome. Although most prices are determined by market forces, rising agricultural subsidies from the European Union have distorted land values.

		Score	Rank	1-Year Change
OPEN MARKETS	Trade Freedom	87.8	11th	+1.0
	Investment Freedom	55.0	96th	0
	Financial Freedom	60.0	41st	0

EU members have a low 1.1 percent average tariff rate and, in general, few non-tariff barriers to trade. Bulgaria's legal and regulatory systems may be difficult for foreign investors to navigate. Although the financial sector as a whole has managed to cope well with the challenging external environment, the level of non-performing loans has been rising in recent years. The top five banks account for about half of total assets in the banking sector.

Long-Term Score Change (since 1995)

RULE OF LAW		GOVERNMENT SIZE		REGULATORY EFFICIENCY		OPEN MARKETS	
Property Rights	**-20.0**	Fiscal Freedom	**+45.2**	Business Freedom	**+18.5**	Trade Freedom	**+15.4**
Freedom from Corruption	**+5.2**	Government Spending	**+13.9**	Labor Freedom	**-0.1**	Investment Freedom	**-15.0**
				Monetary Freedom	**+53.3**	Financial Freedom	**+10.0**

BURKINA FASO

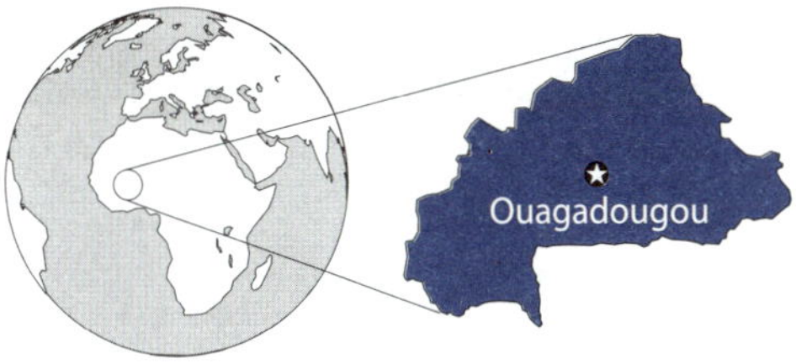

World Rank: **98** Regional Rank: **13**

Economic Freedom Score

Burkina Faso's economic freedom score is 58.9, making its economy the 98th freest in the 2014 *Index*. Its overall score has decreased by 1 point since last year due to declines in financial freedom, trade freedom, monetary freedom, and labor freedom. Burkina Faso is ranked 13th out of 46 countries in the Sub-Saharan Africa region, and its overall score is above the world average.

Over the 20-year history of the *Index*, Burkina Faso has advanced its economic freedom by 9.4 points. It has recorded notable improvements in seven of the 10 economic freedom categories including freedom from corruption, business freedom, and monetary freedom, the scores for which have improved by about 20 points or more since the *Index* began assessing the country's economic freedom in 1995.

Nonetheless, Burkina Faso has been largely confined to the ranks of the "mostly unfree" over the past 20 years. The lack of capable public institutions and weak rule of law continue to undermine the successful implementation of other critical reforms. Tariff and non-tariff barriers, coupled with burdensome investment regulations, continue to hamper development of a more dynamic private sector and interfere with diversification of the country's economic base.

BACKGROUND: President Blaise Compaoré seized power in 1987, and the constitutional council has ruled that the constitutionally mandated two-term limit does not apply to him. Compaoré was re-elected to the presidency in 2010. Army revolts and mass protests contributed to a highly unstable political climate in 2011, but order has been restored. Burkina Faso has sent 500 troops to Mali to help secure the northern half of the country from Tuareg separatists and al-Qaeda-linked groups. Burkina Faso relies heavily on cotton and gold exports for revenue. Approximately 90 percent of the population depends on subsistence agriculture. Lack of adequate infrastructure, a low literacy rate, and an economy that is vulnerable to external shocks are long-standing problems.

Freedom Trend

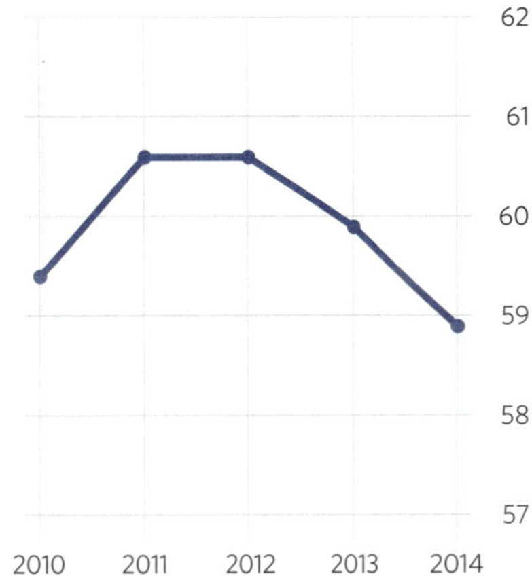

Country Comparisons

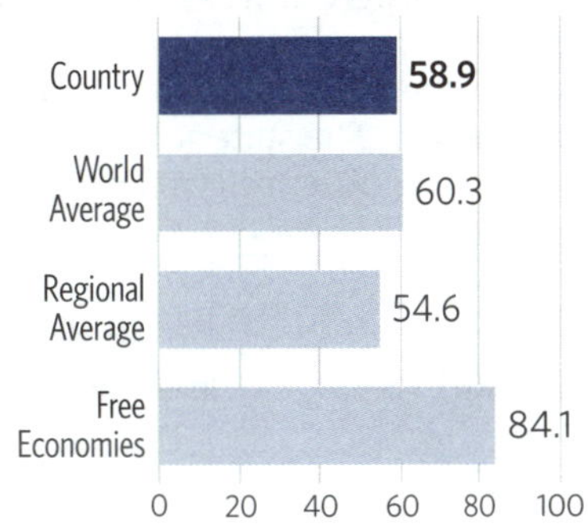

Quick Facts

Population: 17.4 million
GDP (PPP): $24.3 billion
8.0% growth in 2012
5-year compound annual growth 5.7%
$1,399 per capita
Unemployment: 77.0% (2007)
Inflation (CPI): 3.6%
FDI Inflow: $40.1 million
Public Debt: 27.7% of GDP

2012 data unless otherwise noted.
Data compiled as of September 2013.

How Do We Measure Economic Freedom?
See page 471 for an explanation of the methodology or visit the *Index* Web site at *heritage.org/index*.

THE TEN ECONOMIC FREEDOMS

Legend: Country | World Average

RULE OF LAW

	Score	Rank	1-Year Change
Property Rights	30.0	93rd	0
Freedom from Corruption	31.3	98th	+1.3

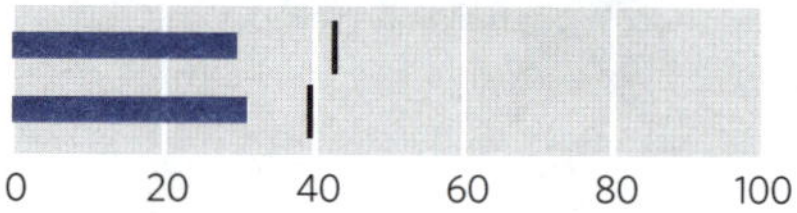

Although the government stepped up anticorruption efforts in 2012, corruption remains widespread. Government procurement can be irregular, and public funds are not well accounted for. The judiciary is weak, judges can be removed arbitrarily, and legal codes are outdated. Civil servants, especially in the police and customs, may demand bribes. Members of the presidential family and the ruling party control key economic activities.

GOVERNMENT SIZE

	Score	Rank	1-Year Change
Fiscal Freedom	83.0	64th	+1.6
Government Spending	82.3	44th	+0.3

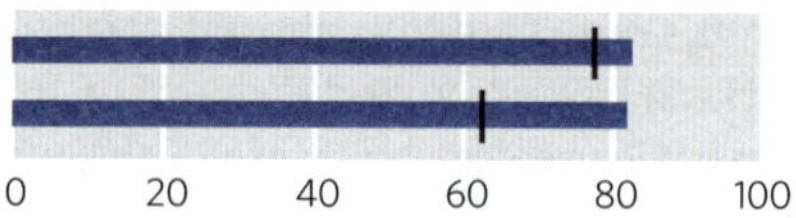

With a cut in the top corporate tax, the individual and corporate income taxes are both 27.5 percent. Other taxes include a value-added tax (VAT). The overall tax burden is 13.7 percent of total domestic income. Government expenditures are around 24 percent of GDP, and public finances have been boosted by strong growth and agricultural exports. Public debt has fallen below 30 percent of GDP.

REGULATORY EFFICIENCY

	Score	Rank	1-Year Change
Business Freedom	60.7	108th	-0.5
Labor Freedom	55.0	115th	-1.4
Monetary Freedom	78.8	51st	-1.8

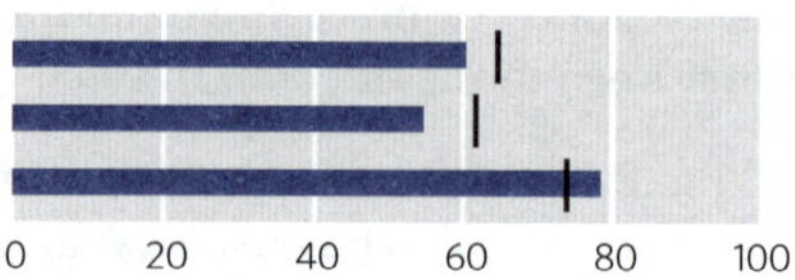

Overall progress in easing regulatory constraints lags behind other developing countries. Getting necessary licenses costs over three times the level of average annual income. The labor market remains underdeveloped, and a large portion of the workforce is employed in the informal sector. The state subsidizes fuels and electricity, maintains price supports for cotton, and influences other prices through the public sector.

OPEN MARKETS

	Score	Rank	1-Year Change
Trade Freedom	67.8	136th	-4.7
Investment Freedom	60.0	80th	+5.0
Financial Freedom	40.0	107th	-10.0

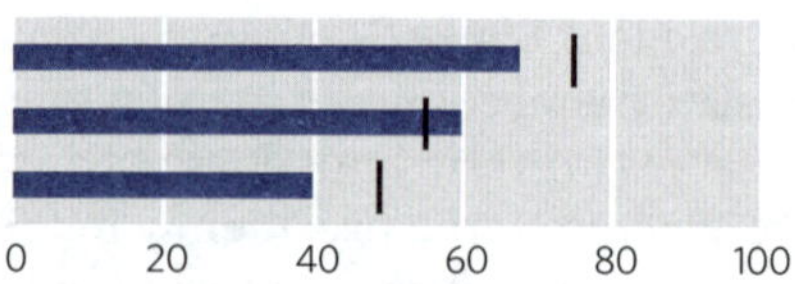

Burkina Faso has an average tariff rate of 8.6 percent. Importing is costly and time-consuming. In general, government policies do not discriminate against foreign investors. The financial system continues to evolve. The government has pursued banking liberalization and restructuring, encouraging competition in the financial sector. The use of credit has increased, reaching a level equivalent to over 20 percent of GDP in recent years.

Long-Term Score Change (since 1996)

RULE OF LAW		GOVERNMENT SIZE		REGULATORY EFFICIENCY		OPEN MARKETS	
Property Rights	0	Fiscal Freedom	+16.3	Business Freedom	+20.7	Trade Freedom	+12.8
Freedom from Corruption	+21.3	Government Spending	-2.0	Labor Freedom	+11.3	Investment Freedom	-10.0
				Monetary Freedom	+19.7	Financial Freedom	+10.0

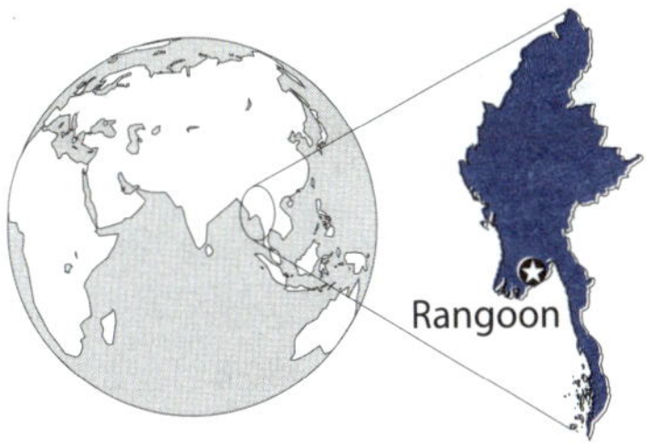

BURMA

World Rank: **162** Regional Rank: **36**

Economic Freedom Score

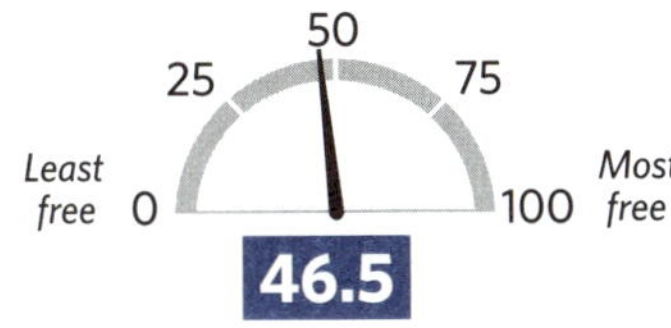

Burma's economic freedom score is 46.5, making its economy the 162nd freest in the 2014 *Index*. Its score is 7.3 points better than last year due to positive changes in investment freedom, business freedom, and labor freedom. Burma is ranked 36th out of 42 countries in the Asia–Pacific region, and its overall score is much lower than the regional average.

Over the 20-year history of the *Index*, Burma's progress toward greater economic freedom has been patchy and modest. The overall score improvement has been merely 1.4 points, with gains in trade and monetary freedoms offset by deteriorations in four of the 10 economic freedoms including property rights and financial freedom, the scores for which have declined by 20 points each. Burma has been considered a "repressed" economy throughout the history of the *Index*.

Offering some hope for the future, a number of notable changes in Burma's economic environment have occurred since the second half of 2011. Economic sanctions have been eased or lifted, and a new foreign investment law, which permits foreign firms' full ownership and eases restrictions on land leases, has been enacted.

BACKGROUND: Burma has been a military dictatorship since 1962. Since 2010, it has pursued limited political and economic reform, including releases of political prisoners, relaxation of media censorship, limited labor protections, and exchange rate reform. National League for Democracy leader and Nobel Peace Prize winner Aung San Suu Kyi was released from jail in November 2010 and won a seat in parliament in 2012. The United States and the European Union have responded by lifting or relaxing sanctions, but recent outbreaks of violence against ethnic minorities have led many to urge caution before fully embracing the government. Burma is richly endowed with natural resources, but government intervention in the economy has made it one of the world's poorest countries.

Freedom Trend

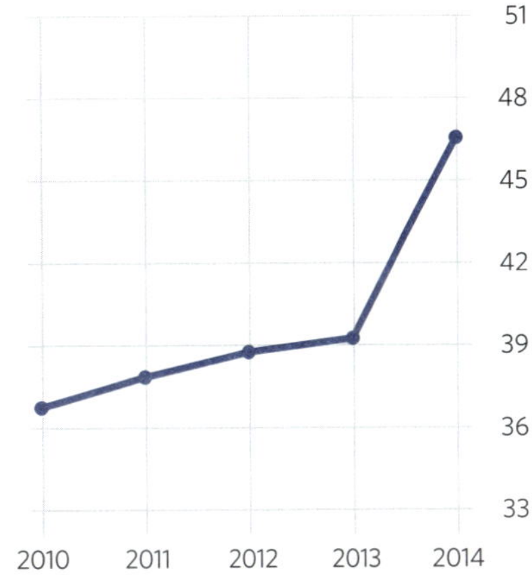

Country Comparisons

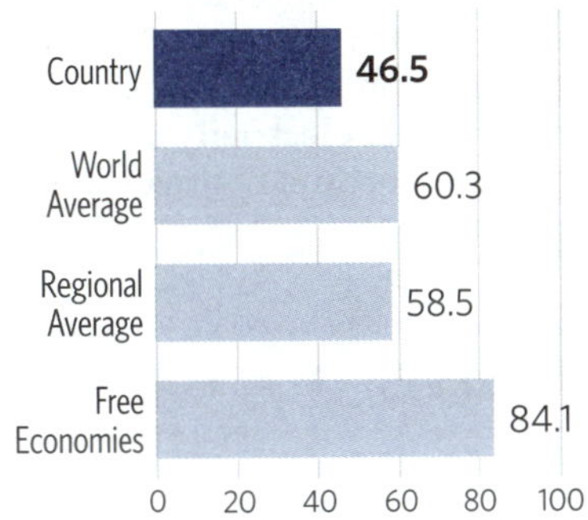

Quick Facts

Population: 63.7 million
GDP (PPP): $89.5 billion
6.3% growth in 2012
5-year compound annual growth 5.2%
$1,405 per capita
Unemployment: 4.0%
Inflation (CPI): 6.1%
FDI Inflow: $2.2 billion
Public Debt: 47.5% of GDP

2012 data unless otherwise noted.
Data compiled as of September 2013.

How Do We Measure Economic Freedom?
See page 471 for an explanation of the methodology or visit the *Index* Web site at *heritage.org/index*.

THE TEN ECONOMIC FREEDOMS

		Score	Rank	1-Year Change
RULE OF LAW	Property Rights	10.0	166th	0
	Freedom from Corruption	11.6	180th	-3.4

Although the government has promised to pursue a course of political and economic liberalization, corruption remains pervasive and continues to be a serious barrier to sustained economic development. The strengthening of the enfeebled judiciary and the introduction of rule of law have been painfully slow. Private property is not protected. The Burmese military has yet to be held accountable for human rights violations.

		Score	Rank	1-Year Change
GOVERNMENT SIZE	Fiscal Freedom	86.9	43rd	+5.0
	Government Spending	89.2	16th	-7.6

The top individual income tax rate has fallen to 20 percent, and the corporate tax rate remains at 30 percent. Other taxes include a commercial tax and a capital gains tax. Overall tax revenue is estimated at just under 4 percent of GDP. Opposition leader Aung San Suu Kyi has called for tax reforms as the government opens up the economy. Public expenditures have grown to 19 percent of GDP, and public debt continues to be below 50 percent of GDP.

		Score	Rank	1-Year Change
REGULATORY EFFICIENCY	Business Freedom	28.3	180th	+8.3
	Labor Freedom	75.7	45th	+55.7
	Monetary Freedom	64.8	167th	-0.3

Inconsistent enforcement of laws and bureaucratic red tape hinder the development of a critically needed private sector. The formal labor market remains distorted by state intervention that sets public-sector wages and influences wage-setting in the market. The government administers electricity prices, subsidizes fuel, sets public and some private wages, and imposes other distortionary prices (for example, for rice).

		Score	Rank	1-Year Change
OPEN MARKETS	Trade Freedom	73.6	107th	0
	Investment Freedom	15.0	169th	+15.0
	Financial Freedom	10.0	174th	0

Burma's average tariff rate is 3.2 percent. Numerous non-tariff barriers further impede trade. Many state-owned enterprises remain in operation. A new law governing foreign investment enacted in 2012 allows foreign investors to maintain up to 100 percent ownership in some cases. The underdeveloped financial sector is dominated by state-owned banks. Access to credit remains poor, and the state often requires banks to channel loans to preferred sectors.

Long-Term Score Change (since 1996)

RULE OF LAW		GOVERNMENT SIZE		REGULATORY EFFICIENCY		OPEN MARKETS	
Property Rights	**-20.0**	Fiscal Freedom	**+5.1**	Business Freedom	**-11.7**	Trade Freedom	**+23.6**
Freedom from Corruption	**+1.6**	Government Spending	**+8.0**	Labor Freedom	**+55.7**	Investment Freedom	**-15.0**
				Monetary Freedom	**+11.5**	Financial Freedom	**-20.0**

BURUNDI

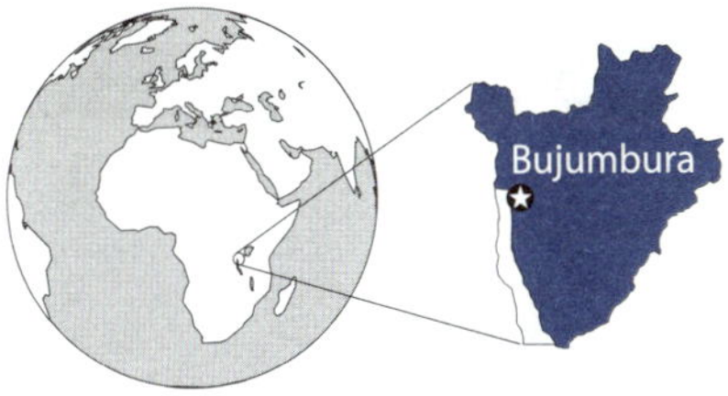

World Rank: **141** Regional Rank: **31**

Economic Freedom Score

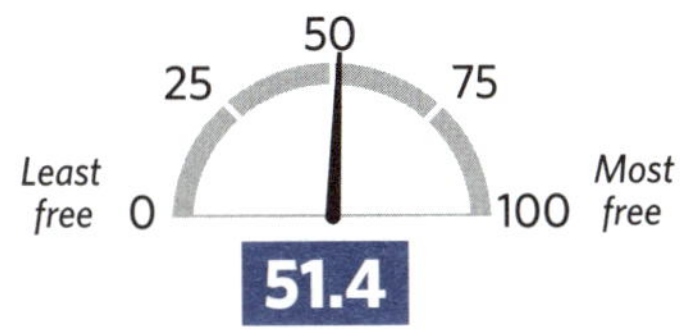

Freedom Trend

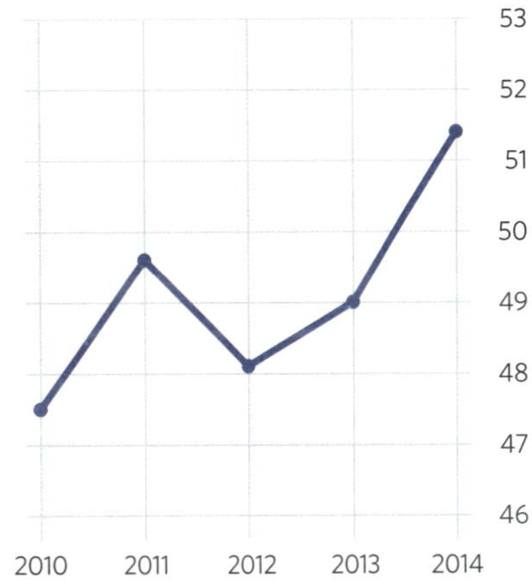

Country Comparisons

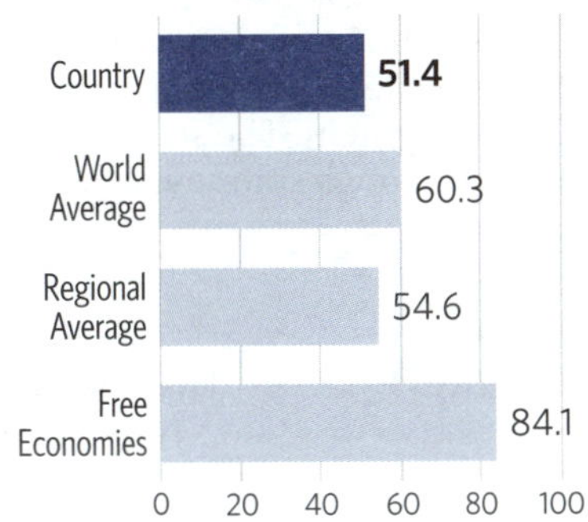

Burundi's economic freedom score is 51.4, making its economy the 141st freest in the 2014 *Index*. Its overall score is 2.4 points better than last year, mainly because of notable improvements in investment freedom and government spending that offset declines in trade freedom, labor freedom, and freedom from corruption. Burundi is ranked 31st out of 46 countries in the Sub-Saharan Africa region, and its score is lower than the world average.

Over the 20-year history of the *Index*, Burundi's economic freedom score has improved by 6 points. Seven of the 10 economic freedoms, notably investment freedom and fiscal freedom, have advanced. However, the scores for property rights and government spending have declined significantly by 10 points and about 30 points, respectively.

Burundi has achieved its highest economic freedom score ever in the 2014 *Index*. Nonetheless, as a "mostly unfree" economy whose foundations of economic freedom remain fragile and uneven across the country, it continues to lack the broad-based economic dynamism that is necessary to ensure long-term economic development. Further reforms in rule of law and financial freedom are urgently needed to improve productivity and raise incomes.

BACKGROUND: The 1993 assassination of Burundi's first Hutu president, Melchior Ndadaye, sparked a civil war between Hutus and Tutsis. The violence following the death of his successor, Cyprien Ntayamira (also a Hutu), and Rwandan President Juvenal Habyarimana in a 1994 plane crash led to the Rwandan genocide carried out by Hutus. Negotiations mediated by South Africa resulted in a power-sharing government in 2001. A new constitution was adopted in 2005, and the National Assembly elected Pierre Nkurunziza president. Together with Uganda, Burundi is active in the African Union's AMISOM peacekeeping mission in Somalia. Agriculture accounts for over 30 percent of GDP and about 90 percent of employment. Political stability and participation in the East African Community have improved aid flows and economic activity, but a lack of political will to build independent institutions is holding back development.

How Do We Measure Economic Freedom?
See page 471 for an explanation of the methodology or visit the *Index* Web site at *heritage.org/index*.

Quick Facts

Population: 8.8 million
GDP (PPP): $5.5 billion
4.0% growth in 2012
5-year compound annual growth 4.1%
$625 per capita
Unemployment: n/a
Inflation (CPI): 11.8%
FDI Inflow: $0.6 million
Public Debt: 32.0% of GDP

2012 data unless otherwise noted.
Data compiled as of September 2013.

THE TEN ECONOMIC FREEDOMS

RULE OF LAW

	Score	Rank	1-Year Change
Property Rights	20.0	139th	0
Freedom from Corruption	15.9	175th	-3.1

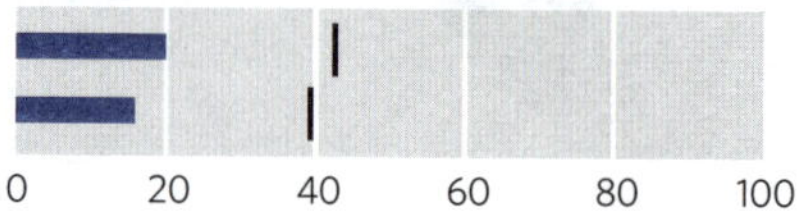

One of the world's poorest nations, Burundi remains the most corrupt country in sub-Saharan Africa. Government procurement is conducted non-transparently amid frequent allegations of cronyism. Customs officials are reportedly very corrupt, extorting bribes from exporters and importers. The judiciary is nominally independent, but judges are vulnerable to political pressure. Private property is subject to government expropriation and armed banditry.

GOVERNMENT SIZE

	Score	Rank	1-Year Change
Fiscal Freedom	73.5	125th	+2.0
Government Spending	51.9	132nd	+29.3

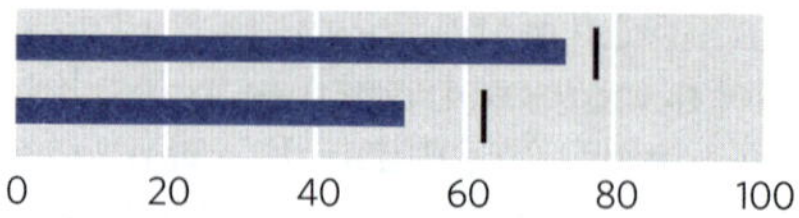

The top individual income and corporate tax rates are 35 percent. Other taxes include a value-added tax (VAT). The overall tax burden is 14.3 percent of GDP. State spending has been falling and is now 40 percent of GDP. Public debt is equivalent to about 30 percent of the domestic economy. The government is still heavily reliant on foreign assistance for about half of its expenditures.

REGULATORY EFFICIENCY

	Score	Rank	1-Year Change
Business Freedom	59.8	113th	+1.4
Labor Freedom	63.1	86th	-3.3
Monetary Freedom	68.2	152nd	-0.5

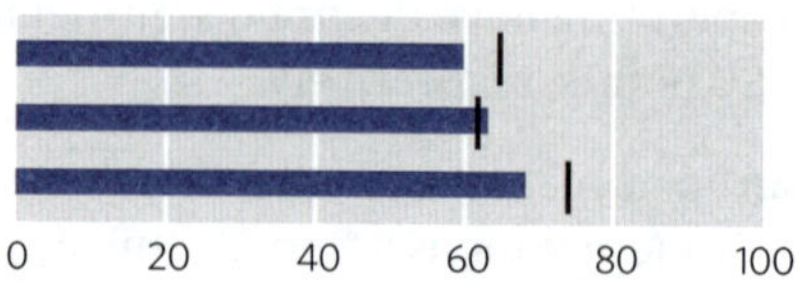

Establishing a business has become less time-consuming and requires fewer than five procedures, but completing licensing requirements continues to be costly, taking more than 10 times the level of average annual income. A large informal economy remains the main source of employment. The state subsidizes fuel, rations subsidized electricity, and influences other prices through state-owned enterprises and agriculture-support programs.

OPEN MARKETS

	Score	Rank	1-Year Change
Trade Freedom	71.8	120th	-7.1
Investment Freedom	60.0	80th	+5.0
Financial Freedom	30.0	132nd	0

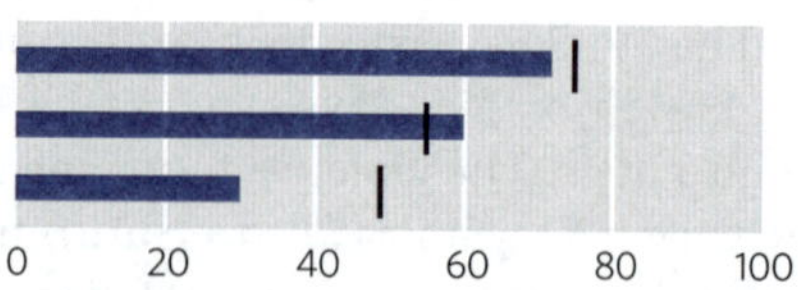

Burundi's average tariff rate is 6.6 percent. Importing is costly and time-consuming. Coffee is the country's leading export, and Burundi has privatized the coffee industry. The financial sector remains dominated by banks, with high levels of non-performing loans and insufficient capitalization. With less than 1 percent of the population having access to bank loans, many rely on microfinancing.

Long-Term Score Change (since 1997)

RULE OF LAW		GOVERNMENT SIZE		REGULATORY EFFICIENCY		OPEN MARKETS	
Property Rights	**-10.0**	Fiscal Freedom	**+29.8**	Business Freedom	**+4.8**	Trade Freedom	**+1.6**
Freedom from Corruption	**+5.9**	Government Spending	**-29.7**	Labor Freedom	**+9.4**	Investment Freedom	**+30.0**
				Monetary Freedom	**+9.6**	Financial Freedom	**0**

CAMBODIA

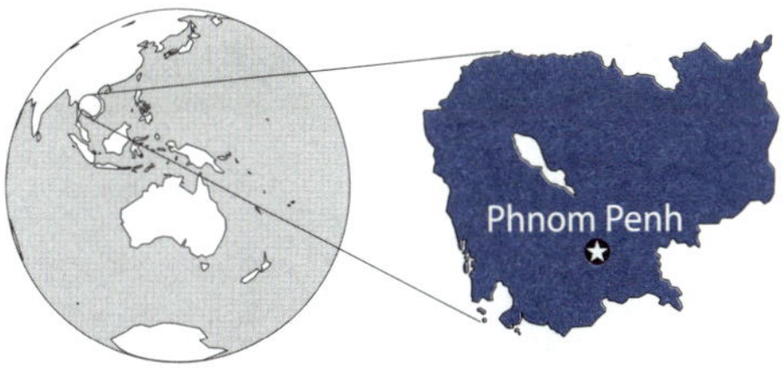

World Rank: 108 **Regional Rank: 23**

Economic Freedom Score

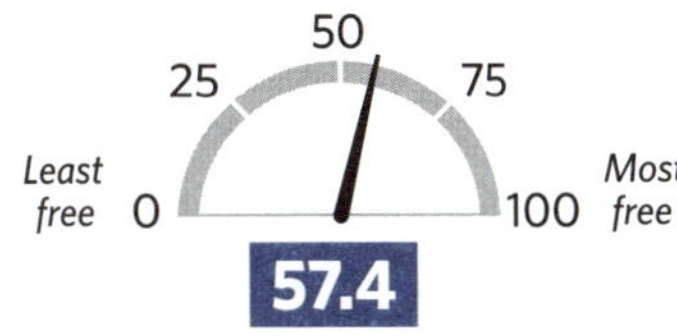

Cambodia's economic freedom score is 57.4, making its economy the 108th freest in the 2014 *Index*. Its overall score is 1.1 points worse than last year due to declines in monetary freedom, business freedom, labor freedom, and freedom from corruption. Cambodia is ranked 23rd out of 42 countries in the Asia–Pacific region, and its overall score is lower than the regional average.

Since Cambodia's economic freedom was first assessed in the 1997 *Index*, its progress in adopting policies that enhance economic freedom has been uneven and modest. The country's overall economic freedom score has improved by only 4.5 points, with advancements in trade freedom, monetary freedom, and investment freedom largely offset by significant declines in business freedom and freedom from corruption.

Cambodia had advanced into the ranks of the "moderately free" during the early 2000s but has fallen back to the status of economically "mostly unfree" since 2006. Substantial challenges remain, particularly in implementing deeper institutional and systemic reforms that are critical to strengthening the foundations of economic freedom. Government interference continues to undermine dynamic flows of investment and overall economic efficiency.

BACKGROUND: Between 1975 and 1979, Pol Pot's Khmer Rouge regime killed an estimated 3 million Cambodians. A tribunal established under an agreement with the United Nations to prosecute senior officials involved in the atrocities has been slow to deliver justice. Now nominally a democracy, Cambodia has been ruled by former Khmer Rouge member and Vietnamese puppet Prime Minister Hun Sen since independent Cambodia held national elections in 1993. Elections have often fallen short of international standards, with the outcome of the most recent, in 2013, hotly contested by the opposition. In 2012, Cambodia took its turn as chair of the Association of Southeast Asian Nations, drawing increased international attention to and criticism of its undemocratic policies and close ties to China. Cambodia's economy depends heavily on tourism and apparel assembly.

How Do We Measure Economic Freedom?
See page 471 for an explanation of the methodology or visit the *Index* Web site at *heritage.org/index*.

Freedom Trend

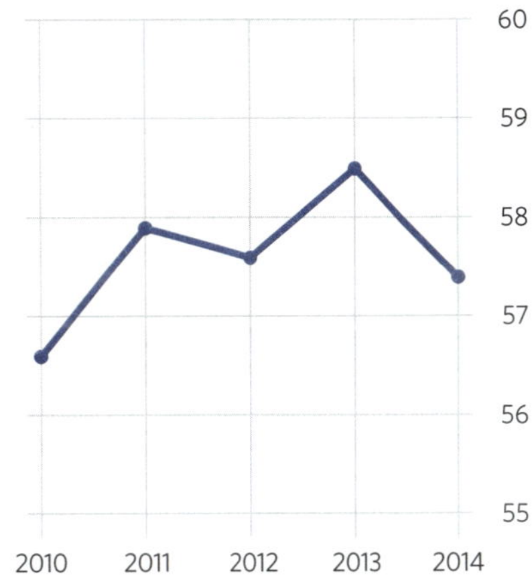

Country Comparisons

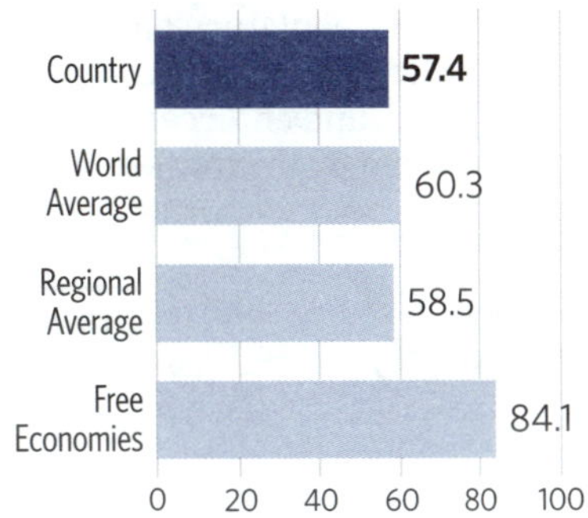

Quick Facts

Population: 15.3 million
GDP (PPP): $36.6 billion
6.5% growth in 2012
5-year compound annual growth 5.2%
$2,402 per capita
Unemployment: 3.5% (2007)
Inflation (CPI): 2.9%
FDI Inflow: $1.6 billion
Public Debt: 28.5% of GDP

2012 data unless otherwise noted.
Data compiled as of September 2013.

THE TEN ECONOMIC FREEDOMS

RULE OF LAW

	Score	Rank	1-Year Change
Property Rights	30.0	93rd	0
Freedom from Corruption	18.7	167th	-2.3

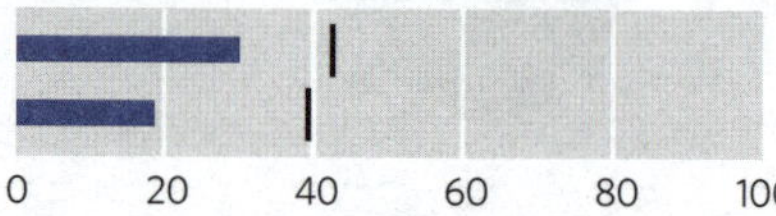

A majority of Cambodians in a 2013 corruption survey said they had paid a bribe in the past year; nearly three-quarters said that personal contacts were needed when dealing with the government. A weak and inconsistent judiciary does not protect private property effectively. Investments in mining, forestry, agriculture, textiles, tourism, hydropower, and real estate frequently involve land grabs by powerful politicians, bureaucrats, and military.

GOVERNMENT SIZE

	Score	Rank	1-Year Change
Fiscal Freedom	90.8	31st	-0.1
Government Spending	88.4	20th	0

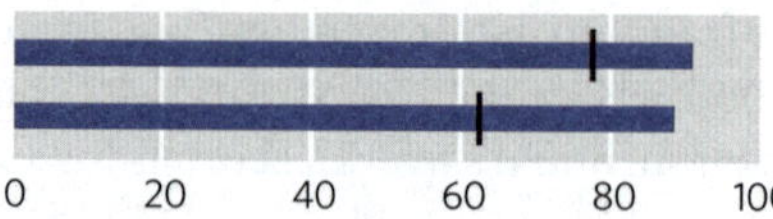

The top individual income tax rate has fallen to 20 percent. The top corporate tax rate remains at 20 percent for most businesses but 30 percent for the petroleum and gas sectors. Other taxes include a value-added tax (VAT) and an excise tax. The overall tax burden has remained steady at about 10.9 percent of GDP. Expenditures remain around 20 percent of the domestic economy, and public debt has stabilized at about 29 percent of GDP.

REGULATORY EFFICIENCY

	Score	Rank	1-Year Change
Business Freedom	36.6	172nd	-2.8
Labor Freedom	50.2	135th	-4.0
Monetary Freedom	77.9	65th	-3.4

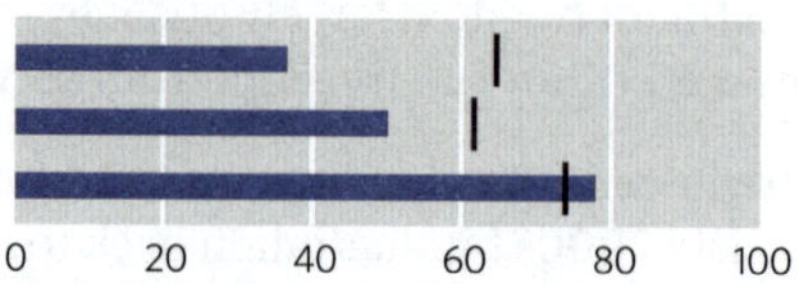

The overall freedom to establish and run a private enterprise is constrained significantly by the inefficient regulatory environment. Starting a business remains time-consuming, and completing licensing requirements takes more than 500 days. The formal labor market is not fully developed, and enforcement of many aspects of the labor codes is ineffective. Most prices are determined by the market, but the state has been increasing subsidies for fuel.

OPEN MARKETS

	Score	Rank	1-Year Change
Trade Freedom	71.0	125th	+0.8
Investment Freedom	60.0	80th	0
Financial Freedom	50.0	69th	0

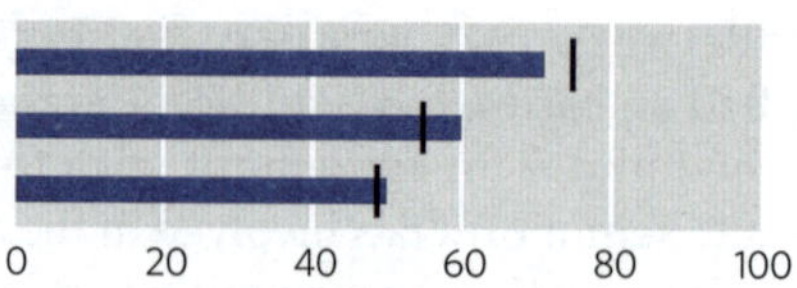

Cambodia has an average tariff rate of 9.5 percent. The country's underdeveloped legal system is a deterrent to foreign investment. The financial system remains segmented and subject to government influence. There is only one company listed in the country's first stock market, which opened in 2012 after years of delay.

Long-Term Score Change (since 1997)

RULE OF LAW		GOVERNMENT SIZE		REGULATORY EFFICIENCY		OPEN MARKETS	
Property Rights	**0**	Fiscal Freedom	**-0.8**	Business Freedom	**-18.4**	Trade Freedom	**+56.0**
Freedom from Corruption	**-11.3**	Government Spending	**-3.4**	Labor Freedom	**+6.3**	Investment Freedom	**+10.0**
				Monetary Freedom	**+15.8**	Financial Freedom	**0**

CAMEROON

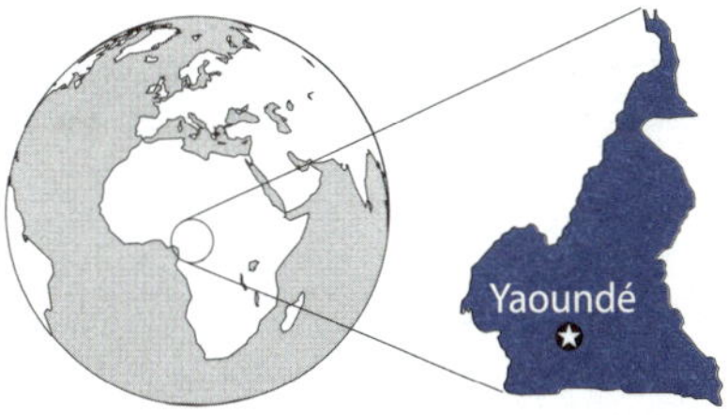

World Rank: **136** Regional Rank: **29**

Economic Freedom Score

Cameroon's economic freedom score is 52.6, making its economy the 136th freest in the 2014 *Index*. Its overall score is 0.3 point better than last year, reflecting gains in trade freedom and fiscal freedom. Cameroon is ranked 29th out of 46 countries in the Sub-Saharan Africa region, and its overall score is lower than the regional average.

Over the 20-year history of the *Index*, Cameroon's economic freedom has been stagnant near the lower boundary of the "mostly unfree" category, and its overall score has improved only 1.3 points. Deteriorations in half of the 10 economic freedoms, including property rights, investment freedom, and monetary freedom, have counterbalanced notable improvements in trade freedom and fiscal freedom.

Substantial challenges remain in the struggle to promote stable long-term economic development, and lingering institutional weaknesses call for much greater commitment to reform, particularly in two areas. Cameroon continues to score below the world average in freedom from corruption and the protection of property rights, and marginal reforms in these critical areas have failed to generate much improvement.

BACKGROUND: President Paul Biya has held office since 1982 and was re-elected in October 2011. Though he claimed 78 percent of the vote, the election was marred by irregularities. Relative stability has allowed Cameroon to develop limited infrastructure to support its emerging oil sector. Although the government claims to maintain strong civil-rights laws, charges of discrimination and abuse of human rights are abundant. In 2012, Cameroon tightened its border security with Nigeria after attacks by the Nigerian terrorist group Boko Haram. Cameroon's economy, highly dependent on commodity exports and subject to burdensome regulation, has been seriously affected by the global economic slowdown. The International Monetary Fund is calling for reforms to reverse the hostile business environment and attract more infrastructure investment.

Freedom Trend

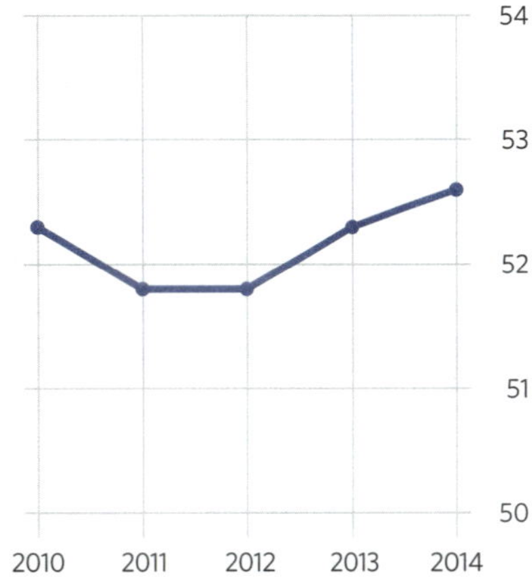

Country Comparisons

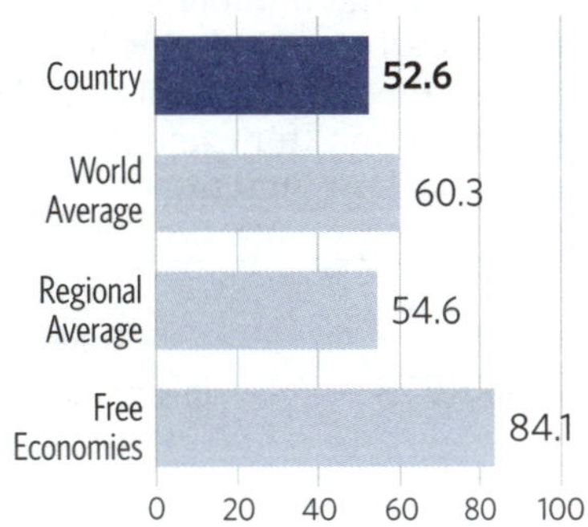

Quick Facts

Population: 21.5 million
GDP (PPP): $50.8 billion
4.7% growth in 2012
5-year compound annual growth 3.5%
$2,366 per capita
Unemployment: n/a
Inflation (CPI): 3.0%
FDI Inflow: $507.0 million
Public Debt: 14.9% of GDP

2012 data unless otherwise noted.
Data compiled as of September 2013.

How Do We Measure Economic Freedom?
See page 471 for an explanation of the methodology or visit the *Index* Web site at *heritage.org/index.*

THE TEN ECONOMIC FREEDOMS

		Score	Rank	1-Year Change
RULE OF LAW	Property Rights	30.0	93rd	0
	Freedom from Corruption	21.9	151st	-3.1

Corruption remains endemic in Cameroon and raises the costs and risks of doing business. President Biya's long tenure in office has encouraged cronyism, and members of his Beti ethnic group dominate many key positions. Protection of real property rights is weak due to pervasive corruption and a slow, inefficient judicial system that is vulnerable to political interference. Intellectual property rights are routinely violated.

		Score	Rank	1-Year Change
GOVERNMENT SIZE	Fiscal Freedom	71.7	131st	+2.4
	Government Spending	86.0	28th	-1.1

Cameroon's top individual income tax rate has risen to 35 percent. The top effective corporate tax rate is 38.5 percent (35 percent plus a 10 percent surcharge). Other taxes include a value-added tax (VAT) and an inheritance tax. The overall tax burden is 11 percent of GDP. Public expenditures are 22 percent of GDP, and public debt amounts to about 15 percent of gross domestic income.

		Score	Rank	1-Year Change
REGULATORY EFFICIENCY	Business Freedom	45.0	162nd	-1.8
	Labor Freedom	56.1	110th	+0.6
	Monetary Freedom	69.4	146th	-0.5

The time and number of procedures required to launch a business have been reduced over the years, but completing licensing requirements still costs over 10 times the average level of annual income. The labor market does not function efficiently. The government's excessive subsidization (for example, for fuel and electricity) and inefficient public financial management systems limit public infrastructure investment.

		Score	Rank	1-Year Change
OPEN MARKETS	Trade Freedom	61.2	155th	+6.3
	Investment Freedom	35.0	142nd	0
	Financial Freedom	50.0	69th	0

Cameroon's average tariff rate is 11.9 percent. As with other members of the Central African Economic and Monetary Community, it may take weeks to import cargo. The legal and regulatory systems can be difficult for foreign investors to navigate. The financial sector is dominated by multi-service banks. Despite efforts to shore up financial intermediation, access to credit remains limited in rural areas, and the cost of long-term financing is high.

Long-Term Score Change (since 1995)

RULE OF LAW		GOVERNMENT SIZE		REGULATORY EFFICIENCY		OPEN MARKETS	
Property Rights	-20.0	Fiscal Freedom	+20.6	Business Freedom	-10.0	Trade Freedom	+36.2
Freedom from Corruption	+11.9	Government Spending	-3.9	Labor Freedom	+4.1	Investment Freedom	-15.0
				Monetary Freedom	-11.6	Financial Freedom	0

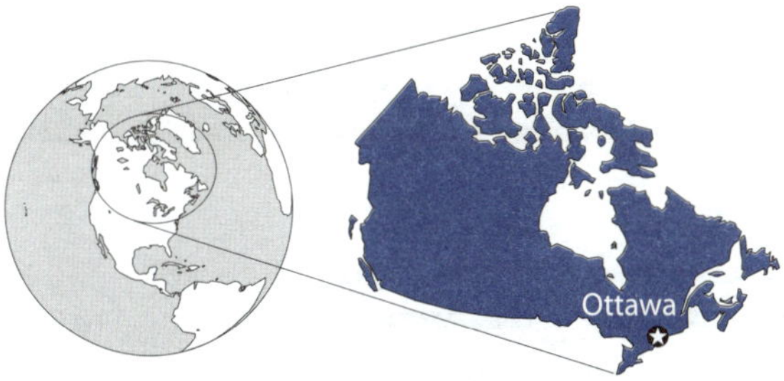

CANADA

Economic Freedom Score

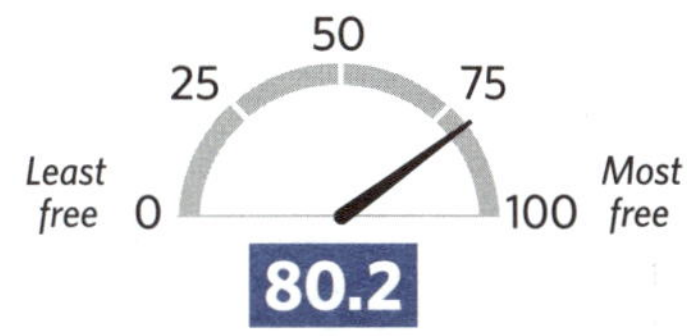

Freedom Trend

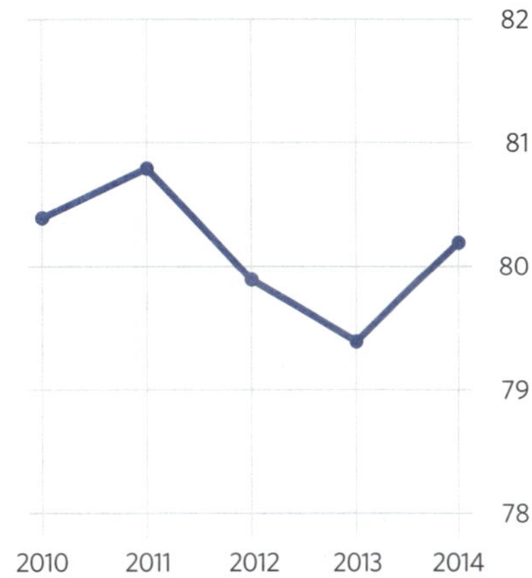

Country Comparisons

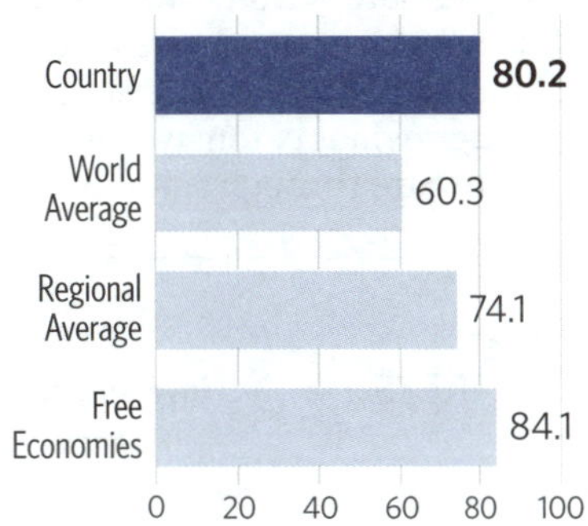

Canada's economic freedom score is 80.2, making its economy the 6th freest in the 2014 *Index*. Its overall score is 0.8 point better than last year, reflecting improvements in investment freedom, the management of government spending, and monetary freedom. Canada continues to be the freest economy in the North America region.

Over the 20-year history of the *Index*, Canada has advanced its economic freedom score by 10.7 points, the third biggest improvement among developed economies. Substantial score increases in seven of the 10 economic freedoms, including investment freedom, fiscal freedom, and the management of public spending, have enabled Canada to elevate its economic freedom status from "moderately free" 20 years ago to "free" today.

A transparent and stable business climate makes Canada one of the world's most attractive investment destinations. Openness to global trade and commerce is firmly institutionalized, and the economy has rebounded relatively quickly from the global recession. The financial system has remained stable, and prudent regulations have allowed banks to withstand the global financial turmoil with little disruption.

BACKGROUND: Prime Minister Stephen Harper governs with a solid Conservative Party majority in Parliament. The Liberal Party, which dominated politics in Canada for decades but suffered a crushing defeat in 2011 in which it lost to the New Democratic Party even the status of official opposition, has achieved renewed popularity under the leadership of Justin Trudeau, son of former Prime Minister Pierre Trudeau. Canada's large and diverse land mass is reflected in a democratic system that provides substantial autonomy to its 13 provinces and territories. The 20 percent of Canadians for whom French is the native language are heavily concentrated in Quebec. Canada's economy is closely linked to that of the United States. The country is a major exporter of oil, minerals, automobiles, manufactured goods, and forest products.

Quick Facts

Population: 34.8 million
GDP (PPP): $1.5 trillion
1.8% growth in 2012
5-year compound annual growth 1.2%
$42,734 per capita
Unemployment: 7.3%
Inflation (CPI): 1.5%
FDI Inflow: $45.4 billion
Public Debt: 85.6% of GDP

2012 data unless otherwise noted.
Data compiled as of September 2013.

How Do We Measure Economic Freedom?
See page 471 for an explanation of the methodology or visit the *Index* Web site at *heritage.org/index.*

THE TEN ECONOMIC FREEDOMS

Score | Country | World Average | Rank | 1-Year Change

RULE OF LAW

	Score	Rank	1-Year Change
Property Rights	90.0	2nd	0
Freedom from Corruption	87.7	10th	+0.7

Canada has long had a reputation for honest, responsible, and responsive government that vigorously prosecutes corruption. Its foundations of economic freedom rest on a judicial system that has an impeccable record of independence and transparency. Private property is well protected. Enforcement of contracts is very reliable, and expropriation is highly unusual. Protection of intellectual property rights is consistent with world standards.

GOVERNMENT SIZE

	Score	Rank	1-Year Change
Fiscal Freedom	79.7	89th	-0.1
Government Spending	47.3	139th	+2.5

The top federal income tax has been cut to 29 percent, and the top corporate tax remains at 15 percent. Other taxes include a value-added tax (VAT) and a property tax. The overall tax burden is 31 percent of GDP. Expenditures have continued to fall to 41.9 percent of domestic output as the Conservative-led government attempts to balance the budget by 2015. Public debt is equivalent to 86 percent of GDP.

REGULATORY EFFICIENCY

	Score	Rank	1-Year Change
Business Freedom	89.3	16th	-2.4
Labor Freedom	83.1	18th	+0.8
Monetary Freedom	76.3	80th	+1.1

The regulatory framework is efficient. With no minimum capital requirement, incorporating a business takes one procedure and less than one week. Licensing requirements are not burdensome. The labor market remains relatively flexible, and labor costs are moderate. The government provides extensive energy and agricultural subsidies and controls virtually all prices for health care through a mandatory "single-payer" nationalized program.

OPEN MARKETS

	Score	Rank	1-Year Change
Trade Freedom	88.3	9th	+0.1
Investment Freedom	80.0	23rd	+5.0
Financial Freedom	80.0	4th	0

Canada's average tariff rate is a low 0.9 percent. Canada is unilaterally eliminating tariffs on many inputs while negotiating several trade agreements. Foreign investment in some sectors of the economy may be screened. The financial sector provides a full range of competitive services and remains dynamic. The six main banks continue to dominate the sector, although it has become easier for foreign banks to enter the market.

Long-Term Score Change (since 1995)

RULE OF LAW		GOVERNMENT SIZE		REGULATORY EFFICIENCY		OPEN MARKETS	
Property Rights	0	Fiscal Freedom	+15.5	Business Freedom	+4.3	Trade Freedom	+13.1
Freedom from Corruption	-2.3	Government Spending	+32.6	Labor Freedom	+0.8	Investment Freedom	+30.0
				Monetary Freedom	-9.6	Financial Freedom	+10.0

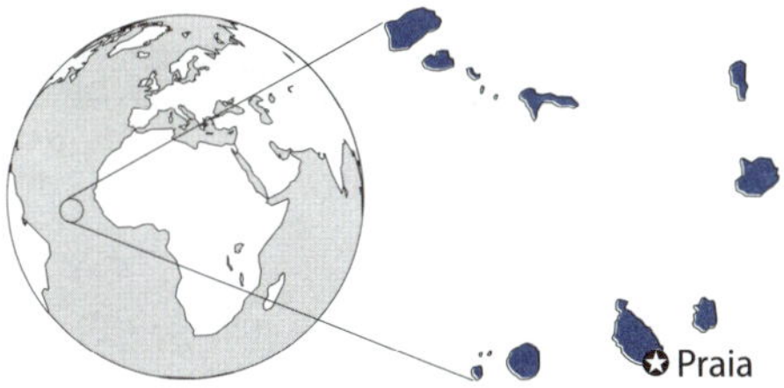

CAPE VERDE

World Rank: 60 **Regional Rank: 3**

Economic Freedom Score

Freedom Trend

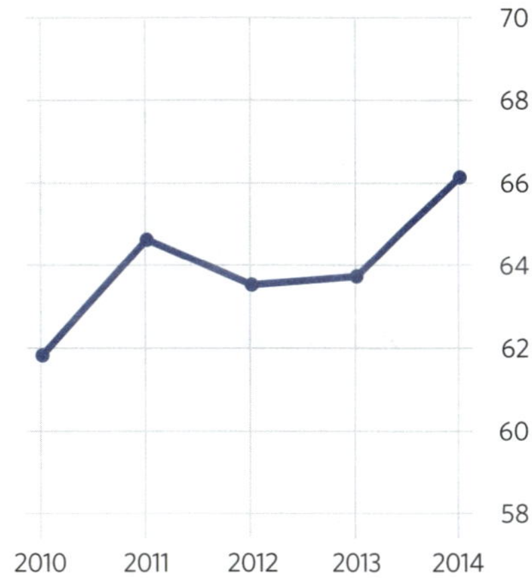

Country Comparisons

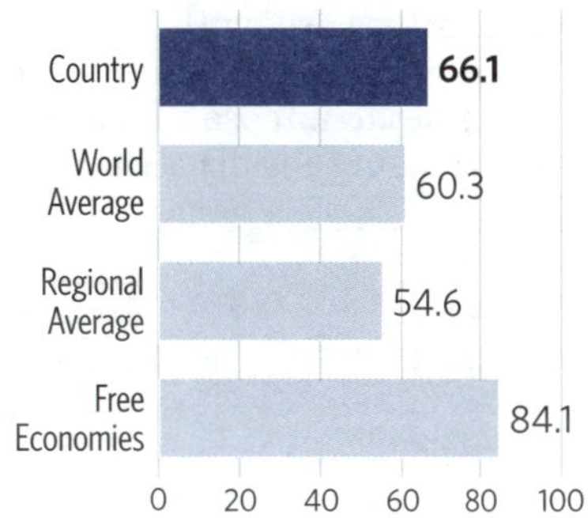

Quick Facts

Population: 0.5 million
GDP (PPP): $2.2 billion
4.3% growth in 2012
5-year compound annual growth 4.9%
$4,133 per capita
Unemployment: 10.0%
Inflation (CPI): 2.5%
FDI Inflow: $70.9 million
Public Debt: 103.4% of GDP

2012 data unless otherwise noted.
Data compiled as of September 2013.

Cape Verde's economic freedom score is 66.1, making its economy the 60th freest in the 2014 *Index*. Its overall score is 2.4 points better than last year, with substantial gains in labor freedom, business freedom, investment freedom, and the management of government spending. Cape Verde is ranked 3rd out of 46 countries in the Sub-Saharan Africa region, and its overall score is higher than the global and regional averages.

Over the 20-year history of the *Index*, Cape Verde has advanced its economic freedom score by 16.4 points, a top 20 improvement. The overall increase has been broad-based in seven of the 10 economic freedoms including trade freedom, financial freedom, the management of government spending, and freedom from corruption, scores for which have improved approximately 25 points or more.

Achieving its highest economic freedom score ever in the 2014 *Index*, Cape Verde has advanced well into the ranks of the "moderately free." While moving toward higher levels of economic freedom, it has made considerable progress in income growth and poverty reduction. The government continues to support policies that promote free trade and open markets.

BACKGROUND: Cape Verde is a stable, multi-party parliamentary democracy. Jose Maria Neves of the African Party for the Independence of Cape Verde became prime minister after the February 2011 legislative elections, and opposition leader Jorge Carlos Fonseca won the presidency later that year. Cape Verde has few natural resources and is subject to frequent droughts and serious water shortages. Services dominate the economy, and about 82 percent of food is imported. Cape Verde has close economic and political ties to the European Union, which has granted it special partnership status. Its currency is pegged to the euro, and it joined the World Trade Organization in 2008. Remittances account for over 20 percent of GDP. Current economic reforms are aimed at lowering regulatory hurdles for business and driving down high unemployment.

How Do We Measure Economic Freedom?
See page 471 for an explanation of the methodology or visit the *Index* Web site at *heritage.org/index*.

THE TEN ECONOMIC FREEDOMS

Legend: Country | World Average

RULE OF LAW

	Score	Rank	1-Year Change
Property Rights	70.0	27th	0
Freedom from Corruption	54.9	40th	-0.1

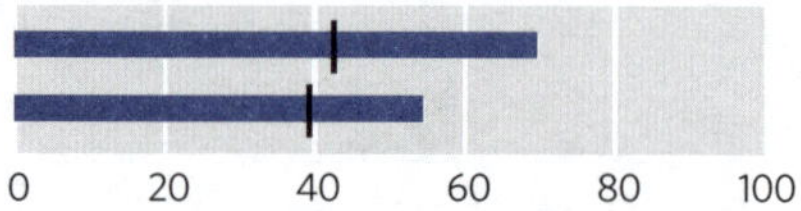

Private property is reasonably well protected. Political and economic governance is generally regarded as among the region's best. The government is creating a reliable and easily accessible land registration system that is expected to strengthen the investment climate. The constitutional provision for an independent judiciary is generally respected, but the judicial system is inefficient, and the case backlog causes significant delays.

GOVERNMENT SIZE

	Score	Rank	1-Year Change
Fiscal Freedom	77.4	107th	-0.5
Government Spending	68.6	93rd	+3.2

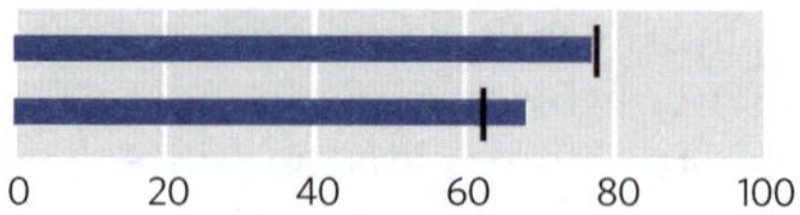

The top individual income tax rate is 35 percent, and the top corporate tax rate is 25 percent. Other taxes include a value-added tax (VAT). The overall tax burden has risen to 20.2 percent of GDP, and government expenditures amount to 32.3 percent of gross domestic output. Public debt continues to climb and has reached over 100 percent of GDP. The government's most recent budget increased the VAT tax on the tourism sector.

REGULATORY EFFICIENCY

	Score	Rank	1-Year Change
Business Freedom	63.8	97th	+4.9
Labor Freedom	48.0	145th	+7.7
Monetary Freedom	79.1	47th	+1.1

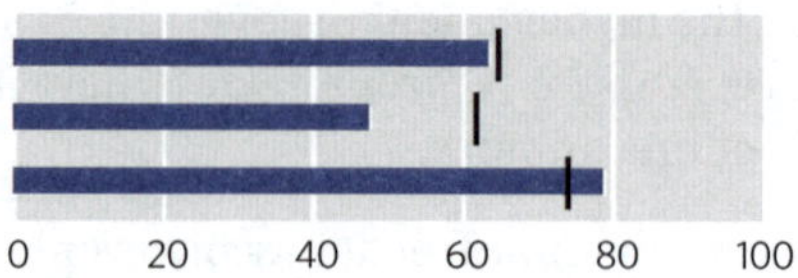

The regulatory framework has been modernized. The business start-up process is now more straightforward, with lower minimum capital requirements, but licensing requirements remain time-consuming and costly. Despite reform efforts, the rigidity of the labor market continues to impose a high cost on businesses. The market determines most prices, but the government subsidizes electricity and water as well as an unprofitable state-owned airline.

OPEN MARKETS

	Score	Rank	1-Year Change
Trade Freedom	69.6	130th	+2.7
Investment Freedom	70.0	46th	+5.0
Financial Freedom	60.0	41st	0

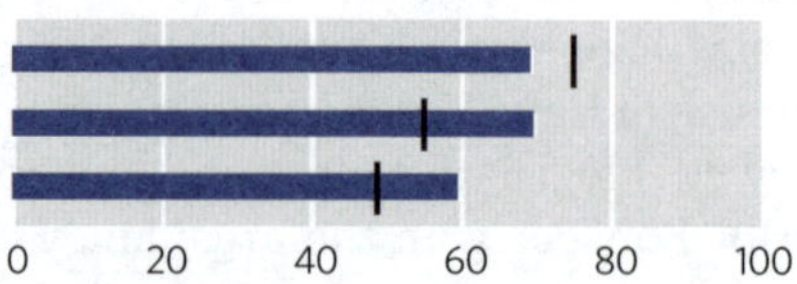

Cape Verde's average tariff rate is 10.2 percent. It is easy to import goods compared to other countries in the region. Several state-owned companies have been privatized with participation from foreign investors. The financial system is dominated by banking, and banking assets constitute over 90 percent of financial sector assets. The share of non-bank financial institutions is negligible except for the state-owned pension fund.

Long-Term Score Change (since 1996)

RULE OF LAW		GOVERNMENT SIZE		REGULATORY EFFICIENCY		OPEN MARKETS	
Property Rights	0	Fiscal Freedom	+13.1	Business Freedom	+8.8	Trade Freedom	+24.6
Freedom from Corruption	+24.9	Government Spending	+37.7	Labor Freedom	-8.8	Investment Freedom	0
				Monetary Freedom	+6.8	Financial Freedom	+50.0

CENTRAL AFRICAN REPUBLIC

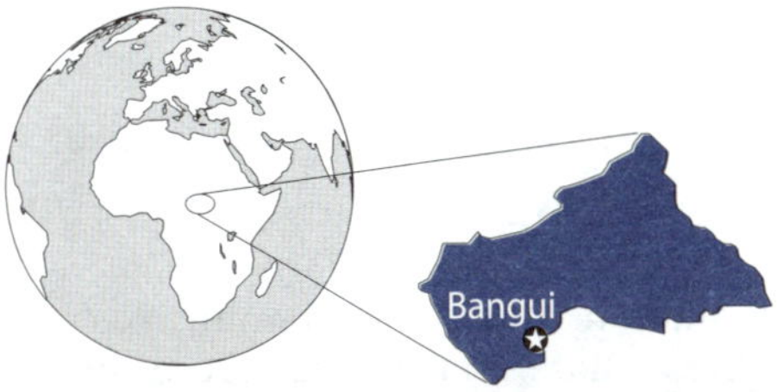

World Rank: **161** Regional Rank: **40**

The Central African Republic's economic freedom score is 46.7, making its economy the 161st freest in the 2014 *Index*. Its overall score is 3.7 points lower than last year, primarily due to significant declines in property rights, trade freedom, investment freedom, and labor freedom. The CAR is ranked 40th out of 46 countries in the Sub-Saharan Africa region, and its overall score is lower than the regional average.

Since the Central African Republic's economic freedom was first assessed in the 2002 *Index*, progress toward greater economic freedom has been uneven. Overall, the country's economic freedom score has declined by 13.1 points, one of the biggest score drops in the history of the *Index*. Scores for eight of the 10 economic freedoms, including property rights, investment freedom, and financial freedom, have deteriorated by 20 points or more.

Consequently, the overall entrepreneurial environment remains severely constrained. An overbearing regulatory framework, exacerbated by poor access to credit and high financing costs, stifles economic activity and hurts business expansion and the development of a vibrant private sector.

BACKGROUND: An agreement between General François Bozizé, opposition leaders, and some rebel groups established a consensus government in 2008, but Bozizé and parliament remained in office beyond their term limits. Bozizé was re-elected in March 2011, but in 2012, rebel groups accused the government of not abiding by the peace agreement. They captured the capital of Bangui in March 2013 despite the presence of international troops. Bozizé was forced to flee the country, and rebel leader Michael Djotodia declared himself president. More than half of the population lives in rural areas and depends on subsistence farming and forestry. Despite timber, diamonds (about 50 percent of exports), gold, uranium, and prospects for oil exploration, the CAR is one of the world's least-developed countries. Anti-market economic policies inhibit investment, resulting in poverty, an uneducated workforce, and shoddy infrastructure.

How Do We Measure Economic Freedom?
See page 471 for an explanation of the methodology or visit the *Index* Web site at *heritage.org/index*.

Economic Freedom Score

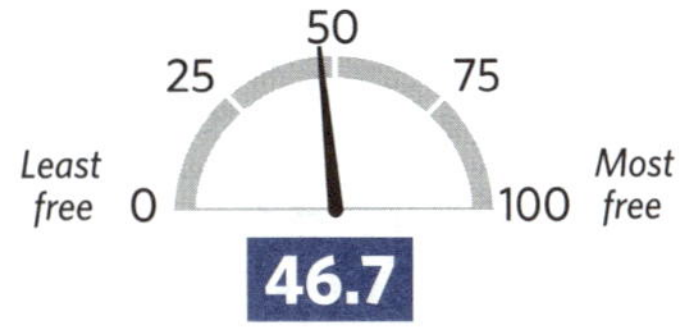

Freedom Trend

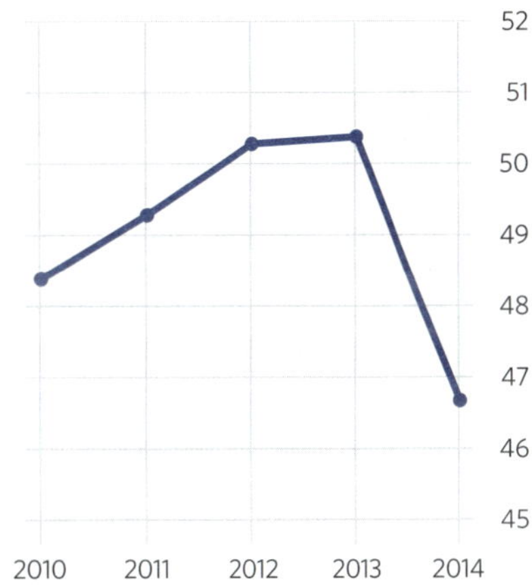

Country Comparisons

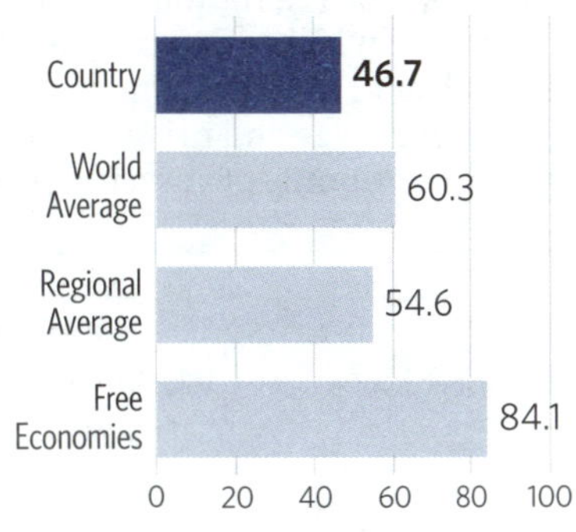

Quick Facts

Population: 4.9 million
GDP (PPP): $3.9 billion
4.1% growth in 2012
5-year compound annual growth 2.8%
$800 per capita
Unemployment: n/a
Inflation (CPI): 5.2%
FDI Inflow: $71.2 million
Public Debt: 30.6% of GDP

2012 data unless otherwise noted.
Data compiled as of September 2013.

THE TEN ECONOMIC FREEDOMS

RULE OF LAW

	Score	Rank	1-Year Change
Property Rights	10.0	166th	-10.0
Freedom from Corruption	20.6	156th	-1.4

A coalition of rebel insurgents seized power in 2013. They have disrupted the economy, exacerbated the precarious humanitarian situation, and amplified a state of lawlessness, resulting in the spread of violence, looting, and human-rights violations. Corruption remains pervasive. Diamonds account for about half of export earnings, but many sales circumvent official channels. Protection of property rights is weak.

GOVERNMENT SIZE

	Score	Rank	1-Year Change
Fiscal Freedom	65.1	156th	0
Government Spending	92.6	3rd	+0.2

The top individual income tax rate has fallen to 50 percent, and the top corporate tax rate is 30 percent. Other taxes include a value-added tax (VAT). The overall tax burden is 9.4 percent of GDP. Government spending has moderated to 16 percent of the domestic economy, and public debt amounts to about 30 percent of GDP.

REGULATORY EFFICIENCY

	Score	Rank	1-Year Change
Business Freedom	33.9	176th	-1.3
Labor Freedom	40.4	167th	-7.5
Monetary Freedom	72.5	127th	-5.6

Burdensome regulations continue to hinder private-sector development. Overall, the regulatory system lacks transparency and clarity, and regulations are enforced inconsistently. The formal labor market is underdeveloped. Government distortions of the economy through subsidies and wage and price controls are aggravated by political instability that undermines the basic functioning of state institutions.

OPEN MARKETS

	Score	Rank	1-Year Change
Trade Freedom	51.8	174th	-6.0
Investment Freedom	50.0	109th	-5.0
Financial Freedom	30.0	132nd	0

The Central African Republic's average tariff rate is 16.6 percent. As with other members of the Central African Economic and Monetary Community, it may take weeks to import cargo. Political instability is a deterrent to foreign investment. The high cost of credit and scarce access to financing hold back development of the private sector. A large part of the population remains outside of the formal banking sector.

Long-Term Score Change (since 2002)

RULE OF LAW		GOVERNMENT SIZE		REGULATORY EFFICIENCY		OPEN MARKETS	
Property Rights	-40.0	Fiscal Freedom	-0.2	Business Freedom	-21.1	Trade Freedom	+3.6
Freedom from Corruption	-9.4	Government Spending	+4.6	Labor Freedom	-9.3	Investment Freedom	-20.0
				Monetary Freedom	-9.5	Financial Freedom	-20.0

CHAD

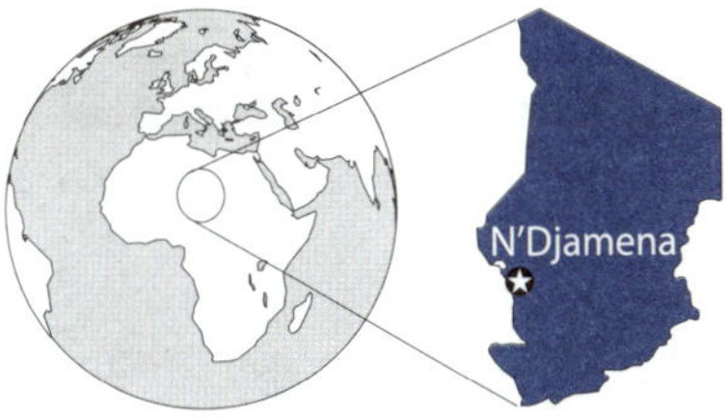

World Rank: **167** Regional Rank: **41**

Economic Freedom Score

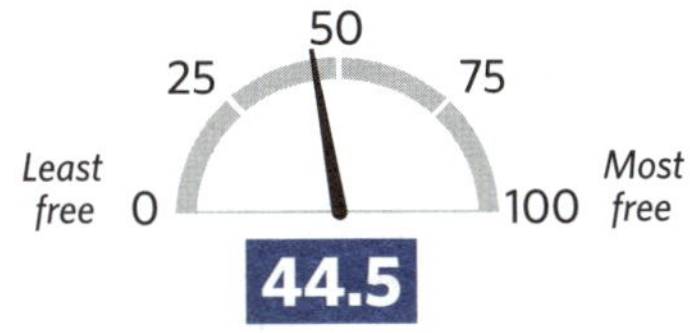

Chad's economic freedom score is 44.5, making its economy the 167th freest in the 2014 *Index*. Its overall score is 0.7 point lower than last year, with substantial deteriorations in freedom from corruption, fiscal freedom, and monetary freedom. Chad is ranked 41st out of 46 countries in the Sub-Saharan Africa region, and its overall score is lower than the regional average.

Over the 20-year history of the *Index*, Chad's economic freedom has been largely stagnant. Despite notable score improvements in the areas of open markets measured by trade freedom, investment freedom, and financial freedom, the country's overall gain has been largely offset by declines in business freedom, the management of government spending, and property rights. In the absence of lasting progress toward greater economic freedom, Chad remains one of the economically "repressed" countries in the *Index*.

The government is largely ineffective, but the state continues to interfere in the market for key goods through price controls. Poor maintenance of the rule of law perpetuates systemic corruption and lax enforcement of property rights and undermines prospects for long-term economic development.

BACKGROUND: President Idriss Déby, who seized power in 1990, won a fourth term in 2011 in a highly dubious election. Due to recent terrorist activity in the Sahel, Chad sent a task force to Mali to help secure the northern half of the country from Tuareg separatists and al-Qaeda–linked groups. In May 2013, state security forces foiled a developing coup. Conflict in eastern Chad and unrest in Sudan's Darfur region have generated hundreds of thousands of internally displaced Chadian and Sudanese refugees in the country. Over 80 percent of Chad's people depend on subsistence agriculture, herding, and fishing. Oil revenues and investments by American and Chinese companies have fueled recent economic growth, and oil accounts for about half of GDP. Chad's most important bilateral economic partnerships are with China and India.

Freedom Trend

Country Comparisons

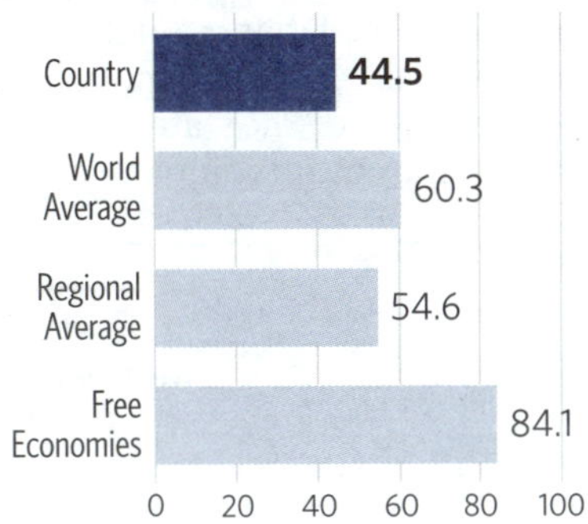

Quick Facts

Population: 10.7 million
GDP (PPP): $20.7 billion
5.0% growth in 2012
5-year compound annual growth 3.7%
$1,924 per capita
Unemployment: n/a
Inflation (CPI): 7.7%
FDI Inflow: $323.5 million
Public Debt: 34.5% of GDP

2012 data unless otherwise noted.
Data compiled as of September 2013.

How Do We Measure Economic Freedom?
See page 471 for an explanation of the methodology or visit the *Index* Web site at *heritage.org/index*.

THE TEN ECONOMIC FREEDOMS

RULE OF LAW

	Score	Rank	1-Year Change
Property Rights	20.0	139th	0
Freedom from Corruption	15.9	175th	-4.1

Corruption is rampant within President Déby's inner circle, who siphon off the nation's oil wealth. The rule of law and the judicial system remain weak, and the courts are heavily influenced by the political leadership. The constitution guarantees judicial independence, but most key judicial officials are named by the president. Protection of private property is weak, and fraud is common in property transactions.

GOVERNMENT SIZE

	Score	Rank	1-Year Change
Fiscal Freedom	46.2	179th	-4.2
Government Spending	80.0	51st	+4.5

The top individual income tax rate has increased to 60 percent, and the top corporate tax rate has risen to 45 percent. Other taxes include a value-added tax (VAT) and a property tax. Overall, the tax burden is 5.1 percent of GDP. Government expenditures have been steady at around 26 percent of the domestic economy, and public debt is 35 percent of GDP.

REGULATORY EFFICIENCY

	Score	Rank	1-Year Change
Business Freedom	24.9	181st	-0.3
Labor Freedom	43.3	161st	+2.8
Monetary Freedom	69.8	143rd	-4.8

Progress in improving the inefficient business framework has been slow and uneven. Although burdensome labor regulations are not generally enforced, the labor market remains poorly developed. Most of the population remains employed outside of the formal sector, primarily in agriculture. The state subsidizes retail fuel prices and such public enterprises as electricity, water and cotton companies, an oil refinery, and a tractor assembly plant.

OPEN MARKETS

	Score	Rank	1-Year Change
Trade Freedom	55.2	169th	-0.4
Investment Freedom	50.0	109th	0
Financial Freedom	40.0	107th	0

Chad's average tariff rate is 14.9 percent. As with other members of the Central African Economic and Monetary Community, it may take weeks to import cargo. There are few formal barriers to foreign investment, but state-owned enterprises operate in several sectors of the economy. Poor access to credit hinders private-sector growth. The banking system remains highly dependent on the government and state-owned companies.

Long-Term Score Change (since 1997)

RULE OF LAW		GOVERNMENT SIZE		REGULATORY EFFICIENCY		OPEN MARKETS	
Property Rights	-10.0	Fiscal Freedom	0	Business Freedom	-30.1	Trade Freedom	+1.8
Freedom from Corruption	+5.9	Government Spending	-9.1	Labor Freedom	0	Investment Freedom	+20.0
				Monetary Freedom	+7.4	Financial Freedom	+10.0

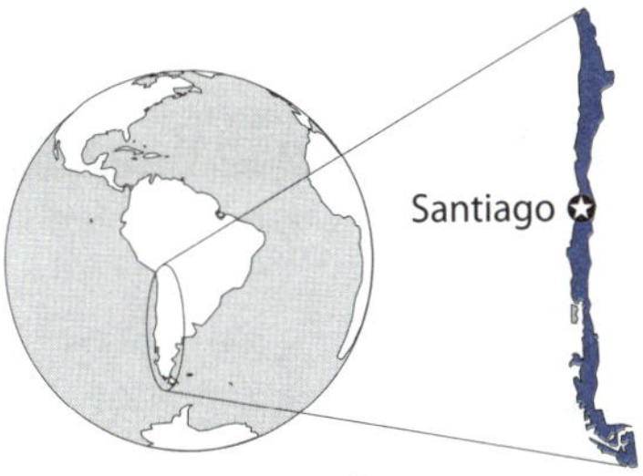

CHILE

Economic Freedom Score

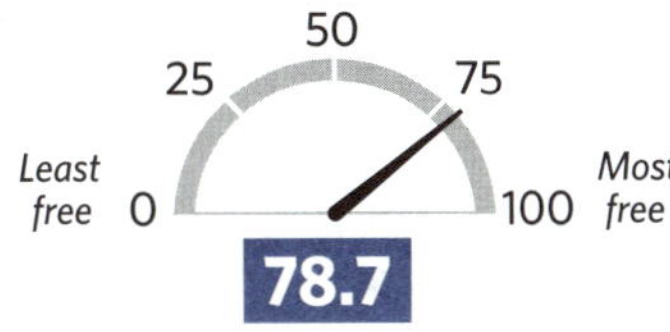

Freedom Trend

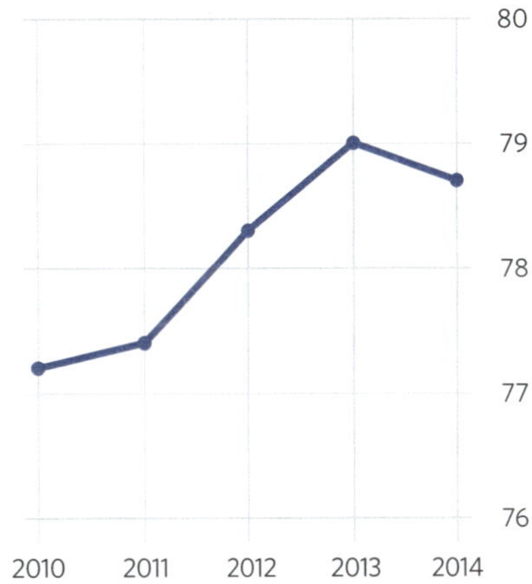

Country Comparisons

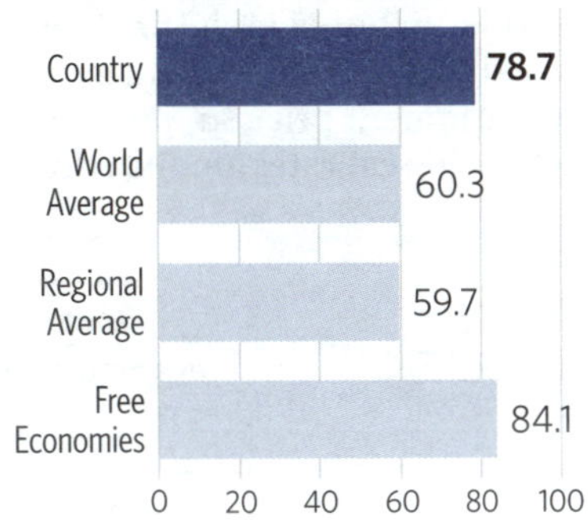

Chile's economic freedom score is 78.7, making its economy the 7th freest in the 2014 *Index*. Its overall score is slightly lower than last year, with an improvement in investment freedom offset by combined declines in labor freedom, business freedom, and fiscal freedom. Continuing as one of the 10 freest economies in the *Index*, Chile enjoys the highest degree of economic freedom in the South and Central America/Caribbean region.

Over the 20-year history of the *Index*, Chile has been consistently rated one of the "mostly free" economies, achieving economic freedom scores above 70. Three of the country's 10 economic freedoms—freedom from corruption, investment freedom, and financial freedom—have recorded score gains of 20 points or more since 1995. Sustaining Chile's high level of regulatory efficiency and market openness, monetary freedom and trade freedom have notably improved as well.

As a global leader in economic freedom, Chile continues to uphold principles of limited government through prudent public finance management that has kept public debt and budget deficits under control. The country's active participation in the ongoing Trans-Pacific Partnership negotiations reflects its steady commitment to trade and investment liberalization.

BACKGROUND: From 1990 to 2009, left-of-center governments largely maintained the market-based institutions and economic policies established under the 17-year rule of General Augusto Pinochet. However, under the center-right Alianza coalition, which took power in 2010, President Sebastian Piñera has raised corporate taxes and personally intervened to stop the construction of a coal-fired electric plant that had cleared all regulatory hurdles. None of that has satisfied the left, and large street protests have become an ongoing problem for the government. Despite Piñera's clumsy political leadership, Chile still has the region's best reputation among foreign investors. It is the first South American country to join the Organisation for Economic Co-operation and Development. Chile is the world's leading producer of copper. The economy is very open to imports but is also an export powerhouse in minerals, wood, fruit, seafood, and wine.

How Do We Measure Economic Freedom?
See page 471 for an explanation of the methodology or visit the *Index* Web site at *heritage.org/index*.

Quick Facts

Population: 17.4 million
GDP (PPP): $320.5 billion
5.5% growth in 2012
5-year compound annual growth 3.8%
$18,419 per capita
Unemployment: 6.5%
Inflation (CPI): 3.0%
FDI Inflow: $30.3 billion
Public Debt: 11.2% of GDP

2012 data unless otherwise noted.
Data compiled as of September 2013.

CHILE (continued)

THE TEN ECONOMIC FREEDOMS

Legend: Country | World Average

RULE OF LAW

	Score	Rank	1-Year Change
Property Rights	90.0	2nd	0
Freedom from Corruption	72.3	22nd	+0.3

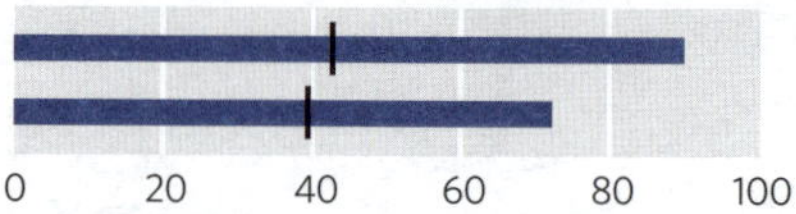

The constitution provides for an independent judiciary, and the courts are generally free from political interference. In the past decade, the Chilean Congress passed significant anti-corruption, transparency, and campaign-finance laws that contributed to Chile's reputation for good governance. Property rights are strongly respected, and expropriation is rare. Crime rates have declined significantly in the period from 2009 to 2013.

GOVERNMENT SIZE

	Score	Rank	1-Year Change
Fiscal Freedom	76.5	113th	-1.1
Government Spending	83.8	37th	+0.1

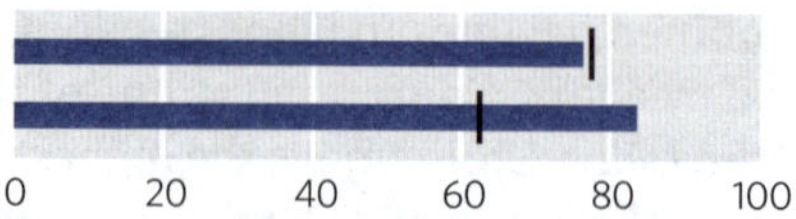

Chile's top individual income tax rate has been lowered to 40 percent, and the corporate tax rate has risen to 20 percent to cover new education spending. Other taxes include a value-added tax (VAT) and a property tax. Overall tax revenue amounts to 18.7 percent of GDP. Falling commodity prices could tighten revenue, but government expenditure has been stable at 23.2 percent of GDP. Public debt is about 11 percent of the domestic economy.

REGULATORY EFFICIENCY

	Score	Rank	1-Year Change
Business Freedom	69.3	81st	-1.2
Labor Freedom	69.3	67th	-4.9
Monetary Freedom	84.1	7th	-0.5

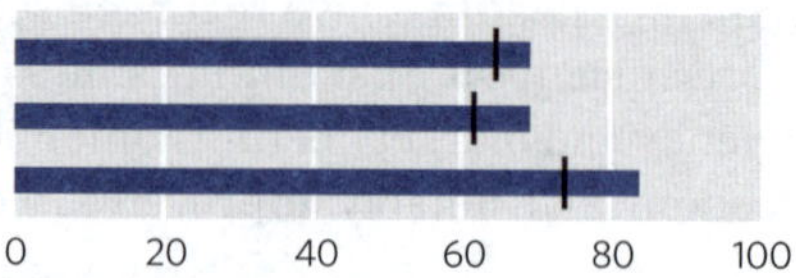

Incorporating a business takes less than 10 procedures, with no paid-in minimum capital required, but completing licensing requirements remains time-consuming and somewhat costly. Minimum wage increases have exceeded overall productivity growth in recent years. Government price supports for agriculture are less than 5 percent of total farm receipts, one of the lowest rates among OECD countries.

OPEN MARKETS

	Score	Rank	1-Year Change
Trade Freedom	82.0	64th	0
Investment Freedom	90.0	2nd	+5.0
Financial Freedom	70.0	19th	0

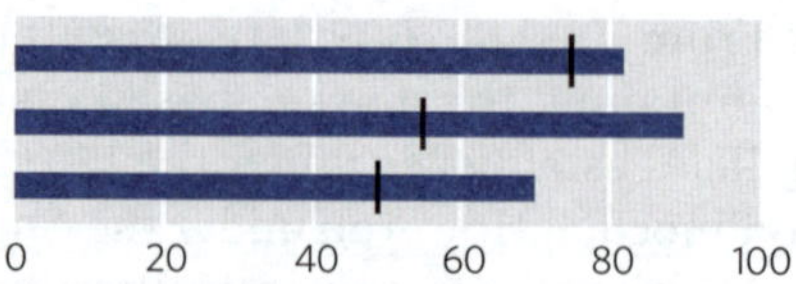

Chile has a 4 percent average tariff rate. It recently joined the Pacific Alliance, which, if counted as a single country, would be the world's ninth-largest economy. Foreign investment is welcomed. The dynamic financial system facilitates high levels of bank usage and provides relatively efficient access to financing. Reforms to improve capital market liquidity and enhance access to financial services for small companies have progressed gradually.

Long-Term Score Change (since 1995)

RULE OF LAW		GOVERNMENT SIZE		REGULATORY EFFICIENCY		OPEN MARKETS	
Property Rights	0	Fiscal Freedom	-2.9	Business Freedom	-15.7	Trade Freedom	+19.0
Freedom from Corruption	+22.3	Government Spending	-3.2	Labor Freedom	-8.0	Investment Freedom	+20.0
				Monetary Freedom	+18.0	Financial Freedom	+20.0

CHINA

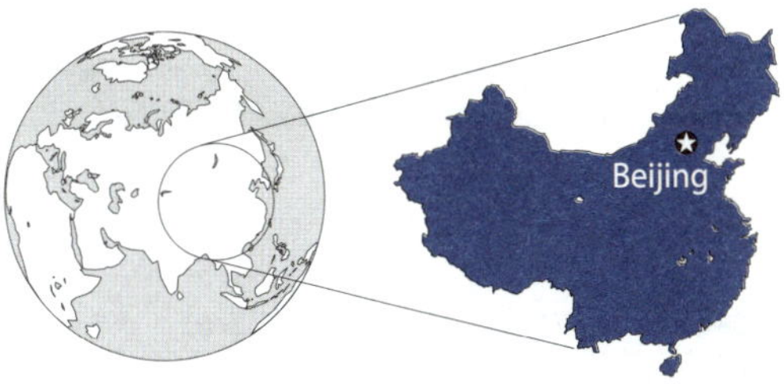

World Rank: **137** Regional Rank: **29**

Economic Freedom Score

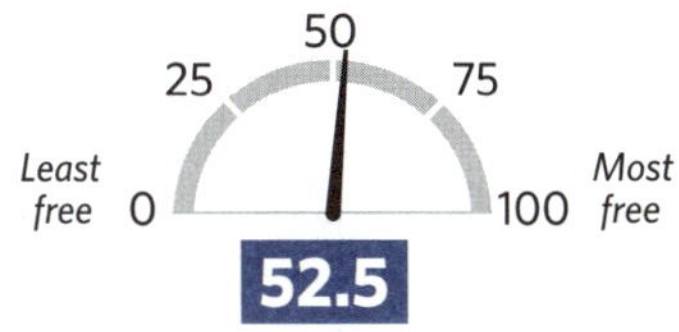

Freedom Trend

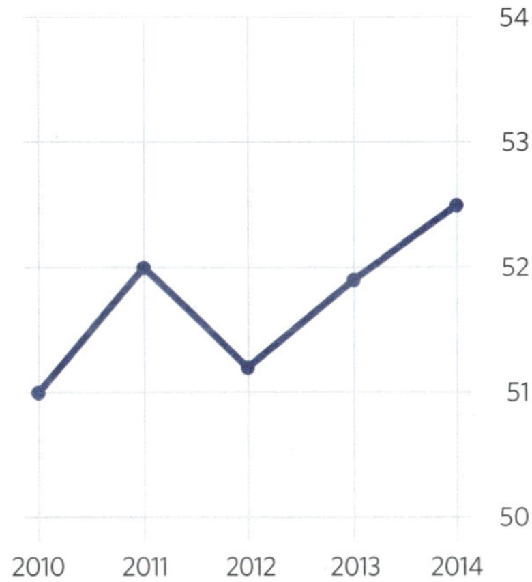

Country Comparisons

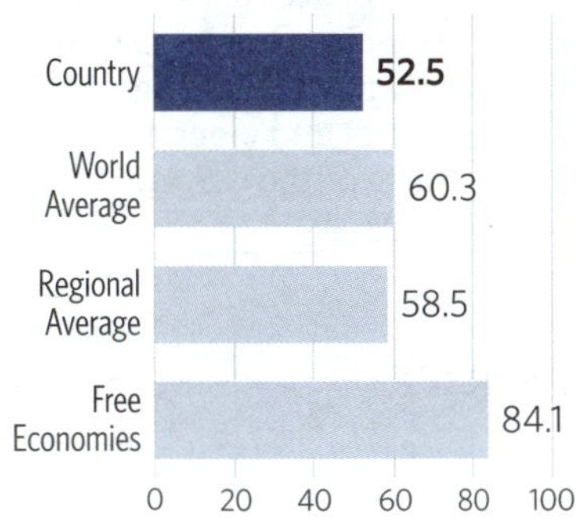

China's economic freedom score is 52.5, making its economy the 137th freest in the 2014 *Index*. Its overall score is 0.6 point higher than last year, with modest improvements in investment freedom, business freedom, and monetary freedom outweighing declines in freedom from corruption, labor freedom, and the management of government spending. China is ranked 29th out of 42 countries in the Asia–Pacific region, and its overall score continues to be lower than the global and regional averages.

Over the 20-year history of the *Index*, China's economic freedom has been almost unchanged, stuck near the lower boundary of the "mostly unfree" category. However, the overall stagnation masks major changes in certain categories of economic freedom: Trade freedom has improved by over 50 points, while scores for investment freedom, financial freedom, property rights, and the control of government spending have all suffered double-digit declines. Although the boost in trade freedom has undoubtedly helped spur China's high overall growth rates, the deterioration in other categories indicates that major economic reforms are still needed to create a more balanced and sustainable economy.

The lack of political will to undertake more fundamental restructuring of the economy has led to continued overreliance on public investment. The Communist Party's ultimate authority throughout the economic system undermines the rule of law, and institutionalized cronyism remains pervasive.

BACKGROUND: China's Communist Party maintains tight control of speech, religion, and assembly. There is some hope for economic reform from the new government led by Communist Party General Secretary Xi Jinping, but meaningful political reform is highly unlikely. Environmental degradation and an aging society fuel popular discontent. China liberalized parts of its economy starting in the late 1970s and again in the early 1990s and achieved impressive GDP growth in part through greater integration into the world trading and financial systems. The size of its industrial and manufacturing sector now rivals that of the United States, though China lags far behind in other areas.

How Do We Measure Economic Freedom?
See page 471 for an explanation of the methodology or visit the *Index* Web site at *heritage.org/index*.

Quick Facts

Population: 1,354.0 million
GDP (PPP): $12.4 trillion
7.8% growth in 2012
5-year compound annual growth 9.3%
$9,162 per capita
Unemployment: 4.1%
Inflation (CPI): 2.7%
FDI Inflow: $121.1 billion
Public Debt: 22.8% of GDP

2012 data unless otherwise noted.
Data compiled as of September 2013.

THE TEN ECONOMIC FREEDOMS

RULE OF LAW

	Score	Rank	1-Year Change
Property Rights	20.0	139th	0
Freedom from Corruption	35.0	77th	-1.0

Many anti-corruption whistleblowers face physical violence or intimidation from those they expose and enjoy little protection from the police or the internal disciplinary investigators of the ruling Chinese Communist Party. Various forms of corruption severely affect banking, finance, government procurement, and construction. China's weak judicial system is highly vulnerable to political influence and corruption. All land is state-owned.

GOVERNMENT SIZE

	Score	Rank	1-Year Change
Fiscal Freedom	69.9	136th	-0.3
Government Spending	82.9	42nd	-0.4

The top individual income tax rate is 45 percent, and the top corporate tax rate is 25 percent. Other taxes include a value-added tax (VAT) and a real estate tax. The overall tax burden is 19 percent of GDP. Total government expenditures account for 24 percent of GDP, and reported public debt is 23 percent of gross domestic output. The new government has responded to a slowing economy with temporary small-business tax cuts and stimulus spending.

REGULATORY EFFICIENCY

	Score	Rank	1-Year Change
Business Freedom	49.7	153rd	+1.7
Labor Freedom	61.9	91st	-0.7
Monetary Freedom	73.3	120th	+1.7

It takes 13 procedures and over a month to launch a business. Completing licensing requirements remains time-consuming and costs over three times the level of average annual income. Relatively rigid labor regulations still hinder overall employment growth. The state provides massive fuel and electricity subsidies; agricultural subsidies (estimated at $160 billion) are twice those of the U.S. and the EU combined.

OPEN MARKETS

	Score	Rank	1-Year Change
Trade Freedom	71.8	121st	-0.2
Investment Freedom	30.0	152nd	+5.0
Financial Freedom	30.0	132nd	0

China's average tariff rate is 4.1 percent. The prevalence of state-owned enterprises and government subsidies continues to distort the economy. The state continues its tight control of the financial system as its primary means for managing the rest of the economy. The government owns all large financial institutions, which lend according to state priorities and directives and favor large state enterprises.

Long-Term Score Change (since 1995)

RULE OF LAW		GOVERNMENT SIZE		REGULATORY EFFICIENCY		OPEN MARKETS	
Property Rights	**-10.0**	Fiscal Freedom	**-0.7**	Business Freedom	**-5.3**	Trade Freedom	**+51.8**
Freedom from Corruption	**+5.0**	Government Spending	**-10.8**	Labor Freedom	**-3.1**	Investment Freedom	**-20.0**
				Monetary Freedom	**+5.0**	Financial Freedom	**-20.0**

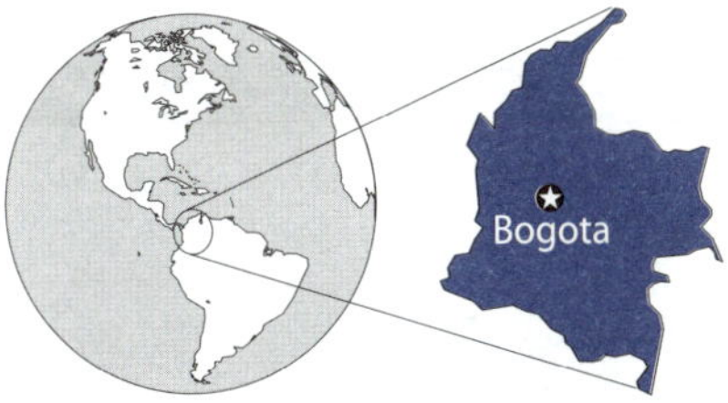

COLOMBIA

World Rank: **34** Regional Rank: **3**

Economic Freedom Score

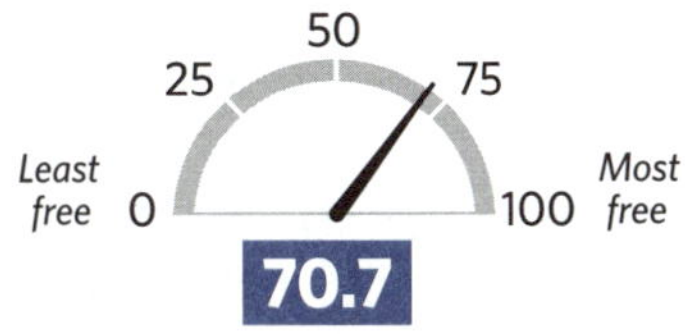

Freedom Trend

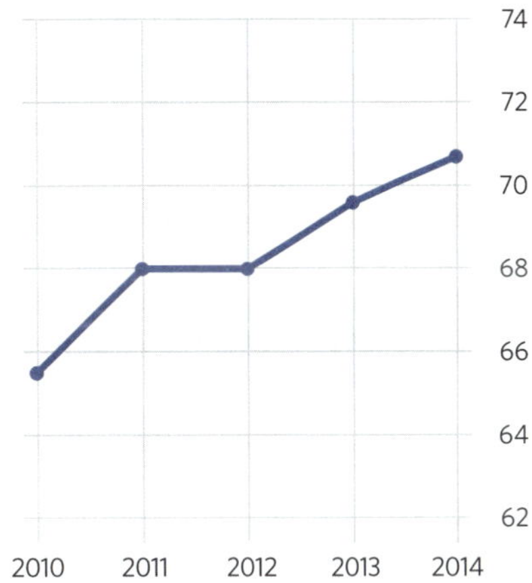

Country Comparisons

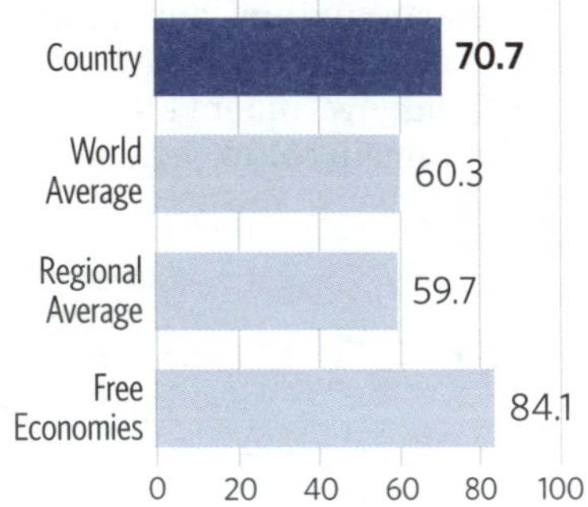

Quick Facts

Population: 46.6 million
GDP (PPP): $502.9 billion
4.0% growth in 2012
5-year compound annual growth 4.0%
$10,792 per capita
Unemployment: 10.4%
Inflation (CPI): 3.2%
FDI Inflow: $15.8 billion
Public Debt: 32.8% of GDP

2012 data unless otherwise noted.
Data compiled as of September 2013.

Colombia's economic freedom score is 70.7, making its economy the 34th freest in the 2014 *Index*. Its overall score is 1.1 points higher than last year, reflecting improvements in trade freedom, investment freedom, and fiscal freedom. Colombia has advanced to 3rd out of 29 countries in the South and Central America/Caribbean region.

Over the 20-year history of the *Index*, Colombia has improved its economic freedom score by 6.2 points. Score increases have been achieved in seven of the 10 economic freedoms, notably trade freedom, monetary freedom, labor freedom, and freedom from corruption, the scores for which have improved by over 10 points. Achieving its highest economic freedom score ever in the 2014 *Index*, Colombia has become a "mostly free" economy for the first time.

Recent reforms have put greater emphasis on improving regulatory efficiency and enhancing financial-sector competitiveness. More important, continued reform efforts are needed to solidify the foundations of economic freedom and ensure vibrant economic development. The judicial system remains inefficient and vulnerable to political interference, and corruption, perceived as widespread, remains a cause for concern.

BACKGROUND: The "democratic security" policy pursued by former President Alvaro Uribe (2002–2010) significantly reduced crime and violence and increased government control of national territory. Uribe also helped to re-establish business confidence. Former Defense Minister Juan Manuel Santos, elected president in June 2010, has engaged in controversial peace talks with the rebel group FARC. He has also emphasized global economic integration. The U.S.–Colombia Free Trade Agreement entered into force in May 2012 and has encouraged job creation and investment. Colombia has pursued free trade agreements with dozens of other nations and is one of four members in the Pacific Alliance. Colombia's economy depends heavily on exports of petroleum, coffee, and cut flowers and is positioned to surpass Argentina as South America's second-largest economy. Poverty has been reduced thanks to robust economic growth.

How Do We Measure Economic Freedom?
See page 471 for an explanation of the methodology or visit the *Index* Web site at *heritage.org/index*.

THE TEN ECONOMIC FREEDOMS

Score — Country | World Average — Rank — 1-Year Change

RULE OF LAW

	Score	Rank	1-Year Change
Property Rights	50.0	53rd	0
Freedom from Corruption	33.2	89th	-0.8

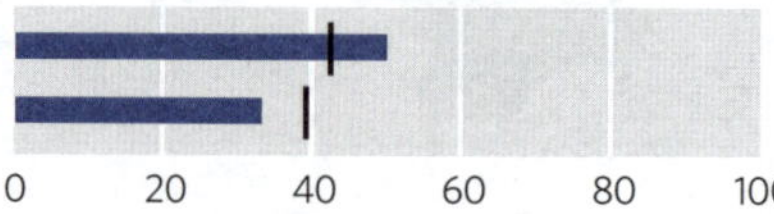

Corruption scandals have emerged in recent years in many government agencies. In 2012, a decade-long scheme to embezzle more than $2 billion from the national health system was uncovered. Despite improvements in fighting corruption and narcotics trafficking, concerns remain over criminal influence on the police, the military, and lower levels of the judiciary and civil service. Property rights are generally respected.

GOVERNMENT SIZE

	Score	Rank	1-Year Change
Fiscal Freedom	80.6	79th	+4.5
Government Spending	74.9	70th	-0.3

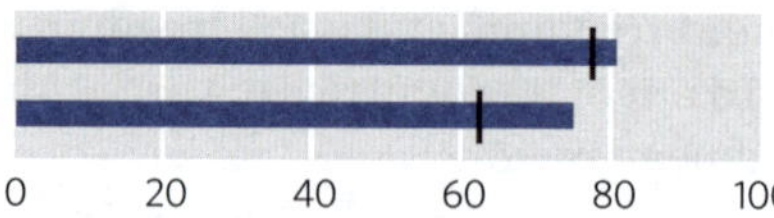

The top individual income tax rate has risen to 33 percent, and the top corporate tax rate has been cut to 25 percent. Other taxes include a value-added tax (VAT) and a financial transactions tax. Overall tax revenue is 15.1 percent of GDP, and government spending is 29 percent of the domestic economy. Public debt remains at around 33 percent of GDP.

REGULATORY EFFICIENCY

	Score	Rank	1-Year Change
Business Freedom	85.2	23rd	-5.0
Labor Freedom	80.5	25th	+1.2
Monetary Freedom	78.8	53rd	+0.1

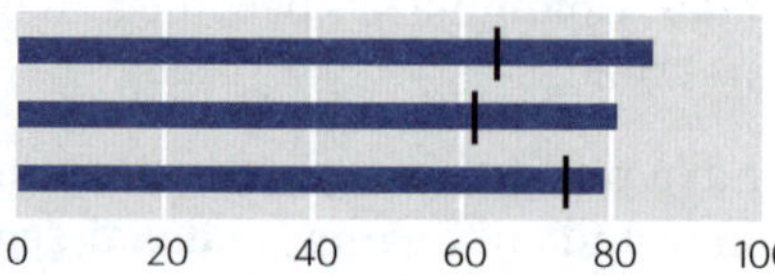

Colombia has few regulatory bottlenecks. It takes less than 10 procedures to start a business, with no minimum capital required. Bankruptcy procedures are relatively streamlined. The non-salary cost of hiring is moderate, but the informal labor market remains sizable. In April 2013, the government increased subsidies to coffee farmers, although levels of other state subsidies remain below regional averages.

OPEN MARKETS

	Score	Rank	1-Year Change
Trade Freedom	78.8	76th	+6.6
Investment Freedom	75.0	35th	+5.0
Financial Freedom	70.0	19th	0

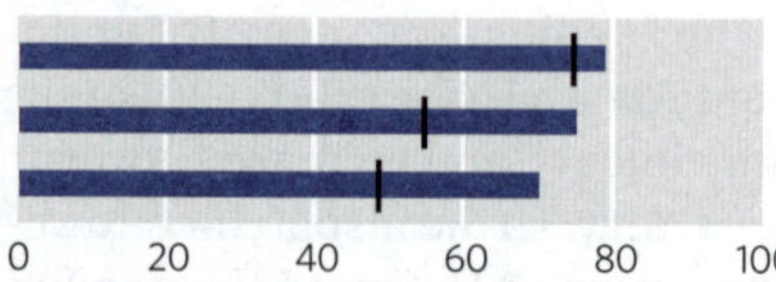

Colombia's average tariff rate is 5.6 percent. It recently joined the Pacific Alliance, which, if counted as a single country, would be the world's ninth-largest economy. Colombia welcomes foreign investment and has resisted calls to implement capital controls. The financial sector remains resilient. Reforms continue to promote the development of capital markets by enhancing flexibility and competition in the market.

Long-Term Score Change (since 1995)

RULE OF LAW		GOVERNMENT SIZE		REGULATORY EFFICIENCY		OPEN MARKETS	
Property Rights	0	Fiscal Freedom	+0.1	Business Freedom	+0.2	Trade Freedom	+13.8
Freedom from Corruption	+23.2	Government Spending	-11.1	Labor Freedom	+17.7	Investment Freedom	+5.0
				Monetary Freedom	+15.0	Financial Freedom	0

COMOROS

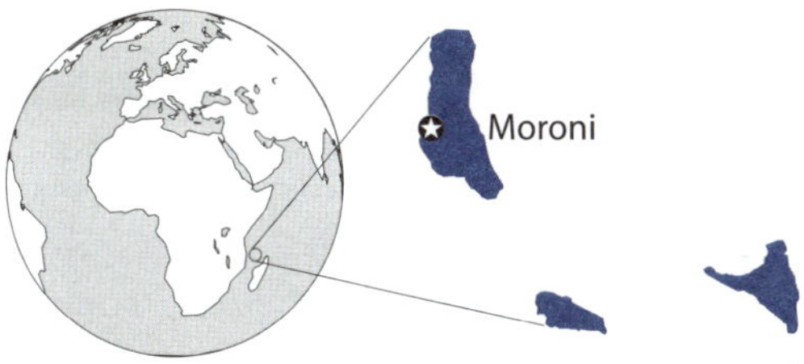

World Rank: **142** Regional Rank: **32**

Economic Freedom Score

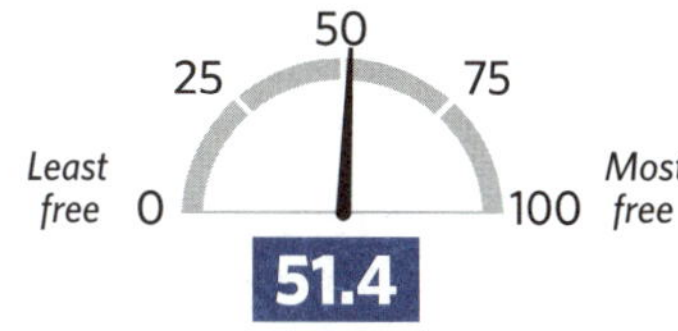

Comoros's economic freedom score is 51.4, making its economy the 142nd freest in the 2013 *Index*. Its overall score is 3.9 points higher than last year due to noteworthy advancements in investment freedom, financial freedom, trade freedom, and business freedom. Comoros is ranked 32nd out of 46 countries in the Sub-Saharan Africa region, and its overall score is lower than the regional average.

Since its economic freedom was first assessed in the 2009 *Index*, Comoros has advanced its overall economic freedom score by 8 points, with particularly notable gains in the area of market openness measured through trade freedom, investment freedom, and financial freedom. Comoros has achieved its highest economic freedom score ever in the 2014 *Index* and has moved out of the ranks of the economically "repressed."

Despite significant progress, Comoros continues to lag in promoting the effective rule of law. The judicial system remains vulnerable to political interference, and property rights are not strongly protected. Lingering corruption further undermines freedom and hampers the emergence of more vibrant economic activity.

BACKGROUND: The three-island Union of the Comoros has endured more than 20 coups d'états since independence in 1975. Under a 2001 constitution granting each island increased autonomy, the presidency rotates among the three islands every four years, and the transfer of power to Ikililou Dhoinine in 2010 was peaceful. The International Monetary Fund and World Bank gave Comoros $176 million in debt relief in 2012. Remittances are an important source of income. Fishing, agriculture, and forestry employ approximately 80 percent of the workforce and provide over 40 percent of GDP. Only about 10 percent of the economy is industrialized. Comoros is a leading producer of ylang-ylang, cloves, and vanilla.

Freedom Trend

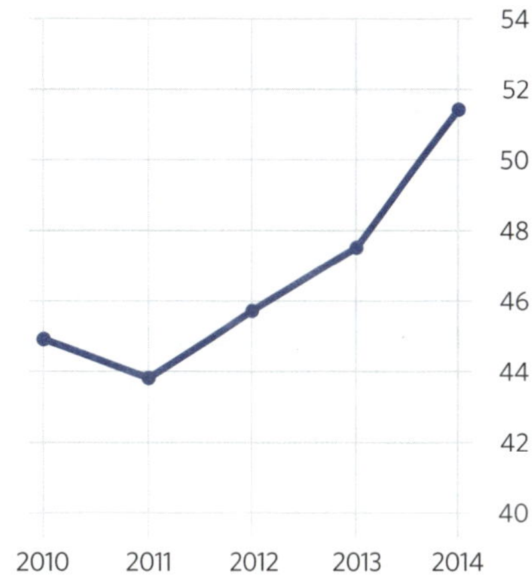

Country Comparisons

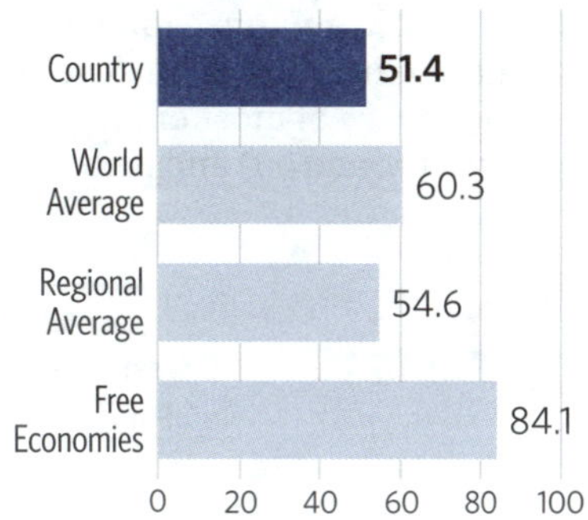

Quick Facts

Population: 0.7 million
GDP (PPP): $0.9 billion
2.5% growth in 2012
5-year compound annual growth 1.9%
$1,258 per capita
Unemployment: n/a
Inflation (CPI): 6.0%
FDI Inflow: $17.0 million
Public Debt: 42.6% of GDP

2012 data unless otherwise noted.
Data compiled as of September 2013.

How Do We Measure Economic Freedom?
See page 471 for an explanation of the methodology or visit the *Index* Web site at *heritage.org/index.*

THE TEN ECONOMIC FREEDOMS

RULE OF LAW

	Score	Rank	1-Year Change
Property Rights	30.0	93rd	0
Freedom from Corruption	22.1	149th	-1.9

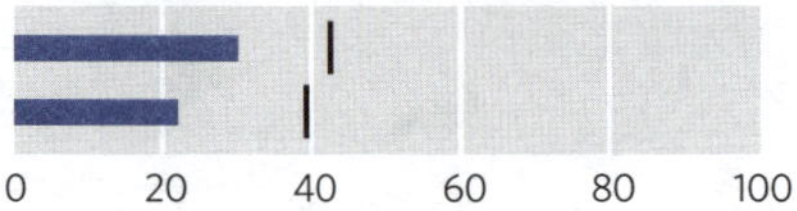

Corruption remains a major problem, affecting all levels of the government, judiciary, and civil service, as well as the police and security forces. In 2013, protestors on the island of Mohéli denounced bad governance, misuse of public funds, and unfair procurement practices. The judicial system is ineffective, contracts are weakly enforced, and courts are relatively inexperienced in commercial litigation.

GOVERNMENT SIZE

	Score	Rank	1-Year Change
Fiscal Freedom	64.5	159th	-0.2
Government Spending	85.3	32nd	+2.9

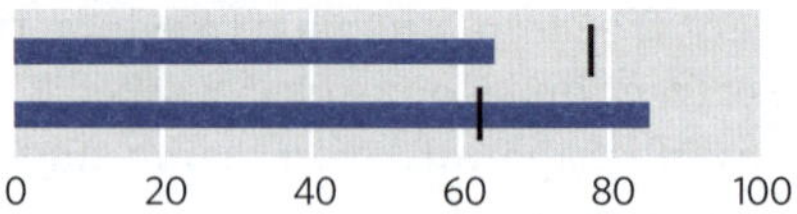

The individual income tax rate is 30 percent, and the corporate tax rate is 50 percent. Other taxes include a value-added tax (VAT) and an insurance tax. The overall tax burden is 12.4 percent of GDP. Government spending is equivalent to 22.1 percent of the domestic economy. Public debt has declined to below 45 percent of GDP as the government completes its debt reduction under the Heavily Indebted Poor Countries Initiative.

REGULATORY EFFICIENCY

	Score	Rank	1-Year Change
Business Freedom	49.4	154th	+4.7
Labor Freedom	50.1	136th	-1.1
Monetary Freedom	74.5	110th	-0.1

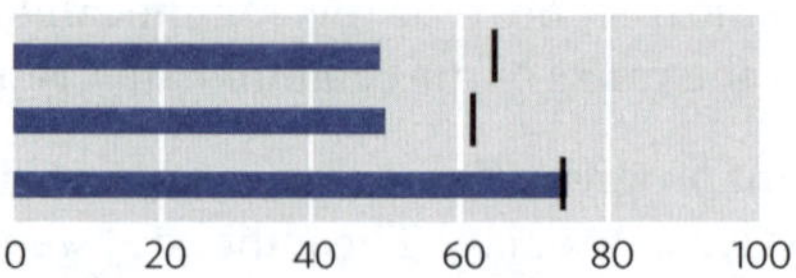

Despite some progress, the regulatory environment still imposes significant burdens on entrepreneurs. Minimum capital requirements to launch a company exceed twice the average level of annual income. With development of a modern labor market lagging, the informal sector is the source of most employment. The government subsidizes state-owned utilities (water, electricity, and oil) and controls other prices.

OPEN MARKETS

	Score	Rank	1-Year Change
Trade Freedom	72.7	116th	+3.9
Investment Freedom	35.0	142nd	+20.0
Financial Freedom	30.0	132nd	+10.0

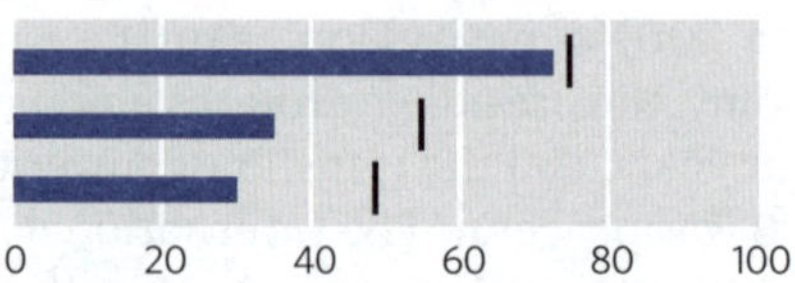

Comoros has an average tariff rate of 6.2 percent. Historically, foreign investors have found the environment challenging, although the government does allow them to repatriate profits freely. The financial system remains underdeveloped, but the banking sector has recorded modest expansion. Non-performing loans have declined steadily in recent years. Privatization of the Development Bank of the Comoros has progressed.

Long-Term Score Change (since 2009)

RULE OF LAW		GOVERNMENT SIZE		REGULATORY EFFICIENCY		OPEN MARKETS	
Property Rights	**0**	Fiscal Freedom	**-0.1**	Business Freedom	**+2.9**	Trade Freedom	**+45.5**
Freedom from Corruption	**-3.9**	Government Spending	**-2.8**	Labor Freedom	**+18.3**	Investment Freedom	**+15.0**
				Monetary Freedom	**-4.4**	Financial Freedom	**+10.0**

DEMOCRATIC REPUBLIC OF CONGO

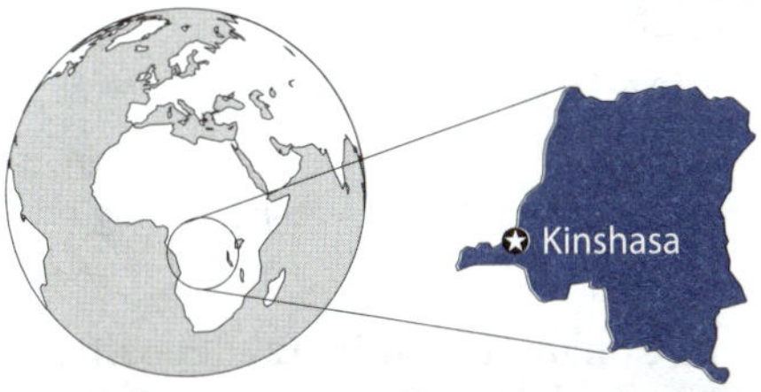

World Rank: 172 **Regional Rank: 44**

Economic Freedom Score

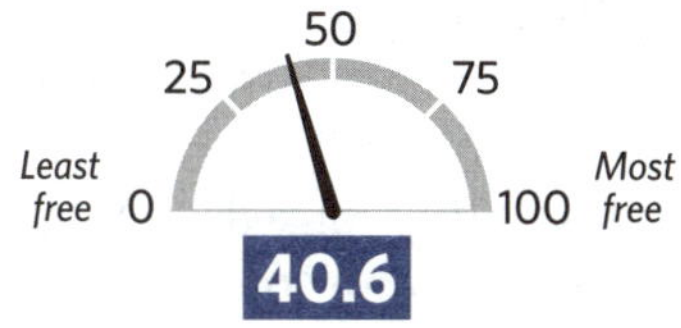

Freedom Trend

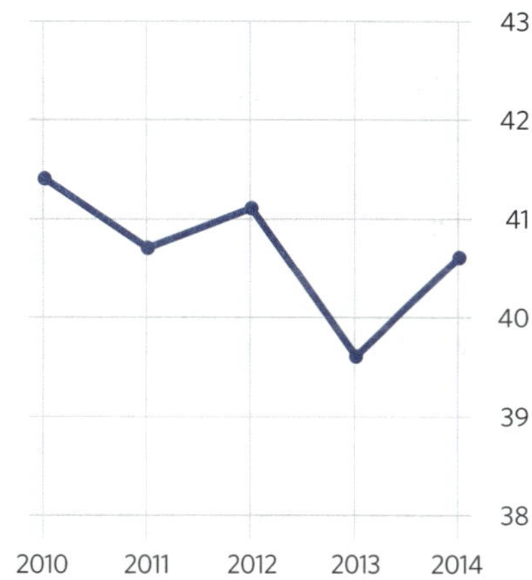

Country Comparisons

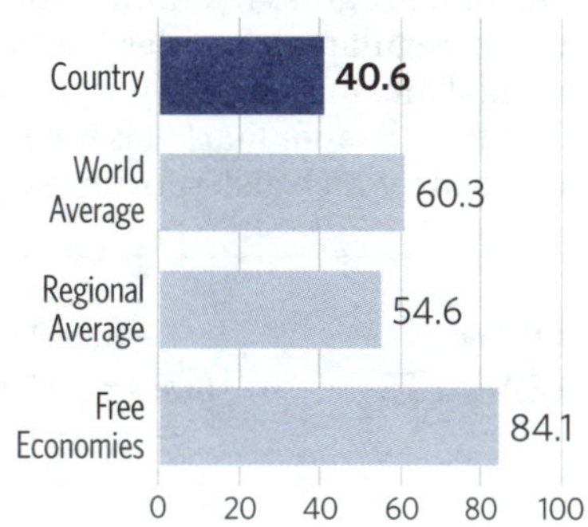

The Democratic Republic of Congo (DRC) has an economic freedom score of 40.6, making it the 172nd freest economy in the 2014 *Index*. Its overall score is 1 point better than last year, with improved scores for government spending, monetary freedom, and labor freedom partially offset by a decline in business freedom. The DRC is ranked 44th out of 46 countries in the Sub-Saharan Africa region, and its score is far below the regional average.

Over the 20-year history of the *Index*, the DRC's economic freedom score has declined by 0.8 point. Significant declines have occurred in five of the 10 economic freedoms, notably property rights and business freedom, the scores for which have deteriorated by 25 points or more. Bright spots include a significant improvement in monetary stability and a modest increase in trade freedom. Grading of the country was temporarily suspended from 2001 to 2008 due to internal conflicts.

Political risk continues to be high, severely undermining prospects for diversified growth and trapping a majority of the population in poverty. The slow pace of reform, coupled with ongoing political instability, has left the capacity of public institutions inadequate to support private-sector development and long-term economic expansion.

BACKGROUND: In 2006, Joseph Kabila won the first multiparty election in 40 years. He was re-elected in December 2011 in a flawed and violent election. Rebel groups that include the Lord's Resistance Army, M23, and the Democratic Forces for the Liberation of Rwanda remain active in the northeastern region. In February 2013, 11 neighboring countries signed a U.N.-backed accord aimed at stabilizing the country. The DRC's immense natural resources, including copper, cobalt, and diamonds, have fueled conflict, forcing foreign businesses to limit their operations. Corruption and costly policy errors discourage participation in the formal sector. The DRC has had positive economic expansion for 10 straight years, but an uncertain legal framework, corruption, and a lack of policy transparency remain serious problems.

How Do We Measure Economic Freedom?
See page 471 for an explanation of the methodology or visit the *Index* Web site at *heritage.org/index*.

Quick Facts

Population: 74.7 million
GDP (PPP): $27.6 billion
7.1% growth in 2012
5-year compound annual growth 6.0%
$369 per capita
Unemployment: n/a
Inflation (CPI): 9.3%
FDI Inflow: $3.3 billion
Public Debt: 36.0% of GDP

2012 data unless otherwise noted.
Data compiled as of September 2013.

THE TEN ECONOMIC FREEDOMS

RULE OF LAW

	Score	Rank	1-Year Change
Property Rights	10.0	166th	0
Freedom from Corruption	17.6	171st	-2.4

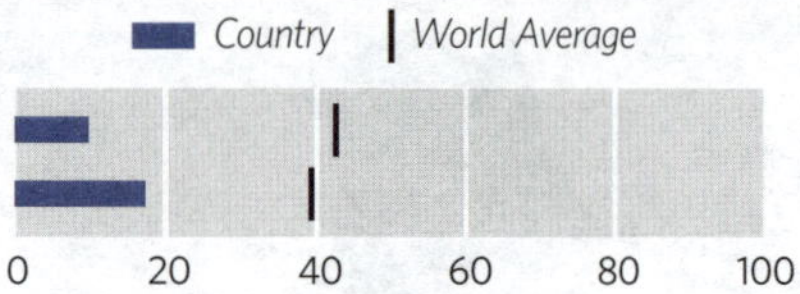

Instability caused by the ongoing fight for control of eastern Congo's rich mineral deposits, continuing entrenched corruption, and general mismanagement of government pose severe obstacles to the rule of law. Protection of property rights remains weak and dependent on a currently dysfunctional public administration and judicial system. Human rights abuses and banditry deter economic activity.

GOVERNMENT SIZE

	Score	Rank	1-Year Change
Fiscal Freedom	69.4	139th	-2.0
Government Spending	74.6	73rd	+14.5

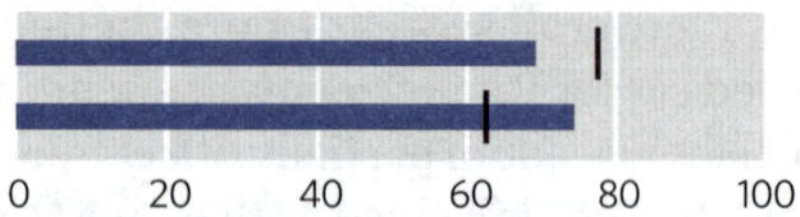

The top individual income tax rate is 30 percent, and the top corporate tax rate is 40 percent. Other taxes include a rental tax and a tax on vehicles. Overall tax revenue amounts to 23.6 percent of GDP. Total government expenditures equal 29 percent of gross domestic output. Debt levels remain relatively low at below 40 percent of GDP.

REGULATORY EFFICIENCY

	Score	Rank	1-Year Change
Business Freedom	30.0	178th	-8.7
Labor Freedom	38.5	171st	+2.2
Monetary Freedom	63.0	173rd	+6.5

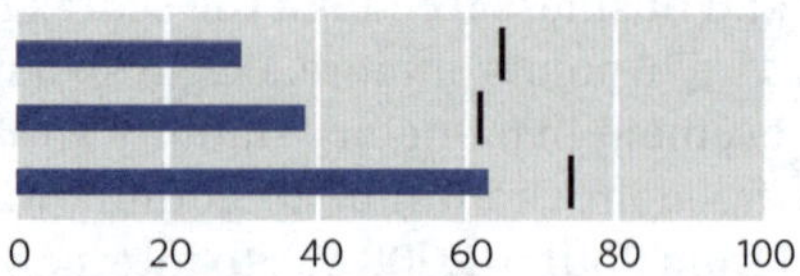

Despite progress in simplifying the business start-up process, private enterprises still face costly regulatory hurdles. Launching a company costs more than twice the level of average annual income, and the cost of completing licensing requirements is over 10 times that level. The formal labor market is not fully developed. Prices are controlled and regulated by the government, which also subsidizes electricity.

OPEN MARKETS

	Score	Rank	1-Year Change
Trade Freedom	63.0	150th	0
Investment Freedom	20.0	164th	0
Financial Freedom	20.0	163rd	0

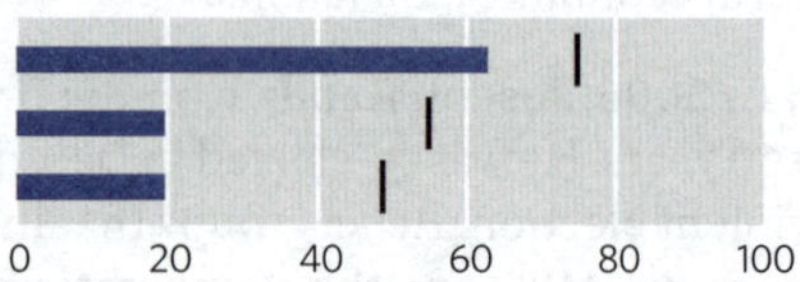

The Democratic Republic of Congo's average tariff rate is 11 percent. It can take several weeks to import goods. The legal and regulatory systems can be difficult for foreign investors to navigate. The financial sector remains limited in scope and depth, with only 2 percent of the population using banks and companies having very limited access to financial services. The majority of bank loans are for short terms only.

Long-Term Score Change (since 1995)

RULE OF LAW		GOVERNMENT SIZE		REGULATORY EFFICIENCY		OPEN MARKETS	
Property Rights	-40.0	Fiscal Freedom	+18.5	Business Freedom	-25.0	Trade Freedom	+14.0
Freedom from Corruption	+7.6	Government Spending	-22.6	Labor Freedom	+4.0	Investment Freedom	-10.0
				Monetary Freedom	+63.0	Financial Freedom	-10.0

REPUBLIC OF CONGO

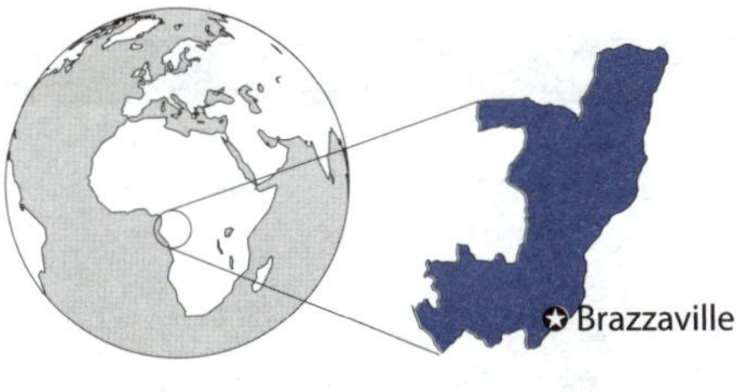

World Rank: **169** Regional Rank: **43**

Economic Freedom Score

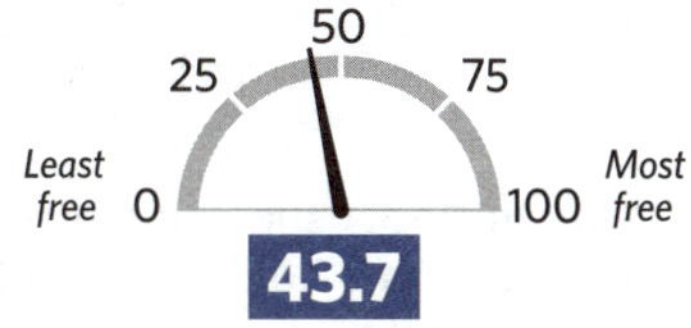

The Republic of Congo's economic freedom score is 43.7, making its economy the 169th freest in the 2014 *Index*. Its overall score is 0.2 point better than last year, with improvements in fiscal freedom, business freedom, and labor freedom offsetting declines in trade freedom, monetary freedom, and freedom from corruption. Congo is ranked 43rd out of 46 countries in the Sub-Saharan Africa region, and its overall score is much lower than the global and regional averages.

Over the 20-year history of the *Index*, the Republic of Congo has been rated a "repressed" economy. Its overall economic freedom score has improved by only 3.4 points during that period, with double-digit score gains in monetary freedom, the management of public finance, and freedom from corruption offset by declines in property rights, business freedom, and investment freedom.

The lack of progress in advancing economic freedom continues to trap many Congolese people in persistent poverty. Substantial challenges remain in the struggle to promote stable long-term economic development, and lingering institutional weaknesses call for much greater commitment to reform. Heavy state involvement in the leading economic sectors has dampened private-sector dynamism and led to uneven economic development.

BACKGROUND: Congo became independent in 1960. After seizing power in 1979, President Denis Sassou-Nguesso governed the country as a Marxist–Leninist state before moderating economic policy and allowing multi-party elections in 1992. He lost that election to Pascal Lissouba but seized power again following a 1997 civil war. He won a flawed election in 2002 and was re-elected in 2009. The 2003 and 2007 peace agreements with rebel groups curtailed unrest, but many rebels have turned to banditry and criminality. Congo is one of Africa's largest petroleum producers, but production is declining. Iron ore mines entering production in 2013 may add as much as $1 billion to annual government revenue. Industry contributes the most to GDP, but much of the population is engaged in subsistence agriculture.

How Do We Measure Economic Freedom?
See page 471 for an explanation of the methodology or visit the *Index* Web site at *heritage.org/index*.

Freedom Trend

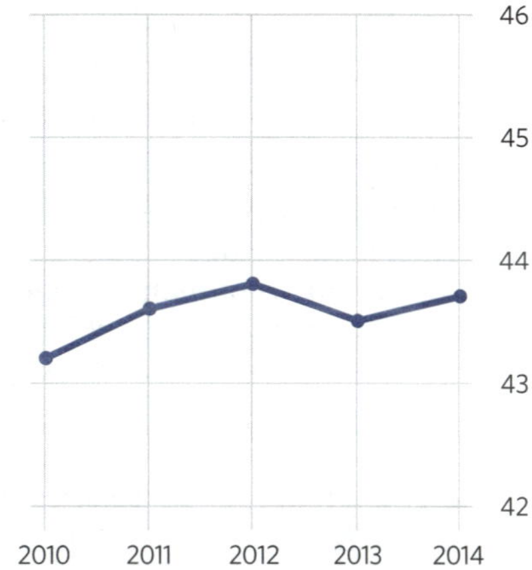

Country Comparisons

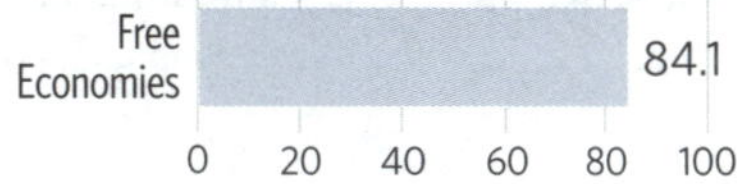

Quick Facts

Population: 4.1 million
GDP (PPP): $19.1 billion
3.8% growth in 2012
5-year compound annual growth 5.8%
$4,667 per capita
Unemployment: 53.0%
Inflation (CPI): 5.0%
FDI Inflow: $2.8 billion
Public Debt: 21.1% of GDP

2012 data unless otherwise noted.
Data compiled as of September 2013.

REPUBLIC OF CONGO (continued)

THE TEN ECONOMIC FREEDOMS

		Score	Rank	1-Year Change
RULE OF LAW	Property Rights	10.0	166th	0
	Freedom from Corruption	20.6	156th	-1.4

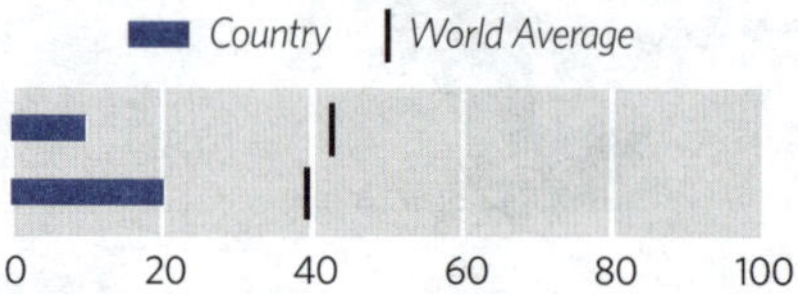

Corruption, especially in the extractive industries, remains pervasive and strengthens the ruling party's hold on the political system. The government will not release oil revenue data, and the state oil company is directly controlled by the president's family and advisers. Congo's underfunded judiciary is crippled by institutional weakness and a lack of technical capability. Contracts are not enforced reliably.

		Score	Rank	1-Year Change
GOVERNMENT SIZE	Fiscal Freedom	67.5	149th	+6.1
	Government Spending	79.6	55th	-0.7

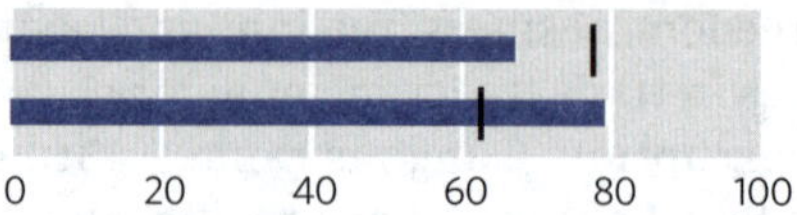

The top individual income tax rate is 45 percent, and the top corporate tax rate is 34 percent. Other taxes include a value-added tax (VAT), a tax on rental values, and an apprenticeship tax. The overall tax burden is equal to 8.4 percent of gross domestic output. Government spending is 26.1 percent of GDP. Public debt amounts to just below a quarter of the domestic economy. Rebels continue to undermine tax collection and government functions.

		Score	Rank	1-Year Change
REGULATORY EFFICIENCY	Business Freedom	35.1	174th	+3.6
	Labor Freedom	47.0	150th	+2.2
	Monetary Freedom	72.0	132nd	-2.3

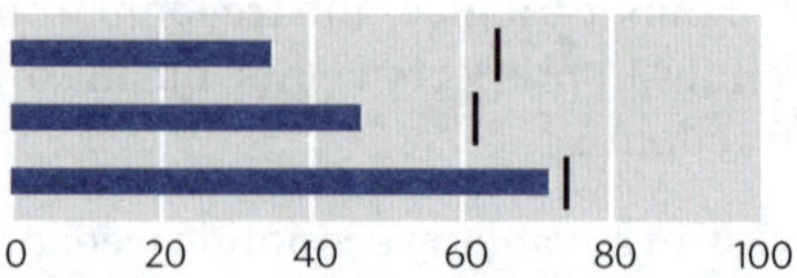

It takes over 150 days to incorporate a company, and the cost of completing licensing requirements exceeds 10 times the level of average annual income. Informal labor activity is widespread, and outmoded employment regulations hinder the development of a modern labor market. The prices of a range of goods and services are affected by government ownership and subsidization of the large public sector.

		Score	Rank	1-Year Change
OPEN MARKETS	Trade Freedom	55.6	166th	-5.1
	Investment Freedom	20.0	164th	0
	Financial Freedom	30.0	132nd	0

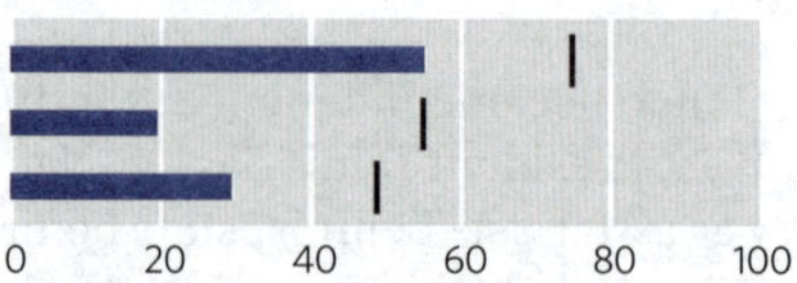

The average tariff rate for the Republic of Congo is 14.7 percent. As with other members of the Central African Economic and Monetary Community, it may take weeks to import cargo. Foreign investment requires government approval. The underdeveloped financial system remains dominated by banks. Despite the increase in the number of banks, financial intermediation is low.

Long-Term Score Change (since 1996)

RULE OF LAW		GOVERNMENT SIZE		REGULATORY EFFICIENCY		OPEN MARKETS	
Property Rights	**-20.0**	Fiscal Freedom	**+17.9**	Business Freedom	**-19.9**	Trade Freedom	**+3.2**
Freedom from Corruption	**+10.6**	Government Spending	**+24.8**	Labor Freedom	**+3.1**	Investment Freedom	**-10.0**
				Monetary Freedom	**+21.1**	Financial Freedom	**0**

COSTA RICA

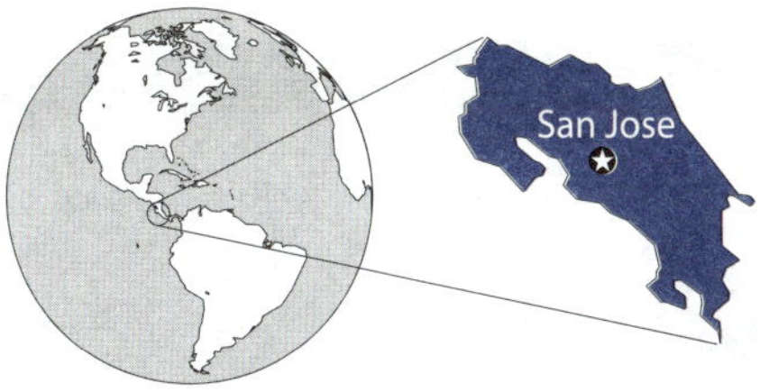

World Rank: **53** Regional Rank: **9**

Economic Freedom Score

Costa Rica's economic freedom score is 66.9, making its economy the 53rd freest in the 2014 *Index*. Its overall score remains virtually unchanged from last year, with improvements in freedom from corruption, business freedom, and momentary freedom offset by the erosion of labor freedom, fiscal freedom, and trade freedom. Costa Rica is ranked 9th out of 29 countries in the South and Central America/Caribbean region, and its overall score is higher than the global and regional averages.

Over the 20-year history of the *Index*, Costa Rica has been consistently rated a "moderately free" economy. Improvements in three of the country's 10 economic freedoms, including trade freedom and monetary freedom, have been offset by deteriorations in labor freedom, business freedom, and fiscal freedom, and its overall score has declined over the 20-year period by 1.1 points.

Costa Rica continues to lag in promoting the effective rule of law. The judicial system, while transparent, remains vulnerable to political interference, and property rights are not strongly protected. Lingering corruption further undermines the emergence of more vibrant economic activity.

BACKGROUND: Costa Rica's history of democratic stability has contributed to one of Latin America's highest levels of foreign direct investment per capita. The portion of the population living in poverty, however, has remained above 20 percent for nearly two decades, and the social safety net has begun to unravel due to growing fiscal constraints on public spending. President Laura Chinchilla has come under increasing criticism for corruption and her government's lack of transparency. While Costa Rica remains safer than many of its neighbors, it is experiencing rising crime rates. It also has an ongoing border dispute with Nicaragua. Costa Rica has benefited from foreign investments in electronics and health care, and the Central America–Dominican Republic–United States Free Trade Agreement (CAFTA–DR) has opened insurance and telecommunications to private investors.

Freedom Trend

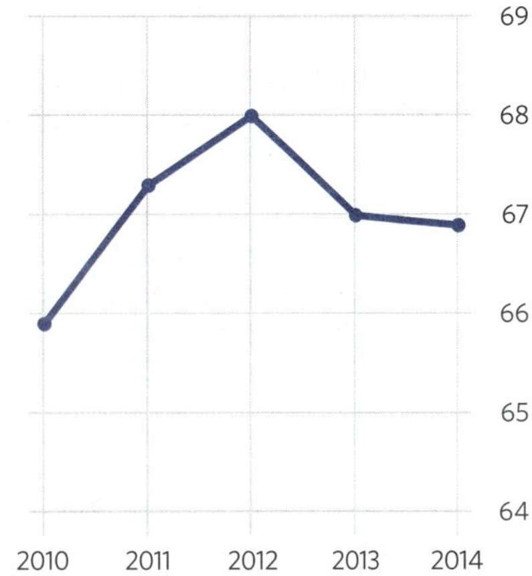

Country Comparisons

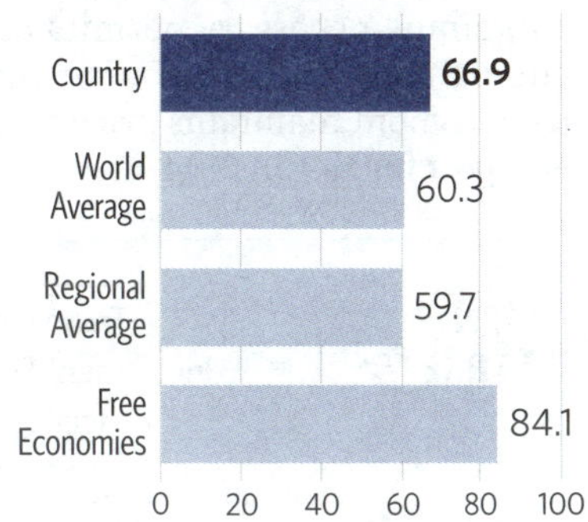

Quick Facts

Population: 4.7 million
GDP (PPP): $58.8 billion
5.0% growth in 2012
5-year compound annual growth 3.1%
$12,606 per capita
Unemployment: 7.5%
Inflation (CPI): 4.5%
FDI Inflow: $2.3 billion
Public Debt: 34.8% of GDP

2012 data unless otherwise noted.
Data compiled as of September 2013.

How Do We Measure Economic Freedom?
See page 471 for an explanation of the methodology or visit the *Index* Web site at *heritage.org/index*.

THE TEN ECONOMIC FREEDOMS

RULE OF LAW

	Score	Rank	1-Year Change
Property Rights	50.0	53rd	0
Freedom from Corruption	50.9	46th	+2.9

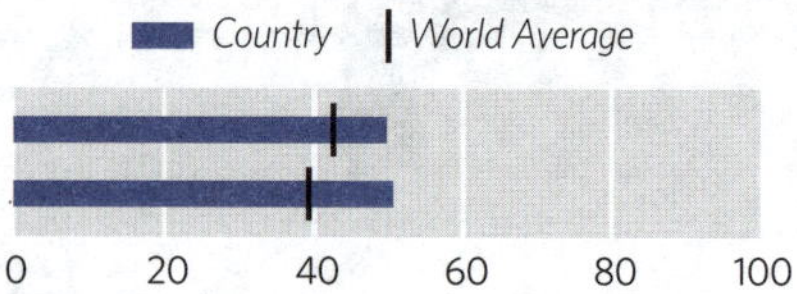

Enforcement of Costa Rica's laws against corruption has sometimes been limited, but a series of high-profile cases in recent years involving directors of state-owned enterprises as well as two ex-presidents has resulted in some convictions. The judicial branch is independent, but there are often substantial delays in the judicial process. Property rights are secure, and contracts are generally upheld.

GOVERNMENT SIZE

	Score	Rank	1-Year Change
Fiscal Freedom	80.0	86th	-2.9
Government Spending	90.0	11th	-0.1

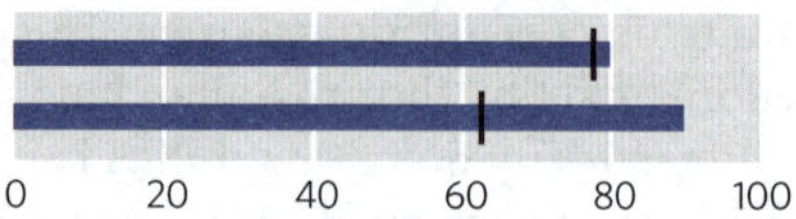

Costa Rica's top individual income tax rate is 25 percent, and the corporate tax rate is 30 percent. Other taxes include a general sales tax and a real property tax. Total tax revenue is 21.9 percent of GDP. Government expenditures are 18.2 percent of GDP, and public debt has been around 35 percent of GDP.

REGULATORY EFFICIENCY

	Score	Rank	1-Year Change
Business Freedom	64.9	92nd	+6.6
Labor Freedom	53.3	123rd	-7.1
Monetary Freedom	76.3	82nd	+0.9

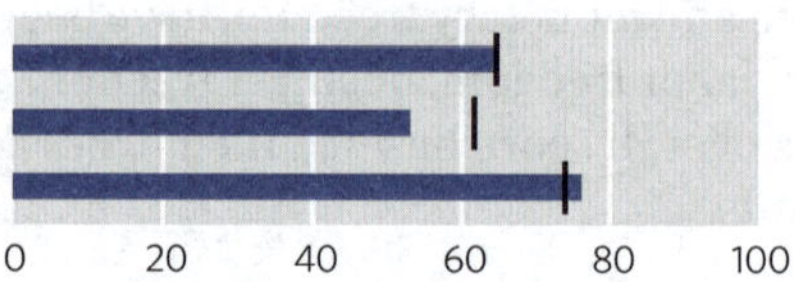

No minimum capital is required to start a company, but it takes almost two months to do so. Obtaining necessary permits takes over 100 days and costs more than the level of average annual income. Rigid labor regulations continue to hamper dynamic employment growth. The government maintains price controls but announced in June 2013 that it will eliminate price support for rice in 2014.

OPEN MARKETS

	Score	Rank	1-Year Change
Trade Freedom	83.8	52nd	-1.3
Investment Freedom	70.0	46th	0
Financial Freedom	50.0	69th	0

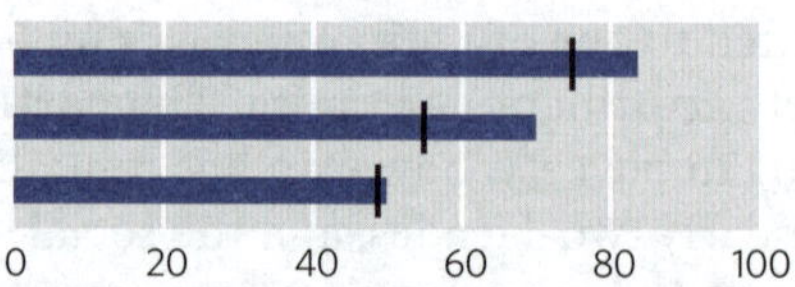

Costa Rica's average tariff rate is 3.1 percent. Foreign investors can find the country's legal and regulatory systems difficult to navigate in a timely manner. The financial sector remains relatively resilient and continues to expand. Despite increased market competition, however, state-owned financial institutions dominate the sector and influence lending.

Long-Term Score Change (since 1995)

RULE OF LAW		GOVERNMENT SIZE		REGULATORY EFFICIENCY		OPEN MARKETS	
Property Rights	**0**	Fiscal Freedom	**-2.6**	Business Freedom	**-5.1**	Trade Freedom	**+5.8**
Freedom from Corruption	**+0.9**	Government Spending	**-0.8**	Labor Freedom	**-7.8**	Investment Freedom	**0**
				Monetary Freedom	**+5.3**	Financial Freedom	**0**

CÔTE D'IVOIRE

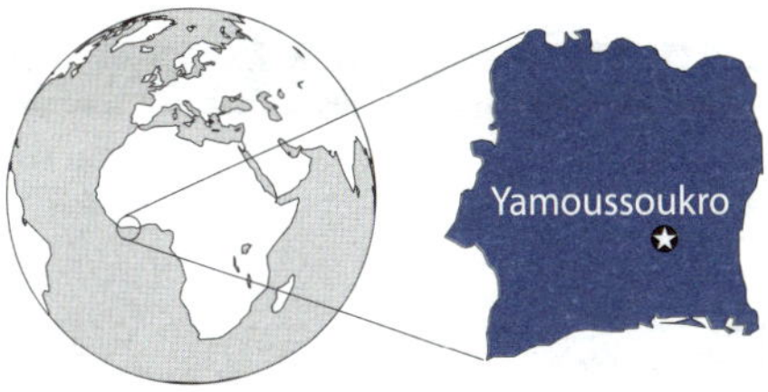

Economic Freedom Score

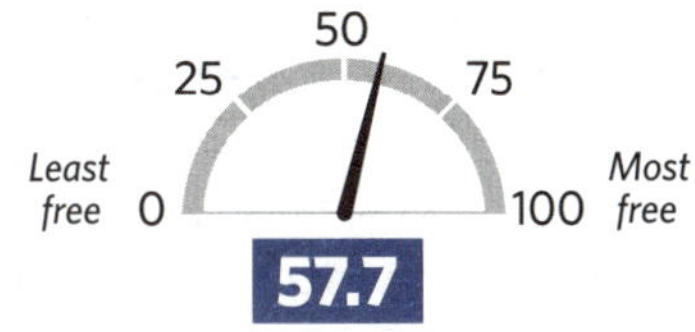

World Rank: **107** Regional Rank: **16**

Côte d'Ivoire's economic freedom score is 57.7, making its economy the 107th freest in the 2014 *Index*. Its score is 3.6 points better than last year, with improvements in all of the 10 economic freedoms except for financial freedom. Registering one of the 10 biggest score increases of the year, Côte d'Ivoire has advanced to 16th out of 46 countries in the Sub-Saharan Africa region, and its overall score is now slightly above the regional average.

Over the 20-year history of the *Index*, Côte d'Ivoire's economic freedom has grown only modestly. The country has recorded notable advancements in trade freedom and fiscal freedom, the scores for which have improved by 20 points or more. However, those gains have been largely offset by substantial score declines in the area of the rule of law measured by property rights and freedom from corruption. Business freedom has also declined.

Côte d'Ivoire continues to be ranked as one of the "mostly unfree" economies in the *Index*. The overall business and investment climate, hampered by political instability and regulatory inefficiency, remains unfavorable to private investment, retarding much-needed economic growth.

BACKGROUND: In 2002, civil war split Côte d'Ivoire between a rebel-controlled North and a government-controlled South. Laurent Gbagbo, ousted from the presidency in April 2011 by French-backed forces, is currently jailed in The Hague, charged with four counts of crimes against humanity for his role in presidential election violence in 2010. Current President Alassane Ouattara gained a parliamentary majority in elections held in December 2011. In June 2012, militias and supporters of ex-President Gbagbo were caught in an attempt to overthrow the government. The largely market-based economy relies heavily on cash-crop agriculture and is highly sensitive to international prices for coffee and palm oil, its top revenue earners. The International Monetary Fund and World Bank have provided $4.4 billion in debt relief under the Heavily Indebted Poor Countries Initiative.

Freedom Trend

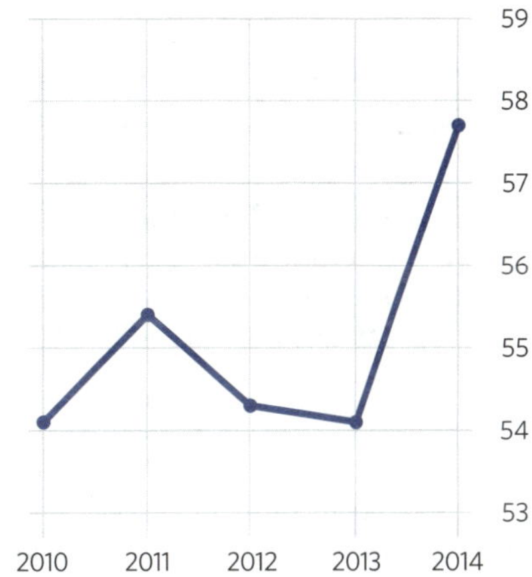

Country Comparisons

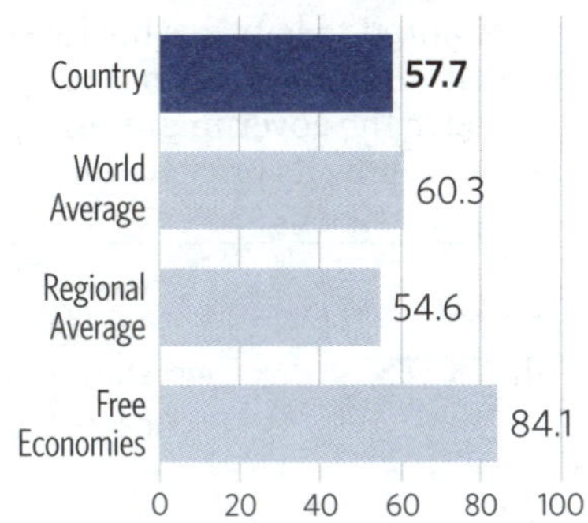

Quick Facts

Population: 23.4 million
GDP (PPP): $40.3 billion
9.8% growth in 2012
5-year compound annual growth 2.6%
$1,727 per capita
Unemployment: n/a
Inflation (CPI): 1.3%
FDI Inflow: $478.4 million
Public Debt: 49.1% of GDP

2012 data unless otherwise noted.
Data compiled as of September 2013.

How Do We Measure Economic Freedom?
See page 471 for an explanation of the methodology or visit the *Index* Web site at *heritage.org/index.*

THE TEN ECONOMIC FREEDOMS

Score ■ Country | World Average

RULE OF LAW

	Score	Rank	1-Year Change
Property Rights	30.0	93rd	+5.0
Freedom from Corruption	22.1	148th	+0.1

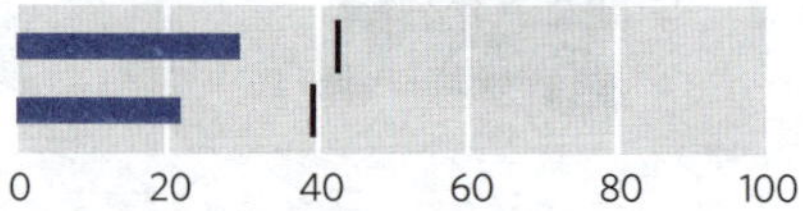

While the law provides criminal penalties for corruption by officials, they frequently engage in corrupt practices with impunity. Tender offers are irregularly publicized. Contract terms are not transparent, and bribes are regularly solicited. Protection of property rights is fragile. Despite the pervasiveness of corruption, the government appears to be making some progress in putting in place mechanisms to address the challenges.

GOVERNMENT SIZE

	Score	Rank	1-Year Change
Fiscal Freedom	79.1	99th	+1.2
Government Spending	79.8	52nd	0

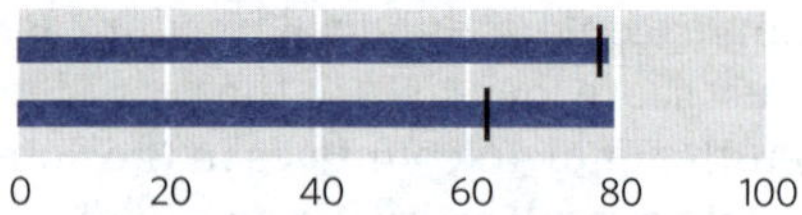

The individual income tax rate is 36 percent, and the corporate tax rate is 25 percent. Other taxes include a value-added tax (VAT) and a tax on interest. The overall tax burden is just over 13 percent of GDP. Government expenditures are around 26 percent of GDP. The Paris Club of rich nations has agreed to cancel nearly all of Côte d'Ivoire's outstanding debt by 2014.

REGULATORY EFFICIENCY

	Score	Rank	1-Year Change
Business Freedom	55.1	138th	+11.8
Labor Freedom	59.0	106th	+4.4
Monetary Freedom	80.6	25th	+2.8

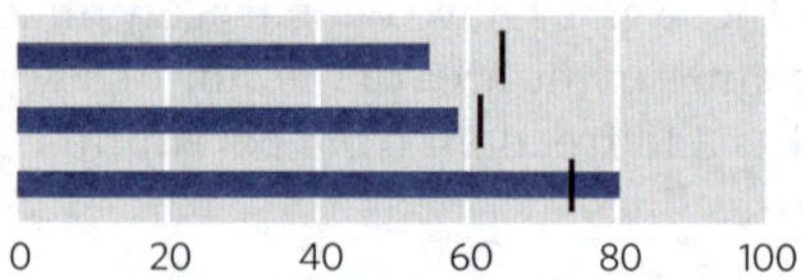

The process for establishing a company is now more streamlined, but paid-in minimum capital required to launch a business equals almost twice the level of average annual income. The formal labor market is not fully developed, and cumbersome labor codes hinder job growth. Although the government regulates many prices, it recently abandoned price setting for cocoa and will allow its price to fluctuate in response to world market conditions.

OPEN MARKETS

	Score	Rank	1-Year Change
Trade Freedom	71.4	123rd	+1.1
Investment Freedom	50.0	109th	+10.0
Financial Freedom	50.0	69th	0

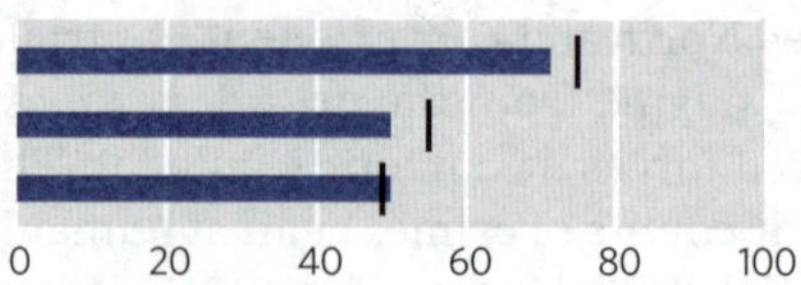

The average tariff rate for Côte d'Ivoire is 6.8 percent. The government screens investment from outside the West Africa Economic and Monetary Union, and foreign investors may find it difficult to enforce contracts. The financial sector remains vulnerable to government influence. The state owns or holds shares in several domestic financial institutions and continues to influence the allocation of credit.

Long-Term Score Change (since 1995)

RULE OF LAW		GOVERNMENT SIZE		REGULATORY EFFICIENCY		OPEN MARKETS	
Property Rights	**–20.0**	Fiscal Freedom	**+26.8**	Business Freedom	**–14.9**	Trade Freedom	**+58.8**
Freedom from Corruption	**–7.9**	Government Spending	**–6.3**	Labor Freedom	**–0.8**	Investment Freedom	**0**
				Monetary Freedom	**+0.9**	Financial Freedom	**0**

CROATIA

World Rank: **87** Regional Rank: **36**

Economic Freedom Score

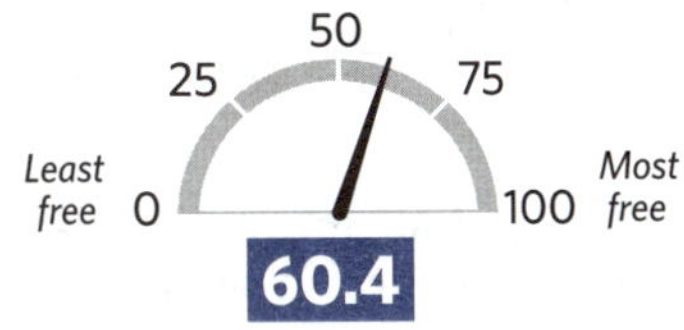

Freedom Trend

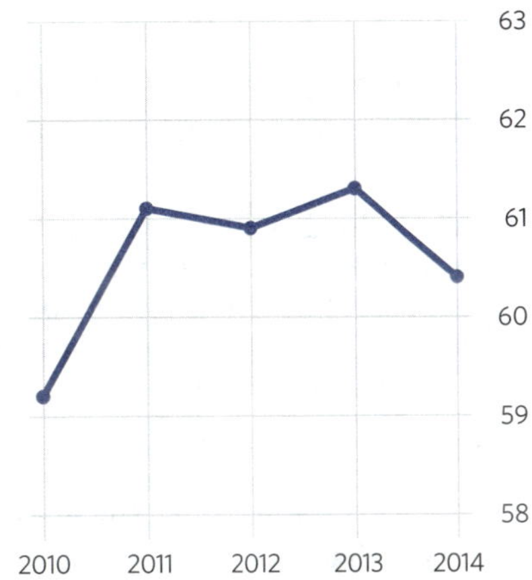

Country Comparisons

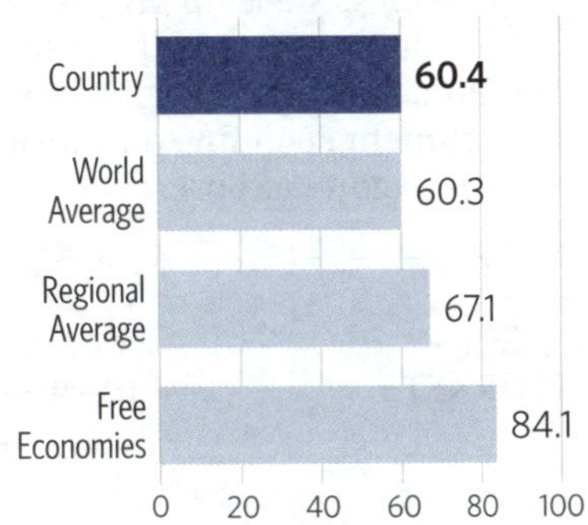

Croatia's economic freedom score is 60.4, making its economy the 87th freest in the 2014 *Index*. Its overall score is 0.9 point lower than last year, with deteriorations in six of the 10 economic freedoms including the control of government spending, fiscal freedom, monetary freedom, and business freedom. Croatia continues to fall behind other emerging economies in the region, and its overall score remains below the regional average.

Over the 20-year history of the *Index*, Croatia's economic freedom score has improved by 12.4 points, with notable score gains in market openness as measured by investment freedom, trade freedom, and financial freedom. These improvements, together with greater regulatory efficiency driven by enhancements in business freedom and monetary freedom, have enabled Croatia to climb gradually up to the ranks of the "moderately free" from economically "repressed" two decades ago.

By sharp contrast, Croatia's rule of law has deteriorated and remains fragile, undermined by substantial continuing corruption. Deeper systemic reforms to strengthen the independence of the judiciary are critically needed to ensure the country's continuing progress toward greater economic freedom.

BACKGROUND: Croatia declared its independence in 1991, contributing to the breakup of Yugoslavia along ethnic and religious lines. Years of conflict between Croats and Serbs ended formally in 1995 with the Dayton Peace Accords. Croatia joined NATO in April 2009 and the European Union in July 2013. Former Prime Minister Jadranka Kosor, credited with making the final push toward EU accession, was defeated by center-left Zoran Milanovic in December 2011. Turnout for Croatia's first-ever elections for the EU Parliament, held in April 2013, was only 20.8 percent. The Croatian economy has been hurt by the global financial crisis and overreliance on tourism. The slow pace of privatization of state-owned businesses hinders growth.

Quick Facts

Population: 4.4 million
GDP (PPP): $78.4 billion
-2.0% growth in 2012
5-year compound annual growth -1.9%
$17,810 per capita
Unemployment: 15.0%
Inflation (CPI): 3.4%
FDI Inflow: $1.3 billion
Public Debt: 56.3% of GDP

2012 data unless otherwise noted.
Data compiled as of September 2013.

How Do We Measure Economic Freedom?
See page 471 for an explanation of the methodology or visit the *Index* Web site at *heritage.org/index*.

THE TEN ECONOMIC FREEDOMS

Score ■ *Country* | *World Average* *Rank* *1-Year Change*

RULE OF LAW

	Score	Rank	1-Year Change
Property Rights	40.0	70th	0
Freedom from Corruption	41.1	66th	+1.1

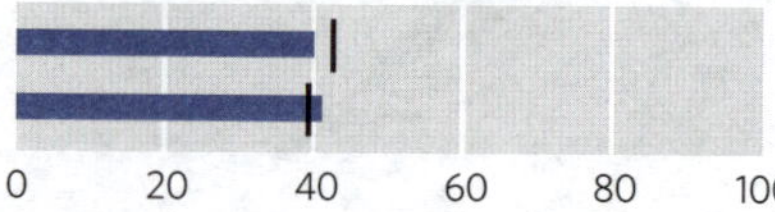

A former prime minister and his deputy were convicted on corruption charges in 2012. High levels of corruption in public companies, universities, public procurement systems, and land registry offices and the lack of meaningful reforms in the judiciary suggest that Croatia's 2013 EU membership may not bring immediate benefits. The court system is cumbersome and inefficient, and backlogs cause business disputes to drag on for years.

GOVERNMENT SIZE

	Score	Rank	1-Year Change
Fiscal Freedom	69.4	140th	-6.0
Government Spending	45.8	142nd	-2.9

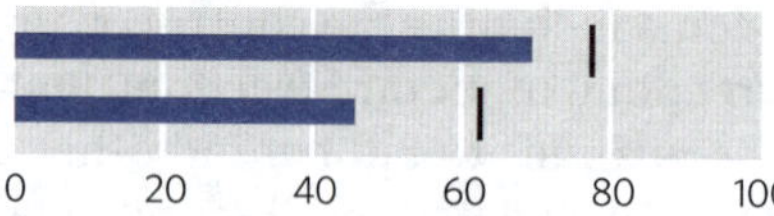

The individual income tax rate in Croatia is 40 percent, and the corporate tax rate is 20 percent. Other taxes include a value-added tax (VAT) and excise taxes. The overall tax burden is 32.6 percent of total domestic income. Government expenditures remain steady at about 43 percent of the domestic economy. Croatia will begin contributing to the EU budget in 2013. Public debt is about 56 percent of GDP.

REGULATORY EFFICIENCY

	Score	Rank	1-Year Change
Business Freedom	61.4	107th	-1.6
Labor Freedom	39.4	170th	-3.0
Monetary Freedom	79.2	45th	-1.9

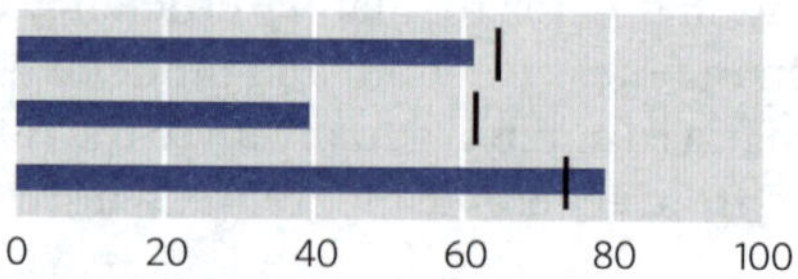

The business start-up process has become less burdensome, taking less than 10 procedures, but obtaining necessary permits takes over 200 days and costs over four times the level of average annual income. Despite ongoing reform efforts, the labor market remains relatively rigid. Government spending on subsidies surged in 2013. The state influences price levels through the still-significant presence of state-owned enterprises.

OPEN MARKETS

	Score	Rank	1-Year Change
Trade Freedom	87.4	36th	-0.1
Investment Freedom	80.0	23rd	+5.0
Financial Freedom	60.0	41st	0

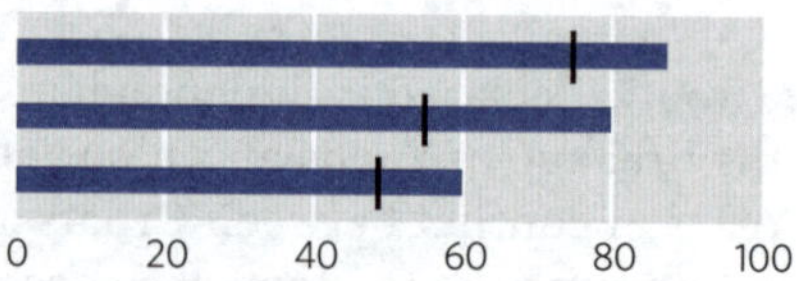

Croatia's average tariff rate in 2011 was 1.3 percent. The country joined the EU effective July 1, 2013. The complex legal and regulatory systems may be challenging for foreign investors. The banking sector is relatively well developed and open to competition, although non-performing loans have increased in recent years. Privatization in the financial sector has progressed well, with only one state-owned bank remaining.

Long-Term Score Change (since 1996)

RULE OF LAW		GOVERNMENT SIZE		REGULATORY EFFICIENCY		OPEN MARKETS	
Property Rights	**-10.0**	Fiscal Freedom	**-8.0**	Business Freedom	**+6.4**	Trade Freedom	**+18.4**
Freedom from Corruption	**+11.1**	Government Spending	**-4.7**	Labor Freedom	**-4.9**	Investment Freedom	**+30.0**
				Monetary Freedom	**+79.2**	Financial Freedom	**+10.0**

CUBA

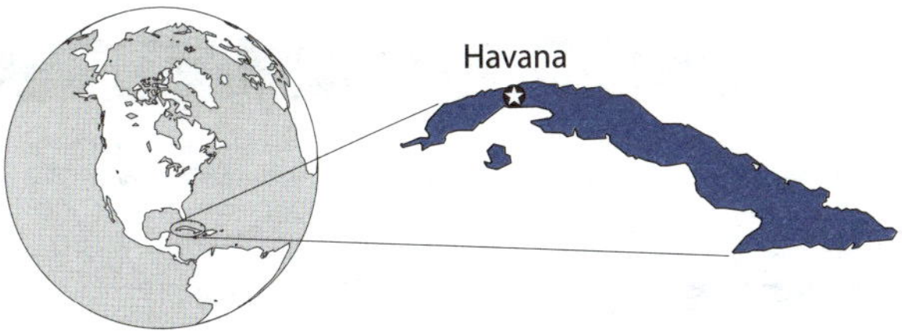

World Rank: **177** Regional Rank: **29**

Economic Freedom Score

Cuba's economic freedom score is 28.7, making its economy one of the world's least free. Its overall score is 0.2 point higher than last year, with deteriorations in trade freedom, fiscal freedom, monetary freedom, and freedom from corruption counterbalanced by an improvement in business freedom. Cuba is ranked least free of 29 countries in the South and Central America/Caribbean region, and its overall score is significantly lower than the regional average.

Over the 20-year history of the *Index*, Cuba's economic freedom has been stagnant near the bottom of the "repressed" category. Its overall score improvement has been less than 1 point over the past two decades, with score gains in fiscal freedom and freedom from corruption offset by double-digit declines in business freedom and investment freedom.

Despite some progress in restructuring the state sector since 2010, the private sector remains constrained by heavy regulations and tight state controls. Open-market policies are not in place to spur growth in trade and investment, and the lack of competition continues to stifle dynamic economic expansion. A watered-down reform package endorsed by the Cuban Communist Party has trimmed the number of state workers and expanded the list of approved professions, but many details of the reform remain obscure.

BACKGROUND: A one-party Communist state, Cuba depends on external assistance (chiefly oil subsidies provided by Venezuela and remittances from Cuban émigrés) and a captive labor force to survive. Property rights are severely restricted. Fidel Castro's 82-year-old brother Raul continues to guide both the government and the Cuban Communist Party. Many workers earn only poverty-level wages, agriculture is a shambles, mining is depressed, and tourism revenue is volatile. Though the Communist government maintains strict control of the economy, it recently loosened restraints on local enterprises in an attempt to maximize their commercial potential. Restrictions on foreign travel have been eased, but the state continues to monitor it closely.

Freedom Trend

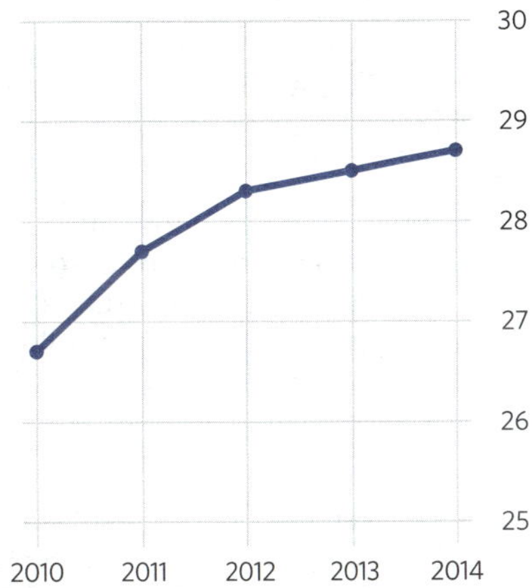

Country Comparisons

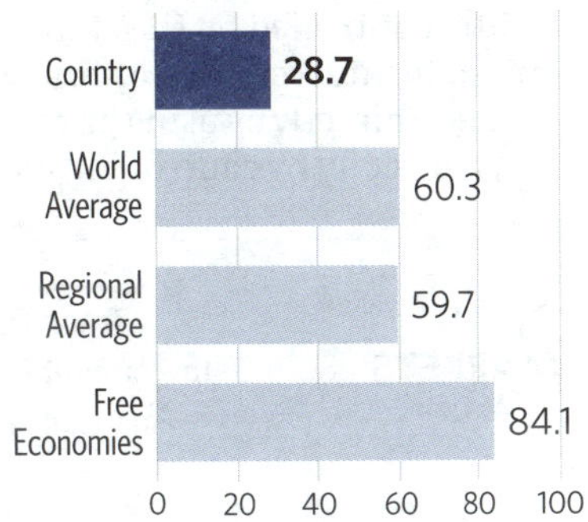

Quick Facts

Population: 11.2 million
GDP (PPP): $126.3 billion
3.0 % growth in 2012
5-year compound annual growth n/a
$11,313 per capita
Unemployment: n/a
Inflation (CPI): 5.5%
FDI Inflow: n/a
Public Debt: 35.3% of GDP

2012 data unless otherwise noted.
Data compiled as of September 2013.

How Do We Measure Economic Freedom?
See page 471 for an explanation of the methodology or visit the *Index* Web site at *heritage.org/index.*

THE TEN ECONOMIC FREEDOMS

Legend: Country | World Average

RULE OF LAW

	Score	Rank	1-Year Change
Property Rights	10.0	166th	0
Freedom from Corruption	41.2	65th	-0.8

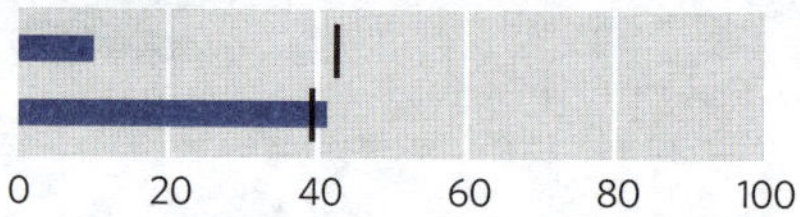

Official corruption remains a serious problem, with a culture of illegality shrouding the mixture of limited private enterprise and a vast state-controlled economy in a country where there is little respect for the rule of law. Only state enterprises can enter into economic agreements with foreigners as minority partners; ordinary citizens cannot participate. Most means of production are owned by the state.

GOVERNMENT SIZE

	Score	Rank	1-Year Change
Fiscal Freedom	60.0	169th	-2.7
Government Spending	0.0	177th	0

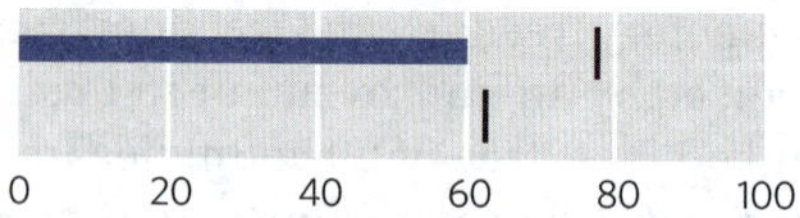

The top individual income tax rate is 50 percent. The top corporate tax rate is 30 percent (35 percent for wholly foreign-owned companies). Other taxes include a tax on property transfers and a sales tax. The overall tax burden is 24.4 percent of GDP. Government spending is around 67 percent of GDP, and public debt is around 35 percent of the domestic economy. Despite reforms, the government continues to play a large role in the economy.

REGULATORY EFFICIENCY

	Score	Rank	1-Year Change
Business Freedom	20.0	182nd	+10.0
Labor Freedom	20.0	183rd	0
Monetary Freedom	65.8	163rd	-1.6

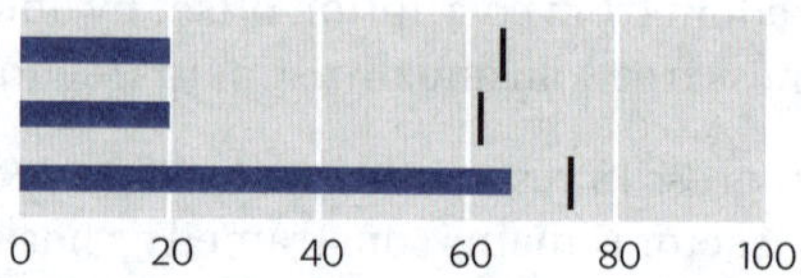

Despite reform measures introduced in recent years, private entrepreneurship is limited and tightly controlled by the state. The public sector remains the major source of employment, and state intervention continues to distort the labor market. The government tries to contain inflation directly by using price controls and regulating the limited areas of free-market activity and indirectly by controlling monetary expansion.

OPEN MARKETS

	Score	Rank	1-Year Change
Trade Freedom	60.0	161st	-2.7
Investment Freedom	0.0	178th	0
Financial Freedom	10.0	174th	0

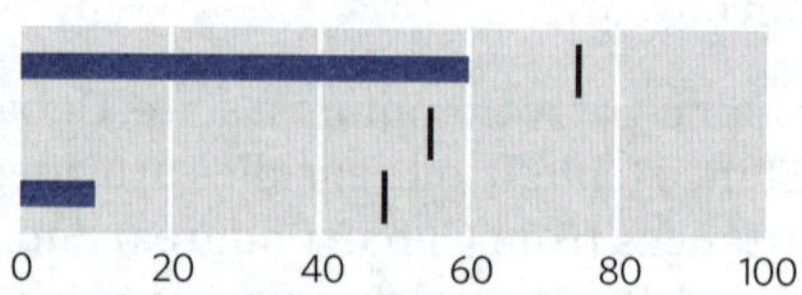

Cuba's average tariff rate is 10 percent. The country's planned economy deters foreign trade and investment. The financial sector remains heavily regulated, and access to credit for entrepreneurial activity is seriously impeded by the shallowness of the financial market. The state maintains strict capital and exchange controls.

Long-Term Score Change (since 1995)

RULE OF LAW		GOVERNMENT SIZE		REGULATORY EFFICIENCY		OPEN MARKETS	
Property Rights	0	Fiscal Freedom	**+12.4**	Business Freedom	**-20.0**	Trade Freedom	**0**
Freedom from Corruption	**+31.2**	Government Spending	**0**	Labor Freedom	**0**	Investment Freedom	**-10.0**
				Monetary Freedom	**+2.9**	Financial Freedom	**0**

CYPRUS

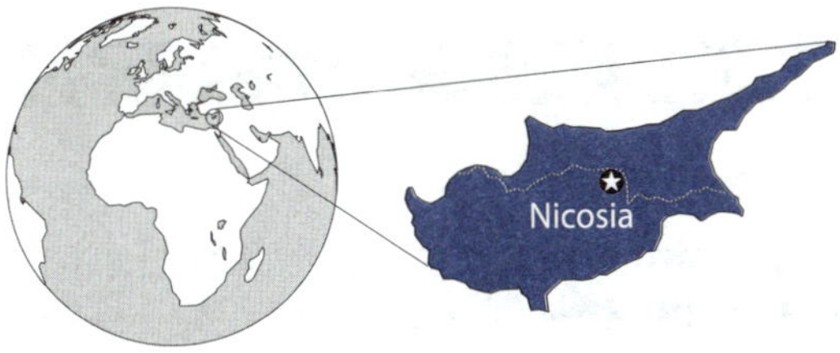

World Rank: 46 | **Regional Rank: 21**

Economic Freedom Score

Cyprus's economic freedom score is 67.6, making its economy the 46th freest in the 2014 *Index*. Its overall score is down by 1.4 points from last year, with notable declines in financial freedom, investment freedom, and monetary freedom. Cyprus is ranked 21st out of 43 countries in the Europe region.

Over the 20-year history of the *Index*, Cyprus's economic freedom has remained virtually unchanged, with hard-won gains in earlier years largely eroded by recent declines in financial freedom and control of government spending. The country had been rated one of the "mostly free" economies throughout the 2000s and had even advanced into the ranks of the world's 20 freest in 2011. However, since 2012, Cyprus has been on a declining path of economic freedom and has fallen back to the status of "moderately free," recording its second lowest score ever in the 2014 *Index*.

Significant problems continue in several areas of economic freedom, and Cyprus's score for control of government spending is far below the world average. The public sector has ballooned to encompass over 45 percent of the small island economy. Undermining the overall entrepreneurial environment, business freedom and investment freedom have also diminished as the pace of reform has slowed significantly.

BACKGROUND: A U.N. buffer zone has separated the Greek Cypriot Republic of Cyprus from the Turkish Republic of Northern Cyprus since 1974. The Republic of Cyprus is a member of the European Union and acts as the island's internationally recognized administration. Despite deep hostility, Greek and Turkish leaders continue to negotiate on possible reunification through U.N.-brokered talks. Center-right politician Nicos Anastasiades became president of Cyprus in February 2013, defeating leftist Stavos Malas. A major economic crisis hit Cyprus in 2013. In March 2013, a €10 billion EU bailout plan centered on bank restructuring. However, draconian measures that include taxing bank deposits were imposed as part of the bailout. Unemployment has risen dramatically, especially among youth.

Freedom Trend

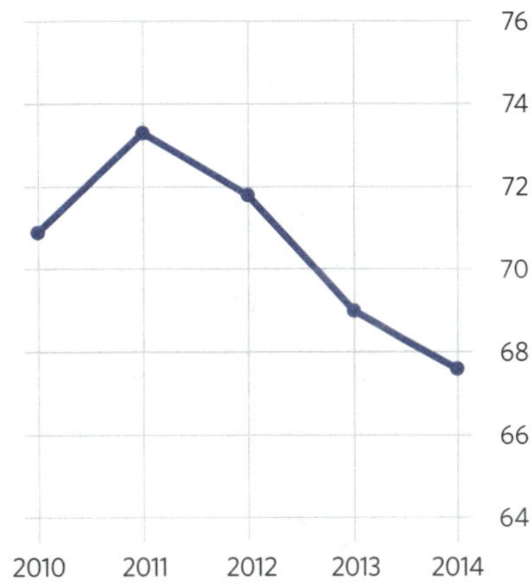

Country Comparisons

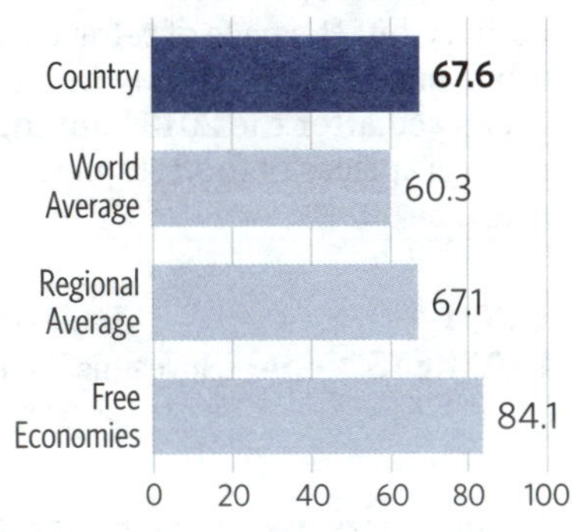

Quick Facts

Population: 0.9 million
GDP (PPP): $23.6 billion
-2.4% growth in 2012
5-year compound annual growth 0.2%
$27,086 per capita
Unemployment: 12.1%
Inflation (CPI): 3.1%
FDI Inflow: $848.6 million
Public Debt: 86.2% of GDP

2012 data unless otherwise noted.
Data compiled as of September 2013.

How Do We Measure Economic Freedom?
See page 471 for an explanation of the methodology or visit the *Index* Web site at *heritage.org/index*.

THE TEN ECONOMIC FREEDOMS

RULE OF LAW

	Score	Rank	1-Year Change
Property Rights	70.0	27th	0
Freedom from Corruption	64.0	30th	+1.0

The absence of a political settlement in the northern area administered by Turkish Cypriots, where corruption, patronage, and lack of transparency continue, poses inherent risks for foreign investors. The March 2013 bailout by the EU that was intended to flush dirty Russian money from Cyprus's bloated banks had the unintended consequence of giving Russian oligarchs majority ownership, at least on paper, of the Bank of Cyprus.

GOVERNMENT SIZE

	Score	Rank	1-Year Change
Fiscal Freedom	79.7	90th	-0.1
Government Spending	36.2	157th	+3.5

The top individual income tax rate is 35 percent, and the top corporate tax rate is 10 percent. Other taxes include a value-added tax (VAT) and a real estate tax. Overall tax revenue is equal to 26.5 percent of GDP. Government spending has been steady at 46.1 percent of GDP, but the eurozone crisis has put severe strains on the government's budget, forcing it to seek a bailout. Public debt has accelerated past 85 percent of the domestic economy.

REGULATORY EFFICIENCY

	Score	Rank	1-Year Change
Business Freedom	79.7	34th	-1.0
Labor Freedom	70.2	63rd	+7.4
Monetary Freedom	78.8	52nd	-5.3

The regulatory process has become streamlined and relatively supportive of entrepreneurial activity, but the pace of reform has slowed in comparison to other comparable economies. The labor market is relatively flexible, but union power is quite strong. EU subsidies to Cyprus increased after the 2013 banking crisis, and the government mandates a minimum wage and controls prices of food staples.

OPEN MARKETS

	Score	Rank	1-Year Change
Trade Freedom	82.8	56th	+1.0
Investment Freedom	65.0	68th	-10.0
Financial Freedom	50.0	69th	-10.0

EU members have a low 1.1 percent average tariff rate and, in general, few non-tariff barriers to trade. Cyprus maintains some additional barriers affecting the services and biotech sectors. The government imposed capital controls in 2013. The financial system continues to be under strain. Despite reorganizations following the March 2013 bailout that averted the country's financial collapse, the banking sector remains unstable and plagued by uncertainty.

Long-Term Score Change (since 1996)

RULE OF LAW		GOVERNMENT SIZE		REGULATORY EFFICIENCY		OPEN MARKETS	
Property Rights	+20.0	Fiscal Freedom	+7.8	Business Freedom	-5.3	Trade Freedom	+14.4
Freedom from Corruption	+14.0	Government Spending	-31.7	Labor Freedom	+0.2	Investment Freedom	-5.0
				Monetary Freedom	+2.8	Financial Freedom	-20.0

CZECH REPUBLIC

World Rank: **26** Regional Rank: **15**

Economic Freedom Score

The Czech Republic's economic freedom score is 72.2, making its economy the 26th freest in the 2014 *Index*. Its overall score is 1.3 points better than last year, with notable improvements in half of the 10 economic freedoms, including investment freedom, business freedom, and freedom from corruption. The Czech Republic is ranked 15th out of 43 countries in the Europe region, and its overall score is higher than the regional and global averages.

Over the 20-year history of the *Index*, the Czech Republic has steadily enhanced its economic freedom to advance to the ranks of "mostly free" economies achieving scores above 70. A series of major reform measures has enabled it to register score improvements of 10 points or more in half of the 10 economic freedoms, including fiscal freedom, labor freedom, and trade freedom. Gains in the area of government size, which measures tax burden and public spending, have also contributed to the Czech Republic's impressive transition to a market economy.

Facilitated by further improvements in open-market policies, the Czech Republic has recorded its highest economic freedom score ever in the 2014 *Index*. Continued reform to strengthen the independence of the judiciary and effectively eradicate corruption will be indispensable to ensuring vibrant economic development in the coming years.

BACKGROUND: The 1989 Velvet Revolution peacefully overthrew a Communist dictatorship and led to the election of dissident playwright Vaclav Havel as president of a democratic Czechoslovakia. The Czech Republic separated from Slovakia in the "velvet divorce," becoming an independent nation in 1993 and joining the European Union in 2004. Although prospects for adoption of the euro are uncertain because of the EU economic crisis, recent legislation and presidential positions indicate that the government is moving toward closer alignment with the eurozone. The Civic Democrats Party was defeated in January 2013, and the Social-Democratic Political Party under President Milos Zeman came to power. The government is trying to pursue pension reform and other measures to shrink government.

How Do We Measure Economic Freedom?
See page 471 for an explanation of the methodology or visit the *Index* Web site at *heritage.org/index.*

Freedom Trend

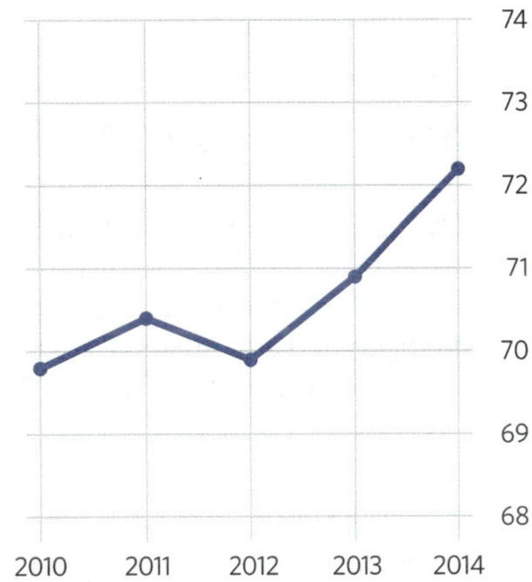

Country Comparisons

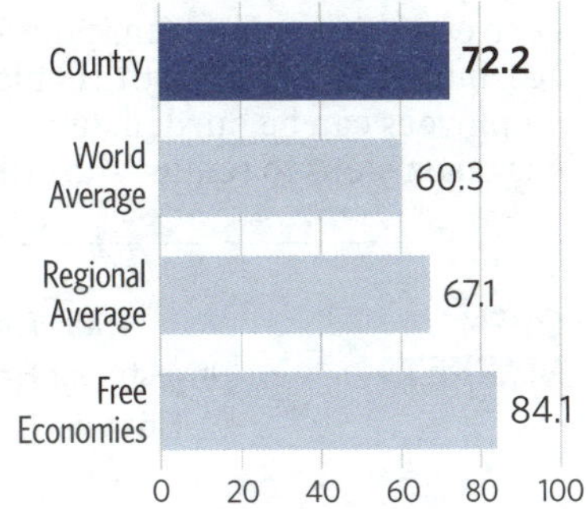

Quick Facts

Population: 10.6 million
GDP (PPP): $287.0 billion
-1.2% growth in 2012
5-year compound annual growth 0.3%
$27,191 per capita
Unemployment: 7.0%
Inflation (CPI): 3.3%
FDI Inflow: $10.6 billion
Public Debt: 43.1% of GDP

2012 data unless otherwise noted.
Data compiled as of September 2013.

THE TEN ECONOMIC FREEDOMS

RULE OF LAW

	Score	Rank	1-Year Change
Property Rights	70.0	27th	0
Freedom from Corruption	45.3	55th	+1.3

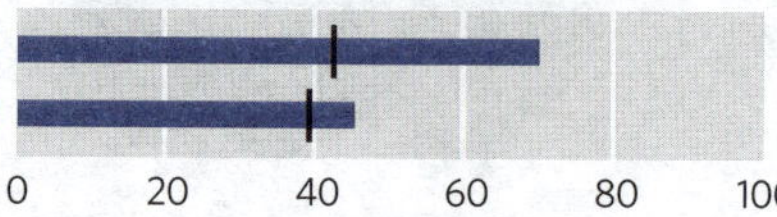

In 2012, several scandals involving senior government officials highlighted ongoing corruption and lack of transparency and caused the European Commission to cut around $650 million of EU aid to the Czech Republic. The judiciary's independence is largely respected, though its complexity and multilayered composition lead to the slow delivery of judgments. Property rights are relatively well protected, and contracts are generally secure.

GOVERNMENT SIZE

	Score	Rank	1-Year Change
Fiscal Freedom	81.7	71st	-0.3
Government Spending	43.8	144th	+0.3

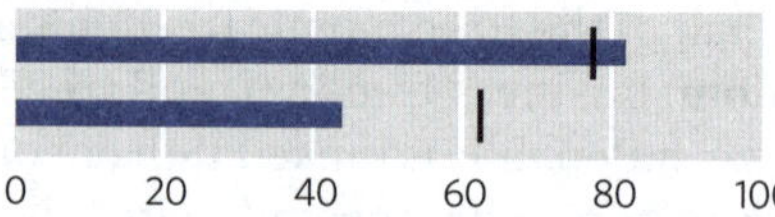

The Czech Republic's top individual income tax rate is 15 percent, and the corporate tax rate remains at 19 percent. Other taxes include a value-added tax (VAT) and an inheritance tax. The overall tax burden is equivalent to 35.3 percent of GDP. Tax increases and budget cuts have yielded surpluses in recent years, and government spending has stabilized at 43 percent of GDP. Public debt is around 45 percent of the domestic economy.

REGULATORY EFFICIENCY

	Score	Rank	1-Year Change
Business Freedom	70.1	75th	+4.3
Labor Freedom	84.0	14th	-1.5
Monetary Freedom	79.4	42nd	-2.3

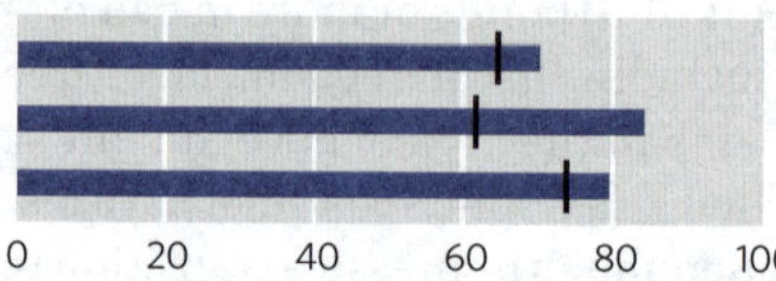

Incorporating a business has become less time-consuming, and licensing requirements have been eased. The minimum capital requirement is now less than 30 percent of the level of average annual income. Labor regulations are relatively flexible, although the non-salary cost of employees can be burdensome. Although a range of price controls are maintained, the state has taken steps to reduce subsidies for state pensions and green energy.

OPEN MARKETS

	Score	Rank	1-Year Change
Trade Freedom	87.8	11th	+1.0
Investment Freedom	80.0	23rd	+10.0
Financial Freedom	80.0	4th	0

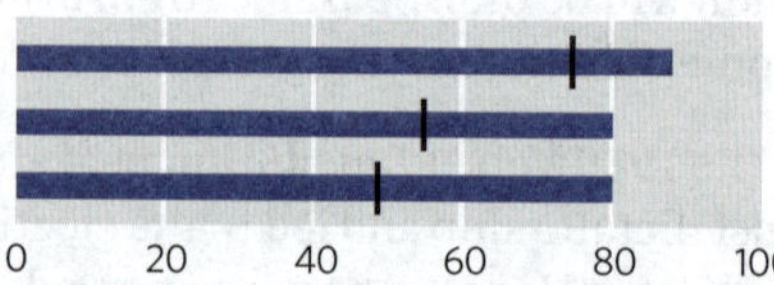

EU members have a low 1.1 percent average tariff rate and, in general, few non-tariff barriers to trade. Restrictions on foreign land ownership have been phased out. The relatively well-regulated financial market continues to grow steadily. The banking sector remains competitive and resilient, offering a wider range of financial products.

Long-Term Score Change (since 1995)

RULE OF LAW		GOVERNMENT SIZE		REGULATORY EFFICIENCY		OPEN MARKETS	
Property Rights	0	Fiscal Freedom	+35.0	Business Freedom	-29.9	Trade Freedom	+11.8
Freedom from Corruption	-4.7	Government Spending	+5.6	Labor Freedom	+26.4	Investment Freedom	+10.0
				Monetary Freedom	+10.2	Financial Freedom	-10.0

DENMARK

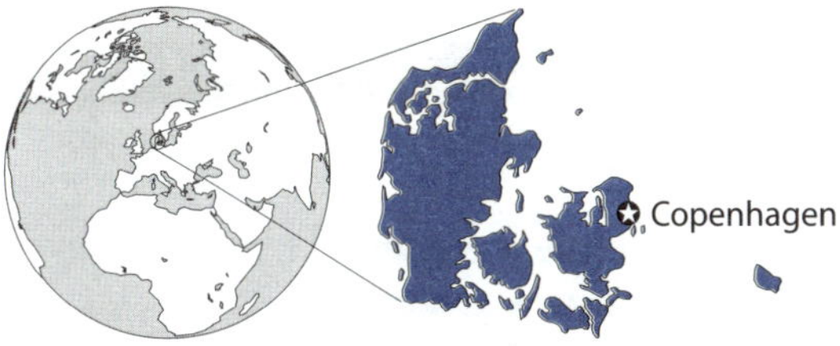

World Rank: **10** Regional Rank: **3**

Economic Freedom Score

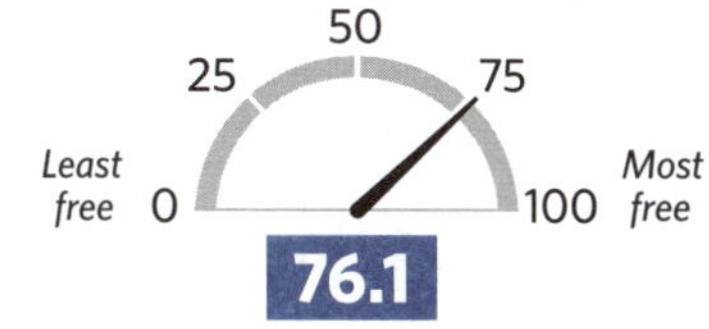

Denmark's economic freedom score is 76.1, making its economy the 10th freest in the 2014 *Index*. Its overall score is the same as last year, with improvements in investment freedom and trade freedom counterbalanced by declines in the management of public spending and fiscal freedom. Trailing Switzerland and Ireland, Denmark is ranked 3rd out of 43 countries in the Europe region.

Over the 20-year history of the *Index*, Denmark's economic freedom score has advanced by nearly 9 points, a top 10 improvement among developed economies. Leading the way have been notable score improvements of 20 points in investment freedom and financial freedom. Overall, Denmark's economic freedom score has remained the same or increased in all but two areas: labor freedom and monetary freedom. Charting a relatively steady rise in economic freedom over two decades, Denmark reached "mostly free" status in 2002 and achieved its highest score of 79.6 in 2009.

Strongly underpinning Denmark's economic dynamism, the judicial system, independent and free of corruption, enforces contracts reliably. Openness to global trade and investment has enabled Denmark to become one of the world's most competitive and flexible economies. On the other hand, the overall tax regime that finances Denmark's large-scale government programs remains burdensome and complex.

BACKGROUND: Helle Thorning-Schmidt became prime minister after a center-left coalition led by Social Democrats defeated Prime Minister Lars Løkke Rasmussen in the September 2011 parliamentary elections. She is Denmark's first female prime minister. Denmark has been a member of the European Union since 1973. Its economy depends heavily on foreign trade, and the private sector is characterized by many small and medium-size companies. Increased immigration spurred by the 2011 uprisings in North Africa has caused the government to consider more restrictive immigration laws. Although not party to the euro, Denmark has felt the impact of the European economic crisis. Growth is sluggish, but unemployment remains relatively low.

How Do We Measure Economic Freedom?
See page 471 for an explanation of the methodology or visit the *Index* Web site at *heritage.org/index.*

Freedom Trend

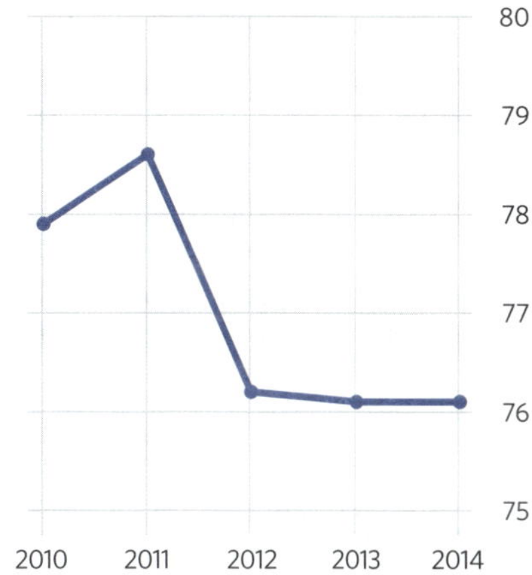

Country Comparisons

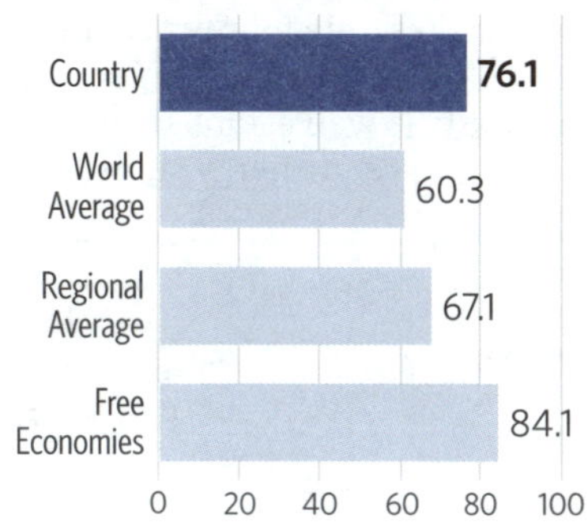

Quick Facts

Population: 5.6 million
GDP (PPP): $210.1 billion
-0.6% growth in 2012
5-year compound annual growth -0.9%
$37,657 per capita
Unemployment: 7.6%
Inflation (CPI): 2.4%
FDI Inflow: $2.9 billion
Public Debt: 50.1% of GDP

2012 data unless otherwise noted.
Data compiled as of September 2013.

THE TEN ECONOMIC FREEDOMS

RULE OF LAW

	Score	Rank	1-Year Change
Property Rights	90.0	2nd	0
Freedom from Corruption	93.7	2nd	-0.3

Levels of corruption are generally very low in Denmark, which consistently receives some of the highest marks in Transparency International's Corruption Perceptions Index. Protections for property rights are strongly enforced, with an independent judicial system institutionalized throughout the economy. Intellectual property rights are respected, and enforcement is consistent with world standards.

GOVERNMENT SIZE

	Score	Rank	1-Year Change
Fiscal Freedom	39.3	182nd	-0.5
Government Spending	0.5	176th	-5.4

The top individual income tax rate is 56 percent, and the corporate tax rate is 25 percent. Other taxes include a value-added tax (VAT) and a tax on fatty foods. The overall tax burden is equivalent to 48 percent of GDP. Public expenditures finance 57.6 percent of the domestic economy, and public debt is about 50 percent of GDP. The eurozone crisis has slowed growth, hurting public finances.

REGULATORY EFFICIENCY

	Score	Rank	1-Year Change
Business Freedom	98.1	2nd	-0.3
Labor Freedom	91.2	5th	+0.1
Monetary Freedom	80.0	30th	0

Denmark's regulatory environment remains one of the world's most efficient. Starting a business takes only four procedures, and minimum capital requirements have been reduced. Relatively flexible hiring and dismissal regulations sustain an efficient labor market. Monetary stability is well established, but rents are controlled, and medications are heavily subsidized. In 2013, green energy subsidies were reduced.

OPEN MARKETS

	Score	Rank	1-Year Change
Trade Freedom	87.8	11th	+1.0
Investment Freedom	90.0	2nd	+5.0
Financial Freedom	90.0	1st	0

EU members have a low 1.1 percent average tariff rate and, in general, few non-tariff barriers to trade. Denmark is very open to foreign investment as well. The financial sector is competitive and diversified. After undergoing a period of uncertainty, the banking sector has become more stable. Banks' dependence on state guarantees has been reduced, and prudential banking regulations have been strengthened.

Long-Term Score Change (since 1996)

RULE OF LAW		GOVERNMENT SIZE		REGULATORY EFFICIENCY		OPEN MARKETS	
Property Rights	0	Fiscal Freedom	+7.8	Business Freedom	+13.1	Trade Freedom	+10.0
Freedom from Corruption	+3.7	Government Spending	+0.5	Labor Freedom	-8.7	Investment Freedom	+20.0
				Monetary Freedom	-11.4	Financial Freedom	+20.0

DJIBOUTI

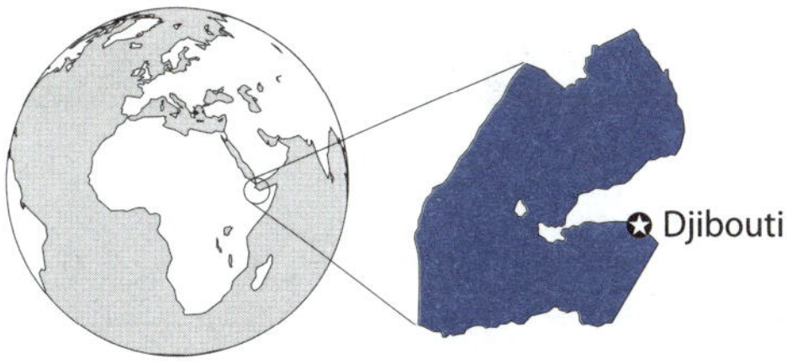

World Rank: **118** Regional Rank: **20**

Economic Freedom Score

Djibouti's economic freedom score is 55.9, making its economy the 118th freest in the 2014 *Index*. Its overall score is 2 points better than last year, with declines in financial freedom and trade freedom outweighed by improvements in six of the 10 economic freedoms including the control of government spending, business freedom, and labor freedom. Djibouti is ranked 20th out of 46 countries in the Sub-Saharan Africa region.

Over the 18 years in which Djibouti has been graded in the *Index*, its economic freedom has remained largely stagnant, with its overall score improving by only 1.5 points. Six of the 10 economic freedoms have increased, including investment freedom and the management of government spending, whose scores have recorded double-digit improvements, but the combined score gains have been largely offset by declines in property rights, business freedom, and fiscal freedom. Djibouti has been rated a "mostly unfree" economy throughout its history in the *Index*.

Effective implementation of deeper institutional reforms remains critical to sustaining dynamic economic growth and ensuring broad-based economic development. Systemic weaknesses linger in the protection of property rights and the enforcement of anti-corruption measures. The judiciary remains vulnerable to political influence.

BACKGROUND: President Ismael Omar Guelleh, whose multi-party, multi-ethnic coalition controls all levels of government, was re-elected by a wide margin in April 2011. Djibouti is strategically located at the mouth of the Red Sea, and its economy is centered on port facilities, the railway, and French, Japanese, and American military facilities. Djibouti is an international partner in combating piracy in the Gulf of Aden. The population is concentrated in the capital city. Food prices stabilized somewhat in 2012 but remain very high. Djibouti depends heavily on food imports, has few natural resources and little industry, and relies on foreign assistance to help support its balance of payments and finance development projects. A nearly 60 percent formal-sector unemployment rate and a lack of fresh water are ongoing challenges.

How Do We Measure Economic Freedom?
See page 471 for an explanation of the methodology or visit the *Index* Web site at *heritage.org/index*.

Freedom Trend

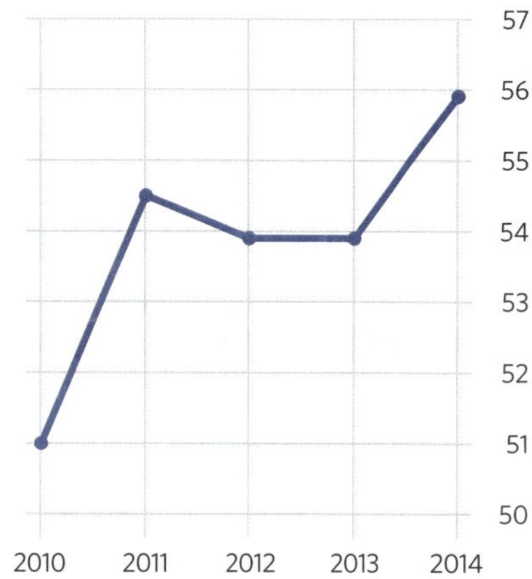

Country Comparisons

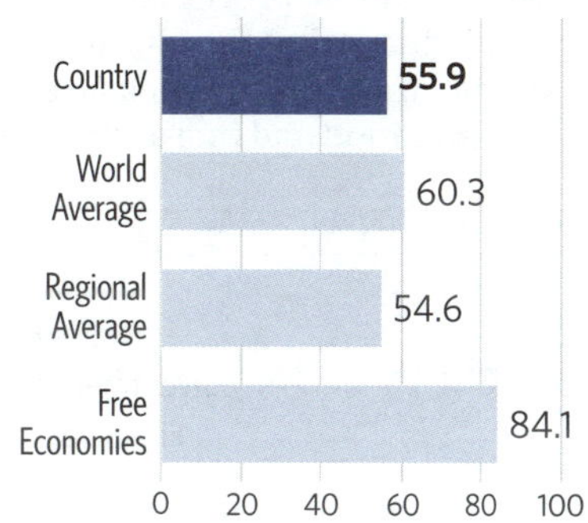

Quick Facts

Population: 0.9 million
GDP (PPP): $2.4 billion
4.8% growth in 2012
5-year compound annual growth 4.7%
$2,677 per capita
Unemployment: 59.0% (2007)
Inflation (CPI): 3.7%
FDI Inflow: $100.0 million
Public Debt: 38.6% of GDP

2012 data unless otherwise noted.
Data compiled as of September 2013.

THE TEN ECONOMIC FREEDOMS

Score ▬ Country | World Average

RULE OF LAW

	Score	Rank	1-Year Change
Property Rights	30.0	93rd	0
Freedom from Corruption	30.9	100th	+0.9

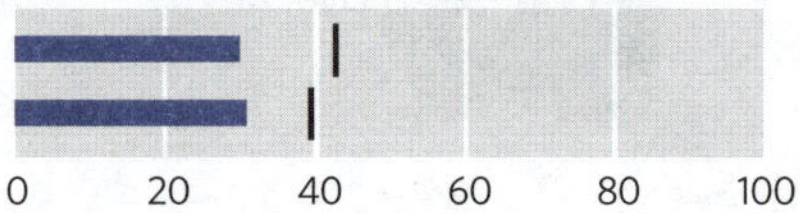

Efforts to curb corruption have met with little success. Power is heavily concentrated in the hands of the president. Public officials are not required to disclose their assets. Trials and judicial proceedings are time-consuming and subject to corruption and political manipulation. Protection of private property is weak. The judicial system is based on the French civil code, although Sharia law prevails in family matters.

GOVERNMENT SIZE

	Score	Rank	1-Year Change
Fiscal Freedom	80.6	78th	+1.2
Government Spending	62.8	110th	+14.0

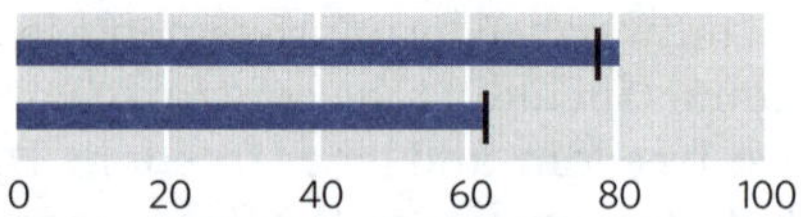

Djibouti's individual income tax rate is 30 percent, and its corporate tax rate is 25 percent. Other taxes include a property tax and an excise tax. The overall tax burden is 20.3 percent of GDP. Government expenditures amount to over one-third of the domestic economy, and public debt is close to 40 percent of GDP.

REGULATORY EFFICIENCY

	Score	Rank	1-Year Change
Business Freedom	42.7	166th	+12.7
Labor Freedom	65.1	80th	+5.5
Monetary Freedom	77.2	71st	+0.6

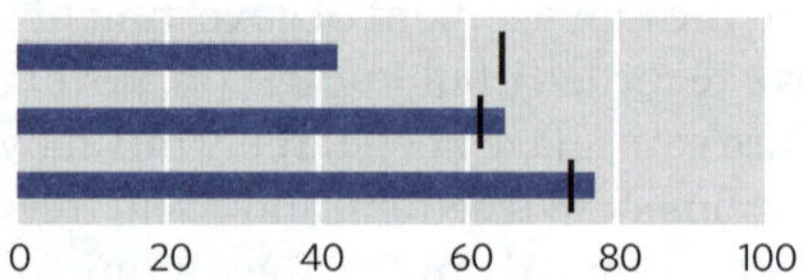

Administrative procedures have been streamlined, and the cost of launching a business has been reduced, but the minimum capital requirement to start a company remains high. Recent labor-market reform measures have not been fully enforced. The government continues to subsidize food and fuel and subjects a range of goods and services to price controls.

OPEN MARKETS

	Score	Rank	1-Year Change
Trade Freedom	54.8	170th	-4.8
Investment Freedom	65.0	68th	0
Financial Freedom	50.0	69th	-10.0

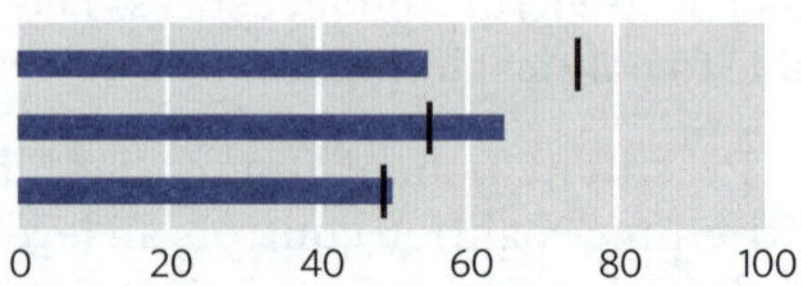

Djibouti's average tariff rate is 17.6 percent, and other non-tariff barriers further constrain trade flows. Although laws do not generally discriminate against foreign investors, some sectors of the economy are restricted. The financial sector generates an increasing share of GDP. Despite establishment of new banks, the sector remains dominated by the two main banks.

Long-Term Score Change (since 1997)

RULE OF LAW		GOVERNMENT SIZE		REGULATORY EFFICIENCY		OPEN MARKETS	
Property Rights	**-20.0**	Fiscal Freedom	**-3.5**	Business Freedom	**-12.3**	Trade Freedom	**+3.8**
Freedom from Corruption	**+0.9**	Government Spending	**+18.3**	Labor Freedom	**+5.4**	Investment Freedom	**+15.0**
				Monetary Freedom	**+1.7**	Financial Freedom	**0**

DOMINICA

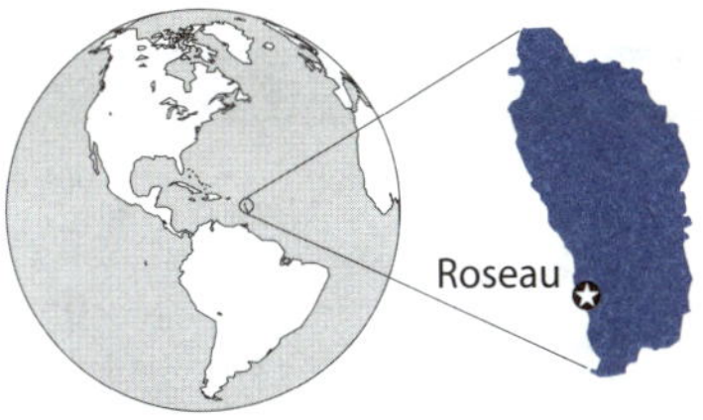

World Rank: **63** Regional Rank: **12**

Dominica's economic freedom score is 65.2, making its economy the 63rd freest in the 2014 *Index*. Its overall score is 1.3 points higher than last year, with improvements in half of the 10 economic freedoms, including the control of government spending, labor freedom, and freedom from corruption. Dominica is ranked 12th out of 29 countries in the South and Central America/Caribbean region, and its overall score is above the world average.

Since Dominica's economic freedom was first assessed in the 2009 *Index*, it has increased only modestly. Improvements in five of the 10 economic freedoms, including investment freedom and the management of public spending, the scores for which have grown by about 10 points each, have been offset somewhat by declines in freedom from corruption, business freedom, and trade freedom.

Still, Dominica has achieved its highest score ever in the 2014 *Index*. Recent reform measures, including simplification of the business start-up process and reduction of the corporate tax rate, have helped to improve the overall investment framework.

BACKGROUND: Dominica has a unicameral parliamentary government with a president and prime minister. Labour Party Prime Minister Roosevelt Skerrit took office in 2004. In 2008, the government joined the Bolivarian Alliance for the Americas (ALBA), a restrictive trade organization led by socialist Venezuela. ALBA's interference in the Caribbean Community (CARICOM) threatens to undermine progress in free-market democratic institutions and regional integration. In 2010, Dominica entered into an economic union with other members of the Organization of Eastern Caribbean States. Bananas, citrus, coconuts, coconut soap, and cocoa dominate the economy, and 40 percent of the labor force works in agriculture. The government encourages investments in coffee, patchouli, aloe vera, exotic fruits, and cut flowers. Dominica's natural beauty inspires eco-tourism, which could further diversify the economy.

How Do We Measure Economic Freedom?
See page 471 for an explanation of the methodology or visit the *Index* Web site at *heritage.org/index*.

Economic Freedom Score

Freedom Trend

Country Comparisons

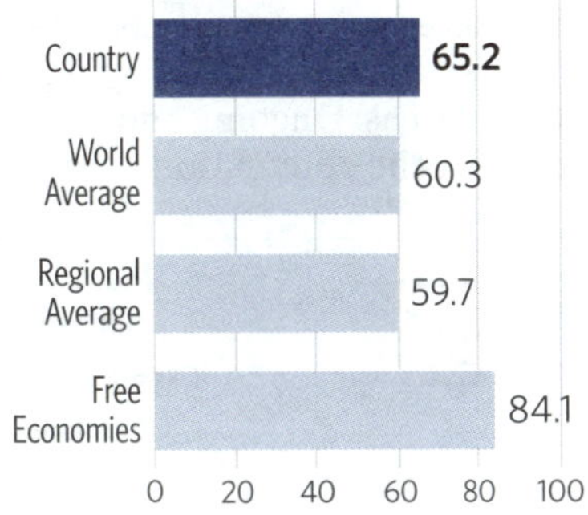

Quick Facts

Population: 0.1 million
GDP (PPP): $1.0 billion
0.4% growth in 2012
5-year compound annual growth 2.0%
$14,166 per capita
Unemployment: n/a
Inflation (CPI): 2.3%
FDI Inflow: $19.7 million
Public Debt: 72.2% of GDP

2012 data unless otherwise noted.
Data compiled as of September 2013.

THE TEN ECONOMIC FREEDOMS

RULE OF LAW

	Score	Rank	1-Year Change
Property Rights	60.0	41st	0
Freedom from Corruption	53.5	43rd	+1.5

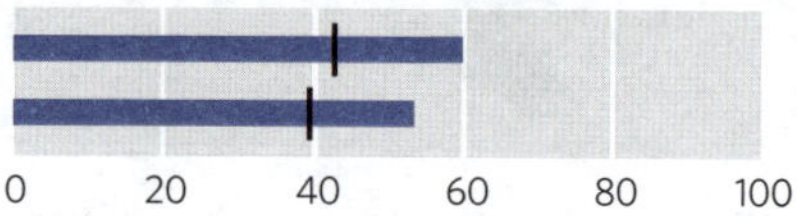

Dominica does not have a major corruption problem, although anti-corruption statutes are sometimes not implemented effectively. The country has an independent judiciary based on English common law, and private property rights are generally respected. Public trials are considered fair. Pirated copyrighted material is sold openly. Non-bank financial institutions are monitored to combat money laundering and the financing of terrorism.

GOVERNMENT SIZE

	Score	Rank	1-Year Change
Fiscal Freedom	72.9	127th	+0.9
Government Spending	61.7	116th	+11.6

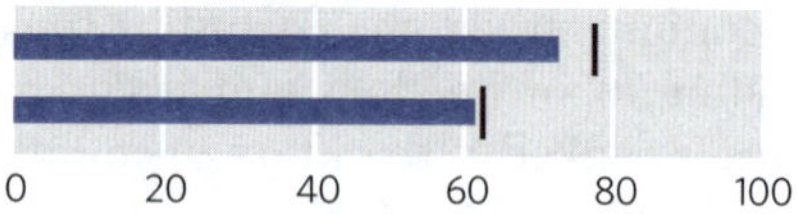

The top individual income tax rate is 35 percent, and the top corporate tax rate is 30 percent. Other taxes include a value-added tax (VAT) and an environmental tax. The overall tax burden is 24.2 percent of GDP. Government spending is 36 percent of the domestic economy. Fiscal stimulus has accelerated debt pressures in recent years, and public debt has reached almost 73 percent of GDP.

REGULATORY EFFICIENCY

	Score	Rank	1-Year Change
Business Freedom	75.0	49th	-2.0
Labor Freedom	70.7	62nd	+1.9
Monetary Freedom	85.8	4th	+0.5

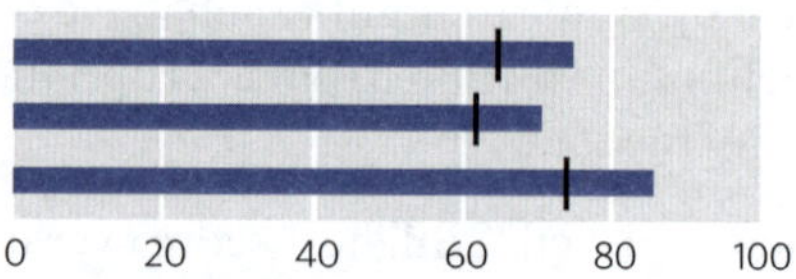

Launching a business takes only five procedures, and no minimum capital is required. Obtaining necessary permits costs less than 10 percent of the level of average annual income. The non-salary cost of employing a worker is moderate, but the labor market lacks flexibility in other areas. Ongoing and comprehensive government attempts to restructure the economy include the elimination of price controls.

OPEN MARKETS

	Score	Rank	1-Year Change
Trade Freedom	72.7	114th	-1.6
Investment Freedom	70.0	46th	0
Financial Freedom	30.0	132nd	0

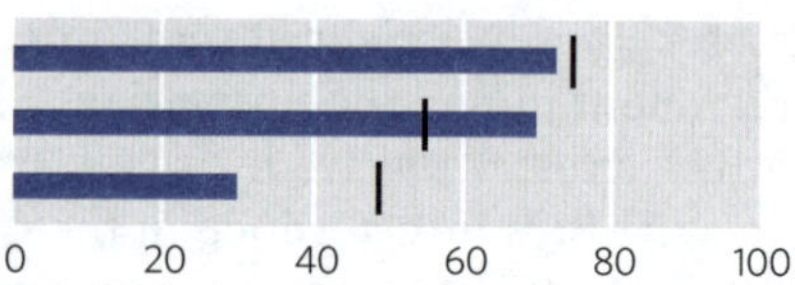

Dominica's average tariff rate is 8.6 percent. New investment is screened by the government, but in general, foreign and domestic investors are treated equally under the law. Administration of the investment regime remains bureaucratic. The financial sector remains underdeveloped. Shallow markets and a lack of available financial instruments restrict overall access to credit.

Long-Term Score Change (since 2009)

RULE OF LAW		GOVERNMENT SIZE		REGULATORY EFFICIENCY		OPEN MARKETS	
Property Rights	0	Fiscal Freedom	+5.5	Business Freedom	-1.4	Trade Freedom	-1.5
Freedom from Corruption	-2.5	Government Spending	+9.5	Labor Freedom	+0.7	Investment Freedom	+10.0
				Monetary Freedom	+6.0	Financial Freedom	0

DOMINICAN REPUBLIC

World Rank: **80** Regional Rank: **16**

Economic Freedom Score

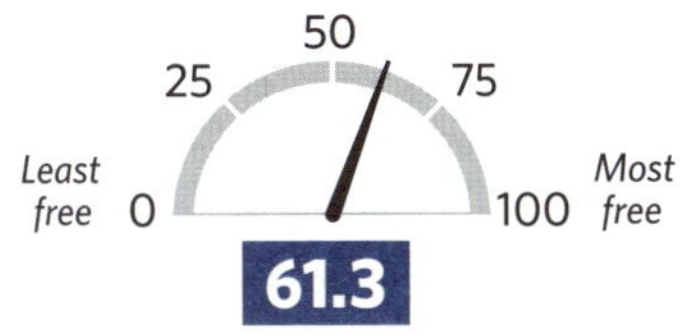

Freedom Trend

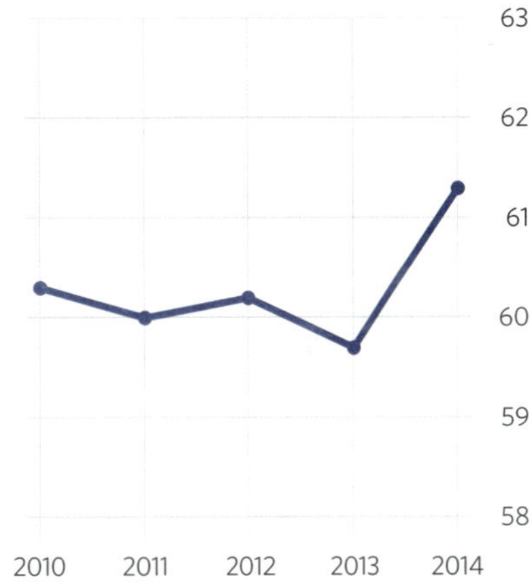

Country Comparisons

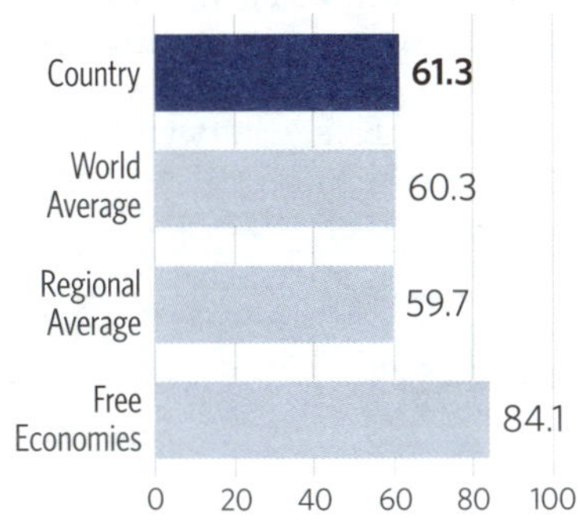

The Dominican Republic's economic freedom score is 61.3, making its economy the 80th freest in the 2014 *Index*. Its overall score is 1.6 points higher than last year due to improvements in investment freedom, monetary freedom, business freedom, and freedom from corruption. The Dominican Republic is ranked 16th out of 29 countries in the South and Central America/Caribbean region, and its score is just above the regional average.

Over the 20-year history of the *Index*, the Dominican Republic's economic freedom score has risen by over 5 points, driven by gains in only three of the 10 economic freedoms. Most improved is the area of market openness. The trade freedom score increase of more than 45 points is one of the largest gains in that category since the founding of the *Index*. The Dominican Republic has advanced into the ranks of the "moderately free" over the past five years.

Nevertheless, the lack of deeper institutional reforms remains a serious impediment to further improvements in economic freedom. The most visible constraints on private-sector development involve excessive administrative bureaucracy and a lack of respect for contracts. Government inefficiency and widespread corruption affect much of the economy.

BACKGROUND: In August 2012, Danilo Medina of the center-left Dominican Liberation Party won the presidency, succeeding three-term President Leonel Fernández. Before the 2008–2009 global financial crisis, there had been a surge in economic growth led by tourism, telecommunications, and maquiladora manufacturing. The economy rebounded somewhat in 2010, and moderate growth has continued. The DR has a nearly $1.7 billion IMF standby agreement. The Central America–Dominican Republic–United States Free Trade Agreement (CAFTA–DR) has helped to boost investment and exports and minimize market-share losses to Asian textile manufacturers. Corruption, wasteful government spending, and unreliable electric service reduce investment returns and contribute to high unemployment. Drug and human trafficking persist. Approximately one-tenth of GDP is supported by remittances from the U.S.

How Do We Measure Economic Freedom?
See page 471 for an explanation of the methodology or visit the *Index* Web site at *heritage.org/index*.

Quick Facts

Population: 10.2 million
GDP (PPP): $98.7 billion
3.9% growth in 2012
5-year compound annual growth 5.0%
$9,646 per capita
Unemployment: 13.0%
Inflation (CPI): 3.7%
FDI Inflow: $3.6 billion
Public Debt: 33.5% of GDP

2012 data unless otherwise noted.
Data compiled as of September 2013.

DOMINICAN REPUBLIC (continued)

THE TEN ECONOMIC FREEDOMS

		Score	Rank	1-Year Change
RULE OF LAW	Property Rights	30.0	93rd	0
	Freedom from Corruption	27.3	120th	+1.3

Official corruption remains a serious problem in the security forces, civilian government, and private sector, and officials can engage in corrupt practices with impunity. The Dominican Republic is a major transit hub for narco-traffickers. The judiciary is politicized and riddled with corruption, and the legal system offers little recourse to those without money or influence. Enforcement of intellectual property rights remains poor.

		Score	Rank	1-Year Change
GOVERNMENT SIZE	Fiscal Freedom	83.7	60th	0
	Government Spending	92.3	7th	-0.3

The top individual income tax rate is 25 percent, and the top corporate tax rate is 29 percent. Other taxes include a value-added tax (VAT), an estate tax, and a net wealth tax. Overall tax revenue is up slightly to 13 percent of GDP. Expenditures have been steady at around 16 percent of GDP. This has put pressure on public finances. Public debt is about 34 percent of gross domestic output.

		Score	Rank	1-Year Change
REGULATORY EFFICIENCY	Business Freedom	56.1	132nd	+2.4
	Labor Freedom	55.2	113th	-0.4
	Monetary Freedom	75.7	87th	+2.8

Incorporating a business takes more than two weeks, and licensing requirements cost over half the level of average annual income. The non-salary cost of employing a worker is moderate, but restrictions on work hours are rigid. By 2012, the government had replaced universal subsidies on gas and electricity with targeted subsidies, higher electricity tariffs, and conditional cash transfers.

		Score	Rank	1-Year Change
OPEN MARKETS	Trade Freedom	77.8	82nd	0
	Investment Freedom	75.0	35th	+10.0
	Financial Freedom	40.0	107th	0

The average tariff rate for the Dominican Republic is 6.1 percent. Foreign investors may not be able to rely fully on enforcement of laws and regulations. The small financial sector remains relatively stable and continues to evolve in a positive manner. Distortions in the foreign exchange market have gradually been eliminated, and a range of credit instruments is available for the private sector.

Long-Term Score Change (since 1995)

RULE OF LAW		GOVERNMENT SIZE		REGULATORY EFFICIENCY		OPEN MARKETS	
Property Rights	0	Fiscal Freedom	-0.7	Business Freedom	+1.1	Trade Freedom	+46.8
Freedom from Corruption	-2.7	Government Spending	-3.1	Labor Freedom	-1.7	Investment Freedom	+25.0
				Monetary Freedom	-0.5	Financial Freedom	-10.0

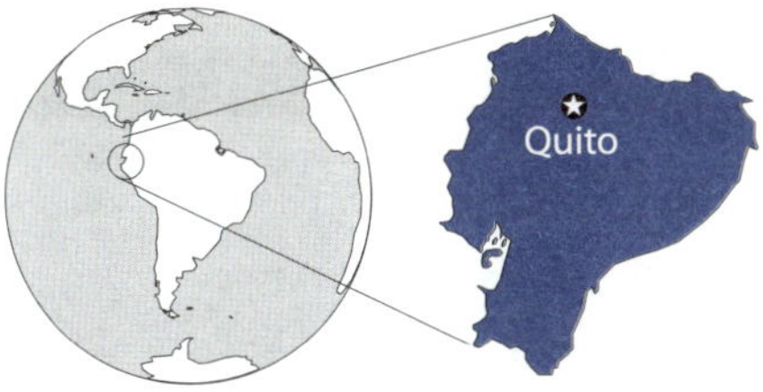

ECUADOR

World Rank: 159 **Regional Rank: 26**

Economic Freedom Score

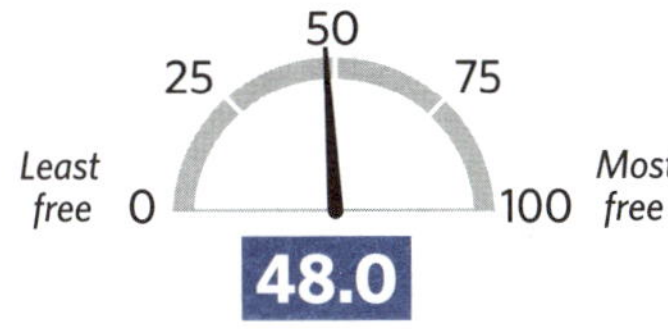

Freedom Trend

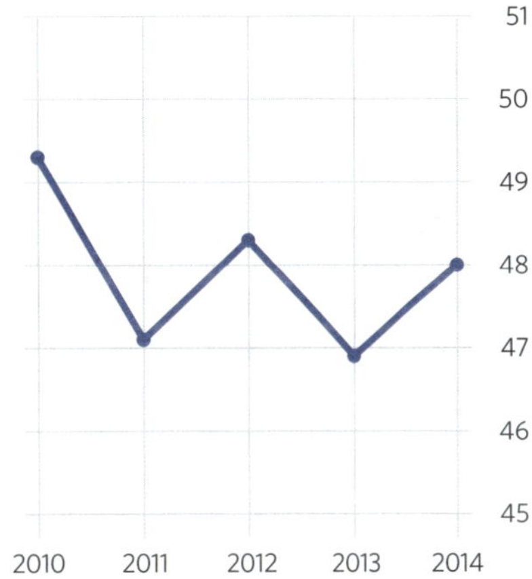

Country Comparisons

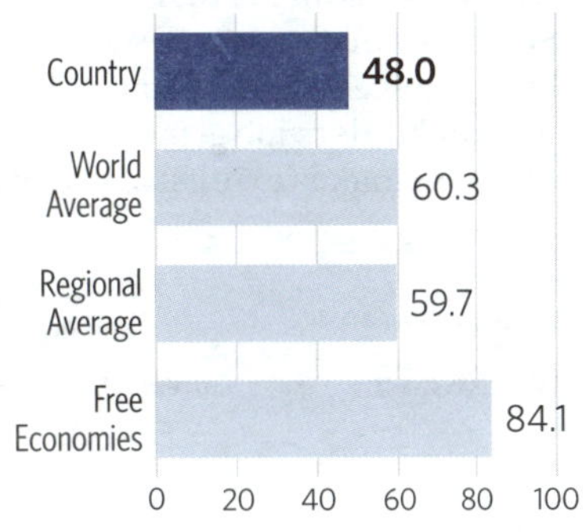

Ecuador's economic freedom score is 48.0, making its economy the 159th freest in the 2014 *Index*. Its overall score is 1.1 points higher than last year, with deteriorations in the management of government spending and freedom from corruption offset by improvements in investment freedom, trade freedom, and labor freedom. Ecuador is ranked 26th out of 29 countries in the South and Central America/Caribbean region, and its overall score is far below the world and regional averages.

Over the 20-year history of the *Index*, Ecuador's economic freedom has fallen nearly 10 points, the fifth largest drop of any country. Investment freedom, government spending, and property rights have deteriorated 30 points or more. Ecuador's economic freedom rose to "moderately free" during the second half of the 1990s but has fallen steadily since then. Over the past five years, Ecuador has been downgraded to a "repressed" economy.

Ecuador continues to lag notably in promoting the rule of law and strengthening the legal framework. The judicial system remains vulnerable to political interference, with corruption further exacerbating institutional shortcomings. Expansionary public spending threatens fiscal sustainability.

BACKGROUND: President Rafael Correa, re-elected in 2013 for the third time, wants to return to international credit markets in 2014 for the first time since Ecuador's $3.2 billion default in 2008 but first will have to negotiate a deal with creditors who in 2009 rejected terms of the country's debt swap. Constitutional amendments passed in 2011 increased Correa's control of the media and the judicial system. He has also worked to undercut the Inter-American Human Rights Commission. Ecuador is part of the ALBA group, led by socialist Venezuela, and has strengthened its relations with Iran. Oil revenues and borrowing from China have counterbalanced declining foreign investment from the West and continued capital flight. Economic growth has moderated significantly. Ecuador is the world's largest banana exporter and has important petroleum reserves. Correa has stiffened contract terms with foreign oil producers and advanced resource nationalism. Approximately one-third of the population lives below the poverty line.

Quick Facts

Population: 15.2 million
GDP (PPP): $153.2 billion
5.0% growth in 2012
5-year compound annual growth 4.7%
$10,056 per capita
Unemployment: 5.3%
Inflation (CPI): 5.1%
FDI Inflow: $586.5 million
Public Debt: 18.6% of GDP

2012 data unless otherwise noted.
Data compiled as of September 2013.

How Do We Measure Economic Freedom?
See page 471 for an explanation of the methodology or visit the *Index* Web site at *heritage.org/index*.

THE TEN ECONOMIC FREEDOMS

Score ▬ Country | World Average

		Score	Rank	1-Year Change
RULE OF LAW	Property Rights	20.0	139th	0
	Freedom from Corruption	26.0	128th	-1.0

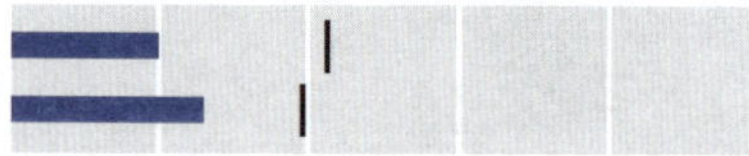

Ecuador has long suffered from political instability and corruption. The weak and politicized judiciary and lack of investigative capacity in government oversight agencies contribute to an atmosphere of impunity. Illicit payments for official favors and theft of public funds reportedly take place frequently. Expropriation is a problem, and the government is constitutionally empowered to control strategic sectors such as natural resources.

		Score	Rank	1-Year Change
GOVERNMENT SIZE	Fiscal Freedom	79.8	88th	-0.3
	Government Spending	41.8	149th	-5.5

Ecuador's top individual income tax rate is 35 percent. The top corporate tax rate has been reduced to 22 percent, and the special rate for reinvested profits remains at 15 percent. Other taxes include a value-added tax (VAT) and an inheritance tax. The overall tax burden is 17.6 percent of GDP. Government spending has risen to 44 percent of GDP. Public debt is low, but the economy continues to suffer from a debt default in 2008.

		Score	Rank	1-Year Change
REGULATORY EFFICIENCY	Business Freedom	52.8	146th	+1.3
	Labor Freedom	52.0	130th	+4.0
	Monetary Freedom	66.1	159th	-0.8

Despite ongoing reform efforts, the overall regulatory environment remains burdensome. Starting a business takes almost two months, but the cost of obtaining necessary permits has been reduced to about half of the level of average annual income. Lack of flexibility in the labor market hinders job growth. Although dollarization produces a modicum of monetary stability, the state makes extensive use of subsidies and price controls.

		Score	Rank	1-Year Change
OPEN MARKETS	Trade Freedom	71.8	121st	+3.7
	Investment Freedom	30.0	152nd	+10.0
	Financial Freedom	40.0	107th	0

Ecuador's average tariff rate is 4.1 percent, and non-tariff barriers continue to interfere with trade. In 2012, the International Centre for Settlement of Investment Disputes (ICSID) hit Ecuador with the largest penalty in the ICSID's history for expropriating property. Government interference in the underdeveloped financial sector is growing, and state banks have become more dominant.

Long-Term Score Change (since 1995)

RULE OF LAW		GOVERNMENT SIZE		REGULATORY EFFICIENCY		OPEN MARKETS	
Property Rights	**-30.0**	Fiscal Freedom	**-2.0**	Business Freedom	**-2.2**	Trade Freedom	**+10.8**
Freedom from Corruption	**+16.0**	Government Spending	**-53.0**	Labor Freedom	**+12.3**	Investment Freedom	**-40.0**
				Monetary Freedom	**+19.8**	Financial Freedom	**-10.0**

EGYPT

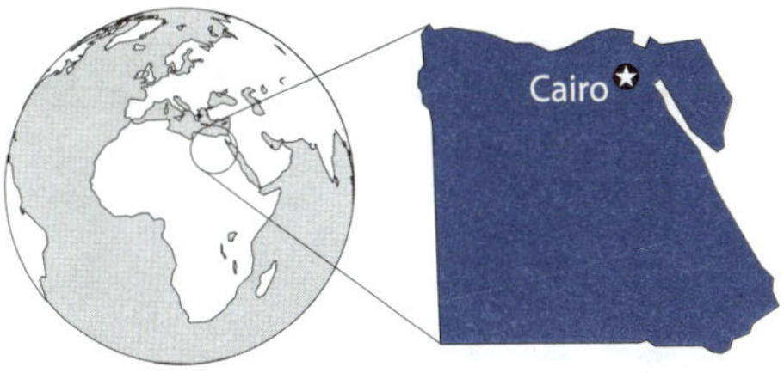

World Rank: **135** Regional Rank: **13**

Economic Freedom Score

Egypt's economic freedom score is 52.9, making its economy the 135th freest in the 2014 *Index*. Its overall score is 1.9 points lower than last year, reflecting declines in half of the 10 economic freedoms including investment freedom, property rights, and freedom from corruption. Egypt is ranked 13th out of 15 countries in the Middle East/North Africa region, and its overall score is below the world and regional averages.

Over the 20-year history of the *Index*, Egypt's economic freedom score has risen over 7 points, reflecting advancements in fiscal freedom and trade freedom. However, overall improvement has been held back by considerable deterioration in other areas, particularly the rule of law as measured through property rights and freedom from corruption. The country's uneven reform progress has largely stalled in recent years, and scores for investment freedom and financial freedom have fallen back as well. Egypt is now on a downward path of economic freedom, registering its lowest score in 12 years in the 2014 *Index*.

Egypt's lack of progress in advancing economic freedom has trapped many of its citizens in poverty and economic stagnation. As noted in earlier editions of the *Index*, institutional reforms are critically needed to ensure Egypt's transition to a functioning market economy under an effective rule of law.

BACKGROUND: The Egyptian army ousted President Hosni Mubarak in February 2011 after massive protests destabilized his government. The Supreme Council of the Armed Forces assumed power pending election of a new civilian government. The parliament was dissolved in June 2012 after the Supreme Constitutional Court ruled that one-third of its members had won their seats illegitimately. Mohamed Morsi of the Muslim Brotherhood's Freedom and Justice Party won the June 2012 presidential election and granted himself sweeping new powers in November. This led to his ouster in mid-2013. Domestic instability and political uncertainty have hurt tourism and foreign investment, both of which are important sources of foreign exchange. There have been limited market reforms, but the government still heavily subsidizes food, energy, and other key commodities.

How Do We Measure Economic Freedom?
See page 471 for an explanation of the methodology or visit the *Index* Web site at *heritage.org/index*.

Freedom Trend

Country Comparisons

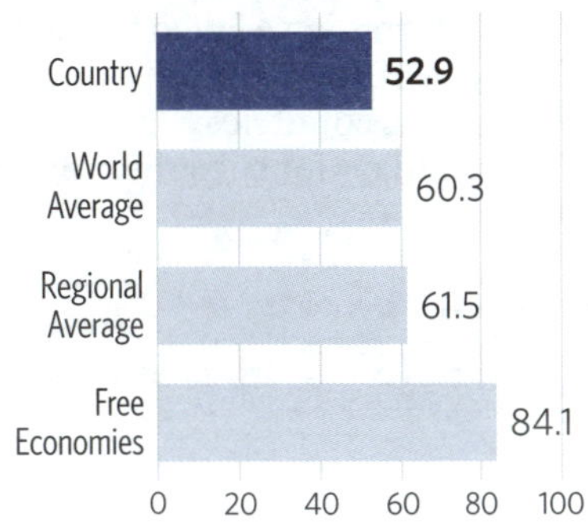

Quick Facts

Population: 82.5 million
GDP (PPP): $540.0 billion
2.2% growth in 2012
5-year compound annual growth 4.2%
$6,545 per capita
Unemployment: 12.3%
Inflation (CPI): 8.6%
FDI Inflow: $2.8 billion
Public Debt: 80.2% of GDP

2012 data unless otherwise noted.
Data compiled as of September 2013.

THE TEN ECONOMIC FREEDOMS

RULE OF LAW

	Score	Rank	1-Year Change
Property Rights	20.0	139th	-15.0
Freedom from Corruption	28.6	113th	-0.4

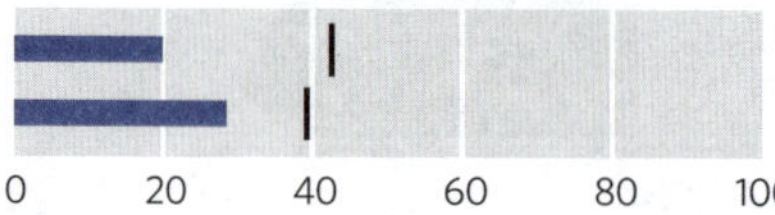

Corruption is pervasive at all levels of government and has eroded trust in the economic system. The rule of law has been highly unstable across the country, and the judicial system's independence is poorly institutionalized. Judicial procedures tend to be protracted, costly, and subject to political pressure. Property rights are not protected effectively, and titles to real property may be difficult to establish.

GOVERNMENT SIZE

	Score	Rank	1-Year Change
Fiscal Freedom	85.6	50th	0
Government Spending	69.6	90th	+0.2

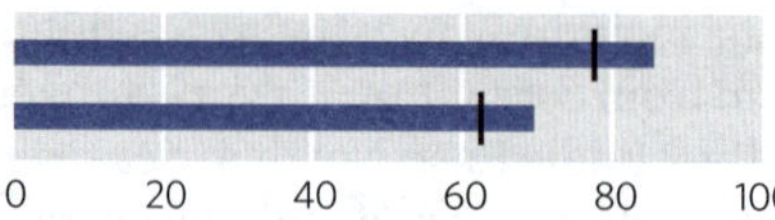

The top individual income and corporate tax rates are 25 percent. Other taxes include a property tax and a general sales tax. The total tax burden is 13.8 percent of GDP. Government spending is 32 percent of the domestic economy, and public debt, now over 80 percent of GDP, continues to rise. International support has buoyed delicate public finances amid political instability.

REGULATORY EFFICIENCY

	Score	Rank	1-Year Change
Business Freedom	62.7	100th	-0.6
Labor Freedom	45.7	153rd	+2.4
Monetary Freedom	60.5	175th	+2.1

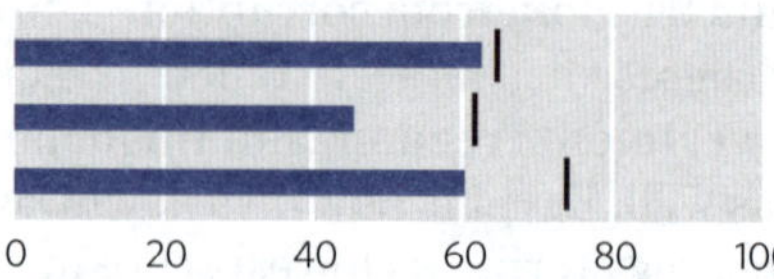

Launching a company and organizing new investment remain burdensome. Previous regulatory reforms have failed to create real momentum for dynamic entrepreneurial growth. In the absence of a well-functioning labor market, informal labor activity persists. Among energy-importing countries, Egypt has one of the highest levels of electricity and fuel subsidies; in 2012, outlays for subsidies soared by 42 percent.

OPEN MARKETS

	Score	Rank	1-Year Change
Trade Freedom	71.4	124th	-2.4
Investment Freedom	45.0	125th	-5.0
Financial Freedom	40.0	107th	0

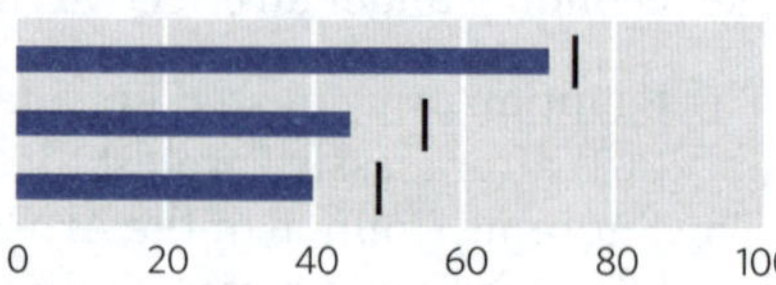

Egypt's average tariff rate is a relatively high 9.3 percent. Political unrest discourages new foreign investment. Investment flows have slowed significantly due to the challenging economic and political situation. The state-dominated financial system has been under stress, with negative impacts from the global economic slowdown exacerbated by domestic turbulence. Banking-sector reform programs have been stalled or derailed.

Long-Term Score Change (since 1995)

RULE OF LAW		GOVERNMENT SIZE		REGULATORY EFFICIENCY		OPEN MARKETS	
Property Rights	**-10.0**	Fiscal Freedom	**+39.6**	Business Freedom	**+7.7**	Trade Freedom	**+46.4**
Freedom from Corruption	**-1.4**	Government Spending	**+16.0**	Labor Freedom	**-13.9**	Investment Freedom	**-5.0**
				Monetary Freedom	**-11.5**	Financial Freedom	**-10.0**

EL SALVADOR

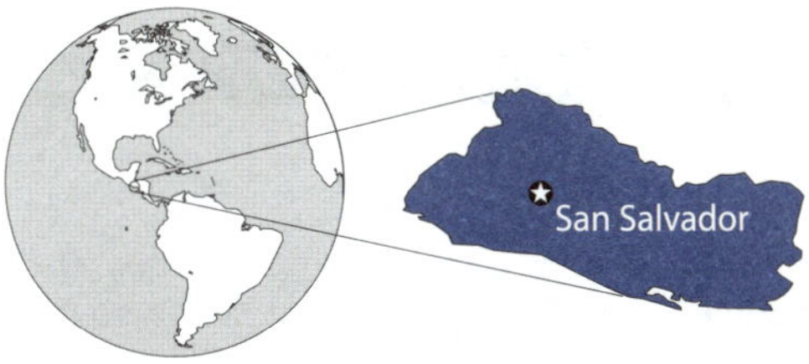

World Rank: 59 **Regional Rank: 11**

Economic Freedom Score

El Salvador's economic freedom score is 66.2, making its economy the 59th freest in the 2014 *Index*. Its overall score is 0.5 point lower than last year due to declines in business freedom and fiscal freedom. El Salvador is ranked 11th out of 29 countries in the South and Central America/Caribbean region, and its overall score remains above the world average.

Over the 20-year history of the *Index*, El Salvador's economic freedom has been stagnant, with hard-won gains in earlier years wiped out by more recent declines in the areas of the rule of law, government size, and regulatory efficiency. Scores for eight of the 10 economic freedoms, notably freedom from corruption, property rights, business freedom, and government spending, have deteriorated markedly over the past two decades.

El Salvador reached its highest economic freedom score in 2000 and achieved the rank of a "mostly free" economy from 1996 to 2005. However, the Salvadorian economy has fallen back to the category of "moderately free" since 2006 and registers its lowest score ever in the 2014 *Index*.

BACKGROUND: After the end of El Salvador's 12-year civil war in 1992, three successive presidents from the National Republican Alliance (ARENA) maintained free-market policies that delivered economic growth and reduced poverty. A fourth ARENA president, Antonio Saca, was less interested in economic reform and the rule of law. Mauricio Funes of the leftist Farabundo Marti Liberation Front (FMLN), elected in 2009, has failed either to reduce growing public debt or to reverse the upward trend in food prices. His policies have repelled foreign investors. The state is plagued by corruption and violence. The government brokered a truce between the country's two major rival gangs, and in little more than a year, homicides dropped approximately 41 percent. However, Security Minister David Mungia Payes, who oversaw the truce, was forced to resign, and a return of gang violence is feared.

Freedom Trend

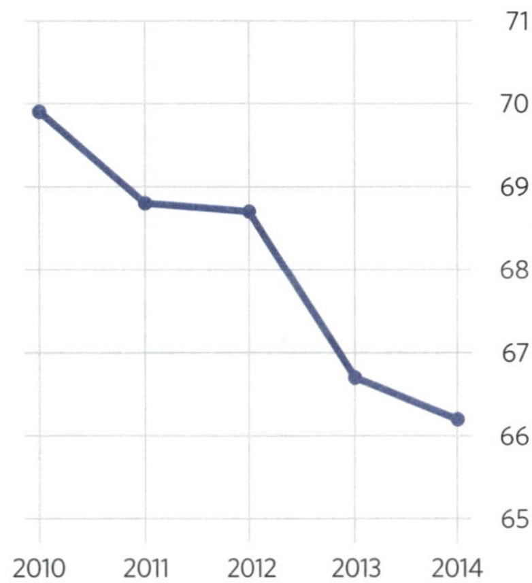

Country Comparisons

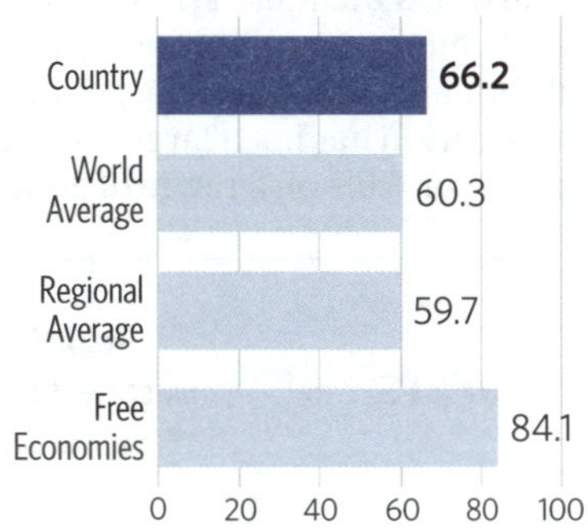

Quick Facts

Population: 6.2 million
GDP (PPP): $46.3 billion
1.6% growth in 2012
5-year compound annual growth 0.6%
$7,438 per capita
Unemployment: 5.7%
Inflation (CPI): 1.7%
FDI Inflow: $515.8 million
Public Debt: 52.2% of GDP

2012 data unless otherwise noted.
Data compiled as of September 2013.

How Do We Measure Economic Freedom?
See page 471 for an explanation of the methodology or visit the *Index* Web site at *heritage.org/index*.

THE TEN ECONOMIC FREEDOMS

Legend: Country | World Average

RULE OF LAW

	Score	Rank	1-Year Change
Property Rights	40.0	70th	0
Freedom from Corruption	34.3	78th	+0.3

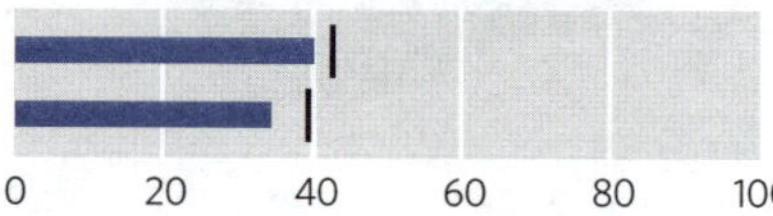

Corruption remains a serious problem in El Salvador, but few high-level public officials have been charged or convicted. The judicial system has demonstrated its independence but is still subject to corruption and obstructionism. Property rights are not strongly respected, and law enforcement is inefficient and uneven. Violent crime, much of it gang-related, continues to be a problem.

GOVERNMENT SIZE

	Score	Rank	1-Year Change
Fiscal Freedom	79.6	93rd	-6.1
Government Spending	85.8	30th	+0.4

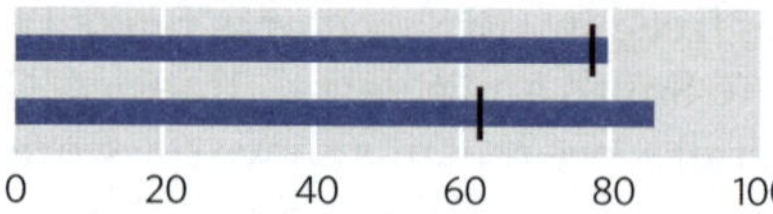

The top marginal individual income and corporate tax rates have risen to 30 percent. Other taxes include a value-added tax (VAT) and excise taxes. The overall tax burden is 15.4 percent of GDP. Government expenditures have reached 22 percent of the economy. Public debt is now 52 percent of GDP, and deteriorating debt forecasts have led some rating agencies to cut credit ratings.

REGULATORY EFFICIENCY

	Score	Rank	1-Year Change
Business Freedom	59.6	115th	-2.2
Labor Freedom	63.3	84th	+1.3
Monetary Freedom	80.0	32nd	+0.4

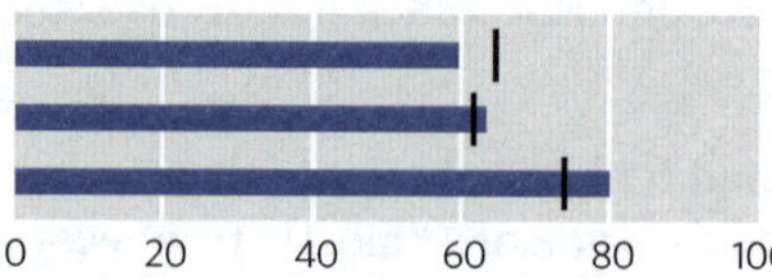

Starting a business still takes more than two weeks, and completing the necessary permits costs more than the level of average annual income. The inefficient labor market lacks flexibility, and imbalances persist in the demand and supply of skilled workers. Although electric generation has been largely privatized, the government partially subsidizes fuels and imposes price controls on a range of goods and services.

OPEN MARKETS

	Score	Rank	1-Year Change
Trade Freedom	79.0	75th	0
Investment Freedom	70.0	46th	0
Financial Freedom	70.0	19th	0

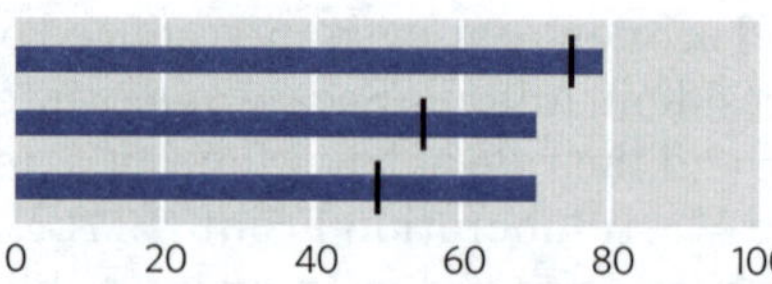

El Salvador's average tariff rate is 5.5 percent. Foreign investors can find the legal and regulatory systems challenging. The financial sector is dominated by banks, which are mostly owned by foreign financial institutions. Two of the banks operating in the country, focusing on mortgages and financial services to the agricultural sector, are state-owned. Overall, the banking sector remains relatively stable.

Long-Term Score Change (since 1995)

RULE OF LAW		GOVERNMENT SIZE		REGULATORY EFFICIENCY		OPEN MARKETS	
Property Rights	**-10.0**	Fiscal Freedom	**-4.1**	Business Freedom	**-10.4**	Trade Freedom	**+14.0**
Freedom from Corruption	**-15.7**	Government Spending	**-7.8**	Labor Freedom	**-4.8**	Investment Freedom	**0**
				Monetary Freedom	**+10.6**	Financial Freedom	**0**

EQUATORIAL GUINEA

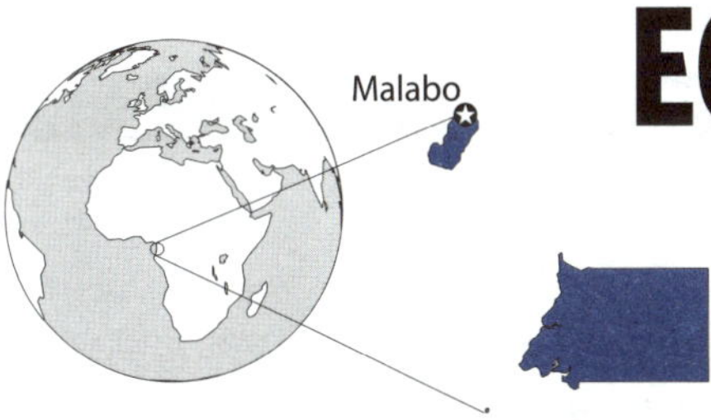

World Rank: 168 **Regional Rank: 42**

Economic Freedom Score

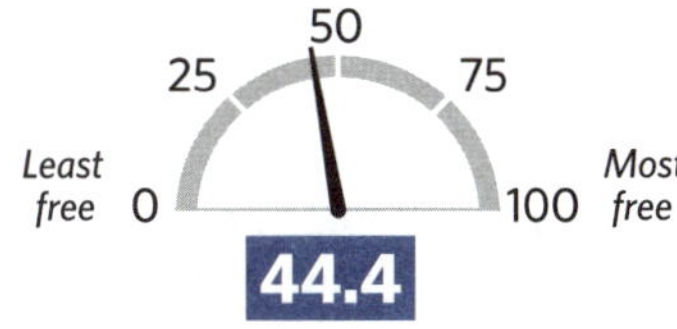

Equatorial Guinea's economic freedom score is 44.4, making its economy the 168th freest in the 2014 *Index*. Its overall score has risen by 2.1 points, with improvements in investment freedom and government spending overcoming deteriorations in trade freedom, property rights, and freedom from corruption. Equatorial Guinea is ranked 42nd out of 46 countries in the Sub-Saharan Africa region, and its score is below the regional and world averages.

Over the 16 years during which Equatorial Guinea has been graded in the *Index*, its economic freedom has remained largely stagnant. Improvements in financial freedom, investment freedom, monetary freedom, and freedom from corruption have been outweighed by double-digit declines in government spending, fiscal freedom, and business freedom. Equatorial Guinea had moved out of the ranks of the "repressed" from 2003 to 2009 but has fallen back to that status since 2010.

Equatorial Guinea's overall economic performance is undermined by poor institutional performance in some of the foundational areas of economic freedom. The judiciary is vulnerable to political interference, the rule of law is weak, and corruption is pervasive. A substantial reform effort will be required to encourage broad-based economic development.

BACKGROUND: President Teodoro Obiang Nguema Mbasogo seized power in 1979 and continues to control the military and the government. Equatorial Guinea is a significant oil producer and one of Africa's fastest-growing economies. In 2007, oil accounted for 91 percent of GDP, 91 percent of government revenue, and 99 percent of exports. Foreign investment in the oil industry is extensive, but government management of oil wealth is not transparent. Corruption is high. Average living standards are low. Most people still rely on subsistence farming, hunting, and fishing. Undeveloped natural resources include zinc, diamonds, gold, and other precious metals. Forestry and farming also contribute modestly to GDP. The president's son, Minister of Agriculture and Forestry Nguema Obiang Mangue, has been accused of embezzling public funds to buy property in France.

Freedom Trend

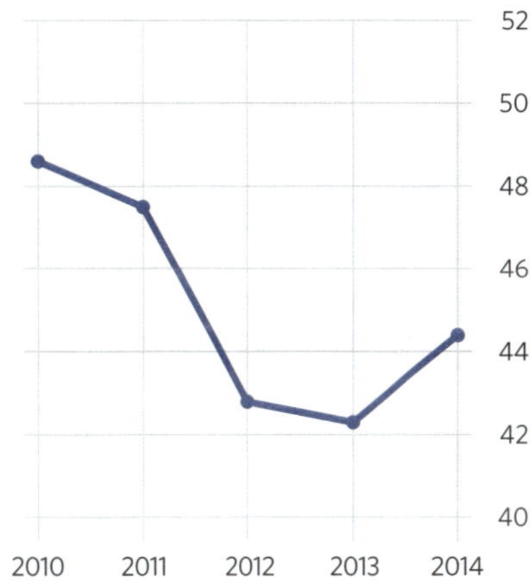

Country Comparisons

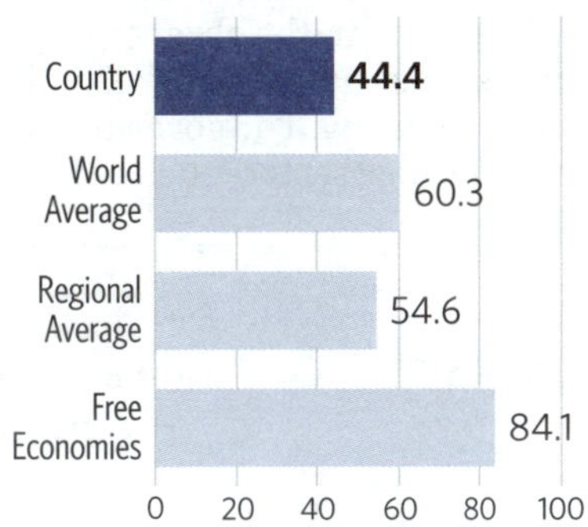

Quick Facts

Population: 0.7 million
GDP (PPP): $19.3 billion
2.0% growth in 2012
5-year compound annual growth 2.7%
$25,929 per capita
Unemployment: 22.3% (2009)
Inflation (CPI): 5.5%
FDI Inflow: $2.1 billion
Public Debt: 8.2% of GDP

2012 data unless otherwise noted.
Data compiled as of September 2013.

How Do We Measure Economic Freedom?
See page 471 for an explanation of the methodology or visit the *Index* Web site at *heritage.org/index*.

THE TEN ECONOMIC FREEDOMS

RULE OF LAW

	Score	Rank	1-Year Change
Property Rights	10.0	166th	-5.0
Freedom from Corruption	16.6	173rd	-2.4

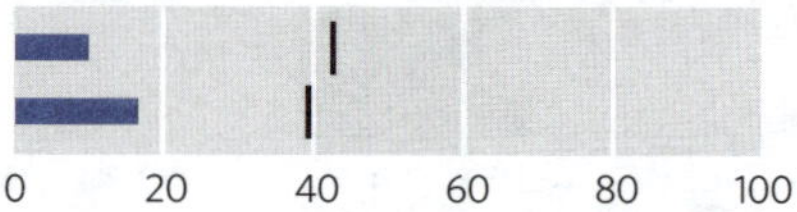

President Obiang and his inner circle dominate Equatorial Guinea's economic landscape, and graft is rampant. Most major business transactions cannot transpire without involving an individual connected to the regime. The judiciary is not independent, and judges in sensitive cases reportedly consult with the president's office before making decisions. Protection of property rights is poor.

GOVERNMENT SIZE

	Score	Rank	1-Year Change
Fiscal Freedom	75.5	117th	+0.1
Government Spending	62.6	112th	+23.3

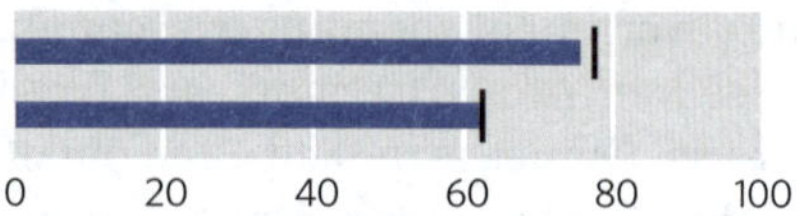

The top individual income and corporate tax rates are 35 percent. Other taxes include a value-added tax (VAT) and a tax on inheritance. The overall tax burden remains a low 1.5 percent of GDP. Public expenditures are 35 percent of the gross domestic economy. Oil revenue continues to be a main supporter of public finances, keeping public debt below 10 percent of GDP.

REGULATORY EFFICIENCY

	Score	Rank	1-Year Change
Business Freedom	43.4	163rd	-1.0
Labor Freedom	41.5	165th	-1.6
Monetary Freedom	75.4	94th	+2.6

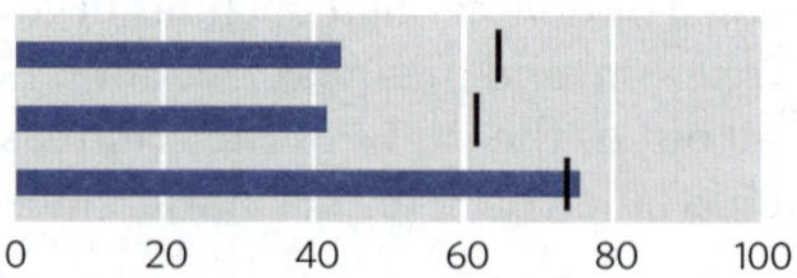

Cumbersome procedures and high compliance costs continue to be impediments to starting a business. In the absence of private-sector employment opportunities, an organized labor market has not emerged. Existing labor regulations are outmoded and create challenging barriers to hiring. The government has misused its substantial oil revenues by using state funds to subsidize sectors such as fisheries, agriculture, and eco-tourism.

OPEN MARKETS

	Score	Rank	1-Year Change
Trade Freedom	53.8	172nd	-5.0
Investment Freedom	35.0	142nd	+10.0
Financial Freedom	30.0	132nd	0

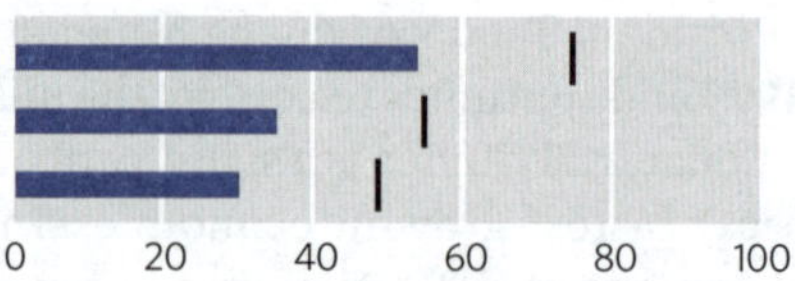

Equatorial Guinea's average tariff rate was 15.6 percent as of 2007. As with other members of the Central African Economic and Monetary Community, it may take weeks to import cargo. The government plays a role in foreign investment decisions. The financial sector remains subject to heavy state interference. Access to financing is limited. The government controls long-term lending through the state-owned development bank.

Long-Term Score Change (since 1999)

RULE OF LAW		GOVERNMENT SIZE		REGULATORY EFFICIENCY		OPEN MARKETS	
Property Rights	0	Fiscal Freedom	-13.8	Business Freedom	-11.6	Trade Freedom	-0.6
Freedom from Corruption	+6.6	Government Spending	-18.8	Labor Freedom	-5.9	Investment Freedom	+5.0
				Monetary Freedom	+9.4	Financial Freedom	+20.0

ERITREA

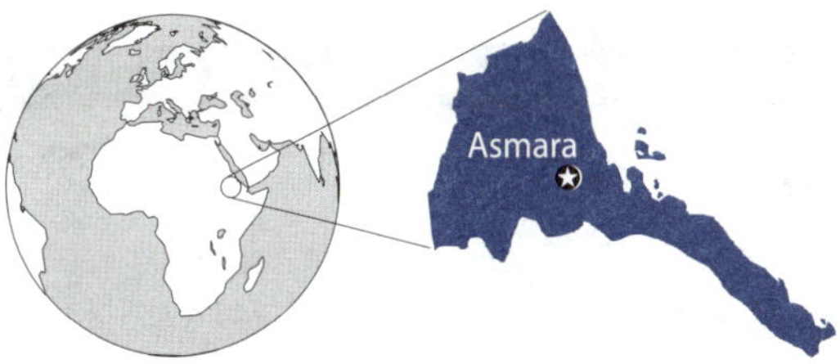

World Rank: 174 **Regional Rank: 45**

Economic Freedom Score

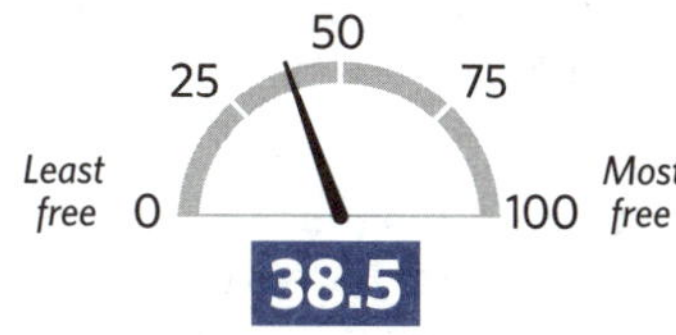

Eritrea's economic freedom score is 38.5, making its economy one of the least free in the 2014 *Index*. Its overall score is 2.2 points better than last year due to improvements in the control of government spending, labor freedom, and monetary freedom that offset a decline in freedom from corruption. Eritrea is ranked 45th out of the 46 countries in the Sub-Saharan Africa region.

Eritrea's economic freedom was first assessed in the 2009 *Index* and has remained stagnant near the bottom of the *Index* rankings. Score improvements in government spending and business have been completely offset by deteriorations in six of the 10 economic freedoms including investment freedom, labor freedom, and fiscal freedom. Scores for financial freedom and property rights have not changed. The country continues to be stuck in the "repressed" category, but its 2014 score tied its highest level ever over the six-year period.

Strong GDP growth has been led by increased foreign investment in the mining industry, but substantial mineral revenues benefit only a narrow segment of the population. The public sector remains the largest source of employment. Chronic deficits due to large military spending plague public finance, worsening already fragile monetary stability. A repressive central government continues to marginalize the domestic private sector, perpetuating an uncertain investment climate.

BACKGROUND: Eritrea won its independence from Ethiopia in 1993, but relations between the two countries remain hostile. Ethiopia launched an incursion into Eritrea in March 2012, citing President Isaias Afwerki's support for terrorist activity as justification. Afwerki has ruled without elections since 1993. The judiciary is politicized, and journalists and others have been held without trial for speaking against the government. Eritrea is subject to U.N. military and economic sanctions for supporting armed opposition groups in Horn of Africa countries. Roughly three-quarters of Eritreans depend on small-scale agriculture and fishing, and up to two-thirds reportedly rely on government assistance. Copper and gold drive economic growth, but military spending drains resources from public development and investment plans. Public debt is at 125 percent of GDP.

How Do We Measure Economic Freedom?
See page 471 for an explanation of the methodology or visit the *Index* Web site at *heritage.org/index*.

Freedom Trend

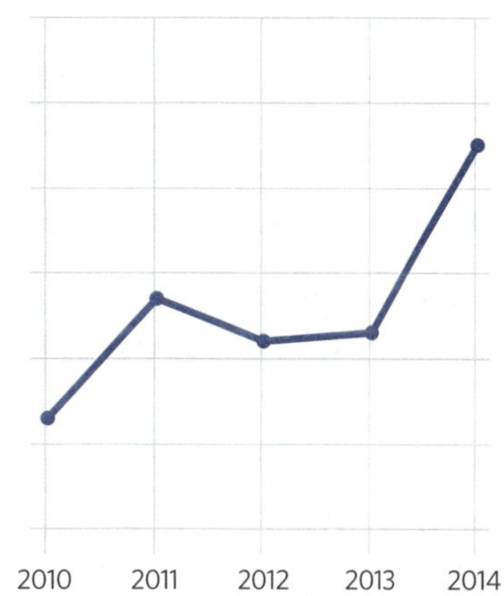

Country Comparisons

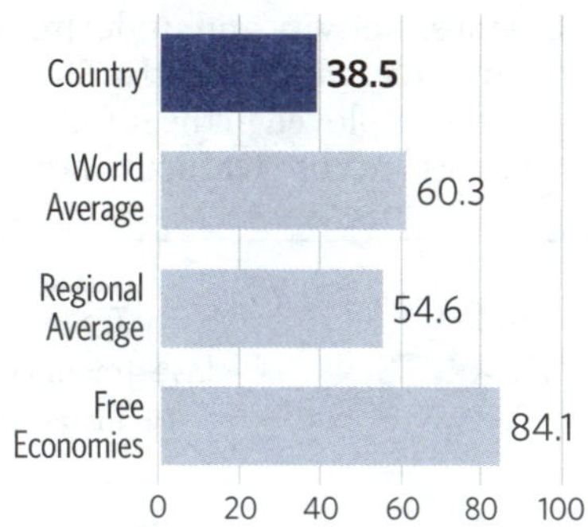

Quick Facts

Population: 5.7 million
GDP (PPP): $4.4 billion
7.0% growth in 2012
5-year compound annual growth 2.2%
$777 per capita
Unemployment: n/a
Inflation (CPI): 12.3%
FDI Inflow: $73.7 million
Public Debt: 125.8% of GDP

2012 data unless otherwise noted.
Data compiled as of September 2013.

THE TEN ECONOMIC FREEDOMS

		Score	Rank	1-Year Change
RULE OF LAW	Property Rights	10.0	166th	0
	Freedom from Corruption	22.9	144th	-2.1

Corruption is a major problem. The president and his small circle of senior advisers and military commanders exercise almost complete political control. The politicized judiciary, understaffed and unprofessional, has never ruled against the government. Protection of property rights is poor. The government has a history of expropriating houses, businesses, and other private property without notice, explanation, or compensation.

		Score	Rank	1-Year Change
GOVERNMENT SIZE	Fiscal Freedom	57.0	171st	0
	Government Spending	66.1	97th	+11.5

The top individual income and corporate tax rates are 30 percent. Other taxes include a 2 percent tax on dual citizens, targeted at Eritrea's large diaspora. The overall tax burden is 50 percent of GDP. Government spending has moderated to 34 percent of GDP. Public debt is large relative to the size of the economy, at over 125 percent of gross domestic output, but has fallen slightly.

		Score	Rank	1-Year Change
REGULATORY EFFICIENCY	Business Freedom	18.6	183rd	+1.3
	Labor Freedom	63.6	82nd	+9.0
	Monetary Freedom	57.6	178th	+2.1

Inconsistent enforcement of regulations and other institutional shortcomings often impede business activity and undermine economic development. Launching a business takes more than 80 days and is costly. The labor market remains underdeveloped, and much of the labor force is employed in the informal sector. Monetary stability has been weak. Subsidies and price controls are core features of the country's command economy.

		Score	Rank	1-Year Change
OPEN MARKETS	Trade Freedom	69.1	132nd	0
	Investment Freedom	0.0	178th	0
	Financial Freedom	20.0	163rd	0

Eritrea's average tariff rate was 5.4 percent as of 2006. It can take several weeks to import goods. State domination of the economy acts as a deterrent to foreign investment. The financial system, consisting mainly of a small banking sector, remains severely underdeveloped and subject to heavy state control. Private-sector participation in the system remains constrained.

Long-Term Score Change (since 2009)

RULE OF LAW		GOVERNMENT SIZE		REGULATORY EFFICIENCY		OPEN MARKETS	
Property Rights	0	Fiscal Freedom	-29.4	Business Freedom	+0.3	Trade Freedom	-0.1
Freedom from Corruption	-5.1	Government Spending	+56.2	Labor Freedom	-10.3	Investment Freedom	-10.0
				Monetary Freedom	-1.5	Financial Freedom	0

ESTONIA

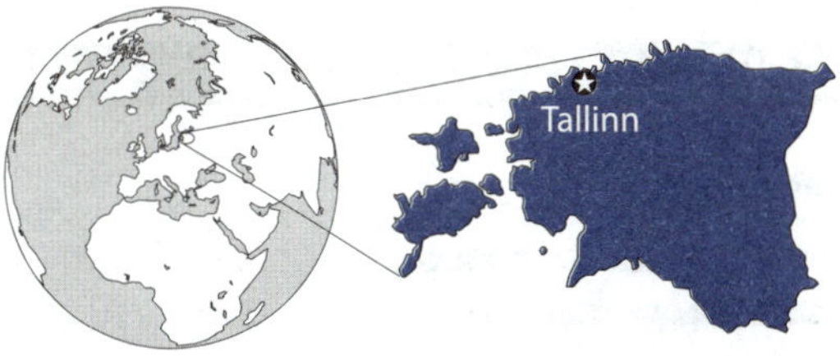

World Rank: 11 **Regional Rank: 4**

Economic Freedom Score

Estonia's economic freedom score is 75.9, making its economy the 11th freest in the 2014 *Index*. Its overall score is 0.6 point higher than last year, with improvements in property rights and trade freedom offsetting a small combined decline in business freedom and the management of public spending. Estonia is ranked 4th out of 43 countries in the Europe region, and its overall score is well above the regional and world averages.

Over the 20-year history of the *Index*, Estonia has recorded an impressive score improvement of nearly 11 points, lifting the economy from the ranks of the "moderately free" to the "mostly free." The country has recorded advancements in six of the 10 economic freedoms, including property rights, freedom from corruption, monetary freedom, trade freedom, and financial freedom, the scores for which have improved by double digits. Market openness has been significantly enhanced and has facilitated Estonia's impressive transition to a free-market economy.

In a challenging global and regional environment, the Estonian economy has demonstrated a high level of resilience and achieved swift economic rebound. Persistent efforts to restore fiscal stability by revitalizing the commitment to limited government have borne fruit. Decisive fiscal consolidation measures have narrowed budget deficits and kept public debt under control.

BACKGROUND: Estonia regained its independence from the Soviet Union in 1991 and is a stable multi-party democracy. It joined NATO and the European Union in 2004 and the Organisation for Economic Co-operation and Development in 2010. In 2011, it adopted the euro, making it the first ex-Soviet state to do so. With a liberal investment climate, foreign investments have risen substantially. Prime Minister Andrus Ansip of the Reform Party has held office since 2005, providing stability and implementing market-oriented policies. Estonia has become one of the world's most dynamic and modern economies. It profits from strong electronics and telecommunication sectors and has strong trade relations with Russia, Germany, Sweden, and Finland.

How Do We Measure Economic Freedom?
See page 471 for an explanation of the methodology or visit the *Index* Web site at *heritage.org/index*.

Freedom Trend

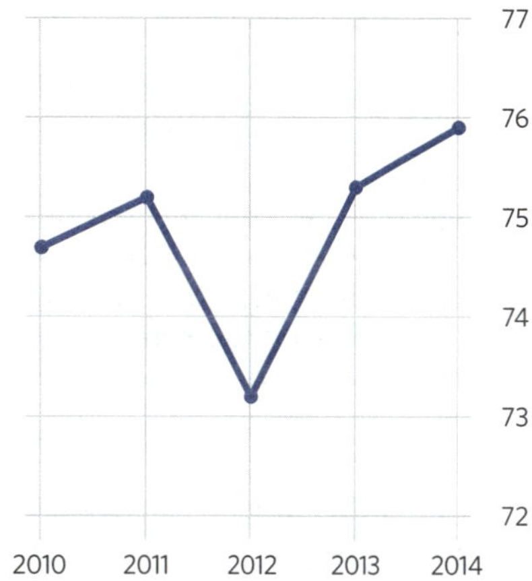

Country Comparisons

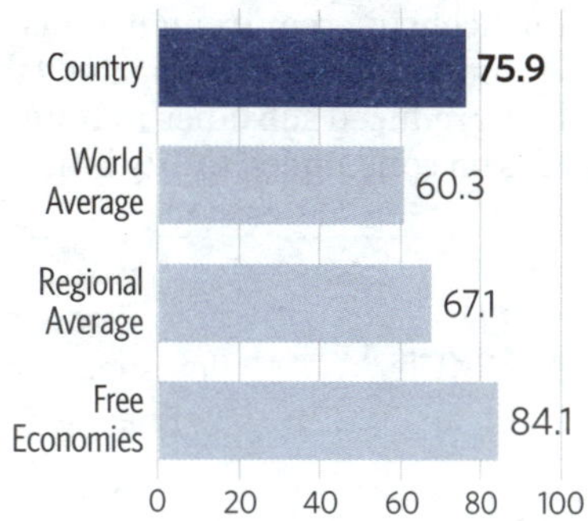

Quick Facts

Population: 1.3 million
GDP (PPP): $29.1 billion
3.2% growth in 2012
5-year compound annual growth –1.0%
$21,713 per capita
Unemployment: 9.8%
Inflation (CPI): 4.2%
FDI Inflow: $1.5 billion
Public Debt: 8.5% of GDP

2012 data unless otherwise noted.
Data compiled as of September 2013.

THE TEN ECONOMIC FREEDOMS

RULE OF LAW

	Score	Rank	1-Year Change
Property Rights	90.0	2nd	+5.0
Freedom from Corruption	64.2	29th	+0.2

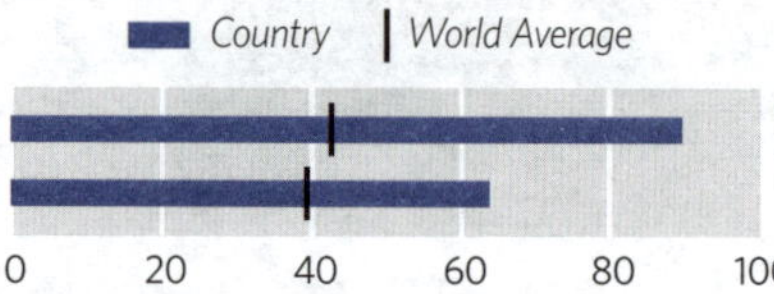

Although there are occasional problems with government corruption in Estonia, the parliament strengthened already tough anti-corruption laws in 2012 to increase transparency and strengthen requirements for politicians to declare their assets. The judiciary is effectively insulated from government influence. Property rights and contracts are well enforced and secure. Commercial codes are applied consistently.

GOVERNMENT SIZE

	Score	Rank	1-Year Change
Fiscal Freedom	80.4	81st	+0.7
Government Spending	56.0	124th	-0.2

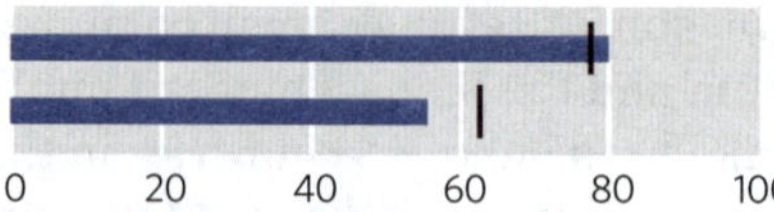

The top individual income tax rate is 21 percent. The top corporate tax rate is also 21 percent on the gross amount of profit distribution. Other taxes include a value-added tax (VAT) and excise taxes. The overall tax burden is 32.8 percent of total domestic income. Government expenditures are around 38 percent of GDP, and public debt is less than 10 percent of the size of the economy. Austerity measures have put the national debt on a sustainable path.

REGULATORY EFFICIENCY

	Score	Rank	1-Year Change
Business Freedom	77.6	37th	-0.6
Labor Freedom	55.9	111th	-0.1
Monetary Freedom	76.9	74th	-0.2

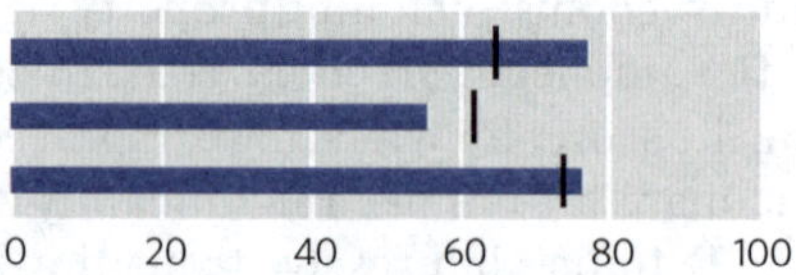

The business start-up process is straightforward and takes about a week. The cost of completing licensing requirements has been cut to less than a quarter of the level of average annual income. The recently enacted labor law aims to reduce costs of dismissal. In 2013, the government reduced subsidies to renewable-energy producers that were being financed by monthly fees on consumers' utility bills.

OPEN MARKETS

	Score	Rank	1-Year Change
Trade Freedom	87.8	11th	+1.0
Investment Freedom	90.0	2nd	0
Financial Freedom	80.0	4th	0

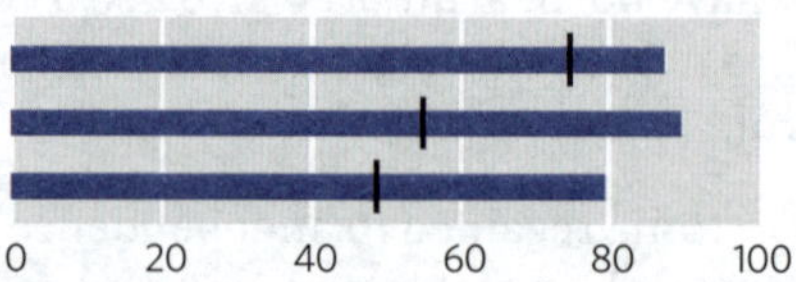

EU members have a low 1.1 percent average tariff rate and, in general, few non-tariff barriers to trade. There are few formal barriers to foreign investment. The financial sector remains supported by efficient supervisory frameworks. With little state intervention in place, the competitive banking sector provides a wide range of financial services. Non-performing loans represent only about 4 percent of total loans.

Long-Term Score Change (since 1995)

RULE OF LAW		GOVERNMENT SIZE		REGULATORY EFFICIENCY		OPEN MARKETS	
Property Rights	**+20.0**	Fiscal Freedom	**-1.6**	Business Freedom	**-7.4**	Trade Freedom	**+10.8**
Freedom from Corruption	**+14.2**	Government Spending	**-7.3**	Labor Freedom	**+8.5**	Investment Freedom	**0**
				Monetary Freedom	**+76.9**	Financial Freedom	**+10.0**

ETHIOPIA

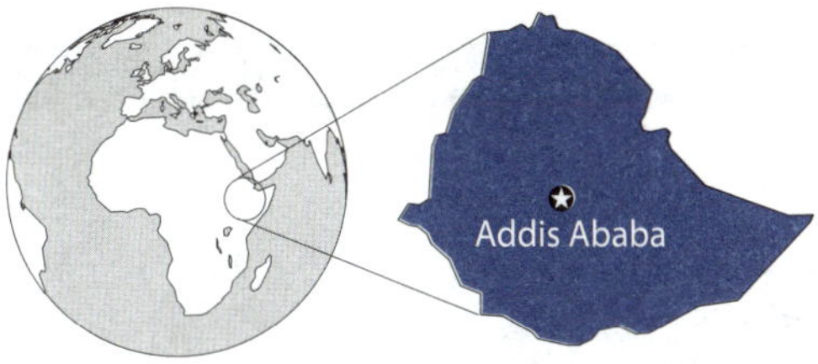

World Rank: **151** Regional Rank: **35**

Ethiopia's economic freedom score is 50.0, making its economy the 151st freest in the 2014 *Index*. Its overall score is 0.6 point higher than last year due to improvements in five of the 10 economic freedoms, including business freedom, labor freedom, and fiscal freedom. Ethiopia is ranked 35th out of 46 countries in the Sub-Saharan Africa region, and its overall score continues to be below the regional average.

Over the 20-year history of the *Index*, Ethiopia has advanced its economic freedom score by over 7 points. The country has recorded improvements in half of the 10 economic freedoms, including trade freedom, fiscal freedom, and investment freedom, scores for which have advanced by 10 points or more. Over the past decade, Ethiopia has fluctuated within the lower ranks of the "mostly unfree" economies.

Reflecting the lack of progress in structural and institutional reforms, Ethiopia continues to underperform in many areas critical to advancing overall economic freedom. The quality and efficiency of government services have been poor and are further undermined by the weak rule of law and pervasive corruption. Monetary stability has been hampered by state distortions in prices.

BACKGROUND: Long-term Prime Minister Meles Zenawi died in August 2012 and was succeeded by Haile Mariam Desalegn. The Ethiopian People's Revolutionary Democratic Front and allied parties hold all but two seats in parliament. In 2008, the U.N. terminated the peacekeeping mission it had established after war with Eritrea in the 1990s. Ethiopia invaded Somalia in support of Somalia's Transitional Federal Government in 2006 and withdrew in 2009. In 2012, Ethiopia sent forces into Eritrea after European tourists were killed by terrorists that Ethiopia claims were trained in Eritrea. Agriculture accounts for 46 percent of GDP and 85 percent of total employment. Although GDP growth is high and the economy has been growing steadily for the past 10 years, per capita income remains among the world's lowest. Construction of the Grand Renaissance Dam on the Nile to develop electricity has increased tensions with Egypt.

Economic Freedom Score

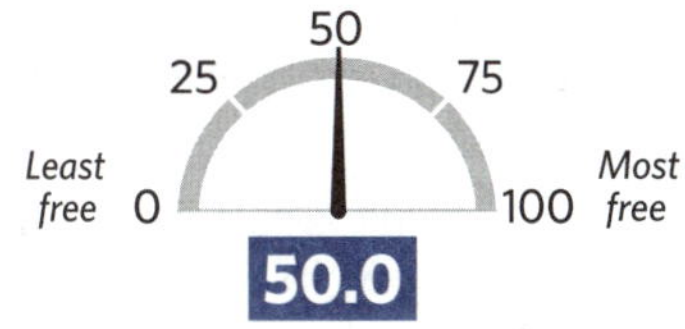

Freedom Trend

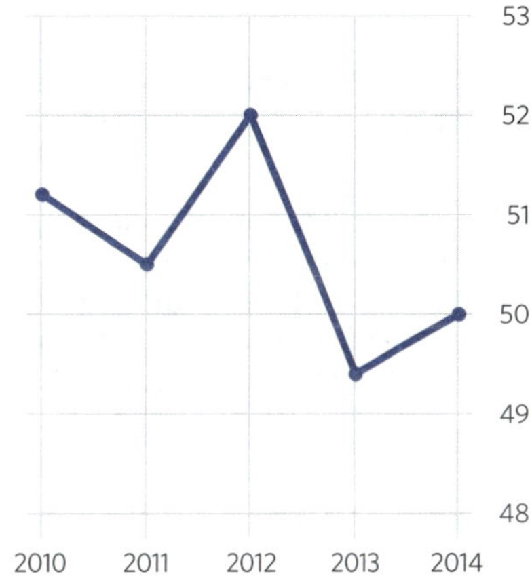

Country Comparisons

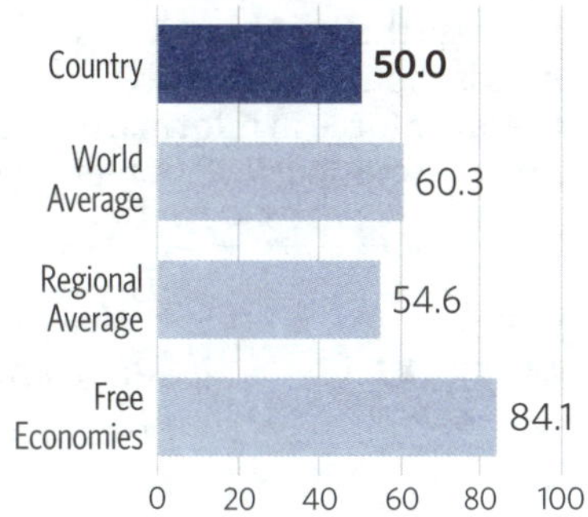

Quick Facts

Population: 86.8 million
GDP (PPP): $103.3 billion
7.0% growth in 2012
5-year compound annual growth 8.7%
$1,191 per capita
Unemployment: n/a
Inflation (CPI): 22.8%
FDI Inflow: $970.4 million
Public Debt: 21.6% of GDP

2012 data unless otherwise noted.
Data compiled as of September 2013.

How Do We Measure Economic Freedom?
See page 471 for an explanation of the methodology or visit the *Index* Web site at *heritage.org/index*.

THE TEN ECONOMIC FREEDOMS

RULE OF LAW

	Score	Rank	1-Year Change
Property Rights	30.0	93rd	0
Freedom from Corruption	27.0	122nd	0

Corruption is a significant problem in Ethiopia. The underdeveloped judiciary is officially independent, but its judgments rarely deviate from government policy. All land is owned by the state but can be leased for up to 99 years. Property and contractual rights are recognized, but enforcement is weak. State-owned and party-owned businesses receive preferential access to land leases and credit.

GOVERNMENT SIZE

	Score	Rank	1-Year Change
Fiscal Freedom	77.5	106th	+3.3
Government Spending	89.9	12th	+0.3

Ethiopia's top individual income tax rate is 35 percent. The top corporate tax rate has fallen to 30 percent. Other taxes include a value-added tax (VAT) and a capital gains tax. The overall tax burden is 11.3 percent of gross domestic income. Public expenditures are 18 percent of gross domestic output. Government debt has remained low since Ethiopia benefited from Heavily Indebted Poor Country debt relief in 2006.

REGULATORY EFFICIENCY

	Score	Rank	1-Year Change
Business Freedom	57.8	126th	+5.4
Labor Freedom	54.7	119th	+7.8
Monetary Freedom	59.0	177th	-5.7

Incorporating a business has become less time-consuming, but other regulatory requirements increase the overall cost of conducting business. The minimum capital required to start a business is about twice the average annual income. The underdeveloped labor market traps much of the labor force in informal economic activity. Monetary stability has been weak, and subsidies for the state-led development model hinder private-sector growth.

OPEN MARKETS

	Score	Rank	1-Year Change
Trade Freedom	64.2	147th	+0.2
Investment Freedom	20.0	164th	-5.0
Financial Freedom	20.0	163rd	0

Ethiopia has a 10.4 percent average tariff rate, and it can take several weeks to import goods. Investment in several sectors of the economy is restricted by the government. The government strongly influences lending and funds state-led development projects by forcing private banks to purchase treasury bills. Foreign ownership in the banking sector is still prohibited.

Long-Term Score Change (since 1995)

RULE OF LAW		GOVERNMENT SIZE		REGULATORY EFFICIENCY		OPEN MARKETS	
Property Rights	0	Fiscal Freedom	+36.5	Business Freedom	+2.8	Trade Freedom	+37.2
Freedom from Corruption	-3.0	Government Spending	+1.4	Labor Freedom	-6.9	Investment Freedom	+10.0
				Monetary Freedom	-13.0	Financial Freedom	-10.0

FIJI

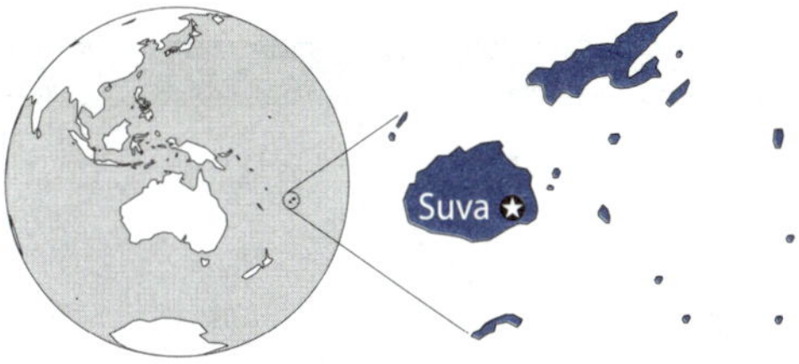

World Rank: **99** Regional Rank: **20**

Economic Freedom Score

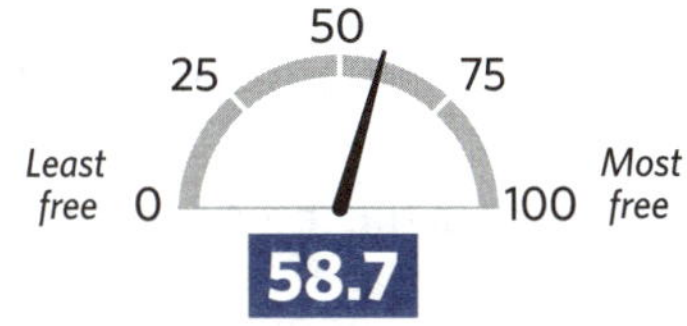

Fiji's economic freedom score is 58.7, making its economy the 99th freest in the 2014 *Index*. Its overall score is 1.5 points higher than last year due to improvements in investment freedom, fiscal freedom, trade freedom, and monetary freedom. Fiji is ranked 20th out of 42 countries in the Asia–Pacific region, and its overall score is below the world and regional averages.

Over the 20-year history of the *Index*, Fiji's economic freedom score has advanced by nearly 4 points. Improvements have occurred in four of the 10 categories, including notable improvements in fiscal freedom and trade freedom. However, these improvements have been counterbalanced by considerable deteriorations in the rule of law as measured by property rights and freedom from corruption. Fiji had risen to the status of economically "moderately free" from 2007 to 2011 but has fallen back into the ranks of the "mostly unfree" since 2012.

Fiji's judiciary continues to be vulnerable to political interference. Corruption has become a serious concern, undermining prospects for broad-based long-term economic development.

BACKGROUND: The Pacific island nation of Fiji is ruled by military strongman Commodore Frank Bainimarama, who has dominated island politics for a decade. Fiji has long suffered from ethnic tension between the indigenous, mostly Christian population and a large minority of Hindu or Muslim Indo–Fijians. Sanctions were imposed in 2006 by Fiji's main trading partners, including the European Union and Australia, in reaction to the coup that installed Bainimarama. These sanctions hurt the vital agriculture, clothing, and fishing industries. In September 2009, Fiji was suspended from the Commonwealth of Nations. In July 2012, Australia and New Zealand restored diplomatic ties with Fiji in response to its preparations for democratic elections in 2014. An industrial reform, begun in 2010, has done little to improve Fiji's slowing economy.

Freedom Trend

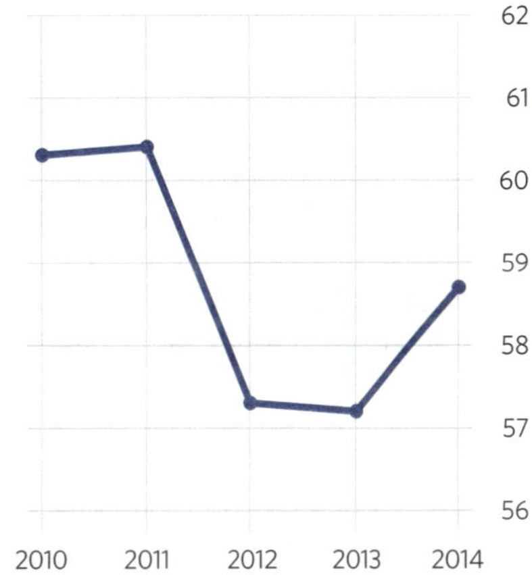

Country Comparisons

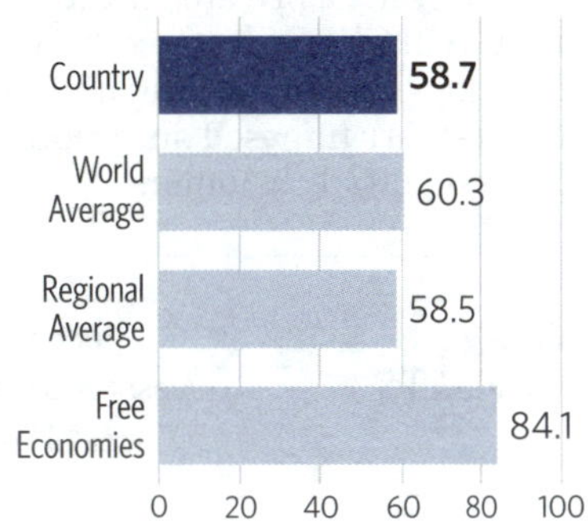

Quick Facts

Population: 0.9 million
GDP (PPP): $4.3 billion
2.1% growth in 2012
5-year compound annual growth 0.8%
$4,786 per capita
Unemployment: 7.0%
Inflation (CPI): 4.3%
FDI Inflow: $267.9 million
Public Debt: 51.6% of GDP

2012 data unless otherwise noted.
Data compiled as of September 2013.

How Do We Measure Economic Freedom?
See page 471 for an explanation of the methodology or visit the *Index* Web site at *heritage.org/index.*

THE TEN ECONOMIC FREEDOMS

RULE OF LAW

	Score	Rank	1-Year Change
Property Rights	25.0	135th	0
Freedom from Corruption	20.0	161st	0

Although the interim government has pledged to eradicate pervasive corruption and improve bureaucratic efficiency, official corruption remains widespread. The suspension of the constitution in 2009 and the related dismissal of judges and their replacement by appointees of the interim government raised serious questions about judicial independence. Protection of property is highly uncertain, and obtaining land titles is difficult.

GOVERNMENT SIZE

	Score	Rank	1-Year Change
Fiscal Freedom	82.3	67th	+4.3
Government Spending	76.2	63rd	-1.8

The top individual income tax rate is 29 percent, and the top corporate tax has fallen to 20 percent. Other taxes include a value-added tax (VAT) and a land sales tax. The overall tax burden equals 23 percent of GDP. Government expenditures are 28 percent of total domestic output, and public debt remains slightly larger than half the size of the domestic economy.

REGULATORY EFFICIENCY

	Score	Rank	1-Year Change
Business Freedom	64.9	92nd	-0.8
Labor Freedom	73.1	53rd	-1.8
Monetary Freedom	75.2	99th	+2.4

Establishing a private enterprise takes almost two months, although no minimum capital is required. Obtaining necessary permits takes 16 procedures and 142 days. The recent labor reform consolidated and updated the labor codes, but labor regulations remain rigid. Price controls are imposed on various goods, and the government continues to subsidize electricity for residential customers.

OPEN MARKETS

	Score	Rank	1-Year Change
Trade Freedom	70.2	128th	+2.2
Investment Freedom	50.0	109th	+10.0
Financial Freedom	50.0	69th	0

Fiji has a 9.9 percent average tariff rate and few formal non-tariff barriers to trade. Restrictions on foreign exchange have been relaxed somewhat in recent years. The government has withdrawn from commercial banking, and foreign participation is significant. Foreign exchange controls have been eased but still limit repatriation of capital and profits.

Long-Term Score Change (since 1995)

RULE OF LAW		GOVERNMENT SIZE		REGULATORY EFFICIENCY		OPEN MARKETS	
Property Rights	**-25.0**	Fiscal Freedom	**+25.2**	Business Freedom	**+9.9**	Trade Freedom	**+17.6**
Freedom from Corruption	**-10.0**	Government Spending	**+3.7**	Labor Freedom	**-10.5**	Investment Freedom	**0**
				Monetary Freedom	**-0.4**	Financial Freedom	**0**

FINLAND

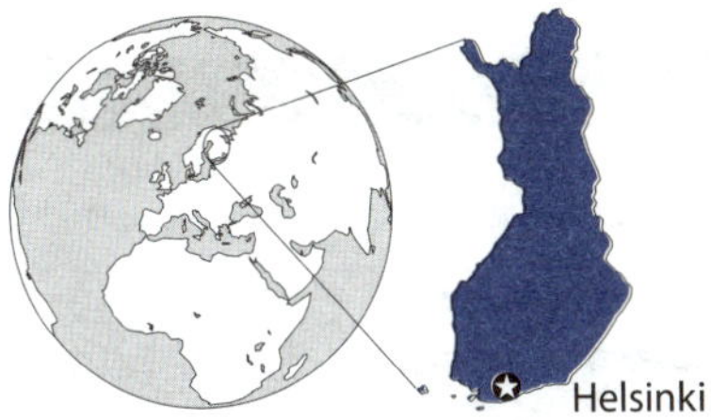

World Rank: **19** Regional Rank: **9**

Economic Freedom Score

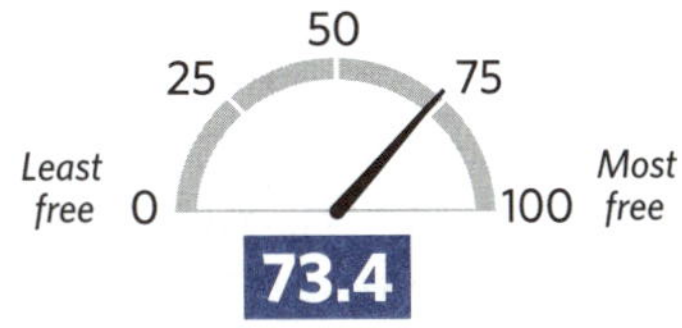

Finland's economic freedom score is 73.4, making its economy the 19th freest in the 2014 *Index*. Its score is 0.6 point worse than last year, due primarily to deteriorations in fiscal freedom, business freedom, and the management of government spending. Finland is ranked 9th out of 43 countries in the Europe region, and its overall score is well above the world average.

Over the 20-year history of the *Index*, Finland has advanced its economic freedom score by 9.7 points, the sixth best performance among advanced economies. Improved scores for seven of the 10 economic freedoms, led by notable enhancements in the area of market openness measured through trade freedom, investment freedom, and financial freedom, have enabled Finland to advance to the ranks of the "mostly free."

As reflected in the steady rise of its economic freedom over the past two decades, Finland's strong competitiveness is built on flexibility and openness. The economy continues to be among the world leaders in several of the 10 economic freedoms including business freedom, property rights, and freedom from corruption. The sound regulatory environment encourages entrepreneurial activity and innovation. Commercial operations are handled with transparency and speed, and corruption is perceived as almost nonexistent.

BACKGROUND: Finland is sparsely populated. About one-fourth of its land mass is above the Arctic Circle. In April 2011, the center-right National Coalition Party formed a six-party governing coalition with Jyrki Katainen as prime minister. In the February 2012 presidential elections, the National Coalition Party's Sauli Niinistö won in the second round of voting, ending 30 years of Social Democrat presidencies. Finland became a member of NATO's Partnership for Peace in 1994 and sits on the Euro–Atlantic Council, but it has not pursued full NATO membership because of its neutral military status and lack of popular support. It joined the European Union in 1995 and adopted the euro as its currency in 1999. Although economic growth remains sluggish, Finland's economy is modern and competitive, with vibrant information and communications-technology sectors.

How Do We Measure Economic Freedom?
See page 471 for an explanation of the methodology or visit the *Index* Web site at *heritage.org/index.*

Freedom Trend

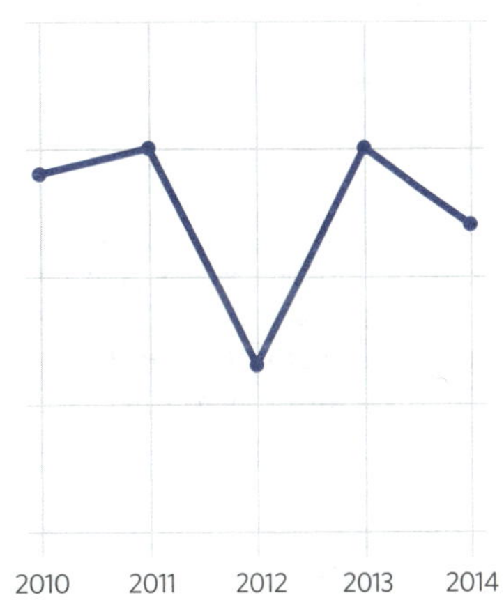

Country Comparisons

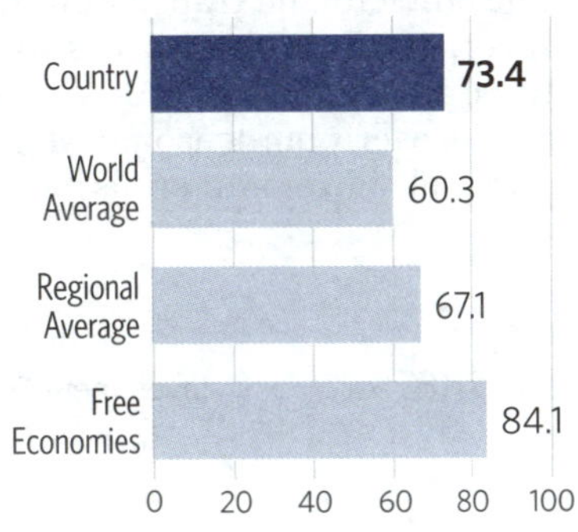

Quick Facts

Population: 5.4 million
GDP (PPP): $197.5 billion
-0.2% growth in 2012
5-year compound annual growth -0.6%
$36,395 per capita
Unemployment: 7.7%
Inflation (CPI): 3.2%
FDI Inflow: -$1.8 billion
Public Debt: 53.3% of GDP

2012 data unless otherwise noted.
Data compiled as of September 2013.

THE TEN ECONOMIC FREEDOMS

Score ▬ Country | World Average

RULE OF LAW

	Score	Rank	1-Year Change
Property Rights	90.0	2nd	0
Freedom from Corruption	93.4	3rd	-0.6

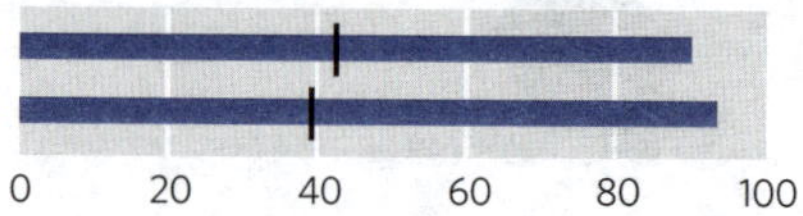

Corruption is not a significant problem in Finland, which consistently ranks among the top performers in Transparency International's Corruption Perceptions Index. Secured interests in property are recognized and enforced. Contractual agreements are strictly honored. The quality of the judiciary is generally high. Finland adheres to numerous international agreements that aim to protect intellectual property.

GOVERNMENT SIZE

	Score	Rank	1-Year Change
Fiscal Freedom	65.1	157th	-1.8
Government Spending	8.9	174th	-3.3

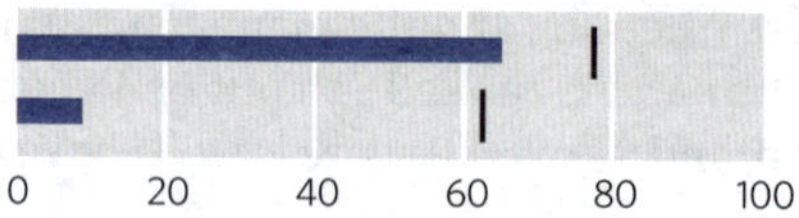

The top individual income tax rate has been increased to 31.8 percent, and the top corporate tax rate remains at 24.5 percent. Other taxes include a value-added tax (VAT) and a flat 28 percent tax on capital income. The overall tax burden is 43.4 percent of GDP. Government expenditures are 55 percent of the domestic economy. The government is working to stop debt growth by 2015. Public debt comprises 53 percent of GDP.

REGULATORY EFFICIENCY

	Score	Rank	1-Year Change
Business Freedom	93.6	7th	-1.2
Labor Freedom	46.5	151st	+1.2
Monetary Freedom	78.9	49th	-0.6

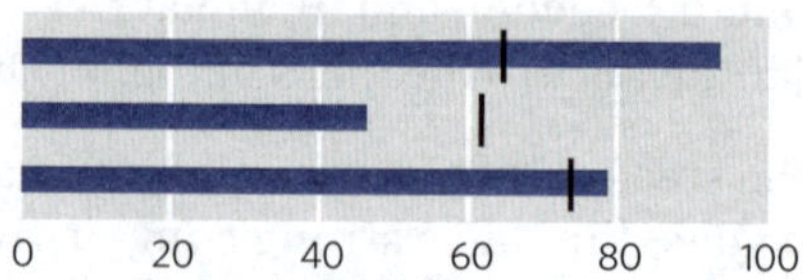

The efficient and transparent business framework continues to support the private sector. Incorporating a business costs about 1 percent of the level of average annual income and takes three procedures. The non-salary cost of employing a worker is high, and severance payments are not overly burdensome. Monetary stability has been well maintained, although the government subsidizes numerous biogas, wind, and solar energy projects.

OPEN MARKETS

	Score	Rank	1-Year Change
Trade Freedom	87.8	11th	+1.0
Investment Freedom	90.0	2nd	0
Financial Freedom	80.0	4th	0

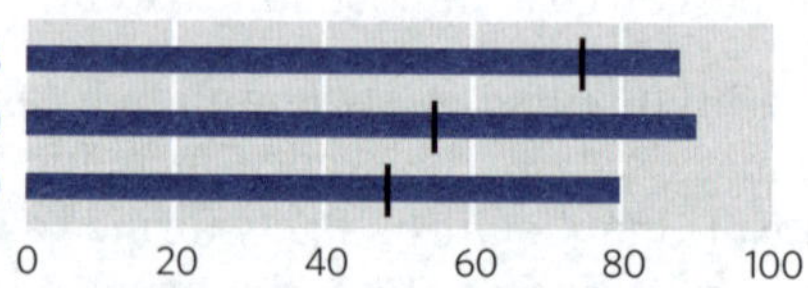

EU members have a low 1.1 percent average tariff rate and, in general, few non-tariff barriers to trade. Investment in some sectors of the economy may be screened by the government. Nonetheless, overall investment regulations are transparent and efficient. The well-developed financial system is competitive and provides a wide range of services. Banking remains generally sound and well-capitalized.

Long-Term Score Change (since 1996)

RULE OF LAW		GOVERNMENT SIZE		REGULATORY EFFICIENCY		OPEN MARKETS	
Property Rights	0	Fiscal Freedom	+6.7	Business Freedom	+38.6	Trade Freedom	+10.0
Freedom from Corruption	+3.4	Government Spending	+8.9	Labor Freedom	-3.4	Investment Freedom	+20.0
				Monetary Freedom	-3.4	Financial Freedom	+30.0

FRANCE

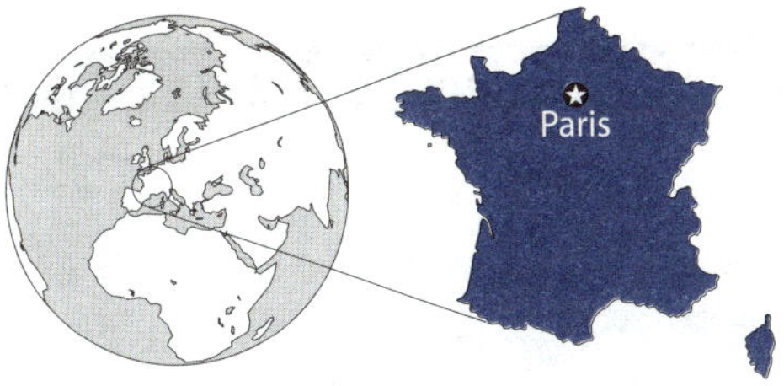

World Rank: **70** Regional Rank: **33**

Economic Freedom Score

France's economic freedom score is 63.5, making its economy the 70th freest in the 2014 *Index*. Its overall score has decreased by 0.7 point due to declines in monetary freedom, fiscal freedom, and business freedom. France is ranked 33rd out of 43 countries in the Europe region, and its overall score is slightly higher than the world average but below the regional average.

Over the 20-year history of the *Index*, France's economic freedom has been stagnant, recording the fifth worst performance among advanced economies. Despite notable score improvements in property rights and market openness as measured by trade freedom, investment freedom, and financial freedom, France's overall economic freedom has been undermined by substantial declines of over 10 points each in freedom from corruption, fiscal freedom, and government spending.

France had been rated one of the "moderately free" economies for most of the *Index* history but dropped into the "mostly unfree" category from 1997 to 2003. The government still dominates major sectors of the economy as a large shareholder, and government spending accounts for over half of GDP. The government has pursued various reform measures to increase the competitiveness and flexibility of the economy, but overall progress has been slow.

BACKGROUND: Socialist François Hollande was elected president in May 2012, and the Socialist Party won control of the National Assembly. By October 2013, less than a third of French citizens approved of Hollande's performance as president. Formally reintegrated into NATO's military command structures, France was a leading participant in NATO's March 2011 military engagement in Libya. It remains apart from NATO's Nuclear Planning Group. France was a founding member of the European Union and has struggled to maintain its traditional influence over EU policy as membership has grown. It has a diversified economy but also is the top recipient of market-distorting agricultural subsidies under the EU's Common Agricultural Policy. Unemployment remains high, and union strikes are a persistent problem. In May 2013, France entered its second recession in four years.

How Do We Measure Economic Freedom?
See page 471 for an explanation of the methodology or visit the *Index* Web site at *heritage.org/index*.

Freedom Trend

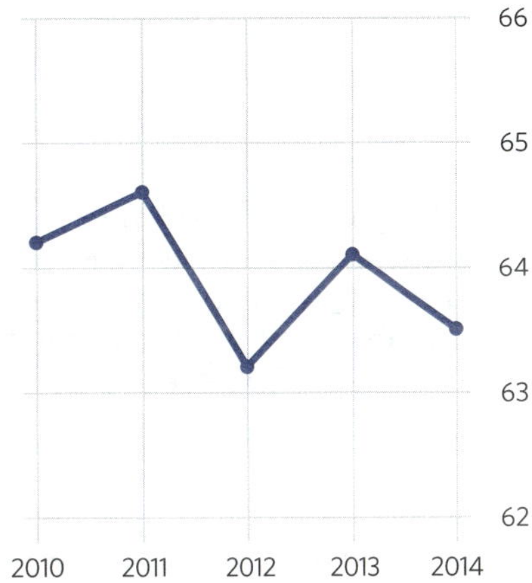

Country Comparisons

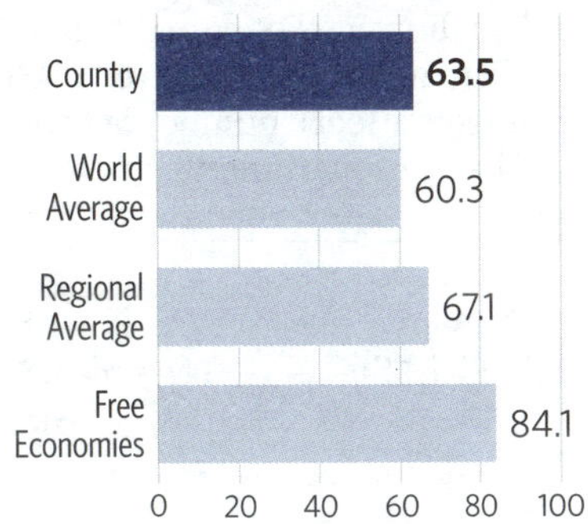

Quick Facts

Population: 63.4 million
GDP (PPP): $2.3 trillion
0.0% growth in 2012
5-year compound annual growth 0.0%
$35,548 per capita
Unemployment: 10.2%
Inflation (CPI): 2.0%
FDI Inflow: $25.1 billion
Public Debt: 90.3% of GDP

2012 data unless otherwise noted.
Data compiled as of September 2013.

THE TEN ECONOMIC FREEDOMS

		Score	Rank	1-Year Change
RULE OF LAW	Property Rights	80.0	20th	0
	Freedom from Corruption	69.9	26th	-0.1

France has an independent judiciary, and the rule of law is firmly established. Property rights and contract enforcement are secure. Intellectual property rights are respected in accordance with international standards. Although anti-corruption measures are in place to ensure transparency and government integrity, a 2012 OECD report called for increased prosecution of French officials who bribe foreign officials to win contracts.

		Score	Rank	1-Year Change
GOVERNMENT SIZE	Fiscal Freedom	48.4	178th	-4.6
	Government Spending	5.6	175th	0

The top individual income tax rate is up to 45 percent, and the top corporate tax rate has been lowered to 34.3 percent. Efforts to increase the top marginal tax rate to 75 percent were ruled unconstitutional. Other taxes include a value-added tax (VAT). The overall tax burden equals 44.2 percent of gross national income. Government expenditures continue to make up over half of the domestic economy, and public debt has reached over 90 percent of GDP.

		Score	Rank	1-Year Change
REGULATORY EFFICIENCY	Business Freedom	79.9	33rd	-4.1
	Labor Freedom	51.8	132nd	+1.3
	Monetary Freedom	76.1	83rd	-5.0

The business start-up process is relatively straightforward, with no minimum capital required. The labor market continues to be stagnant. Ostensibly protecting workers, the labor code's rigid regulations appear instead to have hurt competitiveness and employment prospects. Price controls affect a number of products and services, and state subsidies have increased under the Hollande government.

		Score	Rank	1-Year Change
OPEN MARKETS	Trade Freedom	82.8	56th	+1.0
	Investment Freedom	70.0	46th	+5.0
	Financial Freedom	70.0	19th	0

EU members have a low 1.1 percent average tariff rate and, in general, few non-tariff barriers to trade. France's government limits the freedom to enjoy foreign-language films and songs. The government screens investment in some sectors of the economy. The financial sector remains under relatively strong state influence, with a small number of foreign banks operating.

Long-Term Score Change (since 1995)

RULE OF LAW		GOVERNMENT SIZE		REGULATORY EFFICIENCY		OPEN MARKETS	
Property Rights	+10.0	Fiscal Freedom	-12.4	Business Freedom	-5.1	Trade Freedom	+5.0
Freedom from Corruption	-20.1	Government Spending	-10.1	Labor Freedom	-2.5	Investment Freedom	+20.0
				Monetary Freedom	-4.3	Financial Freedom	+20.0

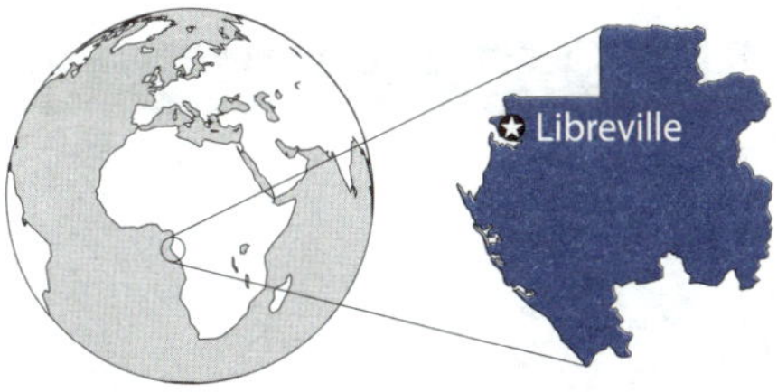

GABON

World Rank: **105** Regional Rank: **14**

Economic Freedom Score

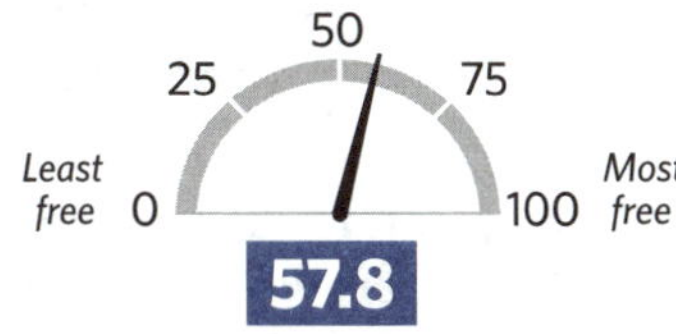

Gabon's economic freedom score is 57.8, making its economy the 105th freest in the 2014 *Index*. Its overall score is unchanged from last year, with improvements in business freedom and the management of government spending counterbalanced by deteriorations in freedom from corruption and monetary freedom. Gabon is ranked 14th out of 46 countries in the Sub-Saharan Africa region, and its overall score is lower than the world average.

Over the 20-year history of the *Index*, Gabon's economic freedom has stagnated, advancing less than 1 point. Marked improvements of over 25 points in trade freedom and fiscal freedom have been offset by declines in six of the 10 economic freedoms, notably declines of 10 points or more in property rights, freedom from corruption, and investment freedom. Gabon has been mired in the ranks of the "mostly unfree" for two decades. Its score in the 2014 *Index* is the same as the previous year but remains its highest in a decade.

Gabon's commitment to structural and institutional reform remains uneven and fragile. More political will is needed to foster an economic environment in which potential entrepreneurs or investors can thrive. Heavy reliance on the oil sector makes the economy highly vulnerable to external shocks and undermines stable economic expansion.

BACKGROUND: President Omar Bongo ruled Gabon from 1967 until his death in 2009 when his son, Ali Ben Bongo, replaced him. Reforms under a 1991 constitution included multi-party democracy with freedom of assembly and the press, but the democratic process remains deeply flawed. In December 2011, Bongo's Gabonese Democratic Party won elections that were boycotted by opposition parties. In February 2012, Raymond Ndong Sima became prime minister. In 2006, oil accounted for over 50 percent of GDP, over 60 percent of government revenues, and over 80 percent of exports. Oil revenue is controlled by the state, and investment has stagnated. Forestry and minerals are also important. The government has pledged to increase transparency and is trying to diversify the economy. GDP grew more than 6 percent per year between 2010 and 2012.

How Do We Measure Economic Freedom?
See page 471 for an explanation of the methodology or visit the *Index* Web site at *heritage.org/index*.

Freedom Trend

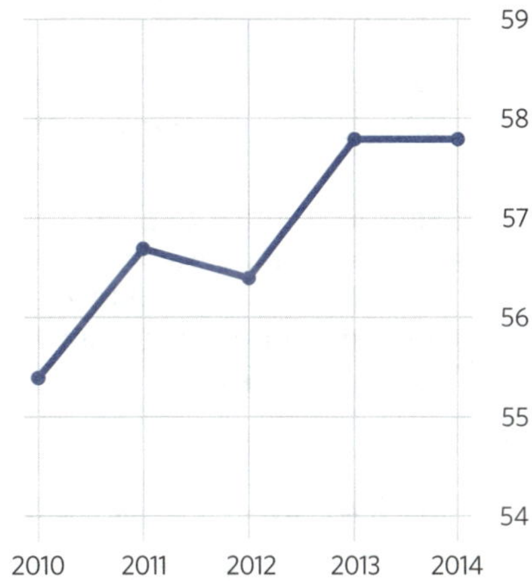

Country Comparisons

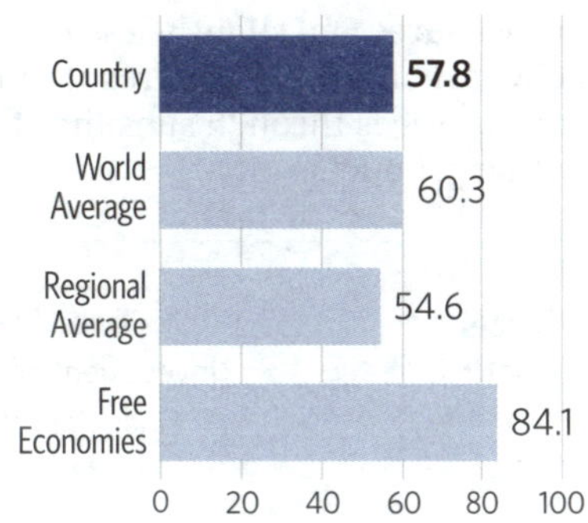

Quick Facts

Population: 1.5 million
GDP (PPP): $25.5 billion
6.2% growth in 2012
5-year compound annual growth 3.6%
$16,548 per capita
Unemployment: 21.0% (2006)
Inflation (CPI): 3.0%
FDI Inflow: $702.4 million
Public Debt: 22.0% of GDP

2012 data unless otherwise noted.
Data compiled as of September 2013.

THE TEN ECONOMIC FREEDOMS

RULE OF LAW

	Score	Rank	1-Year Change
Property Rights	40.0	70th	0
Freedom from Corruption	29.1	109th	-0.9

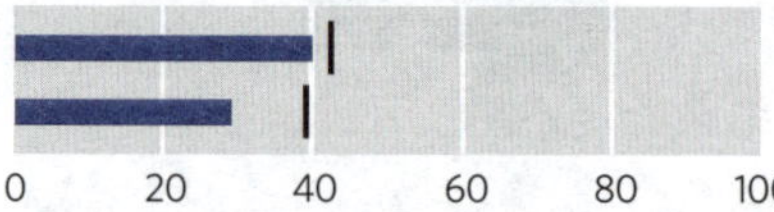

Corruption is widespread, and rampant graft prevents the country's significant natural resource revenues from benefiting most citizens. The judiciary is inefficient and not independent. Judges may deliver summary verdicts in some cases, and prosecutions of former government officials appear to target opposition members. Protections for property rights and contracts are not strongly enforced.

GOVERNMENT SIZE

	Score	Rank	1-Year Change
Fiscal Freedom	74.5	120th	+0.3
Government Spending	81.7	47th	+1.6

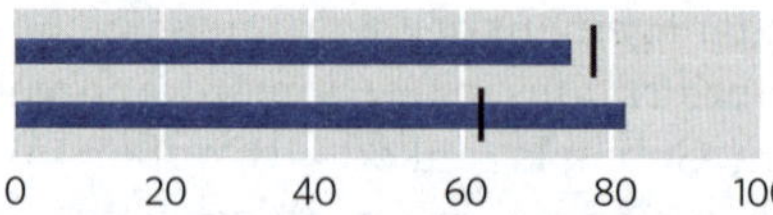

Gabon's top individual income and corporate tax rates are 35 percent. Oil and land development companies are taxed at separate rates of 35 percent and 25 percent, respectively. Other taxes include a value-added tax (VAT). The overall tax burden is 10.1 percent of GDP. Public spending is just under a quarter of gross domestic output. Public debt recently reached over 20 percent of GDP.

REGULATORY EFFICIENCY

	Score	Rank	1-Year Change
Business Freedom	58.9	120th	+2.4
Labor Freedom	63.0	88th	-0.1
Monetary Freedom	75.1	100th	-2.4

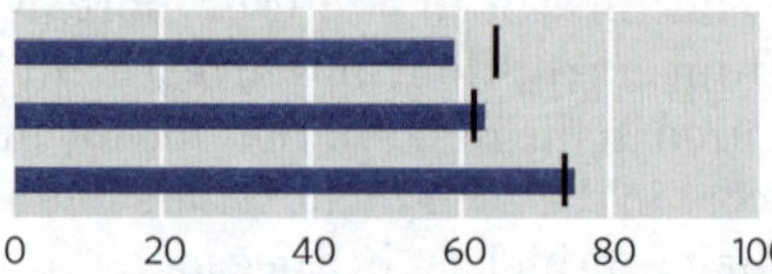

The overall business environment remains burdensome. Starting a new business takes seven procedures and slightly less than a month on average. Licensing requirements take over 150 days to complete. Labor regulations are outdated and not applied consistently. The state influences prices through subsidies to state-owned enterprises and direct control of the prices of other products.

OPEN MARKETS

	Score	Rank	1-Year Change
Trade Freedom	61.0	157th	-0.1
Investment Freedom	55.0	96th	0
Financial Freedom	40.0	107th	0

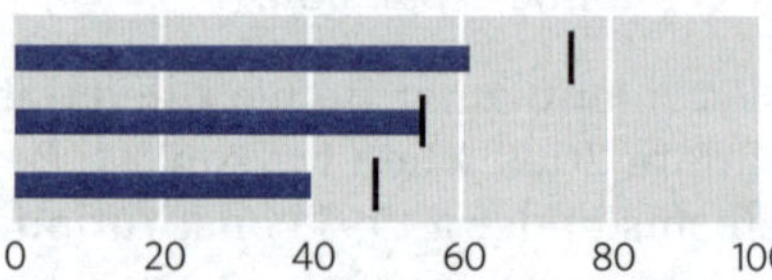

Gabon's average tariff rate is 14.5 percent. Foreign investors may have a difficult time navigating the country's legal and regulatory systems. The underdeveloped financial sector, dominated by banks, remains state-controlled. Credit costs are high, and access to financing is scarce. The government controls long-term lending through the state-owned development bank.

Long-Term Score Change (since 1995)

RULE OF LAW		GOVERNMENT SIZE		REGULATORY EFFICIENCY		OPEN MARKETS	
Property Rights	**-10.0**	Fiscal Freedom	**+25.0**	Business Freedom	**-11.1**	Trade Freedom	**+37.4**
Freedom from Corruption	**-20.9**	Government Spending	**+5.7**	Labor Freedom	**+2.8**	Investment Freedom	**-15.0**
				Monetary Freedom	**-3.8**	Financial Freedom	**-10.0**

THE GAMBIA

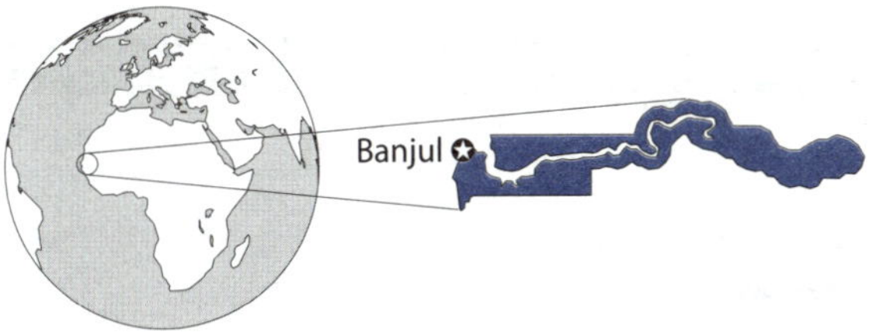

World Rank: **92** Regional Rank: **11**

Economic Freedom Score

The Gambia's economic freedom score is 59.5, making its economy the 92nd freest in the 2014 *Index*. Its overall score is 0.7 point higher than last year, reflecting gains in trade freedom, labor freedom, and fiscal freedom offset partially by declines in business freedom, control of government spending, and freedom from corruption. The Gambia is ranked 11th out of out of 46 countries in the Sub-Saharan Africa region, and its overall score is just below the world average.

The Gambia was first graded in the 1997 *Index*, and its economic freedom has advanced since then by over 6 points. Scores for seven of the 10 economic freedoms, including trade freedom, investment freedom, and financial freedom categories that account for market openness, have improved. A large decline in property rights has held back overall progress. The Gambia has been rated a "mostly unfree" economy throughout its history in the *Index* but has achieved its highest score ever in the 2014 *Index*.

Although progress has been made in streamlining bankruptcy procedures, establishing and running a business still requires overcoming numerous bureaucratic hurdles. The application of commercial law is non-transparent and not always consistent. The judiciary is subject to pervasive political interference, and there is corruption in many parts of the economy.

BACKGROUND: Yahya Jammeh ousted President Sir Dawda Kairaba Jawara in a military coup in 1994 and won flawed multi-party presidential elections in 1996, 2001, 2006, and 2011. Jammeh's Alliance for Patriotic Reorientation and Construction won a major victory in the 2012 legislative elections, which were boycotted by opposition parties. Government restraints on civil liberties and political opponents remain problematic. The Gambia has few natural resources. Agriculture employs 75 percent of the labor force and accounts for 22 percent of GDP. Groundnuts are a major export. Unfavorable weather patterns caused the agriculture sector to shrink in 2012. Industry and services account for approximately 12 percent and 59 percent of GDP, respectively. Tourism is an important source of foreign exchange.

Freedom Trend

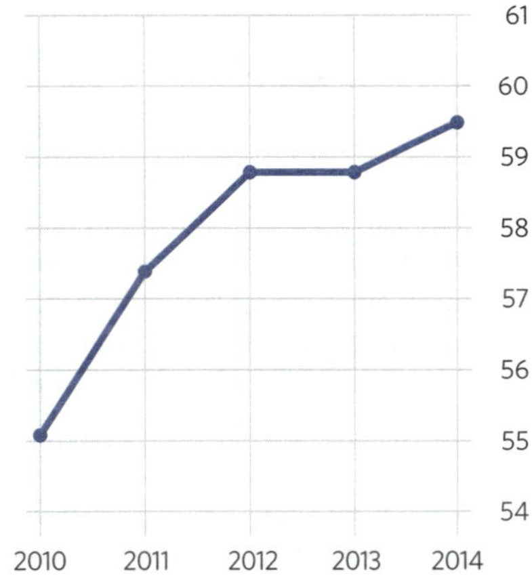

Country Comparisons

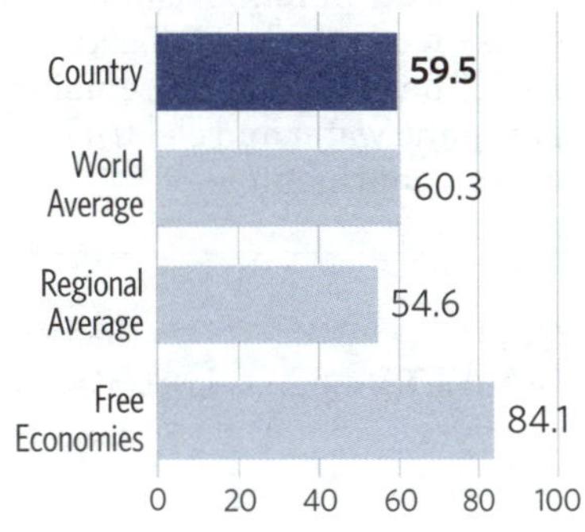

Quick Facts

Population: 1.8 million
GDP (PPP): $3.4 billion
3.9% growth in 2012
5-year compound annual growth 3.6%
$1,864 per capita
Unemployment: n/a
Inflation (CPI): 4.6%
FDI Inflow: $78.8 million
Public Debt: 77.2% of GDP

2012 data unless otherwise noted.
Data compiled as of September 2013.

How Do We Measure Economic Freedom?
See page 471 for an explanation of the methodology or visit the *Index* Web site at *heritage.org/index*.

THE TEN ECONOMIC FREEDOMS

Score | Country | World Average | Rank | 1-Year Change

RULE OF LAW

	Score	Rank	1-Year Change
Property Rights	30.0	93rd	0
Freedom from Corruption	31.7	95th	-3.3

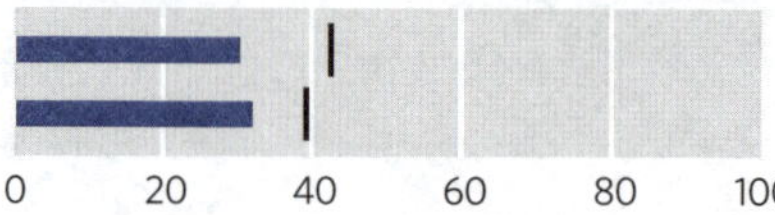

President Jammeh retains a firm grip on power through a combination of patronage and repression. Although the constitution provides for an independent judiciary, the president has the authority to select and dismiss judges. The judicial system recognizes customary law and Sharia law, primarily with regard to personal status and family matters. Impunity for members of the country's security forces is a serious problem.

GOVERNMENT SIZE

	Score	Rank	1-Year Change
Fiscal Freedom	79.0	101st	+3.9
Government Spending	79.8	54th	-2.9

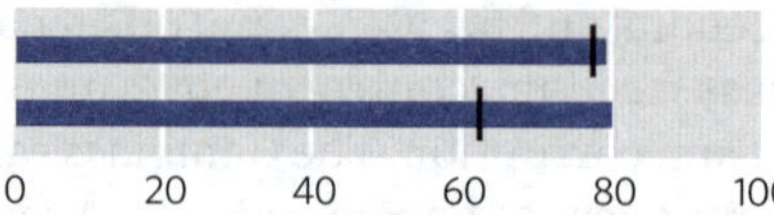

The top individual income tax rate has dropped to 30 percent, and the top corporate tax rate is 32 percent. Other taxes include a capital gains tax and a sales tax. The overall tax burden accounts for 13.2 percent of the domestic economy. Government spending is 26 percent of GDP, and government debt is equivalent to nearly 80 percent of the economy. Drought-induced crop failures have affected revenue collection in the past year.

REGULATORY EFFICIENCY

	Score	Rank	1-Year Change
Business Freedom	57.4	128th	-2.1
Labor Freedom	65.8	76th	+6.5
Monetary Freedom	71.3	137th	+0.2

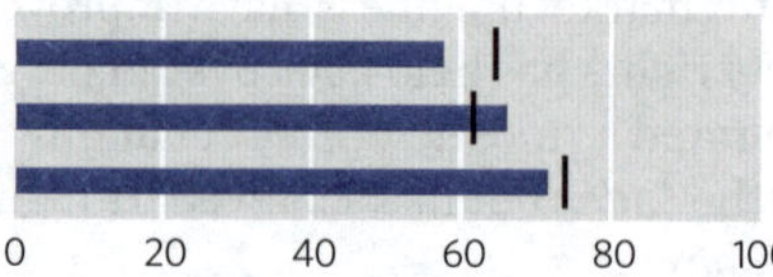

There is no minimum capital requirement for incorporating a company, but business start-up costs exceed the level of average annual income. Obtaining necessary permits takes over 100 days. The labor market remains inefficient. Although the government heavily subsidizes the parastatal water and electricity companies, they are among the least efficient operators on the African continent.

OPEN MARKETS

	Score	Rank	1-Year Change
Trade Freedom	65.0	143rd	+4.5
Investment Freedom	65.0	68th	0
Financial Freedom	50.0	69th	0

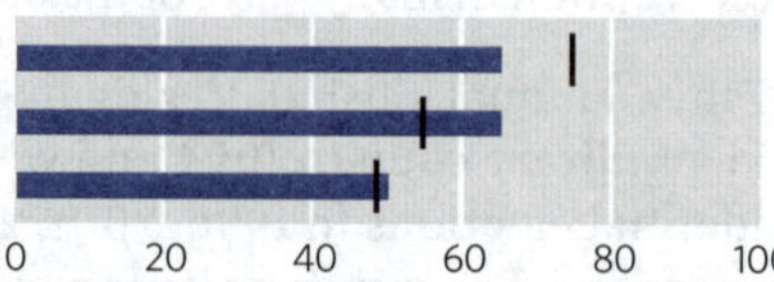

The Gambia's average tariff rate is 12.5 percent. In general, foreign and domestic investors are treated equally under the law. The financial sector has gradually expanded and benefited from increased competition. Almost all commercial banks are majority-owned by foreign banks, and credit to the private sector has been rising. Capital markets remain underdeveloped, and there is no stock exchange.

Long-Term Score Change (since 1997)

RULE OF LAW		GOVERNMENT SIZE		REGULATORY EFFICIENCY		OPEN MARKETS	
Property Rights	-40.0	Fiscal Freedom	+6.5	Business Freedom	+2.4	Trade Freedom	+7.0
Freedom from Corruption	+21.7	Government Spending	-1.0	Labor Freedom	-9.2	Investment Freedom	+35.0
				Monetary Freedom	+1.3	Financial Freedom	+20.0

GEORGIA

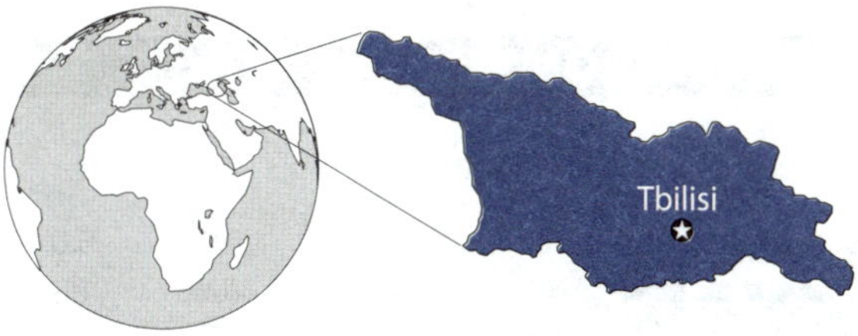

World Rank: 22 | **Regional Rank: 12**

Georgia's economic freedom score is 72.6, making its economy the 22nd freest in the 2014 *Index*. Its overall score is 0.4 point higher than last year, with improvements in six of the 10 economic freedoms including the management of public finance, investment freedom, monetary freedom, and property rights. Georgia is ranked 12th out of 43 countries in the Europe region, and its score is well above the regional average.

Over the 19 years that Georgia has been graded in the *Index*, its economic freedom has advanced over 28 points, the third best of any country. The impressive rise of Georgia's economic freedom has been propelled by broad-based score improvements in such critical areas as regulatory efficiency and market openness. Notable structural reforms have included trade liberalization, privatization, implementation of competitive flat tax rates, and modernization of the regulatory environment. With the effective maintenance of low inflation, greater monetary stability has also been achieved.

From a "repressed" economy almost two decades ago, Georgia has gradually advanced to the ranks of the economically "mostly free," achieving its highest score ever in the 2014 *Index*. Nonetheless, deeper institutional reforms to eradicate lingering corruption and increase judicial independence are critical to ensuring greater economic freedom in Georgia.

BACKGROUND: Georgia gained independence in 1991 and is a leading economic reformer among the post-Soviet countries. It has been particularly effective in reducing regulations, taxes, and corruption. After a civil war in 1992, Russian-supported Abkhazia and South Ossetia seceded. A 2008 military effort to regain the lost territories resulted in a stinging defeat. Georgia left the Commonwealth of Independent States in 2009. Relations with Russia remain difficult, but Georgia has taken unilateral steps to improve them. In 2012, billionaire Bidzina Ivanishvili, who made his fortune in Russia, and his Georgian Dream coalition defeated President Mikheil Saakashvili's United National Movement, paving the way for Ivanishvili to become prime minister. The economic recovery that began in 2010 continues, but foreign direct investment has not fully recovered since the 2008 conflict.

How Do We Measure Economic Freedom?
See page 471 for an explanation of the methodology or visit the *Index* Web site at *heritage.org/index*.

Economic Freedom Score

Freedom Trend

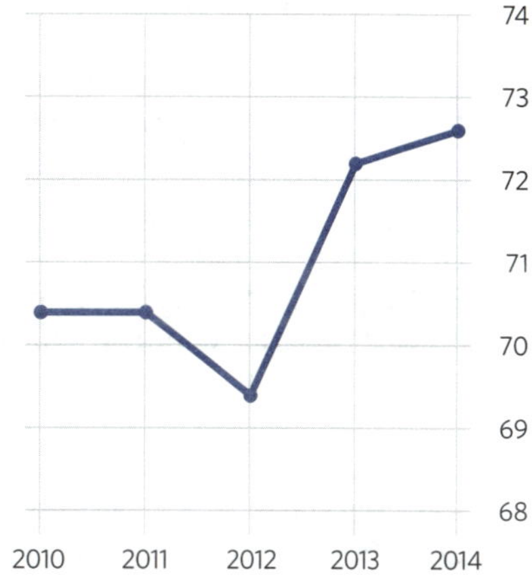

Country Comparisons

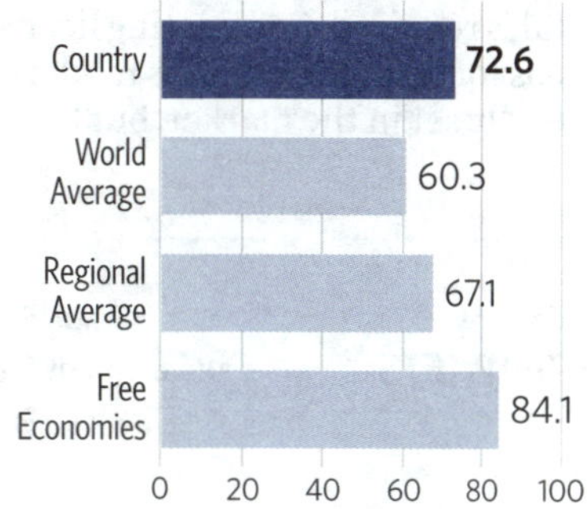

Quick Facts

Population: 4.5 million
GDP (PPP): $26.7 billion
6.5% growth in 2012
5-year compound annual growth 3.6%
$5,930 per capita
Unemployment: 14.6%
Inflation (CPI): -0.9%
FDI Inflow: $866.1 million
Public Debt: 32.7% of GDP

2012 data unless otherwise noted.
Data compiled as of September 2013.

THE TEN ECONOMIC FREEDOMS

Score | Country | World Average | Rank | 1-Year Change

RULE OF LAW

	Score	Rank	1-Year Change
Property Rights	40.0	70th	-5.0
Freedom from Corruption	42.8	62nd	+1.8

In 2013, several ministers from the outgoing United National Movement government of Mikheil Saakashvili were charged with various corruption-related crimes by authorities from the new Georgian Dream coalition government. President Saakashvili called the charges politically motivated. Georgia continues to struggle with the lingering effects of Soviet-era corruption. There are ongoing efforts to improve the security of property rights.

GOVERNMENT SIZE

	Score	Rank	1-Year Change
Fiscal Freedom	87.3	39th	-0.9
Government Spending	69.7	89th	+0.8

The individual income and corporate tax rates are a flat 20 percent and 15 percent, respectively. Other taxes include a value-added tax (VAT) and a tax on dividends. The overall tax burden is 25.4 percent of GDP. Government spending has been falling and is now at 32 percent of the gross domestic economy. This has had a positive impact on public debt, now reduced to less than 33 percent of GDP.

REGULATORY EFFICIENCY

	Score	Rank	1-Year Change
Business Freedom	87.8	18th	-2.8
Labor Freedom	91.2	5th	+0.1
Monetary Freedom	78.4	60th	+5.8

Incorporating a new company takes only two procedures and two days, and no minimum capital is required. Completing licensing requirements still takes over two months. The non-salary cost of hiring a worker is moderate, and regulations on work hours are flexible. Prices are generally set in the market, but the state maintains price-control measures and subsidizes fuel.

OPEN MARKETS

	Score	Rank	1-Year Change
Trade Freedom	88.6	8th	-0.6
Investment Freedom	80.0	23rd	+5.0
Financial Freedom	60.0	41st	0

Georgia has a low 0.7 percent average tariff rate and relatively few non-tariff trade barriers. With the exception of some restrictions on foreign land ownership, foreign investment is generally welcomed. The financial sector remains dominated by banks. The state does not hold any stake in banks. The growing banking sector offers improved access to financing, although the stock exchange remains relatively small and underdeveloped.

Long-Term Score Change (since 1996)

RULE OF LAW		GOVERNMENT SIZE		REGULATORY EFFICIENCY		OPEN MARKETS	
Property Rights	+10.0	Fiscal Freedom	-4.7	Business Freedom	+32.8	Trade Freedom	+19.6
Freedom from Corruption	+32.8	Government Spending	+8.3	Labor Freedom	+24.5	Investment Freedom	+30.0
				Monetary Freedom	+78.4	Financial Freedom	+30.0

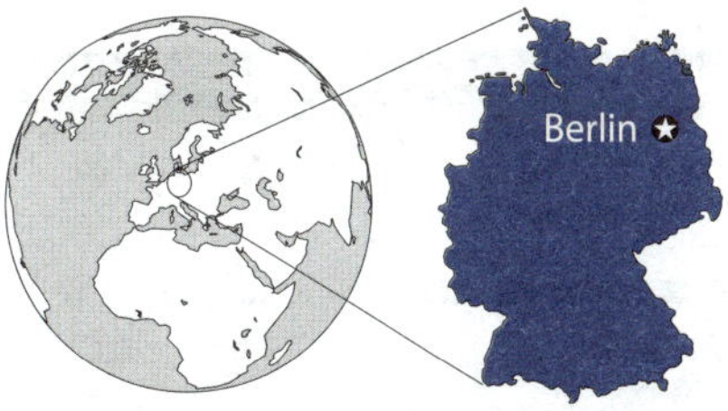

GERMANY

World Rank: 18 | **Regional Rank: 8**

Germany's economic freedom score is 73.4, making its economy the 18th freest in the 2014 *Index*. Its overall score is 0.6 point better than last year, reflecting modest improvements in investment freedom, labor freedom, and trade freedom. Germany is ranked 8th out of 43 countries in the Europe region, and its score exceeds the world and regional averages.

Over the 20-year history of the *Index,* Germany's economic freedom has advanced by nearly 4 points. Its 2014 score is its highest ever. Double-digit gains have been achieved in the areas of market openness and limited government. High levels of trade freedom and investment freedom continue to underpin Germany's competitiveness in global commerce and ensure dynamic economic growth.

During the first half of its history in the *Index,* Germany was rated one of the "moderately free" economies, but since 2006, it has steadily advanced to the ranks of the "mostly free" as one of the top 20 freest economies. Though its overall progress has been good, labor freedom remains significantly below world averages, and business freedom has slipped a bit from previous highs.

BACKGROUND: Chancellor Angela Merkel's Christian Democratic Union won the biggest share of the national vote in the September 2013 election, but its coalition partner, the economically liberal Free Democratic Party, failed to cross the 5 percent threshold and is no longer in the Bundestag. As of October 2013, coalition negotiations with the Social Democrat Party and the Green Party were ongoing. Economic reforms remain stalled because of an almost exclusive focus on rescuing the euro. Germany has funded the lion's share of large rescue packages for fellow eurozone members Greece and Cyprus. Germany and France have been the key proponents of the European Union's January 2013 Fiscal Compact Treaty. Germany's industrialized economy, the largest in Europe, is well integrated into the global marketplace and generates average per capita incomes that are among the highest in the world. Germany has one of the lowest unemployment rates in Europe and remains, both politically and economically, the most influential nation in the EU.

How Do We Measure Economic Freedom?
See page 471 for an explanation of the methodology or visit the *Index* Web site at *heritage.org/index.*

Economic Freedom Score

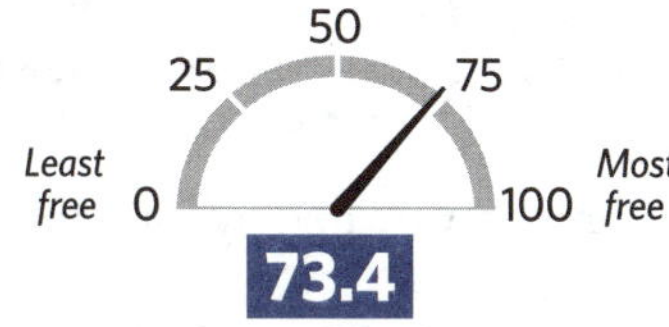

Freedom Trend

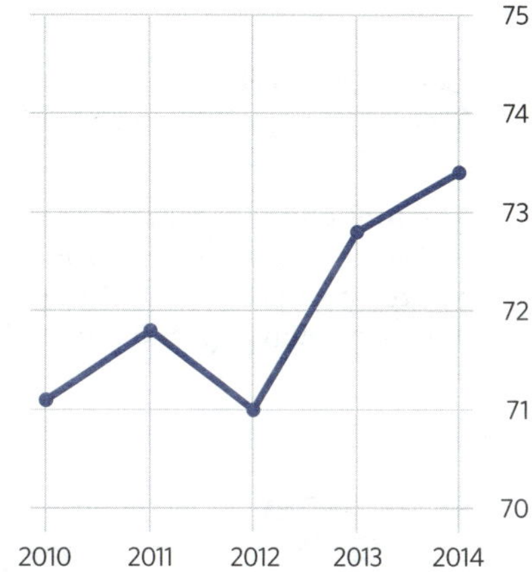

Country Comparisons

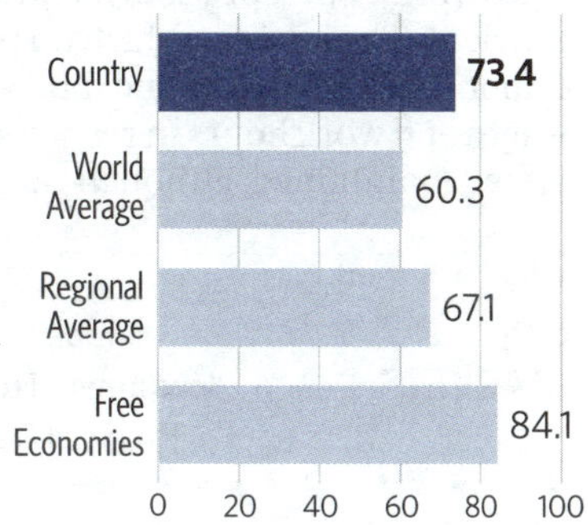

Quick Facts

Population: 81.9 million
GDP (PPP): $3.2 trillion
0.9% growth in 2012
5-year compound annual growth 0.7%
$39,028 per capita
Unemployment: 5.5%
Inflation (CPI): 2.1%
FDI Inflow: $6.6 billion
Public Debt: 82.0% of GDP

2012 data unless otherwise noted.
Data compiled as of September 2013.

THE TEN ECONOMIC FREEDOMS

RULE OF LAW

	Score	Rank	1-Year Change
Property Rights	90.0	2nd	0
Freedom from Corruption	80.1	14th	+0.1

Property owned by foreigners is fully protected under German law, and secured interests in property are recognized and enforced. Although government transparency is high and anti-corruption measures are enforced effectively, the construction and health sectors and public contracting represent areas of continued concern, particularly in conjunction with questionable political party influence and party donations.

GOVERNMENT SIZE

	Score	Rank	1-Year Change
Fiscal Freedom	61.2	166th	-0.6
Government Spending	38.2	155th	+0.9

The top individual income tax rate has risen to 47.5 percent, and the top corporate tax rate remains at 15.8 percent. Other taxes include a value-added tax (VAT) and a capital gains tax. Tax revenue is equal to 37 percent of GDP. Public spending has stabilized at 45 percent of the domestic economy, and public debt has remained steady at around 80 percent of GDP.

REGULATORY EFFICIENCY

	Score	Rank	1-Year Change
Business Freedom	89.9	13th	-2.2
Labor Freedom	46.4	152nd	+2.6
Monetary Freedom	80.8	23rd	-0.4

The overall entrepreneurial environment remains one of the world's most transparent and efficient. The business start-up process is straightforward, with no minimum capital required. Labor relations are sound, and employers and workers have worked cooperatively to adjust wages and work hours in response to the changing economic environment. Monetary stability is well maintained, although the government subsidizes the cost of renewable power.

OPEN MARKETS

	Score	Rank	1-Year Change
Trade Freedom	87.8	11th	+1.0
Investment Freedom	90.0	2nd	+5.0
Financial Freedom	70.0	19th	0

EU members have a low 1.1 percent average tariff rate and, in general, few non-tariff barriers to trade. Investment in a few sectors of the economy may be subject to government screening, but the government generally does not discriminate against foreign investment. The competitive financial sector remains largely stable, offering a full range of services. The traditional three-tiered system of private, public, and cooperative banks remains intact.

Long-Term Score Change (since 1995)

RULE OF LAW		GOVERNMENT SIZE		REGULATORY EFFICIENCY		OPEN MARKETS	
Property Rights	0	Fiscal Freedom	+28.0	Business Freedom	+4.9	Trade Freedom	+10.0
Freedom from Corruption	-9.9	Government Spending	+7.6	Labor Freedom	-2.3	Investment Freedom	+20.0
				Monetary Freedom	-0.9	Financial Freedom	0

GHANA

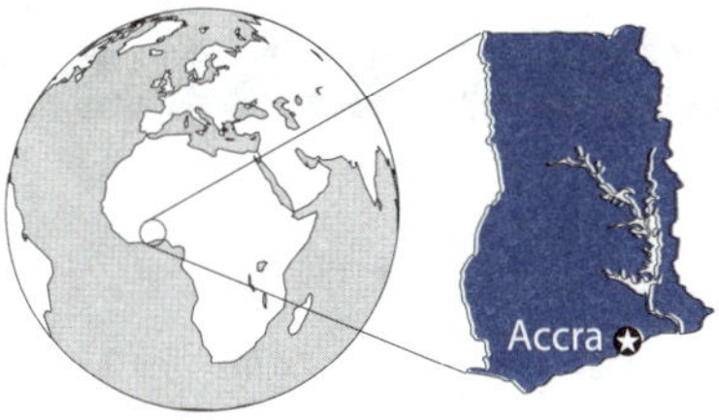

World Rank: 66 **Regional Rank: 5**

Economic Freedom Score

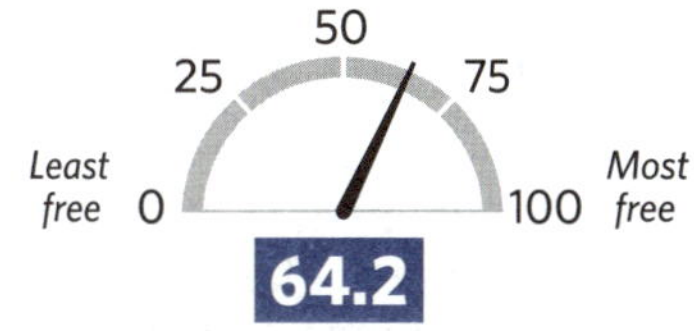

Ghana's economic freedom score is 64.2, making its economy the 66th freest in the 2014 *Index*. Its overall score is 2.9 points better than last year, reflecting notable improvements in the control of government spending, freedom from corruption, and business freedom. Ghana is ranked 5th out of 46 countries in the Sub-Saharan Africa region, and its overall score has risen above the world average.

Over the 20-year history of the *Index*, Ghana's economic freedom has advanced by nearly 9 points. With improvements in seven of the 10 areas measured, Ghana's overall economic freedom has been undermined only by declines in freedom from corruption and monetary freedom. In the area of market openness that measures trade freedom, investment freedom, and financial freedom, Ghana has made particularly notable progress. Categorized as a "mostly unfree" economy for much of its history in the *Index*, Ghana has achieved "moderately free" status in four of the past five years.

Lingering institutional impediments to advancing economic freedom include the inefficient protection of property rights and the weak rule of law. Corruption remains a serious deterrent to translating economic growth into sustained and broad-based economic development throughout the country.

BACKGROUND: Ghana has been a stable democracy since 1992. Long-time opposition candidate John Atta Mills was elected president in December 2008 but died in 2012. Former Vice President John Dramani Mahama won a special election in December 2012. Ghana is considered a regional model for political and economic reform. It is rich in natural resources, including gold, diamonds, manganese ore, and bauxite, and oil production began in 2010. Challenges include managing new oil revenue while maintaining fiscal discipline and resisting debt accumulation. Estimated oil reserves have jumped to almost 700 million barrels. The industrial sector (about 30 percent of GDP in 2007) is more developed than in other African countries, but agriculture accounts for 50 percent of employment and 39 percent of exports.

Freedom Trend

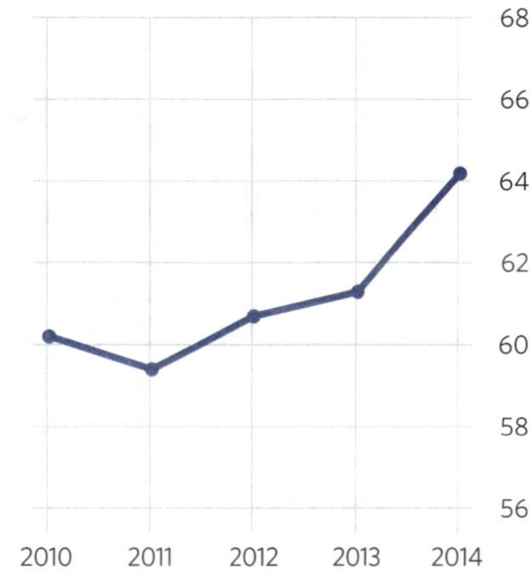

Country Comparisons

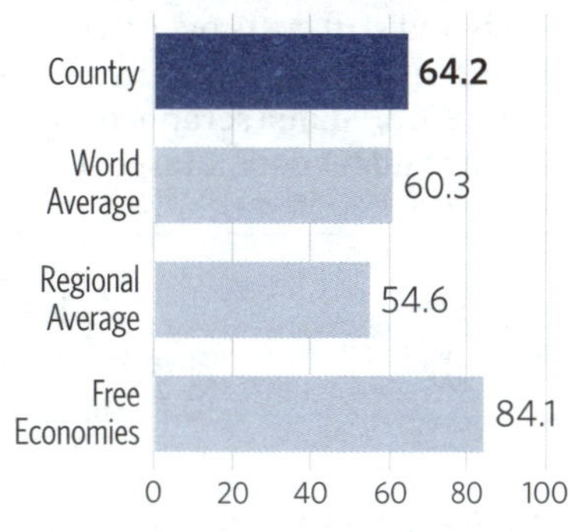

Quick Facts

Population: 24.9 million
GDP (PPP): $82.4 billion
7.0% growth in 2012
5-year compound annual growth 8.3%
$3,305 per capita
Unemployment: n/a
Inflation (CPI): 9.2%
FDI Inflow: $3.3 billion
Public Debt: 56.5% of GDP

2012 data unless otherwise noted.
Data compiled as of September 2013.

How Do We Measure Economic Freedom?
See page 471 for an explanation of the methodology or visit the *Index* Web site at *heritage.org/index*.

THE TEN ECONOMIC FREEDOMS

RULE OF LAW

	Score	Rank	1-Year Change
Property Rights	50.0	53rd	0
Freedom from Corruption	40.4	67th	+1.4

Government corruption remains a significant problem, and anti-corruption laws are rarely implemented effectively. Scarce budgetary resources compromise and delay the judicial process, and poorly paid judges are tempted by bribes. The process for gaining clear title to land is often difficult, complicated, and lengthy. Some progress has been made in recent years in improving the protection of intellectual property.

GOVERNMENT SIZE

	Score	Rank	1-Year Change
Fiscal Freedom	85.4	51st	-0.6
Government Spending	83.3	39th	+30.8

Ghana's top individual income and corporate tax rates are 25 percent. Other taxes include a value-added tax (VAT), a national insurance levy, and a capital gains tax. The overall tax burden equals 14.6 percent of total domestic income. Government expenditures are 24 percent of gross domestic output, and public debt remains over 55 percent of the size of the economy.

REGULATORY EFFICIENCY

	Score	Rank	1-Year Change
Business Freedom	62.6	101st	+1.1
Labor Freedom	60.2	100th	-1.4
Monetary Freedom	65.8	164th	+1.0

The business start-up process takes two weeks, but obtaining necessary permits takes over 200 days and still costs over twice the level of average annual income. Despite ongoing efforts to modernize the labor code, a large share of the labor force remains in the informal economy. In May 2013, Ghana scrapped costly fuel subsidies to help restore fiscal stability after overshooting its budget deficit target by nearly 100 percent in 2012.

OPEN MARKETS

	Score	Rank	1-Year Change
Trade Freedom	64.8	144th	-3.0
Investment Freedom	70.0	46th	0
Financial Freedom	60.0	41st	0

Ghana has a 10.1 percent average tariff rate, and non-tariff barriers further impede trade. Foreign investment is officially welcomed, but investors may face restrictions in certain sectors of the economy. The financial sector has undergone restructuring through privatizations, but the banking sector is undercapitalized, and access to financing remains limited.

Long-Term Score Change (since 1995)

RULE OF LAW		GOVERNMENT SIZE		REGULATORY EFFICIENCY		OPEN MARKETS	
Property Rights	0	Fiscal Freedom	+19.0	Business Freedom	+7.6	Trade Freedom	+33.6
Freedom from Corruption	-29.6	Government Spending	+1.4	Labor Freedom	+10.0	Investment Freedom	+40.0
				Monetary Freedom	-0.4	Financial Freedom	+10.0

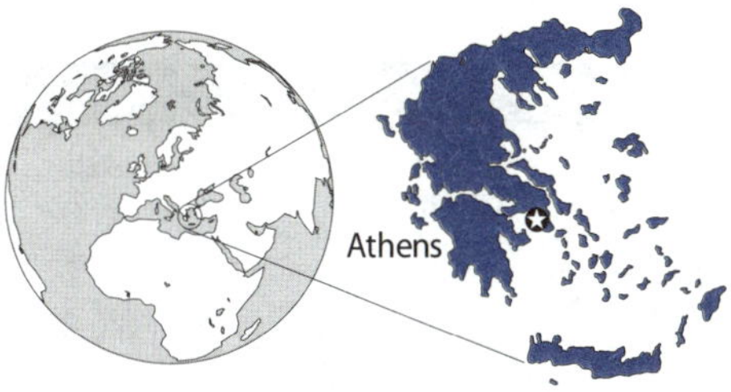

GREECE

Greece's economic freedom score is 55.7, making its economy the 119th freest in the 2014 *Index*. Its score is only slightly better than last year, with improvements in labor freedom and monetary freedom almost completely offset by deteriorations in investment freedom, the control of government spending, business freedom, and freedom from corruption. Greece is ranked 40th out of 43 countries in the Europe region, and its overall score is below the world and regional averages.

Over the 20-year history of the *Index*, Greece's economic freedom score has declined by over 5 points. Despite improvements in five of the 10 economic freedoms, large declines in property rights, freedom from corruption, government spending, and investment freedom have more than offset any gains.

Greece has fluctuated between the ranks of the "moderately free" and the "mostly unfree" throughout the history of the *Index*. It achieved its highest level of economic freedom in 2010, but its scores have plummeted dramatically since then. Major fiscal weaknesses aggravated by the debt and unemployment crises have not been sufficiently addressed, and the relatively poor economic performance associated with levels of economic freedom that are significantly below other members of the EU has led to a loss of competitiveness and even to political volatility.

BACKGROUND: Greece joined NATO in 1952 and the European Union in 1981. It adopted the euro in 2002. To confront a sovereign debt crisis in 2010, the European Central Bank and the International Monetary Fund provided emergency loans in exchange for necessary but long-delayed austerity measures. A year later, after a series of violent protests, the government collapsed. A caretaker government was formed in November 2011. When elections in May 2012 failed to produce a government, new elections in June 2012 led to formation of a "pro-Euro" coalition led by the center-right New Democracy party along with the center-left Pan-Hellenic Socialist Movement and the Democratic Left Party. Greece's economy, which depends heavily on shipping, tourism, and services, has contracted for 19 straight quarters.

How Do We Measure Economic Freedom?
See page 471 for an explanation of the methodology or visit the *Index* Web site at *heritage.org/index*.

Economic Freedom Score

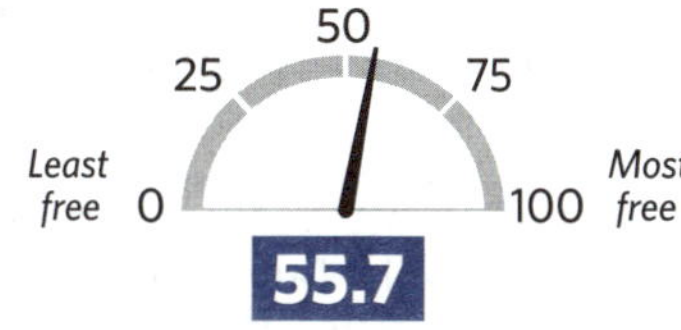

Freedom Trend

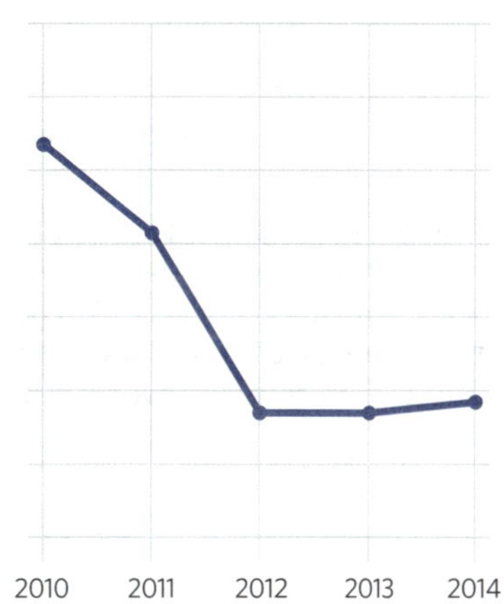

Country Comparisons

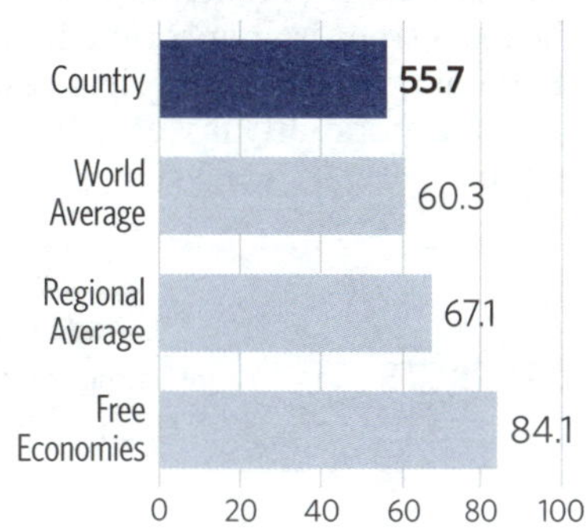

Quick Facts

Population: 11.3 million
GDP (PPP): $276.9 billion
-6.4% growth in 2012
5-year compound annual growth -4.4%
$24,505 per capita
Unemployment: 24.2%
Inflation (CPI): 1.0%
FDI Inflow: $2.9 billion
Public Debt: 158.5% of GDP

2012 data unless otherwise noted.
Data compiled as of September 2013.

THE TEN ECONOMIC FREEDOMS

RULE OF LAW

	Score	Rank	1-Year Change
Property Rights	40.0	70th	0
Freedom from Corruption	33.2	89th	-0.8

Corruption remains a problem in Greece. In April 2012, a former minister of defense was charged with taking millions of euros in bribes from European armaments manufacturers. An October 2012 press report detailed extensive tax evasion by wealthy Greek citizens. The judiciary is independent, and the constitution provides for public trials. Protection of property rights is not strongly enforced.

GOVERNMENT SIZE

	Score	Rank	1-Year Change
Fiscal Freedom	65.9	153rd	-0.3
Government Spending	19.2	172nd	-5.5

The top individual income tax rate has been reduced to 42 percent, and the top corporate tax rate is 26 percent. Other taxes include a value-added tax (VAT) and a real estate tax. The overall tax burden is nearly 31.2 percent of GDP. Public spending has stabilized at 52 percent of the domestic economy. Economic recession continues to put pressure on public accounts, and public debt remains over 150 percent of GDP.

REGULATORY EFFICIENCY

	Score	Rank	1-Year Change
Business Freedom	75.8	45th	-1.3
Labor Freedom	53.9	121st	+11.8
Monetary Freedom	76.3	79th	+2.9

The process for launching a company is fairly streamlined and takes only five procedures, but licensing requirements remain burdensome and time-consuming. With high non-salary costs to employ a worker and rigid restrictions on work hours, the labor market remains stagnant. Monetary stability is weak, and Greece is receiving substantial subsidies from the European Union.

OPEN MARKETS

	Score	Rank	1-Year Change
Trade Freedom	82.8	56th	+1.0
Investment Freedom	60.0	80th	-5.0
Financial Freedom	50.0	69th	0

EU members have a low 1.1 percent average tariff rate and, in general, few non-tariff barriers to trade. Greece's government procurement policies sometimes favor domestic companies. Economic uncertainty continues to deter foreign investment. The overall stability of the financial system has been severely undermined, and the banking sector continues to be under strain.

Long-Term Score Change (since 1995)

RULE OF LAW		GOVERNMENT SIZE		REGULATORY EFFICIENCY		OPEN MARKETS	
Property Rights	**-30.0**	Fiscal Freedom	**+3.4**	Business Freedom	**+5.8**	Trade Freedom	**+5.0**
Freedom from Corruption	**-16.8**	Government Spending	**-36.1**	Labor Freedom	**-2.2**	Investment Freedom	**-10.0**
				Monetary Freedom	**+11.0**	Financial Freedom	**+20.0**

GUATEMALA

World Rank: **83** Regional Rank: **17**

Economic Freedom Score

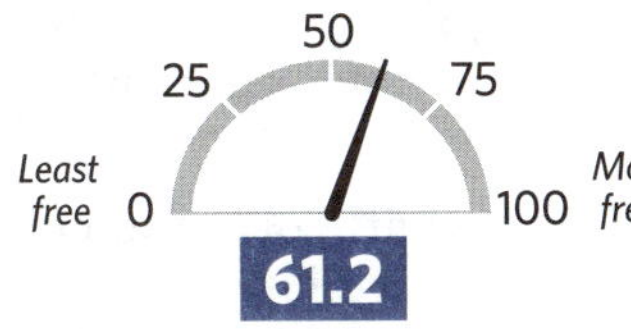

Guatemala's economic freedom score is 61.2, making its economy the 83rd freest in the 2014 *Index*. Its score has increased by 1.2 points, reflecting improvements in six of the 10 economic freedoms including business freedom, investment freedom, and freedom from corruption. Guatemala is ranked 17th out of 29 countries in the South and Central America/Caribbean region, and its overall score is above the regional and world averages.

Over the 20-year history of the *Index*, Guatemala's economic freedom has largely stagnated. Improvements in trade freedom, investment freedom, and business freedom have been undermined by an expansion of government spending and taxation and double-digit declines in property rights and freedom from corruption. Reflecting the lack of a consistent governmental commitment to structural reform, the Guatemalan economy has fluctuated in the ranks of the "moderately free" and the "mostly unfree" throughout the history of the *Index*.

Guatemala enjoys a relatively high degree of market openness but continues to lag in promoting the effective rule of law. The judicial system remains vulnerable to political interference, and lingering serious corruption further undermines the emergence of a more vibrant private sector.

BACKGROUND: Former General Otto Perez Molina won the presidency in 2011, replacing social democrat Alvaro Colom, whose four-year term was marked by internal political feuding, skyrocketing corruption, and mounting insecurity. Guatemala is the administrative hub for the Central American Integration System, which aims to improve regional economic cooperation. Agriculture accounts for 13 percent of Guatemala's GDP. Exports include coffee, bananas, sugar, and apparel. The economy was seriously damaged during the global recession but rebounded slightly in 2012. More than half of the population lives below the poverty line. Guatemala works closely with the U.S. on security issues, but drug trafficking persists, and Mexican cartels continue to expand their influence in the country.

Freedom Trend

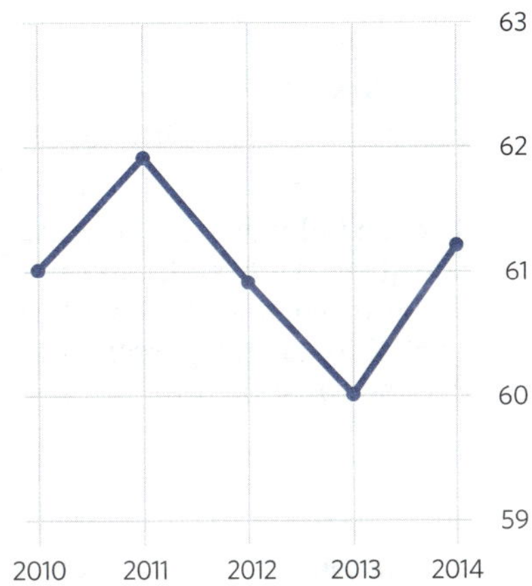

Country Comparisons

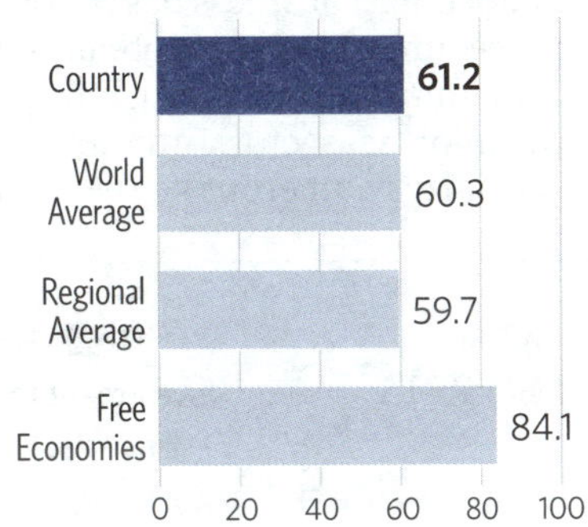

Quick Facts

Population: 15.1 million
GDP (PPP): $78.7 billion
3.0% growth in 2012
5-year compound annual growth 2.8%
$5,209 per capita
Unemployment: 4.1% (2011)
Inflation (CPI): 3.8%
FDI Inflow: $1.2 billion
Public Debt: 25.1% of GDP

2012 data unless otherwise noted.
Data compiled as of September 2013.

How Do We Measure Economic Freedom?
See page 471 for an explanation of the methodology or visit the *Index* Web site at *heritage.org/index.*

THE TEN ECONOMIC FREEDOMS

RULE OF LAW

	Score	Rank	1-Year Change
Property Rights	25.0	135th	-5.0
Freedom from Corruption	28.7	112th	+1.7

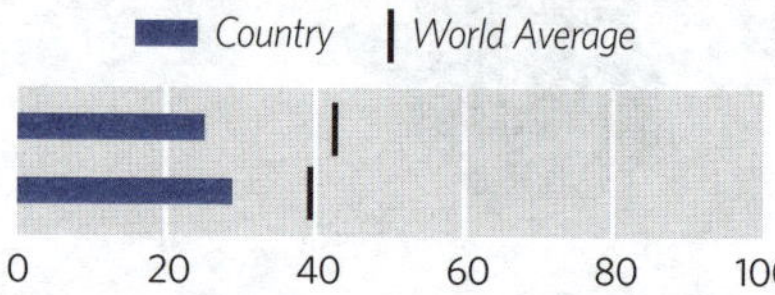

Despite anti-corruption efforts, serious problems remain. In May 2013, former President Alfonso Portillo was extradited to the United States to face charges of using U.S. banks to launder millions of dollars allegedly embezzled while he was in office. Drug-trafficking and related violence are increasing. The judiciary is troubled by corruption, inefficiency, capacity shortages, and intimidation of judges, prosecutors, and witnesses.

GOVERNMENT SIZE

	Score	Rank	1-Year Change
Fiscal Freedom	79.6	94th	0
Government Spending	93.6	1st	0

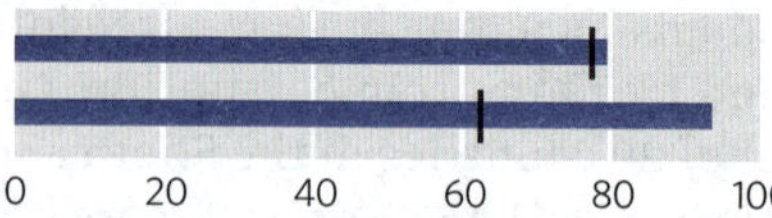

The top individual income and corporate tax rates are 31 percent. Other taxes include a value-added tax (VAT) and a tax on real estate. The overall tax burden amounts to 11 percent of gross domestic income. Public expenditures are around 15 percent of the domestic economy. In 2006, the U.S. forgave 20 percent of Guatemala's debt in exchange for protection of rain forests. Public debt now rests at around 25 percent of GDP.

REGULATORY EFFICIENCY

	Score	Rank	1-Year Change
Business Freedom	58.4	122nd	+7.6
Labor Freedom	49.3	142nd	+0.6
Monetary Freedom	76.7	75th	+1.2

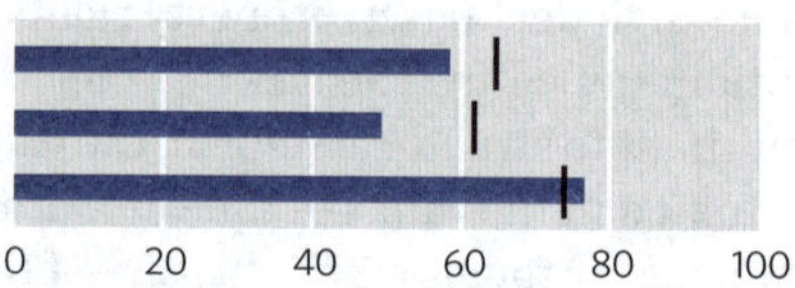

Launching a business has become more streamlined and takes about 20 days and less than 10 procedures. The cost of obtaining necessary licenses remains about four times the level of average annual income. The labor market is inefficient, and much of the labor force is employed in the informal sector. Inflation has abated slightly. The state maintains few price controls but subsidizes numerous key economic activities and products.

OPEN MARKETS

	Score	Rank	1-Year Change
Trade Freedom	85.4	47th	+0.2
Investment Freedom	65.0	68th	+5.0
Financial Freedom	50.0	69th	0

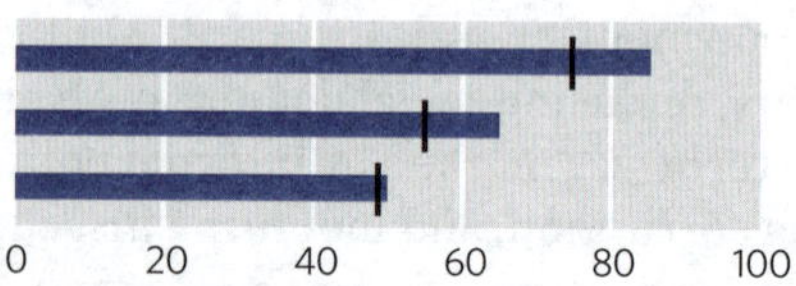

Guatemala's average tariff rate is 2.3 percent. The regulatory and legal systems may be challenging for foreign investors to navigate. The small financial system, which has been reorganized in recent years, is dominated by banks. The banking sector remains relatively stable and well capitalized, and the number of non-performing loans is declining. A recently enacted insurance law opened the insurance market to foreign firms.

Long-Term Score Change (since 1995)

RULE OF LAW		GOVERNMENT SIZE		REGULATORY EFFICIENCY		OPEN MARKETS	
Property Rights	**-25.0**	Fiscal Freedom	**-7.2**	Business Freedom	**+3.4**	Trade Freedom	**+33.0**
Freedom from Corruption	**-21.3**	Government Spending	**-3.0**	Labor Freedom	**-11.3**	Investment Freedom	**+15.0**
				Monetary Freedom	**+9.8**	Financial Freedom	**0**

GUINEA

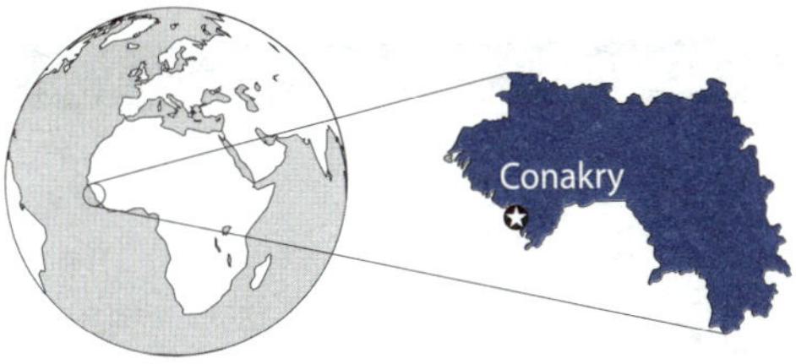

Economic Freedom Score

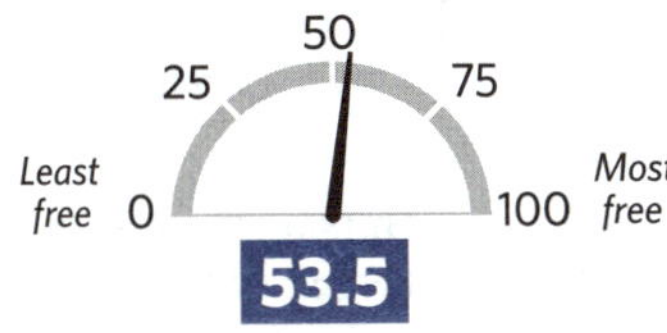

World Rank: **133** Regional Rank: **27**

Guinea's economic freedom score is 53.5, making its economy the 133rd freest in the 2014 *Index*. Its overall score is 2.3 points higher than last year, with notable improvement in half of the 10 economic freedoms including investment freedom, labor freedom, and business freedom. Guinea is ranked 27th out of 46 countries in the Sub-Saharan Africa region, and its overall score is below the world and regional averages.

Over the 20 year-history of the *Index*, Guinea's progress toward greater economic freedom has been uneven but generally downward. Overall, its economic freedom score has declined by 5.9 points, one of the 20 biggest drops in the history of the *Index*. Its scores for property rights, business freedom, monetary freedom, and financial freedom have deteriorated by more than 10 points.

The overall entrepreneurial environment remains severely constrained. An overbearing regulatory framework, exacerbated by poor access to credit and high financing costs, stifles economic activity and hurts business expansion and the development of a vibrant private sector. Corruption, perceived as widespread, is a serious problem.

BACKGROUND: In 2008, a military junta led by Captain Moussa Dadis Camara seized power and suspended the constitution. The first free democratic presidential election since independence in 1958 took place in November 2010. Alpha Conde won the presidency and was inaugurated in December after a court challenge. Political violence erupted in February 2013, and parliamentary elections, the results of which were not immediately available, were delayed until September. Guinea is host to hundreds of thousands of refugees from Côte d'Ivoire, Sierra Leone, and Liberia. Electricity and water shortages are common, and much of the workforce is engaged in subsistence agriculture. Despite possessing two-thirds of the world's bauxite reserves and large deposits of iron ore, gold, and diamonds, the population remains impoverished due to the absence of property rights, rampant corruption, poor government administration, poor infrastructure, and political instability.

How Do We Measure Economic Freedom?
See page 471 for an explanation of the methodology or visit the *Index* Web site at *heritage.org/index*.

Freedom Trend

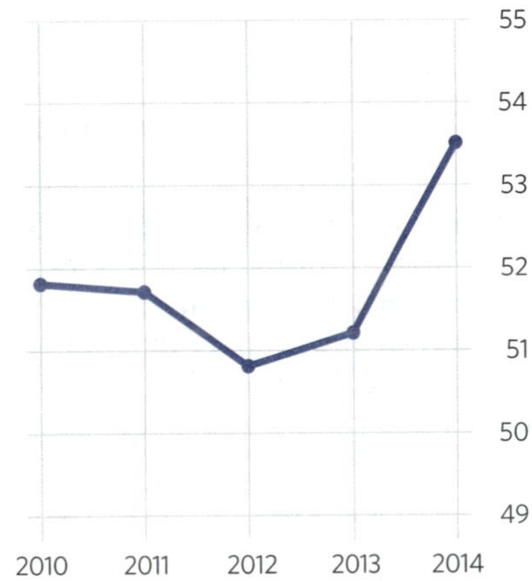

Country Comparisons

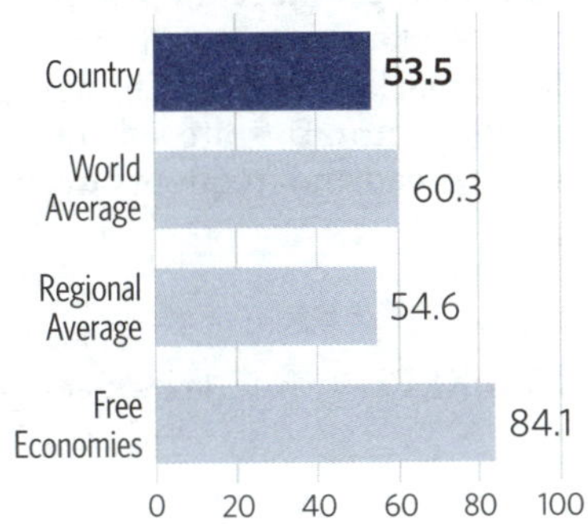

Quick Facts

Population: 10.9 million
GDP (PPP): $12.2 billion
3.9% growth in 2012
5-year compound annual growth 2.9%
$1,121 per capita
Unemployment: n/a
Inflation (CPI): 15.2%
FDI Inflow: $743.8 million
Public Debt: 43.0% of GDP

2012 data unless otherwise noted.
Data compiled as of September 2013.

THE TEN ECONOMIC FREEDOMS

RULE OF LAW

	Score	Rank	1-Year Change
Property Rights	20.0	139th	0
Freedom from Corruption	19.2	165th	-1.8

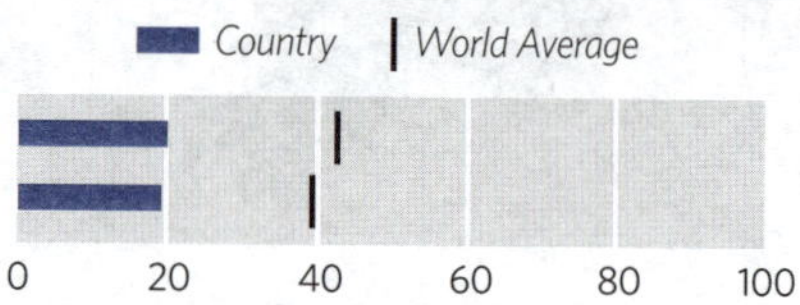

Corruption is a serious problem, and many government activities are shrouded in secrecy. Guinea has rich natural resources, yet the majority of the population lives in poverty. Despite demonstrating a modest degree of independence in the past few years, the court system remains subject to political interference and lacks transparency. The rule of law is uneven, and protection of property rights is very weak.

GOVERNMENT SIZE

	Score	Rank	1-Year Change
Fiscal Freedom	69.3	141st	-0.3
Government Spending	86.2	26th	+3.6

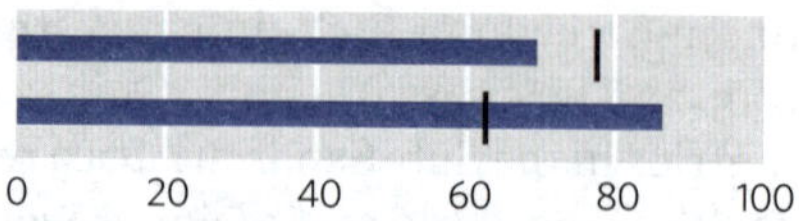

The top individual income tax rate is 40 percent, and the top corporate tax rate is 35 percent. Other taxes include a value-added tax (VAT) and an inheritance tax. The overall tax burden is 15.6 percent of GDP. Government expenditures are 22 percent of gross domestic output. In 2012, Guinea benefited from a $2 billion IMF-financed debt relief that cut public debt from 105 percent of GDP to below 45 percent in four years.

REGULATORY EFFICIENCY

	Score	Rank	1-Year Change
Business Freedom	51.8	149th	+5.7
Labor Freedom	73.4	51st	+9.6
Monetary Freedom	64.1	169th	+1.3

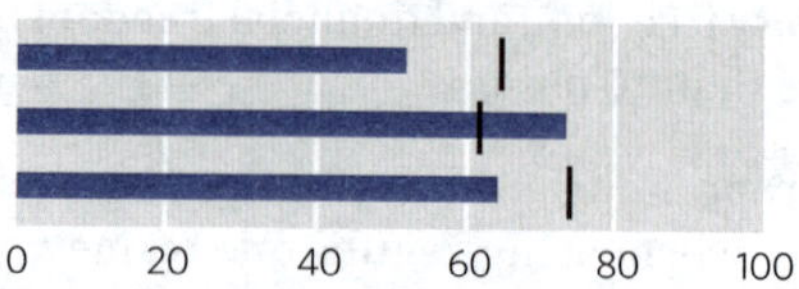

The business start-up process still takes 16 days on average. Completing licensing requirements takes more than 150 days and costs about the level of average annual income. With the labor market relatively underdeveloped, most formal employment remains confined to the public sector. Despite substantial subsidies provided to the state electrical utility, there are widespread and frequent power shortages.

OPEN MARKETS

	Score	Rank	1-Year Change
Trade Freedom	61.2	155th	0
Investment Freedom	50.0	109th	+5.0
Financial Freedom	40.0	107th	0

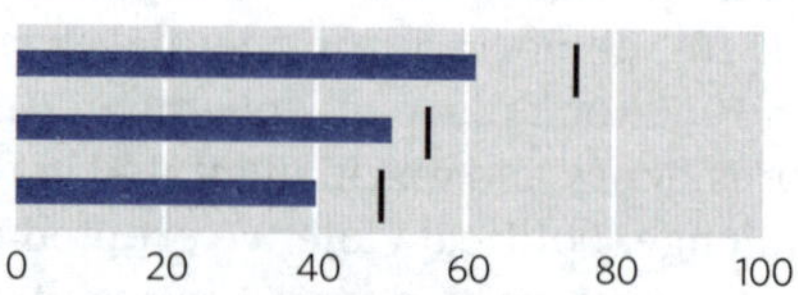

The average tariff rate for Guinea is 11.9 percent. Imports of rice, flour, and sugar are not allowed. The legal and regulatory systems are a challenge for foreign investors to navigate. The financial sector remains underdeveloped, providing a very limited range of services. Many people still rely on informal lending and have no bank accounts.

Long-Term Score Change (since 1995)

RULE OF LAW		GOVERNMENT SIZE		REGULATORY EFFICIENCY		OPEN MARKETS	
Property Rights	**-30.0**	Fiscal Freedom	**-2.0**	Business Freedom	**-18.2**	Trade Freedom	**+10.2**
Freedom from Corruption	**+9.2**	Government Spending	**-0.2**	Labor Freedom	**+2.9**	Investment Freedom	**0**
				Monetary Freedom	**-11.8**	Financial Freedom	**-30.0**

GUINEA–BISSAU

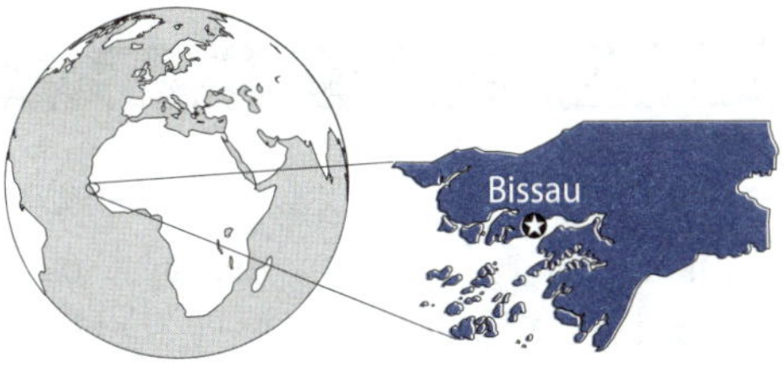

World Rank: 143 **Regional Rank: 33**

Economic Freedom Score

Guinea–Bissau's economic freedom score is 51.3, making its economy the 143rd freest in the 2014 *Index*. Its score has increased by 0.2 point, with improvements in labor freedom and the management of government spending outweighing declines in investment freedom, trade freedom, and freedom from corruption. Guinea–Bissau is ranked 33rd out of 46 countries in the Sub-Saharan Africa region, and its overall score remains well below the world and regional averages.

Guinea–Bissau was first graded in the 1999 *Index*, and its economic freedom has advanced since then by nearly 18 points. With no decline in any of the 10 economic freedoms and dramatic score improvements in the area of market openness as measured by trade freedom and financial freedom, the country advanced out of the ranks of the "repressed" in 2012 and recorded its highest score ever in 2014.

Guinea–Bissau's progress toward greater economic freedom will require deeper institutional reforms to ensure an effective transition to an open market economy under the rule of law. Corruption and weak enforcement of property rights drain economic resources, and the judicial system lacks transparency and independence.

BACKGROUND: President Joao Vieira, ousted in 1998, won the presidency in 2005 but was assassinated in March 2009. Malam Bacai Sanha, who won an emergency election in June 2009, died in January 2012, and a military coup in April prevented an election to determine his successor. Manuel Serifo Nhamadjo became acting president in May 2012 as part of a transitional arrangement. Guinea–Bissau remains highly dependent on subsistence agriculture, the export of cashew nuts (the country's most important commercial crop), and foreign assistance. Agriculture employs over 80 percent of the labor force and accounts for over 60 percent of GDP and about 90 percent of exports. The country is a major transit point for drugs and arms trafficking by international criminal gangs. GDP contracted by 1.5 percent last year.

Freedom Trend

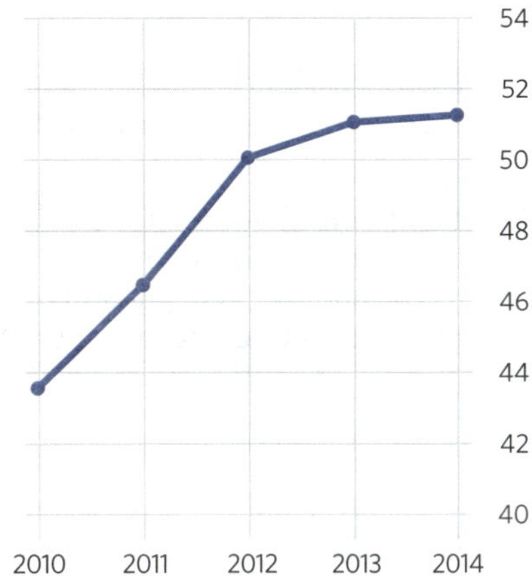

Country Comparisons

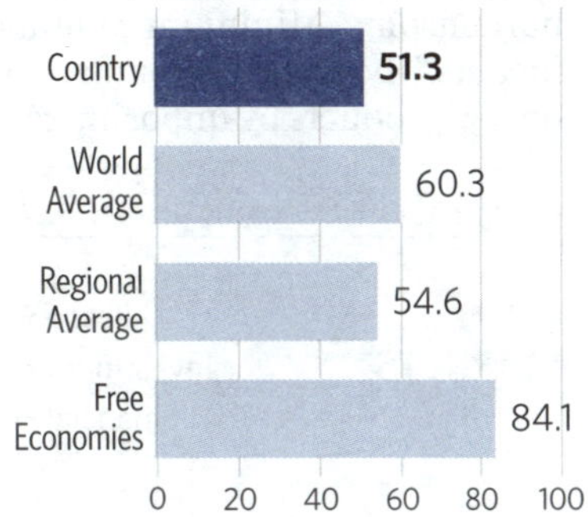

Quick Facts

Population: 1.6 million
GDP (PPP): $1.9 billion
-1.5% growth in 2012
5-year compound annual growth 2.7%
$1,223 per capita
Unemployment: n/a
Inflation (CPI): 2.2%
FDI Inflow: $16.2 million
Public Debt: 59.8% of GDP

2012 data unless otherwise noted.
Data compiled as of September 2013.

How Do We Measure Economic Freedom?
See page 471 for an explanation of the methodology or visit the *Index* Web site at *heritage.org/index*.

GUINEA-BISSAU (continued)

THE TEN ECONOMIC FREEDOMS

Score ■ Country | World Average

RULE OF LAW

	Score	Rank	1-Year Change
Property Rights	20.0	139th	0
Freedom from Corruption	20.2	159th	-1.8

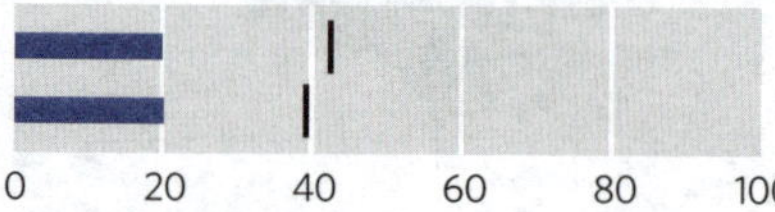

Corruption is pervasive, driven in large part by the illicit drug trade. With weak institutions and porous borders, Guinea-Bissau has become a major transit point for Latin American drug traffickers moving cocaine to Europe. Scant resources and endemic corruption severely challenge judicial independence. Judges and magistrates are poorly trained, irregularly paid, and highly susceptible to corruption and political pressure.

GOVERNMENT SIZE

	Score	Rank	1-Year Change
Fiscal Freedom	89.0	36th	-0.1
Government Spending	86.6	24th	+4.6

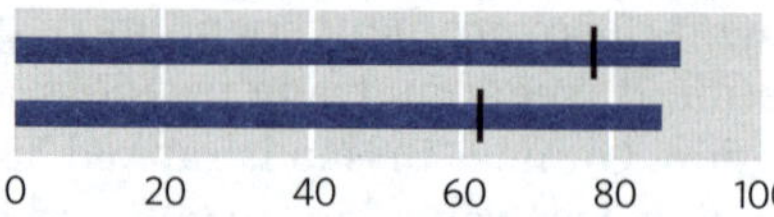

The top individual income tax rate is 20 percent, and the top corporate tax rate is 25 percent. Other taxes include a sales tax. The overall tax burden is 8.6 percent of GDP. Government spending is 21 percent of gross domestic output. Public debt has been rising and recently reached about 60 percent of GDP. Fiscal uncertainty remains high after a coup in 2012.

REGULATORY EFFICIENCY

	Score	Rank	1-Year Change
Business Freedom	40.5	168th	-0.8
Labor Freedom	61.4	93rd	+7.4
Monetary Freedom	74.4	112th	+1.7

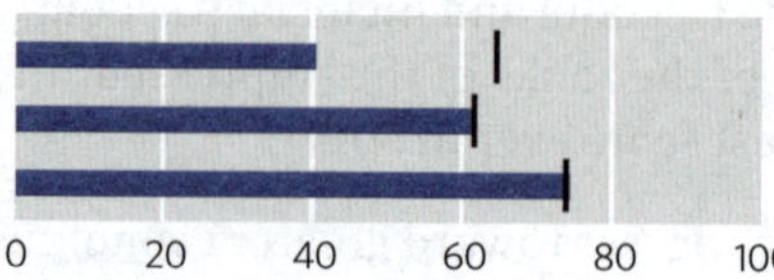

Establishing a business has become streamlined, but other regulatory requirements remain burdensome. Minimum capital requirements exceed three times the average level of annual income. The formal labor market is underdeveloped. The government maintains price controls on key products by imposing reference prices for fuel and basic foods.

OPEN MARKETS

	Score	Rank	1-Year Change
Trade Freedom	61.4	154th	-3.9
Investment Freedom	30.0	152nd	-5.0
Financial Freedom	30.0	132nd	0

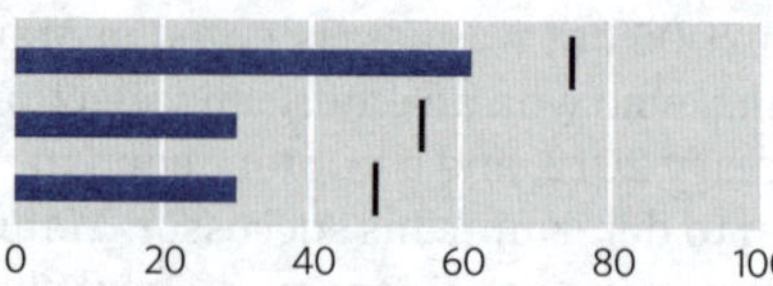

Guinea-Bissau's average tariff rate is 11.8 percent. Political unrest has been a deterrent to foreign investment. The underdeveloped financial sector is a serious impediment to private-sector growth. Most economic activity remains outside of the formal banking sector, and medium-term and long-term financing is not easily accessible.

Long-Term Score Change (since 1999)

RULE OF LAW		GOVERNMENT SIZE		REGULATORY EFFICIENCY		OPEN MARKETS	
Property Rights	+10.0	Fiscal Freedom	+23.5	Business Freedom	+0.5	Trade Freedom	+32.0
Freedom from Corruption	+10.2	Government Spending	+20.6	Labor Freedom	+9.7	Investment Freedom	0
				Monetary Freedom	+33.8	Financial Freedom	+20.0

GUYANA

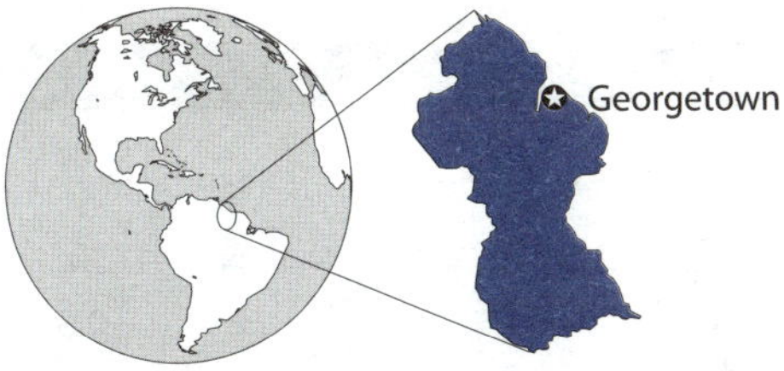

World Rank: **121** Regional Rank: **22**

Economic Freedom Score

Freedom Trend

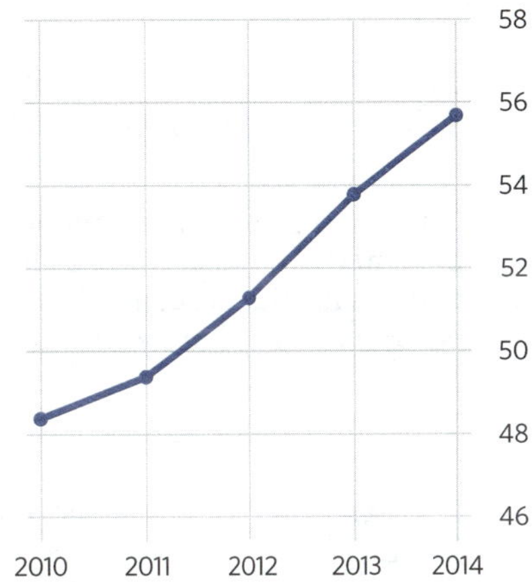

Country Comparisons

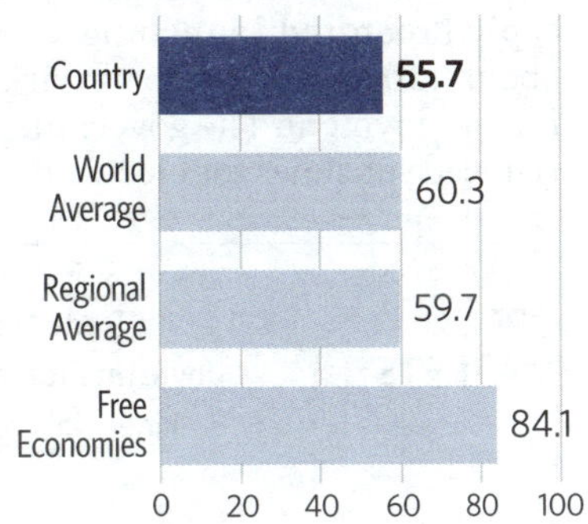

Guyana's economic freedom score is 55.7, making its economy the 121st freest in the 2014 *Index*. Its overall score is 1.9 points higher than last year, reflecting notable score increases in control of government spending and investment freedom. Guyana is ranked 22nd out of 29 countries in the South and Central America/Caribbean region, and its overall score is well below the world and regional averages.

Over the 20-year history of the *Index*, Guyana has advanced its economic freedom score by 10 points. This overall increase has been achieved by enhancements in seven of the 10 economic freedoms, notably the management of public spending, freedom from corruption, and monetary freedom, the scores for which have improved by 10 points or more.

Guyana slipped back into economically "repressed" status during the late 2000s but has risen out of that category since 2012 and recorded its highest score in eight years in the 2014 *Index*. Nevertheless, broad-based economic growth continues to be held back by institutional weaknesses in the economy. Long-standing constraints on economic freedom include fragile protection of property rights and below-average levels of openness and integration into world markets.

BACKGROUND: Since independence in 1966, Guyana has been ruled mostly by left-wing populist governments. President Donald Ramotar was elected in 2011. Reform has been attempted only under framework agreements with international organizations. Although the risk of political violence is the lowest since the early 1990s, relations between the ruling People's Progressive Party/Civic and the People's National Congress/Reform remain hostile. Guyana is one of the Western Hemisphere's poorest countries, and its state-dominated economy, dependent mainly on agriculture and mining, has been stagnant for many years. The economy relies heavily on exports of sugar, gold, bauxite, shrimp, timber, and rice, which represent nearly 60 percent of GDP and are susceptible to weather conditions and fluctuations in commodity prices. Violent crime and drug trafficking are endemic.

Quick Facts

Population: 0.8 million
GDP (PPP): $6.2 billion
3.3% growth in 2012
5-year compound annual growth 3.7%
$7,939 per capita
Unemployment: 11.0% (2007)
Inflation (CPI): 3.0%
FDI Inflow: $230.9 million
Public Debt: 60.3% of GDP

2012 data unless otherwise noted.
Data compiled as of September 2013.

How Do We Measure Economic Freedom?
See page 471 for an explanation of the methodology or visit the *Index* Web site at *heritage.org/index*.

THE TEN ECONOMIC FREEDOMS

RULE OF LAW

	Score	Rank	1-Year Change
Property Rights	30.0	93rd	0
Freedom from Corruption	24.4	135th	–0.6

Guyana is a transshipment point for South American cocaine destined for North America and Europe, and counter-narcotics efforts are undermined by corruption that reaches into high levels of the government. Crime is a major problem. The judicial system is generally perceived as slow and ineffective in enforcing contracts or resolving disputes. Protection of property rights is insufficient.

GOVERNMENT SIZE

	Score	Rank	1-Year Change
Fiscal Freedom	68.4	147th	+0.5
Government Spending	71.8	81st	+10.7

Guyana's top individual income tax rate is 33.3 percent, and its top corporate tax rate is 40 percent. Other taxes include a property tax and a value-added tax (VAT). The overall tax burden equals 21.2 percent of gross domestic income. Government spending remains around 30 percent of GDP. Public debt is around 60 percent of GDP.

REGULATORY EFFICIENCY

	Score	Rank	1-Year Change
Business Freedom	64.3	95th	–2.0
Labor Freedom	72.6	58th	–2.8
Monetary Freedom	78.1	62nd	+2.2

The overall pace of regulatory reform has lagged behind other countries. With no minimum capital required, launching a business takes eight procedures and 20 days. Licensing takes about 200 days. The labor market is underdeveloped, and many rely on the informal sector for employment. The government influences prices through state-owned enterprises but has reduced subsidies for electricity and transportation significantly.

OPEN MARKETS

	Score	Rank	1-Year Change
Trade Freedom	72.0	118th	+0.8
Investment Freedom	45.0	125th	+10.0
Financial Freedom	30.0	132nd	0

Guyana's average tariff rate is 6.5 percent. Political unrest has been a deterrent to foreign investment. The financial sector is small and underdeveloped. Banking remains plagued by inefficiency and a poor financial regulatory framework. High credit costs and scarce access to financing remain barriers to generating more dynamic entrepreneurial activity.

Long-Term Score Change (since 1995)

RULE OF LAW		GOVERNMENT SIZE		REGULATORY EFFICIENCY		OPEN MARKETS	
Property Rights	–20.0	Fiscal Freedom	+12.6	Business Freedom	+9.3	Trade Freedom	+6.0
Freedom from Corruption	+14.4	Government Spending	+41.5	Labor Freedom	+10.1	Investment Freedom	–5.0
				Monetary Freedom	+14.1	Financial Freedom	0

HAITI

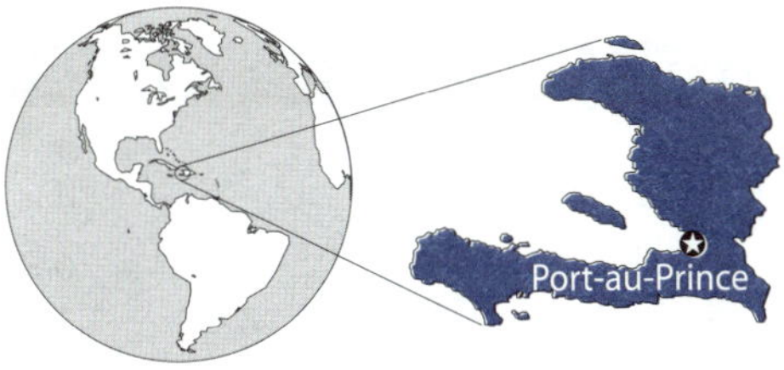

World Rank: **156** Regional Rank: **24**

Economic Freedom Score

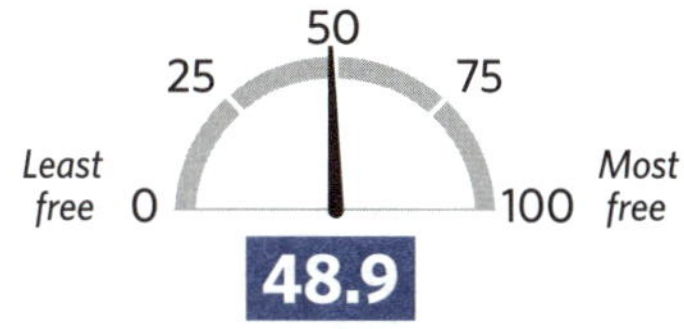

Haiti's economic freedom score is 48.9, making its economy the 156th freest in the 2014 *Index*. Its overall score has increased by 0.8 point since last year due to notable improvements in investment freedom and labor freedom. Haiti is ranked 24th out of 29 countries in the South and Central America/Caribbean region, and its overall score is far below the regional average.

Over the 20-year history of the *Index*, Haiti has advanced its economic freedom score by nearly 6 points. The overall score improvement has been relatively broad based, driven by improvements in six of the 10 economic freedoms including investment freedom, monetary freedom, and financial freedom.

Nonetheless, reforms to improve the business and investment climates have been largely undermined in practice because of pervasive corruption and the inefficient judicial framework. Governing institutions remain weak, and overall progress in post-earthquake reconstruction has been limited. The effectiveness of public spending has been reduced by ongoing political volatility that undermines the already fragile foundations of the rule of law.

BACKGROUND: President Michel Martelly was elected in 2011. Though Martelly won the runoff election with a strong majority, his party lacks majority support in the legislature. Prime Minister Laurent Lamothe took office in May 2012 after a four-month vacancy following his predecessor's resignation. Despite the presence of a U.N. Stability Mission since 2004 and improvements in the training and equipping of the national police force, civil unrest remains a constant threat. Several thousand former members of the disbanded Forces Armées d'Haiti (FADH) have formed rogue paramilitary units. Haiti is poor, corrupt, and without dependable rule of law. Drug trafficking is a major destabilizing factor. Haiti suffered a massive earthquake with a magnitude of 7.0 in 2010, complicating efforts to restore public order and jump-start development.

Freedom Trend

Country Comparisons

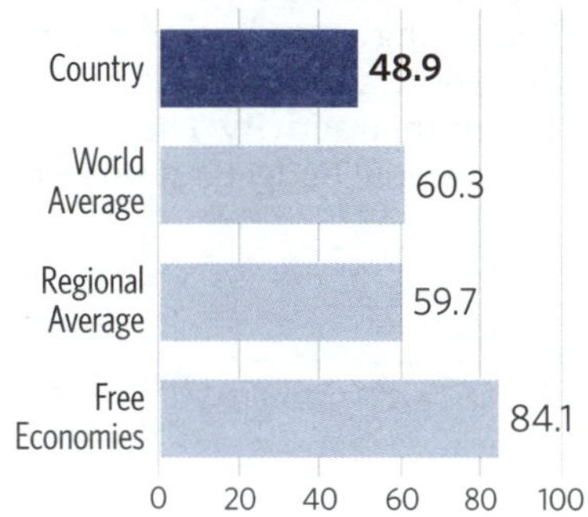

Quick Facts

Population: 10.4 million
GDP (PPP): $12.9 billion
2.8% growth in 2012
5-year compound annual growth 1.3%
$1,243 per capita
Unemployment: 40.6% (2010)
Inflation (CPI): 6.8%
FDI Inflow: $178.8 million
Public Debt: 15.4% of GDP

2012 data unless otherwise noted.
Data compiled as of September 2013.

How Do We Measure Economic Freedom?
See page 471 for an explanation of the methodology or visit the *Index* Web site at *heritage.org/index*.

THE TEN ECONOMIC FREEDOMS

RULE OF LAW

	Score	Rank	1-Year Change
Property Rights	10.0	166th	0
Freedom from Corruption	16.9	172nd	-1.1

Endemic corruption continues to limit Haiti's political and economic development. Smuggling is a major problem. The judicial system is underfunded, inefficient, corrupt, and burdened by a large backlog of cases, outdated legal codes, and poor facilities. Most commercial disputes are settled out of court if at all. There is no comprehensive civil registry. Bona fide and undisputed property titles are virtually nonexistent.

GOVERNMENT SIZE

	Score	Rank	1-Year Change
Fiscal Freedom	80.3	83rd	-0.4
Government Spending	66.3	96th	0

The top individual income and corporate tax rates are 30 percent. Other taxes include a value-added tax (VAT) and a capital gains tax. The overall tax burden is 13.1 percent of gross domestic income. Government expenditures are around one-third of the domestic economy, but the government has relied heavily on foreign aid since the 2010 earthquake. Public debt is below 20 percent of GDP.

REGULATORY EFFICIENCY

	Score	Rank	1-Year Change
Business Freedom	33.3	177th	-0.1
Labor Freedom	68.5	70th	+4.9
Monetary Freedom	73.6	117th	-0.6

Haiti's already poor regulatory efficiency is undercut by economic and political uncertainty. Launching a new business is costly and time-consuming. Completing licensing requirements takes over 1,000 days. A considerable portion of the workforce is underemployed or dependent on informal activity. The state-owned and-subsidized electrical utility consumes 12 percent of the national budget but serves only 25 percent of the population.

OPEN MARKETS

	Score	Rank	1-Year Change
Trade Freedom	70.4	126th	-4.4
Investment Freedom	40.0	132nd	+10.0
Financial Freedom	30.0	132nd	0

The average tariff rate for Haiti is 7.3 percent. Civil unrest has been a deterrent to foreign investment, and investment in some sectors of the economy is subject to government screening. The underdeveloped financial sector does not provide adequate support for the private sector. Most financial transactions are handled informally, and credit for new business ventures remains severely constrained.

Long-Term Score Change (since 1995)

RULE OF LAW		GOVERNMENT SIZE		REGULATORY EFFICIENCY		OPEN MARKETS	
Property Rights	0	Fiscal Freedom	+1.7	Business Freedom	-6.7	Trade Freedom	-9.6
Freedom from Corruption	+6.9	Government Spending	-29.3	Labor Freedom	+6.6	Investment Freedom	+30.0
				Monetary Freedom	+20.8	Financial Freedom	+20.0

HONDURAS

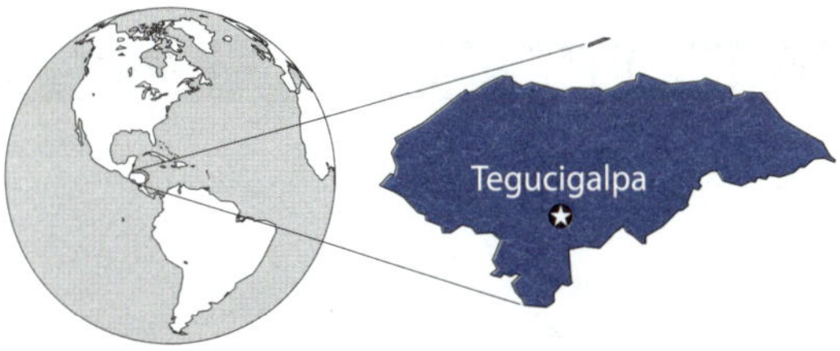

World Rank: **112** Regional Rank: **19**

Economic Freedom Score

Honduras's economic freedom score is 57.1, making its economy the 112th freest in the 2014 *Index*. Its overall score is 1.3 points worse than last year due to deteriorations in six of the 10 economic freedoms including investment freedom, business freedom, freedom from corruption, and trade freedom. Honduras is ranked 19th out of 29 countries in the South and Central America/Caribbean region, and its overall score is lower than the world and regional averages.

Over the 20-year history of the *Index*, Honduras's economic freedom has been stagnant. Scores for six of the 10 economic freedoms, notably in the area of market openness assessed by trade freedom, investment freedom, and financial freedom, have improved. However, considerable deteriorations in the management of public spending and the rule of law, measured by property rights and freedom from corruption, have offset these gains. Briefly rated a "moderately free" economy in 2003, Honduras has been ranked "mostly unfree" for the rest of the history of the *Index*.

Business regulations are relatively benign except in the area of labor relations. The government has been developing the idea of "charter cities" to stimulate the economy, but broader implementation of deeper institutional reforms is critical to spurring more dynamic economic growth.

BACKGROUND: In June 2009, the legislature ordered the military to arrest President Manuel Zelaya after he violated the constitution by trying to amend it to run for another term. The military deported Zelaya to Costa Rica, and Honduras was expelled from the Organization of American States. Zelaya returned later that year and was not prosecuted. National Party candidate Porfirio Lobo won the presidency in November 2009, and Honduras returned to the OAS two years later. The constitutional crisis continued in 2012–2013, however, with the removal of high-court judges by the legislature. Political polarization, drug trafficking, violent crime, and youth gangs are ongoing concerns. The economy, based traditionally on exports of coffee and bananas, has diversified to include shrimp, melons, tourism, and textiles, but Honduras remains one of Latin America's poorest countries.

How Do We Measure Economic Freedom?
See page 471 for an explanation of the methodology or visit the *Index* Web site at *heritage.org/index*.

Freedom Trend

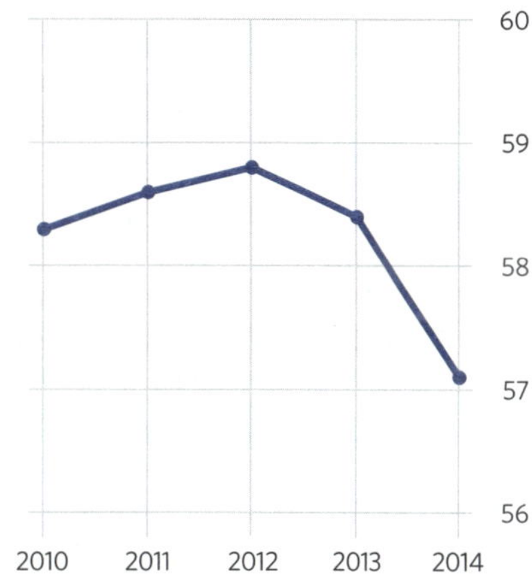

Country Comparisons

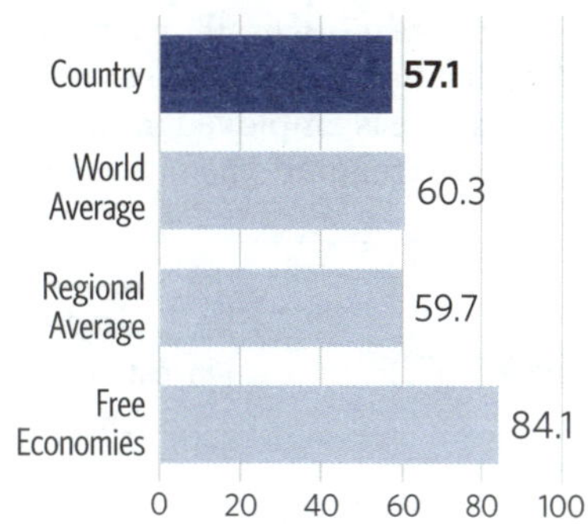

Quick Facts

Population: 8.2 million
GDP (PPP): $37.8 billion
3.3% growth in 2012
5-year compound annual growth 2.5%
$4,610 per capita
Unemployment: 4.4%
Inflation (CPI): 5.2%
FDI Inflow: $1.1 billion
Public Debt: 34.7% of GDP

2012 data unless otherwise noted.
Data compiled as of September 2013.

THE TEN ECONOMIC FREEDOMS

RULE OF LAW

	Score	Rank	1-Year Change
Property Rights	30.0	93rd	0
Freedom from Corruption	23.7	140th	-2.3

Weak institutions and corruption limit the country's economic potential, and intensifying gang and drug-related violence continues to pose a significant risk of political and social instability. The court system is weak and inefficient, and resolution of disputed cases can take years. Laws and practices regarding real estate differ substantially from those in more developed countries, and fraudulent deeds and titles are common.

GOVERNMENT SIZE

	Score	Rank	1-Year Change
Fiscal Freedom	84.9	54th	-0.4
Government Spending	79.8	53rd	+0.6

The top individual income and corporate tax rates are 25 percent. A 5 percent temporary social contribution tax for corporations will be phased out by 2015. Other taxes include a capital gains tax and a general sales tax. The overall tax burden equals 16.1 percent of GDP. Public expenditures equal around a quarter of gross domestic income, and government debt is 35 percent of GDP. Growing deficits have eroded the country's credit rating.

REGULATORY EFFICIENCY

	Score	Rank	1-Year Change
Business Freedom	55.4	136th	-5.6
Labor Freedom	26.5	181st	-0.3
Monetary Freedom	75.1	102nd	+1.2

Earlier reforms have reduced the number of days and procedures required to launch a new business, but overall progress in easing regulatory constraints lags behind other countries. Getting necessary licenses costs over twice the level of average annual income. Much of the workforce is employed in the informal sector. The government subsidizes electricity and continues to regulate the prices of key products (for example, fuel) and services.

OPEN MARKETS

	Score	Rank	1-Year Change
Trade Freedom	75.4	96th	-1.7
Investment Freedom	60.0	80th	-5.0
Financial Freedom	60.0	41st	0

The average tariff rate for Honduras is 7.3 percent. Foreign investors sometimes find it difficult to have contracts enforced through the judicial system. The financial sector remains relatively stable and continues to expand. There are two state-owned banks, but private banks dominate the banking sector. There are few legal and regulatory barriers to entry, but most foreign banks' participation has been at a regional rather than national level.

Long-Term Score Change (since 1995)

RULE OF LAW		GOVERNMENT SIZE		REGULATORY EFFICIENCY		OPEN MARKETS	
Property Rights	-20.0	Fiscal Freedom	+19.4	Business Freedom	+0.4	Trade Freedom	+14.4
Freedom from Corruption	-6.3	Government Spending	-3.6	Labor Freedom	-18.2	Investment Freedom	+10.0
				Monetary Freedom	+7.3	Financial Freedom	+10.0

HONG KONG

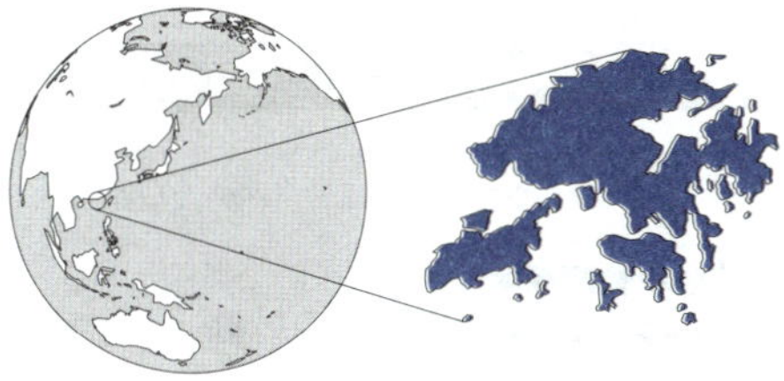

World Rank: **1** Regional Rank: **1**

Economic Freedom Score

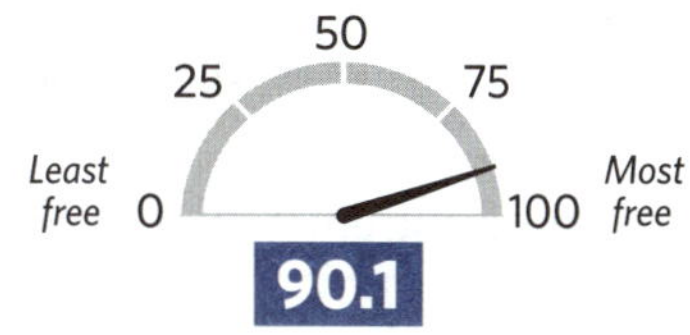

Hong Kong's economic freedom score is 90.1, making it the top-rated economy in the *Index* for the 20th consecutive year. Its overall score is slightly better than last year due to improvements in government size and regulatory efficiency that offset a decline in freedom from corruption. Hong Kong is ranked 1st out of 42 countries in the Asia–Pacific region and 1st in the world.

Throughout the 20-year history of the *Index*, Hong Kong has been rated the world's freest economy, but its strong commitment to economic freedom has become somewhat less exceptional as average world economic freedom has advanced. This year, Hong Kong recorded its second highest economic freedom score ever. In recent years, populist policies that increase spending and empower the administrative bureaucracy, as well as an increasing level of perceived corruption, have held back Hong Kong's overall rating.

Yet the territory has effectively navigated global booms and busts, recording an overall score improvement of 1.6 points over the past two decades. A high degree of market openness, as measured by trade freedom, investment freedom, and financial freedom, has been complemented by a transparent regulatory environment and competitive tax regime. A highly motivated workforce and a high level of labor freedom have added to Hong Kong's economic dynamism and resilience.

BACKGROUND: The Special Administrative Region of Hong Kong is part of the People's Republic of China but self-governing on a day-to-day basis, and its people enjoy a wide range of freedoms under its Basic Law. Implementation of promised democratic reforms, including universal suffrage, has been slow. Chief Executive Leung Chun-ying, who took office in 2012, was chosen by a 1,200-member Election Committee and formally appointed by the mainland government. Hong Kong has one of the world's most prosperous economies, thanks to a commitment to small government, low taxes, and light regulation. Major industries include financial services and shipping; manufacturing has largely migrated to the mainland. Current concerns include cronyism in policymaking, state control of land, and restrictions on information flows.

How Do We Measure Economic Freedom?
See page 471 for an explanation of the methodology or visit the *Index* Web site at *heritage.org/index*.

Freedom Trend

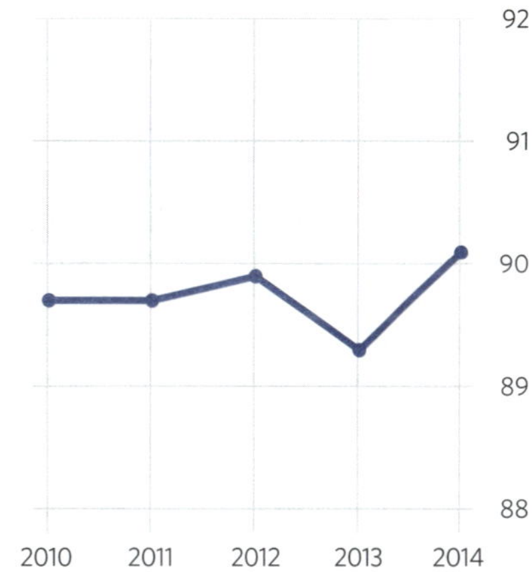

Country Comparisons

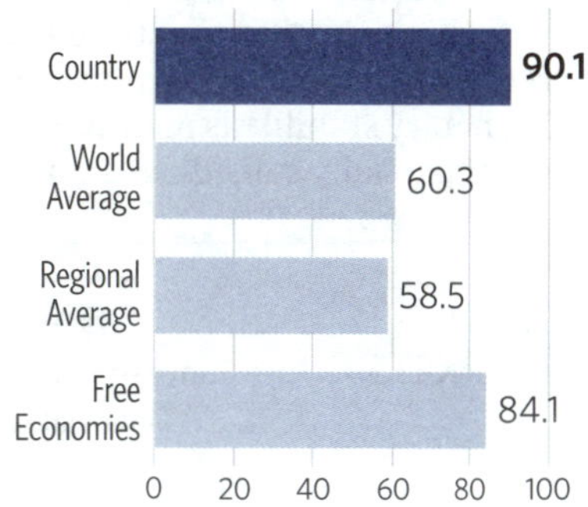

Quick Facts

Population: 7.2 million
GDP (PPP): $369.4 billion
1.4% growth in 2012
5-year compound annual growth 2.5%
$51,494 per capita
Unemployment: 3.3%
Inflation (CPI): 4.1%
FDI Inflow: $74.6 billion
Public Debt: 0.5% of GDP

2012 data unless otherwise noted.
Data compiled as of September 2013.

THE TEN ECONOMIC FREEDOMS

Legend: Country | World Average

RULE OF LAW

	Score	Rank	1-Year Change
Property Rights	90.0	2nd	0
Freedom from Corruption	82.3	13th	-1.7

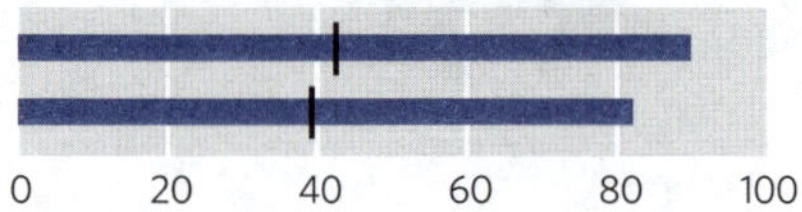

Hong Kong enjoys low rates of corruption, although business interests exercise a strong influence in the unicameral legislature and executive branch. The judiciary is efficient and independent, and the rule of law is respected. Property rights are well protected, and the government devotes significant attention and resources to enforcement of intellectual property laws.

GOVERNMENT SIZE

	Score	Rank	1-Year Change
Fiscal Freedom	93.0	17th	+0.1
Government Spending	89.7	14th	+0.8

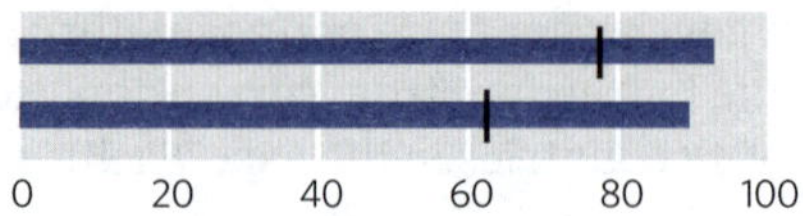

The standard individual income tax rate is 15 percent, and the top corporate tax rate is 16.5 percent. The tax system is simple and efficient, and the overall tax burden is around 14 percent of GDP. Government spending remains equivalent to slightly under one-fifth of the domestic economy. Public debt is virtually nonexistent, and a budget surplus has been maintained even in light of increased government spending and tax rebates.

REGULATORY EFFICIENCY

	Score	Rank	1-Year Change
Business Freedom	98.9	1st	0
Labor Freedom	95.5	4th	+9.3
Monetary Freedom	82.0	13th	-0.1

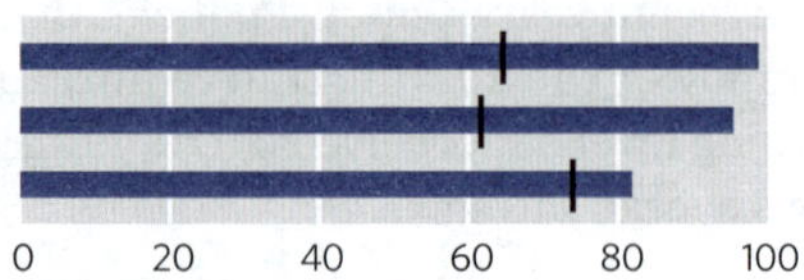

The competitive regulatory regime aids business formation and innovation. The process for launching a business is straightforward, and no minimum capital is required. The impact of the recently introduced statutory minimum wage on the labor market has been relatively subdued. Monetary stability is maintained through the exchange-rate peg to the U.S. dollar. The government partially subsidizes small and medium enterprises.

OPEN MARKETS

	Score	Rank	1-Year Change
Trade Freedom	90.0	1st	0
Investment Freedom	90.0	2nd	0
Financial Freedom	90.0	1st	0

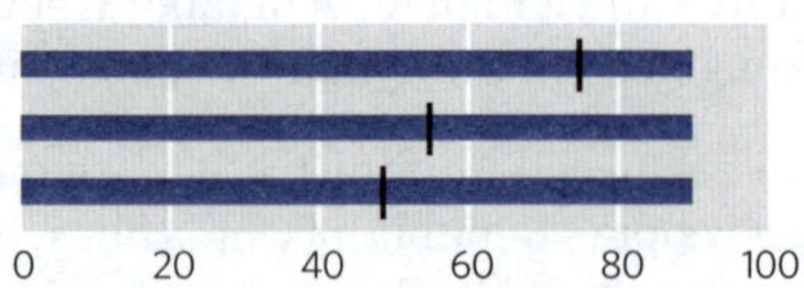

Hong Kong is very open to international commerce, with a 0 percent average tariff rate and few barriers to foreign investment. A robust and transparent investment framework, in place for many years, continues to attract foreign investment. The financial sector remains highly competitive and well capitalized, serving as a leading global hub. There are no restrictions on foreign banks, which are treated the same as domestic banks.

Long-Term Score Change (since 1995)

RULE OF LAW		GOVERNMENT SIZE		REGULATORY EFFICIENCY		OPEN MARKETS	
Property Rights	**0**	Fiscal Freedom	**0**	Business Freedom	**-1.1**	Trade Freedom	**0**
Freedom from Corruption	**-7.7**	Government Spending	**-3.8**	Labor Freedom	**+9.0**	Investment Freedom	**0**
				Monetary Freedom	**+1.2**	Financial Freedom	**+20.0**

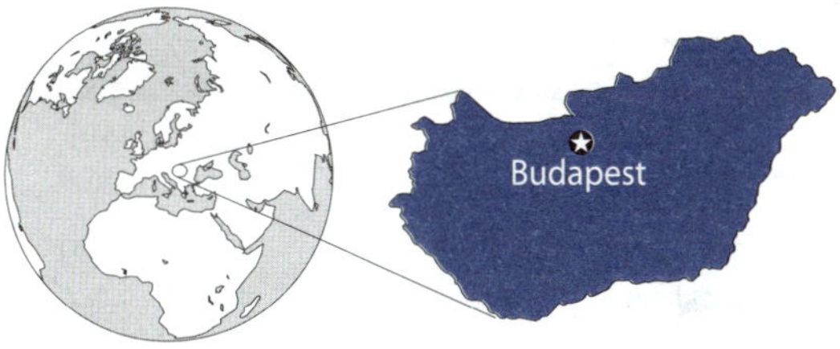

HUNGARY

Economic Freedom Score

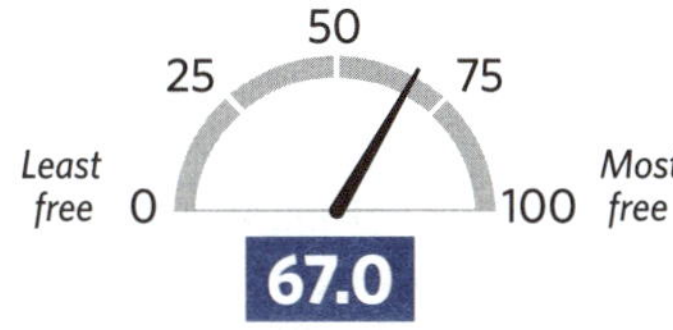

World Rank: **51** Regional Rank: **24**

Hungary's economic freedom score is 67.0, making its economy the 51st freest in the 2014 *Index*. Its score has decreased by 0.3 point, with declines in property rights, the control of public spending, and monetary freedom outweighing improvements in freedom from corruption and fiscal freedom. Hungary is ranked 24th out of 43 countries in the Europe region, and its overall score is well above the world average and about the regional average.

Over the 20-year history of the *Index*, Hungary has advanced its economic freedom score by nearly 12 points. The overall score improvement has been broad-based, driven by advancements in six of the 10 economic freedoms including double-digit growth in scores for trade freedom, financial freedom, monetary freedom, fiscal freedom, and the management of public spending. For the past 15 years, Hungary has achieved the status of a "moderately free" economy.

The rule of law and consistent protection of private property have contributed to Hungary's long-term competitiveness and growth. Steps have been taken to improve fiscal transparency, but further fiscal consolidation and better management of public finance remain critical to ensuring Hungary's successful transition to a freer market economy.

BACKGROUND: The center-right FIDESZ party won a two-thirds parliamentary majority in April 2010 but got into trouble with the European Union and the Council of Europe because of government overcentralization, failure to address human rights problems, and racist rhetoric by the extreme nationalist Jobbik party. Prime Minister Viktor Orbán inherited significant public and private-sector debt. Despite electoral support, Orbán so far has achieved only limited success. He rejected a €15 billion International Monetary Fund bailout plan, avoiding an IMF austerity program, but has yet to address the debt problem. Growth remains anemic, and three major credit rating agencies have downgraded Hungarian debt to junk bond status amid doubts about the independence of Hungary's central bank.

How Do We Measure Economic Freedom?
See page 471 for an explanation of the methodology or visit the *Index* Web site at *heritage.org/index*.

Freedom Trend

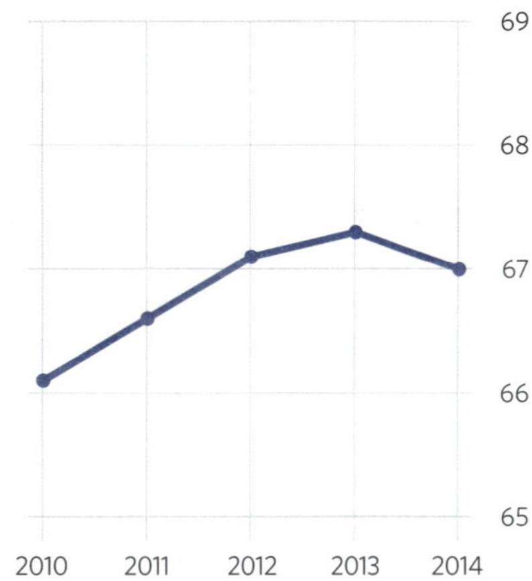

Country Comparisons

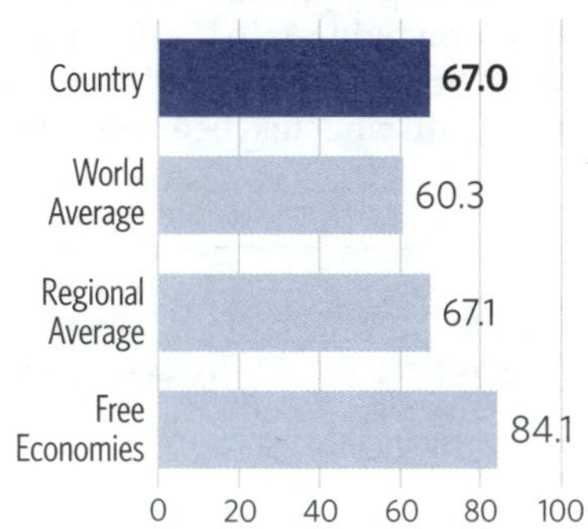

Quick Facts

Population: 10.0 million
GDP (PPP): $195.6 billion
-1.7% growth in 2012
5-year compound annual growth -1.0%
$19,638 per capita
Unemployment: 11.0%
Inflation (CPI): 5.7%
FDI Inflow: $13.5 billion
Public Debt: 79.0% of GDP

2012 data unless otherwise noted.
Data compiled as of September 2013.

THE TEN ECONOMIC FREEDOMS

Legend: Country | World Average

		Score	Rank	1-Year Change
RULE OF LAW	Property Rights	60.0	41st	-5.0
	Freedom from Corruption	48.6	50th	+2.6

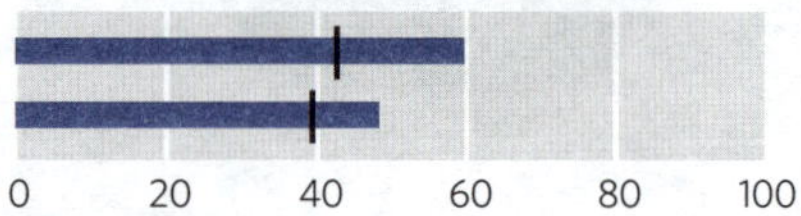

Rampant collusion has been reported between the public sector and privileged private businesses. In December 2012, the constitution was amended to bar foreigners and non-farmer Hungarian citizens from buying farmland. The independence of the judiciary has come under scrutiny following the adoption of a reform package granting extensive judicial administrative powers to an agency whose leadership is elected by parliament.

		Score	Rank	1-Year Change
GOVERNMENT SIZE	Fiscal Freedom	81.1	72nd	+1.4
	Government Spending	26.8	164th	-2.9

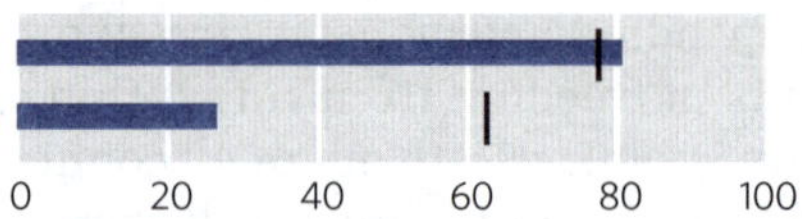

The individual income tax rate is a flat 16 percent, and the top corporate tax rate is 19 percent. Other taxes include a value-added tax (VAT) and a property tax. The overall tax burden is equal to 35.7 percent of gross domestic income. Government spending is 49.4 percent of gross domestic income. The EU has excused Hungary from budget monitoring despite limited progress in controlling spending. Public debt is now about 80 percent of GDP.

		Score	Rank	1-Year Change
REGULATORY EFFICIENCY	Business Freedom	79.3	35th	+0.2
	Labor Freedom	65.7	77th	+1.3
	Monetary Freedom	75.6	88th	-1.5

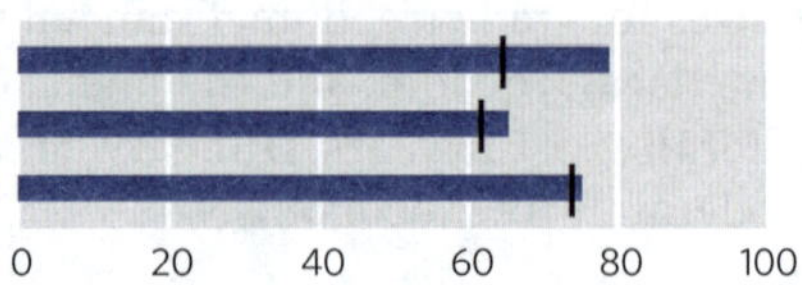

Launching a business takes four procedures and five days, and the minimum capital required has been reduced to less than 10 percent of the level of average annual income. Restrictions on work hours remain rigid, and the overall labor code lacks flexibility. The state has reinserted itself into what had been one of the few fully privatized natural-gas industry sectors in Europe.

		Score	Rank	1-Year Change
OPEN MARKETS	Trade Freedom	87.8	11th	+1.0
	Investment Freedom	75.0	35th	0
	Financial Freedom	70.0	19th	0

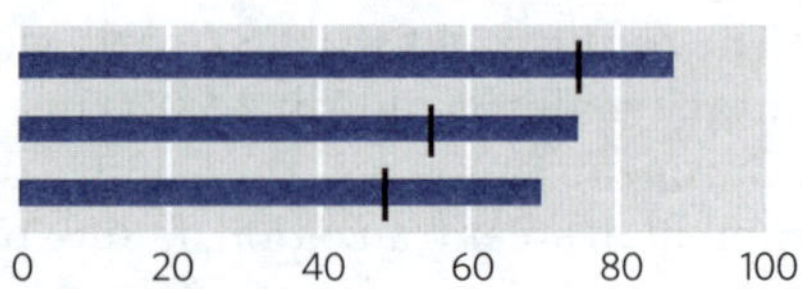

EU members have a low 1.1 percent average tariff rate and, in general, few non-tariff barriers to trade. In 2012, the government amended the constitution to prohibit people from selling their agricultural land to foreigners. The growing financial sector is open to competition, and the state has largely withdrawn from banking. Capital markets are relatively developed, and foreign investors participate freely.

Long-Term Score Change (since 1995)

RULE OF LAW		GOVERNMENT SIZE		REGULATORY EFFICIENCY		OPEN MARKETS	
Property Rights	**-10.0**	Fiscal Freedom	**+34.3**	Business Freedom	**-5.7**	Trade Freedom	**+26.8**
Freedom from Corruption	**-1.4**	Government Spending	**+26.8**	Labor Freedom	**-2.4**	Investment Freedom	**+5.0**
				Monetary Freedom	**+11.4**	Financial Freedom	**+20.0**

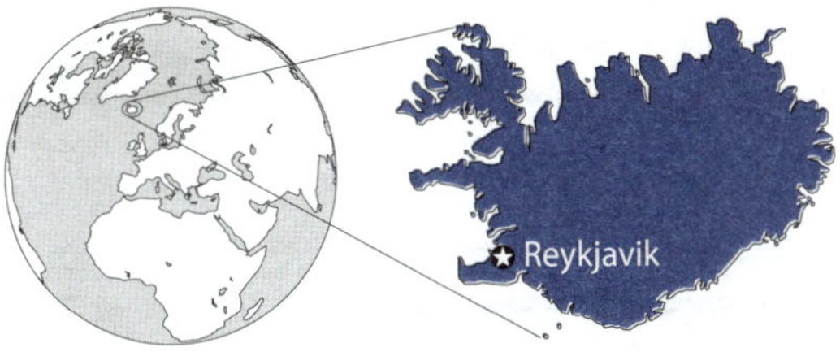

ICELAND

World Rank: **23** Regional Rank: **13**

Economic Freedom Score

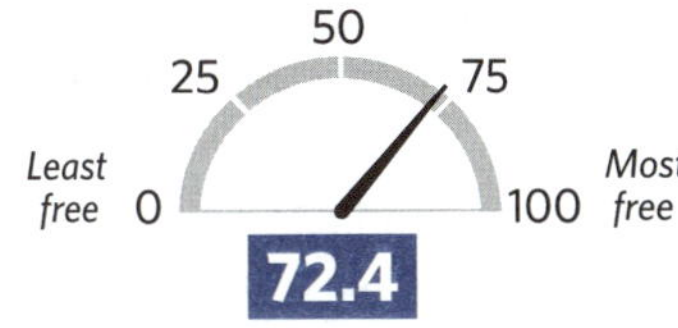

Iceland's economic freedom score is 72.4, making its economy the 23rd freest in the 2014 *Index*. Its overall score is 0.3 point better than last year, with improvements in six of the 10 economic freedoms, including investment freedom and freedom from corruption, overcoming declines in the management of government spending and business freedom. Iceland is ranked 13th out of 43 countries in the Europe region, and its overall score remains well above the world and regional averages.

Iceland's economic freedom was first assessed in the 1997 *Index*, and its economy has been largely rated "mostly free." Gains in four of the 10 economic freedoms, including business freedom and fiscal freedom, which have improved by more than 10 points, have helped Iceland's overall economic freedom to advance by about 2 points over its history in the *Index*.

Iceland has demonstrated a strong commitment to restoring sound public finance and policy credibility. Regulatory efficiency and open-market policies underpin efforts to restore positive momentum. However, the emergency economic measures, particularly capital controls, implemented by the socialist government during the financial crisis are being unwound only slowly and constitute a serious barrier to greater economic dynamism.

BACKGROUND: The collapse of Iceland's banking sector in 2008 sparked a currency crisis and a substantial contraction of the economy. The pro–European Union Social Democrats lost the April 2013 parliamentary elections. Sigmundur Davíð Gunnlaugsson of the Progressive Party was elected prime minister in a coalition government consisting of the Progressive Party and Independence Party. The new governing coalition indefinitely suspended accession talks with the EU in May 2013. In order to join the EU, the government must win a public referendum, and public opinion remains divided. Iceland already enjoys EU-related benefits that include free trade and movement of capital, labor, goods, and services within the region. It also has membership in the Schengen zone, which allows visa-free travel in 26 European countries.

How Do We Measure Economic Freedom?
See page 471 for an explanation of the methodology or visit the *Index* Web site at *heritage.org/index*.

Freedom Trend

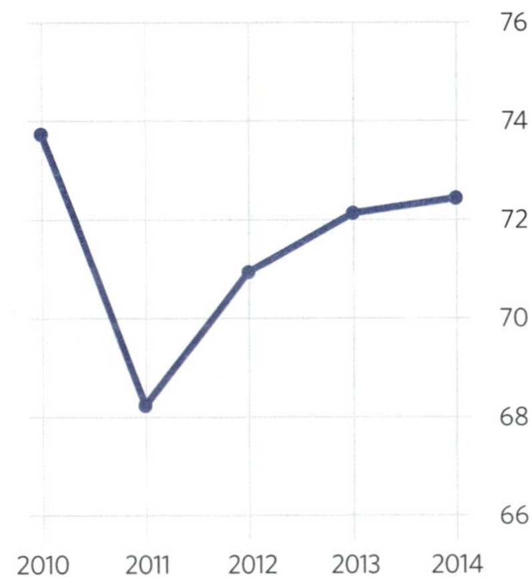

Country Comparisons

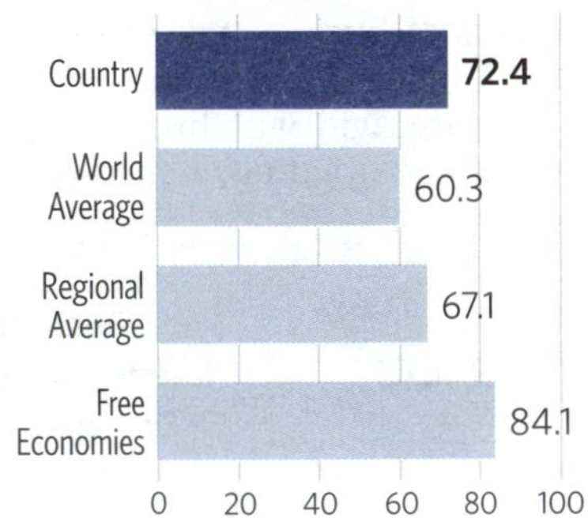

Quick Facts

Population: 0.3 million
GDP (PPP): $12.8 billion
1.6% growth in 2012
5-year compound annual growth -1.1%
$39,224 per capita
Unemployment: 5.8%
Inflation (CPI): 5.2%
FDI Inflow: $510.7 million
Public Debt: 99.1% of GDP

2012 data unless otherwise noted.
Data compiled as of September 2013.

THE TEN ECONOMIC FREEDOMS

RULE OF LAW

	Score	Rank	1-Year Change
Property Rights	90.0	2nd	0
Freedom from Corruption	84.2	11th	+1.2

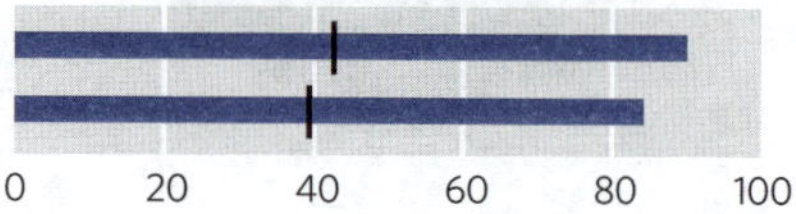

Corruption is not a serious problem, although there have been a few politically tinged business-fraud scandals in recent years. A 1,000-year history of parliamentary government has engendered the institutionalization of accountability and transparency. Private property is well protected. The constitution provides for an independent judiciary, and trials are generally public and fair.

GOVERNMENT SIZE

	Score	Rank	1-Year Change
Fiscal Freedom	72.9	126th	+0.2
Government Spending	32.9	158th	-3.3

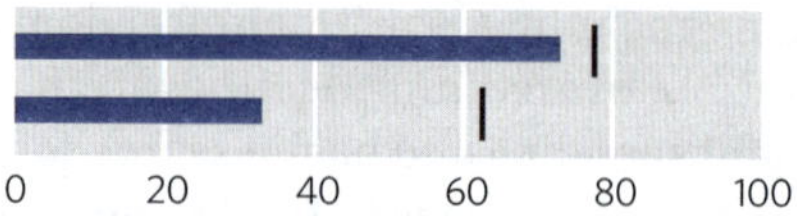

The top individual income tax rate is 31.8 percent, and the top corporate tax rate is 20 percent. Other taxes include a value-added tax (VAT) and an estate tax. The overall tax burden is 36 percent of gross domestic income. Government expenditures equal 47 percent of the domestic economy. Iceland continues to emerge from austerity brought on by the financial crisis, but public debt remains near 100 percent of GDP.

REGULATORY EFFICIENCY

	Score	Rank	1-Year Change
Business Freedom	91.2	10th	-0.3
Labor Freedom	59.1	104th	+0.2
Monetary Freedom	76.0	85th	+0.2

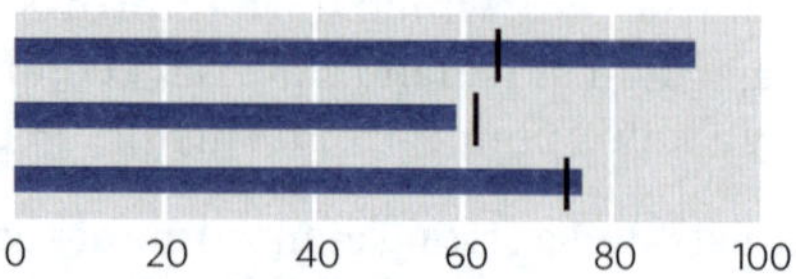

The regulatory regime continues to sustain innovative business formation and operation. Starting a business takes five procedures and five days on average and costs about 3 percent of the level of average annual income. Bankruptcy proceedings are relatively easy. Labor regulations are rigid, with broad wage settlements and high unionization. Despite the challenging economic situation, monetary stability remains relatively well maintained.

OPEN MARKETS

	Score	Rank	1-Year Change
Trade Freedom	87.9	10th	+0.1
Investment Freedom	70.0	46th	+5.0
Financial Freedom	60.0	41st	0

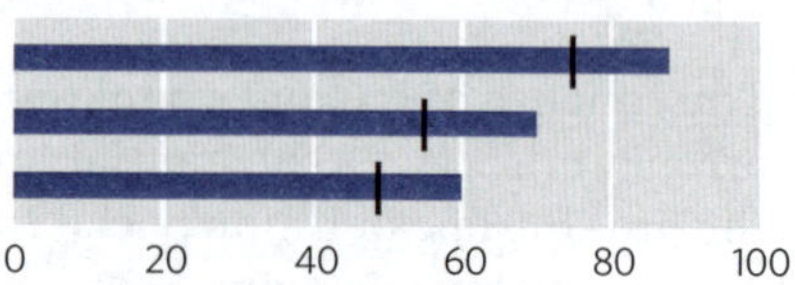

Iceland's average tariff rate is only 1 percent, but trade barriers restrict imports of meat and dairy products. Capital controls that were put in place in 2008 have discouraged foreign investment, but they have been slated for elimination. The financial sector remains dominated by banking. After a period of intense strain, the banking sector has been largely recapitalized, and Iceland has returned to the global bond market.

Long-Term Score Change (since 1997)

RULE OF LAW		GOVERNMENT SIZE		REGULATORY EFFICIENCY		OPEN MARKETS	
Property Rights	0	Fiscal Freedom	+11.3	Business Freedom	+21.2	Trade Freedom	+7.1
Freedom from Corruption	-5.8	Government Spending	-7.7	Labor Freedom	-5.5	Investment Freedom	0
				Monetary Freedom	-5.3	Financial Freedom	+10.0

INDIA

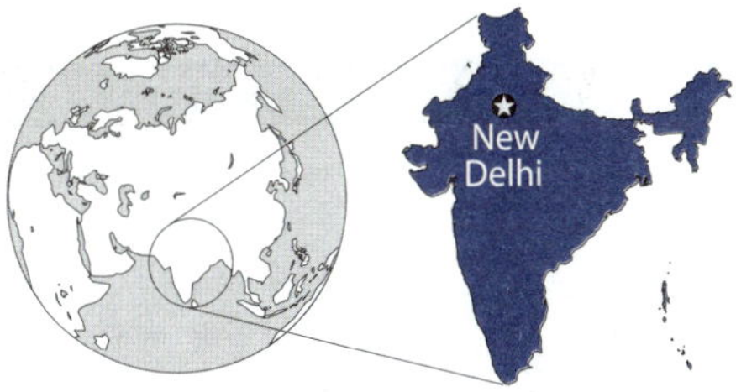

World Rank: **120** Regional Rank: **25**

Economic Freedom Score

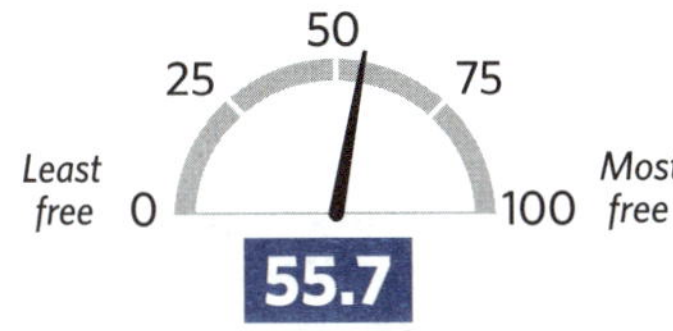

India's economic freedom score is 55.7, making its economy the 120th freest in the 2014 *Index*. Its score is 0.5 point higher than last year, reflecting modest improvements in six of the 10 economic freedoms including trade freedom and fiscal freedom. India is ranked 25th out of 41 countries in the Asia–Pacific region, and its overall score is below the regional and world averages.

Over the 20-year history of the *Index*, India has advanced its economic freedom score by nearly 11 points. From a low base, it has achieved double-digit improvements in half of the 10 economic freedoms, most notably trade freedom, which improved by over 65 points. Although India continues to be rated a "mostly unfree" economy, the country has achieved its highest score ever in the 2014 *Index*.

Institutional shortcomings continue to undermine India's chances for long-term economic development. The government's presence in the economy remains extensive through state-owned enterprises and wasteful subsidy programs that result in chronically high budget deficits. In September 2012, the government lifted foreign direct investment restrictions in several sectors including retail and aviation. However, the overall regulatory environment remains burdened by administrative bureaucracy. Non-tariff barriers and burdensome investment regulations hamper private-sector development and modernization of the economic base.

BACKGROUND: India is a relatively stable democracy, but its size and diversity (more than 80 percent of its population is Hindu, but its Muslim population is one of the world's largest) are challenges to effective governance. A Maoist insurgency still plagues central and eastern India, as evidenced by an attack on Congress Party workers in late May 2013. Prime Minister Manmohan Singh's government has been undermined by corruption scandals and a faltering economy, with growth at a 10-year low. The ruling Congress Party is focusing on populist policies to shore up votes for parliamentary elections in 2014 and has avoided the implementation of much-needed economic reforms. India is a significant force in world trade, but its economy continues to operate far below its potential.

How Do We Measure Economic Freedom?
See page 471 for an explanation of the methodology or visit the *Index* Web site at *heritage.org/index*.

Freedom Trend

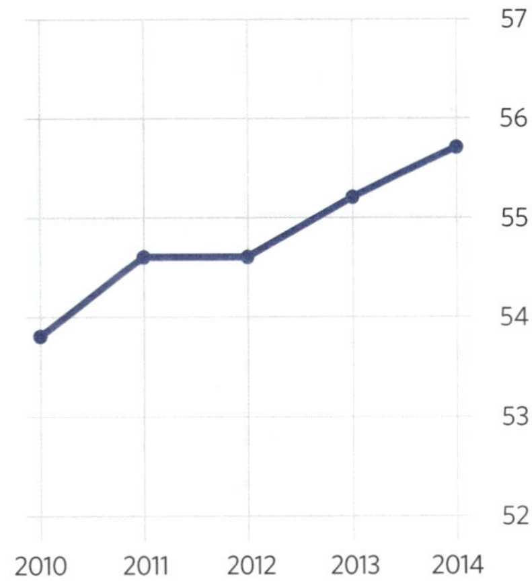

Country Comparisons

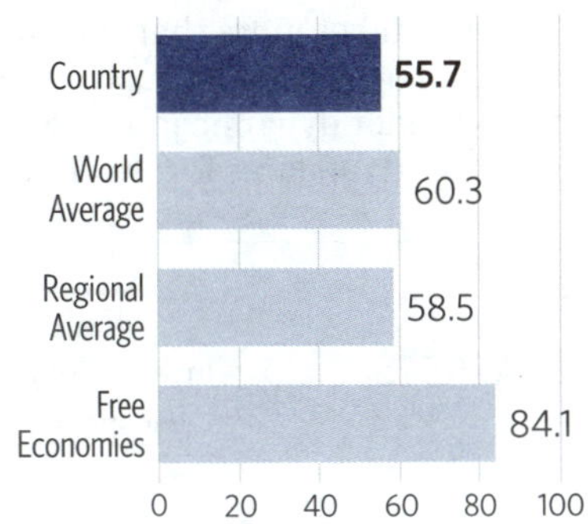

Quick Facts

Population: 1,223.2 million
GDP (PPP): $4.7 trillion
4.0% growth in 2012
5-year compound annual growth 6.8%
$3,830 per capita
Unemployment: 8.5%
Inflation (CPI): 9.3%
FDI Inflow: $25.5 billion
Public Debt: 66.8% of GDP

2012 data unless otherwise noted.
Data compiled as of September 2013.

THE TEN ECONOMIC FREEDOMS

Score — Country | World Average

		Score	Rank	1-Year Change
RULE OF LAW	Property Rights	50.0	53rd	0
	Freedom from Corruption	31.5	97th	+0.5

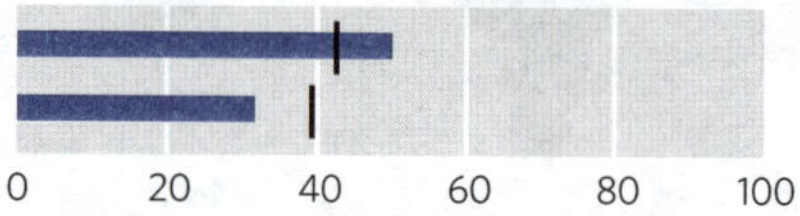

Recent anti-corruption legislation was spurred by domestic and international pressure to counter the effects of graft on government efficiency and economic performance. The judiciary is independent of the executive branch, but judicial procedures tend to be protracted, costly, and subject to political pressure. Enforcement of intellectual property rights protection laws is weak, and piracy of copyrighted materials is widespread.

		Score	Rank	1-Year Change
GOVERNMENT SIZE	Fiscal Freedom	79.4	95th	+1.1
	Government Spending	77.8	62nd	-0.1

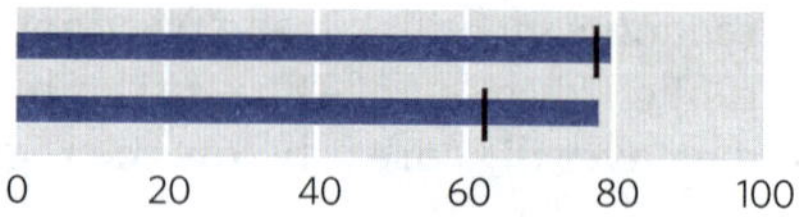

The top individual income tax rate is 30.9 percent, which includes an additional 3 percent levy for education. The top corporate tax rate is 32.4 percent, although domestic corporations pay only 30 percent. Surcharges push the effective rates higher. Other taxes include a value-added tax (VAT). The overall tax burden is 7 percent of GDP. Government expenditures are 27 percent of gross domestic output, and public debt is about 67 percent of GDP.

		Score	Rank	1-Year Change
REGULATORY EFFICIENCY	Business Freedom	37.7	171st	+0.4
	Labor Freedom	74.0	49th	+0.4
	Monetary Freedom	65.5	166th	+0.2

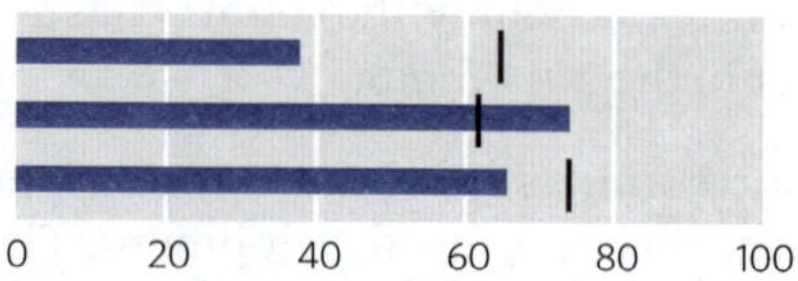

Progress in improving the entrepreneurial environment has been only modest. Launching a business takes more than 25 days on average, and licensing requirements cost almost 10 times the level of average annual income. The labor market lacks flexibility, and its complex regulations hinder dynamic job growth. In September 2012, the government reduced fuel subsidies and raised rail fares for the first time in a decade.

		Score	Rank	1-Year Change
OPEN MARKETS	Trade Freedom	65.6	142nd	+2.0
	Investment Freedom	35.0	142nd	0
	Financial Freedom	40.0	107th	0

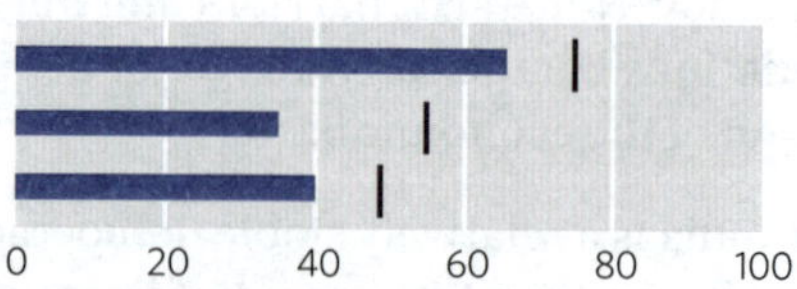

India's average tariff rate is 7.2 percent, and non-tariff barriers, including tariff-rate quotas on corn and dairy imports, significantly impede trade. There are many bureaucratic barriers to foreign investment. The financial system remains subject to government interference, and the state retains considerable ownership in the banking sector. All domestic banks are required to do priority-sector lending as directed by the government.

Long-Term Score Change (since 1995)

RULE OF LAW		GOVERNMENT SIZE		REGULATORY EFFICIENCY		OPEN MARKETS	
Property Rights	0	Fiscal Freedom	+32.7	Business Freedom	-17.3	Trade Freedom	+65.6
Freedom from Corruption	+21.5	Government Spending	-14.6	Labor Freedom	+12.3	Investment Freedom	-15.0
				Monetary Freedom	-6.1	Financial Freedom	+10.0

INDONESIA

World Rank: **100** Regional Rank: **21**

Economic Freedom Score

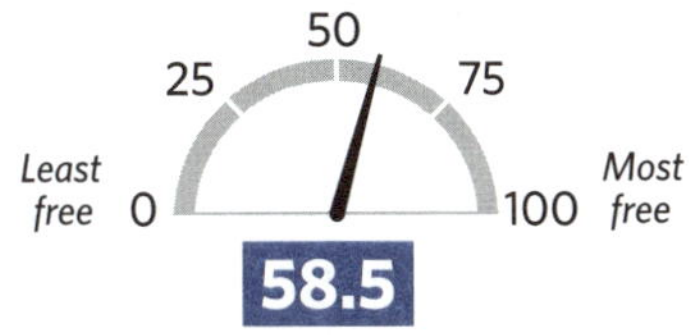

Indonesia's economic freedom score is 58.5, making its economy the 100th freest in the 2014 *Index*. Its score is 1.6 points better than last year due to notable improvements in business freedom, investment freedom, and financial freedom that offset small declines in labor freedom and freedom from corruption. Indonesia is ranked 21st out of 42 countries in the Asia–Pacific region, and its overall score is the same as the regional average but below the world average.

Over the 20-year history of the *Index*, Indonesia has advanced its economic freedom score by about 4 points. This modest overall score increase has been relatively broad-based, facilitated by improvements in six of the 10 economic freedoms including trade freedom, freedom from corruption, and fiscal freedom, each of which gained 10 points or more.

Nonetheless, the Indonesian economy continues to be considered "mostly unfree" due to the lack of progress in other critical areas of economic freedom. Indonesia has lagged in promoting the effective rule of law. The judicial system remains vulnerable to political interference, and property rights are not strongly protected. Despite some progress, lingering corruption continues to undermine enforcement of the rule of law and hampers the realization of Indonesia's full growth potential.

BACKGROUND: Indonesia is the world's most populous Muslim-majority democracy. Since 1998, when long-standing authoritarian ruler General Suharto stepped down, Indonesia's nearly 250 million people have enjoyed a widening range of political freedoms, and participation in the political process is high. President Susilo Bambang Yudhoyono has tried to address corruption and encourage much-needed foreign investment, but the weak rule of law remains a major impediment to attracting capital. As a member of the G-20 and a driving force within the Association of Southeast Asian Nations, Indonesia plays a growing role at the multilateral level. The increasingly modern and diversified economy has recovered from the global recession.

How Do We Measure Economic Freedom?
See page 471 for an explanation of the methodology or visit the *Index* Web site at *heritage.org/index*.

Freedom Trend

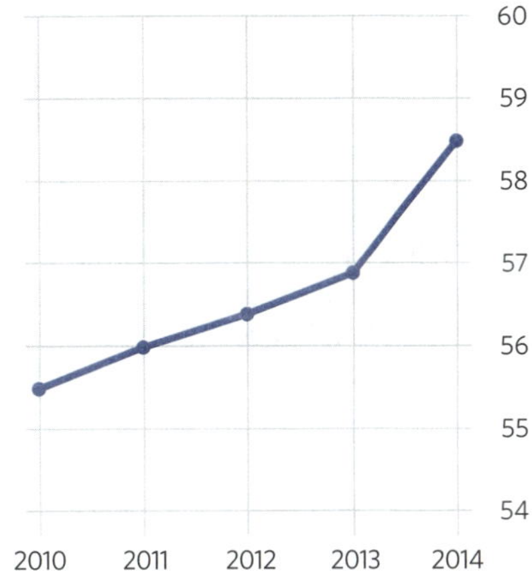

Country Comparisons

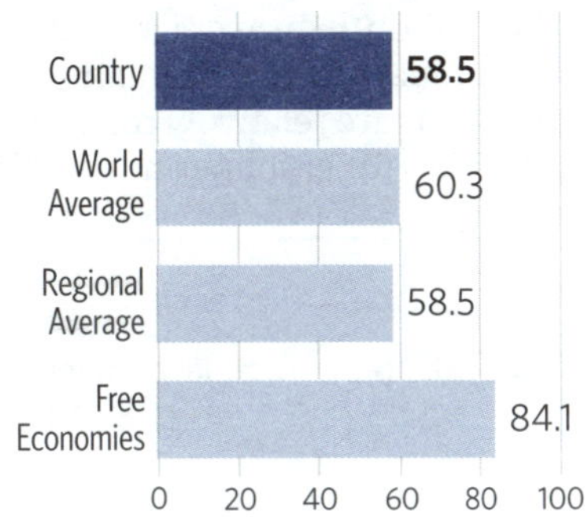

Quick Facts

Population: 244.5 million
GDP (PPP): $1.2 trillion
6.2% growth in 2012
5-year compound annual growth 5.9%
$4,977 per capita
Unemployment: 6.2%
Inflation (CPI): 4.3%
FDI Inflow: $19.9 billion
Public Debt: 24.0% of GDP

2012 data unless otherwise noted.
Data compiled as of September 2013.

THE TEN ECONOMIC FREEDOMS

RULE OF LAW

	Score	Rank	1-Year Change
Property Rights	30.0	93rd	0
Freedom from Corruption	28.0	118th	-2.0

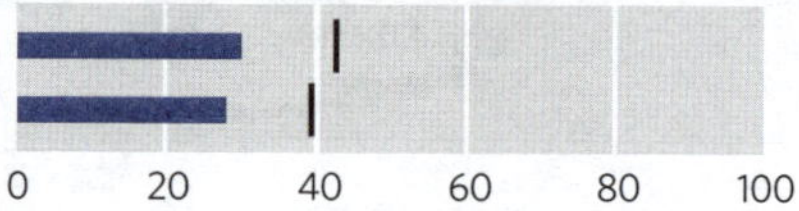

Corruption remains endemic. In 2013, the chief oil-and-gas regulator was arrested on corruption charges. In 2012, there were several high-profile convictions for bribery and money laundering. The judiciary has demonstrated its independence in some cases, but the court system remains plagued by corruption and other weaknesses. Property rights are generally respected, but enforcement is inefficient and uneven.

GOVERNMENT SIZE

	Score	Rank	1-Year Change
Fiscal Freedom	83.4	62nd	0
Government Spending	89.8	13th	+0.6

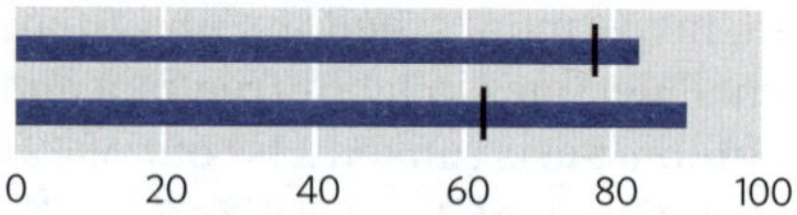

The top individual income tax rate is 30 percent, and the top corporate tax rate is 25 percent. Other taxes include a value-added tax (VAT) and a property tax. The overall tax burden is 11.8 percent of gross domestic income. Public spending is 19 percent of GDP, and public debt has fallen to 24 percent of gross domestic output. The government has raised subsidized fuel prices to help narrow fiscal shortfalls.

REGULATORY EFFICIENCY

	Score	Rank	1-Year Change
Business Freedom	54.8	139th	+4.6
Labor Freedom	47.8	146th	-3.0
Monetary Freedom	76.4	78th	+0.9

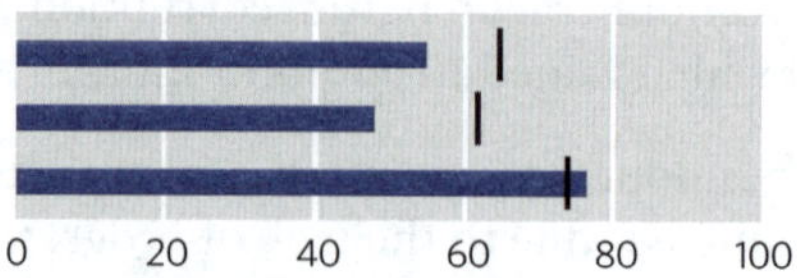

Despite some progress, overall regulatory efficiency is weak. Launching a business takes more than a month on average, and licensing requirements cost slightly less than the level of average annual income. Regulations concerning the creation and termination of employment relationships are relatively costly. In June 2013, the legislature voted to reduce costly government subsidies for gasoline and diesel fuel.

OPEN MARKETS

	Score	Rank	1-Year Change
Trade Freedom	74.8	102nd	-0.2
Investment Freedom	40.0	132nd	+5.0
Financial Freedom	60.0	41st	+10.0

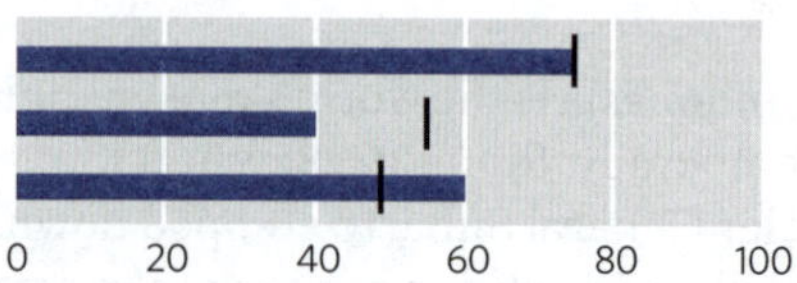

Indonesia's average tariff rate is only 2.6 percent, but import licensing and quotas further restrict trade. Foreign investment in several sectors of the economy requires government approval. The financial sector remains stable, and a Financial Services Authority has been formed to improve regulatory efficiency. The government has allowed more foreign involvement in the financial sector, although limits remain.

Long-Term Score Change (since 1995)

RULE OF LAW		GOVERNMENT SIZE		REGULATORY EFFICIENCY		OPEN MARKETS	
Property Rights	-20.0	Fiscal Freedom	+10.2	Business Freedom	-0.2	Trade Freedom	+29.8
Freedom from Corruption	+18.0	Government Spending	+0.1	Labor Freedom	-1.3	Investment Freedom	-10.0
				Monetary Freedom	+5.6	Financial Freedom	+10.0

IRAN

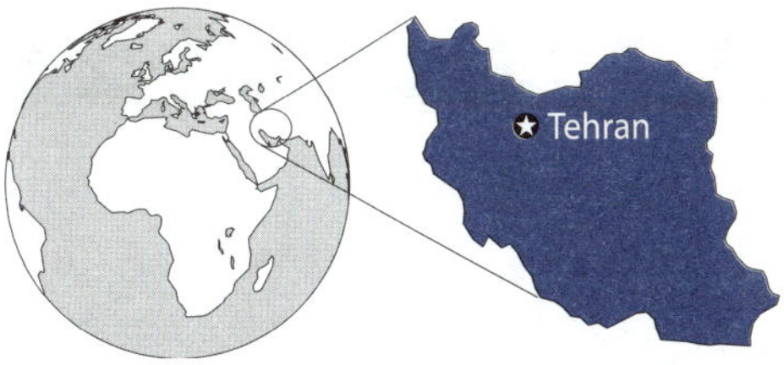

World Rank: **173** Regional Rank: **15**

Economic Freedom Score

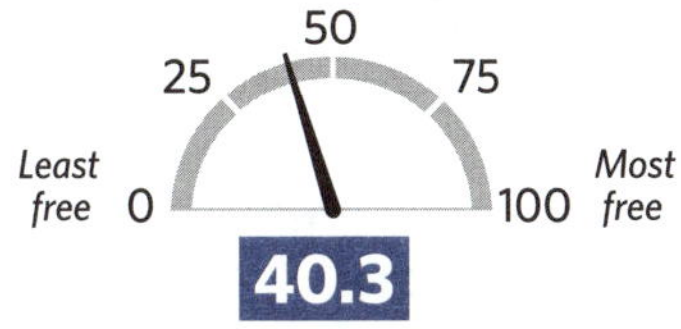

Iran's economic freedom score is 40.3, making its economy the 173rd freest in the 2014 *Index*. Its score has decreased by 2.9 points from last year, reflecting deteriorations in six of the 10 economic freedoms including labor freedom, monetary freedom, trade freedom, and freedom from corruption. Iran is ranked last out of 15 countries in the Middle East/North Africa region, and its overall score is well below the world and regional averages.

Over the 19 years during which Iran has been graded in the *Index*, its economic freedom has advanced by about 4 points. Score improvements have occurred in just three of the 10 economic freedoms, most notably in fiscal freedom and freedom from corruption. A large drop in labor freedom, compounded by deterioration in most measures of market openness, has undermined overall progress and kept the country generally in the ranks of the "repressed" economies rated in the *Index*.

Heavy state interference in many aspects of private economic activity has resulted in economic stagnation in Iran's non-oil sector and a serious lack of overall economic dynamism. A restrictive business and investment environment continues to hamper development of a viable private sector. Private firms, largely marginalized by the burdensome regulatory environment, are further undermined by government inefficiency and mismanagement.

BACKGROUND: Iran had one of the Middle East's most advanced economies before the 1979 Islamic revolution. Today, the economy is in shambles thanks to a policy agenda characterized by large subsidies to favored sectors, a bloated public sector, and high inflation. Corruption is also a serious problem. The effects of sanctions imposed by the U.S. and European Union in 2012 in response to Iran's illicit nuclear weapons program have been devastating. Petroleum exports, which provide about 85 percent of government revenues, declined to about 1.5 million barrels per day in 2012 from about 2.5 million barrels per day in 2011. President Hassan Rowhani, elected in June 2013, faces a difficult task in reviving Iran's faltering economy.

How Do We Measure Economic Freedom?
See page 471 for an explanation of the methodology or visit the *Index* Web site at *heritage.org/index.*

Freedom Trend

Country Comparisons

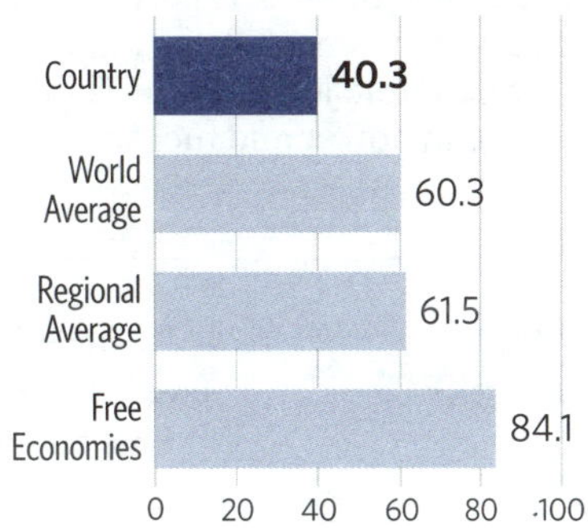

Quick Facts

Population: 76.1 million
GDP (PPP): $999.2 billion
–1.9% growth in 2012
5-year compound annual growth 2.3%
$13,127 per capita
Unemployment: 12.5%
Inflation (CPI): 30.6%
FDI Inflow: $4.9 billion
Public Debt: 10.7% of GDP

2012 data unless otherwise noted.
Data compiled as of September 2013.

IRAN (continued)

THE TEN ECONOMIC FREEDOMS

RULE OF LAW

	Score	Rank	1-Year Change
Property Rights	10.0	166th	0
Freedom from Corruption	23.4	141st	-3.6

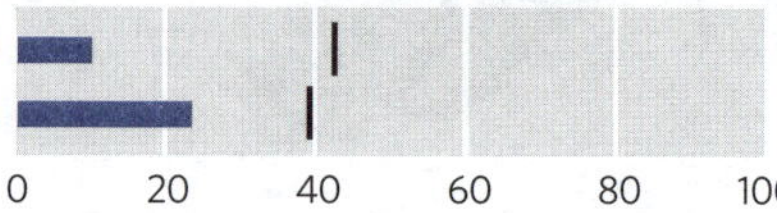

Corruption is pervasive. The hard-line clerical establishment has gained great wealth through control of tax-exempt foundations that dominate many economic sectors. The government long ago abolished independent financial watchdogs. The judicial system is not independent; the supreme leader directly appoints the head of the judiciary, who appoints the senior judges. The government has confiscated property belonging to religious minorities.

GOVERNMENT SIZE

	Score	Rank	1-Year Change
Fiscal Freedom	80.6	76th	-0.2
Government Spending	85.9	29th	+5.4

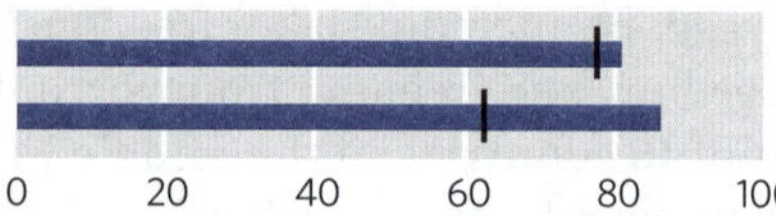

The top individual income tax rate is 35 percent, and the top corporate tax rate is 25 percent. A standard tax applies to all property transfers. Other taxes include a value-added tax (VAT). The overall tax burden equals 9.3 percent of GDP. Government expenditures remain around 22 percent of gross domestic output, and public debt has fallen to about 11 percent of GDP. Sanctions on the oil industry continue to put pressure on public finances.

REGULATORY EFFICIENCY

	Score	Rank	1-Year Change
Business Freedom	62.3	103rd	-3.0
Labor Freedom	41.7	164th	-13.3
Monetary Freedom	47.3	181st	-10.7

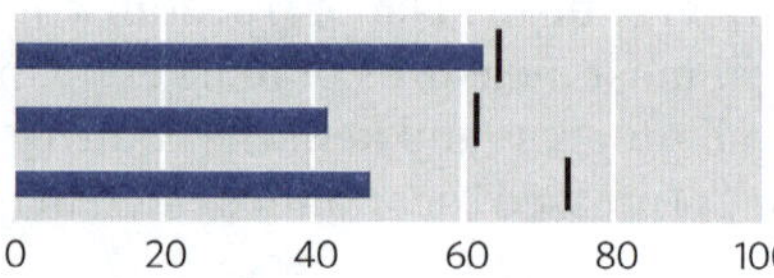

Obtaining operating permits takes more than 300 days and costs over twice the level of annual average income. Labor market rigidity, exacerbated by state interference, continues to discourage dynamic job growth. Tight government controls distort price levels. In 2011, Iran led the world in power and fuel subsidies, spending over $80 billion to lower consumer prices.

OPEN MARKETS

	Score	Rank	1-Year Change
Trade Freedom	41.4	178th	-4.3
Investment Freedom	0.0	178th	0
Financial Freedom	10.0	174th	0

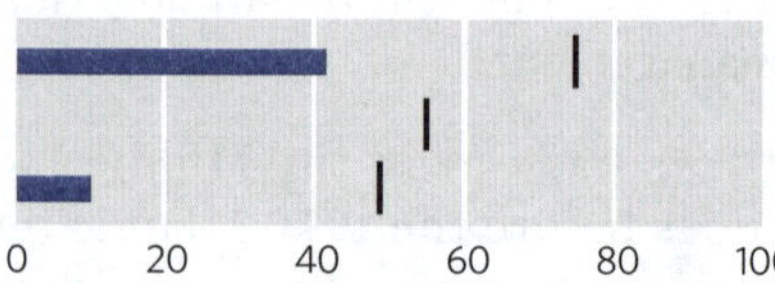

Iran's average tariff rate is a relatively high 21.8 percent. Foreign investment is screened by the government, and there are restrictions on investment in several sectors of the economy. State-owned commercial banks account for a majority of total banking-sector assets, and credit allocation is directed by the government. Capital markets are not fully developed.

Long-Term Score Change (since 1996)

RULE OF LAW		GOVERNMENT SIZE		REGULATORY EFFICIENCY		OPEN MARKETS	
Property Rights	0	Fiscal Freedom	+39.1	Business Freedom	+7.3	Trade Freedom	-3.6
Freedom from Corruption	+13.4	Government Spending	-6.2	Labor Freedom	-34.7	Investment Freedom	-10.0
				Monetary Freedom	-4.0	Financial Freedom	0

IRAQ

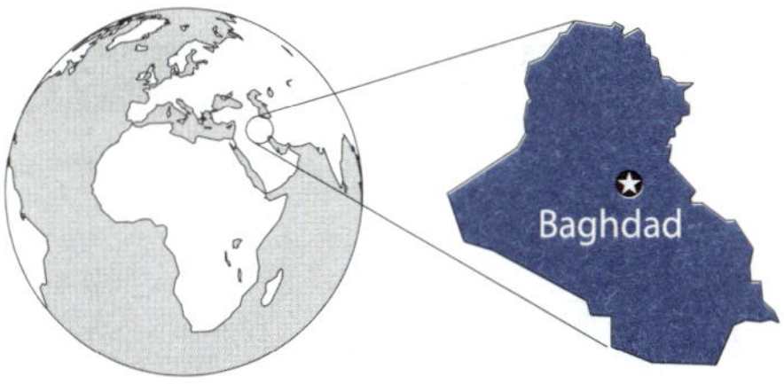

World Rank: Not Ranked   Regional Rank: Not Ranked

Economic Freedom Score

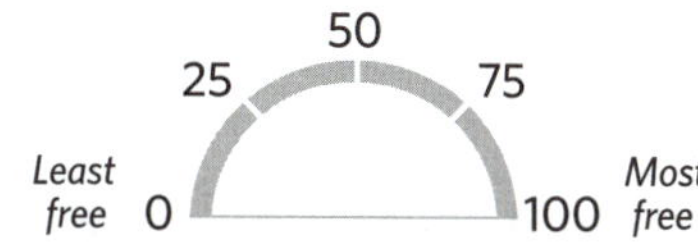

This economy is not graded

Freedom Trend

Country Comparisons

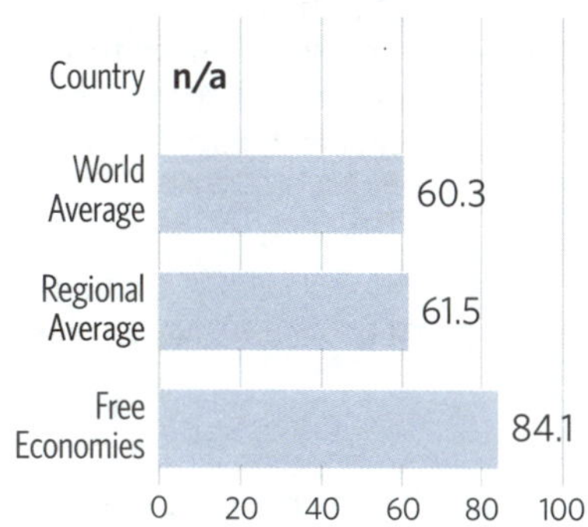

Iraq remains unranked in the 2014 *Index* because of the lack of sufficiently reliable data on economic freedom within the country. The Iraqi economy has slowly recovered from the hostilities that began in 2003, but progress has been uneven, and the country faces continuing political and security challenges. Iraq was last graded in the 2002 *Index*, when it received an overall score of 15.6.

With its economic growth highly volatile, Iraq's ongoing economic reconstruction, though facilitated by the oil sector and foreign economic aid, has been fragile. Political instability and corruption continue to undermine the limited progress made in past years.

Operating well below potential, the Iraqi economy is burdened by systemic problems. A lack of transparency exacerbates the negative impact on entrepreneurial activity of inefficient business regulations, forestalling the emergence of a dynamic private sector. The economy lacks effective monetary and fiscal policies. The weak state of the financial system, coupled with its limited role within the economy, hampers investment and the everyday operation of businesses.

BACKGROUND: Prime Minister Nuri al-Maliki's Shia-dominated coalition government has lost support among Sunni Arabs and Kurds, who charge that he has adopted a sectarian agenda. The Sunni Arab minority staged a series of protests beginning in 2012 that threatened to devolve into a renewed civil war unless their complaints of marginalization were addressed. Iraq's state-dominated economy grew by over 9 percent in 2011 and over 10 percent in 2012, propelled by high oil prices and the recovery of the oil industry, which provides more than 90 percent of government revenue. Oil exports rose to 2.6 million barrels per day, a 30-year high. Inadequate infrastructure, weak property rights, bureaucratic red tape, and widespread corruption continue to impede development.

Quick Facts

Population: 33.7 million

GDP (PPP): $238.6 billion

8.4% growth in 2012

5-year compound annual growth 7.1%

$7,080 per capita

Unemployment: 16.0%

Inflation (CPI): 6.1%

FDI Inflow: $2.5 billion

Public Debt: 34.2% of GDP

2012 data unless otherwise noted.
Data compiled as of September 2013.

How Do We Measure Economic Freedom?
See page 471 for an explanation of the methodology or visit the *Index* Web site at *heritage.org/index*.

THE TEN ECONOMIC FREEDOMS

RULE OF LAW

	Score	Rank	1-Year Change
Property Rights	n/a	—	n/a
Freedom from Corruption	13.7	177th	-4.3

Corruption is pervasive at all levels of government. There are widespread reports of demands by officials for bribes, mismanagement of public funds, payments to "ghost" employees, salary skimming, and nepotism. Although judicial independence is guaranteed in the constitution, judges are subject to immense political and sectarian pressure and are viewed by the public as corrupt or ineffective. Property rights are not well protected.

GOVERNMENT SIZE

	Score	Rank	1-Year Change
Fiscal Freedom	95.5	12th	n/a
Government Spending	40.3	150th	n/a

Iraq's individual and corporate income tax rates are 15 percent. Oil and gas companies pay a higher rate. Few other taxes exist. The overall tax burden is less than 2 percent of gross domestic income. Public expenditures are over 40 percent of GDP, and public debt is 34 percent of the domestic economy. The government relies heavily on oil revenues.

REGULATORY EFFICIENCY

	Score	Rank	1-Year Change
Business Freedom	56.9	131st	+9.9
Labor Freedom	73.4	51st	+3.3
Monetary Freedom	70.0	140th	n/a

Application of existing regulations has been inconsistent and non-transparent. Starting a new business has become easier, but obtaining operating licenses takes over four months. In the absence of a well-functioning labor market, informal labor activity persists. The state uses oil revenues to subsidize basic services such as water and housing, and total subsidies for oil, natural gas, and electricity equal nearly 20 percent of GDP.

OPEN MARKETS

	Score	Rank	1-Year Change
Trade Freedom	n/a	—	n/a
Investment Freedom	n/a	—	n/a
Financial Freedom	n/a	—	n/a

Trade flows remain far below potential as broad-based commercial activity is still suppressed. Numerous non-tariff barriers add to the cost of trade. Iraq is open to foreign investment in principle, but bureaucratic inertia, policy uncertainty, and security concerns deter investment growth. State banks dominate credit markets, and the largely cash-based economy lacks the infrastructure of a fully functioning modern financial system.

Long-Term Score Change: n/a

RULE OF LAW		GOVERNMENT SIZE		REGULATORY EFFICIENCY		OPEN MARKETS	
Property Rights	n/a	Fiscal Freedom	n/a	Business Freedom	n/a	Trade Freedom	n/a
Freedom from Corruption	n/a	Government Spending	n/a	Labor Freedom	n/a	Investment Freedom	n/a
				Monetary Freedom	n/a	Financial Freedom	n/a

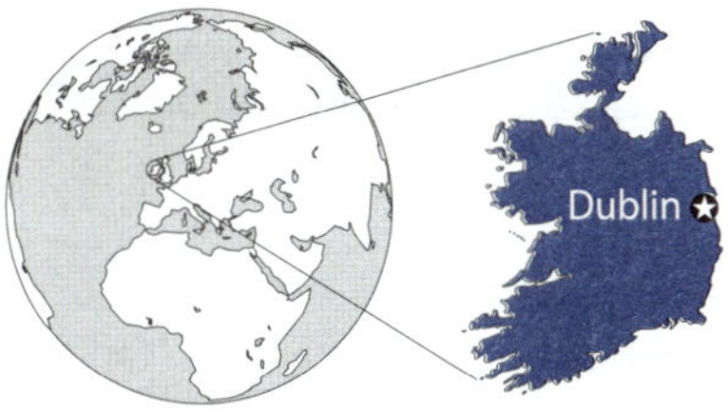

IRELAND

Economic Freedom Score

World Rank: **9** Regional Rank: **2**

Ireland's economic freedom score is 76.2, making its economy the 9th freest in the 2014 *Index*. Its score has increased by 0.5 point from last year due to improvements in trade freedom, labor freedom, and the management of public finance that offset small declines in monetary freedom and freedom from corruption. The Irish economy has become the second freest economy in the Europe region and has regained a place among the world's top 10 freest economies.

Over the 20-year history of the *Index*, Ireland has advanced its economic freedom score by almost 8 points, one of the 10 best improvements among developed countries. Score increases have occurred in five of the 10 economic freedoms, including improvements of 20 points or more in freedom from corruption, fiscal freedom, and investment freedom. Ireland ranked among the world's "free" economies from 2001 to 2010 and, while it has fallen back to "mostly free" status in recent years, is again on an upward trajectory.

Despite its recent difficulties, Ireland's overall level of economic freedom has been consistently competitive, sustained by such institutional strengths as strong protection of property rights, a low level of corruption, efficient business regulations, and competitive tax rates.

BACKGROUND: Ireland is a member of the eurozone and ratified the European Union's Lisbon Treaty in October 2009. Prime Minister Enda Kenny's Fine Gael government was elected in February 2011. Ireland's modern, highly industrialized economy performed extraordinarily well throughout the 1990s and most of the next decade, encouraged by free-market policies that attracted investment capital, but in 2008, a speculative housing bubble burst. A 2010 National Recovery Plan, implemented after the government nationalized several banks and accepted a $90 billion European Union–International Monetary Fund rescue package, aims to get the economy back on a solid footing by 2015. In February 2013, Ireland reached agreement with the European Central Bank to restructure loans and ease the debt burden incurred when Anglo Irish Bank was nationalized in 2009.

How Do We Measure Economic Freedom?
See page 471 for an explanation of the methodology or visit the *Index* Web site at *heritage.org/index*.

Freedom Trend

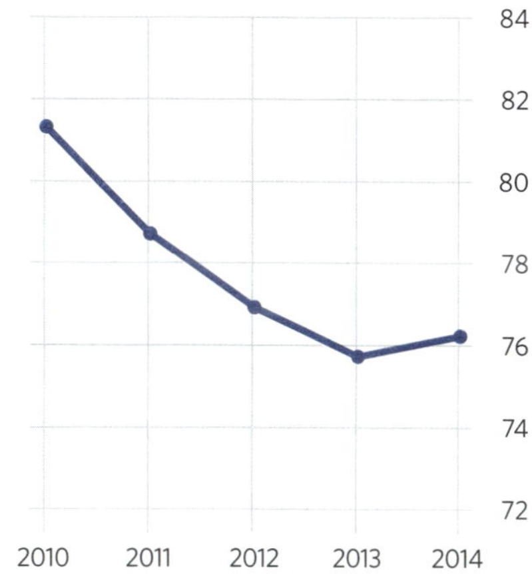

Country Comparisons

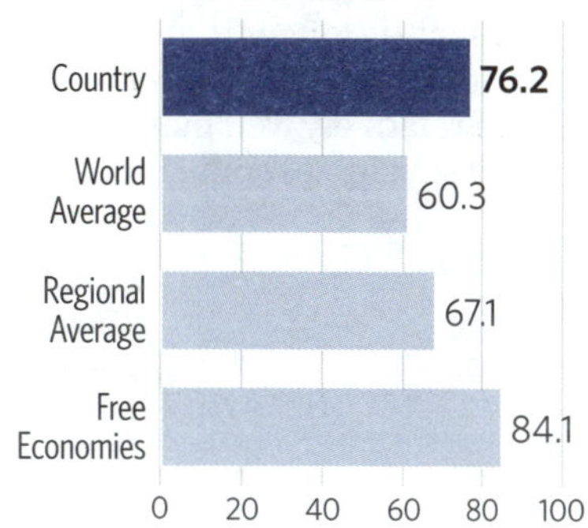

Quick Facts

Population: 4.6 million
GDP (PPP): $192.2 billion
0.9% growth in 2012
5-year compound annual growth -1.2%
$41,921 per capita
Unemployment: 14.7%
Inflation (CPI): 1.9%
FDI Inflow: $29.3 billion
Public Debt: 117.1% of GDP

2012 data unless otherwise noted.
Data compiled as of September 2013.

THE TEN ECONOMIC FREEDOMS

RULE OF LAW

	Score	Rank	1-Year Change
Property Rights	90.0	2nd	0
Freedom from Corruption	74.8	19th	-0.2

Contracts are secure and expropriation is rare, but corruption, including cronyism, political patronage, and illegal donations, is a recurring problem. In 2012, a former prime minister resigned from his political party due to perceptions of corruption. Ireland's legal system is based on common law, and the judiciary is independent. An efficient, non-discriminatory legal system protects the acquisition and disposition of all property rights.

GOVERNMENT SIZE

	Score	Rank	1-Year Change
Fiscal Freedom	74.0	122nd	+0.2
Government Spending	30.6	160th	+1.8

The top individual income tax rate is 41 percent, and the top corporate tax rate is 12.5 percent. Other taxes include a value-added tax (VAT) and a capital gains tax. The total tax burden is 27.6 percent of gross domestic income. Government spending is 48.1 percent of the domestic economy. Public debt still exceeds 117 percent of GDP, but ratings agencies have raised Ireland's debt outlook in response to austerity measures.

REGULATORY EFFICIENCY

	Score	Rank	1-Year Change
Business Freedom	83.4	26th	0
Labor Freedom	79.5	30th	+2.9
Monetary Freedom	81.7	15th	-1.1

With no minimum capital requirement, incorporating a business takes only four procedures and slightly longer than one week. Completing licensing requirements is not burdensome. The labor market remains relatively flexible, and labor costs are moderate. Monetary stability has been relatively well maintained, and prices are generally set by market forces, but the government subsidizes some industries (for example, wind energy).

OPEN MARKETS

	Score	Rank	1-Year Change
Trade Freedom	87.8	11th	+1.0
Investment Freedom	90.0	2nd	0
Financial Freedom	70.0	19th	0

EU members have a low 1.1 percent average tariff rate. Ireland has few barriers to international trade and investment. Domestic and foreign firms generally receive equal treatment under a competitive and efficient investment regime. The structure of the banking sector has changed significantly through massive recapitalization and restructuring. Considerable consolidation has taken place among domestic lenders.

Long-Term Score Change (since 1995)

RULE OF LAW		GOVERNMENT SIZE		REGULATORY EFFICIENCY		OPEN MARKETS	
Property Rights	0	Fiscal Freedom	+24.9	Business Freedom	-1.6	Trade Freedom	+10.0
Freedom from Corruption	+24.8	Government Spending	-8.1	Labor Freedom	+1.3	Investment Freedom	+20.0
				Monetary Freedom	-4.4	Financial Freedom	0

ISRAEL

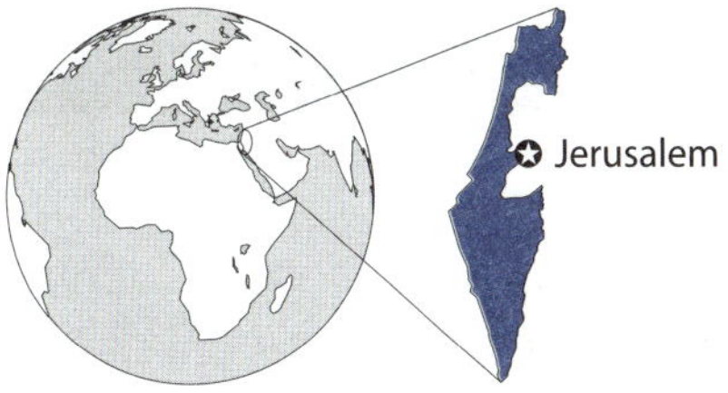

World Rank: 44 **Regional Rank: 5**

Economic Freedom Score

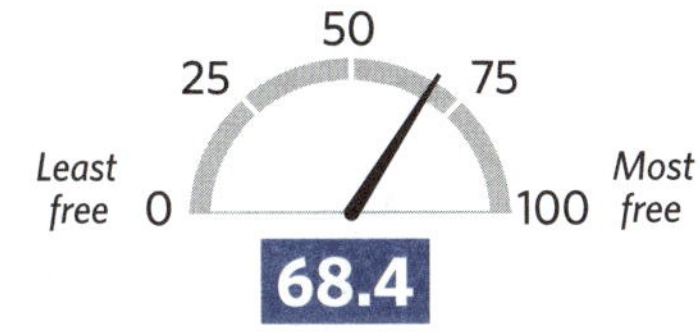

Israel's economic freedom score is 68.4, making its economy the 44th freest in the 2014 *Index*. Its overall score has increased by 1.5 points due to improvements in half of the 10 economic freedoms including business freedom, property rights, monetary freedom, and freedom from corruption. Israel is ranked 5th out of 15 countries in the Middle East/North Africa region.

Over the 20-year history of the *Index*, Israel has been consistently rated a "moderately free" economy, and its score has increased by almost 7 points. Improvements have been recorded in seven of the 10 economic freedoms, notably financial freedom, freedom from corruption, and fiscal freedom, which have advanced by double digits. However, Israel has lagged in enhancing regulatory efficiency.

Despite the challenging global economic environment, the Israeli economy has been on a path of well-balanced recovery. With the productive base increasingly diversified and structural reforms ongoing, Israel has achieved steady growth of over 3 percent annually over the past five years. Its economic competitiveness is anchored in strong protection of property rights and relatively low levels of corruption and facilitated by openness to global trade and investment.

BACKGROUND: Israel gained independence in 1948, and its vibrant democracy remains unique in the region. Prime Minister Benjamin Netanyahu, re-elected in January 2013, leads a right-of-center coalition government. Israel has developed a modern economy that attracts considerable foreign investment because of reliable property rights. The discovery of large offshore natural gas deposits has improved Israel's energy security and balance-of-payments prospects. Domestic production was expected to meet domestic natural gas needs by the end of 2013. Exports of goods and services generate about 40 percent of GDP. Despite the 2006 war against Hezbollah in Lebanon, the December 2008 war against Hamas in Gaza, and the constant threat of terrorism, Israel recovered faster than most other countries from the global financial crisis in 2008–2009.

How Do We Measure Economic Freedom?
See page 471 for an explanation of the methodology or visit the *Index* Web site at *heritage.org/index*.

Freedom Trend

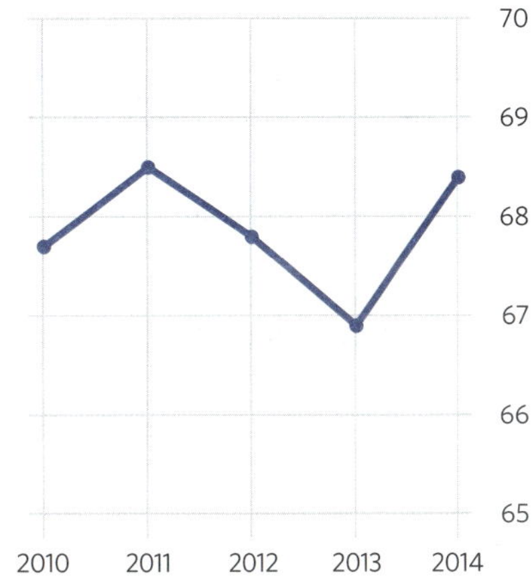

Country Comparisons

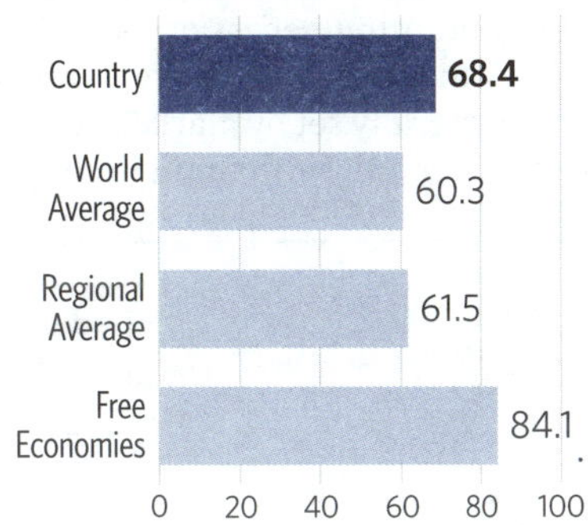

Quick Facts

Population: 7.7 million
GDP (PPP): $248.7 billion
3.1% growth in 2012
5-year compound annual growth 3.6%
$32,312 per capita
Unemployment: 6.9%
Inflation (CPI): 1.7%
FDI Inflow: $10.4 billion
Public Debt: 74.6% of GDP

2012 data unless otherwise noted.
Data compiled as of September 2013.

THE TEN ECONOMIC FREEDOMS

RULE OF LAW

	Score	Rank	1-Year Change
Property Rights	75.0	25th	+5.0
Freedom from Corruption	59.3	37th	+1.3

Bribery and other forms of corruption are illegal, and relatively effective anti-corruption measures help to strengthen the foundations of economic freedom. Israel's modern and independent legal system is based on British common law and provides effective enforcement of property and contractual rights. Courts are independent. Contracts are enforced effectively, and protection of intellectual property has improved.

GOVERNMENT SIZE

	Score	Rank	1-Year Change
Fiscal Freedom	60.1	168th	-0.1
Government Spending	40.3	151st	+1.0

Israel's top individual income tax rate is 48 percent, and its top corporate tax rate remains at 25 percent. Other taxes include a value-added tax (VAT) and a capital gains tax. The overall tax burden is 32.6 percent of gross domestic income. Public expenditures amount to 45 percent of GDP. Government debt is equal to about 75 percent of gross domestic income.

REGULATORY EFFICIENCY

	Score	Rank	1-Year Change
Business Freedom	73.2	63rd	+7.1
Labor Freedom	63.0	87th	-0.7
Monetary Freedom	80.6	26th	+2.0

Launching a business takes five procedures on average, and no minimum capital is required, but obtaining necessary permits involves about 20 procedures and takes over 200 days. The labor market needs more flexibility to accommodate rapid economic transformation. Prices are generally set by market forces, but the government subsidizes some political priorities such as West Bank settlement housing and green energy initiatives.

OPEN MARKETS

	Score	Rank	1-Year Change
Trade Freedom	82.9	54th	-0.1
Investment Freedom	80.0	23rd	0
Financial Freedom	70.0	19th	0

Israel has a 3.5 percent average tariff rate, and there are some additional barriers to agricultural imports. Foreign investment is generally welcomed on a non-discriminatory basis. The financial sector has undergone tremendous change in recent years. Financial institutions offer a wide range of services, and credit is readily available on market terms. Capital markets continue to evolve.

Long-Term Score Change (since 1995)

RULE OF LAW		GOVERNMENT SIZE		REGULATORY EFFICIENCY		OPEN MARKETS	
Property Rights	**+5.0**	Fiscal Freedom	**+15.3**	Business Freedom	**-11.8**	Trade Freedom	**+2.5**
Freedom from Corruption	**+29.3**	Government Spending	**+10.3**	Labor Freedom	**-1.1**	Investment Freedom	**-10.0**
				Monetary Freedom	**+7.4**	Financial Freedom	**+20.0**

ITALY

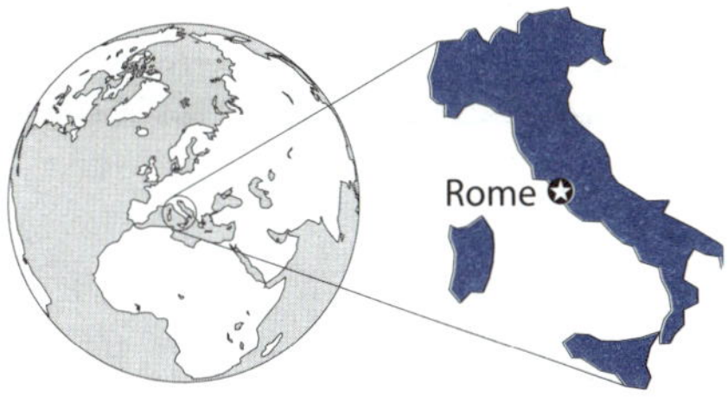

Economic Freedom Score

World Rank: **86** Regional Rank: **35**

Freedom Trend

Country Comparisons

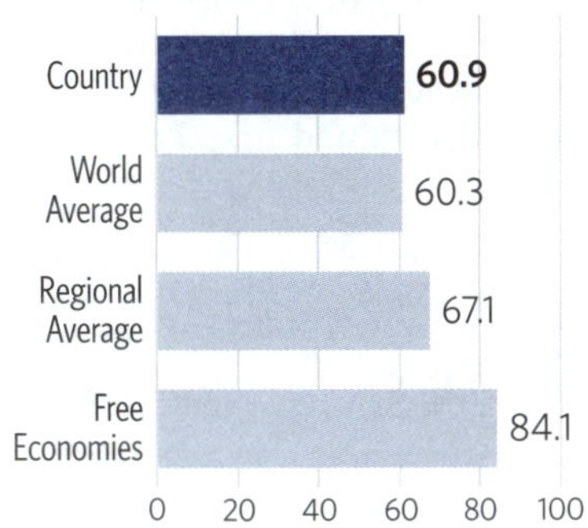

Italy's economic freedom score is 60.9, making its economy the 86th freest in the 2014 *Index*. Its overall score is 0.3 point higher than last year, with improvements in investment freedom and trade freedom counterbalanced by modest declines in monetary freedom, business freedom, and freedom from corruption. Italy is ranked 35th out of 43 countries in the Europe region, and its score is above the world average.

Over the 20-year history of the *Index*, Italy's economic freedom score has been stagnant. Gains in market openness and government fiscal policy have been undermined by significant declines in property rights, freedom from corruption, and labor freedom. Italy has been rated a "moderately free" economy through most of the history of the *Index*. Its 2014 score is its highest in four years.

Despite repeated reform attempts, short-term legislative reforms have not been implemented effectively, and the economy remains burdened by political interference, corruption, high levels of taxation, and a rigid labor market. Due to the complexity of the regulatory framework and the high cost of conducting business, a considerable amount of economic activity remains in the informal sector.

BACKGROUND: Italy held general elections in February 2013 to elect a new parliament. No clear winner emerged in the voting, but center-left Democratic Party leader Enrico Letta was eventually chosen prime minister. He leads a coalition government consisting of the Democratic Party, the center-right People of Freedom Party led by former Prime Minister Silvio Berlusconi, and the centrist Civic Choice Party. The election showcased a strong protest vote against austerity measures put in place under former technocratic Prime Minister Mario Monti. Persistent problems for the government include organized crime, a large informal sector, unemployment, and the long-standing imbalance between the prosperous, industrialized North and the less-developed, agricultural South.

Quick Facts

Population: 60.8 million
GDP (PPP): $1.8 trillion
-2.4% growth in 2012
5-year compound annual growth -1.4%
$30,136 per capita
Unemployment: 10.6%
Inflation (CPI): 3.3%
FDI Inflow: $9.6 billion
Public Debt: 127.0% of GDP

2012 data unless otherwise noted.
Data compiled as of September 2013.

How Do We Measure Economic Freedom?
See page 471 for an explanation of the methodology or visit the *Index* Web site at *heritage.org/index*.

THE TEN ECONOMIC FREEDOMS

RULE OF LAW

	Score	Rank	1-Year Change
Property Rights	50.0	53rd	0
Freedom from Corruption	38.5	70th	-0.5

Corruption and a culture of lawlessness and tax evasion remain central issues. In 2012, a court sentenced former Prime Minister Silvio Berlusconi to prison for tax fraud. He is appealing the sentence. The legal system is vulnerable to political interference. Property rights and contracts are secure, but court procedures are extremely slow. Many companies choose to settle out of court. Protection of intellectual property is below EU norms.

GOVERNMENT SIZE

	Score	Rank	1-Year Change
Fiscal Freedom	55.5	173rd	0
Government Spending	25.6	166th	+0.3

The top individual income tax rate is 43 percent, and the top corporate tax rate is 27.5 percent. Other taxes include a value-added tax (VAT) and an inheritance tax. The overall tax burden is 43 percent of GDP. Public expenditures amount to about 50 percent of the domestic economy. Italy has struggled to meet budget goals to rein in its burdensome public debt, which has grown to 127 percent of GDP.

REGULATORY EFFICIENCY

	Score	Rank	1-Year Change
Business Freedom	75.5	47th	-1.4
Labor Freedom	52.5	128th	+0.5
Monetary Freedom	78.9	48th	-1.3

Completing licensing requirements takes over 200 days and costs more than the level of average annual income. Serious labor market rigidities constrain job growth, and the informal labor market accounts for a large proportion of employment. Monetary stability has been relatively well maintained, and the government has reduced subsidies for renewable energy sources.

OPEN MARKETS

	Score	Rank	1-Year Change
Trade Freedom	87.8	11th	+1.0
Investment Freedom	85.0	13th	+5.0
Financial Freedom	60.0	41st	0

EU members have a low 1.1 percent average tariff rate and, in general, few non-tariff barriers to trade. Investment in some sectors of Italy's economy may be screened by the government. The financial sector provides a relatively wide range of services but remains subject to political interference. The banking sector has been strained by the European sovereign debt crisis.

Long-Term Score Change (since 1995)

RULE OF LAW		GOVERNMENT SIZE		REGULATORY EFFICIENCY		OPEN MARKETS	
Property Rights	-20.0	Fiscal Freedom	+11.9	Business Freedom	-9.5	Trade Freedom	+10.0
Freedom from Corruption	-31.5	Government Spending	+22.0	Labor Freedom	-22.0	Investment Freedom	+15.0
				Monetary Freedom	-2.2	Financial Freedom	+10.0

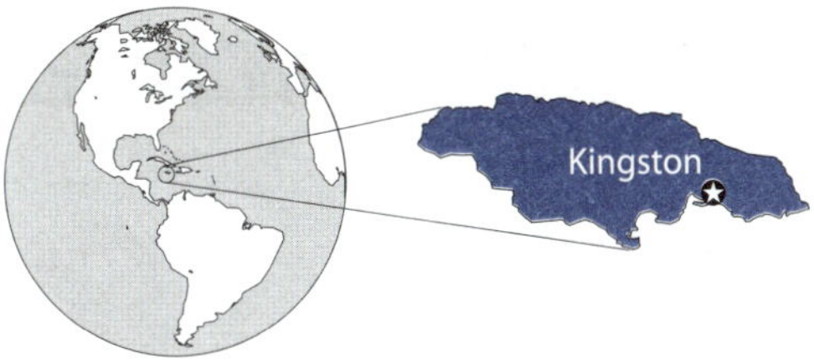

JAMAICA

Economic Freedom Score

World Rank: **56** Regional Rank: **10**

Jamaica's economic freedom score is 66.7, making its economy the 56th freest in the 2014 *Index*. Its score is essentially unchanged from last year, with combined improvements in five of the 10 economic freedoms, including labor freedom and the control of government spending, offset by declines in financial freedom and fiscal freedom. Jamaica ranks 10th out of 29 countries in the South and Central America/Caribbean region.

Over the 20-year history of the *Index*, Jamaica has advanced its economic freedom score by only 2.3 points. Regulatory efficiency, measured through business freedom, labor freedom, and monetary freedom, has improved notably, and both trade freedom and investment freedom have recorded double-digit improvements. Counterbalancing these gains, however, have been substantial deteriorations in the rule of law, as assessed by property rights and freedom from corruption, and financial freedom.

Jamaica's critical development challenges include lingering corruption and relatively high government spending. Public debt has surpassed 145 percent of GDP. Reducing the bloated public sector, following through on plans to privatize loss-making state-owned enterprises, and enforcing expenditure restraint are all essential in order to meet fiscal targets.

BACKGROUND: Prime Minister Portia Simpson-Miller's People's National Party was re-elected in December 2011 with a large parliamentary majority. In her second term, Simpson-Miller has maintained market-friendly policies, but high interest rates and excessive government debt burden the economy. A $1.27 billion standby agreement with the International Monetary Fund for balance of payment support, signed in 2010, required a commitment to major fiscal reforms that have been slow to materialize. An extended IMF agreement was approved in 2013. Services account for more than 60 percent of GDP. Most foreign exchange comes from remittances, tourism, and bauxite production, all of which declined sharply in the 2009 recession. Tourism receipts have recovered slightly, but unemployment and underemployment in the formal sector remain high. Violent crime and the drug trade remain serious problems.

How Do We Measure Economic Freedom?
See page 471 for an explanation of the methodology or visit the *Index* Web site at *heritage.org/index*.

Freedom Trend

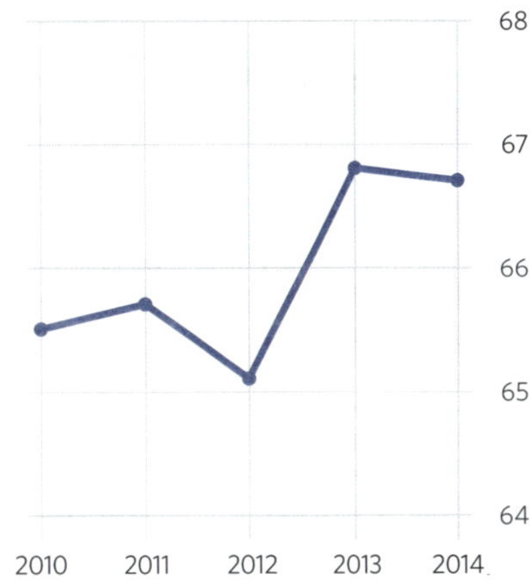

Country Comparisons

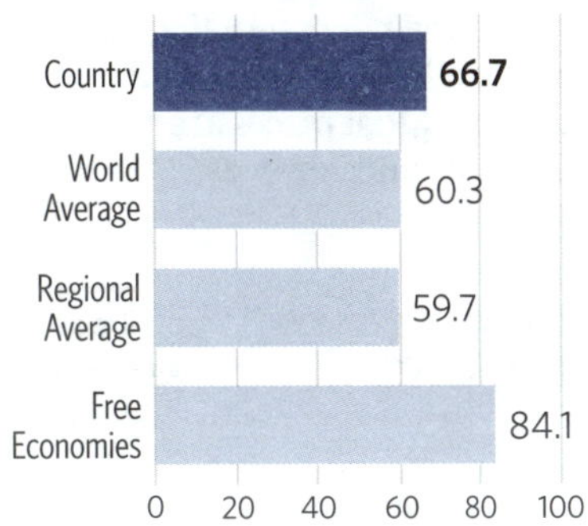

Quick Facts

Population: 2.8 million
GDP (PPP): $25.2 billion
0.1% growth in 2012
5-year compound annual growth −0.8%
$9,159 per capita
Unemployment: 13.0%
Inflation (CPI): 7.3%
FDI Inflow: $362.2 million
Public Debt: 146.6% of GDP

2012 data unless otherwise noted.
Data compiled as of September 2013.

THE TEN ECONOMIC FREEDOMS

RULE OF LAW

	Score	Rank	1-Year Change
Property Rights	40.0	70th	0
Freedom from Corruption	33.0	91st	0

Corruption remains a serious problem, and many citizens view the police as endemically corrupt. Jamaica has one of the Western Hemisphere's highest murder rates, driven in part by drug trafficking. An inefficient legal system weakens the security of property rights and the rule of law. The judiciary lacks adequate resources, and trials can be delayed for years. The Trinidad-based Caribbean Court of Justice is the highest appellate court.

GOVERNMENT SIZE

	Score	Rank	1-Year Change
Fiscal Freedom	77.2	109th	-0.3
Government Spending	69.4	91st	+1.7

The top individual income tax rate is 25 percent, and the top corporate tax rate is 33.3 percent. Other taxes include a property transfer tax and a general consumption tax. The overall tax burden is 23.4 percent of gross domestic income. Government spending amounts to 32 percent of gross domestic output. Public debt is high at over 145 percent of GDP, and the government has had to seek IMF assistance.

REGULATORY EFFICIENCY

	Score	Rank	1-Year Change
Business Freedom	84.6	25th	+0.3
Labor Freedom	75.6	46th	+6.3
Monetary Freedom	77.3	70th	+1.2

The business start-up process is straightforward, with no minimum capital required, but obtaining necessary licenses still takes more than four months and costs over 200 percent of the level of average annual income. Rigid employment regulations are not conducive to job growth. Most prices are set by the market, but the government regulates the prices of a number of goods and services.

OPEN MARKETS

	Score	Rank	1-Year Change
Trade Freedom	75.1	100th	+0.1
Investment Freedom	85.0	13th	0
Financial Freedom	50.0	69th	-10.0

Tariffs average 7.5 percent and are a significant source of revenue. Some agricultural products face higher tariffs. There are few legal barriers to foreign investment, but bureaucratic red tape can discourage investors. The financial system continues to grow. However, while the overall banking sector appears to be sound, its excessive exposure to public debt, which represents about 20 percent of total assets, is a serious weakness.

Long-Term Score Change (since 1995)

RULE OF LAW		GOVERNMENT SIZE		REGULATORY EFFICIENCY		OPEN MARKETS	
Property Rights	**-10.0**	Fiscal Freedom	**-0.3**	Business Freedom	**+14.6**	Trade Freedom	**+10.1**
Freedom from Corruption	**-17.0**	Government Spending	**-7.0**	Labor Freedom	**+7.2**	Investment Freedom	**+15.0**
				Monetary Freedom	**+26.4**	Financial Freedom	**-20.0**

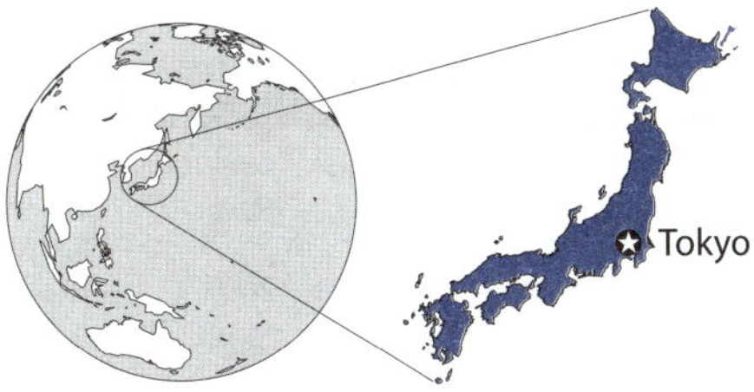

JAPAN

World Rank: 25 **Regional Rank: 6**

Economic Freedom Score

Japan's economic freedom score is 72.4, making its economy the 25th freest in the 2014 *Index*. Its score is 0.6 point higher than last year, reflecting improvements in trade freedom, investment freedom, and control of government spending that outweigh deteriorations in freedom from corruption, monetary freedom, and business freedom. Japan is ranked 6th out of 41 countries in the Asia–Pacific region.

Over the 20-year history of the *Index*, Japan's economic freedom has regressed, with its score falling by nearly 3 points. Declines have been recorded in six of the 10 economic freedoms, with double-digit declines in financial freedom, property rights, freedom from corruption, and control of government spending. The decline of Japan's overall economic freedom score over the past two decades is the third worst among advanced economies.

Japan continues to be one of the "mostly free" economies. However, as reflected in the lack of progress toward greater economic freedom over the history of the *Index*, it continues to fall behind other countries in pursuing and implementing critical reform measures. A large and growing public debt has taken a toll on private-sector economic activity, preventing more dynamic growth. Disparities in productivity between different segments of the economy have continued to widen. Japan has lagged behind other countries in pursuing free trade agreements.

BACKGROUND: The Liberal Democratic Party retook control of the lower house of parliament in 2012, returning Prime Minister Shinzo Abe to office. The LDP's resurgence was due in large part to the electorate's rejection of the Democratic Party of Japan for its ineptitude and corruption scandals. Voters also view Abe as more likely to stand up to an increasingly aggressive China, which claims sovereignty over Japan's Senkaku Islands. Although Abe has proposed pragmatic changes in Japan's defense forces, his revisionist comments about its wartime actions have angered others in the region. The LDP won another landslide victory in the July 2013 election for the upper house, largely on popular hopes that "Abenomics" would rejuvenate the economy.

How Do We Measure Economic Freedom?
See page 471 for an explanation of the methodology or visit the *Index* Web site at *heritage.org/index.*

Freedom Trend

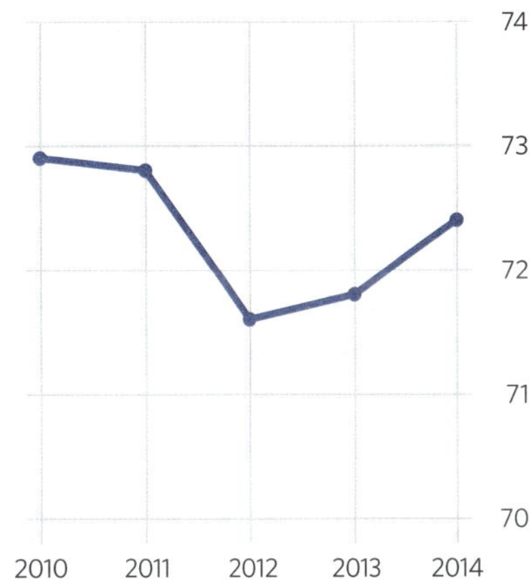

Country Comparisons

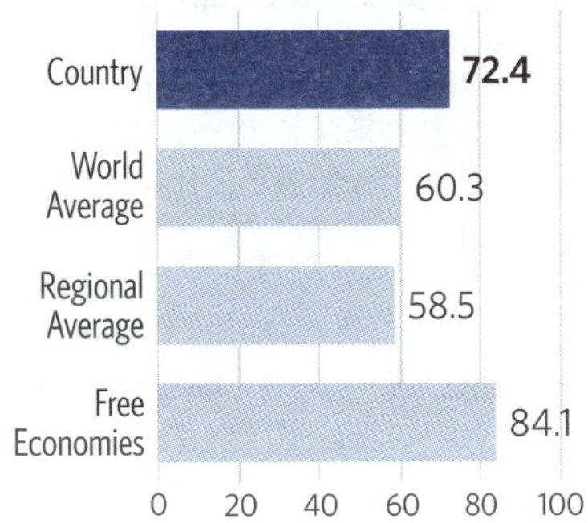

Quick Facts

Population: 127.6 million
GDP (PPP): $4.6 trillion
2.0% growth in 2012
5-year compound annual growth -0.2%
$36,266 per capita
Unemployment: 4.4%
Inflation (CPI): 0.0%
FDI Inflow: $1.7 billion
Public Debt: 237.9% of GDP

2012 data unless otherwise noted.
Data compiled as of September 2013.

THE TEN ECONOMIC FREEDOMS

		Score	Rank	1-Year Change
RULE OF LAW	Property Rights	80.0	20th	0
	Freedom from Corruption	77.8	16th	-2.2

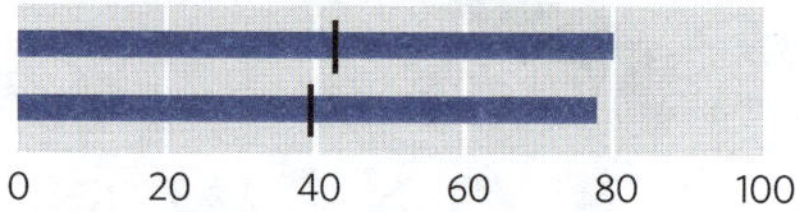

Significant efforts have been made to fight Japan's relatively modest level of corruption by reforming the "iron triangle" system, mostly by loosening ties between the government and big business. The judiciary is independent, and its solid multi-level institutional framework, although at times inefficient, provides secure protection of real and intellectual property. Obtaining and protecting patents and trademarks can be time-consuming and costly.

		Score	Rank	1-Year Change
GOVERNMENT SIZE	Fiscal Freedom	69.2	142nd	0
	Government Spending	47.1	141st	+2.1

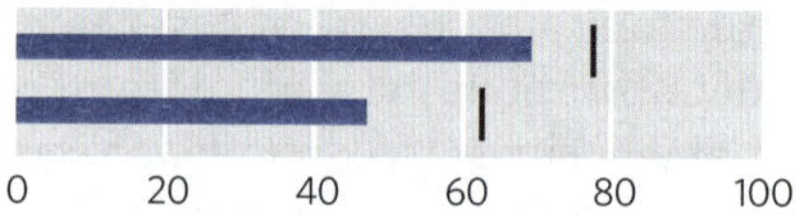

The top individual income tax rate has been raised to 40.8 percent, and the top corporate tax rate has been lowered to 25.5 percent. A fiscal surtax exists for the next three fiscal years, bringing the effective tax rate to 28.05 percent. Local and enterprise taxes can also raise rates significantly. The overall tax burden is 27.6 percent of GDP. Government spending is 42 percent of GDP, and public debt amounts to well over twice the size of the economy.

		Score	Rank	1-Year Change
REGULATORY EFFICIENCY	Business Freedom	80.0	32nd	-1.3
	Labor Freedom	79.8	29th	-0.5
	Monetary Freedom	87.5	2nd	-3.1

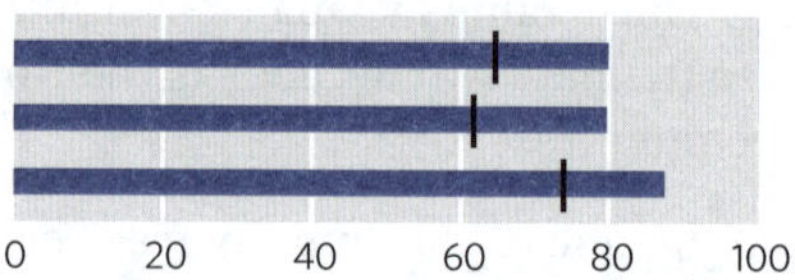

With no minimum capital required, business formation takes less than 10 procedures, but burdensome licensing requirements discourage dynamic entrepreneurial growth. A tendency to grant lifetime employment guarantees hurts productivity and impedes the development of a more flexible labor market. Prices are generally set by market forces, but the government subsidizes numerous industries and sectors.

		Score	Rank	1-Year Change
OPEN MARKETS	Trade Freedom	82.4	62nd	+0.6
	Investment Freedom	70.0	46th	+10.0
	Financial Freedom	50.0	69th	0

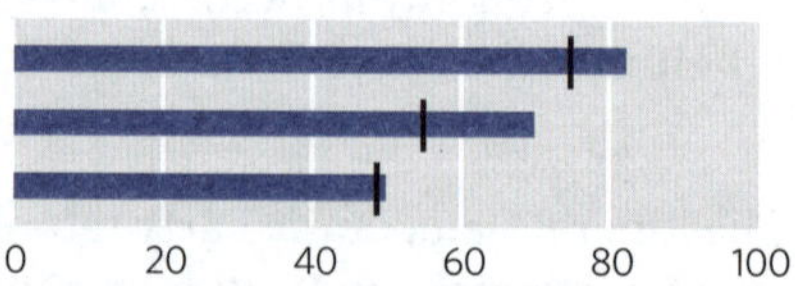

Japan has a relatively low 1.3 percent average tariff rate, but significant non-tariff barriers restrict many agricultural imports. Investment in several sectors of the economy may be screened by the government. The financial sector is subject to political influence and lacks dynamic growth. Reform of the state-owned postal savings system has been largely derailed since late 2009.

Long-Term Score Change (since 1995)

RULE OF LAW		GOVERNMENT SIZE		REGULATORY EFFICIENCY		OPEN MARKETS	
Property Rights	**-10.0**	Fiscal Freedom	**+15.6**	Business Freedom	**-5.0**	Trade Freedom	**+0.4**
Freedom from Corruption	**-12.2**	Government Spending	**-20.6**	Labor Freedom	**-3.6**	Investment Freedom	**+20.0**
				Monetary Freedom	**+0.4**	Financial Freedom	**-20.0**

JORDAN

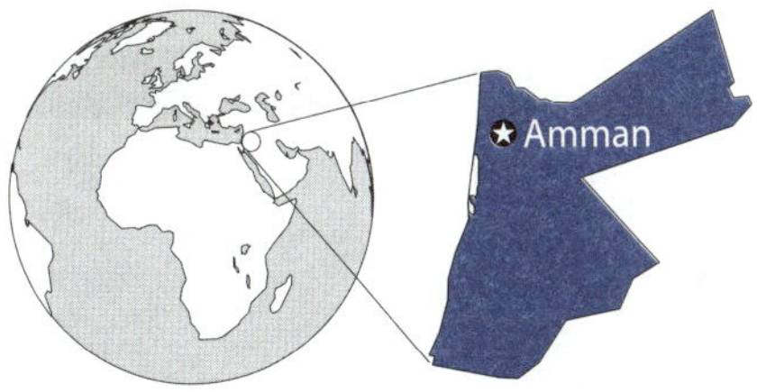

World Rank: **39** Regional Rank: **4**

Economic Freedom Score

Jordan's economic freedom score is 69.2, making its economy the 39th freest in the 2014 *Index*. Its score is 1.2 points worse than last year, due primarily to a deterioration in regulatory efficiency as measured by business freedom, labor freedom, and monetary freedom. Jordan is ranked 4th out of 15 countries in the Middle East/North Africa region, and its overall score continues to be well above the world and regional averages.

Over the 20-year history of the *Index*, Jordan has advanced its economic freedom score by nearly 7 points, with increases in four of the 10 economic freedoms. Double-digit improvements of over 15 points in freedom from corruption, fiscal freedom, and trade freedom have offset declines in such areas as property rights and financial freedom. Jordan has been rated generally "moderately free" over the past two decades.

Despite the region's ongoing political and security challenges, Jordan's economy has been resilient. The economy has benefited from earlier years' reform agenda in the areas of privatization and public finance management. High levels of trade freedom and investment freedom continue to sustain market openness, keeping the economy relatively competitive. Promoting the transition to a more open and flexible economy, the financial sector has taken steps to meet international standards.

BACKGROUND: Jordan is a constitutional monarchy with relatively few natural resources. Its economy is supported by foreign loans, international aid, and remittances from expatriate workers. In 2011, King Abdullah responded to "Arab Spring" demonstrations by dismissing his cabinet and ceding greater authority to the judiciary and parliament. The government also implemented two economic relief packages and a supplementary budget to subsidize the middle class and the poor. In 2000, Jordan joined the World Trade Organization and signed a free trade agreement with the United States; in 2001, it signed an association agreement with the European Union. Jordan negotiated a $2.1 billion standby arrangement with the International Monetary Fund in 2012 to finance its budgetary and balance-of-payments deficits. The presence of hundreds of thousands of Syrian refugees poses serious administrative and resource problems for the government.

How Do We Measure Economic Freedom?
See page 471 for an explanation of the methodology or visit the *Index* Web site at *heritage.org/index*.

Freedom Trend

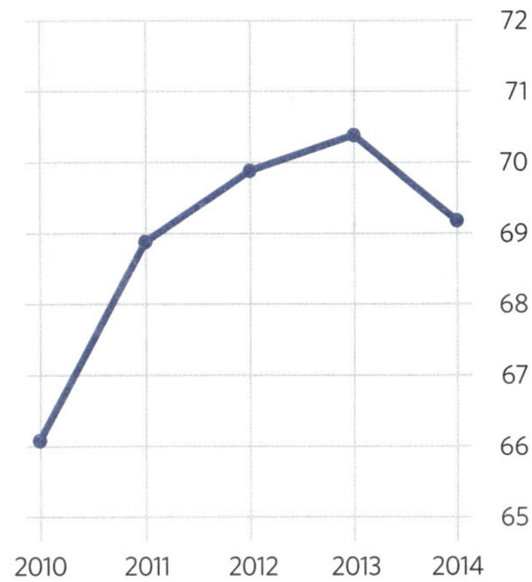

Country Comparisons

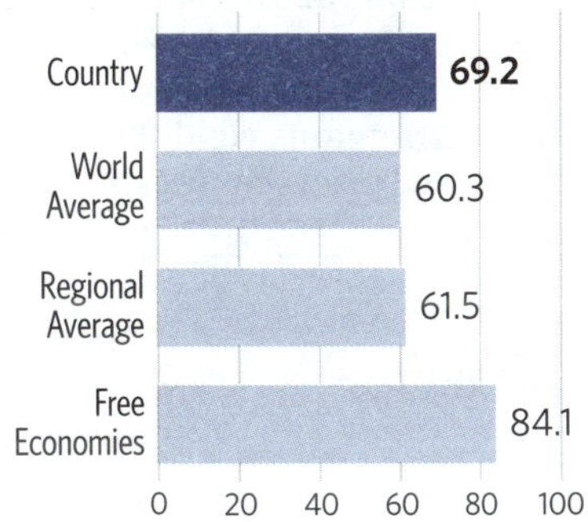

Quick Facts

Population: 6.4 million
GDP (PPP): $38.7 billion
2.8% growth in 2012
5-year compound annual growth 4.1%
$6,042 per capita
Unemployment: 12.2%
Inflation (CPI): 4.8%
FDI Inflow: $1.4 billion
Public Debt: 79.6% of GDP

2012 data unless otherwise noted.
Data compiled as of September 2013.

THE TEN ECONOMIC FREEDOMS

RULE OF LAW

	Score	Rank	1-Year Change
Property Rights	60.0	41st	0
Freedom from Corruption	45.6	54th	+0.6

Influence peddling and lack of transparency undermine the fairness of government procurement and dispute settlement. The use of family, business, and other personal connections to advance business interests is regarded as a normal aspect of the culture. Anti-corruption efforts have had mixed results. Property rights are respected for the most part. The judiciary is generally independent, but the king is the ultimate authority.

GOVERNMENT SIZE

	Score	Rank	1-Year Change
Fiscal Freedom	94.0	16th	+0.4
Government Spending	66.9	95th	-1.9

The top individual income and corporate tax rates are 14 percent. Other taxes include a value-added tax (VAT) and a property tax. The overall tax burden is 14.4 percent of gross domestic income. Government spending is 33 percent of GDP. Public debt continues to climb and has reached about 80 percent of gross domestic income.

REGULATORY EFFICIENCY

	Score	Rank	1-Year Change
Business Freedom	62.0	105th	-7.2
Labor Freedom	72.9	55th	-2.6
Monetary Freedom	81.3	19th	-0.7

With no minimum capital required, launching a business takes 12 days, but licensing requirements remain burdensome, costing about five times the level of average annual income. Progress toward reforming bloated public-sector employment has been dismal, and the labor market remains rigid. Faced with budget deficits, the government reduced subsidies and increased prices for fuel in 2012 and plans to do the same for electricity.

OPEN MARKETS

	Score	Rank	1-Year Change
Trade Freedom	79.6	72nd	0
Investment Freedom	70.0	46th	0
Financial Freedom	60.0	41st	0

Jordan has a 5.2 percent average tariff rate. Licenses are required for some agricultural products. New investment may be subject to government screening. The evolving financial sector remains relatively stable. Along with financial-sector policies that are intended to enhance competition and efficiency, the banking sector is guided by regulations that generally conform to international standards. The state owns no commercial banks.

Long-Term Score Change (since 1995)

RULE OF LAW		GOVERNMENT SIZE		REGULATORY EFFICIENCY		OPEN MARKETS	
Property Rights	-10.0	Fiscal Freedom	+47.4	Business Freedom	-8.0	Trade Freedom	+20.4
Freedom from Corruption	+15.6	Government Spending	-3.7	Labor Freedom	-1.0	Investment Freedom	0
				Monetary Freedom	+3.8	Financial Freedom	-10.0

KAZAKHSTAN

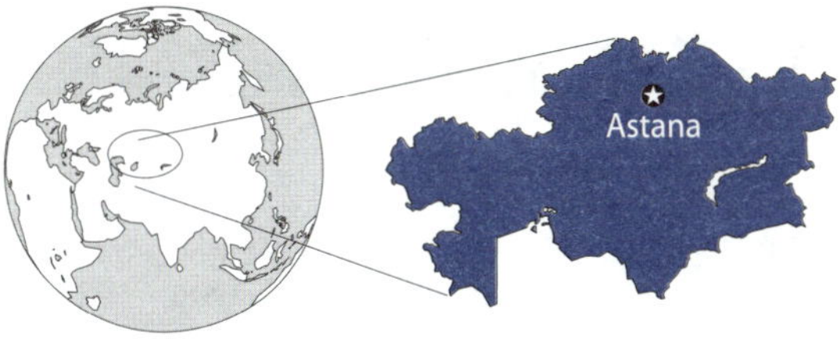

World Rank: 67 | **Regional Rank: 11**

Kazakhstan's economic freedom score is 63.7, making its economy the 67th freest in the 2014 *Index*. Its score is 0.7 point higher than last year, with notable improvements in investment freedom, business freedom, and monetary freedom partially counterbalanced by deterioration in the rule of law as measured by property rights and freedom from corruption. Kazakhstan ranks 11th out of 42 countries in the Asia–Pacific region, and its overall score is above the world and regional averages.

Over the 17 years that Kazakhstan has been graded in the *Index*, its economic freedom has advanced by 22 points, one of the 20 best improvements recorded by any country. This increase has been facilitated especially by improvements in regulatory efficiency and market openness. Scores for seven of the 10 economic freedoms, including monetary freedom, trade freedom, financial freedom, fiscal freedom, and business freedom, have increased by double digits. Once considered a "repressed" economy, Kazakhstan has risen to "moderately free" since 2008.

Looking ahead, deeper structural reforms will be critical in overcoming challenges associated with the need to reduce dependence on the energy sector and achieve more diversified growth. Property rights and freedom from corruption remain far below average world levels.

BACKGROUND: Kazakhstan is a founding member of the Customs Union with Russia and Belarus and plans to join the Eurasian Union in 2015. President Nursultan Nazarbayev won a fifth five-year term with over 95.5 percent of the vote in 2011, and his Nur Otan party holds 80.7 percent of the seats in parliament. In June 2013, Kazakhstan reached out to Uzbekistan in an effort to defuse tensions over disputed segments of the border and water rights. Oil production is projected to reach 3 million barrels per day by 2030. Kazakhstan is also the world's largest producer of uranium. There is heavy dependence on commodity exports, but manufacturing also has shown solid growth, as has trade with China.

How Do We Measure Economic Freedom?
See page 471 for an explanation of the methodology or visit the *Index* Web site at *heritage.org/index*.

Economic Freedom Score

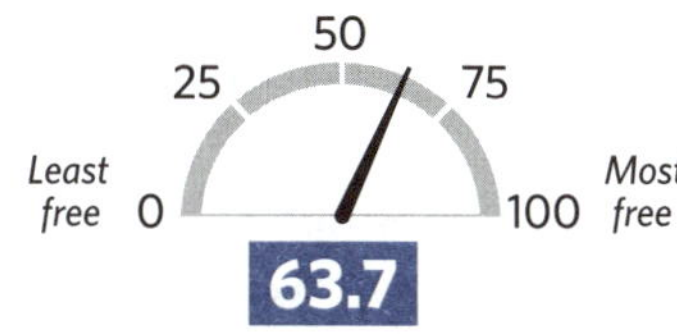

Freedom Trend

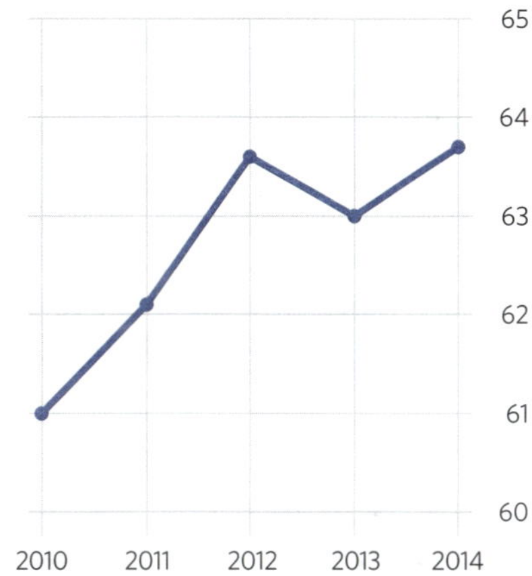

Country Comparisons

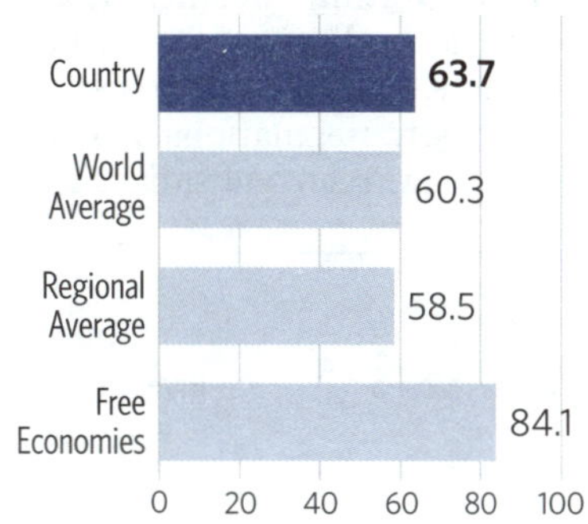

Quick Facts

Population: 16.7 million
GDP (PPP): $231.8 billion
5.0% growth in 2012
5-year compound annual growth 4.8%
$13,893 per capita
Unemployment: 5.4%
Inflation (CPI): 5.1%
FDI Inflow: $14.0 billion
Public Debt: 12.3% of GDP

2012 data unless otherwise noted.
Data compiled as of September 2013.

KAZAKHSTAN (continued)

THE TEN ECONOMIC FREEDOMS

		Score	Rank	1-Year Change
RULE OF LAW	Property Rights	30.0	93rd	-5.0
	Freedom from Corruption	25.7	129th	-1.3

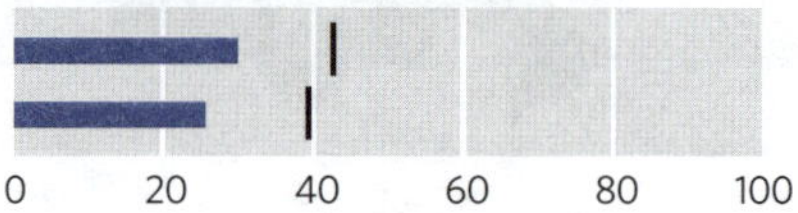

Corruption, bribery, and graft are widespread at all levels of government as evidenced by several high-profile cases in the past year. The judiciary is constitutionally subservient to the executive branch. Judges are subject to political bias, and corruption pervades the judicial system. Courts cannot protect property rights effectively, and infringements of intellectual property rights are rife.

		Score	Rank	1-Year Change
GOVERNMENT SIZE	Fiscal Freedom	92.9	19th	-0.3
	Government Spending	85.0	33rd	+0.5

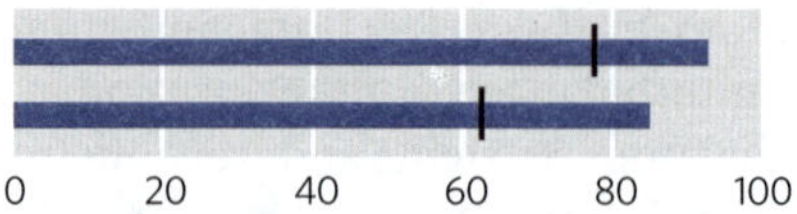

The individual income tax rate is a flat 10 percent, and the corporate tax rate is 20 percent. Other taxes include a value-added tax (VAT) and excise taxes. The overall tax burden is 14.6 percent of gross domestic income. Government expenditures make up 22 percent of the domestic economy. Large oil reserves help to boost public accounts, keeping public debt low at about 12 percent of GDP.

		Score	Rank	1-Year Change
REGULATORY EFFICIENCY	Business Freedom	74.4	54th	+2.6
	Labor Freedom	86.7	11th	-1.7
	Monetary Freedom	74.4	113th	+2.2

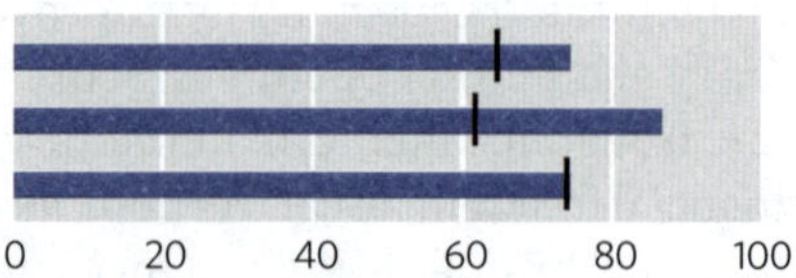

Incorporating a business takes six procedures, with no minimum capital required. However, completing licensing requirements takes almost four months. Labor regulations are relatively flexible. The non-salary cost of employing a worker is moderate, and dismissing an employee is not costly. Regulations on work hours can be rigid. Monetary stability is well maintained, but the government subsidizes agriculture and imposes price control measures on fuel.

		Score	Rank	1-Year Change
OPEN MARKETS	Trade Freedom	78.2	81st	0
	Investment Freedom	40.0	132nd	+10.0
	Financial Freedom	50.0	69th	0

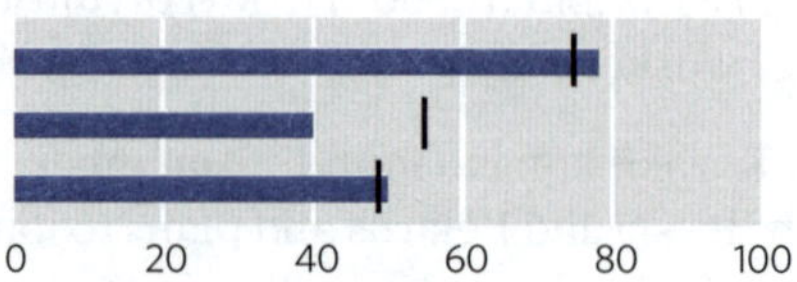

The average tariff rate is 3.4 percent. It is costly and time-consuming to import goods. Foreign investors sometimes find it difficult to navigate the legal and regulatory systems. The financial sector has experienced deeper reforms than other areas of the economy. However, capital markets remain underdeveloped, although the bond market has been growing. Troubled banks have been recapitalized.

Long-Term Score Change (since 1998)

RULE OF LAW		GOVERNMENT SIZE		REGULATORY EFFICIENCY		OPEN MARKETS	
Property Rights	**0**	Fiscal Freedom	**+19.6**	Business Freedom	**+19.4**	Trade Freedom	**+17.2**
Freedom from Corruption	**+15.7**	Government Spending	**-0.7**	Labor Freedom	**+4.1**	Investment Freedom	**+10.0**
				Monetary Freedom	**+74.4**	Financial Freedom	**+20.0**

KENYA

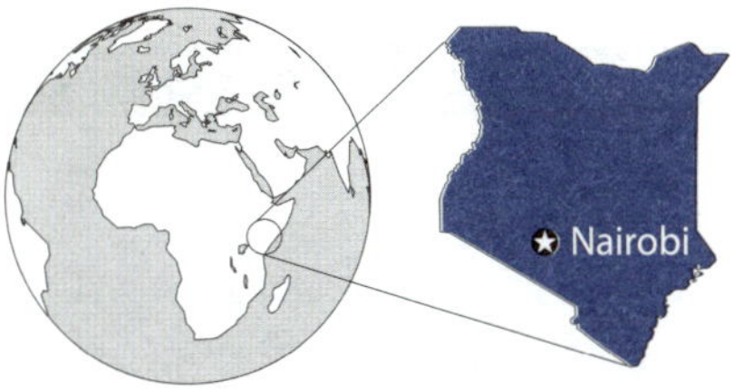

World Rank: 111 Regional Rank: **17**

Kenya's economic freedom score is 57.1, making its economy the 111th freest in the 2014 *Index*. Its score has increased by 1.2 points since last year, with notable advancements in trade freedom, labor freedom, and monetary freedom outweighing declines in business freedom and freedom from corruption. Kenya is ranked 17th out of 46 countries in the Sub-Saharan Africa region, and its overall score is below the world average but above the regional average.

Over the 20-year history of the *Index*, Kenya has advanced its economic freedom score by 2.7 points. Measures have been implemented to improve public financial management, and the government has pursued reforms related to business development and easing the customs process. Score increases have been recorded in six of the 10 economic freedoms, notably monetary freedom, trade freedom, and the management of government spending.

These gains, however, have been largely eroded by significant deterioration in the rule of law as measured by property rights and freedom from corruption. Kenya has been rated a "mostly unfree" economy during most of its history in the *Index* and was ranked "moderately free" only once, in 1997.

BACKGROUND: In March 2013, Uhuru Kenyatta and his running mate William Ruto won the first presidential election under the new constitution, adopted in 2010. Both face charges of crimes against humanity related to violence in the aftermath of the 2007 presidential election. In November 2011, Kenya launched a military incursion into Somalia in response to terrorist activity and kidnappings. In September 2013, it suffered its largest terrorist attack since the 1998 U.S. embassy bombing. Economic growth, hindered for decades by poor government administration, weak property rights, and corruption, picked up in 2009. The government employs one-third of the formal labor force. Agriculture accounts for about 25 percent of GDP and employs a majority of the workforce. In 2012, Kenya launched the $25.5 billion Lamu Port South Sudan Ethiopia Corridor project.

How Do We Measure Economic Freedom?
See page 471 for an explanation of the methodology or visit the *Index* Web site at *heritage.org/index*.

Economic Freedom Score

Freedom Trend

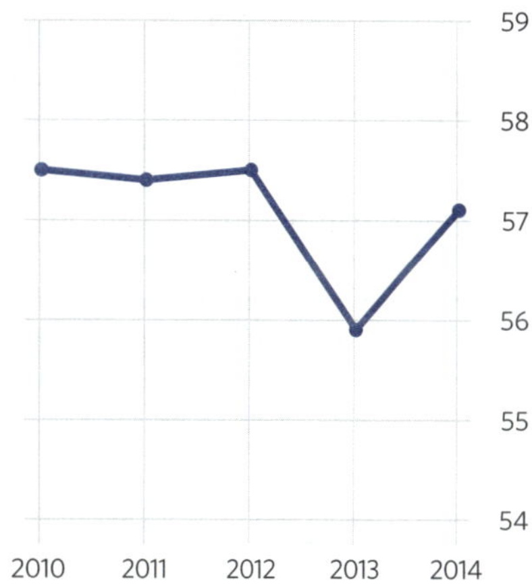

Country Comparisons

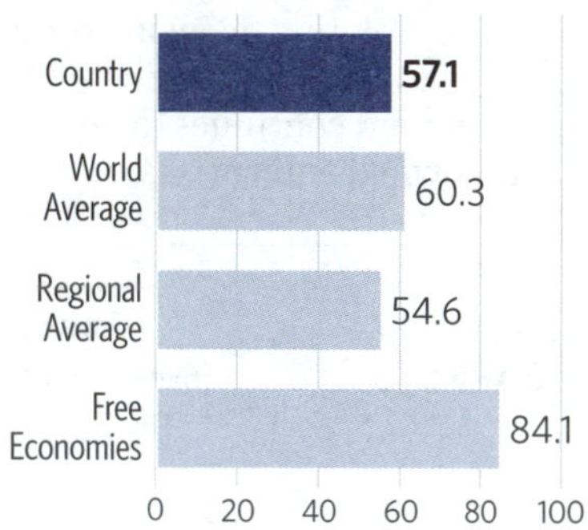

Quick Facts

Population: 42.1 million
GDP (PPP): $75.9 billion
4.7% growth in 2012
5-year compound annual growth 3.8%
$1,802 per capita
Unemployment: 40.0% (2008)
Inflation (CPI): 9.4%
FDI Inflow: $258.6 million
Public Debt: 48.2% of GDP

2012 data unless otherwise noted.
Data compiled as of September 2013.

KENYA (continued)

THE TEN ECONOMIC FREEDOMS

RULE OF LAW

	Score	Rank	1-Year Change
Property Rights	30.0	93rd	0
Freedom from Corruption	21.0	155th	-1.0

Kenya's 2010 constitution provides for increased accountability and transparency to combat pervasive corruption, but no top officials have been successfully prosecuted for corruption since 2002. The police, the judiciary, and the Ministry of Defense have been identified as some of the country's most corrupt institutions. Although the judiciary is independent, the courts are understaffed and underfinanced, leading to delays.

GOVERNMENT SIZE

	Score	Rank	1-Year Change
Fiscal Freedom	78.0	104th	+0.5
Government Spending	74.6	72nd	+1.1

The top individual income and corporate tax rates are 30 percent. Other taxes include a value-added tax (VAT) and a tax on interest. The overall tax burden is equal to 20.1 percent of gross domestic income. Government spending amounts to 29 percent of the domestic economy. Public debt has edged down to 48 percent of GDP. The new government has focused on capital gains tax enforcement to boost revenue.

REGULATORY EFFICIENCY

	Score	Rank	1-Year Change
Business Freedom	55.8	133rd	-2.2
Labor Freedom	64.0	81st	+6.9
Monetary Freedom	74.9	107th	+1.1

The business start-up process takes 10 procedures, and no minimum capital is required. However, completing licensing requirements takes more than 100 days and costs about twice the level of average annual income. Much of the labor force is employed in the public sector. The government continues to regulate prices through subsidies, agricultural marketing boards, and state-owned enterprises.

OPEN MARKETS

	Score	Rank	1-Year Change
Trade Freedom	72.8	113th	+6.1
Investment Freedom	50.0	109th	0
Financial Freedom	50.0	69th	0

Kenya's average tariff rate is 6.1 percent. In general, laws do not discriminate against foreign investors, but new investment is screened by the government. The financial sector remains relatively stable. Non-performing loans, particularly from state-owned banks to state-owned enterprises, have been declining. About 20 percent of the adult population has bank accounts and access to formal financial services. Capital markets are relatively small.

Long-Term Score Change (since 1995)

RULE OF LAW		GOVERNMENT SIZE		REGULATORY EFFICIENCY		OPEN MARKETS	
Property Rights	-20.0	Fiscal Freedom	+9.9	Business Freedom	+0.8	Trade Freedom	+19.2
Freedom from Corruption	-29.0	Government Spending	+11.6	Labor Freedom	+4.6	Investment Freedom	0
				Monetary Freedom	+24.5	Financial Freedom	0

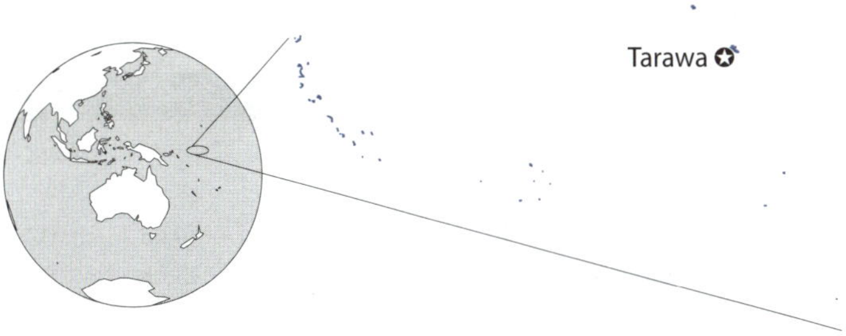

KIRIBATI

World Rank: **164** Regional Rank: **38**

Economic Freedom Score

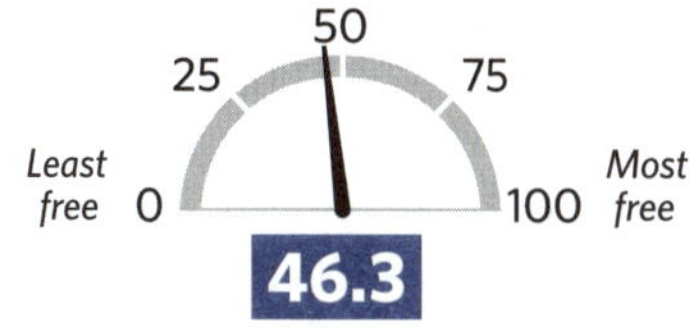

Kiribati's economic freedom score is 46.3, making its economy the 164th freest in the 2014 *Index*. Its score is 0.4 point higher than last year, reflecting modest improvements in monetary freedom, labor freedom, and fiscal freedom that outweigh declines in business freedom and freedom from corruption. Kiribati is ranked 38th out of 42 countries in the Asia–Pacific region, and its overall score is below the world and regional averages.

Kiribati was first graded in the 2009 *Index*, and its economic freedom has advanced since then by less than 1 point. Score increases have occurred in only two of the 10 economic freedoms, including a gain of nearly 30 points in fiscal freedom. Considered a "repressed" economy throughout its history in the *Index*, Kiribati recorded its highest economic freedom score in 2012.

Kiribati's public sector accounts for two-thirds of formal employment and about half of GDP. Only a small proportion of the total labor force is employed on salaries; the rest work in subsistence farming or fishing. The economy relies heavily on foreign assistance and remittances. Progress in decentralizing economic activity away from the main islands has been very limited. The financial sector remains underdeveloped, and much of the population lacks formal access to banking services.

BACKGROUND: The Pacific archipelago of Kiribati gained its independence from Britain in 1979 and is a democracy. President Anote Tong was elected to a third and final term in January 2012. Kiribati was once rich in phosphates and highly dependent on mining, but deposits were exhausted in 1979. Today, it depends on a $500 million Revenue Equalization Reserve Fund created with the profits from phosphates earnings, as well as foreign assistance, remittances from overseas, sale of fishing licenses, exports of fish and coconuts, and tourism. Crippling algae in the corals surrounding Kiribati seriously threaten the fishing industry, and preservation of the coral ecosystem, the South Pacific's largest marine reserve, continues to be a priority.

Freedom Trend

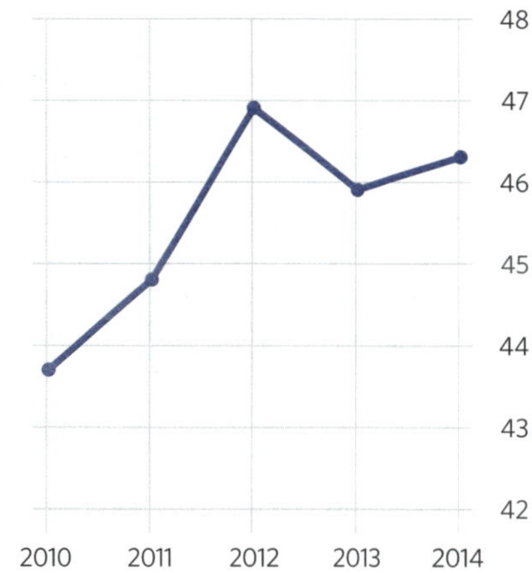

Country Comparisons

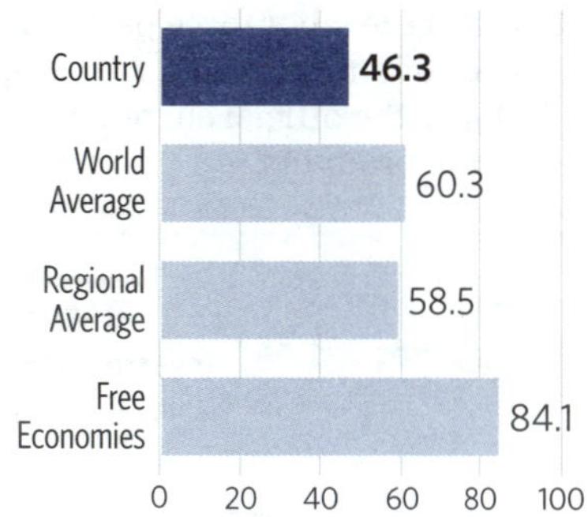

Quick Facts

Population: 0.1 million
GDP (PPP): $0.6 billion
2.5% growth in 2012
5-year compound annual growth 0.3%
$5,973 per capita
Unemployment: n/a
Inflation (CPI): 2.0%
FDI Inflow: –$1.7 million
Public Debt: 10.0% of GDP

2012 data unless otherwise noted.
Data compiled as of September 2013.

How Do We Measure Economic Freedom?
See page 471 for an explanation of the methodology or visit the *Index* Web site at *heritage.org/index*.

THE TEN ECONOMIC FREEDOMS

Score ■ Country | World Average

RULE OF LAW

	Score	Rank	1-Year Change
Property Rights	30.0	93rd	0
Freedom from Corruption	29.2	108th	-1.8

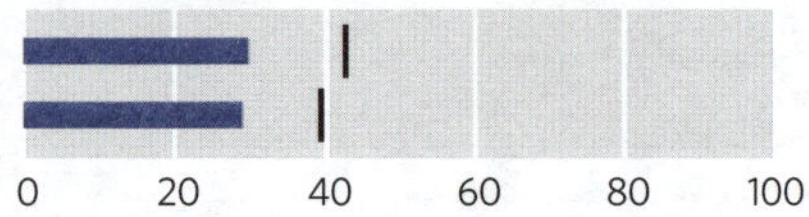

Official corruption and abuse are serious problems, and international donors have demanded improved governance and transparency. The judicial system is modeled on English common law and provides adequate due process rights, although the rule of law remains uneven. Traditional custom permits corporal punishment. Contracts are weakly enforced, and courts are relatively inexperienced in commercial litigation.

GOVERNMENT SIZE

	Score	Rank	1-Year Change
Fiscal Freedom	71.4	133rd	+0.2
Government Spending	0.0	177th	0

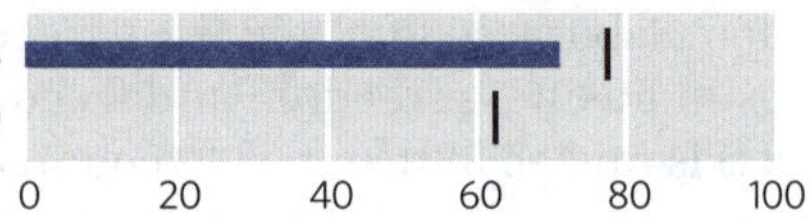

The top individual income and corporate tax rates are 35 percent. Taxation remains erratic and poorly enforced among Kiribati's 32 islands. The overall tax burden is 20.2 percent of gross domestic income. Government expenditures make up a sizable portion of the domestic economy at 92 percent of GDP. Public debt remained low at 10 percent of GDP in the most recent year.

REGULATORY EFFICIENCY

	Score	Rank	1-Year Change
Business Freedom	57.0	129th	-2.2
Labor Freedom	83.6	17th	+5.1
Monetary Freedom	81.3	18th	+2.9

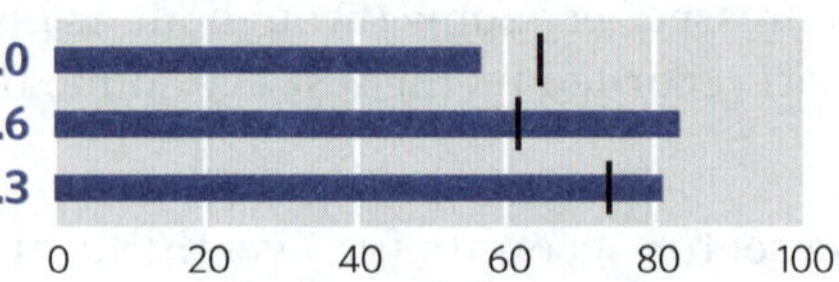

The costs of launching a business and completing licensing requirements remain high. A small share of the labor force participates in the formal economy, and the public sector is the major source of employment. Although monetary instability is mitigated by use of the Australian dollar as the official currency, the government funds price-distorting subsidies for some agricultural products.

OPEN MARKETS

	Score	Rank	1-Year Change
Trade Freedom	55.4	168th	0
Investment Freedom	25.0	159th	0
Financial Freedom	30.0	132nd	0

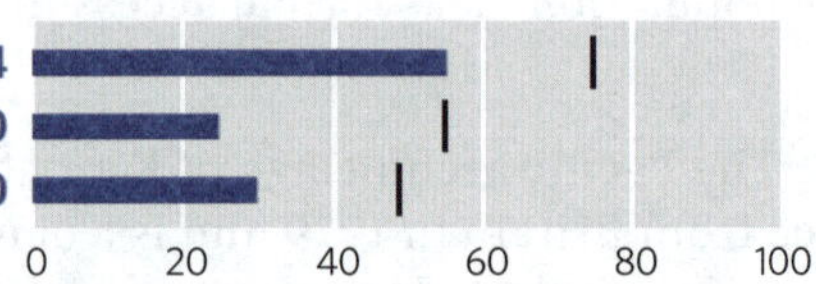

The average tariff rate was 17.3 percent as of 2006. Tariffs have been a significant source of revenue. New foreign investment may be subject to government screening. The financial sector remains underdeveloped, leaving much of the population without formal access to banking services. Constrained access to financing severely impedes entrepreneurial activity and private-sector development.

Long-Term Score Change (since 2009)

RULE OF LAW		GOVERNMENT SIZE		REGULATORY EFFICIENCY		OPEN MARKETS	
Property Rights	0	Fiscal Freedom	+29.3	Business Freedom	-5.5	Trade Freedom	+0.4
Freedom from Corruption	-3.8	Government Spending	0	Labor Freedom	-2.1	Investment Freedom	-5.0
				Monetary Freedom	-7.4	Financial Freedom	0

NORTH KOREA

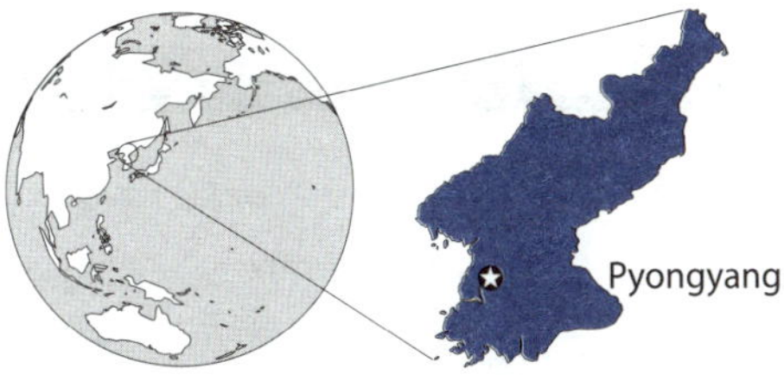

World Rank: 178 | **Regional Rank: 42**

Economic Freedom Score

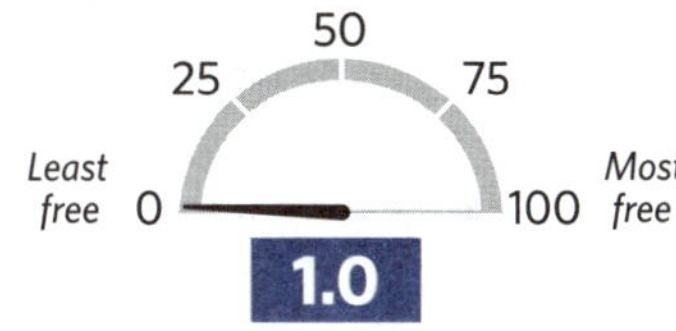

North Korea remains isolated from most of the rest of the world. Data collection is extremely challenging, and reported statistics on the economy remain largely speculative, requiring careful evaluation. North Korea's economic freedom score of 1.0 is 0.5 point lower than last year due to a worsened rating for freedom from corruption.

Over the 20-year history of the *Index*, North Korea has remained an unreformed and essentially closed dictatorial state. Despite experimenting with a few market reforms, the world's most repressed economy adheres firmly to a system of state command and control that upholds the regime's longstanding *songun* ("military first") policy. Every aspect of economic activity is tightly controlled by the Communist Party. The state-run rationing system has deteriorated significantly in recent years. The North Korean economy has been rated the least free throughout the history of the *Index*.

North Korea may be attempting to open its economy slightly by encouraging limited foreign direct investment, but the dominant military establishment and ongoing leadership transition make any near-term substantial changes unlikely. Normal foreign trade is minimal, with China and South Korea being the most important trading partners.

BACKGROUND: The death of Kim Jong-il in 2011 and the ascent of the Western-educated Kim Jong-un generated predictions that North Korea would implement political and economic reforms while moderating its threatening foreign policy. Although the new leader displayed a change in style, he has maintained Pyongyang's aggressive rhetoric, international provocations, and resistance to market-based reforms. North Korea continues to conduct nuclear and missile tests in violation of U.N. Security Council resolutions and has threatened nuclear attacks on the United States and its allies. Pyongyang has typically escalated, then lowered tensions in attempts to garner diplomatic and economic benefits. The Obama Administration, along with South Korea and Japan, has expressed unwillingness to resume negotiations without tangible signs of change in North Korean policy.

How Do We Measure Economic Freedom?
See page 471 for an explanation of the methodology or visit the *Index* Web site at *heritage.org/index*.

Freedom Trend

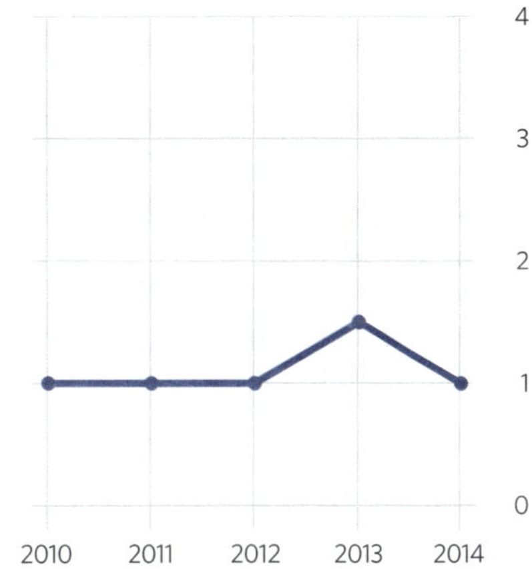

Country Comparisons

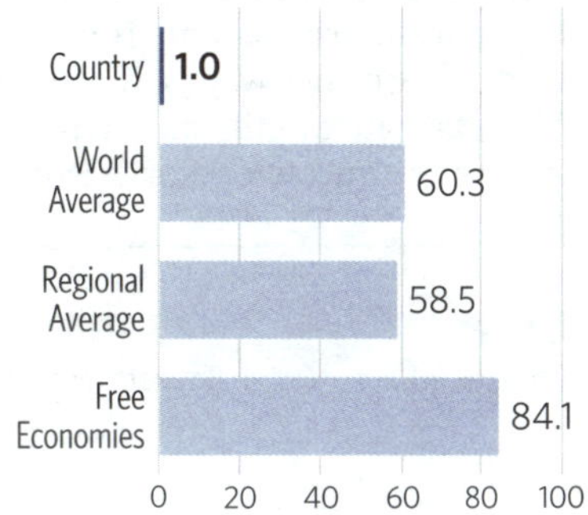

Quick Facts

Population: 24.7 million
GDP (PPP): $40.0 billion (2011)
0.8% growth in 2011
5-year compound annual growth n/a
$1,800 per capita (2011)
Unemployment: n/a
Inflation (CPI): n/a
FDI Inflow: $79.0 million
Public Debt: n/a

2012 data unless otherwise noted.
Data compiled as of September 2013.

NORTH KOREA (continued)

THE TEN ECONOMIC FREEDOMS

		Score	Rank	1-Year Change
RULE OF LAW	Property Rights	5.0	179th	0
	Freedom from Corruption	5.0	184th	-5.0

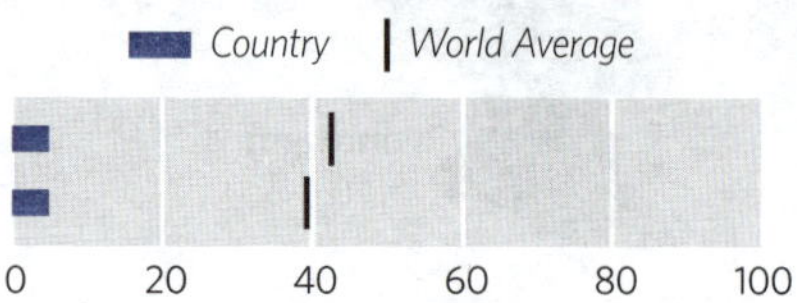

Corruption is endemic at every level of the state and economy. A modern judicial system does not exist. The Workers' Party, the Korean People's Army, and members of the cabinet run companies that compete to earn foreign exchange. Property rights are not guaranteed. Almost all property belongs to the state, and government control extends even to chattel property (domestically produced goods and all imports and exports).

		Score	Rank	1-Year Change
GOVERNMENT SIZE	Fiscal Freedom	0.0	183rd	0
	Government Spending	0.0	177th	0

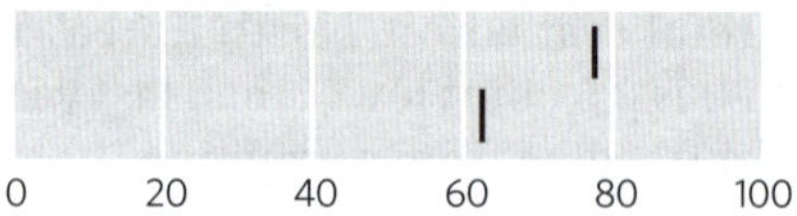

No effective tax system is in place. The government commands and dictates almost every part of the economy. It sets production levels for most products, and state-owned industries account for nearly all GDP. The state directs all significant economic activity. Large military spending further drains scarce resources. Despite the state's attempts to crack down on them, black markets have grown.

		Score	Rank	1-Year Change
REGULATORY EFFICIENCY	Business Freedom	0.0	184th	0
	Labor Freedom	0.0	184th	0
	Monetary Freedom	0.0	183rd	0

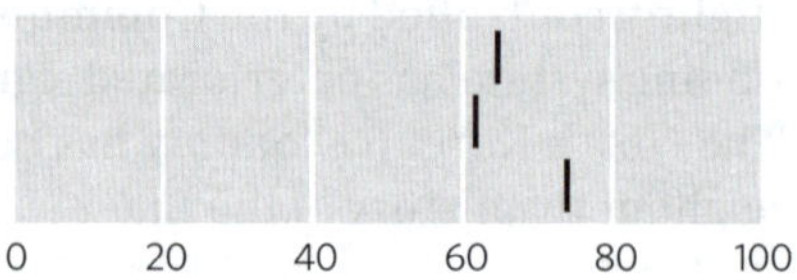

The state continues to regulate the economy heavily through central planning and control. Entrepreneurial activity remains virtually impossible. As the main source of employment, the state determines wages. It also tightly controls the labor market and the movement of people. Monetary instability and hyperinflation stemming from the botched currency revaluation in 2009 continue, with North Koreans preferring to conduct transactions using Chinese yuan.

		Score	Rank	1-Year Change
OPEN MARKETS	Trade Freedom	0.0	180th	0
	Investment Freedom	0.0	178th	0
	Financial Freedom	0.0	181st	0

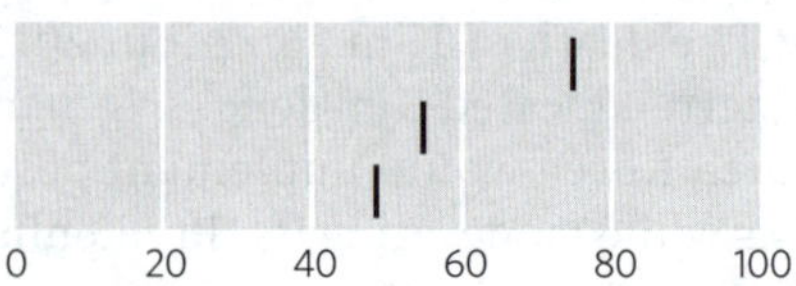

North Korea's citizens are highly isolated from other countries. International trade and investment are tightly controlled by the government. Limited foreign participation is allowed in the economy through special economic zones where investment is approved on a case-by-case basis. The financial sector is firmly controlled by the state.

Long-Term Score Change (since 1995)

RULE OF LAW		GOVERNMENT SIZE		REGULATORY EFFICIENCY		OPEN MARKETS	
Property Rights	-5.0	Fiscal Freedom	0	Business Freedom	-40.0	Trade Freedom	0
Freedom from Corruption	-5.0	Government Spending	0	Labor Freedom	0	Investment Freedom	-10.0
				Monetary Freedom	0	Financial Freedom	-10.0

SOUTH KOREA

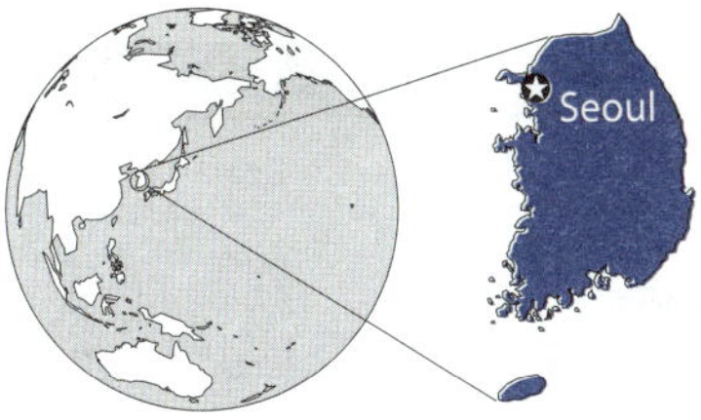

World Rank: **31** | Regional Rank: **8**

Economic Freedom Score

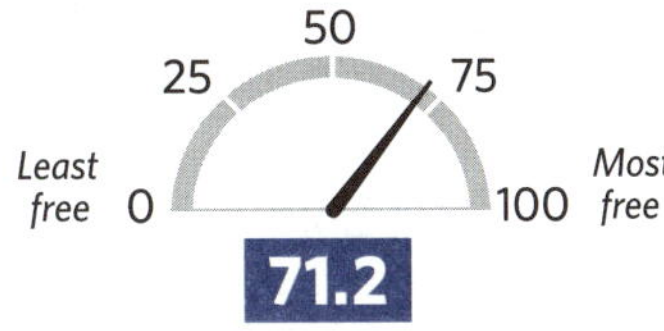

South Korea's economic freedom score is 71.2, making its economy the 31st freest in the 2014 *Index*. Its score is 0.9 point higher than last year, with improvements in financial freedom and monetary freedom outweighing modest declines in business freedom, labor freedom, and fiscal freedom. South Korea is ranked 8th out of 42 countries in the Asia–Pacific region.

Over the 20-year history of the *Index*, South Korea's economic freedom has been largely stagnant. Notable gains in market openness, which measures trade freedom, investment freedom, and financial freedom, have been undercut by declines in property rights, freedom from corruption, and the management of public spending. South Korea's economy, rated "moderately free" through most of the history of the *Index*, has advanced to "mostly free" in the past two years.

A dynamic private sector, reinforced by a well-educated labor force and high capacity for innovation, has capitalized on openness to global trade and investment. A sound legal framework is in place, although corruption continues to undermine equity and trust in government. South Korea's long-term economic dynamism hinges on the outcome of ongoing debates about the proper scope of government in the free market and welfare policies.

BACKGROUND: Conservative President Park Geun-hye assumed office in February 2013 vowing a new approach to North Korea. Her "trustpolitik" strategy balances enhancing South Korean defense capabilities to deter North Korean attacks with a willingness to engage Pyongyang in conditional, reciprocal diplomacy. North Korea has shown no sign of accepting Park's outreach without massive unconditional benefits. Her election, however, turned more on economic issues. Park pledged a mixture of business-friendly economic policies to jump-start the economy and increased government "social welfarism" to redress economic disparities. South Korea, the world's 15th-largest economy, has enjoyed decades of impressive economic growth and is a world leader in electronics, telecommunications, automobile production, and shipbuilding.

How Do We Measure Economic Freedom?
See page 471 for an explanation of the methodology or visit the *Index* Web site at *heritage.org/index*.

Freedom Trend

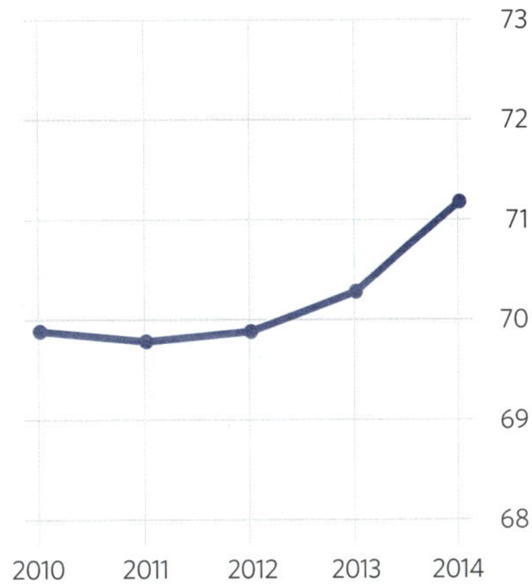

Country Comparisons

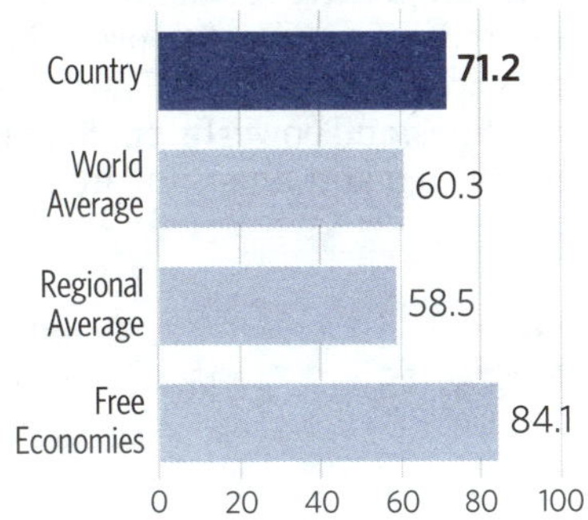

Quick Facts

Population: 50.0 million
GDP (PPP): $1.6 trillion
2.0% growth in 2012
5-year compound annual growth 2.9%
$32,272 per capita
Unemployment: 3.3%
Inflation (CPI): 2.2%
FDI Inflow: $9.9 billion
Public Debt: 33.7% of GDP

2012 data unless otherwise noted. Data compiled as of September 2013.

THE TEN ECONOMIC FREEDOMS

		Score	Rank	1-Year Change
RULE OF LAW	Property Rights	70.0	27th	0
	Freedom from Corruption	54.0	42nd	0

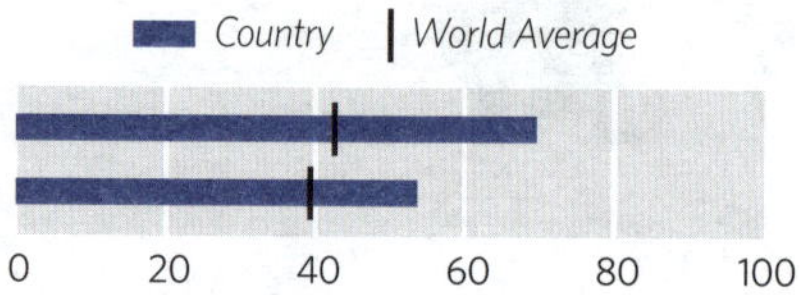

Despite the political system's overall health, bribery, influence peddling, and extortion remain present in politics, business, and everyday life. In 2012, the speaker of South Korea's National Assembly resigned after allegations surfaced that he had obtained his post through bribery. A well-functioning modern legal framework ensures strong protection of private property rights. The rule of law is effective, and the judicial system is efficient.

		Score	Rank	1-Year Change
GOVERNMENT SIZE	Fiscal Freedom	72.6	128th	-0.4
	Government Spending	72.6	78th	-0.2

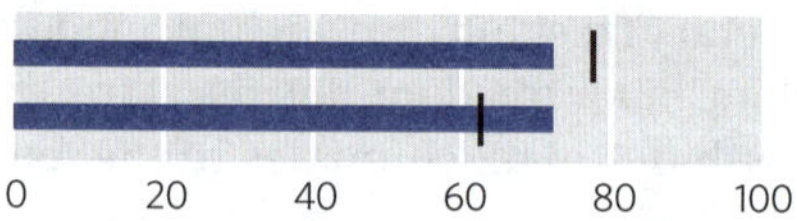

The top individual income tax rate is 35 percent, and the top corporate tax rate is 22 percent. A 10 percent surtax on individual and corporate rates and a value-added tax (VAT) bring the overall tax burden to 25.9 percent of GDP. Government spending is equivalent to 30.2 percent of total domestic output. The budget balance has been in small surplus, and public debt remains below 35 percent of GDP.

		Score	Rank	1-Year Change
REGULATORY EFFICIENCY	Business Freedom	92.8	8th	-0.8
	Labor Freedom	47.8	147th	-0.9
	Monetary Freedom	79.6	39th	+1.7

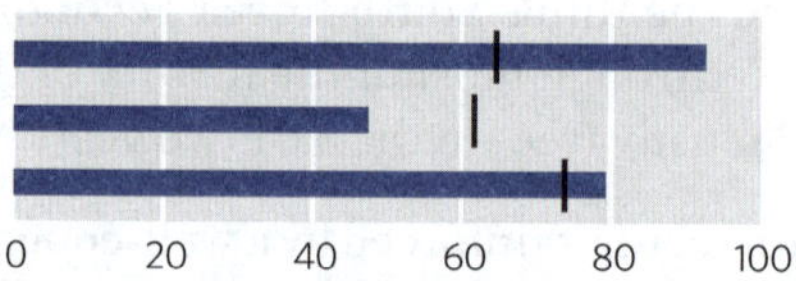

The competitive regulatory framework facilitates business formation and innovation. Launching a company takes five procedures, and no minimum capital is required. Bankruptcy proceedings are relatively easy. The labor market remains dynamic, but there are lingering regulatory rigidities, and powerful trade unions add to the cost of conducting business. Monetary stability has been maintained, and inflationary pressures have eased.

		Score	Rank	1-Year Change
OPEN MARKETS	Trade Freedom	72.6	117th	0
	Investment Freedom	70.0	46th	0
	Financial Freedom	80.0	4th	+10.0

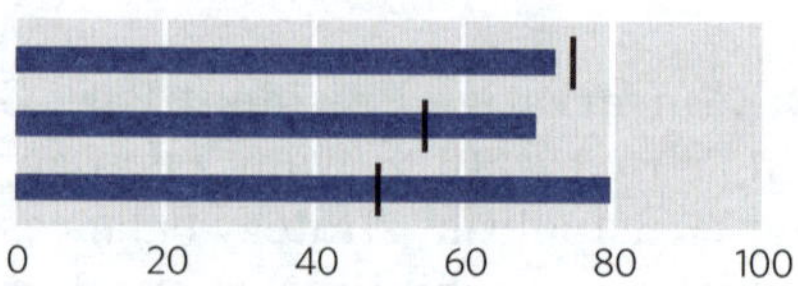

South Korea's average tariff rate is 8.7 percent. The country has completed several free trade agreements and is pursuing agreements with Australia, China, and Canada. Foreign ownership in some sectors of the economy is capped at different levels. The financial sector is sophisticated and well developed, with its assets valued at about nine times GDP. Financial institutions have gained more autonomy from the state, ensuring greater market competition.

Long-Term Score Change (since 1995)

RULE OF LAW		GOVERNMENT SIZE		REGULATORY EFFICIENCY		OPEN MARKETS	
Property Rights	-20.0	Fiscal Freedom	+9.3	Business Freedom	+22.8	Trade Freedom	+3.4
Freedom from Corruption	-16.0	Government Spending	-13.0	Labor Freedom	-8.8	Investment Freedom	+20.0
				Monetary Freedom	-0.6	Financial Freedom	+10.0

KOSOVO

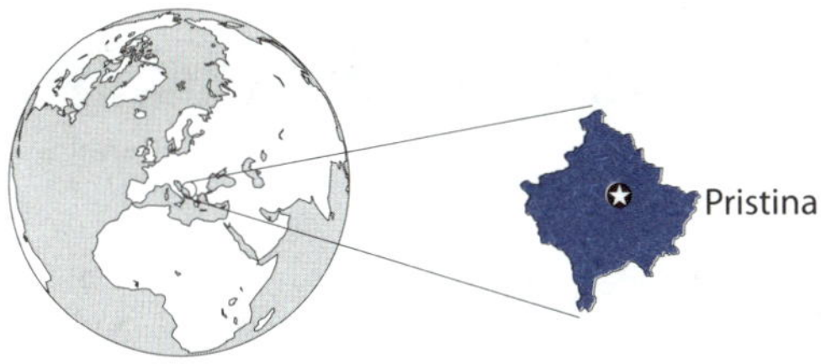

World Rank: Not Ranked   Regional Rank: Not Ranked

Economic Freedom Score

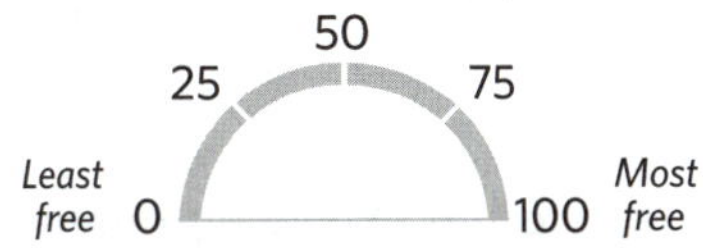

This economy is not graded

Freedom Trend

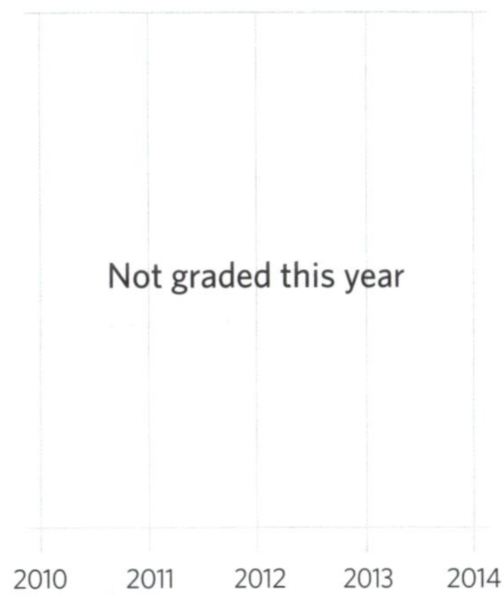

Kosovo's economy is not graded in the 2014 *Index* due to insufficient data. Those facets of economic freedom for which data are available have been individually scored. Kosovo will receive an overall economic freedom score and ranking in future editions as more information becomes available.

Kosovo has been transitioning from a centrally planned economy to a more market-based economy. Privatizing many of its state-owned assets, the young nation has opened its borders to global trade and investment, with services and manufacturing accounting for a large majority of economic activity. Other bold reforms have included implementation of competitively low tax rates, which has contributed to the gradual emergence of entrepreneurial dynamism.

Despite this progress, institutional capacity remains weak, and greater political commitment is needed to implement the significant reforms necessary to jump-start the economy. Weak protection of property rights and widespread corruption discourage vibrant entrepreneurial activity, undermining the rule of law. The judiciary is subject to political interference and lacks the resources to prosecute complex crimes. Intrusive bureaucracy and costly registration procedures reflect a history of central planning.

BACKGROUND: In the late 1990s, a NATO intervention stopped a Serb-initiated campaign of ethnic cleansing against Kosovo Albanians. After Serbian forces left, Kosovo was administered by the United Nations until declaring full independence in 2008. Today, approximately 5,000 international soldiers are based in Kosovo as part of a NATO-led peacekeeping mission. In early 2013, Kosovo signed an agreement aimed at normalization of relations with Serbia. Kosovo has been transitioning slowly to a market-based economy, but huge economic challenges remain. The formal-sector unemployment rate is around 45 percent. Kosovo is a member of the World Bank, the International Monetary Fund, and the Central Europe Free Trade Area and has long-term ambitions of joining NATO and the European Union.

Country Comparisons

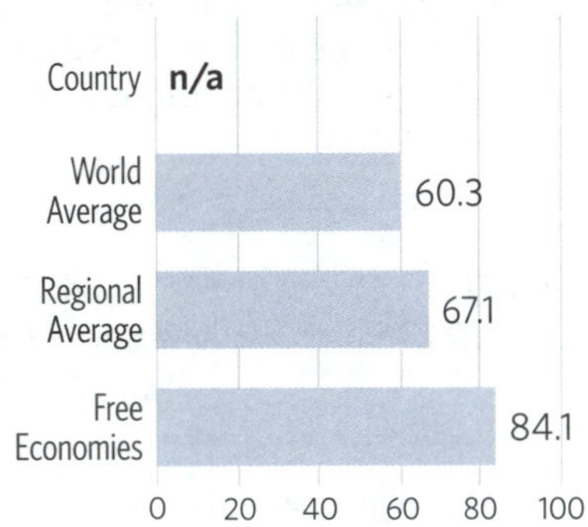

Quick Facts

Population: 1.8 million

GDP (PPP): $13.4 billion

2.1% growth in 2012

5-year compound annual growth 4.1%

$7,427 per capita

Unemployment: 45.3% (2011)

Inflation (CPI): 2.5%

FDI Inflow: $293.2 million

Public Debt: 5.5% of GDP (2011)

2012 data unless otherwise noted.
Data compiled as of September 2013.

How Do We Measure Economic Freedom?
See page 471 for an explanation of the methodology or visit the *Index* Web site at *heritage.org/index*.

THE TEN ECONOMIC FREEDOMS

RULE OF LAW

	Score	Rank	1-Year Change
Property Rights	30.0	93rd	0
Freedom from Corruption	28.6	114th	-0.4

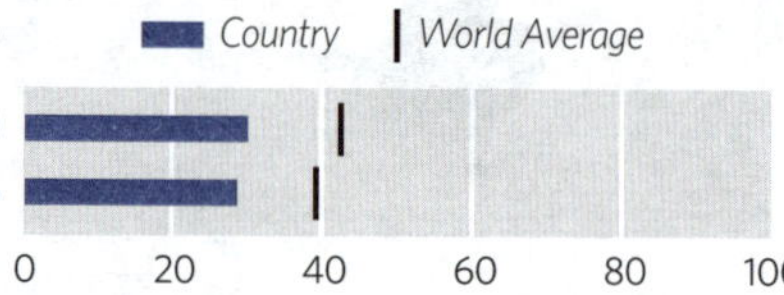

A steadily expanding bureaucracy increases opportunities for corruption, which is widespread in many areas of government including the judiciary and law enforcement. Despite reforms in 2012 that improved judicial independence, the courts are understaffed, case backlogs remain high, and enforcement of judgments is weak.

GOVERNMENT SIZE

	Score	Rank	1-Year Change
Fiscal Freedom	92.7	21st	-0.8
Government Spending	73.0	77th	0

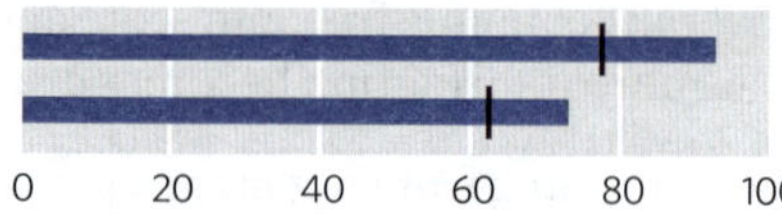

The top individual income and corporate tax rates are 10 percent. Other taxes include a value-added tax (VAT) and a property tax. The overall tax burden is 23.1 percent of gross domestic income. Government spending is 30 percent of GDP. The budget is still dependent on IMF support, aid, and diaspora remittances. Public debt remains below 10 percent of the domestic economy.

REGULATORY EFFICIENCY

	Score	Rank	1-Year Change
Business Freedom	58.1	124th	+5.7
Labor Freedom	71.3	61st	-6.4
Monetary Freedom	72.7	126th	n/a

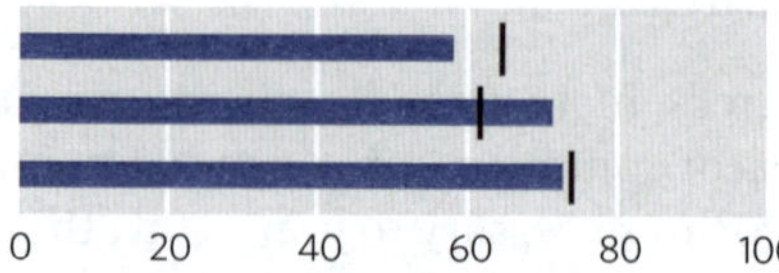

Incorporating a business takes 30 days on average, and no minimum capital is required. Despite some progress, completing licensing requirements still costs almost five times the level of average annual income and takes over three months. Agricultural and energy-related subsidies by the government and international donors amount to more than one-third of GDP.

OPEN MARKETS

	Score	Rank	1-Year Change
Trade Freedom	n/a	—	n/a
Investment Freedom	65.0	68th	0
Financial Freedom	n/a	—	n/a

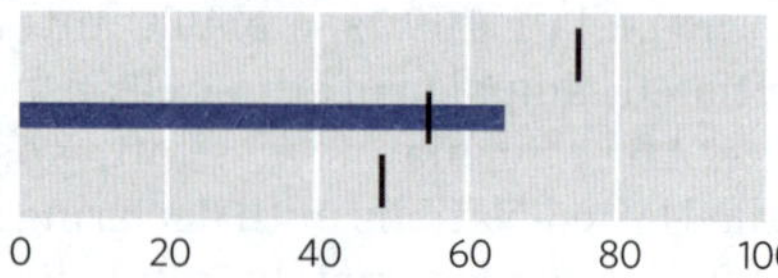

Most goods originating from outside the Central European Free Trade Agreement region are subject to a 10 percent tariff. There are few official barriers to foreign investment, but the legal and regulatory systems are complex. The financial system continues to evolve, with the level of financial intermediation gradually increasing. The banking sector remains relatively stable and well capitalized.

Long-Term Score Change: n/a

RULE OF LAW		GOVERNMENT SIZE		REGULATORY EFFICIENCY		OPEN MARKETS	
Property Rights	n/a	Fiscal Freedom	n/a	Business Freedom	n/a	Trade Freedom	n/a
Freedom from Corruption	n/a	Government Spending	n/a	Labor Freedom	n/a	Investment Freedom	n/a
				Monetary Freedom	n/a	Financial Freedom	n/a

KUWAIT

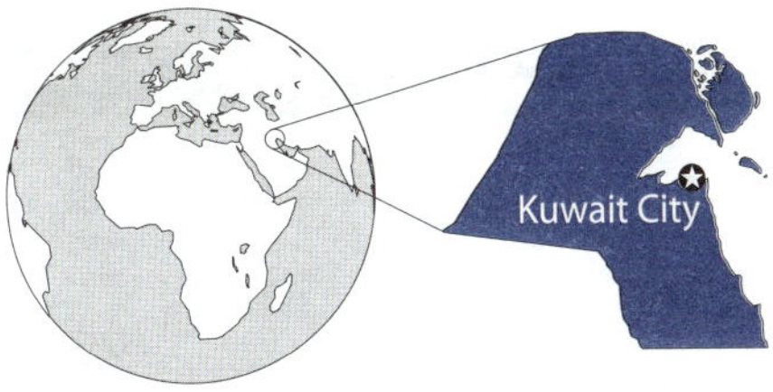

World Rank: **76** Regional Rank: **7**

Economic Freedom Score

Kuwait's economic freedom score is 62.3, making its economy the 76th freest in the 2014 *Index*. Its score is 0.8 point lower than last year, with small improvements in monetary freedom and labor freedom outweighed by declining scores for freedom from corruption, fiscal freedom, and the control of government spending. Kuwait is ranked 7th out of 15 countries in the Middle East/North Africa region.

Kuwait's economic freedom score has dropped by about 4 points over the 19 years it has been graded in the *Index*. Large score improvements in the categories of government spending and investment freedom have been offset by declines in seven other economic freedoms, including declines of over 20 points in property rights, freedom from corruption, and business freedom. Kuwait has been consistently ranked a "moderately free" economy, achieving its highest score in 1999.

Kuwait has benefited from open-market policies that facilitate global trade and investment flows. The country's scores for trade freedom and investment freedom have been above the world averages. High oil revenues, however, have delayed privatization and other deep structural reforms that would diversify the economy and help a more vibrant private sector to emerge.

BACKGROUND: Kuwait, one of the richest Arab nations, is a constitutional monarchy ruled by the al-Sabah dynasty. During the "Arab Spring" of 2011, young activists called for political reforms, and undocumented residents demanded citizenship and jobs. After Islamists scored major gains in parliamentary elections in February 2012, Amir Sabah al-Ahmad al-Jabr al-Sabah annulled the results and changed the election laws. This sparked protests and triggered a boycott of new elections in December 2012. The results of that election were annulled by the Constitutional Court, and in new balloting held in July 2013, pro-government Sunni candidates achieved a significant majority. Kuwait controls roughly 7 percent of the world's oil reserves. Oil accounts for nearly 50 percent of GDP and 95 percent of export revenues.

Freedom Trend

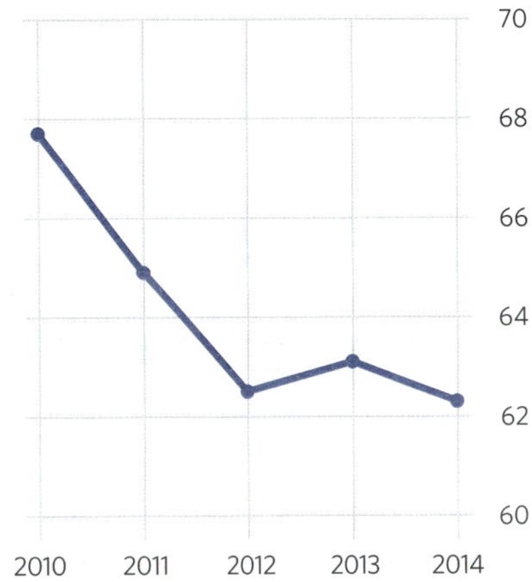

Country Comparisons

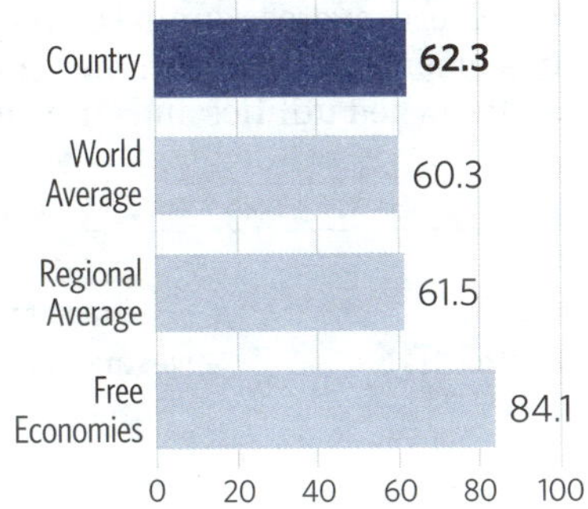

Quick Facts

Population: 3.8 million
GDP (PPP): $151.0 billion
5.1% growth in 2012
5-year compound annual growth 0.8%
$39,889 per capita
Unemployment: 2.1%
Inflation (CPI): 2.9%
FDI Inflow: $1.9 billion
Public Debt: 7.3% of GDP

2012 data unless otherwise noted.
Data compiled as of September 2013.

How Do We Measure Economic Freedom?
See page 471 for an explanation of the methodology or visit the *Index* Web site at *heritage.org/index.*

THE TEN ECONOMIC FREEDOMS

Score ▬ Country | World Average

RULE OF LAW

	Score	Rank	1-Year Change
Property Rights	50.0	53rd	0
Freedom from Corruption	43.7	59th	-2.3

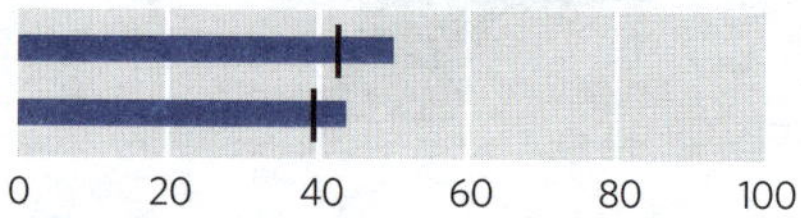

Corruption remains a dominant political issue, and although lawmakers have pressured the government to address the problem, the public prosecutor formally ended the state's inquiry into allegations in August 2011 that up to 18 members of parliament received large cash deposits into their personal bank accounts. The legal framework is not well developed, and the rule of law remains weak.

GOVERNMENT SIZE

	Score	Rank	1-Year Change
Fiscal Freedom	97.7	6th	-2.2
Government Spending	55.6	127th	-5.9

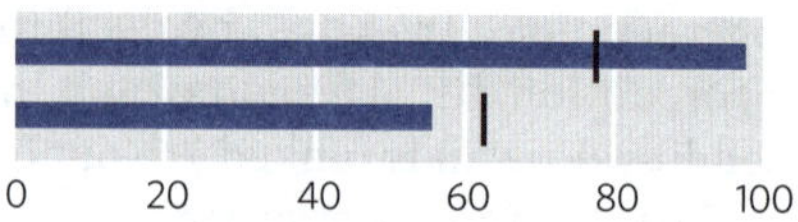

Kuwait has no individual income tax. Foreign-owned companies pay a 15 percent corporate tax on net profits, but there are exemptions for foreign investment. Most other revenue is collected from the state's sovereign wealth fund. The overall tax burden is less than 1 percent of GDP. Government expenditures are 39 percent of gross domestic output. Public debt is relatively low at about 7 percent of GDP.

REGULATORY EFFICIENCY

	Score	Rank	1-Year Change
Business Freedom	57.7	127th	0
Labor Freedom	63.6	83rd	+0.8
Monetary Freedom	73.2	121st	+1.6

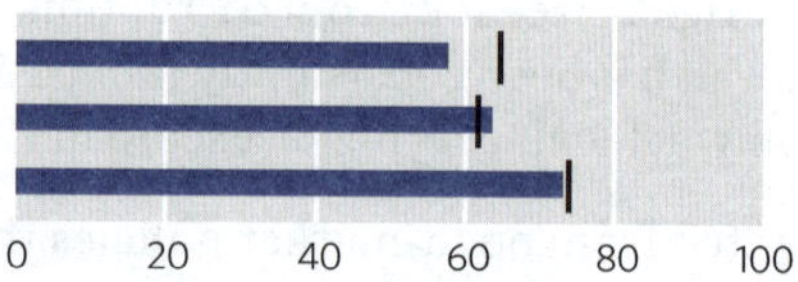

Starting a business takes about a month. Completing licensing requirements, which costs about the level of average annual income, faces bureaucratic hurdles. The labor market remains highly segmented. The government has an extensive system of subsidies and price controls through state-owned utilities and enterprises in an effort to keep a lid on overall inflation.

OPEN MARKETS

	Score	Rank	1-Year Change
Trade Freedom	76.7	89th	-0.1
Investment Freedom	55.0	96th	0
Financial Freedom	50.0	69th	0

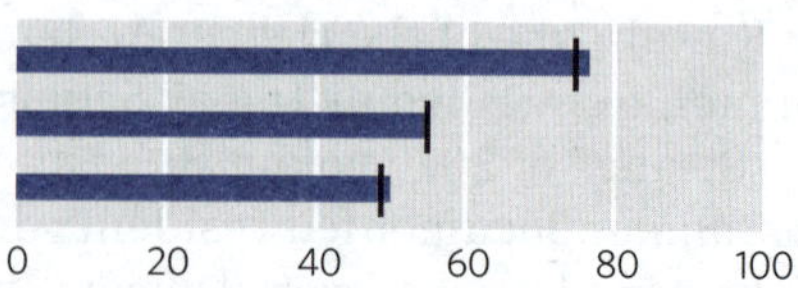

Kuwait's average tariff rate is 4.1 percent. There are additional restrictions on imported meat, used vehicles, and other products. Foreign ownership levels in some sectors of the economy are capped. The financial sector continues to evolve. With non-performing loans declining, the banking sector remains well capitalized. The central bank is not completely independent.

Long-Term Score Change (since 1996)

RULE OF LAW		GOVERNMENT SIZE		REGULATORY EFFICIENCY		OPEN MARKETS	
Property Rights	**-40.0**	Fiscal Freedom	**-2.2**	Business Freedom	**-27.3**	Trade Freedom	**-0.3**
Freedom from Corruption	**-26.3**	Government Spending	**+44.7**	Labor Freedom	**-16.6**	Investment Freedom	**+25.0**
				Monetary Freedom	**-8.5**	Financial Freedom	**0**

KYRGYZ REPUBLIC

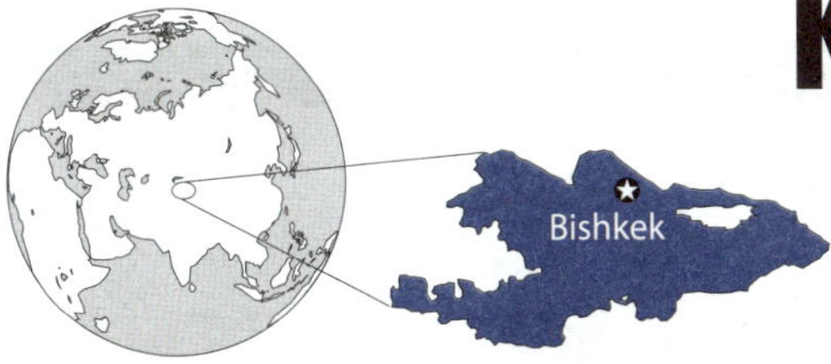

World Rank: 85 **Regional Rank: 15**

Economic Freedom Score

The Kyrgyz Republic's economic freedom score is 61.1, making its economy the 85th freest in the 2014 *Index*. Its score is 1.5 points better than last year, reflecting substantial advancements in investment freedom, monetary freedom, and the control of government spending. The Kyrgyz Republic is ranked 15th out of 42 countries in the Asia–Pacific region.

The Kyrgyz Republic was first graded in the 1998 *Index*, and its economic freedom has advanced since then by 9.3 points. Its overall score increase has been facilitated by improvements in six of the 10 economic freedoms, including gains of over 20 points in monetary freedom and fiscal freedom and gains of about 10 points in trade freedom and investment freedom. The Kyrgyz Republic has been mostly rated "moderately free" during the second half of its history in the *Index*.

The country has lagged, however, in promoting the effective rule of law. The judicial system remains vulnerable to political interference, and property rights are not strongly protected. Corruption continues to undermine enforcement of the rule of law and hampers prospects for long-term economic growth and development.

BACKGROUND: The Kyrgyz Republic is one of Central Asia's poorest and least stable countries. President Kurmanbek Bakiyev, ousted in April 2010 following violent unrest after a rise in fuel prices, was succeeded briefly by interim President Roza Otunbayeva. In October 2011, with Moscow's support, former Prime Minister Almazbek Atambayev was elected president with over 60 percent of the vote. Challenges include extremist threats, high levels of external debt, dependence on foreign aid, organized crime, and corruption. The country attracts strong foreign investment, and domestic demand is robust. The parliament voted in June 2013 to terminate U.S. military use of the Manas international airport by July 2014. This will eliminate a key geostrategic point for the movement of U.S. troops and supplies into and out of Afghanistan.

Freedom Trend

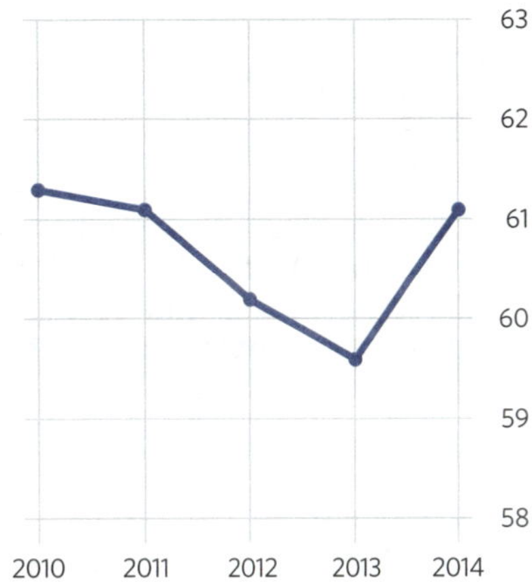

Country Comparisons

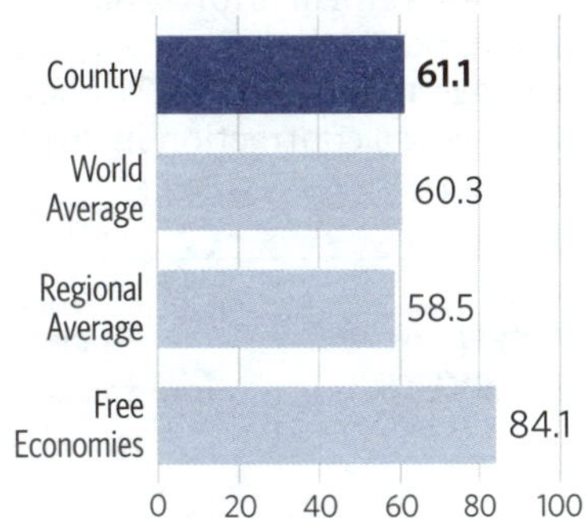

Quick Facts

Population: 5.6 million
GDP (PPP): $13.3 billion
-0.9% growth in 2012
5-year compound annual growth 3.0%
$2,376 per capita
Unemployment: 7.7%
Inflation (CPI): 2.8%
FDI Inflow: $372.2 million
Public Debt: 48.9% of GDP

2012 data unless otherwise noted.
Data compiled as of September 2013.

How Do We Measure Economic Freedom?
See page 471 for an explanation of the methodology or visit the *Index* Web site at *heritage.org/index.*

THE TEN ECONOMIC FREEDOMS

Legend: Country | World Average

RULE OF LAW

	Score	Rank	1-Year Change
Property Rights	20.0	139th	0
Freedom from Corruption	19.2	165th	-1.8

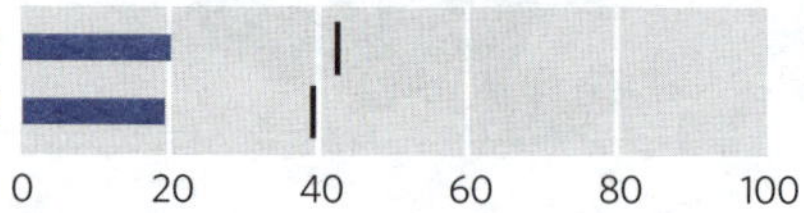

Corruption is pervasive from the family and associates of former President Bakiyev on down. In 2012, the former president's brother was due to stand trial for corruption but escaped from a clinic where he had supposedly been receiving treatment. Courts are largely unreformed, judges are often corrupt, and the legal framework is weak. Licensing, registration, and enforcement of contracts are prone to dispute.

GOVERNMENT SIZE

	Score	Rank	1-Year Change
Fiscal Freedom	94.6	15th	-0.2
Government Spending	60.2	119th	+3.8

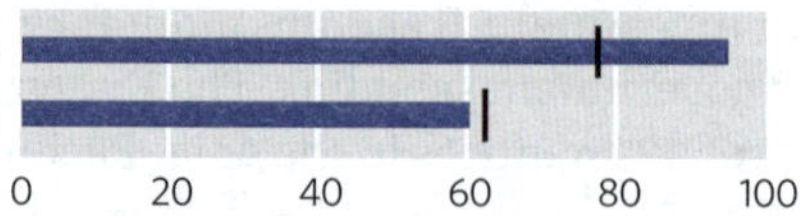

The individual income and corporate tax rates are a flat 10 percent. Other taxes include a value-added tax (VAT). The overall tax burden has reached 18.5 percent of gross domestic income. Government expenditures are 36 percent of GDP. Public debt is equivalent to slightly less than 50 percent of the domestic economy. A new aid package sponsored by Western countries, China, and Russia has boosted spending.

REGULATORY EFFICIENCY

	Score	Rank	1-Year Change
Business Freedom	74.2	58th	+1.0
Labor Freedom	83.8	15th	-4.8
Monetary Freedom	73.7	116th	+7.0

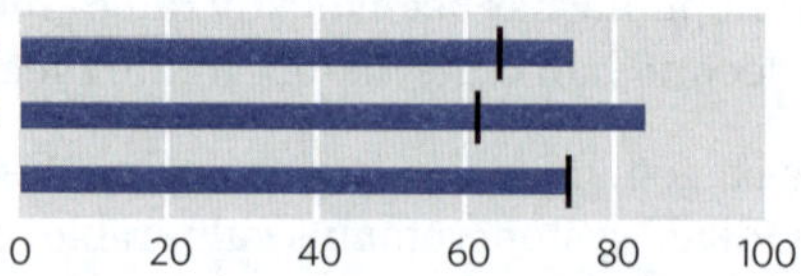

Despite reform efforts, bureaucratic impediments hamper private-sector production and investment. Obtaining necessary licenses takes over 140 days and costs more than the level of average annual income. The labor market remains inefficient. Monetary stability has improved following a contraction in 2012 caused by disruptions in gold production, but vulnerabilities remain.

OPEN MARKETS

	Score	Rank	1-Year Change
Trade Freedom	75.2	99th	-0.2
Investment Freedom	60.0	80th	+10.0
Financial Freedom	50.0	69th	0

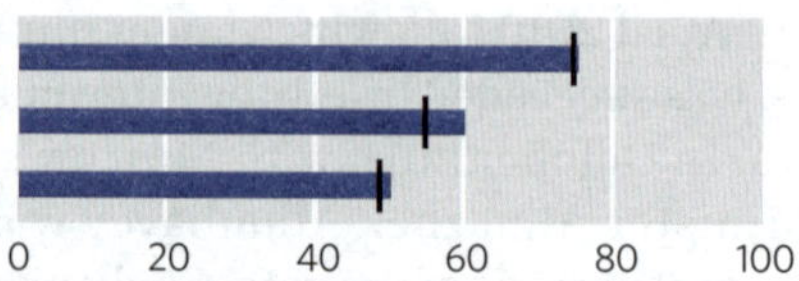

The average tariff rate is 2.4 percent. Importation of goods is expensive and time-consuming. Legal protections for investors may be difficult to enforce in the courts in a timely manner. The financial sector remains vulnerable to state interference, although the level of financial intermediation continues to increase. Some progress has been made in strengthening microfinance.

Long-Term Score Change (since 1998)

RULE OF LAW		GOVERNMENT SIZE		REGULATORY EFFICIENCY		OPEN MARKETS	
Property Rights	**-10.0**	Fiscal Freedom	**+22.3**	Business Freedom	**+19.2**	Trade Freedom	**+10.2**
Freedom from Corruption	**-10.8**	Government Spending	**-12.4**	Labor Freedom	**+19.0**	Investment Freedom	**+10.0**
				Monetary Freedom	**+32.7**	Financial Freedom	**0**

LAOS

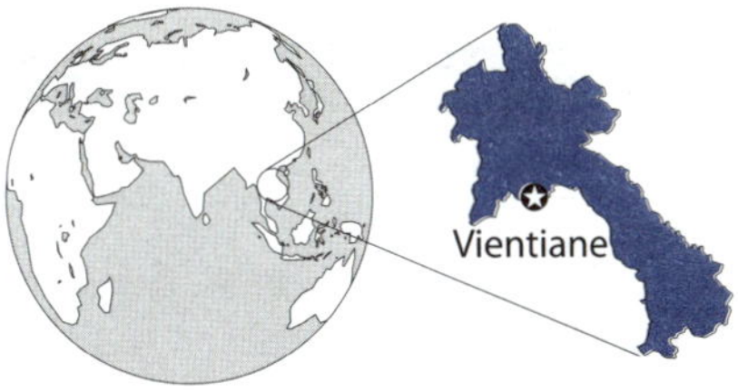

World Rank: **144** Regional Rank: **31**

Economic Freedom Score

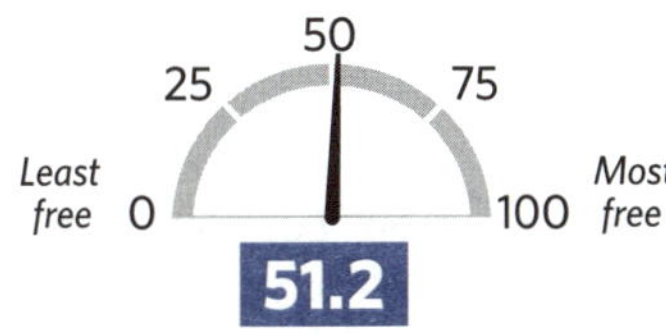

Laos's economic freedom score is 51.2, making its economy the 144th freest in the 2014 *Index*. Its overall score is 1.1 points higher than last year, with improvements in five of the 10 economic freedoms, including investment freedom, fiscal freedom, and monetary freedom, outweighing declines in business freedom and freedom from corruption. Laos is ranked 31st out of 42 countries in the Asia–Pacific region, and its overall score is below the world and regional averages.

Over the 19 years during which Laos has been graded in the *Index*, its economic freedom score has advanced by nearly 13 points. Its overall score improvement has been broad, occurring in seven of the 10 economic freedoms. Notable score gains have been recorded in fiscal freedom, business freedom, and investment freedom, scores for which have increased by over 20 points. Laos has been out of the ranks of the economically "repressed" since 2007.

Despite this progress, however, economic freedom in Laos is still held back by poor institutional development and the lack of much-needed economic reform. Protection of property rights and enforcement of the rule of law remain weak, and significant corruption burdens individuals and entrepreneurs.

BACKGROUND: Laos's Communist government, in power since 1975, devastated the economy in the early years of its rule. Slow liberalization, begun in 1986, has had limited success. Corruption is endemic, the law is applied erratically, and the country remains highly dependent on international aid. Basic human rights are heavily restricted. Seventy-five percent of the workforce is employed in subsistence farming. In 2013, following a 15-year negotiation process, Laos became a member of the World Trade Organization.

Freedom Trend

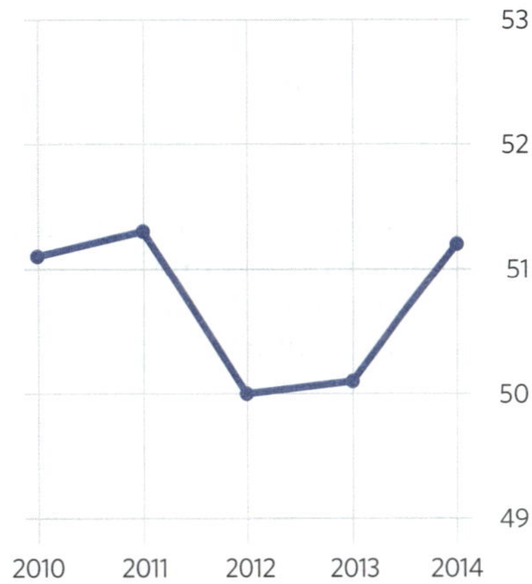

Country Comparisons

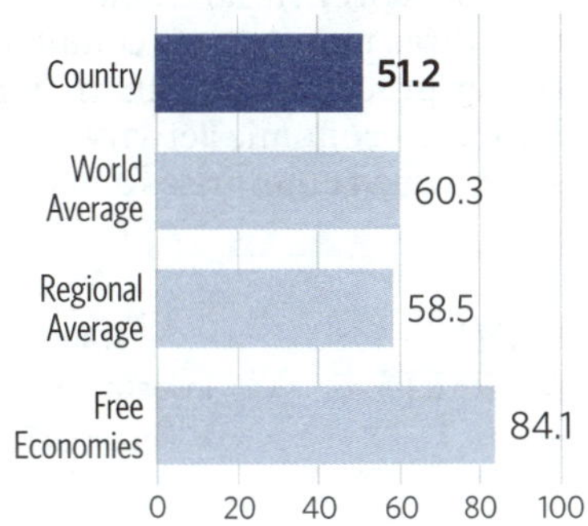

Quick Facts

Population: 6.4 million

GDP (PPP): $19.2 billion

8.3% growth in 2012

5-year compound annual growth 8.0%

$3,011 per capita

Unemployment: 2.5% (2009)

Inflation (CPI): 4.3%

FDI Inflow: $294.4 million

Public Debt: 53.1% of GDP

2012 data unless otherwise noted.
Data compiled as of September 2013.

How Do We Measure Economic Freedom?
See page 471 for an explanation of the methodology or visit the *Index* Web site at *heritage.org/index*.

THE TEN ECONOMIC FREEDOMS

RULE OF LAW

	Score	Rank	1-Year Change
Property Rights	15.0	159th	0
Freedom from Corruption	18.6	168th	-3.4

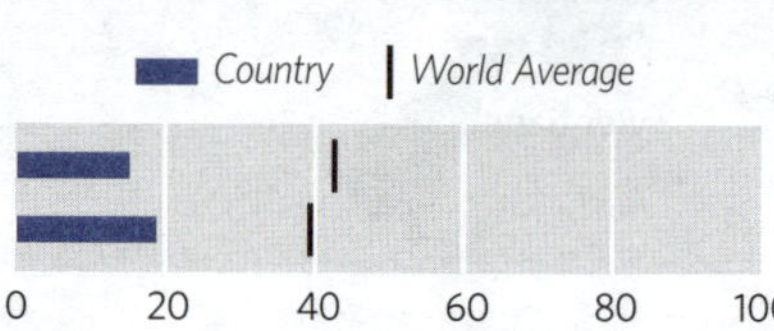

Government corruption is widespread. Anti-graft laws are rarely enforced, and government regulation of virtually every facet of life provides many opportunities for bribery. Senior government and military officials are frequently involved with Chinese and Vietnamese businessmen in commercial logging, mining, and other extractive enterprises. The judicial system is inefficient, and protections for property rights are not enforced effectively.

GOVERNMENT SIZE

	Score	Rank	1-Year Change
Fiscal Freedom	86.6	45th	+6.9
Government Spending	86.7	23rd	+0.9

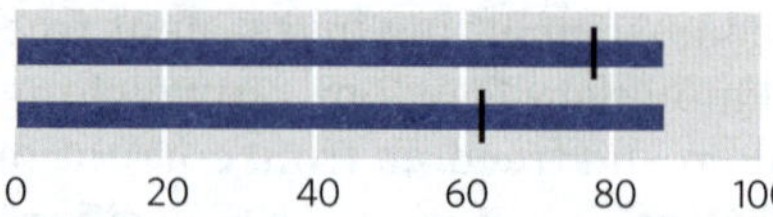

The top individual income and corporate tax rates have fallen to 24 percent. Other taxes include a vehicle tax and excise taxes. The overall tax burden is 13.7 percent of GDP. Overall government expenditures are 21 percent of the size of the economy. Public debt has dropped slightly to 53 percent of GDP.

REGULATORY EFFICIENCY

	Score	Rank	1-Year Change
Business Freedom	60.7	108th	-1.4
Labor Freedom	54.9	118th	+0.2
Monetary Freedom	75.5	90th	+2.5

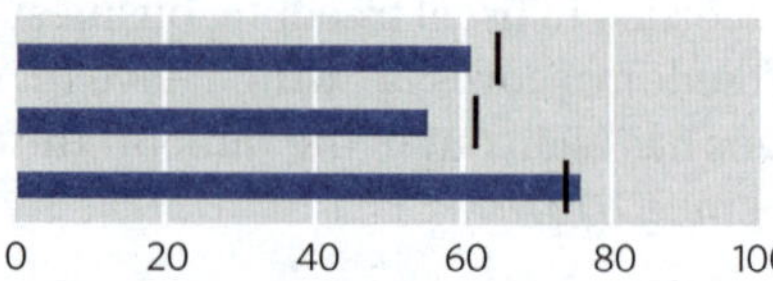

The entrepreneurial framework lacks transparency and efficiency. Starting a business takes over three months, and completing licensing requirements takes more than 100 days. Bankruptcy procedures are inefficient. The rigid labor market has resulted in a large amount of informal economic activity. The government influences many prices through subsidies and state-owned enterprises and utilities.

OPEN MARKETS

	Score	Rank	1-Year Change
Trade Freedom	58.6	165th	-0.1
Investment Freedom	35.0	142nd	+5.0
Financial Freedom	20.0	163rd	0

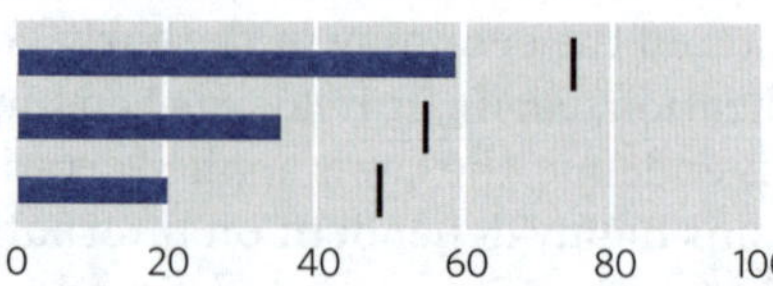

The average tariff rate is 13.2 percent. Laos's still-developing legal system is a barrier to international commerce, and foreign investment may be screened by the government. Financial-sector reforms are ongoing, and the first stock market opened in 2011, but high credit costs and scarce access to financing severely impede private-sector development. Much of the population remains outside of the formal banking sector.

Long-Term Score Change (since 1996)

RULE OF LAW		GOVERNMENT SIZE		REGULATORY EFFICIENCY		OPEN MARKETS	
Property Rights	**+5.0**	Fiscal Freedom	**+54.3**	Business Freedom	**+20.7**	Trade Freedom	**-22.4**
Freedom from Corruption	**+8.6**	Government Spending	**-3.4**	Labor Freedom	**-6.4**	Investment Freedom	**+25.0**
				Monetary Freedom	**+12.8**	Financial Freedom	**+10.0**

LATVIA

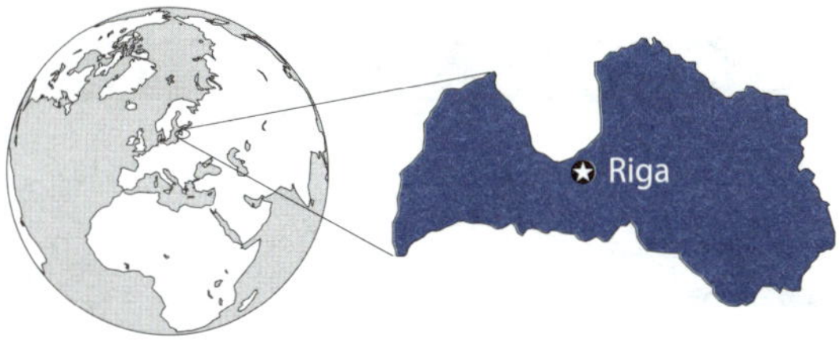

World Rank: **42** Regional Rank: **19**

Economic Freedom Score

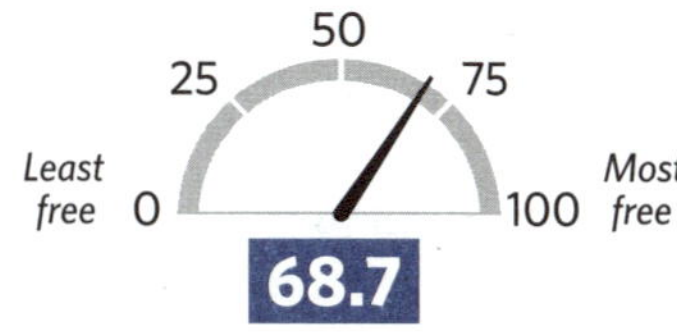

Latvia's economic freedom score is 68.7, making its economy the 42nd freest in the 2014 *Index*. Its score is 2.2 points better than last year, reflecting broad-based improvements in eight of the 10 economic freedoms, notably business freedom, labor freedom, investment freedom, and freedom from corruption. Latvia is ranked 19th out of 43 countries in the Europe region, and its overall score is above the regional and world averages.

Over the 19 years during which it has been graded in the *Index*, Latvia has advanced its economic freedom score by nearly 14 points, a top-20 improvement. Score increases in seven of the 10 economic freedoms have been driven by trade liberalization, privatization, implementation of competitively low tax rates, and modernization of the regulatory environment. Recording its highest economic freedom score ever in the 2014 *Index*, Latvia's economy remains "moderately free."

Latvia's transition to a more dynamic and market-oriented economy has been facilitated by openness to global commerce and efficient regulation designed to promote entrepreneurial activity. However, continued reforms, particularly to strengthen the independence of the judiciary and eradicate corruption, are needed to ensure progress toward greater prosperity.

BACKGROUND: Latvia regained its independence from the Soviet Union in 1991 and joined the European Union and NATO in 2004. After the October 2011 early elections, the Unity party, a center-right coalition led by Valdis Dombrovskis, formed a coalition with the pro-Russian Harmony Center and the Reform Party, allowing Dombrovskis to remain prime minister. A referendum on making Russian an official language failed in February 2012, reflecting Latvia's deep ethnic divisions. Financial and transportation services, along with banking and electronics manufacturing, are developing despite the 2008 economic crisis. Given its International Monetary Fund–backed fiscal adjustment programs and compliance with Maastricht criteria, Latvia is planning to adopt the euro as its currency in 2014.

How Do We Measure Economic Freedom?
See page 471 for an explanation of the methodology or visit the *Index* Web site at *heritage.org/index*.

Freedom Trend

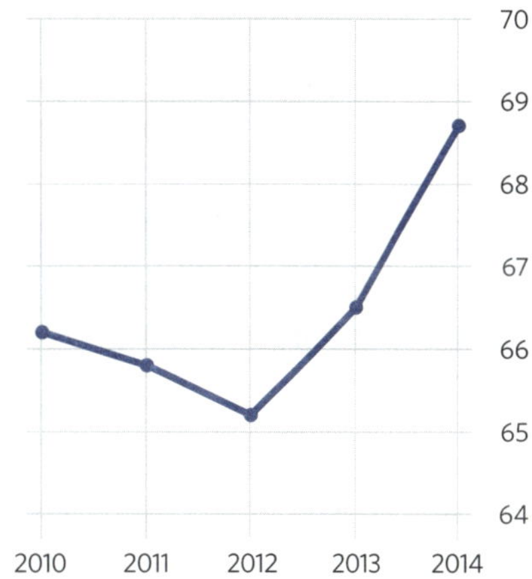

Country Comparisons

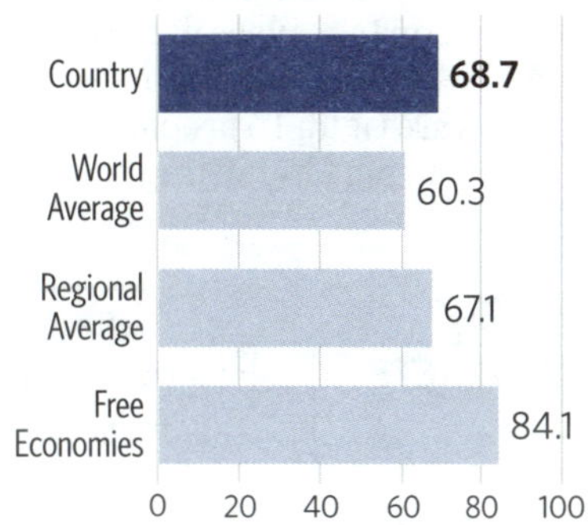

Quick Facts

Population: 2.0 million
GDP (PPP): $37.3 billion
5.6% growth in 2012
5-year compound annual growth -2.6%
$18,255 per capita
Unemployment: 14.9%
Inflation (CPI): 2.3%
FDI Inflow: $987.6 million
Public Debt: 36.4% of GDP

2012 data unless otherwise noted.
Data compiled as of September 2013.

THE TEN ECONOMIC FREEDOMS

Score ▬ Country | World Average

		Score	Rank	1-Year Change
RULE OF LAW	Property Rights	50.0	53rd	0
	Freedom from Corruption	43.6	61st	+1.6

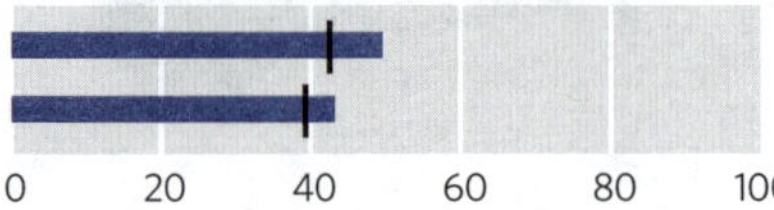

Corruption exists at every level of government. Despite laws strengthened in 2009, money laundering continues, linked especially to tax evasion and the proceeds from Russian organized crime. Judicial independence is generally respected, but inefficiency, politicization, and corruption remain problems. A legal framework for the protection of intellectual property is in place, but enforcement is weak.

		Score	Rank	1-Year Change
GOVERNMENT SIZE	Fiscal Freedom	84.6	58th	+0.2
	Government Spending	54.9	129th	+1.3

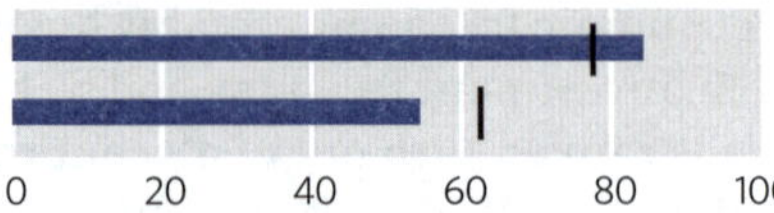

The top individual income tax rate has fallen to 24 percent, and the top corporate tax rate is 15 percent. The individual rate is set to fall incrementally to 20 percent by 2015. Other taxes include a value-added tax (VAT) and excise taxes. The overall tax burden is 27.2 percent of gross domestic income. Government spending is 39 percent of GDP. Public debt is below 40 percent of gross domestic income.

		Score	Rank	1-Year Change
REGULATORY EFFICIENCY	Business Freedom	82.5	29th	+6.8
	Labor Freedom	68.5	69th	+4.1
	Monetary Freedom	79.7	37th	+1.4

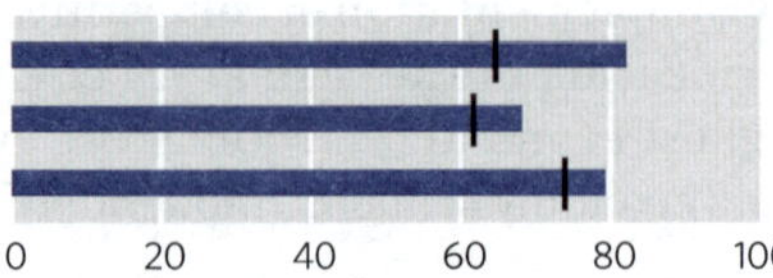

The efficient regulatory framework supports entrepreneurial activity. Business formation and operation take place without bureaucratic interference. Despite some progress, the labor market lacks flexibility; non-salary costs of employing workers are high, and restrictions on work hours are rigid. To prepare for adoption of the euro in 2014, the government reduced its budget deficit in part by cutting state spending on subsidies.

		Score	Rank	1-Year Change
OPEN MARKETS	Trade Freedom	87.8	11th	+1.0
	Investment Freedom	85.0	13th	+5.0
	Financial Freedom	50.0	69th	0

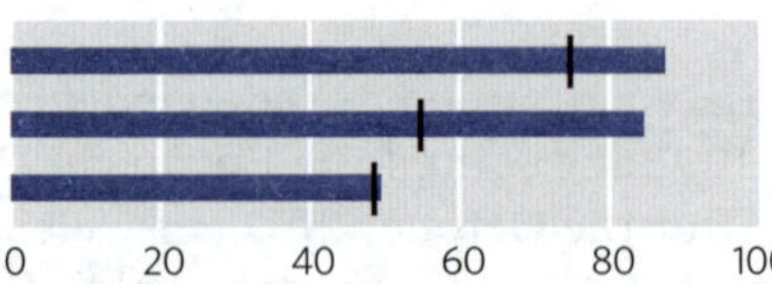

EU members have a low 1.1 percent average tariff rate and, in general, few non-tariff barriers to trade. Latvia provides a relatively favorable environment for foreign investors. The financial sector has undertaken significant regulatory adjustments since early 2009, and the government has supported the sector through capital injections. New legislation has accelerated the process of liquidating ailing banks.

Long-Term Score Change (since 1996)

RULE OF LAW		GOVERNMENT SIZE		REGULATORY EFFICIENCY		OPEN MARKETS	
Property Rights	0	Fiscal Freedom	+6.6	Business Freedom	+12.5	Trade Freedom	+32.8
Freedom from Corruption	-6.4	Government Spending	+4.1	Labor Freedom	+5.0	Investment Freedom	+35.0
				Monetary Freedom	+38.5	Financial Freedom	0

LEBANON

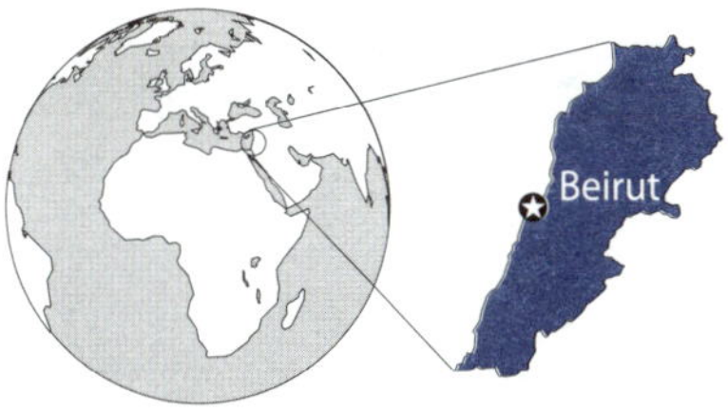

World Rank: **96** Regional Rank: **9**

Lebanon's economic freedom score is 59.4, making its economy the 96th freest in the 2014 *Index*. Its score is essentially unchanged from last year, with small improvements in business freedom and labor freedom offset by declines in trade freedom, monetary freedom, and the control of government spending. Lebanon is ranked 9th out of 15 countries in the Middle East/North Africa region, and its overall score is just below the world average.

Over the 19 years during which it has been graded in the *Index*, Lebanon's economic freedom score has decreased by nearly 4 points. Modest improvements in four of the 10 economic freedoms, including monetary freedom, investment freedom, and freedom from corruption, have been overwhelmed by substantial declines in property rights, financial freedom, and business freedom. Once considered "moderately free," Lebanon's economy has fallen back to "mostly unfree" over the past two years.

Lebanon's overall entrepreneurial environment is hampered by political instability and regulatory inefficiency. Commercial regulations and bureaucratic red tape are burdensome. Property rights are severely undermined by an inefficient judiciary, which is vulnerable to corruption. Effective implementation of institutional reforms is critical for long-term economic development.

BACKGROUND: Since 1975, Lebanon's economy has been disrupted by civil war, Syrian occupation, Hezbollah clashes with Israel, political uncertainty, and growing sectarian tensions. Syria was forced to withdraw its army in 2005 after its government was implicated in the assassination of former Lebanese Prime Minister Rafiq Hariri. In 2006, Lebanon-based Hezbollah forces instigated a conflict with Israel. Hariri's son, Saad Hariri, was elected prime minister in June 2009, but his government collapsed in January 2011 when Hezbollah engineered the elevation of Najib Mikati as prime minister. Mikati resigned in March 2013, and Tammam Salam was asked to form a caretaker government until new elections, slated for 2014. Economic growth has fallen dramatically.

How Do We Measure Economic Freedom?
See page 471 for an explanation of the methodology or visit the *Index* Web site at *heritage.org/index.*

Economic Freedom Score

Freedom Trend

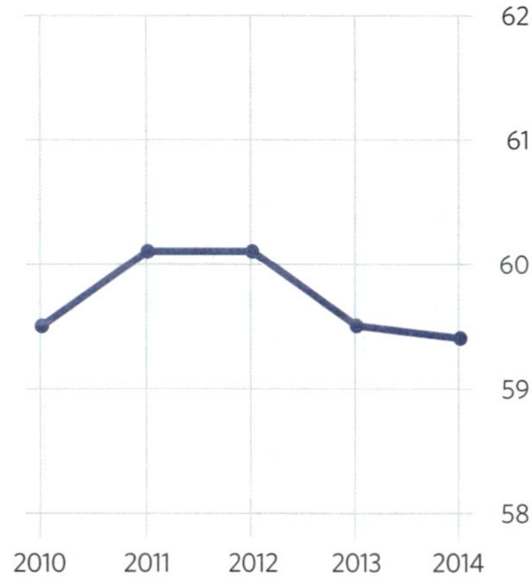

Country Comparisons

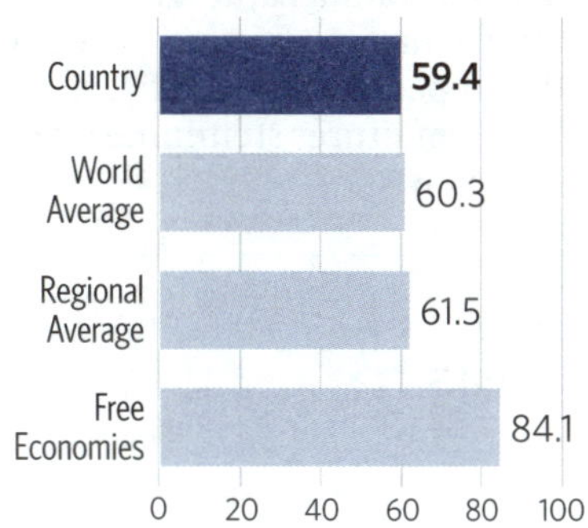

Quick Facts

Population: 4.0 million
GDP (PPP): $63.2 billion
1.5% growth in 2012
5-year compound annual growth 5.5%
$15,757 per capita
Unemployment: n/a
Inflation (CPI): 6.6%
FDI Inflow: $3.8 billion
Public Debt: 139.5% of GDP

2012 data unless otherwise noted.
Data compiled as of September 2013.

LEBANON (continued)

THE TEN ECONOMIC FREEDOMS

Score ■ Country | World Average

RULE OF LAW

	Score	Rank	1-Year Change
Property Rights	20.0	139th	0
Freedom from Corruption	24.5	134th	-0.5

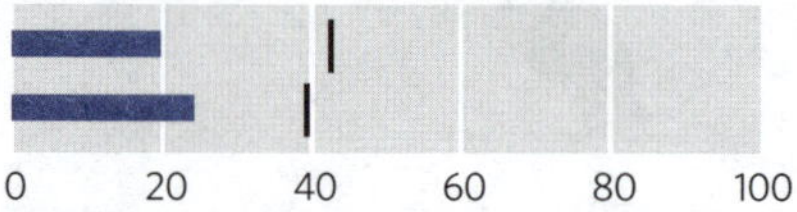

The sectarian political system and the powerful role of foreign patrons limit the public accountability of elected officials. Political and bureaucratic corruption is widespread, businesses routinely pay bribes and cultivate ties with politicians to win contracts, and anti-corruption laws are enforced only loosely. The judiciary, ostensibly independent, is subject to heavy political influence in practice.

GOVERNMENT SIZE

	Score	Rank	1-Year Change
Fiscal Freedom	90.9	30th	+0.1
Government Spending	73.7	76th	-0.9

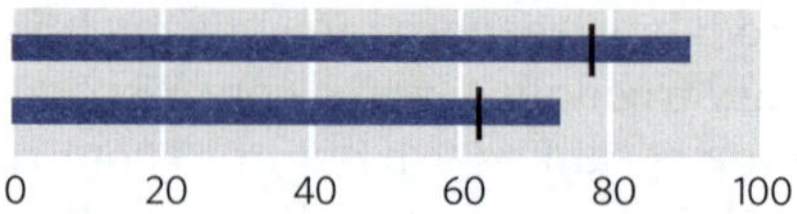

The top individual income tax rate is 20 percent, and the top corporate tax rate is 15 percent. Other taxes include a value-added tax (VAT) and an inheritance tax. The overall tax burden equals 17 percent of gross national income. Government spending remains around 30 percent of GDP. Capital flight, political instability, and Syria's civil war have hurt the budget outlook. Public debt is steady at around 140 percent of the economy.

REGULATORY EFFICIENCY

	Score	Rank	1-Year Change
Business Freedom	55.6	134th	+5.3
Labor Freedom	58.7	107th	+1.5
Monetary Freedom	74.5	111th	-2.0

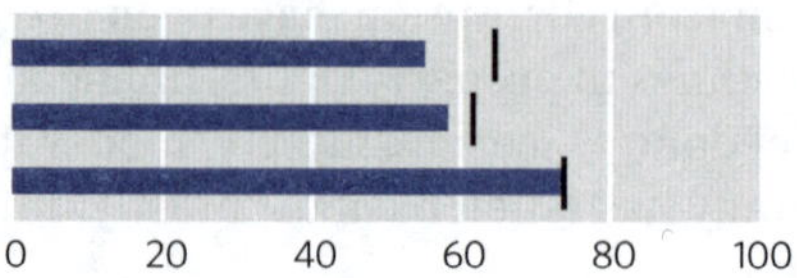

The minimum capital needed to launch a business equals 35 percent of the level of average annual income. Licensing requirements remain time-consuming. The labor market is underdeveloped. The overall fiscal deficit reached 8.7 percent of GDP in 2012, driven by a sharp rise in expenditures stemming from public-sector wages and increased subsidies to the electricity company.

OPEN MARKETS

	Score	Rank	1-Year Change
Trade Freedom	75.8	92nd	-4.6
Investment Freedom	60.0	80th	0
Financial Freedom	60.0	41st	0

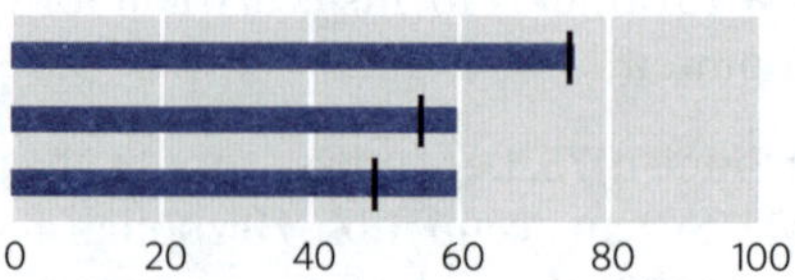

Lebanon's average tariff rate is 7.1 percent. Non-tariff barriers are not a significant impediment to trade. The legal and regulatory systems are sometimes challenging for foreign investors to navigate. Regional unrest deters investment. The financial sector is relatively well developed for the region. The state retains no ownership in any commercial bank.

Long-Term Score Change: n/a

RULE OF LAW		GOVERNMENT SIZE		REGULATORY EFFICIENCY		OPEN MARKETS	
Property Rights	-30.0	Fiscal Freedom	-7.1	Business Freedom	-14.4	Trade Freedom	+0.8
Freedom from Corruption	+14.5	Government Spending	-6.2	Labor Freedom	-0.5	Investment Freedom	+10.0
				Monetary Freedom	+8.2	Financial Freedom	-10.0

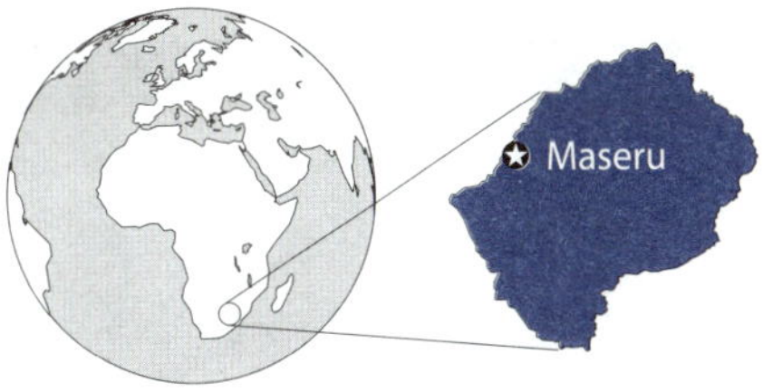

LESOTHO

World Rank: 154 **Regional Rank: 37**

Economic Freedom Score

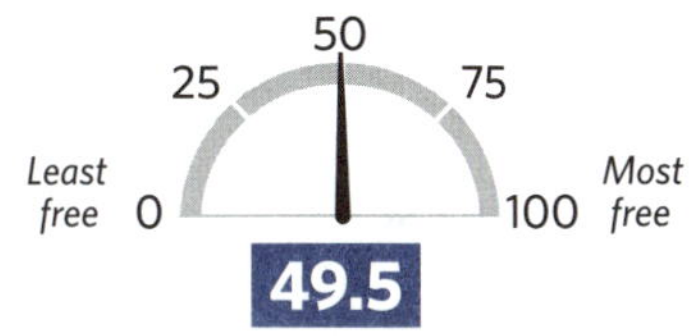

Freedom Trend

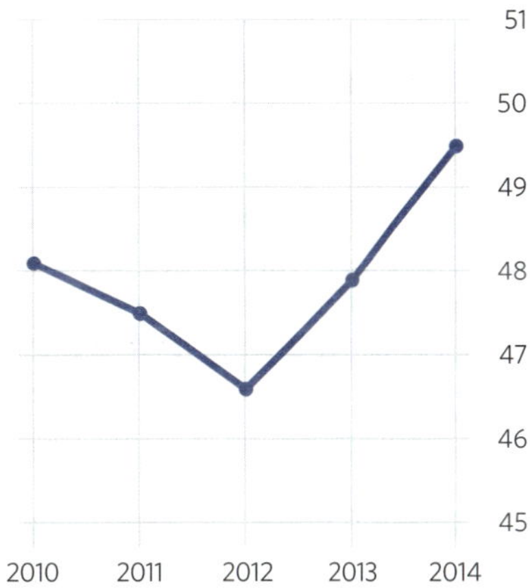

Lesotho's economic freedom score is 49.5, making its economy the 154th freest in the 2014 *Index*. Its score is 1.6 points better than last year, with improvements in fiscal freedom, investment freedom, and freedom from corruption outweighing a substantial drop in business freedom. Lesotho is ranked 37th out of 46 countries in the Sub-Saharan Africa region, and its overall score is below the world average.

Over Lesotho's 19-year history in the *Index*, its economic freedom has been stagnant, and its overall score has improved only 2.5 points. Improvements in half of the 10 economic freedoms, including trade freedom, monetary freedom, and financial freedom, have been undermined by deteriorations in labor freedom, property rights, and the control of government spending.

Considerable challenges remain in the struggle to promote stable long-term economic development, and lingering institutional weaknesses call for much greater commitment to reform, particularly in two areas. Lesotho continues to score below the world averages in freedom from corruption and the protection of property rights, and marginal reforms have failed to generate much improvement.

BACKGROUND: Lesotho became independent in 1966, but instability in the 1990s led to military intervention by South Africa and Botswana. An interim authority overhauled the government and oversaw elections in 2002. King Letsie III is ceremonial head of state. Prime Minister Thomas Thabane heads a coalition government that ousted former Prime Minister Bethuel Mosisili after close elections in May 2012. Lesotho is geographically surrounded by and economically integrated with South Africa, and it relies on customs duties from the Southern Africa Customs Union for revenue and on remittances from laborers employed in South Africa for much of its national income. Trade with the United States is important, and apparel exports have grown significantly with the help of the U.S. African Growth and Opportunity Act.

Country Comparisons

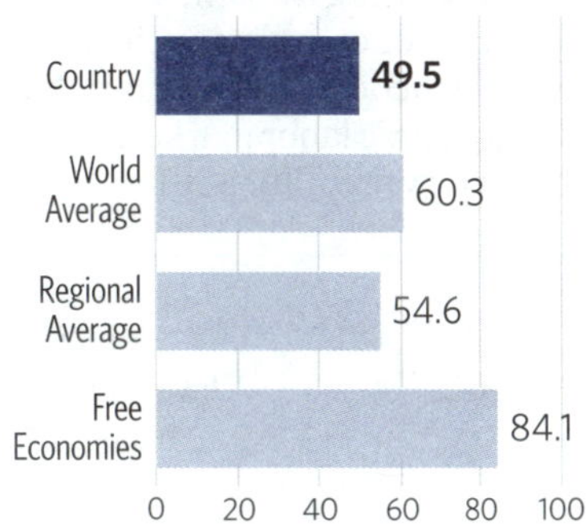

Quick Facts

Population: 1.9 million
GDP (PPP): $4.1 billion
4.0% growth in 2012
5-year compound annual growth 5.2%
$2,138 per capita
Unemployment: 25.0% (2008)
Inflation (CPI): 5.3%
FDI Inflow: $172.3 million
Public Debt: 41.9% of GDP

2012 data unless otherwise noted.
Data compiled as of September 2013.

How Do We Measure Economic Freedom?
See page 471 for an explanation of the methodology or visit the *Index* Web site at *heritage.org/index*.

LESOTHO (continued)

THE TEN ECONOMIC FREEDOMS

RULE OF LAW

	Score	Rank	1-Year Change
Property Rights	40.0	70th	0
Freedom from Corruption	37.1	75th	+2.1

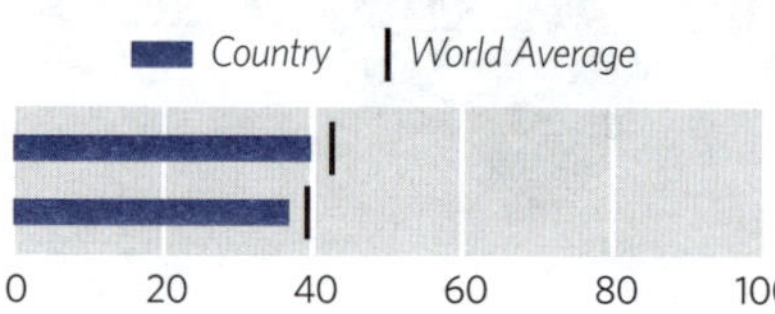

In 2013, Lesotho's prime minister described corruption as the country's worst public enemy after HIV/AIDS. Corruption affects all sectors of government, and cronyism is prevalent in state bidding procedures. The judiciary is relatively independent but politicized and chronically underfunded. There are insufficient mechanisms to hold authorities accountable. Protection of private property rights is ineffective, although expropriation is unlikely.

GOVERNMENT SIZE

	Score	Rank	1-Year Change
Fiscal Freedom	67.4	150th	+19.2
Government Spending	0.0	177th	0

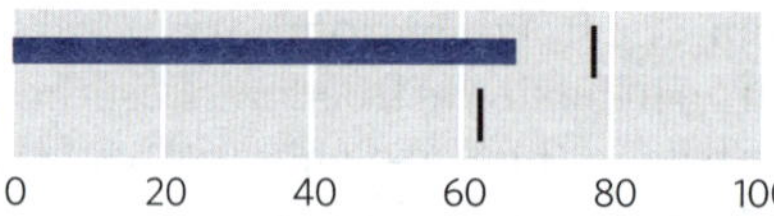

The top individual income tax rate is 35 percent, and the top corporate tax rate is 25 percent. Other taxes include a value-added tax (VAT) and a tax on dividends. Overall tax revenue is equal to 37.6 percent of gross domestic income. Government spending dominates the economy and equals 63 percent of GDP. Public debt is about 42 percent of gross domestic income.

REGULATORY EFFICIENCY

	Score	Rank	1-Year Change
Business Freedom	54.0	142nd	-9.7
Labor Freedom	62.4	89th	-0.4
Monetary Freedom	75.5	92nd	-0.2

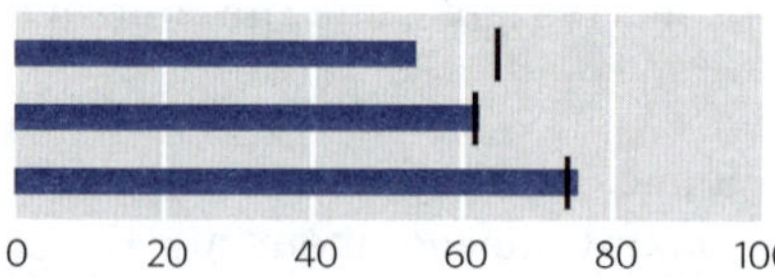

Incorporating a business still takes almost a month, although no minimum capital is required. The cost of completing licensing requirements remains over eight times the level of average annual income, taking more than 300 days. Outmoded labor laws undermine the development of a dynamic labor market. The government influences prices through state-owned enterprises. Monetary stability is affected by inflationary pressures in South Africa.

OPEN MARKETS

	Score	Rank	1-Year Change
Trade Freedom	68.6	135th	-0.5
Investment Freedom	50.0	109th	+5.0
Financial Freedom	40.0	107th	0

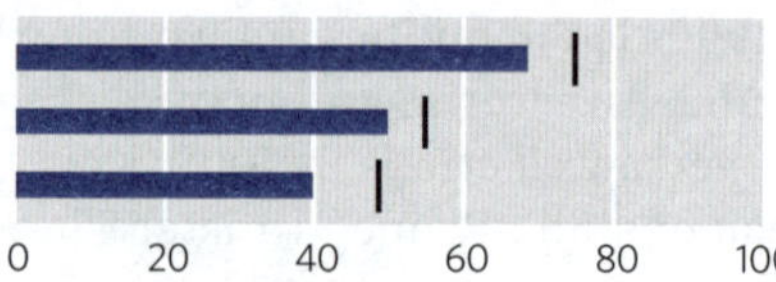

Lesotho's average tariff rate is 10.7 percent. Imports of some agricultural products and used clothing and autos may face additional barriers. Foreign investment is allowed but may be screened by the government. Much of the population lacks adequate access to banking services. The high cost of credit hinders entrepreneurial activity and the development of a vibrant private sector.

Long-Term Score Change (since 1996)

RULE OF LAW		GOVERNMENT SIZE		REGULATORY EFFICIENCY		OPEN MARKETS	
Property Rights	**-10.0**	Fiscal Freedom	**+8.2**	Business Freedom	**-1.0**	Trade Freedom	**+23.6**
Freedom from Corruption	**+7.1**	Government Spending	**-38.7**	Labor Freedom	**-9.5**	Investment Freedom	**0**
				Monetary Freedom	**+10.2**	Financial Freedom	**+10.0**

LIBERIA

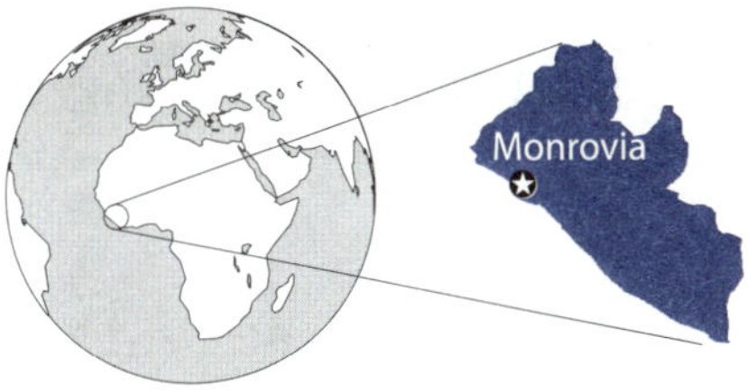

World Rank: **138** Regional Rank: **30**

Economic Freedom Score

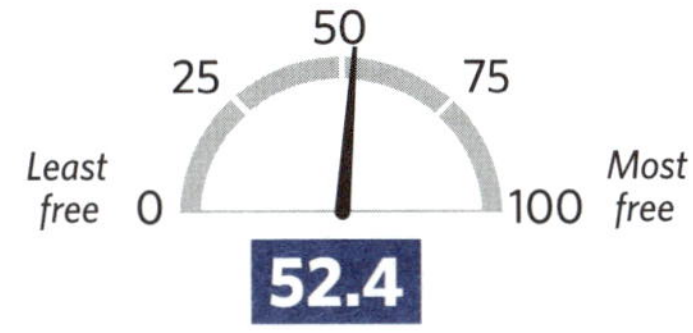

Liberia's economic freedom score is 52.4, making its economy the 138th freest in the 2014 *Index*. Its score is 3.1 points better than last year, with notable improvements in investment freedom, fiscal freedom, business freedom, and trade freedom. Liberia is ranked 30th out of 46 countries in the Sub-Saharan Africa region, and its overall rating remains significantly below the world and regional averages.

Liberia's economic freedom was first assessed in the 2009 *Index*. Since then, its overall score has advanced by 4.3 points, with improvements in seven of the 10 economic freedoms and scores for business freedom, trade freedom, investment freedom, and freedom from corruption rising by 10 points or more. Liberia has achieved its highest economic freedom score ever in the 2014 *Index*, moving out of the ranks of the economically "repressed."

Despite significant progress, Liberia still lags in promoting the effective rule of law. The judicial system remains vulnerable to political interference, and property rights are not strongly protected. Lingering corruption further undermines freedom and hampers the emergence of more vibrant economic activity.

BACKGROUND: Liberia is Africa's oldest republic. Charles Taylor, elected president in 1997 after an eight-year civil war, was forced to resign in 2003 and was convicted of war crimes by the Special Court for Sierra Leone in 2012. Ellen Johnson Sirleaf was elected president in 2005 and re-elected in 2011. In September 2012, the U.N. Security Council called for a 50 percent reduction in the number of U.N. troops in Liberia. Formal-sector unemployment and illiteracy are high, and political instability and international sanctions have destroyed most large businesses and driven out many foreign investors. Rubber exports and the world's second-largest maritime registry generate major income. Despite over $4.6 billion in debt relief from official creditors in 2010, about 85 percent of the population continues to live below the poverty line.

Freedom Trend

Country Comparisons

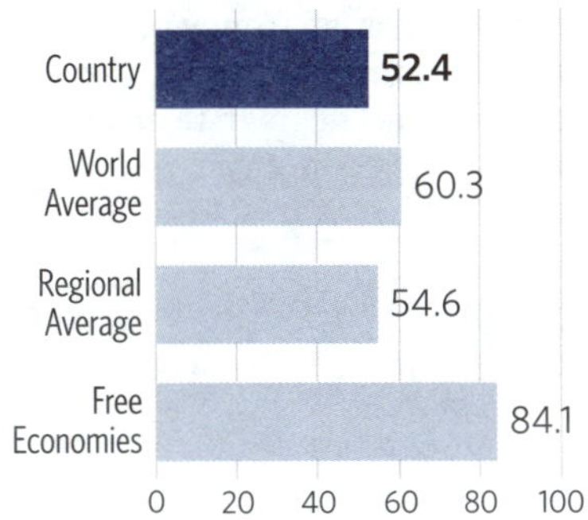

Quick Facts

Population: 4.0 million
GDP (PPP): $2.7 billion
8.3% growth in 2012
5-year compound annual growth 6.8%
$673 per capita
Unemployment: n/a
Inflation (CPI): 6.8%
FDI Inflow: $1.4 billion
Public Debt: 29.1% of GDP

2012 data unless otherwise noted.
Data compiled as of September 2013.

How Do We Measure Economic Freedom?
See page 471 for an explanation of the methodology or visit the *Index* Web site at *heritage.org/index*.

THE TEN ECONOMIC FREEDOMS

RULE OF LAW

	Score	Rank	1-Year Change
Property Rights	30.0	93rd	0
Freedom from Corruption	33.8	84th	+1.8

Some progress has been made in curbing corruption through code of conduct requirements, though the problem remains endemic. Property rights are not strongly protected, and the rule of law remains uneven across the country. The judiciary lacks adequate facilities. The government is drafting a Land Rights Policy to reconcile the statutory and customary land tenure systems.

GOVERNMENT SIZE

	Score	Rank	1-Year Change
Fiscal Freedom	83.6	61st	+7.0
Government Spending	70.5	86th	-7.3

With a cut in the individual income tax rate, both the top marginal income and the flat corporate tax rates are now 25 percent. Other taxes include a property tax and a goods and services tax. The overall tax burden is 19.8 percent of GDP. Government spending is 31 percent of gross domestic income, and public debt continues to fall below 30 percent of GDP.

REGULATORY EFFICIENCY

	Score	Rank	1-Year Change
Business Freedom	62.3	103rd	+5.8
Labor Freedom	47.0	149th	-0.2
Monetary Freedom	72.9	124th	+0.9

The requirements for starting a business have been simplified, but regulatory inefficiency and a lack of transparency persist. Licensing requirements still cost over three times the level of average annual income. The labor market remains inefficient, and informal labor activity is quite high. The near-term effectiveness of monetary policy is limited, given the high dollarization of the economy.

OPEN MARKETS

	Score	Rank	1-Year Change
Trade Freedom	64.1	148th	+2.7
Investment Freedom	40.0	132nd	+20.0
Financial Freedom	20.0	163rd	0

Liberia's average tariff rate is 10.4 percent. The government restricts foreign investment in several sectors. The financial sector remains vulnerable to political influence and institutional instability. The scarce access to financing continues to impede much-needed entrepreneurial activity and private-sector development. The financial sector is dominated by banking, but a large part of the population remains outside of the formal banking sector.

Long-Term Score Change (since 2009)

RULE OF LAW		GOVERNMENT SIZE		REGULATORY EFFICIENCY		OPEN MARKETS	
Property Rights	+5.0	Fiscal Freedom	+9.8	Business Freedom	+22.1	Trade Freedom	+10.3
Freedom from Corruption	+12.8	Government Spending	-26.7	Labor Freedom	-2.8	Investment Freedom	+10.0
				Monetary Freedom	+2.8	Financial Freedom	0

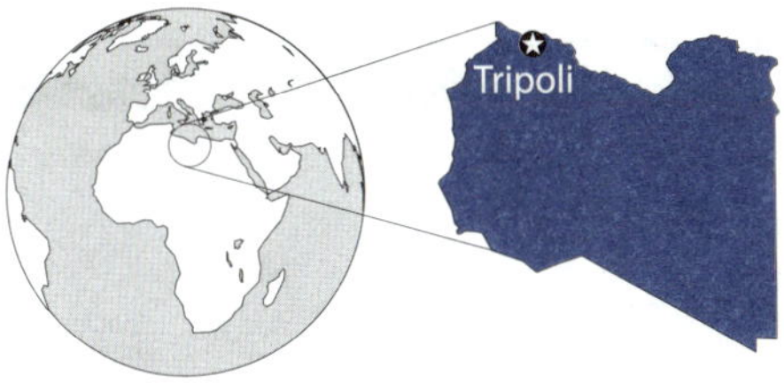

LIBYA

World Rank: Not Ranked | Regional Rank: Not Ranked

Economic Freedom Score

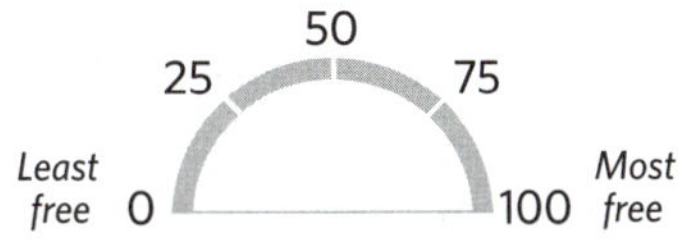

This economy is not graded

Numerical grading of Libya's overall economic freedom remains suspended in the 2014 *Index* because of political turmoil that has resulted in civil unrest and the deteriorating quality of publicly available economic statistics. Those facets of economic freedom for which data are still available have been individually scored. As a "repressed" economy with a score of 35.9, Libya was ranked last in the Middle East/North Africa region when it was last graded in the 2012 *Index*.

Before the downfall of the Qadhafi regime in 2011, the weak rule of law and systemic corruption had largely marginalized private-sector activity in the formal economy. Libya, overly dependent on the oil sector, had undertaken only limited reforms to diversify its economy.

Libya's near-term challenge is to ensure a peaceful political transition while maintaining macroeconomic stability. The government needs to stabilize the economic environment and implement much-needed reforms following the revolution. The economic infrastructure was significantly degraded during the civil war, and economic uncertainty remains very high as the weak interim government struggles to restore the rule of law and establish a new system of effective governance.

BACKGROUND: After the 2011 overthrow of dictator Muammar Qadhafi by rebels backed by the U.N. Security Council and a NATO bombing campaign, elections were held in July 2012. The new government led by President Mohammed Magarief and Prime Minister Ali Zeidan has struggled to rein in fiercely independent militias fighting for control of territory and resources. Oil and natural gas provide about 80 percent of GDP, 95 percent of export revenues, and 99 percent of government revenues. Economic recovery, which began in 2012, has been driven by the energy sector, which is producing at pre-war levels. The government faces major challenges in disarming and demobilizing militias, imposing the rule of law, and reforming the state-dominated socialist economy.

Freedom Trend

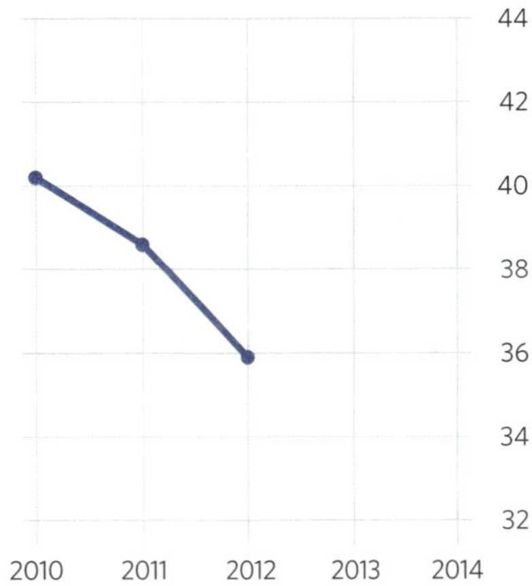

Country Comparisons

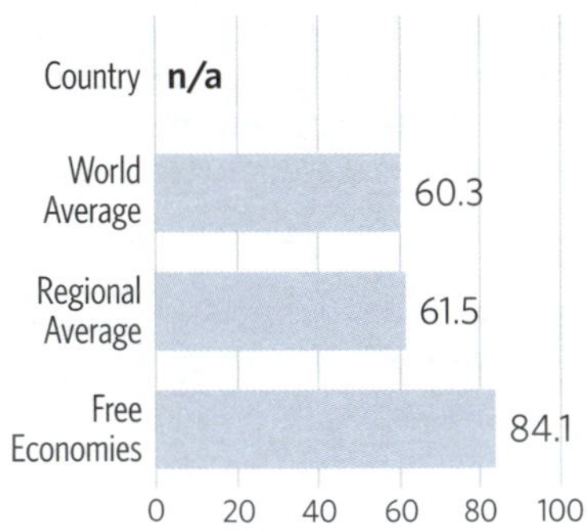

Quick Facts

Population: 6.4 million
GDP (PPP): $77.4 billion
104.5% growth in 2012
5-year compound annual growth -3.7%
$12,066 per capita
Unemployment: n/a
Inflation (CPI): 6.1%
FDI Inflow: n/a
Public Debt: 0.0% of GDP

2012 data unless otherwise noted.
Data compiled as of September 2013.

How Do We Measure Economic Freedom?
See page 471 for an explanation of the methodology or visit the *Index* Web site at *heritage.org/index.*

THE TEN ECONOMIC FREEDOMS

RULE OF LAW

	Score	Rank	1-Year Change
Property Rights	10.0	166th	0
Freedom from Corruption	18.3	169th	-1.7

Corruption has long been pervasive in the private sector and in government. The fall of the Qadhafi regime raised some hopes that the level of graft would decline, but oil interests, foreign governments, smuggling groups, and armed militias often still wield undue influence, especially in the South, and opportunities for corruption abound in the absence of effective fiscal, judicial, and commercial institutions.

GOVERNMENT SIZE

	Score	Rank	1-Year Change
Fiscal Freedom	95.0	14th	n/a
Government Spending	0.0	177th	n/a

The top individual income tax rate has fallen to 10 percent, and the top corporate tax rate remains 20 percent. A 4 percent surcharge for the "Jihad" fund is applied to corporations. Oil revenues have helped to bolster public finances even though taxation has been enforced only erratically since the beginning of 2011. The overall tax burden is about 1 percent of GDP. Public expenditures are around 67 percent of GDP. Libya has no public debt.

REGULATORY EFFICIENCY

	Score	Rank	1-Year Change
Business Freedom	50.1	152nd	n/a
Labor Freedom	77.9	39th	n/a
Monetary Freedom	66.9	157th	+2.1

Regulatory efficiency is very poor, and only limited private entrepreneurial activity has been successful. Application of regulations is inconsistent and non-transparent. The labor market remains destabilized, and the informal sector is large. Increased spending on public-sector wages adds to inflationary pressure, which the government attempts to mitigate through extensive (and price-distorting) food, fuel, and electricity subsidies.

OPEN MARKETS

	Score	Rank	1-Year Change
Trade Freedom	n/a	—	n/a
Investment Freedom	5.0	174th	-5.0
Financial Freedom	20.0	163rd	0

Libya has a 0 percent average tariff rate, but civil unrest is a significant deterrent to international trade and investment. The financial system continues to function relatively normally, but limited access to financing has severely impeded any meaningful private business development. Commercial banking has been dominated by four main banks.

Long-Term Score Change: n/a

RULE OF LAW		GOVERNMENT SIZE		REGULATORY EFFICIENCY		OPEN MARKETS	
Property Rights	n/a	Fiscal Freedom	n/a	Business Freedom	n/a	Trade Freedom	n/a
Freedom from Corruption	n/a	Government Spending	n/a	Labor Freedom	n/a	Investment Freedom	n/a
				Monetary Freedom	n/a	Financial Freedom	n/a

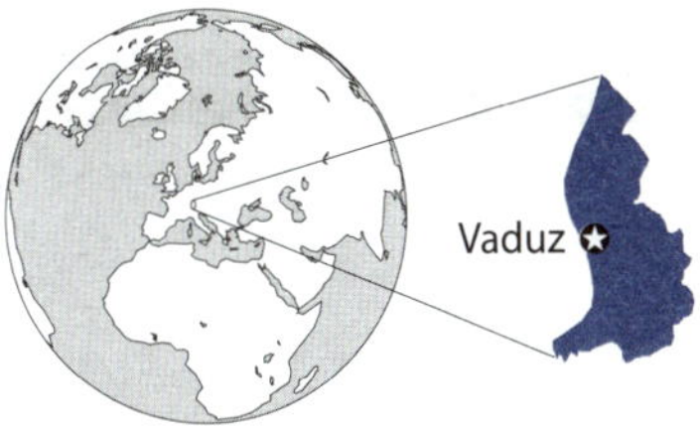

LIECHTENSTEIN

World Rank: Not Ranked | Regional Rank: Not Ranked

Economic Freedom Score

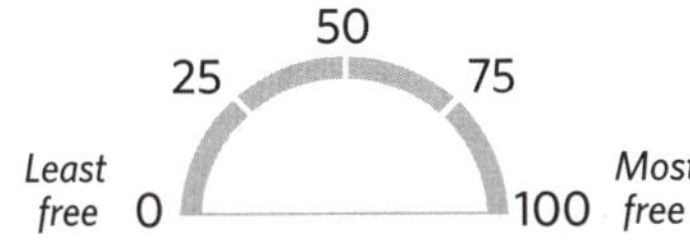

This economy is not graded

Freedom Trend

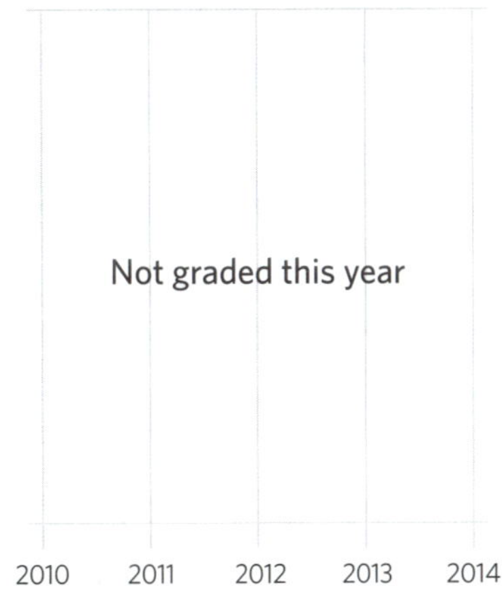

Country Comparisons

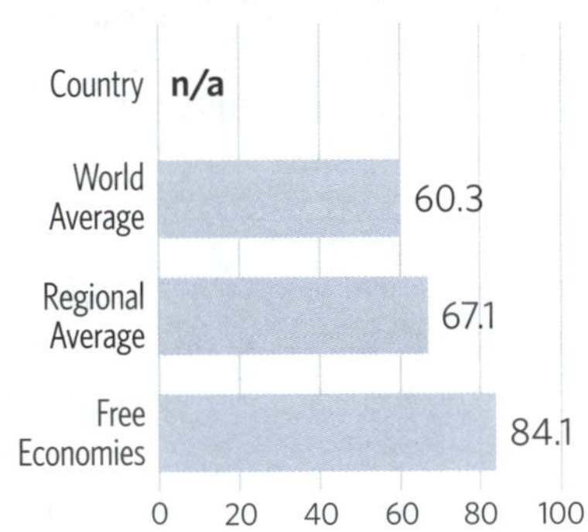

Liechtenstein's overall economic freedom remains unrated in the 2014 *Index* because of a lack of sufficient comparable data. Those facets of economic freedom for which data are available have been individually scored. The country will receive an overall economic freedom score and ranking in future editions as more information becomes available.

Flexibility and openness to global commerce are the cornerstones of Liechtenstein's modern and diversified economy. Barriers to trade and investment are minimal, and a straightforward, transparent, and streamlined regulatory system supports an innovative entrepreneurial sector. Competitive tax rates and sound labor regulations further promote dynamic business activity.

Liechtenstein's steady macroeconomic and regulatory environments have contributed to its position as an attractive place in which to do business. The banking sector has benefited from the country's high political and social stability as well as its sound and transparent judicial system. Liechtenstein's vigorous defense of property rights, even intellectual property rights, and the near total absence of corruption minimize potential drags on its dynamic economy.

BACKGROUND: Prince of Liechtenstein Hans-Adam II is head of state and wields considerable power. The center-right Progressive Citizens' Party won the March 2013 parliamentary elections, and Prime Minister Adrian Hasler now heads the government. Liechtenstein has a vibrant free-enterprise economy. Low taxes and traditions of strict bank secrecy (now relaxed) have contributed significantly to the ability of financial institutions to attract funds, although the worldwide financial crisis led to a sharp contraction in the banking sector. In 2009, the Organisation for Economic Co-operation and Development removed Liechtenstein from its list of uncooperative tax havens. The principality's economy is closely linked to Switzerland, whose currency it shares, and to the European Union. Liechtenstein is a member of the European Free Trade Association and the European Economic Area, but it is not a member of the EU.

Quick Facts

Population: 37,009
GDP (PPP): $3.2 billion (2009)
-0.5% growth in 2009
5-year compound annual growth n/a
$89,400 per capita (2009)
Unemployment: 2.5% (2011)
Inflation (CPI): 0.2% (2011)
FDI Inflow: n/a
Public Debt: n/a

2012 data unless otherwise noted.
Data compiled as of September 2013.

How Do We Measure Economic Freedom?
See page 471 for an explanation of the methodology or visit the *Index* Web site at *heritage.org/index*.

THE TEN ECONOMIC FREEDOMS

RULE OF LAW

	Score	Rank	1-Year Change
Property Rights	n/a	—	n/a
Freedom from Corruption	n/a	—	n/a

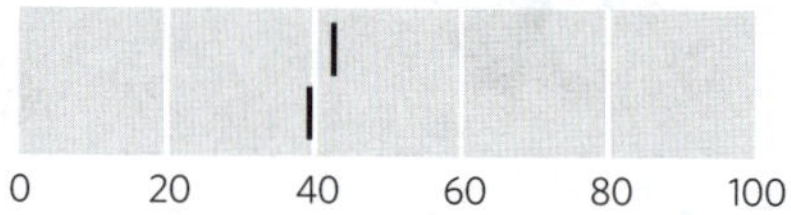

Liechtenstein is largely free of corruption and continues to work to prevent money laundering in its banking system. In its first report on Liechtenstein, released in October 2012, the Group of States Against Corruption said that the country is "in the early stages of implementing effective anti-corruption measures." Property rights and contracts are secure. Intellectual property laws are based on Switzerland's IPR protection regimes.

GOVERNMENT SIZE

	Score	Rank	1-Year Change
Fiscal Freedom	n/a	—	n/a
Government Spending	n/a	—	n/a

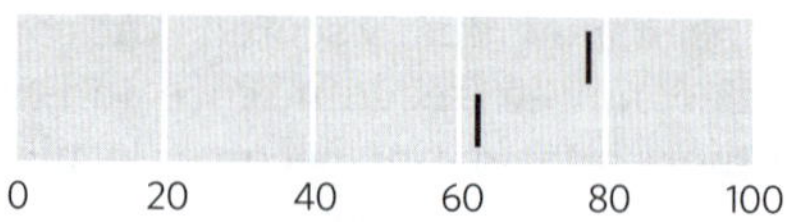

The tax reform act that came into effect in 2011 has kept rates low and modernized the tax system. The top individual income tax rate is 7 percent, and the top corporate tax rate is 12.5 percent. Other taxes include a value-added tax (VAT) administered by Switzerland. The fiscal system lacks some transparency, but government fiscal management has been relatively sound, with minimal administrative bureaucracy.

REGULATORY EFFICIENCY

	Score	Rank	1-Year Change
Business Freedom	n/a	—	n/a
Labor Freedom	n/a	—	n/a
Monetary Freedom	n/a	—	n/a

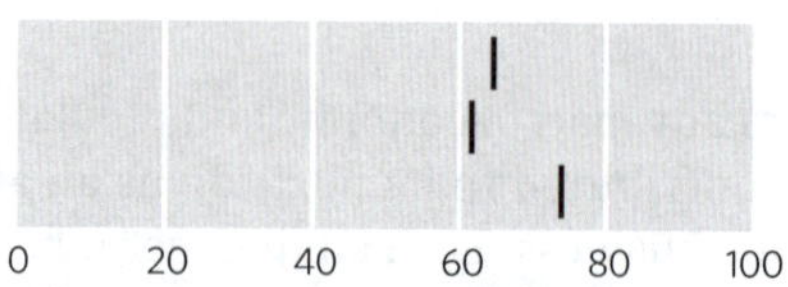

The overall freedom to conduct a business is well protected under the transparent regulatory environment. Administrative procedures are straightforward and applied consistently. The labor market is dynamic, and unemployment traditionally has been very low. Liechtenstein has a de facto monetary union with Switzerland, although the principality has no vote in the Swiss National Bank's monetary policy.

OPEN MARKETS

	Score	Rank	1-Year Change
Trade Freedom	90.0	1st	0
Investment Freedom	85.0	13th	n/a
Financial Freedom	80.0	4th	0

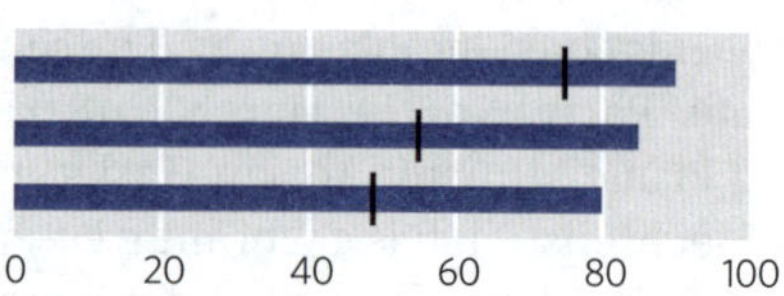

Liechtenstein has a 0 percent average tariff rate and is relatively open to international trade and investment. It is a major financial center, particularly in private banking. Major financial services include private asset management, international asset structuring, investment funds, insurance, and reinsurance. Resident and non-resident clients enjoy equal access. Financial services account for about 30 percent of GDP.

Long-Term Score Change: n/a

RULE OF LAW		GOVERNMENT SIZE		REGULATORY EFFICIENCY		OPEN MARKETS	
Property Rights	n/a	Fiscal Freedom	n/a	Business Freedom	n/a	Trade Freedom	n/a
Freedom from Corruption	n/a	Government Spending	n/a	Labor Freedom	n/a	Investment Freedom	n/a
				Monetary Freedom	n/a	Financial Freedom	n/a

LITHUANIA

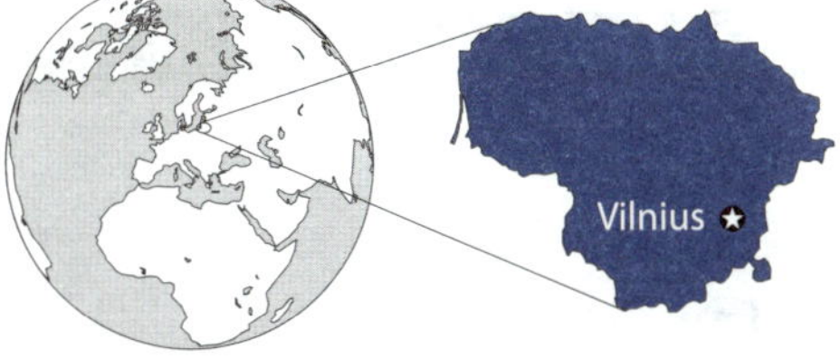

World Rank: **21** Regional Rank: **11**

Economic Freedom Score

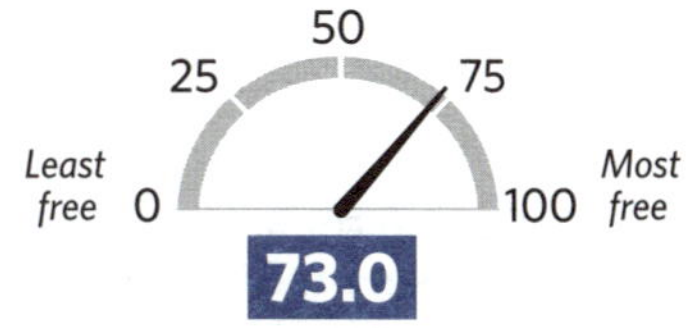

Lithuania's economic freedom score is 73.0, making its economy the 21st freest in the 2014 *Index*. Its overall score has risen by 0.9 point, with notable improvements in business freedom and the management of public finance outweighing a deterioration in labor freedom. Lithuania is ranked 11th out of 43 countries in the Europe region, and its overall score is well above the world and regional averages.

Lithuania's economic freedom score has advanced by 20 points over the 19 years it has been graded in the *Index*. Score improvements have occurred particularly in the areas of market openness, regulatory efficiency, and the rule of law. Effective implementation of critical reforms has facilitated the emergence of a vibrant private sector. Overall regulatory efficiency is further enhanced by open-market policies that support increased trade and investment flows. Once considered "repressed," Lithuania's economy has risen to the status of "mostly free," achieving its highest economic freedom score ever in the 2014 *Index*.

Despite the challenging economic situation, Lithuania has demonstrated a commitment to restoring the soundness of public finance and the credibility of its policies. Bringing down government spending through deficit-cutting efforts has helped to sustain the momentum for economic recovery.

BACKGROUND: Lithuania, largest of the Baltic States, regained its independence from the Soviet Union in 1991. It joined the European Union and NATO in 2004. Former Finance Minister Dalia Grybauskaite won the presidential elections by a landslide in July 2009. Under her leadership, the country has worked on a more transparent system of parliamentary elections, judicial reforms, and energy and financial security. Lithuania and Poland are exploring the possibility of gas interconnectors between the two countries to lessen dependence on Russian gas. There has been growth in the construction, financial services, and retail sectors.

How Do We Measure Economic Freedom?
See page 471 for an explanation of the methodology or visit the *Index* Web site at *heritage.org/index*.

Freedom Trend

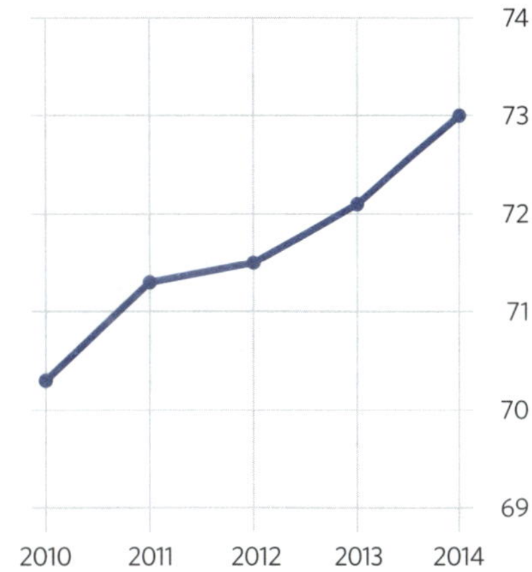

Country Comparisons

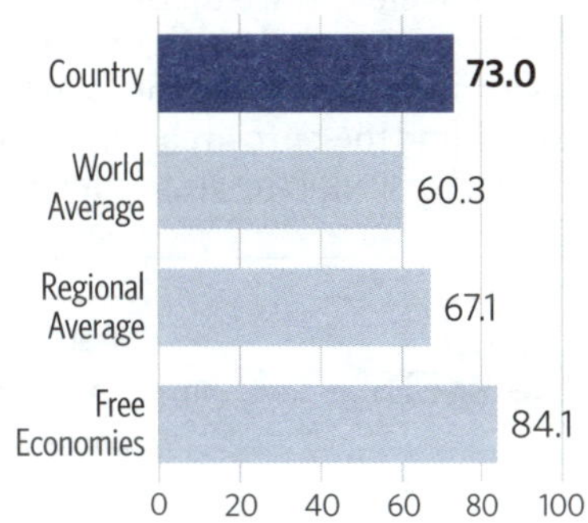

Quick Facts

Population: 3.0 million
GDP (PPP): $65.0 billion
3.6% growth in 2012
5-year compound annual growth −0.5%
$21,615 per capita
Unemployment: 13.2%
Inflation (CPI): 3.2%
FDI Inflow: $835.1 million
Public Debt: 40.0% of GDP

2012 data unless otherwise noted.
Data compiled as of September 2013.

THE TEN ECONOMIC FREEDOMS

Score ▬ *Country* | *World Average*

		Score	Rank	1-Year Change
RULE OF LAW	Property Rights	60.0	41st	0
	Freedom from Corruption	49.9	47th	+1.9

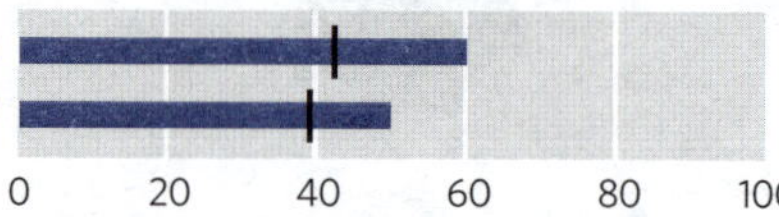

Corruption remains a problem, although many officials suspected of abusing their power have been prosecuted. Regulation of commerce by more than 50 government institutions creates many opportunities for corruption. The constitution guarantees judicial independence, which is respected in practice and has been strengthened by EU membership, but an inefficient legal framework inhibits effective contract enforcement.

		Score	Rank	1-Year Change
GOVERNMENT SIZE	Fiscal Freedom	92.9	18th	+0.1
	Government Spending	55.9	126th	+2.3

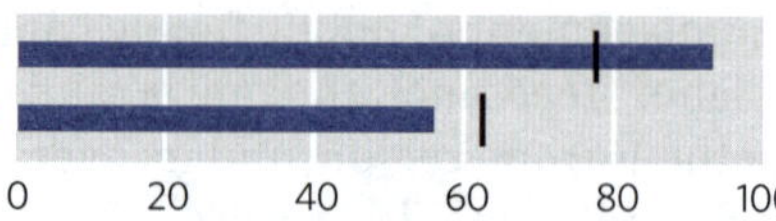

Lithuania's top individual income and corporate tax rates are 15 percent. Small companies are subject to a 5 percent rate. Other taxes include an inheritance tax and a value-added tax (VAT). The overall tax burden is 16 percent of gross domestic income. Government spending equals 38 percent of GDP, and public debt equates to 40 percent of the economy. The government was recently released from the EU's excessive deficit procedure.

		Score	Rank	1-Year Change
REGULATORY EFFICIENCY	Business Freedom	85.7	20th	+8.1
	Labor Freedom	59.0	105th	-5.1
	Monetary Freedom	78.6	57th	+0.3

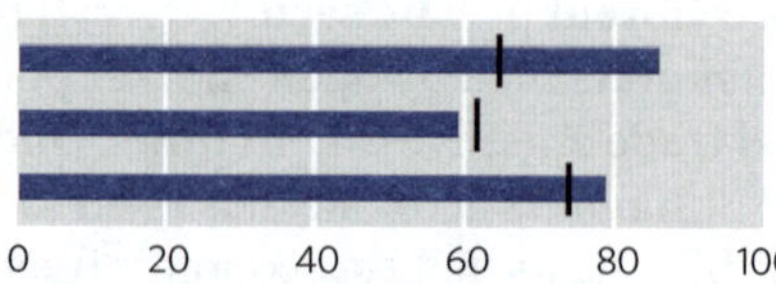

The business start-up process has become more straightforward, and no minimum capital is required. Fees related to completing licensing requirements have been reduced considerably. Despite some reform, the labor market remains relatively rigid. Realization of Lithuania's goal of joining the euro area will require additional fiscal discipline to reduce the public debt ratio, in part by reducing state subsidies.

		Score	Rank	1-Year Change
OPEN MARKETS	Trade Freedom	87.8	11th	+1.0
	Investment Freedom	80.0	23rd	0
	Financial Freedom	80.0	4th	0

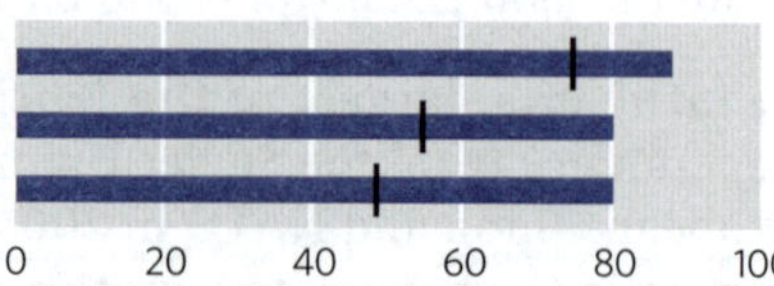

EU members have a low 1.1 percent average tariff rate and, in general, few non-tariff barriers to trade. The government does not generally allow foreign investors to buy agricultural land. The last state-owned bank was privatized almost a decade ago, and most commercial banks are foreign-owned. Offering a wide range of financial services, the financial sector remains competitive and stable. Capital markets are small but function well.

Long-Term Score Change (since 1996)

RULE OF LAW		GOVERNMENT SIZE		REGULATORY EFFICIENCY		OPEN MARKETS	
Property Rights	**+10.0**	Fiscal Freedom	**+16.3**	Business Freedom	**+15.7**	Trade Freedom	**+22.8**
Freedom from Corruption	**+19.9**	Government Spending	**-6.5**	Labor Freedom	**+3.3**	Investment Freedom	**+30.0**
				Monetary Freedom	**+65.8**	Financial Freedom	**+50.0**

LUXEMBOURG

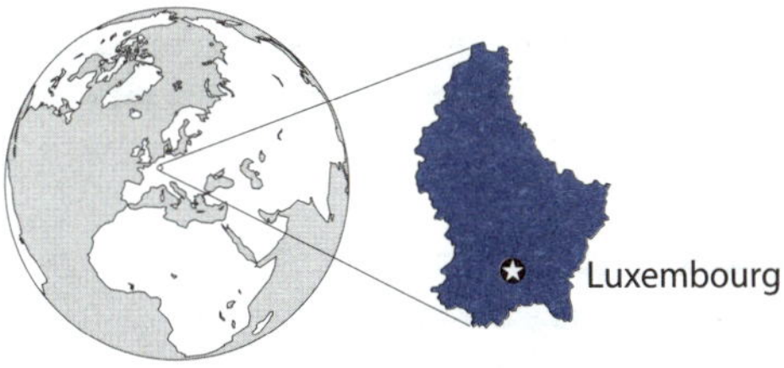

World Rank: **16** Regional Rank: **7**

Economic Freedom Score

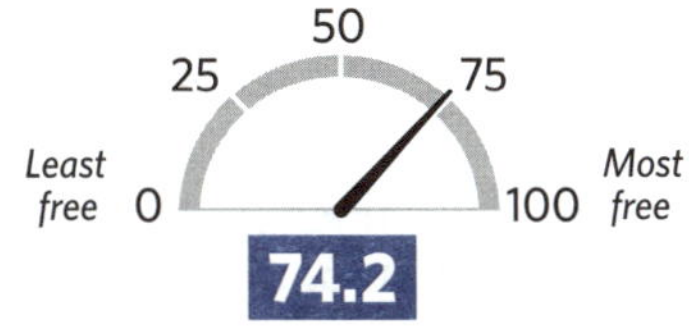

Luxembourg's economic freedom score is 74.2, making its economy the 16th freest in the 2014 *Index*. Its overall score is unchanged from last year, with improvements in labor freedom and trade freedom offset by declines in business freedom and fiscal freedom. Luxembourg is ranked 7th out of 43 countries in the Europe region.

Over the 19 years since Luxembourg was first graded in the 1996 *Index*, its economic freedom score has improved by 1.7 points. Recording score improvements in half of the 10 economic freedoms, including investment freedom, the management of public finance, and financial freedom, Luxembourg has been rated one of the "mostly free" economies.

Openness to global trade and investment has been the cornerstone of Luxembourg's efficient and dynamic economy. A high degree of macroeconomic stability minimizes uncertainty, and the transparent regulatory framework supports the operation of private enterprises, making Luxembourg an attractive place in which to conduct global business. Financial services represent an important economic sector in Luxembourg.

BACKGROUND: A founding member of the European Union in 1957, the Grand Duchy of Luxembourg was also a founding member of the euro in 1999. It continues to promote European integration. Jean-Claude Juncker of the center-right Christian Social People's Party has been prime minister since 1995. Luxembourgers have one of the world's highest income levels, although the global economic crisis provoked the first recession in 60 years in 2009. During the 20th century, Luxembourg evolved from an industrial economy into a mixed manufacturing and services economy with a very strong financial services industry. The government is trying to diversify the economy by promoting Luxembourg as an information technology and e-commerce hub. The country has a skilled workforce and well-developed infrastructure.

Freedom Trend

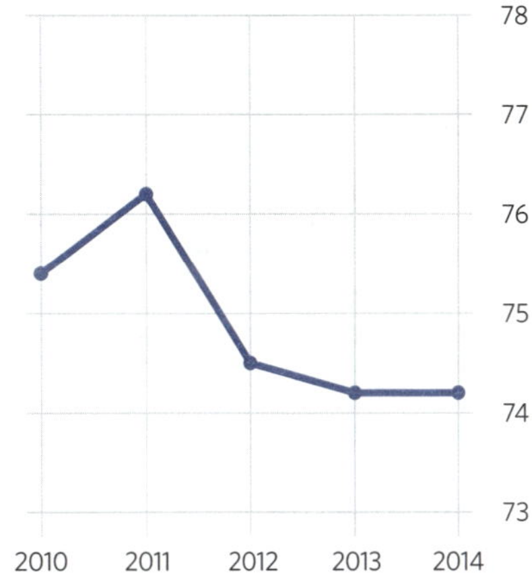

Country Comparisons

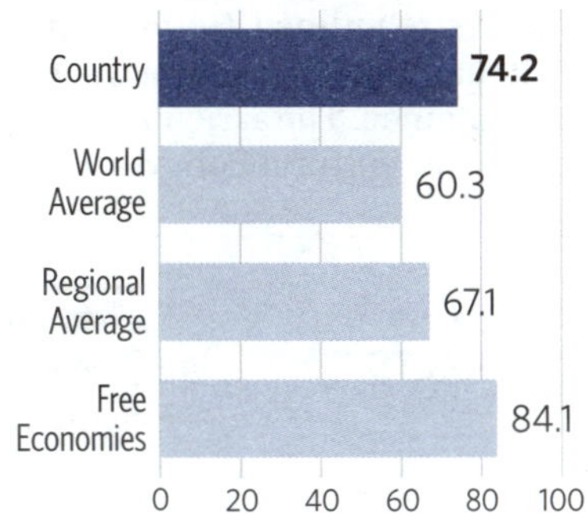

Quick Facts

Population: 0.5 million
GDP (PPP): $42.2 billion
0.1% growth in 2012
5-year compound annual growth −0.1%
$79,785 per capita
Unemployment: 6.0%
Inflation (CPI): 2.9%
FDI Inflow: $27.9 billion
Public Debt: 21.1% of GDP

2012 data unless otherwise noted.
Data compiled as of September 2013.

How Do We Measure Economic Freedom?
See page 471 for an explanation of the methodology or visit the *Index* Web site at *heritage.org/index.*

LUXEMBOURG (continued)

THE TEN ECONOMIC FREEDOMS

RULE OF LAW

	Score	Rank	1-Year Change
Property Rights	90.0	2nd	0
Freedom from Corruption	84.1	12th	-0.9

The government is largely free from corruption. Anti-corruption laws are enforced effectively, and the minimum tolerance for corruption encourages transparency and honest government. The judiciary is independent, and the legal framework strongly supports the rule of law. Private property rights are well protected, and contracts are secure. Luxembourg adheres to key international agreements on intellectual property rights.

GOVERNMENT SIZE

	Score	Rank	1-Year Change
Fiscal Freedom	62.8	164th	-2.2
Government Spending	47.6	138th	+0.5

The top individual income tax rate has risen to 43.6 percent, and the top corporate tax rate remains 21 percent. Individuals and corporations also pay a 7 percent to 9 percent surtax for the unemployment fund. Other taxes include a value-added tax (VAT) and an inheritance tax. The overall tax burden is 37 percent of gross domestic income. Government spending amounts to 42 percent of GDP.

REGULATORY EFFICIENCY

	Score	Rank	1-Year Change
Business Freedom	72.6	66th	-2.2
Labor Freedom	43.1	162nd	+4.1
Monetary Freedom	78.9	50th	-0.4

The overall regulatory framework is relatively efficient, and the business start-up process has been streamlined. Completing licensing requirements is less costly but still takes more than 150 days. The minimum wage is one of the region's highest. Monetary stability has been well maintained. The agricultural sector is highly subsidized by the state and through the EU's Common Agricultural Policy.

OPEN MARKETS

	Score	Rank	1-Year Change
Trade Freedom	87.8	11th	+1.0
Investment Freedom	95.0	1st	0
Financial Freedom	80.0	4th	0

EU members have a low 1.1 percent average tariff rate and, in general, few non-tariff barriers to trade. Luxembourg generally welcomes foreign investment. As a global financial hub, Luxembourg's sophisticated banking sector is well capitalized and competitive. Regulations are transparent and effective. Many of the world's leading banks have subsidiaries in Luxembourg.

Long-Term Score Change (since 1996)

RULE OF LAW		GOVERNMENT SIZE		REGULATORY EFFICIENCY		OPEN MARKETS	
Property Rights	0	Fiscal Freedom	+16.3	Business Freedom	-12.4	Trade Freedom	+8.8
Freedom from Corruption	-5.9	Government Spending	+10.5	Labor Freedom	-8.3	Investment Freedom	+25.0
				Monetary Freedom	-5.9	Financial Freedom	+10.0

MACAU

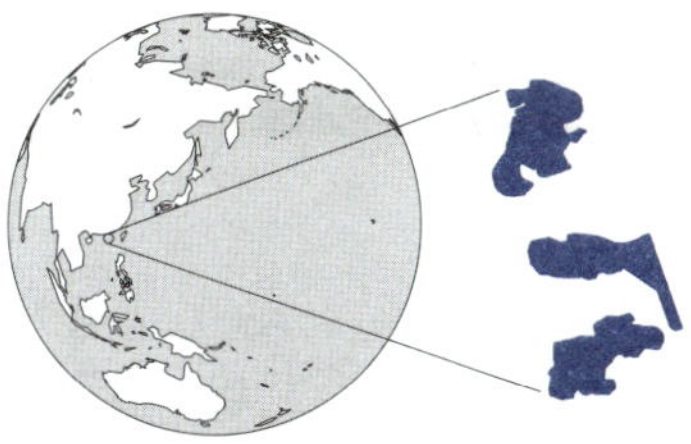

World Rank: **29** Regional Rank: **7**

Economic Freedom Score

Freedom Trend

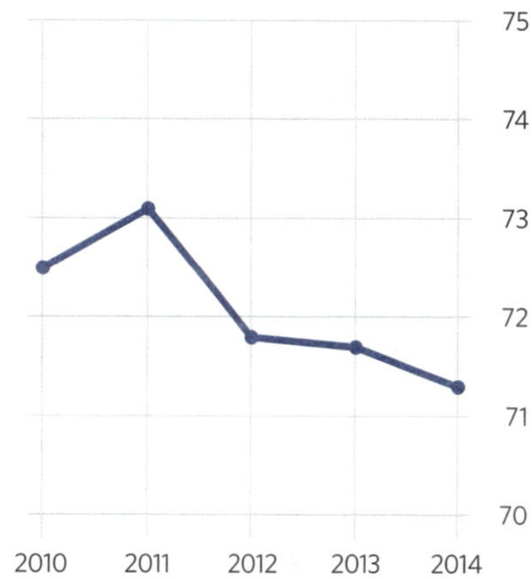

Country Comparisons

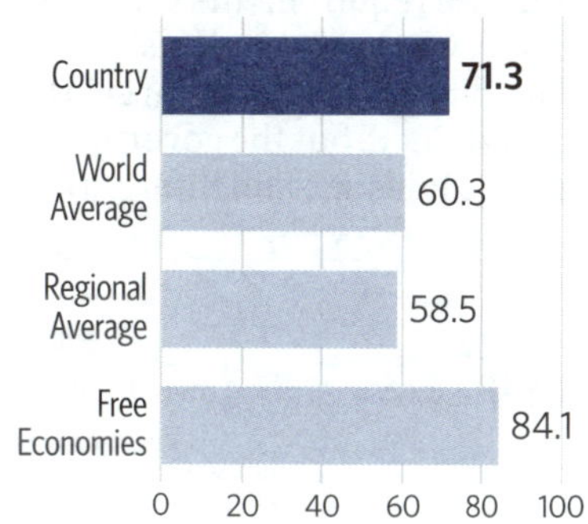

Macau's economic freedom score is 71.3, making its economy the 29th freest in the 2014 *Index*. Its overall score is 0.4 point lower than last year due to declines in fiscal freedom, monetary freedom, and freedom from corruption. Macau is ranked 7th out of 42 countries in the Asia–Pacific region, and its overall score is well above the world and regional averages.

Macau's economic freedom was first graded in the 2009 *Index*, and its progress in implementing more targeted reforms to advance economic freedom has been stagnant at best. Modest declines in half of the 10 economic freedoms, including freedom from corruption, government spending, and labor freedom, have resulted in a six-year combined score loss of less than 1 point. Only investment freedom has advanced, further enhancing market openness.

Macau's economy has been rated "mostly free" throughout its history in the *Index*. The free port city has long benefited from global trade and investment. The entrepreneurial environment is generally efficient and streamlined, and property rights are relatively well respected. The services sector accounts for almost 90 percent of GDP and over 70 percent of total employment. Investment in resort and entertainment projects and related infrastructure has transformed Macau's small economy into one of the world's leading tourism destinations.

BACKGROUND: Macau became a Special Administrative Region of China in 1999, but it retains much of its historic political governance structure and economic system. Its chief executive is appointed by Beijing. Gambling revenues reportedly amounted to $23.5 billion in 2010, and direct taxes on gambling account for well over half of all government revenue. Manufacturing of textiles and garments, once the mainstay of the economy, has largely migrated to the mainland. Macau's currency enjoys full convertibility with the Hong Kong dollar, which in turn is pegged to the U.S. dollar.

Quick Facts

Population: 0.6 million
GDP (PPP): $43.6 billion
9.9% growth in 2012
5-year compound annual growth n/a
$78,275 per capita
Unemployment: 1.9%
Inflation (CPI): 6.1%
FDI Inflow: $1.5 billion
Public Debt: 0.0% of GDP

2012 data unless otherwise noted.
Data compiled as of September 2013.

How Do We Measure Economic Freedom?
See page 471 for an explanation of the methodology or visit the *Index* Web site at *heritage.org/index*.

MACAU (continued)

THE TEN ECONOMIC FREEDOMS

Country | World Average

RULE OF LAW

	Score	Rank	1-Year Change
Property Rights	60.0	41st	0
Freedom from Corruption	49.7	48th	-1.3

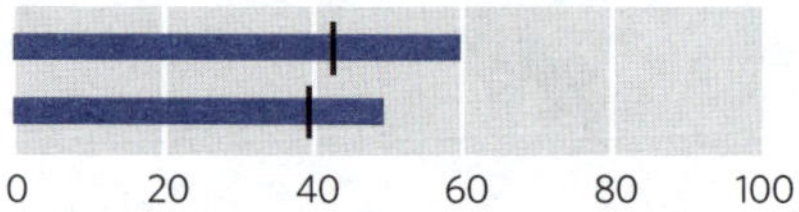

In 2013, China pressed Macau to step up efforts against money laundering in casinos and adopt other anti-corruption measures. Macau has its own judicial system with a high court; the legal framework is based largely on Portuguese law. Property rights and commercial contracts are secure. In 2012, the Legislative Assembly strengthened the copyright law by extending protections to Internet and digital technology.

GOVERNMENT SIZE

	Score	Rank	1-Year Change
Fiscal Freedom	71.4	132nd	-2.1
Government Spending	91.7	8th	+0.2

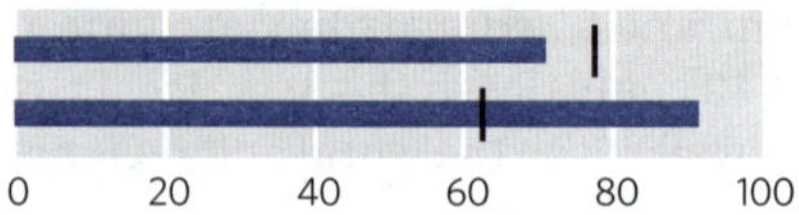

The top individual income tax rate is 12 percent, and the top corporate tax rate is 39 percent. Taxes on gaming and gambling constitute a large portion of overall tax revenue, which is equal to 34.5 percent of gross domestic income. Budget surpluses have been the norm in recent years. Public expenditures are 16.6 percent of gross domestic income. There is no public debt.

REGULATORY EFFICIENCY

	Score	Rank	1-Year Change
Business Freedom	60.0	111th	0
Labor Freedom	55.0	116th	0
Monetary Freedom	79.8	36th	-1.5

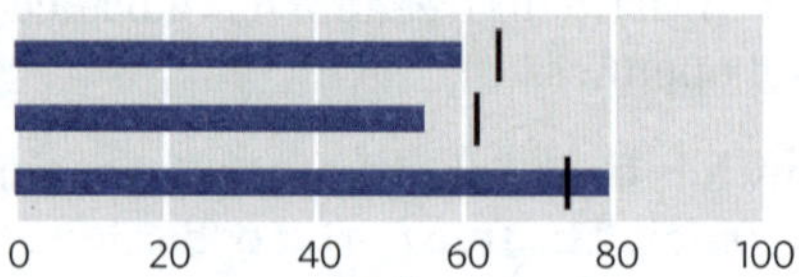

License requirements vary by type of economic activity, but general business activities such as retail, wholesale, and business consultancies do not require a license. The lack of a broad-based labor market is due in part to the absence of serious reform. Monetary stability is relatively well maintained, but the government funds numerous subsidies such as those for pension benefits, public housing, and international convention tourism.

OPEN MARKETS

	Score	Rank	1-Year Change
Trade Freedom	90.0	1st	0
Investment Freedom	85.0	13th	0
Financial Freedom	70.0	19th	0

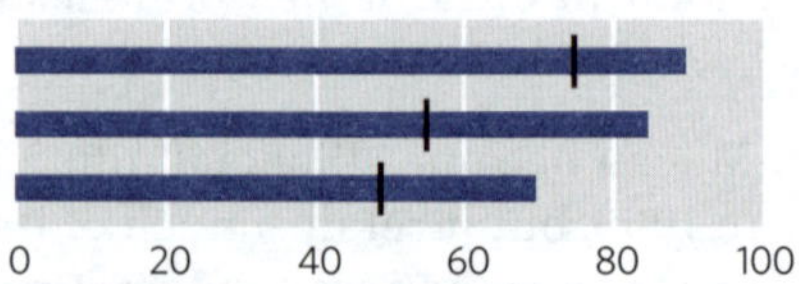

Macao has a 0 percent average tariff rate and few non-tariff barriers. There are few restrictions on foreign investment. The small financial system, dominated by banks, functions without undue government influence. Credit is allocated on market terms, and relatively sound regulation and supervision assure free flows of financial resources. Easy access to financing is available for private-sector activity.

Long-Term Score Change (since 2009)

RULE OF LAW		GOVERNMENT SIZE		REGULATORY EFFICIENCY		OPEN MARKETS	
Property Rights	0	Fiscal Freedom	-7.9	Business Freedom	0	Trade Freedom	0
Freedom from Corruption	-7.3	Government Spending	-1.5	Labor Freedom	-5.0	Investment Freedom	+15.0
				Monetary Freedom	-0.5	Financial Freedom	0

MACEDONIA

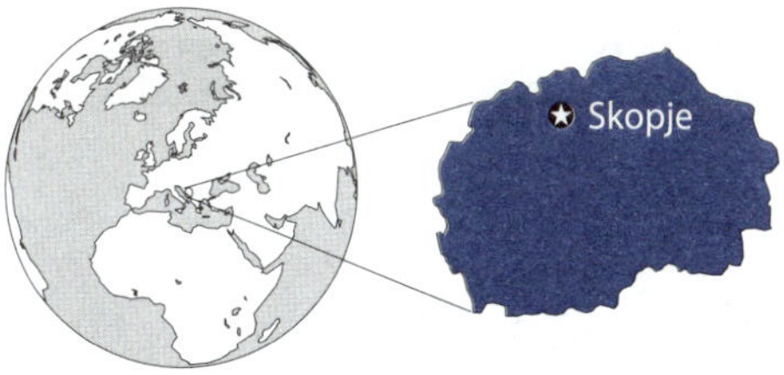

World Rank: **43** Regional Rank: **20**

Economic Freedom Score

Macedonia's economic freedom score is 68.6, making its economy the 43rd freest in the 2014 *Index*. Its overall score has increased by 0.4 point from last year, reflecting improvements in trade freedom, business freedom, and the control of public spending. Macedonia is ranked 20th out of 43 countries in the Europe region, and its overall score is above the world and regional averages.

Macedonia was first assessed in the 2002 *Index*, and its economic freedom score has advanced since then by nearly 11 points. Its transition to a more open and flexible economic system has been facilitated by substantial restructuring measures, which have been quite comprehensive. Score improvements in nine of the 10 economic freedoms include double-digit gains in fiscal freedom, business freedom, labor freedom, trade freedom, and investment freedom. Once considered a "mostly unfree" economy, Macedonia joined the ranks of the "moderately free" in 2007 and has achieved its highest economic freedom score ever in the 2014 *Index*.

The banking sector has weathered the global financial crisis relatively well, and monetary stability has been sustained. Systemic weaknesses persist, however, in the protection of property rights and enforcement of anti-corruption measures. The judicial system is weak, undercut by lingering corruption, and vulnerable to political influence.

BACKGROUND: The Republic of Macedonia gained its independence from the former Yugoslavia in 1991 and has achieved a considerable degree of political and economic stability in recent years. The Social Democrats called for early parliamentary elections in June 2011, and Prime Minister Nikola Gruevski maintained control in a coalition with the Democratic Union for Integration. Macedonia has fulfilled NATO's Membership Action Plan, but Greece has unilaterally blocked its accession to the alliance because it objects to Macedonia's constitutional name. This dispute is expected to delay Macedonia's accession to the European Union as well.

Freedom Trend

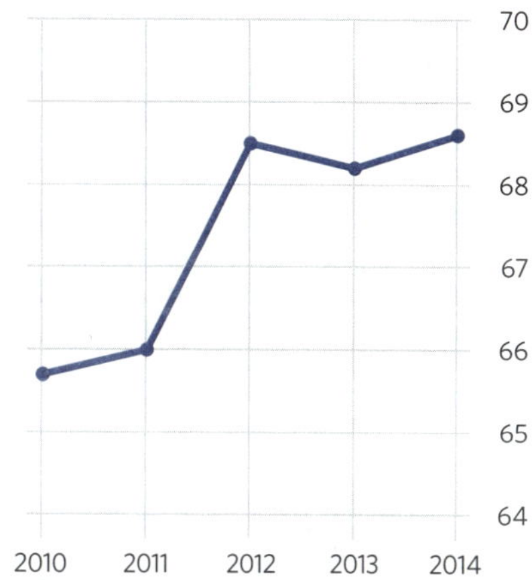

Country Comparisons

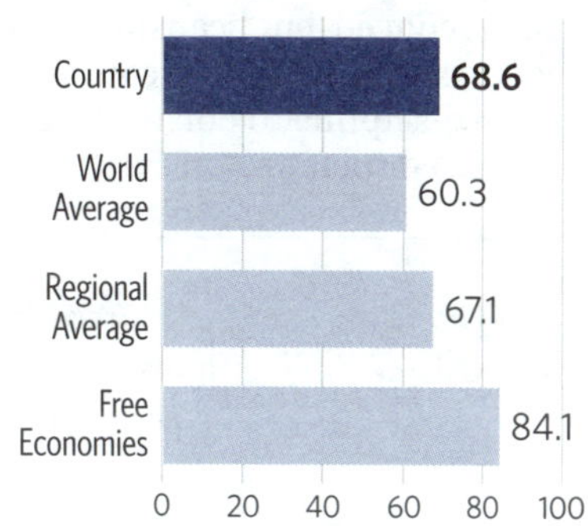

Quick Facts

Population: 2.1 million
GDP (PPP): $21.9 billion
-0.3% growth in 2012
5-year compound annual growth 1.9%
$10,579 per capita
Unemployment: 31.3%
Inflation (CPI): 3.3%
FDI Inflow: $134.6 million
Public Debt: 33.3% of GDP

2012 data unless otherwise noted.
Data compiled as of September 2013.

How Do We Measure Economic Freedom?
See page 471 for an explanation of the methodology or visit the *Index* Web site at *heritage.org/index*.

THE TEN ECONOMIC FREEDOMS

		Score	Rank	1-Year Change
RULE OF LAW	Property Rights	35.0	92nd	0
	Freedom from Corruption	39.6	68th	+0.6

Corruption is a serious problem, particularly in public procurement. Enforcement of anti-corruption legislation is weak. The government has not implemented a new judicial reform strategy. In a 2012 report, the European Commission noted that little progress has been made on judicial independence, impartiality, and competence. Uncertainties in registering real property and obtaining land titles continue to undermine economic freedom.

		Score	Rank	1-Year Change
GOVERNMENT SIZE	Fiscal Freedom	91.4	26th	0
	Government Spending	70.7	85th	+1.6

The personal income and corporate tax rates are a flat 10 percent. Other taxes include a value-added tax (VAT) and a property transfer tax. Overall, tax revenue constitutes 25.6 percent of gross domestic income. Public expenditures are around 31 percent of GDP. Government debt is about 33 percent of gross domestic income. There has been popular opposition to recent increases in government spending.

		Score	Rank	1-Year Change
REGULATORY EFFICIENCY	Business Freedom	81.0	30th	+0.7
	Labor Freedom	78.8	33rd	+0.4
	Monetary Freedom	83.5	8th	-0.5

Procedures for launching a business have been streamlined, and licensing requirements have been reduced, but licensing can cost over five times the level of average annual income. Labor codes lack flexibility, discouraging dynamic job creation. The government has tried to maintain fiscal discipline to bolster its case for eventual membership in the euro-zone, but in 2013, it increased spending on agricultural subsidies, social transfers, and pensions.

		Score	Rank	1-Year Change
OPEN MARKETS	Trade Freedom	85.9	43rd	+1.3
	Investment Freedom	60.0	80th	0
	Financial Freedom	60.0	41st	0

Macedonia's average tariff rate is 2 percent. There are few non-tariff trade barriers, and the government does not discriminate against foreign investors. The financial sector has strengthened in recent years, with the government's role limited primarily to regulatory enforcement. Bank competition has increased, and the foreign presence in the financial system accounts for more than 70 percent of total bank assets.

Long-Term Score Change (since 2002)

RULE OF LAW		GOVERNMENT SIZE		REGULATORY EFFICIENCY		OPEN MARKETS	
Property Rights	**+5.0**	Fiscal Freedom	**+10.5**	Business Freedom	**+26.0**	Trade Freedom	**+22.9**
Freedom from Corruption	**+6.6**	Government Spending	**+7.4**	Labor Freedom	**+22.5**	Investment Freedom	**+10.0**
				Monetary Freedom	**+6.4**	Financial Freedom	**-10.0**

MADAGASCAR

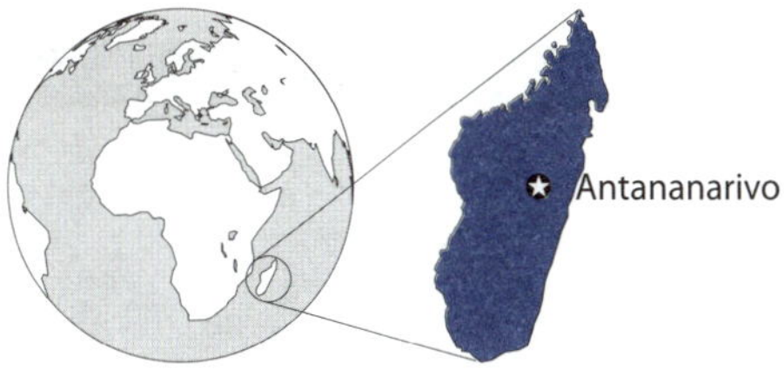

World Rank: **79** Regional Rank: **7**

Economic Freedom Score

Freedom Trend

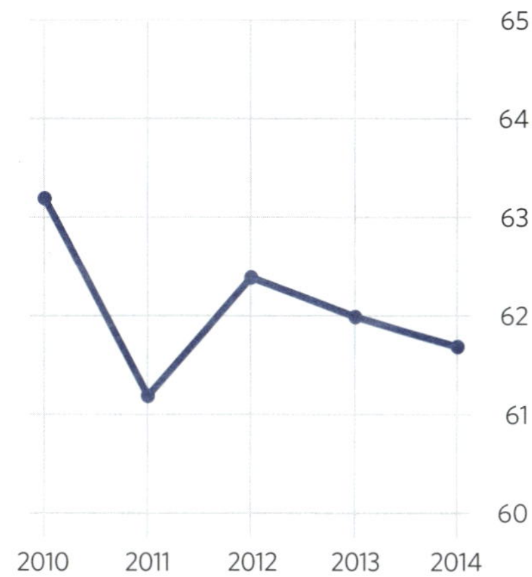

Country Comparisons

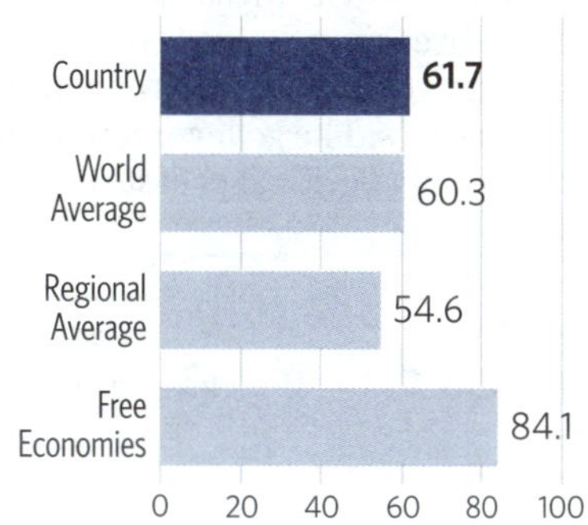

Madagascar's economic freedom score is 61.7, making its economy the 79th freest in the 2014 *Index*. Its score has decreased by 0.3 point from last year, with small declines in labor freedom, freedom from corruption, and control of government spending outweighing modest gains in trade freedom and monetary freedom. Madagascar is ranked 7th out of 46 countries in the Sub-Saharan Africa region, and its overall score is above the world and regional averages.

Over the 20-year history of the *Index*, Madagascar has improved its economic freedom score by over 10 points. In addition to notable advancements in the areas of rule of law, market openness, and government size, double-digit growth has been recorded in half of the 10 economic freedoms including freedom from corruption, fiscal freedom, financial freedom, property rights, and trade freedom. Once considered "mostly unfree," Madagascar's economy has been rated "moderately free" since 2003.

Despite some progress toward much-needed economic development, the combined impact of poor economic management and the ongoing risk of political instability has severely undermined much of the progress made in reducing poverty. The judicial system is underdeveloped, and convoluted administrative procedures facilitate corruption.

BACKGROUND: Both former President Didier Ratsiraka and opposition candidate Marc Ravalomanana claimed victory in the 2001 elections, and the resulting violence and economic disruption ended only when Ratsiraka fled in 2002. Ravalomanana won a second term in 2006 but stepped down in 2009 after a power struggle with the opposition. Opposition leader Andry Rajoelina seized power with military backing and declared himself president of the High Transitional Authority. A presidential election set for 2012 was postponed until October 2013. Some donors have suspended aid, and the African Union and Southern African Development Community have suspended Madagascar's membership. The political crisis has discouraged investors and contributed to economic stagnation.

How Do We Measure Economic Freedom?
See page 471 for an explanation of the methodology or visit the *Index* Web site at *heritage.org/index*.

Quick Facts

Population: 22.4 million
GDP (PPP): $21.4 billion
1.9% growth in 2012
5-year compound annual growth 1.4%
$955 per capita
Unemployment: n/a
Inflation (CPI): 6.5%
FDI Inflow: $894.7 million
Public Debt: 38.3% of GDP

2012 data unless otherwise noted.
Data compiled as of September 2013.

MADAGASCAR (continued)

THE TEN ECONOMIC FREEDOMS

RULE OF LAW

	Score	Rank	1-Year Change
Property Rights	40.0	70th	0
Freedom from Corruption	27.3	120th	-2.7

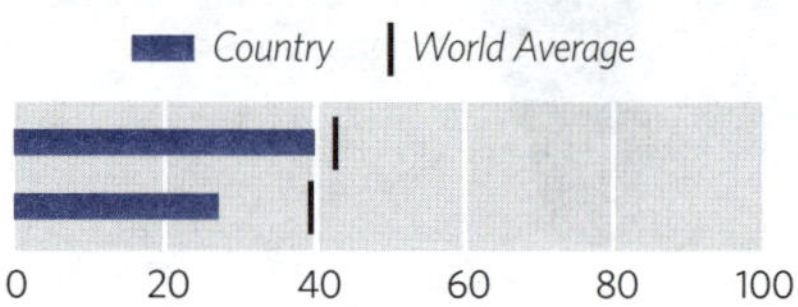

Pervasive corruption remains a major problem as repercussions continue to be felt in the wake of the 2009 coup. In 2011, the Extractive Industries Transparency Initiative suspended Madagascar. The judiciary is susceptible to corruption and executive influence. The coup highlighted institutional weaknesses, and subsequent judicial decisions were tainted by frequent intimidation. Enforcement of contracts cannot be guaranteed.

GOVERNMENT SIZE

	Score	Rank	1-Year Change
Fiscal Freedom	90.8	32nd	+0.8
Government Spending	92.3	5th	-2.3

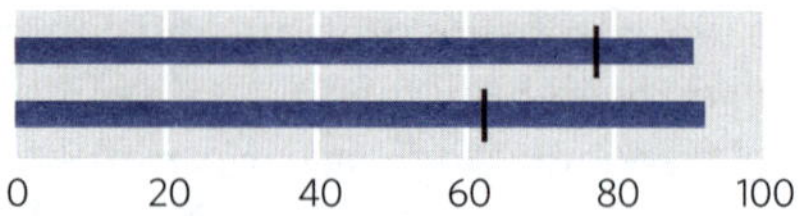

The top individual income and corporate tax rates have fallen to 20 percent. Other taxes include a value-added tax (VAT) and a capital gains tax. The overall tax burden amounts to 11.1 percent of gross domestic income. Public expenditures are 16 percent of GDP. Public debt is around 38 percent of gross domestic income. Cuts in aid flows in recent years have put pressure on public spending.

REGULATORY EFFICIENCY

	Score	Rank	1-Year Change
Business Freedom	62.8	99th	-0.7
Labor Freedom	43.9	159th	-3.5
Monetary Freedom	77.6	67th	+2.7

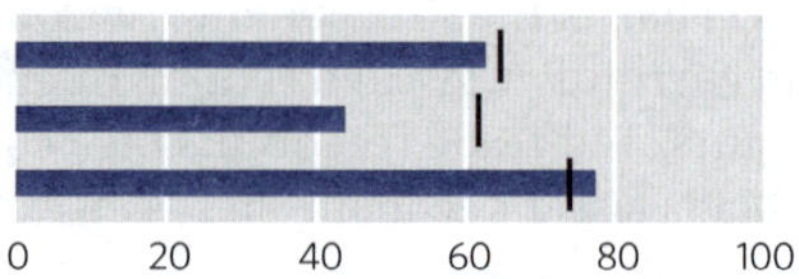

Launching a business has become more straightforward, but licensing requirements still take over three months and cost more than 10 times the level of average annual income. The labor market remains poorly developed. Inflation has averaged 10 percent over the most recent three years. The government's maintenance of fiscal and monetary discipline is coming under increasing political pressure.

OPEN MARKETS

	Score	Rank	1-Year Change
Trade Freedom	77.8	83rd	+3.2
Investment Freedom	55.0	96th	0
Financial Freedom	50.0	69th	0

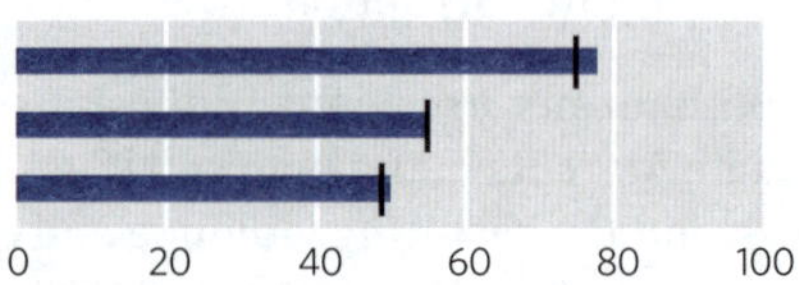

Madagascar's average tariff rate is 6.1 percent, and there are relatively few non-tariff barriers to trade. The unstable political climate deters investment. Less than 5 percent of the population has access to comprehensive financial services. The relatively high costs of financing and scarce access to credit are barriers to private-sector development. Capital markets remain underdeveloped, and there is no stock market.

Long-Term Score Change (since 1995)

RULE OF LAW		GOVERNMENT SIZE		REGULATORY EFFICIENCY		OPEN MARKETS	
Property Rights	+10.0	Fiscal Freedom	+16.0	Business Freedom	-7.2	Trade Freedom	+40.2
Freedom from Corruption	+17.3	Government Spending	+4.4	Labor Freedom	-4.9	Investment Freedom	+5.0
				Monetary Freedom	+3.6	Financial Freedom	+20.0

MALAWI

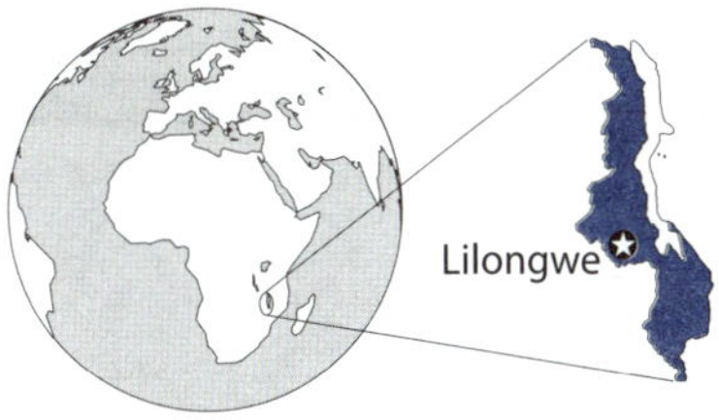

Economic Freedom Score

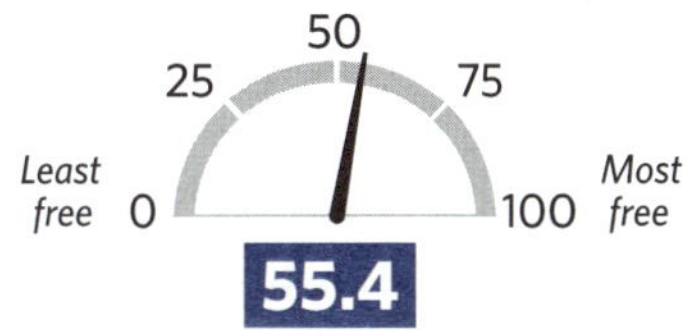

World Rank: 124 | **Regional Rank: 22**

Malawi's economic freedom score is 55.4, making its economy the 124th freest in the 2014 *Index*. Its score is essentially unchanged from last year, with improvements in property rights, labor freedom and the control of government spending undermined by a significant loss of monetary stability. Malawi is ranked 22nd out of 46 countries in the Sub-Saharan Africa region, and its overall score is below the world average.

Over the 20-year history of the *Index*, Malawi's economic freedom has been largely stagnant. Despite notable score improvements in trade freedom, monetary freedom, and fiscal freedom, its overall gain has been largely offset by a notable decline in business freedom and a smaller decline in property rights.

Malawi's economy continues to be rated "mostly unfree." It lags in competitiveness and the promotion of the broad-based economic growth so essential to the reduction of poverty. The poor quality of much of the basic infrastructure and the government's inefficiency in delivering public goods have been serious impediments to vibrant economic development.

BACKGROUND: Malawi achieved independence in 1964 and was ruled as a one-party state by Dr. Hastings Kamuzu Banda for 30 years. President Bingu wa Mutharika, elected in 2004 and re-elected in 2009, died in April 2012 and was replaced by Vice President Joyce Banda. Malawi is one of Africa's most densely populated countries. Over 85 percent of the population depends on subsistence agriculture, and the agricultural sector accounts for over 35 percent of GDP and over 80 percent of exports. Tobacco, tea, and sugar are the most important exports. Foreign donors, who provided an average of 36 percent of government revenue since 2006, suspended general budget support for Malawi in 2011. In a bid to have donor funding restored, Banda has reversed several of her predecessor's anti-market economic policies.

Freedom Trend

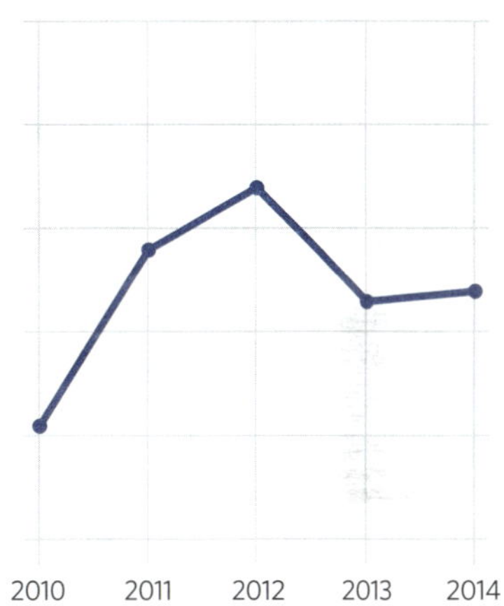

Country Comparisons

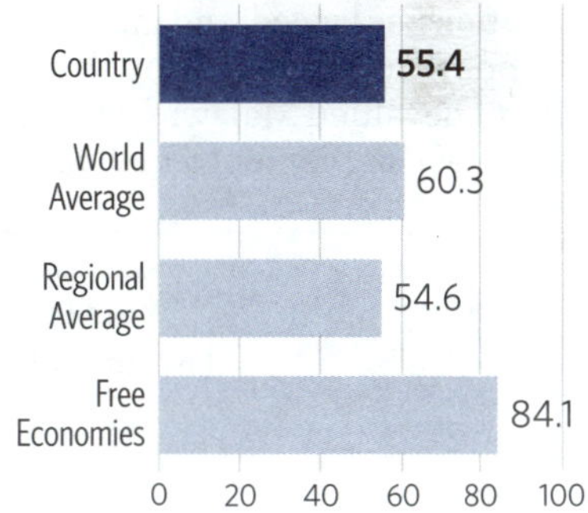

Quick Facts

Population: 16.6 million
GDP (PPP): $14.3 billion
1.9% growth in 2012
5-year compound annual growth 6.0%
$858 per capita
Unemployment: n/a
Inflation (CPI): 21.3%
FDI Inflow: $129.5 million
Public Debt: 54.9% of GDP

2012 data unless otherwise noted.
Data compiled as of September 2013.

How Do We Measure Economic Freedom?
See page 471 for an explanation of the methodology or visit the *Index* Web site at *heritage.org/index*.

THE TEN ECONOMIC FREEDOMS

Country | World Average

RULE OF LAW

	Score	Rank	1-Year Change
Property Rights	45.0	68th	+5.0
Freedom from Corruption	31.9	94th	+1.9

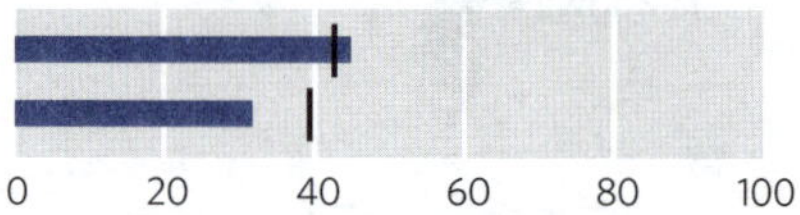

Although the constitution provides for the separation of powers among the judicial, executive, and legislative branches of government, the effectiveness of checks and balances has varied. President Banda's administration has been praised for efforts to reduce waste and fight corruption. A law that limited the power of the courts to issue injunctions was repealed, and the head of the national police was replaced.

GOVERNMENT SIZE

	Score	Rank	1-Year Change
Fiscal Freedom	78.0	103rd	-0.4
Government Spending	63.0	109th	+3.0

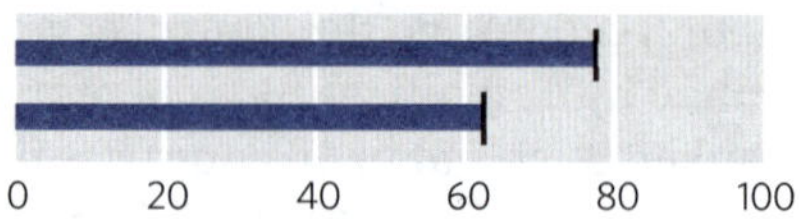

The top individual income and corporate tax rates are 30 percent. Other taxes include a value-added tax (VAT) and a capital gains tax. Overall tax revenue is about 20 percent of the domestic economy. Government expenditures equate to 35 percent of GDP. Public debt reached about 55 percent of the domestic economy in 2013. Public finances have been under stress, and the new government has looked to tighten spending.

REGULATORY EFFICIENCY

	Score	Rank	1-Year Change
Business Freedom	38.9	169th	-2.2
Labor Freedom	60.3	98th	+1.5
Monetary Freedom	64.1	168th	-8.4

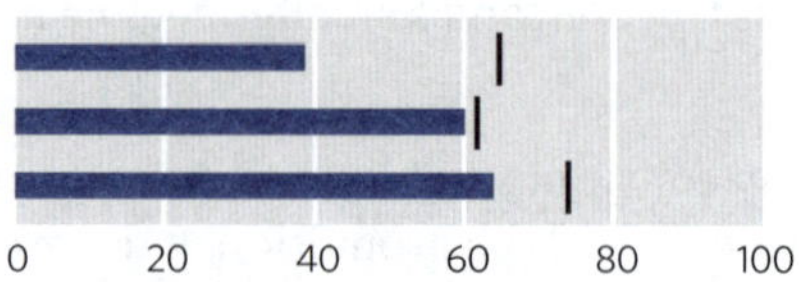

Commercial regulations have not been implemented or enforced effectively. Economic diversification has lagged, and much private-sector activity takes place outside of the formal economy. Labor regulations, although not fully enforced, are relatively rigid. In 2012, the new government devalued Malawi's currency to allow a market-determined exchange rate. A new three-year IMF agreement worth $157 million soon followed.

OPEN MARKETS

	Score	Rank	1-Year Change
Trade Freedom	72.7	115th	+0.9
Investment Freedom	50.0	109th	0
Financial Freedom	50.0	69th	0

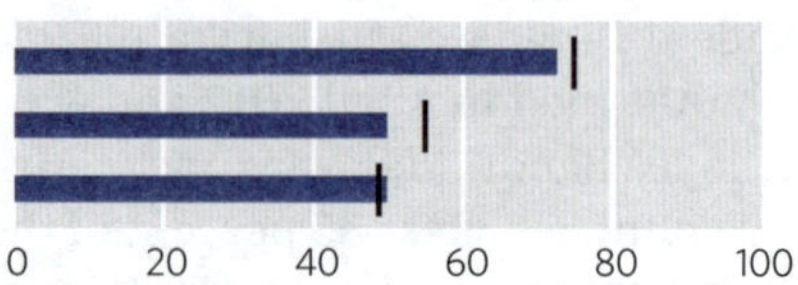

Malawi's average tariff rate is 6.2 percent. Importing goods is costly and time-consuming. Access to foreign exchange can be difficult at times. The financial sector, dominated by banking, remains underdeveloped, and a full range of modern financing tools is not readily available. Capital transactions and foreign exchange accounts are also limited.

Long-Term Score Change (since 1995)

RULE OF LAW		GOVERNMENT SIZE		REGULATORY EFFICIENCY		OPEN MARKETS	
Property Rights	**-5.0**	Fiscal Freedom	**+8.7**	Business Freedom	**-16.1**	Trade Freedom	**+8.7**
Freedom from Corruption	**+1.9**	Government Spending	**-1.0**	Labor Freedom	**+2.4**	Investment Freedom	**0**
				Monetary Freedom	**+3.9**	Financial Freedom	**0**

MALAYSIA

World Rank: **37** Regional Rank: **9**

Economic Freedom Score

Freedom Trend

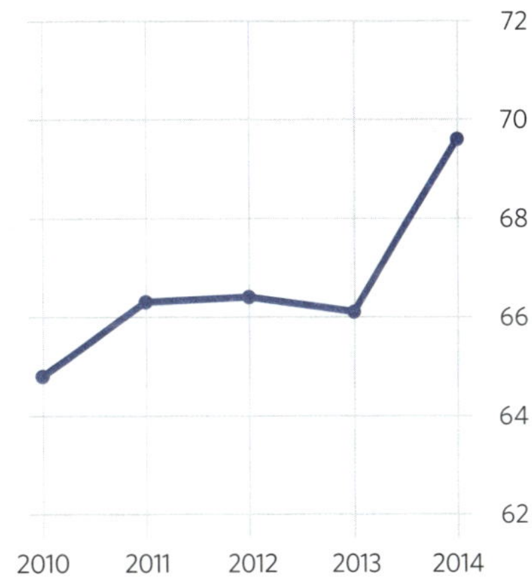

Country Comparisons

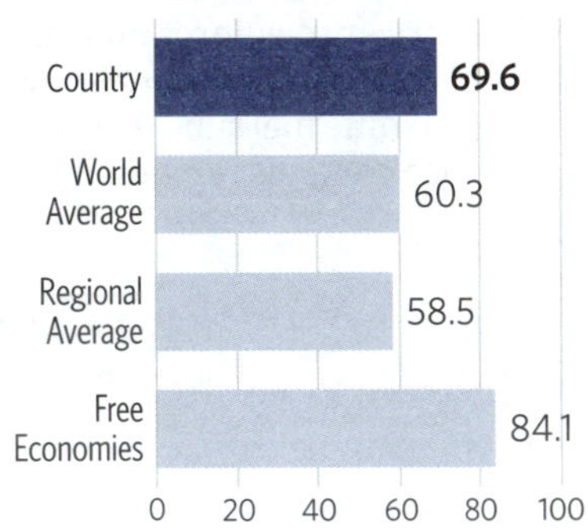

Malaysia's economic freedom score is 69.6, making its economy the 37th freest in the 2014 *Index*. Its score is 3.5 points higher than last year, with impressive improvements in seven of the 10 economic freedoms including financial freedom, investment freedom, labor freedom, and business freedom. Malaysia is ranked 9th out of 42 countries in the Asia–Pacific region, and its overall score is above the world and regional averages.

Over the 20-year history of the *Index*, Malaysia's economic freedom score has declined by 2.3 points. Declines have been recorded in five of the 10 economic freedoms, including property rights, freedom from corruption, and investment freedom. Most notably, freedom from corruption has declined by over 25 points, undermining the rule of law. Over the past two decades, Malaysia's economy has mostly been rated "moderately free."

Registering one of the 10 best score improvements in the 2014 *Index*, Malaysia has charted an upward trajectory of economic freedom for the past five years. It has undertaken wide-ranging reforms to address various structural weaknesses and improve competitiveness. Recent reforms have put greater emphasis on improving regulatory efficiency, enhancing regional competitiveness, and modernizing the financial sector.

BACKGROUND: The ethnically and religiously diverse constitutional monarchy of Malaysia has been ruled by the United Malays National Organization since independence in 1957, but dissatisfaction with pro-Malay affirmative-action programs and corruption generated important opposition gains in the March 2008 elections. The trend continued with the 2013 elections, in which the UMNO-led coalition retained power but failed for the first time to win more than 50 percent of the popular vote. Despite significant steps toward liberalizing the economy, the government maintains investments in such key sectors as banking, media, automobiles, and airlines. Malaysia is a leading exporter of electronics and information technology products; other industries include agricultural products and automobiles.

How Do We Measure Economic Freedom?
See page 471 for an explanation of the methodology or visit the *Index* Web site at *heritage.org/index*.

Quick Facts

Population: 29.5 million
GDP (PPP): $498.5 billion
5.6% growth in 2012
5-year compound annual growth 4.2%
$16,922 per capita
Unemployment: 3.0%
Inflation (CPI): 1.7%
FDI Inflow: $10.1 billion
Public Debt: 55.5% of GDP

2012 data unless otherwise noted.
Data compiled as of September 2013.

THE TEN ECONOMIC FREEDOMS

Country | World Average

RULE OF LAW

		Score	Rank	1-Year Change
RULE OF LAW	Property Rights	55.0	51st	0
	Freedom from Corruption	44.3	56th	+1.3

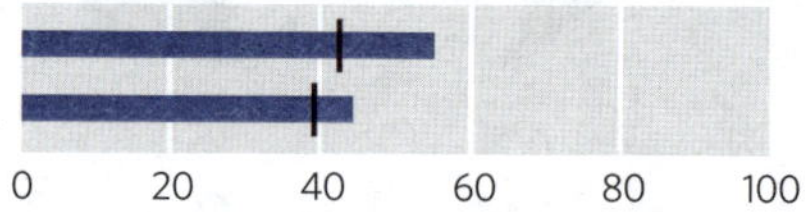

Several high-level government officials and law enforcement bodies figured in corruption scandals in the past year, and the government has taken steps to address the problem. Judicial independence is undermined by extensive executive influence, and arbitrary or politically motivated verdicts can occur. Private property is protected effectively. Corporate lawsuits face lengthy delays.

GOVERNMENT SIZE

		Score	Rank	1-Year Change
GOVERNMENT SIZE	Fiscal Freedom	84.6	57th	-0.5
	Government Spending	75.6	66th	+2.1

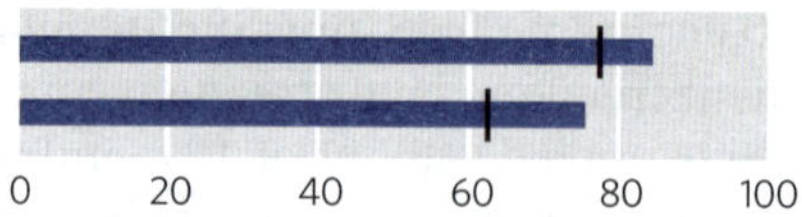

The top individual income tax rate is 26 percent, and the top corporate tax rate is 25 percent. Other taxes include a capital gains tax. The overall tax burden equals 15.3 percent of the domestic economy. Government spending is equivalent to 29 percent of GDP, and public debt has increased slightly to about 56 percent of the domestic economy. In 2013, the government moved to reduce fuel subsidies in order to narrow budget imbalances.

REGULATORY EFFICIENCY

		Score	Rank	1-Year Change
REGULATORY EFFICIENCY	Business Freedom	85.6	21st	+5.7
	Labor Freedom	78.5	36th	+6.2
	Monetary Freedom	81.0	21st	+1.2

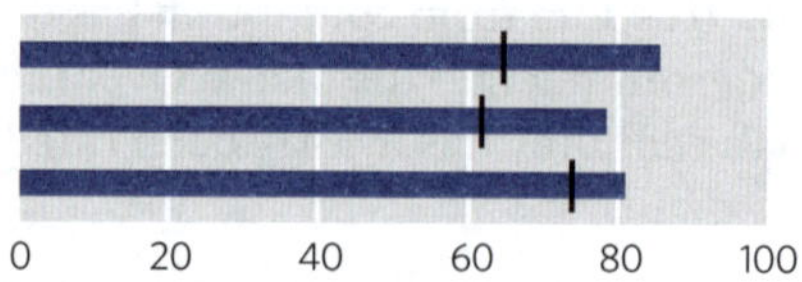

Steps to introduce greater regulatory efficiency have been implemented in recent years. It takes three procedures and six days on average to incorporate a business, and no minimum capital is required. Despite some improvement, labor market rigidity persists. The government reduced some fuel subsidies in 2013, but numerous other economically distortionary subsidies and price controls remain in place.

OPEN MARKETS

		Score	Rank	1-Year Change
OPEN MARKETS	Trade Freedom	76.4	90th	-0.6
	Investment Freedom	55.0	96th	+10.0
	Financial Freedom	60.0	41st	+10.0

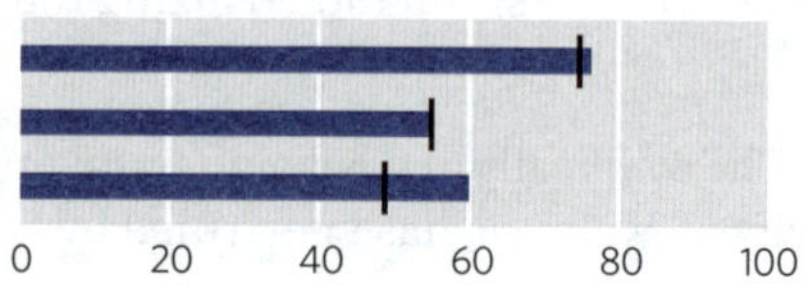

Malaysia's average tariff rate is 4.3 percent, and non-tariff barriers impede imports of agricultural goods and automobiles. The foreign investment regime has been liberalized, but the government still screens manufacturing projects. The financial sector remains stable, offering a comprehensive array of financial services. Measures to open the banking sector to greater competition have been implemented.

Long-Term Score Change (since 1995)

RULE OF LAW		GOVERNMENT SIZE		REGULATORY EFFICIENCY		OPEN MARKETS	
Property Rights	**-15.0**	Fiscal Freedom	**+10.6**	Business Freedom	**+0.6**	Trade Freedom	**+9.4**
Freedom from Corruption	**-25.7**	Government Spending	**-2.7**	Labor Freedom	**+6.5**	Investment Freedom	**-15.0**
				Monetary Freedom	**-1.6**	Financial Freedom	**+10.0**

MALDIVES

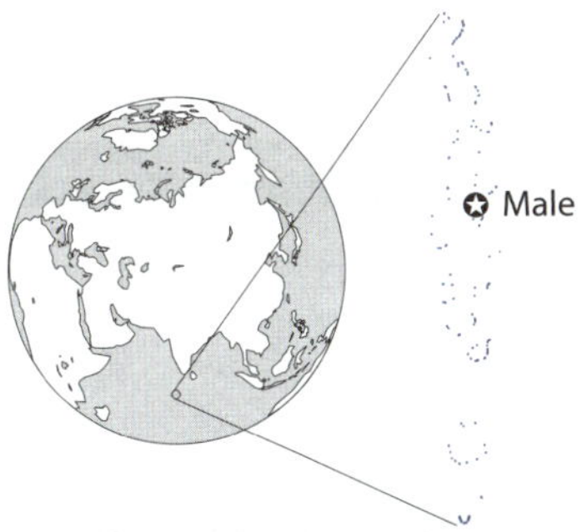

World Rank: **145** Regional Rank: **32**

The Maldives' economic freedom score is 51.0, making its economy the 145th freest in the 2014 *Index*. Its score has increased by 2.0 points, with a significant improvement in the control of government spending and labor freedom outweighing declines in investment freedom, property rights, and freedom from corruption. The Maldives is ranked 32nd out of 42 countries in the Asia–Pacific region, and its overall score is below the world and regional averages.

The Maldives' economic freedom was first assessed in the 2009 *Index*, and there has been no overall progress since then. Declines in six of the 10 economic freedoms, notably labor freedom, monetary freedom, and investment freedom, have offset significant improvement in the control of government spending. The rule of law, measured through property rights and freedom from corruption, has deteriorated substantially. The Maldives' economy is rated "mostly unfree," the same as it was six years ago.

With no system of direct taxation, the government relies heavily on import taxes, tourism taxes, and income generated by state-owned enterprises. Weaknesses include chronically high government spending, an inefficient and outsized public sector, and widespread corruption. The state still plays a large role in the economy through state-owned enterprises, limiting private-sector activity. Public ownership is widespread in every sector except tourism and remains the largest source of employment, hiring over one-third of the formal labor force.

BACKGROUND: The military forced President Mohammed Nasheed to step down in February 2012 after several weeks of anti-government street protests instigated by former dictator Maumoon Abdul Gayoom. Fresh elections in September 2013 were annulled by the Supreme Court due to voting irregularities and were to be rescheduled by the end of the year. Tourism is the centerpiece of the economy, contributing 28 percent of GDP and over 90 percent of government tax revenue.

How Do We Measure Economic Freedom?
See page 471 for an explanation of the methodology or visit the *Index* Web site at *heritage.org/index*.

Economic Freedom Score

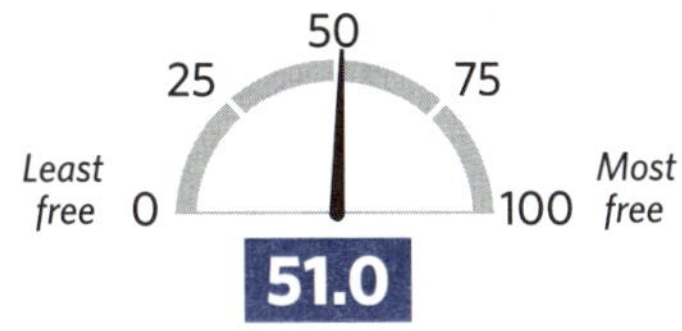

Freedom Trend

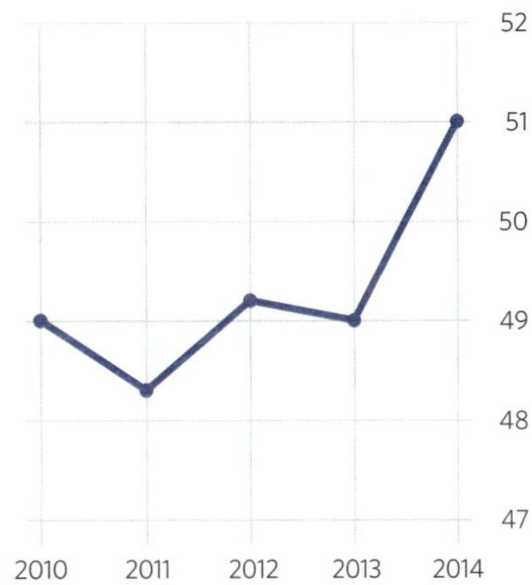

Country Comparisons

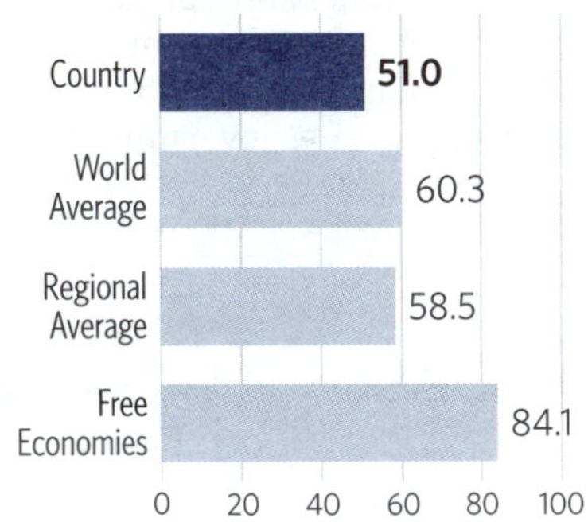

Quick Facts

Population: 0.3 million
GDP (PPP): $3.1 billion
3.5% growth in 2012
5-year compound annual growth 5.1%
$9,235 per capita
Unemployment: 28.0%
Inflation (CPI): 10.9%
FDI Inflow: $284.0 million
Public Debt: 77.5% of GDP

2012 data unless otherwise noted.
Data compiled as of September 2013.

THE TEN ECONOMIC FREEDOMS

RULE OF LAW

	Score	Rank	1-Year Change
Property Rights	20.0	139th	-5.0
Freedom from Corruption	21.9	153rd	-3.1

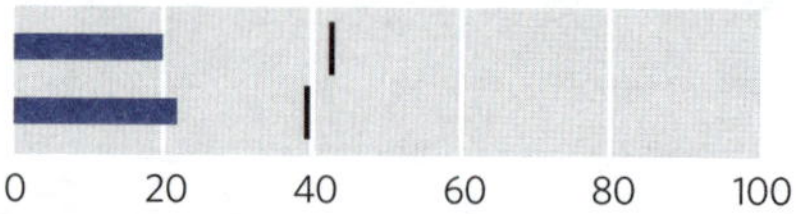

In recent years, a new, independent auditor general has provided greater transparency and shed light on pervasive corruption. The tumultuous political situation in the wake of the removal at gunpoint of the president and replacement by his vice president in 2012, however, at times has paralyzed the government. The rule of law remains uneven, and the inefficient judicial system is subject to political influence.

GOVERNMENT SIZE

	Score	Rank	1-Year Change
Fiscal Freedom	97.4	8th	-1.4
Government Spending	43.8	143rd	+29.3

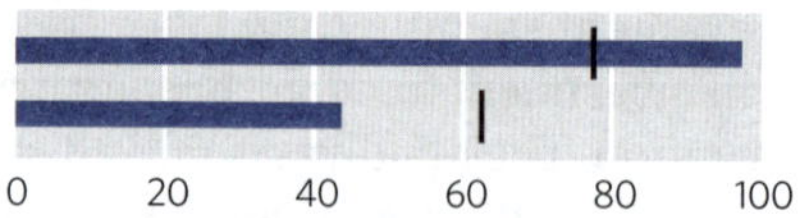

The Maldives has no corporate or individual income tax. Commercial banks are subject to a 25 percent tax. The overall tax burden is 16.2 percent of gross domestic income. Government expenditures continue to rise at 43 percent of GDP. Public debt reached about 78 percent of the size of the domestic economy in the most recent year. Political uncertainty and expanding security spending have increased budgetary uncertainty.

REGULATORY EFFICIENCY

	Score	Rank	1-Year Change
Business Freedom	87.4	19th	-1.3
Labor Freedom	71.7	60th	+7.7
Monetary Freedom	69.4	144th	-1.0

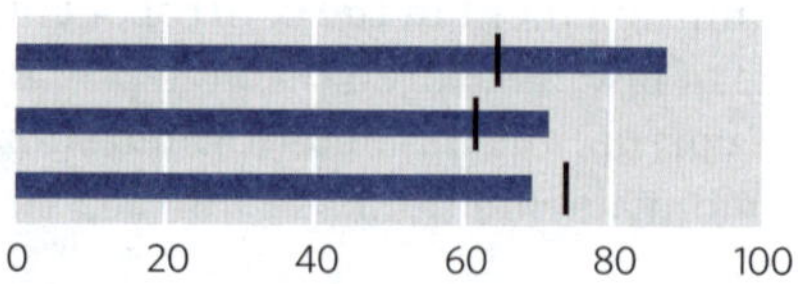

The non-transparent and costly regulatory framework continues to discourage the emergence of entrepreneurial dynamism. Labor regulations are not enforced effectively, and there is no efficient countrywide labor market. A large share of the workforce is employed in the informal sector. The new government has increased spending and the inflation rate remains over 10 percent.

OPEN MARKETS

	Score	Rank	1-Year Change
Trade Freedom	43.8	177th	+0.1
Investment Freedom	25.0	159th	-5.0
Financial Freedom	30.0	132nd	0

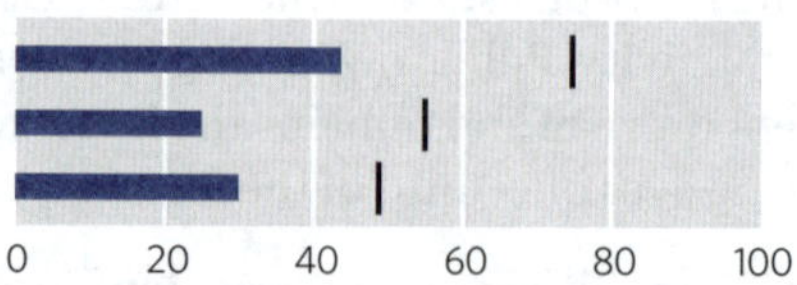

The average tariff rate is 20.6 percent, and import quotas are imposed on some agricultural imports. Political unrest deters foreign investment. Banking has expanded, but costs are high and access to financial services is limited. As part of efforts to enhance private-sector development, the state, which owns over half of the largest telecommunications company, has embarked on a mobile phone banking project.

Long-Term Score Change (since 2009)

RULE OF LAW		GOVERNMENT SIZE		REGULATORY EFFICIENCY		OPEN MARKETS	
Property Rights	**-10.0**	Fiscal Freedom	**+1.6**	Business Freedom	**+4.2**	Trade Freedom	**-0.2**
Freedom from Corruption	**-11.1**	Government Spending	**+43.8**	Labor Freedom	**-18.4**	Investment Freedom	**-5.0**
				Monetary Freedom	**-7.1**	Financial Freedom	**0**

MALI

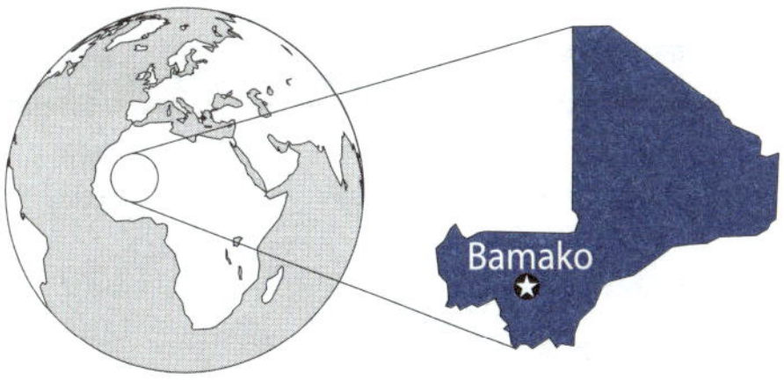

World Rank: **122** Regional Rank: **21**

Economic Freedom Score

Mali's economic freedom score is 55.5, making its economy the 122nd freest in the 2014 *Index*. Its score has decreased by 0.9 point from last year, mainly reflecting declines in property rights and five other economic freedoms that outweigh a notable gain in investment freedom. Mali is ranked 21st out of 46 countries in the Sub-Saharan Africa region, and its score is below the world average.

Over the 20-year history of the *Index*, Mali has advanced its economic freedom score by just over 3 points. Gains from score increases in five of the 10 economic freedoms, including freedom from corruption, fiscal freedom, government spending, trade freedom, and financial freedom, have been largely eroded by deteriorations in investment freedom, property rights, and business freedom. Rated "moderately free" from 2000 to 2002, Mali's economy has fallen back to "mostly unfree."

Overall institutional weaknesses continue to perpetuate the stagnation of economic freedom and limit economic dynamism. Corruption undermines the rule of law, and the inefficient judicial system remains vulnerable to political influence.

BACKGROUND: President Amadou Toumani Touré was ousted in a March 2012 coup, and former National Assembly speaker Dioncounda Traore became interim president after a brief period of military rule. Tuareg separatists and al-Qaeda–linked militants continue to dominate much of northern Mali. In January 2013, French armed forces restored government control in the major cities, and Tuareg rebels signed a peace accord in June. Ex-Prime Minister Ibrahim Boubacar Keita won the presidential election in a second-round ballot in August. Terrorism remains a grave concern; French forces are scheduled to be reduced to 1,000 troops in 2014 and are being replaced by an African Union peacekeeping force. Subsistence agriculture, livestock, and fishing employ 80 percent of the workforce and account for about a third of GDP. Mineral resources remain underexploited, and infrastructure is inadequate.

How Do We Measure Economic Freedom?
See page 471 for an explanation of the methodology or visit the *Index* Web site at *heritage.org/index*.

Freedom Trend

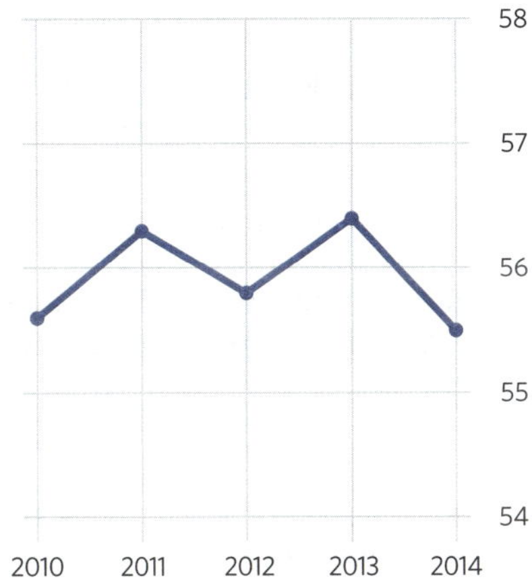

Country Comparisons

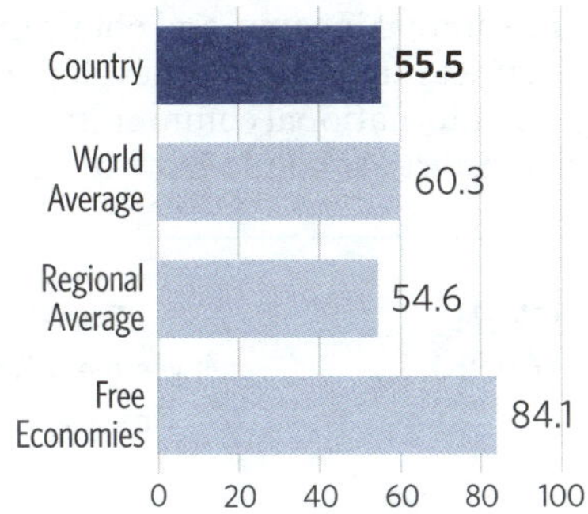

Quick Facts

Population: 16.3 million
GDP (PPP): $18.0 billion
-1.2% growth in 2012
5-year compound annual growth 3.3%
$1,100 per capita
Unemployment: 30.0% (2009)
Inflation (CPI): 5.3%
FDI Inflow: $310.5 million
Public Debt: 32.0% of GDP

2012 data unless otherwise noted.
Data compiled as of September 2013.

THE TEN ECONOMIC FREEDOMS

		Score	Rank	1-Year Change
RULE OF LAW	Property Rights	20.0	139th	-10.0
	Freedom from Corruption	27.7	119th	-0.3

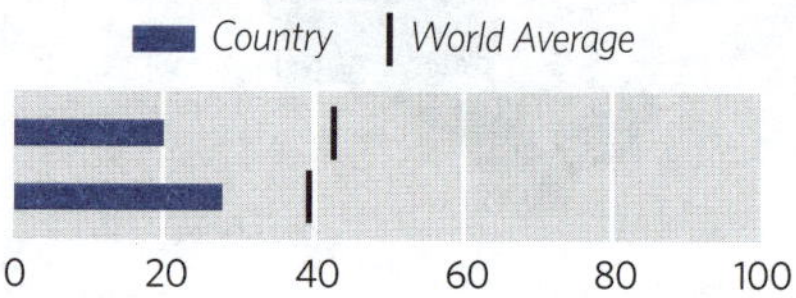

Before President Touré's removal in March 2012, a number of anti-corruption initiatives had been launched, including the creation of a general auditor's office. However, corruption remained a problem in government, public procurement, and public and private contracting. Even before the coup, Mali's judicial system was considered notoriously inefficient and corrupted by bribery and influence-peddling.

		Score	Rank	1-Year Change
GOVERNMENT SIZE	Fiscal Freedom	69.8	137th	+0.2
	Government Spending	81.7	46th	-2.2

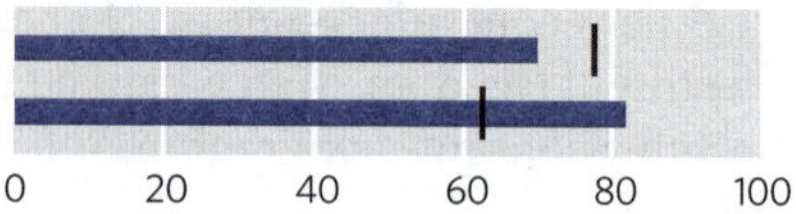

The top individual income tax rate is 40 percent, and the top corporate tax rate is 35 percent. Other taxes include a value-added tax (VAT). The overall tax burden is 14 percent of gross domestic income. Violence and political uncertainty have made tax collection difficult. Public expenditures equate to 25 percent of GDP, and government debt is 31 percent of gross domestic income.

		Score	Rank	1-Year Change
REGULATORY EFFICIENCY	Business Freedom	48.0	155th	-2.1
	Labor Freedom	63.2	85th	-1.4
	Monetary Freedom	76.7	76th	-3.2

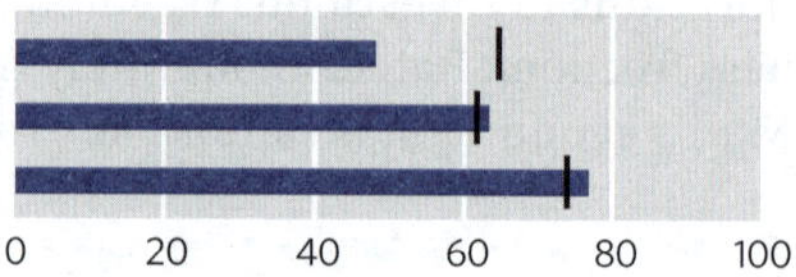

The minimum capital required for launching a business is about three times the level of average annual income, and obtaining necessary licenses is time-consuming and costly. The labor market remains underdeveloped. As Mali seeks to return to political stability with the help of the international community, the government must strengthen public financial management to restart economic growth.

		Score	Rank	1-Year Change
OPEN MARKETS	Trade Freedom	73.2	109th	0
	Investment Freedom	55.0	96th	+10.0
	Financial Freedom	40.0	107th	0

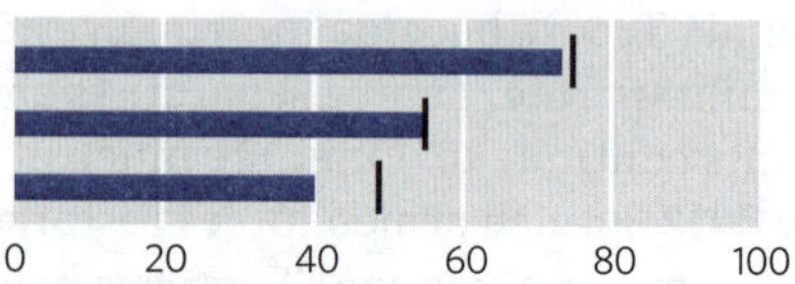

Mali's average tariff rate is 8.4 percent. Foreign and domestic investors are generally treated equally under the law. Civil unrest deters foreign investment. Financial intermediation remains low, and access to financing is limited. The inefficient legal framework is an impediment to enhancing the financial system. Much of the population relies on informal lending.

Long-Term Score Change (since 1995)

RULE OF LAW		GOVERNMENT SIZE		REGULATORY EFFICIENCY		OPEN MARKETS	
Property Rights	**-10.0**	Fiscal Freedom	**+20.9**	Business Freedom	**-7.0**	Trade Freedom	**+8.2**
Freedom from Corruption	**+17.7**	Government Spending	**+1.1**	Labor Freedom	**-0.1**	Investment Freedom	**-15.0**
				Monetary Freedom	**-5.4**	Financial Freedom	**+10.0**

MALTA

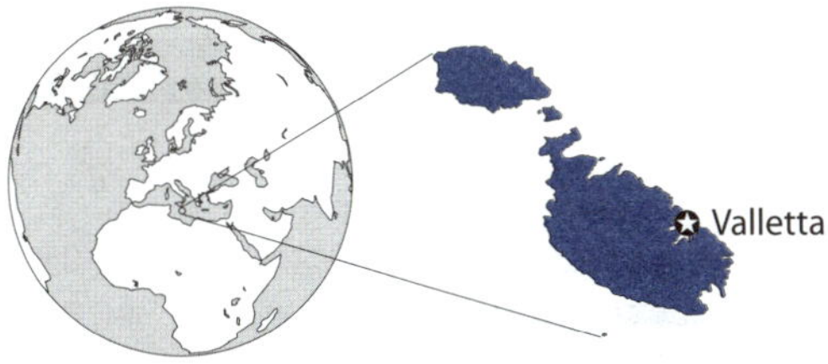

Economic Freedom Score

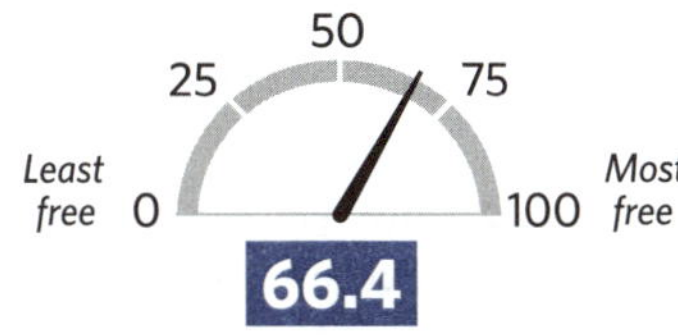

World Rank: **58** Regional Rank: **27**

Freedom Trend

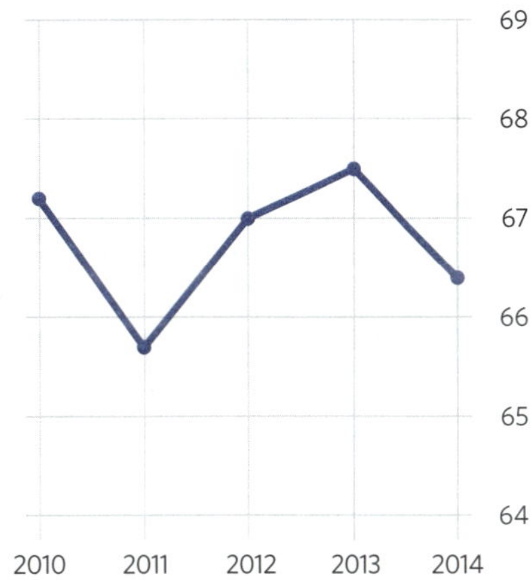

Country Comparisons

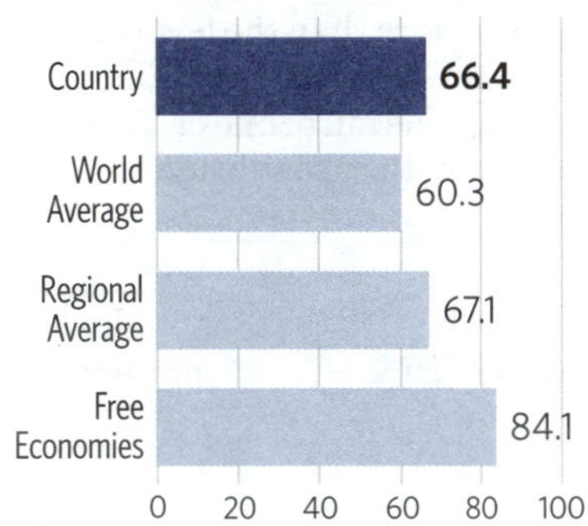

Malta's economic freedom score is 66.4, making its economy the 58th freest in the 2014 *Index*. Its overall score is 1.1 points lower than last year, with declines in labor freedom and investment freedom outweighing improvements in fiscal freedom, control of government spending, and business freedom. Malta ranks 27th out of 43 countries in the Europe region, and its overall score is below the regional average.

Over the 20-year history of the *Index*, Malta has advanced its economic freedom score by over 10 points, the fifth largest improvement among developed countries. Improvements in six of the 10 economic freedoms include notable gains in the rule of law as measured by property rights and freedom from corruption. Measures of market openness, including trade freedom, investment freedom, and financial freedom, also have improved markedly. Malta's economy, once rated "mostly unfree," advanced to "moderately free" as of 2001.

Despite its institutional competitiveness, Malta remains weak in several areas. Relatively high tax rates and government spending are a drag on economic activity. Lingering corruption and rigid labor regulations add to the cost of conducting business.

BACKGROUND: Malta joined the European Union in 2004 and the eurozone in 2008. Labour Party leader Joseph Muscat won the March 2013 elections and became prime minister. With few natural resources, Malta imports most of its food and fresh water and 100 percent of its energy supply. The economy depends on tourism, trade, and manufacturing. Well-trained workers, low labor costs, and membership in the EU attract foreign investment, but the government maintains a sprawling socialist bureaucracy, with the majority of spending allocated to housing, education, and health care. In early 2013, excessive public borrowing led to an EU warning to reduce the budget deficit, which exceeded EU guidelines. Regional instability and large immigration flows from North Africa are concerns.

How Do We Measure Economic Freedom?
See page 471 for an explanation of the methodology or visit the *Index* Web site at *heritage.org/index*.

Quick Facts

Population: 0.4 million
GDP (PPP): $11.3 billion
0.8% growth in 2012
5-year compound annual growth 1.3%
$27,022 per capita
Unemployment: 6.3%
Inflation (CPI): 3.2%
FDI Inflow: $157.2 million
Public Debt: 72.5% of GDP

2012 data unless otherwise noted.
Data compiled as of September 2013.

MALTA (continued)

THE TEN ECONOMIC FREEDOMS

RULE OF LAW

	Score	Rank	1-Year Change
Property Rights	75.0	25th	0
Freedom from Corruption	55.8	39th	-0.2

A 2012 study revealed that 88 percent of Maltese saw corruption as a major problem in both politics and business. Malta lacks appropriate institutions to implement and monitor anti-corruption activities. The judiciary is independent constitutionally and in practice. Property rights are protected, and expropriation is unlikely. Foreigners do not have full rights to buy property on the island.

GOVERNMENT SIZE

	Score	Rank	1-Year Change
Fiscal Freedom	63.7	161st	+2.5
Government Spending	47.2	140th	+3.1

The top individual income and corporate tax rates are 35 percent. The new budget proposal envisions cutting the top personal tax rate to 25 percent by 2015. Other taxes include a value-added tax (VAT) and a capital gains tax. The overall tax burden equals 34.4 percent of gross domestic income. Government expenditure amounts to 42 percent of GDP, and public debt has risen to about 73 percent of gross domestic output.

REGULATORY EFFICIENCY

	Score	Rank	1-Year Change
Business Freedom	62.4	102nd	+1.3
Labor Freedom	53.2	124th	-12.2
Monetary Freedom	79.1	46th	-1.3

Incorporating a business takes 40 days on average, and completing licensing requirements costs more than the level of average annual income. The labor market remains relatively rigid, and the government mandates a minimum wage. Malta maintained macroeconomic stability during the eurozone crisis but faces deteriorating public finances and needs to reform pension and health care subsidies.

OPEN MARKETS

	Score	Rank	1-Year Change
Trade Freedom	87.8	11th	+1.0
Investment Freedom	80.0	23rd	-5.0
Financial Freedom	60.0	41st	0

EU members have a low 1.1 percent average tariff rate and, in general, few non-tariff barriers to trade. Malta generally welcomes foreign investment, but investment in companies producing goods for the domestic market may be screened. The financial sector has undergone gradual restructuring. The banking sector has become more open to foreign banks and has withstood the global financial turmoil relatively well.

Long-Term Score Change (since 1995)

RULE OF LAW

Property Rights	+25.0
Freedom from Corruption	+45.8

GOVERNMENT SIZE

Fiscal Freedom	-4.5
Government Spending	-4.6

REGULATORY EFFICIENCY

Business Freedom	-7.6
Labor Freedom	-6.8
Monetary Freedom	+5.7

OPEN MARKETS

Trade Freedom	+24.2
Investment Freedom	+10.0
Financial Freedom	+10.0

MAURITANIA

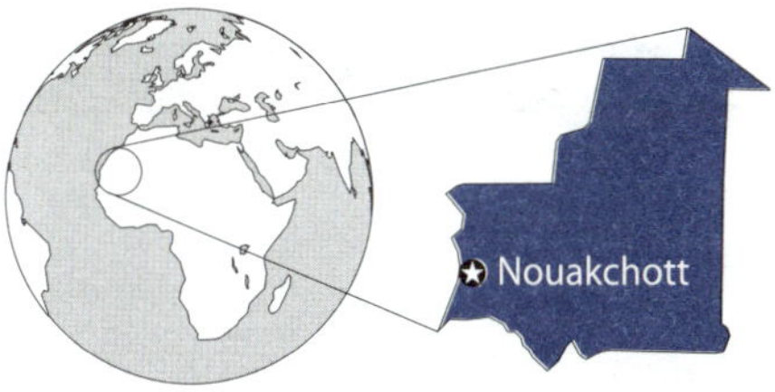

World Rank: **134** Regional Rank: **28**

Economic Freedom Score

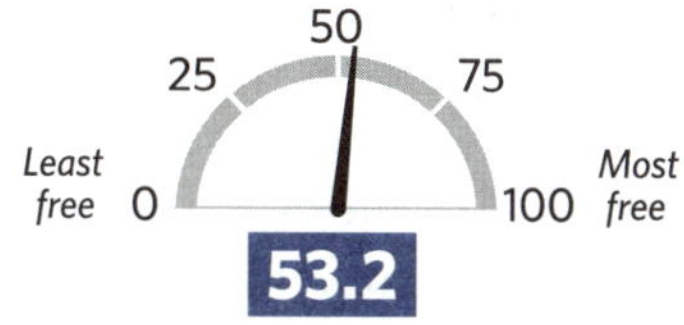

Mauritania's economic freedom score is 53.2, making its economy the 134th freest in the 2014 *Index*. Its score has increased by 0.9 point since last year, with improvements in six of the 10 economic freedoms including investment freedom, trade freedom, and labor freedom. Mauritania is ranked 28th out of 46 countries in the Sub-Saharan Africa region, and its overall score is below the world and regional averages.

Mauritania has advanced its economic freedom score by nearly 8 points over the 19 years during which it has been graded in the *Index*. It has improved notably in the area of market openness as assessed by trade freedom, investment freedom, and financial freedoms. Rated "moderately free" in 2005, Mauritania's economy has since fallen back to "mostly unfree."

Although the Mauritanian economy has expanded its limited productive base, it suffers from serious institutional weaknesses, and growth remains fragile. Court enforcement of property rights is subject to pervasive political interference. Corruption and a lack of transparency increase uncertainty and risk.

BACKGROUND: A military junta ruled Mauritania from 1978 until 1992, when the first multi-party elections were held. In 2008, General Mohamed Ould Abdel Aziz overthrew President Sidi Ould Cheikh Abdallahi. Aziz won elections in July 2009, but popular discontent threatened his parliamentary alliance in the run-up to elections scheduled for October 2011, which were repeatedly postponed. There are recurring ethnic tensions within the mixed population of Moors and black Africans. Aziz sustained injuries from an accidental shooting by his own troops in October 2012 but has continued to maintain his authority. Mining and fishing dominate the economy. Offshore oil production began in 2006, but substantial economic gains have been slow to materialize. Mauritania faces the growing threat of terrorism, drought, and poor harvests. Formal-sector unemployment is persistently high.

How Do We Measure Economic Freedom?
See page 471 for an explanation of the methodology or visit the *Index* Web site at *heritage.org/index*.

Freedom Trend

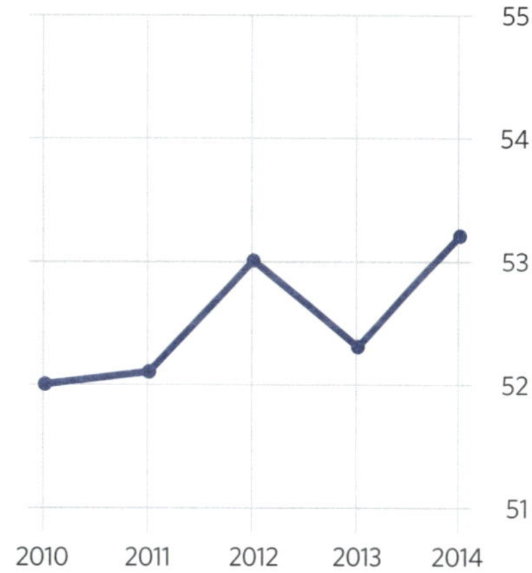

Country Comparisons

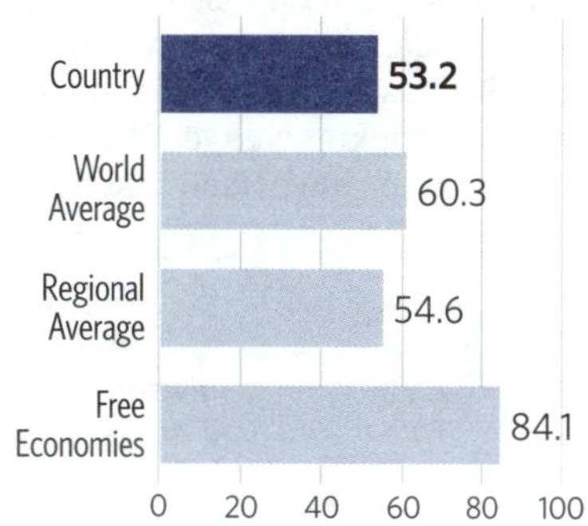

Quick Facts

Population: 3.6 million
GDP (PPP): $7.7 billion
6.4% growth in 2012
5-year compound annual growth 3.5%
$2,122 per capita
Unemployment: 30.0% (2008)
Inflation (CPI): 4.9%
FDI Inflow: $1.2 billion
Public Debt: 79.7% of GDP

2012 data unless otherwise noted.
Data compiled as of September 2013.

THE TEN ECONOMIC FREEDOMS

		Score	Rank	1-Year Change
RULE OF LAW	Property Rights	25.0	135th	0
	Freedom from Corruption	23.9	137th	-0.1

Corruption is a serious problem, and political instability has undermined fiscal transparency. Several senior officials were charged with corruption for the first time in recent years, but either the cases were dismissed or the officials were ordered to reimburse the government for the amount they supposedly embezzled with no further legal ramifications. The chaotic and corrupt judicial system is heavily influenced by the government.

		Score	Rank	1-Year Change
GOVERNMENT SIZE	Fiscal Freedom	81.7	70th	+1.4
	Government Spending	75.8	64th	+1.1

The top individual income tax rate has been reduced to 30 percent, and the top corporate tax rate remains 25 percent. Other taxes include a value-added tax (VAT). The overall tax burden is 17.5 percent of gross domestic income. Public expenditures are 28 percent of GDP. Government debt continues to fall and has reached a level equal to about 80 percent of the domestic economy.

		Score	Rank	1-Year Change
REGULATORY EFFICIENCY	Business Freedom	38.0	170th	-5.3
	Labor Freedom	53.1	125th	+2.0
	Monetary Freedom	75.5	89th	+0.4

Launching a business takes nine procedures and 19 days, but completing licensing requirements takes more than two months and remains costly. The absence of a well-functioning labor market has led to chronically high unemployment and severe underemployment. The government has acknowledged the need to shrink the public sector and reduce food and fuel subsidies, but no steps have been taken.

		Score	Rank	1-Year Change
OPEN MARKETS	Trade Freedom	69.0	133rd	+4.2
	Investment Freedom	50.0	109th	+5.0
	Financial Freedom	40.0	107th	0

Mauritania's average tariff rate is 8 percent. Imports of some goods may require "special authorization." The legal system moves slowly, which can discourage foreign investment. Limited access to credit and the high costs of financing continue to impede entrepreneurial activity. Progress in modernizing the financial sector has been sluggish and limited. The banking sector dominates the financial system.

Long-Term Score Change (since 1996)

RULE OF LAW		GOVERNMENT SIZE		REGULATORY EFFICIENCY		OPEN MARKETS	
Property Rights	-5.0	Fiscal Freedom	+31.9	Business Freedom	-17.0	Trade Freedom	+14.0
Freedom from Corruption	-6.1	Government Spending	-4.6	Labor Freedom	+6.0	Investment Freedom	+20.0
				Monetary Freedom	+6.0	Financial Freedom	+30.0

MAURITIUS

World Rank: **8** Regional Rank: **1**

Economic Freedom Score

Freedom Trend

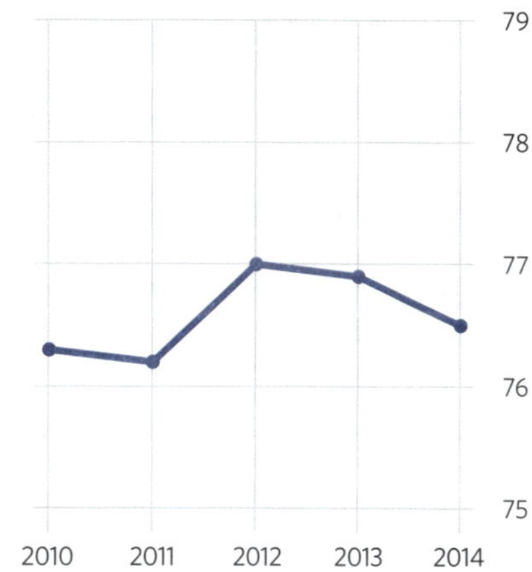

Country Comparisons

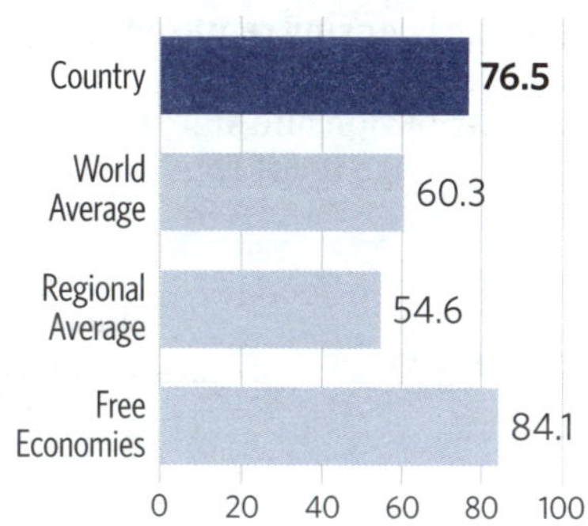

Mauritius's economic freedom score is 76.5, making its economy the 8th freest in the 2014 *Index*. Its overall score is 0.4 point lower than last year, with declines in investment freedom, property rights, and business freedom that outweigh improvements in labor freedom, freedom from corruption, and monetary freedom. Mauritius is ranked 1st out of 46 countries in the Sub-Saharan Africa region.

Mauritius was first graded in the 1999 *Index*, and its economic freedom score has advanced since then by 8 points. Improvements in six of the 10 categories of economic freedom include double-digit growth in scores for trade freedom, investment freedom, and fiscal freedom. Mauritius was ranked "mostly free" for the first time in 2009 and since 2012 has been rated one of the world's 10 freest economies.

Mauritius is a regional leader in economic freedom. Efficient and transparent regulations underpin a dynamic entrepreneurial environment and support diversified economic development. An open trade regime and relatively well-protected property rights further bolster the island economy's engagement in global commerce.

BACKGROUND: Independent since 1968, Mauritius has one of Sub-Saharan Africa's strongest economies and is the only African country ranked as a "full democracy" in the Economist Intelligence Unit Democracy Index. Navin Ramgoolam of the Mauritius Labour Party has been prime minister since 2005. The government is trying to encourage modernization of the sugar and textile industries while promoting diversification into such areas as information and communications technology, financial and business services, seafood processing, and exports. Services and tourism remain the economic drivers. The government still owns utilities and controls imports of rice, flour, petroleum products, and cement. Mauritius has made maritime security a priority and in 2012 signed a deal with Britain's Royal Navy for the transfer of suspected pirates captured by Britain to Mauritius for prosecution.

Quick Facts

Population: 1.3 million
GDP (PPP): $20.2 billion
3.3% growth in 2012
5-year compound annual growth 3.9%
$15,592 per capita
Unemployment: 8.0%
Inflation (CPI): 3.9%
FDI Inflow: $360.9 million
Public Debt: 50.3% of GDP

2012 data unless otherwise noted.
Data compiled as of September 2013.

How Do We Measure Economic Freedom?
See page 471 for an explanation of the methodology or visit the *Index* Web site at *heritage.org/index*.

MAURITIUS (continued)

THE TEN ECONOMIC FREEDOMS

RULE OF LAW

	Score	Rank	1-Year Change
Property Rights	65.0	40th	-5.0
Freedom from Corruption	53.4	44th	+2.4

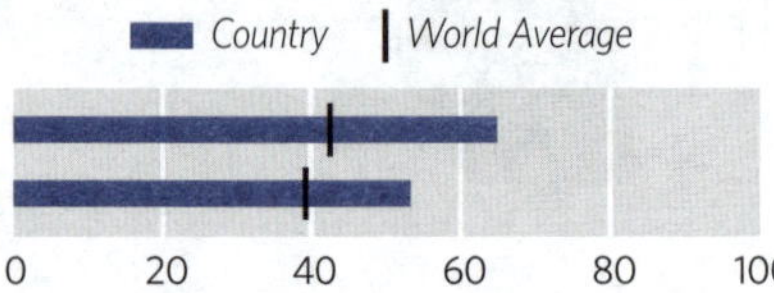

Mauritius's reputation for transparency and accountability was damaged by scandal in the wake of arrests of two prominent government officials in 2011, as well as by allegations that the ruling party has used a government anti-corruption commission as a political tool. The judiciary continues to be independent, however, and the legal system is generally non-discriminatory and transparent.

GOVERNMENT SIZE

	Score	Rank	1-Year Change
Fiscal Freedom	92.2	24th	+0.1
Government Spending	81.8	45th	-0.1

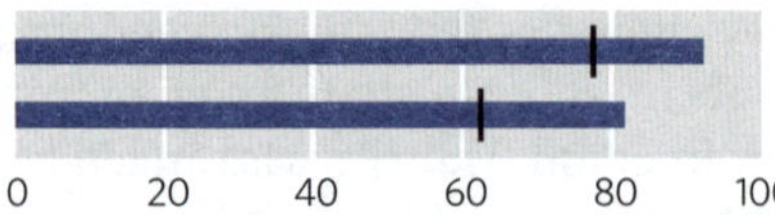

The top individual income and corporate tax rates are 15 percent. Other taxes include a value-added tax (VAT). The overall tax burden is equal to 18.3 percent of gross domestic income. Government expenditures are 25 percent of GDP. Public debt is steady at 50 percent of the domestic economy. Sound public financial management has prompted credit rating upgrades in the past year.

REGULATORY EFFICIENCY

	Score	Rank	1-Year Change
Business Freedom	74.4	54th	-3.8
Labor Freedom	78.0	38th	+5.7
Monetary Freedom	76.7	77th	+1.3

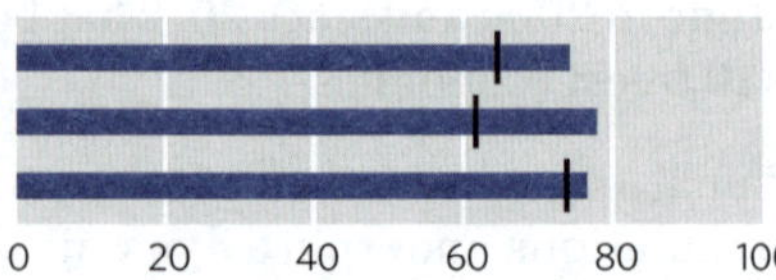

Launching a business takes six procedures, and no minimum capital is required. However, completing licensing requirements remains time-consuming. Labor regulations are not rigid, and costs to terminate employment are relatively low. Recent budgets reflect a switch away from redistribution and state intervention and toward private-sector–led economic growth.

The average tariff rate for Mauritius is 0.7 percent, and there are few non-tariff barriers to

---

OPEN MARKETS

	Score	Rank	1-Year Change
Trade Freedom	88.6	7th	+0.7
Investment Freedom	85.0	13th	-5.0
Financial Freedom	70.0	19th	0

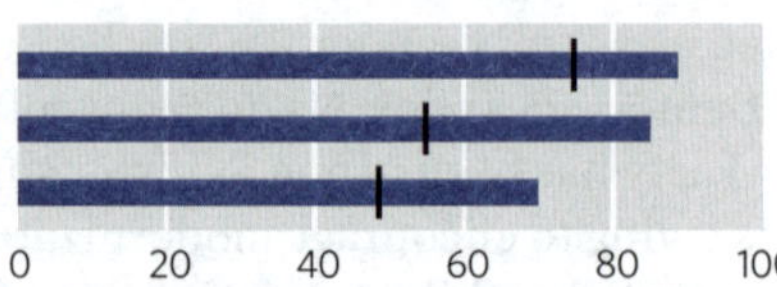

trade. Purchases of land by foreign investors require government approval. The growing financial sector, dominated by private commercial banks, is competitive. The number of non-performing loans is declining, and banks continue to be well capitalized and resilient despite ongoing global financial turbulence.

Long-Term Score Change (since 1999)

RULE OF LAW		GOVERNMENT SIZE		REGULATORY EFFICIENCY		OPEN MARKETS	
Property Rights	**-5.0**	Fiscal Freedom	**+16.2**	Business Freedom	**-10.6**	Trade Freedom	**+31.6**
Freedom from Corruption	**+3.4**	Government Spending	**-3.3**	Labor Freedom	**+1.6**	Investment Freedom	**+35.0**
				Monetary Freedom	**+3.0**	Financial Freedom	**0**

MEXICO

World Rank: 55 **Regional Rank: 3**

Economic Freedom Score

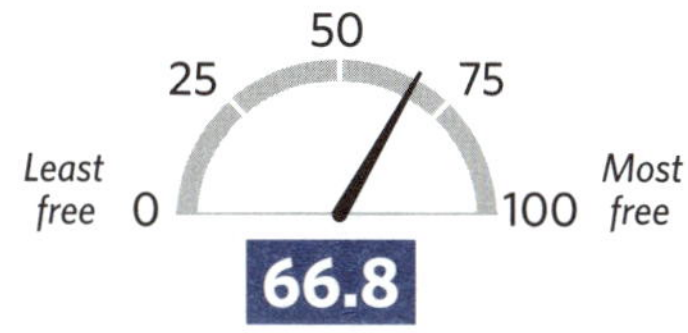

Mexico's economic freedom score is 66.8, making its economy the 55th freest in the 2014 *Index*. Its score is slightly lower than last year, with a notable improvement in trade freedom offset by declines in the areas of regulatory efficiency and government size and intrusiveness. Mexico is ranked 3rd out of three countries in the North America region, but its score is well above the world average.

Over the 20-year history of the *Index*, Mexico has advanced its economic freedom score by nearly 4 points. Improvements in half of the 10 economic freedoms include strong gains in fiscal freedom, business freedom, trade freedom, and financial freedom. Double-digit declines in property rights and freedom from corruption have limited overall progress. Mexico's economy has generally been rated "moderately free" in the *Index*, dropping below that level only briefly in the late 1990s.

Despite some progress, Mexico's overall economic freedom is still constrained by institutional weaknesses including corruption and labor market rigidity. The government's reform agenda has been extensive, but progress has been sluggish. The judicial system is slow to resolve cases and vulnerable to corruption.

BACKGROUND: The Institutional Revolutionary Party (PRI), which ruled Mexico for 71 years before the election of center-right National Action Party Presidents Vicente Fox (2000–2006) and Felipe Calderon (2006–2012), returned to power under President Enrique Peña Nieto, who took office on December 1, 2012. In his first year, Peña Nieto made commitments to second-generation reforms in education, energy, telecommunications, and fiscal policy. It is too early to tell whether his government will go far enough to make the economy truly competitive. Foreign investment rebounded in the first quarter of 2013, bringing in $4.99 billion, and emigration to the U.S. has slowed, but Mexico still struggles with formal-sector unemployment and poverty. Drug trafficking remains a serious problem.

Freedom Trend

Country Comparisons

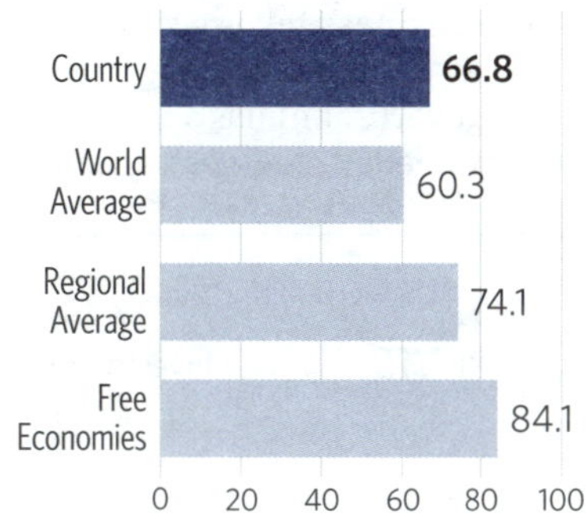

Quick Facts

Population: 114.9 million
GDP (PPP): $1.7 trillion
3.9% growth in 2012
5-year compound annual growth 1.6%
$15,312 per capita
Unemployment: 4.8%
Inflation (CPI): 4.1%
FDI Inflow: $12.7 billion
Public Debt: 43.5% of GDP

2012 data unless otherwise noted.
Data compiled as of September 2013.

How Do We Measure Economic Freedom?
See page 471 for an explanation of the methodology or visit the *Index* Web site at *heritage.org/index*.

THE TEN ECONOMIC FREEDOMS

Legend: Country | World Average

RULE OF LAW

	Score	Rank	1-Year Change
Property Rights	50.0	53rd	0
Freedom from Corruption	29.7	103rd	-0.3

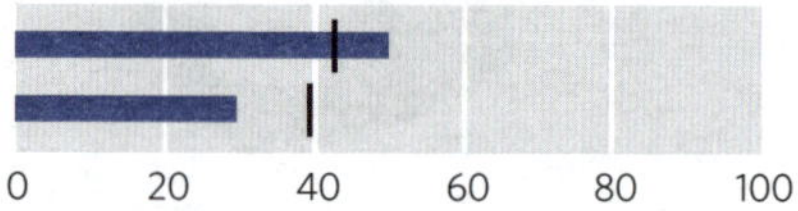

Corruption is deeply embedded culturally and remains pervasive at all levels of society, fed by and entrenching the power of monopolists, party bosses, and other mafias. Billions of narco-dollars enter Mexico each year from the U.S., affecting politics particularly at the state and local levels. Contracts are generally upheld, but courts are inefficient and vulnerable to political interference.

GOVERNMENT SIZE

	Score	Rank	1-Year Change
Fiscal Freedom	80.9	74th	-0.2
Government Spending	78.9	56th	-0.5

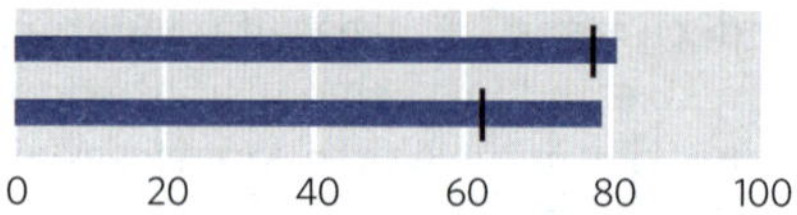

The top individual income and corporate tax rates are 30 percent. The corporate income tax is set to decline to 29 percent in 2014 and 28 percent in 2015. Other taxes include a value-added tax (VAT). The overall tax burden is 10.6 percent of gross domestic income. Government spending equates to 27 percent of GDP, and public debt is equal to 43 percent of domestic output. The new government has proposed a tax overhaul.

REGULATORY EFFICIENCY

	Score	Rank	1-Year Change
Business Freedom	76.8	40th	-4.6
Labor Freedom	58.3	108th	-1.4
Monetary Freedom	77.4	69th	-0.3

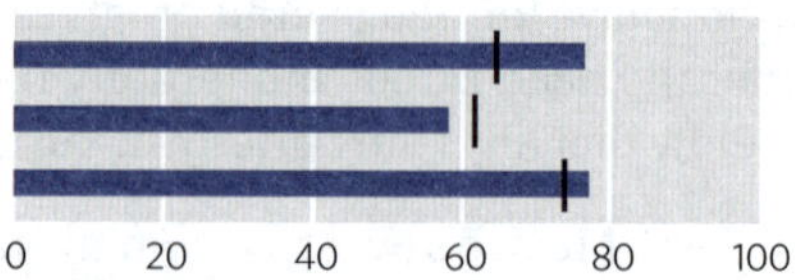

The overall start-up process has been simplified, and no minimum capital is required. Launching a business takes six procedures and six days on average, but licensing requirements take over two months to complete. A recent labor reform bill was watered down to protect unions. The government has announced ambitious energy and fiscal reform plans but has yet to make many needed changes to reduce subsidies.

OPEN MARKETS

	Score	Rank	1-Year Change
Trade Freedom	85.6	45th	+5.0
Investment Freedom	70.0	46th	0
Financial Freedom	60.0	41st	0

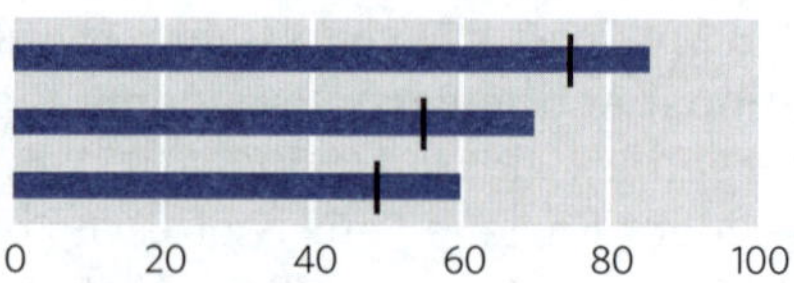

Mexico has a 2.2 percent average tariff rate, and non-tariff barriers have been reduced unilaterally and through numerous trade agreements. The government restricts foreign investment in several sectors of the economy. Reforms have strengthened the regulatory framework and increased openness in the financial system, but domestic bank credit to the private sector equals less than 20 percent of GDP.

Long-Term Score Change (since 1995)

RULE OF LAW		GOVERNMENT SIZE		REGULATORY EFFICIENCY		OPEN MARKETS	
Property Rights	-20.0	Fiscal Freedom	+8.5	Business Freedom	+21.8	Trade Freedom	+19.4
Freedom from Corruption	-20.3	Government Spending	-7.9	Labor Freedom	-3.1	Investment Freedom	0
				Monetary Freedom	+9.7	Financial Freedom	+30.0

MICRONESIA

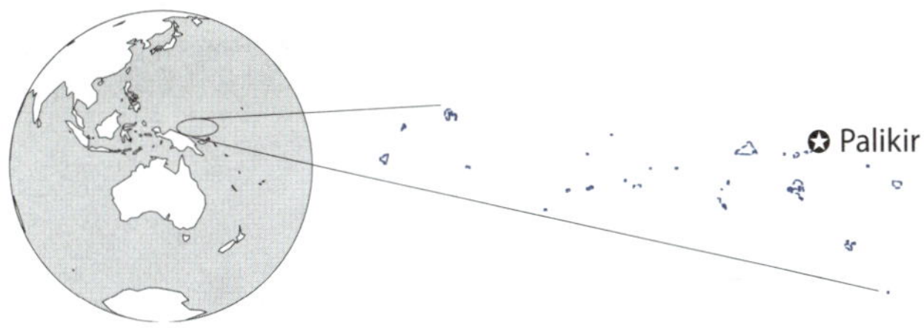

World Rank: 153 **Regional Rank: 35**

Economic Freedom Score

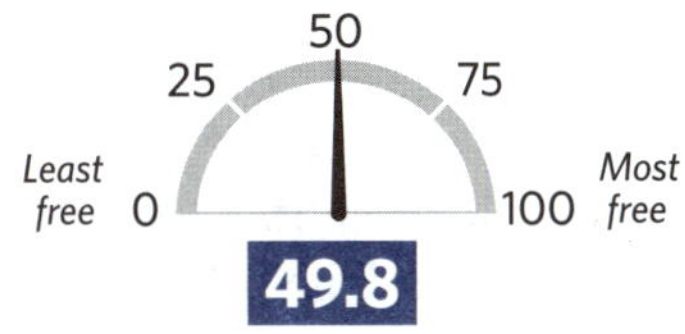

Micronesia's economic freedom score is 49.8, making its economy the 153rd freest in the 2014 *Index*. Its score has decreased by 0.3 point since last year, with declines in business freedom, labor freedom, and monetary freedom outweighing an improvement in investment freedom. Micronesia is ranked 35th out of 42 countries in the Asia–Pacific region, and its overall score is lower than the world and regional averages.

Micronesia was first graded in the 2009 *Index*, and its economic freedom score has dropped since then by nearly 2 points. In addition to a decline in investment freedom, notable deteriorations have been recorded in the area of regulatory efficiency as measured by business freedom, labor freedom, and monetary freedom. Rated "mostly unfree" for the previous five years, Micronesia's economy has fallen to the status of "repressed" in the 2014 *Index*.

Micronesia's lack of commitment to structural reform is hampering much-needed economic development. Faced with the non-transparent and onerous regulatory framework, the private sector has been marginalized to a great extent in an economically stagnant environment. Open-market policies are not in place to spur dynamic growth of trade and attract new investment.

BACKGROUND: Politically organized as a confederation of four states—the island groups of Pohnpei, Chuuk, Yap, and Kosrae—the 607-island South Pacific archipelago of Micronesia has a central government with limited powers. The president is elected by the small unicameral legislature from among its at-large members. Formerly administered by the United States as a U.N. Trust Territory, Micronesia became independent in 1986 and signed a Compact of Free Association with the United States. Under an amended compact, it receives about $130 million annually in direct assistance from the U.S. The government sector employs more than half of the workforce. Economic development is hampered by poor infrastructure in electricity and water.

Freedom Trend

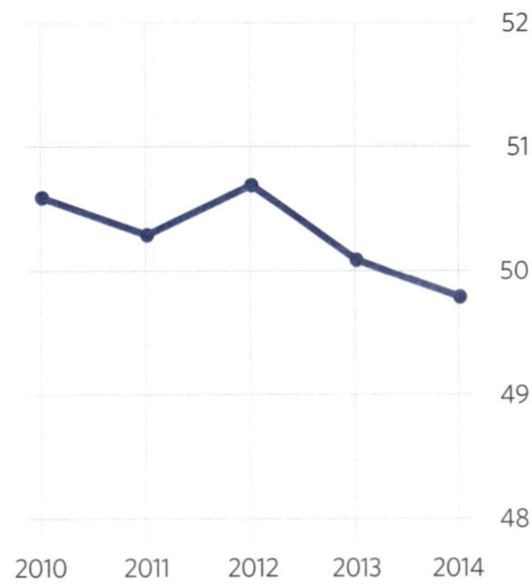

Country Comparisons

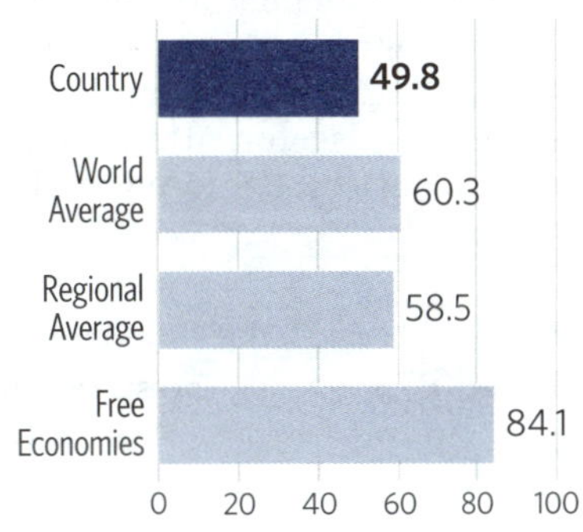

Quick Facts

Population: 0.1 million
GDP (PPP): $0.8 billion
1.4% growth in 2012
5-year compound annual growth 0.9%
$7,346 per capita
Unemployment: n/a
Inflation (CPI): 5.6%
FDI Inflow: $0.8 million
Public Debt: 27% of GDP

2012 data unless otherwise noted.
Data compiled as of September 2013.

How Do We Measure Economic Freedom?
See page 471 for an explanation of the methodology or visit the *Index* Web site at *heritage.org/index.*

THE TEN ECONOMIC FREEDOMS

		Score	Rank	1-Year Change
RULE OF LAW	Property Rights	30.0	93rd	0
	Freedom from Corruption	30.0	102nd	0

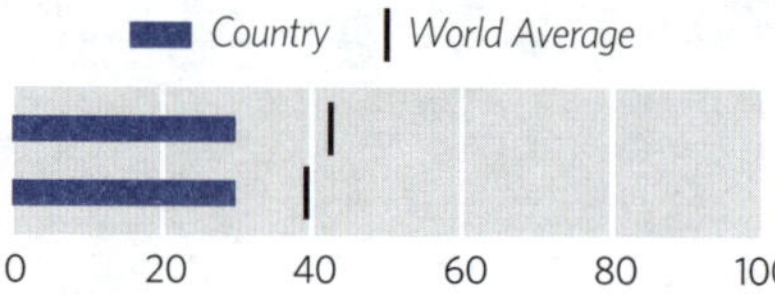

Official corruption is a major source of public discontent. In September 2012, the public auditor reported many fundamental weaknesses in the government payroll system, with paychecks going to employees who had been fired and overpayments for unauthorized work hours among the problems. The rule of law remains uneven across the islands, and a well-functioning, consistent legal framework is not in place.

		Score	Rank	1-Year Change
GOVERNMENT SIZE	Fiscal Freedom	97.5	7th	0
	Government Spending	0.0	177th	0

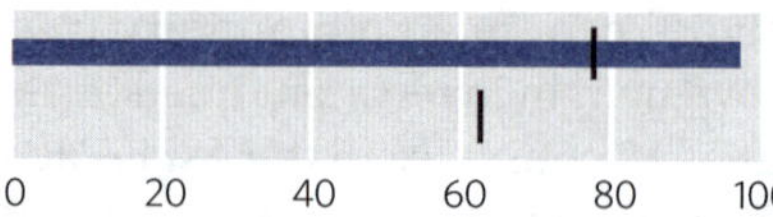

The top individual income tax rate is 10 percent, and the top corporate tax rate is 3 percent. Tax laws are administered erratically among the nation's 607 islands. The overall tax burden equals 12 percent of gross domestic product. Public expenditures amount to 65 percent of the domestic economy, and public debt is 27 percent of GDP.

		Score	Rank	1-Year Change
REGULATORY EFFICIENCY	Business Freedom	51.7	150th	-2.4
	Labor Freedom	77.9	41st	-4.6
	Monetary Freedom	75.2	98th	-0.9

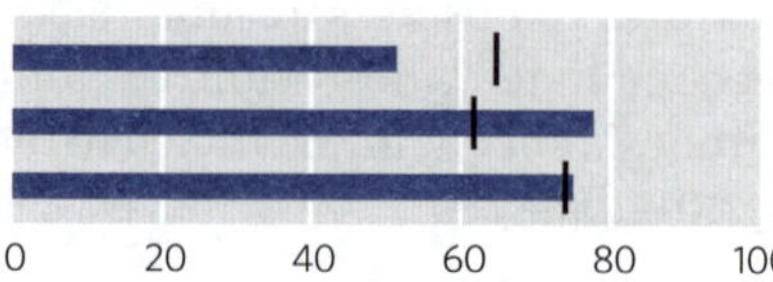

The overall regulatory environment is not conducive to business formation and operation. Launching a business takes seven procedures on average, but licensing requirements are time-consuming. The labor market is underdeveloped. Much of the labor force is employed in the large public sector. Attempts to implement public-sector reforms have been undermined by dependence on U.S. foreign aid.

		Score	Rank	1-Year Change
OPEN MARKETS	Trade Freedom	81.0	69th	0
	Investment Freedom	25.0	159th	+5.0
	Financial Freedom	30.0	132nd	0

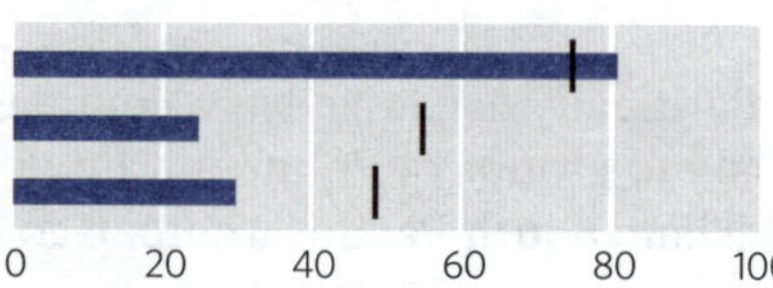

Micronesia's average tariff rate was 4.5 percent as of 2006. Foreign investors may not own land. Federal and state regulations discourage new foreign investment. The financial sector remains rudimentary, forcing much of the population to operate outside of the formal banking sector. High credit costs and scarce access to financing continue to constrain the small private sector.

Long-Term Score Change (since 2009)

RULE OF LAW		GOVERNMENT SIZE		REGULATORY EFFICIENCY		OPEN MARKETS	
Property Rights	0	Fiscal Freedom	+0.1	Business Freedom	-8.1	Trade Freedom	0
Freedom from Corruption	0	Government Spending	0	Labor Freedom	-4.4	Investment Freedom	-5.0
				Monetary Freedom	-1.5	Financial Freedom	0

MOLDOVA

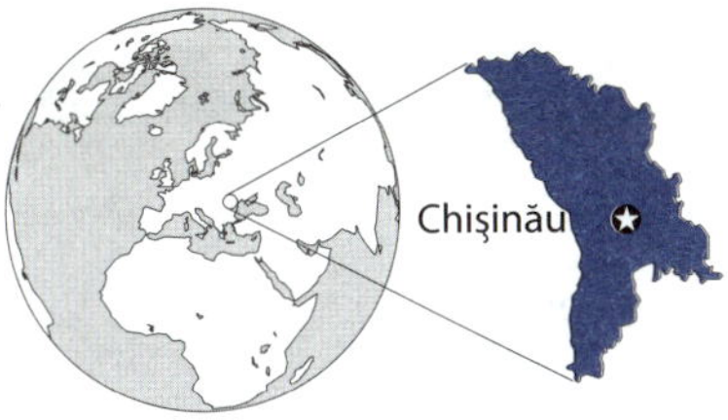

World Rank: 110 **Regional Rank: 39**

Economic Freedom Score

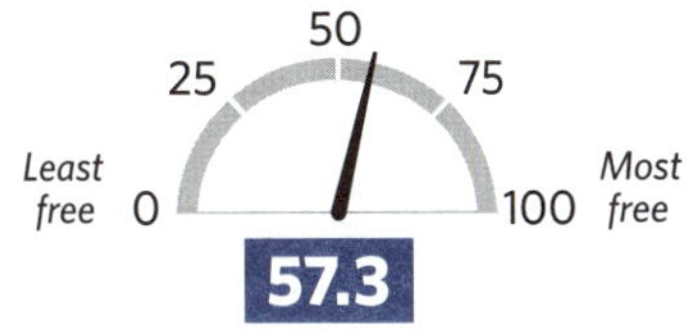

Moldova's economic freedom score is 57.3, making its economy the 110th freest in the 2014 *Index*. Its score has increased by 1.8 points, reflecting improvements in six of the 10 economic freedoms including investment freedom, control of government spending, monetary freedom, and business freedom. Moldova is ranked 39th among 43 countries in the Europe region, and its overall score is below the regional and world averages.

Over the 20-year history of the *Index*, Moldova has advanced its economic freedom score by over 24 points, the sixth largest improvement of any country. Its overall score increase has been driven by seven of the 10 economic freedoms, most notably a 75-point improvement in monetary freedom and a 63-point gain in trade freedom. Moldova reached "moderately free" status with its highest economic freedom score ever in the 2004 *Index* but has fallen back to "mostly unfree" since then.

Realization of growth potential remains constrained by state interference in the private sector, which has left the economy vulnerable in a changing political environment. Political instability has left fiscal policy fragmented, and corruption is significant in most areas of the bureaucracy.

BACKGROUND: Moldova gained independence after the collapse of the Soviet Union in 1991 and continues to face a secessionist pro-Russian movement in its Transnistria region. It remains poor, with a large percentage of the population working in Russia and the EU. The reformed Communist Party, which dominated Moldovan politics for most of 2000–2009, supported European integration and did not reverse market reforms instituted in the early 1990s. Since 2010, the center-right Liberal Democrat Party under Prime Minister Vlad Filat has increased foreign investment by 25 percent. In March 2012, the parliament elected pro-European integration Judge Nicolae Timofti as president. Foodstuffs, wine, and agricultural products are the main exports, although the technology sector is developing.

How Do We Measure Economic Freedom?
See page 471 for an explanation of the methodology or visit the *Index* Web site at *heritage.org/index*.

Freedom Trend

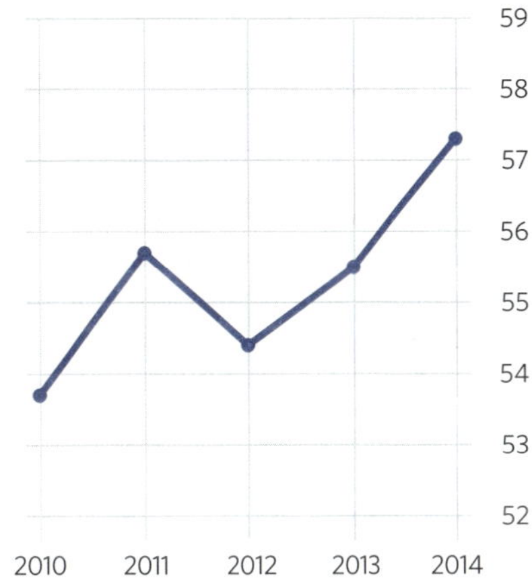

Country Comparisons

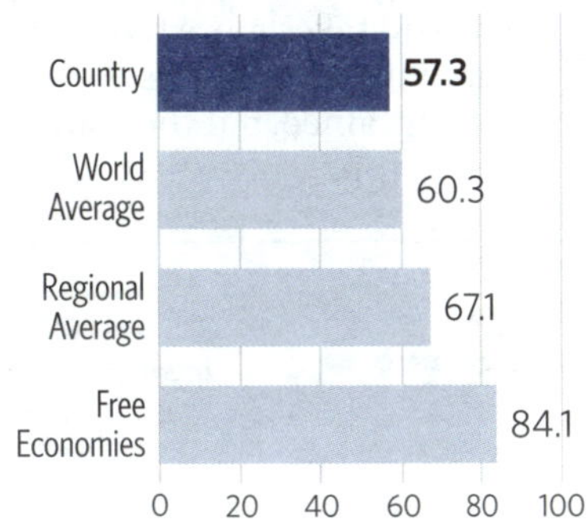

Quick Facts

Population: 3.6 million
GDP (PPP): $12.2 billion
-0.8% growth in 2012
5-year compound annual growth 2.8%
$3,415 per capita
Unemployment: 5.5% (2008)
Inflation (CPI): 4.7%
FDI Inflow: $159.2 million
Public Debt: 23.8% of GDP

2012 data unless otherwise noted.
Data compiled as of September 2013.

THE TEN ECONOMIC FREEDOMS

RULE OF LAW

	Score	Rank	1-Year Change
Property Rights	40.0	70th	0
Freedom from Corruption	29.5	104th	+0.5

Corruption is a major problem, especially in law enforcement, the judicial system, public service, political parties, the educational system, and the legislature. Leading politicians regularly trade accusations of graft and illegal business activity. The judiciary is constitutionally independent, but the legal framework is ineffective, and reform efforts suffer from lack of funds. Enforcement of intellectual property rights is sporadic.

GOVERNMENT SIZE

	Score	Rank	1-Year Change
Fiscal Freedom	85.8	48th	-1.4
Government Spending	54.4	130th	+4.3

The top individual income tax rate is 18 percent. The corporate tax, which was eliminated in 2008, has been reinstated at a 12 percent rate. Other taxes include a value-added tax (VAT). The overall tax burden is just over 30.8 percent of GDP. The government is continuing fiscal consolidation, and spending has fallen to 39 percent of GDP. Public debt is equal to about 24 percent of the domestic economy.

REGULATORY EFFICIENCY

	Score	Rank	1-Year Change
Business Freedom	70.1	75th	+0.4
Labor Freedom	37.9	172nd	-3.0
Monetary Freedom	75.0	106th	+1.6

Launching a business takes six procedures and seven days, but completing licensing requirements still takes more than 100 days. Labor market rigidity continues to discourage dynamic job growth. Restrictions on work hours are stringent. Monetary stability has been relatively well maintained, but the state has increased agricultural subsidies in support of eventual EU membership.

OPEN MARKETS

	Score	Rank	1-Year Change
Trade Freedom	80.1	70th	+0.1
Investment Freedom	50.0	109th	+15.0
Financial Freedom	50.0	69th	0

Moldova has a 2.5 percent average tariff rate, and non-tariff barriers further impede trade. Efforts to privatize state-owned enterprises are ongoing. Rapid credit growth has supported private-sector growth, but long-term financing remains difficult. Overall, the financial sector remains constrained by structural impediments. Banks are the main source of business financing; non-banking financial sectors are underdeveloped.

Long-Term Score Change (since 1995)

RULE OF LAW		GOVERNMENT SIZE		REGULATORY EFFICIENCY		OPEN MARKETS	
Property Rights	-10.0	Fiscal Freedom	+48.6	Business Freedom	+0.1	Trade Freedom	+62.5
Freedom from Corruption	+19.5	Government Spending	-17.7	Labor Freedom	-26.8	Investment Freedom	+20.0
				Monetary Freedom	+75.0	Financial Freedom	+40.0

MONGOLIA

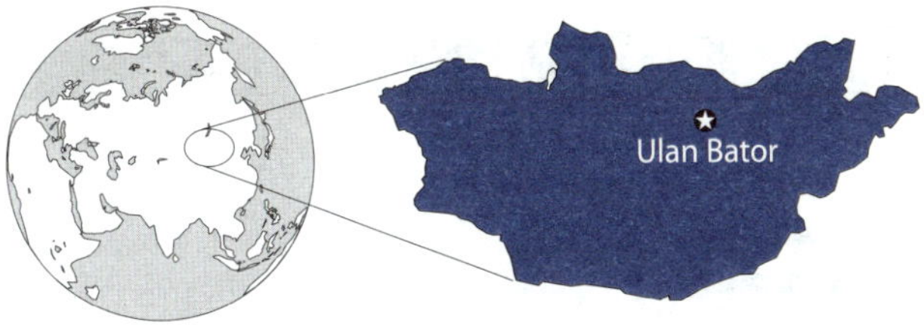

World Rank: **97** Regional Rank: **19**

Economic Freedom Score

Freedom Trend

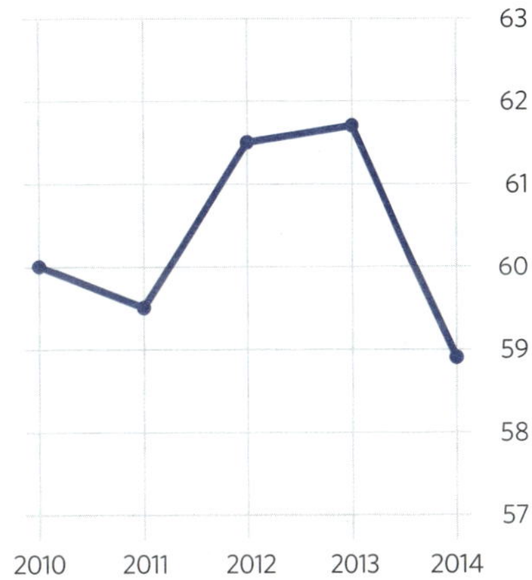

Country Comparisons

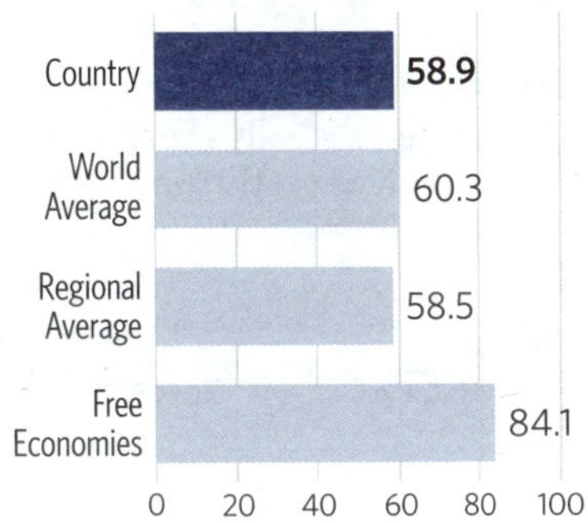

Mongolia's economic freedom score is 58.9, making its economy the 97th freest in the 2014 *Index*. Its overall score is 2.8 points lower than last year, with deteriorations in the control of government spending, trade freedom, and monetary freedom outweighing small improvements in business freedom and labor freedom. Mongolia is ranked 19th out of 42 countries in the Asia–Pacific region, and its overall score is above the regional average.

Over the 20-year history of the *Index*, Mongolia has advanced its economic freedom score by over 11 points. Despite ups and downs, its relatively broad-based overall score improvement has been facilitated by advancements in seven of the 10 economic freedoms including monetary freedom, fiscal freedom, and trade freedom. The rule of law has lagged, however. Once considered a "repressed" economy, Mongolia had risen to "moderately free" before falling back this year.

Despite notable strides made over the past decade, the momentum for deeper institutional reform has largely stalled. Prospects for enhancing economic freedom remain curtailed by a lack of institutional commitment to strong protection of property rights and by ineffectiveness in fighting corruption. The judicial framework remains vulnerable to political interference.

BACKGROUND: Mongolia's transition from a Soviet Socialist Republic to democracy has been characterized by the gradual introduction of political and free-market reforms. Despite political tensions, the country has enjoyed relative stability in recent years. Tsakhiagiin Elbegdorj, whose Democratic Party coalition controls parliament, was re-elected to a second and final term as president in June 2013. Agriculture and mining are the most important sectors of the economy, although tourism and construction are growing in importance. With its abundant mineral resources attracting foreign investment, Mongolia has become one of the world's fastest-growing economies. While improving overall relations with the U.S., Japan, and South Korea, it has also sought to strengthen ties with Russia and China.

How Do We Measure Economic Freedom?
See page 471 for an explanation of the methodology or visit the *Index* Web site at *heritage.org/index*.

Quick Facts

Population: 2.8 million
GDP (PPP): $15.2 billion
12.3% growth in 2012
5-year compound annual growth 8.6%
$5,372 per capita
Unemployment: 6.8%
Inflation (CPI): 15.0%
FDI Inflow: $4.5 billion
Public Debt: 41.3% of GDP

2012 data unless otherwise noted.
Data compiled as of September 2013.

THE TEN ECONOMIC FREEDOMS

Score ■ *Country* | *World Average* *Rank* *1-Year Change*

RULE OF LAW

	Score	Rank	1-Year Change
Property Rights	30.0	93rd	0
Freedom from Corruption	28.2	116th	+1.2

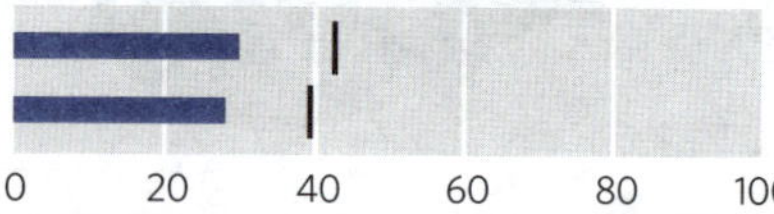

Corruption is viewed as pervasive. Graft is endemic, and weak institutions do not enforce anti-corruption measures effectively. The judiciary is independent but inefficient and vulnerable to political interference. Corruption persists among judges. Property and contractual rights are recognized, but enforcement is weak. The government lacks the capacity to enforce intellectual property rights laws.

GOVERNMENT SIZE

	Score	Rank	1-Year Change
Fiscal Freedom	81.8	69th	-0.7
Government Spending	39.1	152nd	-23.5

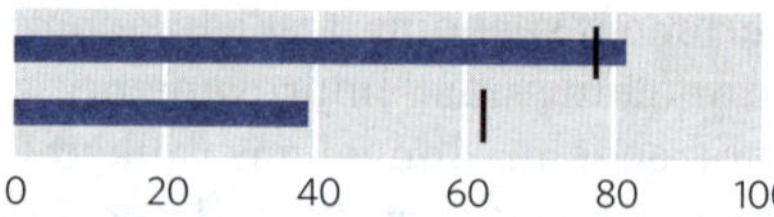

The top individual income tax rate is 10 percent, and the top corporate tax rate is 25 percent. Other taxes include a value-added tax (VAT) and an excise tax. The overall tax burden is 33.1 percent of gross domestic income. Government expenditures equal 45 percent of GDP, and public debt stood at 41 percent of gross domestic income in the most recent year. The government receives substantial revenues from the growing mining sector.

REGULATORY EFFICIENCY

	Score	Rank	1-Year Change
Business Freedom	71.8	67th	+1.4
Labor Freedom	81.1	24th	+1.9
Monetary Freedom	72.4	129th	-3.2

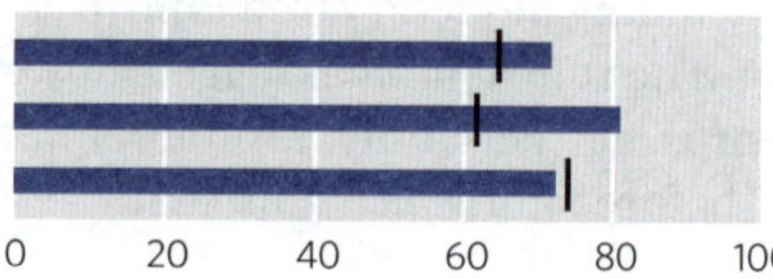

Despite some progress in modernizing the regulatory framework, time-consuming and costly requirements continue to reduce overall regulatory efficiency. The labor market remains inefficient, and chronic unemployment and underemployment continue. At the end of 2012, the IMF noted a steady erosion of fiscal discipline as the government increased spending on subsidies such as costly universal cash transfers.

OPEN MARKETS

	Score	Rank	1-Year Change
Trade Freedom	74.7	103rd	-5.1
Investment Freedom	50.0	109th	0
Financial Freedom	60.0	41st	0

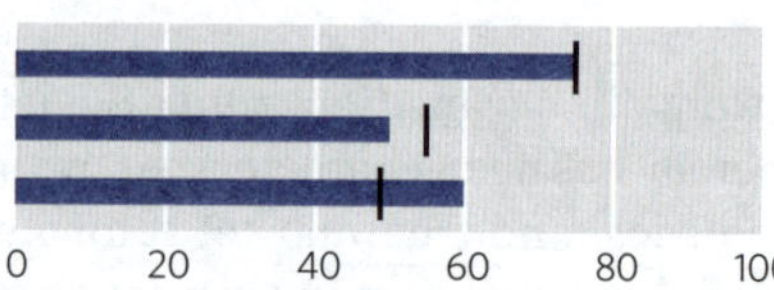

Mongolia has a 5.1 percent average tariff rate. It is costly and time-consuming to import goods. The "Strategic Entities Foreign Investment Law," enacted in 2012, limits investment in strategic industries. The financial system has undergone rigorous modernization. Weathering the strain caused by the global financial turmoil, the banking sector has stabilized.

Long-Term Score Change (since 1995)

RULE OF LAW		GOVERNMENT SIZE		REGULATORY EFFICIENCY		OPEN MARKETS	
Property Rights	**-40.0**	Fiscal Freedom	**+34.2**	Business Freedom	**+1.8**	Trade Freedom	**+19.7**
Freedom from Corruption	**-21.8**	Government Spending	**+21.8**	Labor Freedom	**+10.7**	Investment Freedom	**-20.0**
				Monetary Freedom	**+72.4**	Financial Freedom	**+10.0**

MONTENEGRO

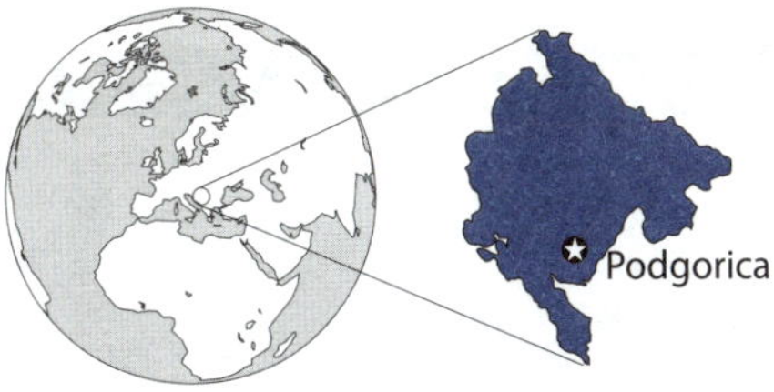

Economic Freedom Score

World Rank: **68** Regional Rank: **31**

Montenegro's economic freedom score is 63.6, making its economy the 68th freest in the 2014 *Index*. Its score is 1.0 point higher than last year, with notable gains in business freedom and investment freedom outweighing declines in labor freedom, monetary freedom, and freedom from corruption. Montenegro is ranked 31st out of 43 countries in the Europe region, and its overall score is above the world average.

Montenegro was first graded in the 2009 *Index* and has advanced its economic freedom by over 5 points since then. Six of the 10 economic freedoms, including investment freedom, labor freedom, business freedom, and freedom from corruption, have improved, with investment freedom gaining 25 points. Tying its highest overall score ever, Montenegro remains "moderately free."

However, economic freedom is still curtailed by the lack of institutional commitment to the strong protection of property rights and an effective fight against corruption. The court system remains inefficient and vulnerable to political interference.

BACKGROUND: The Republic of Montenegro declared its independence from Serbia in 2006. In 1996, Montenegro had adopted its own economic policy and even adopted the German mark as its currency. Upon gaining independence, it introduced significant privatization and adopted the euro as its legal tender despite not being a member of the eurozone. The Coalition for European Montenegro, an alliance between the Democratic Party of Socialists of Montenegro and two other center-left parties, won the October 2012 parliamentary elections. Its leader, Milo Đukanović, became prime minister in December 2012. Montenegro was invited to undertake a NATO Membership Action Plan in 2009, became a candidate for membership in the European Union in 2010, and became a member of the World Trade Organization in 2011. Its economy relies heavily on tourism and exports of refined metals. Unprofitable state companies burden public finances, and unemployment is high.

Freedom Trend

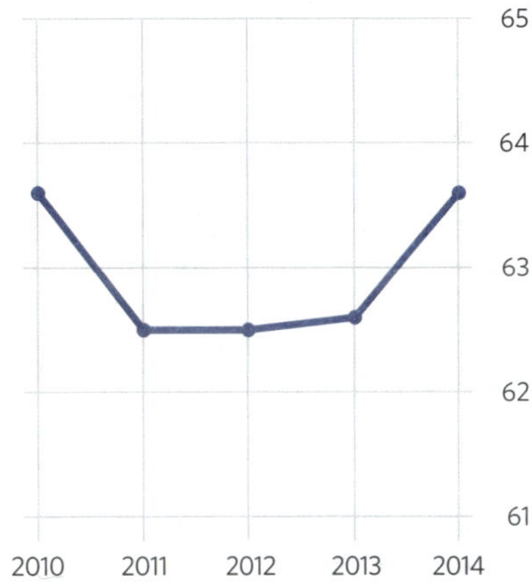

Country Comparisons

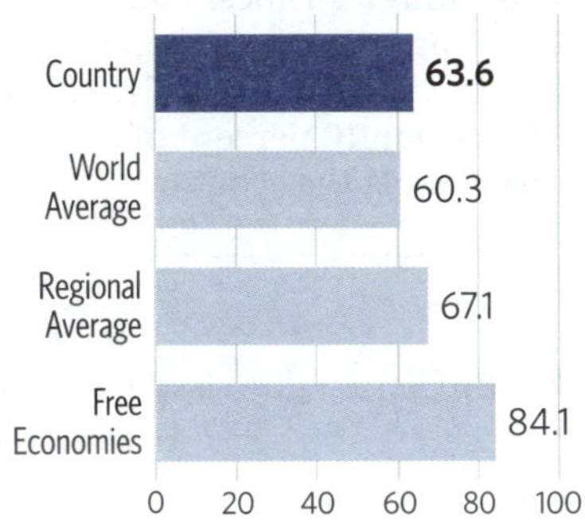

Quick Facts

Population: 0.6 million
GDP (PPP): $7.3 billion
0.0% growth in 2012
5-year compound annual growth 1.3%
$11,800 per capita
Unemployment: 19.1%
Inflation (CPI): 3.6%
FDI Inflow: $609.5 million
Public Debt: 51.1% of GDP

2012 data unless otherwise noted.
Data compiled as of September 2013.

How Do We Measure Economic Freedom?
See page 471 for an explanation of the methodology or visit the *Index* Web site at *heritage.org/index*.

THE TEN ECONOMIC FREEDOMS

RULE OF LAW

	Score	Rank	1-Year Change
Property Rights	40.0	70th	0
Freedom from Corruption	37.8	73rd	-2.2

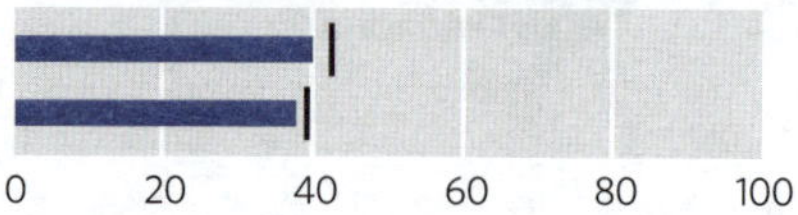

Corruption remains pervasive in the executive and judicial branches and is partly a legacy of the struggle against the Milošević regime in the 1990s, when the small republic turned to various forms of smuggling to finance government operations. Although the European Commission cited progress on judicial reform in 2012, the constitutionally independent judiciary remains inefficient and subject to political interference.

GOVERNMENT SIZE

	Score	Rank	1-Year Change
Fiscal Freedom	92.5	22nd	+0.1
Government Spending	42.6	146th	+1.1

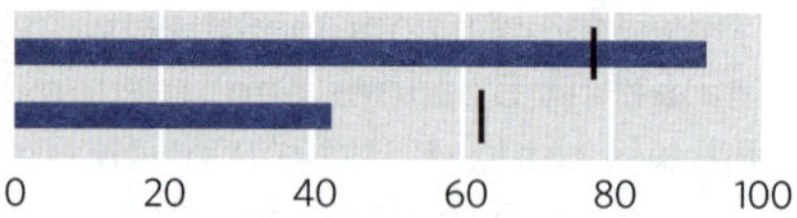

The individual income and corporate tax rates are a flat 9 percent. Other taxes include a value-added tax (VAT) and an inheritance tax. The overall tax burden equals 24.2 percent of gross domestic income. Government expenditures equate to 44 percent of GDP, and public debt has risen to over 50 percent of gross domestic income. The budget has come under pressure as the government seeks to cover the losses of a failing aluminum plant.

REGULATORY EFFICIENCY

	Score	Rank	1-Year Change
Business Freedom	77.6	37th	+4.9
Labor Freedom	68.6	68th	-2.8
Monetary Freedom	78.6	58th	-1.3

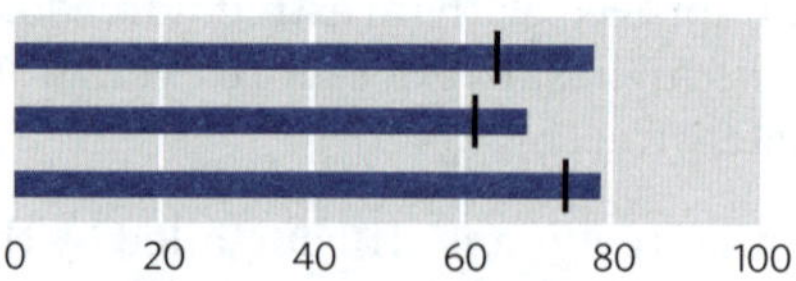

Launching a business takes six procedures and 10 days, and no minimum capital is required, but licensing takes more than 100 days and costs over 10 times the level of average annual income. Labor regulations lack flexibility, discouraging more dynamic job creation. Massive subsidies (more than 10 percent of GDP), mainly for a state-supported Communist-era aluminum factory, distort the economy.

OPEN MARKETS

	Score	Rank	1-Year Change
Trade Freedom	83.1	53rd	+0.1
Investment Freedom	65.0	68th	+10.0
Financial Freedom	50.0	69th	0

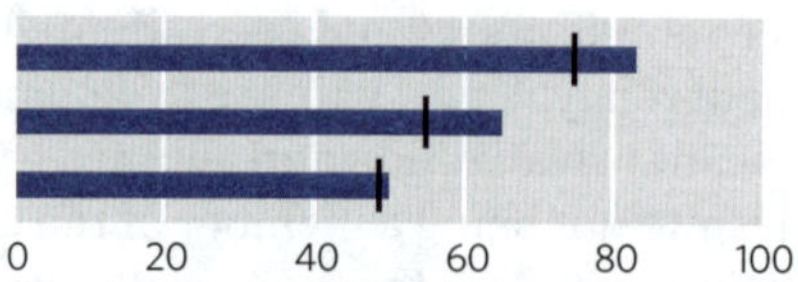

Montenegro's average tariff rate is 3.5 percent. Foreign and domestic investors are treated equally under the law, and several state-owned enterprises have been privatized. The financial sector, though small and underdeveloped, is becoming more competitive. Foreign banks' participation and investment are significant. Despite growing competition, credit prices remain fairly high. The non-banking financial sector remains underdeveloped.

Long-Term Score Change (since 2009)

RULE OF LAW		GOVERNMENT SIZE		REGULATORY EFFICIENCY		OPEN MARKETS	
Property Rights	**0**	Fiscal Freedom	**+3.4**	Business Freedom	**+8.9**	Trade Freedom	**+2.9**
Freedom from Corruption	**+4.8**	Government Spending	**-2.7**	Labor Freedom	**+11.4**	Investment Freedom	**+25.0**
				Monetary Freedom	**-0.3**	Financial Freedom	**0**

MOROCCO

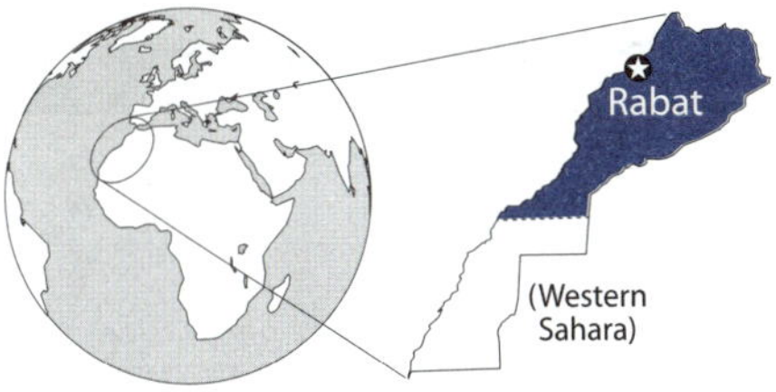

World Rank: **103** Regional Rank: **10**

Economic Freedom Score

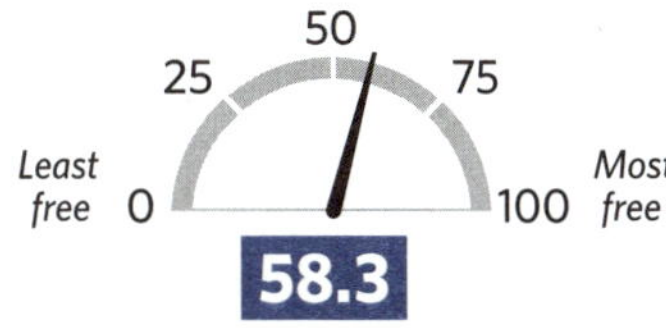

Morocco's economic freedom score is 58.3, making its economy the 103rd freest in the 2014 *Index*. Its score is 1.3 points worse than last year due to declines in trade freedom, freedom from corruption, and monetary freedom. Morocco is ranked 10th out of 15 countries in the Middle East/North Africa region, and its overall score is just below the world average.

Over the 20-year history of the *Index*, Morocco's economic freedom score has dropped by nearly 5 points, one of the 20 largest declines. Modest gains in half of the economic freedoms, including fiscal freedom, trade freedom, and financial freedom, have been overwhelmed by declines, particularly in property rights and freedom from corruption. Once ranked "moderately free," Morocco's economy is now rated "mostly unfree."

Morocco has tried to integrate its economy into the global marketplace, but overall progress toward greater economic freedom has been uneven. Critical challenges include widespread corruption and relatively high government spending. Budget deficits continue, and public debt has risen to almost 60 percent of GDP. The judicial system remains inefficient and vulnerable to political influence.

BACKGROUND: Morocco, a constitutional monarchy with an elected parliament, has been a key ally in the international struggle against Islamist extremism. Constitutional amendments proposed by a commission authorized by King Mohammed VI and approved by referendum in 2011 are designed to increase the power and independence of the prime minister and provide protections for human rights. In November 2011, the Justice and Development Party became the first Islamist party to lead a Moroccan government, although the king retains significant power as chief executive. Morocco has a large tourism industry and a growing manufacturing sector. Agriculture accounts for about 15 percent of GDP and employs almost 45 percent of the labor force. High prices for fuel, which is heavily subsidized, have worsened the current account deficit.

Freedom Trend

Country Comparisons

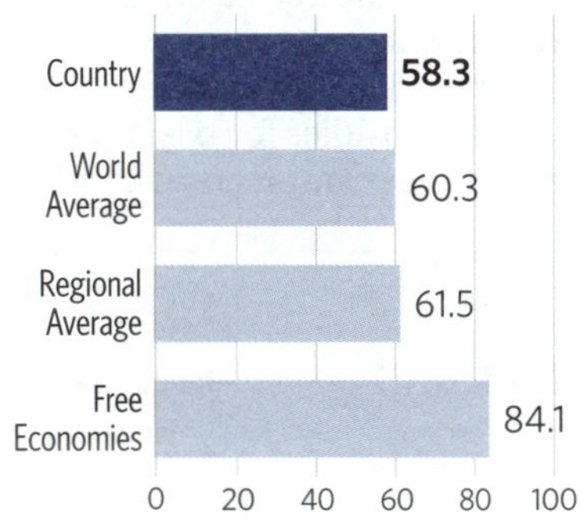

Quick Facts

Population: 32.5 million
GDP (PPP): $171.2 billion
3.0% growth in 2012
5-year compound annual growth 4.4%
$5,265 per capita
Unemployment: 8.8%
Inflation (CPI): 1.3%
FDI Inflow: $2.8 billion
Public Debt: 59.6% of GDP

2012 data unless otherwise noted.
Data compiled as of September 2013.

How Do We Measure Economic Freedom?
See page 471 for an explanation of the methodology or visit the *Index* Web site at *heritage.org/index.*

THE TEN ECONOMIC FREEDOMS

		Score	Rank	1-Year Change
RULE OF LAW	Property Rights	40.0	70th	0
	Freedom from Corruption	33.3	88th	-0.7

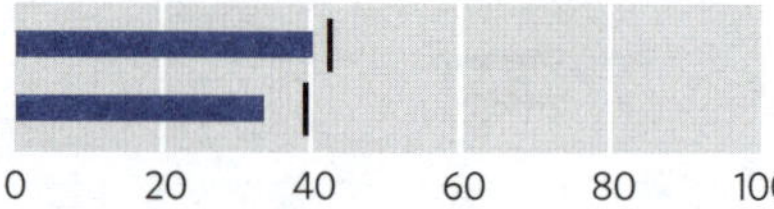

Despite government rhetoric about combating corruption, it remains widespread in public life and in the business world. The government has tried to improve the transparency of public tenders and now requires that senior government officials declare their assets at the beginning and end of their government service. The judiciary is influenced by the king, and adjudication of cases can be slow.

		Score	Rank	1-Year Change
GOVERNMENT SIZE	Fiscal Freedom	71.3	134th	-0.1
	Government Spending	64.1	103rd	-0.2

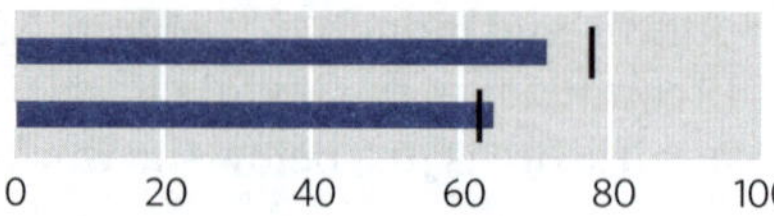

The top individual income tax rate is 38 percent, and the top corporate tax rate is 30 percent. Other taxes include a value-added tax (VAT) and a gift tax. The overall tax burden is about 23 percent of GDP. Government spending accounts for 35 percent of the domestic economy. Public debt has reached almost 60 percent of GDP, and social spending has been rising in response to "Arab Spring" pressure.

		Score	Rank	1-Year Change
REGULATORY EFFICIENCY	Business Freedom	76.2	44th	-0.2
	Labor Freedom	31.5	176th	+1.4
	Monetary Freedom	78.1	61st	-0.8

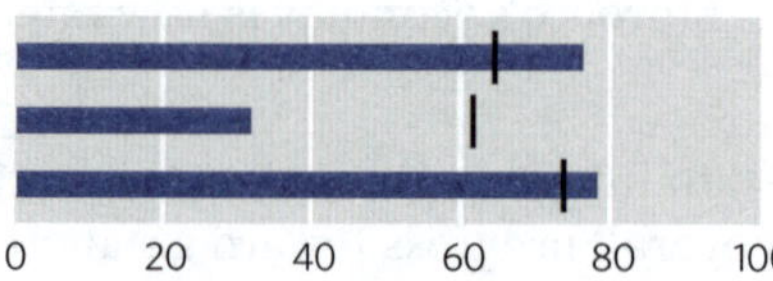

Burdensome requirements continue to hurt regulatory efficiency. Completing licensing requirements takes over 100 days and costs twice the level of annual average income. The labor market remains inefficient, and chronic unemployment and underemployment continue. Costly subsidies for basic commodities (estimated at 6.5 percent of GDP in 2012) have placed heavy pressure on government spending.

		Score	Rank	1-Year Change
OPEN MARKETS	Trade Freedom	58.8	164th	-12.0
	Investment Freedom	70.0	46th	0
	Financial Freedom	60.0	41st	0

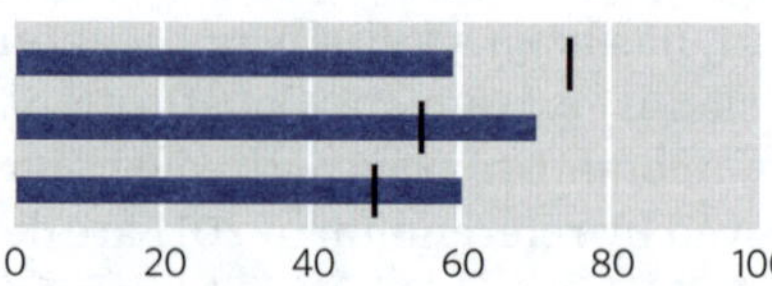

Morocco's average tariff rate is 13.1 percent. Tariffs provide around 7 percent of the government's revenue. Investors often find the legal and regulatory systems difficult to navigate. The financial sector is fairly well developed in comparison to other economies in the region, and banking intermediation is increasing gradually. Credit costs remain relatively high.

Long-Term Score Change (since 1995)

RULE OF LAW		GOVERNMENT SIZE		REGULATORY EFFICIENCY		OPEN MARKETS	
Property Rights	**-30.0**	Fiscal Freedom	**+13.8**	Business Freedom	**+6.2**	Trade Freedom	**+9.0**
Freedom from Corruption	**-16.7**	Government Spending	**-8.7**	Labor Freedom	**-10.6**	Investment Freedom	**0**
				Monetary Freedom	**+3.1**	Financial Freedom	**+10.0**

MOZAMBIQUE

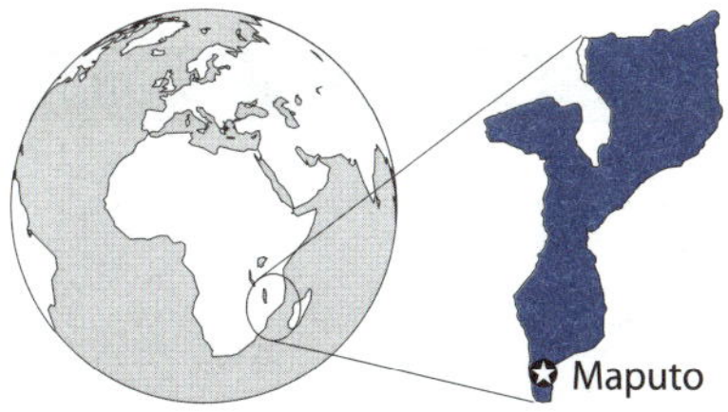

World Rank: **128** Regional Rank: **25**

Economic Freedom Score

Freedom Trend

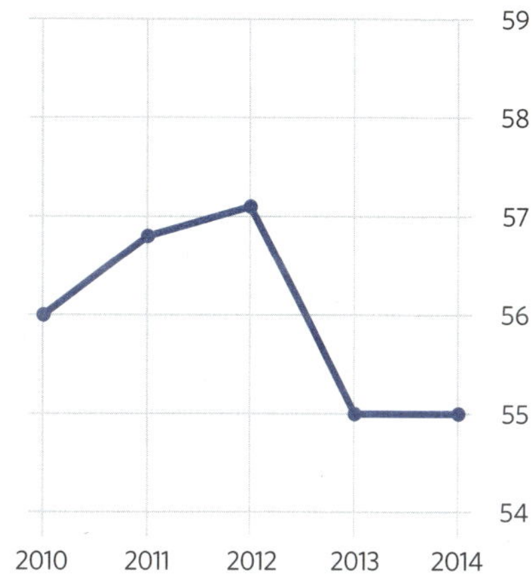

Country Comparisons

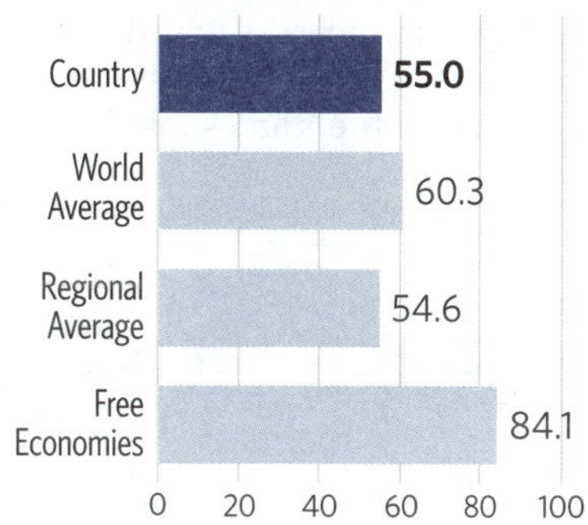

Mozambique's economic freedom score is 55.0, making its economy the 128th freest in the 2014 *Index*. Its overall score is unchanged from last year, with improvements in monetary freedom, business freedom, and trade freedom offset by declines in investment freedom, labor freedom, fiscal freedom, and freedom from corruption. Mozambique is ranked 25th out of 46 countries in the Sub-Saharan Africa region, and its overall score is just above the regional average.

Over the 20-year history of the *Index*, Mozambique has advanced its economic freedom score by nearly 10 points. Scores have improved in eight of the 10 economic freedoms, with a decline only in the management of public spending. Most notable is a 37-point improvement in monetary freedom. No longer rated economically "repressed," Mozambique moved into the "mostly unfree" category as of 2000.

Institutional problems continue to limit overall economic freedom and long-term economic development. The judiciary is subject to corruption and political influence. The inefficient regulatory environment, despite some progress in recent years, remains burdensome, and a dynamic labor market has not been fully developed.

BACKGROUND: Mozambique promotes itself as a model for development. However, when President Armando Guebuza was re-elected in 2009, the elections were widely regarded as corrupt and unfair, and Freedom House has removed Mozambique from its list of electoral democracies. In 2012, the government passed a law restricting the personal business activities of politicians and public servants. Economic growth has been generally strong since the mid-1990s, but the economy is burdened by state-sanctioned monopolies and inefficient public services. Small-scale agriculture, fishing, and forestry employ about 80 percent of the workforce, but more than 90 percent of the arable land is still uncultivated. The informal sector accounts for most employment. Major exports include aluminum, shrimp, and cash crops. Significant natural gas reserves are being developed.

Quick Facts

Population: 22.5 million
GDP (PPP): $26.3 billion
7.5% growth in 2012
5-year compound annual growth 7.0%
$1,169 per capita
Unemployment: 17.0% (2007)
Inflation (CPI): 2.1%
FDI Inflow: $5.2 billion
Public Debt: 46.6% of GDP

2012 data unless otherwise noted.
Data compiled as of September 2013.

How Do We Measure Economic Freedom?
See page 471 for an explanation of the methodology or visit the *Index* Web site at *heritage.org/index*.

MOZAMBIQUE (continued)

THE TEN ECONOMIC FREEDOMS

Score ▬ Country | World Average — Rank — 1-Year Change

RULE OF LAW

	Score	Rank	1-Year Change
Property Rights	30.0	93rd	0
Freedom from Corruption	26.2	125th	-0.8

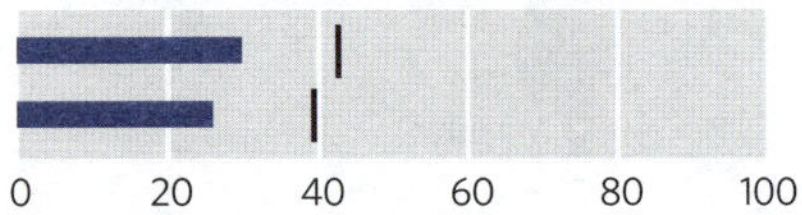

Corruption in government and business remains pervasive. Corruption, scarce resources, and poor training undermine judicial independence. The judicial system is further challenged by a lack of qualified judges and a backlog of cases. Without an efficient legal framework, court rulings can be arbitrary and inconsistent. Property rights are not strongly respected, and law enforcement is inefficient and uneven.

GOVERNMENT SIZE

	Score	Rank	1-Year Change
Fiscal Freedom	75.7	116th	-0.5
Government Spending	64.6	101st	+0.1

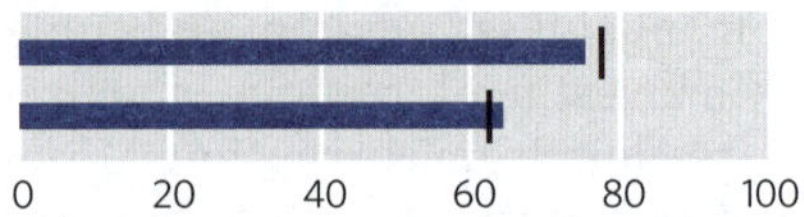

The top individual income and corporate tax rates are 32 percent. Other taxes include a value-added tax (VAT) and an inheritance tax. The overall tax burden equals 19.6 percent of gross domestic income. Government spending accounts for 34 percent of GDP. Public debt equals about 47 percent of gross domestic income. Recent discoveries of large natural gas reserves off the coast should bolster public finances.

REGULATORY EFFICIENCY

	Score	Rank	1-Year Change
Business Freedom	65.2	90th	+1.3
Labor Freedom	36.7	173rd	-1.2
Monetary Freedom	80.8	24th	+6.1

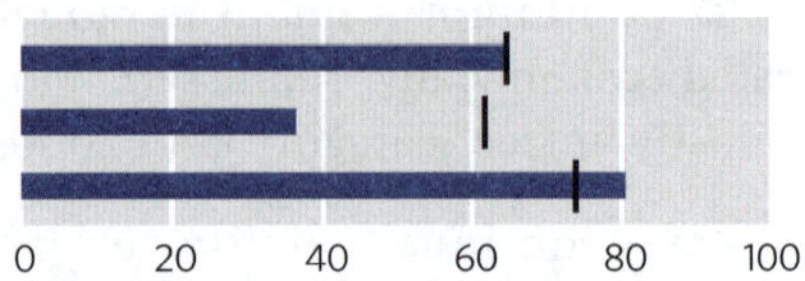

Considerable efforts have been made to modernize the regulatory framework. The business start-up process is now more straightforward, and no minimum capital is required. Licensing requirements, though still costly, have been eased. The government maintains administered prices for fuels and subsidizes state-owned enterprises such as the electricity company.

OPEN MARKETS

	Score	Rank	1-Year Change
Trade Freedom	75.5	94th	+0.1
Investment Freedom	45.0	125th	-5.0
Financial Freedom	50.0	69th	0

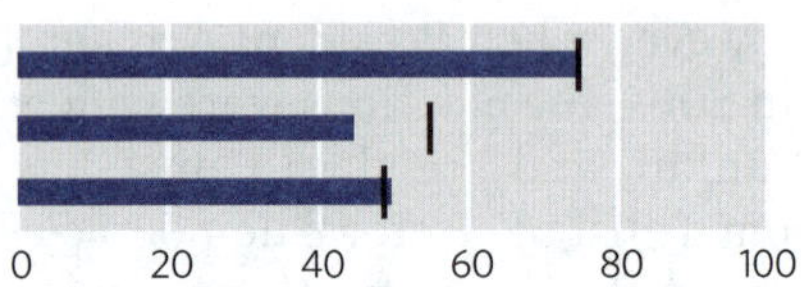

Mozambique has a 4.8 percent average tariff rate. The government is involved in several agricultural sectors where trade barriers remain high. There are domestic ownership requirements for some new foreign investment. Dominated by banking, the small financial sector has been evolving, but most people and businesses lack adequate access to financial services. High borrowing costs discourage entrepreneurship.

Long-Term Score Change (since 1995)

RULE OF LAW		GOVERNMENT SIZE		REGULATORY EFFICIENCY		OPEN MARKETS	
Property Rights	0	Fiscal Freedom	+15.2	Business Freedom	+10.2	Trade Freedom	+0.5
Freedom from Corruption	+16.2	Government Spending	-10.2	Labor Freedom	+1.6	Investment Freedom	+15.0
				Monetary Freedom	+36.9	Financial Freedom	+20.0

NAMIBIA

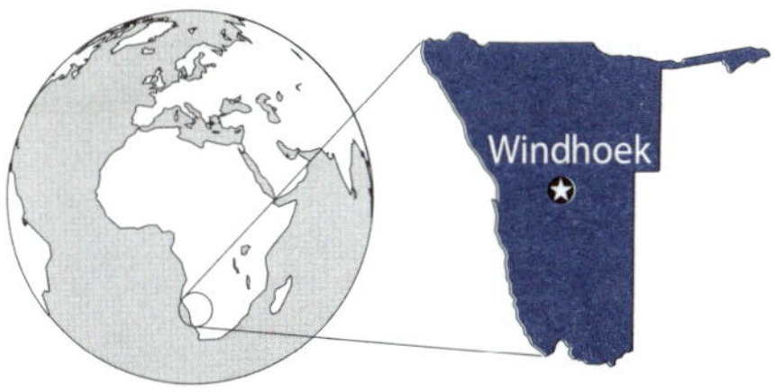

World Rank: **94** Regional Rank: **12**

Economic Freedom Score

Namibia's economic freedom score is 59.4, making its economy the 94th freest in the 2014 *Index*. Its score is 0.9 point worse than last year, with declines in the control of government spending and business freedom outweighing improvements in labor freedom, trade freedom, and fiscal freedom. Namibia is ranked 12th out of 46 countries in the Sub-Saharan Africa region, and its overall score is above the regional average.

Namibia was first graded in the 1997 *Index*, and its economic freedom score has dropped since then by over 2 points. A gain of over 45 points in trade freedom has been more than offset by declines in seven of the 10 economic freedoms, including large declines in property rights, financial freedom, and investment freedom. Namibia's economy is now rated "mostly unfree."

Namibia's overall economic freedom remains constrained by institutional weaknesses and an absence of commitment to deeper reforms. Namibia is weak in protecting property rights and ineffective in eliminating corruption. The judicial system is inconsistent in contract enforcement and vulnerable to political influence. Corruption is perceived as significant.

BACKGROUND: President Hifikepunye Pohamba won a second five-year term in 2009. Namibia is rich in minerals, but weak property rights and poor infrastructure impede growth, and unemployment in the formal economy remains a serious problem. About a third of Namibians depend on subsistence agriculture and herding; the services sector employs most workers in the formal economy and contributes the most to GDP. Namibia receives 30–40 percent of its revenues from the Southern African Customs Union. Economic growth depends largely on the price of uranium. There has been official pressure on white and foreign landowners to sell their property to the government so that "historically disadvantaged" and landless Namibians can be resettled. The state owns many enterprises in key sectors.

Freedom Trend

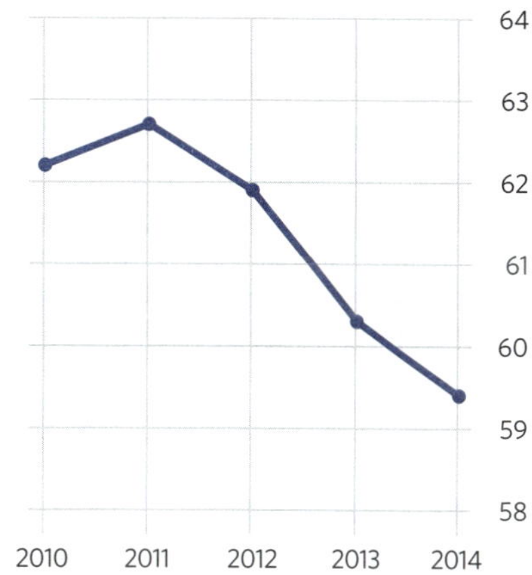

Country Comparisons

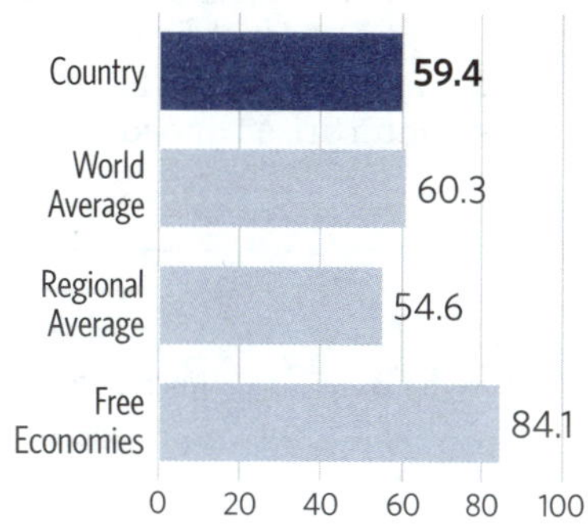

Quick Facts

Population: 2.2 million
GDP (PPP): $16.8 billion
4.0% growth in 2012
5-year compound annual growth 3.5%
$7,772 per capita
Unemployment: n/a
Inflation (CPI): 6.7%
FDI Inflow: $357.5 million
Public Debt: 26.6% of GDP

2012 data unless otherwise noted.
Data compiled as of September 2013.

How Do We Measure Economic Freedom?
See page 471 for an explanation of the methodology or visit the *Index* Web site at *heritage.org/index.*

THE TEN ECONOMIC FREEDOMS

RULE OF LAW

	Score	Rank	1-Year Change
Property Rights	30.0	93rd	0
Freedom from Corruption	44.2	57th	+0.2

Official corruption remains a problem, and investigations of major cases proceed slowly. Public office is often given as a reward for political service, and tribal affiliation is a factor. The rule of law remains weak, and access to justice is obstructed by economic and geographic barriers, a shortage of public defenders, and delays. Property rights are not protected effectively.

GOVERNMENT SIZE

	Score	Rank	1-Year Change
Fiscal Freedom	66.9	151st	+0.5
Government Spending	58.8	121st	-12.7

The top individual income tax rate is 37 percent, and the top corporate tax rate is 34 percent. Other taxes include a value-added tax (VAT). The overall tax burden is equal to 28 percent of gross domestic income. Public expenditures equate to 37 percent of GDP. Public debt has risen to a level equivalent to over a quarter of the gross domestic economy.

REGULATORY EFFICIENCY

	Score	Rank	1-Year Change
Business Freedom	64.4	94th	-4.0
Labor Freedom	81.9	21st	+5.2
Monetary Freedom	75.0	105th	+0.1

There is no minimum capital requirement for starting a business, but completing licensing requirements now takes over 100 days. The public and energy sectors employ much of the formal labor force. The labor market continues to lack flexibility. Wasteful subsidies to state-owned enterprises impede efficiency, and rising inflation threatens monetary stability.

OPEN MARKETS

	Score	Rank	1-Year Change
Trade Freedom	82.9	55th	+1.4
Investment Freedom	50.0	109th	0
Financial Freedom	40.0	107th	0

Namibia has a low 1.1 percent average tariff rate. Imports of several agricultural products face additional non-tariff barriers. New foreign investment can be subject to government screening. The financial sector is not fully developed. Financial intermediation remains uneven across the country, and scarce access to credit and banking services discourages entrepreneurial activity.

Long-Term Score Change (since 1997)

RULE OF LAW		GOVERNMENT SIZE		REGULATORY EFFICIENCY		OPEN MARKETS	
Property Rights	**-40.0**	Fiscal Freedom	**-0.8**	Business Freedom	**+9.4**	Trade Freedom	**+46.7**
Freedom from Corruption	**-5.8**	Government Spending	**-1.6**	Labor Freedom	**-4.7**	Investment Freedom	**-20.0**
				Monetary Freedom	**+0.1**	Financial Freedom	**-30.0**

NEPAL

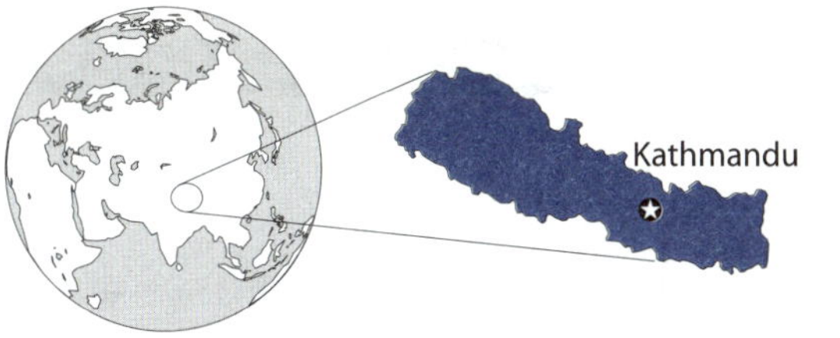

World Rank: 149 | **Regional Rank: 34**

Economic Freedom Score

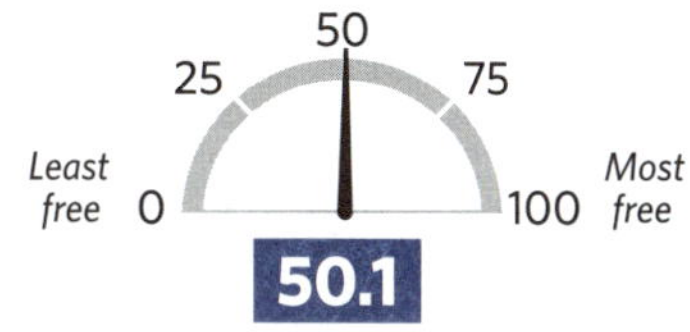

Nepal's economic freedom score is 50.1, making its economy the 149th freest in the 2014 *Index*. Its score has decreased by 0.3 point since last year, with modest improvements in business freedom, monetary freedom, and the control of government spending outweighed by declines in investment freedom and freedom from corruption. Nepal is ranked 34th out of 42 countries in the Asia–Pacific region, and its score remains far below world and regional averages.

Nepal was first graded in the 1996 *Index*, and its economic freedom score since then has been largely stagnant, declining overall by less than half a point. Improvements in four of the 10 economic freedoms, including freedom from corruption, business freedom, monetary freedom, and trade freedom, have been more than offset by deterioration in other areas, particularly a 25-point decrease in investment freedom. Considered a "mostly unfree" economy throughout its history in the *Index*, Nepal achieved its highest score in 2007.

Overall, a statist approach to economic management and development is a serious drag on business activity. A lack of transparency, corruption, and a burdensome approval process impede much-needed private investment and production. Property rights are undermined by the inefficient judicial system, which is subject to substantial corruption and political influence.

BACKGROUND: Seven years after the end of a Maoist insurgency and abolition of the monarchy, political instability continues to plague Nepal. In May 2012, interim Prime Minister Baburam Bhattarai dissolved the Constituent Assembly after the political parties failed to meet a deadline to form a new constitution. Elections scheduled for November 2012 were postponed. The reintegration of former Maoist fighters into the national army remains a controversial issue. Nepal is among the world's poorest and least developed countries and benefits from very little foreign direct investment. The main industry is agriculture, which accounts for one-third of GDP.

Freedom Trend

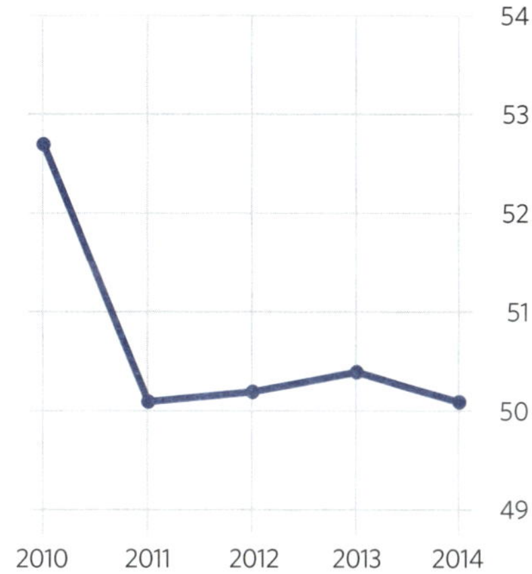

Country Comparisons

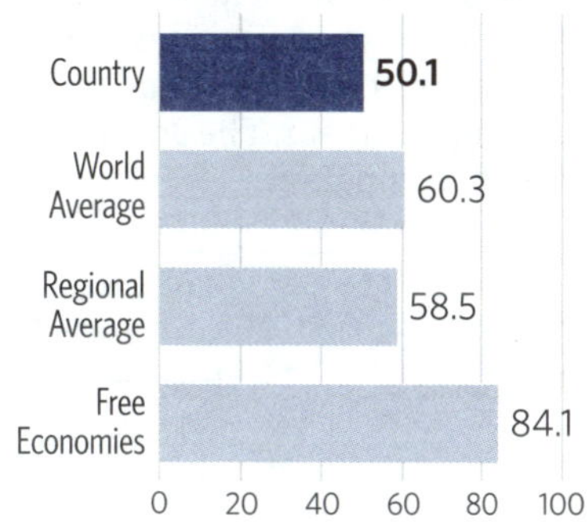

Quick Facts

Population: 31.0 million
GDP (PPP): $40.6 billion
4.6% growth in 2012
5-year compound annual growth 4.8%
$1,308 per capita
Unemployment: n/a
Inflation (CPI): 8.3%
FDI Inflow: $92.0 million
Public Debt: 33.1% of GDP

2012 data unless otherwise noted.
Data compiled as of September 2013.

How Do We Measure Economic Freedom?
See page 471 for an explanation of the methodology or visit the *Index* Web site at *heritage.org/index.*

THE TEN ECONOMIC FREEDOMS

RULE OF LAW

	Score	Rank	1-Year Change
Property Rights	30.0	93rd	0
Freedom from Corruption	21.3	154th	-0.7

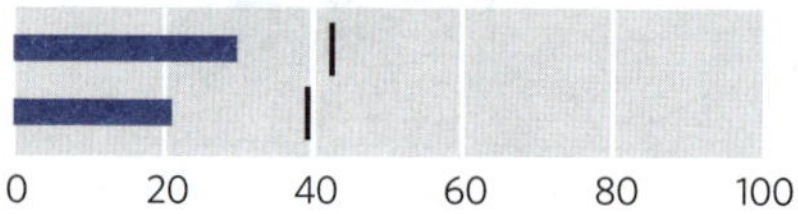

Corruption is endemic in politics and government. Many members of the legislature have been accused or convicted of corruption in the past, but high-level officials are rarely prosecuted. Graft is particularly prevalent in the judiciary, with frequent payoffs to judges for favorable rulings, and in the police force, which has been accused of extensive involvement in organized crime. Protections for property rights are not enforced effectively.

GOVERNMENT SIZE

	Score	Rank	1-Year Change
Fiscal Freedom	85.9	47th	+0.1
Government Spending	89.6	15th	+0.4

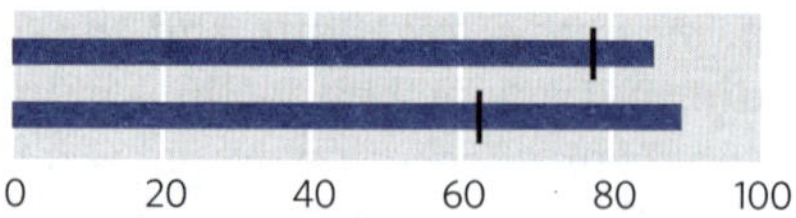

The top individual income and corporate tax rates are 25 percent. Other taxes include a value-added tax (VAT) and a property tax. The overall tax burden is 12.6 percent of gross domestic income. Government expenditures are steady at around 19 percent of GDP. Public debt is about 33 percent of the domestic economy. The government's ability to produce a budget has come into question because of political instability.

REGULATORY EFFICIENCY

	Score	Rank	1-Year Change
Business Freedom	58.5	121st	+1.3
Labor Freedom	43.8	160th	-0.5
Monetary Freedom	76.3	81st	+1.2

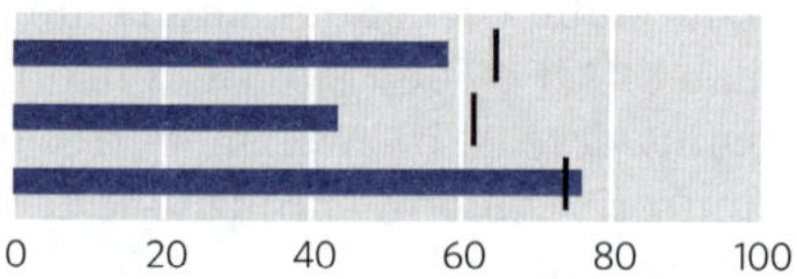

Bureaucracy and a lack of transparency often make business formation and operation costly and burdensome. Business start-up is now more streamlined, but obtaining necessary licenses continues to be time-consuming. Labor regulations are rigid, and restrictions on work hours remain stringent. The government provides extensive subsidies to the state-owned electricity and oil companies.

OPEN MARKETS

	Score	Rank	1-Year Change
Trade Freedom	61.0	157th	+0.2
Investment Freedom	5.0	174th	-5.0
Financial Freedom	30.0	132nd	0

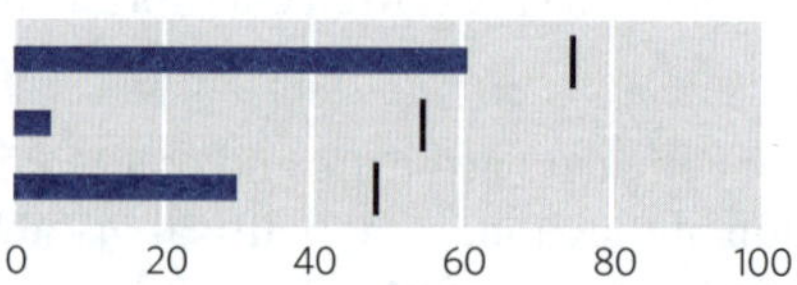

Nepal's average tariff rate is 12 percent. Tariffs are a significant source of government revenue. Consumers are not allowed to import used products. Foreign investors face government screening and a challenging economic environment. The financial sector remains fragmented, and government ownership and influence in the allocation of credit remain substantial.

Long-Term Score Change (since 1996)

RULE OF LAW		GOVERNMENT SIZE		REGULATORY EFFICIENCY		OPEN MARKETS	
Property Rights	0	Fiscal Freedom	-0.5	Business Freedom	+3.5	Trade Freedom	+7.8
Freedom from Corruption	+11.3	Government Spending	-1.7	Labor Freedom	-3.6	Investment Freedom	-25.0
				Monetary Freedom	+9.3	Financial Freedom	0

NETHERLANDS

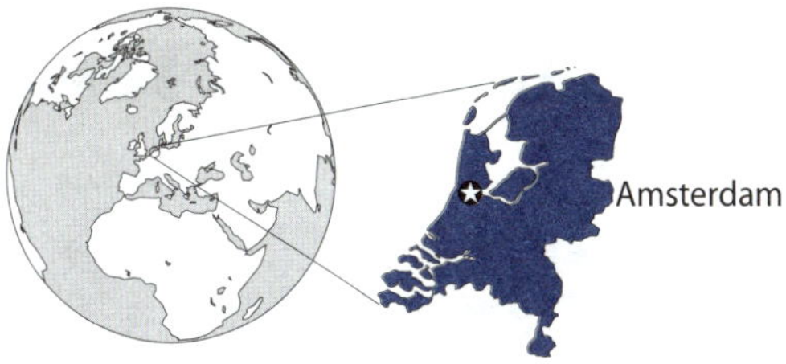

World Rank: **15** | Regional Rank: **6**

Economic Freedom Score

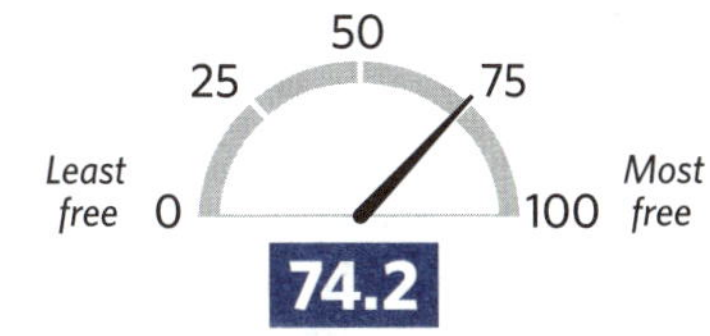

The Netherlands' economic freedom score is 74.2, making its economy the 15th freest in the 2014 *Index*. Its score is 0.7 point better than last year, with a strong improvement in business freedom more than balancing modest declines in several other freedoms. The Netherlands is ranked 6th out of 43 countries in the Europe region.

Over the 20-year history of the *Index*, the Netherlands' economic freedom score has advanced by over 4 points. Improvements in half of the 10 economic freedoms, including significant gains in fiscal freedom, control of government spending, trade freedom, and investment freedom, have been partially offset by declines in monetary freedom and financial freedom. Considered "moderately free" in the 1990s, the Netherlands' economy has been rated "mostly free" since 2000.

Open to global commerce, the Netherlands has long benefited from a high degree of regulatory efficiency that facilitates entrepreneurial activity. The judicial system provides strong protection for property rights. However, public spending continues to be quite high, and the overall tax regime is burdensome and complex.

BACKGROUND: In June 2010, Mark Rutte of the Peoples Party for Freedom and Democracy became prime minister as head of a center-right coalition. In April 2012, the coalition collapsed when the Freedom Party's Geert Wilders refused to back Rutte's austerity package. In early elections in September 2012, Rutte's party and its principal coalition partner won increased support to maintain power. Under Rutte's leadership, the Netherlands has been one of the staunchest supporters in the EU for turning power back to member states. The Netherlands is a center of international commerce. Rotterdam is one of the world's largest ports and Europe's largest in terms of cargo tonnage handled. The economy is sensitive to global market conditions, and in 2013, the Netherlands was one of nine members of the eurozone to be in recession.

Freedom Trend

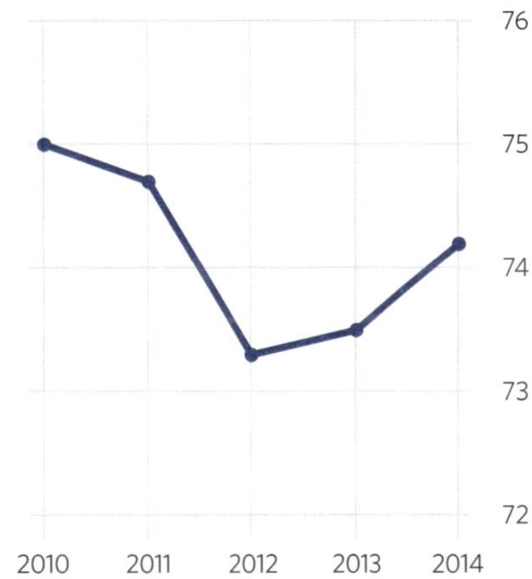

Country Comparisons

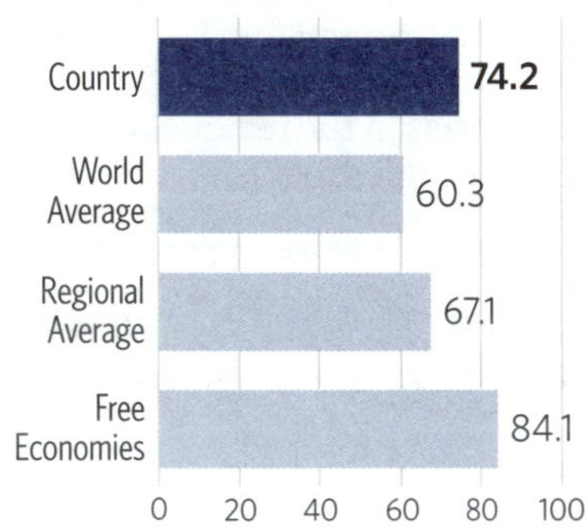

Quick Facts

Population: 16.8 million
GDP (PPP): $707.0 billion
-0.9% growth in 2012
5-year compound annual growth 0.0%
$42,194 per capita
Unemployment: 5.3%
Inflation (CPI): 2.8%
FDI Inflow: -$244.1 million
Public Debt: 71.7% of GDP

2012 data unless otherwise noted.
Data compiled as of September 2013.

How Do We Measure Economic Freedom?
See page 471 for an explanation of the methodology or visit the *Index* Web site at *heritage.org/index*.

THE TEN ECONOMIC FREEDOMS

		Score	Rank	1-Year Change
RULE OF LAW	Property Rights	90.0	2nd	0
	Freedom from Corruption	88.0	8th	-1.0

The legal framework ensures strong protection of private property rights and enforcement of contracts. Citizens and foreigners purchasing real property receive equal treatment. Independent of political interference, the judiciary is respected and provides fair adjudication of disputes. Intellectual property rights are relatively well protected. Effective anti-corruption measures and minimal tolerance for corruption ensure government integrity.

		Score	Rank	1-Year Change
GOVERNMENT SIZE	Fiscal Freedom	51.7	175th	-0.4
	Government Spending	25.6	166th	+0.9

The top individual income tax rate is 52 percent, and the top corporate tax rate is 25 percent. Other taxes include a value-added tax (VAT) and environmental taxes. The overall tax burden takes up 38.7 percent of gross domestic income. Public expenditures amount to about half the size of the domestic economy. The government has been in breach of EU deficit rules since 2009, and debt levels have reached over 70 percent of GDP.

		Score	Rank	1-Year Change
REGULATORY EFFICIENCY	Business Freedom	89.7	15th	+6.7
	Labor Freedom	59.6	102nd	+1.0
	Monetary Freedom	79.9	34th	-1.2

The entrepreneurial framework is transparent and efficient. Starting a business takes four procedures and four days on average, but licensing can be time-consuming. The labor market lacks flexibility, but the non-salary cost of employment is not high in comparison to other countries in the region. Monetary stability has been well maintained, and the government has cut subsidies to offshore wind power projects.

		Score	Rank	1-Year Change
OPEN MARKETS	Trade Freedom	87.8	11th	+1.0
	Investment Freedom	90.0	2nd	0
	Financial Freedom	80.0	4th	0

EU members have a low 1.1 percent average tariff rate and, in general, few non-tariff barriers to trade. Foreign and domestic investors in the Netherlands are treated equally under the law. The well-developed financial sector has been competitive but has been forced to restructure drastically since 2009. The government has remained involved in the banking sector through ownership, guarantees, and capital injections.

Long-Term Score Change (since 1996)

RULE OF LAW		GOVERNMENT SIZE		REGULATORY EFFICIENCY		OPEN MARKETS	
Property Rights	0	Fiscal Freedom	**+17.9**	Business Freedom	**+4.7**	Trade Freedom	**+10.0**
Freedom from Corruption	**-2.0**	Government Spending	**+19.0**	Labor Freedom	**-1.9**	Investment Freedom	**+20.0**
				Monetary Freedom	**-4.6**	Financial Freedom	**-10.0**

NEW ZEALAND

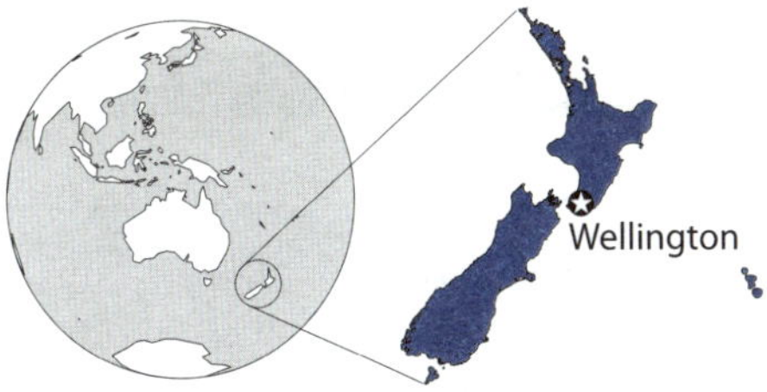

World Rank: **5** Regional Rank: **4**

Economic Freedom Score

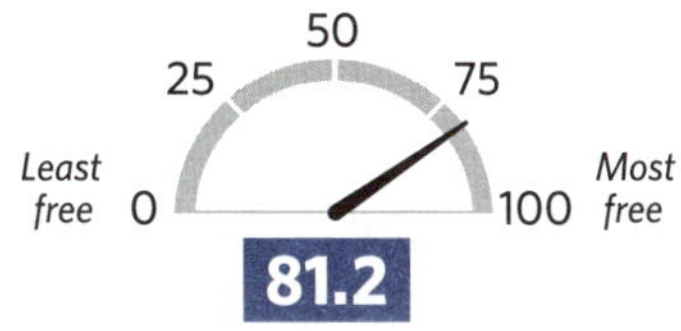

New Zealand's economic freedom score is 81.2, making its economy the 5th freest in the 2014 *Index*. Its score is slightly lower than last year, reflecting modest declines in four economic freedoms, including business freedom and freedom from corruption, that outweigh improvements in monetary freedom and labor freedom. New Zealand is ranked 4th out of 42 countries in the Asia–Pacific region.

New Zealand was first graded in the 1996 *Index*, and its economic freedom score has advanced since then by over 3 points. Improvements in seven of the 10 economic freedoms, including business freedom, investment freedom, trade freedom, and fiscal freedom, have enabled New Zealand to move from "mostly free" almost 20 years ago to "free" today. Since 2007, New Zealand has been rated one of the world's five freest economies.

New Zealand's modern and competitive economy benefits from a strong commitment to open-market policies that facilitate engagement in global commerce. Transparent and efficient regulations are applied evenly in most cases, encouraging dynamic private-sector entrepreneurial activity. Buttressed by a strong tradition of minimum tolerance for corruption, New Zealand's vigorous defense of effective rule of law sustains the foundations of economic freedom and contributes to the high level of lasting prosperity.

BACKGROUND: New Zealand is a parliamentary democracy and one of the Asia–Pacific region's most prosperous countries. After 10 years of Labor Party–dominated governments, the center-right National Party, led by Prime Minister John Key, returned to power in November 2008 and was re-elected in November 2011. Far-reaching liberalization in the 1980s and 1990s largely deregulated the economy. It is powered mainly by agriculture but also benefits from a flourishing manufacturing sector, thriving tourism, and a strong renewable geothermal energy resource base. Following a sizable financial contraction during the global economic recession, the economy has been expanding since 2010.

Freedom Trend

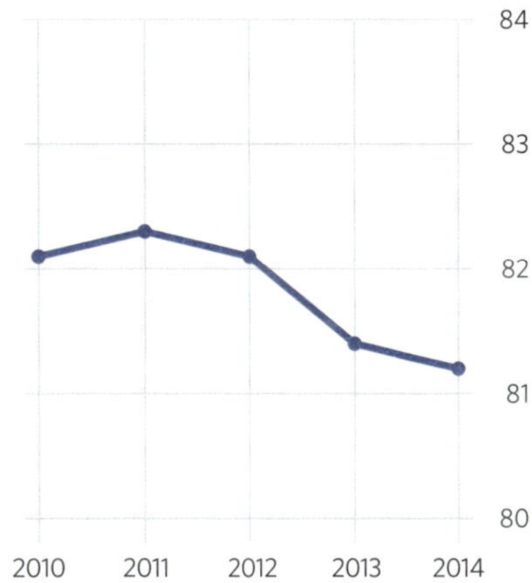

Country Comparisons

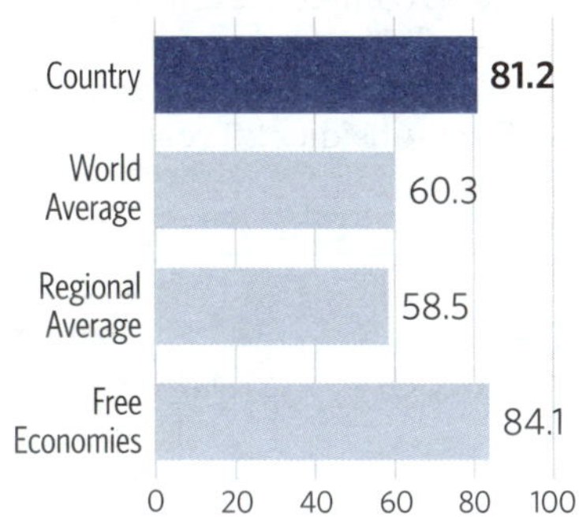

Quick Facts

Population: 4.4 million
GDP (PPP): $132.0 billion
2.5% growth in 2012
5-year compound annual growth 0.6%
$29,730 per capita
Unemployment: 6.9%
Inflation (CPI): 1.1%
FDI Inflow: $2.9 billion
Public Debt: 38.2% of GDP

2012 data unless otherwise noted.
Data compiled as of September 2013.

How Do We Measure Economic Freedom?
See page 471 for an explanation of the methodology or visit the *Index* Web site at *heritage.org/index*.

THE TEN ECONOMIC FREEDOMS

RULE OF LAW

	Score	Rank	1-Year Change
Property Rights	95.0	1st	0
Freedom from Corruption	94.0	1st	-1.0

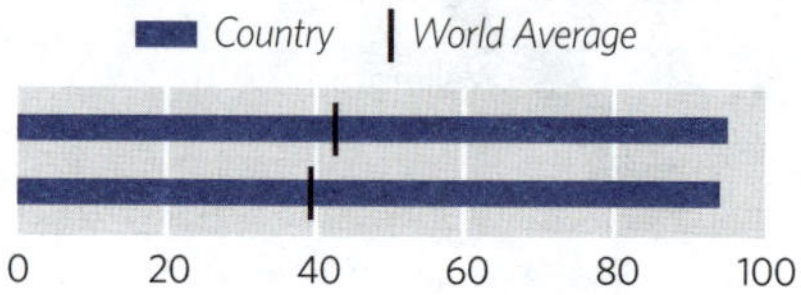

New Zealand is renowned for its efforts to ensure transparent, competitive, and corruption-free government procurement. Stiff penalties against bribery of government officials and those who accept bribes are strictly enforced. The judicial system is independent and functions well. Private property rights are strongly protected, and contracts are notably secure. Enforcement of intellectual property rights is solid.

GOVERNMENT SIZE

	Score	Rank	1-Year Change
Fiscal Freedom	71.2	135th	-0.3
Government Spending	32.3	159th	-0.9

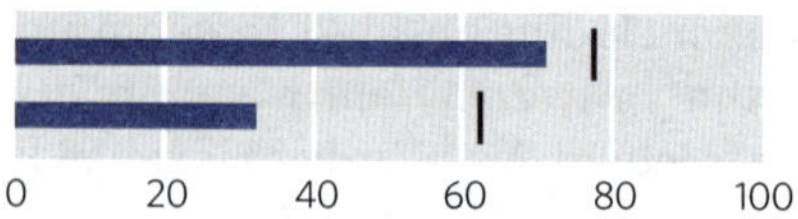

The top individual income tax rate is 33 percent, and the top corporate tax rate is 28 percent. Other taxes include a goods and services tax (GST) and environmental taxes. The overall tax burden equals 31.7 percent of gross domestic income. Government spending equates to about 47.5 percent of GDP, and public debt is steady at 38 percent of GDP. Ongoing earthquake recovery and rebuilding burden the government's budget.

REGULATORY EFFICIENCY

	Score	Rank	1-Year Change
Business Freedom	96.1	4th	-3.8
Labor Freedom	90.2	8th	+0.7
Monetary Freedom	86.3	3rd	+3.0

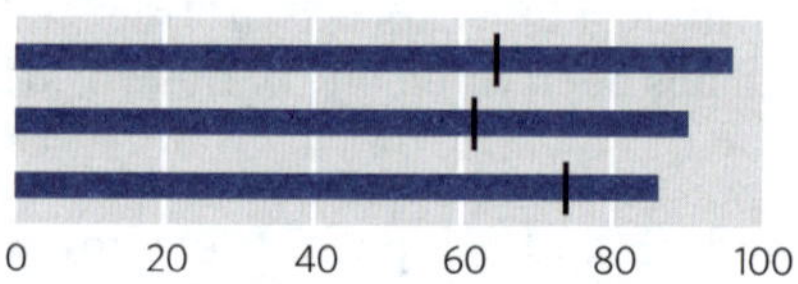

Start-up companies enjoy great flexibility under licensing and other regulatory frameworks. It takes only one procedure to start a business, and no minimal capital is required. Flexible labor regulations facilitate a dynamic labor market, increasing overall productivity. The removal of all farm subsidies 20 years ago spurred the development of a vibrant and diversified agriculture sector.

OPEN MARKETS

	Score	Rank	1-Year Change
Trade Freedom	86.8	40th	0
Investment Freedom	80.0	23rd	0
Financial Freedom	80.0	4th	0

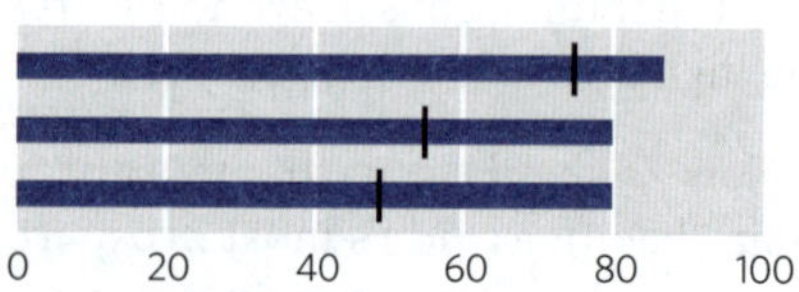

New Zealand's average tariff rate is 1.6 percent, and there are few non-tariff barriers to trade. The government screens foreign investment in certain sectors. The well-developed financial sector offers a wide range of financing instruments. The financial system has remained stable, and prudent regulations allowed banks to withstand the global financial turmoil with little disruption.

Long-Term Score Change (since 1996)

RULE OF LAW		GOVERNMENT SIZE		REGULATORY EFFICIENCY		OPEN MARKETS	
Property Rights	**+5.0**	Fiscal Freedom	**+6.1**	Business Freedom	**+11.1**	Trade Freedom	**+8.2**
Freedom from Corruption	**+4.0**	Government Spending	**-16.3**	Labor Freedom	**-0.9**	Investment Freedom	**+10.0**
				Monetary Freedom	**+0.3**	Financial Freedom	**-10.0**

NICARAGUA

Economic Freedom Score

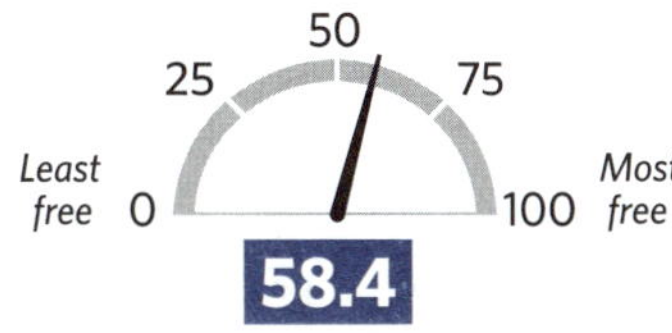

Nicaragua's economic freedom score is 58.4, making its economy the 102nd freest in the 2014 *Index*. Its score is 1.8 points better than last year, with significant improvements in investment freedom and the control of government spending offsetting declines in labor freedom and freedom from corruption. Nicaragua is ranked 18th out of 29 countries in the South and Central America/Caribbean region, and its overall score is below the world average.

Over the 20-year history of the *Index*, Nicaragua has advanced its economic freedom score by nearly 16 points, a top-20 improvement facilitated especially by gains in the area of market openness as measured by trade freedom, investment freedom, and financial freedom. Scores for three of the 10 economic freedoms, notably monetary freedom, have advanced by 20 points or more. Nicaragua reached its highest economic freedom score in 2006 and was rated "moderately free" during most of the 2000s.

Since 2009, however, Nicaragua's economy has fallen back to "mostly unfree." Anti–free market policies are bolstered by economic and political populism that drives class warfare. Institutional weaknesses persist in protection of property rights and combating corruption.

BACKGROUND: Despite a constitutional prohibition, Sandinista President Daniel Ortega was re-elected in November 2011. He is aligned with the Bolivarian Alliance for the Americas (ALBA), an anti-American trade organization organized by Venezuela. Ortega has weathered domestic opposition due to economic assistance from Venezuela and a divided opposition. The Central America–Dominican Republic–United States Free Trade Agreement (CAFTA–DR) has helped to diversify the economy. Agricultural goods and textile production account for 50 percent of exports. Nicaragua remains one of the least developed and poorest countries in the Americas. Much of the workforce is underemployed in the formal sector. The government has granted a Chinese company a concession to begin construction of an Atlantic/Pacific canal in Nicaragua.

Freedom Trend

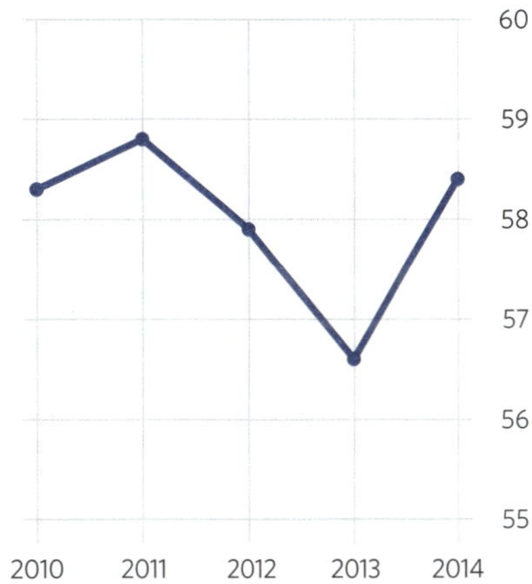

Country Comparisons

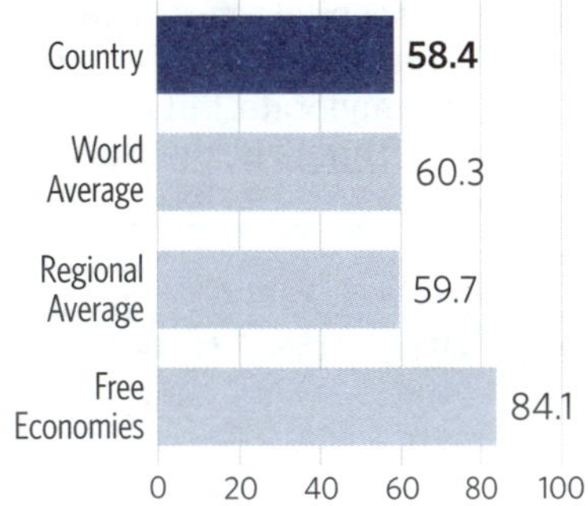

Quick Facts

Population: 6.0 million
GDP (PPP): $26.7 billion
5.2% growth in 2012
5-year compound annual growth 3.2%
$4,458 per capita
Unemployment: 7.8%
Inflation (CPI): 7.9%
FDI Inflow: $810.0 million
Public Debt: 52.1% of GDP

2012 data unless otherwise noted.
Data compiled as of September 2013.

How Do We Measure Economic Freedom?
See page 471 for an explanation of the methodology or visit the *Index* Web site at *heritage.org/index.*

THE TEN ECONOMIC FREEDOMS

RULE OF LAW

	Score	Rank	1-Year Change
Property Rights	15.0	159th	0
Freedom from Corruption	24.1	136th	-0.9

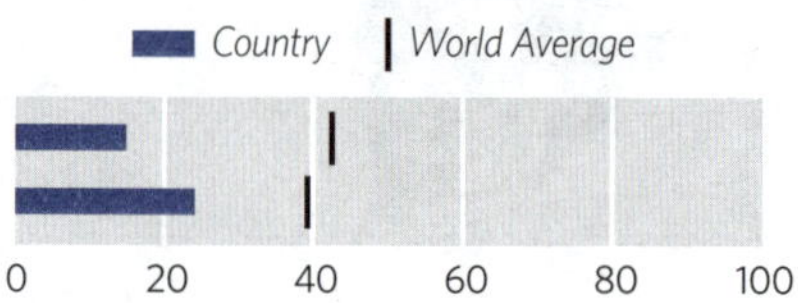

Corruption cases against opposition figures and private entities appear to be politically motivated. There are persistent concerns about the transparency of funds flowing to Nicaragua from the Venezuela-funded Bolivarian Alliance. The judicial system is not independent from political interference. Protection of private property rights is not enforced effectively, and contracts are not always secure.

GOVERNMENT SIZE

	Score	Rank	1-Year Change
Fiscal Freedom	78.6	102nd	-0.1
Government Spending	80.0	50th	+14.9

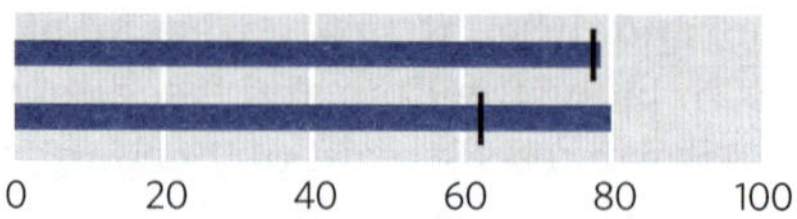

The top individual income and corporate tax rates are 30 percent. Other taxes include a value-added tax (VAT) and a capital gains tax. The overall tax burden is 18.4 percent of gross national income. Government spending is 26 percent of GDP. Public debt has fallen to half the size of the domestic economy. The government still relies on development assistance, but donors withdrew some support after flawed 2008 elections.

REGULATORY EFFICIENCY

	Score	Rank	1-Year Change
Business Freedom	52.6	147th	+1.4
Labor Freedom	60.3	99th	-1.9
Monetary Freedom	72.8	125th	-0.4

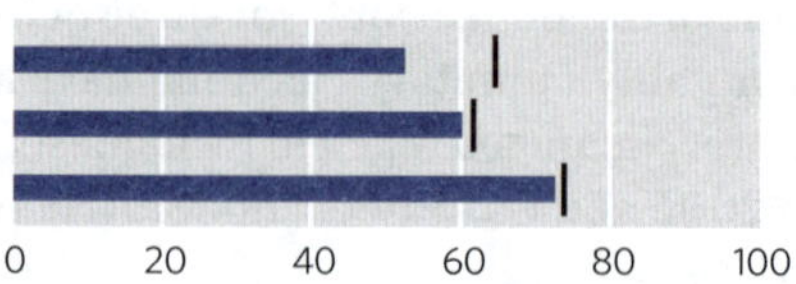

The entrepreneurial environment remains burdened by costly regulatory procedures. The minimum capital requirement for starting a business has been eliminated, but licensing costs still average over twice the level of average annual income. The non-salary cost of employing a worker is moderate, but regulations on work hours are restrictive. Substantial energy and cash subsidies from Venezuela distort domestic prices.

OPEN MARKETS

	Score	Rank	1-Year Change
Trade Freedom	85.4	48th	0
Investment Freedom	65.0	68th	+5.0
Financial Freedom	50.0	69th	0

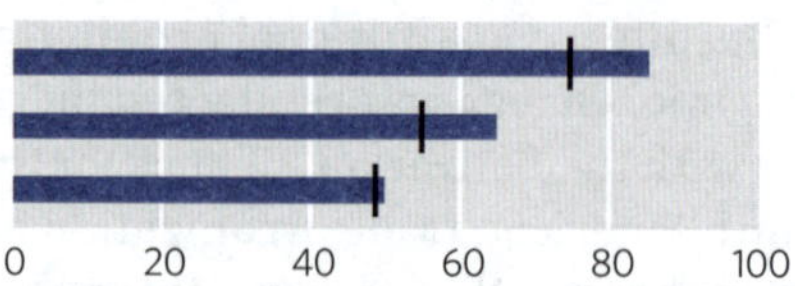

Nicaragua's average tariff rate is 2.3 percent. There are no significant non-tariff barriers to trade. Foreign investors must contend with legal and regulatory systems that are affected by political connections. The financial sector is concentrated in urban areas and not fully developed. The small banking sector is highly dollarized and provides a limited range of financial services. The cost of long-term financing is high.

Long-Term Score Change (since 1995)

RULE OF LAW		GOVERNMENT SIZE		REGULATORY EFFICIENCY		OPEN MARKETS	
Property Rights	**-15.0**	Fiscal Freedom	**+0.3**	Business Freedom	**-2.4**	Trade Freedom	**+31.0**
Freedom from Corruption	**+14.1**	Government Spending	**+4.8**	Labor Freedom	**-12.6**	Investment Freedom	**+15.0**
				Monetary Freedom	**+72.8**	Financial Freedom	**+20.0**

NIGER

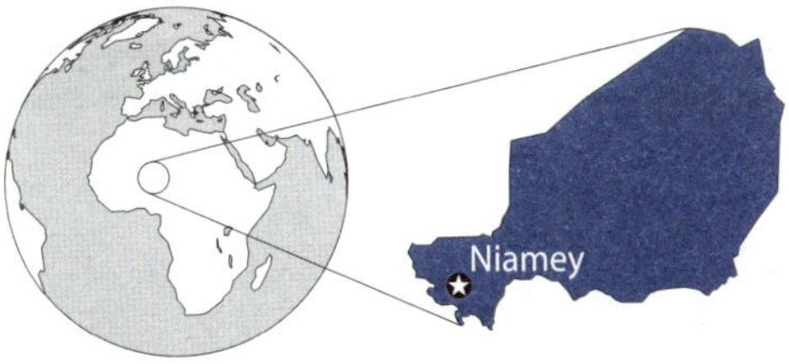

Economic Freedom Score

World Rank: **127** Regional Rank: **24**

Niger's economic freedom score is 55.1, making its economy the 127th freest in the 2014 *Index*. Its score has increased by 1.2 points since last year, with improvements in the control of government spending, labor freedom, monetary freedom, and freedom from corruption outweighing a substantial decline in trade freedom. Niger is ranked 24th out of 46 countries in the Sub-Saharan Africa region, and its overall score is slightly above the regional average.

Niger was first graded in the 1996 *Index* and since then has advanced its economic freedom score by over 9 points, reaching its highest score ever in the 2014 *Index*. Its scores have improved in seven of the 10 categories of economic freedom, especially market openness as measured through trade freedom, investment freedom, and financial freedom, although its business freedom has lagged compared to other countries.

Effective implementation of deeper institutional reforms is critical to sustaining Niger's high levels of economic growth and ensuring long-term development. Systemic weaknesses linger in the protection of property rights and the effective enforcement of anti-corruption measures. The judiciary remains vulnerable to political influence.

BACKGROUND: President Mamadou Tandja was overthrown in 2010. Opposition leader Mahamadou Issoufou won elections in March 2011 and was inaugurated as president in April 2011. His political coalition also won a majority in the National Assembly. A Tuareg rebellion in northern Niger, spillover violence from conflicts in Libya and Mali, and the growing presence of al-Qaeda–linked groups remain serious threats. Niger is one of the world's poorest countries. With the exception of uranium, its substantial mineral resources, including petroleum and gold, have yet to be exploited. About 80 percent of the population depends on subsistence agriculture and herding. Infrastructure is poor, and extended periods of drought hinder food production. Niger is a major transit point for human trafficking.

Freedom Trend

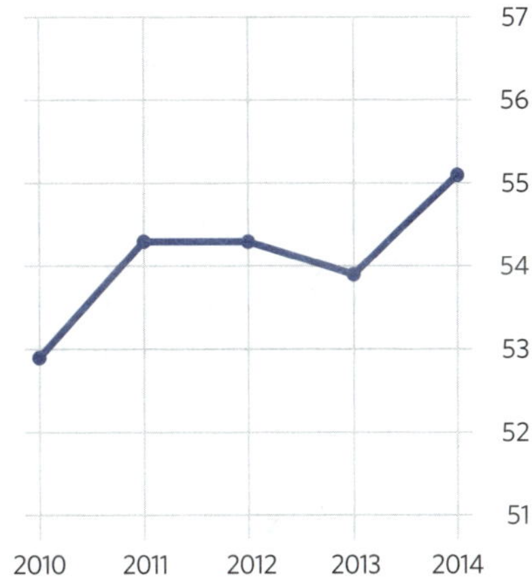

Country Comparisons

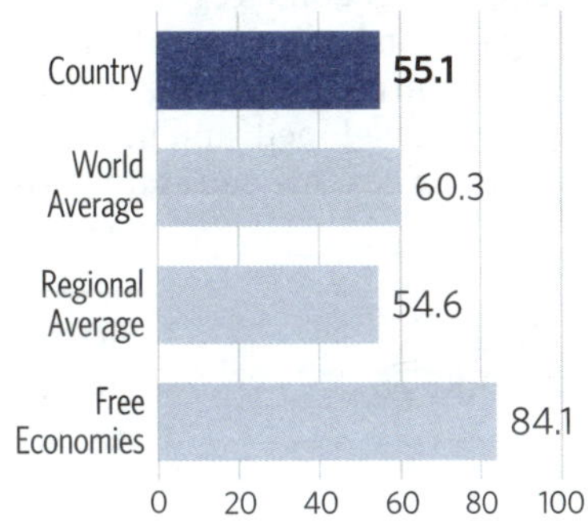

Quick Facts

Population: 16.1 million
GDP (PPP): $13.1 billion
11.2% growth in 2012
5-year compound annual growth 6.4%
$815 per capita
Unemployment: n/a
Inflation (CPI): 0.5%
FDI Inflow: $793.4 million
Public Debt: 31.1% of GDP

2012 data unless otherwise noted.
Data compiled as of September 2013.

How Do We Measure Economic Freedom?
See page 471 for an explanation of the methodology or visit the *Index* Web site at *heritage.org/index*.

THE TEN ECONOMIC FREEDOMS

		Score	Rank	1-Year Change
RULE OF LAW	Property Rights	30.0	93rd	0
	Freedom from Corruption	26.0	127th	+1.0

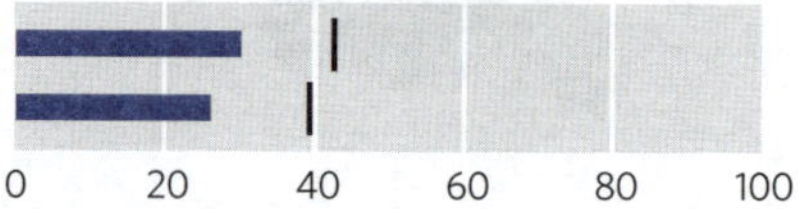

The civilian government that took office in 2011 has committed itself to improving governance, implementing reforms, and supporting national reconciliation. However, corruption remains a serious problem, and observers have raised concerns regarding uranium-mining contracts. The rule of law is hampered by an ineffective judicial framework, and a weak court system remains vulnerable to political interference.

		Score	Rank	1-Year Change
GOVERNMENT SIZE	Fiscal Freedom	76.8	112th	-0.2
	Government Spending	88.4	19th	+8.3

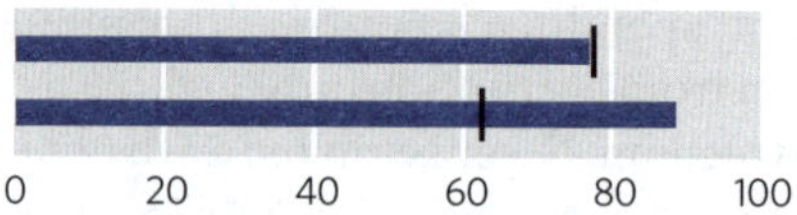

The top individual income tax rate is 35 percent, and the top corporate tax rate is 30 percent. Other taxes include a tax on interest and a capital gains tax. The overall tax burden equals 14.1 percent of gross domestic income. Government spending is equivalent to 20 percent of the domestic economy. Public debt has reached over 30 percent of GDP. Strong uranium-mining revenue should help the government cope with a recurring food crisis.

		Score	Rank	1-Year Change
REGULATORY EFFICIENCY	Business Freedom	35.2	173rd	0
	Labor Freedom	45.4	155th	+6.1
	Monetary Freedom	88.3	1st	+2.9

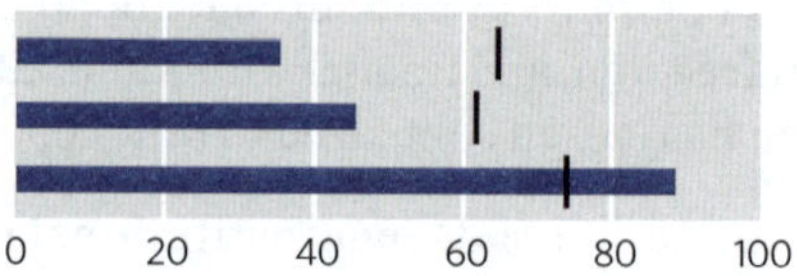

The burdensome regulatory framework hampers private-sector development. Inconsistent regulations impose substantial costs on business operations. The cost of completing licensing requirements is still over 10 times the level of annual average income. The labor market is poorly developed, and much of the labor force works in the informal sector. The state influences prices through state-owned utilities.

		Score	Rank	1-Year Change
OPEN MARKETS	Trade Freedom	65.6	141st	-6.1
	Investment Freedom	55.0	96th	0
	Financial Freedom	40.0	107th	0

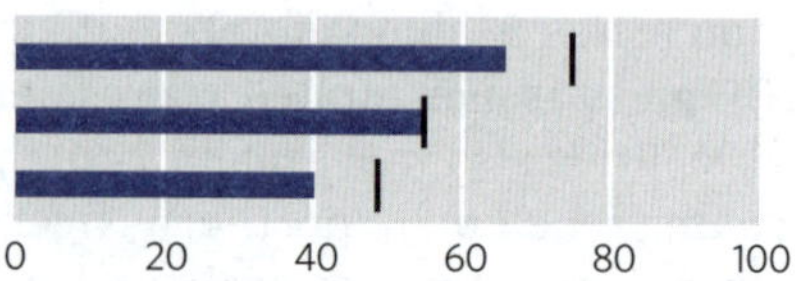

Niger's average tariff rate is 9.7 percent. Tariffs are highest on products that compete with domestic industries. It can take weeks to import goods. The country's laws generally treat domestic and foreign investors equally. Some progress has been made toward modernizing the financial sector, but the number of available financial options for starting and expanding private businesses is limited.

Long-Term Score Change (since 1996)

RULE OF LAW		GOVERNMENT SIZE		REGULATORY EFFICIENCY		OPEN MARKETS	
Property Rights	0	Fiscal Freedom	+30.6	Business Freedom	-19.8	Trade Freedom	+0.6
Freedom from Corruption	+16.0	Government Spending	-3.6	Labor Freedom	+1.2	Investment Freedom	+25.0
				Monetary Freedom	+33.8	Financial Freedom	+10.0

NIGERIA

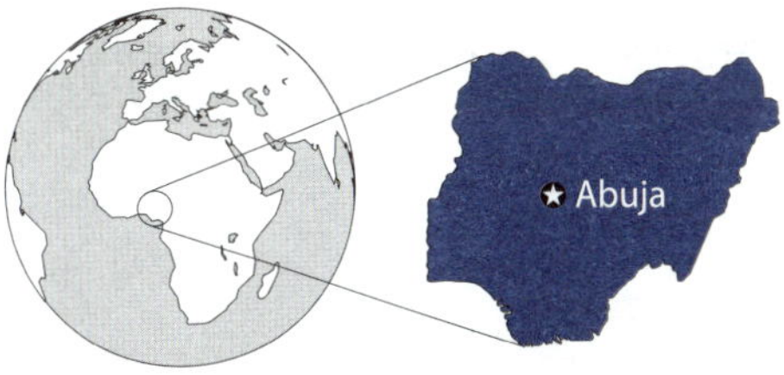

World Rank: **129** Regional Rank: **26**

Economic Freedom Score

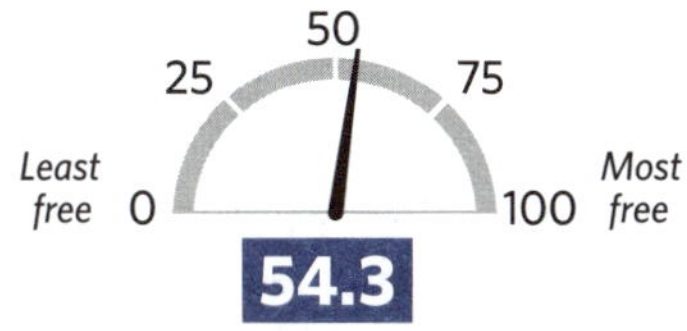

Nigeria's economic freedom score is 54.3, making its economy the 129th freest in the 2014 *Index*. Its score is 0.8 point lower than last year, reflecting deteriorations in six of the 10 economic freedoms including business freedom, freedom from corruption, and labor freedom. Nigeria is ranked 26th out of 46 countries in the Sub-Saharan Africa region, and its overall score is below the world average.

Over the 20-year history of the *Index*, Nigeria has advanced its economic freedom score by 7 points. Scores for the control of government spending, monetary freedom, and trade freedom have improved by double digits, although these gains have been largely undercut by declines in six of the 10 economic freedoms including business freedom, labor freedom, investment freedom, and financial freedom. Scores for property rights and freedom from corruption have declined by 20 points or more.

For two decades, Nigeria has fluctuated between "repressed" and "mostly unfree." The state intrudes heavily into private-sector activity. Regulatory barriers still prevent broad-based private-sector development, and much of the population remains engaged in subsistence agriculture.

BACKGROUND: President Goodluck Jonathan was re-elected in a contested election in 2011. Ethnic and regional violence, aggravated by the imposition of Islamic law in a number of states, has taken a heavy toll on the nation. Violence by the domestic terrorist group Boko Haram in the predominately Muslim North led the government to declare a state of emergency in May 2013. Nigeria is Africa's most populous nation. It is also Africa's leading oil producer, although sabotage of oil facilities and pipelines in the Niger Delta continues to impede operations. Oil and gas account for about 90 percent of export earnings and 80 percent of government revenue. Nigeria ranks 6th in the world in oil exports and 10th in natural gas reserves. The informal economy is extensive.

Freedom Trend

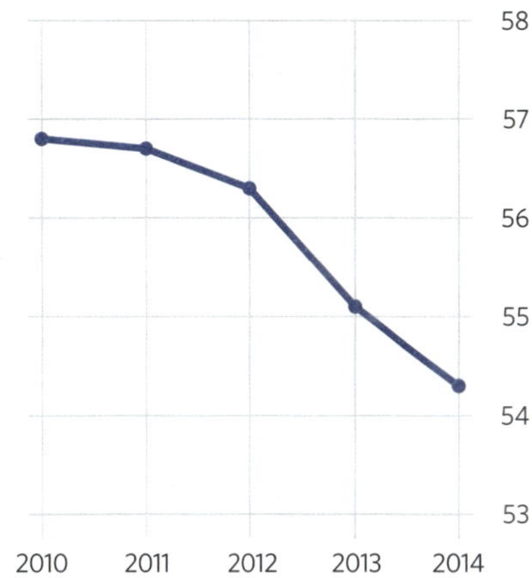

Country Comparisons

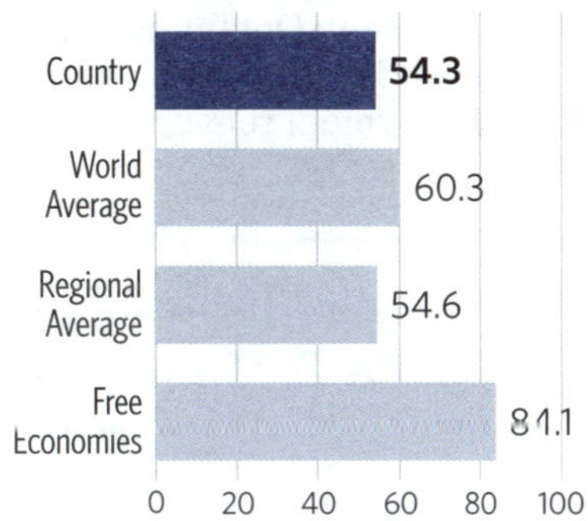

Quick Facts

Population: 164.8 million
GDP (PPP): $448.1 billion
6.3% growth in 2012
5-year compound annual growth 6.9%
$2,720 per capita
Unemployment: 23.9% (2011)
Inflation (CPI): 12.2%
FDI Inflow: $7.0 billion
Public Debt: 17.8% of GDP

2012 data unless otherwise noted.
Data compiled as of September 2013.

How Do We Measure Economic Freedom?
See page 471 for an explanation of the methodology or visit the *Index* Web site at *heritage.org/index.*

THE TEN ECONOMIC FREEDOMS

RULE OF LAW

	Score	Rank	1-Year Change
Property Rights	30.0	93rd	0
Freedom from Corruption	22.7	145th	-1.3

Corruption is pervasive, and government efforts to improve transparency and reduce graft have been inadequate. It is estimated that 100,000 barrels of oil are stolen every day from pipelines, ports, and storage tanks with the connivance of government officials. One of the world's least efficient property registration systems makes acquiring and maintaining rights to real property difficult. Enforcement of copyrights, patents, and trademarks is deficient.

GOVERNMENT SIZE

	Score	Rank	1-Year Change
Fiscal Freedom	85.0	53rd	+2.4
Government Spending	74.5	74th	-0.1

The top individual income tax rate is 24 percent, and the top corporate tax rate is 30 percent. Other taxes include a value-added tax (VAT) and a capital gains tax. The overall tax burden is equal to 4.7 percent of gross domestic income. Government spending is 29 percent of GDP. Public debt is equivalent to about 18 percent of the domestic economy. The government remains highly dependent on oil revenues to finance public accounts.

REGULATORY EFFICIENCY

	Score	Rank	1-Year Change
Business Freedom	48.0	155th	-7.7
Labor Freedom	66.4	75th	-0.8
Monetary Freedom	73.1	122nd	-0.2

Red tape and inconsistent enforcement of commercial regulations burden the entrepreneurial environment. Obtaining necessary permits still takes more than 100 days and costs over 30 times the level of average annual income. The underdeveloped labor market is inefficient, and unemployment remains high. The government subsidizes and administers the prices of fuel and electricity.

OPEN MARKETS

	Score	Rank	1-Year Change
Trade Freedom	63.8	149th	-0.1
Investment Freedom	40.0	132nd	0
Financial Freedom	40.0	107th	0

The average tariff rate for Nigeria is 10.6 percent. High tariffs apply to imports that compete with domestically made goods. Political instability is a deterrent to foreign investment. The financial system remains weak and inefficient. Overall banking development is still hindered by bureaucracy and a cash-based economy. Banks interact with a very limited portion of the population, and access to financing is limited.

Long-Term Score Change (since 1995)

RULE OF LAW		GOVERNMENT SIZE		REGULATORY EFFICIENCY		OPEN MARKETS	
Property Rights	**-20.0**	Fiscal Freedom	**+9.6**	Business Freedom	**-7.0**	Trade Freedom	**+18.8**
Freedom from Corruption	**-27.3**	Government Spending	**+74.5**	Labor Freedom	**-6.8**	Investment Freedom	**-10.0**
				Monetary Freedom	**+22.9**	Financial Freedom	**-10.0**

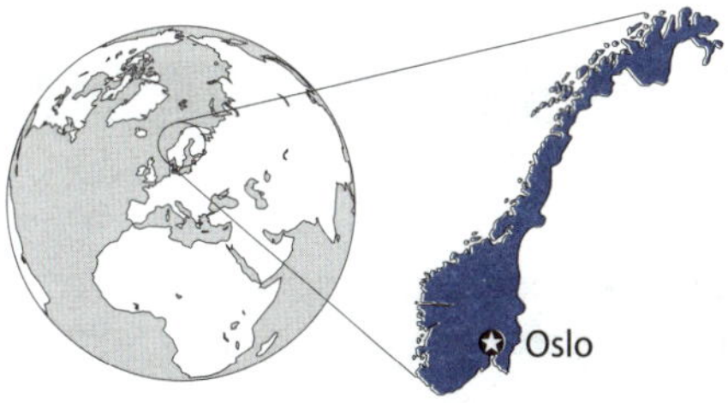

NORWAY

World Rank: **32** Regional Rank: **16**

Economic Freedom Score

Norway's economic freedom score is 70.9, making its economy the 32nd freest in the 2014 *Index*. Its score has increased by 0.4 point since last year, with improvements in investment freedom, the management of government spending, and monetary freedom partially offset by declines in freedom from corruption and business freedom. Norway is ranked 16th out of 43 countries in the Europe region, and its overall score is well above the world and regional averages.

Norway was first rated in the 1996 *Index* and since then has advanced its economic freedom score by 5.5 points. Improved scores for half of the 10 economic freedoms, led by notable gains in the area of market openness measured through trade freedom, investment freedom, and financial freedom, have enabled Norway to prosper despite declines in fiscal freedom, labor freedom, and monetary freedom. Norway's economy, recording its highest score ever in the 2014 *Index*, is now considered "mostly free."

Norway's strong competitiveness is built on flexibility and openness. The economy continues to be a world leader in several of the 10 economic freedoms including trade freedom, property rights, and freedom from corruption. The sound regulatory environment encourages entrepreneurial activity and innovation. Commercial operations are handled with transparency and efficiency.

BACKGROUND: Prime Minister Jens Stoltenberg heads a labor–socialist government. Norway has been a member of NATO since 1949, but voters have twice rejected membership in the European Union; the country instead interacts with EU members under a European Free Trade Association agreement. Norway is one of the world's most prosperous countries. Fisheries, metal, and oil are the most important commodities. Norway saves a large portion of its petroleum-sector revenues, such as dividends from the partially state-owned Statoil and taxes from oil and gas companies operating in Norway, in its Government Pension Fund-Global.

How Do We Measure Economic Freedom?
See page 471 for an explanation of the methodology or visit the *Index* Web site at *heritage.org/index*.

Freedom Trend

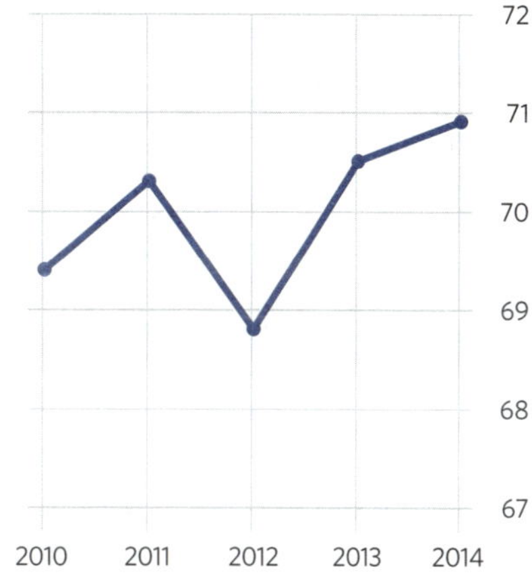

Country Comparisons

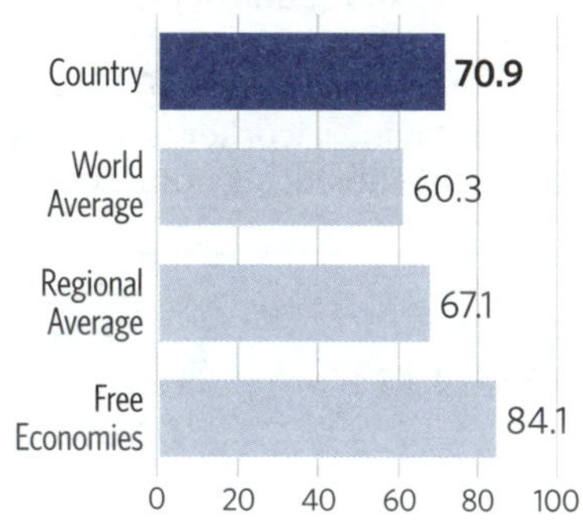

Quick Facts

Population: 5.0 million
GDP (PPP): $277.1 billion
3.0% growth in 2012
5-year compound annual growth 0.6%
$55,009 per capita
Unemployment: 3.2%
Inflation (CPI): 0.7%
FDI Inflow: $12.8 billion
Public Debt: 34.1% of GDP

2012 data unless otherwise noted.
Data compiled as of September 2013.

THE TEN ECONOMIC FREEDOMS

RULE OF LAW

	Score	Rank	1-Year Change
Property Rights	90.0	2nd	0
Freedom from Corruption	88.1	7th	-1.9

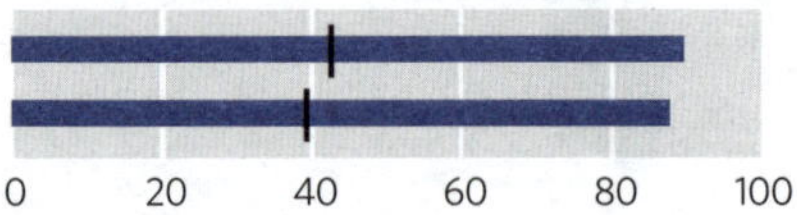

Norway remains one of the world's least corrupt countries. Well-established anti-corruption measures reinforce a cultural emphasis on government integrity. Transparency is a key institutional asset. The judiciary is independent, and the court system, headed by the Supreme Court, operates fairly at the local and national levels. Private property rights are securely protected, and commercial contracts are reliably enforced.

GOVERNMENT SIZE

	Score	Rank	1-Year Change
Fiscal Freedom	50.6	177th	-0.4
Government Spending	42.2	148th	+1.9

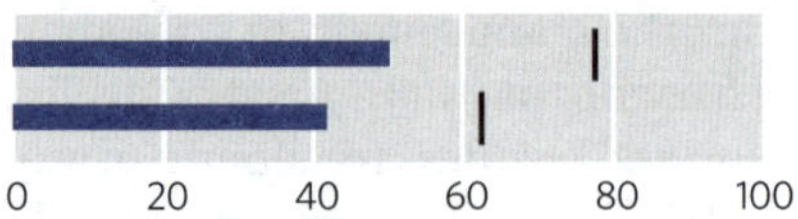

The top individual income tax rate is 47.8 percent, and the top corporate tax rate is 28 percent. Other taxes include a value-added tax (VAT), a tax on net wealth, and environmental taxes. The overall tax burden equals 43.2 percent of gross domestic income. Government spending equals 44 percent of GDP, and public debt equals 34 percent of the domestic economy. Public finances are partially funded by a $750 billion sovereign wealth fund.

REGULATORY EFFICIENCY

	Score	Rank	1-Year Change
Business Freedom	90.9	12th	-1.7
Labor Freedom	44.6	158th	-0.1
Monetary Freedom	78.7	56th	+1.8

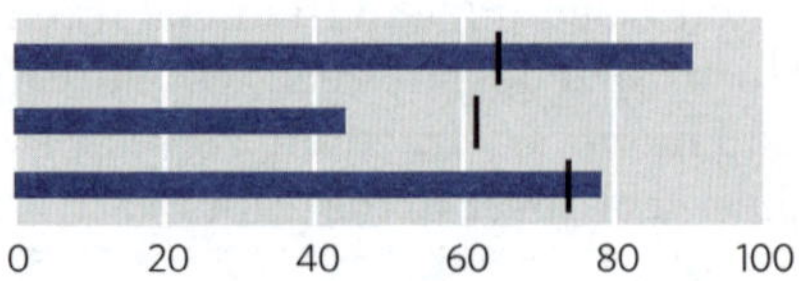

The overall regulatory framework is transparent and competitive. Launching a business is subject to minimum capital requirements but takes only five procedures. Bankruptcy procedures are modern and efficient. Labor regulations are relatively rigid, and the non-salary cost of employing a worker is high. Monetary stability has been well maintained, although the government subsidizes numerous renewable energy projects.

OPEN MARKETS

	Score	Rank	1-Year Change
Trade Freedom	89.1	6th	-0.2
Investment Freedom	75.0	35th	+5.0
Financial Freedom	60.0	41st	0

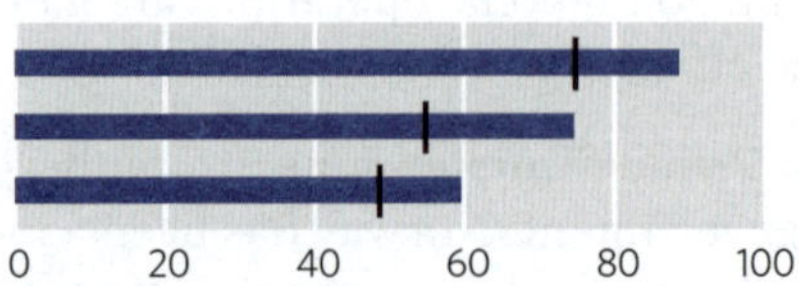

Norway has a low 0.5 percent average tariff rate. There are few government barriers to international trade and investment, but investment in some sectors may be screened. The financial sector is market-driven, although the state retains ownership of the largest financial institution. Supervision of the banking sector is prudent, and regulations are largely consistent with international norms. Credit is allocated on market terms.

Long-Term Score Change (since 1996)

RULE OF LAW		GOVERNMENT SIZE		REGULATORY EFFICIENCY		OPEN MARKETS	
Property Rights	0	Fiscal Freedom	-8.3	Business Freedom	+20.9	Trade Freedom	+20.1
Freedom from Corruption	-1.9	Government Spending	+33.3	Labor Freedom	-4.8	Investment Freedom	+5.0
				Monetary Freedom	-3.1	Financial Freedom	+10.0

OMAN

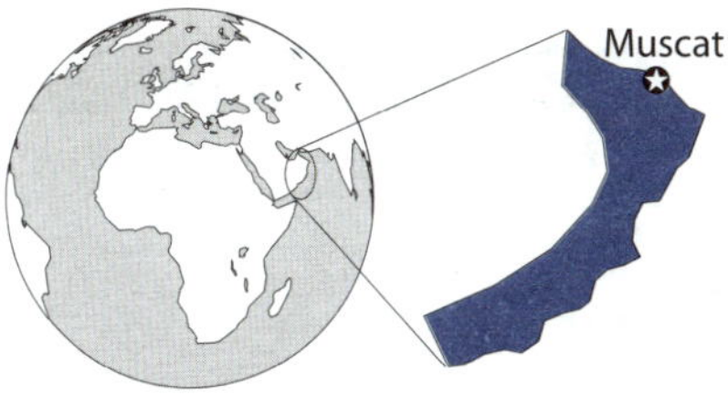

World Rank: **48** Regional Rank: **6**

Economic Freedom Score

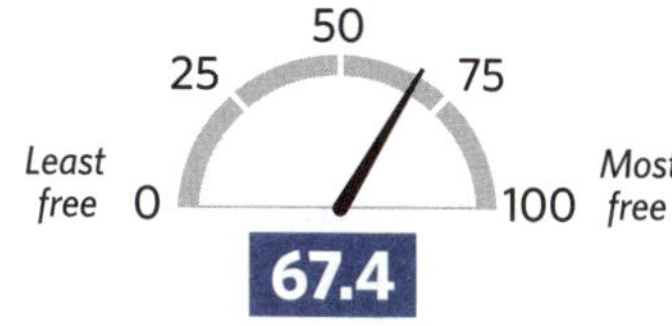

Oman's economic freedom score is 67.4, making its economy the 48th freest in the 2014 *Index*. Its score is 0.7 point lower than last year due to declines in the management of government spending and labor freedom that outweigh improvements in investment freedom and monetary freedom. Oman is ranked 6th out of 15 countries in the Middle East/North Africa region, and its overall score is above the world and regional averages.

Over the 20-year history of the *Index*, Oman's economic freedom has dropped by nearly 3 points. Improvements in five of the 10 economic freedoms, including fiscal freedom, investment freedom, and trade freedom, have been more than offset by declines in rule of law and regulatory efficiency. Scores for freedom from corruption, property rights, and business freedom have deteriorated by over 15 points. Oman's economy has been rated "moderately free" for the past 19 years.

Overall economic freedom remains constrained by state involvement in the economy through public enterprises. Reliance on a large state-owned energy sector that boosted economic expansion over the past decade has left Oman vulnerable to external shocks.

BACKGROUND: In early 2011, in response to turmoil throughout the region, Sultan Qabus bin Said changed cabinet ministers and promised political and economic changes and more government jobs. A Consultative Council elected in October 2011 has expanded regulatory and legislative powers. Municipal councils elected in December 2012 will advise the executive branch on local needs. Oman is a relatively small oil exporter. The government is trying to expand exports of natural gas, develop gas-based industries, and encourage foreign investment in petrochemicals, electric power, and telecommunications. It also stresses "Omanization" (replacing foreign workers with local staff to reduce chronically high unemployment). Oman joined the World Trade Organization in 2000 and signed a free trade agreement with the United States in 2006.

Freedom Trend

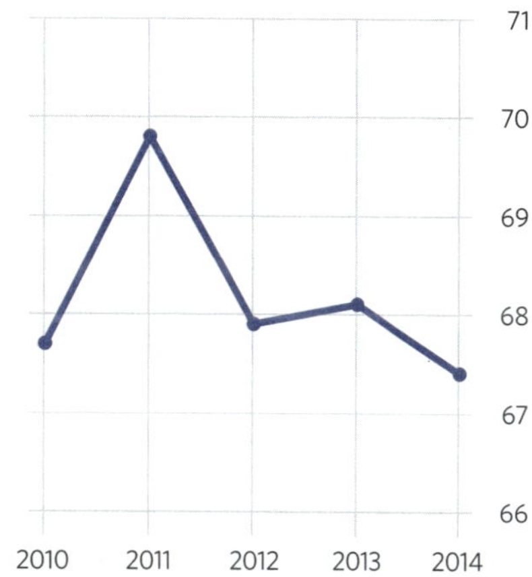

Country Comparisons

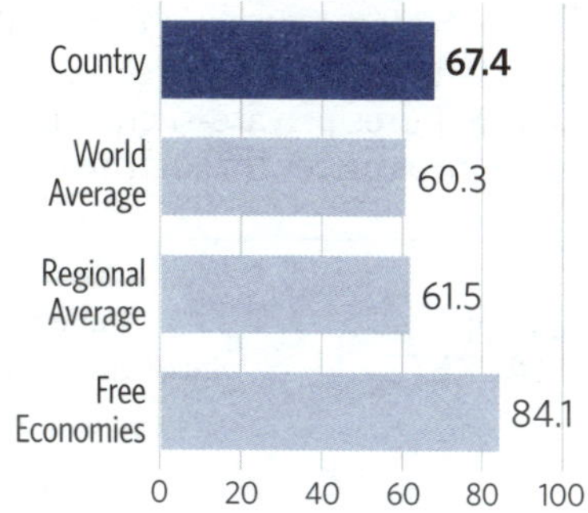

Quick Facts

Population: 3.1 million
GDP (PPP): $90.1 billion
5.0% growth in 2012
5-year compound annual growth 6.3%
$29,166 per capita
Unemployment: n/a
Inflation (CPI): 2.9%
FDI Inflow: $1.5 billion
Public Debt: 6.1% of GDP

2012 data unless otherwise noted.
Data compiled as of September 2013.

How Do We Measure Economic Freedom?
See page 471 for an explanation of the methodology or visit the *Index* Web site at *heritage.org/index.*

OMAN (continued)

THE TEN ECONOMIC FREEDOMS

		Score	Rank	1-Year Change
RULE OF LAW	Property Rights	50.0	53rd	0
	Freedom from Corruption	48.2	52nd	+0.2

Although corruption has not been perceived as serious, the public has recently shown heightened awareness of it despite the lack of freedom of information provisions in the legal code. In 2012, public-sector employees became subject to financial disclosure requirements. The judiciary is not independent and remains subordinate to the sultan and the Ministry of Justice. Property rights are well protected.

		Score	Rank	1-Year Change
GOVERNMENT SIZE	Fiscal Freedom	98.5	5th	0
	Government Spending	56.0	123rd	-13.1

Oman has no income tax, and the corporate tax rate is 12 percent. There is also no consumption tax or value-added tax (VAT). The overall tax burden is 2.2 percent of gross domestic income. Government expenditures equal about 38 percent of GDP. Oil and gas revenues, which constitute 84 percent of total revenue, have helped to keep public debt low at less than 10 percent of GDP.

		Score	Rank	1-Year Change
REGULATORY EFFICIENCY	Business Freedom	68.3	83rd	+0.2
	Labor Freedom	75.5	47th	-5.4
	Monetary Freedom	73.6	118th	+0.9

Launching a business takes five procedures, but minimum capital requirements equal over twice the level of average annual income. Obtaining necessary permits takes more than 150 days. Discouraging more dynamic job growth, labor laws enforce the "Omanization" policy that requires private-sector firms to meet quotas for hiring native Omani workers. The state influences prices through an extensive subsidy system.

		Score	Rank	1-Year Change
OPEN MARKETS	Trade Freedom	78.7	78th	0
	Investment Freedom	65.0	68th	+10.0
	Financial Freedom	60.0	41st	0

Oman's average tariff rate is 3.2 percent. Licensing procedures for several products deter imports. Foreign investors may not own land. The financial sector continues to evolve, and commercial banks perform well. Most credit is offered at market rates, but the government uses subsidized loans to promote investment. The Muscat Securities Market is active and open to foreign investors.

Long-Term Score Change (since 1995)

RULE OF LAW		GOVERNMENT SIZE		REGULATORY EFFICIENCY		OPEN MARKETS	
Property Rights	**-20.0**	Fiscal Freedom	**+23.6**	Business Freedom	**-16.7**	Trade Freedom	**+5.7**
Freedom from Corruption	**-21.8**	Government Spending	**+3.3**	Labor Freedom	**+1.7**	Investment Freedom	**+15.0**
				Monetary Freedom	**-12.1**	Financial Freedom	**-10.0**

PAKISTAN

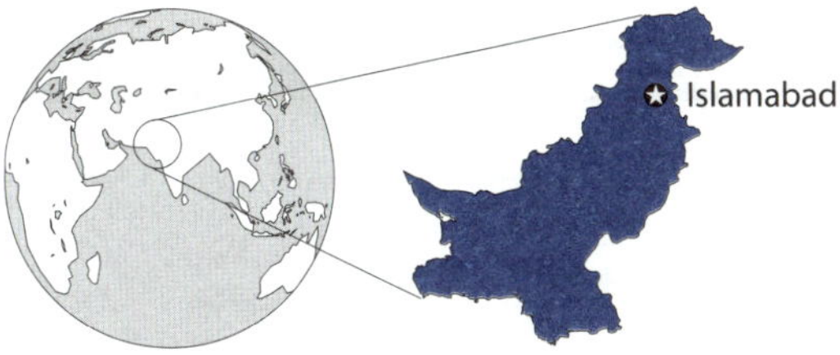

World Rank: **126** Regional Rank: **26**

Economic Freedom Score

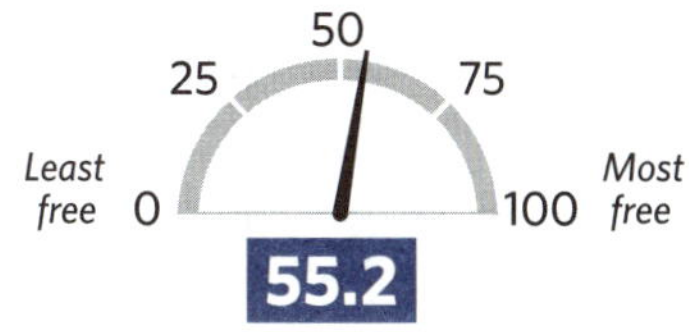

Pakistan's economic freedom score is 55.2, making its economy the 126th freest in the 2014 *Index*. Its score is essentially the same as last year, with modest improvements in investment freedom and monetary freedom largely offset by deteriorations in freedom from corruption, business freedom, and trade freedom. Pakistan is ranked 26th out of 42 countries in the Asia–Pacific region, and its overall score is below the world and regional averages.

Over the 20-year history of the *Index*, Pakistan's economic freedom score has declined by over 2 points. Scores have deteriorated in five of the 10 economic freedoms, including property rights, investment freedom, and financial freedom. Most notably, a 40-point decline in property rights has severely undermined Pakistan's performance in the rule of law. Pakistan's economy has consistently been rated "mostly unfree."

Social and political instability undercuts meaningful progress toward a stable macroeconomic environment. Corruption, endemic throughout the economy, remains a serious drag on long-term economic development. The overall regulatory environment continues to be affected by convoluted administrative bureaucracy, and there is little commitment to opening markets.

BACKGROUND: The victory of the Pakistan Muslim League/Nawaz party led by two-time Prime Minister Nawaz Sharif in the May 2013 elections represents a boost for civilian as opposed to military control, but the two power centers will continue to jockey for control as the nation faces terrorism, sectarian violence, and a well-organized insurgency along the border with Afghanistan. U.S.–Pakistan relations started to recover in late 2012 from an all-time low after the May 2011 U.S. raid that killed Osama bin Laden and a November 2011 NATO air strike that accidentally killed 24 Pakistani soldiers. Pakistan has privatized some state-run industries, but the economy is still heavily regulated, and the security situation discourages foreign investment. Other problems include increasing energy shortages and rising food prices.

How Do We Measure Economic Freedom?
See page 471 for an explanation of the methodology or visit the *Index* Web site at *heritage.org/index*.

Freedom Trend

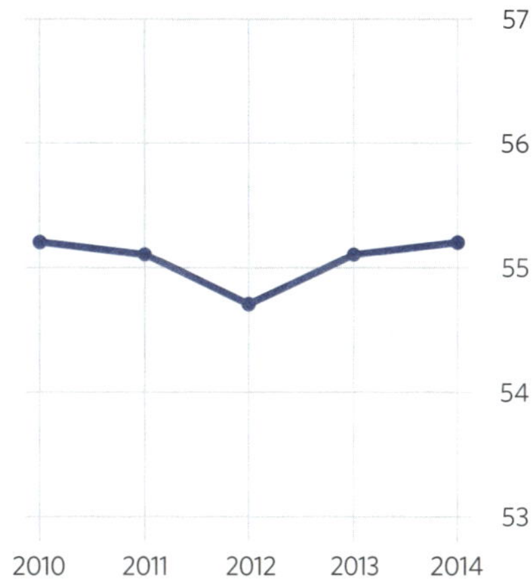

Country Comparisons

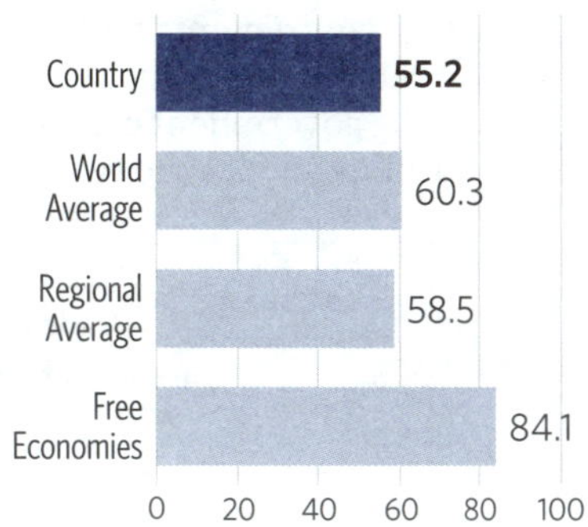

Quick Facts

Population: 178.9 million
GDP (PPP): $515.4 billion
3.7% growth in 2012
5-year compound annual growth 3.0%
$2,881 per capita
Unemployment: 7.7%
Inflation (CPI): 11.0%
FDI Inflow: $846.7 million
Public Debt: 62.1% of GDP

2012 data unless otherwise noted.
Data compiled as of September 2013.

THE TEN ECONOMIC FREEDOMS

		Score	Rank	1-Year Change
RULE OF LAW	Property Rights	30.0	93rd	0
	Freedom from Corruption	22.7	145th	-2.3

Pakistan's government operates with limited transparency and accountability. Corruption is pervasive at all levels of politics and the bureaucracy, and oversight mechanisms to ensure transparency remain weak. Hundreds of politicians, diplomats, and officials have been granted immunity in ongoing corruption cases. Property rights are not protected effectively. The legal system performs poorly.

		Score	Rank	1-Year Change
GOVERNMENT SIZE	Fiscal Freedom	80.6	76th	+0.1
	Government Spending	88.3	21st	-0.7

The top individual income tax rate is 25 percent, although salaried employees are subject to a lesser rate. The top corporate tax rate is 35 percent. Other taxes include a general sales tax (GST) and an interest tax. The overall tax burden is 9.3 percent of domestic output. The government has been tightening spending to qualify for IMF funding, and spending is now 20 percent of GDP. Public debt equates to 62 percent of the domestic economy.

		Score	Rank	1-Year Change
REGULATORY EFFICIENCY	Business Freedom	69.4	80th	-1.3
	Labor Freedom	47.3	148th	-0.6
	Monetary Freedom	68.5	149th	+1.5

Starting a business takes an average of 21 days, but no minimum capital is required. Completing licensing requirements still costs almost twice the level of average annual income. The labor market remains stagnant. A large portion of the workforce is underemployed in the informal sector. The government controls fuel prices but was taking steps in 2013 to reduce its substantial subsidies for electricity.

		Score	Rank	1-Year Change
OPEN MARKETS	Trade Freedom	64.8	144th	-1.2
	Investment Freedom	40.0	132nd	+5.0
	Financial Freedom	40.0	107th	0

The average tariff rate is 10.1 percent. Imports of agricultural and manufactured products may face additional non-tariff barriers. Economic uncertainty has discouraged foreign investment. The financial sector, dominated by commercial banks, remains vulnerable to state interference. Large segments of the population and small businesses still do not use banking services, and lending to individuals accounts for only 9 percent of private-sector credit.

Long-Term Score Change (since 1995)

RULE OF LAW		GOVERNMENT SIZE		REGULATORY EFFICIENCY		OPEN MARKETS	
Property Rights	-40.0	Fiscal Freedom	+21.6	Business Freedom	+14.4	Trade Freedom	+32.4
Freedom from Corruption	+12.7	Government Spending	+6.1	Labor Freedom	-12.2	Investment Freedom	-30.0
				Monetary Freedom	-1.5	Financial Freedom	-30.0

PANAMA

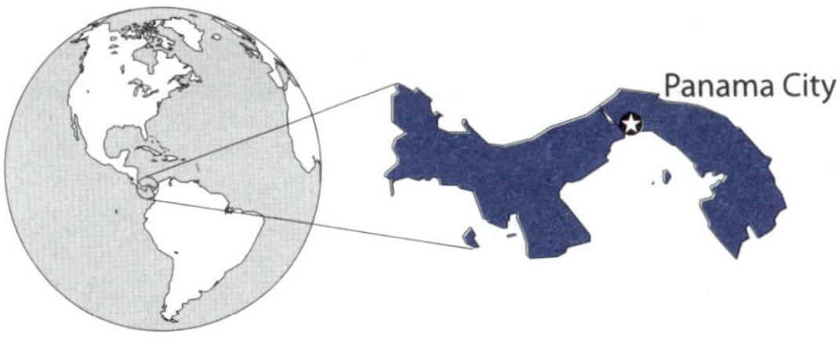

World Rank: **71** Regional Rank: **13**

Economic Freedom Score

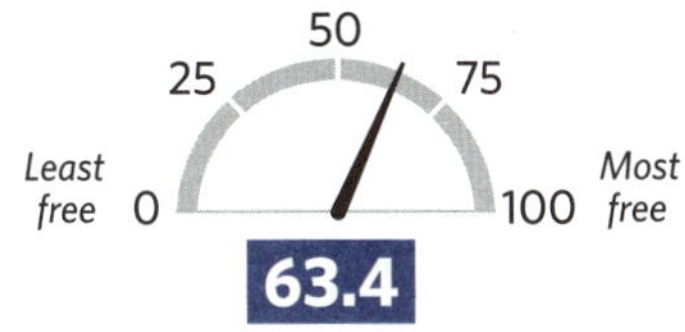

Freedom Trend

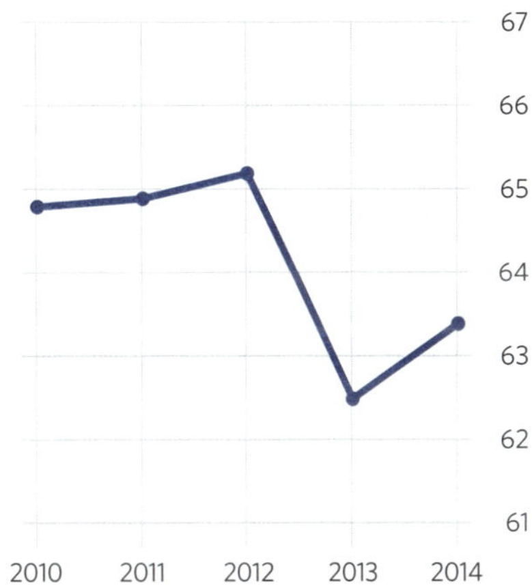

Country Comparisons

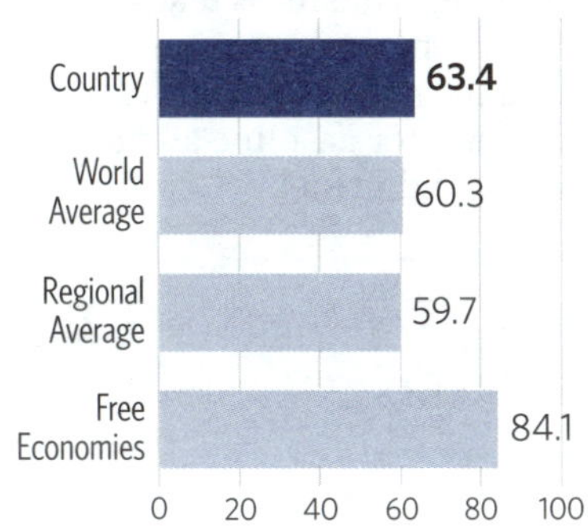

Panama's economic freedom score is 63.4, making its economy the 71st freest in the 2014 *Index*. Its score is 0.9 point better than last year, reflecting improvements in investment freedom, freedom from corruption, and the control of government spending that outweigh small declines in fiscal freedom and three other freedoms. Panama is ranked 13th out of 29 countries in the South and Central America/Caribbean region, and its overall score is above the world average.

Over the 20-year history of the *Index*, Panama's economic freedom score has dropped by about 8 points, one of the 10 largest declines measured. Modest gains in four of the 10 economic freedoms, including fiscal freedom, trade freedom, and investment freedom, have been overwhelmed by declines, particularly in the rule of law as measured by property rights and freedom from corruption. Panama's economy, once rated "mostly free," is now rated "moderately free."

Panama has been generally well integrated into the global marketplace as an international business and banking hub, but its overall progress has been uneven. Anti-corruption laws seem to have little impact, and the judicial system remains vulnerable to political interference.

BACKGROUND: Since the opening of the Panama Canal in 1914, Panama has been a strategic hub for commerce and security in the Americas. Panama now has sole responsibility for operating the canal and plans to double its capacity by 2015. President Ricardo Martinelli of the center-right Democratic Change party employs pro-business, pro-growth rhetoric but is fond of big government projects. His authoritarian style, disregard for the rule of law, and attempt to pack the high court in 2012 have drawn intense criticism. There has been high growth due to successful transportation facilities and infrastructure development, and banking and services account for 80 percent of jobs. The U.S.–Panama Trade Promotion Agreement was approved by the U.S. Congress in 2011.

Quick Facts

Population: 3.7 million
GDP (PPP): $57.1 billion
10.7% growth in 2012
5-year compound annual growth 8.6%
$15,617 per capita
Unemployment: 4.2%
Inflation (CPI): 5.7%
FDI Inflow: $3.0 billion
Public Debt: 38.8% of GDP

2012 data unless otherwise noted.
Data compiled as of September 2013.

How Do We Measure Economic Freedom?
See page 471 for an explanation of the methodology or visit the *Index* Web site at *heritage.org/index*.

THE TEN ECONOMIC FREEDOMS

RULE OF LAW

	Score	Rank	1-Year Change
Property Rights	30.0	93rd	0
Freedom from Corruption	34.0	81st	+1.0

Corruption remains widespread, and the fight against it is hampered by the government's refusal to dismantle Panama's dictatorship-era libel and contempt laws. The judicial system remains overburdened, inefficient, politicized, and prone to corruption. Its capacity to resolve contractual and property disputes is weak. The majority of land in Panama, and almost all land outside of Panama City, is not titled.

GOVERNMENT SIZE

	Score	Rank	1-Year Change
Fiscal Freedom	84.3	59th	-1.9
Government Spending	78.7	57th	+0.9

The top individual income and corporate tax rates are 25 percent. Other taxes include a value-added tax (VAT) and a capital gains tax. The overall tax burden is 17.8 percent of gross domestic income. Public expenditures equal 26.6 percent of GDP. Government debt is equivalent to about 39 percent of the gross domestic economy.

REGULATORY EFFICIENCY

	Score	Rank	1-Year Change
Business Freedom	73.0	64th	+0.5
Labor Freedom	39.4	169th	-0.7
Monetary Freedom	75.1	103rd	-0.8

Starting a business takes five procedures, and no minimum capital is required, but licensing requirements continue to be time-consuming and costly. The labor market lacks flexibility, and the non-salary cost of hiring a worker is relatively high. The government maintains price ceilings for gasoline and diesel and has extensive subsidy programs for electricity, housing, and cooking fuel.

OPEN MARKETS

	Score	Rank	1-Year Change
Trade Freedom	74.2	105th	-0.6
Investment Freedom	75.0	35th	+10.0
Financial Freedom	70.0	19th	0

The average tariff rate is 7.9 percent, but non-tariff barriers are not a significant impediment to trade. Foreign investment in some sectors is restricted by the state. As a regional financial hub, the financial sector provides a wide range of services, and the banking sector has been stable. Foreign and domestic banks are treated equally. Capital markets are relatively sophisticated, although the stock market trades primarily in government debt.

Long-Term Score Change (since 1995)

RULE OF LAW		GOVERNMENT SIZE		REGULATORY EFFICIENCY		OPEN MARKETS	
Property Rights	-20.0	Fiscal Freedom	+6.9	Business Freedom	+3.0	Trade Freedom	+9.8
Freedom from Corruption	-16.0	Government Spending	-5.3	Labor Freedom	-5.8	Investment Freedom	+5.0
				Monetary Freedom	-13.6	Financial Freedom	-20.0

PAPUA NEW GUINEA

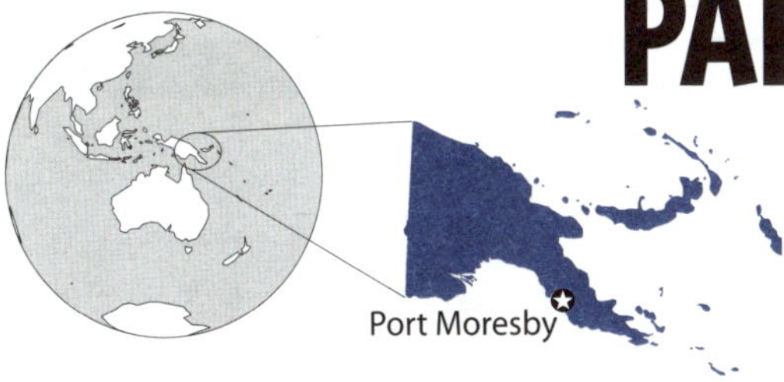

World Rank: **132** Regional Rank: **28**

Economic Freedom Score

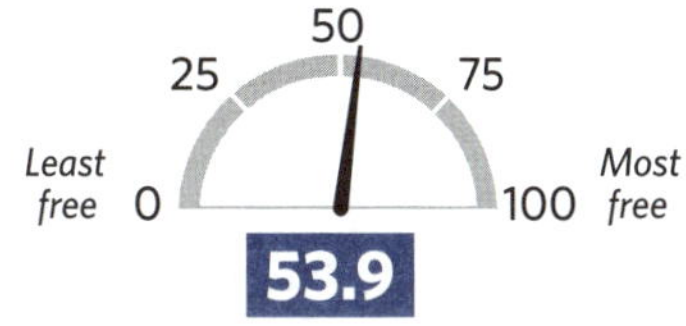

Papua New Guinea's economic freedom score is 53.9, making its economy the 132nd freest in the 2014 *Index*. Its score is 0.3 point higher than last year, with improvements in the control of government spending and monetary freedom counterbalanced by declines in freedom from corruption, business freedom, and fiscal freedom. Papua New Guinea is ranked 28th out of 42 countries in the Asia–Pacific region, and its overall score is lower than the world average.

Over Papua New Guinea's 19-year history in the *Index*, its economic freedom score has declined by almost 5 points, one of the 20 worst losses. Seven of the 10 economic freedoms, notably property rights, freedom from corruption, investment freedom, and business freedom, have declined. Grading was suspended from 2002 to 2008; since 2009, Papua New Guinea's economy has been rated "mostly unfree."

Papua New Guinea's economy includes a formal sector based on exports of natural resources and a large informal sector that relies on subsistence farming and other small-scale economic activity. The economy has been expanding due to high commodity prices and a construction boom, but an inefficient legal system and lingering corruption undercut the rule of law.

BACKGROUND: Papua New Guinea is a parliamentary democracy with nearly 7 million people speaking over 840 different languages. A year-long constitutional crisis seemingly came to an end in August 2012 with the re-election of Prime Minister Peter O'Neill, whose People's National Congress Party won the most seats in parliament. Sir Michael Somare, O'Neill's chief rival, announced that they would form a joint government. Gold and copper mining, oil, and natural gas dominate the formal economy, but the vast majority of Papua New Guineans depend on subsistence hunting or agriculture and the informal economy. Australia provides around US$480 million a year in assistance. The country is plagued by corruption, weak governance, crime, and poverty.

Freedom Trend

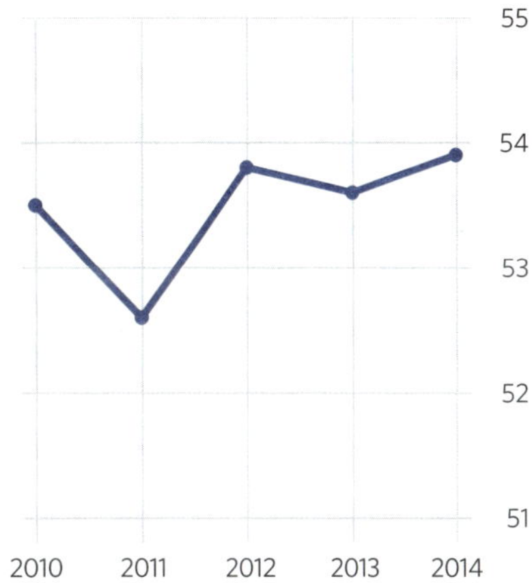

Country Comparisons

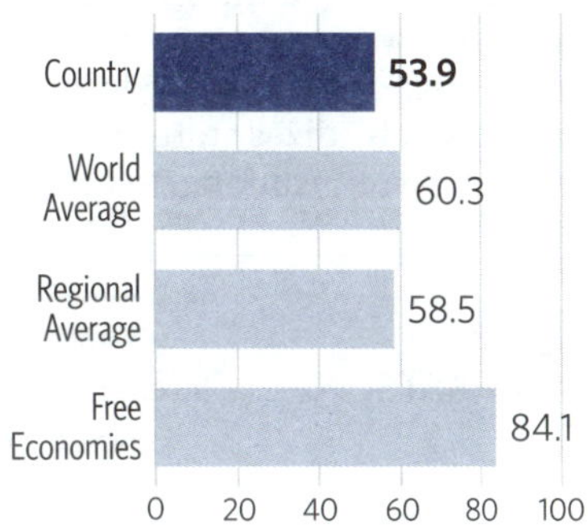

Quick Facts

Population: 6.8 million
GDP (PPP): $19.1 billion
9.1% growth in 2012
5-year compound annual growth 8.1%
$2,797 per capita
Unemployment: 1.9% (2008)
Inflation (CPI): 4.0%
FDI Inflow: $28.8 million
Public Debt: 14.1% of GDP

2012 data unless otherwise noted.
Data compiled as of September 2013.

How Do We Measure Economic Freedom?
See page 471 for an explanation of the methodology or visit the *Index* Web site at *heritage.org/index.*

THE TEN ECONOMIC FREEDOMS

RULE OF LAW

	Score	Rank	1-Year Change
Property Rights	20.0	139th	0
Freedom from Corruption	20.2	159th	-1.8

Official abuse and corruption, particularly misappropriation of public funds and nepotism, are widespread. The risk of domestic corruption is likely to be enhanced as rapid economic growth continues, fueled by large-scale foreign investment in mining and petroleum. A modern and well-functioning judicial framework is not firmly in place, and land is often held communally.

GOVERNMENT SIZE

	Score	Rank	1-Year Change
Fiscal Freedom	66.7	152nd	-0.7
Government Spending	75.4	67th	+3.1

Papua New Guinea's top individual income tax rate is 42 percent, and its top corporate tax rate is 30 percent. Other taxes include a value-added tax (VAT) and an excise tax. The overall tax burden equals 25.8 percent of domestic income. Government spending amounts to 29 percent of GDP. Public debt in the most recent year was about 14 percent of GDP.

REGULATORY EFFICIENCY

	Score	Rank	1-Year Change
Business Freedom	57.0	129th	-1.3
Labor Freedom	73.7	50th	+0.3
Monetary Freedom	75.5	91st	+3.1

Progress toward the structural changes needed to promote entrepreneurial activity has been limited. Private enterprises face numerous time-consuming bureaucratic hurdles. The formal labor market is not fully developed, and informal labor activity is substantial. The government heavily subsidizes state-owned enterprises that provide substandard service in such areas as power, water, banking, telecommunications, air travel, and seaports.

OPEN MARKETS

	Score	Rank	1-Year Change
Trade Freedom	85.1	49th	+0.1
Investment Freedom	35.0	142nd	0
Financial Freedom	30.0	132nd	0

The average tariff rate for Papua New Guinea is 2.5 percent, and there are few non-tariff barriers to trade. New foreign investment may be screened by the government, and foreign investment in some sectors of the economy is restricted. The availability of financial services is inconsistent throughout the economy, and much of the population remains underserved by the formal banking sector.

Long-Term Score Change (since 1996)

RULE OF LAW		GOVERNMENT SIZE		REGULATORY EFFICIENCY		OPEN MARKETS	
Property Rights	-30.0	Fiscal Freedom	-14.8	Business Freedom	-13.0	Trade Freedom	+39.3
Freedom from Corruption	-29.8	Government Spending	+6.2	Labor Freedom	-7.5	Investment Freedom	-15.0
				Monetary Freedom	-5.7	Financial Freedom	0

PARAGUAY

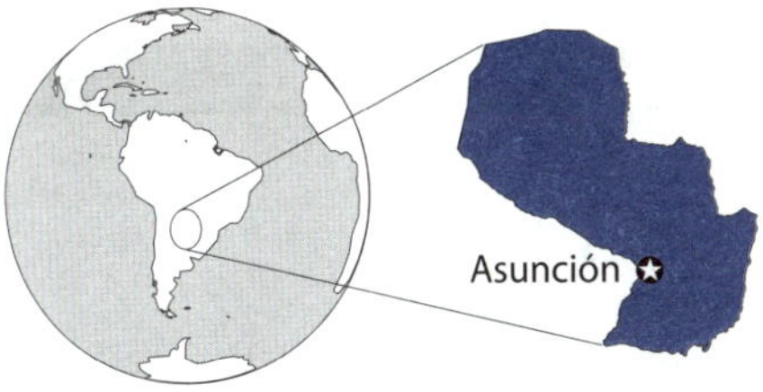

Economic Freedom Score

World Rank: 78 **Regional Rank: 15**

Freedom Trend

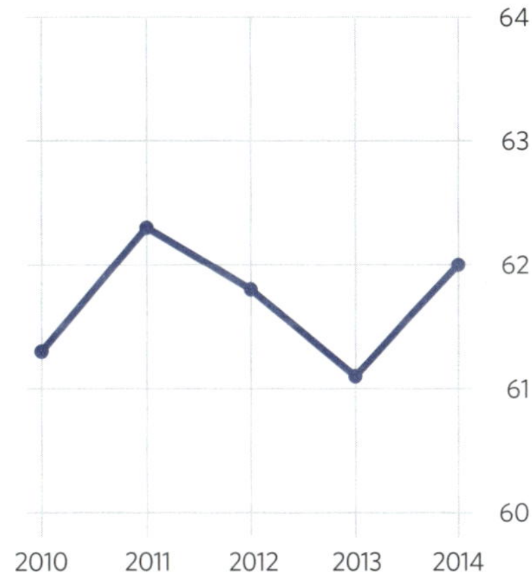

Paraguay's economic freedom score is 62.0, making its economy the 78th freest in the 2014 *Index*. Its score is 0.9 point higher than last year, with improvements in half of the 10 economic freedoms, including investment freedom, the management of public finance, and labor freedom, partially offset by declines in trade freedom and freedom from corruption. Paraguay is ranked 15th out of 29 countries in the South and Central America/Caribbean region, and its overall score is above the world average.

Over the 20 year-history of the *Index*, Paraguay's progress toward greater economic freedom has been uneven. Overall, its economic freedom score has declined by 3.9 points. Improvements in half of the 10 economic freedoms have been outweighed by score declines of more than 10 points in property rights, business freedom, and investment freedom.

The overall entrepreneurial environment remains constrained. An overbearing regulatory framework, exacerbated by poor access to credit and high financing costs, stifles economic activity and retards the development of a vibrant private sector. Corruption is perceived as widespread.

BACKGROUND: Horacio Cartes of the traditionally dominant Colorado Party won the presidency in 2013, succeeding Federico Franco, who had served temporarily following the impeachment of left-leaning President Fernando Lugo in 2012. Lugo was removed lawfully but under protest from his ideological allies in the region, and Paraguay has been suspended from the main regional trade bloc (MERCOSUR) and has not been allowed to participate in the summits of the South American Union (UNASUR). Paraguay is a major exporter of soy. The extensive informal economy is geared to the re-export of consumer goods to neighboring countries. Institutional impediments to the market economy are considerable. Corruption is pervasive, and government attempts to reduce smuggling and scrutinize suspected terrorist groups in the tri-border area with Brazil and Argentina have met with little success.

Country Comparisons

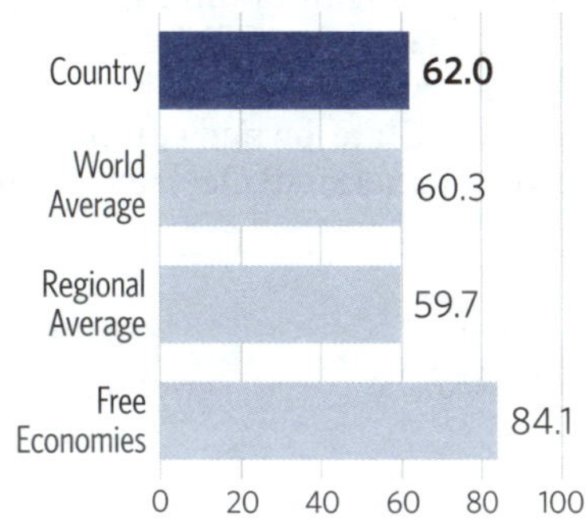

Quick Facts

Population: 6.7 million
GDP (PPP): $40.9 billion
-1.2% growth in 2012
5-year compound annual growth 3.6%
$6,136 per capita
Unemployment: 5.8%
Inflation (CPI): 3.8%
FDI Inflow: $319.9 million
Public Debt: 11.4% of GDP

2012 data unless otherwise noted.
Data compiled as of September 2013.

How Do We Measure Economic Freedom?
See page 471 for an explanation of the methodology or visit the *Index* Web site at *heritage.org/index.*

THE TEN ECONOMIC FREEDOMS

		Score	Rank	1-Year Change
RULE OF LAW	Property Rights	30.0	93rd	0
	Freedom from Corruption	20.5	158th	-1.5

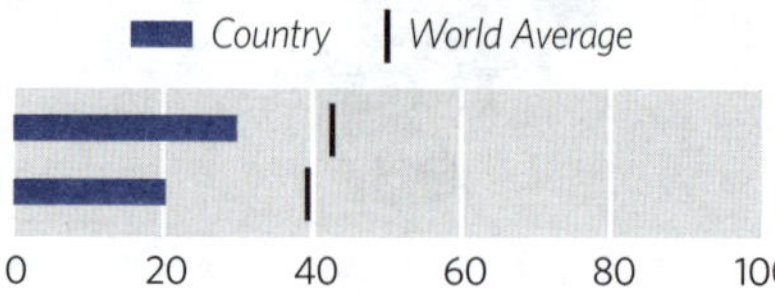

Corruption cases languish in the courts for years without resolution, and corruption often goes unpunished as judges favor the powerful and wealthy. Before he was abruptly (and constitutionally) removed from power in 2012, former President Lugo had pledged greater transparency in government and a reduction in corruption, specifically in the judiciary, but no progress was made in depoliticizing the corrupt Supreme Court.

		Score	Rank	1-Year Change
GOVERNMENT SIZE	Fiscal Freedom	96.2	11th	+0.3
	Government Spending	89.0	18th	+3.6

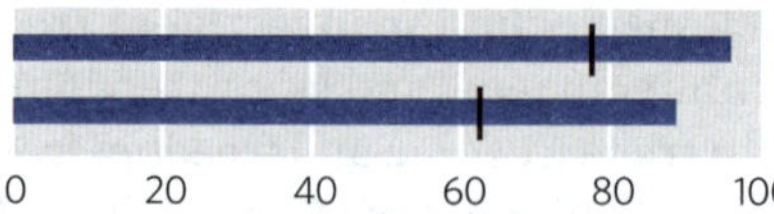

The top individual income and corporate tax rates are 10 percent. Other taxes include a value-added tax (VAT) and a property tax. The overall tax burden equals 13.4 percent of gross domestic income. Government spending makes up one-fifth of the domestic economy. Public debt is a modest 11 percent of GDP.

		Score	Rank	1-Year Change
REGULATORY EFFICIENCY	Business Freedom	58.0	125th	-1.1
	Labor Freedom	28.9	179th	+3.3
	Monetary Freedom	80.9	22nd	+1.1

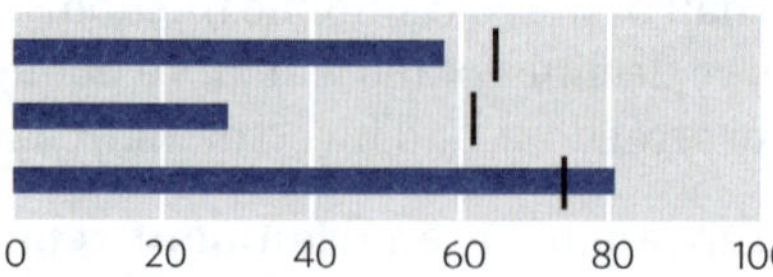

There is no minimum capital requirement for starting a business, but the process still takes more than a month. The cost of completing licensing requirements remains almost twice the level of average annual income. The labor market's lack of flexibility hurts formal-sector job growth. State-owned companies have monopolies for petroleum products and (100 percent hydro-generated) electricity markets.

		Score	Rank	1-Year Change
OPEN MARKETS	Trade Freedom	81.1	68th	-1.6
	Investment Freedom	75.0	35th	+5.0
	Financial Freedom	60.0	41st	0

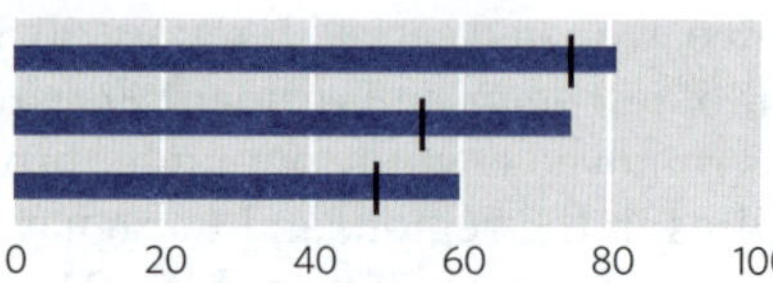

Paraguay's average tariff rate is 4.5 percent. Tariffs provide about 13 percent of government revenue. The judicial and regulatory bureaucracies deter foreign investment. The level of financial intermediation has been improving gradually, but an inefficient legal framework remains a considerable impediment to the creation of a more dynamic financial sector. Capital markets remain underdeveloped.

Long-Term Score Change (since 1995)

RULE OF LAW		GOVERNMENT SIZE		REGULATORY EFFICIENCY		OPEN MARKETS	
Property Rights	**-20.0**	Fiscal Freedom	**+6.1**	Business Freedom	**-12.0**	Trade Freedom	**+22.7**
Freedom from Corruption	**+10.5**	Government Spending	**-2.5**	Labor Freedom	**+0.8**	Investment Freedom	**-15.0**
				Monetary Freedom	**+17.8**	Financial Freedom	**-10.0**

PERU

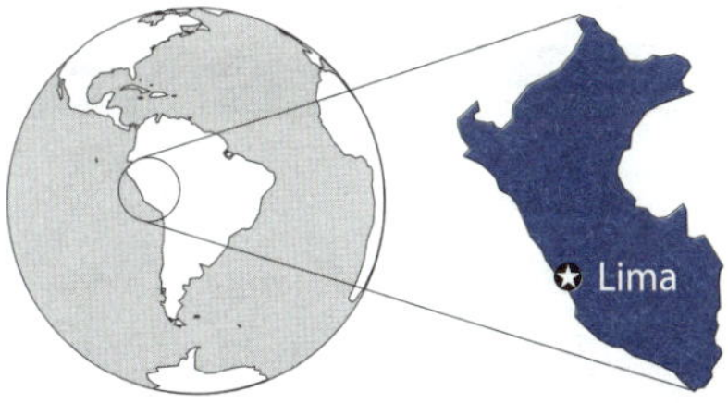

Economic Freedom Score

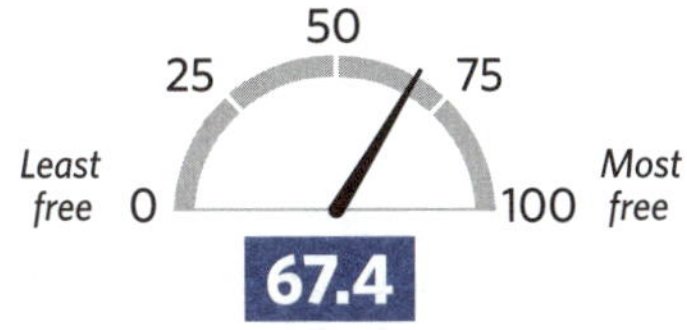

World Rank: 47 **Regional Rank: 7**

Peru's economic freedom score is 67.4, making its economy the 47th freest in the 2014 *Index*. Its score is 0.8 point lower than last year, with an improvement in trade freedom outweighed by deteriorations in labor freedom and business freedom. Peru is ranked 7th out of 29 countries in the South and Central America/Caribbean region, and its overall score is above the world average.

Over the 20-year history of the *Index*, Peru has advanced its economic freedom score by nearly 11 points. It has achieved double-digit improvements in half of the 10 economic freedoms, most notably in monetary freedom and trade freedom, which have improved by over 35 points and provide a stable foundation to improve the economy's engagement in global commerce. Peru's economy continues to be rated "moderately free."

Nonetheless, institutional shortcomings continue to undermine Peru's chances for long-term economic development, slowing the transition to greater economic freedom. Property rights are only moderately well protected, and the judicial system is relatively inefficient.

BACKGROUND: Free-market and economic liberalization policies implemented by former President Alan Garcia (2006–2011) and continued by current President Ollanta Humala of the leftist Peruvian Nationalist Party have attracted significant foreign investment and lifted millions out of poverty. Humala, who once led a failed uprising against former president Alberto Fujimori, ran for office on a platform of more state intervention in the economy to help the poor. However, he has governed moderately and has respected the rule of law. Significant natural resources include gold, copper, and silver. Less than 30 percent of Peruvians now live below the poverty line, and economic growth has been well above the Latin American average. The U.S.–Peru Free Trade Agreement has expanded trade and employment. Peru has also entered into numerous other free trade agreements and is a founding member of the Pacific Alliance.

How Do We Measure Economic Freedom?
See page 471 for an explanation of the methodology or visit the *Index* Web site at *heritage.org/index*.

Freedom Trend

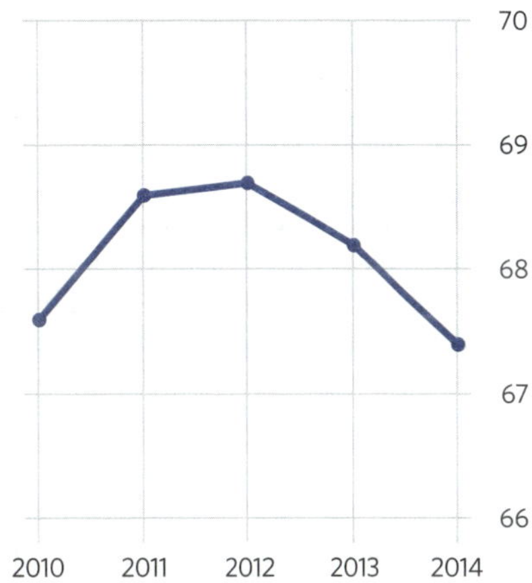

Country Comparisons

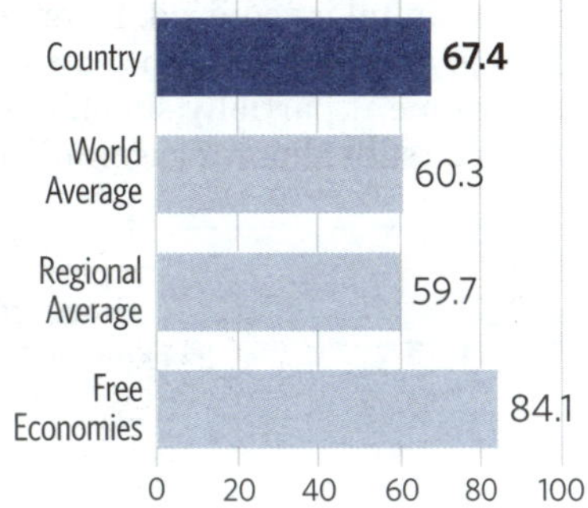

Quick Facts

Population: 30.5 million
GDP (PPP): $326.7 billion
6.3% growth in 2012
5-year compound annual growth 6.5%
$10,719 per capita
Unemployment: 6.8%
Inflation (CPI): 3.7%
FDI Inflow: $12.2 billion
Public Debt: 19.8% of GDP

2012 data unless otherwise noted.
Data compiled as of September 2013.

PERU (continued)

THE TEN ECONOMIC FREEDOMS

RULE OF LAW

	Score	Rank	1-Year Change
Property Rights	40.0	70th	0
Freedom from Corruption	34.0	81st	0

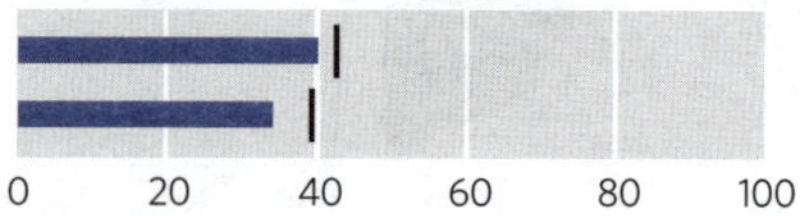

Corruption is a serious problem. Although corruption was rated the most negative aspect of former President Alan García's administration, a congressional commission charged with investigating corruption among García administration officials produced few criminal accusations in 2012. Dozens of sitting members of Congress are under investigation for corrupt practices. The judiciary is widely distrusted and prone to corruption scandals.

GOVERNMENT SIZE

	Score	Rank	1-Year Change
Fiscal Freedom	79.1	97th	-0.8
Government Spending	89.1	17th	0

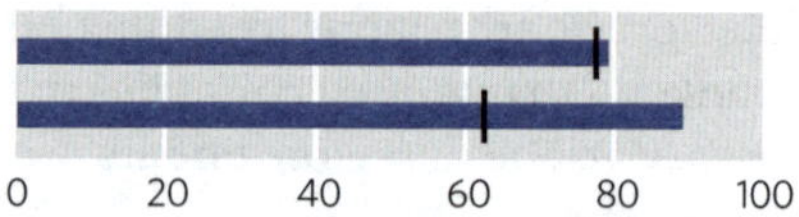

The top individual income and corporate tax rates are 30 per cent. Other taxes include a value-added tax (VAT) and a financial transactions tax. The overall tax burden amounts to 17 percent of gross domestic income. The leftist government has shown a surprising commitment to prudent fiscal policies, with government spending falling to 19 percent of GDP and public debt shrinking below 20 percent of GDP.

REGULATORY EFFICIENCY

	Score	Rank	1-Year Change
Business Freedom	70.6	74th	-1.7
Labor Freedom	61.4	94th	-5.7
Monetary Freedom	83.3	9th	-1.0

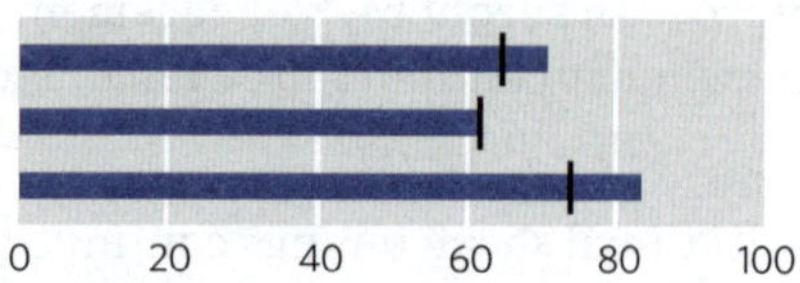

Starting a business now takes five procedures and slightly less than a month, and no minimum capital is required. Licensing requirements continue to be costly and time-consuming. Employment regulations continue to evolve, but more slowly than in other economies. The government partially subsidizes electricity and automotive and cooking fuels, although it reduced subsidies for gasoline in 2013.

OPEN MARKETS

	Score	Rank	1-Year Change
Trade Freedom	87.0	37th	+2.0
Investment Freedom	70.0	46th	0
Financial Freedom	60.0	41st	0

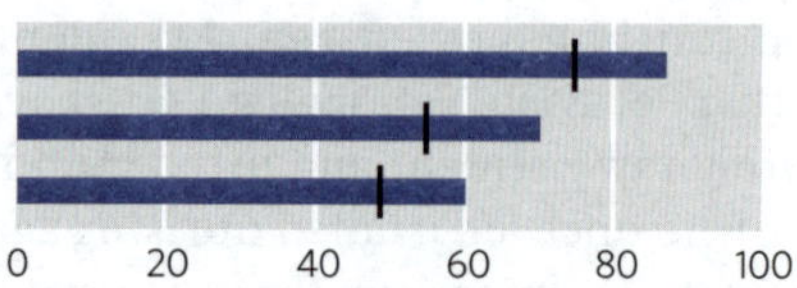

Peru's average tariff rate is 1.5 percent. In 2013, Peru, Mexico, Chile, and Columbia created the Pacific Alliance free-trade area. The government restricts imports of used clothing and vehicles. Foreign and domestic investment are treated equally under the constitution. Credit to the private sector has increased steadily, and banking remains stable and well-capitalized. Non-performing loans represent fewer than 5 percent of total loans.

Long-Term Score Change (since 1995)

RULE OF LAW		GOVERNMENT SIZE		REGULATORY EFFICIENCY		OPEN MARKETS	
Property Rights	**-10.0**	Fiscal Freedom	**-1.9**	Business Freedom	**+15.6**	Trade Freedom	**+36.0**
Freedom from Corruption	**+24.0**	Government Spending	**-0.4**	Labor Freedom	**+15.5**	Investment Freedom	**0**
				Monetary Freedom	**+47.4**	Financial Freedom	**-10.0**

PHILIPPINES

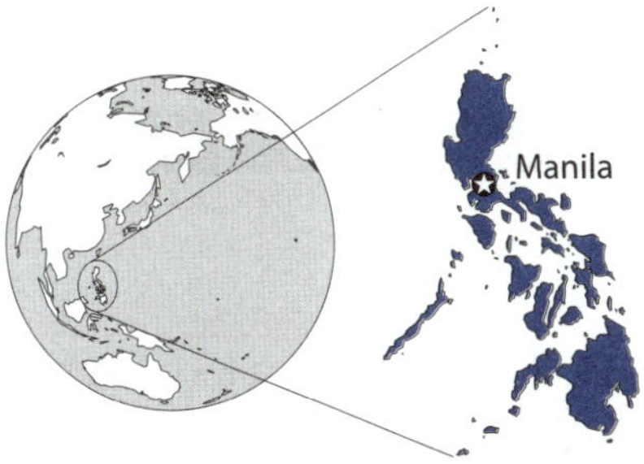

World Rank: **89** Regional Rank: **16**

Economic Freedom Score

The Philippines' economic freedom score is 60.1, making its economy the 89th freest in the 2014 *Index*. Its score is 1.9 points higher than last year, reflecting notable improvements in investment freedom, business freedom, monetary freedom, and the control of government spending. The Philippines ranks 16th out of 42 countries in the Asia–Pacific region, and its overall score is slightly below the world average.

Over the 20-year history of the *Index*, the Philippines' economic freedom score has advanced by 5.1 points. Improvements in seven of the 10 economic freedoms, including significant gains in trade freedom, investment freedom, and freedom from corruption, have been partially offset by a deterioration in property rights. With its third consecutive year of overall score improvement, the Philippines has risen back to "moderately free" in the 2014 *Index*.

Demonstrating a high degree of resilience, the Philippine economy has recorded average annual growth of around 5 percent over the past five years. The government has pursued a series of legislative reforms to enhance the investment environment and incentivize broader-based private-sector job growth. Despite progress, lingering institutional challenges will not be overcome without a deeper commitment to reform. Although the perceived level of corruption has declined, more effective anti-corruption measures need to be firmly institutionalized.

BACKGROUND: The Philippines has a diverse population that speaks more than 80 languages and dialects and is spread over 7,000 islands in the Western Pacific. The country returned to democracy in 1986 after two decades of autocratic rule. President Benigno Aquino III took office in 2010 with a mandate to address pervasive corruption and has launched investigations into abuses of power by prior administrations. While agriculture is still significant, industrial production in areas like electronics, apparel, and shipbuilding has been growing rapidly. Remittances from overseas workers are equivalent to more than 10 percent of GDP.

Freedom Trend

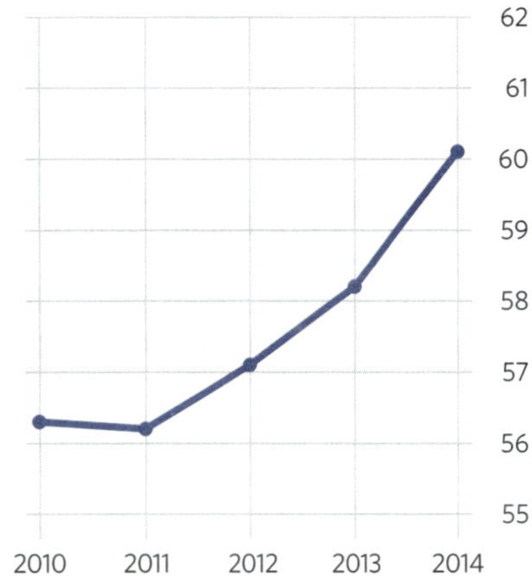

Country Comparisons

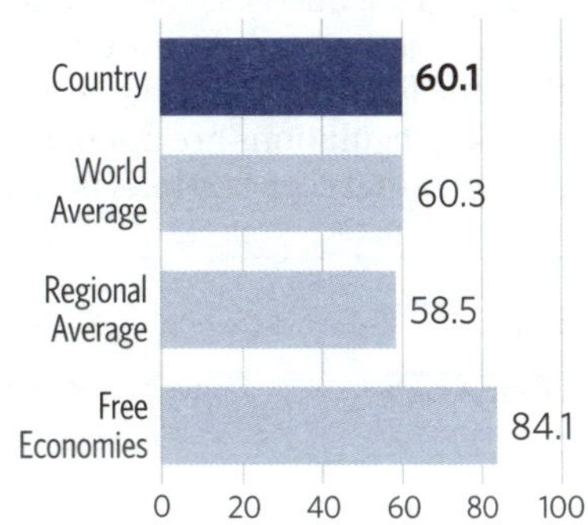

Quick Facts

Population: 95.8 million

GDP (PPP): $424.4 billion

6.6% growth in 2012

5-year compound annual growth 4.7%

$4,430 per capita

Unemployment: 7.0%

Inflation (CPI): 3.1%

FDI Inflow: $2.8 billion

Public Debt: 41.9% of GDP

2012 data unless otherwise noted.
Data compiled as of September 2013.

How Do We Measure Economic Freedom?
See page 471 for an explanation of the methodology or visit the *Index* Web site at *heritage.org/index*.

THE TEN ECONOMIC FREEDOMS

		Score	Rank	1-Year Change
RULE OF LAW	Property Rights	30.0	93rd	0
	Freedom from Corruption	26.1	126th	+0.1

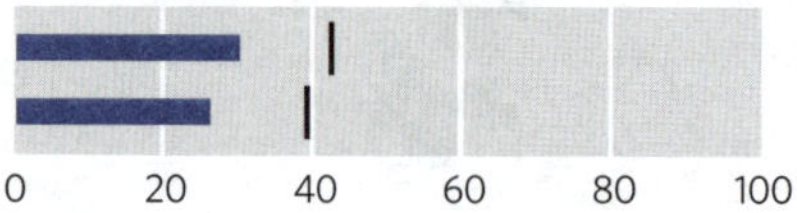

Corruption and cronyism are rife in business and government, with a few dozen leading families holding an outsized share of wealth and political power. Judicial independence has traditionally been strong, but the rule of law is generally weak. A culture of impunity, stemming in part from a case backlog in the judicial system, hampers the fight against corruption. Delays and uncertainty negatively affect property rights.

		Score	Rank	1-Year Change
GOVERNMENT SIZE	Fiscal Freedom	79.2	96th	-0.1
	Government Spending	92.3	4th	+2.1

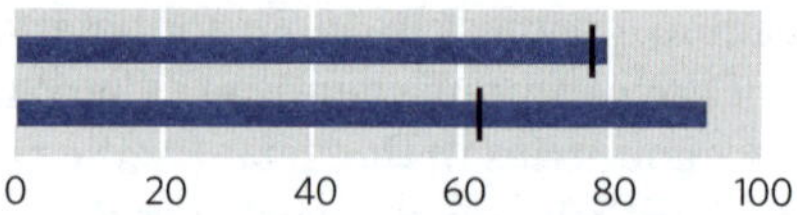

The top individual income tax rate is 32 percent, and the top corporate tax rate is 30 percent. Other taxes include a value-added tax (VAT) and an environmental tax. The overall tax burden equals 12.3 percent of gross domestic income. Government expenditures equate to 12.3 percent of GDP. Total public debt is equal to about 42 percent of the total size of the domestic economy.

		Score	Rank	1-Year Change
REGULATORY EFFICIENCY	Business Freedom	59.9	112th	+6.8
	Labor Freedom	49.7	141st	-1.3
	Monetary Freedom	78.0	64th	+1.4

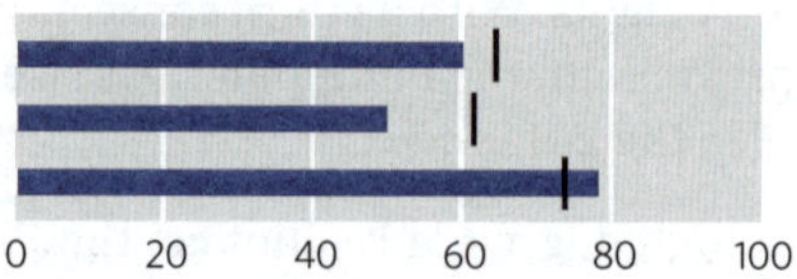

Launching a business takes 15 procedures and 35 days. The time needed to deal with licensing requirements has been notably reduced, and the cost of completing them has been cut to less than the level of average annual income. The labor market remains structurally rigid, although existing regulations are not particularly burdensome. The government subsidizes state-owned or controlled corporations in the power, food, health care, and agriculture sectors.

		Score	Rank	1-Year Change
OPEN MARKETS	Trade Freedom	75.5	95th	0
	Investment Freedom	60.0	80th	+10.0
	Financial Freedom	50.0	69th	0

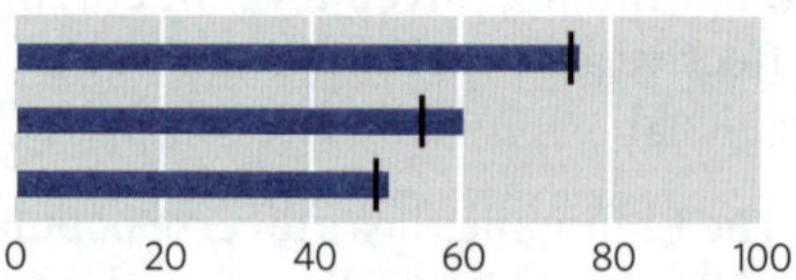

The average tariff rate is 4.8 percent. Tariffs provide over 20 percent of government revenue. Tariff-rate quotas restrict some agricultural imports. The legal and regulatory systems may be difficult for foreign investors to navigate. The relatively small financial sector, dominated by banking, has been expanding strongly with greater market competition in recent years. The percentage of non-performing loans has gradually declined.

Long-Term Score Change (since 1995)

RULE OF LAW		GOVERNMENT SIZE		REGULATORY EFFICIENCY		OPEN MARKETS	
Property Rights	**-20.0**	Fiscal Freedom	**+6.0**	Business Freedom	**+4.9**	Trade Freedom	**+33.5**
Freedom from Corruption	**+16.1**	Government Spending	**+4.0**	Labor Freedom	**-3.7**	Investment Freedom	**+10.0**
				Monetary Freedom	**+1.3**	Financial Freedom	**0**

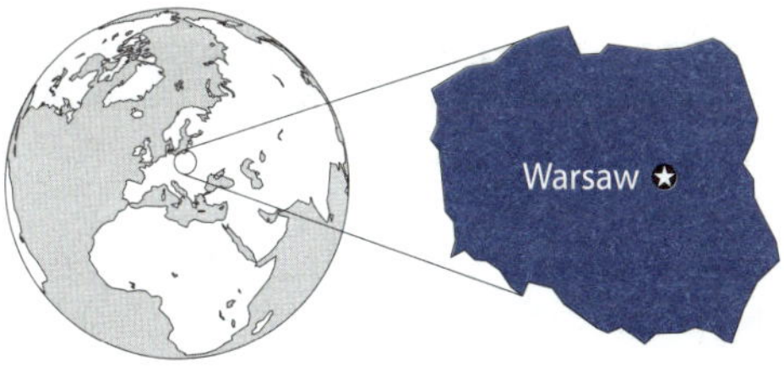

POLAND

Economic Freedom Score

World Rank: **50** Regional Rank: **23**

Poland's economic freedom score is 67.0, making its economy the 50th freest in the 2014 *Index*. Its score is 1.0 point better than last year, reflecting improvements in six of the 10 economic freedoms including business freedom, investment freedom, and trade freedom. Poland is ranked 23rd out of 43 countries in the Europe region, and its overall score is above the world average.

Over the 20-year history of the *Index*, Poland's economic freedom score has advanced by about 16 points, a top-20 improvement. With increases in nine of the 10 economic freedoms and no declines, Poland has risen since 2002 to the rank of "moderately free." Structural reforms include trade liberalization, privatization, implementation of a competitively low corporate tax rate, and modernization of the regulatory environment. Poland has achieved its highest economic freedom score ever in the 2014 *Index*.

Poland has taken steps to restore fiscal discipline despite a challenging economic environment. Continued reform, particularly to strengthen the independence of the judiciary and eradicate corruption, is needed to solidify the foundations of economic freedom and ensure progress toward greater prosperity.

BACKGROUND: Poland joined NATO in 1999 and the European Union in 2004. In April 2010, the majority of its top leadership died when the presidential plane crashed in Russia. Center-right leader Bronislaw Komorowski won the ensuing presidential election, and Prime Minister Donald Tusk of the center-right Civic Platform party was re-elected in October 2011. With a flexible exchange rate, approval of an IMF credit line, access to international markets, and healthy economic policies, Poland weathered the 2008 economic crisis better than its neighbors did. Agriculture is held back by inefficiency, structural problems, and low investment, but the automotive, pharmaceutical, aviation, steel, and machinery sectors have made Poland one of the EU's strongest economic performers. The private sector now accounts for two-thirds of GDP.

How Do We Measure Economic Freedom?
See page 471 for an explanation of the methodology or visit the *Index* Web site at *heritage.org/index*.

Freedom Trend

Country Comparisons

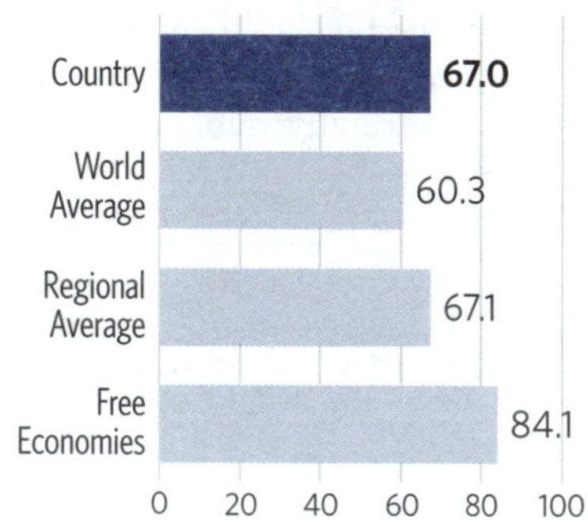

Quick Facts

Population: 38.9 million
GDP (PPP): $800.9 billion
2.0% growth in 2012
5-year compound annual growth 3.4%
$20,592 per capita
Unemployment: 10.3%
Inflation (CPI): 3.7%
FDI Inflow: $3.4 billion
Public Debt: 55.2% of GDP

2012 data unless otherwise noted.
Data compiled as of September 2013.

THE TEN ECONOMIC FREEDOMS

RULE OF LAW

	Score	Rank	1-Year Change
Property Rights	60.0	41st	0
Freedom from Corruption	54.8	41st	-0.2

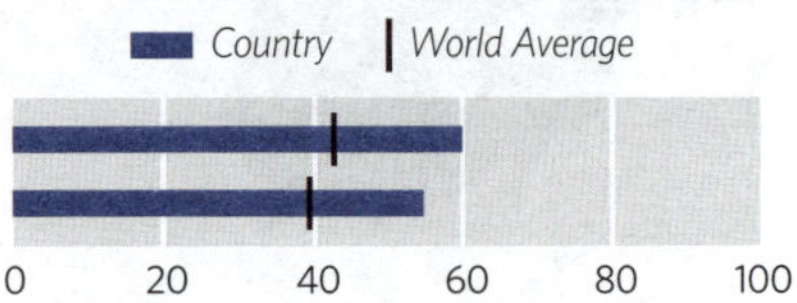

Anti-corruption laws are not always implemented effectively, and official corruption remains a problem. The legal system protects rights to acquire and dispose of property, and the judiciary is independent, but the courts are notorious for delays in adjudicating cases. Prosecutors' slow action on corruption investigations has prompted concerns that they are subject to political pressure.

GOVERNMENT SIZE

	Score	Rank	1-Year Change
Fiscal Freedom	76.1	114th	+0.1
Government Spending	43.2	145th	+0.2

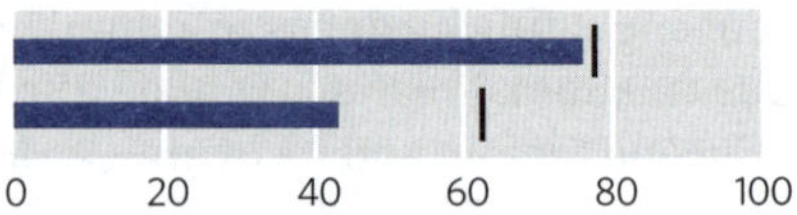

The top individual income tax rate is 32 percent, and the top corporate tax rate is 19 percent. Other taxes include a value-added tax (VAT) and a property tax. The overall tax burden equals 32 percent of domestic output. Public expenditures equal 43.5 percent of the economy, and government debt equals about 55 percent of GDP. The government has indicated that it plans to relax its fiscal rules in hopes of boosting growth.

REGULATORY EFFICIENCY

	Score	Rank	1-Year Change
Business Freedom	70.1	75th	+6.1
Labor Freedom	60.4	97th	-2.5
Monetary Freedom	77.8	66th	+0.1

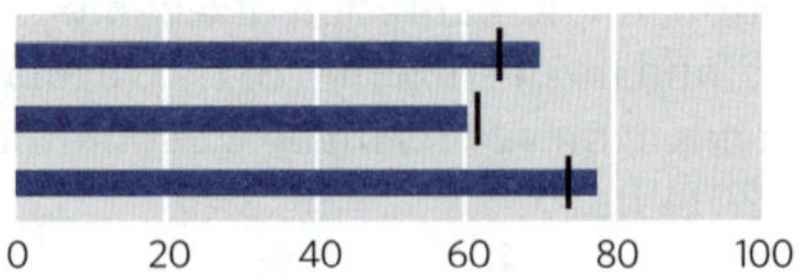

Launching a business takes only four procedures, and the cost of completing licensing requirements has been reduced considerably. Labor regulations are more stringent than those of other countries in the region. The government's transformation of Poland's coal mining sector into a commercially viable industry is a textbook case of success in reducing politically sensitive subsidies.

OPEN MARKETS

	Score	Rank	1-Year Change
Trade Freedom	87.8	11th	+1.0
Investment Freedom	70.0	46th	+5.0
Financial Freedom	70.0	19th	0

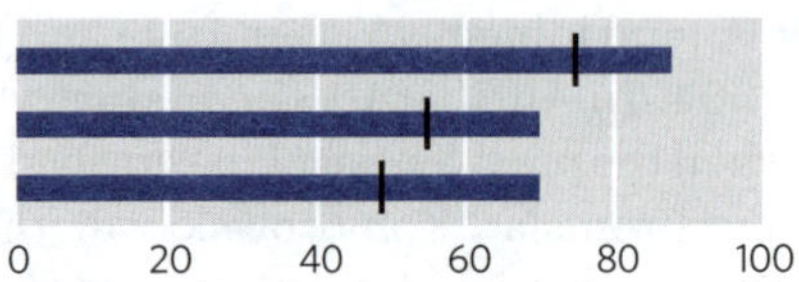

EU members have a low 1.1 percent average tariff rate and, in general, few non-tariff barriers to trade. Foreign investment levels for some sectors of the economy are capped. The financial sector continues to expand. Credit is available on market terms, and foreign investors can access domestic financial markets. Restrictions on capital flows have been removed, and capital markets have become more sophisticated.

Long-Term Score Change (since 1995)

RULE OF LAW		GOVERNMENT SIZE		REGULATORY EFFICIENCY		OPEN MARKETS	
Property Rights	+10.0	Fiscal Freedom	+25.1	Business Freedom	+0.1	Trade Freedom	+30.8
Freedom from Corruption	+4.8	Government Spending	+33.7	Labor Freedom	+0.4	Investment Freedom	0
				Monetary Freedom	+29.1	Financial Freedom	+20.0

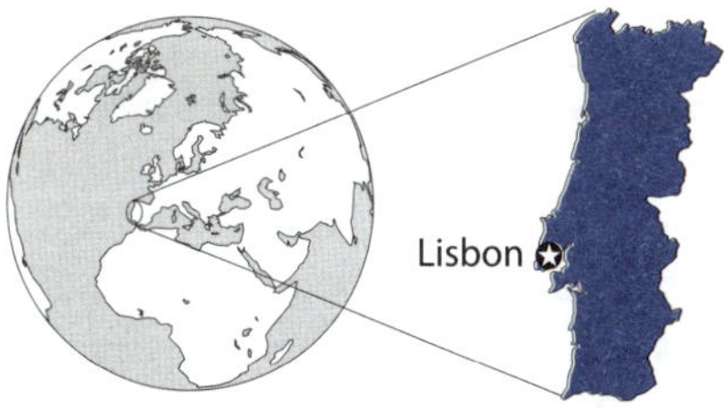

PORTUGAL

World Rank: 69 **Regional Rank: 32**

Economic Freedom Score

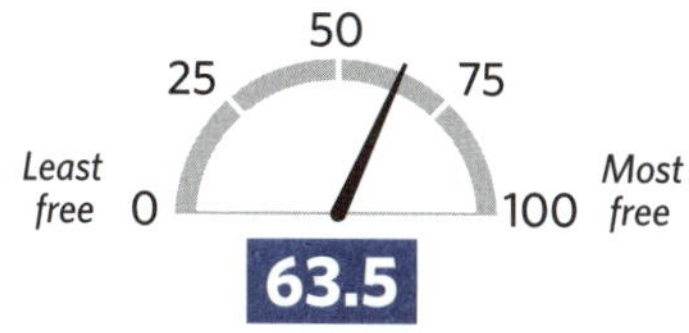

Portugal's economic freedom score is 63.5, making its economy the 69th freest in the 2014 *Index*. Its score is 0.4 point higher than last year, reflecting improvements in labor freedom, business freedom, and trade freedom that outweigh declines in the control of public finance and monetary freedom. Portugal is ranked 32nd out of 43 countries in the Europe region, and its overall score is above the world average.

Over the 20-year history of the *Index*, Portugal's economic freedom score has been stagnant at best. Significant gains in market openness and regulatory efficiency have been undermined by declines in property rights and the management of public finance and a level of labor freedom that is far below average. Portugal's economy has been rated "moderately free" throughout the history of the *Index*. Its 2014 score is its highest in three years.

Short-term legislative reforms have not been implemented effectively. Ongoing efforts have focused on reducing the inefficient and oversized government sector, better managing public finance, and reforming loss-making state-owned enterprises. However, the economy remains burdened by political interference, corruption, a rigid labor market, and uncertainty in the eurozone.

BACKGROUND: Portugal joined the European Union in 1986 and the eurozone in 2002. By 2011, a sovereign debt crisis threatened to sink the economy. The center-right Social Democrats led by Pedro Passos Coelho defeated Prime Minister Jose Socrates' Socialist Party in the 2011 general elections. In May 2011, Portugal accepted a €78 billion European Union–International Monetary Fund bailout plan. Despite cuts in state spending, Portugal is still in deep recession, thanks in part to tax increases. The economy is based primarily on services and industrial production. Some state enterprises have been privatized. In the first quarter of 2013, unemployment reached an all-time high of 17.7 percent, and youth unemployment was 42 percent.

How Do We Measure Economic Freedom?
See page 471 for an explanation of the methodology or visit the *Index* Web site at *heritage.org/index*.

Freedom Trend

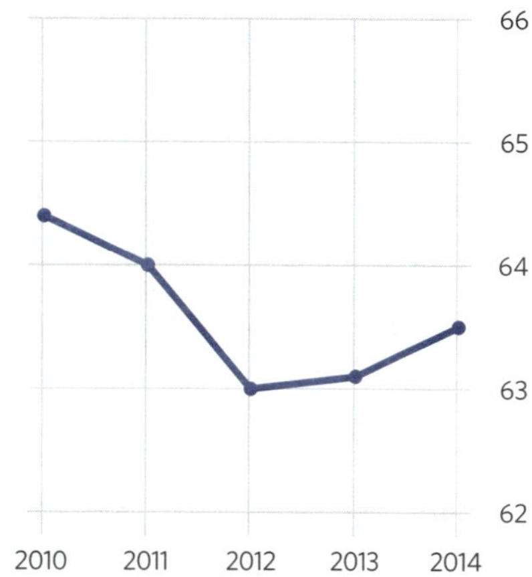

Country Comparisons

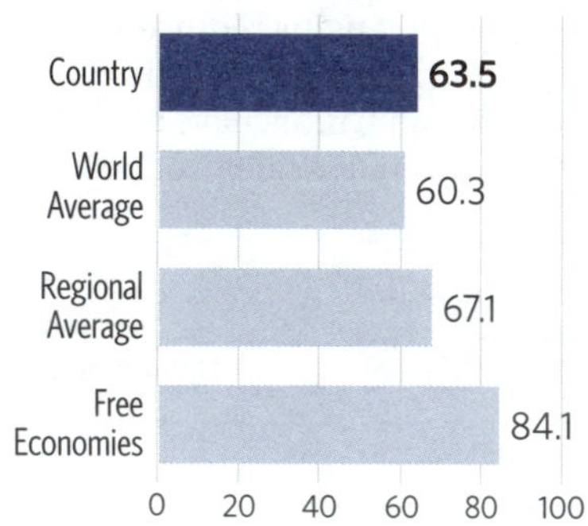

Quick Facts

Population: 10.5 million
GDP (PPP): $246.5 billion
-3.2% growth in 2012
5-year compound annual growth -1.2%
$23,385 per capita
Unemployment: 15.7%
Inflation (CPI): 2.8%
FDI Inflow: $8.9 billion
Public Debt: 123.0% of GDP

2012 data unless otherwise noted.
Data compiled as of September 2013.

THE TEN ECONOMIC FREEDOMS

RULE OF LAW

	Score	Rank	1-Year Change
Property Rights	70.0	27th	0
Freedom from Corruption	61.1	33rd	+0.1

Portugal continued to struggle with corruption issues in the past year as more than 30 former government officials faced trial charged with graft, money laundering, and influence peddling in cases dating to 2009. The constitution provides for an independent judiciary, but staff shortages and inefficiency have contributed to a considerable backlog of pending trials.

GOVERNMENT SIZE

	Score	Rank	1-Year Change
Fiscal Freedom	60.1	167th	-1.5
Government Spending	26.8	164th	-1.5

The top individual income tax rate has risen to 48 percent, and the top corporate tax rate has risen to 26.5 percent, including a surcharge of up to 5 percent levied on companies with over 7.5 million euros in profits. Other taxes include a value-added tax (VAT). The overall tax burden equals 31.3 percent of gross domestic income. Public expenditures amount to 49 percent of the size of the economy. Debt has stabilized at below 130 percent of GDP.

REGULATORY EFFICIENCY

	Score	Rank	1-Year Change
Business Freedom	84.9	24th	+2.1
Labor Freedom	34.6	174th	+3.6
Monetary Freedom	79.3	43rd	-0.1

The overall regulatory framework generally supports entrepreneurial activity. However, completing licensing requirements still costs almost four times the level of average annual income. Several revisions in Portugal's labor regulations, which had been among the least flexible in the European Union, have been implemented recently. In 2013, the government reduced subsidies paid to small-scale producers of power from solar energy by 30 percent.

OPEN MARKETS

	Score	Rank	1-Year Change
Trade Freedom	87.8	11th	+1.0
Investment Freedom	70.0	46th	0
Financial Freedom	60.0	41st	0

EU members have a low 1.1 percent average tariff rate and, in general, few non-tariff barriers to trade. Foreign investment in some sectors of the economy is screened by the government. Restructuring of the banking sector has progressed over the past year, but the overall financial system remains under considerable strain. Banks have become highly dependent on the European Central Bank for liquidity.

Long-Term Score Change (since 1995)

RULE OF LAW		GOVERNMENT SIZE		REGULATORY EFFICIENCY		OPEN MARKETS	
Property Rights	0	Fiscal Freedom	-0.4	Business Freedom	+14.9	Trade Freedom	+10.0
Freedom from Corruption	-8.9	Government Spending	-9.2	Labor Freedom	-6.6	Investment Freedom	+20.0
				Monetary Freedom	+1.7	Financial Freedom	+10.0

QATAR

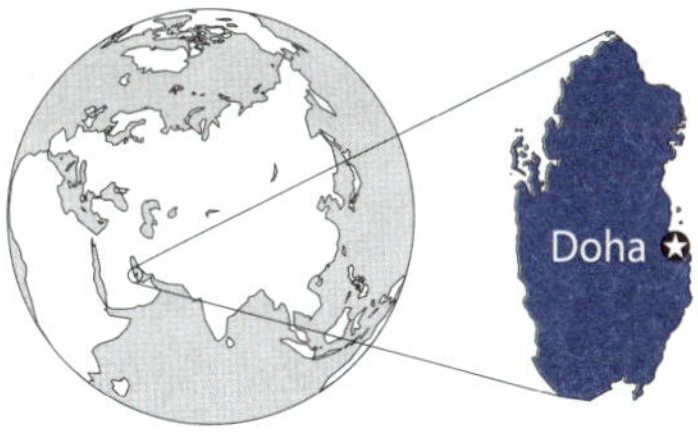

World Rank: **30** Regional Rank: **3**

Economic Freedom Score

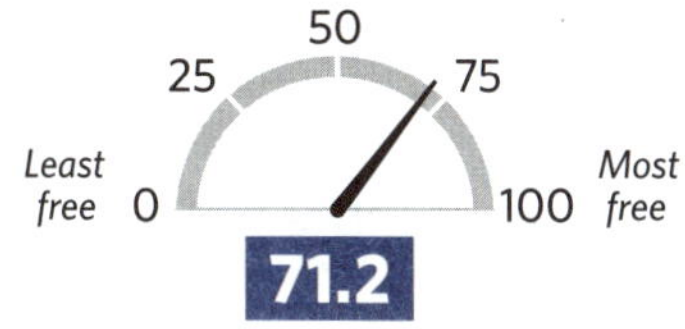

Qatar's economic freedom score is 71.2, making its economy the 30th freest in the 2014 *Index*. Its score is essentially unchanged from last year, with improvements in half of the 10 economic freedoms, including business freedom, labor freedom, and monetary freedom, offset by declines in the control of government spending and trade freedom. Qatar is ranked 3rd out of 15 countries in the Middle East/North Africa region, and its overall score is above the world average.

Qatar was first graded in the 1999 *Index* and since then has advanced its economic freedom score by over 9 points, reaching its second highest score ever in the 2014 *Index*. Scores for eight of the 10 categories of economic freedom have improved. Market openness, measured through trade freedom and financial freedom, has advanced significantly, and gains in business freedom, labor freedom, and monetary freedom have improved overall regulatory efficiency.

Deeper institutional reforms are needed to sustain high levels of economic growth and ensure long-term development. Systemic weaknesses linger in the enforcement of anti-corruption measures, although Qatar's anti-corruption record remains much better than the world average.

BACKGROUND: Qatar has been ruled by the Al-Thani family since independence from Great Britain in 1971. Political reforms promised by current Sheikh Hamad bin Khalifa al-Thani have largely stalled. Qatar is endowed with 25 billion barrels of proven oil reserves and the world's third-largest natural gas reserves. Oil and gas account for about 85 percent of export revenues and more than 50 percent of GDP. Qatar has permitted extensive foreign investment in its natural gas industry and in 2007 became the world's largest exporter of liquefied natural gas. With one of the world's highest per capita incomes and almost no poverty, Qatar has largely avoided the political instability that other Middle Eastern countries have suffered as a result of the "Arab Spring."

Freedom Trend

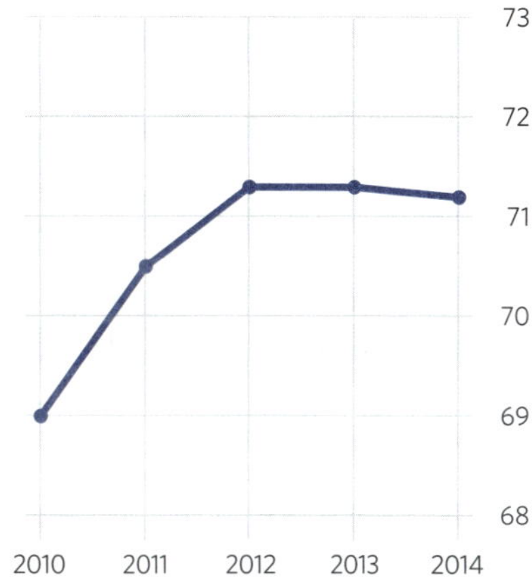

Country Comparisons

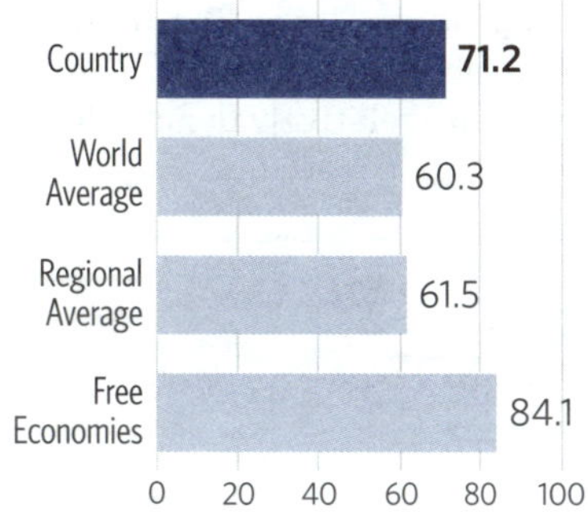

Quick Facts

Population: 1.8 million
GDP (PPP): $187.9 billion
6.6% growth in 2012
5-year compound annual growth 13.1%
$102,211 per capita
Unemployment: 0.5%
Inflation (CPI): 1.9%
FDI Inflow: $326.9 million
Public Debt: 37.8% of GDP

2012 data unless otherwise noted.
Data compiled as of September 2013.

How Do We Measure Economic Freedom?
See page 471 for an explanation of the methodology or visit the *Index* Web site at *heritage.org/index*.

QATAR (continued)

THE TEN ECONOMIC FREEDOMS

Legend: Country | World Average (scale 0–100)

RULE OF LAW

	Score	Rank	1-Year Change
Property Rights	70.0	27th	0
Freedom from Corruption	72.4	21st	+0.4

Although critics continue to complain of a lack of transparency in government procurement, Qatar's anti-corruption record is among the best in the Middle East. The rule of law has been solidly respected. A well-functioning legal framework is in place, but the judiciary is susceptible to political influence and can be bureaucratic. Foreigners are generally not allowed to own property.

GOVERNMENT SIZE

	Score	Rank	1-Year Change
Fiscal Freedom	99.9	1st	+0.1
Government Spending	72.1	80th	-9.1

Qatar has no individual income tax or corporate tax. There are no other major taxes apart from customs duties. The overall tax burden amounts to 2.9 percent of gross domestic income. Government is funded largely by oil revenues, and public expenditures are equal to 31 percent of GDP. Public debt amounts to less than 40 percent of the size of the economy.

REGULATORY EFFICIENCY

	Score	Rank	1-Year Change
Business Freedom	71.7	68th	+2.3
Labor Freedom	70.0	65th	+6.6
Monetary Freedom	81.2	20th	+0.9

Launching a business takes eight procedures and slightly more than a week. However, despite some progress, completing licensing requirements continues to be relatively time-consuming. The labor force consists primarily of expatriate workers, and immigration and employment rules are relatively flexible. The government does not mandate a minimum wage.

OPEN MARKETS

	Score	Rank	1-Year Change
Trade Freedom	79.8	71st	-2.7
Investment Freedom	45.0	125th	0
Financial Freedom	50.0	69th	0

Qatar's average tariff rate is 5.1 percent. Government procurement policies favor domestic producers. With some exceptions, foreign investment levels are capped at 49 percent. The financial sector, in which the state continues to retain some ownership, has undergone modernization. The Qatar Financial Center, opened in 2005, has attracted major financial firms and rivals other regional financial hubs.

Long-Term Score Change (since 1999)

RULE OF LAW		GOVERNMENT SIZE		REGULATORY EFFICIENCY		OPEN MARKETS	
Property Rights	**+20.0**	Fiscal Freedom	**+12.4**	Business Freedom	**+16.7**	Trade Freedom	**+4.8**
Freedom from Corruption	**-17.6**	Government Spending	**+24.3**	Labor Freedom	**+10.0**	Investment Freedom	**-5.0**
				Monetary Freedom	**+8.5**	Financial Freedom	**+20.0**

ROMANIA

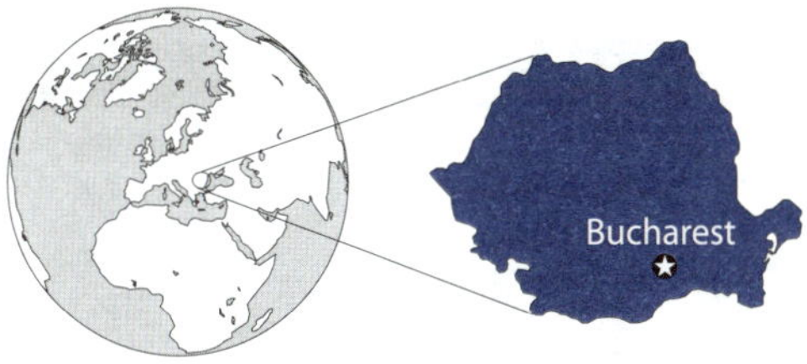

World Rank: 62 **Regional Rank: 29**

Economic Freedom Score

Romania's economic freedom score is 65.5, making its economy the 62nd freest in the 2014 *Index*. Its score is 0.4 point better this year due to small improvements in half of the 10 economic freedoms, including monetary freedom, freedom from corruption, and trade freedom. Romania is ranked 29th out of 43 countries in the Europe region, and its overall score is higher than the world average.

Over the 20-year history of the *Index*, Romania's economic freedom score has advanced by about 23 points, the eighth best improvement of any country. With gains in nine of the 10 economic freedoms, Romania has made tremendous strides in eliminating economically repressive policies. Structural reforms to enhance regulatory efficiency and market openness have advanced the economy to "moderately free." In the 2014 *Index*, Romania has achieved its highest economic freedom score ever.

Deeper institutional reforms, particularly related to eradicating corruption and ensuring judicial independence, remain critical to ensuring Romania's ongoing transition to a more resilient market-oriented economy and to improved economic growth.

BACKGROUND: Romania is a member of the European Union and NATO. Center-right politician Traian Basescu won the presidency in 2009 for a second time and has survived a series of impeachment attempts, the most recent led by center-left Prime Minister Victor Ponta in July 2012. The results of a July 2012 impeachment referendum were struck down by the Constitutional Court due to low voter turnout. Romania experienced a deep recession as a result of the 2008 global financial crisis. Modest economic growth has resumed. The government is pursuing significant privatization of major state corporations such as railway freight company CFR Marfa, chemical producer Oltchim, copper mines, and energy companies. Geostrategically positioned on the Black Sea, Romania has extensive natural resources, a productive agriculture sector, and the potential for growth in industry and tourism.

How Do We Measure Economic Freedom?
See page 471 for an explanation of the methodology or visit the *Index* Web site at *heritage.org/index.*

Freedom Trend

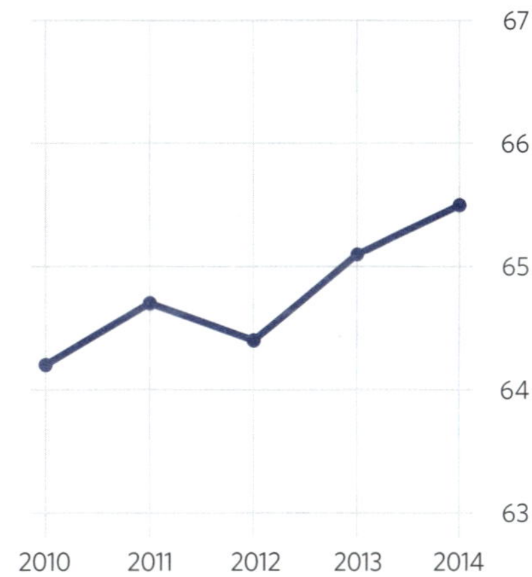

Country Comparisons

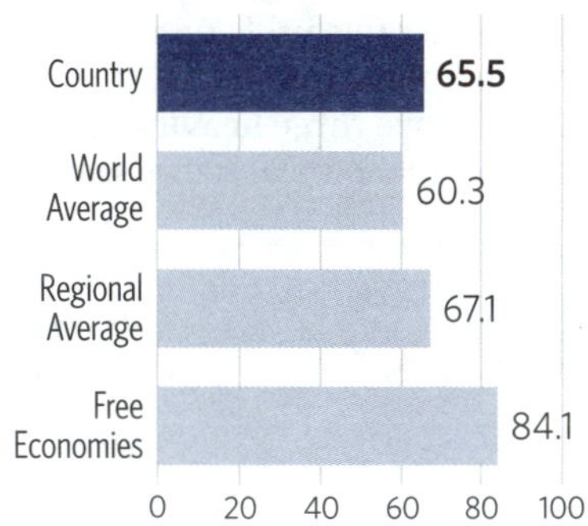

Quick Facts

Population: 21.3 million
GDP (PPP): $273.4 billion
0.3% growth in 2012
5-year compound annual growth 0.3%
$12,808 per capita
Unemployment: 7.0%
Inflation (CPI): 3.3%
FDI Inflow: $2.2 billion
Public Debt: 37.0% of GDP

2012 data unless otherwise noted.
Data compiled as of September 2013.

ROMANIA (continued)

THE TEN ECONOMIC FREEDOMS

RULE OF LAW

	Score	Rank	1-Year Change
Property Rights	40.0	70th	0
Freedom from Corruption	37.7	74th	+1.7

Romania has struggled to meet EU anti-corruption requirements. A 2012 EU report cited problems with follow-up by administrative and judicial bodies and a pattern of minimum or suspended sentences. Judicial independence was threatened in 2012 by political pressure surrounding the presidential impeachment effort, and courts continue to suffer from corruption, political influence, staffing shortages, and inefficient resources.

GOVERNMENT SIZE

	Score	Rank	1-Year Change
Fiscal Freedom	87.0	41st	-0.9
Government Spending	59.2	120th	-3.0

The top individual income and corporate tax rates are 16 percent. Other taxes include a value-added tax (VAT) and an environmental tax. The overall tax burden is equal to 28 percent of GDP. Government spending amounts to 37 percent of GDP. Public debt is equivalent to 37 percent of the domestic economy. The government has been receiving EU and IMF loans to temper the effects of the eurozone crisis.

REGULATORY EFFICIENCY

	Score	Rank	1-Year Change
Business Freedom	71.0	71st	+0.6
Labor Freedom	65.2	79th	+1.7
Monetary Freedom	77.1	72nd	+2.4

The processes for business formation and operation have been streamlined. Launching a business takes five procedures and about 8 days. Labor regulations remain rigid, although several amendments to improve the flexibility of the labor code have been made. Government efforts to privatize three heavily subsidized loss-making state-owned enterprises in the rail, mining, and petrochemical sectors are still in progress.

OPEN MARKETS

	Score	Rank	1-Year Change
Trade Freedom	87.8	11th	+1.0
Investment Freedom	80.0	23rd	0
Financial Freedom	50.0	69th	0

EU members have a low 1.1 percent average tariff rate and, in general, few non-tariff barriers to trade. Romania's legal and regulatory systems can be difficult for foreign investors to navigate. The evolving financial sector is open to competition, and foreign-owned banks dominate the banking sector. The banking system remains liquid and well capitalized, but significant vulnerabilities remain in light of the ongoing eurozone turmoil.

Long-Term Score Change (since 1995)

RULE OF LAW		GOVERNMENT SIZE		REGULATORY EFFICIENCY		OPEN MARKETS	
Property Rights	+10.0	Fiscal Freedom	+47.6	Business Freedom	+16.0	Trade Freedom	+8.8
Freedom from Corruption	+27.7	Government Spending	+7.0	Labor Freedom	+9.7	Investment Freedom	+10.0
				Monetary Freedom	+77.1	Financial Freedom	0

RUSSIA

Economic Freedom Score

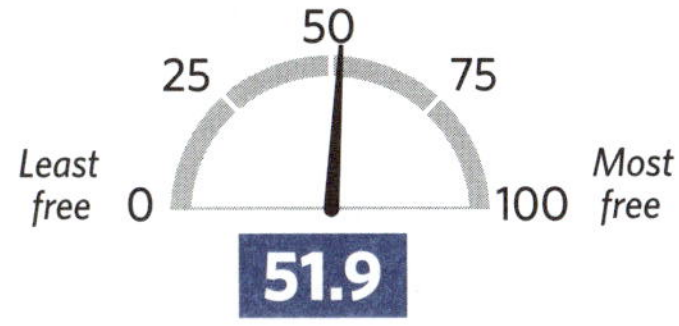

World Rank: **140** Regional Rank: **41**

Russia's economic freedom score is 51.9, making its economy the 140th freest in the 2014 *Index*. Its score is 0.8 point higher this year, with improvements in four of the 10 economic freedoms, including control of government spending, counterbalanced by declines in trade freedom, freedom from corruption, and fiscal freedom. Russia is ranked 41st out of 43 countries in the Europe region, and its overall score is below the world average.

Over the 20-year history of the *Index*, Russia's economic freedom has been stagnant, with its score improving less than 1 point. Overall, notable improvements in trade freedom and monetary freedom have been largely offset by substantial declines in investment freedom, financial freedom, business freedom, and property rights, and Russia's economy remains "mostly unfree."

The foundations for sustainable economic development remain fragile, exacerbated by the poor legal framework. Corruption, endemic throughout the economy, is becoming ever more debilitating. The state maintains an extensive presence in many sectors through state-owned enterprises.

BACKGROUND: Former President and Prime Minister Vladimir Putin was re-elected president in March 2012 on the heels of hotly disputed December 2011 Duma elections. Political repression is on the rise. Prominent opposition figures have been forced to leave the country, and others have been prosecuted on what appear to be trumped-up charges. Sergey Magnitsky, an anti-corruption crusader and whistleblower, died in jail. The state has reasserted its dominance in the aerospace, mining, and oil and gas industries, and the state budget remains heavily dependent on exports of natural resources, especially hydrocarbons. Russia's reputation for cronyism and corruption and an inhospitable regulatory environment have damaged its investment climate as well as its emerging small-business community. Russia became a member of the World Trade Organization in August 2012 and is making a bid to join the Organisation for Economic Co-operation and Development.

How Do We Measure Economic Freedom?
See page 471 for an explanation of the methodology or visit the *Index* Web site at *heritage.org/index*.

Freedom Trend

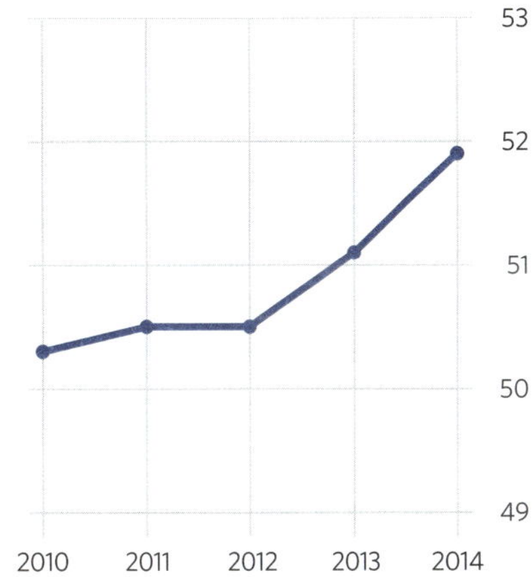

Country Comparisons

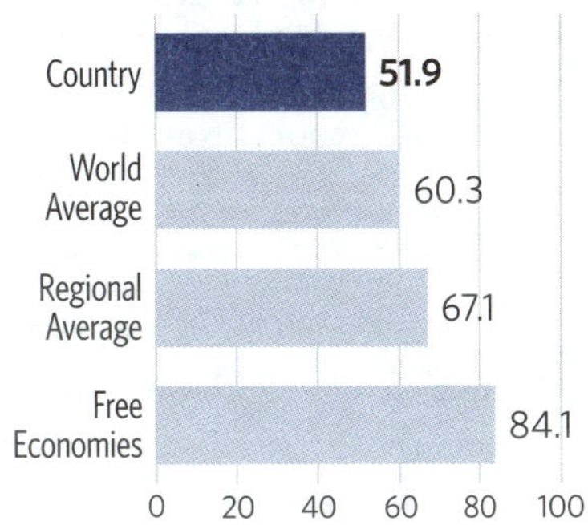

Quick Facts

Population: 141.9 million
GDP (PPP): $2.5 trillion
3.4% growth in 2012
5-year compound annual growth 1.8%
$17,709 per capita
Unemployment: 6.0%
Inflation (CPI): 5.1%
FDI Inflow: $51.4 billion
Public Debt: 10.9% of GDP

2012 data unless otherwise noted.
Data compiled as of September 2013.

THE TEN ECONOMIC FREEDOMS

RULE OF LAW

	Score	Rank	1-Year Change
Property Rights	25.0	135th	0
Freedom from Corruption	22.1	149th	-1.9

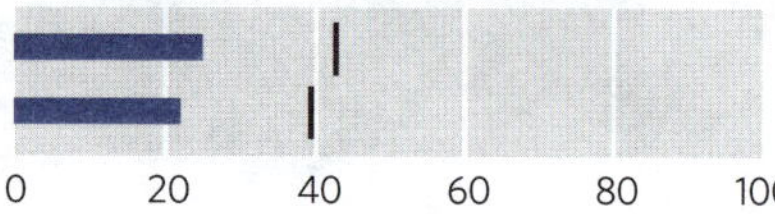

Corruption in government and business is pervasive, and a growing lack of accountability enables bureaucrats to act with impunity. The leadership frequently announces anticorruption campaigns, but they are typically superficial in nature. The rule of law is not maintained uniformly across the country, and the judiciary is vulnerable to political pressure and inconsistent in applying the law. Protection of private property rights is weak.

GOVERNMENT SIZE

	Score	Rank	1-Year Change
Fiscal Freedom	85.6	49th	-1.3
Government Spending	61.5	117th	+7.1

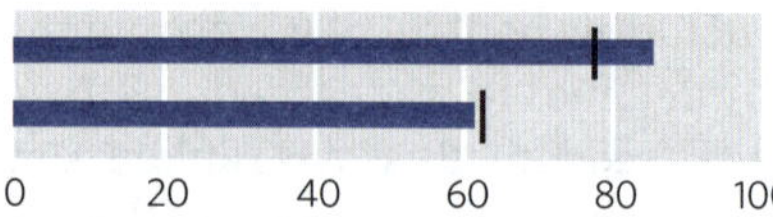

The top individual income tax rate is 13 percent, and the top corporate tax rate is 20 percent. Other taxes include a value-added tax (VAT) and an environmental tax. The overall tax burden is 29.5 percent of GDP. Government spending is 36 percent of GDP. Public debt remains modest at just over 10 percent of GDP. Reduced oil and gas revenues have put pressure on public finances.

REGULATORY EFFICIENCY

	Score	Rank	1-Year Change
Business Freedom	70.0	78th	+0.8
Labor Freedom	55.8	112th	+3.2
Monetary Freedom	69.4	145th	+2.7

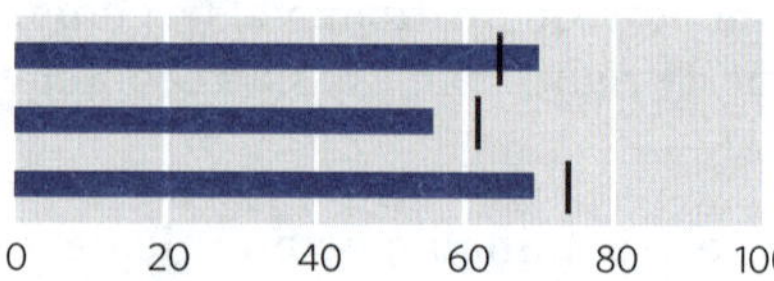

Bureaucratic obstacles and inconsistent enforcement of regulations continue to inject considerable uncertainty into entrepreneurial decision-making. The outmoded labor code continues to limit employment growth. The government uses extensive subsidies, numerous state-owned companies, export taxes on petroleum products, and other means to influence domestic prices.

OPEN MARKETS

	Score	Rank	1-Year Change
Trade Freedom	74.6	104th	-2.8
Investment Freedom	25.0	159th	0
Financial Freedom	30.0	132nd	0

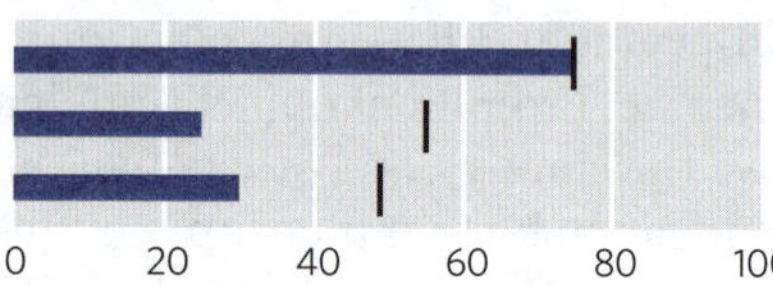

Russia's average tariff rate is 5.2 percent. Russia joined the World Trade Organization in 2012, but some non-tariff barriers such as tariff-rate quotas on agricultural products continue to impede imports. The government screens foreign investment in several sectors of the economy. Large state-owned institutions have increased their domination in the financial sector, outweighing domestic private and foreign banks.

Long-Term Score Change (since 1995)

RULE OF LAW		GOVERNMENT SIZE		REGULATORY EFFICIENCY		OPEN MARKETS	
Property Rights	**-25.0**	Fiscal Freedom	**+10.1**	Business Freedom	**-15.0**	Trade Freedom	**+22.6**
Freedom from Corruption	**+12.1**	Government Spending	**-5.7**	Labor Freedom	**-6.0**	Investment Freedom	**-45.0**
				Monetary Freedom	**+69.4**	Financial Freedom	**-20.0**

RWANDA

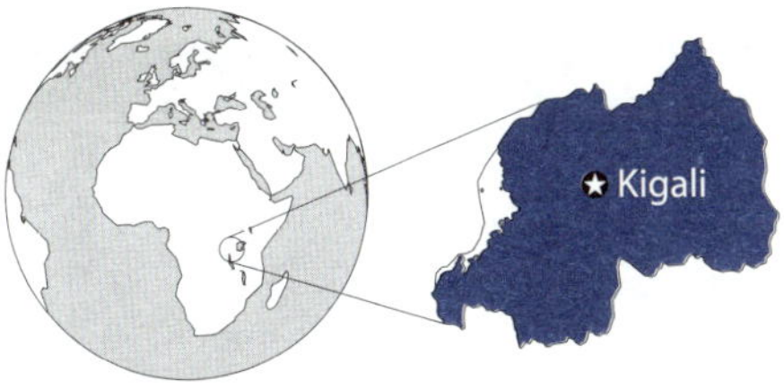

World Rank: 65 | **Regional Rank: 4**

Economic Freedom Score

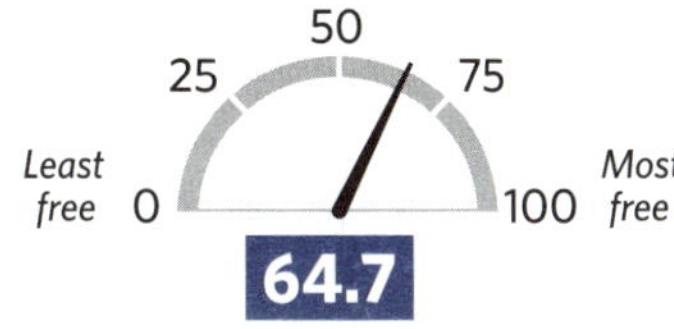

Rwanda's economic freedom score is 64.7, making its economy the 65th freest in the 2014 *Index*. Its score is 0.6 point better than last year, reflecting improvements in the management of government spending, business freedom, and labor freedom. Rwanda is ranked 4th out of 46 countries in the Sub-Saharan Africa region, and its score exceeds the world average.

Over the 20-year history of the *Index*, Rwanda has improved its economic freedom score by 26.4 points, the fifth-best increase of any country. Recording score improvements in nine of the 10 economic freedoms, Rwanda has advanced from economic repression 20 years ago to a "moderately free" economy today.

Nonetheless, substantial challenges remain, particularly in implementing deeper institutional and systemic reforms that are critical to strengthening the foundations of economic freedom. While the security situation is more stable, the absence of a well-functioning legal system undermines protection of property rights and efforts to eradicate corruption.

BACKGROUND: Decades of ethnic tension culminated in April 1994 in the genocidal slaughter of an estimated one million Tutsis and moderate Hutus. After now-President Paul Kagame's Tutsi-led Rwandan Patriotic Front seized power in July 1994, millions of Hutus fled to the Democratic Republic of Congo. Kagame was elected president in 2000 and re-elected in August 2010 amid allegations of fraud, voter intimidation, and violence. He has since focused on political reconciliation and rebuilding Rwanda's shattered economy. In September 2013 parliamentary elections, the RPF gained a resounding victory. In July 2012, the U.N. criticized Kagame for supporting the M23 rebel group in the DRC, and the U.S., the Netherlands, and Germany suspended aid. Economic reforms have encouraged recovery, but the government has constrained political and media freedoms. Despite strong growth based on tourism and exports of coffee and tea, there is widespread poverty. Over 80 percent of Rwandans depend on subsistence agriculture.

How Do We Measure Economic Freedom?
See page 471 for an explanation of the methodology or visit the *Index* Web site at *heritage.org/index*.

Freedom Trend

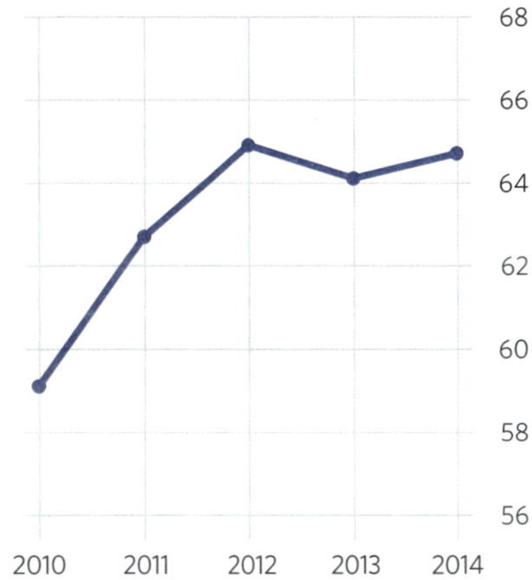

Country Comparisons

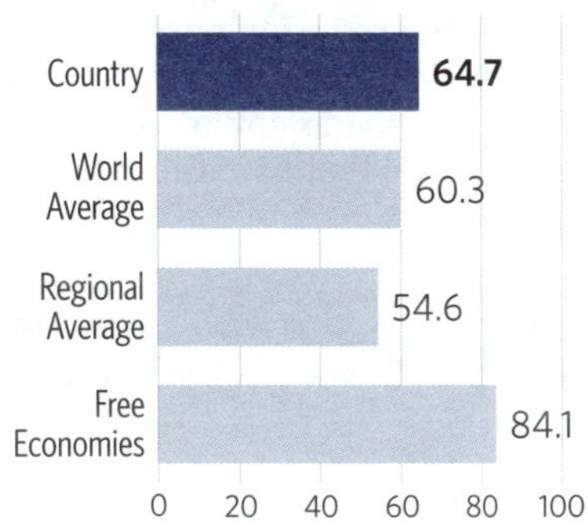

Quick Facts

Population: 10.4 million
GDP (PPP): $15.5 billion
7.7% growth in 2012
5-year compound annual growth 8.5%
$1,486 per capita
Unemployment: n/a
Inflation (CPI): 6.3%
FDI Inflow: $159.8 million
Public Debt: 28.0% of GDP

2012 data unless otherwise noted.
Data compiled as of September 2013.

THE TEN ECONOMIC FREEDOMS

Score — Country | World Average — *Rank* — *1-Year Change*

RULE OF LAW

	Score	Rank	1-Year Change
Property Rights	30.0	93rd	0
Freedom from Corruption	46.9	53rd	-3.1

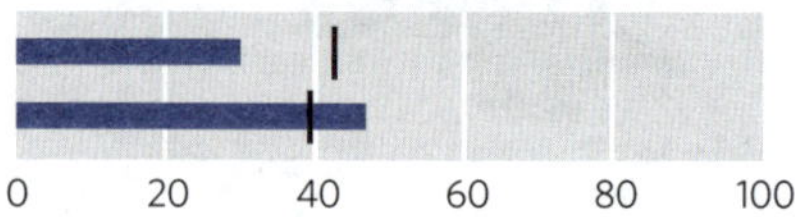

Government countermeasures have helped to limit corruption, though graft remains a problem. In recent years, a number of senior government officials have been fired and have faced prosecution for alleged corruption, embezzlement, and abuse of power. Recent improvements in the judicial system include improved training and revisions of the legal code, but the judiciary has yet to secure full independence from the executive.

GOVERNMENT SIZE

	Score	Rank	1-Year Change
Fiscal Freedom	80.3	83rd	-0.1
Government Spending	78.2	60th	+2.3

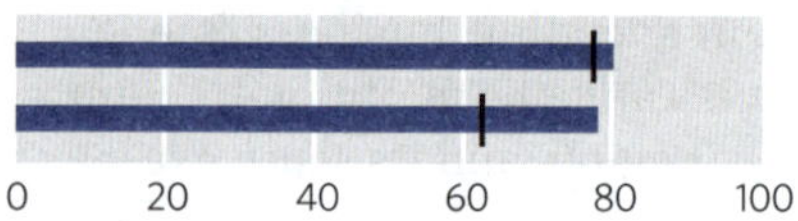

The top individual income and corporate tax rates are 30 percent. Other taxes include a value-added tax (VAT) and a property transfer tax. the overall tax burden equals 13.1 percent of the domestic economy. The government is still reliant on aid flows; however, domestic revenue has reached new highs. Public expenditures are 27 percent of GDP, and government debt is below 30 percent of the size of the economy.

REGULATORY EFFICIENCY

	Score	Rank	1-Year Change
Business Freedom	69.6	79th	+4.0
Labor Freedom	84.1	13th	+3.8
Monetary Freedom	74.8	108th	-0.7

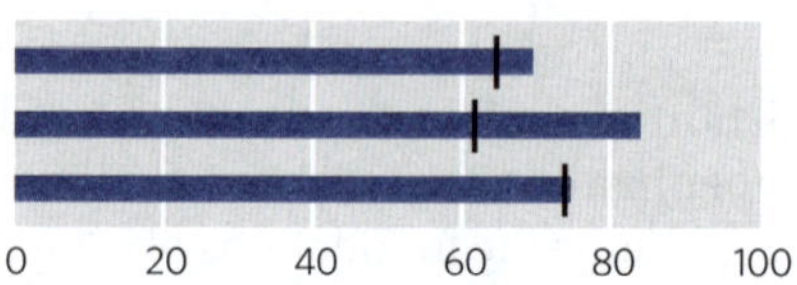

Launching a company takes two procedures and two days, and no minimum capital is required. Licensing requirements still cost over three times the level of average annual income. With relatively flexible labor regulations in place, the labor market continues to evolve. The government sets maximum prices for automotive fuels and subsidizes power for the 20 percent of the population that has access to electricity.

OPEN MARKETS

	Score	Rank	1-Year Change
Trade Freedom	77.7	84th	-0.3
Investment Freedom	65.0	68th	0
Financial Freedom	40.0	107th	0

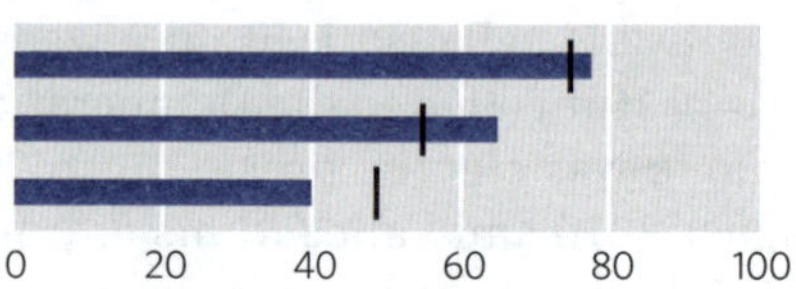

The average tariff rate for Rwanda is 6.1 percent, and there are few formal non-tariff barriers to trade. Foreign and domestic investors are formally treated equally under the law, but some mining companies have made allegations of expropriation without full compensation. The financial sector is small but growing. Despite progress, the high costs of financing and limited access to credit remain serious challenges for entrepreneurs.

Long-Term Score Change (since 1997)

RULE OF LAW		GOVERNMENT SIZE		REGULATORY EFFICIENCY		OPEN MARKETS	
Property Rights	+20.0	Fiscal Freedom	+12.4	Business Freedom	+29.6	Trade Freedom	+43.7
Freedom from Corruption	+36.9	Government Spending	-14.1	Labor Freedom	+26.1	Investment Freedom	+35.0
				Monetary Freedom	+24.0	Financial Freedom	+30.0

SAINT LUCIA

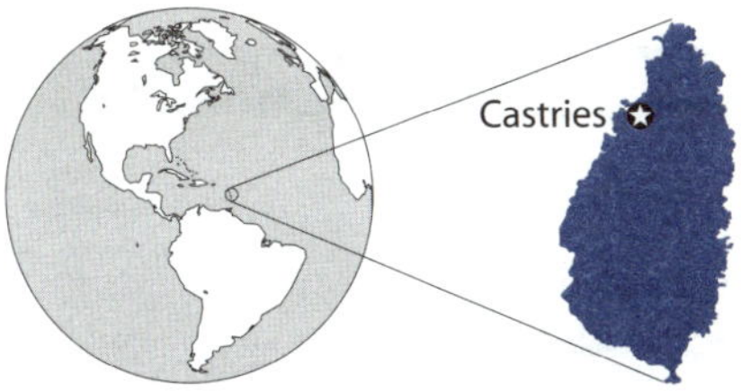

World Rank: **33** Regional Rank: **2**

Economic Freedom Score

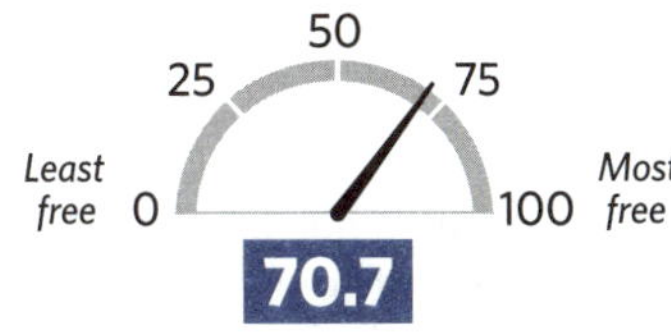

Saint Lucia's economic freedom score is 70.7, making its economy the 33rd freest in the 2014 *Index*. Its score is 0.3 point better than last year, with improvements in labor freedom and freedom from corruption offsetting combined declines in business freedom, monetary freedom, and fiscal freedom. Saint Lucia is ranked 2nd out of 29 countries in the South and Central America/Caribbean region, and its overall score is above the world average.

Saint Lucia was first graded in the 2009 *Index*, and its economic freedom score since then has increased only modestly. Improvements in four of the 10 economic freedoms, led by a 25-point advance in investment freedom, have been undermined by declines in the management of government spending, business freedom, and monetary freedom.

Saint Lucia has been rated "mostly free" since 2010. Its economy scores above the world average in many of the 10 economic freedoms, including property rights, business freedom, freedom from corruption, and monetary freedom. Greater access to financing opportunities remains critical to private-sector development, and there is considerable scope for further development and better regulation of the financial sector.

BACKGROUND: In late 2011, former Prime Minister Kenny D. Anthony and his Saint Lucia Labour Party defeated Prime Minister Stephenson King's more business-friendly United Workers Party. Saint Lucia is a member of the Community of Latin American and Caribbean States (CELAC) and the Caribbean Community (CARICOM) and home to the Organization of Eastern Caribbean States. Its economy depends primarily on tourism (65 percent of GDP), banana production, and light manufacturing. An educated workforce and reliable infrastructure and port facilities attract foreign investment in tourism, petroleum storage, and transshipment. A decline in tourism during the 2009 recession, fluctuations in banana prices, and reduced European Union banana trade preferences have motivated greater economic diversification in cocoa, mangos, and avocados. Violent crime threatens tourism.

How Do We Measure Economic Freedom?
See page 471 for an explanation of the methodology or visit the *Index* Web site at *heritage.org/index*.

Freedom Trend

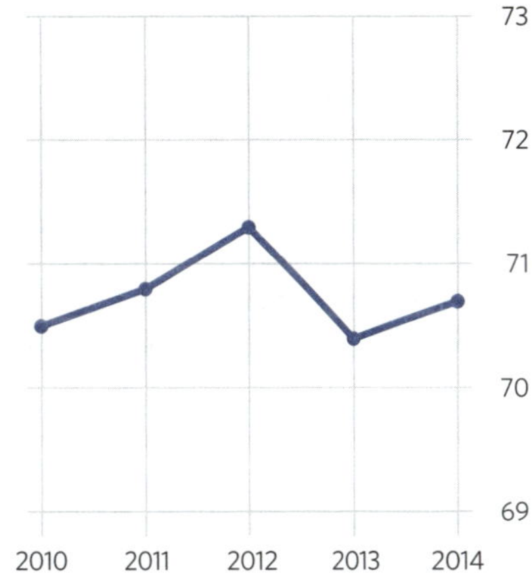

Country Comparisons

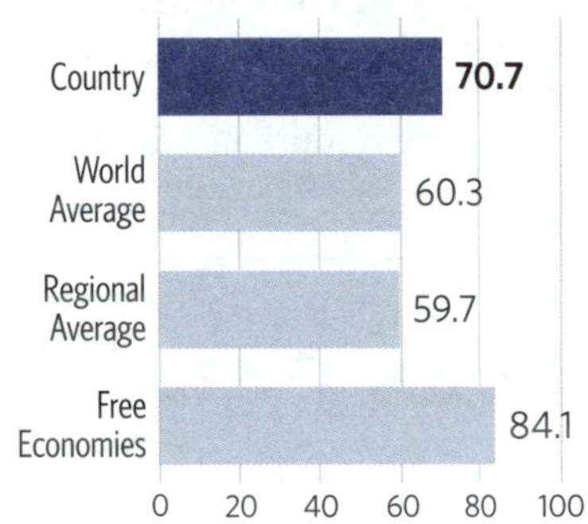

Quick Facts

Population: 0.2 million
GDP (PPP): $2.2 billion
-0.4% growth in 2012
5-year compound annual growth 1.3%
$13,104 per capita
Unemployment: n/a
Inflation (CPI): 4.3%
FDI Inflow: $112.8 million
Public Debt: 78.4% of GDP

2012 data unless otherwise noted.
Data compiled as of September 2013.

THE TEN ECONOMIC FREEDOMS

RULE OF LAW

	Score	Rank	1-Year Change
Property Rights	70.0	27th	0
Freedom from Corruption	70.6	25th	+0.6

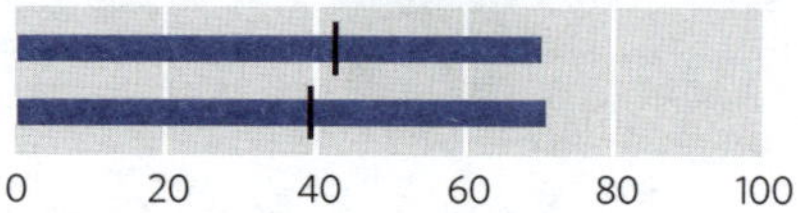

Saint Lucia has low levels of corruption. Access to information is legally guaranteed, and government officials are legally required to present their financial assets annually to the Integrity Commission. The judicial system is independent, conducts generally fair public trials, and includes a high court under the Saint Lucia–based Eastern Caribbean Supreme Court. Enforcement of intellectual property rights has been weak.

GOVERNMENT SIZE

	Score	Rank	1-Year Change
Fiscal Freedom	75.7	115th	-1.2
Government Spending	63.6	106th	0

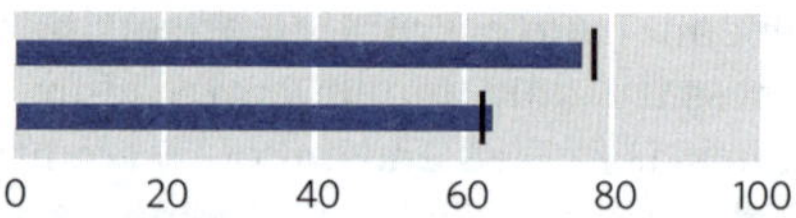

Saint Lucia's top personal income and corporate tax rates are 30 percent. Other taxes include a consumption tax and a property transfer tax. The overall tax burden is 25 percent of GDP. Government spending amounts to 35 percent of GDP. Public debt has been rising, reaching a level greater than 75 percent of the size of the domestic economy.

REGULATORY EFFICIENCY

	Score	Rank	1-Year Change
Business Freedom	83.1	27th	-2.2
Labor Freedom	84.5	12th	+8.1
Monetary Freedom	82.7	10th	-2.0

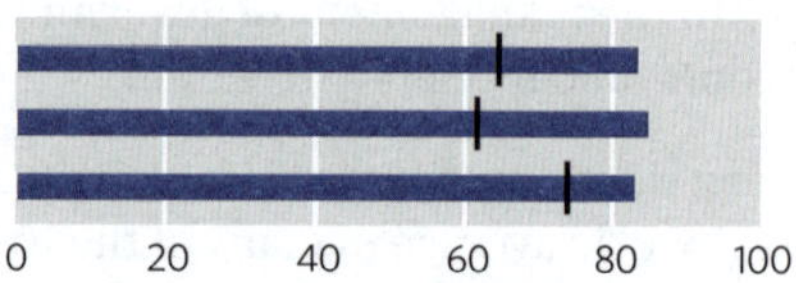

Enforcement of commercial regulations is relatively effective and consistent. It takes five procedures to incorporate a business, and no minimum capital is required. A well-functioning labor market has not been fully developed, and much of the labor force is employed in agriculture and tourism. In June 2013, the government reduced bulk rice, flour, and brown sugar subsidies by 50 per cent.

OPEN MARKETS

	Score	Rank	1-Year Change
Trade Freedom	71.9	119th	0
Investment Freedom	65.0	68th	0
Financial Freedom	40.0	107th	0

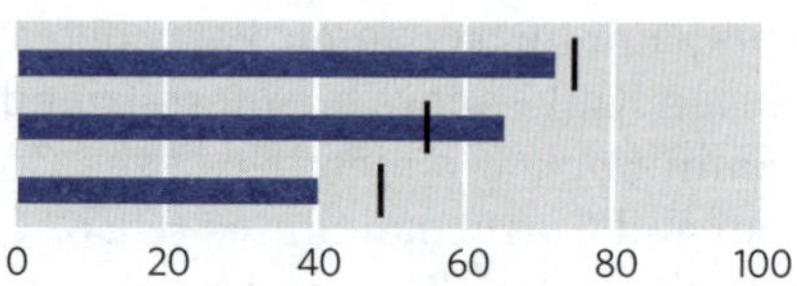

Saint Lucia's average tariff rate is 9 percent. There are few non-tariff barriers to trade, and the government generally treats foreign and domestic investors equally. New foreign investment may require government approval. A considerable portion of the population does not use the formal banking sector, and access to financing is limited. There is a small offshore financial sector, and the banking sector is dominated by commercial banking.

Long-Term Score Change (since 2009)

RULE OF LAW		GOVERNMENT SIZE		REGULATORY EFFICIENCY		OPEN MARKETS	
Property Rights	0	Fiscal Freedom	+1.7	Business Freedom	-4.6	Trade Freedom	-0.1
Freedom from Corruption	+2.6	Government Spending	-4.9	Labor Freedom	+1.7	Investment Freedom	+25.0
				Monetary Freedom	-2.4	Financial Freedom	0

SAINT VINCENT AND THE GRENADINES

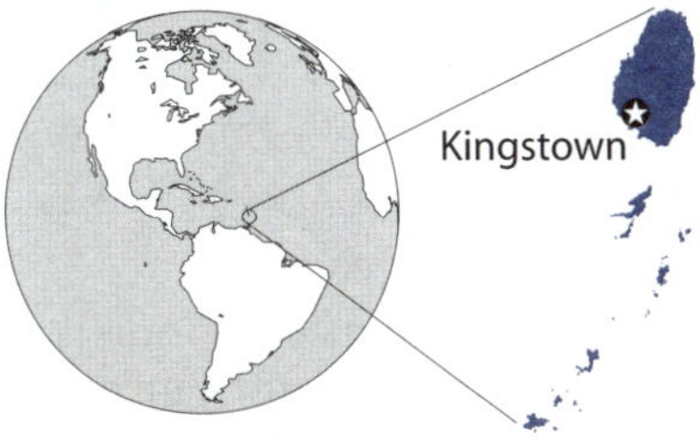

Economic Freedom Score

World Rank: 52 **Regional Rank: 8**

Freedom Trend

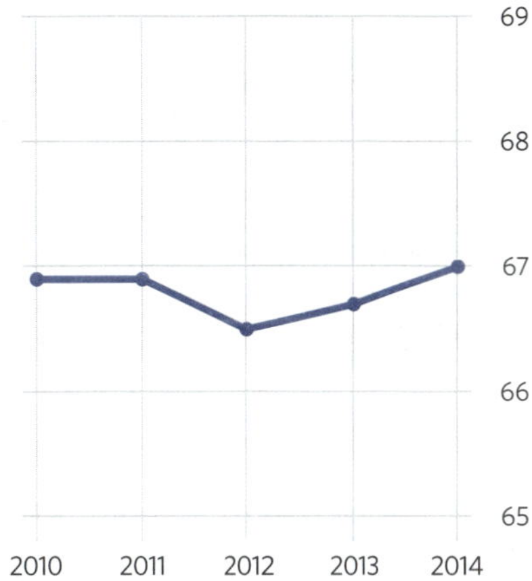

Saint Vincent and the Grenadines' economic freedom score is 67.0, making its economy the 52nd freest in the 2014 *Index*. Its score is 0.3 point higher than last year, with improvements in the control of government spending, labor freedom, and freedom from corruption that outweigh declines in trade freedom and business freedom. Saint Vincent and the Grenadines ranks 8th out of 29 countries in the South and Central America/Caribbean region, and its score is above the world average.

Saint Vincent and the Grenadines' economic freedom was first assessed in the 2009 *Index*, and its score has advanced since then by about 3 points, with improvements in six of the 10 economic freedoms including investment freedom, the management of public finance, and monetary freedom. The country remains "moderately free" and has achieved its highest economic freedom score ever in the 2014 *Index*.

By and large, Saint Vincent and the Grenadines has flexible labor regulations, an efficient legal system, and macroeconomic stability. However, tariff and non-tariff barriers undercut trade freedom, and private-sector growth remains stifled by an underdeveloped financial sector.

BACKGROUND: Prime Minister Ralph Gonsalves' Unity Labour Party has governed since 2001 and retained a slim majority in the December 2010 parliamentary elections. Saint Vincent and the Grenadines is a parliamentary democracy and part of the British Commonwealth. It is also a member of the Caribbean Community (CARICOM) and the Organization of Eastern Caribbean States. The economy is supported by the U.S. Caribbean Basin Initiative, which allows goods to enter the United States duty-free. Agriculture and tourism employ a significant portion of the workforce, but high formal-sector unemployment has caused many to emigrate. The economy is vulnerable to global price fluctuations and natural disasters. Tourism has not recovered from the 2009 recession, and nearly one-third of all revenue is directed toward servicing the high government debt.

Country Comparisons

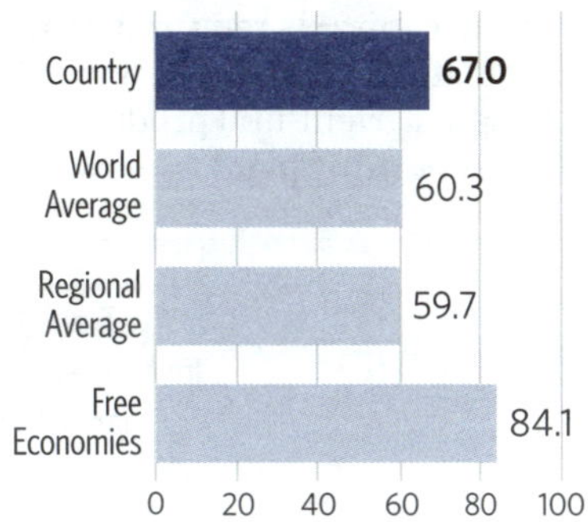

Quick Facts

Population: 0.1 million
GDP (PPP): $1.3 billion
0.5% growth in 2012
5-year compound annual growth -0.8%
$11,776 per capita
Unemployment: n/a
Inflation (CPI): 2.6%
FDI Inflow: $125.5 million
Public Debt: 70.2% of GDP

2012 data unless otherwise noted.
Data compiled as of September 2013.

How Do We Measure Economic Freedom?
See page 471 for an explanation of the methodology or visit the *Index* Web site at *heritage.org/index*.

THE TEN ECONOMIC FREEDOMS

Score | Country | World Average | Rank | 1-Year Change

RULE OF LAW

	Score	Rank	1-Year Change
Property Rights	70.0	27th	0
Freedom from Corruption	61.1	34th	+3.1

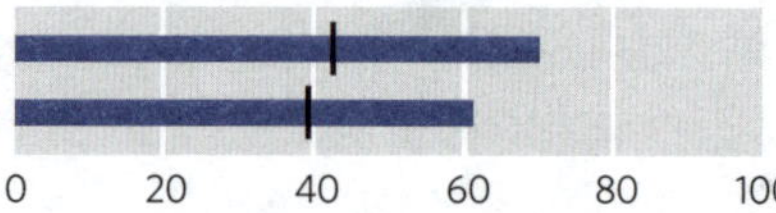

Compared to some neighboring countries, the rule of law remains strong, and corruption is not pervasive. There have been some allegations of money laundering through Saint Vincent banks and drug-related corruption within the government and police, but the government has taken action to prosecute such crimes. The relatively independent and efficient judicial system is based on British common law.

GOVERNMENT SIZE

	Score	Rank	1-Year Change
Fiscal Freedom	73.7	124th	-0.5
Government Spending	72.4	79th	+5.3

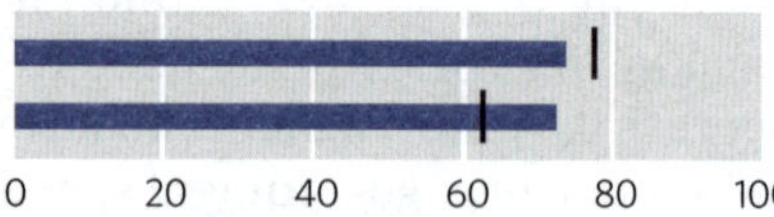

The top individual income tax rate is 32.5 percent, and the top corporate tax rate has risen to 33 percent. Other taxes include a property tax and a value-added tax (VAT). The overall tax burden amounts to 22 percent of the total domestic economy. Public expenditures equal 30 percent of GDP. Government debt equates to about 70 percent of gross domestic income.

REGULATORY EFFICIENCY

	Score	Rank	1-Year Change
Business Freedom	76.3	41st	-1.3
Labor Freedom	78.7	34th	+2.1
Monetary Freedom	79.8	35th	-0.5

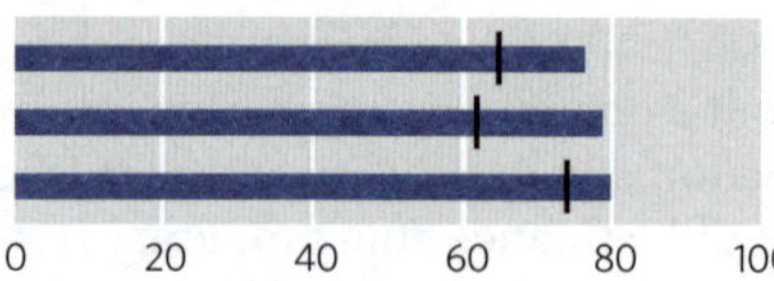

It takes seven procedures and about 10 days on average to incorporate a business, and no minimum capital is required. However, modern bankruptcy procedures are not in place. Labor regulations are relatively flexible, but their application is uneven. Several subsidy programs benefit agricultural products such as bananas and state-owned enterprises such as a coconut-water bottling plant.

OPEN MARKETS

	Score	Rank	1-Year Change
Trade Freedom	67.6	138th	-5.7
Investment Freedom	50.0	109th	0
Financial Freedom	40.0	107th	0

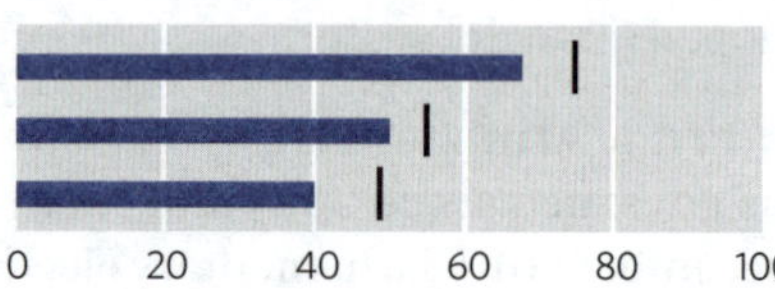

The average tariff rate in Saint Vincent and the Grenadines is 11.2 percent. Non-tariff barriers to trade are relatively low. A license for foreign investment is required if foreign ownership levels will exceed 50 percent. Foreign investment in land is regulated. The developing financial system is dominated by banks. Capital markets are underdeveloped, and local entrepreneurs lack adequate access to a wide variety of financing instruments.

Long-Term Score Change (since 2009)

RULE OF LAW		GOVERNMENT SIZE		REGULATORY EFFICIENCY		OPEN MARKETS	
Property Rights	0	Fiscal Freedom	+8.9	Business Freedom	-1.9	Trade Freedom	-6.0
Freedom from Corruption	+0.1	Government Spending	+11.5	Labor Freedom	+0.2	Investment Freedom	+10.0
				Monetary Freedom	+4.2	Financial Freedom	0

SAMOA

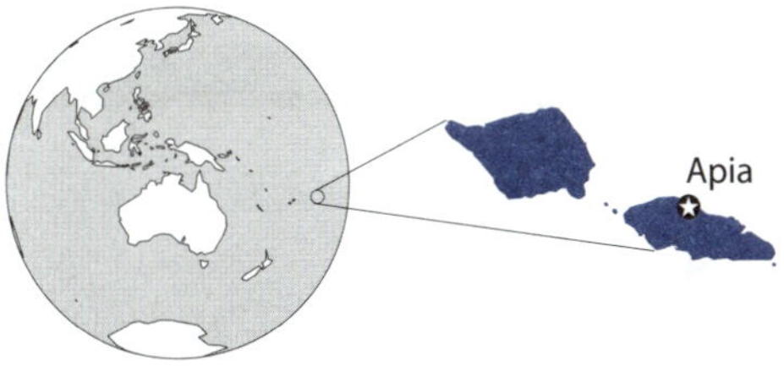

World Rank: 84 **Regional Rank: 14**

Economic Freedom Score

Samoa's economic freedom score is 61.1, making its economy the 84th freest in the 2014 *Index*. Its score is 4 points better this year due to significant improvements in four of the 10 economic freedoms including investment freedom, trade freedom, and the control of government spending. Samoa is ranked 14th out of 42 countries in the Asia–Pacific region, and its overall score is above the world and regional averages.

Samoa was first rated in the 1997 *Index*, and its economic freedom score has advanced since then by over 13 points, with gains in eight of the 10 economic freedoms including fiscal freedom, the control of government spending, and especially trade freedom, which improved by 75 points. Grading of Samoa was suspended from 2002 to 2008, and much of this progress has occurred since 2009 when the *Index* resumed assessing its economic freedom.

Recording its highest economic freedom score ever in the 2014 *Index*, Samoa has regained its "moderately free" status. Nevertheless, it still lags in promoting the effective rule of law. The judicial system remains vulnerable to political interference, and property rights are not strongly protected. Corruption further undermines enforcement of the rule of law.

BACKGROUND: Samoa is a small South Pacific archipelago with a population of less than 200,000. Independent since 1962, it is now a multi-party democracy dominated politically by the Human Rights Protection Party. After the 2011 parliamentary elections, a few politicians were found guilty of bribery, but the HRPP remained in power. The economy is based mostly on fishing, agriculture, and tourism. Remittances from Samoans working abroad account for about 24 percent of national income. A sizable tsunami in 2009 killed over 200 people and significantly damaged infrastructure and property. To facilitate better trade with Australia and New Zealand, Samoa officially moved west of the International Date Line in 2011.

Freedom Trend

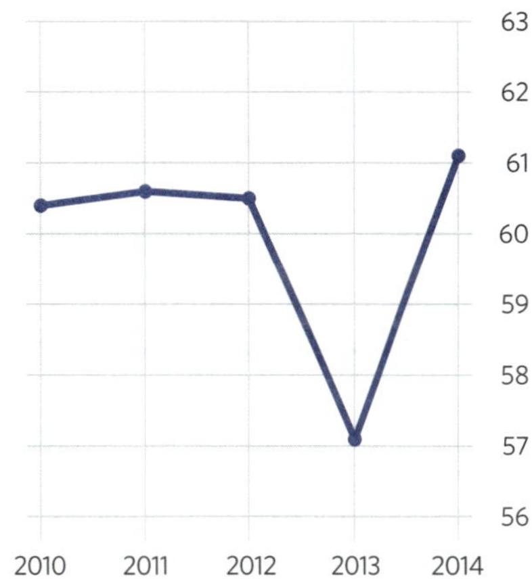

Country Comparisons

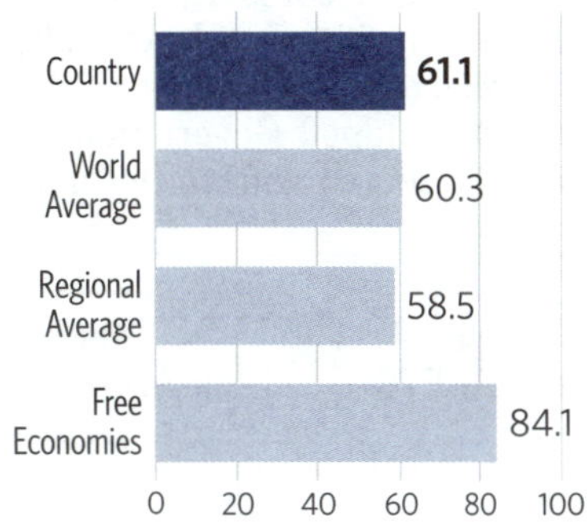

Quick Facts

Population: 0.2 million
GDP (PPP): $1.1 billion
1.2% growth in 2012
5-year compound annual growth 0.5%
$6,149 per capita
Unemployment: n/a
Inflation (CPI): 6.2%
FDI Inflow: $21.5 million
Public Debt: 53.6% of GDP

2012 data unless otherwise noted.
Data compiled as of September 2013.

How Do We Measure Economic Freedom?
See page 471 for an explanation of the methodology or visit the *Index* Web site at *heritage.org/index*.

THE TEN ECONOMIC FREEDOMS

RULE OF LAW

	Score	Rank	1-Year Change
Property Rights	60.0	41st	0
Freedom from Corruption	38.0	71st	-1.0

Official corruption and abuses are a source of increasing public discontent. The English common law–based judiciary is independent and upholds the right to a fair trial. However, a modern and well-functioning legal framework for land ownership and enforcement of property rights is not firmly in place. More than 80 percent of the land is owned by extended families represented by their chiefs.

GOVERNMENT SIZE

	Score	Rank	1-Year Change
Fiscal Freedom	79.9	87th	-0.7
Government Spending	42.2	147th	+7.9

Samoa's top individual income and corporate tax rates are 27 percent. Other taxes include a value-added tax (VAT) and an excise tax. The overall tax burden equals 23.4 percent of the domestic economy. Government expenditures equate to 44 percent of GDP. Public debt in the most recent year amounted to about 54 percent of gross domestic income.

REGULATORY EFFICIENCY

	Score	Rank	1-Year Change
Business Freedom	73.7	59th	+1.3
Labor Freedom	80.3	27th	-0.1
Monetary Freedom	76.1	84th	-2.4

Launching a company takes only four procedures, and no minimum capital is required. The regulatory framework generally supports entrepreneurial activity, but application of the commercial codes is not always straightforward. A well-functioning modern labor market is not fully developed. Government subsidies funded by international donors spiked in the wake of a devastating cyclone in December 2012.

OPEN MARKETS

	Score	Rank	1-Year Change
Trade Freedom	75.8	93rd	+9.8
Investment Freedom	55.0	96th	+25.0
Financial Freedom	30.0	132nd	0

Samoa's average tariff rate was 7.1 percent as of 2006. Some sectors of the economy are reserved for domestic investors, and new foreign investment is screened by the government. Samoa's small and underdeveloped financial sector is dominated by banking. Although bank lending to the private sector has increased rapidly in recent years, a significant portion of the population remains outside the formal banking sector.

Long-Term Score Change (since 1996)

RULE OF LAW		GOVERNMENT SIZE		REGULATORY EFFICIENCY		OPEN MARKETS	
Property Rights	+10.0	Fiscal Freedom	+15.4	Business Freedom	+3.7	Trade Freedom	+75.8
Freedom from Corruption	-32.0	Government Spending	+40.1	Labor Freedom	+0.1	Investment Freedom	+5.0
				Monetary Freedom	+4.0	Financial Freedom	-20.0

SÃO TOMÉ AND PRÍNCIPE

World Rank: **157** Regional Rank: **38**

Economic Freedom Score

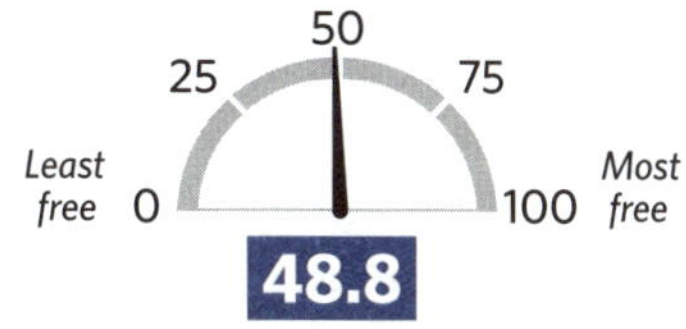

São Tomé and Príncipe's economic freedom score is 48.8, making its economy the 157th freest in the 2014 *Index*. Its score has increased by 0.8 point from last year, with improvements in freedom from corruption, labor freedom, monetary freedom, and trade freedom largely offset by a significant deterioration in the control of government spending. São Tomé and Príncipe is ranked 38th out of 46 countries in the Sub-Saharan Africa region, and its score is below the world and regional averages.

São Tomé and Príncipe's economic freedom was first assessed in the 2009 *Index*, and its score has advanced since then by 5 points. Notable score improvements have occurred in seven of the 10 economic freedoms, with significant gains in trade freedom, fiscal freedom, and investment freedom. These improvements have been partially offset by a decline in property rights.

The island economy has fallen back to the rank of economically "repressed" in recent years. The poor judicial system and lax protection of property rights are damaging prospects for much-needed sustainable economic development and have undermined past years' gains in regulatory efficiency.

BACKGROUND: President Manual Pinto da Costa, who served as president for 15 years following independence from Portugal in 1975, returned to office in 2011. Under São Tomé and Príncipe's democratic constitution, the president shares power with a prime minister who requires the confidence of the parliament to retain power. Prime Minister Gabriel Costa, who took office in 2012, is regarded as a consensus builder who may be able to bring stability to an office that has seen 15 incumbents since 1990. Agriculture, particularly cocoa and coffee, dominates the economy, with cocoa accounting for about 95 percent of exports. The government has been encouraging economic diversification and hopes to exploit the billions of barrels of oil that are thought to lie off the coast.

Freedom Trend

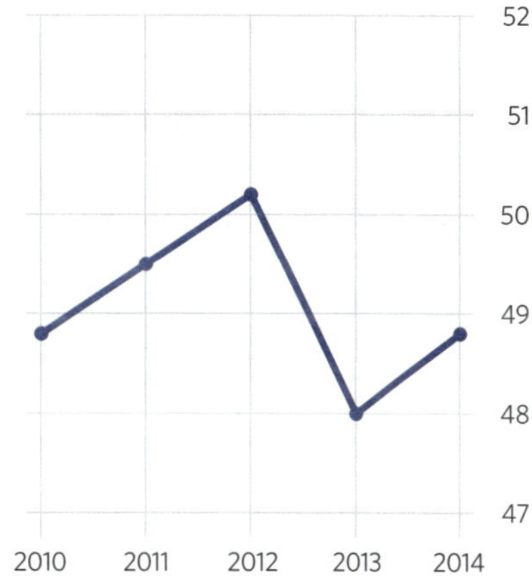

Country Comparisons

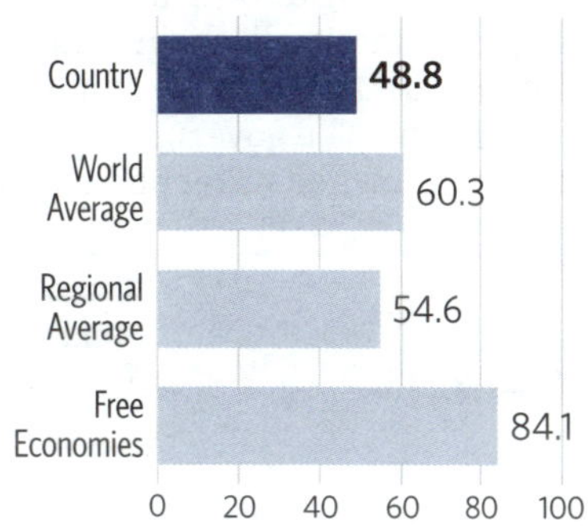

Quick Facts

Population: 0.2 million
GDP (PPP): $0.4 billion
4.0% growth in 2012
5-year compound annual growth 5.3%
$2,337 per capita
Unemployment: 14.2%
Inflation (CPI): 10.6%
FDI Inflow: $49.5 million
Public Debt: 75.5% of GDP

2012 data unless otherwise noted.
Data compiled as of September 2013.

How Do We Measure Economic Freedom?
See page 471 for an explanation of the methodology or visit the *Index* Web site at *heritage.org/index*.

SÃO TOMÉ AND PRÍNCIPE (continued)

THE TEN ECONOMIC FREEDOMS

		Score	Rank	1-Year Change
RULE OF LAW	Property Rights	20.0	139th	0
	Freedom from Corruption	32.5	93rd	+2.5

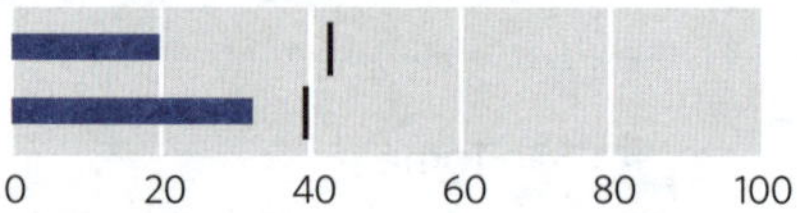

Development aid and potential oil wealth have fueled corruption among the ruling elite. Bribery, embezzlement, and mismanagement of public funds are regarded as endemic. The judiciary is independent but weak, underfunded, understaffed, inefficient, and susceptible to persistent political influence. There is no separate commercial court, and backlogs of civil cases cause long delays. Property rights are not protected effectively.

		Score	Rank	1-Year Change
GOVERNMENT SIZE	Fiscal Freedom	86.9	42nd	0
	Government Spending	27.9	162nd	-17.4

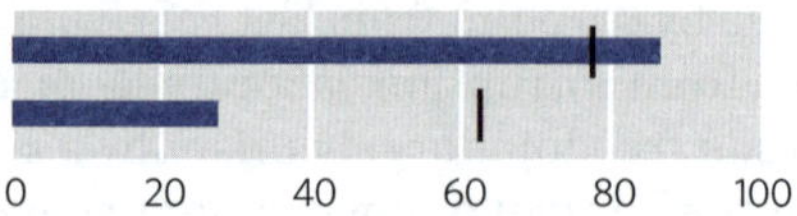

The top individual income tax rate is 20 percent, and the top corporate tax rate is 25 percent. Other taxes include a sales tax and a dividend tax. The overall tax burden equals 16.8 percent of total domestic income. Government spending is equal to about half of the size of the domestic economy. Public debt is equal to 75 percent of GDP. The approval of a Public Debt Management Law may help to establish positive fiscal policies.

		Score	Rank	1-Year Change
REGULATORY EFFICIENCY	Business Freedom	52.6	147th	-0.9
	Labor Freedom	44.7	157th	+6.1
	Monetary Freedom	68.3	151st	+2.3

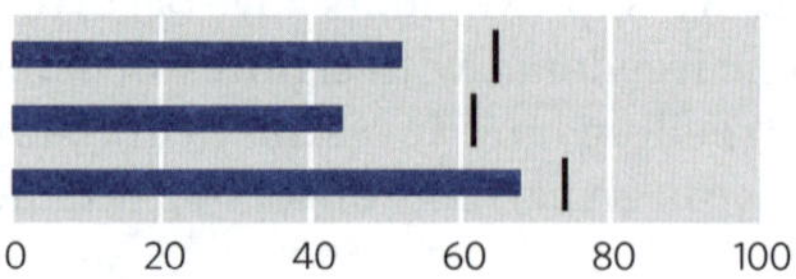

Incorporating a company takes less than a week, and no minimum capital is required. However, completing licensing requirements still costs about four times the level of average annual income. In the absence of a well-functioning labor market, informal labor activity remains significant. The government says it wants to cut fuel and power subsidies and fix problems in the state-owned water and electricity firm, but progress is very slow.

		Score	Rank	1-Year Change
OPEN MARKETS	Trade Freedom	75.3	98th	+15.3
	Investment Freedom	50.0	109th	0
	Financial Freedom	30.0	132nd	0

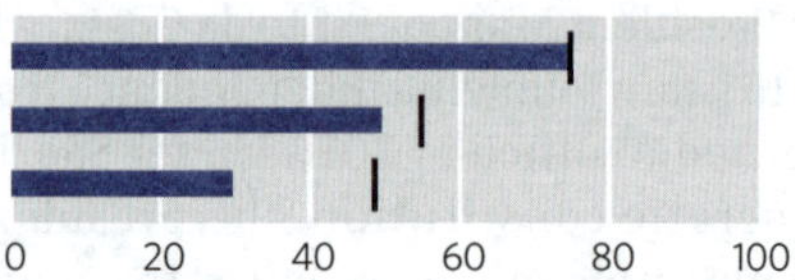

São Tomé and Principe's average tariff rate was 7.4 percent as of 2008. Pork imports are not allowed. Foreign investment is generally treated the same as domestic investment under the law, and most sectors of the economy are open to investment. The underdeveloped financial sector, dominated by banks, does not provide adequate access to banking services for a large portion of the population.

Long-Term Score Change (since 2009)

RULE OF LAW		GOVERNMENT SIZE		REGULATORY EFFICIENCY		OPEN MARKETS	
Property Rights	**-10.0**	Fiscal Freedom	**+11.9**	Business Freedom	**+7.5**	Trade Freedom	**+15.3**
Freedom from Corruption	**+5.5**	Government Spending	**+5.9**	Labor Freedom	**-3.3**	Investment Freedom	**+10.0**
				Monetary Freedom	**+6.9**	Financial Freedom	**0**

SAUDI ARABIA

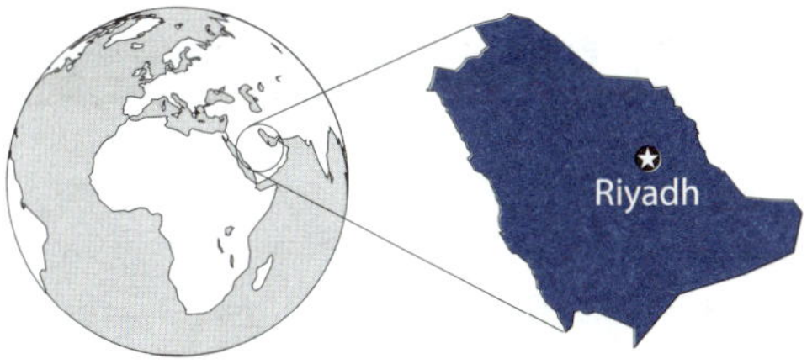

World Rank: **77** Regional Rank: **8**

Economic Freedom Score

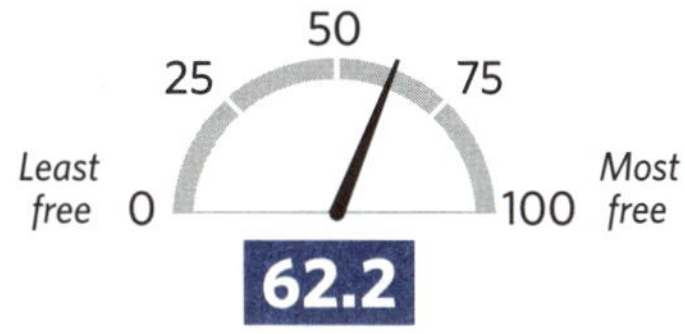

Saudi Arabia's economic freedom score is 62.2, making its economy the 77th freest in the 2014 *Index*. Its score is 1.6 points better than last year, reflecting improvements in the control of government spending, labor freedom, and monetary freedom that outweigh combined score declines in trade freedom and business freedom. Saudi Arabia is ranked 8th out of 15 countries in the Middle East/North Africa region, and its overall score remains above the world average.

Saudi Arabia was first graded in the 1996 *Index*, and its economic freedom score has declined since then by 6.1 points. Rating gains in trade freedom, investment freedom, and the management of government spending have been overwhelmed by substantial double-digit declines in property rights, freedom from corruption, and overall regulatory efficiency.

Reflecting the lack of progress toward greater economic freedom, Saudi Arabia's economy has been rated only "moderately free" throughout the country's 19-year history in the *Index*. The kingdom's overall economic freedom remains constrained by institutional shortcomings. The perceived level of corruption has increased, and the legal system remains susceptible to political influence. Saudi Arabia's property rights score is now lower than the world average.

BACKGROUND: Saudi Arabia is an absolute monarchy ruled by King Abdallah bin Abdul Aziz Al Saud. Pro-reform "Arab Spring" demonstrations in 2011 drew few crowds outside of eastern Saudi Arabia, where the Shia minority population is concentrated. Most of the Sunni majority appeared to be satisfied with increased economic handouts and the king's promise of greater political participation. As a leading oil producer and exporter, Saudi Arabia dominates the Organization of Petroleum Exporting Countries. Oil revenues account for about 90 percent of export earnings and about 80 percent of government revenues. Saudi Arabia joined the World Trade Organization in 2005 as part of an effort to promote foreign investment and economic diversification.

Freedom Trend

Country Comparisons

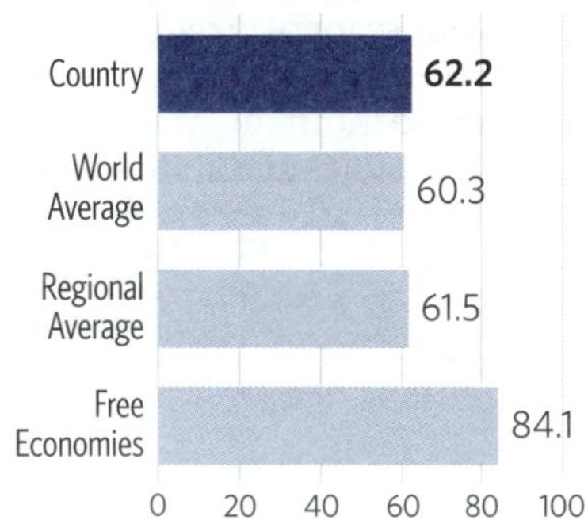

Quick Facts

Population: 29.0 million
GDP (PPP): $906.8 billion
6.8% growth in 2012
5-year compound annual growth 6.6%
$31,275 per capita
Unemployment: 10.6%
Inflation (CPI): 2.9%
FDI Inflow: $12.2 billion
Public Debt: 3.6% of GDP

2012 data unless otherwise noted.
Data compiled as of September 2013.

How Do We Measure Economic Freedom?
See page 471 for an explanation of the methodology or visit the *Index* Web site at *heritage.org/index*.

SAUDI ARABIA (continued)

THE TEN ECONOMIC FREEDOMS

RULE OF LAW

	Score	Rank	1-Year Change
Property Rights	40.0	70th	0
Freedom from Corruption	43.7	59th	-0.3

Corruption remains significant. A 2011 royal decree established an anti-corruption commission to monitor government departments, but administrative obstacles have continued to hinder the commission's success. The slow and non-transparent judiciary is not independent and must coordinate its decisions with the executive branch. Laws protecting private property transactions are subject to Islamic practices.

GOVERNMENT SIZE

	Score	Rank	1-Year Change
Fiscal Freedom	99.7	3rd	+0.1
Government Spending	63.1	108th	+10.9

Saudi nationals and Gulf Cooperation Council citizens are not subject to any income tax, but a 2.5 percent zakat, or religious tax mandated by Islamic law, is levied on all Saudi citizens' net worth. Non-Saudi companies are subject to a 20 percent corporate income tax. The overall tax burden equals 3.7 percent of GDP. Government expenditures make up 35 percent of gross domestic income, and public debt is less than 5 percent of GDP.

REGULATORY EFFICIENCY

	Score	Rank	1-Year Change
Business Freedom	67.3	87th	-0.9
Labor Freedom	75.8	44th	+6.6
Monetary Freedom	68.7	147th	+3.0

Incorporating a business takes nine procedures and about three weeks on average, and no minimum capital is required. Obtaining necessary permits costs about a quarter of the level of average annual income. A new employment quota system enforces "Saudiisation." There is no mandated minimum wage. In 2013, the Minister of Economy admitted that extensive government subsidies and state-owned enterprises distort the economy.

OPEN MARKETS

	Score	Rank	1-Year Change
Trade Freedom	74.0	106th	-3.3
Investment Freedom	40.0	132nd	0
Financial Freedom	50.0	69th	0

Saudi Arabia's average tariff rate is 5.5 percent. Non-tariff barriers affect several categories of imports. The government limits foreign investment in several sectors of the economy. The financial sector has undergone gradual transformation, and some restrictions on foreign investment in financial services have been eased. The government retains majority shares in the largest bank and offers subsidized credit to preferred sectors.

Long-Term Score Change (since 1996)

RULE OF LAW		GOVERNMENT SIZE		REGULATORY EFFICIENCY		OPEN MARKETS	
Property Rights	**-50.0**	Fiscal Freedom	**+0.3**	Business Freedom	**-17.7**	Trade Freedom	**+15.0**
Freedom from Corruption	**-26.3**	Government Spending	**+16.7**	Labor Freedom	**-9.4**	Investment Freedom	**+10.0**
				Monetary Freedom	**-16.1**	Financial Freedom	**0**

SENEGAL

World Rank: **125** Regional Rank: **23**

Economic Freedom Score

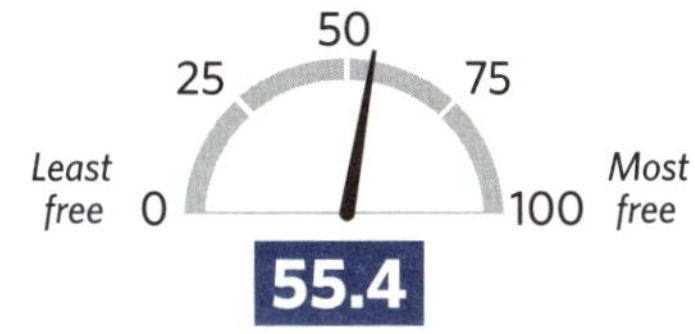

Senegal's economic freedom score is 55.4, making its economy the 125th freest in the 2014 *Index*. Its score is essentially the same as last year, with improvements in monetary freedom, trade freedom, and investment freedom offset by a considerable decline in business freedom. Senegal is ranked 23rd out of 46 countries in the Sub-Saharan Africa region, and its score is below the world average.

Senegal was first graded in the 1996 *Index*, and its economic freedom score has declined since then by over 2.5 points. Ratings have deteriorated in six of the 10 economic freedoms, including property rights, freedom from corruption, the control of government spending, and financial freedom. Most notably, property rights has declined by 30 points. Over its 19-year history in the *Index*, Senegal's economy has been largely rated "mostly unfree."

Corruption, endemic throughout the economy and exacerbated by the weak legal framework, remains a serious drag on long-term economic development. Hindering dynamic engagement in global commerce, the absence of strong commitment to open-market polices continues to undermine the emergence of a more vibrant private sector.

BACKGROUND: Former president Abdoulaye Wade amended Senegal's constitution over a dozen times to augment executive power and weaken the opposition, but his run for a third term ended in his defeat by Macky Sall in a March 2012 runoff election. In September 2012, lawmakers voted to abolish the Senate and the vice presidency to save money for disaster management. Sporadic fighting between the government and separatists continues in the southern Casamance region. Economic reforms have proceeded slowly. Some 75 percent of the workforce is engaged in agriculture or fishing. In 2010, frequent power cuts sparked protests, and in 2012, the government announced plans for construction of a new 250-megawatt power plant. High formal-sector unemployment is a major factor in high rates of Senegalese emigration to Europe.

Freedom Trend

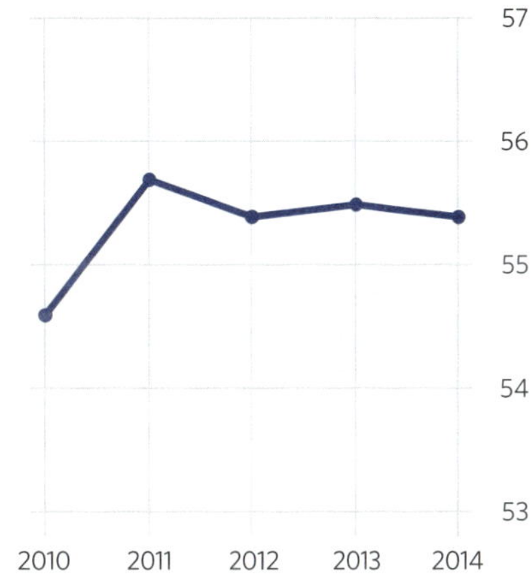

Country Comparisons

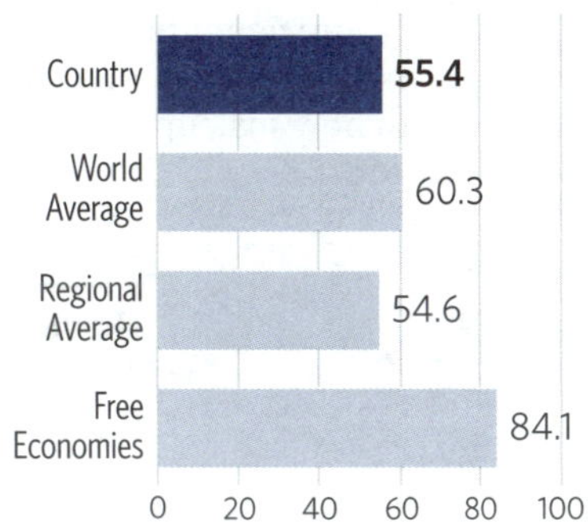

Quick Facts

Population: 13.1 million
GDP (PPP): $26.6 billion
3.5% growth in 2012
5-year compound annual growth 3.3%
$2,027 per capita
Unemployment: n/a
Inflation (CPI): 1.1%
FDI Inflow: $337.7 million
Public Debt: 45.0% of GDP

2012 data unless otherwise noted.
Data compiled as of September 2013.

How Do We Measure Economic Freedom?
See page 471 for an explanation of the methodology or visit the *Index* Web site at *heritage.org/index*.

THE TEN ECONOMIC FREEDOMS

RULE OF LAW

	Score	Rank	1-Year Change
Property Rights	**40.0**	*70th*	0
Freedom from Corruption	**29.5**	*104th*	+0.5

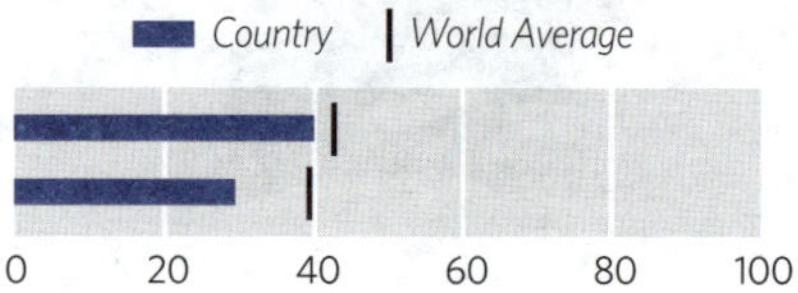

Corruption has long been a serious problem and has provoked growing public outrage. The judiciary is independent by law, but inadequate pay and lack of tenure expose judges to external influences and prevent the courts from providing a proper check on the other branches of government. Commercial courts are inefficient, and rulings can be arbitrary and inconsistent. Property titling procedures are uneven across the country.

GOVERNMENT SIZE

	Score	Rank	1-Year Change
Fiscal Freedom	**65.1**	*155th*	-0.1
Government Spending	**75.4**	*68th*	-0.2

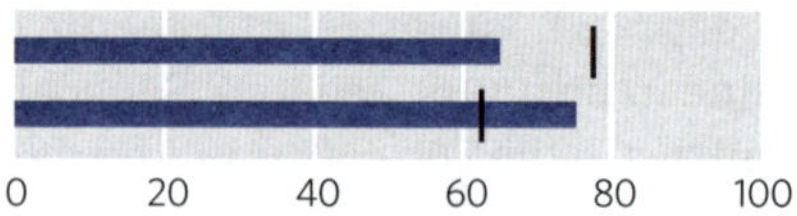

The top individual income tax rate is 50 percent, and the top corporate tax rate is 25 percent. Other taxes include a value-added tax (VAT) and an insurance tax. Overall tax revenue equals 19 percent of the domestic economy. Public expenditures equal 29 percent of gross domestic income. Government debt is equivalent to 47 percent of GDP. The new government has promised to rein in spending after a decade of high deficits.

REGULATORY EFFICIENCY

	Score	Rank	1-Year Change
Business Freedom	**47.5**	*157th*	-9.2
Labor Freedom	**41.5**	*166th*	+0.2
Monetary Freedom	**81.8**	*14th*	+2.2

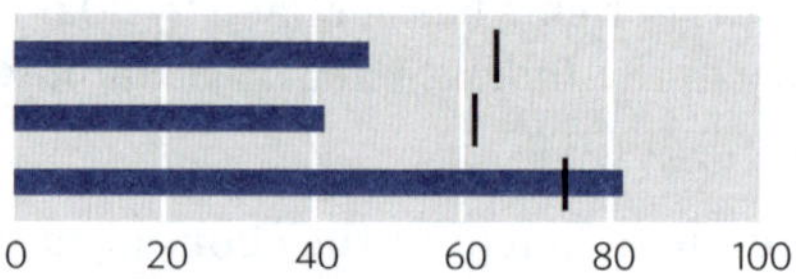

Launching a business takes about twice the level of average annual income, and completing licensing requirements is time-consuming. A formal urban labor market has been slow to emerge. Senegal provides an example of the burden and inertia effects of energy subsidy outlays, which now soak up more funds than are allocated for new capital expenditures on health or education.

OPEN MARKETS

	Score	Rank	1-Year Change
Trade Freedom	**73.2**	*111th*	+1.0
Investment Freedom	**60.0**	*80th*	+5.0
Financial Freedom	**40.0**	*107th*	0

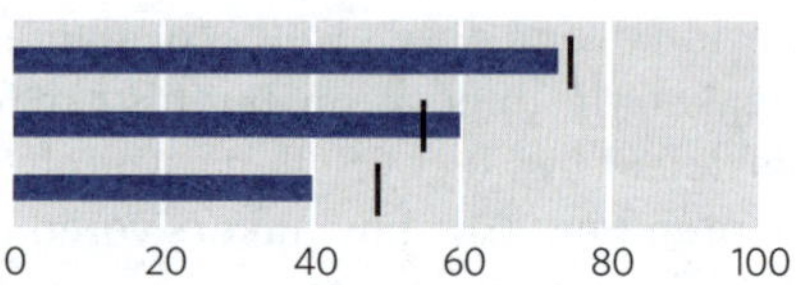

Senegal's average tariff rate is 8.4 percent. Imports of some agricultural products face additional non-tariff barriers. Foreign ownership levels in some sectors of the economy are capped. The underdeveloped financial system is dominated by the banking sector, which is highly concentrated with three banks holding about two-thirds of deposits. In recent years, bank supervision has gradually been strengthened.

Long-Term Score Change (since 1996)

RULE OF LAW		GOVERNMENT SIZE		REGULATORY EFFICIENCY		OPEN MARKETS	
Property Rights	**-30.0**	Fiscal Freedom	**+4.4**	Business Freedom	**-7.5**	Trade Freedom	**+28.2**
Freedom from Corruption	**-20.5**	Government Spending	**-11.6**	Labor Freedom	**-2.3**	Investment Freedom	**+10.0**
				Monetary Freedom	**+26.0**	Financial Freedom	**-10.0**

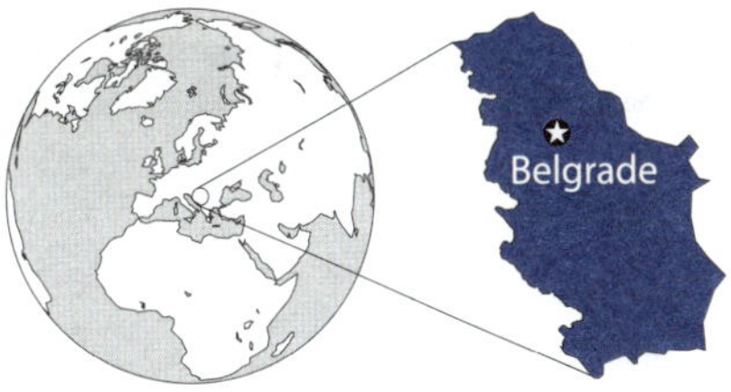

SERBIA

World Rank: **95** Regional Rank: **37**

Economic Freedom Score

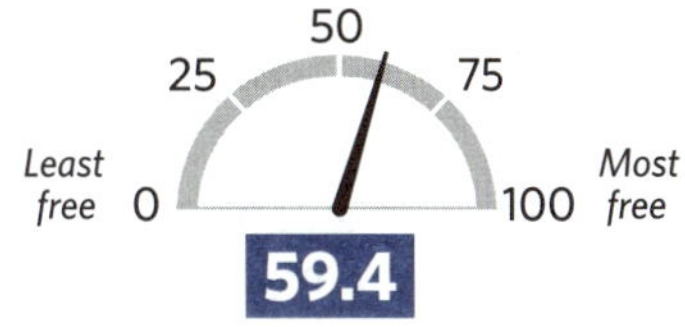

Serbia's economic freedom score is 59.4, making its economy the 95th freest in the 2014 *Index*. Its score is 0.8 point higher than last year, with improvements in investment freedom, monetary freedom, and freedom from corruption balanced by declines in the control of government spending, fiscal freedom, business freedom, and trade freedom. Serbia is ranked 37th out of 43 countries in the Europe region, and its overall score is below the world and regional averages.

Serbia's economic freedom was first graded in the 2009 *Index*, and its score has improved since then by 2.8 points. Four of the 10 economic freedoms, including investment freedom, business freedom, and monetary freedom, have advanced. Most notably, investment freedom has improved by 35 points. These gains, however, have been partially offset by deteriorations in the management of government spending and fiscal freedom.

In the 2014 *Index*, Serbia has achieved its highest economic freedom score ever. Despite significant progress in a few areas, however, it continues to lag in promoting the effective rule of law. Implementation of deeper institutional reform remains critical.

BACKGROUND: Serbia signed a Stability and Association Agreement with the European Union in 2008 and formally applied for membership in 2009. Accession talks were contingent on the arrest of wartime leader Ratko Mladic, who was apprehended in May 2011. In March 2012, Serbia was invited to begin the accession process after agreeing to allow Kosovo to attend West Balkan regional meetings. The center-left Socialist Party of Serbia won the July 2012 parliamentary elections, and Prime Minister Ivica Dačić has pledged to continue working toward Euro–Atlantic integration and membership in the World Trade Organization. Serbia's economy has attracted significant investment in manufacturing and services and has become far more integrated into the international economic system. However, economic growth remains sluggish, and unemployment is a significant problem.

How Do We Measure Economic Freedom?
See page 471 for an explanation of the methodology or visit the *Index* Web site at *heritage.org/index*.

Freedom Trend

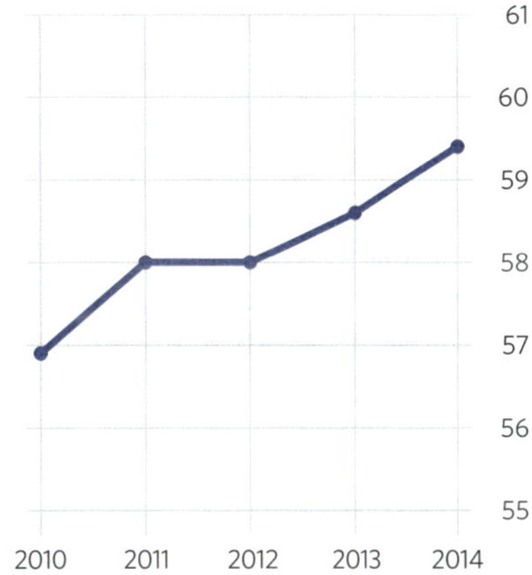

Country Comparisons

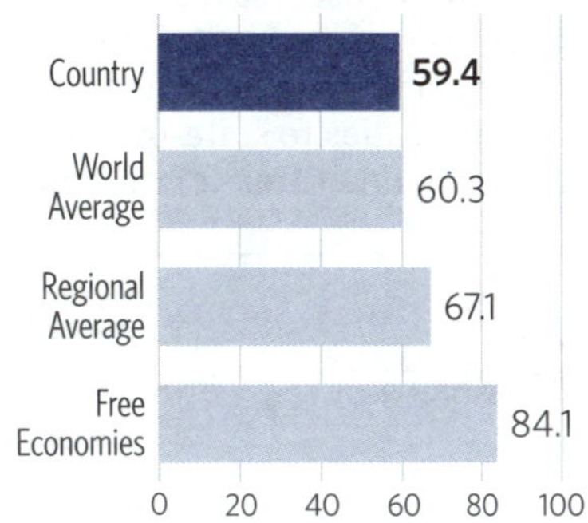

Quick Facts

Population: 7.6 million
GDP (PPP): $78.7 billion
-1.8% growth in 2012
5-year compound annual growth 0.2%
$10,405 per capita
Unemployment: 23.1%
Inflation (CPI): 7.3%
FDI Inflow: $650.4 million
Public Debt: 63.7% of GDP

2012 data unless otherwise noted.
Data compiled as of September 2013.

THE TEN ECONOMIC FREEDOMS

RULE OF LAW

	Score	Rank	1-Year Change
Property Rights	40.0	70th	0
Freedom from Corruption	34.0	79th	+1.0

Corruption remains a serious concern. Graft and misconduct are widespread, especially in public procurement and privatization. The government does not have a track record of investigating and prosecuting corruption, especially in high-profile cases. Although reforms in the legal system have been implemented, including a review of all prosecutorial and judicial positions, independence and accountability need to be improved.

GOVERNMENT SIZE

	Score	Rank	1-Year Change
Fiscal Freedom	83.1	63rd	-1.1
Government Spending	38.6	154th	-1.7

The top individual income and corporate tax rates are 15 percent. (The corporate tax was increased from 10 percent to 15 percent beginning in January 2013.) Other taxes include a value-added tax (VAT) and a property tax. The overall tax burden amounts to 35.2 percent of the domestic economy. Public spending is 45 percent of gross domestic income. Government debt is about 64 percent of GDP.

REGULATORY EFFICIENCY

	Score	Rank	1-Year Change
Business Freedom	59.3	118th	-0.9
Labor Freedom	70.1	64th	-0.3
Monetary Freedom	66.9	158th	+1.6

Starting a business takes six procedures, and no minimum capital is required, but obtaining licenses costs over 14 times the level of average annual income. A fully functioning modern labor market has not developed, and the informal sector remains large. In addition to significant subsidies to state-owned enterprises, the government has funded start-up companies in less developed areas of the country, with little to show for it.

OPEN MARKETS

	Score	Rank	1-Year Change
Trade Freedom	77.0	87th	-0.9
Investment Freedom	75.0	35th	+10.0
Financial Freedom	50.0	69th	0

Serbia's average tariff rate is 6.5 percent. Legal barriers to international trade and investment have been reduced. Foreign and domestic investors are treated equally under the law. Reforms involving privatization and consolidation have revived the banking sector. A wide range of credit instruments is available to the private sector, but the level of financial intermediation is relatively low. Capital markets remain small and underdeveloped.

Long-Term Score Change (since 2009)

RULE OF LAW		GOVERNMENT SIZE		REGULATORY EFFICIENCY		OPEN MARKETS	
Property Rights	0	Fiscal Freedom	**-2.8**	Business Freedom	**+3.3**	Trade Freedom	**-1.0**
Freedom from Corruption	0	Government Spending	**-7.7**	Labor Freedom	**+0.1**	Investment Freedom	**+35.0**
				Monetary Freedom	**+1.1**	Financial Freedom	0

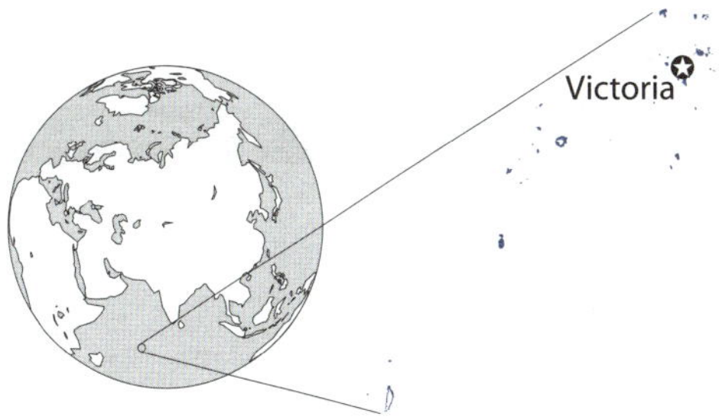

SEYCHELLES

World Rank: **117** Regional Rank: **19**

Economic Freedom Score

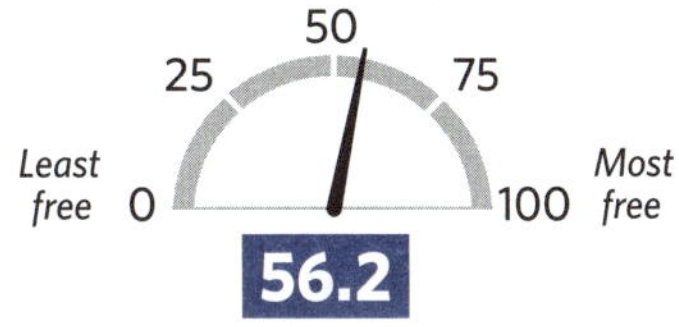

Seychelles' economic freedom score is 56.2, making its economy the 117th freest in the 2014 *Index*. Its score is 1.3 points higher than last year, reflecting notable improvements in four of the 10 economic freedoms including the control of government spending, labor freedom, and investment freedom. Seychelles is ranked 19th among 46 countries in the Sub-Saharan Africa region.

Seychelles' economic freedom was first assessed in the 2009 *Index*, and its score has advanced since then by 8.4 points. Improved scores for six of the 10 economic freedoms, led by notable enhancements in the management of public spending and overall regulatory efficiency, have enabled Seychelles to advance from the status of economically "repressed."

In the 2014 *Index*, Seychelles has achieved its highest economic freedom score ever. In addition to improving overall regulatory efficiency, the government has enhanced the investment regime and cut personal income and corporate tax rates. Implementing deeper institutional reform will be critical to improving competitiveness and ensuring broader-based economic development beyond the tourism sector.

BACKGROUND: The People's Progressive Front has ruled Seychelles since 1977, when France Albert René seized power in a bloodless coup. In 2004, René ceded power to Vice President James Michel. Michel was elected to a third term in May 2011. The economy relies heavily on tourism and fishing, and services account for almost 80 percent of GDP. In early 2013, tropical cyclone Felleng produced torrential rain, flooding, and landslides that destroyed hundreds of houses. Since mid-2008, Seychelles has adhered to an IMF-negotiated economic reform agenda focused on reducing its debt-to-GDP ratio. The country is attempting to implement further reforms, including overhauling the tax system and deregulating the finance and communication sectors. Piracy caused losses of $17 million in 2012, not including lost revenues from fisheries.

Freedom Trend

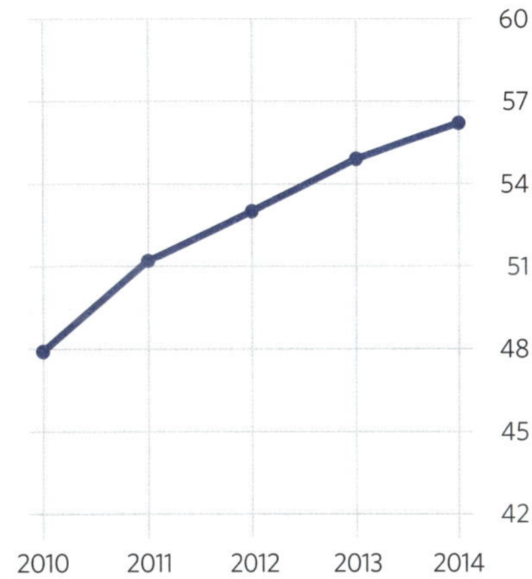

Country Comparisons

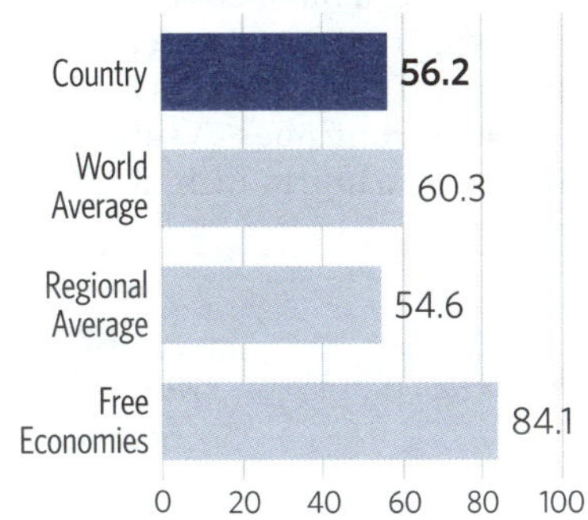

Quick Facts

Population: 0.1 million

GDP (PPP): $2.3 billion

2.8% growth in 2012

5-year compound annual growth 2.2%

$25,229 per capita

Unemployment: 3.7%

Inflation (CPI): 7.1%

FDI Inflow: $114.0 million

Public Debt: 82.5% of GDP

2012 data unless otherwise noted.
Data compiled as of September 2013.

How Do We Measure Economic Freedom?
See page 471 for an explanation of the methodology or visit the *Index* Web site at *heritage.org/index*.

THE TEN ECONOMIC FREEDOMS

		Score	Rank	1-Year Change
RULE OF LAW	Property Rights	50.0	53rd	0
	Freedom from Corruption	48.5	51st	+0.5

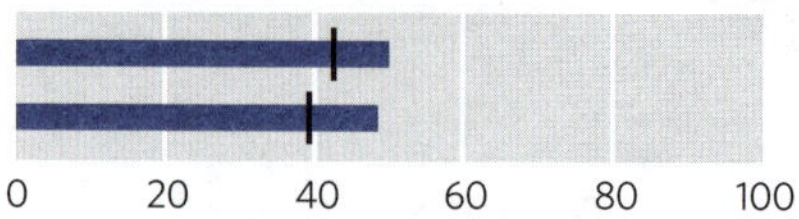

Concerns about government corruption have focused on a lack of transparency in the privatization and allocation of government-owned land. A December 2011 report released by the auditor-general revealed nearly two decades of dysfunction in government finances, including unprofessional bookkeeping, illegal procedures, and embezzlement. Judges generally decide cases fairly but face interference in high-level cases.

		Score	Rank	1-Year Change
GOVERNMENT SIZE	Fiscal Freedom	76.8	111th	-0.8
	Government Spending	61.8	115th	+4.9

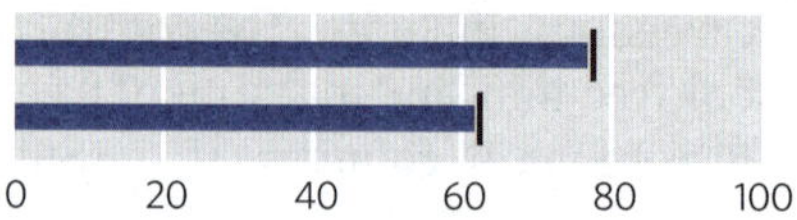

The individual income tax rate is a flat 15 percent, and the top corporate tax rate is 33 percent. Other taxes include a vehicle tax, an interest tax, and (as of January 2013) a new value-added tax (VAT). Overall tax revenue equals 31.7 percent of gross domestic income. Government expenditures amount to 36 percent of GDP. Public debt is equal to over 80 percent of the domestic economy.

		Score	Rank	1-Year Change
REGULATORY EFFICIENCY	Business Freedom	67.6	85th	-1.6
	Labor Freedom	68.5	71st	+5.0
	Monetary Freedom	75.1	104th	-0.5

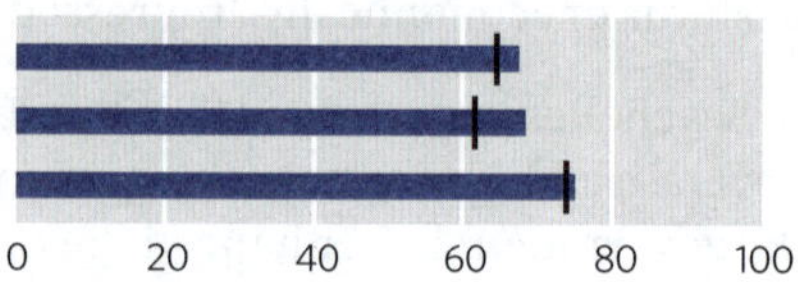

Launching a business takes 10 procedures, but no minimum capital is required. Completing licensing requirements costs less than 25 percent of the level of average annual income, but it takes over three months on average. The formal labor market is not fully developed. The government continues to subsidize the public utility but sold a minority stake in its loss-making national airline to Etihad Airways in 2012.

		Score	Rank	1-Year Change
OPEN MARKETS	Trade Freedom	33.4	179th	0
	Investment Freedom	50.0	109th	+5.0
	Financial Freedom	30.0	132nd	0

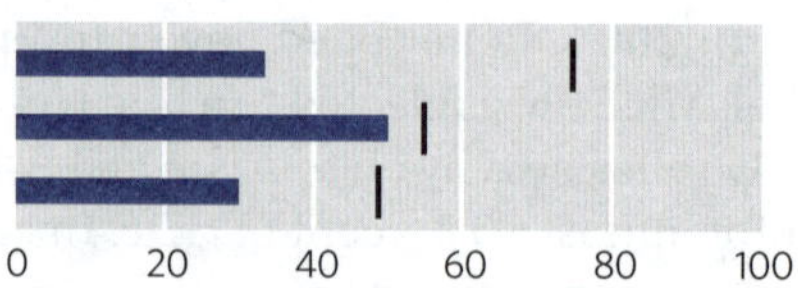

The average tariff rate for Seychelles was 28.3 percent as of 2007. Tariffs are a significant source of government revenue. Foreign investment in some sectors of the economy is controlled by the government. The financial system remains rudimentary. The banking sector consists of both state-owned and foreign financial institutions. A large part of the population lacks access to formal banking services.

Long-Term Score Change (since 2009)

RULE OF LAW		GOVERNMENT SIZE		REGULATORY EFFICIENCY		OPEN MARKETS	
Property Rights	0	Fiscal Freedom	+3.1	Business Freedom	+2.1	Trade Freedom	+5.0
Freedom from Corruption	+3.5	Government Spending	+61.8	Labor Freedom	+11.4	Investment Freedom	0
				Monetary Freedom	-3.0	Financial Freedom	0

SIERRA LEONE

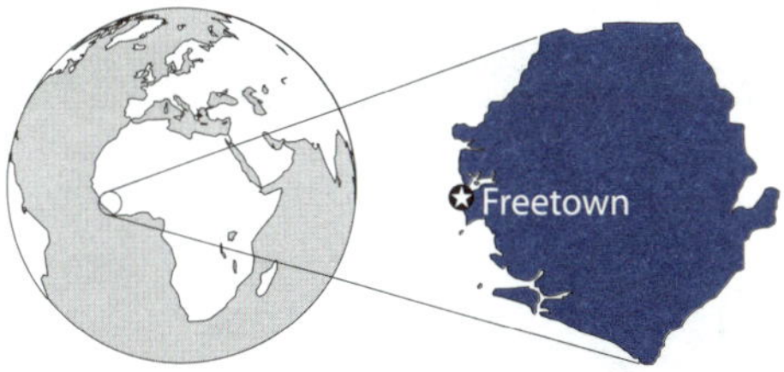

World Rank: **148** Regional Rank: **34**

Economic Freedom Score

Sierra Leone's economic freedom score is 50.5, making its economy the 148th freest in the 2014 *Index*. Its score is 2.2 points higher than last year, with substantial increases in half of the 10 economic freedoms including the control of government spending, property rights, business freedom, and labor freedom. Sierra Leone is ranked 34th out of 46 countries in the Sub-Saharan Africa region, and its overall score is below the world average.

Over the 20-year history of the *Index*, Sierra Leone's economic freedom score has improved by 0.7 point. Improvements in half of the 10 economic freedoms include double digit growth in trade freedom, fiscal freedom, and freedom from corruption. Grading of Sierra Leone was suspended from 2001 to 2002 due to internal conflicts.

Achieving its highest economic freedom score ever in the 2014 *Index*, Sierra Leone has advanced from economically "repressed" for the second time. Reforms have been targeted at improving regulatory efficiency and strengthening the enforcement of contracts. However, weak protection of property rights and pervasive corruption still jeopardize the emergence of a sustainable private sector.

BACKGROUND: Opposition candidate Ernest Bai Koroma was elected president in 2007 in Sierra Leone's first peaceful transition of power since independence in 1961. He was re-elected in 2012. Recovery since the end of the 10-year civil war in 2002 has been fragile, and the military is increasingly involved in state affairs in the name of stability. The U.N. still maintains a peace-building office in the country. Infrastructure remains poor, and corruption is pervasive. Mining is the primary industry and accounts for almost one-quarter of GDP. Mineral exports are the principal foreign exchange earner, with gem-quality diamonds accounting for nearly half of exports. Several offshore oil discoveries were announced in 2009 and 2010, and initial development of these reserves spurred 20 percent GDP growth in 2012.

Freedom Trend

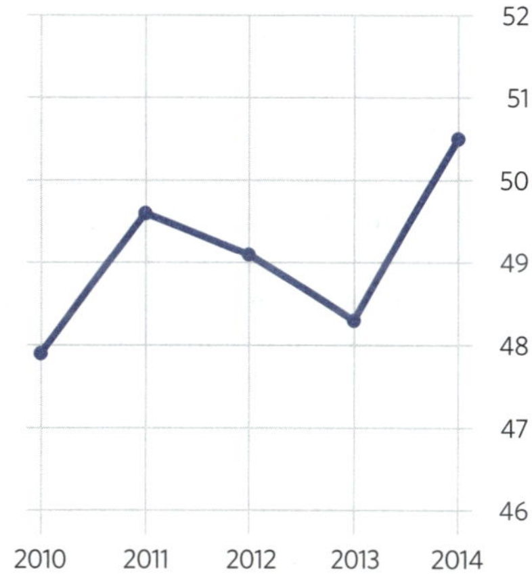

Country Comparisons

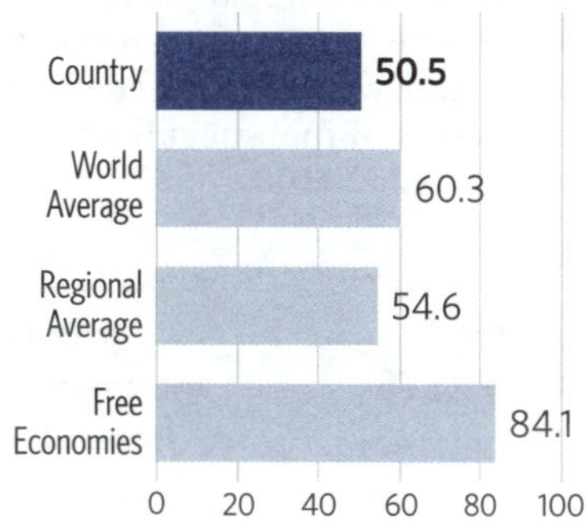

Quick Facts

Population: 6.2 million
GDP (PPP): $8.3 billion
19.8% growth in 2012
5-year compound annual growth 7.8%
$1,344 per capita
Unemployment: n/a
Inflation (CPI): 13.8%
FDI Inflow: $740.1 million
Public Debt: 44.5% of GDP

2012 data unless otherwise noted.
Data compiled as of September 2013.

How Do We Measure Economic Freedom?
See page 471 for an explanation of the methodology or visit the *Index* Web site at *heritage.org/index*.

THE TEN ECONOMIC FREEDOMS

Score ■ Country | World Average

RULE OF LAW

	Score	Rank	1-Year Change
Property Rights	15.0	159th	+5.0
Freedom from Corruption	24.6	132nd	-0.4

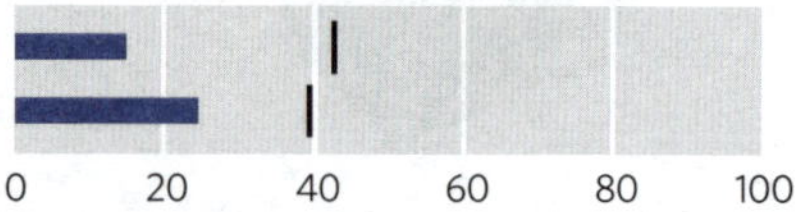

Corruption remains a serious problem, and President Koroma has encouraged and supported the work of the Anti-Corruption Commission. The rule of law is fragile and uneven across the country. In the absence of an effectively functioning legal framework, property rights and contracts are not secure. There is no land titling system, and judicial corruption is significant. Traditional tribal justice systems are still used in rural areas.

GOVERNMENT SIZE

	Score	Rank	1-Year Change
Fiscal Freedom	80.7	75th	0
Government Spending	85.7	31st	+9.8

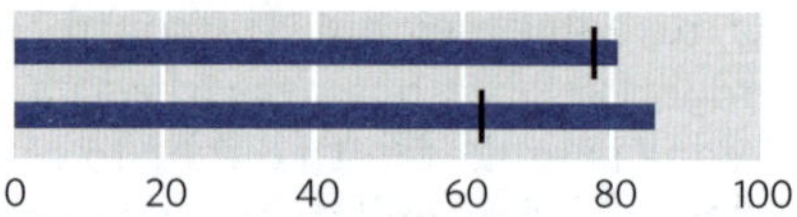

The top individual income and corporate tax rates are 30 percent. Other taxes include a goods and services tax (GST) and an interest tax. Total tax revenue makes up about 11.5 percent of the domestic economy. Government spending equals 22 percent of gross domestic income. Public debt has fallen below 45 percent of GDP. Revenues are projected to get a boost as the economy moves toward resource extraction.

REGULATORY EFFICIENCY

	Score	Rank	1-Year Change
Business Freedom	55.3	137th	+3.8
Labor Freedom	28.7	180th	+2.4
Monetary Freedom	70.2	139th	+1.7

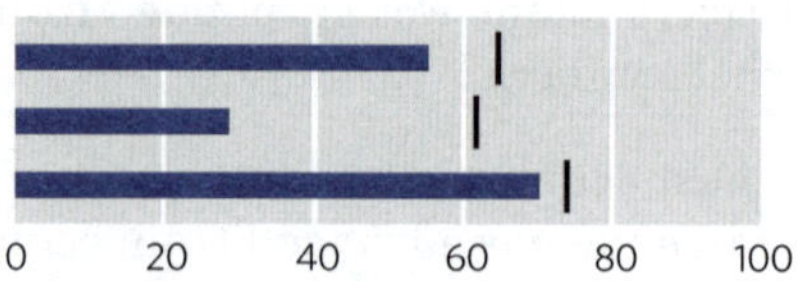

Launching a company takes fewer than 10 procedures, but licensing requirements continue to be time-consuming and costly. Making additional hiring burdensome, an increase in the minimum wage has exceeded labor productivity growth in the formal sector. A plan for gradual reduction of fuel subsidies was suspended in 2012 in advance of elections but was due to be reinstated in 2013.

OPEN MARKETS

	Score	Rank	1-Year Change
Trade Freedom	70.2	127th	0
Investment Freedom	55.0	96th	0
Financial Freedom	20.0	163rd	0

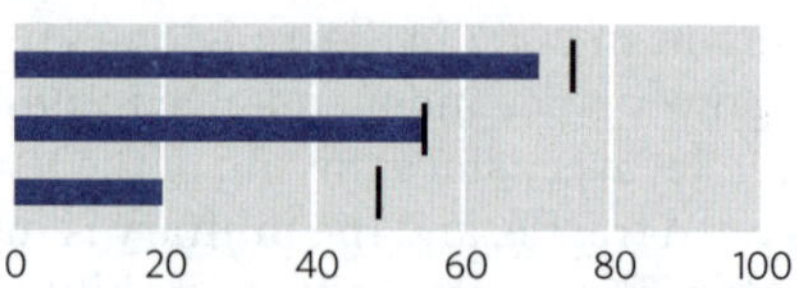

Sierra Leone's average tariff rate is 9.9 percent. Tariffs account for over 20 percent of government revenue. The country's "Agenda for Prosperity" recognizes the benefits of foreign investment in reducing poverty, but Sierra Leone remains a challenging environment for investors. The state controls the majority of bank assets, and much of the population operates outside of the formal banking sector.

Long-Term Score Change (since 1995)

RULE OF LAW		GOVERNMENT SIZE		REGULATORY EFFICIENCY		OPEN MARKETS	
Property Rights	**-35.0**	Fiscal Freedom	**+29.0**	Business Freedom	**-14.7**	Trade Freedom	**+25.2**
Freedom from Corruption	**+14.6**	Government Spending	**-5.9**	Labor Freedom	**-3.9**	Investment Freedom	**+5.0**
				Monetary Freedom	**+20.3**	Financial Freedom	**-10.0**

SINGAPORE

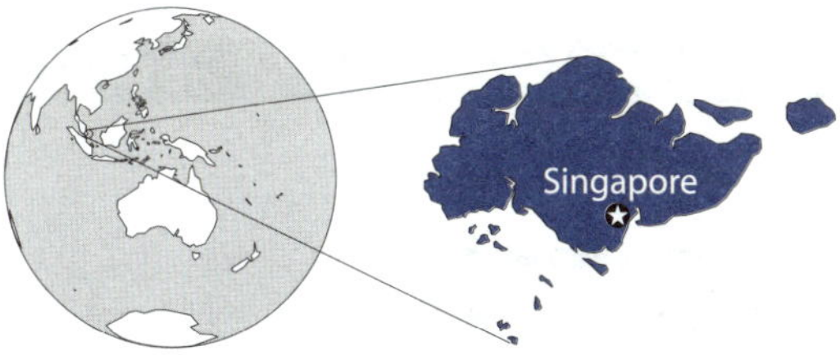

World Rank: **2** Regional Rank: **2**

Economic Freedom Score

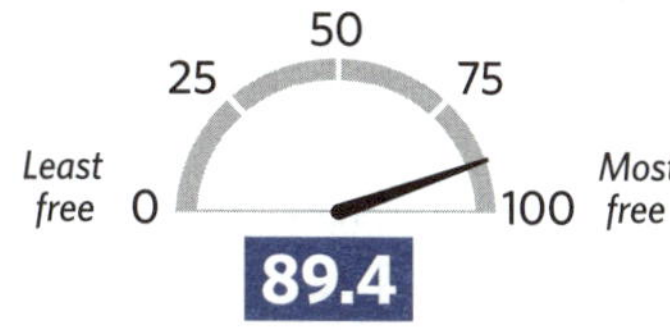

Singapore's economic freedom score is 89.4, making its economy the 2nd freest in the 2014 *Index*. Its score is 1.4 points better than last year, reflecting improvements in investment freedom and labor freedom that outweigh small declines in monetary freedom and business freedom. Singapore is ranked 2nd out of 42 countries in the Asia–Pacific region.

Over the 20-year history of the *Index*, Singapore's economic freedom has advanced by nearly 3 points. The areas of market openness and limited government have advanced by double digits. High levels of trade freedom and regulatory efficiency continue to underpin Singapore's competitiveness in global commerce and ensure resilient economic growth. Recording four consecutive years of score improvements since 2010, Singapore has achieved its highest economic freedom score ever in the 2014 *Index*.

A strong tradition of minimum tolerance for corruption is institutionalized in an efficient judicial framework, sustaining the rule of law in the dynamic economy. Openness to global investment has facilitated the emergence of a more competitive financial sector and continues to ensure economic growth and development. However, state ownership or involvement in key sectors remains considerable, hampering achievement of Singapore's full economic potential.

BACKGROUND: Singapore is a nominally democratic state that has been ruled by the People's Action Party (PAP) since independence in 1965. The PAP won 81 out of 87 seats in the May 2011 elections, although its percentage of the vote (just over 60 percent) was its lowest in history. The opposition won another seat in 2013 during a special election. Certain civil liberties, such as freedom of assembly and freedom of speech, remain restricted, but the PAP has embraced economic liberalization and international trade. Singapore is one of the world's most prosperous nations. Its economy is dominated by services, but the country is also a major manufacturer of electronics and chemicals.

How Do We Measure Economic Freedom?
See page 471 for an explanation of the methodology or visit the *Index* Web site at *heritage.org/index*.

Freedom Trend

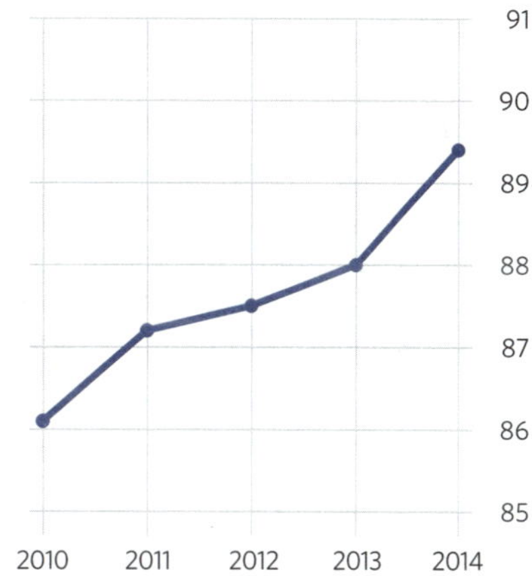

Country Comparisons

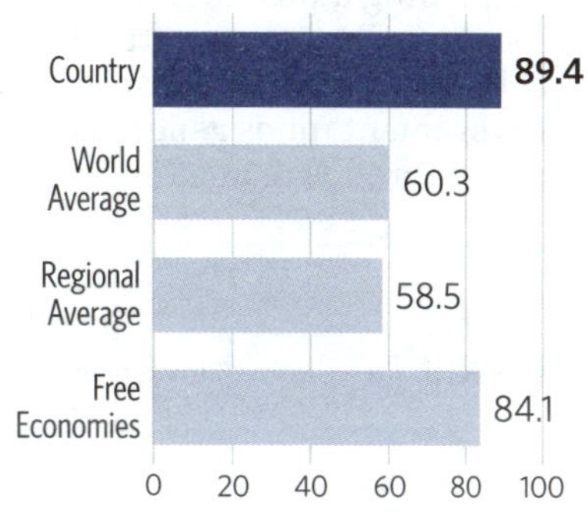

Quick Facts

Population: 5.4 million
GDP (PPP): $326.5 billion
1.3% growth in 2012
5-year compound annual growth 4.3%
$60,410 per capita
Unemployment: 2.0%
Inflation (CPI): 4.6%
FDI Inflow: $56.7 billion
Public Debt: 111.0% of GDP

2012 data unless otherwise noted.
Data compiled as of September 2013.

THE TEN ECONOMIC FREEDOMS

Legend: Country | World Average

RULE OF LAW

	Score	Rank	1-Year Change
Property Rights	90.0	2nd	0
Freedom from Corruption	91.9	5th	-0.1

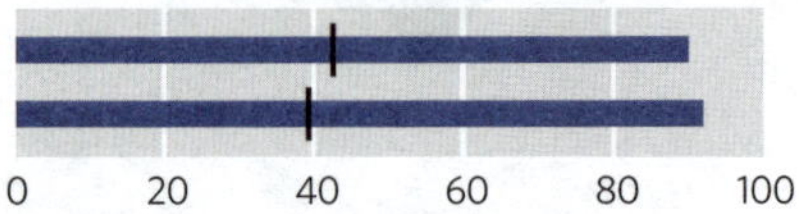

Singapore has traditionally been lauded for its lack of corruption, though transparency remains a concern. The government's overwhelming success in court cases raises concerns about judicial independence. Lawsuits against opposition politicians and parties can bankrupt them. Contracts are secure, there is no expropriation, and commercial courts function well. Singapore has one of Asia's best intellectual property rights regimes.

GOVERNMENT SIZE

	Score	Rank	1-Year Change
Fiscal Freedom	91.2	28th	+0.1
Government Spending	91.2	9th	-0.1

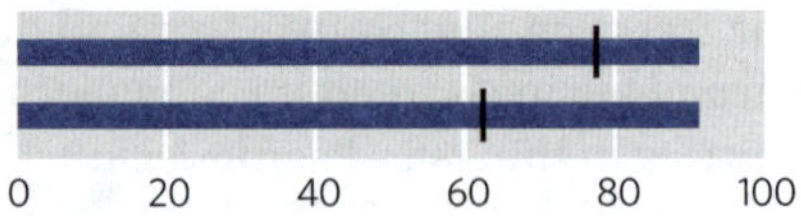

Singapore's top individual income tax rate is 20 percent, and its top corporate tax rate is 17 percent. Other taxes include a value-added tax (VAT) and a property tax. Overall tax revenues make up 13.8 percent of the total domestic economy. Government expenditures amount to 17 percent of GDP. Changes in some property and excise taxes appear to have targeted the wealthy.

REGULATORY EFFICIENCY

	Score	Rank	1-Year Change
Business Freedom	96.8	3rd	-0.3
Labor Freedom	96.5	2nd	+5.1
Monetary Freedom	81.5	17th	-0.5

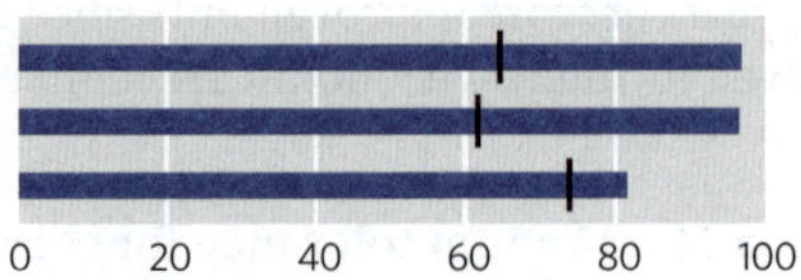

Launching a business takes three days and three procedures, and no minimum capital is required. There is no statutory minimum wage, but wage adjustments are guided by the National Wage Council. Inflation is under control despite the challenging external environment. The government funds generous housing and health care subsidy programs and influences other prices through regulation and state-linked enterprises.

OPEN MARKETS

	Score	Rank	1-Year Change
Trade Freedom	90.0	1st	0
Investment Freedom	85.0	13th	+10.0
Financial Freedom	80.0	4th	0

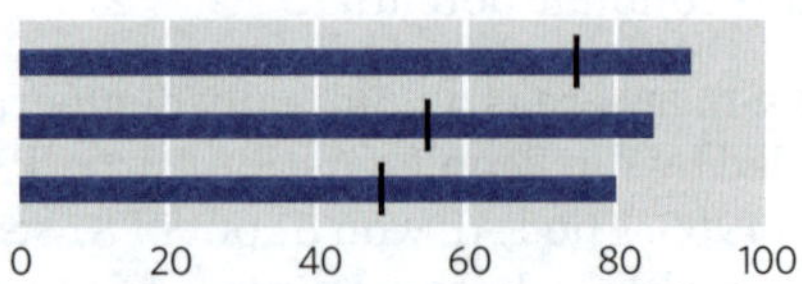

Singapore's average tariff rate is 0 percent, and there are few non-tariff barriers. Foreign investment in several economic sectors is restricted by the government. As a leading global financial center, the highly competitive financial sector offers a wide range of financing options. The government has been opening the domestic market to foreign banks; over 115 of 122 commercial banks are now foreign.

Long-Term Score Change (since 1995)

RULE OF LAW		GOVERNMENT SIZE		REGULATORY EFFICIENCY		OPEN MARKETS	
Property Rights	0	Fiscal Freedom	+10.5	Business Freedom	-3.2	Trade Freedom	+7.0
Freedom from Corruption	+1.9	Government Spending	+3.1	Labor Freedom	-1.7	Investment Freedom	-5.0
				Monetary Freedom	-3.8	Financial Freedom	+10.0

SLOVAKIA

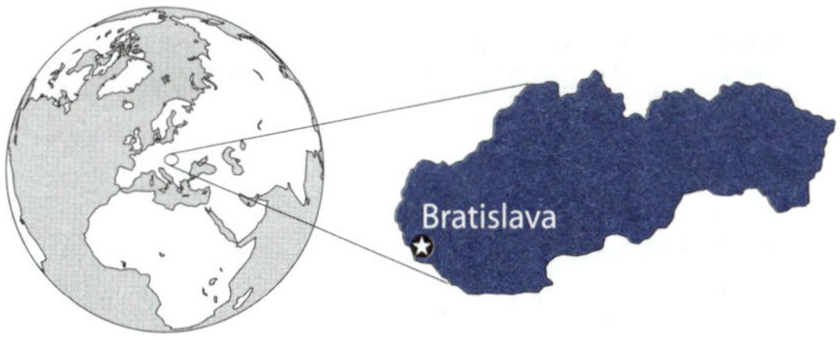

World Rank: **57** Regional Rank: **26**

Economic Freedom Score

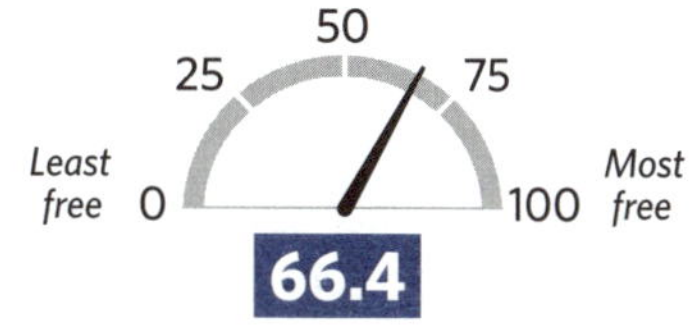

Slovakia's economic freedom score is 66.4, making its economy the 57th freest in the 2014 *Index*. Its score has decreased by 2.3 points from last year, reflecting considerable declines in labor freedom, fiscal freedom, and business freedom that outweigh improvements in trade freedom, freedom from corruption, and investment freedom. Slovakia is ranked 26th out of 43 countries in the Europe region, and its overall score is higher than the world average.

Over the 20-year history of the *Index*, Slovakia's economic freedom score has advanced by 6 points. Six of the 10 economic freedoms, including the trade freedom, investment freedom, and financial freedom categories that account for market openness, have advanced by 10 points or more. Overall improvement, however, has been undermined by deteriorations in the rule of law and regulatory efficiency. Slovakia's economy has generally been rated "moderately free" since 2004.

Deeper systemic reforms to strengthen the legal framework are critically needed to ensure Slovakia's progress toward greater economic freedom. Although the regulatory environment is generally consistent with a market economy, corruption and red tape slow entrepreneurial dynamism. Regaining fiscal discipline in light of recent large fiscal deficits is another significant challenge.

BACKGROUND: After independence in 1993, market reforms made Slovakia one of Europe's most attractive destinations for capital. Initially, however, the pace of reform slowed significantly due to poor monetary policies and cronyism under former Prime Minister Vladimír Mečiar (1993–1998). Slovakia joined the European Union and NATO in 2004 and adopted the euro as its currency in 2009. After a political corruption scandal in late 2011, the center-left Social Democrats won 44 percent of the vote in the March 2012 parliamentary elections. Former Prime Minister Robert Fico returned to office in April 2012. Strong automotive and agricultural sectors have enabled moderate economic growth despite the slowdown in many other EU member states.

Freedom Trend

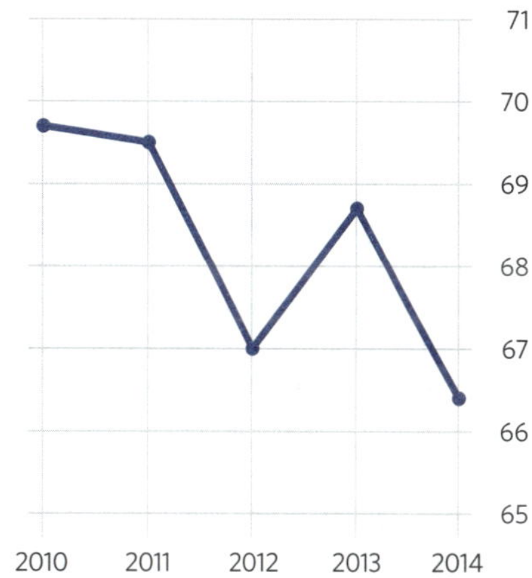

Country Comparisons

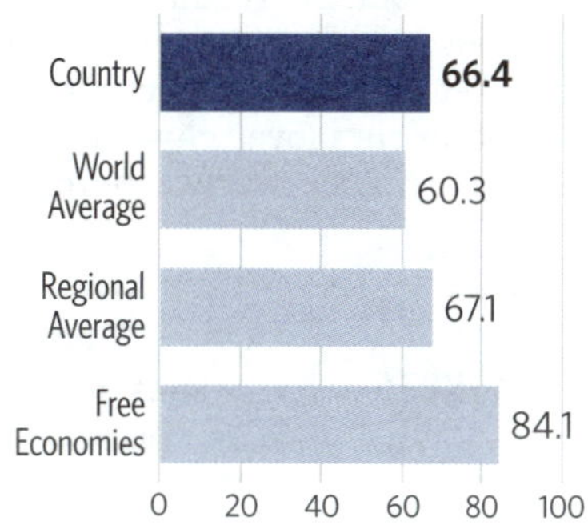

Quick Facts

Population: 5.4 million
GDP (PPP): $131.9 billion
2.0% growth in 2012
5-year compound annual growth 2.0%
$24,249 per capita
Unemployment: 14.0%
Inflation (CPI): 3.7%
FDI Inflow: $2.8 billion
Public Debt: 52.3% of GDP

2012 data unless otherwise noted.
Data compiled as of September 2013.

How Do We Measure Economic Freedom?
See page 471 for an explanation of the methodology or visit the *Index* Web site at *heritage.org/index*.

THE TEN ECONOMIC FREEDOMS

RULE OF LAW

	Score	Rank	1-Year Change
Property Rights	50.0	53rd	0
Freedom from Corruption	41.8	63rd	+1.8

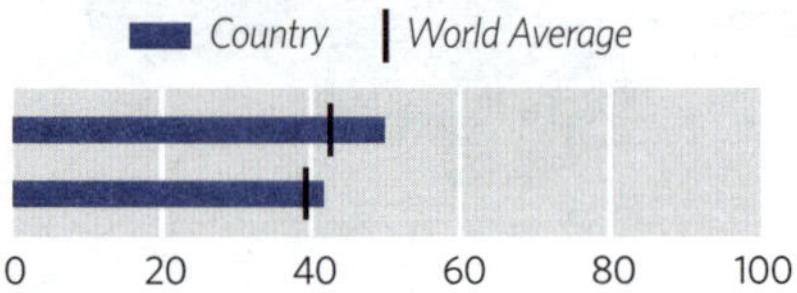

Corruption is significant, particularly in public procurement and the health care sector. Many state-owned companies do not publish even basic information. The constitution provides for an independent judiciary, but the court system, despite some reforms, continues to suffer from corruption, intimidation of judges, and a significant backlog of cases. Secured interests in property and contractual rights are recognized and enforced.

GOVERNMENT SIZE

	Score	Rank	1-Year Change
Fiscal Freedom	80.2	85th	-4.5
Government Spending	56.0	124th	-2.0

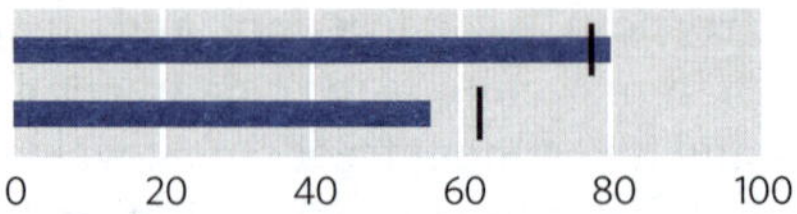

The top individual income tax rate has risen to 25 percent, and the top corporate tax rate has risen to 23 percent. Other taxes include a value-added tax (VAT) and a property tax. The overall tax burden amounts to 28.8 percent of gross domestic income. Government spending is 38.3 percent of GDP. Public debt has reached half of the size of the domestic economy. The eurozone crisis continues to affect the country's finances.

REGULATORY EFFICIENCY

	Score	Rank	1-Year Change
Business Freedom	67.0	88th	-4.0
Labor Freedom	53.6	122nd	-18.6
Monetary Freedom	78.1	63rd	-1.0

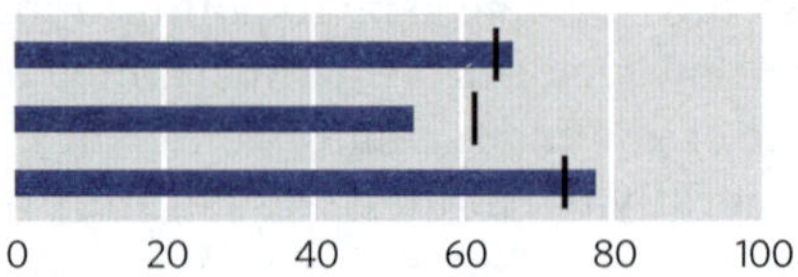

The competitive regulatory framework strongly supports commercial activity, but the pace of improvements in regulatory efficiency has slowed in comparison to other economies. The labor market lacks flexibility, contributing to an unemployment rate of over 10 percent. Although the government moved closer to heavily subsidized "single payer" health care in 2013, it also took steps to reduce overly generous renewable-energy subsidies.

OPEN MARKETS

	Score	Rank	1-Year Change
Trade Freedom	87.8	11th	+1.0
Investment Freedom	80.0	23rd	+5.0
Financial Freedom	70.0	19th	0

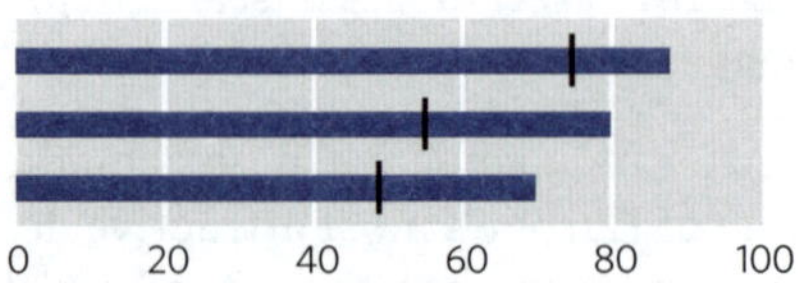

EU members have a low 1.1 percent average tariff rate and, in general, few non-tariff barriers to trade. Slovakia's legal and regulatory systems can be a challenge for foreign investors to navigate. The financial system is still dominated by the banking sector but has become increasingly diversified as insurance and securities companies have grown. Capital markets remain relatively small and continue to evolve.

Long-Term Score Change (since 1995)

RULE OF LAW		GOVERNMENT SIZE		REGULATORY EFFICIENCY		OPEN MARKETS	
Property Rights	-20.0	Fiscal Freedom	+22.5	Business Freedom	-18.0	Trade Freedom	+12.8
Freedom from Corruption	-8.2	Government Spending	+33.7	Labor Freedom	-22.1	Investment Freedom	+10.0
				Monetary Freedom	+14.7	Financial Freedom	+20.0

SLOVENIA

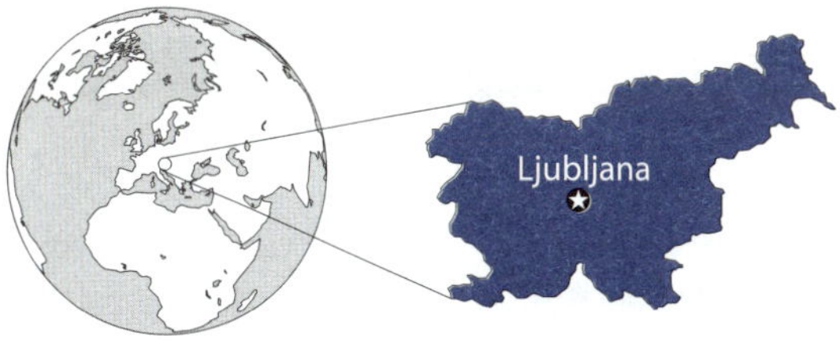

World Rank: **74** Regional Rank: **34**

Economic Freedom Score

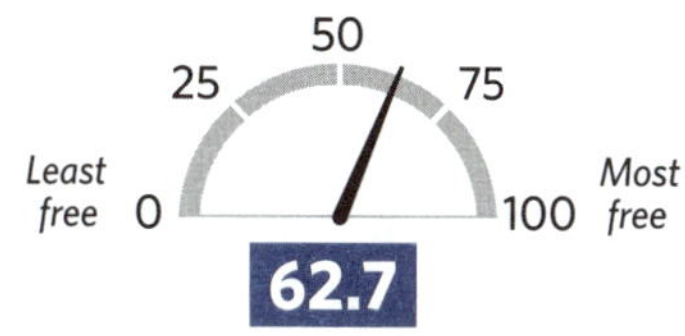

Slovenia's economic freedom score is 62.7, making its economy the 74th freest in the 2014 *Index*. Its score has increased by 1.0 point since last year, with substantial improvements in labor freedom, business freedom, and freedom from corruption outweighing declines in fiscal freedom and monetary freedom. Slovenia is ranked 34th out of 43 countries in the Europe region, and its overall score is above the world average.

Slovenia was first graded in the 1996 *Index*, and its economic freedom score has advanced since then by 12.3 points, the best improvement among advanced economies. The overall increase has been broad-based in seven of the 10 economic freedoms, including investment freedom, trade freedom, property rights, and freedom from corruption, all of which have improved by about 30 points or more. These substantial gains, however, have been partially offset by deteriorations in the management of public finance and financial freedom.

Despite several setbacks over its 19-year history in the *Index*, Slovenia's economy has been largely rated "moderately free." Further growth in economic freedom in Slovenia calls for strengthened management of public finance as well as implementation of deeper institutional reform to advance the rule of law. The judicial system remains inefficient and vulnerable to political interference, and corruption remains a cause for concern.

BACKGROUND: In March 2013, Prime Minister Alenka Bratušek formed a new center-left coalition government consisting of her Positive Slovenia Party and the Social Democrats, Civic List, and Democratic Party of Pensioners of Slovenia. Bratušek seeks to sell state-owned companies and restructure banks. Her government has opted to raise taxes rather than cut spending. Slovenia joined the European Union and NATO in 2004, adopted the euro in 2007, and joined the Organisation for Economic Co-operation and Development in 2010. Considered the gateway to the Balkans, Slovenia has excellent infrastructure and an educated workforce.

Freedom Trend

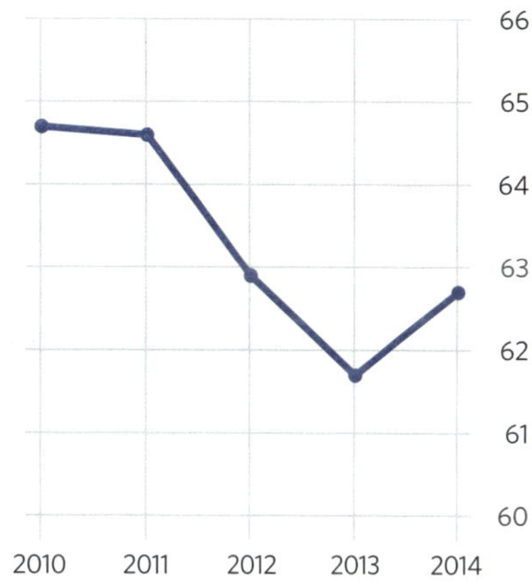

Country Comparisons

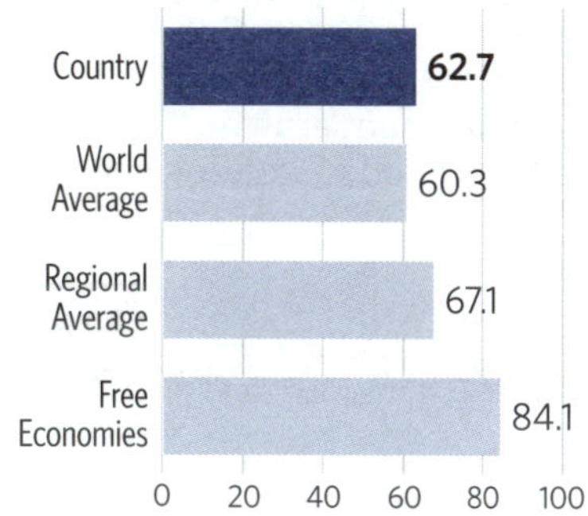

Quick Facts

Population: 2.1 million
GDP (PPP): $58.0 billion
-2.3% growth in 2012
5-year compound annual growth -1.1%
$28,195 per capita
Unemployment: 9.0%
Inflation (CPI): 2.6%
FDI Inflow: $144.8 million
Public Debt: 52.6% of GDP

2012 data unless otherwise noted.
Data compiled as of September 2013.

How Do We Measure Economic Freedom?
See page 471 for an explanation of the methodology or visit the *Index* Web site at *heritage.org/index.*

THE TEN ECONOMIC FREEDOMS

RULE OF LAW

	Score	Rank	1-Year Change
Property Rights	60.0	41st	0
Freedom from Corruption	61.0	35th	+2.0

Corruption, while less extensive than in some other Central European countries, remains a problem in Slovenia, usually taking the form of conflicts of interest and contracting links between government officials and private businesses. The judicial framework remains vulnerable to political interference. Private property rights are constitutionally guaranteed, but the courts are inadequately staffed and slow.

GOVERNMENT SIZE

	Score	Rank	1-Year Change
Fiscal Freedom	58.9	170th	-6.8
Government Spending	22.6	169th	+0.3

The top individual income tax rate has risen to 50 percent, and the top corporate tax rate has fallen to 16 percent as the government deals with fallout from the eurozone crisis. Other taxes include a value-added tax (VAT) and a property transfer tax. The overall tax burden equals 36.8 percent of gross domestic income. Public expenditures equal 51 percent of GDP. Public debt is equivalent to about 50 percent of gross domestic income.

REGULATORY EFFICIENCY

	Score	Rank	1-Year Change
Business Freedom	85.4	22nd	+4.7
Labor Freedom	51.0	133rd	+10.6
Monetary Freedom	80.3	28th	-1.3

The business environment is generally conducive to entrepreneurial activity, with the process for incorporating a business taking less than a week, but completing licensing requirements still takes over 150 days. Despite some progress, rigid labor regulations hamper dynamic employment growth. The small agricultural sector is highly subsidized, but the government plans to sell 15 state-owned companies, including the largest telecommunications operator.

OPEN MARKETS

	Score	Rank	1-Year Change
Trade Freedom	87.8	11th	+1.0
Investment Freedom	70.0	46th	0
Financial Freedom	50.0	69th	0

EU members have a low 1.1 percent average tariff rate and, in general, few non-tariff barriers to trade. State-owned enterprises remain prevalent in several sectors of the economy. The financial sector remains dominated by banks. Despite some progress, privatization of state-owned financial institutions has been uneven. Equity financing remains difficult for start-ups and smaller companies. Capital markets are relatively small.

Long-Term Score Change (since 1996)

RULE OF LAW		GOVERNMENT SIZE		REGULATORY EFFICIENCY		OPEN MARKETS	
Property Rights	+30.0	Fiscal Freedom	-10.4	Business Freedom	+15.4	Trade Freedom	+28.8
Freedom from Corruption	+31.0	Government Spending	-12.0	Labor Freedom	+10.7	Investment Freedom	+40.0
				Monetary Freedom	+19.8	Financial Freedom	-20.0

SOLOMON ISLANDS

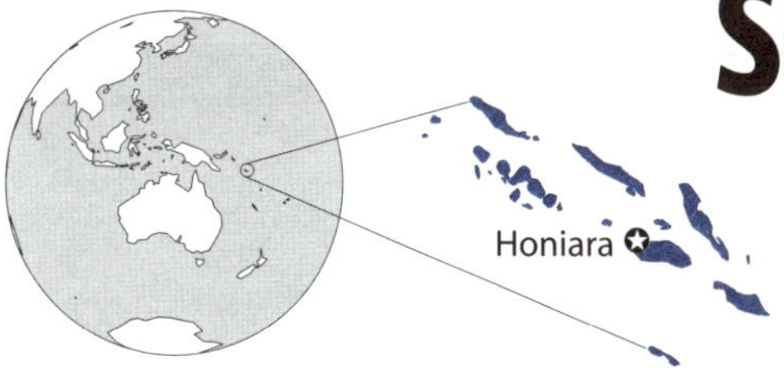

World Rank: 165 | **Regional Rank: 39**

Economic Freedom Score

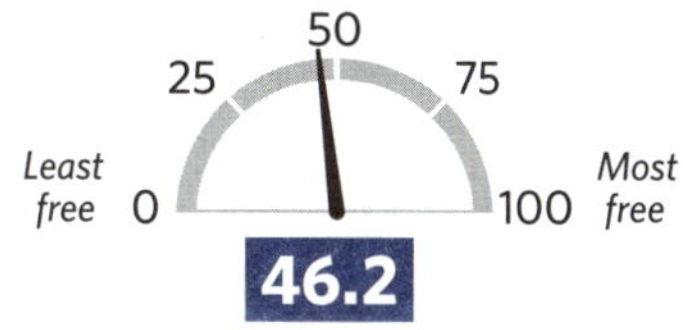

Freedom Trend

Country Comparisons

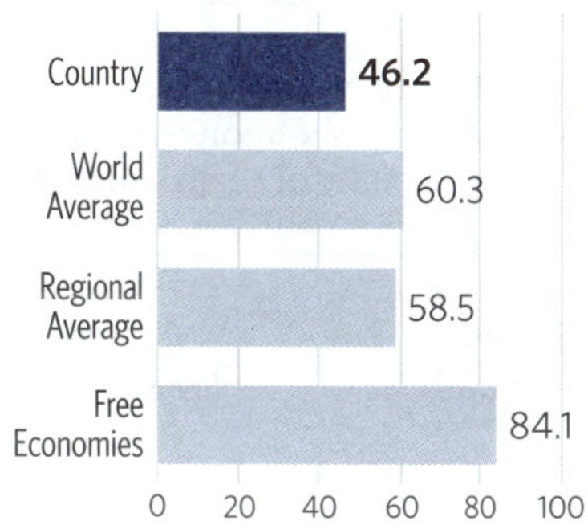

The Solomon Islands' economic freedom score is 46.2, making its economy the 165th freest in the 2014 *Index*. Its score is 1.2 points higher than last year, with advancements in the control of government spending, investment freedom, and trade freedom partially offset by deteriorations in fiscal freedom, freedom from corruption, business freedom, and labor freedom. The Solomon Islands is ranked 39th out of 42 countries in the Asia–Pacific region, and its overall score is far below the world average.

The Solomon Islands was first graded in the 2009 *Index*, and its economic freedom score remains essentially unchanged. Improvements in three of the 10 economic freedoms include a gain of over 20 points in the management of government spending, but deteriorations in fiscal freedom, investment freedom, and overall regulatory efficiency have offset any gains. The Solomon Islands remains economically "repressed."

Economic dynamism and development remain stifled by serious deficiencies that include poor governance and an inefficient public sector. Private-sector development is undermined by underdeveloped legal and physical infrastructure, political instability, the government's outsized role in the economy, and the lack of political will to reform the poor regulatory framework.

BACKGROUND: The Solomon Islands is a parliamentary democracy and one of Asia's poorest nations. Danny Philip's election as prime minister in 2010 appeared to have stabilized a chaotic political environment. However, following allegations of corruption, Philip resigned in 2011 rather than face a motion of no confidence, and Gordon Darcy Lilo was elected shortly thereafter. Australia has had to intervene several times to defuse ethnic conflict that has held back economic development. Australia, the European Union, Japan, New Zealand, and the Republic of China provide significant financial aid. Most of the population lives in rural communities, and three-fourths of the workforce is engaged in subsistence farming and fishing. Growth depends largely on logging and timber exports.

How Do We Measure Economic Freedom?
See page 471 for an explanation of the methodology or visit the *Index* Web site at *heritage.org/index*.

Quick Facts

Population: 0.6 million
GDP (PPP): $1.9 billion
5.5% growth in 2012
5-year compound annual growth 5.1%
$3,345 per capita
Unemployment: n/a
Inflation (CPI): 5.1%
FDI Inflow: $69.3 million
Public Debt: 18.2% of GDP

2012 data unless otherwise noted.
Data compiled as of September 2013.

SOLOMON ISLANDS (continued)

THE TEN ECONOMIC FREEDOMS

RULE OF LAW

	Score	Rank	1-Year Change
Property Rights	30.0	93rd	0
Freedom from Corruption	25.0	131st	-2.0

Corruption is rampant, and public offices are seen as opportunities for personal enrichment. Many current and former lawmakers have faced a variety of corruption charges. Threats against judges and prosecutors have weakened the independence and rigor of the judicial system. Judges and prosecutors have also been implicated in scandals relating to corruption and abuse of power. Land ownership is reserved for citizens.

GOVERNMENT SIZE

	Score	Rank	1-Year Change
Fiscal Freedom	61.4	165th	-4.8
Government Spending	21.3	171st	+15.2

The top individual income tax rate is 40 percent, and the top corporate tax rate is 30 percent. Other taxes include a property tax and a sales tax. Overall tax revenue is equivalent to 37 percent of the domestic economy. Government expenditures amount to just over 51 percent of gross domestic output. Public debt is below 20 percent of GDP.

REGULATORY EFFICIENCY

	Score	Rank	1-Year Change
Business Freedom	65.2	90th	-1.4
Labor Freedom	65.2	78th	-1.2
Monetary Freedom	75.4	93rd	0

The business environment discourages entrepreneurship and new investment. Completing licensing requirements still costs over twice the level of average annual income and takes about three months. The labor market is underdeveloped, and informal labor activity remains substantial. About one-third of total public spending subsidizes infrastructure development projects, many of them funded by international donors.

OPEN MARKETS

	Score	Rank	1-Year Change
Trade Freedom	73.0	112th	+0.4
Investment Freedom	15.0	169th	+5.0
Financial Freedom	30.0	132nd	0

The average tariff rate for the Solomon Islands is 8.5 percent, and exports of some natural resources are taxed. Foreign investment is screened by the government, and investment in some sectors of the economy is prohibited. The underdeveloped financial sector is dominated by banking. A large part of the population remains outside the formal banking system. Access to credit, particularly long-term credit, continues to be very limited.

Long-Term Score Change (since 2009)

RULE OF LAW		GOVERNMENT SIZE		REGULATORY EFFICIENCY		OPEN MARKETS	
Property Rights	0	Fiscal Freedom	-7.5	Business Freedom	-2.0	Trade Freedom	+6.6
Freedom from Corruption	-3.0	Government Spending	+21.3	Labor Freedom	-11.1	Investment Freedom	-5.0
				Monetary Freedom	+1.9	Financial Freedom	0

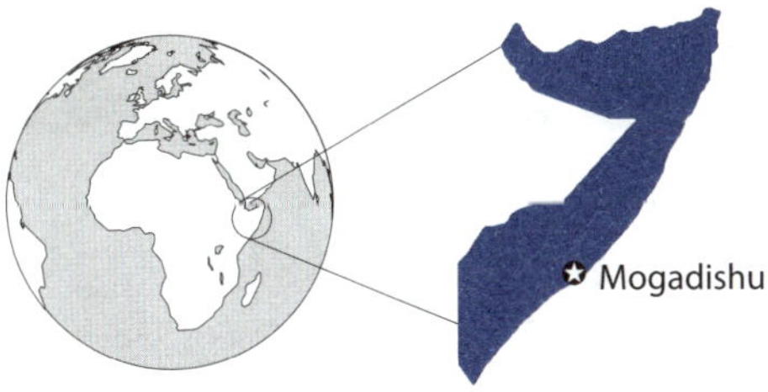

SOMALIA

World Rank: Not Ranked   Regional Rank: Not Ranked

Economic Freedom Score

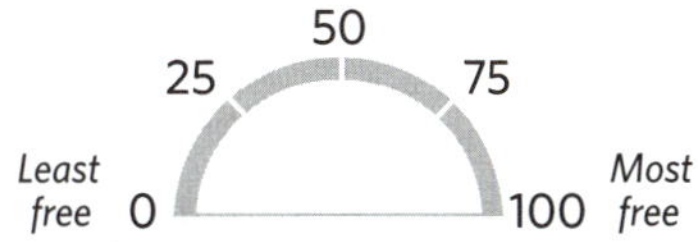

This economy is not graded

Freedom Trend

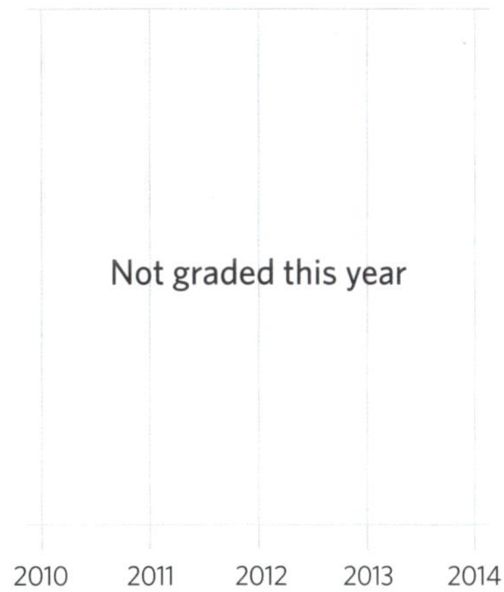

Country Comparisons

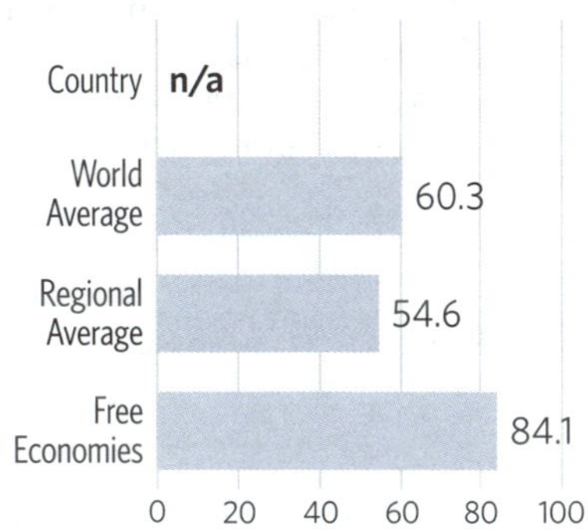

Somalia's economic freedom remains unrated due to a severe lack of reliable data caused by the country's ongoing political instability. The last time Somalia was fully graded was in the 2000 *Index* when it received a score of only 27.8.

The 2013 *Index* included Somalia for the first time since 2001. Over the past decade, prolonged political instability and lawlessness have wracked Somalia and ruined the country's prospects for long-term investment and economic development. Economic collapse has resulted in massive human migrations, and much of the population lives in conditions of severe poverty.

The territory under the federal government's control has gradually expanded. However, progress toward economic normalization and recovery remains severely impeded by continuing security threats. In the absence of an effectively functioning central government, numerous armed groups and militias control different parts of the country. Although local authorities or elders sometimes enforce laws based on traditional customs, Islamic Sharia law has become more entrenched since 2009.

BACKGROUND: Somalia has been in chaos since the collapse of the Siad Barre regime in 1991 and the subsequent civil war. When a U.N. humanitarian mission's mandate ended in 1995, the Transitional Federal Government was forced to rely on the African Union's peacekeeping mission to Somalia to protect civilians. A new provisional constitution was passed in August 2012, and the end of the TFG mandate in September led to the establishment of the Federal Government of Somalia. Somalia's economy is based largely on agriculture and livestock herding, which account for 60 percent of GDP. The population is dependent on overseas remittances and foreign aid. However, economic growth is slowly expanding from Mogadishu, which has been in recovery since the terrorist group Al-Shabaab retreated to rural parts of Somalia in 2011. The African Union peacekeeping force continues to conduct operations against al-Shabaab.

Quick Facts

Population: 9.1 million
GDP (PPP): $6.1 billion
2.6% growth in 2012
5-year compound annual growth n/a
$600 per capita
Unemployment: n/a
Inflation (CPI): n/a
FDI Inflow: $107.3 million
Public Debt: n/a

2012 data unless otherwise noted.
Data compiled as of September 2013.

How Do We Measure Economic Freedom?
See page 471 for an explanation of the methodology or visit the *Index* Web site at *heritage.org/index.*

SOMALIA (continued)

THE TEN ECONOMIC FREEDOMS

Legend: Country | World Average

RULE OF LAW

	Score	Rank	1-Year Change
Property Rights	n/a	—	n/a
Freedom from Corruption	5.0	184th	-5.0

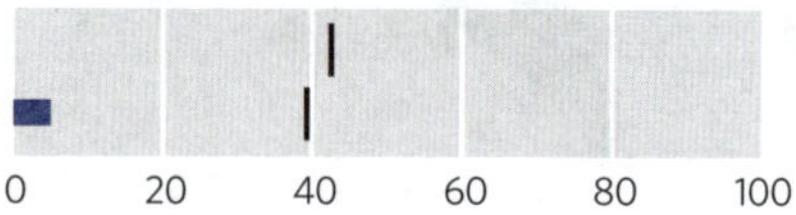

Corruption in Somalia is rampant. A U.N. report could not account for 70 percent of revenues to Somalia between 2009 and 2010. There is no functioning national judicial system. Authorities in Mogadishu administer a mix of Sharia law and traditional justice. In areas controlled by al-Shabaab, some people convicted of theft or other minor crimes have been flogged or have had their limbs amputated, usually in public.

GOVERNMENT SIZE

	Score	Rank	1-Year Change
Fiscal Freedom	n/a	—	n/a
Government Spending	n/a	—	n/a

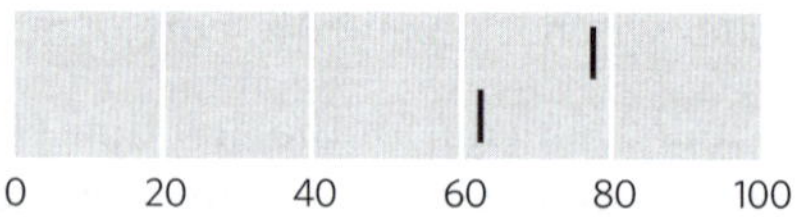

Somalia lacks an effective central government and administration that can provide basic services and collect taxes. Although some duties and taxes are collected, there is little effective fiscal policy in place. Most of the federal government is financed through aid. Militias and warlords continue to collect levies from the population, particularly in the southern portion of the country.

REGULATORY EFFICIENCY

	Score	Rank	1-Year Change
Business Freedom	n/a	—	n/a
Labor Freedom	n/a	—	n/a
Monetary Freedom	n/a	—	n/a

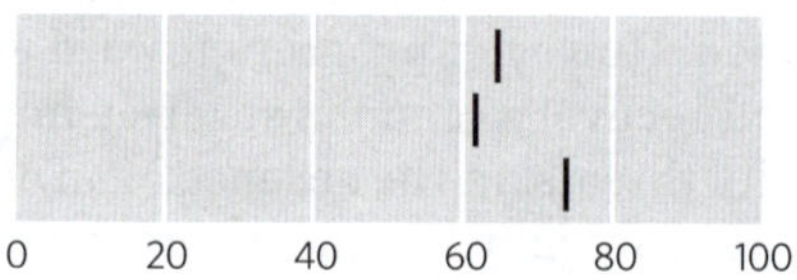

Political instability, an outmoded regulatory environment, and inadequate infrastructure significantly deter the formation and operation of businesses. The labor market is dominated by the agricultural sector and informal hiring practices. Despite almost nonexistent national governance, Somalia's informal agricultural, financial, and telecommunications sectors have flourished without subsidies.

OPEN MARKETS

	Score	Rank	1-Year Change
Trade Freedom	n/a	—	n/a
Investment Freedom	n/a	—	n/a
Financial Freedom	n/a	—	n/a

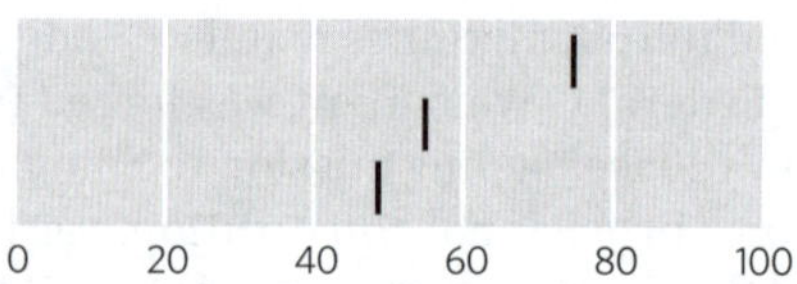

Violence in Somalia has been a deterrent to international trade and investment flows. The government is working to update its laws to attract foreign investment. In October 2012, a new Islamic banking bill was signed into law, paving the way for private commercial banks to start operating in the country.

Long-Term Score Change: n/a

RULE OF LAW		GOVERNMENT SIZE		REGULATORY EFFICIENCY		OPEN MARKETS	
Property Rights	n/a	Fiscal Freedom	n/a	Business Freedom	n/a	Trade Freedom	n/a
Freedom from Corruption	n/a	Government Spending	n/a	Labor Freedom	n/a	Investment Freedom	n/a
				Monetary Freedom	n/a	Financial Freedom	n/a

SOUTH AFRICA

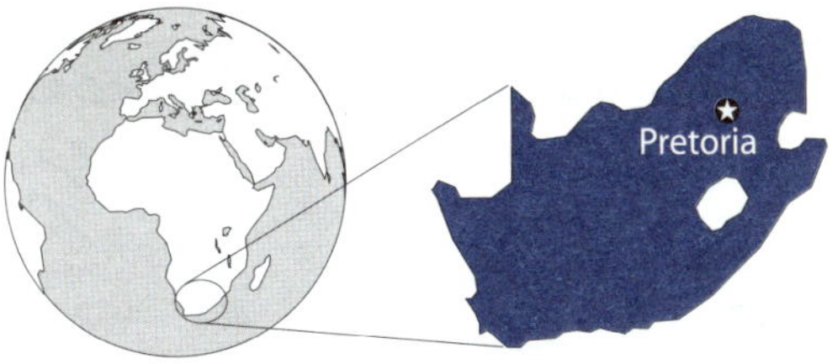

World Rank: **75** Regional Rank: **6**

South Africa's economic freedom score is 62.5, making its economy the 75th freest in the 2014 *Index*. Its score is 0.7 point higher than last year, with improvements in investment freedom and freedom from corruption offset by declines in six areas including fiscal freedom, labor freedom, and monetary freedom. South Africa is ranked 6th out of 46 countries in the Sub-Saharan Africa region, and its overall score is higher than the world and regional averages.

Over the 20-year history of the *Index*, South Africa's economic freedom score has advanced by 1.8 points. Gains in market openness, measured through trade freedom and financial freedom, and the management of public finance have been corroded by declines in freedom from corruption, business freedom, and investment freedom that keep the economy "moderately free."

South Africa achieved its highest economic freedom score in 2003 and has failed to show further progress. Its transition to a more open economic system, helped by a relatively competitive trade regime, has been undermined by the failure of structural reforms to diversify the economic base.

BACKGROUND: Jacob Zuma of the African National Congress was elected president by the National Assembly in May 2009. The ANC has dominated politics since the end of apartheid in 1994. South Africa is Sub-Saharan Africa's largest economy and one of the world's largest producers and exporters of gold and platinum. Mining, services, manufacturing, and agriculture rival similar sectors in the developed world. However, formal-sector unemployment and crime are high, poverty is widespread, public education is poor, and much of the population lacks access to infrastructure and basic services. Economic policy is focused on controlling inflation and the budget deficit. Services contribute the most to GDP and employment. The government aims to increase black South African farmland ownership to 30 percent by 2014, but its affirmative-action mandates threaten private property rights.

How Do We Measure Economic Freedom?
See page 471 for an explanation of the methodology or visit the *Index* Web site at *heritage.org/index*.

Economic Freedom Score

Freedom Trend

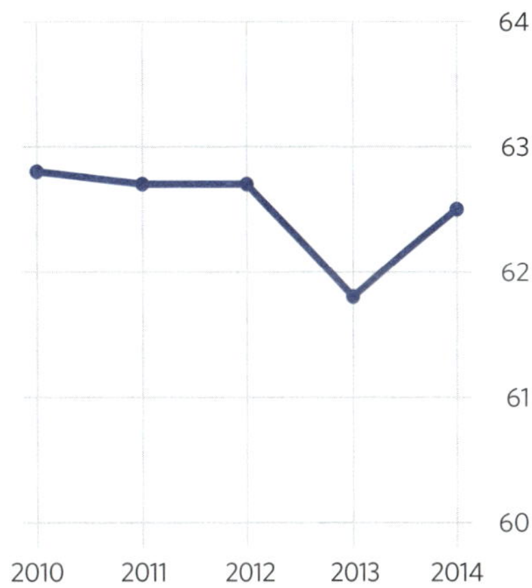

Country Comparisons

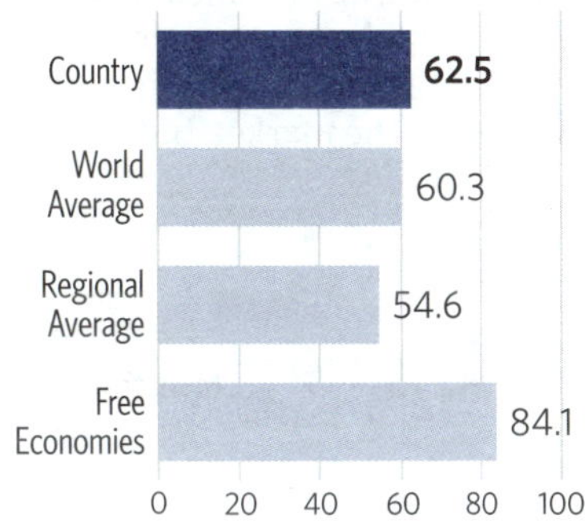

Quick Facts

Population: 51.2 million
GDP (PPP): $582.4 billion
2.5% growth in 2012
5-year compound annual growth 2.2%
$11,375 per capita
Unemployment: 25.2%
Inflation (CPI): 5.7%
FDI Inflow: $4.6 billion
Public Debt: 42.3% of GDP

2012 data unless otherwise noted.
Data compiled as of September 2013.

THE TEN ECONOMIC FREEDOMS

Country | World Average

RULE OF LAW

	Score	Rank	1-Year Change
Property Rights	50.0	53rd	0
Freedom from Corruption	41.6	64th	+0.6

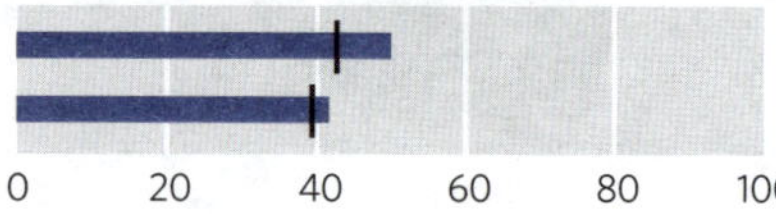

Enforcement of anti-corruption statutes is inadequate. Public servants often do not declare their business interests as required by law. The ruling ANC allegedly charges fees for access to top government officials. The public procurement process is often politically driven and opaque, and the delivery of government services is undermined by poor administration. Property rights are relatively well-protected. Contracts are generally secure.

GOVERNMENT SIZE

	Score	Rank	1-Year Change
Fiscal Freedom	68.7	146th	-1.8
Government Spending	69.1	92nd	-0.1

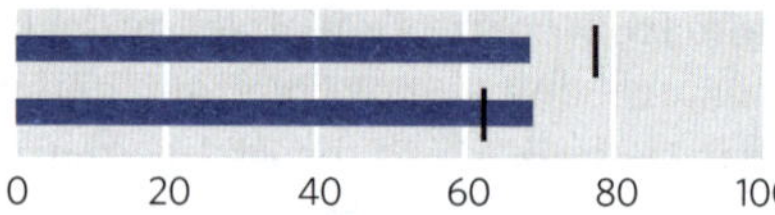

The top individual income tax rate is 40 percent, and the top corporate tax rate is 28 percent. Other taxes include a value-added tax (VAT) and a capital gains tax. The overall tax burden equals 27.3 percent of gross domestic income. Government expenditures equal 32 percent of GDP. Public debt amounts to around 42 percent of the domestic economy. Commodity market slowdowns and labor unrest are putting pressure on government finances.

REGULATORY EFFICIENCY

	Score	Rank	1-Year Change
Business Freedom	74.5	52nd	-0.2
Labor Freedom	54.4	120th	-1.2
Monetary Freedom	75.3	97th	-0.5

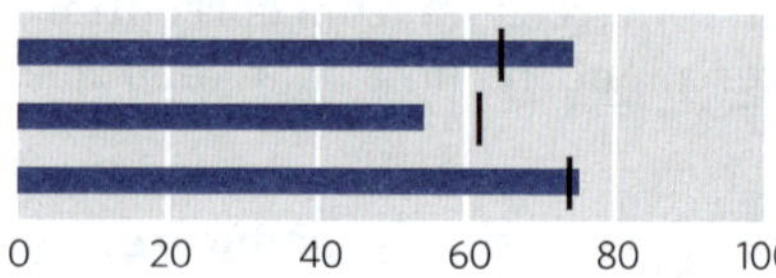

Incorporating a business takes five procedures and 19 days, and no minimum capital is required. However, obtaining necessary licenses still takes more than two months on average. Labor regulations are not applied effectively, and the labor market lacks flexibility. Prices are generally set by the market, but the government controls the prices of fuels and other basic products.

OPEN MARKETS

	Score	Rank	1-Year Change
Trade Freedom	76.1	91st	-0.2
Investment Freedom	55.0	96th	+10.0
Financial Freedom	60.0	41st	0

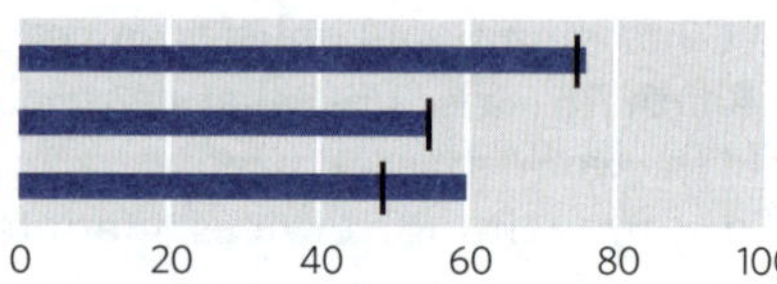

South Africa's average tariff rate is 4.5 percent. Anti-dumping measures and other non-tariff barriers further impede trade. Foreign investment in several sectors of the economy is screened by the government. The evolving financial sector has been increasingly open and deregulated over the past decade and is one of the largest and most well-developed among emerging markets.

Long-Term Score Change (since 1995)

RULE OF LAW		GOVERNMENT SIZE		REGULATORY EFFICIENCY		OPEN MARKETS	
Property Rights	**0**	Fiscal Freedom	**+7.6**	Business Freedom	**-10.5**	Trade Freedom	**+33.1**
Freedom from Corruption	**-8.4**	Government Spending	**+5.9**	Labor Freedom	**-4.3**	Investment Freedom	**-15.0**
				Monetary Freedom	**+1.5**	Financial Freedom	**+10.0**

SPAIN

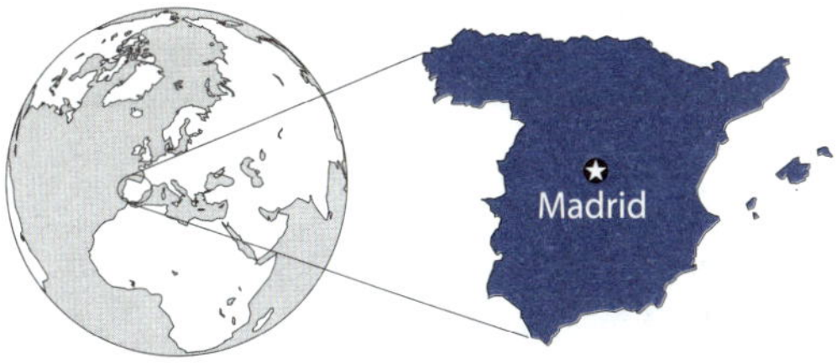

World Rank: **49** Regional Rank: **22**

Economic Freedom Score

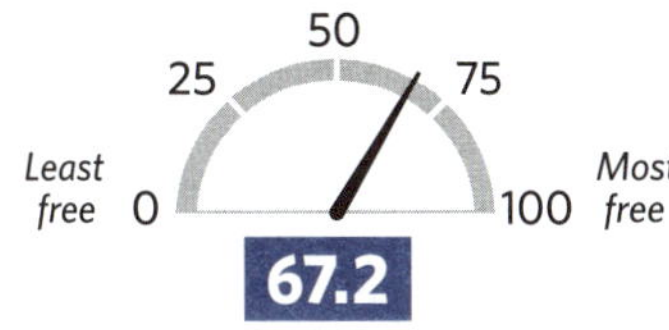

Spain's economic freedom score is 67.2, making its economy the 49th freest in the 2014 *Index*. Its score is 0.8 point lower than last year due to declines in the management of government spending, business freedom, and labor freedom that outweigh small improvements in trade freedom and freedom from corruption. Spain is ranked 22nd out of 43 countries in the Europe region.

Over the 20-year history of the *Index*, Spain has improved its economic freedom score by 4.4 points. Almost all of the 10 economic freedoms have shown some improvement, with the greatest gains in the areas of market openness and freedom from corruption. Regulatory efficiency and the rule of law have been relatively well maintained.

Modest long-term gains, however, mask the erratic path of Spain's economic freedom over the past two decades. Still ranked "moderately free" and recording its second lowest economic freedom score in 10 years, Spain continues to score below the world averages in fiscal freedom, government spending, and labor freedom.

BACKGROUND: The burst of a housing-market bubble in 2008 meant that the global economic crisis hit Spain hard. Actions taken by the Spanish Socialist Workers Party, then in power, made the economic situation worse. The conservative Popular Party, led by Mariano Rajoy, won the November 2011 election and has since introduced the largest budget deficit–reduction plan in Spain's history. Good progress has been made toward the EU standard of 3 percent of GDP, although the government is not there yet. In 2012, Spain received a €41 billion loan from the EU to bail out its banking sector. Thanks to high unemployment, emigration is also a long-term problem. In 2013, Spain appears to have pulled out of its double-dip recession, but growth remains low. Spain's steadily increasing unemployment rate stands at 27 percent, and youth unemployment stands at an estimated 55 percent.

Freedom Trend

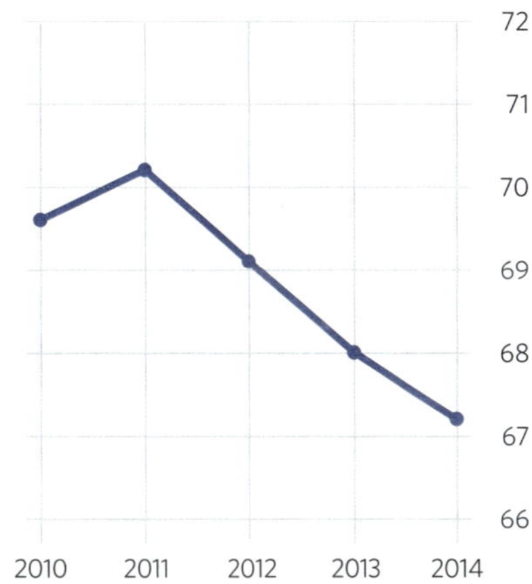

Country Comparisons

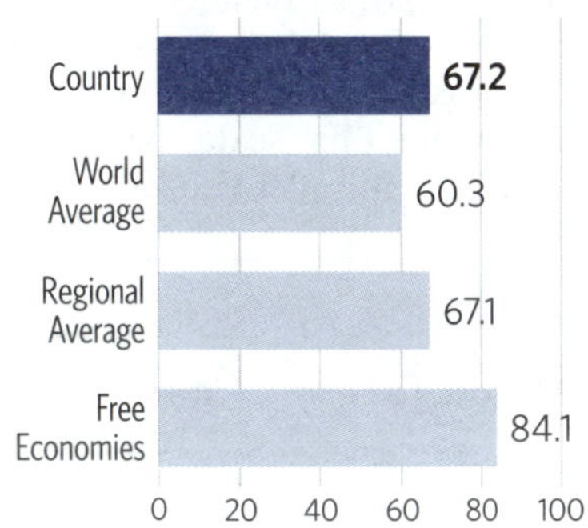

Quick Facts

Population: 46.2 million
GDP (PPP): $1.4 trillion
-1.4% growth in 2012
5-year compound annual growth -0.8%
$30,557 per capita
Unemployment: 25.0%
Inflation (CPI): 2.4%
FDI Inflow: $27.7 billion
Public Debt: 84.1% of GDP

2012 data unless otherwise noted.
Data compiled as of September 2013.

How Do We Measure Economic Freedom?
See page 471 for an explanation of the methodology or visit the *Index* Web site at *heritage.org/index*.

THE TEN ECONOMIC FREEDOMS

RULE OF LAW

	Score	Rank	1-Year Change
Property Rights	70.0	27th	0
Freedom from Corruption	62.6	31st	+0.6

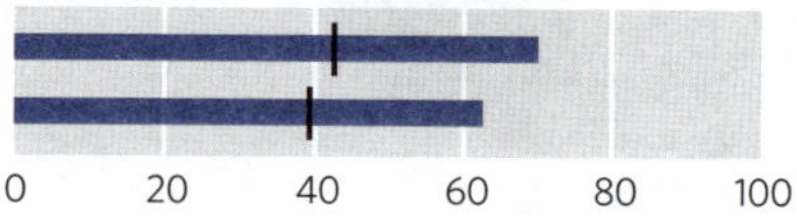

In recent years, increased incidents of political corruption and the downturn in the economy have exposed the relations between politicians and construction magnates that fed a disastrous housing bubble. The judiciary is independent in practice, but bureaucratic obstacles are significant. Contracts are secure, although enforcement is very slow. Patent, copyright, and trademark laws approximate or exceed EU levels of IPR protection.

GOVERNMENT SIZE

	Score	Rank	1-Year Change
Fiscal Freedom	54.0	174th	+0.1
Government Spending	38.7	153rd	-4.3

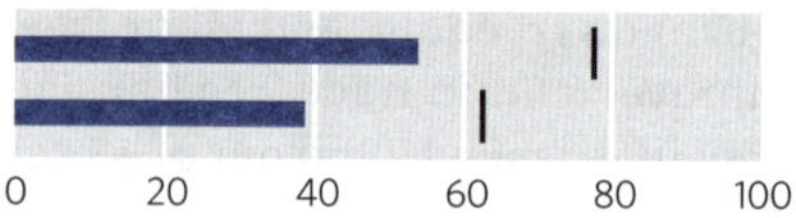

The top individual income tax rate is 52 percent, and the top corporate tax rate is 30 percent. Other taxes include a value-added tax (VAT) and a capital gains tax. The overall tax burden amounts to 31.6 percent of the domestic economy. Public expenditures are 45 percent of gross domestic income. Government debt is now equal to over 80 percent of GDP. Public finances continue to feel pressure from bailouts of the financial sector and high unemployment.

REGULATORY EFFICIENCY

	Score	Rank	1-Year Change
Business Freedom	77.3	39th	-3.0
Labor Freedom	52.2	129th	-2.1
Monetary Freedom	79.9	33rd	0

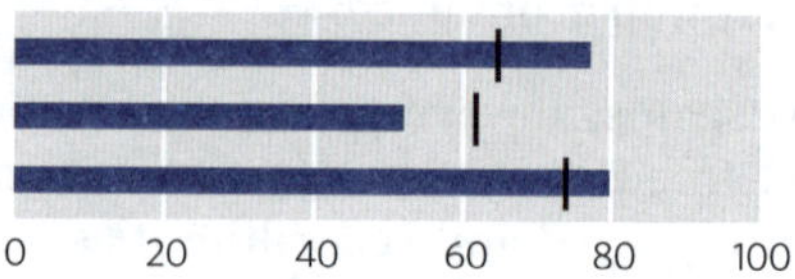

Incorporating a business takes 10 procedures and about three weeks, but completing licensing requirements takes over seven months and costs more than the level of average annual income. Labor regulations remain largely inflexible hindering job growth in the private sector. The government has scaled back once-generous solar-energy subsidies that have contributed to a massive public debt burden.

OPEN MARKETS

	Score	Rank	1-Year Change
Trade Freedom	87.8	11th	+1.0
Investment Freedom	80.0	23rd	0
Financial Freedom	70.0	19th	0

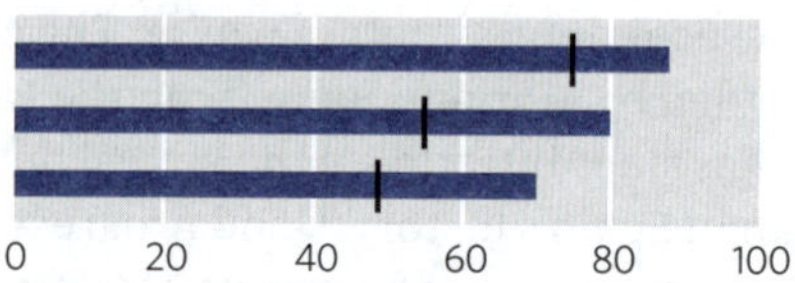

EU members have a low 1.1 percent average tariff rate and, in general, few non-tariff barriers to trade. Spain has few restrictions on foreign investment. With the banking sector under growing strain since 2012, the overall stability of the financial system has deteriorated. Savings banks have been under severe pressure. The overall cost of the bailout for troubled banks has been substantial.

Long-Term Score Change (since 1995)

RULE OF LAW		GOVERNMENT SIZE		REGULATORY EFFICIENCY		OPEN MARKETS	
Property Rights	0	Fiscal Freedom	+8.7	Business Freedom	+7.3	Trade Freedom	+10.0
Freedom from Corruption	+12.6	Government Spending	+1.9	Labor Freedom	+3.4	Investment Freedom	+10.0
				Monetary Freedom	+4.1	Financial Freedom	0

SRI LANKA

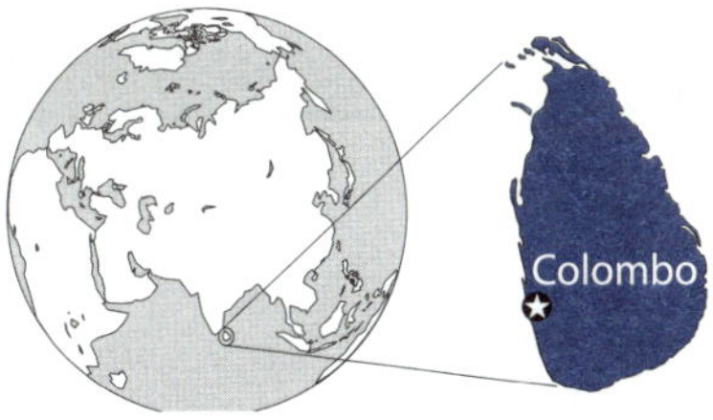

World Rank: 90 **Regional Rank: 17**

Economic Freedom Score

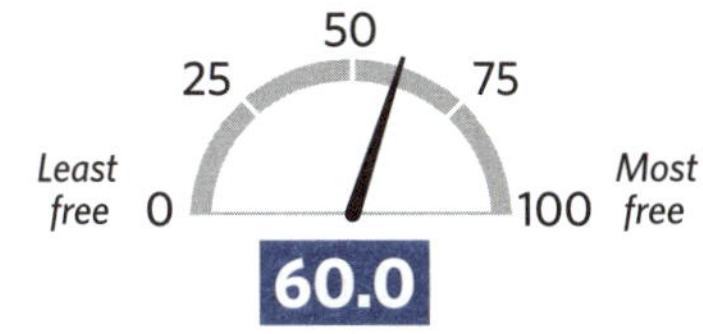

Sri Lanka's economic freedom score is 60.0, making its economy the 90th freest in the 2014 *Index*. Its score is 0.7 point lower than last year, reflecting modest declines in five of the 10 economic freedoms including trade freedom, business freedom, labor freedom, and monetary freedom. Sri Lanka is ranked 17th out of 42 countries in the Asia–Pacific region, and its score is just below the world average.

Over the 20-year history of the *Index*, Sri Lanka's economic freedom has been largely stagnant. Despite notable score improvements in trade freedom and fiscal freedom, overall progress has been stifled by declines in five areas of economic freedom, including a 30-point decline in financial freedom. In the absence of lasting progress toward greater economic freedom, Sri Lanka's economy has been rated "mostly unfree" in recent years.

Notable reforms in past years have included the easing of foreign exchange controls and the reduction of both individual and corporate marginal income tax rates below 30 percent. Substantial challenges remain, however, in the struggle to promote sustainable economic development. Institutional weaknesses cannot be addressed without a firmer political commitment to reform. Sri Lanka continues to score below the world average in the area of rule of law as measured by freedom from corruption and the protection of property rights.

BACKGROUND: In May 2009, the Sri Lankan military defeated the rebel Liberation Tigers of Tamil Eelam, ending 26 years of civil war and contributing to President Mahinda Rajapakse's April 2010 re-election. The international outcry over the deaths of thousands of civilians in the final days of the war has largely died down. Agriculture, apparel, and tourism are the main economic sectors. Sri Lanka depends heavily on foreign assistance and remittances from workers, primarily in the Middle East. China has become a significant lender for infrastructure projects.

Freedom Trend

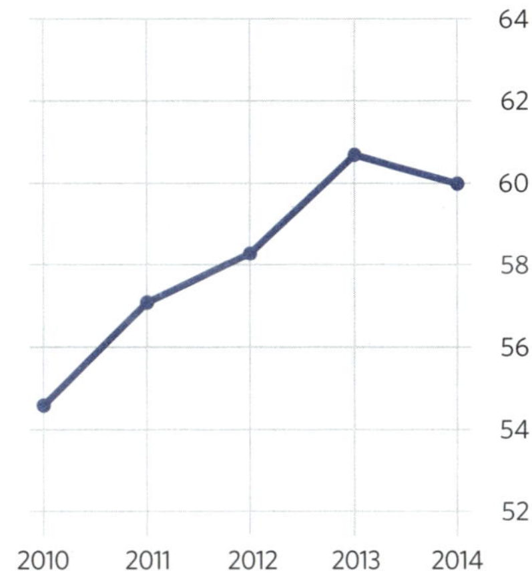

Country Comparisons

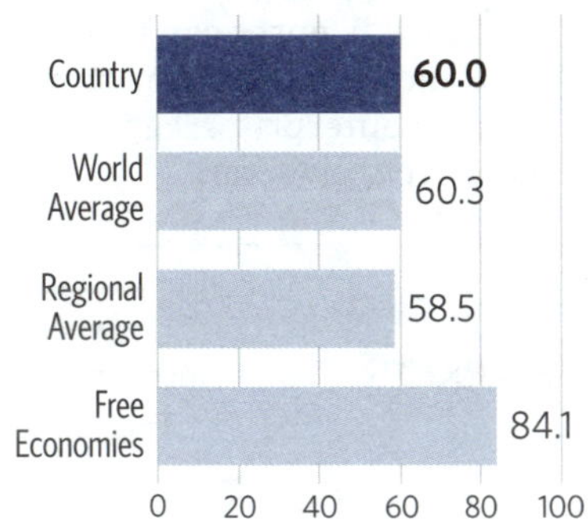

Quick Facts

Population: 20.7 million
GDP (PPP): $126.3 billion
6.4% growth in 2012
5-year compound annual growth 6.4%
$6,107 per capita
Unemployment: 4.9%
Inflation (CPI): 7.5%
FDI Inflow: $775.5 million
Public Debt: 77.7% of GDP

2012 data unless otherwise noted.
Data compiled as of September 2013.

How Do We Measure Economic Freedom?
See page 471 for an explanation of the methodology or visit the *Index* Web site at *heritage.org/index.*

THE TEN ECONOMIC FREEDOMS

RULE OF LAW

	Score	Rank	1-Year Change
Property Rights	40.0	70th	0
Freedom from Corruption	33.4	87th	+0.4

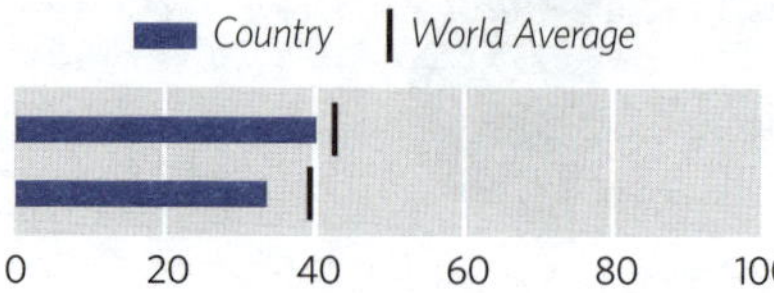

Official corruption worsened during the past year. The administrative framework does not promote integrity or punish corrupt behavior effectively. Increasing threats, intimidation, and political interference culminated in a significant assault on judicial independence in November 2012 when the parliament impeached the chief justice. A fairly reliable registration system exists for private property but is marred by fraud and forged documents.

GOVERNMENT SIZE

	Score	Rank	1-Year Change
Fiscal Freedom	84.9	55th	+0.2
Government Spending	86.3	25th	-0.2

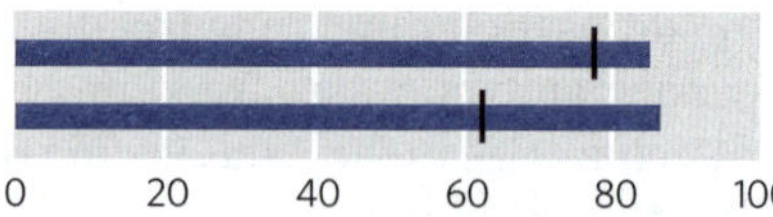

The top individual income tax rate is 24 percent, and the top corporate tax rate is 28 percent. Other taxes include a value-added tax (VAT). Total tax revenue makes up about 12.4 percent of the gross domestic economy. Government spending is 21 percent of GDP, and public debt amounts to 78 percent of GDP. Government is subject to fiscal targets set under an IMF loan agreement.

REGULATORY EFFICIENCY

	Score	Rank	1-Year Change
Business Freedom	74.4	54th	-2.6
Labor Freedom	59.2	103rd	-1.6
Monetary Freedom	68.0	153rd	-1.1

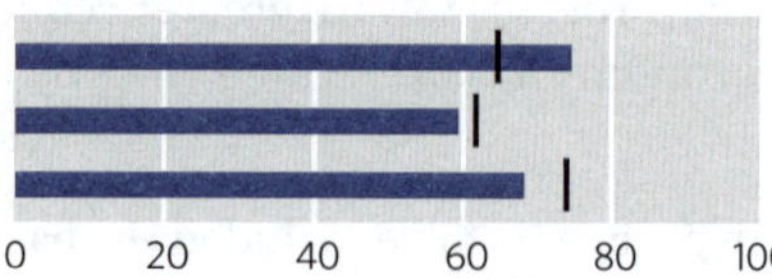

Launching a business takes eight days, and no minimum capital is required, but obtaining necessary licenses can take more than 150 days. Inefficiency in the labor market causes an imbalance between labor supply and demand. The government is heavily subsidizing small and medium enterprises, agriculture, and infrastructure projects, in part to repair damage from the 26-year civil war.

OPEN MARKETS

	Score	Rank	1-Year Change
Trade Freedom	73.6	108th	-2.6
Investment Freedom	40.0	132nd	0
Financial Freedom	40.0	107th	0

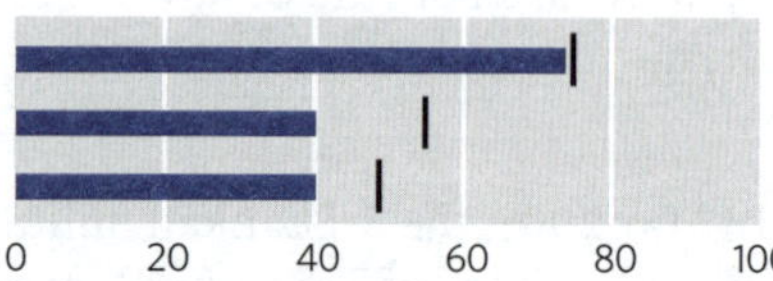

Sri Lanka's average tariff rate is 5.7 percent. Government policies based on import replacement and agricultural self-sufficiency distort trade. Investment in several sectors of the economy is subject to government screening. The financial system, dominated by banking, remains vulnerable to state influence. The central bank is not fully independent. High credit costs continue to discourage more dynamic business activity.

Long-Term Score Change (since 1995)

RULE OF LAW		GOVERNMENT SIZE		REGULATORY EFFICIENCY		OPEN MARKETS	
Property Rights	**-10.0**	Fiscal Freedom	**+20.6**	Business Freedom	**+4.4**	Trade Freedom	**+19.4**
Freedom from Corruption	**+3.4**	Government Spending	**+8.0**	Labor Freedom	**-8.3**	Investment Freedom	**-10.0**
				Monetary Freedom	**-10.4**	Financial Freedom	**-30.0**

SUDAN

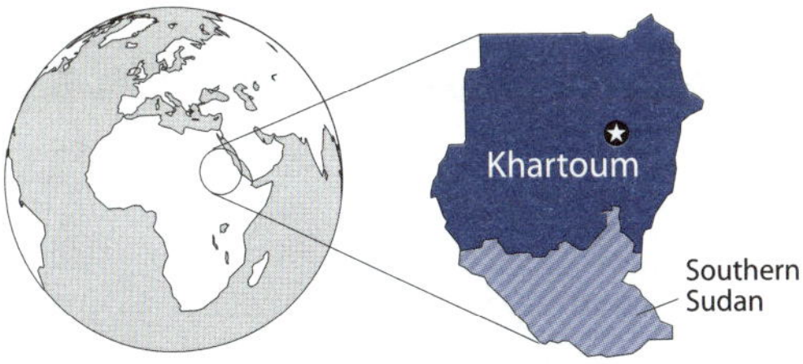

World Rank: Not Ranked | Regional Rank: Not Ranked

Sudan's economic freedom remains unrated due to the lack of reliable data. Those facets of economic freedom for which data are available have been individually scored. The last time Sudan was fully graded was in 2000, when it received a score of 47.2.

Sudan's economic freedom was assessed for the first six years of the 20-year history of the *Index*. Since 2000, when the country reached its highest economic freedom score, grading of Sudan has been suspended due to its internal conflicts and the deficient availability of economic data. Despite the political settlement that established a breakaway Republic of Sudan in July 2011, security and political uncertainty remain formidable challenges. The rule of law remains fragile and uneven.

Outside of the hydrocarbon sector, economic development is very limited by the ongoing instability in Sudan. Attempts to develop and diversify the economy are constrained by a lack of basic institutional capacity. The large informal economy has been an important source of employment in the fragile economy.

BACKGROUND: In April 2010, President Omar Hassan al-Bashir, who came to power in a 1989 military coup, won Sudan's first multi-party elections in 24 years. Even as president, however, he still faces a 2009 indictment by the International Criminal Court for crimes against humanity in Darfur, where over 2 million people were displaced and over 200,000 killed. In July 2011, southern Sudan became the independent Republic of Sudan, also known as South Sudan. Cross-border violence, political instability, poor infrastructure, weak property rights, a 46 percent unemployment rate, and corruption hinder development in Sudan. Export growth, other than oil, is largely stagnant, and 80 percent of the workforce is employed in agriculture. With two-thirds of its oil revenue lost to the South, Sudan is struggling to maintain economic stability and has begun austerity measures to reduce spending.

How Do We Measure Economic Freedom?
See page 471 for an explanation of the methodology or visit the *Index* Web site at *heritage.org/index.*

Economic Freedom Score

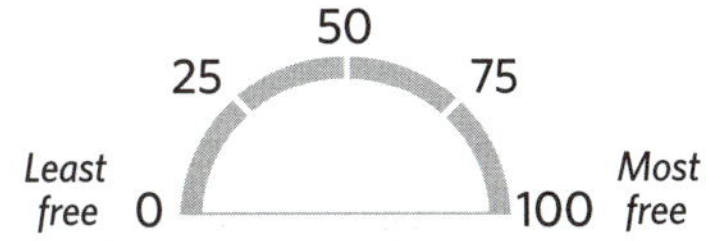

This economy is not graded

Freedom Trend

Country Comparisons

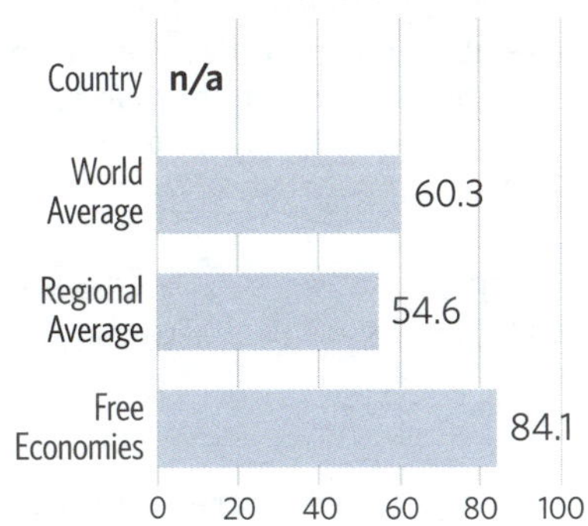

Quick Facts

Population: 33.5 million
GDP (PPP): $85.3 billion
-4.4% growth in 2012
5-year compound annual growth 0.8%
$2,545 per capita
Unemployment: 10.8%
Inflation (CPI): 35.6%
FDI Inflow: $2.5 billion
Public Debt: 97.6% of GDP

2012 data unless otherwise noted.
Data compiled as of September 2013.

THE TEN ECONOMIC FREEDOMS

Legend: Country | World Average

RULE OF LAW

	Score	Rank	1-Year Change
Property Rights	n/a	—	n/a
Freedom from Corruption	9.8	182nd	-6.2

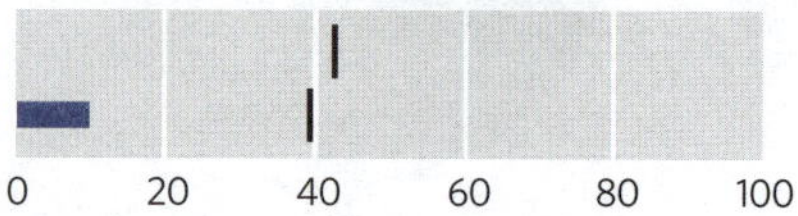

Sudan is considered one of the world's most corrupt countries. Power and resources are concentrated in and around Khartoum, and outlying states are neglected and impoverished. Members of the ruling party tightly control the national economy and use their wealth to buy political support. There is little respect for private property, and the legal framework is severely hampered by years of political conflict.

GOVERNMENT SIZE

	Score	Rank	1-Year Change
Fiscal Freedom	85.1	52nd	n/a
Government Spending	90.3	10th	+0.4

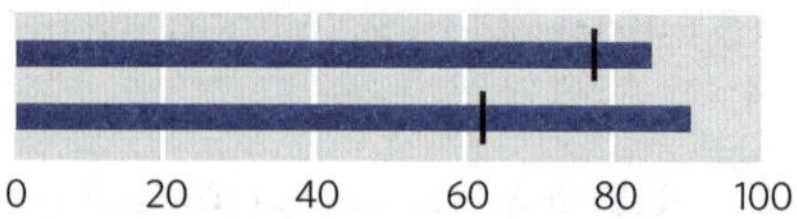

The top individual income tax rate has been increased to 15 percent. Corporate tax rates differ by sector, but the top rate is 35 percent for companies engaged in the oil and gas sector, a major part of the economy. Other taxes include a value-added tax (VAT) and a capital gains tax. Overall tax revenue amounts to 6.7 percent of GDP. Government spending is 18 percent of gross domestic income. Public debt is close to 100 percent of GDP.

REGULATORY EFFICIENCY

	Score	Rank	1-Year Change
Business Freedom	54.5	141st	-2.9
Labor Freedom	49.1	143rd	-16.3
Monetary Freedom	55.8	179th	-8.7

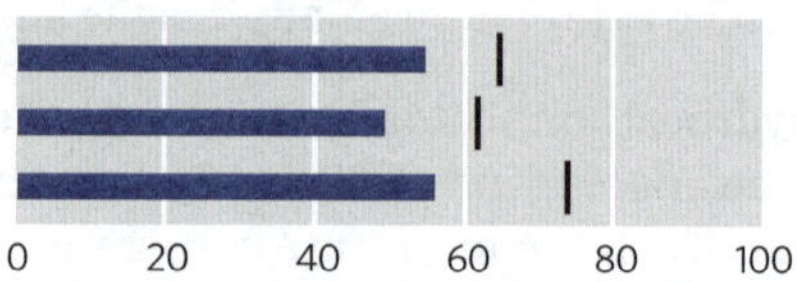

Launching a business takes 10 procedures and more than a month on average. Completing licensing requirements still costs over twice the level of average annual income. The labor market remains underdeveloped, and much of the labor force is employed in the informal sector. In 2013, the government made dramatic cuts in fuel and other subsidies in the face of a runaway budget deficit, sparking violent demonstrations.

OPEN MARKETS

	Score	Rank	1-Year Change
Trade Freedom	55.6	166th	n/a
Investment Freedom	15.0	169th	0
Financial Freedom	n/a	—	n/a

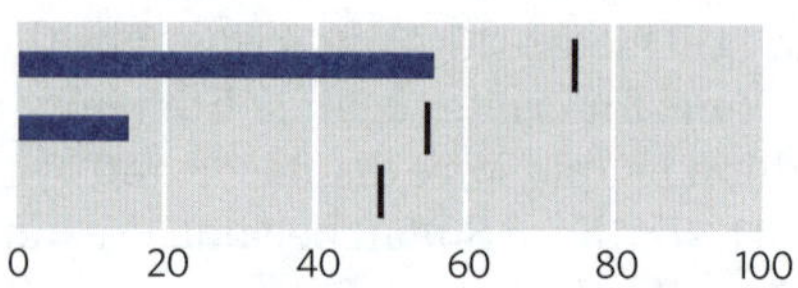

Sudan's average tariff rate is 14.7 percent. Violence and instability interfere with trade and investment flows. Foreign investment is not allowed in several sectors of the economy. A large portion of the population remains outside of the formal banking sector, and access to credit remains severely limited. The government continues to direct the allocation of credit, and nonperforming loans are a problem.

Long-Term Score Change: n/a

RULE OF LAW		GOVERNMENT SIZE		REGULATORY EFFICIENCY		OPEN MARKETS	
Property Rights	n/a	Fiscal Freedom	n/a	Business Freedom	n/a	Trade Freedom	n/a
Freedom from Corruption	n/a	Government Spending	n/a	Labor Freedom	n/a	Investment Freedom	n/a
				Monetary Freedom	n/a	Financial Freedom	n/a

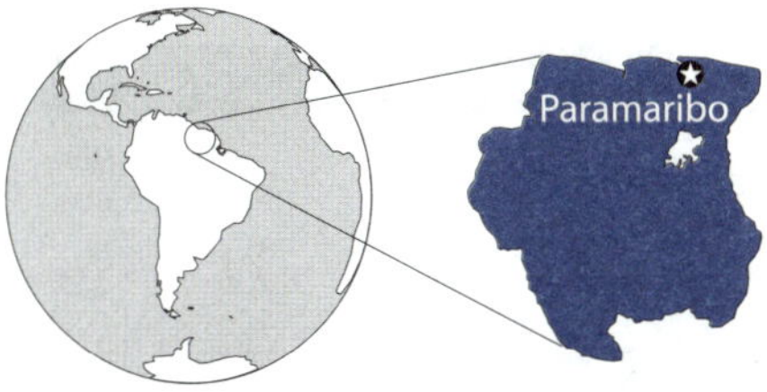

SURINAME

World Rank: **130** Regional Rank: **23**

Economic Freedom Score

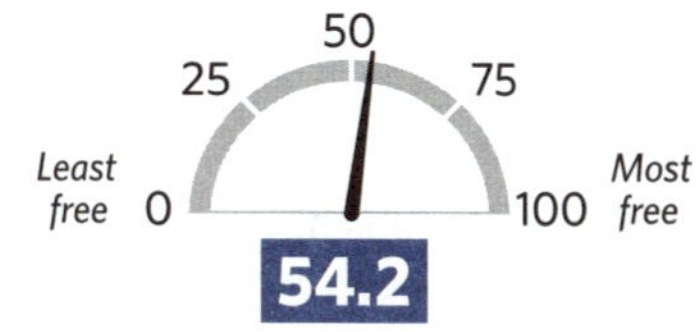

Suriname's economic freedom score is 54.2, making its economy the 130th freest in the 2014 *Index*. Its score is 2.2 points better than last year due to improvements in six of the 10 economic freedoms including the control of government spending, monetary freedom, investment freedom, and labor freedom. Suriname is ranked 23rd out of 29 countries in the South and Central America/Caribbean region, and its overall score is lower than the world and regional averages.

Suriname's economic freedom was first graded in the 1996 *Index*, and its score has improved since then by 17.5 points. Score improvements have been achieved in half of the 10 economic freedoms, notably monetary freedom, trade freedom, and the management of public spending. Reform measures have enabled Sudan to advance from economically "repressed" since 2005.

Nonetheless, overall private-sector growth continues to be hampered by the state's heavy presence in Suriname's economy. Privatization has been slow and uneven. Direct state involvement in the economy through ownership or control remains considerable. Pervasive corruption continues to undermine the judicial system and the rule of law.

BACKGROUND: In 2010, former dictator Desi Bouterse of the National Democratic Party, running in a coalition with the economic reform–oriented New Front, was returned to power as president. In 1999, he had been convicted in absentia of narcotics trafficking by a Dutch court. In May 2012, Suriname's unicameral legislature amended an amnesty law to absolve him of murders committed during the military coup he led in 1982. Suriname remains one of South America's poorest and least-developed countries. The economy is dominated by exports of natural resources, especially alumina, oil, and gold, and is highly vulnerable to commodity price fluctuations. Continued commitment to responsible monetary and fiscal policies and introduction of structural reforms to liberalize markets and promote competition will be crucial to economic progress.

How Do We Measure Economic Freedom?
See page 471 for an explanation of the methodology or visit the *Index* Web site at *heritage.org/index*.

Freedom Trend

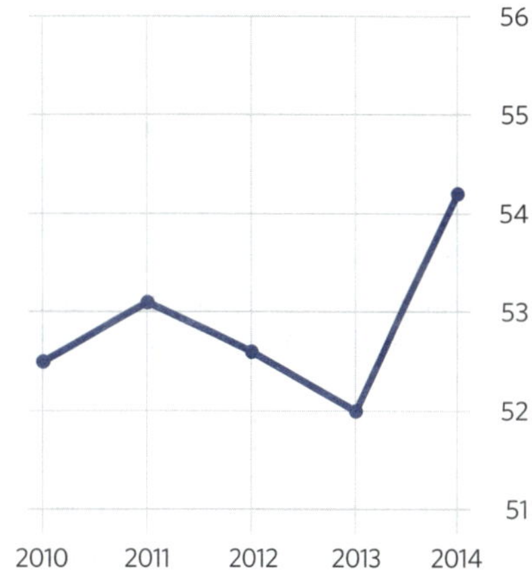

Country Comparisons

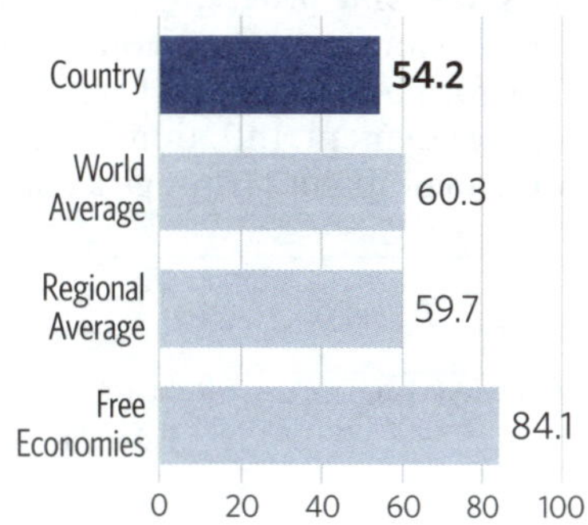

Quick Facts

Population: 0.5 million
GDP (PPP): $6.8 billion
4.5% growth in 2012
5-year compound annual growth 4.1%
$12,398 per capita
Unemployment: 9.0% (2008)
Inflation (CPI): 5.0%
FDI Inflow: $70.1 million
Public Debt: 20.5% of GDP

2012 data unless otherwise noted.
Data compiled as of September 2013.

THE TEN ECONOMIC FREEDOMS

RULE OF LAW

	Score	Rank	1-Year Change
Property Rights	40.0	70th	0
Freedom from Corruption	32.9	92nd	+2.9

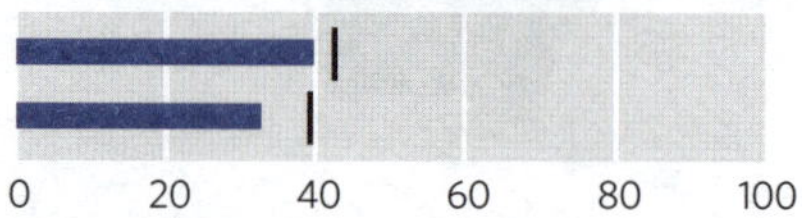

Suriname has been plagued by corruption cases in recent years, and organized crime and drug networks continue to hamper governance and undermine the judicial system. Corruption is most pervasive in government procurement, license issuance, land policy, and taxation. The judiciary is susceptible to political influence and suffers from a significant shortage of judges and a large backlog of cases. Property rights are not well protected.

GOVERNMENT SIZE

	Score	Rank	1-Year Change
Fiscal Freedom	69.0	143rd	-2.6
Government Spending	78.3	58th	+5.8

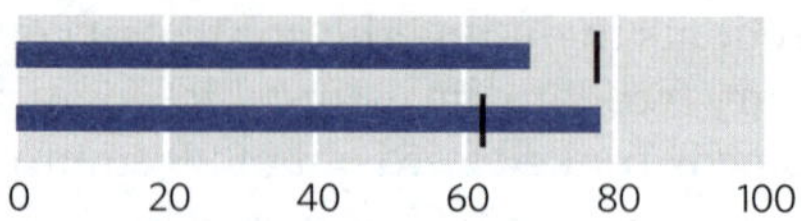

The top individual income tax rate is 38 percent, and the top corporate tax rate is 36 percent. Other taxes include a property tax, a tax on dividends, and an excise tax. The overall tax burden equals 19 percent of the domestic economy. Overall public spending is 27 percent of GDP. Public debt amounts to about 20 percent of gross domestic output. The country is debating creating a sovereign wealth fund, which could buoy public finances.

REGULATORY EFFICIENCY

	Score	Rank	1-Year Change
Business Freedom	41.8	167th	+1.6
Labor Freedom	81.8	22nd	+4.3
Monetary Freedom	71.8	133rd	+5.1

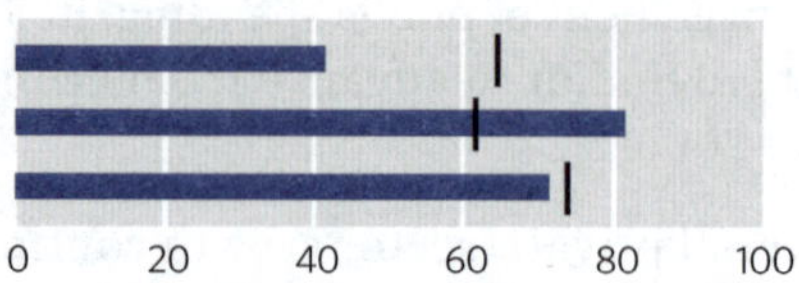

Despite some progress, licensing requirements are burdensome, and procedures for launching a business are time-consuming. Bankruptcy proceedings are difficult and often prolonged. The formal labor market is not fully developed, and the public sector remains a major source of employment. Inflation has been extremely volatile. The government supports state-owned utility companies through a complicated web of cross subsidies and transfers.

OPEN MARKETS

	Score	Rank	1-Year Change
Trade Freedom	66.2	139th	-0.1
Investment Freedom	30.0	152nd	+5.0
Financial Freedom	30.0	132nd	0

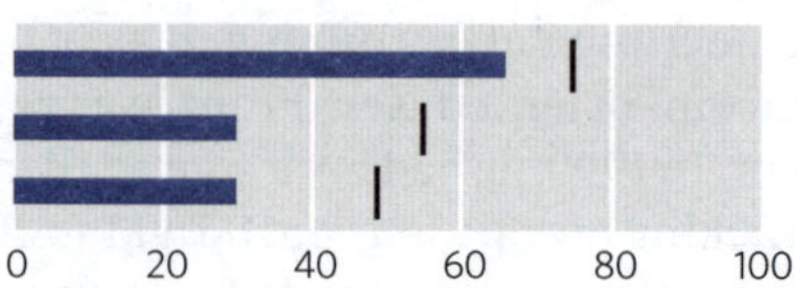

Suriname's average tariff rate is 11.9 percent. Foreign investment is screened by the government, and the legal system may move slowly in adjudicating contract disputes. The financial sector remains underdeveloped and vulnerable to government influence. Financial regulations are antiquated, and supervision is poor. Capital markets offer only a narrow range of government and other securities.

Long-Term Score Change (since 1996)

RULE OF LAW		GOVERNMENT SIZE		REGULATORY EFFICIENCY		OPEN MARKETS	
Property Rights	-10.0	Fiscal Freedom	+19.5	Business Freedom	-28.2	Trade Freedom	+41.2
Freedom from Corruption	+22.9	Government Spending	+32.5	Labor Freedom	-3.9	Investment Freedom	-20.0
				Monetary Freedom	+71.8	Financial Freedom	0

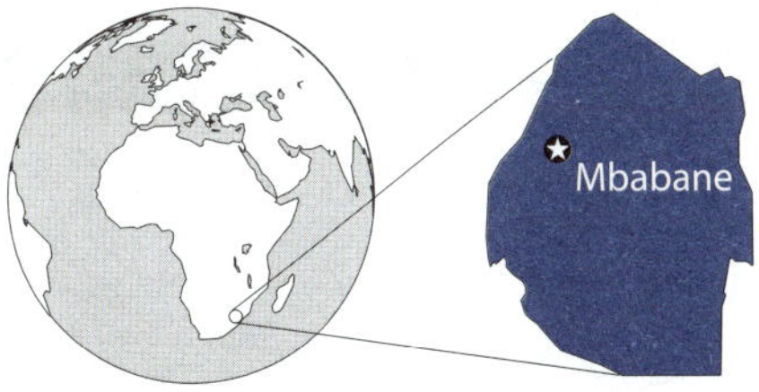

SWAZILAND

World Rank: **82** Regional Rank: **8**

Economic Freedom Score

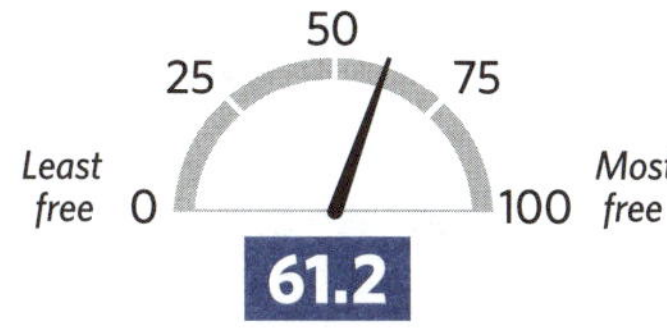

Swaziland's economic freedom score is 61.2, making its economy the 82nd freest in the 2014 *Index*. Its score has improved by 4.0 points since last year, primarily due to improvements in the control of government spending, trade freedom, and investment freedom. Swaziland is ranked 8th out of 46 countries in the Sub-Saharan Africa region, and its overall score is just above the world average.

Swaziland was first rated in the 1996 *Index*, and its economic freedom score has dropped since then by 2.1 points. Improvements in five of the 10 economic freedoms, including double-digit increases in trade freedom and fiscal freedom, have been more than offset by significant declines, including declines of 10 points or more in freedom from corruption, property rights, and financial freedom.

Swaziland had been on a generally downward path of economic freedom since 1995. In 2014, however, it has achieved its highest economic freedom score in eight years and is again rated "moderately free." Deeper institutional reforms are critical to ensuring sustainable economic development and greater poverty reduction.

BACKGROUND: King Mswati III rules Africa's last monarchy under a constitution that includes some democratic elements and protections for human rights. September 2013 parliamentary elections were criticized because political parties were not allowed to participate. Swaziland is part of the Southern African Customs Union and the Common Monetary Area. Its currency is pegged to the South African rand, and South Africa is its largest trading partner. Subsistence agriculture employs 70 percent of the workforce. The soft-drink concentrate, textile, and cane sugar industries are the leading export earners and the largest private-sector manufacturers. Coal and diamonds are also exported. Swaziland qualified for the African Growth and Opportunity Act's apparel provision in 2001, and 30,000 new jobs in its apparel industry have since been created. Swaziland has one of the world's highest HIV/AIDS rates.

Freedom Trend

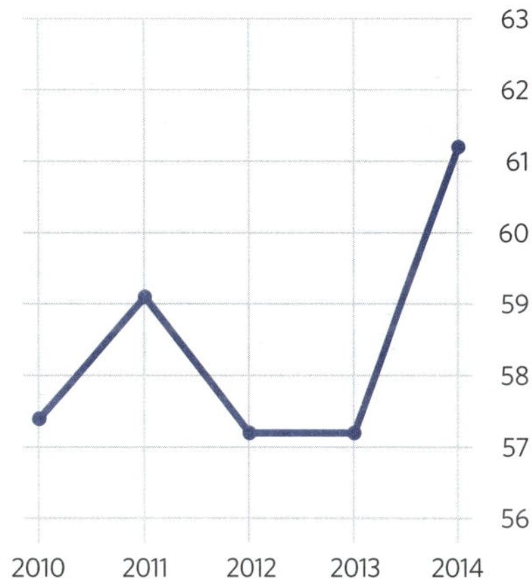

Country Comparisons

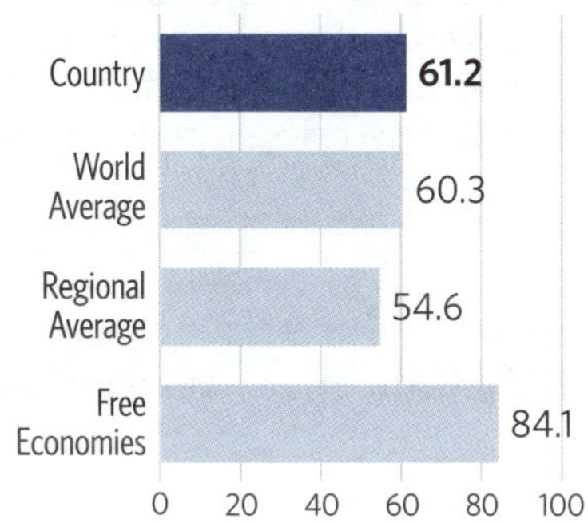

Quick Facts

Population: 1.1 million
GDP (PPP): $6.2 billion
-1.5% growth in 2012
5-year compound annual growth 1.0%
$5,782 per capita
Unemployment: n/a
Inflation (CPI): 8.9%
FDI Inflow: $89.6 million
Public Debt: 19.0% of GDP

2012 data unless otherwise noted.
Data compiled as of September 2013.

How Do We Measure Economic Freedom?
See page 471 for an explanation of the methodology or visit the *Index* Web site at *heritage.org/index*.

THE TEN ECONOMIC FREEDOMS

RULE OF LAW

	Score	Rank	1-Year Change
Property Rights	40.0	70th	0
Freedom from Corruption	31.6	96th	+0.6

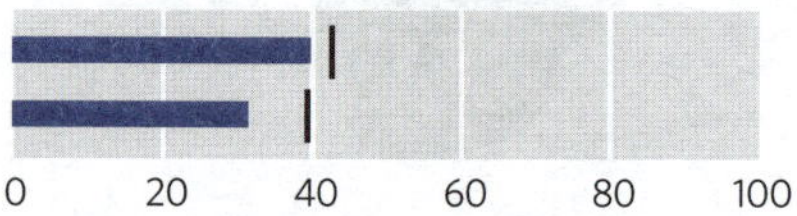

Corruption is a major problem, and government corruption was widely blamed for contributing to Swaziland's current economic problems. The dual judicial system includes courts based on Roman–Dutch law and traditional courts using customary law. The judiciary is independent in most civil cases, though the king has ultimate judicial powers, and the royal family and government often refuse to respect rulings with which they disagree.

GOVERNMENT SIZE

	Score	Rank	1-Year Change
Fiscal Freedom	74.7	119th	+0.3
Government Spending	70.9	84th	+19.6

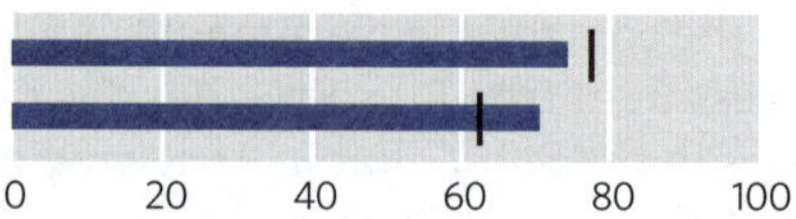

The top individual income tax rate is 33 percent, and the top corporate tax rate is 30 percent. Other taxes include a fuel tax and a sales tax. Overall tax revenue amounts to about 23.3 percent of the domestic economy. Government expenditures amount to 31 percent of the economy. Public debt has risen to almost 20 percent of GDP. Windfall revenues from the South African Customs Union have failed to shore up public finances.

REGULATORY EFFICIENCY

	Score	Rank	1-Year Change
Business Freedom	64.2	96th	-1.8
Labor Freedom	71.7	59th	+1.4
Monetary Freedom	72.3	130th	-2.4

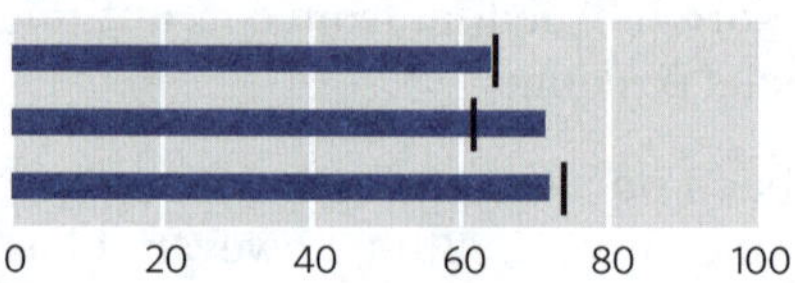

It takes 12 procedures and more than a month to launch a business, and completing licensing requirements costs more than the level of average annual income. A formal labor market has not been fully developed, and informal labor activity remains substantial. The state continues to influence prices through numerous state-owned enterprises and utilities.

OPEN MARKETS

	Score	Rank	1-Year Change
Trade Freedom	81.5	66th	+11.8
Investment Freedom	65.0	68th	+10.0
Financial Freedom	40.0	107th	0

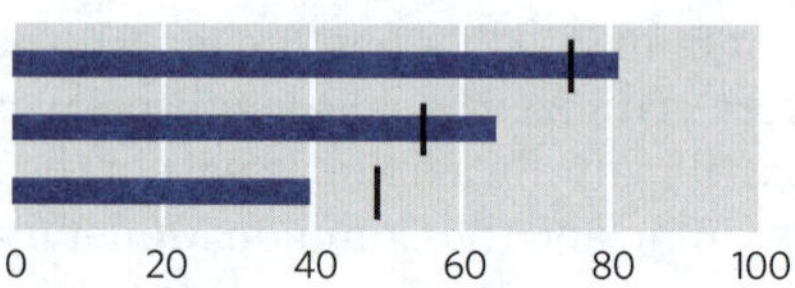

Swaziland has an average tariff rate of 4.2 percent. Foreign investment is allowed in most sectors of the economy, with ownership levels of up to 100 percent. The financial sector remains underdeveloped, and most of the population still lacks access to formal credit. Overall supervision of the banking sector is weak, and the sector remains subject to government influence. Capital markets are small.

Long-Term Score Change (since 1995)

RULE OF LAW		GOVERNMENT SIZE		REGULATORY EFFICIENCY		OPEN MARKETS	
Property Rights	**-30.0**	Fiscal Freedom	**+11.2**	Business Freedom	**-5.8**	Trade Freedom	**+23.5**
Freedom from Corruption	**-18.4**	Government Spending	**+1.6**	Labor Freedom	**+2.5**	Investment Freedom	**-5.0**
				Monetary Freedom	**+2.9**	Financial Freedom	**-10.0**

SWEDEN

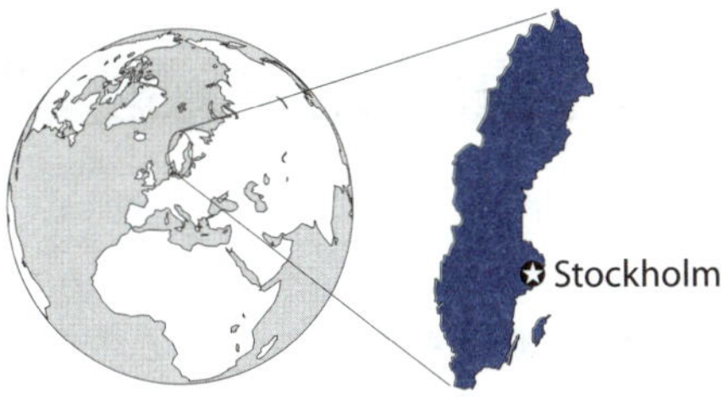

Economic Freedom Score

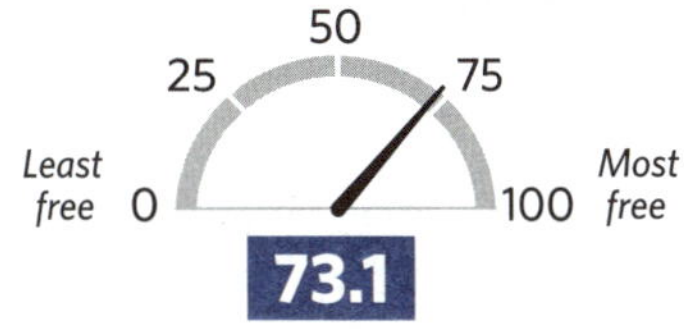

World Rank: **20** Regional Rank: **10**

Freedom Trend

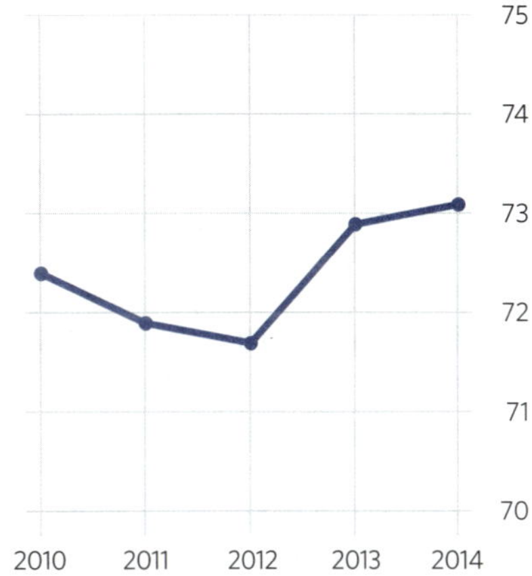

Sweden's economic freedom score is 73.1, making its economy the 20th freest in the 2014 *Index*. Its score has increased by 0.2 point since last year, with improvements in fiscal freedom and trade freedom outweighing combined small declines in business freedom, labor freedom, and freedom from corruption. Sweden is ranked 10th out of 43 countries in the Europe region, and its overall score is above the world and regional averages.

Over the 20-year history of the *Index*, Sweden has advanced its economic freedom score by 11.7 points, the second best improvement among developed economies. Substantial increases in eight of the 10 economic freedoms, including financial freedom, the management of public spending, business freedom, and investment freedom, have enabled the economy to advance from "moderately free" to "mostly free." In the 2014 *Index*, Sweden has achieved its highest economic freedom score ever.

Country Comparisons

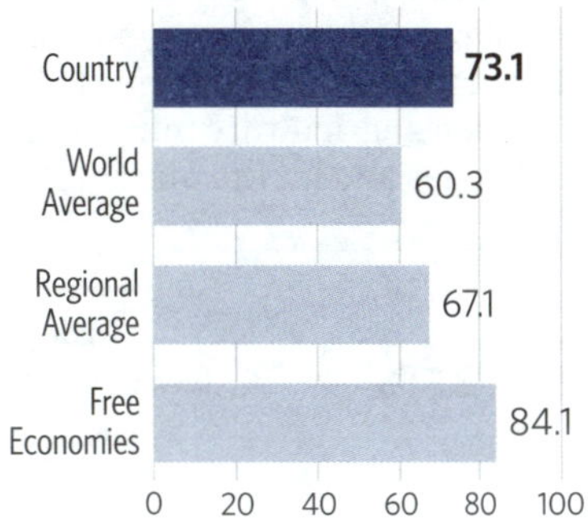

Openness to global trade and commerce has propelled economic dynamism, and Sweden has rebounded relatively quickly from the global recession. The financial system remains stable, and prudent regulations allowed banks to withstand the global financial turmoil with little disruption. Sweden has long benefited from institutional strengths that include strong protection of property rights and minimum tolerance for corruption.

BACKGROUND: Sweden joined the European Union in 1995 but rejected adoption of the euro in 2003, and its public remains hostile to eurozone membership. The center-right Alliance for Sweden headed by the Moderate Party, led by Fredrik Reinfeldt, currently leads a minority government. There were riots in the largely immigrant suburbs outside of Stockholm in May 2013. Sweden's economy was healthy before the international financial crisis, but a downturn in 2009 led to a slight increase in unemployment. Banks are well capitalized, and Sweden has weathered the financial crisis relatively well. Principal exports include automobiles, telecommunications products, construction equipment, and other investment goods.

Quick Facts

Population: 9.5 million
GDP (PPP): $393.0 billion
1.2% growth in 2012
5-year compound annual growth 1.0%
$41,191 per capita
Unemployment: 7.9%
Inflation (CPI): 0.9%
FDI Inflow: $13.7 billion
Public Debt: 38.0% of GDP

2012 data unless otherwise noted.
Data compiled as of September 2013.

How Do We Measure Economic Freedom?
See page 471 for an explanation of the methodology or visit the *Index* Web site at *heritage.org/index.*

THE TEN ECONOMIC FREEDOMS

RULE OF LAW

	Score	Rank	1-Year Change
Property Rights	90.0	2nd	0
Freedom from Corruption	92.3	4th	-0.7

Corruption rates are generally low, and anti-corruption measures discourage bribery of public officials and uphold government integrity. However, Sweden was admonished by the OECD in 2012 for insufficient enforcement of its foreign bribery laws. The rule of law is well maintained. The judicial system operates independently and impartially, with consistent application of laws. Property rights and contract enforcement are very secure.

GOVERNMENT SIZE

	Score	Rank	1-Year Change
Fiscal Freedom	42.9	181st	+3.3
Government Spending	21.4	170th	+0.4

The top individual income tax rate is 57 percent, and the top corporate tax rate has been cut to 22 percent. Other taxes include a value-added tax (VAT) and a capital gains tax. The overall tax burden is 44.5 percent of GDP. Public expenditures make up about half of GDP, and public debt is below 40 percent of GDP. The government is attempting to expand investment in infrastructure and research while reining in welfare spending.

REGULATORY EFFICIENCY

	Score	Rank	1-Year Change
Business Freedom	91.1	11th	-2.1
Labor Freedom	52.9	127th	-0.7
Monetary Freedom	82.5	12th	+0.4

It takes three procedures and 16 days to incorporate a business, but completing licensing requirements can be time-consuming and costly. Bankruptcy procedures are straightforward. Labor regulations continue to be rigid, with the non-salary cost of hiring a worker considerable. Sweden's agriculture minister has led a courageous fight to eliminate all European Union farm subsidies and let the markets dictate food prices.

OPEN MARKETS

	Score	Rank	1-Year Change
Trade Freedom	87.8	11th	+1.0
Investment Freedom	90.0	2nd	0
Financial Freedom	80.0	4th	0

EU members have a low 1.1 percent average tariff rate and, in general, few non-tariff barriers to trade. Sweden generally treats foreign and domestic investors equally. The economy includes several state-owned enterprises. The well-developed financial sector accounts for about 4 percent of GDP and continues to fare quite well, with stability firmly in place. Banking regulations are sensible, and lending practices have been prudent.

Long-Term Score Change (since 1995)

RULE OF LAW		GOVERNMENT SIZE		REGULATORY EFFICIENCY		OPEN MARKETS	
Property Rights	+20.0	Fiscal Freedom	-1.2	Business Freedom	+21.1	Trade Freedom	+10.8
Freedom from Corruption	+2.3	Government Spending	+21.4	Labor Freedom	-12.3	Investment Freedom	+20.0
				Monetary Freedom	+1.0	Financial Freedom	+30.0

SWITZERLAND

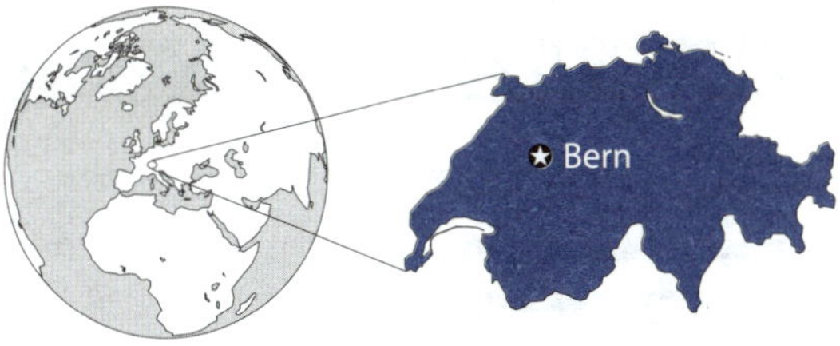

World Rank: **4** Regional Rank: **1**

Economic Freedom Score

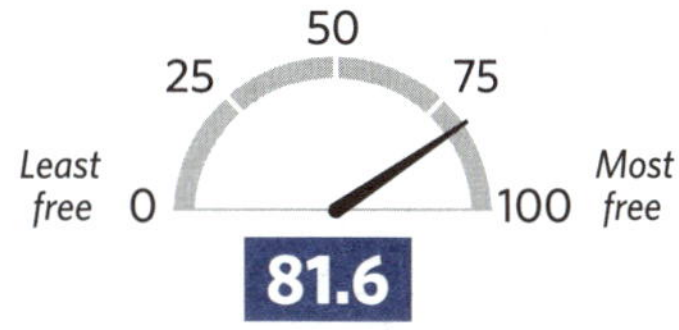

Switzerland's economic freedom score is 81.6, making its economy the 4th freest for the first time ever in the 2014 *Index*. Its score is 0.6 point higher than last year, with improvements in trade freedom and the management of public spending partially offset by declines in monetary freedom and labor freedom. Switzerland is ranked 1st out of 43 countries in the Europe region.

Switzerland was first graded in the 1996 *Index*, and its economic freedom score has advanced since then by 4.8 points. Improved ratings for six of the 10 economic freedoms, led by the sound management of public spending and notable enhancements in the area of market openness as measured through trade freedom and financial freedom, have enabled Switzerland to advance to economically "free" since 2010.

As reflected in the steady rise of its economic freedom over the 19 years it has been graded, Switzerland's strong competitiveness is built on flexibility and openness. The sound regulatory environment encourages entrepreneurial activity and innovation. Banking regulations and lending practices are prudent and sensible. The judicial system, independent and free of corruption, provides strong protection of property rights.

BACKGROUND: Switzerland's federal system of government disperses power widely, and executive authority is exercised collectively by the seven-member Federal Council. Switzerland has a long tradition of openness to the world but jealously guards its independence and neutrality. It did not join the United Nations until 2002, and two referenda on membership in the European Union have failed by wide margins. Membership in the European Economic Area was rejected by referendum in 1992. Switzerland is one of the world's richest and most investment-friendly countries and has a well-developed financial services industry. In addition to banking, the economy relies heavily on precision manufacturing, metals, pharmaceuticals, chemicals, and electronics. Economic growth was solid but slow in 2013. Unemployment is around 3 percent.

How Do We Measure Economic Freedom?
See page 471 for an explanation of the methodology or visit the *Index* Web site at *heritage.org/index.*

Freedom Trend

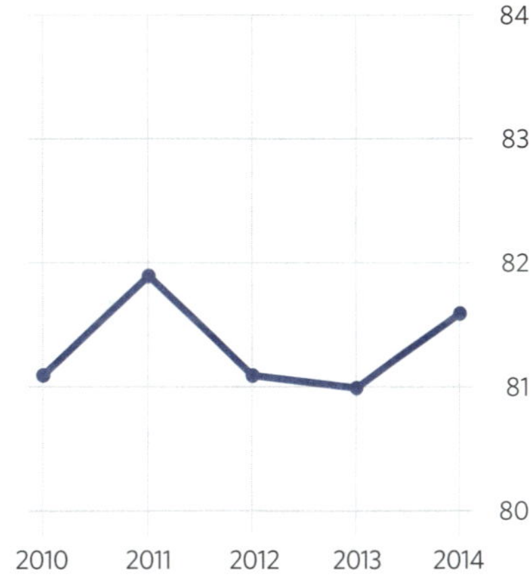

Country Comparisons

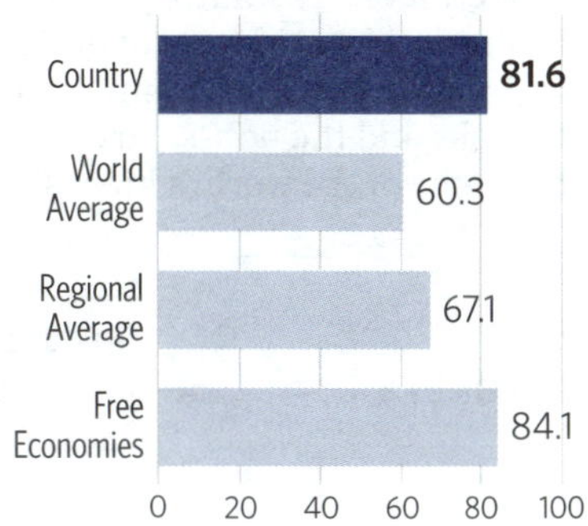

Quick Facts

Population: 8.0 million
GDP (PPP): $363.4 billion
1.0% growth in 2012
5-year compound annual growth 1.2%
$45,418 per capita
Unemployment: 2.9%
Inflation (CPI): -0.7%
FDI Inflow: $3.6 billion
Public Debt: 49.1% of GDP

2012 data unless otherwise noted.
Data compiled as of September 2013.

THE TEN ECONOMIC FREEDOMS

RULE OF LAW

	Score	Rank	1-Year Change
Property Rights	90.0	2nd	0
Freedom from Corruption	88.1	6th	+0.1

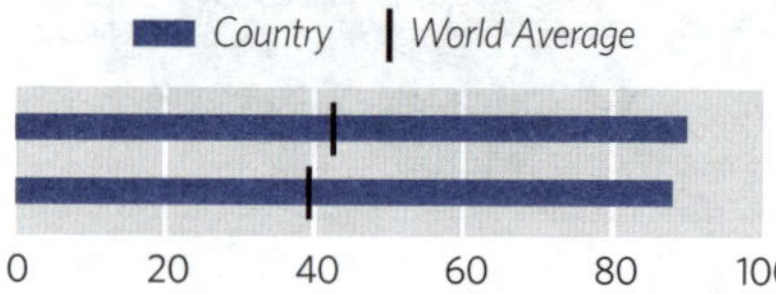

In 2013, the government broadened anti-corruption laws to make bribery almost always a criminal offense. Protection of property rights is strongly enforced, and an independent and fair judicial system is institutionalized throughout the economy. Commercial and bankruptcy laws are applied consistently and efficiently. Intellectual property rights are respected, and enforcement is consistent with world standards.

GOVERNMENT SIZE

	Score	Rank	1-Year Change
Fiscal Freedom	68.9	144th	+0.8
Government Spending	65.7	99th	+1.9

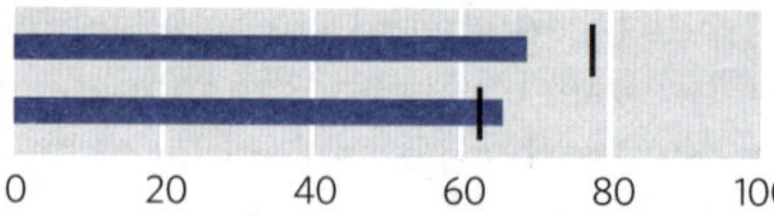

Switzerland's tax regime remains more burdensome at the cantonal level than at the federal level. The top federal income tax rate is 11.5 percent, with a combined tax rate that can reach 41.5 percent. The federal corporate tax rate is 8.5 percent, which, combined with cantonal taxes, can reach 24 percent. The overall tax burden is 28.5 percent of GDP. Government spending accounts for 33.8 percent of the economy.

REGULATORY EFFICIENCY

	Score	Rank	1-Year Change
Business Freedom	75.4	48th	-0.4
Labor Freedom	87.4	9th	-0.5
Monetary Freedom	85.2	5th	-1.0

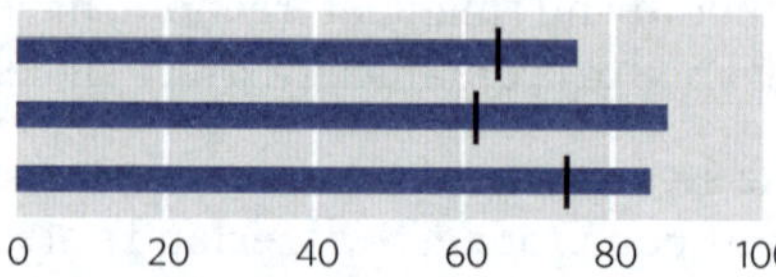

The efficient regulatory framework strongly facilitates entrepreneurial activity, allowing business formation and operation to be dynamic. The government generally takes a hands-off approach in sectors dominated by small businesses. Overall labor regulations are relatively flexible, and the non-salary cost of hiring a worker is moderate. Proportionately, Switzerland has some of the world's highest agricultural subsidies.

OPEN MARKETS

	Score	Rank	1-Year Change
Trade Freedom	90.0	1st	0
Investment Freedom	85.0	13th	+5.0
Financial Freedom	80.0	4th	0

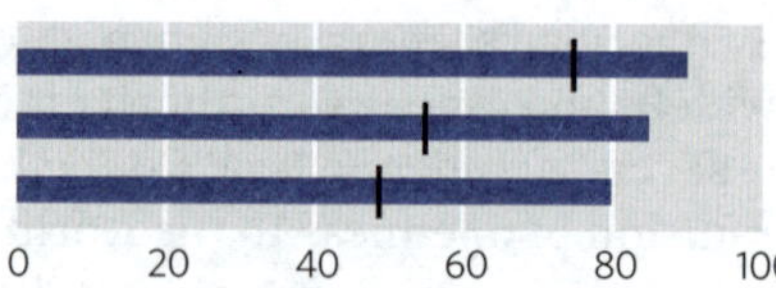

Switzerland has a 0 percent average tariff rate. Some non-tariff barriers impede agricultural imports. Foreign investment is not screened, and the government generally treats foreign and domestic investors equally. As a leading financial center, the highly developed financial sector provides a wide range of financing instruments for foreign and domestic investors. Despite the challenging external environment, banks remain well-capitalized.

Long-Term Score Change (since 1996)

RULE OF LAW		GOVERNMENT SIZE		REGULATORY EFFICIENCY		OPEN MARKETS	
Property Rights	**+20.0**	Fiscal Freedom	**-9.1**	Business Freedom	**+5.4**	Trade Freedom	**+12.0**
Freedom from Corruption	**-1.9**	Government Spending	**+12.3**	Labor Freedom	**+10.2**	Investment Freedom	**-5.0**
				Monetary Freedom	**-6.4**	Financial Freedom	**+10.0**

SYRIA

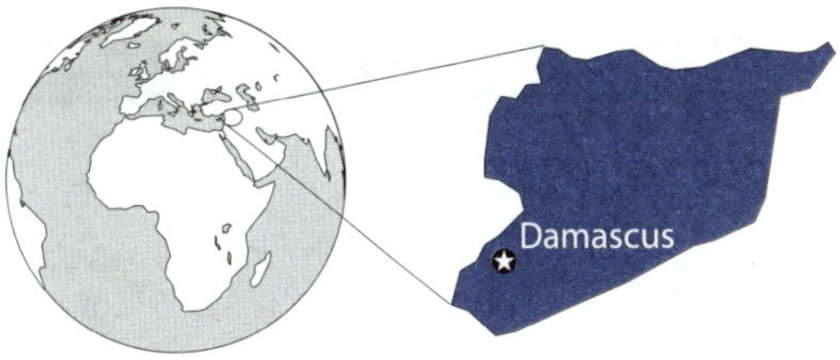

World Rank: Not Ranked Regional Rank: Not Ranked

Economic Freedom Score

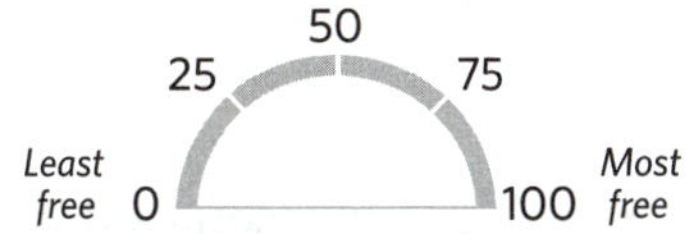

This economy is not graded

Numerical grading of Syria's overall economic freedom remains suspended because of the ongoing political turmoil that has led to civil unrest and a significant deterioration in the quality of publicly available economic statistics. Those facets of economic freedom for which data are still available have been individually scored. As a "mostly unfree" economy with a score of 51.2, Syria was ranked fourth lowest in the Middle East/North Africa region when it was last graded in the 2012 *Index*.

Before grading was suspended, the fragility of the foundations of economic freedom in Syria had been documented in very low scores for property rights and freedom from corruption. The state has long dominated economic activity, and the repressive environment has marginalized the private sector and prevented any sustainable development.

The Bashar al-Assad regime's brutal actions to maintain its hold on power have destroyed the rule of law and destabilized the region. Over 2 million refugees are registered by the United Nations, and it is estimated that 4 million people have been displaced internally. More than 100,000 people have been killed, and the degradation of health services has been highlighted by outbreaks of polio.

BACKGROUND: The Assad family's iron grip on Syria, which it has ruled since Hafez al-Assad's coup in 1970, faces serious challenges. Bashar al-Assad, who succeeded his father in 2000, has failed to deliver on promises to reform Syria's socialist economy and ease political repression. Anti-government "Arab Spring" protests in 2011 were met with brutal crackdowns. By 2012, the uprising against Assad had spiraled into a sectarian civil war. With Sunni-dominated rebels pitted against the Alawite-dominated regime, the fighting had killed more than 90,000 by June 2013 and triggered a severe economic recession. Syria's economy is also hobbled by a large state bureaucracy, falling oil production, rising budget deficits, and inflation.

How Do We Measure Economic Freedom?
See page 471 for an explanation of the methodology or visit the *Index* Web site at *heritage.org/index*.

Freedom Trend

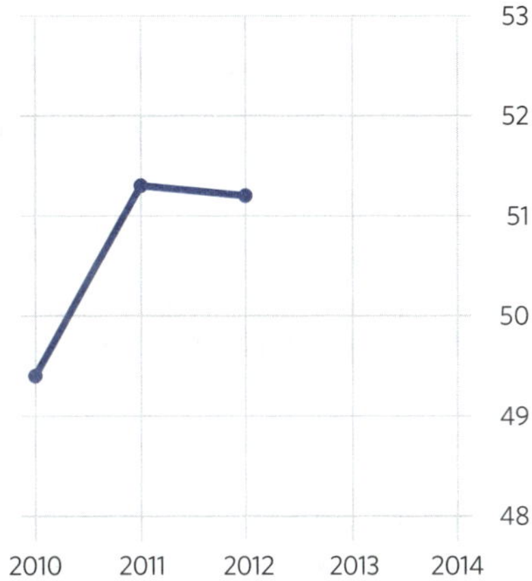

Country Comparisons

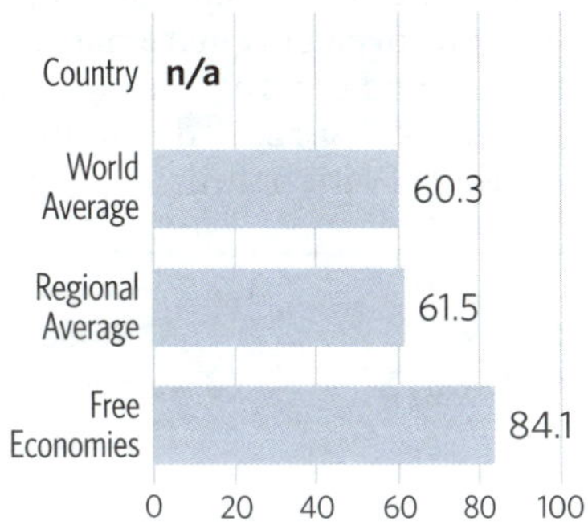

Quick Facts

Population: n/a
GDP (PPP): $107.6 billion (2011)
n/a growth in 2012
5-year compound annual growth n/a
n/a per capita
Unemployment: n/a
Inflation (CPI): 40.2%
FDI Inflow: n/a
Public Debt: n/a

2012 data unless otherwise noted.
Data compiled as of September 2013.

THE TEN ECONOMIC FREEDOMS

		Score	Rank	1-Year Change
RULE OF LAW	Property Rights	10.0	166th	-10.0
	Freedom from Corruption	23.3	142nd	-2.7

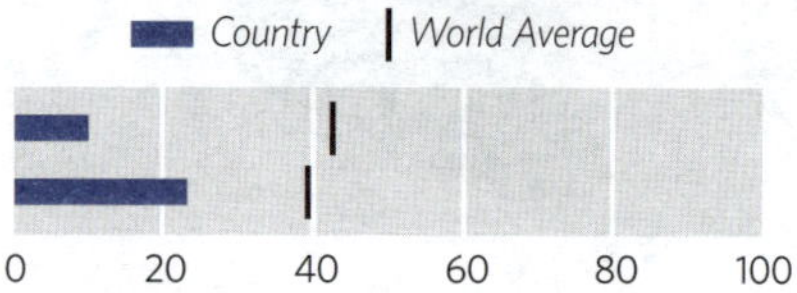

Corruption is widespread and rarely carries serious punishment, and bribery is often necessary to navigate the bureaucracy. Regime officials and their families benefit from a range of illicit economic activities. Syria's legal system is a mix of Ottoman and French civil law with Islamic law. The constitution requires that Islamic jurisprudence be a main source of legislation. The judiciary is neither transparent nor independent.

		Score	Rank	1-Year Change
GOVERNMENT SIZE	Fiscal Freedom	n/a	—	n/a
	Government Spending	n/a	—	n/a

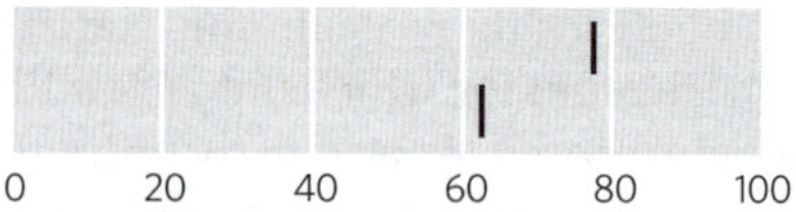

The top individual income tax rate is 22 percent, and the top corporate tax rate is 28 percent. Other taxes include an inheritance tax and a property transfer tax. Overall tax revenue equals 10.4 percent of the domestic economy. Public debt is 29 percent of GDP. The ongoing civil war continues to interfere with public administration and the implementation of fiscal policy.

		Score	Rank	1-Year Change
REGULATORY EFFICIENCY	Business Freedom	60.4	110th	+1.1
	Labor Freedom	55.1	114th	+6.2
	Monetary Freedom	n/a	—	n/a

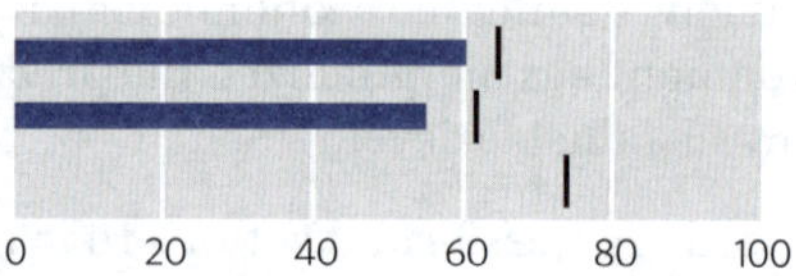

Before the ongoing civil unrest, the business environment, lacking transparency and efficiency, had improved only marginally. The labor market, which had already suffered from state interference and control, has been severely affected by the devastating conflicts. Inflation surged substantially in 2013 due to shortages and wide-ranging subsidy reductions despite the introduction of ration cards.

		Score	Rank	1-Year Change
OPEN MARKETS	Trade Freedom	n/a	—	n/a
	Investment Freedom	0.0	178th	-10.0
	Financial Freedom	20.0	163rd	0

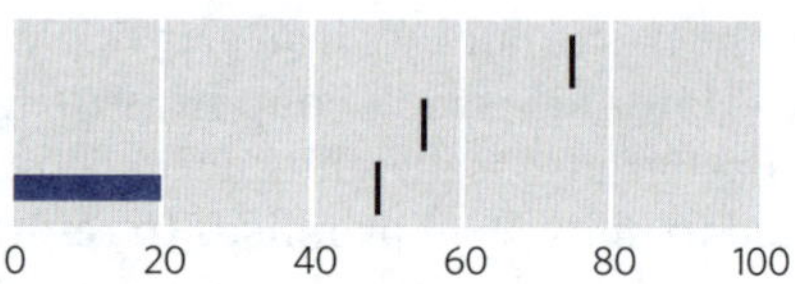

Syria has a 6.1 percent average tariff rate, and foreign investment is subject to government screening. Civil unrest is a major barrier to international trade and investment. Political uncertainty and repression have severely weakened the financial system. The central bank has imposed restrictions on the sale of foreign currency by banks to individuals.

Long-Term Score Change: n/a

RULE OF LAW		GOVERNMENT SIZE		REGULATORY EFFICIENCY		OPEN MARKETS	
Property Rights	n/a	Fiscal Freedom	n/a	Business Freedom	n/a	Trade Freedom	n/a
Freedom from Corruption	n/a	Government Spending	n/a	Labor Freedom	n/a	Investment Freedom	n/a
				Monetary Freedom	n/a	Financial Freedom	n/a

TAIWAN

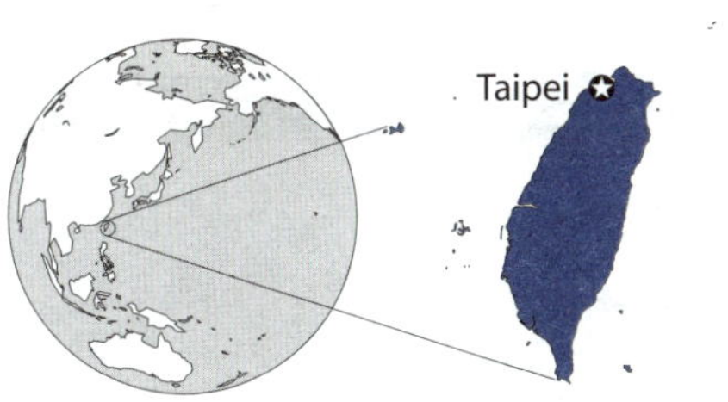

World Rank: 17 **Regional Rank: 5**

Economic Freedom Score

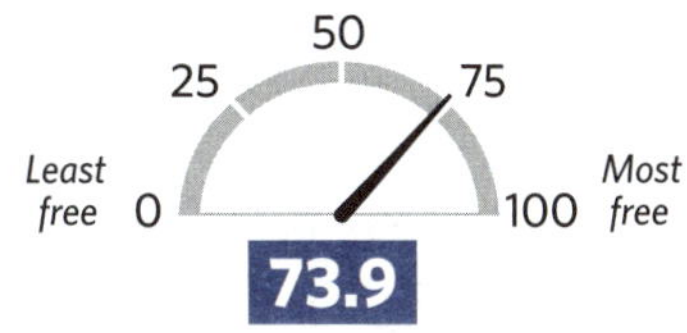

Freedom Trend

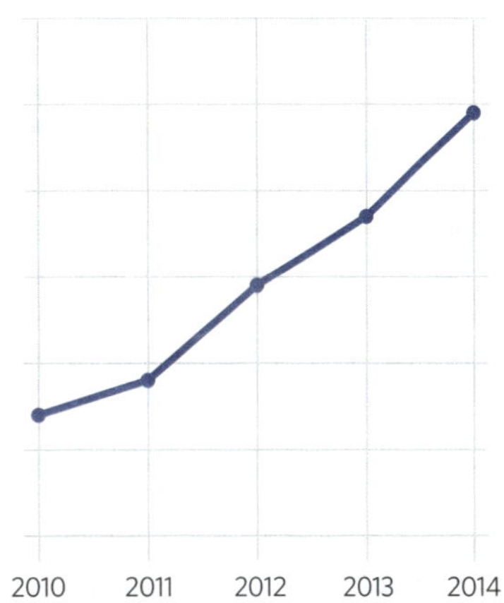

Country Comparisons

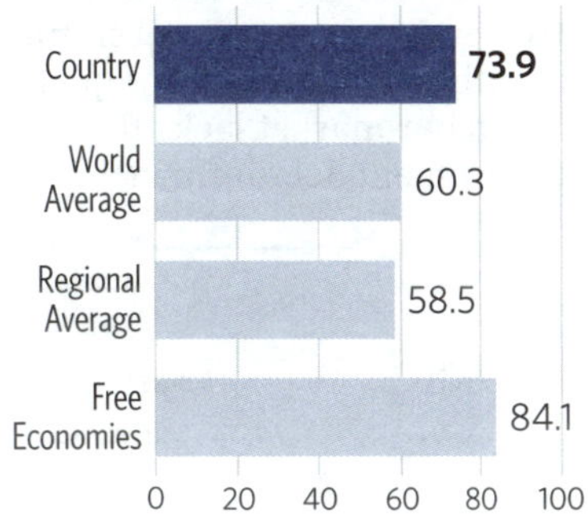

Taiwan's economic freedom score is 73.9, making its economy the 17th freest in the 2014 *Index*. Its score is 1.2 points higher than last year, with significant improvements in financial freedom and investment freedom outweighing small declines in six of the 10 economic freedoms including freedom from corruption. Taiwan is ranked 5th out of 42 economies in the Asia–Pacific region, and its overall score is higher than the world average.

Over the 20-year history of the *Index*, Taiwan's economy has generally been rated "mostly free" with an economic freedom score hovering near 70 points. Market openness, measured through trade freedom, investment freedom, and financial freedom, has improved by 10 points or more. Taiwan has recorded uninterrupted advancements in economic freedom since 2009 and continues to be ranked one of the world's 20 freest economies.

Taiwan has maintained well-developed legal and commercial infrastructure in the private sector. The corporate tax rate has become more competitive, and small and medium-size enterprises continue to be the backbone of economic dynamism. The level of state involvement in the economy remains considerable, but government spending is under control.

BACKGROUND: Taiwan is a dynamic multi-party democracy. President Ma Ying-jeou, re-elected in 2012 on a platform that promised economic revitalization and a more open economic relationship with China, has relaxed cross-Strait barriers and negotiated a multi-stage formal economic agreement with the mainland. Taiwan remains excluded from membership in the United Nations, other international organizations, and a variety of free trade arrangements as a result of Beijing's efforts to pressure it into unification. Although internal opposition to engaging with China is considerable because of fears that sovereignty will be lost, recent economic arrangements bind the island closer to the PRC. With emphasis on services and high-technology manufacturing, Taiwan's economy is one of the richest in Asia.

Quick Facts

Population: 23.3 million
GDP (PPP): $903.5 billion
1.3% growth in 2012
5-year compound annual growth 2.9%
$38,749 per capita
Unemployment: 4.2%
Inflation (CPI): 1.9%
FDI Inflow: $3.2 billion
Public Debt: 40.9% of GDP

2012 data unless otherwise noted.
Data compiled as of September 2013.

How Do We Measure Economic Freedom?
See page 471 for an explanation of the methodology or visit the *Index* Web site at *heritage.org/index.*

THE TEN ECONOMIC FREEDOMS

RULE OF LAW

	Score	Rank	1-Year Change
Property Rights	70.0	27th	0
Freedom from Corruption	59.7	36th	-1.3

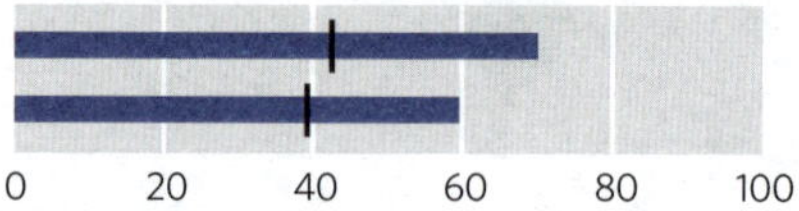

Corruption remains a problem, though significantly less pervasive than in the past, and politics and big business are closely intertwined. The judiciary is independent, and the court system is free of political interference. A new law enacted in July 2012 established a rating and removal system to address concerns about corrupt or incompetent judges. Property rights are generally protected, and the judiciary enforces contracts effectively.

GOVERNMENT SIZE

	Score	Rank	1-Year Change
Fiscal Freedom	80.3	82nd	-0.2
Government Spending	84.7	34th	-0.2

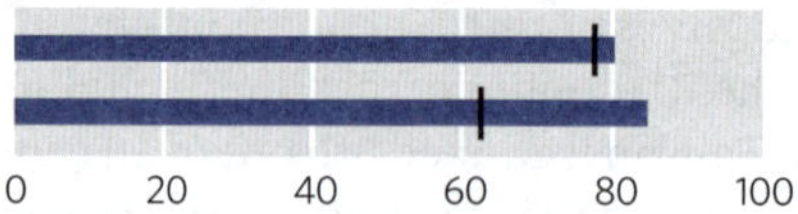

The top individual income tax rate is 40 percent, and the top corporate tax rate is 17 percent. Other taxes include a value-added tax (VAT) and an interest tax. The overall tax burden amounts to 8.8 percent of gross domestic income. Government spending accounts for 23 percent of GDP, and public debt remains steady at about 40 percent of the gross domestic economy.

REGULATORY EFFICIENCY

	Score	Rank	1-Year Change
Business Freedom	93.9	6th	-0.4
Labor Freedom	53.1	126th	-0.2
Monetary Freedom	81.7	16th	-1.2

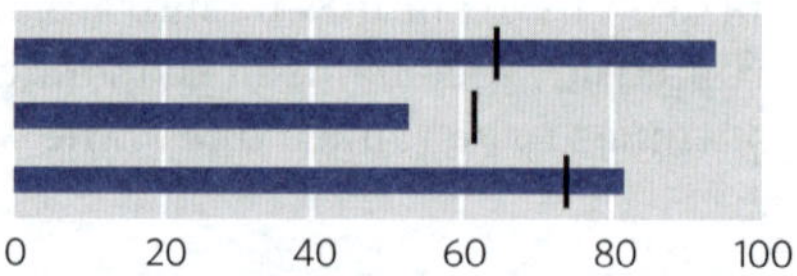

It takes three procedures on average to start a company, and no minimum capital is required. However, licensing requirements remain relatively time-consuming and take over three months on average to complete. Bankruptcy proceedings are fairly easy and straightforward. The labor market lacks flexibility. Prices are market-determined for the most part, but the government does influence some prices (for example, through fluctuating fuel subsidies).

OPEN MARKETS

	Score	Rank	1-Year Change
Trade Freedom	85.8	44th	+0.8
Investment Freedom	70.0	46th	+5.0
Financial Freedom	60.0	41st	+10.0

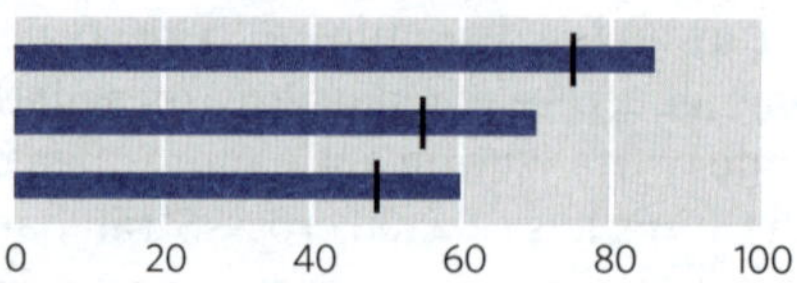

The average tariff rate is 2.1 percent. Tariff-rate quotas are imposed on some categories of imports. New foreign investment may be screened by the government, and investment in some sectors of the economy is subject to limits. The financial sector, dominated by banking, has gradually become more competitive, although it is subject to state interference. A variety of financial instruments are available to investors on market terms.

Long-Term Score Change (since 1995)

RULE OF LAW		GOVERNMENT SIZE		REGULATORY EFFICIENCY		OPEN MARKETS	
Property Rights	**-20.0**	Fiscal Freedom	**+6.2**	Business Freedom	**+8.9**	Trade Freedom	**+10.6**
Freedom from Corruption	**-30.3**	Government Spending	**+14.9**	Labor Freedom	**+7.0**	Investment Freedom	**+20.0**
				Monetary Freedom	**-1.7**	Financial Freedom	**+10.0**

TAJIKISTAN

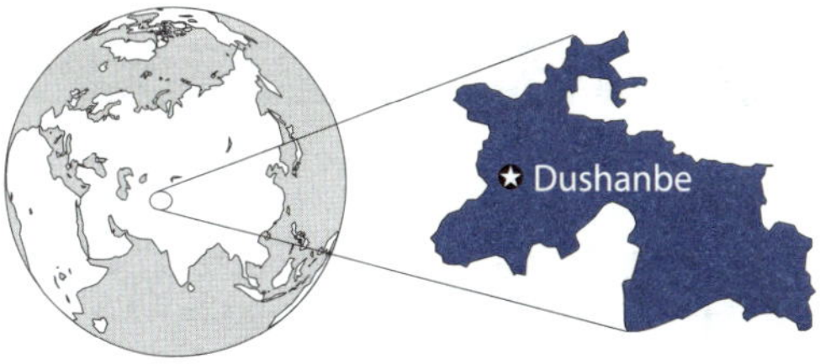

World Rank: 139 | **Regional Rank: 30**

Tajikistan's economic freedom score is 52.0, making its economy the 139th freest in the 2014 *Index*. It score has decreased by 1.4 points since last year, with relatively large declines in labor freedom, trade freedom, freedom from corruption, and business freedom offsetting an improvement in investment freedom. Tajikistan is ranked 30th out of 42 countries in the Asia–Pacific region, and its overall score is lower than the world average.

Tajikistan's economic freedom was first rated in the 1998 *Index*, and its score has advanced since then by nearly 11 points. From a low base, it has achieved double-digit score improvements in three of the 10 economic freedoms, most notably an increase of more than 65 points in monetary freedom, which contributed strongly to lifting Tajikistan out of the "repressed" category. However, potential economic gains from these improvements have been undermined considerably by deteriorations in labor freedom, the control of government spending, and property rights.

Institutional shortcomings, particularly in the area of rule of law, continue to undermine Tajikistan's chances for long-term economic development, slowing down its transition to a more market-oriented economy. Lagging far behind many other developing countries in terms of economic and human development, Tajikistan's economy remains "mostly unfree."

BACKGROUND: Tajikistan's post-Communist transition has been stunted ever since the 1992–1997 civil war between an Islamist/democratic coalition and the ruling Communists. President Emomali Rahmon has been in power for over 20 years, dominating all three branches of government. Social and economic challenges include political corruption, Islamist terrorism, spillover from the war in Afghanistan, and tensions with neighboring Uzbekistan. Government abuses of human rights are widespread. Tajikistan is heavily dependent on revenues from aluminum and cotton exports. The drug trade and remittances from its 1 million migrant workers, primarily in Russia, account for over 45 percent of GDP.

How Do We Measure Economic Freedom?
See page 471 for an explanation of the methodology or visit the *Index* Web site at *heritage.org/index*.

Economic Freedom Score

Freedom Trend

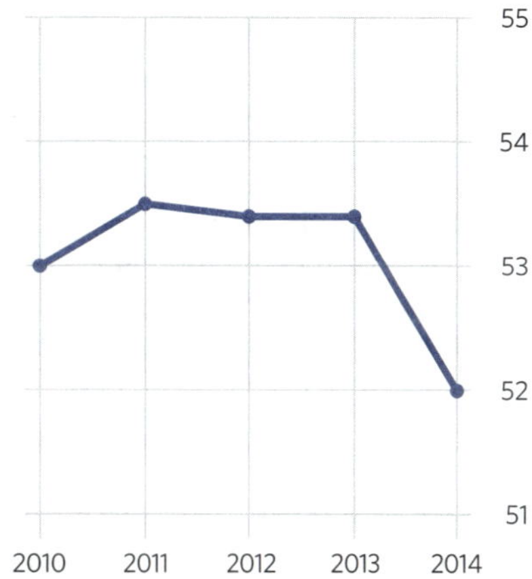

Country Comparisons

Quick Facts

Population: 8.0 million
GDP (PPP): $17.7 billion
7.5% growth in 2012
5-year compound annual growth 6.7%
$2,229 per capita
Unemployment: 2.5%
Inflation (CPI): 5.8%
FDI Inflow: $289.9 million
Public Debt: 32.5% of GDP

2012 data unless otherwise noted.
Data compiled as of September 2013.

THE TEN ECONOMIC FREEDOMS

RULE OF LAW

	Score	Rank	1-Year Change
Property Rights	20.0	139th	0
Freedom from Corruption	19.4	163rd	-3.6

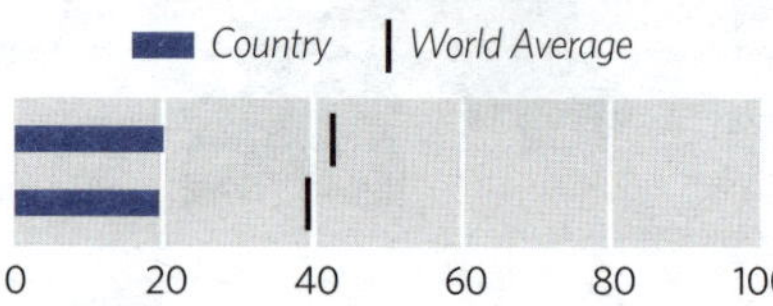

Corruption is pervasive. Patronage networks and regional affiliations are central to political life. At least two of President Rahmon's children hold senior government posts, and various family members reportedly maintain extensive business interests. The judiciary lacks independence. Many judges are poorly trained and inexperienced, and bribery is reportedly widespread. Under Tajik law, all land belongs to the state.

GOVERNMENT SIZE

	Score	Rank	1-Year Change
Fiscal Freedom	92.3	23rd	-0.5
Government Spending	78.1	61st	0

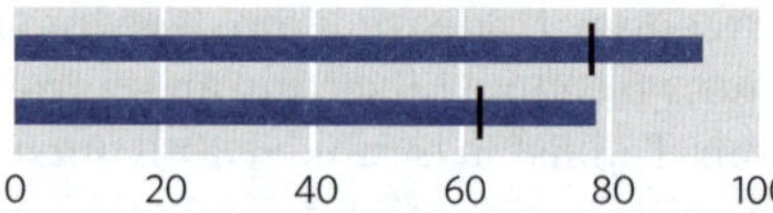

The top individual income tax rate is 13 percent, and the top corporate tax rate is 15 percent. A 25 percent tax is applied to companies in the transportation, telecommunications, and service industries. Other taxes include a value-added tax (VAT) and a sales tax. Overall tax revenue amounts to 19.5 percent of the domestic economy. Public expenditures are 27 percent of GDP. Government debt is 33 percent of gross domestic output.

REGULATORY EFFICIENCY

	Score	Rank	1-Year Change
Business Freedom	58.4	122nd	-3.3
Labor Freedom	45.5	154th	-10.0
Monetary Freedom	67.7	156th	+3.1

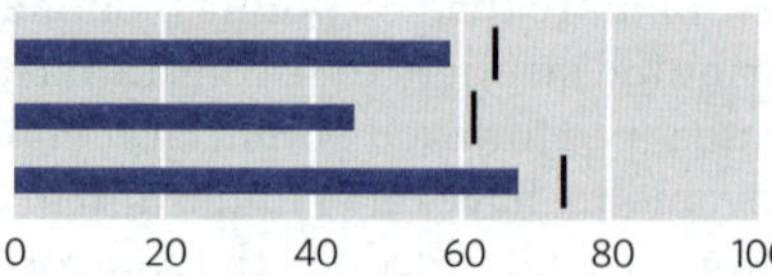

With no minimum capital required, launching a business takes five procedures and over a month. State interference increases regulatory costs. Completing licensing requirements takes more than 200 days and costs over six times the level of average annual income. The labor market remains underdeveloped. The government influences prices through regulation and subsidies provided to numerous state-owned and state trading enterprises.

OPEN MARKETS

	Score	Rank	1-Year Change
Trade Freedom	73.2	109th	-5.0
Investment Freedom	25.0	159th	+5.0
Financial Freedom	40.0	107th	0

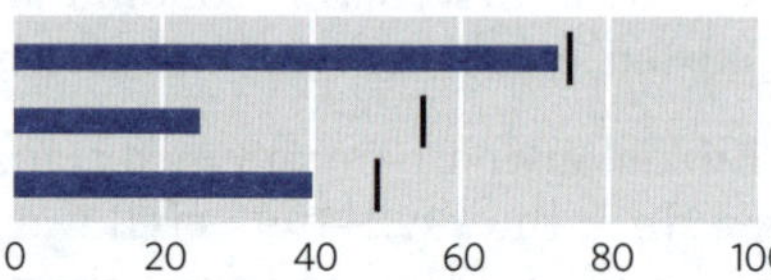

The average tariff rate for Tajikistan is 5.9 percent. Although Tajikistan joined the World Trade Organization in 2013, it remains costly and time-consuming to import goods. Foreign investment is subject to government screening. The financial sector remains underdeveloped and subject to heavy state control. Continued government interference and the sector's limited overall capacity pose serious handicaps to private-sector development.

Long-Term Score Change (since 1998)

RULE OF LAW		GOVERNMENT SIZE		REGULATORY EFFICIENCY		OPEN MARKETS	
Property Rights	-10.0	Fiscal Freedom	+34.8	Business Freedom	+3.4	Trade Freedom	+4.8
Freedom from Corruption	+9.4	Government Spending	-11.2	Labor Freedom	-14.8	Investment Freedom	-5.0
				Monetary Freedom	+67.7	Financial Freedom	+10.0

TANZANIA

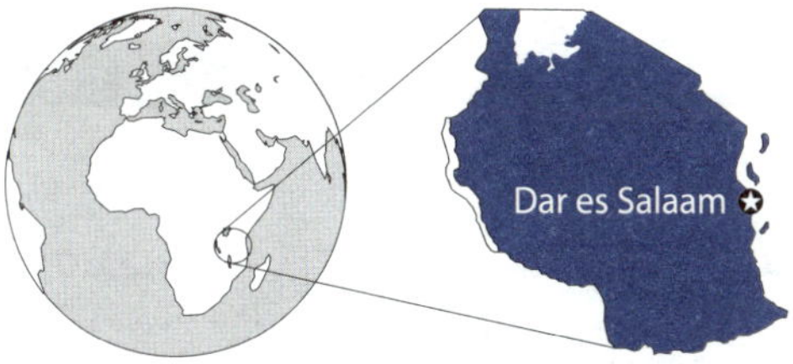

World Rank: **106** Regional Rank: **15**

Economic Freedom Score

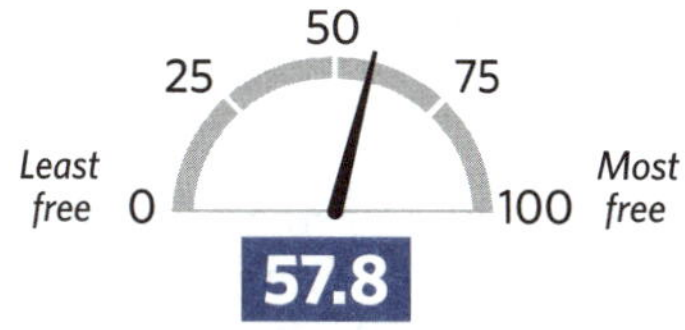

Freedom Trend

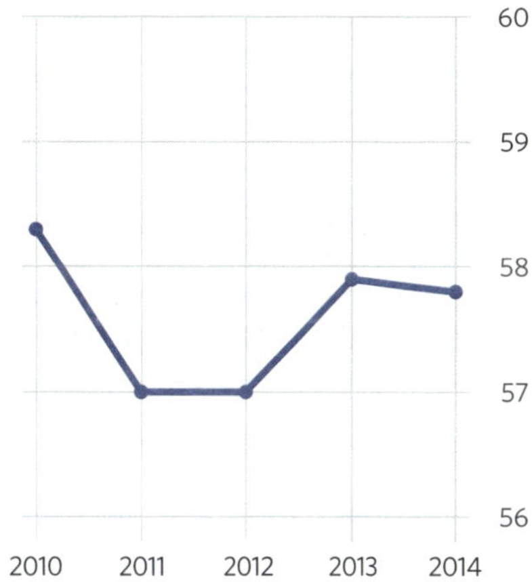

Country Comparisons

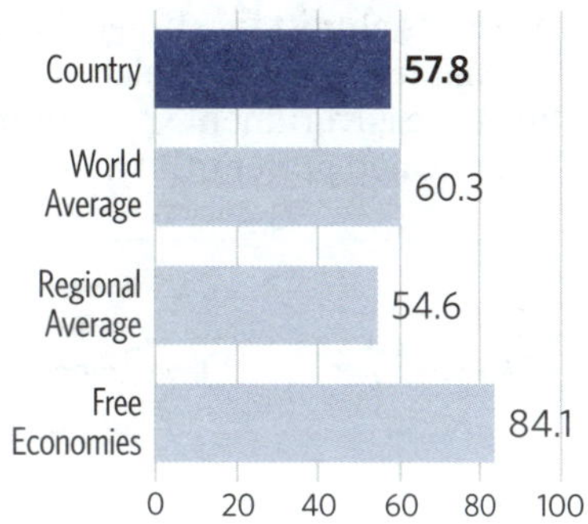

Quick Facts

Population: 47.1 million
GDP (PPP): $73.9 billion
6.9% growth in 2012
5-year compound annual growth 6.8%
$1,567 per capita
Unemployment: n/a
Inflation (CPI): 16.0%
FDI Inflow: $1.7 billion
Public Debt: 41.4% of GDP

2012 data unless otherwise noted.
Data compiled as of September 2013.

Tanzania's economic freedom score is 57.8, making its economy the 106th freest in the 2014 *Index*. Its score is essentially the same as last year, with improvements in investment freedom and trade freedom largely offset by combined deteriorations in monetary freedom, business freedom, and freedom from corruption. Tanzania is ranked 15th out of 46 countries in the Sub-Saharan Africa region, and its overall score is lower than the world average.

Over the 20-year history of the *Index*, Tanzania's economic freedom has been stagnant near the upper boundary of the "mostly unfree" category. Its overall score has increased slightly, but declines in the management of government spending, business freedom, and property rights have largely canceled out double-digit improvements in trade freedom and investment freedom.

Tanzania's notable economic expansion in recent years has been facilitated by open-market policies related to global commerce. The financial sector and the investment framework are relatively well developed for the region. Nevertheless, Tanzania appears to lack any strong commitment to the further institutional reforms that are essential to the development of a strong private sector. Private property rights are weakly protected and poorly defined, deterring sustainable investment.

BACKGROUND: President Jakaya Kikwete was elected in December 2005 and re-elected in October 2010. Tanzania's historically state-led economy has transitioned to a market-based economy but remains hindered by weak property rights, poor infrastructure, and a high HIV/AIDS rate. Thirty percent of the budget depends on donor assistance. The financial sector has expanded, and foreign-owned banks account for 48 percent of banking assets. Foreign investment has led to improvements in efficiency. A 50-year-old border dispute with Malawi resurfaced in 2012 when Malawi gave a British firm exploration rights for oil in Lake Malawi. Agriculture is the most important sector of the economy, providing about 27 percent of GDP and 80 percent of employment.

How Do We Measure Economic Freedom?
See page 471 for an explanation of the methodology or visit the *Index* Web site at *heritage.org/index*.

THE TEN ECONOMIC FREEDOMS

		Score	Rank	1-Year Change
RULE OF LAW	Property Rights	30.0	93rd	0
	Freedom from Corruption	28.8	110th	-1.2

Corruption remains pervasive in all aspects of political and commercial life, especially in the energy and natural resources sectors. Tanzania's judiciary remains subject to political influence and suffers from underfunding and corruption, in part due to increasing problems stemming from narcotics trafficking. Complex land laws have led to a high incidence of land disputes.

		Score	Rank	1-Year Change
GOVERNMENT SIZE	Fiscal Freedom	79.7	91st	-0.2
	Government Spending	78.3	59th	+0.4

The top individual income and corporate tax rates are 30 percent. Other taxes include a value-added tax (VAT) and an interest tax. The overall tax burden equals 15.2 percent of gross domestic income. Overall government expenditures amount to 27 percent of GDP, and public debt equals about 41 percent of the size of the economy. Institutional and policy reforms have begun to lay the foundation for prudent public finances.

		Score	Rank	1-Year Change
REGULATORY EFFICIENCY	Business Freedom	47.0	159th	-1.6
	Labor Freedom	61.1	95th	-0.8
	Monetary Freedom	66.0	160th	-5.8

Although requirements for launching a business are not time-consuming, the licensing process still costs almost five times the level of average annual income and takes more than 200 days to complete. Labor regulations are not efficient enough to support a vibrant labor market. In 2013, the government spent more than 1 percent of GDP to subsidize losses at TANESCO, the state-owned power utility.

		Score	Rank	1-Year Change
OPEN MARKETS	Trade Freedom	76.8	88th	+3.3
	Investment Freedom	60.0	80th	+5.0
	Financial Freedom	50.0	69th	0

Tanzania's average tariff rate is 6.6 percent. Bureaucratic delays in the judicial and regulatory systems may discourage foreign investment. The small financial sector has been evolving. Credit is allocated largely at market rates, and a variety of commercial credit instruments are available to the private sector. However, capital markets are rudimentary, reflecting the lack of efficiency and depth in the financial sector.

Long-Term Score Change (since 1995)

RULE OF LAW		GOVERNMENT SIZE		REGULATORY EFFICIENCY		OPEN MARKETS	
Property Rights	**-20.0**	Fiscal Freedom	**+1.8**	Business Freedom	**-8.0**	Trade Freedom	**+23.0**
Freedom from Corruption	**-1.2**	Government Spending	**-12.3**	Labor Freedom	**+13.2**	Investment Freedom	**+10.0**
				Monetary Freedom	**+7.5**	Financial Freedom	**0**

THAILAND

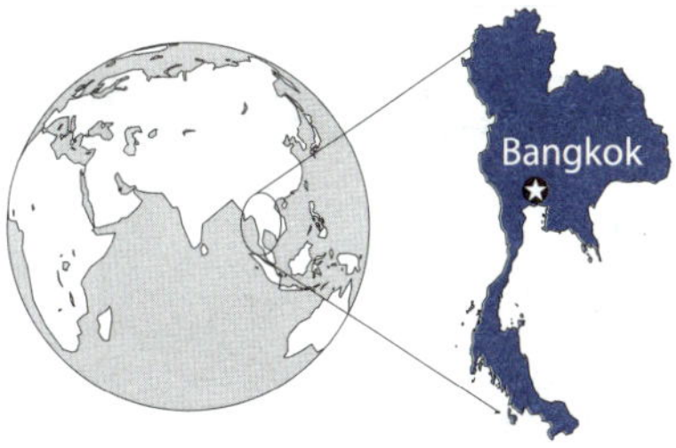

Economic Freedom Score

World Rank: 72 | **Regional Rank: 12**

Thailand's economic freedom score is 63.3, making its economy the 72nd freest in the 2014 *Index*. Its score is 0.8 point worse than last year due to continuing declines in labor freedom, the control of government spending, and freedom from corruption. Business freedom has recorded a score decline as well. Thailand is ranked 12th out of 42 countries in the Asia–Pacific region, and its overall score is higher than the world and regional averages.

Over the 20-year history of the *Index*, Thailand's economic freedom score has declined by 7.9 points, one of the 20 biggest deteriorations. Rating gains in financial freedom, fiscal freedom, and trade freedom have been overwhelmed by substantial double-digit declines in the rule of law as measured by property rights and freedom from corruption. Progress toward greater regulatory efficiency has been relatively slow. Since 1997, Thailand has been downgraded to the ranks of the "moderately free" economies.

Although economic fundamentals remain relatively solid, serious challenges require deeper institutional reforms. As reflected in the country's long-term score decline, Thailand's overall economic freedom remains constrained by institutional shortcomings. The perceived level of corruption has increased, and the legal system remains susceptible to political influence.

BACKGROUND: Thailand has had 18 military coups since becoming a constitutional monarchy in 1932. The government returned to democratic civilian control in December 2007, but political turmoil has continued. In the July 2011 parliamentary elections, Peua Thai, the opposition party of exiled leader Thaksin Shinawatra, won an outright majority, and Shinawatra's sister, Yingluck Shinawatra, became prime minister. About 40 percent of the population is engaged in agriculture, but a thriving manufacturing sector, including the manufacture of such high-technology products as integrated circuits, contributes significantly to export-led growth.

Freedom Trend

Country Comparisons

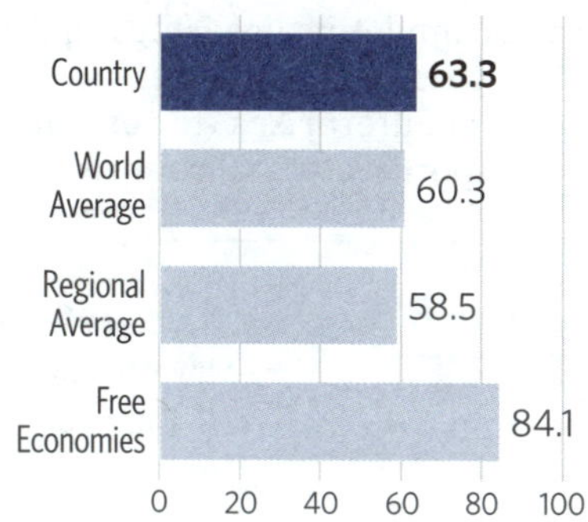

Quick Facts

Population: 64.4 million
GDP (PPP): $651.9 billion
6.4% growth in 2012
5-year compound annual growth 2.8%
$10,126 per capita
Unemployment: 0.5%
Inflation (CPI): 3.0%
FDI Inflow: $8.6 billion
Public Debt: 44.3% of GDP

2012 data unless otherwise noted.
Data compiled as of September 2013.

How Do We Measure Economic Freedom?
See page 471 for an explanation of the methodology or visit the *Index* Web site at *heritage.org/index*.

THE TEN ECONOMIC FREEDOMS

RULE OF LAW

	Score	Rank	1-Year Change
Property Rights	45.0	68th	0
Freedom from Corruption	33.6	85th	-0.4

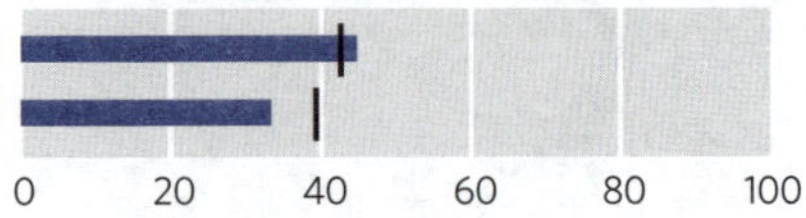

Corruption is widespread at all levels of Thai society. The country has an independent judiciary that generally is effective in enforcing property and contractual rights but remains vulnerable to political interference. Private property is generally protected, but the legal process is slow, and judgments can be affected through extralegal means. Infringements of intellectual property rights are substantial.

GOVERNMENT SIZE

	Score	Rank	1-Year Change
Fiscal Freedom	79.7	92nd	+0.8
Government Spending	83.6	38th	-0.1

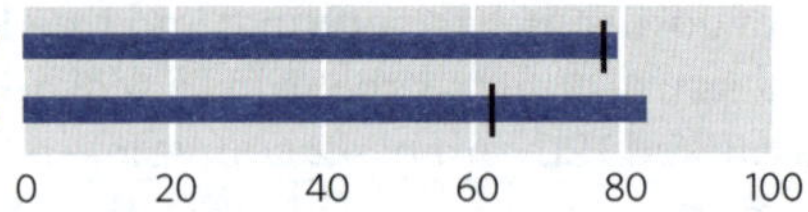

Thailand's top individual income tax rate is 37 percent, and its top corporate tax rate has fallen to 20 percent. Other taxes include a value-added tax (VAT) and a property tax. The overall tax burden is equal to 16 percent of gross domestic income. Government expenditures equate to 23 percent of GDP. Public debt is equivalent to about 45 percent of the domestic economy.

REGULATORY EFFICIENCY

	Score	Rank	1-Year Change
Business Freedom	71.4	70th	-1.8
Labor Freedom	61.6	92nd	-11.3
Monetary Freedom	68.6	148th	+0.3

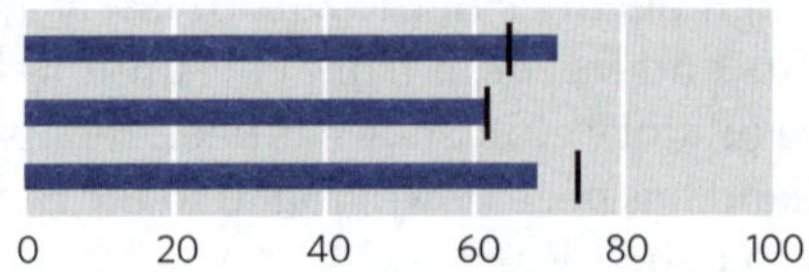

There is no minimum capital requirement, but incorporating a business takes almost a month, and completing licensing requirements continues to be time-consuming. Reform of the relatively rigid labor market has lagged, and informal labor activity remains substantial. State-owned enterprises (for example, in the utility, energy, telecom, banking, agriculture, and transport sectors) account for more than 40 percent of GDP.

OPEN MARKETS

	Score	Rank	1-Year Change
Trade Freedom	75.0	101st	-0.2
Investment Freedom	45.0	125th	+5.0
Financial Freedom	70.0	19th	0

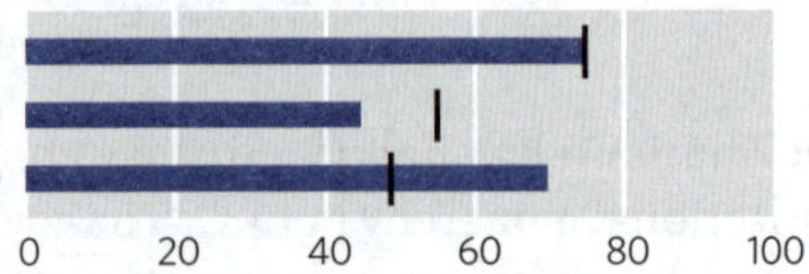

Thailand's average tariff rate is 5 percent. Tariff-rate quotas, import license requirements, and government subsidies distort trade. Foreign investment may be subject to government screening, and investment in several sectors of the economy is limited. The financial sector, dominated by banks, is relatively small but diversified. State-owned specialized financial institutions have become more prominent. The banking sector remains sound.

Long-Term Score Change (since 1995)

RULE OF LAW		GOVERNMENT SIZE		REGULATORY EFFICIENCY		OPEN MARKETS	
Property Rights	**-45.0**	Fiscal Freedom	**+5.1**	Business Freedom	**+1.4**	Trade Freedom	**+8.6**
Freedom from Corruption	**-36.4**	Government Spending	**-9.2**	Labor Freedom	**-15.2**	Investment Freedom	**-5.0**
				Monetary Freedom	**-9.1**	Financial Freedom	**+20.0**

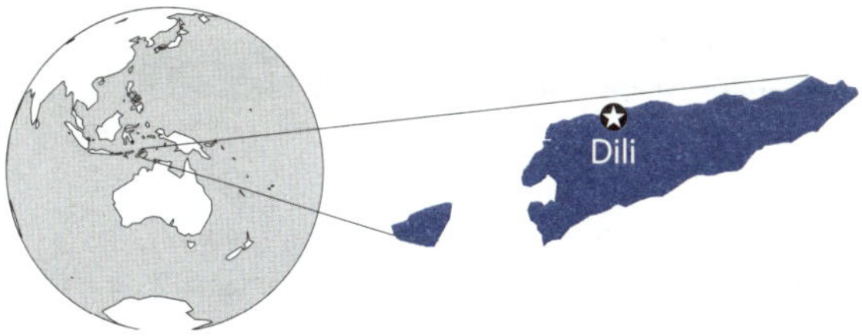

TIMOR-LESTE

Economic Freedom Score

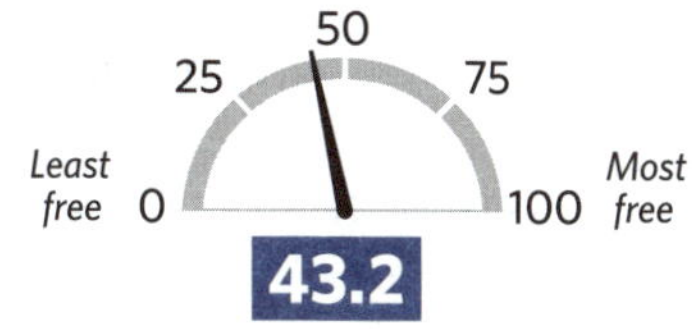

World Rank: 170 **Regional Rank: 40**

Timor-Leste's economic freedom score is 43.2, making its economy the 170th freest in the 2014 *Index*. Its score has decreased by 0.5 point from last year, reflecting declines in trade freedom, labor freedom, and monetary freedom that outweigh improvements in investment freedom and freedom from corruption. Timor-Leste is ranked 40th out of 42 countries in the Asia–Pacific region, and its overall score is well below the world and regional averages.

Since 2009, when Timor-Leste's economic freedom was first assessed in the *Index*, its score has declined by over 7 points. Large score improvements in investment freedom and labor freedom have been offset by substantial declines in five other economic freedoms including a very large deterioration in the management of government spending. Public spending that is huge relative to non-oil GDP reflects the state's outsized role in the economy.

Economic freedom remains severely constrained in Timor-Leste. Since 2010, Timor-Leste has been mired in the ranks of the "repressed" economies. The economic base is narrow, and widespread corruption unchecked by a weak judicial system has been a considerable drag on economic activity.

BACKGROUND: The Democratic Republic of Timor-Leste became independent in 2002, and successive governments have struggled to pacify the country. Revolutionary leader Xanana Gusmao, who served as its first president, has headed the government as prime minister since 2007. Economic liberalization has mostly stalled, and the economy depends heavily on foreign aid. Infrastructure is very poor, and corruption is pervasive. Timor-Leste remains primarily an agricultural economy. Oil and gas profits account for more than 95 percent of government revenue. The government deposits all oil income in a Petroleum Fund that is not counted as part of GDP but is reflected in government revenue figures. In 2011, with Indonesia's support, Timor-Leste applied for membership in the Association of Southeast Asian Nations.

Freedom Trend

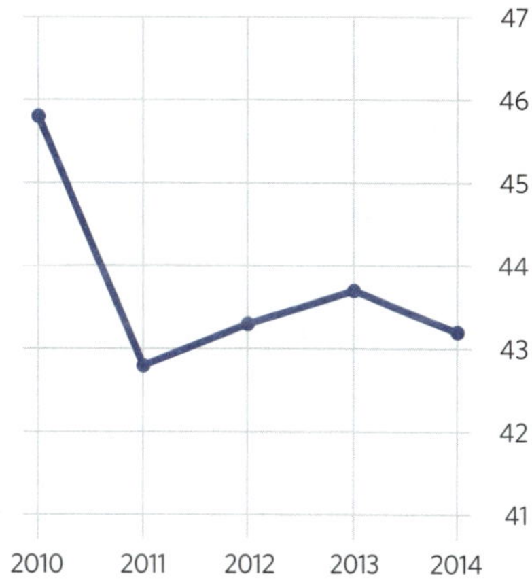

Country Comparisons

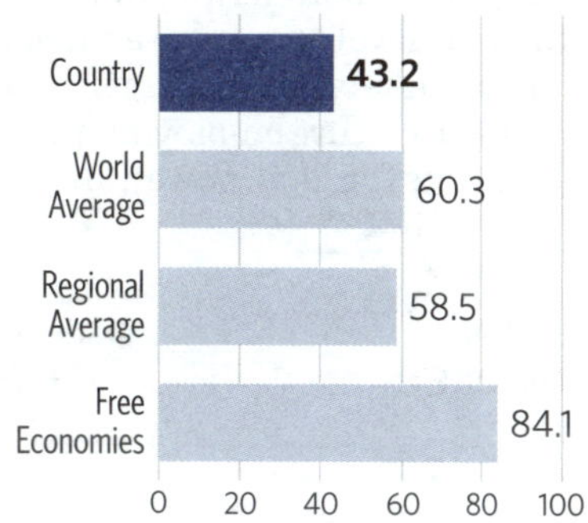

Quick Facts

Population: 1.1 million
GDP (PPP): $11.0 billion
10.0% growth in 2012
5-year compound annual growth 11.5%
$9,873 per capita
Unemployment: 18.4% (2010)
Inflation (CPI): 11.8%
FDI Inflow: $42.0 million
Public Debt: 0.0% of GDP

2012 data unless otherwise noted.
Data compiled as of September 2013.

How Do We Measure Economic Freedom?
See page 471 for an explanation of the methodology or visit the *Index* Web site at *heritage.org/index*.

THE TEN ECONOMIC FREEDOMS

Legend: Country | World Average

RULE OF LAW

		Score	Rank	1-Year Change
RULE OF LAW	Property Rights	20.0	139th	0
	Freedom from Corruption	25.4	130th	+1.4

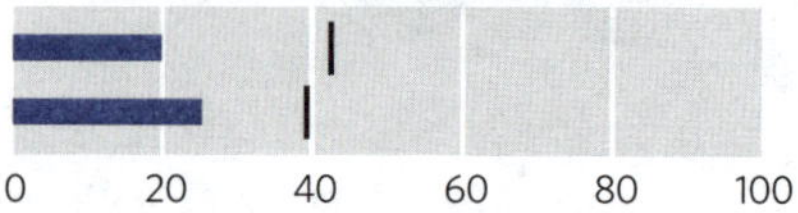

Corruption and nepotism have plagued governments of both major parties, but efforts are underway to establish internal discipline and performance standards. The country suffers from weak rule of law and a prevailing culture of impunity. There is a considerable backlog in the understaffed court system. Community property comprises approximately 90 percent of the land in East Timor, and land reform remains a contentious issue.

GOVERNMENT SIZE

		Score	Rank	1-Year Change
GOVERNMENT SIZE	Fiscal Freedom	64.7	158th	0
	Government Spending	0.0	177th	0

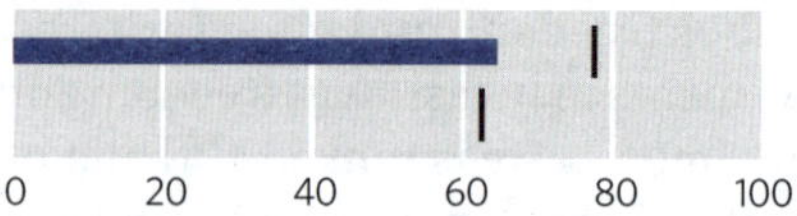

The top individual income and corporate tax rates are 10 percent. The majority of government revenues come from offshore oil and gas production in the Timor Sea. Tax revenue equals almost three times the size of the domestic economy. Government spending is nearly 140 percent of GDP. The government reserves all income from the oil sector in its Petroleum Fund, which makes government revenue quite large.

REGULATORY EFFICIENCY

		Score	Rank	1-Year Change
REGULATORY EFFICIENCY	Business Freedom	45.4	160th	+0.6
	Labor Freedom	79.2	31st	-2.0
	Monetary Freedom	68.3	150th	-1.0

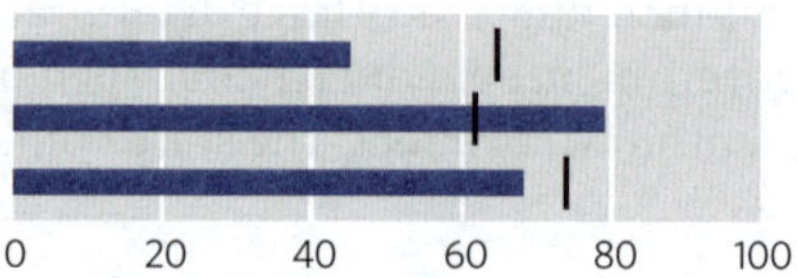

Despite reductions, the minimum capital requirement for starting a business remains more than the level of average annual income. Incorporating a business still takes over 90 days. The labor market remains largely underdeveloped, and the public sector accounts for about half of non-agriculture employment. The state uses its substantial oil revenues to fund large subsidy programs for food, power, and fuel.

OPEN MARKETS

		Score	Rank	1-Year Change
OPEN MARKETS	Trade Freedom	64.4	146th	-8.6
	Investment Freedom	45.0	125th	+5.0
	Financial Freedom	20.0	163rd	0

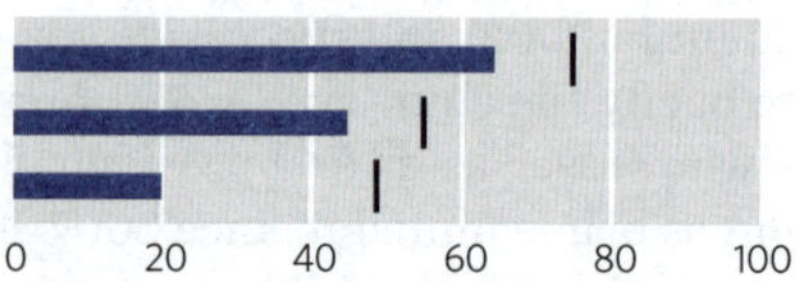

The simple average tariff rate for Timor-Leste was 10.3 percent in 2011. Restrictions on foreign land ownership and a slow-moving bureaucracy deter foreign investment. The financial sector is still at a nascent stage of development. Modest progress has been made in establishing an effective banking system. Access to credit remains limited, and the commercial banking sector remains very small.

Long-Term Score Change (since 2009)

RULE OF LAW		GOVERNMENT SIZE		REGULATORY EFFICIENCY		OPEN MARKETS	
Property Rights	0	Fiscal Freedom	0	Business Freedom	-1.6	Trade Freedom	-8.6
Freedom from Corruption	-0.6	Government Spending	-84.0	Labor Freedom	+13.2	Investment Freedom	+15.0
				Monetary Freedom	-5.8	Financial Freedom	0

TOGO

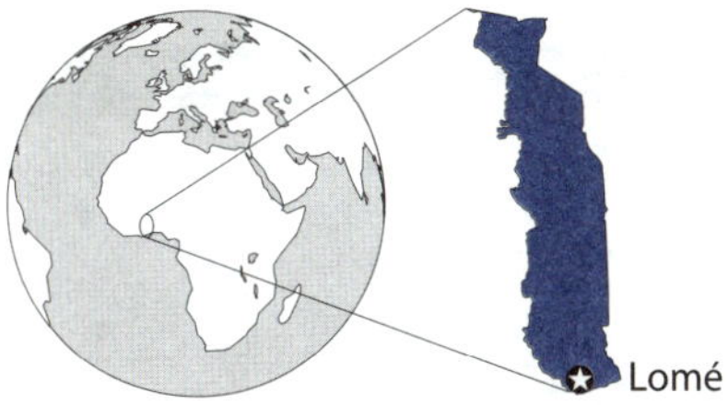

World Rank: 152 | **Regional Rank: 36**

Economic Freedom Score

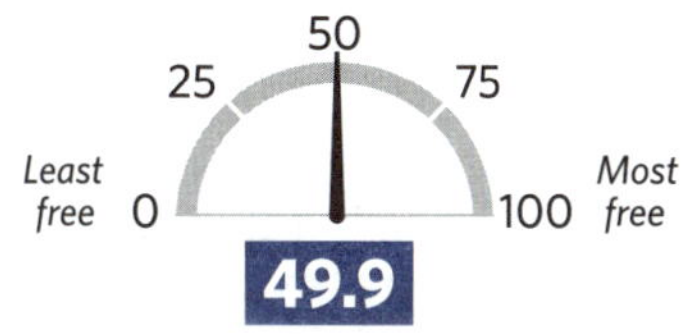

Togo's economic freedom score is 49.9, making its economy the 152nd freest in the 2014 *Index*. Its score has increased by 1.1 points since last year, reflecting improvement in half of the 10 economic freedoms including trade freedom, business freedom, and fiscal freedom. Togo is ranked 36th out of 46 countries in the Sub-Saharan Africa region, and its overall score is well below the world and regional averages.

Togo's economic freedom was first assessed in the 1999 *Index*, and its score has improved since then by less than 2 points. Modest gains in market openness, regulatory efficiency, and freedom from corruption have been undermined by declines in the management of public finance. Togo's economy has been rated "repressed" throughout the history of the *Index*. Its 2014 score is its highest in three years.

Sustaining steady growth remains challenging because of the lack of economic dynamism stemming from Togo's patchy progress toward greater economic freedom. The economy remains highly vulnerable to external shocks, and the inefficient regulatory environment still constrains commercial operations and investment.

BACKGROUND: The military appointed Faure Gnassingbé to the presidency in 2005 following the death of his father, who had ruled for 38 years. Faced with sanctions by the Economic Community of West African States and the African Union, he stepped down two months later and called for an election, which he won. Legislative elections were held in 2007, and Gnassingbé was re-elected in 2010. Togo is the world's fourth-largest producer of phosphate. Cocoa, coffee, and cotton generate about 40 percent of export earnings. Services, especially re-exports from the Lomé port facility, are also important. Agriculture employs 65 percent of the workforce. Togo completed the International Monetary Fund Extended Credit Facility in 2011, and 95 percent of its debt has been forgiven. It continues to work on IMF-designed reforms.

Freedom Trend

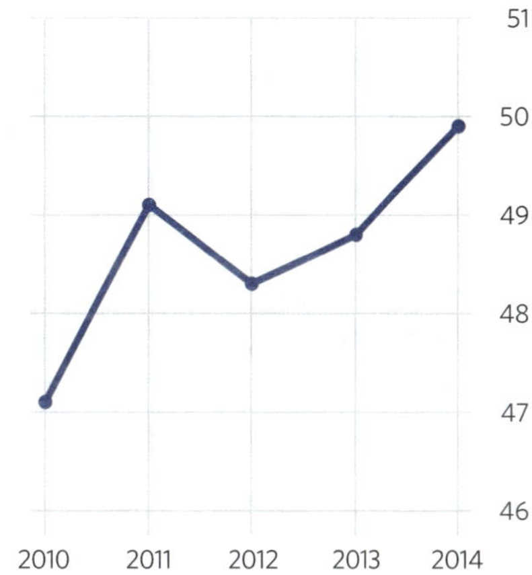

Country Comparisons

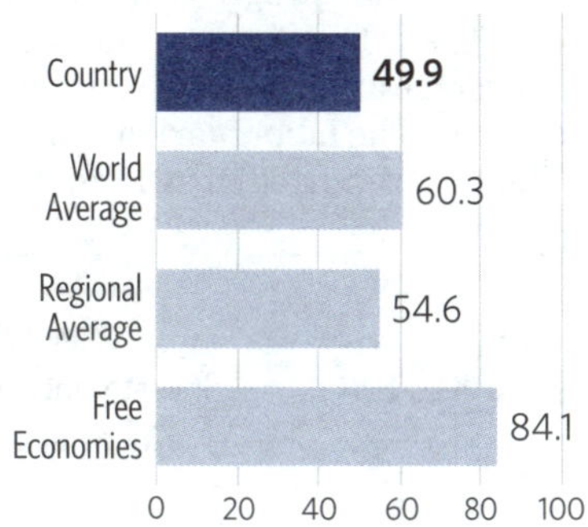

Quick Facts

Population: 6.3 million
GDP (PPP): $6.9 billion
5.0% growth in 2012
5-year compound annual growth 4.0%
$1,096 per capita
Unemployment: n/a
Inflation (CPI): 2.6%
FDI Inflow: $166.3 million
Public Debt: 46.7% of GDP

2012 data unless otherwise noted.
Data compiled as of September 2013.

How Do We Measure Economic Freedom?
See page 471 for an explanation of the methodology or visit the *Index* Web site at *heritage.org/index*.

THE TEN ECONOMIC FREEDOMS

		Score	Rank	1-Year Change
RULE OF LAW	Property Rights	30.0	93rd	0
	Freedom from Corruption	23.8	138th	-0.2

Corruption is a serious problem, and providing cash or other gifts to expedite business transactions remains a common practice, reportedly shortening delays for obtaining registrations, permits, and licenses. The judicial system is vulnerable to strong influence from the executive and does not provide independent protection of private property. Contracts are difficult to enforce. Ownership of physical property is frequently disputed.

		Score	Rank	1-Year Change
GOVERNMENT SIZE	Fiscal Freedom	69.7	138th	+1.2
	Government Spending	82.4	43rd	+0.8

The top individual income tax rate remains 45 percent, but the top corporate tax rate has fallen to 27 percent. Other taxes include a value-added tax (VAT) and a property tax. The overall tax burden amounts to 16.7 percent of the domestic economy. Government spending equals 24 percent of GDP. Public debt is 47 percent of gross domestic output. Improved tax collection has helped to ease the fiscal situation.

		Score	Rank	1-Year Change
REGULATORY EFFICIENCY	Business Freedom	43.3	165th	+3.4
	Labor Freedom	42.8	163rd	-1.4
	Monetary Freedom	79.3	44th	+0.8

Despite some progress, the overall business framework remains quite burdensome. It takes 19 days to start a company, and the minimum capital requirement costs over three times the level of average annual income. Completing licensing requirements takes more than four months on average. The labor market is underdeveloped, and informal labor activity remains substantial. The IMF reported in 2013 that fuel subsidies remain in effect.

		Score	Rank	1-Year Change
OPEN MARKETS	Trade Freedom	62.8	151st	+6.1
	Investment Freedom	35.0	142nd	0
	Financial Freedom	30.0	132nd	0

Togo's average tariff rate is 11.1 percent. Nearly 25 percent of government revenue is generated by tariffs. Foreign investors may find the legal and regulatory systems to be slow-moving and inefficient. The financial system is rudimentary, and a considerable portion of the population has no access to credit. The underdeveloped banking system lacks liquidity. Capital transactions are subject to some controls or government approval.

Long-Term Score Change (since 1999)

RULE OF LAW		GOVERNMENT SIZE		REGULATORY EFFICIENCY		OPEN MARKETS	
Property Rights	0	Fiscal Freedom	-7.8	Business Freedom	+3.3	Trade Freedom	-0.2
Freedom from Corruption	+13.8	Government Spending	-4.2	Labor Freedom	-4.0	Investment Freedom	+5.0
				Monetary Freedom	+12.3	Financial Freedom	0

TONGA

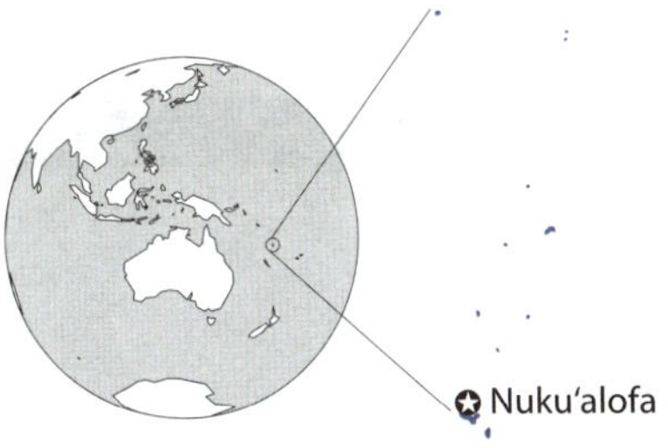

World Rank: **104** Regional Rank: **22**

Economic Freedom Score

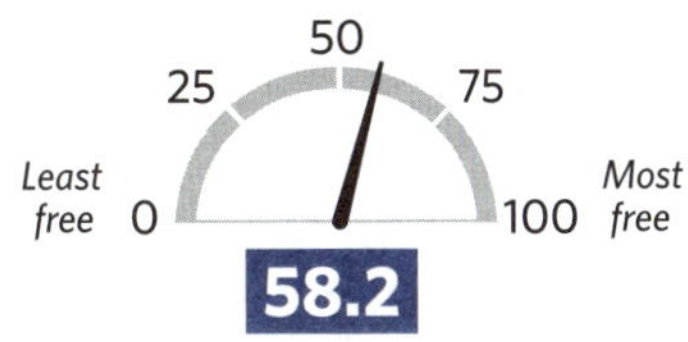

Tonga's economic freedom score is 58.2, making its economy the 104th freest in the 2014 *Index*. Its score is 2.2 points higher than last year, reflecting substantial improvements in the control of government spending, labor freedom, investment freedom, and trade freedom. Tonga is ranked 22nd out of 42 countries in the Asia–Pacific region, and its score is below the world average.

Tonga's economic freedom was first assessed in the 2009 *Index*, and its score has advanced since then by about 4 points. Improvements in half of the 10 economic freedoms, notably in trade freedom, the management of public spending, and freedom from corruption, have been undermined by declines in investment freedom and overall regulatory efficiency, and Tonga remains "mostly unfree," but the country has achieved its highest economic freedom score ever in the 2014 *Index*,.

The Tongan economy remains heavily dependent on foreign aid and overseas workers. The public sector's dominance has contributed to a low level of economic dynamism despite a well-educated workforce. More dynamic entrepreneurial investment is stifled by a largely opaque regulatory environment. Property rights are weakly enforced, and a high level of perceived corruption hampers private-sector growth.

BACKGROUND: The island Kingdom of Tonga is the South Pacific's last Polynesian monarchy. Tonga has been independent since 1970, and its political life is dominated by the royal family, hereditary nobles, and a few other landholders. Tonga held its first elections in November 2010 in its drive to become a constitutional monarchy. The Friendly Islands Democratic Party won a plurality in parliament, and Lord Siale'ataonga Tu'ivakano became Tonga's first elected prime minister. Tonga boasts a 99 percent literacy rate, although more than half of the population lives abroad, mostly in New Zealand. Agriculture is the principal productive sector of the economy, and remittances from abroad are the primary source of income.

Freedom Trend

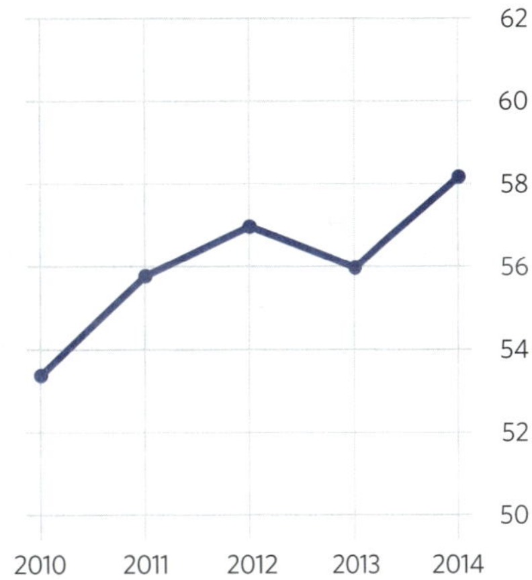

Country Comparisons

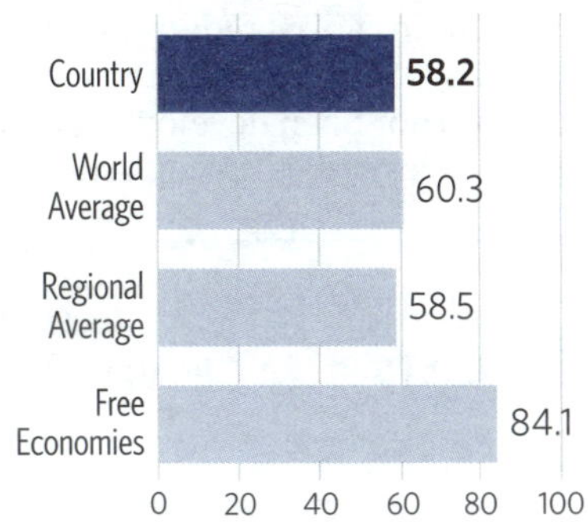

Quick Facts

Population: 0.1 million
GDP (PPP): $0.8 billion
1.4% growth in 2012
5-year compound annual growth 1.2%
$7,548 per capita
Unemployment: n/a
Inflation (CPI): 4.5%
FDI Inflow: $6.6 million
Public Debt: 42.8% of GDP

2012 data unless otherwise noted.
Data compiled as of September 2013.

How Do We Measure Economic Freedom?
See page 471 for an explanation of the methodology or visit the *Index* Web site at *heritage.org/index*.

THE TEN ECONOMIC FREEDOMS

RULE OF LAW

	Score	Rank	1-Year Change
Property Rights	20.0	139th	0
Freedom from Corruption	28.6	115th	-2.4

Corruption is widespread, and royals, nobles, and their top associates allegedly have used state assets for personal benefit. Transparency and accountability are lacking. The judicial system is based on British common law and is generally independent, although a shortage of judges has created serious case backlogs. Property rights are uncertain, and enforcement of them is weak.

GOVERNMENT SIZE

	Score	Rank	1-Year Change
Fiscal Freedom	86.7	44th	-0.4
Government Spending	74.8	71st	+10.1

The top individual income tax rate is 20 percent, and the top corporate tax rate is 25 percent. Other taxes include a value-added tax (VAT) and an interest tax. The overall tax burden equals 17.5 percent of gross domestic income. Foreign aid donations cover 55 percent of government expenditures, which make up about 29 percent of GDP. Public debt equaled 43 percent of the domestic economy in the most recent year.

REGULATORY EFFICIENCY

	Score	Rank	1-Year Change
Business Freedom	74.6	51st	-2.0
Labor Freedom	91.2	5th	+6.8
Monetary Freedom	71.3	136th	+0.2

Regulatory codes are relatively sound, but implementation remains ineffective. There is no minimum capital requirement for establishing a business, which takes more than two weeks on average. Although labor codes are favorable to labor market flexibility, an efficient labor market has not been developed and informal labor activity remains substantial. The government influences prices through subsidies for electricity and to loss-making state-owned enterprises.

OPEN MARKETS

	Score	Rank	1-Year Change
Trade Freedom	79.5	73rd	+3.9
Investment Freedom	35.0	142nd	+5.0
Financial Freedom	20.0	163rd	0

Tonga's average tariff rate is 5.3 percent. Foreign investment is screened by the government, and investment in some sectors of the economy is restricted. The underdeveloped legal system and infrastructure continue to impede the development of a modern financial sector. There are no capital markets. Much of the population operates financially outside of the formal banking sector.

Long-Term Score Change (since 2009)

RULE OF LAW		GOVERNMENT SIZE		REGULATORY EFFICIENCY		OPEN MARKETS	
Property Rights	0	Fiscal Freedom	+4.2	Business Freedom	-4.4	Trade Freedom	+23.5
Freedom from Corruption	+11.6	Government Spending	+16.8	Labor Freedom	-8.1	Investment Freedom	-5.0
				Monetary Freedom	+2.4	Financial Freedom	0

TRINIDAD AND TOBAGO

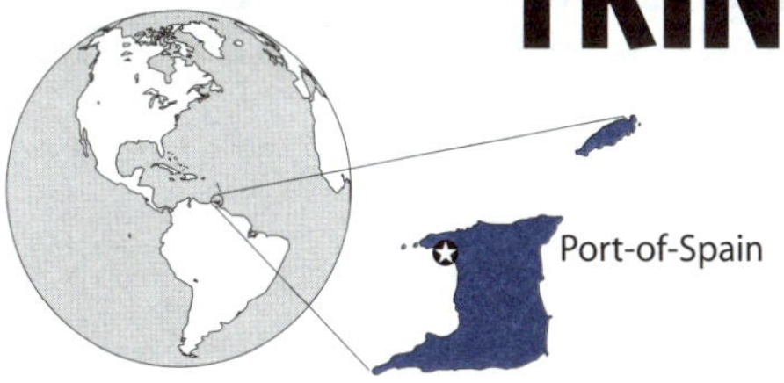

World Rank: **73** Regional Rank: **14**

Economic Freedom Score

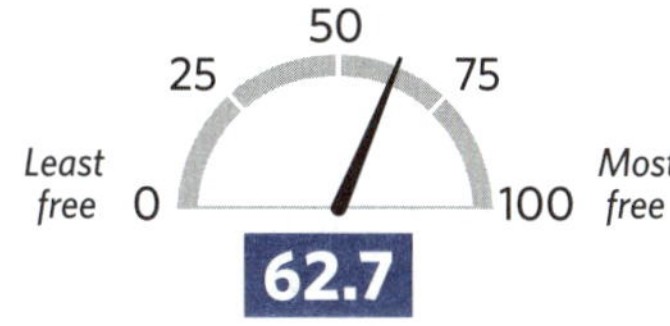

Freedom Trend

Country Comparisons

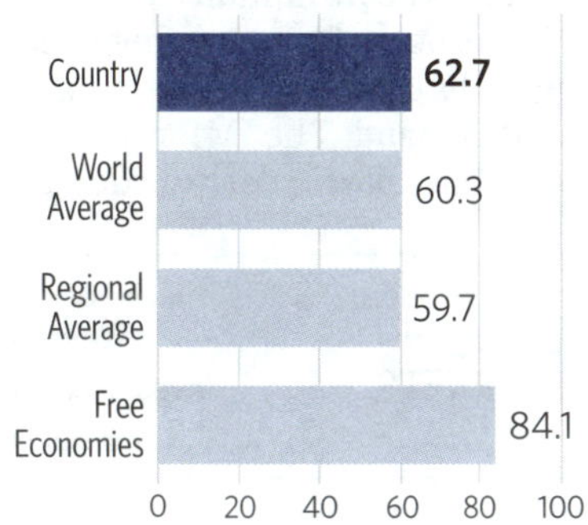

Trinidad and Tobago's economic freedom score is 62.7, making its economy the 73rd freest in the 2014 *Index*. Its score is 0.4 point higher than last year due to improvements in trade freedom, business freedom, and freedom from corruption that outweigh a deterioration in financial freedom. Trinidad and Tobago is ranked 14th out of 29 countries in the South and Central America/Caribbean region, and its score is above the world average.

Trinidad and Tobago's economic freedom was first assessed in the 1996 *Index*, and its score has declined since then by 6.5 points. Despite double-digit score growth in trade freedom and fiscal freedom, serious deteriorations in rule of law, regulatory efficiency, and market openness have kept the once "mostly free" economy among the "moderately free" since 2008.

Dependence on the energy sector for economic growth has undermined competitiveness and private-sector diversification. Fiscal stimulus has included additional subsidies, transfers, and investments in state-owned enterprises. The financial sector has undergone uncertainty and a bailout of one of the largest financial groups. Trinidad and Tobago continues to score below the world average in freedom from corruption, business freedom, and trade freedom.

BACKGROUND: In late 2011, police thwarted a plot to assassinate Prime Minister Kamla Persad-Bissessar and members of her cabinet. The plot was linked to the state of emergency she declared in August 2011 to counter a surge in drug-related violent crime. Trinidad and Tobago's economy has traditionally been agriculturally based, but a shift to petrochemical, liquefied natural gas, and steel production has made it one of the most developed nations in the Caribbean. The economy doubled between 2002 and 2008, with hydrocarbons accounting for more than 40 percent of GDP and 80 percent of exports. Tourism also has the potential to grow significantly, making Trinidad and Tobago a promising place for investors.

Quick Facts

Population: 1.3 million
GDP (PPP): $26.7 billion
0.4% growth in 2012
5-year compound annual growth –0.6%
$20,087 per capita
Unemployment: 5.5%
Inflation (CPI): 9.3%
FDI Inflow: $2.5 billion
Public Debt: 39.7% of GDP

2012 data unless otherwise noted.
Data compiled as of September 2013.

How Do We Measure Economic Freedom?
See page 471 for an explanation of the methodology or visit the *Index* Web site at *heritage.org/index.*

TRINIDAD AND TOBAGO (continued)

THE TEN ECONOMIC FREEDOMS

RULE OF LAW

	Score	Rank	1-Year Change
Property Rights	50.0	53rd	0
Freedom from Corruption	34.0	79th	+2.0

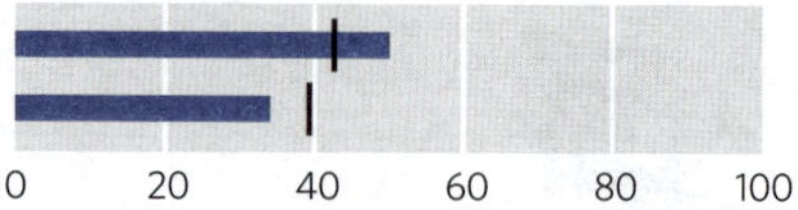

The country is believed to suffer from high-level corruption, much of it drug-related, which extends to the business community and includes money laundering through front companies. Narcotics-related corruption in the police force is endemic. The judicial branch is independent but subject to some political pressure and corruption. Rising crime rates have produced a severe backlog in the court system. Property rights are well protected.

GOVERNMENT SIZE

	Score	Rank	1-Year Change
Fiscal Freedom	84.8	56th	-0.1
Government Spending	62.5	113th	+2.1

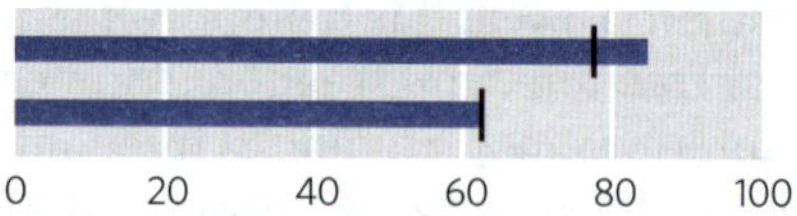

The top individual income and corporate tax rates are 25 percent. Other taxes include a value-added tax (VAT) and a property tax. Overall tax revenue equates to about 16.5 percent of gross domestic income. Government spending amounts to 35 percent of GDP. Public debt is equivalent to about 40 percent of the overall size of the economy. Oil and gas reserves continue to help support public finances.

REGULATORY EFFICIENCY

	Score	Rank	1-Year Change
Business Freedom	59.4	116th	+4.3
Labor Freedom	76.4	43rd	-0.3
Monetary Freedom	71.7	135th	-2.0

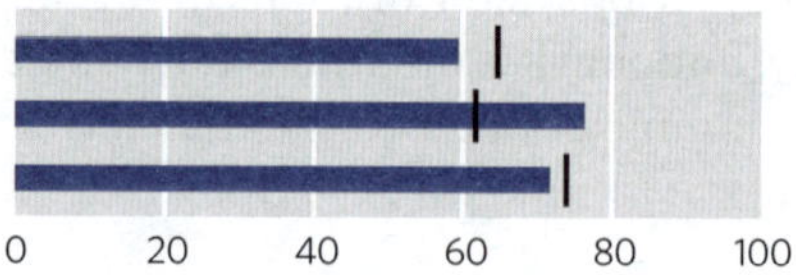

There is no minimum capital requirement, but it takes over a month to incorporate a business. The process for obtaining necessary permits remains time-consuming and takes over seven months on average. The labor market is relatively flexible, facilitating the matching of supply and demand. The IMF reported in 2013 that subsidies are on an unsustainable path, with fuel subsidies particularly difficult to justify.

OPEN MARKETS

	Score	Rank	1-Year Change
Trade Freedom	78.6	80th	+8.7
Investment Freedom	60.0	80th	0
Financial Freedom	50.0	69th	-10.0

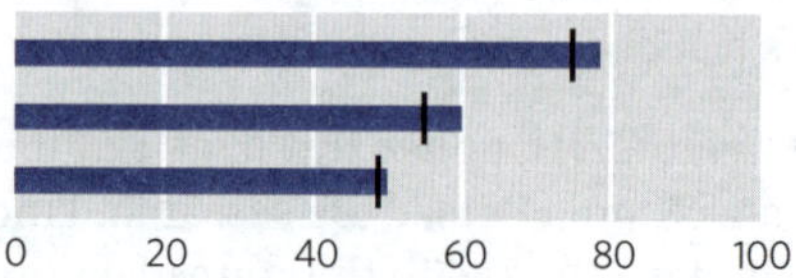

The average tariff rate is 5.7 percent. Customs procedures have been modernized in recent years. A license is required for foreign ownership of land. Modernization of financial regulations is ongoing. State influence in the financial sector is not substantial, and a wide variety of financing instruments are available. The financial sector has been under strain in the aftermath of the collapse of a large financial group and the subsequent bailout.

Long-Term Score Change (since 1996)

RULE OF LAW		GOVERNMENT SIZE		REGULATORY EFFICIENCY		OPEN MARKETS	
Property Rights	**-40.0**	Fiscal Freedom	**+20.3**	Business Freedom	**-10.6**	Trade Freedom	**+43.6**
Freedom from Corruption	**-16.0**	Government Spending	**-15.0**	Labor Freedom	**-2.6**	Investment Freedom	**-30.0**
				Monetary Freedom	**-4.2**	Financial Freedom	**-20.0**

TUNISIA

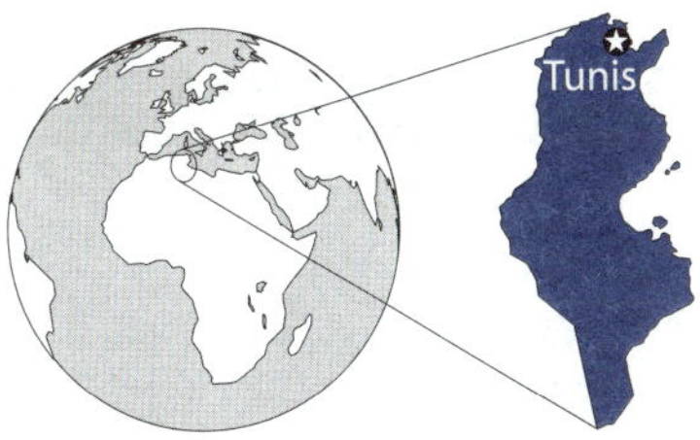

World Rank: 109 | **Regional Rank: 11**

Economic Freedom Score

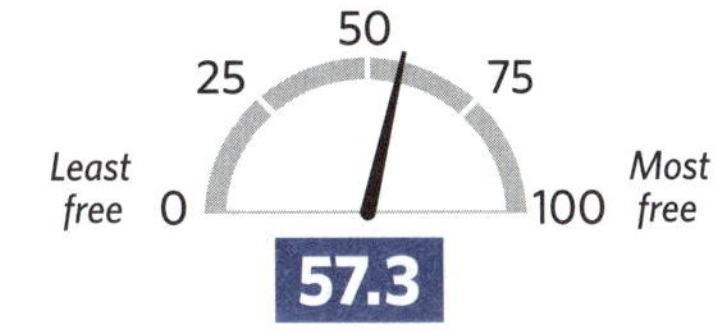

Tunisia's economic freedom score is 57.3, making its economy the 109th freest in the 2014 *Index*. Its score is 0.3 point higher this year, with improvements in trade freedom and labor freedom largely offset by declines in business freedom and monetary freedom. Tunisia is ranked 11th out of 15 countries in the Middle East/North Africa region, and its overall score is below the world average.

Over the 20-year history of the *Index*, Tunisia's economic freedom score has declined by over 6 points, one of the 20 biggest drops in the history of the *Index*. Across the 10 economic freedoms, including the areas of the rule of law, regulatory efficiency, and market openness, Tunisia's ratings have declined substantially. Tunisia's economy was considered "mostly free" during most of the first 10 years of the *Index* but has been largely rated "mostly unfree" since 2003.

The overall entrepreneurial environment remains severely constrained. An overbearing regulatory framework, exacerbated by poor access to credit and high financing costs, stifles economic activity and hurts business expansion and the development of a vibrant private sector. Corruption, which is perceived as widespread, is a serious problem.

BACKGROUND: Tunisia, birthplace of the "Arab Spring," ousted President Zine al-Abidine Ben Ali in January 2011. Moncef Marzouki has served as interim president since December 2011. The formerly banned Islamist Ennhada Party has the largest number of seats in parliament, but the country's governance is still in turmoil. Tunisia's diverse economy is based on manufacturing, tourism, agriculture, and mining. An association agreement with the European Union has helped to create jobs and modernize the economy, but the EU economic slowdown has depressed demand for Tunisian-made goods. Salafi Islamist violence has undermined foreign investment and tourism. Political stability also is threatened by high unemployment, particularly in the impoverished interior of the country.

Freedom Trend

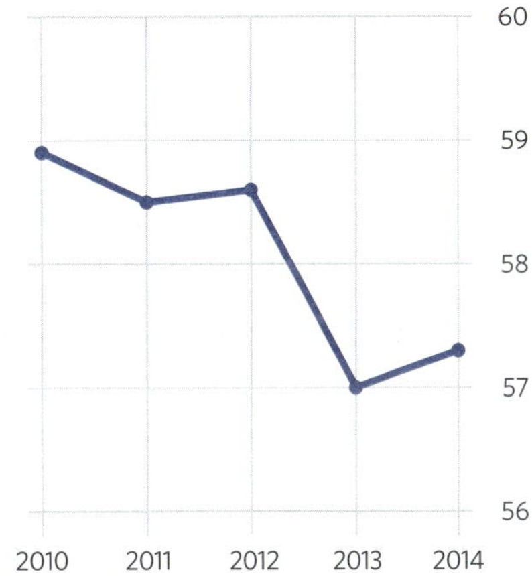

Country Comparisons

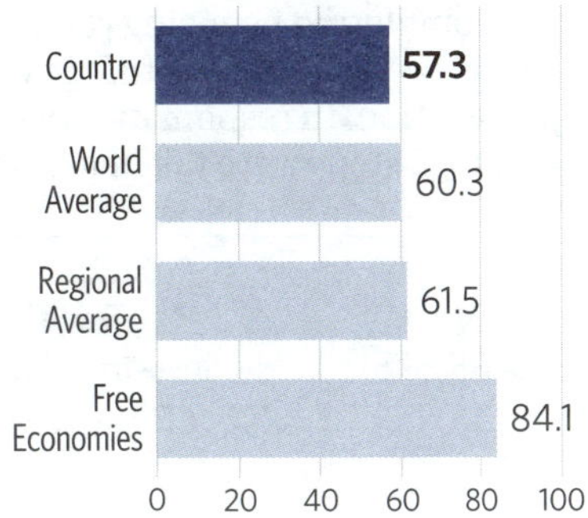

Quick Facts

Population: 10.8 million
GDP (PPP): $105.3 billion
3.6% growth in 2012
5-year compound annual growth 2.5%
$9,775 per capita
Unemployment: 18.9%
Inflation (CPI): 5.6%
FDI Inflow: $1.9 billion
Public Debt: 44.5% of GDP

2012 data unless otherwise noted.
Data compiled as of September 2013.

How Do We Measure Economic Freedom?
See page 471 for an explanation of the methodology or visit the *Index* Web site at *heritage.org/index.*

THE TEN ECONOMIC FREEDOMS

		Score	Rank	1-Year Change
RULE OF LAW	Property Rights	40.0	70th	0
	Freedom from Corruption	39.2	69th	+1.2

Financial investigators are pursuing hundreds of corruption cases from the era of the Ben Ali government that involve activities that include bribery, embezzlement of state assets, contraband and drug-trafficking, and money laundering. Independence and fairness are poorly institutionalized within the judicial system, and law enforcement is uneven across the country. Property rights are not protected effectively.

		Score	Rank	1-Year Change
GOVERNMENT SIZE	Fiscal Freedom	74.3	121st	-0.2
	Government Spending	63.8	105th	+0.1

The top individual income tax rate is 35 percent, and the top corporate tax rate is 30 percent. Other taxes include a value-added tax (VAT) and a property tax. The overall tax burden amounts to 21.1 percent of gross domestic income. Government spending is 35 percent of GDP. Public debt is equal to about 45 percent of the domestic economy. Political instability and security issues continue to weaken economic recovery.

		Score	Rank	1-Year Change
REGULATORY EFFICIENCY	Business Freedom	80.7	31st	-2.1
	Labor Freedom	72.6	57th	+2.5
	Monetary Freedom	75.9	86th	-1.9

It takes less than two weeks to incorporate a business, and no minimum capital is required, but completing licensing requirements costs over twice the level of average annual income. Despite some progress, the rigid labor market still lacks the capacity to facilitate much-needed job creation. In response to the 2011 crisis, the government increased and expanded subsidies, although steps were taken in 2013 to reduce them.

		Score	Rank	1-Year Change
OPEN MARKETS	Trade Freedom	61.8	153rd	+3.7
	Investment Freedom	35.0	142nd	0
	Financial Freedom	30.0	132nd	0

The average tariff rate is 14.1 percent. Non-tariff barriers impede imports of some pharmaceutical and agricultural goods. Foreign investment is subject to government screening. The financial sector, dominated by state-owned banks that account for almost 40 percent of total banking assets, remains fragmented. Modernization and diversification of the financial system has begun, but overall progress has been slow.

Long-Term Score Change (since 1995)

RULE OF LAW		GOVERNMENT SIZE		REGULATORY EFFICIENCY		OPEN MARKETS	
Property Rights	**-10.0**	Fiscal Freedom	**+4.6**	Business Freedom	**-4.3**	Trade Freedom	**+16.4**
Freedom from Corruption	**-10.8**	Government Spending	**-5.3**	Labor Freedom	**+9.8**	Investment Freedom	**-35.0**
				Monetary Freedom	**-5.2**	Financial Freedom	**-20.0**

TURKEY

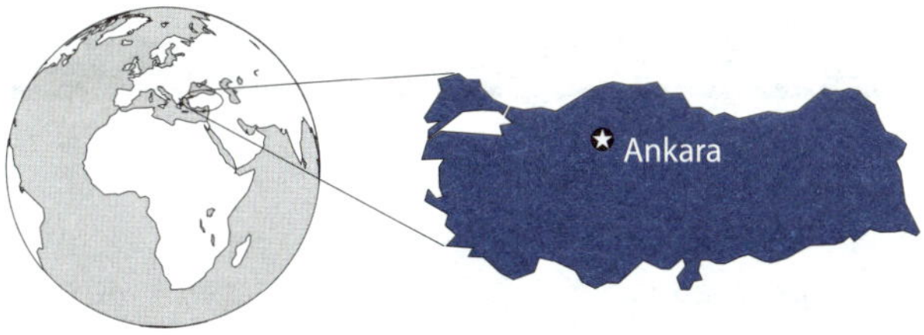

World Rank: 64 | **Regional Rank: 30**

Turkey's economic freedom score is 64.9, making its economy the 64th freest in the 2014 *Index*. Its score is 2.0 points better than last year, with notable improvements in labor freedom, investment freedom, and freedom from corruption partially offset by declines in monetary freedom and the management of public spending. Turkey is ranked 30th out of 43 countries in the Europe region, and its overall score is higher than the world average.

Over the 20-year history of the *Index*, Turkey has advanced its economic freedom score by over 6 points. Its relatively broad-based overall improvement has been facilitated by advancements in six of the 10 economic freedoms, including monetary freedom, freedom from corruption, and fiscal freedom, scores for which have improved by over 30 points. Its overall gain, however, has been undermined by deteriorations in property rights and financial freedom.

Recording score improvements two years in a row, Turkey has achieved its highest economic freedom score ever in the 2014 *Index*. Deeper institutional reform to firmly establish the rule of law and improve regulatory efficiency will be critical to solidifying its transition to a more market-based economy.

BACKGROUND: Turkey is constitutionally secular, but Prime Minister Recep Tayyip Erdogan's Justice and Development Party has been pushing an Islamist agenda and eroding Turkey's Euro–Atlantic connections. The country was rocked by large-scale protests in early 2013. Economic modernization is progressing despite clashes with the media and the slow pace of judicial reform. Turkey has been a member of NATO since 1952. In early 2013, NATO deployed air defense units on Turkey's southern border because of concerns raised by Syria's civil war. The European Union granted Turkey candidate status in 1999, but there is strong opposition from France, Germany, and Austria. Turkey's dispute with Cyprus has also delayed negotiations. Principal exports include foodstuffs, textiles, clothing, iron, and steel.

How Do We Measure Economic Freedom?
See page 471 for an explanation of the methodology or visit the *Index* Web site at *heritage.org/index*.

Economic Freedom Score

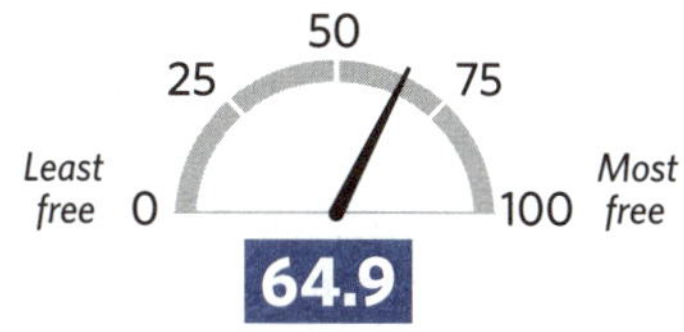

Freedom Trend

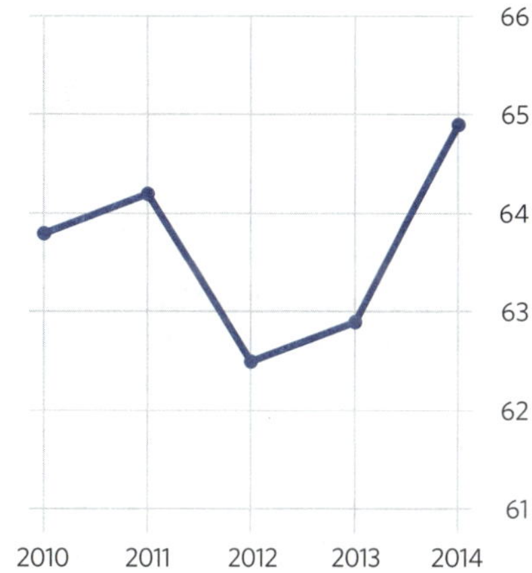

Country Comparisons

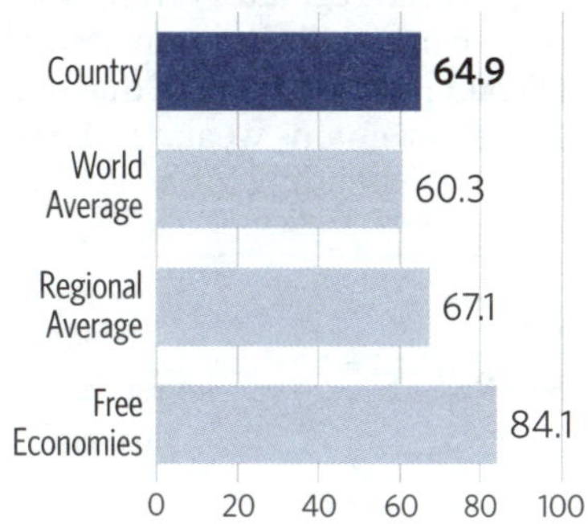

Quick Facts

Population: 74.9 million
GDP (PPP): $1.1 trillion
2.6% growth in 2012
5-year compound annual growth 3.1%
$15,001 per capita
Unemployment: 9.2%
Inflation (CPI): 8.9%
FDI Inflow: $12.4 billion
Public Debt: 36.4% of GDP

2012 data unless otherwise noted.
Data compiled as of September 2013.

THE TEN ECONOMIC FREEDOMS

RULE OF LAW

	Score	Rank	1-Year Change
Property Rights	50.0	53rd	0
Freedom from Corruption	44.0	58th	+2.0

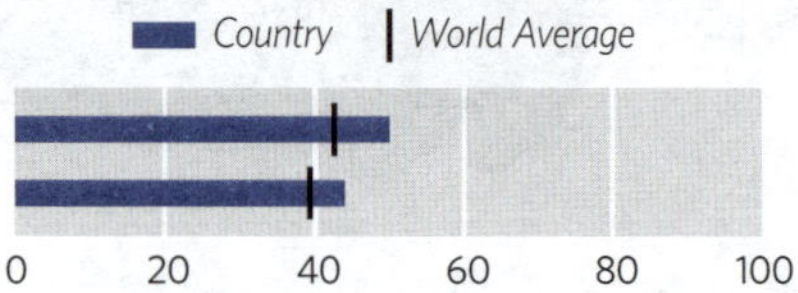

Turkey struggles with corruption, cronyism, and nepotism in government and daily life. The government has adopted some anti-corruption measures, but progress has been limited. The judiciary is independent, but in practice, the government can influence judges through appointments, promotions, and financing. Property rights are generally enforced, but the courts are slow, and judges are not well trained for commercial cases.

GOVERNMENT SIZE

	Score	Rank	1-Year Change
Fiscal Freedom	77.5	105th	+0.5
Government Spending	63.5	107th	-1.4

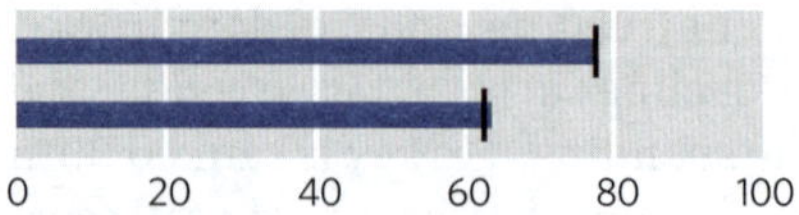

The top individual income tax rate is 35 percent, and the top corporate tax rate is 20 percent. Other taxes include a value-added tax (VAT) and an environment tax. Overall tax revenues equal 25 percent of the size of the economy. Government spending is 35 percent of GDP. Public debt amounts to about 36 percent of gross domestic output. Budget targets are under threat as the government spends in the run-up to elections.

REGULATORY EFFICIENCY

	Score	Rank	1-Year Change
Business Freedom	67.6	85th	-0.6
Labor Freedom	59.7	101st	+16.6
Monetary Freedom	71.8	134th	-1.5

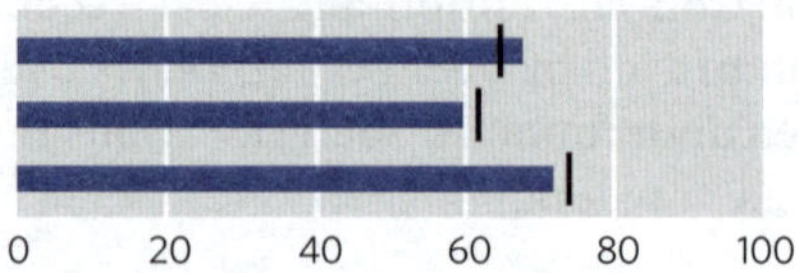

The overall regulatory framework has undergone a series of reforms, but the pace of reform has slowed markedly in comparison to other emerging economies. Despite some progress, the labor market lacks dynamism due to lingering rigidities. A large informal sector persists. Monetary stability remains weak. In the past, the government reduced subsidies for fuel and electricity, but state spending for health care has been increasing.

OPEN MARKETS

	Score	Rank	1-Year Change
Trade Freedom	84.5	51st	-0.7
Investment Freedom	70.0	46th	+5.0
Financial Freedom	60.0	41st	0

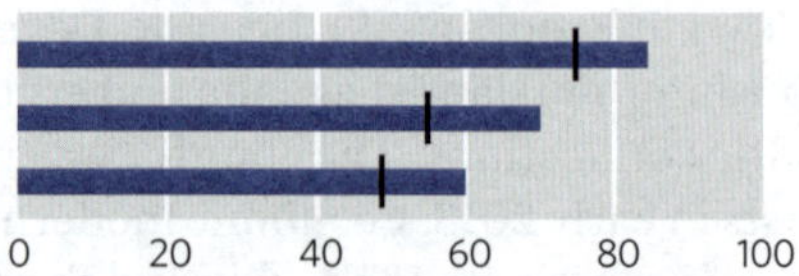

The average tariff rate is 2.7 percent. Agricultural products may face especially high trade barriers. Foreign and domestic investors are generally treated equally under the law, but investment in some sectors is restricted. The financial system continues to evolve, with overall financial intermediation accounting gradually increasing. Banking remains relatively stable, but privatization in the sector has been slow.

Long-Term Score Change (since 1995)

RULE OF LAW		GOVERNMENT SIZE		REGULATORY EFFICIENCY		OPEN MARKETS	
Property Rights	**-20.0**	Fiscal Freedom	**+33.0**	Business Freedom	**-17.4**	Trade Freedom	**+9.7**
Freedom from Corruption	**+34.0**	Government Spending	**+0.3**	Labor Freedom	**+19.0**	Investment Freedom	**0**
				Monetary Freedom	**+33.6**	Financial Freedom	**-10.0**

TURKMENISTAN

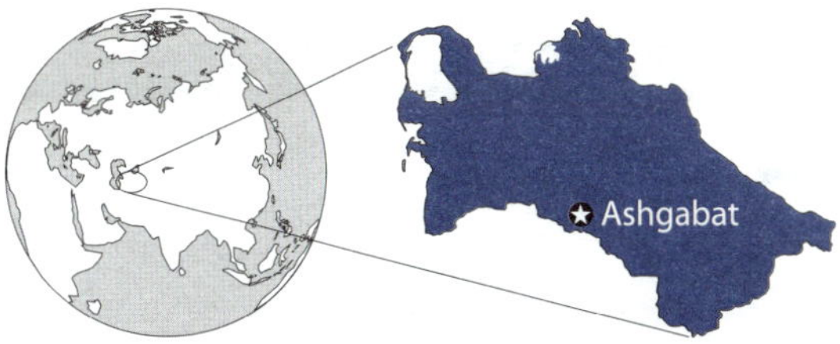

Economic Freedom Score

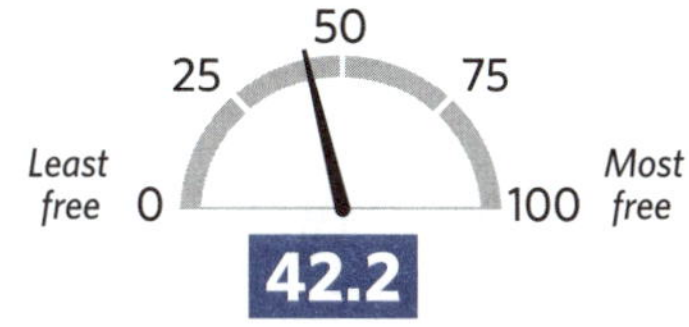

World Rank: 171 **Regional Rank: 41**

Turkmenistan's economic freedom score is 42.2, making its economy the 171st freest in the 2014 *Index*. Its score is 0.4 point lower than last year due to declines in freedom from corruption and monetary freedom. Turkmenistan is ranked 41st out of 42 countries in the Asia–Pacific region, and its overall score is significantly lower than the world and regional averages.

Turkmenistan's economic freedom was first assessed in the 1998 *Index*, and its score has advanced since then by about 7 points. Its overall score increase, driven by very large gains in monetary freedom, trade freedom, and fiscal freedom, masks significant declines in business freedom, investment freedom, and the protection of property rights.

Charting a downward path of economic freedom in recent years, Turkmenistan continues to be mired in the ranks of the "repressed" economies. Reforms intended to improve the business and investment climates have been largely undermined in practice. The economy remains heavily reliant on the energy sector, which is dominated by state-owned enterprises and firms specifically chosen by the government for investment. Corruption continues to erode the business environment, severely undermining the rule of law and encouraging cronyism.

BACKGROUND: President Gurbanguly Berdymukhammedov was re-elected in February 2012 in elections regarded as flawed by international observers. The presidency controls all three branches of government, the economy, social services, and the mass media. Berdymukhammedov's policies are somewhat more open than those of his predecessor, Saparmurad Niyazov (Turkmenbashi), but the government still tends toward isolationism. Berdymukhammedov has encouraged some foreign investment in the energy sector, especially from Russia, China, and Iran. Turkmenistan boasts the world's fifth largest natural gas reserves and has signed a deal to supply Afghanistan, India, and Pakistan with gas through the 1,000-mile TAPI pipeline.

Freedom Trend

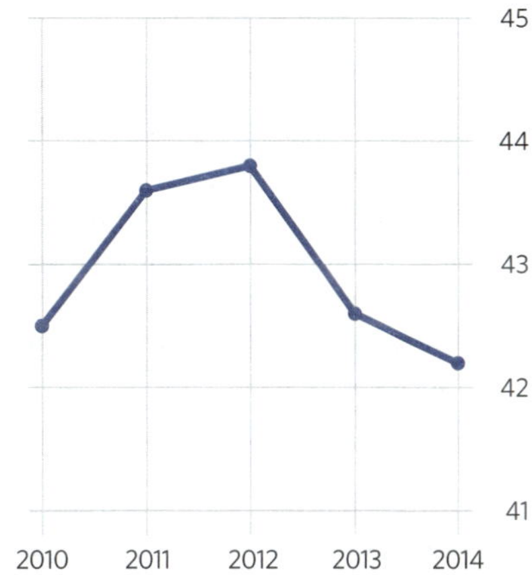

Country Comparisons

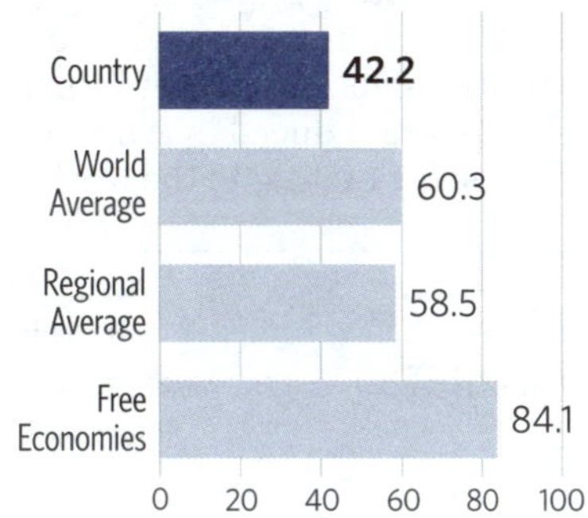

Quick Facts

Population: 5.6 million
GDP (PPP): $48.9 billion
11.0% growth in 2012
5-year compound annual growth 11.1%
$8,718 per capita
Unemployment: n/a
Inflation (CPI): 4.9%
FDI Inflow: $3.2 billion
Public Debt: 15.8% of GDP

2012 data unless otherwise noted.
Data compiled as of September 2013.

How Do We Measure Economic Freedom?
See page 471 for an explanation of the methodology or visit the *Index* Web site at *heritage.org/index*.

TURKMENISTAN (continued)

THE TEN ECONOMIC FREEDOMS

Legend: Country | World Average

		Score	Rank	1-Year Change
RULE OF LAW	Property Rights	5.0	179th	0
	Freedom from Corruption	13.4	178th	-2.6

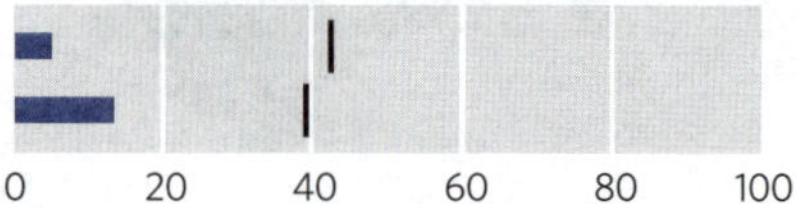

Corruption is widespread, with public officials often forced to bribe their way into their positions. The judicial system is subservient to the president, who appoints and removes judges without legislative review. The legal system does not enforce contracts and property rights effectively. Laws are poorly developed, and judges are poorly trained and open to bribery. All land is owned by the government, and other ownership rights are limited.

		Score	Rank	1-Year Change
GOVERNMENT SIZE	Fiscal Freedom	95.2	13th	+1.2
	Government Spending	93.0	2nd	+1.3

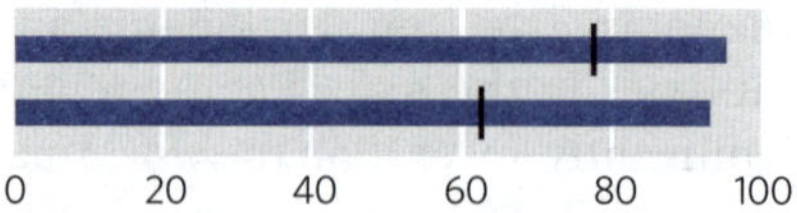

The top individual income tax rate is a flat 10 percent, and the top corporate tax rate is 8 percent. A 20 percent rate applies to legal entities with foreign participation. Other taxes include a value-added tax (VAT) and a property tax. The overall tax burden equals 17.8 percent of gross domestic income. Public expenditures are 15 percent of GDP. Public debt has been rising but is a modest 16 percent of gross domestic output.

		Score	Rank	1-Year Change
REGULATORY EFFICIENCY	Business Freedom	30.0	178th	0
	Labor Freedom	30.0	177th	0
	Monetary Freedom	65.9	161st	-4.7

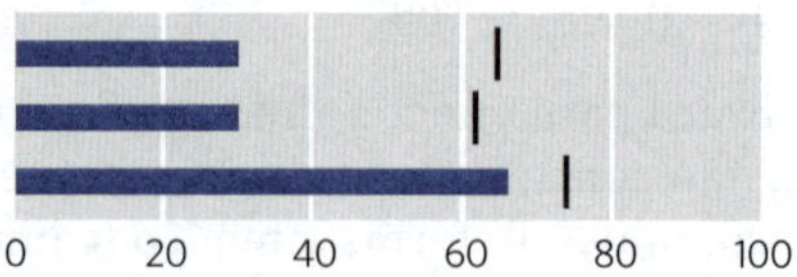

The regulatory system is highly arbitrary, and enforcement is inconsistent. Personal relations with government officials are often required to cut through red tape. The public sector provides most jobs, and the informal sector remains an important source of employment. Although some were reduced in 2013, state subsidies for fuel and food as a percentage of GDP are still among the highest in the world.

		Score	Rank	1-Year Change
OPEN MARKETS	Trade Freedom	79.2	74th	0
	Investment Freedom	0.0	178th	0
	Financial Freedom	10.0	174th	0

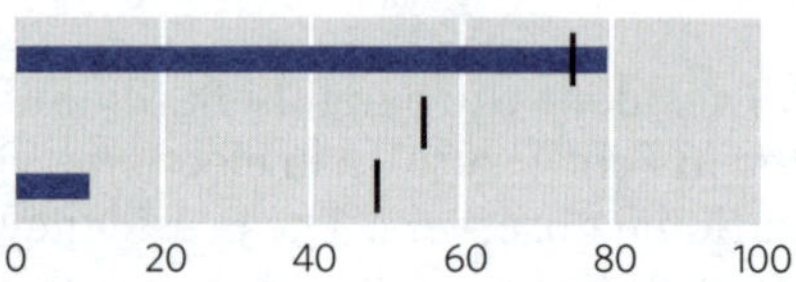

The most recently reported average tariff rate was 2.9 percent. Slow customs procedures impede trade, and the government does not allow people to import cars that are more than five years old. State-owned enterprises dominate several sectors of the economy. The financial system remains heavily government-controlled, and the flow of financial resources is severely restricted. The private sector's access to credit is very limited.

Long-Term Score Change (since 1998)

RULE OF LAW		GOVERNMENT SIZE		REGULATORY EFFICIENCY		OPEN MARKETS	
Property Rights	**-25.0**	Fiscal Freedom	**+39.0**	Business Freedom	**-25.0**	Trade Freedom	**+39.2**
Freedom from Corruption	**+3.4**	Government Spending	**+8.9**	Labor Freedom	**0**	Investment Freedom	**-30.0**
				Monetary Freedom	**+65.9**	Financial Freedom	**0**

UGANDA

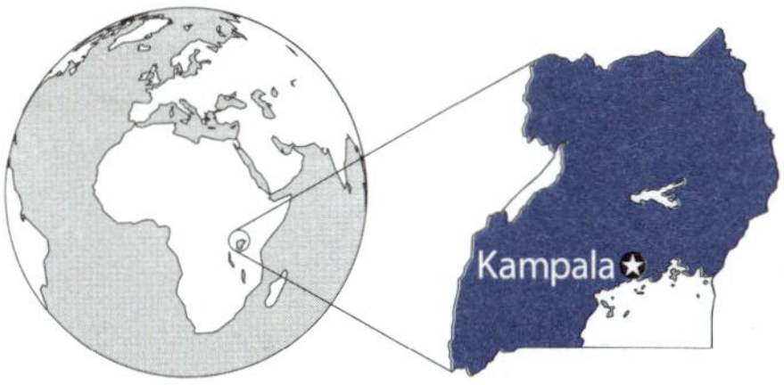

World Rank: **91** Regional Rank: **10**

Uganda's economic freedom score is 59.9, making it the 91st freest economy in the 2014 *Index*. Its score is 1.2 points lower than last year due primarily to deteriorations in financial freedom, monetary freedom, and business freedom. Uganda is ranked 10th out of 46 countries in the Sub-Saharan Africa region, and its overall score is below the world average.

Over the 20-year history of the *Index*, Uganda's economic freedom has been stagnant, with hard-won gains in earlier years wiped out by declines in the rule of law, government size, and regulatory efficiency. Scores for eight of the 10 economic freedoms, notably property rights, business freedom, financial freedom, and investment freedom, have deteriorated markedly.

Recording its second lowest economic freedom score ever in the 2014 *Index*, the Ugandan economy has fallen back to "mostly unfree." There is a serious need for greater institutional reforms to increase the legal framework's efficiency and transparency and improve law enforcement. Widespread corruption erodes entrepreneurial incentives, and political influence undermines the independence and integrity of judicial and regulatory systems.

BACKGROUND: Milton Obote led Uganda to independence in 1962 and was ousted in 1971 by Idi Amin Dada. When Tanzanian forces ousted Amin in 1979, Obote returned to power. In 1986, insurgent leader Yoweri Museveni took power in a military coup. A multi-party government was established in 2005. Museveni won a third term in 2006 and a fourth in 2011. Limited market reforms have produced more than a decade of relatively strong economic growth. Uganda has substantial natural resources, but agriculture and fishing employ over 80 percent of the workforce. Uganda is believed to have 3.5 billion barrels of oil reserves. Instability in South Sudan, Uganda's main export partner, threatens to destabilize the economy. Uganda continues to play a role in peacekeeping operations in Somalia and the fight against terrorism.

How Do We Measure Economic Freedom?
See page 471 for an explanation of the methodology or visit the *Index* Web site at *heritage.org/index*.

Economic Freedom Score

Freedom Trend

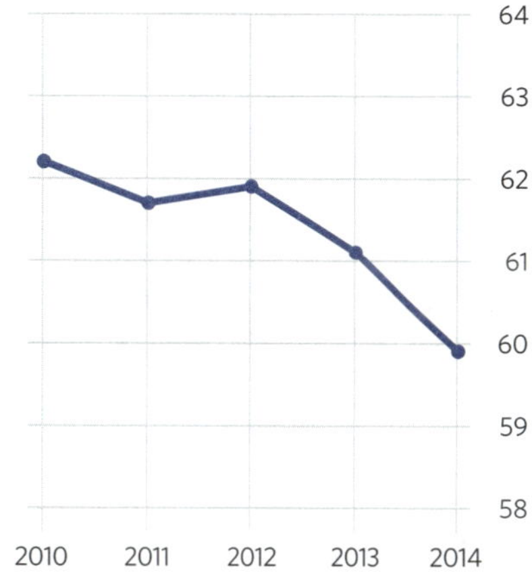

Country Comparisons

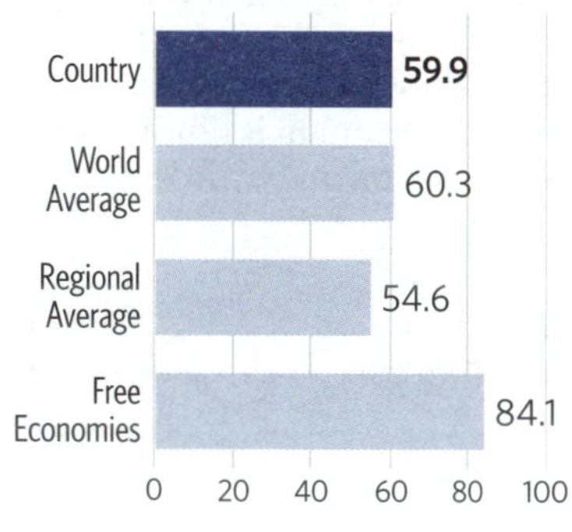

Quick Facts

Population: 35.6 million
GDP (PPP): $50.4 billion
2.6% growth in 2012
5-year compound annual growth 5.9%
$1,415 per capita
Unemployment: n/a
Inflation (CPI): 14.1%
FDI Inflow: $1.7 billion
Public Debt: 34.5% of GDP

2012 data unless otherwise noted.
Data compiled as of September 2013.

THE TEN ECONOMIC FREEDOMS

RULE OF LAW

	Score	Rank	1-Year Change
Property Rights	30.0	93rd	0
Freedom from Corruption	23.8	139th	-0.2

Despite laws and institutions to combat corruption, Uganda remains the most corrupt country in East Africa. In 2012, the EU froze foreign aid after a report that at least $13 million had been embezzled by the prime minister's office. Executive influence undermines judicial independence. The rule of law is weak, and the legal system is too inefficient to provide strong protection of property rights.

GOVERNMENT SIZE

	Score	Rank	1-Year Change
Fiscal Freedom	79.1	97th	-1.5
Government Spending	87.3	22nd	+3.0

The top individual income and corporate tax rates are 30 percent. Other taxes include a value-added tax (VAT) and a property tax. Overall tax revenue amounts to 17 percent of the size of the economy. Government expenditures amount to one-fifth of the domestic economy. The government has expanded borrowing against expected oil revenues, and public debt has risen to about 35 percent of GDP.

REGULATORY EFFICIENCY

	Score	Rank	1-Year Change
Business Freedom	45.1	161st	-3.3
Labor Freedom	87.4	9th	-0.5
Monetary Freedom	71.0	138th	-6.2

The regulatory environment is not conducive to entrepreneurial activity. There is no minimum capital requirement for establishing a business, but requirements for commercial licenses are time-consuming and costly. The formal labor market remains inefficient and lacks dynamism. The government is funding substantial price-distorting subsidies by financing the oil refining/distribution and hydroelectric sectors.

OPEN MARKETS

	Score	Rank	1-Year Change
Trade Freedom	75.4	97th	+1.8
Investment Freedom	60.0	80th	+5.0
Financial Freedom	40.0	107th	-10.0

Uganda's average tariff rate is 7.3 percent. The government does not generally discriminate against foreign investors, but the legal and regulatory systems may be difficult to navigate. The financial system is dominated by banking, which is relatively open to competition but subject to government influence. Bank lending to the private sector has gradually increased. Capital markets are relatively small and underdeveloped.

Long-Term Score Change (since 1995)

RULE OF LAW		GOVERNMENT SIZE		REGULATORY EFFICIENCY		OPEN MARKETS	
Property Rights	-20.0	Fiscal Freedom	-2.4	Business Freedom	-24.9	Trade Freedom	+17.6
Freedom from Corruption	-6.2	Government Spending	-2.3	Labor Freedom	-0.5	Investment Freedom	-10.0
				Monetary Freedom	+3.9	Financial Freedom	-10.0

UKRAINE

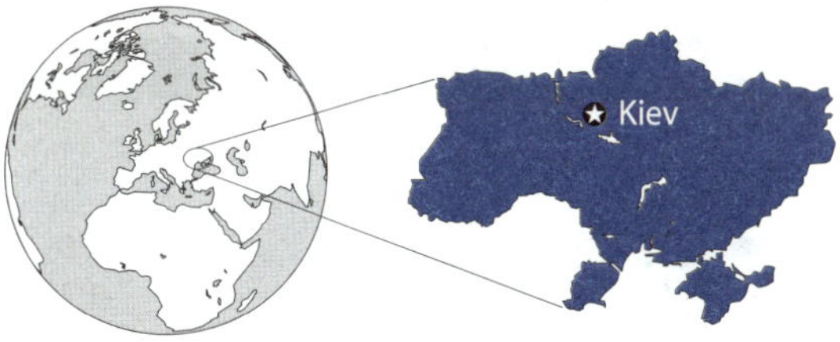

World Rank: **155** Regional Rank: **43**

Economic Freedom Score

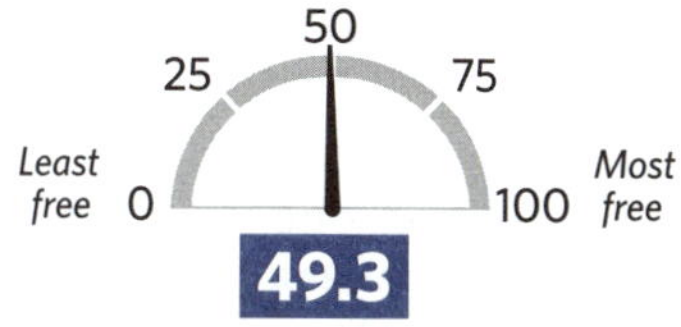

Ukraine's economic freedom score is 49.3, making its economy the 155th freest in the 2014 *Index*. Its score is 3.0 points higher than last year, with notable increases in five of the 10 economic freedoms including business freedom, control of public spending, and monetary freedom. Ukraine is ranked last out of 43 countries in the Europe region, and its overall score is lower than the world average.

Over the 20-year history of the *Index*, Ukraine's economic freedom score has advanced by over 9 points. Score increases in half of the 10 economic freedoms include particular gains in monetary stability and openness to global trade and more moderate progress in fiscal freedom and the elimination of corruption.

Nonetheless, Ukraine's economy remains "repressed." Deeper institutional reforms are critical for the achievement of more broadly based development. The inefficient legal framework remains highly vulnerable to political interference, and corruption further undermines the fragile rule of law.

BACKGROUND: Ukraine gained independence with the collapse of the Soviet Union in 1991. President Victor Yanukovych, in office since 2010, has pursued rapprochement with Russia, harassed the political opposition, and impeded press freedom. Ukraine joined the World Trade Organization in 2008 and the European Union's Eastern Partnership in 2009, and plans for closer cooperation with the EU have been proceeding despite Russian opposition. The government is trying to borrow $4 billion in international capital markets, in part to help service $3 billion owed to the International Monetary Fund and $2 billion owed to Russia's VTO Bank. It also has allowed Chevron and Shell to prospect for gas in the Black Sea. Ukraine has well-developed agricultural and industrial sectors, but dependence on steel and steel-product exports makes it vulnerable to global financial turmoil and Russian pressure. Its geostrategic location provides a vital energy transit route from Russia to Western Europe.

Freedom Trend

Country Comparisons

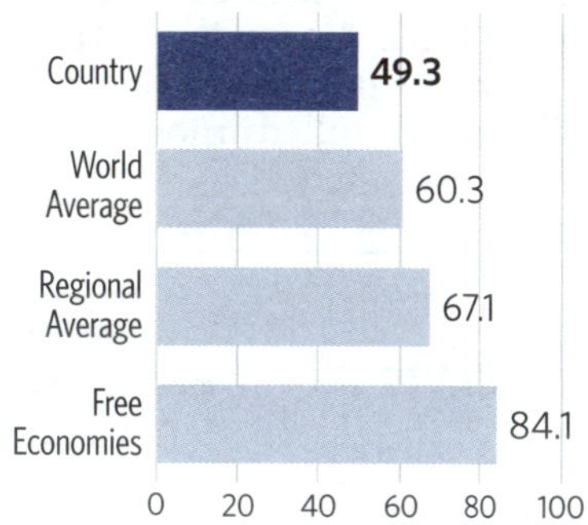

Quick Facts

Population: 45.5 million
GDP (PPP): $335.2 billion
0.2% growth in 2012
5-year compound annual growth -0.9%
$7,374 per capita
Unemployment: 8.0%
Inflation (CPI): 0.6%
FDI Inflow: $7.8 billion
Public Debt: 37.4% of GDP

2012 data unless otherwise noted.
Data compiled as of September 2013.

How Do We Measure Economic Freedom?
See page 471 for an explanation of the methodology or visit the *Index* Web site at *heritage.org/index*.

THE TEN ECONOMIC FREEDOMS

RULE OF LAW

	Score	Rank	1-Year Change
Property Rights	30.0	93rd	0
Freedom from Corruption	21.9	151st	-1.1

Corruption, one of Ukraine's most serious problems, continues to worsen. Business magnates benefit financially from their close association with top politicians. In 2012, a new law eliminated transparency requirements for public procurement. The judiciary is subject to intense political pressure and largely carries out the will of the executive branch. Contracts are not well enforced, and expropriation is always a possibility.

GOVERNMENT SIZE

	Score	Rank	1-Year Change
Fiscal Freedom	79.1	100th	+0.9
Government Spending	37.5	156th	+8.1

The top individual income tax rate is 17 percent, and the corporate tax rate was cut to 19 percent effective January 2013. Other taxes include a value-added tax (VAT) and a property tax. The overall tax burden equals 38 percent of gross domestic income. Public expenditures amount to 46 percent of GDP. Public debt is below 40 percent of gross domestic output. Government finances have been affected by the eurozone slowdown, pushing up deficits.

REGULATORY EFFICIENCY

	Score	Rank	1-Year Change
Business Freedom	59.8	113th	+12.2
Labor Freedom	49.8	139th	-0.1
Monetary Freedom	78.7	55th	+7.7

The business start-up process has been streamlined, but completing licensing requirements is still time-consuming and costs more than six times the level of average annual income. The labor code is outmoded and lacks flexibility. Massive and price-distorting government subsidies have resulted in domestic natural gas prices that are less than one-quarter of the importation cost.

OPEN MARKETS

	Score	Rank	1-Year Change
Trade Freedom	86.2	42nd	+1.8
Investment Freedom	20.0	164th	0
Financial Freedom	30.0	132nd	0

The average tariff rate is 1.9 percent. Government procurement policies sometimes favor domestic firms. Many state-owned enterprises exist, and foreign investment in several sectors is restricted by the government. The weak financial system remains underdeveloped. Restructuring of the banking sector has proceeded slowly in the aftermath of the recent global financial crisis, which has resulted in bailouts and nationalization of several banks.

Long-Term Score Change (since 1995)

RULE OF LAW		GOVERNMENT SIZE		REGULATORY EFFICIENCY		OPEN MARKETS	
Property Rights	0	Fiscal Freedom	+17.2	Business Freedom	+4.8	Trade Freedom	+31.2
Freedom from Corruption	+11.9	Government Spending	-9.5	Labor Freedom	-6.0	Investment Freedom	-30.0
				Monetary Freedom	+78.7	Financial Freedom	-20.0

UNITED ARAB EMIRATES

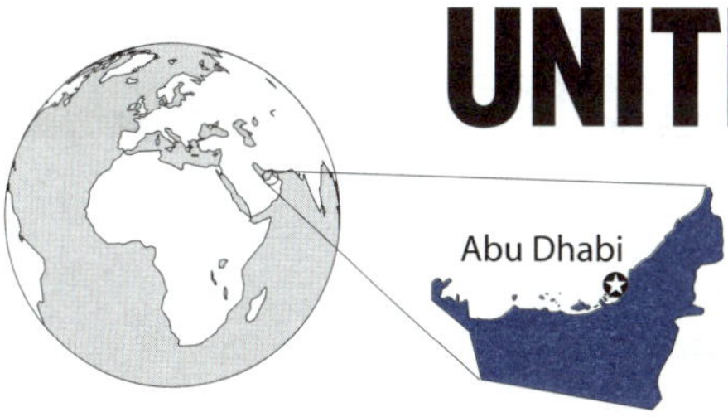

World Rank: **28** Regional Rank: **2**

Economic Freedom Score

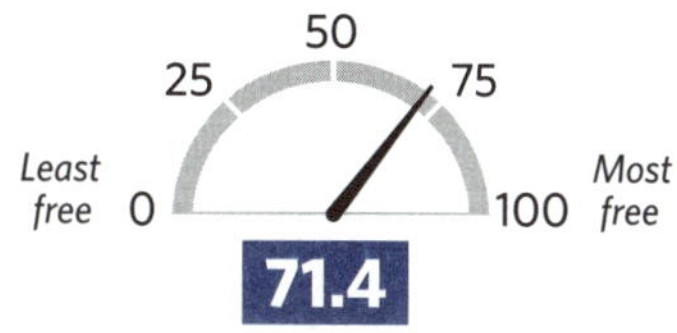

The United Arab Emirates' economic freedom score is 71.4, making its economy the 28th freest in the 2014 *Index*. Its score is 0.3 point higher than last year, with improvements in labor freedom, business freedom, and monetary freedom outweighing declines in the control of government spending and freedom from corruption. The UAE is ranked 2nd out of 15 countries in the Middle East/North Africa region, and its overall score is higher than the world and regional averages.

The UAE was first assessed in the 1996 *Index* and since then has been a regional leader in economic freedom. Improvements in half of the 10 economic freedoms include advancements in the management of public spending and market openness. Significant declines in property rights and freedom from corruption have prevented an overall gain, but the economy has achieved its highest economic freedom score in a decade in the 2014 *Index*.

The UAE can do better in the rule of law. Respect for the rule of law remains undermined by the judicial system's lack of independence and vulnerability to political influence.

BACKGROUND: The United Arab Emirates is a federation of seven monarchies: Abu Dhabi, Ajman, Dubai, Fujairah, Ras Al-Khaimah, Sharjah, and Umm al-Qaiwain. The government responded to demands for reform during the "Arab Spring" by initiating a $1.6 billion program to improve the infrastructure in the poorer northern emirates. It also expanded the number of people allowed to vote in the September 2011 elections for the Federal National Council. Abu Dhabi accounts for about 90 percent of oil production; Dubai is the center of finance, commerce, transportation, and tourism. Free trade zones that permit 100 percent foreign ownership with zero taxation help to diversify the economy. UAE nationals rely heavily on public-sector employment and subsidized services. Oil and gas exports account for roughly 80 percent of government revenues.

Freedom Trend

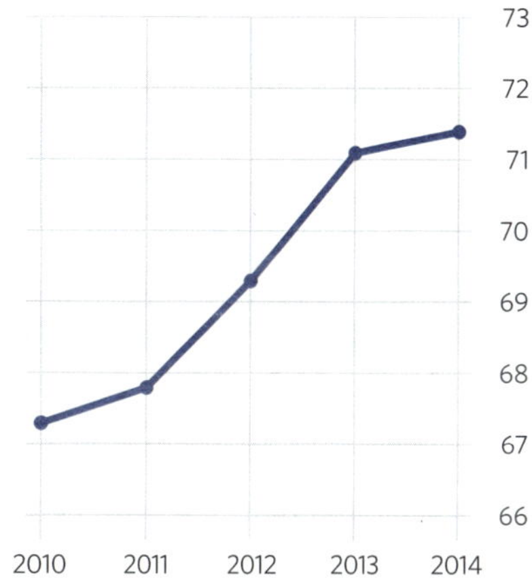

Country Comparisons

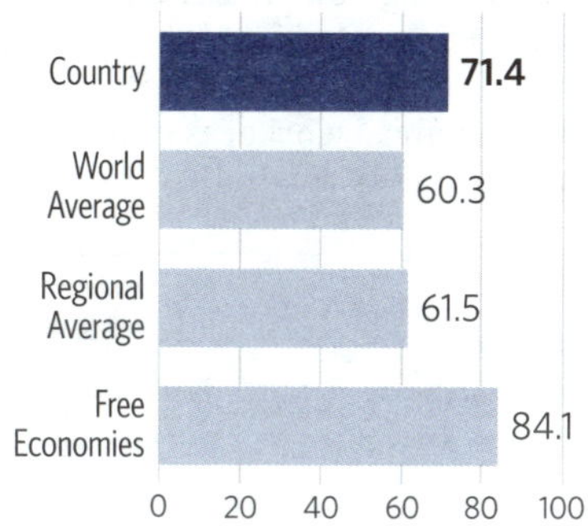

Quick Facts

Population: 5.5 million
GDP (PPP): $271.3 billion
3.9% growth in 2012
5-year compound annual growth 2.1%
$49,012 per capita
Unemployment: n/a
Inflation (CPI): 0.7%
FDI Inflow: $9.6 billion
Public Debt: 17.6% of GDP

2012 data unless otherwise noted.
Data compiled as of September 2013.

How Do We Measure Economic Freedom?
See page 471 for an explanation of the methodology or visit the *Index* Web site at *heritage.org/index*.

UNITED ARAB EMIRATES (continued)

THE TEN ECONOMIC FREEDOMS

		Score	Rank	1-Year Change
RULE OF LAW	Property Rights	55.0	51st	0
	Freedom from Corruption	66.4	28th	-1.6

The UAE is considered one of the least corrupt countries in the Middle East. The rule of law is relatively well-maintained, but the judiciary is not independent, and court rulings are subject to review by the political leadership. All land in Abu Dhabi, largest of the seven emirates, is government-owned. Non-citizens are allowed to own property only in certain areas.

		Score	Rank	1-Year Change
GOVERNMENT SIZE	Fiscal Freedom	99.6	4th	-0.3
	Government Spending	83.1	40th	-2.0

The UAE has no income tax and no federal-level corporate tax. In some emirates, different corporate taxes exist for certain business activities. There are few other taxes, and the overall tax burden is quite low at 6.1 percent of the economy. Government spending is 24 percent of gross domestic output. Public debt is low at about 18 percent of GDP. Oil and gas revenues contribute significantly to public spending.

		Score	Rank	1-Year Change
REGULATORY EFFICIENCY	Business Freedom	74.4	54th	+0.4
	Labor Freedom	82.9	19th	+5.3
	Monetary Freedom	84.6	6th	+0.7

Launching a business takes six procedures and eight days, and no minimum capital is required. Licensing requirements have been streamlined and are less costly, but completing them still takes over a month. Employment regulations are relatively flexible, and the non-salary cost of employing a worker is moderate. Continued restructuring of heavily subsidized and indebted government-related entities (GREs) is needed.

		Score	Rank	1-Year Change
OPEN MARKETS	Trade Freedom	82.5	60th	-0.1
	Investment Freedom	35.0	142nd	0
	Financial Freedom	50.0	69th	0

The UAE's average tariff rate is 3.7 percent. Non-tariff barriers are not a significant deterrent to trade. Foreign ownership in many sectors of the economy is capped at 49 percent. The modern financial sector is efficient and competitive. Banks offer a full range of services. Islamic banking is increasingly prominent. State-owned banks have maintained a strong presence, but foreign banks have over 100 branches around the country.

Long-Term Score Change (since 1996)

RULE OF LAW		GOVERNMENT SIZE		REGULATORY EFFICIENCY		OPEN MARKETS	
Property Rights	**-35.0**	Fiscal Freedom	**-0.3**	Business Freedom	**-10.6**	Trade Freedom	**+5.5**
Freedom from Corruption	**-23.6**	Government Spending	**+36.0**	Labor Freedom	**+8.7**	Investment Freedom	**+5.0**
				Monetary Freedom	**+9.4**	Financial Freedom	**0**

UNITED KINGDOM

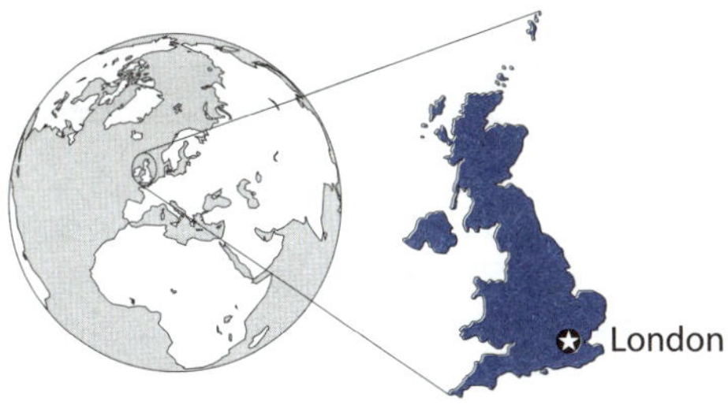

World Rank: **14** Regional Rank: **5**

Economic Freedom Score

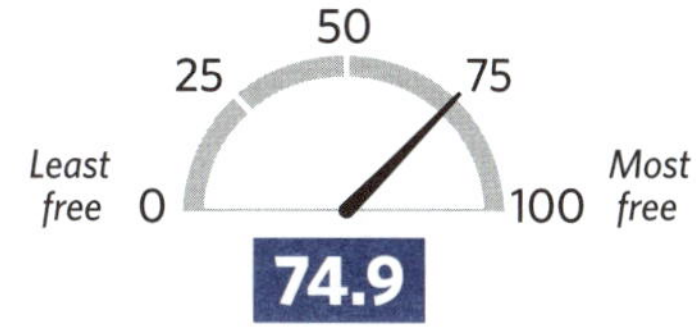

The United Kingdom's economic freedom score is 74.9, making its economy the 14th freest in the 2014 *Index*. Its score is essentially the same as last year, with modest improvements in government spending, labor freedom, monetary freedom, and trade freedom offset by deteriorations in business freedom, freedom from corruption, and fiscal freedom. The U.K. is ranked 5th out of 43 countries in the Europe region.

Over the 20-year history of the *Index*, the U.K.'s economic freedom has declined by 3 points, the second worst performance among advanced economies. Despite notable improvements in trade freedom and investment freedom, the overall gain has been offset by combined declines in the management of public finance and regulatory efficiency.

Britain's economy has been consistently rated one of the world's 20 freest. However, since 2006, when it reached its highest economic freedom score ever, the U.K. has been largely on a path of declining economic freedom. Expansionary public spending has generated significant budgetary pressure. With government debt over 90 percent of the size of the economy, underlying economic fundamentals generally remain weak.

BACKGROUND: Following the market reforms instituted by Prime Minister Margaret Thatcher in the 1980s, Britain experienced steady economic growth throughout the 1990s, but the government's size and spending grew significantly under successive Labour governments. Prime Minister David Cameron's Conservative–Liberal Democrat coalition government, formed after the 2010 general election, has cut public services but maintained spending on the National Health Service and foreign aid. The government's debt continues to increase. The economy was in recession in early 2012 but has bounced back to positive growth. Cameron vetoed Britain's participation in the European Union's Fiscal Compact in 2011 and has been at the forefront of attempts to cap the EU's annual and long-term budgets. He has also promised a referendum for 2017 on continued membership in the EU.

How Do We Measure Economic Freedom?
See page 471 for an explanation of the methodology or visit the *Index* Web site at *heritage.org/index*.

Freedom Trend

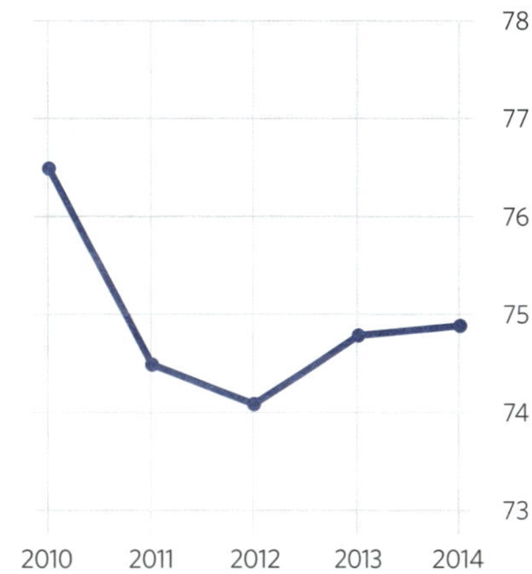

Country Comparisons

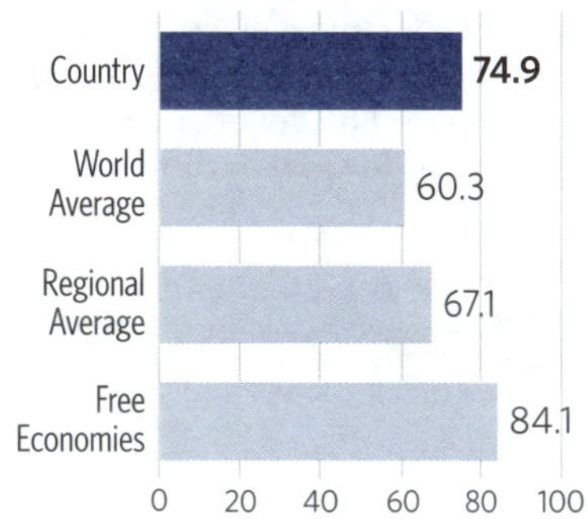

Quick Facts

Population: 63.2 million
GDP (PPP): $2.3 trillion
0.2% growth in 2012
5-year compound annual growth -0.4%
$36,941 per capita
Unemployment: 8.0%
Inflation (CPI): 2.8%
FDI Inflow: $62.4 billion
Public Debt: 90.3% of GDP

2012 data unless otherwise noted.
Data compiled as of September 2013.

THE TEN ECONOMIC FREEDOMS

RULE OF LAW

	Score	Rank	1-Year Change
Property Rights	90.0	2nd	0
Freedom from Corruption	76.4	17th	-1.6

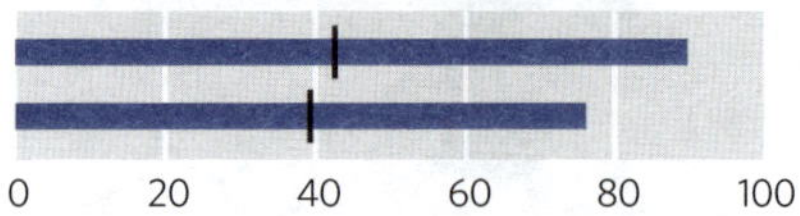

Corruption is not pervasive, but high-profile scandals have damaged political reputations in both major parties. The Bribery Act, considered one of the most sweeping anti-bribery laws in the world, came into force in 2011. The rule of law is well established within an independent legal framework. Private property rights and contracts are very secure, and the court system is efficient. Protection of intellectual property rights is effective.

GOVERNMENT SIZE

	Score	Rank	1-Year Change
Fiscal Freedom	56.6	172nd	-0.4
Government Spending	29.5	161st	+1.8

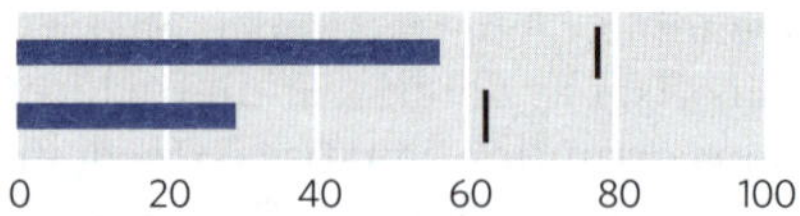

The top individual income tax rate is 50 percent, and the top corporate rate is 24 percent. Other taxes include a value-added tax (VAT) and an environment tax. The overall tax burden amounts to 35.5 percent of gross domestic income. Public expenditures have been falling to 48.5 percent of GDP. However, public debt continues to rise, surpassing 90 percent of gross domestic output.

REGULATORY EFFICIENCY

	Score	Rank	1-Year Change
Business Freedom	92.0	9th	-2.1
Labor Freedom	73.1	54th	+1.5
Monetary Freedom	73.5	119th	+1.1

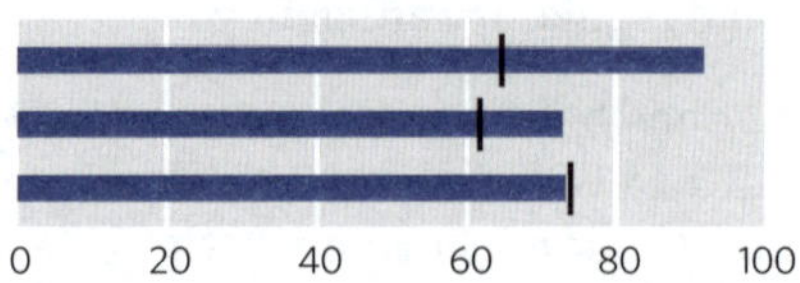

It takes six procedures and 12 days to incorporate a business, and no minimum capital is required. However, completing licensing requirements takes almost three months. The non-salary cost of employing a worker is moderate, and severance payments are not overly burdensome. The government controls virtually all prices for health care services and will triple subsidies for low-carbon power generation by 2020.

OPEN MARKETS

	Score	Rank	1-Year Change
Trade Freedom	87.8	11th	+1.0
Investment Freedom	90.0	2nd	0
Financial Freedom	80.0	4th	0

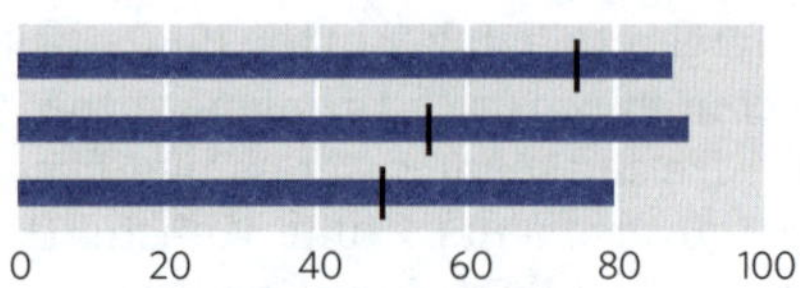

EU members have a low 1.1 percent average tariff rate and, in general, few non-tariff barriers to trade. The United Kingdom has few limitations on foreign investment. The overall stability of the financial system has been restored. However, the state continues to hold stakes in two large banks, Royal Bank of Scotland and Lloyds. The process of selling government shares in these institutions has begun, but progress has been gradual.

Long-Term Score Change (since 1995)

RULE OF LAW		GOVERNMENT SIZE		REGULATORY EFFICIENCY		OPEN MARKETS	
Property Rights	0	Fiscal Freedom	-4.7	Business Freedom	-8.0	Trade Freedom	+10.0
Freedom from Corruption	-13.6	Government Spending	-7.8	Labor Freedom	-5.9	Investment Freedom	+20.0
				Monetary Freedom	-11.5	Financial Freedom	-10.0

UNITED STATES

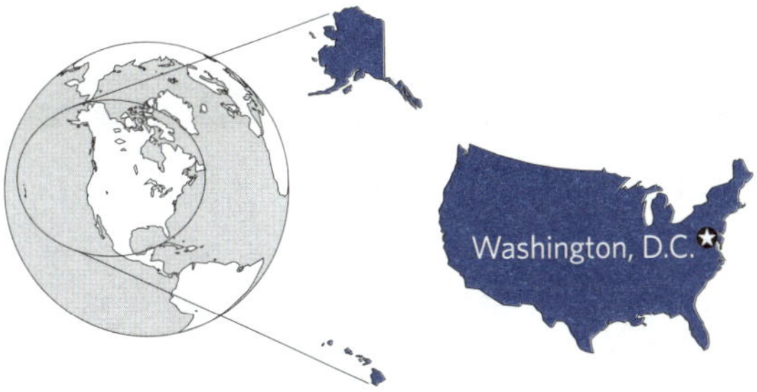

World Rank: **12** Regional Rank: **2**

Economic Freedom Score

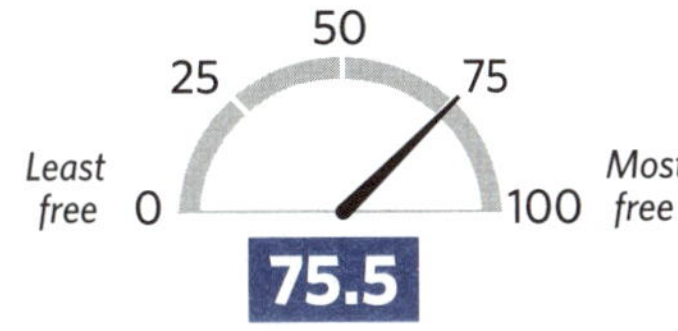

The United States, with an economic freedom score of 75.5, is the 12th freest economy in the 2014 *Index*. Its score is half a point lower than last year, primarily due to deteriorations in property rights, fiscal freedom, and business freedom. The U.S. is ranked 2nd out of three countries in the North America region, and although its score remains well above the world and regional averages, it is no longer one of the top 10 freest economies.

Over the 20-year history of the *Index*, the U.S.'s economic freedom has fluctuated significantly. During the first 10 years, its score rose gradually, and it joined the ranks of the economically "free" in 2006. Since then, it has suffered a dramatic decline of almost 6 points, with particularly large losses in property rights, freedom from corruption, and control of government spending. The U.S. is the only country to have recorded a loss of economic freedom each of the past seven years. The overall U.S. score decline from 1995 to 2014 is 1.2 points, the fourth worst drop among advanced economies.

Substantial expansion in the size and scope of government, including through new and costly regulations in areas like finance and health care, has contributed significantly to the erosion of U.S. economic freedom. The growth of government has been accompanied by increasing cronyism that has undermined the rule of law and perceptions of fairness.

BACKGROUND: President Barack Obama won re-election in 2012, but his efforts to expand government spending and regulation have been partially thwarted by the Republican-controlled House of Representatives. The continuing underperformance of the U.S. economy, by far the world's largest, is a serious concern. The Administration's uncertain responses to foreign policy challenges in Libya, Egypt, Syria, and Iran, among others, have reduced U.S. influence in countering tensions in the Middle East. Implementation of the health care law passed in 2010 has hit major snags and appears to be significantly hurting job creation and full-time employment. Partisan disagreements over spending levels led to a partial shutdown of the federal government in late 2013.

Freedom Trend

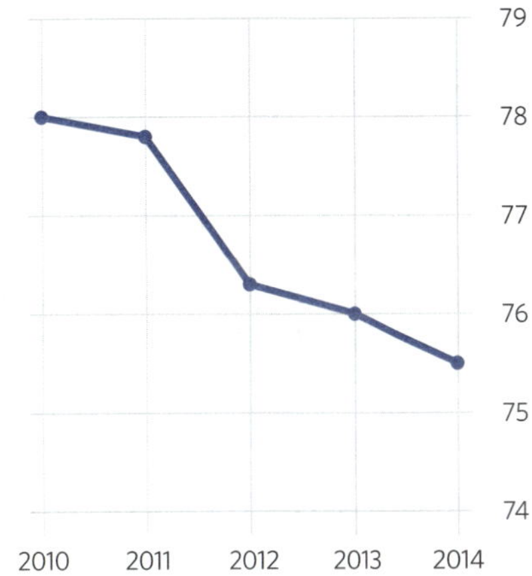

Country Comparisons

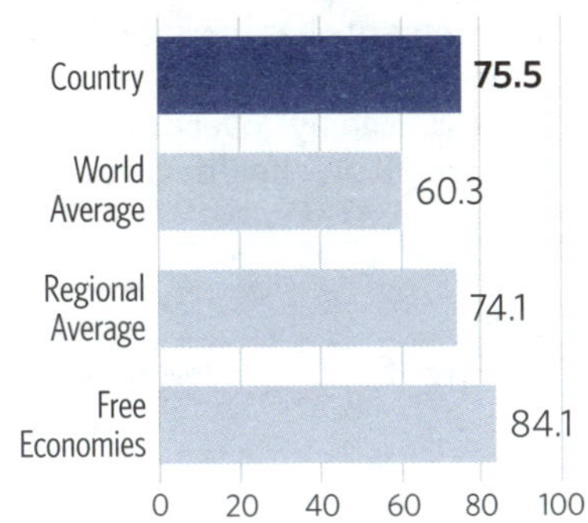

Quick Facts

Population: 314.2 million
GDP (PPP): $15.7 trillion
2.2% growth in 2012
5-year compound annual growth 0.6%
$49,922 per capita
Unemployment: 7.2% (Sept. 2013)
Inflation (CPI): 2.1%
FDI Inflow: $167.6 billion
Public Debt: 106.5% of GDP

2012 data unless otherwise noted.
Data compiled as of September 2013.

How Do We Measure Economic Freedom?
See page 471 for an explanation of the methodology or visit the *Index* Web site at *heritage.org/index*.

THE TEN ECONOMIC FREEDOMS

Score | ■ *Country* | *World Average*

RULE OF LAW		Score	Rank	1-Year Change
	Property Rights	80.0	20th	-5.0
	Freedom from Corruption	72.0	23rd	+1.0

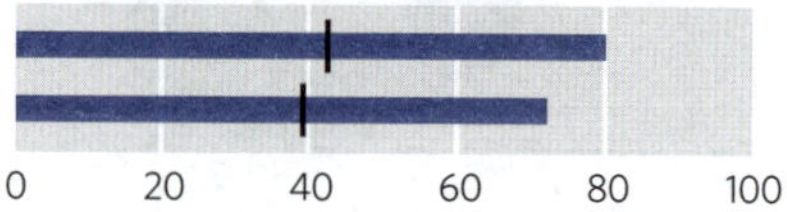

The expansive use of government regulatory agencies to manage economic activity, particularly in the financial, health care, and energy sectors, has opened the door to increased perceptions of cronyism and corruption. Although property rights are guaranteed and the judiciary functions independently and predictably, protection of property rights has been uneven, raising charges of favoritism.

GOVERNMENT SIZE		Score	Rank	1-Year Change
	Fiscal Freedom	65.8	154th	-3.5
	Government Spending	48.1	137th	+0.3

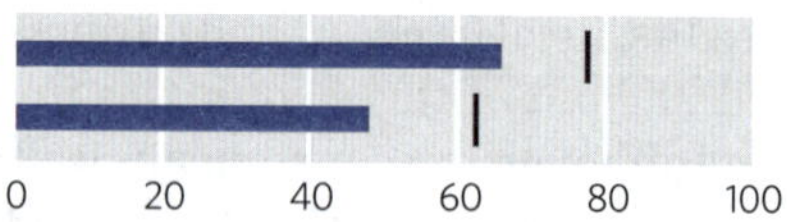

The top individual income tax rate has risen to 39.6 percent, and the top corporate tax rate remains at 35 percent. Other taxes include a capital gains tax and excise taxes. The payroll tax holiday expired at the beginning of 2013. The overall tax burden amounts to 25.1 percent of gross domestic income. General government expenditures are slightly over 40 percent of GDP. Total public debt equals over 100 percent of the size of the economy.

REGULATORY EFFICIENCY		Score	Rank	1-Year Change
	Business Freedom	89.2	17th	-1.3
	Labor Freedom	97.2	1st	+1.7
	Monetary Freedom	75.4	95th	+0.4

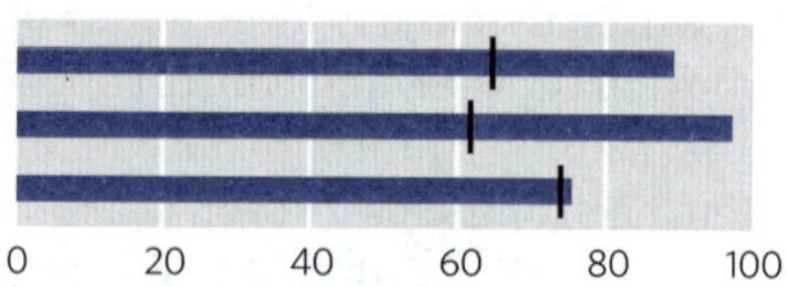

Incorporating a business takes five days on average, but the overall cost of meeting regulatory requirements has increased by over $60 billion since 2009, with more than 130 new regulations imposed. The labor market, primarily regulated at the state level, remains flexible. Price distortions, caused by government interventions such as monetary easing and substantial subsidies for agriculture, health care and other welfare programs, have increased.

OPEN MARKETS		Score	Rank	1-Year Change
	Trade Freedom	86.8	39th	+0.4
	Investment Freedom	70.0	46th	0
	Financial Freedom	70.0	19th	0

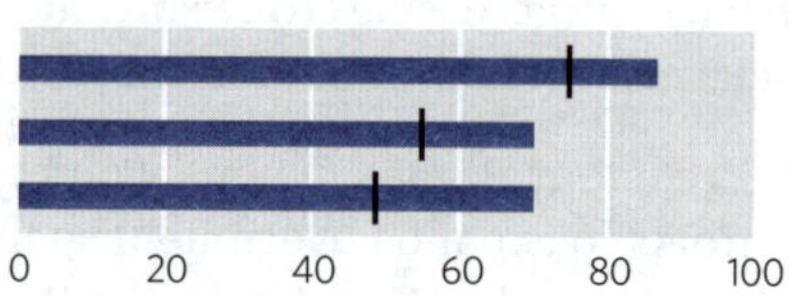

The average tariff rate is 1.3 percent. Relatively new non-tariff barriers include restrictions on tomatoes imported from Mexico. Foreign investment in airlines and media is capped, and the regulatory process can be a deterrent to investment. The full effects of the onerous Dodd–Frank bill, passed three years ago, have yet to be felt. A backlog of ongoing rulemakings has prolonged business uncertainty, impeding economic growth.

Long-Term Score Change (since 1995)

RULE OF LAW		GOVERNMENT SIZE		REGULATORY EFFICIENCY		OPEN MARKETS	
Property Rights	-10.0	Fiscal Freedom	+0.9	Business Freedom	+4.2	Trade Freedom	+8.4
Freedom from Corruption	-18.0	Government Spending	-9.7	Labor Freedom	+1.8	Investment Freedom	0
				Monetary Freedom	-8.4	Financial Freedom	0

URUGUAY

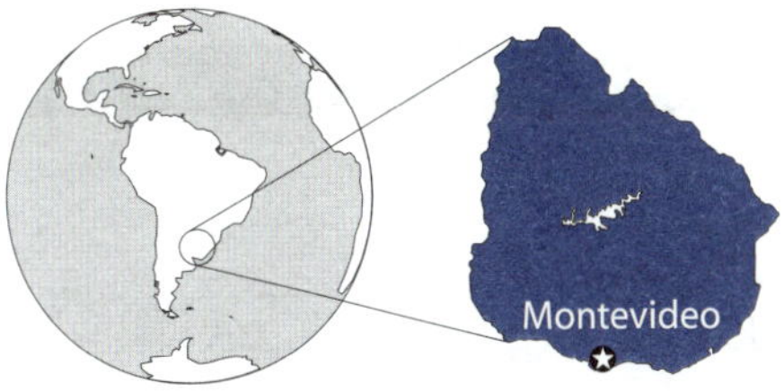

World Rank: **38** Regional Rank: **5**

Economic Freedom Score

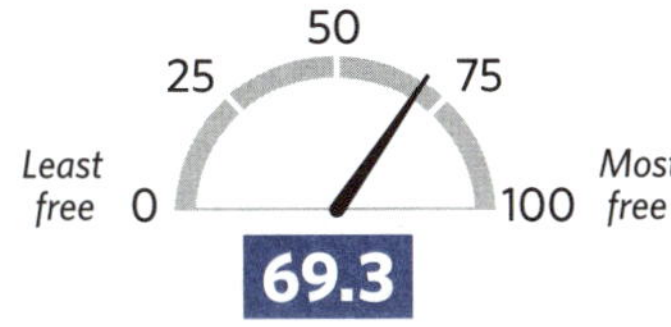

Uruguay's economic freedom score is 69.3, making its economy the 38th freest in the 2014 *Index*. Its score is 0.4 point lower than last year, with declines in fiscal freedom, labor freedom, monetary freedom, and trade freedom outweighing improvements in freedom from corruption, business freedom, and investment freedom. Uruguay is ranked 5th out of 29 countries in the South and Central America/Caribbean region, and its overall score is above the world average.

Over the 20-year history of the *Index,* Uruguay has advanced its economic freedom score by over 6 points. Improvements in six of the 10 economic freedoms include gains in business freedom, investment freedom, trade freedom, monetary freedom, and rule of law as measured by property rights and freedom from corruption, scores for which have improved by 20 points.

Uruguay typically has been ranked near the upper boundary of the "moderately free" category. Government policies promote engagement in global trade and investment, and the private sector contributes to economic growth to an enhanced degree. However, state interference in the financial sector and other areas still constrains development of more dynamic growth.

BACKGROUND: Former guerrilla Jose Mujica was elected president of Uruguay in 2009. After strong growth in 2010 and 2011, the economy has slowed. State involvement in the economy is substantial, and deregulation is needed in telecommunications, energy, and public utilities. Crime and violence are increasing, and drug trafficking is a problem in urban areas. Uruguay is a founding member of MERCOSUR and signed a Trade and Investment Framework Agreement with the United States in 2007. The economy is still based largely on exports of commodities like milk, beef, rice, and wool. Uruguay offers excellent banking services, including branches of some of the world's largest banks, but an information-sharing agreement with Argentina has reduced consumer confidence in the country as a safe haven for assets.

Freedom Trend

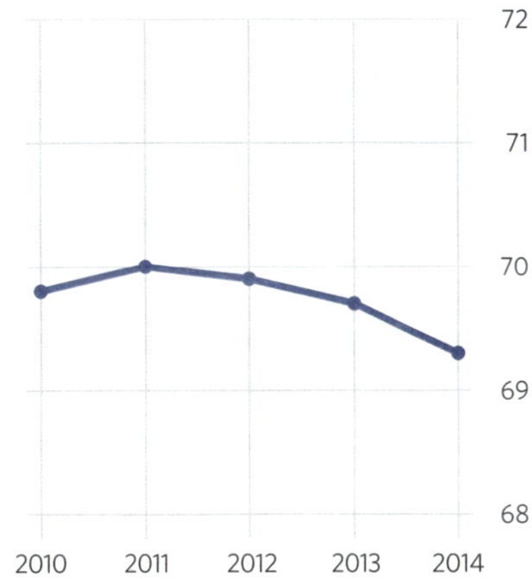

Country Comparisons

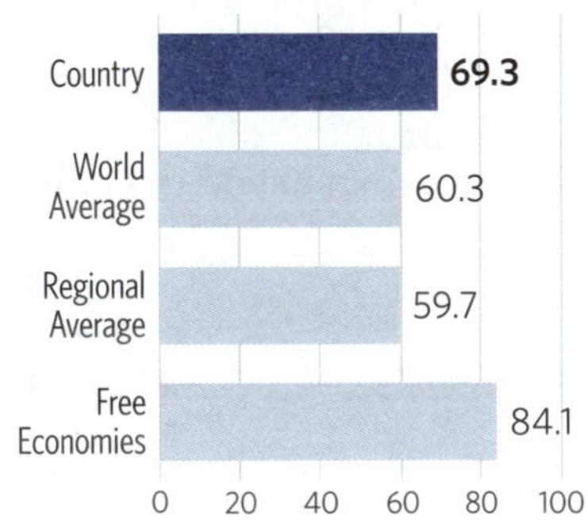

Quick Facts

Population: 3.4 million
GDP (PPP): $53.8 billion
3.8% growth in 2012
5-year compound annual growth 5.6%
$15,911 per capita
Unemployment: 6.1%
Inflation (CPI): 8.1%
FDI Inflow: $2.7 billion
Public Debt: 53.7% of GDP

2012 data unless otherwise noted.
Data compiled as of September 2013.

How Do We Measure Economic Freedom?
See page 471 for an explanation of the methodology or visit the *Index* Web site at *heritage.org/index.*

THE TEN ECONOMIC FREEDOMS

Score ▬ *Country* | *World Average*

RULE OF LAW

	Score	Rank	1-Year Change
Property Rights	70.0	27th	0
Freedom from Corruption	70.6	24th	+0.6

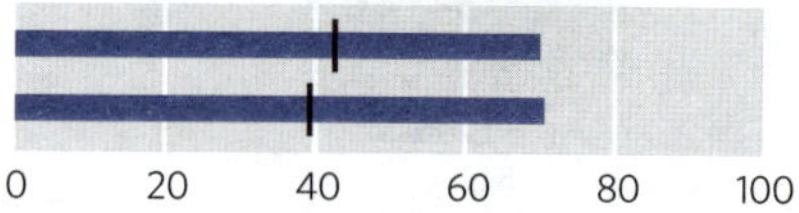

Uruguay is one of Latin America's least corrupt countries. A Transparency Law criminalizes a broad range of potential abuses of power by officeholders, including the laundering of funds related to public corruption cases. The judiciary is relatively independent, but the court system remains severely backlogged. Private property is generally secure, and expropriation is unlikely. Contracts are enforced, and regulations protect IPR.

GOVERNMENT SIZE

	Score	Rank	1-Year Change
Fiscal Freedom	77.4	108th	-6.8
Government Spending	68.0	94th	-0.3

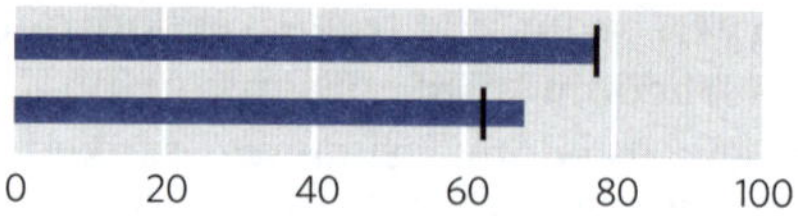

The top individual income tax rate is 30 percent, and the top corporate tax rate is 25 percent. Other taxes include a value-added tax (VAT) and a capital gains tax. Overall tax revenue constitutes 27.2 percent of the economy. Public expenditures are equivalent to one-third of the domestic economy. Government debt is 54 percent of GDP. Regional drought has pushed up energy costs, widening the budget deficit.

REGULATORY EFFICIENCY

	Score	Rank	1-Year Change
Business Freedom	74.5	52nd	+1.1
Labor Freedom	68.1	73rd	-2.6
Monetary Freedom	72.1	131st	-0.4

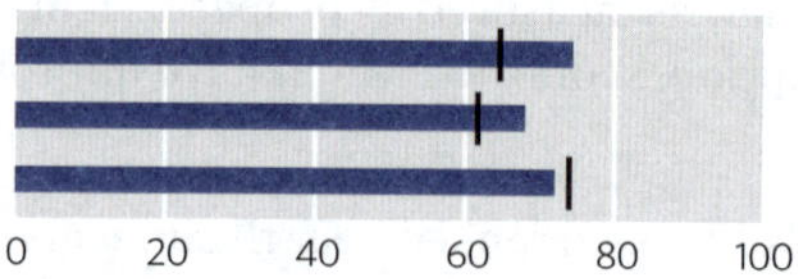

It takes five procedures and seven days to incorporate a business, and no minimum capital is required. The cost of completing licensing requirements is about half the level of average annual income. The non-salary cost of employing a worker is low, but restrictions on work hours are not flexible. The government shut down the state-owned oil refinery in 2011, but subsidies to the state-owned electricity company increased in 2012.

OPEN MARKETS

	Score	Rank	1-Year Change
Trade Freedom	82.5	61st	-0.4
Investment Freedom	80.0	23rd	+5.0
Financial Freedom	30.0	132nd	0

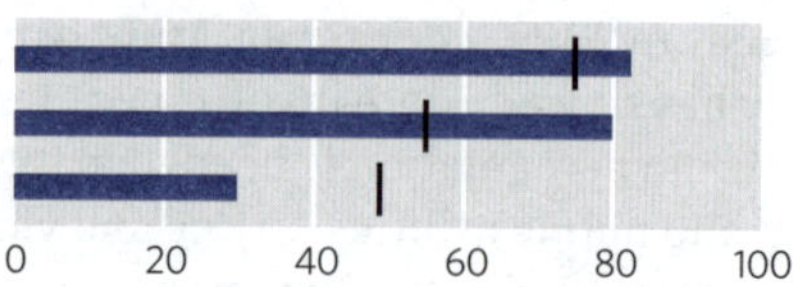

Uruguay's average tariff rate is 3.8 percent. Some imports require licenses. Foreign investors are treated the same as domestic investors under the law, and there generally are no ownership limits. The financial sector continues to evolve, but the government remains heavily involved through ownership and allocation of credit. Capital markets are underdeveloped and concentrate on government debt.

Long-Term Score Change (since 1995)

RULE OF LAW		GOVERNMENT SIZE		REGULATORY EFFICIENCY		OPEN MARKETS	
Property Rights	**+20.0**	Fiscal Freedom	**-7.2**	Business Freedom	**+4.5**	Trade Freedom	**+19.5**
Freedom from Corruption	**+20.6**	Government Spending	**-11.5**	Labor Freedom	**-7.8**	Investment Freedom	**+10.0**
				Monetary Freedom	**+26.9**	Financial Freedom	**-20.0**

UZBEKISTAN

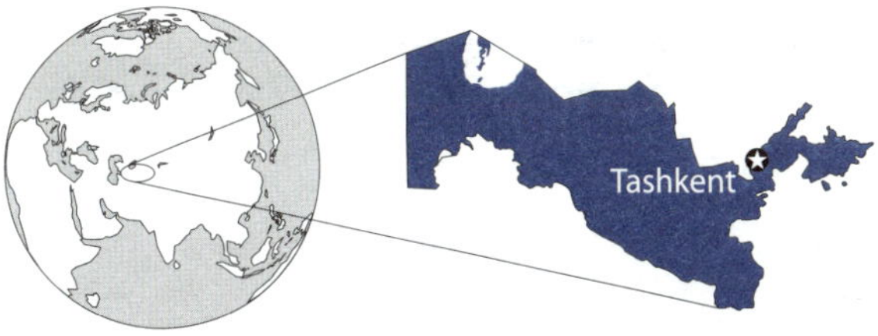

World Rank: **163** Regional Rank: **37**

Economic Freedom Score

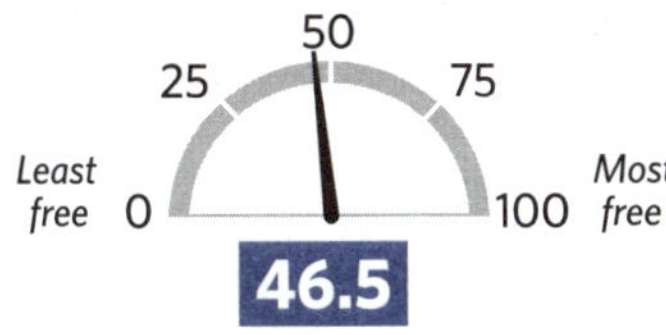

Uzbekistan's economic freedom score is 46.5, making its economy the 163rd freest in the 2014 *Index*. Its score is 0.5 point higher than last year, with improvements in business freedom and the control of government spending outweighing declines in freedom from corruption and labor freedom. Uzbekistan is ranked 37th out of 42 countries in the Asia–Pacific region, and its overall score is much lower than the world average.

Uzbekistan was first ranked in the *Index* in 1998. Since then, its economic freedom score has advanced by about 15 points, one of the top 20 improvements. Overall improvement has been driven by gains in six of the 10 economic freedoms including monetary freedom, business freedom, and fiscal freedom. However, property rights and investment freedom have declined by 15 points or more over the country's history in the *Index*.

Uzbekistan remains economically "repressed." Pervasive state controls persist in many areas, stifling progress in the development of a modern diversified economy. Corruption is widespread, and contract enforcement and protection of property rights are seriously deficient.

BACKGROUND: President Islam Karimov has held power since the late 1980s. Uzbekistan allowed NATO to use its Karshi-Khanabad air base after 9/11 but expelled all U.S. forces in 2005 and moved closer to Russia following Western criticism related to the Andijan incident, in which government troops shot and killed hundreds of Islamist protesters. Recently, relations with the United States and the European Union have improved due to cooperation in fighting Islamist terrorism. Uzbekistan left the Russia-dominated Commonwealth Security Treaty Organization in 2012. Rapprochement with Kazakhstan, if pursued, would shore up regional stability. Uzbekistan is a leading cotton producer and heavily dependent on natural gas, oil, gold, and uranium exports. It has secured a $2.54 billion loan from a consortium of private banks to build the Ustyurt gas and chemical complex.

How Do We Measure Economic Freedom?
See page 471 for an explanation of the methodology or visit the *Index* Web site at *heritage.org/index*.

Freedom Trend

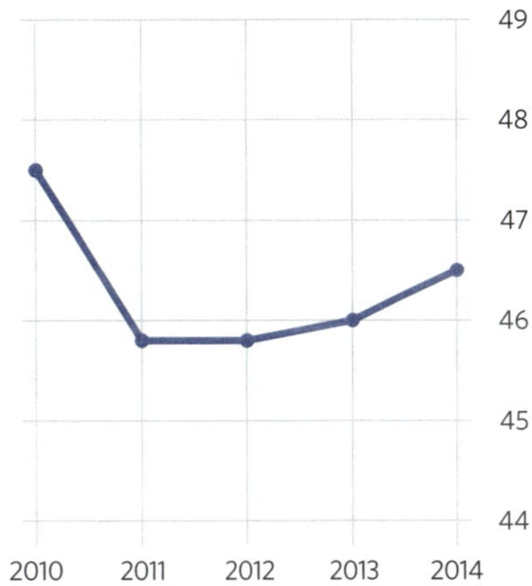

Country Comparisons

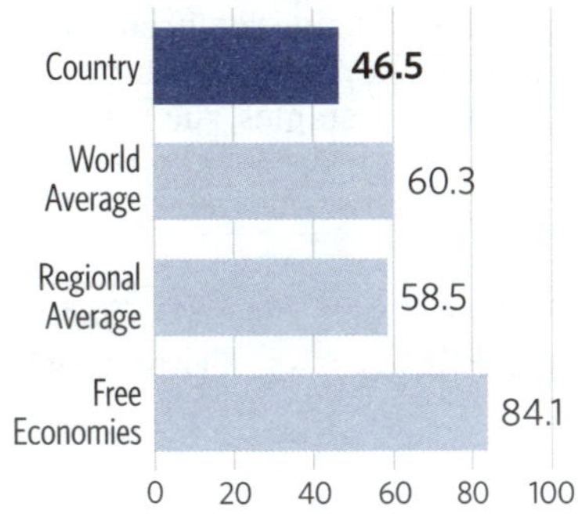

Quick Facts

Population: 29.4 million
GDP (PPP): $104.7 billion
8.0% growth in 2012
5-year compound annual growth 8.4%
$3,555 per capita
Unemployment: 0.2%
Inflation (CPI): 12.1%
FDI Inflow: $1.1 billion
Public Debt: 8.6% of GDP

2012 data unless otherwise noted.
Data compiled as of September 2013.

THE TEN ECONOMIC FREEDOMS

RULE OF LAW

	Score	Rank	1-Year Change
Property Rights	15.0	159th	0
Freedom from Corruption	13.4	178th	-2.6

The judiciary is subservient to the president, who appoints all judges and can remove them at any time. Court procedures fall short of international standards, and expropriation by powerful figures able to act with impunity is possible. Corruption is rampant. Property ownership, generally respected by local and central authorities, can be subverted by the government. There is no general system for registration of liens on chattel property.

GOVERNMENT SIZE

	Score	Rank	1-Year Change
Fiscal Freedom	90.3	33rd	+0.1
Government Spending	70.4	87th	+2.6

The top individual income tax rate is 22 percent, and the top corporate tax rate is 9 percent. Other taxes include a value-added tax (VAT) and a property tax. The overall tax burden equals 20.2 percent of gross domestic income. Government expenditures amount to 31 percent of GDP. Public debt is below 10 percent of gross domestic income. The central government has reported a rare budget surplus due to expanding revenue collection.

REGULATORY EFFICIENCY

	Score	Rank	1-Year Change
Business Freedom	75.7	46th	+4.5
Labor Freedom	60.8	96th	-0.2
Monetary Freedom	63.1	172nd	+0.1

Starting a business takes four procedures, and no minimum capital is required. However, completing licensing requirements still takes over 200 days. The labor market remains stagnant. A large portion of the workforce is in the informal sector. The government administers prices of many basic staples, such as petroleum products, natural gas, utilities, and bread.

OPEN MARKETS

	Score	Rank	1-Year Change
Trade Freedom	66.1	140th	0
Investment Freedom	0.0	178th	0
Financial Freedom	10.0	174th	0

The average tariff rate is 6.9 percent. It is very costly and time-consuming to import goods. It may be difficult for investors to access foreign currency. The government screens new foreign investment and restricts investment in many industries. Banking is dominated by state-owned banks and lacks competition and transparency. State-controlled banks support government economic priorities through subsidized loans offered in specific sectors.

Long-Term Score Change (since 1998)

RULE OF LAW		GOVERNMENT SIZE		REGULATORY EFFICIENCY		OPEN MARKETS	
Property Rights	**-15.0**	Fiscal Freedom	**+32.9**	Business Freedom	**+35.7**	Trade Freedom	**+16.1**
Freedom from Corruption	**+3.4**	Government Spending	**+14.0**	Labor Freedom	**-6.3**	Investment Freedom	**-30.0**
				Monetary Freedom	**+63.1**	Financial Freedom	**0**

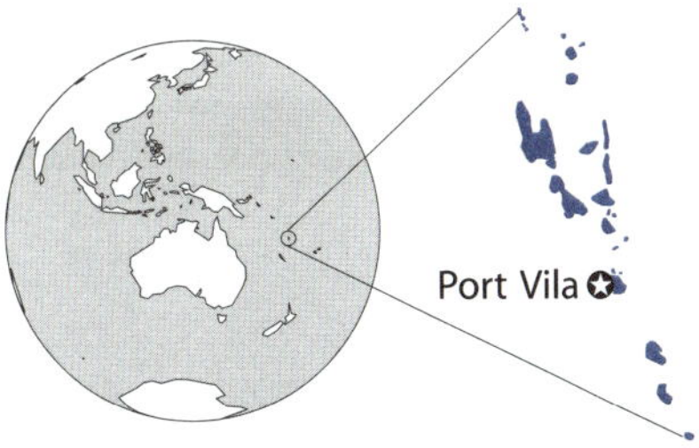

VANUATU

World Rank: **93** Regional Rank: **18**

Economic Freedom Score

Vanuatu's economic freedom score is 59.5, making its economy the 93rd freest in the 2014 *Index*. Its score is 2.9 points better than last year, reflecting a substantial improvement in investment freedom that outweighs combined declines in business freedom, freedom from corruption, and labor freedom. Vanuatu is ranked 18th out of 42 countries in the Asia–Pacific region, and its overall score is just below the world average.

Vanuatu was first assessed in the 2009 *Index*, and its economic freedom has advanced only modestly. Improvements in five of the 10 economic freedoms, including investment freedom, monetary freedom, and labor freedom, have been offset by declines in trade freedom and business freedom. Although it's economy is still ranked "mostly unfree," Vanuatu has achieved its highest score ever in the 2014 *Index*.

Stronger commitment to institutional reform is needed to spark development of a truly dynamic private sector. Property rights are poorly protected, and inadequate legal infrastructure deters investment. Corruption continues to undermine the rule of law. High tariffs and non-tariff barriers to trade hold back integration into the global marketplace.

BACKGROUND: The Republic of Vanuatu, 83 islands spread over 4,500 square miles of the South Pacific, achieved independence in 1980 and is today a parliamentary democracy that remains divided between its English-speaking and French-speaking citizens. In the 2012 elections, 18 parties won seats in the legislature, with the Vanua'aku Pati party winning the most seats at eight. Sato Kilman served as prime minister until March 2013, when several members of parliament crossed the aisle to join the opposition and forced Kilman to resign. The legislature subsequently elected Moana Carcasses Kalosil of the Green Confederation party as prime minister. The economy is dominated by tourism and agriculture, and over 80 percent of the population is involved in farming, which accounts for roughly 20 percent of GDP.

Freedom Trend

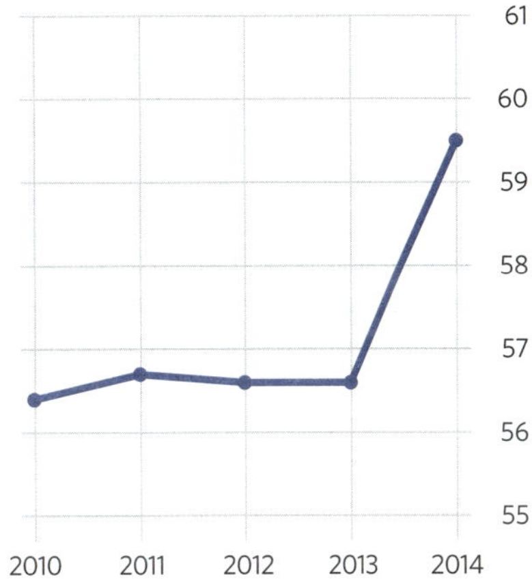

Country Comparisons

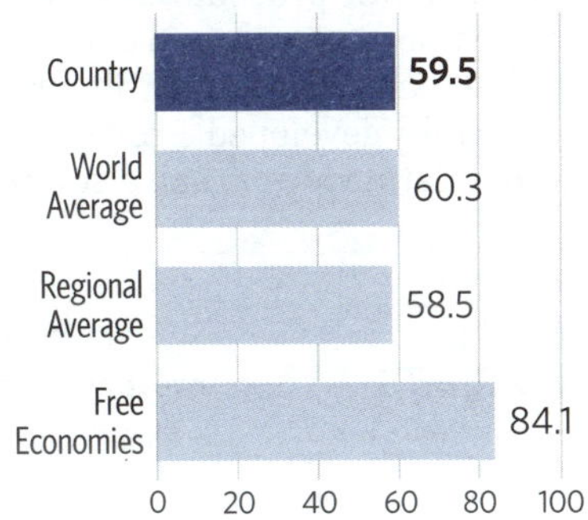

Quick Facts

Population: 0.3 million
GDP (PPP): $1.2 billion
2.7% growth in 2012
5-year compound annual growth 3.1%
$4,916 per capita
Unemployment: n/a
Inflation (CPI): 1.4%
FDI Inflow: $37.7 million
Public Debt: 20.0% of GDP

2012 data unless otherwise noted.
Data compiled as of September 2013.

How Do We Measure Economic Freedom?
See page 471 for an explanation of the methodology or visit the *Index* Web site at *heritage.org/index*.

VANUATU (continued)

THE TEN ECONOMIC FREEDOMS

		Score	Rank	1-Year Change
RULE OF LAW	Property Rights	40.0	70th	0
	Freedom from Corruption	33.5	86th	-1.5

Corruption is a serious problem, and official abuse is serious and widespread. Vanuatu has a fairly effective legal system based on British common law, and the judiciary is largely independent, but a lack of resources that hinders the hiring and retention of qualified judges and prosecutors results in backlogs. Tribal chiefs often adjudicate local disputes. Land disputes are a constant source of tension.

		Score	Rank	1-Year Change
GOVERNMENT SIZE	Fiscal Freedom	97.3	9th	0
	Government Spending	81.7	48th	+1.2

Vanuatu has no individual income or corporate tax. Taxes include a value-added tax (VAT) and import duties. The overall tax burden is 16.4 percent of the size of the domestic economy. In recent years, government spending, which accounts for 25 percent of GDP, has been dominated by the health and education sectors. Public debt is equivalent to 20 percent of gross domestic output.

		Score	Rank	1-Year Change
REGULATORY EFFICIENCY	Business Freedom	54.8	139th	-1.6
	Labor Freedom	56.8	109th	-0.9
	Monetary Freedom	82.7	11th	+1.3

Bureaucratic procedures are complex and lack transparency. Incorporating a business takes more than a month, and completing licensing requirements costs over four times the level of average annual income. Labor regulations are relatively rigid, although the formal labor market is not fully developed. Prudent fiscal and monetary policies have kept fiscal deficits, public debt, and inflation lower than elsewhere in the region.

		Score	Rank	1-Year Change
OPEN MARKETS	Trade Freedom	48.0	176th	0
	Investment Freedom	60.0	80th	+30.0
	Financial Freedom	40.0	107th	0

The average tariff rate is 18.5 percent. Vanuatu is working to upgrade its customs procedures. The government screens new foreign investment, and foreign investors may lease but not own land. The financial sector remains rudimentary. The state-owned National Bank of Vanuatu has the largest branch network in the country. Bank lending has increased in recent years, but access to secure financial services remains poor.

Long-Term Score Change (since 2009)

RULE OF LAW		GOVERNMENT SIZE		REGULATORY EFFICIENCY		OPEN MARKETS	
Property Rights	0	Fiscal Freedom	+2.0	Business Freedom	-14.2	Trade Freedom	-15.0
Freedom from Corruption	+2.5	Government Spending	-2.3	Labor Freedom	+4.2	Investment Freedom	+30.0
				Monetary Freedom	+4.0	Financial Freedom	0

VENEZUELA

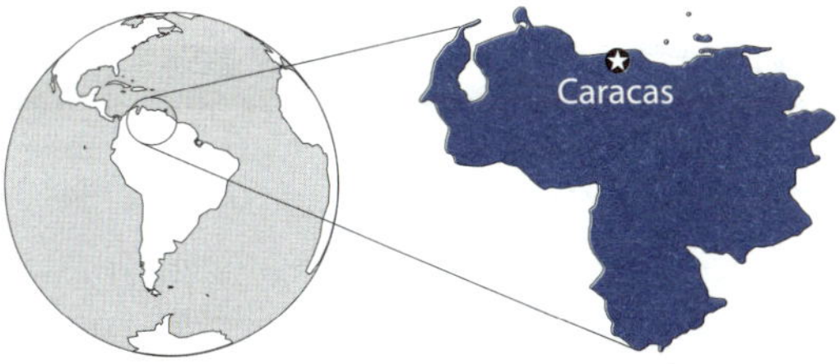

World Rank: 175 **Regional Rank: 28**

Economic Freedom Score

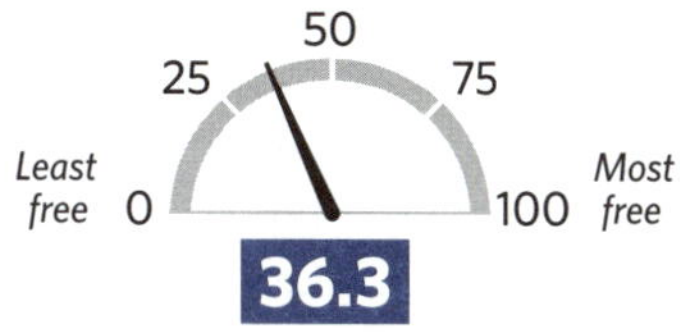

Venezuela's economic freedom score is 36.3, making its economy the 175th freest in the 2014 *Index*. Its score is essentially unchanged from last year, with gains in trade freedom, monetary freedom, and the control of government spending offset by declines in freedom from corruption, business freedom, labor freedom, and fiscal freedom. Venezuela is ranked 28th out of 29 countries in the South and Central America/Caribbean region, and its overall score is far below the world and regional averages.

Over the 20-year history of the *Index*, Venezuela's economic freedom has deteriorated by 23.5 points, the worst decline of any country. Significant losses have occurred in eight of the 10 measured categories, including property rights and the area of market openness, scores for which have plummeted 45 points or more. Regulatory efficiency, measured through business freedom and monetary stability, has diminished greatly as state interference in the economy has grown.

With an economy rated as "repressed" since 2004, Venezuelans have endured economic stagnation and deteriorating living conditions. Oil prices have driven recent strong economic growth, but economic development remains severely constrained by institutional shortcomings. The rule of law, undermined by a weak judiciary subject to political interference, is fragile across the country.

BACKGROUND: The death of Hugo Chávez in early 2013 led to elections won by Chávez's hand-picked successor and former foreign minister Nicolas Maduro. Opposition leader and state governor Henrique Capríles condemned the flawed election, but to no avail. After more than 14 years of "21st-century socialism," economic and political freedom is nonexistent. Food is scarce, inflation is soaring, corruption is rampant, and the capital, Caracas, is one the world's most dangerous cities. Maduro mimics Chávez's style but without his charisma. He has strengthened ties with China, Cuba, Russia, and Iran and persecutes political adversaries and critics. Restrictions on media freedom undermine the opposition.

Freedom Trend

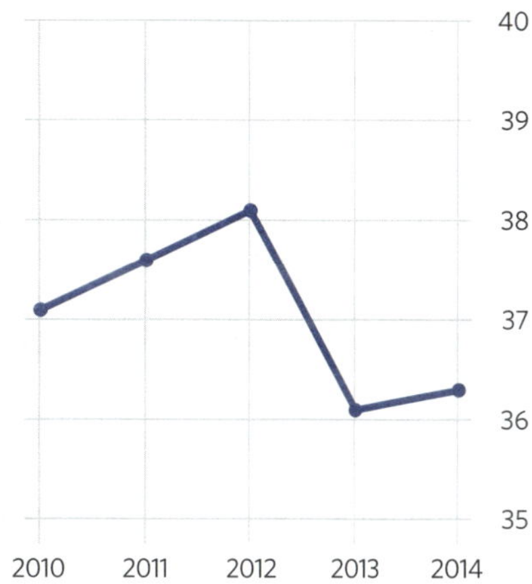

Country Comparisons

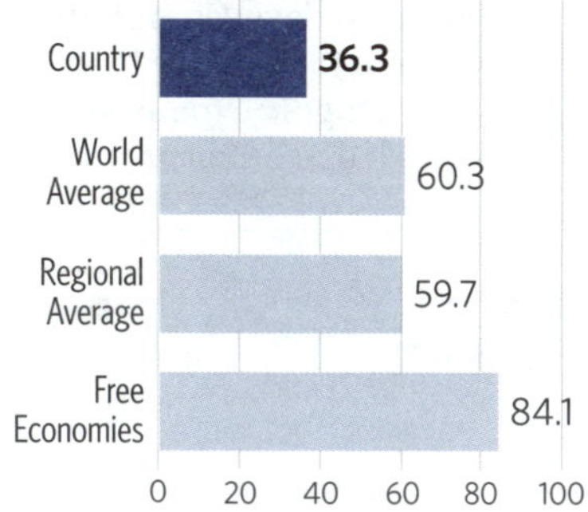

Quick Facts

Population: 29.5 million
GDP (PPP): $401.9 billion
5.5% growth in 2012
5-year compound annual growth 2.0%
$13,616 per capita
Unemployment: 7.8%
Inflation (CPI): 21.1%
FDI Inflow: $3.2 billion
Public Debt: 57.3% of GDP

2012 data unless otherwise noted.
Data compiled as of September 2013.

How Do We Measure Economic Freedom?
See page 471 for an explanation of the methodology or visit the *Index* Web site at *heritage.org/index.*

THE TEN ECONOMIC FREEDOMS

RULE OF LAW

	Score	Rank	1-Year Change
Property Rights	5.0	179th	0
Freedom from Corruption	16.5	174th	-2.5

If there were ever a country where the actors in a national political system could be said to have "perfected" the art of 21st century corruption, it would be Venezuela, where government leaders act with complete impunity. The entire formal economy now operates as a black market, and outside experts estimate that annual inflation far exceeds official estimates. The judiciary is dysfunctional and completely controlled by the executive.

GOVERNMENT SIZE

	Score	Rank	1-Year Change
Fiscal Freedom	75.3	118th	-0.3
Government Spending	51.8	133rd	+1.2

The top individual income and corporate tax rates are 34 percent. Other taxes include a value-added tax (VAT). The overall tax burden amounts to 12.5 percent of the domestic economy. Government spending has reached 40 percent of gross domestic output. Public debt levels continue to rise, reaching close to 60 percent of GDP.

REGULATORY EFFICIENCY

	Score	Rank	1-Year Change
Business Freedom	43.4	163rd	-2.2
Labor Freedom	33.7	175th	-0.8
Monetary Freedom	49.7	180th	+2.4

No minimum capital is required to establish a business, but the process takes 17 procedures and over 100 days. Completing licensing requirements costs about the level of average annual income and takes more than 10 months. The labor market remains state-controlled. The government's highly expansive fiscal and monetary policy, coupled with exchange and price controls, has led to a sharply overvalued official exchange rate.

OPEN MARKETS

	Score	Rank	1-Year Change
Trade Freedom	62.7	152nd	+3.9
Investment Freedom	5.0	174th	0
Financial Freedom	20.0	163rd	0

Venezuela's average tariff rate is 8.6 percent. Non-tariff barriers restrict imports of cars and agricultural products. It may take several weeks to import goods. Restrictive currency controls, expropriation of private property, and other government measures discourage foreign investment. The financial sector, dominated by banks, remains controlled by the state through directed credits and threats of confiscation. Long-term finance is scarce.

Long-Term Score Change (since 1995)

RULE OF LAW		GOVERNMENT SIZE		REGULATORY EFFICIENCY		OPEN MARKETS	
Property Rights	-45.0	Fiscal Freedom	-4.7	Business Freedom	-41.6	Trade Freedom	-2.3
Freedom from Corruption	+6.5	Government Spending	-24.3	Labor Freedom	+1.4	Investment Freedom	-45.0
				Monetary Freedom	-2.3	Financial Freedom	-50.0

VIETNAM

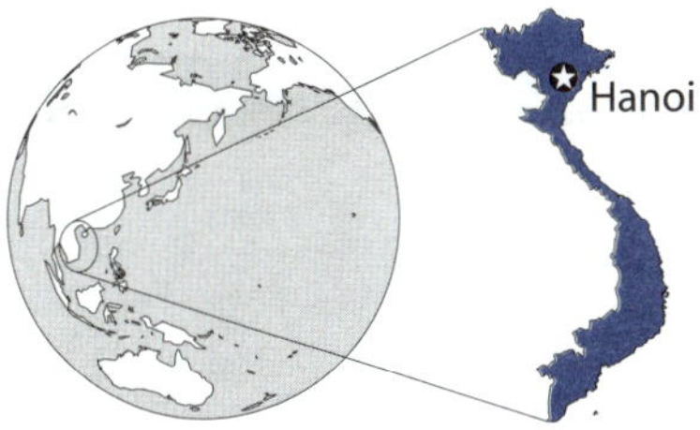

World Rank: **147** Regional Rank: **33**

Economic Freedom Score

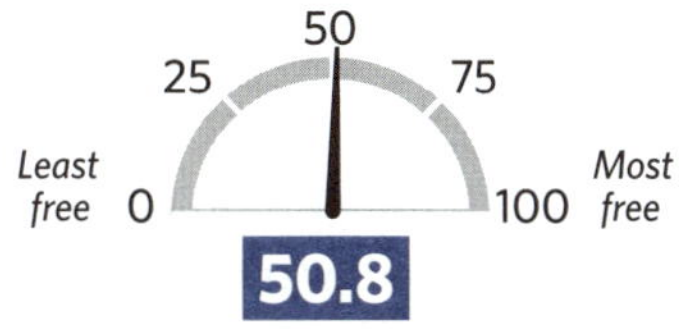

Vietnam's economic freedom score is 50.8, making its economy the 147th freest in the 2014 *Index*. Its score is 0.2 point worse than last year, reflecting declines in freedom from corruption, monetary freedom, and business freedom that outweigh improvements in labor freedom and fiscal freedom. Vietnam is ranked 33rd out of 42 countries in the Asia–Pacific region, and its overall score is lower than the world and regional averages.

Over the 20-year history of the *Index*, Vietnam has advanced its economic freedom score by about 9 points. Improvements in seven of the 10 economic freedoms include gains in trade freedom, business freedom, and freedom from corruption, scores for which have advanced by 10 points or more. Reforms have included partial privatization of state-owned enterprises and increasing recognition of private property rights.

Vietnam has fluctuated within the lower ranks of the "mostly unfree" economies for two decades, constrained by key institutional shortcomings. Although measurable progress has been made in enhancing the rule of law, the weak judiciary continues to be vulnerable to political influence, and corruption remains widespread. The overall regulatory environment, despite ongoing reform efforts, is not particularly efficient or transparent. Investment is hindered by opaque bureaucracy and an unreliable legal system.

BACKGROUND: The Socialist Republic of Vietnam is a Communist dictatorship characterized by political repression and a lack of respect for basic human rights. Economic liberalization began in 1986 with its doi moi reforms, and Vietnam joined the World Trade Organization in 2007. In 2012, Prime Minister Nguyen Tan Dung acknowledged mismanagement of the Vietnamese economy and affirmed his commitment to reforming the state sector, but delays persist. Vietnam's economy is driven primarily by tourism and exports, but inflation is a problem, and the country has struggled to attract more investment in the absence of a transparent legal and regulatory system.

Freedom Trend

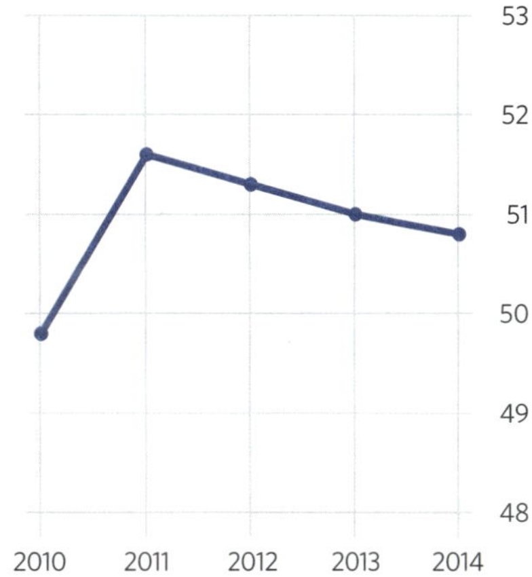

Country Comparisons

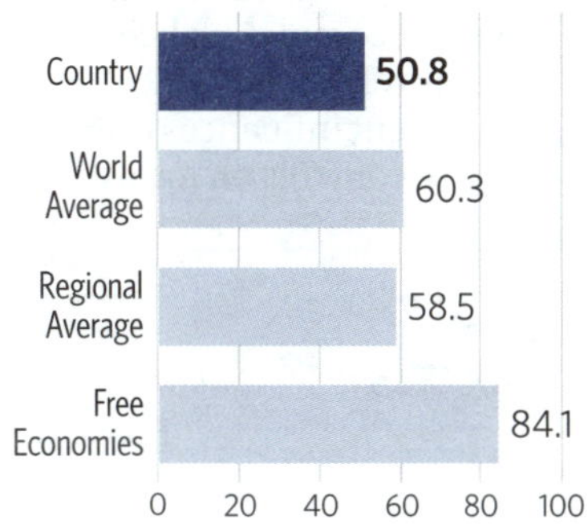

Quick Facts

Population: 90.4 million
GDP (PPP): $320.7 billion
5.0% growth in 2012
5-year compound annual growth 5.9%
$3,548 per capita
Unemployment: 4.5%
Inflation (CPI): 9.1%
FDI Inflow: $8.4 billion
Public Debt: 52.1% of GDP

2012 data unless otherwise noted.
Data compiled as of September 2013.

How Do We Measure Economic Freedom?
See page 471 for an explanation of the methodology or visit the *Index* Web site at *heritage.org/index.*

THE TEN ECONOMIC FREEDOMS

		Score	Rank	1-Year Change
RULE OF LAW	Property Rights	15.0	159th	0
	Freedom from Corruption	26.9	123rd	-2.1

Corruption and abuse of office are serious problems, as are the lack of transparency and the lack of media freedom. Many companies report having to pay bribes for customs clearances. The judiciary is subservient to the ruling Communist Party, which controls courts at all levels. Private property rights are not strongly respected, and resolution of disputes can take years. Infringement of intellectual property rights is common.

		Score	Rank	1-Year Change
GOVERNMENT SIZE	Fiscal Freedom	77.0	110th	+1.4
	Government Spending	71.4	82nd	-1.0

The top individual income tax rate is 35 percent, and the top corporate tax rate is 25 percent. Other taxes include a value-added tax (VAT) and a property tax. The overall tax burden equals 21.1 percent of gross domestic income. Public expenditures amount to 31 percent of GDP. Government debt is equivalent to slightly over 50 percent of the domestic economy.

		Score	Rank	1-Year Change
REGULATORY EFFICIENCY	Business Freedom	62.0	105th	-1.8
	Labor Freedom	68.3	72nd	+2.8
	Monetary Freedom	63.6	171st	-1.7

Launching a business takes 10 procedures on average, and no minimum capital is required. However, completing licensing requirements still takes more than 100 days. The labor market remains relatively rigid, although the non-salary cost of employing a worker is moderate. The government influences prices though state-owned and state-subsidized companies and administrative controls on interest rates.

		Score	Rank	1-Year Change
OPEN MARKETS	Trade Freedom	78.7	77th	+0.1
	Investment Freedom	15.0	169th	0
	Financial Freedom	30.0	132nd	0

Vietnam's average tariff rate is 5.7 percent. Import licensing and tariff-rate quotas impede imports. The role of state-owned enterprises in the economy has declined but remains significant. The financial sector, dominated by banks, continues to expand, with capital markets gradually evolving. The four largest state-owned commercial banks still dominate the banking sector, although their market shares have declined.

Long-Term Score Change (since 1995)

RULE OF LAW		GOVERNMENT SIZE		REGULATORY EFFICIENCY		OPEN MARKETS	
Property Rights	+5.0	Fiscal Freedom	+8.3	Business Freedom	+22.0	Trade Freedom	+34.1
Freedom from Corruption	+16.9	Government Spending	-15.7	Labor Freedom	+4.1	Investment Freedom	-15.0
				Monetary Freedom	+8.4	Financial Freedom	0

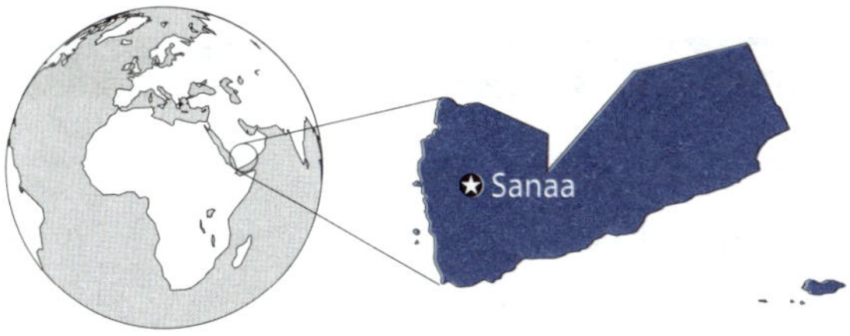

YEMEN

Economic Freedom Score

World Rank: **123** Regional Rank: **12**

Yemen's economic freedom score is 55.5, making its economy the 123rd freest in the 2014 *Index*. Its score is 0.4 point lower than last year, reflecting declines in four of the 10 economic freedoms including monetary freedom, business freedom, and freedom from corruption. Yemen is ranked 12th out of 15 countries in the Middle East/North Africa region, and its overall score is lower than the world and regional averages.

Over the 20-year history of the *Index*, Yemen's progress toward greater economic freedom has been modest, with its score improving by 5.7 points. Gains in trade freedom, monetary stability, fiscal freedom, and the control of corruption have been offset by significant declines in labor freedom, investment freedom, and business freedom. Yemen was considered a "repressed" economy during its first eight years in the *Index* but since 2003 has fluctuated within the ranks of the "mostly unfree."

Despite some reform attempts, the economy remains burdened by institutional shortcomings that include political interference, corruption, and a rigid labor market. Due to the complexity of the regulatory framework and the high cost of conducting business, considerable economic activity remains in the informal sector.

BACKGROUND: Yemen is one of the Arab world's poorest countries. Secessionists, unruly tribes, and Islamist extremists oppose its moderate foreign policy and cooperation with the United States against al-Qaeda. In early 2011, important members of President Ali Abdullah Saleh's government defected to a coalition of opposition forces. Saleh was forced to resign in a deal brokered by the Gulf Cooperation Council. He transferred power to Vice President Abd Rabbuh Mansur al-Hadi after a February 2012 election. The government initiated an economic reform program in 2006, but declining oil production, terrorism, kidnappings, clashes between Sunni and Shia Muslims, tribal rivalries, a strong al-Qaeda presence, and growing water shortages have undermined foreign investment, tourism, and economic growth.

Freedom Trend

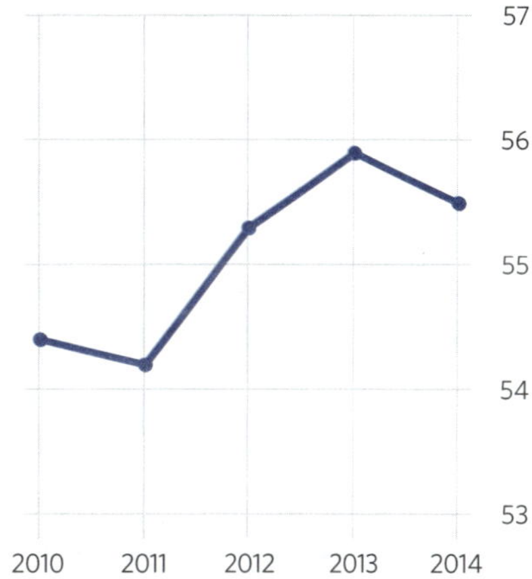

Country Comparisons

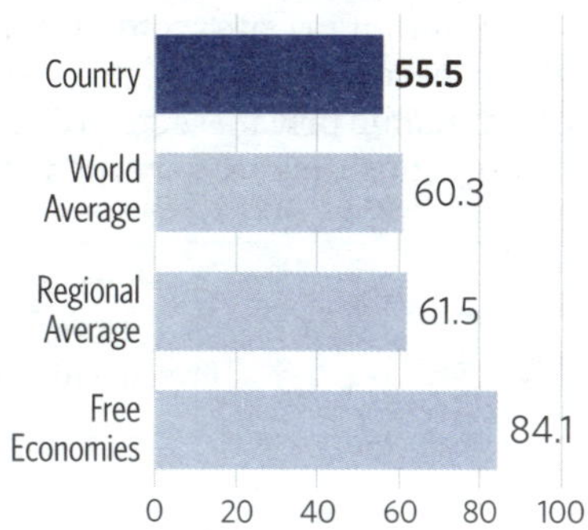

Quick Facts

Population: 25.9 million
GDP (PPP): $59.1 billion
0.1% growth in 2012
5-year compound annual growth 0.8%
$2,283 per capita
Unemployment: n/a
Inflation (CPI): 11.0%
FDI Inflow: $348.8 million
Public Debt: 46.7% of GDP

2012 data unless otherwise noted.
Data compiled as of September 2013.

How Do We Measure Economic Freedom?
See page 471 for an explanation of the methodology or visit the *Index* Web site at *heritage.org/index.*

YEMEN (continued)

THE TEN ECONOMIC FREEDOMS

RULE OF LAW

	Score	Rank	1-Year Change
Property Rights	30.0	93rd	0
Freedom from Corruption	19.4	162nd	-1.6

Corruption is endemic, and bribery of government officials may be required at every step of a project. Despite recent government efforts to fight graft, Yemen lacks most legal safeguards against conflicts of interest. The judiciary is nominally independent but susceptible to interference from the executive branch. Authorities have a poor record of enforcing judicial rulings.

GOVERNMENT SIZE

	Score	Rank	1-Year Change
Fiscal Freedom	91.7	25th	+0.2
Government Spending	74.9	69th	+2.1

The top individual income and corporate tax rates are 20 percent. Other taxes include a general sales tax (GST) and a property tax. The overall tax burden equals 5.3 percent of total domestic income. Government spending is 29 percent of GDP. Public debt is about 47 percent of gross domestic income. The government is still grappling with restoring fiscal balance following the uprising in 2011.

REGULATORY EFFICIENCY

	Score	Rank	1-Year Change
Business Freedom	59.2	119th	-2.1
Labor Freedom	54.9	117th	-0.4
Monetary Freedom	62.1	174th	-3.6

A non-transparent and time-consuming regulatory framework hinders the emergence of a more vibrant private sector. It takes 40 days to launch a business and more than five months to obtain necessary construction permits. Employment regulations remain rigid, and the absence of a dynamic private sector results in chronic underemployment and a large informal sector. Energy subsidies are very high and represent a major drain on the budget.

OPEN MARKETS

	Score	Rank	1-Year Change
Trade Freedom	82.4	63rd	+0.9
Investment Freedom	50.0	109th	0
Financial Freedom	30.0	132nd	0

Yemen's average tariff rate is 3.8 percent. Civil unrest is a deterrent to international trade and investment. The judicial and regulatory systems may be difficult for foreign investors to navigate. The small financial system remains underdeveloped and dominated by the state. The economy is largely cash-based, and the limited availability of financing precludes more vibrant entrepreneurial activity.

Long-Term Score Change (since 1995)

RULE OF LAW		GOVERNMENT SIZE		REGULATORY EFFICIENCY		OPEN MARKETS	
Property Rights	0	Fiscal Freedom	+13.5	Business Freedom	-10.8	Trade Freedom	+37.4
Freedom from Corruption	+9.4	Government Spending	+1.6	Labor Freedom	-21.9	Investment Freedom	-20.0
				Monetary Freedom	+20.3	Financial Freedom	0

ZAMBIA

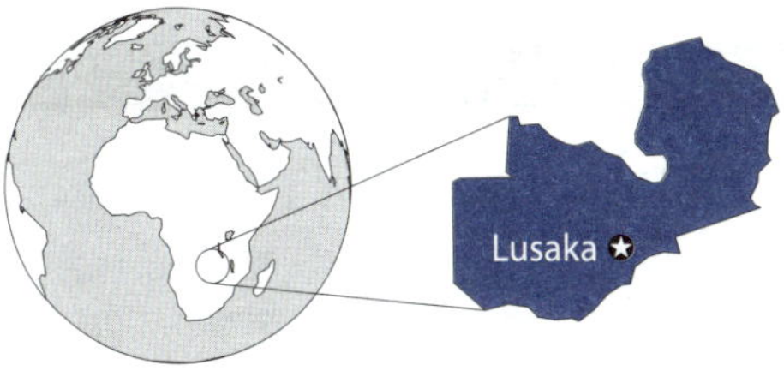

World Rank: **88** Regional Rank: **9**

Economic Freedom Score

Zambia's economic freedom score is 60.4, making its economy the 88th freest in the 2014 *Index*. Its score is 1.7 points higher than last year due to notable improvements in five of the 10 economic freedoms including business freedom, investment freedom, and the management of public spending. Zambia is ranked 9th out of 46 countries in the Sub-Saharan Africa region, and its overall score is just above the world average.

Over the 20-year history of the *Index*, Zambia has advanced its economic freedom score by over 5 points. Improvements in half of the 10 economic freedoms have included double-digit advances in monetary freedom, trade freedom, and business freedom. Achieving its highest economic freedom score since 2001, Zambia has rejoined the ranks of the "moderately free" in the 2014 *Index*.

However, in some critical areas of economic freedom, particularly property rights, financial freedom, and investment freedom, Zambia has lost ground over the history of the *Index*. The perceived level of corruption remains high, further undermining the rule of law.

BACKGROUND: In 1991, the government of Kenneth Kaunda, in power since independence in 1964, enacted a new constitution instituting multi-party democracy. Michael Sata of the Patriotic Front won the presidency in 2011, the first time a candidate from a party other than the Movement for Multiparty Democracy had been successful. In April 2012, Zambia released a draft for yet another new constitution, which included press freedoms, decentralized government, a bill of rights, and a 50 percent-plus-1-vote requirement to win the presidency. Ratification is still pending. Recent increases in copper prices have boosted trade revenues by 30 percent. In 2012, the country made its first foray into international markets with a $750 million bond issue. High rates of HIV/AIDS, unemployment, and market-distorting agricultural policies contribute to high poverty rates. Agriculture employs 85 percent of the workforce.

Freedom Trend

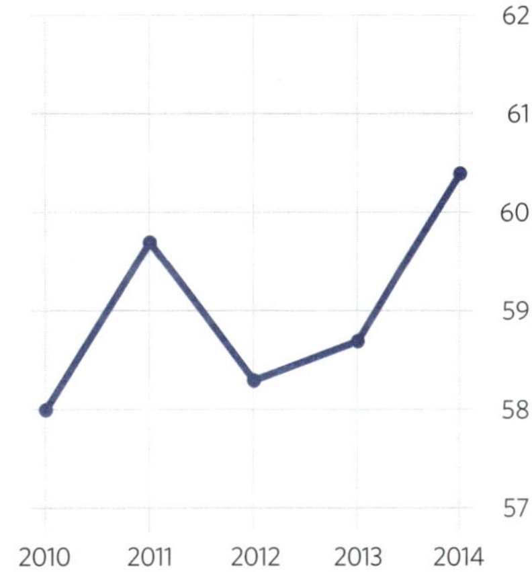

Country Comparisons

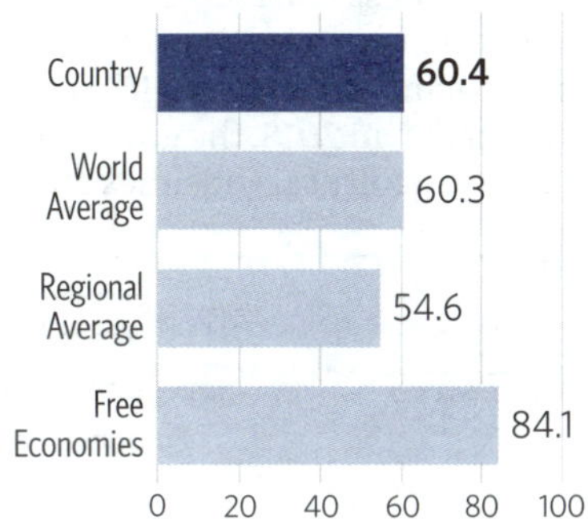

Quick Facts

Population: 13.9 million
GDP (PPP): $24.0 billion
7.3% growth in 2012
5-year compound annual growth 6.8%
$1,722 per capita
Unemployment: n/a
Inflation (CPI): 6.6%
FDI Inflow: $1.1 billion
Public Debt: 26.9% of GDP

2012 data unless otherwise noted.
Data compiled as of September 2013.

How Do We Measure Economic Freedom?
See page 471 for an explanation of the methodology or visit the *Index* Web site at *heritage.org/index*.

THE TEN ECONOMIC FREEDOMS

Score ■ Country | World Average

		Score	Rank	1-Year Change
RULE OF LAW	Property Rights	30.0	93rd	0
	Freedom from Corruption	31.3	99th	-0.7

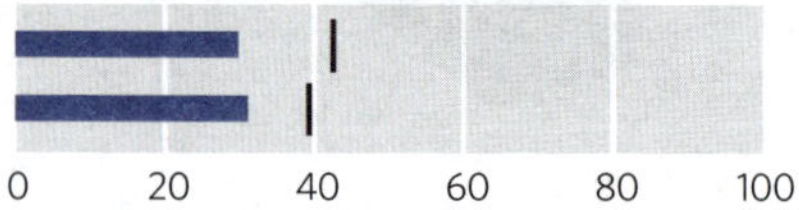

Corruption is believed to be widespread, although the government has taken some steps to fight graft. The rule of law remains uneven. The judicial system suffers from inefficiency, government influence, and a lack of resources. Contract enforcement is weak, and courts are relatively inexperienced in commercial litigation. The government lacks the capacity to enforce intellectual property rights laws effectively.

		Score	Rank	1-Year Change
GOVERNMENT SIZE	Fiscal Freedom	71.8	130th	-1.1
	Government Spending	82.9	41st	+2.6

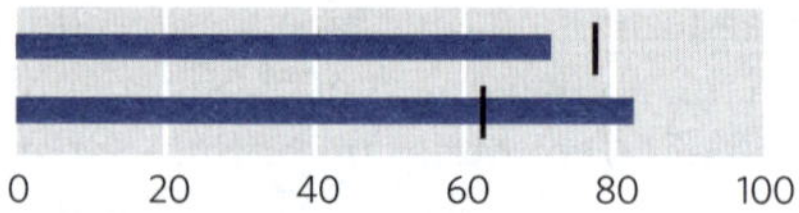

The top individual income and corporate tax rates are 35 percent. Other taxes include a value-added tax (VAT) and a property tax. Overall tax revenue amounts to 19.3 percent of total domestic income. Public expenditures amount to 24 percent of the domestic economy. Public debt is equivalent to 27 percent of GDP. Expansion of the already robust mining sector is expected to help revenues.

		Score	Rank	1-Year Change
REGULATORY EFFICIENCY	Business Freedom	74.9	50th	+14.5
	Labor Freedom	50.1	137th	-8.3
	Monetary Freedom	68.0	154th	+2.0

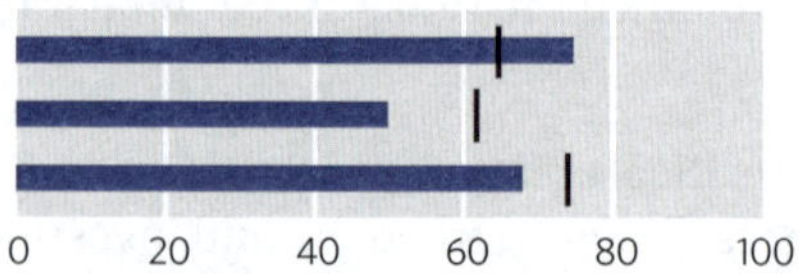

The business start-up process has been simplified, taking about a week. However, completing licensing requirements costs almost twice the level of average annual income and takes more than 120 days. A well-functioning labor market is not fully developed. Although politically unpopular, in 2013, the government decided to remove a 5 percent fuel subsidy and discontinue some agricultural subsidies and price supports.

		Score	Rank	1-Year Change
OPEN MARKETS	Trade Freedom	84.6	50th	+2.3
	Investment Freedom	60.0	80th	+5.0
	Financial Freedom	50.0	69th	0

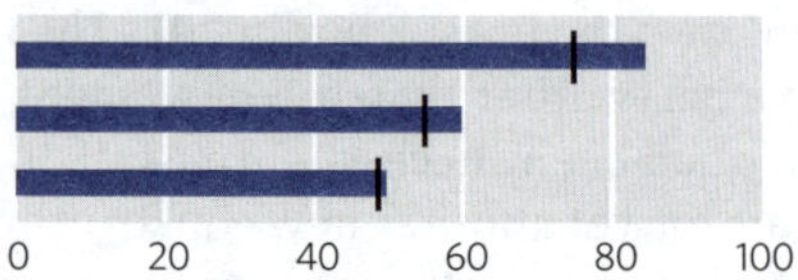

The average tariff rate is 2.7 percent. It is expensive and time-consuming to import goods. Foreign and domestic investors are generally treated equally under the law, but the court system can be slow-moving and unreliable. Zambia has a relatively liberal banking regime, but financial intermediation and credit to the private sector remain low. The banking sector has recorded growth, but high lending rates continue to hinder access to financing.

Long-Term Score Change (since 1995)

RULE OF LAW		GOVERNMENT SIZE		REGULATORY EFFICIENCY		OPEN MARKETS	
Property Rights	**-20.0**	Fiscal Freedom	**-0.7**	Business Freedom	**+19.9**	Trade Freedom	**+23.4**
Freedom from Corruption	**+1.3**	Government Spending	**+8.2**	Labor Freedom	**-2.6**	Investment Freedom	**-10.0**
				Monetary Freedom	**+55.8**	Financial Freedom	**-20.0**

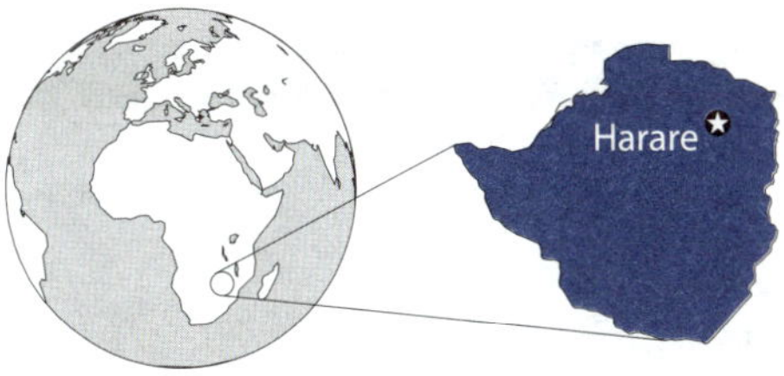

ZIMBABWE

Economic Freedom Score

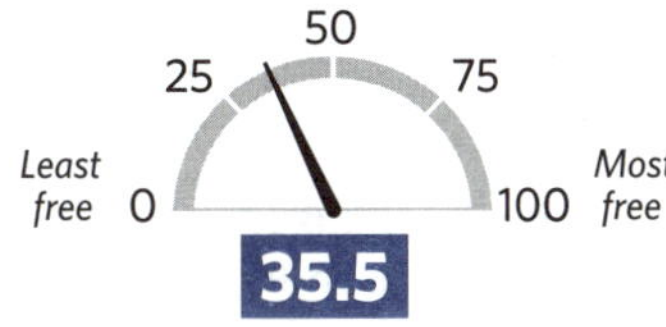

World Rank: **176** Regional Rank: **46**

Zimbabwe's economic freedom score is 35.5, making its economy the 176th freest in the 2014 *Index*. Its score has increased by 6.9 points from last year, reflecting a particularly large score gain in monetary freedom following the end of hyperinflation. Zimbabwe is ranked last out of 46 countries in the Sub-Saharan Africa region and is the third-least free country rated in the 2014 *Index*.

Over the 20-year history of the *Index*, Zimbabwe's economic freedom has deteriorated by 13 points, the fourth worst score drop. Significant declines in seven of the 10 economic freedoms include 40-point drops in scores for property rights and investment freedom. Regulatory efficiency has greatly diminished, as indicated by considerable score declines in business freedom and labor freedom.

Consistently rated a "repressed" economy since 1995, Zimbabwe remains characterized by economic instability and policy volatility. The impacts of years of hyperinflation have crippled entrepreneurial activity, severely undermining realization of the country's economic potential. A corrupt and inefficient judicial system and general lack of transparency severely exacerbate business costs.

BACKGROUND: Zimbabwe gained its independence in 1965 and at that time enjoyed a diversified economy, well-developed infrastructure, and an advanced financial sector. It is now one of Africa's poorest countries. Robert Mugabe became prime minister in 1980 and president in 1987 and has been in power ever since. In 2008, he claimed victory in a run-off election that was marred by political violence that forced opposition leader Morgan Tsvangirai to withdraw. Under a power-sharing agreement, Mugabe remains head of state, the cabinet, and the armed services. In March 2013, voters approved a new constitution that would roll back presidential power. Peaceful but disputed elections held in July 2013 resulted in a landslide victory for Mugabe and his ZANU-PF party. A land reform program has effectively confiscated the property of white landowners.

Freedom Trend

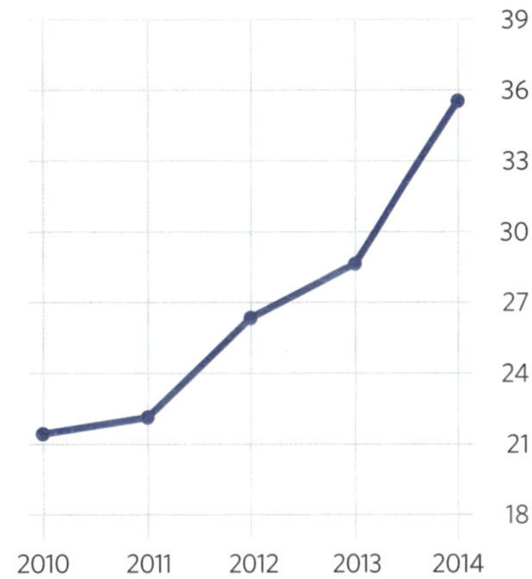

Country Comparisons

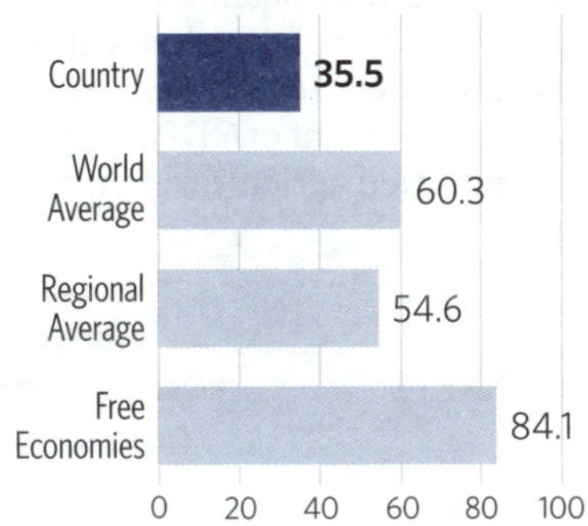

Quick Facts

Population: 13.0 million
GDP (PPP): $7.2 billion
4.4% growth in 2012
5-year compound annual growth 2.5%
$559 per capita
Unemployment: n/a
Inflation (CPI): 3.7%
FDI Inflow: $399.5 million
Public Debt: 60.5% of GDP

2012 data unless otherwise noted.
Data compiled as of September 2013.

How Do We Measure Economic Freedom?
See page 471 for an explanation of the methodology or visit the *Index* Web site at *heritage.org/index*.

THE TEN ECONOMIC FREEDOMS

RULE OF LAW

	Score	Rank	1-Year Change
Property Rights	10.0	166th	0
Freedom from Corruption	19.3	164th	-2.7

Corruption has become endemic, including at the highest levels of government. The IMF reports that $600 million of diamond dividends to the state was initially budgeted for 2012, but only $45 million was actually received in the treasury. Pressure from the executive branch has substantially eroded judicial independence. The government's land reform program, characterized by chaos and violence, badly damaged commercial farming.

GOVERNMENT SIZE

	Score	Rank	1-Year Change
Fiscal Freedom	63.3	163rd	-8.5
Government Spending	64.0	104th	-2.4

The top individual income tax rate is 46.4 percent, and the top corporate tax rate is 25 percent. Other taxes include a value-added tax (VAT) and a capital gains tax. Overall tax revenue accounts for about 30 percent of gross domestic income. Government spending is 35 percent of GDP. Public debt equals about 60 percent of gross domestic income. Mining continues to make significant contributions to the economy and public coffers.

REGULATORY EFFICIENCY

	Score	Rank	1-Year Change
Business Freedom	34.5	175th	+1.1
Labor Freedom	22.2	182nd	+0.3
Monetary Freedom	73.0	123rd	+73.0

Incorporating a business takes nine procedures and 90 days, with no minimum capital required. However, completing licensing requirements costs over 40 times the level of average annual income. The informal sector continues to be the main source of employment. Energy subsidies exceed 4 percent of GDP, and in 2013, the government shifted from price supports to subsidies for imported agricultural inputs.

OPEN MARKETS

	Score	Rank	1-Year Change
Trade Freedom	54.2	171st	+3.8
Investment Freedom	5.0	174th	+5.0
Financial Freedom	10.0	174th	0

The average tariff rate is 15.4 percent. It is expensive and time-consuming to import goods. Foreign investment in several sectors of the economy is capped. Government intervention, inadequate supervision, and political instability have severely undermined the financial system. Many banks suffer from a lack of liquidity. The state has used banks to finance deficit spending and has required loans to state-owned enterprises.

Long-Term Score Change (since 1995)

RULE OF LAW		GOVERNMENT SIZE		REGULATORY EFFICIENCY		OPEN MARKETS	
Property Rights	**-40.0**	Fiscal Freedom	**+13.1**	Business Freedom	**-20.5**	Trade Freedom	**+2.4**
Freedom from Corruption	**-10.7**	Government Spending	**-1.3**	Labor Freedom	**-20.7**	Investment Freedom	**-25.0**
				Monetary Freedom	**+18.3**	Financial Freedom	**-40.0**

Appendix

Index of Economic Freedom Scores, 1995–2014

Country	1995	1996	1997	1998	1999	2000	2001	2002	2003	2004	2005	2006	2007	2008	2009	2010	2011	2012	2013	2014
Afghanistan	-	-	-	-	-	-	-	-	-	-	-	-	-	-	-	-	-	-	-	-
Albania	49.7	53.8	54.8	53.9	53.4	53.6	56.6	56.8	56.8	58.5	57.8	60.3	61.4	62.4	63.7	66.0	64.0	65.1	65.2	66.9
Algeria	55.7	54.5	54.9	55.8	57.2	56.8	57.3	61.0	57.7	58.1	53.2	55.7	55.4	56.2	56.6	56.9	52.4	51.0	49.6	50.8
Angola	27.4	24.4	24.2	24.9	23.7	24.3	-	-	-	-	-	43.5	44.7	46.9	47.0	48.4	46.2	46.7	47.3	47.7
Argentina	68.0	74.7	73.3	70.9	70.6	70.0	68.6	65.7	56.3	53.9	51.7	53.4	54.0	54.2	52.3	51.2	51.7	48.0	46.7	44.6
Armenia	-	42.2	46.7	49.6	56.4	63.0	66.4	68.0	67.3	70.3	69.8	70.6	68.6	69.9	69.9	69.2	69.7	68.8	69.4	68.9
Australia	74.1	74.0	75.5	75.6	76.4	77.1	77.4	77.3	77.4	77.9	79.0	79.9	81.1	82.2	82.6	82.6	82.5	83.1	82.6	82.0
Austria	70.0	68.9	65.2	65.4	64.0	68.4	68.1	67.4	67.6	67.6	68.8	71.1	71.6	71.4	71.2	71.6	71.9	70.3	71.8	72.4
Azerbaijan	-	30.0	34.0	43.1	47.4	49.8	50.3	53.3	54.1	53.4	54.4	53.2	54.6	55.3	58.0	58.8	59.7	58.9	59.7	61.3
The Bahamas	71.8	74.0	74.5	74.5	74.7	73.9	74.8	74.4	73.5	72.1	72.6	72.3	72.0	71.1	70.3	67.3	68.0	68.0	70.1	69.8
Bahrain	76.2	76.4	76.1	75.6	75.2	75.7	75.9	75.6	76.3	75.1	71.2	71.6	71.2	72.2	74.8	76.3	77.7	75.2	75.5	75.1
Bangladesh	40.9	51.1	49.9	52.0	50.0	48.9	51.2	51.9	49.3	50.0	47.5	52.9	46.7	44.2	47.5	51.1	53.0	53.2	52.6	54.1
Barbados	-	62.3	64.5	67.9	66.7	69.5	71.5	73.6	71.3	69.4	70.1	71.9	70.0	71.3	71.5	68.3	68.5	69.0	69.3	68.3
Belarus	40.4	38.7	39.8	38.0	35.4	41.3	38.0	39.0	39.7	43.1	46.7	47.5	47.0	45.3	45.0	48.7	47.9	49.0	48.0	50.1
Belgium	-	66.0	64.6	64.7	62.9	63.5	63.8	67.6	68.1	68.7	69.0	71.8	72.5	71.7	72.1	70.1	70.2	69.0	69.2	69.9
Belize	62.9	61.6	64.3	59.1	60.7	63.3	65.9	65.6	63.5	62.8	64.5	64.7	63.3	63.0	63.0	61.5	63.8	61.9	57.3	56.7
Benin	-	54.5	61.3	61.7	60.6	61.5	60.1	57.3	54.9	54.6	52.3	54.0	55.1	55.2	55.4	55.4	56.0	55.7	57.6	57.1
Bhutan	-	-	-	-	-	-	-	-	-	-	-	-	-	-	57.7	57.0	57.6	56.6	55.0	56.7
Bolivia	56.8	65.2	65.1	68.8	65.6	65.0	68.0	65.1	64.3	64.5	58.4	57.8	54.2	53.1	53.6	49.4	50.0	50.2	47.9	48.4
Bosnia and Herzegovina		-	-	29.4	29.4	45.1	36.6	37.4	40.6	44.7	48.8	55.6	54.4	53.9	53.1	56.2	57.5	57.3	57.3	58.4
Botswana	56.8	61.6	59.1	62.8	62.9	65.8	66.8	66.2	68.6	69.9	69.3	68.8	68.1	68.2	69.7	70.3	68.8	69.6	70.6	72.0
Brazil	51.4	48.1	52.6	52.3	61.3	61.1	61.9	61.5	63.4	62.0	61.7	60.9	56.2	56.2	56.7	55.6	56.3	57.9	57.7	56.9
Brunei	-	-	-	-	-	-	-	-	-	-	-	-	-	-	-	-	-	-	-	69.0
Bulgaria	50.0	48.6	47.6	45.7	46.2	47.3	51.9	57.1	57.0	59.2	62.3	64.1	62.7	63.7	64.6	62.3	64.9	64.7	65.0	65.7
Burkina Faso	-	49.4	54.0	54.5	55.0	55.7	56.7	58.8	58.9	58.0	56.6	55.8	55.1	55.7	59.5	59.4	60.6	60.6	59.9	58.9
Burma	-	45.1	45.4	45.7	46.4	47.9	46.1	45.5	44.9	43.6	40.5	40.0	41.0	39.5	37.7	36.7	37.8	38.7	39.2	46.5
Burundi	-	-	45.4	44.7	41.1	42.6	-	-	-	-	-	48.7	46.9	46.2	48.8	47.5	49.6	48.1	49.0	51.4
Cambodia	-	-	52.8	59.8	59.9	59.3	59.6	60.7	63.7	61.1	60.0	56.7	55.9	55.9	56.6	56.6	57.9	57.6	58.5	57.4

Index of Economic Freedom Scores, 1995–2014

Country	1995	1996	1997	1998	1999	2000	2001	2002	2003	2004	2005	2006	2007	2008	2009	2010	2011	2012	2013	2014
Cameroon	51.3	45.7	44.6	48.0	50.3	49.9	53.3	52.8	52.7	52.3	53.0	54.6	55.6	54.3	53.0	52.3	51.8	51.8	52.3	52.6
Canada	69.4	70.3	67.9	68.5	69.3	70.5	71.2	74.6	74.8	75.3	75.8	77.4	78.0	80.2	80.5	80.4	80.8	79.9	79.4	80.2
Cape Verde	-	49.7	47.7	48.0	50.7	51.9	56.3	57.6	56.1	58.1	57.8	58.6	56.5	57.9	61.3	61.8	64.6	63.5	63.7	66.1
Central African Republic	-	-	-	-	-	-	-	59.8	60.0	57.5	56.5	54.2	50.6	48.6	48.3	48.4	49.3	50.3	50.4	46.7
Chad	-	-	45.1	46.6	47.2	46.8	46.4	49.2	52.6	53.1	52.1	50.0	50.1	47.8	47.5	47.5	45.3	44.8	45.2	44.5
Chile	71.2	72.6	75.9	74.9	74.1	74.7	75.1	77.8	76.0	76.9	77.8	78.0	77.7	78.6	78.3	77.2	77.4	78.3	79.0	78.7
China	52.0	51.3	51.7	53.1	54.8	56.4	52.6	52.8	52.6	52.5	53.7	53.6	52.0	53.1	53.2	51.0	52.0	51.2	51.9	52.5
Colombia	64.5	64.3	66.4	65.5	65.3	63.3	65.6	64.2	64.2	61.2	59.6	60.4	59.9	62.2	62.3	65.5	68.0	68.0	69.6	70.7
Comoros	-	-	-	-	-	-	-	-	-	-	-	-	-	-	43.3	44.9	43.8	45.7	47.5	51.4
Congo, Dem. Rep. of	41.4	39.5	39.5	40.6	34.0	34.8	-	-	-	-	-	-	-	-	42.8	41.4	40.7	41.1	39.6	40.6
Congo, Rep. of	-	40.3	42.2	33.8	41.6	40.6	44.3	45.3	47.7	45.9	46.2	43.8	44.4	45.3	45.4	43.2	43.6	43.8	43.5	43.7
Costa Rica	68.0	66.4	65.6	65.6	67.4	68.4	67.6	67.5	67.0	66.4	66.1	65.9	64.0	64.2	66.4	65.9	67.3	68.0	67.0	66.9
Côte d'Ivoire	53.4	49.9	50.5	51.3	51.7	50.2	54.8	57.3	56.7	57.8	56.6	56.2	54.9	53.9	55.0	54.1	55.4	54.3	54.1	57.7
Croatia	-	48.0	46.7	51.7	53.1	53.6	50.7	51.1	53.3	53.1	51.9	53.6	53.4	54.1	55.1	59.2	61.1	60.9	61.3	60.4
Cuba	27.8	27.8	27.8	28.2	29.7	31.3	31.6	32.4	35.1	34.4	35.5	29.3	28.6	27.5	27.9	26.7	27.7	28.3	28.5	28.7
Cyprus	-	67.7	67.9	68.2	67.8	67.2	71.0	73.0	73.3	74.1	71.9	71.8	71.7	71.3	70.8	70.9	73.3	71.8	69.0	67.6
Czech Republic	67.8	68.1	68.8	68.4	69.7	68.6	70.2	66.5	67.5	67.0	64.6	66.4	67.4	68.1	69.4	69.8	70.4	69.9	70.9	72.2
Denmark	-	67.3	67.5	67.5	68.1	68.3	68.3	71.1	73.2	72.4	75.3	75.4	77.0	79.2	79.6	77.9	78.6	76.2	76.1	76.1
Djibouti	-	-	54.5	55.9	57.1	55.1	58.3	57.8	55.7	55.6	55.2	53.2	52.4	51.2	51.3	51.0	54.5	53.9	53.9	55.9
Dominica	-	-	-	-	-	-	-	-	-	-	-	-	-	-	62.6	63.2	63.3	61.6	63.9	65.2
Dominican Republic	55.8	58.1	53.5	58.1	58.1	59.0	59.1	58.6	57.8	54.6	55.1	56.3	56.8	57.7	59.2	60.3	60.0	60.2	59.7	61.3
Ecuador	57.7	60.1	61.0	62.8	62.9	59.8	55.1	53.1	54.1	54.4	52.9	54.6	55.3	55.2	52.5	49.3	47.1	48.3	46.9	48.0
Egypt	45.7	52.0	54.5	55.8	58.0	51.7	51.5	54.1	55.3	55.5	55.8	53.2	54.4	58.5	58.0	59.0	59.1	57.9	54.8	52.9
El Salvador	69.1	70.1	70.5	70.2	75.1	76.3	73.0	73.0	71.5	71.2	71.5	69.6	68.9	68.5	69.8	69.9	68.8	68.7	66.7	66.2
Equatorial Guinea	-	-	-	-	45.1	45.6	47.9	46.4	53.1	53.3	53.3	51.5	53.2	51.6	51.3	48.6	47.5	42.8	42.3	44.4

Index of Economic Freedom Scores, 1995–2014

Country	1995	1996	1997	1998	1999	2000	2001	2002	2003	2004	2005	2006	2007	2008	2009	2010	2011	2012	2013	2014
Eritrea	-	-	-	-	-	-	-	-	-	-	-	-	-	-	38.5	35.3	36.7	36.2	36.3	38.5
Estonia	65.2	65.4	69.1	72.5	73.8	69.9	76.1	77.6	77.7	77.4	75.2	74.9	78.0	77.9	76.4	74.7	75.2	73.2	75.3	75.9
Ethiopia	42.6	45.9	48.1	49.2	46.7	50.2	48.9	49.8	48.8	54.5	51.1	50.9	53.6	52.5	53.0	51.2	50.5	52.0	49.4	50.0
Fiji	54.7	57.4	58.0	58.2	58.4	57.8	53.7	53.9	54.7	58.0	58.2	58.4	60.8	61.8	61.0	60.3	60.4	57.3	57.2	58.7
Finland	-	63.7	65.2	63.5	63.9	64.3	69.7	73.6	73.7	73.4	71.0	72.9	74.0	74.6	74.5	73.8	74.0	72.3	74.0	73.4
France	64.4	63.7	59.1	58.9	59.1	57.4	58.0	58.0	59.2	60.9	60.5	61.1	62.1	64.7	63.3	64.2	64.6	63.2	64.1	63.5
Gabon	57.5	55.7	58.8	59.2	60.5	58.2	55.0	58.0	58.7	57.1	54.8	56.1	54.8	54.2	55.0	55.4	56.7	56.4	57.8	57.8
The Gambia	-	-	52.9	53.4	52.1	52.7	56.6	57.7	56.3	55.3	56.5	57.3	57.7	56.9	55.8	55.1	57.4	58.8	58.8	59.5
Georgia	-	44.1	46.5	47.9	52.5	54.3	58.3	56.7	58.6	58.9	57.1	64.5	69.3	69.2	69.8	70.4	70.4	69.4	72.2	72.6
Germany	69.8	69.1	67.5	64.3	65.6	65.7	69.5	70.4	69.7	69.5	68.1	70.8	70.8	70.6	70.5	71.1	71.8	71.0	72.8	73.4
Ghana	55.6	57.7	56.7	57.0	57.9	58.1	58.0	57.2	58.2	59.1	56.5	55.6	57.6	57.0	58.1	60.2	59.4	60.7	61.3	64.2
Greece	61.2	60.5	59.6	60.6	61.0	61.0	63.4	59.1	58.8	59.1	59.0	60.1	58.7	60.6	60.8	62.7	60.3	55.4	55.4	55.7
Guatemala	62.0	63.7	65.7	65.8	66.2	64.3	65.1	62.3	62.3	59.6	59.5	59.1	60.5	59.8	59.4	61.0	61.9	60.9	60.0	61.2
Guinea	59.4	58.5	52.9	61.0	59.4	58.2	58.4	52.9	54.6	56.1	57.4	52.8	54.5	52.8	51.0	51.8	51.7	50.8	51.2	53.5
Guinea-Bissau	-	-	-	-	33.5	34.7	42.5	42.3	43.1	42.6	46.0	46.5	46.1	44.4	45.4	43.6	46.5	50.1	51.1	51.3
Guyana	45.7	50.1	53.2	52.7	53.3	52.4	53.3	54.3	50.3	53.0	56.5	56.6	53.7	48.8	48.4	48.4	49.4	51.3	53.8	55.7
Haiti	43.0	41.0	45.8	45.7	45.9	45.7	47.1	47.9	50.6	51.2	48.4	49.2	51.4	49.0	50.5	50.8	52.1	50.7	48.1	48.9
Honduras	57.0	56.6	56.0	56.2	56.7	57.6	57.0	58.7	60.4	55.3	55.3	57.4	59.1	58.9	58.7	58.3	58.6	58.8	58.4	57.1
Hong Kong	88.6	90.5	88.6	88.0	88.5	89.5	89.9	89.4	89.8	90.0	89.5	88.6	89.9	89.7	90.0	89.7	89.7	89.9	89.3	90.1
Hungary	55.2	56.8	55.3	56.9	59.6	64.4	65.6	64.5	63.0	62.7	63.5	65.0	64.8	67.6	66.8	66.1	66.6	67.1	67.3	67.0
Iceland	-	-	70.5	71.2	71.4	74.0	73.4	73.1	73.5	72.1	76.6	75.8	76.0	75.8	75.9	73.7	68.2	70.9	72.1	72.4
India	45.1	47.4	49.7	49.7	50.2	47.4	49.0	51.2	51.2	51.5	54.2	52.2	53.9	54.1	54.4	53.8	54.6	54.6	55.2	55.7
Indonesia	54.9	61.0	62.0	63.4	61.5	55.2	52.5	54.8	55.8	52.1	52.9	51.9	53.2	53.2	53.4	55.5	56.0	56.4	56.9	58.5
Iran	-	36.1	34.5	36.0	36.8	36.1	35.9	36.4	43.2	42.8	50.5	45.0	45.0	45.0	44.6	43.4	42.1	42.3	43.2	40.3
Iraq	-	17.2	17.2	17.2	17.2	17.2	17.2	15.6	-	-	-	-	-	-	-	-	-	-	-	-
Ireland	68.5	68.5	72.6	73.7	74.6	76.1	81.2	80.5	80.9	80.3	80.8	82.2	82.6	82.5	82.2	81.3	78.7	76.9	75.7	76.2
Israel	61.5	62.0	62.7	68.0	68.3	65.5	66.1	66.9	62.7	61.4	62.6	64.4	64.8	66.3	67.6	67.7	68.5	67.8	66.9	68.4
Italy	61.2	60.8	58.1	59.1	61.6	61.9	63.0	63.6	64.3	64.2	64.9	62.0	62.8	62.6	61.4	62.7	60.3	58.8	60.6	60.9

Index of Economic Freedom Scores, 1995–2014

Country	1995	1996	1997	1998	1999	2000	2001	2002	2003	2004	2005	2006	2007	2008	2009	2010	2011	2012	2013	2014
Jamaica	64.4	66.7	67.7	67.1	64.7	65.5	63.7	61.7	67.0	66.7	67.0	66.4	65.5	65.7	65.2	65.5	65.7	65.1	66.8	66.7
Japan	75.0	72.6	70.3	70.2	69.1	70.7	70.9	66.7	67.6	64.3	67.3	73.3	72.7	73.0	72.8	72.9	72.8	71.6	71.8	72.4
Jordan	62.7	60.8	63.6	66.8	67.4	67.5	68.3	66.2	65.3	66.1	66.7	63.7	64.5	64.1	65.4	66.1	68.9	69.9	70.4	69.2
Kazakhstan	-	-	-	41.7	47.3	50.4	51.8	52.4	52.3	49.7	53.9	60.2	59.6	61.1	60.1	61.0	62.1	63.6	63.0	63.7
Kenya	54.5	56.4	60.1	58.4	58.2	59.7	57.6	58.2	58.6	57.7	57.9	59.7	59.6	59.3	58.7	57.5	57.4	57.5	55.9	57.1
Kiribati	-	-	-	-	-	-	-	-	-	-	-	-	-	-	45.7	43.7	44.8	46.9	45.9	46.3
North Korea	8.9	8.9	8.9	8.9	8.9	8.9	8.9	8.9	8.9	8.9	8.0	4.0	3.0	3.0	2.0	1.0	1.0	1.0	1.5	1.0
South Korea	72.0	73.0	69.8	73.3	69.7	69.7	69.1	69.5	68.3	67.8	66.4	67.5	67.8	68.6	68.1	69.9	69.8	69.9	70.3	71.2
Kosovo	-	-	-	-	-	-	-	-	-	-	-	-	-	-	-	-	-	-	-	-
Kuwait	-	66.1	64.8	66.3	69.5	69.7	68.2	65.4	66.7	63.6	64.6	66.5	66.4	68.1	65.6	67.7	64.9	62.5	63.1	62.3
Kyrgyz Republic	-	-	-	51.8	54.8	55.7	53.7	51.7	56.8	58.0	56.6	61.0	60.2	61.1	61.8	61.3	61.1	60.2	59.6	61.1
Laos	-	38.5	35.1	35.2	35.2	36.8	33.5	36.8	41.0	42.0	44.4	47.5	50.3	50.3	50.4	51.1	51.3	50.0	50.1	51.2
Latvia	-	55.0	62.4	63.4	64.2	63.4	66.4	65.0	66.0	67.4	66.3	66.9	67.9	68.3	66.6	66.2	65.8	65.2	66.5	68.7
Lebanon	-	63.2	63.9	59.0	59.1	56.1	61.0	57.1	56.7	56.9	57.2	57.5	60.4	60.0	58.1	59.5	60.1	60.1	59.5	59.4
Lesotho	-	47.0	47.2	48.4	48.2	48.4	50.6	48.9	52.0	50.3	53.9	54.7	53.2	52.1	49.7	48.1	47.5	46.6	47.9	49.5
Liberia	-	-	-	-	-	-	-	-	-	-	-	-	-	-	48.1	46.2	46.5	48.6	49.3	52.4
Libya	-	31.7	28.9	32.0	32.3	34.7	34.0	35.4	34.6	31.5	32.8	33.2	37.0	38.7	43.5	40.2	38.6	35.9	-	-
Liechtenstein	-	-	-	-	-	-	-	-	-	-	-	-	-	-	-	-	-	-	-	-
Lithuania	-	49.7	57.3	59.4	61.5	61.9	65.5	66.1	69.7	72.4	70.5	71.8	71.5	70.9	70.0	70.3	71.3	71.5	72.1	73.0
Luxembourg	-	72.5	72.8	72.7	72.4	76.4	80.1	79.4	79.9	78.9	76.3	75.3	74.6	74.7	75.2	75.4	76.2	74.5	74.2	74.2
Macau	-	-	-	-	-	-	-	-	-	-	-	-	-	-	72.0	72.5	73.1	71.8	71.7	71.3
Macedonia	-	-	-	-	-	-	-	58.0	60.1	56.8	56.1	59.2	60.6	61.1	61.2	65.7	66.0	68.5	68.2	68.6
Madagascar	51.6	52.2	53.8	51.8	52.8	54.4	53.9	56.8	62.8	60.9	63.1	61.0	61.1	62.4	62.2	63.2	61.2	62.4	62.0	61.7
Malawi	54.7	56.2	53.4	54.1	54.0	57.4	56.2	56.9	53.2	53.6	53.6	55.4	52.9	52.7	53.7	54.1	55.8	56.4	55.3	55.4
Malaysia	71.9	69.9	66.8	68.2	68.9	66.0	60.2	60.1	61.1	59.9	61.9	61.6	63.8	63.9	64.6	64.8	66.3	66.4	66.1	69.6
Maldives	-	-	-	-	-	-	-	-	-	-	-	-	-	-	51.3	49.0	48.3	49.2	49.0	51.0
Mali	52.4	57.0	56.4	57.3	58.4	60.3	60.1	61.1	58.6	56.6	57.3	54.1	54.7	55.6	55.6	55.6	56.3	55.8	56.4	55.5
Malta	56.3	55.8	57.9	61.2	59.3	58.3	62.9	62.2	61.1	63.3	68.9	67.3	66.1	66.0	66.1	67.2	65.7	67.0	67.5	66.4

Index of Economic Freedom Scores, 1995–2014

Country	1995	1996	1997	1998	1999	2000	2001	2002	2003	2004	2005	2006	2007	2008	2009	2010	2011	2012	2013	2014
Mauritania	-	45.5	47.0	43.7	42.8	46.0	48.5	52.5	59.0	61.8	59.4	55.7	53.6	55.2	53.9	52.0	52.1	53.0	52.3	53.2
Mauritius	-	-	-	-	68.5	67.2	66.4	67.7	64.4	64.3	67.2	67.4	69.4	72.6	74.3	76.3	76.2	77.0	76.9	76.5
Mexico	63.1	61.2	57.1	57.9	58.5	59.3	60.6	63.0	65.3	66.0	65.2	64.7	66.0	66.2	65.8	68.3	67.8	65.3	67.0	66.8
Micronesia	-	-	-	-	-	-	-	-	-	-	-	-	-	-	51.7	50.6	50.3	50.7	50.1	49.8
Moldova	33.0	52.5	48.9	53.5	56.1	59.6	54.9	57.4	60.0	57.1	57.4	58.0	58.7	57.9	54.9	53.7	55.7	54.4	55.5	57.3
Mongolia	47.8	47.4	52.9	57.3	58.6	58.5	56.0	56.7	57.7	56.5	59.7	62.4	60.3	63.6	62.8	60.0	59.5	61.5	61.7	58.9
Montenegro	-	-	-	-	-	-	-	46.6	43.5	-	-	-	-	-	58.2	63.6	62.5	62.5	62.6	63.6
Morocco	62.8	64.3	64.7	61.1	63.8	63.2	63.9	59.0	57.8	56.7	52.2	51.5	56.4	55.6	57.7	59.2	59.6	60.2	59.6	58.3
Mozambique	45.5	48.4	44.0	43.0	48.9	52.2	59.2	57.7	58.6	57.2	54.6	51.9	54.7	55.4	55.7	56.0	56.8	57.1	55.0	55.0
Namibia	-	-	61.6	66.1	66.1	66.7	64.8	65.1	67.3	62.4	61.4	60.7	63.5	61.4	62.4	62.2	62.7	61.9	60.3	59.4
Nepal	-	50.3	53.6	53.5	53.1	51.3	51.6	52.3	51.5	51.2	51.4	53.7	54.4	54.1	53.2	52.7	50.1	50.2	50.4	50.1
The Netherlands	-	69.7	70.4	69.2	70.2	70.4	73.0	75.1	74.6	74.5	72.9	75.4	75.5	77.4	77.0	75.0	74.7	73.3	73.5	74.2
New Zealand	-	78.1	79.0	79.2	81.7	80.9	81.1	80.7	81.1	81.5	82.3	82.0	81.4	80.7	82.0	82.1	82.3	82.1	81.4	81.2
Nicaragua	42.5	54.1	53.3	53.8	54.0	56.9	58.0	61.1	62.6	61.4	62.5	63.8	62.7	60.8	59.8	58.3	58.8	57.9	56.6	58.4
Niger	-	45.8	46.6	47.5	48.6	45.9	48.9	48.2	54.2	54.6	54.1	52.5	53.2	52.9	53.8	52.9	54.3	54.3	53.9	55.1
Nigeria	47.3	47.4	52.8	52.3	55.7	53.1	49.6	50.9	49.5	49.2	48.4	48.7	55.6	55.1	55.1	56.8	56.7	56.3	55.1	54.3
Norway	-	65.4	65.1	68.0	68.6	70.1	67.1	67.4	67.2	66.2	64.5	67.9	67.9	68.6	70.2	69.4	70.3	68.8	70.5	70.9
Oman	70.2	65.4	64.5	64.9	64.9	64.1	67.7	64.0	64.6	66.9	66.5	63.7	65.8	67.3	67.0	67.7	69.8	67.9	68.1	67.4
Pakistan	57.6	58.4	56.0	53.2	53.0	56.4	56.0	55.8	55.0	54.9	53.3	57.9	57.2	55.6	57.0	55.2	55.1	54.7	55.1	55.2
Panama	71.6	71.8	72.4	72.6	72.6	71.6	70.6	68.5	68.4	65.3	64.3	65.6	64.6	64.7	64.7	64.8	64.9	65.2	62.5	63.4
Papua New Guinea	-	58.6	56.7	55.2	56.3	55.8	57.2	-	-	-	-	-	-	-	54.8	53.5	52.6	53.8	53.6	53.9
Paraguay	65.9	67.1	67.3	65.2	63.7	64.0	60.3	59.6	58.2	56.7	53.4	55.6	58.3	60.0	61.0	61.3	62.3	61.8	61.1	62.0
Peru	56.9	62.5	63.8	65.0	69.2	68.7	69.6	64.8	64.6	64.7	61.3	60.5	62.7	63.8	64.6	67.6	68.6	68.7	68.2	67.4
The Philippines	55.0	60.2	62.2	62.8	61.9	62.5	60.9	60.7	61.3	59.1	54.7	56.3	56.0	56.0	56.8	56.3	56.2	57.1	58.2	60.1
Poland	50.7	57.8	56.8	59.2	59.6	60.0	61.8	65.0	61.8	58.7	59.6	59.3	58.1	60.3	60.3	63.2	64.1	64.2	66.0	67.0
Portugal	62.4	64.5	63.6	65.0	65.6	65.5	66.0	65.4	64.9	64.9	62.4	62.9	64.0	63.9	64.9	64.4	64.0	63.0	63.1	63.5
Qatar	-	-	-	-	62.0	62.0	60.0	61.9	65.9	66.5	63.5	62.4	62.9	62.2	65.8	69.0	70.5	71.3	71.3	71.2
Romania	42.9	46.2	50.8	54.4	50.1	52.1	50.0	48.7	50.6	50.0	52.1	58.2	61.2	61.7	63.2	64.2	64.7	64.4	65.1	65.5

Index of Economic Freedom Scores, 1995–2014

Country	1995	1996	1997	1998	1999	2000	2001	2002	2003	2004	2005	2006	2007	2008	2009	2010	2011	2012	2013	2014
Russia	51.1	51.6	48.6	52.8	54.5	51.8	49.8	48.7	50.8	52.8	51.3	52.4	52.2	49.8	50.8	50.3	50.5	50.5	51.1	51.9
Rwanda	-	-	38.3	39.1	39.8	42.3	45.4	50.4	47.8	53.3	51.7	52.8	52.4	54.2	54.2	59.1	62.7	64.9	64.1	64.7
Saint Lucia	-	-	-	-	-	-	-	-	-	-	-	-	-	-	68.8	70.5	70.8	71.3	70.4	70.7
Saint Vincent & the Grenadines	-	-	-	-	-	-	-	-	-	-	-	-	-	-	64.3	66.9	66.9	66.5	66.7	67.0
Samoa	-	47.6	51.5	49.9	58.7	60.8	63.1	-	-	-	-	-	-	-	59.5	60.4	60.6	60.5	57.1	61.1
São Tomé and Príncipe	-	-	-	-	-	-	-	-	-	-	-	-	-	-	43.8	48.8	49.5	50.2	48.0	48.8
Saudi Arabia	-	68.3	68.7	69.3	65.5	66.5	62.2	65.3	63.2	60.4	63.0	63.0	60.9	62.5	64.3	64.1	66.2	62.5	60.6	62.2
Senegal	-	58.2	58.1	59.7	60.6	58.9	58.7	58.6	58.1	58.9	57.9	56.2	58.1	58.3	56.3	54.6	55.7	55.4	55.5	55.4
Serbia	-	-	-	-	-	-	-	46.6	43.5	-	-	-	-	-	56.6	56.9	58.0	58.0	58.6	59.4
Seychelles	-	-	-	-	-	-	-	-	-	-	-	-	-	-	47.8	47.9	51.2	53.0	54.9	56.2
Sierra Leone	49.8	52.3	45.0	47.7	47.2	44.2	-	-	42.2	43.6	44.8	45.2	47.0	48.3	47.8	47.9	49.6	49.1	48.3	50.5
Singapore	86.3	86.5	87.3	87.0	86.9	87.7	87.8	87.4	88.2	88.9	88.6	88.0	87.1	87.3	87.1	86.1	87.2	87.5	88.0	89.4
Slovak Republic	60.4	57.6	55.5	57.5	54.2	53.8	58.5	59.8	59.0	64.6	66.8	69.8	69.6	70.0	69.4	69.7	69.5	67.0	68.7	66.4
Slovenia	-	50.4	55.6	60.7	61.3	58.3	61.8	57.8	57.7	59.2	59.6	61.9	59.6	60.2	62.9	64.7	64.6	62.9	61.7	62.7
Solomon Islands	-	-	-	-	-	-	-	-	-	-	-	-	-	-	46.0	42.9	45.9	46.2	45.0	46.2
Somalia	-	25.6	25.6	27.8	27.8	27.8	-	-	-	-	-	-	-	-	-	-	-	-	-	-
South Africa	60.7	62.5	63.2	64.3	63.3	63.7	63.8	64.0	67.1	66.3	62.9	63.7	63.5	63.4	63.8	62.8	62.7	62.7	61.8	62.5
Spain	62.8	59.6	59.6	62.6	65.1	65.9	68.1	68.8	68.8	68.9	67.0	68.2	69.2	69.1	70.1	69.6	70.2	69.1	68.0	67.2
Sri Lanka	60.6	62.5	65.5	64.6	64.0	63.2	66.0	64.0	62.5	61.6	61.0	58.7	59.4	58.4	56.0	54.6	57.1	58.3	60.7	60.0
Sudan	39.4	39.2	39.9	38.3	39.6	47.2	-	-	-	-	-	-	-	-	-	-	-	-	-	-
Suriname	-	36.7	35.9	39.9	40.1	45.8	44.3	48.0	46.9	47.9	51.9	55.1	54.8	54.3	54.1	52.5	53.1	52.6	52.0	54.2
Swaziland	63.3	58.6	59.4	62.0	62.1	62.6	63.6	60.9	59.6	58.6	59.4	61.4	60.1	58.4	59.1	57.4	59.1	57.2	57.2	61.2
Sweden	61.4	61.8	63.3	64.0	64.2	65.1	66.6	70.8	70.0	70.1	69.8	70.9	69.3	70.8	70.5	72.4	71.9	71.7	72.9	73.1
Switzerland	-	76.8	78.6	79.0	79.1	76.8	76.0	79.3	79.0	79.5	79.3	78.9	78.0	79.5	79.4	81.1	81.9	81.1	81.0	81.6
Syria	-	42.3	43.0	42.2	39.0	37.2	36.6	36.3	41.3	40.6	46.3	51.2	48.3	47.2	51.3	49.4	51.3	51.2	-	-

Index of Economic Freedom Scores, 1995–2014

Country	1995	1996	1997	1998	1999	2000	2001	2002	2003	2004	2005	2006	2007	2008	2009	2010	2011	2012	2013	2014
Taiwan	74.2	74.1	70.0	70.4	71.5	72.5	72.8	71.3	71.7	69.6	71.3	69.7	69.4	70.3	69.5	70.4	70.8	71.9	72.7	73.9
Tajikistan	-	-	-	41.1	41.2	44.8	46.8	47.3	46.5	48.7	50.4	52.6	53.6	54.4	54.6	53.0	53.5	53.4	53.4	52.0
Tanzania	57.3	57.5	59.3	59.6	60.0	56.0	54.9	58.3	56.9	60.1	56.3	58.5	56.8	56.5	58.3	58.3	57.0	57.0	57.9	57.8
Thailand	71.3	71.0	66.1	67.3	66.9	66.6	68.9	69.1	65.8	63.7	62.5	63.3	63.5	62.3	63.0	64.1	64.7	64.9	64.1	63.3
Timor-Leste	-	-	-	-	-	-	-	-	-	-	-	-	-	-	50.5	45.8	42.8	43.3	43.7	43.2
Togo	-	-	-	-	48.2	46.4	45.3	45.2	46.8	47.0	48.2	47.3	49.7	48.9	48.7	47.1	49.1	48.3	48.8	49.9
Tonga	-	-	-	-	-	-	-	-	-	-	-	-	-	-	54.1	53.4	55.8	57.0	56.0	58.2
Trinidad and Tobago	-	69.2	71.3	72.0	72.4	74.5	71.8	70.1	68.8	71.3	71.5	70.4	70.6	69.5	68.0	65.7	66.5	64.4	62.3	62.7
Tunisia	63.4	63.9	63.8	63.9	61.1	61.3	60.8	60.2	58.1	58.4	55.4	57.5	60.3	60.1	58.0	58.9	58.5	58.6	57.0	57.3
Turkey	58.4	56.7	60.8	60.9	59.2	63.4	60.6	54.2	51.9	52.8	50.6	57.0	57.4	59.9	61.6	63.8	64.2	62.5	62.9	64.9
Turkmenistan	-	-	-	35.0	36.1	37.6	41.8	43.2	51.3	50.7	47.6	43.8	43.0	43.4	44.2	42.5	43.6	43.8	42.6	42.2
Uganda	62.9	66.2	66.6	64.7	64.8	58.2	60.4	61.0	60.1	64.1	62.9	63.9	63.1	63.8	63.5	62.2	61.7	61.9	61.1	59.9
Ukraine	39.9	40.6	43.5	40.4	43.7	47.8	48.5	48.2	51.1	53.7	55.8	54.4	51.5	51.0	48.8	46.4	45.8	46.1	46.3	49.3
United Arab Emirates	-	71.6	71.9	72.2	71.5	74.2	74.9	73.6	73.4	67.2	65.2	62.2	62.6	62.6	64.7	67.3	67.8	69.3	71.1	71.4
United Kingdom	77.9	76.4	76.4	76.5	76.2	77.3	77.6	78.5	77.5	77.7	79.2	80.4	79.9	79.4	79.0	76.5	74.5	74.1	74.8	74.9
United States	76.7	76.7	75.6	75.4	75.5	76.4	79.1	78.4	78.2	78.7	79.9	81.2	81.2	81.0	80.7	78.0	77.8	76.3	76.0	75.5
Uruguay	62.5	63.7	67.5	68.6	68.5	69.3	70.7	68.7	69.8	66.7	66.9	65.3	68.4	67.9	69.1	69.8	70.0	69.9	69.7	69.3
Uzbekistan	-	-	-	31.5	33.8	38.1	38.2	38.5	38.3	39.1	45.8	48.7	51.5	51.9	50.5	47.5	45.8	45.8	46.0	46.5
Vanuatu	-	-	-	-	-	-	-	-	-	-	-	-	-	-	58.4	56.4	56.7	56.6	56.6	59.5
Venezuela	59.8	54.5	52.8	54.0	56.1	57.4	54.6	54.7	54.8	46.7	45.2	44.6	47.9	44.7	39.9	37.1	37.6	38.1	36.1	36.3
Vietnam	41.7	40.2	38.6	40.4	42.7	43.7	44.3	45.6	46.2	46.1	48.1	50.5	49.8	50.4	51.0	49.8	51.6	51.3	51.0	50.8
Yemen	49.8	49.6	48.4	46.1	43.3	44.5	44.3	48.6	50.3	50.5	53.8	52.6	54.1	53.8	56.9	54.4	54.2	55.3	55.9	55.5
Zambia	55.1	59.6	62.1	62.7	64.2	62.8	59.5	59.6	55.3	54.9	55.0	56.8	56.2	56.2	56.6	58.0	59.7	58.3	58.7	60.4
Zimbabwe	48.5	46.7	48.0	44.6	47.2	48.7	38.8	36.7	36.7	34.4	35.2	33.5	32.0	29.5	22.7	21.4	22.1	26.3	28.6	35.5

Methodology

The *Index of Economic Freedom* focuses on four key aspects of the economic environment over which governments typically exercise some policy control:

- **Rule of law,**
- **Government size,**
- **Regulatory efficiency,** and
- **Market openness.**

To provide as comprehensive a picture as possible of conditions in these four categories, the *Index* measures 10 specific components of economic freedom, each of which is graded on a scale from 0 to 100. Scores on these 10 components of economic freedom, which are calculated from a number of sub-variables, are equally weighted and averaged to produce an overall economic freedom score for each economy.

The following sections provide detailed descriptions of the formulas and methodology used to compute the scores for each of the 10 components of economic freedom.

RULE OF LAW

Property Rights

The property rights component is a qualitative assessment of the extent to which a country's legal framework allows individuals to freely accumulate private property, secured by clear laws that are enforced effectively by the government. It measures the degree to which a country's laws protect private property rights and the extent to which those laws are respected. It also assesses the likelihood that private property will be expropriated by the state and analyzes the independence of the judiciary, the existence of corruption within the judiciary, and the ability of individuals and businesses to enforce contracts.

The more effective the legal protection of property, the higher a country's score; similarly, the greater the chances of government expropriation of property or the less independent the judiciary, the lower a country's score.

Each country's property rights score is assessed according to the following criteria:

- **100**—Private property is guaranteed by the government. The court system enforces contracts efficiently and quickly. The justice system punishes those who unlawfully confiscate private property. There is no corruption or expropriation.
- **90**—Private property is guaranteed by the government. The court system enforces contracts efficiently. The justice system punishes those who unlawfully confiscate private property. Corruption is nearly nonexistent, and expropriation is highly unlikely.
- **80**—Private property is guaranteed by the government. The court system enforces contracts efficiently but with some delays. Corruption is minimal, and expropriation is highly unlikely.
- **70**—Private property is guaranteed by the government. The court system is subject to delays and is lax in enforcing contracts. Corruption is possible but rare, and expropriation is unlikely.
- **60**—Enforcement of property rights is lax and subject to delays. Corruption is possible but rare, and the judiciary may be influenced by other branches of government. Expropriation is unlikely.
- **50**—The court system is inefficient and subject to delays. Corruption may be present, and the judiciary may be influenced by other branches of government. Expropriation is possible but rare.
- **40**—The court system is highly inefficient, and delays are so long that they deter the use of the court system. Corruption is present, and the judiciary is influenced by other branches of government. Expropriation is possible.
- **30**—Property ownership is weakly protected. The court system is highly inefficient. Corruption is extensive, and the judiciary is strongly influenced by other branches of government. Expropriation is possible.
- **20**—Private property is weakly protected. The court system is so inefficient and corrupt that outside settlement and arbitration is the norm. Property rights are difficult to enforce. Judicial corruption is extensive. Expropriation is common.
- **10**—Private property is rarely protected, and almost all property belongs to the state. The country is in such chaos (for example, because of ongoing war) that protection of property is almost impossible to enforce. The judiciary is so corrupt that property is not protected effectively. Expropriation is common.
- **0**—Private property is outlawed, and all property belongs to the state. People do not have the right to sue others and do not have access to the courts. Corruption is endemic.

An intermediate score such as 75 or 45 may be assigned to countries whose property rights fall between two adjacent categories.

Sources. Unless otherwise noted, the *Index* relies on the following sources for information on property rights, in order of priority: Economist Intelligence Unit, *Country Commerce*, 2010–2013; U.S. Department of Commerce, *Country Commercial Guide*, 2010–2013; U.S. Department of State, *Country Reports on Human Rights Practices*, 2010–2012; and various news and magazine articles.

Freedom from Corruption

Corruption erodes economic freedom by introducing insecurity and uncertainty into economic relations. It also reduces economic vitality by increasing costs and shifting resources into unproductive activities.

The score for this component is derived primarily from Transparency International's Corruption Perceptions Index (CPI), which measures the level of perceived corruption in 176 countries.

Transparency International revised its CPI methodology in 2012 and now reports CPI scores on a 0–100 scale in which a score of 100 indicates very little perceived corruption. Transparency International has indicated that country scores computed with its new methodology are not directly comparable to its scores for previous years. The *Index* has therefore adjusted its methodological use of CPI data in order to maintain as much comparability as possible between current freedom from corruption scores and scores from prior years. A two-step approach has been used.

First, the *Index* converts the raw CPI data to maintain approximately the same range of scores achieved in the previous *Index*, using the following equation:

$$\text{CORRUPTION}_{xi} = ((10\text{–CPI}_x)/(10\text{–}95)) * 100$$

where CORRUPTION_{xi} represents an initially converted current-year corruption score for country *x*, CPI_x represents Transparency International's CPI score for country *x*, and 10 and 95 represent the previous minimum and maximum values achieved on the *Index*'s freedom from corruption score.

Second, in computing the final 2014 *Index* freedom from corruption scores, each country's initially converted corruption score is averaged with its corruption scores from the previous two *Index* editions (2013 and 2012) so that year-to-year score incompatibility introduced by Transparency International's new methodology is further reduced. Nonetheless, the reader is urged to use caution in comparing the 2014 *Index*'s corruption scores with the previous edition's corruption scores.

For countries that are not covered in the CPI, the freedom from corruption score is determined by using the qualitative information from internationally recognized and reliable sources.[1] This procedure considers the extent to which corruption prevails in a country. As with scores derived from Transparency International data, these scores are averaged with corruption scores from the previous two editions of the *Index*.

Sources. Unless otherwise noted, the *Index* relies on the following sources for information on informal market activities, in order of priority: Transparency International, *Corruption Perceptions Index*, 2010–2012; U.S. Department of Commerce, *Country Commercial Guide*, 2010–2013; Economist Intelligence Unit, *Country Commerce*, 2010–2013; Office of the U.S. Trade Representative, *2013 National Trade Estimate Report on Foreign Trade Barriers*; and official government publications of each country.

GOVERNMENT SIZE

Fiscal Freedom

The fiscal freedom component is a composite measure of the burden of taxes that reflects both marginal tax rates and the overall level of taxation, including direct and indirect taxes imposed by all levels of government, as a percentage of GDP. The component score is derived from three quantitative factors:

- The top marginal tax rate on individual income,
- The top marginal tax rate on corporate income, and
- The total tax burden as a percentage of GDP.

Each of these numerical variables is weighted equally as one-third of the component score. This equal weighting allows a country to achieve a score as high as 67 based on two of the factors even if it receives a score of 0 on the third.

Fiscal freedom scores are calculated with a quadratic cost function to reflect the diminishing revenue returns from very high rates of taxation. The data for each factor are converted to a 100-point scale using the following equation:

$$\text{Fiscal Freedom}_{ij} = 100 - \alpha\,(\text{Factor}_{ij})^2$$

where $\text{Fiscal Freedom}_{ij}$ represents the fiscal freedom in country *i* for factor *j*; Factor_{ij} represents the value (a percentage expressed on a scale of 0 to 100) in country *i* for factor *j*; and α is a coefficient set equal to 0.03. The minimum score for each factor is zero, which is not represented in the printed equation but was utilized because it means that no single high tax burden will make the other two factors irrelevant.

As an example, in the 2014 *Index*, Mauritius has a flat rate of 15 percent for both individual and corporate tax rates, which yields a score of 93.3 for each of the two factors. Mauritius's overall tax burden as a portion of GDP is 18.3 percent, yielding a tax burden factor score of 90.0. When the three factors are averaged together, Mauritius's overall fiscal freedom score becomes 92.2.

Sources. Unless otherwise noted, the *Index* relies on the following sources for information on taxation, in order of priority: Deloitte, *International Tax and Business Guide Highlights*; International Monetary Fund, *Staff Country Report*, "Selected Issues and Statistical Appendix," and *Staff Country Report*, "Article IV Consultation," 2010–2013; PricewaterhouseCoopers, *Worldwide Tax Summaries*, 2010–2013; countries' investment agencies; other government authorities (embassy confirmations and/or the country's treasury or tax authority); and Economist Intelligence Unit, *Country Commerce* and *Country Finance*, 2010–2013.

For information on tax burden as a percentage of GDP, the primary sources (in order of priority) were Organisation for Economic Co-operation and Development data; Eurostat, Government Finance Statistics data; African Development Bank and Organisation for Economic Co-operation and Development, *African Economic Outlook 2013*; International Monetary Fund, *Staff Country Report*, "Selected Issues," and *Staff Country Report*, "Article IV Consultation," 2010–2013; Asian Development Bank, *Key Indicators for Asia and the Pacific*, 2010–2013; and individual contacts from government agencies and multinational organizations such as the IMF and World Bank.

Government Spending

The government spending component captures the burden imposed by government expenditures, which includes consumption by the state and all transfer payments related to various entitlement programs.

No attempt has been made to identify an optimal level of government spending. The ideal level will vary from country to country, depending on factors ranging from culture to geography to level of economic development. However, government spending becomes an unavoidable burden at some point as government grows in scope and size, resulting in both misallocation of resources and loss of economic efficiency. Volumes of research have shown that excessive government spending that causes chronic budget deficits and the accumulation of public debt is one of the most serious drags on economic dynamism.

The *Index* methodology treats zero government spending as the benchmark. Underdeveloped countries, particularly those with little government capacity, may receive artificially high scores as a result. However, such governments, which can provide few if any public goods, are likely to receive low scores on some of the other components of economic freedom (such as property rights, financial freedom, and investment freedom) that measure aspects of government effectiveness.

Government spending has a major impact on economic freedom, but it is just one of many important components. The scale for scoring government spending is non-linear, which means that government spending that is close to zero is lightly penalized, while levels of government spending that exceed 30 percent of GDP lead to much worse scores in a quadratic fashion (for example, doubling spending yields four times less freedom). Only extraordinarily large levels of government spending—for example, over 58 percent of GDP—receive a score of zero.

The equation used for computing a country's government spending score is:

$$GE_i = 100 - \alpha\,(\text{Expenditures}_i)^2$$

where GE_i represents the government expenditure score in country *i*; Expenditures_i represents the total amount of government spending at all levels as a portion of GDP (between 0 and 100); and α is a coefficient to control for variation among scores (set at 0.03). The minimum component score is zero.

In most cases, the *Index* uses general government expenditure data that include all levels of government such as federal, state, and local. In cases where data on general government spending are not available, data on central government expenditures are used instead.

Sources. Unless otherwise noted, the *Index* relies on the following sources for information on government intervention in the economy, in order of priority: Organisation for Economic Co-operation and Development data; Eurostat data; African Development Bank and Organisation for Economic Co-operation and Development, *African Economic Outlook 2013*; International Monetary Fund, *Staff Country Report*, "Selected Issues and Statistical Appendix," *Staff Country Report*, "Article IV Consultation," 2010–2013, and *World Economic Outlook Database 2012*; Asian Development Bank, *Key Indicators for Asia and the Pacific*, 2010–2013; African Development Bank, *The ADB Statistics Pocketbook 2013*; official government publications of each country; and United Nations Economic Commission for Latin America, *Economic Survey of Latin America and the Caribbean*, 2010–2013.

REGULATORY EFFICIENCY

Business Freedom

Business freedom is an overall indicator of the efficiency of government regulation of business. The quantitative score is derived from an array of measurements of the ease of starting, operating, and closing a business.

The business freedom score for each country is a number between 0 and 100, with 100 indicating the freest business environment. The score is based on 10 factors, all weighted equally, using data from the World Bank's *Doing Business* report:

- Starting a business—procedures (number);
- Starting a business—time (days);
- Starting a business—cost (% of income per capita);
- Starting a business—minimum capital (% of income per capita);
- Obtaining a license—procedures (number);[2]
- Obtaining a license—time (days);
- Obtaining a license—cost (% of income per capita);
- Closing a business—time (years);
- Closing a business—cost (% of estate); and
- Closing a business—recovery rate (cents on the dollar).[3]

Each of these factors is converted to a scale of 0 to 100, after which the average of the converted values is computed. The result represents the country's business freedom score in comparison to other countries. Even if a country requires the highest number of procedures for starting a business, which yields a score of zero in that factor, it could still receive a score as high as 90 based on scores in the other nine factors. Singapore, for instance, receives scores of 100 in nine of these 10 factors, but the 11 licensing procedures required by the government equate to a score of 68.2 for that factor, giving Singapore an overall business freedom score of 96.8.

Each factor is converted to a scale of 0 to 100 using the following equation:

$$\text{Factor Score}_i = 50\ \text{factor}_{average}/\text{factor}_i$$

which is based on the ratio of the country data for each factor relative to the world average, multiplied by 50. For example, on average worldwide, it takes 15 procedures to get necessary licenses. Canada's 11 licensing procedures are a factor value better than the average, resulting in a ratio of 1.15. That ratio multiplied by 50 equals the final factor score of 68.2.

For the six countries that are not covered by the World Bank's *Doing Business* report, business freedom is scored by analyzing business regulations based on qualitative information from reliable and internationally recognized sources.[4]

Sources. Unless otherwise noted, the *Index* relies on the following sources in determining business freedom scores, in order of priority: World Bank, *Doing Business 2014*; Economist Intelligence Unit, *Country Commerce*, 2010–2013; U.S. Department of Commerce, *Country Commercial Guide*, 2010–2013; and official government publications of each country.

Labor Freedom

The labor freedom component is a quantitative measure that considers various aspects of the legal and regulatory framework of a country's labor market, including regulations concerning minimum wages, laws inhibiting layoffs, severance requirements, and measurable regulatory restraints on hiring and hours worked.

Six quantitative factors are equally weighted, with each counted as one-sixth of the labor freedom component:[5]

- Ratio of minimum wage to the average value added per worker,
- Hindrance to hiring additional workers,
- Rigidity of hours,
- Difficulty of firing redundant employees,
- Legally mandated notice period, and
- Mandatory severance pay.

Based on data collected in connection with the World Bank's *Doing Business* report, these factors specifically examine labor regulations that affect "the hiring and redundancy of workers and the rigidity of working hours."[6]

In constructing the labor freedom score, each of the six factors is converted to a scale of 0 to 100 based on the following equation:

$$\text{Factor Score}_i = 50 \times \text{factor}_{average}/\text{factor}_i$$

where country *i* data are calculated relative to the world average and then multiplied by 50.

The simple average of the converted values for the six factors is computed for the country's overall labor freedom score. Even if a country had the worst rigidity of hours in the world with a zero score for that factor, it could still get a score as high as 83.3 based on the other five factors.

For the six countries that are not covered by the World Bank's *Doing Business* report, the labor freedom component is scored by looking into labor market flexibility based on qualitative information from other reliable and internationally recognized sources.[7]

Sources. Unless otherwise noted, the *Index* relies on the following sources for data on labor freedom, in order of priority: World Bank, *Doing Business 2014*; Economist Intelligence Unit, *Country Commerce*, 2010–2013; U.S. Department of Commerce, *Country Commercial Guide*, 2010–2013; and official government publications of each country.

Monetary Freedom

Monetary freedom combines a measure of price stability with an assessment of price controls. Both inflation and price controls distort market activity. Price stability without microeconomic intervention is the ideal state for the free market.

The score for the monetary freedom component is based on two factors:

- The weighted average inflation rate for the most recent three years and
- Price controls.

The weighted average inflation rate for the most recent three years serves as the primary input into an equation that generates the base score for monetary freedom. The extent of price controls is then assessed as a penalty deduction of up to 20 points from the base score. The two equations used to convert inflation rates into the final monetary freedom score are:

$$\text{Weighted Avg. Inflation}_i = \theta_1 \text{ Inflation}_{it} + \theta_2 \text{Inflation}_{it-1} + \theta_3 \text{ Inflation}_{it-2}$$

$$\text{Monetary Freedom}_i = 100 - \alpha \sqrt{\text{Weighted Avg. Inflation}_i} - \text{PC penalty}_i$$

where θ_1 through θ_3 (thetas 1–3) represent three numbers that sum to 1 and are exponentially smaller in sequence (in this case, values of 0.665, 0.245, and 0.090, respectively); Inflation_{it} is the absolute value of the annual inflation rate in country *i* during year *t* as measured by the Consumer Price Index; α represents a coefficient that stabilizes the variance of scores; and the price control (PC) penalty is an assigned value of 0–20 penalty points based on the extent of price controls.

The convex (square root) functional form was chosen to create separation among countries with low inflation rates. A concave functional form would essentially treat all hyperinflations as equally bad, whether they were 100 percent price increases annually or 100,000 percent, whereas the square root provides much more gradation. The α coefficient is set to equal 6.333, which converts a 10 percent inflation rate into a freedom score of 80.0 and a 2 percent inflation rate into a score of 91.0.

Sources. Unless otherwise noted, the *Index* relies on the following sources for data on monetary policy, in order of priority: International Monetary Fund, *International Financial Statistics Online*; International Monetary Fund, *World Economic Outlook*, 2013; Economist Intelligence Unit, *ViewsWire*; and official government publications of each country.

OPEN MARKETS

Trade Freedom

Trade freedom is a composite measure of the extent of tariff and non-tariff barriers that affect imports and exports of goods and services. The trade freedom score is based on two inputs:

- The trade-weighted average tariff rate and
- Non-tariff barriers (NTBs).

Different imports entering a country can, and often do, face different tariffs. The weighted average tariff uses weights for each tariff based on the share of imports for each good. Weighted average tariffs are a purely quantitative measure and account for the calculation of the base trade freedom score using the following equation:

$$\text{Trade Freedom}_i = (((\text{Tariff}_{max} - \text{Tariff}_i)/(\text{Tariff}_{max} - \text{Tariff}_{min})) * 100) - \text{NTB}_i$$

where Trade Freedom_i represents the trade freedom in country *i*; Tariff_{max} and Tariff_{min} represent the upper and lower bounds for tariff rates (%); and Tariff_i represents the weighted average tariff rate (%) in country *i*. The minimum tariff is naturally zero percent, and the upper bound was set as 50 percent. An NTB penalty is then subtracted from the base score. The penalty of 5, 10, 15, or 20 points is assigned according to the following scale:

- **20**—NTBs are used extensively across many goods and services and/or act to impede a significant amount of international trade.
- **15**—NTBs are widespread across many goods and services and/or act to impede a majority of potential international trade.
- **10**—NTBs are used to protect certain goods and services and impede some international trade.
- **5**—NTBs are uncommon, protecting few goods and services, and/or have very limited impact on international trade.
- **0**—NTBs are not used to limit international trade.

We determine the extent of NTBs in a country's trade policy regime using both qualitative and quantitative information. Restrictive rules that hinder trade vary widely, and their overlapping and shifting nature makes their complexity difficult to gauge. The categories of NTBs considered in our penalty include:

- **Quantity restrictions**—import quotas; export limitations; voluntary export restraints; import–export embargoes and bans; countertrade, etc.
- **Price restrictions**—antidumping duties; countervailing duties; border tax adjustments; variable levies/tariff rate quotas.
- **Regulatory restrictions**—licensing; domestic content and mixing requirements; sanitary and phytosanitary standards (SPSs); safety and industrial standards regulations; packaging, labeling, and trademark regulations; advertising and media regulations.
- **Investment restrictions**—exchange and other financial controls.
- **Customs restrictions**—advance deposit requirements; customs valuation procedures; customs classification procedures; customs clearance procedures.
- **Direct government intervention**—subsidies and other aid; government industrial policy and regional development measures; government-financed research and other technology policies; national taxes and social insurance; competition policies; immigration policies; government procurement policies; state trading, government monopolies, and exclusive franchises.

As an example, Botswana received a trade freedom score of 79.7. By itself, Botswana's weighted average tariff of 5.2 percent would have yielded a score of 89.7, but the existence of NTBs in Botswana reduced its score by 10 points.

Gathering tariff statistics to make a consistent cross-country comparison is a challenging task. Unlike data on inflation, for instance, countries do not report their weighted average tariff rate or simple average tariff rate every year; in some cases, the most recent year for which a country reported its tariff data could be as far back as 2007.

To preserve consistency in grading the trade freedom component, the *Index* uses the most recently reported weighted average tariff rate for a country from our primary source. If another reliable source reports more updated information on the country's tariff rate, this fact is noted, and the grading of this component may be reviewed if there is strong evidence that the most recently reported weighted average tariff rate is outdated.

The World Bank publishes the most comprehensive and consistent information on weighted average applied tariff rates. When the weighted average applied tariff rate is not available, the *Index* uses the country's average applied tariff rate; and when the country's average applied tariff rate is not available, the weighted average or the simple average of most favored nation (MFN) tariff rates is used.[8] In the very few cases where data on duties and customs revenues are not available, data on international trade taxes or an estimated effective tariff rate are used instead. In all cases, an effort is made to clarify the type of data used in the corresponding write-up for the trade freedom component.

Sources. Unless otherwise noted, the *Index* relies on the following sources to determine scores for trade policy, in order of priority: World Bank, *World Development Indicators 2013*; World Trade Organization, *Trade Policy Review*, 1995–2013; Office of the U.S. Trade Representative, *2013 National Trade Estimate Report on Foreign Trade Barriers*; World Bank, *Doing Business 2012* and *Doing Business 2013*; U.S. Department of Commerce, *Country Commercial Guide*, 2009–2013; Economist Intelligence Unit, *Country Commerce*, 2010–2013; World Bank, *Data on Trade and Import Barriers: Trends in Average Applied Tariff Rates in Developing and Industrial Countries, 1981–2010*; and official government publications of each country.

Investment Freedom

In an economically free country, there would be no constraints on the flow of investment capital. Individuals and firms would be allowed to move their resources into and out of specific activities, both internally and across the country's borders, without restriction. Such an ideal country would receive a score of 100 on the investment freedom component of the *Index*.

In practice, however, most countries have a variety of restrictions on investment. Some have different rules for foreign and domestic investment; some restrict access to foreign exchange; some impose restrictions on payments, transfers, and capital transactions; in some, certain industries are closed to foreign investment.

The *Index* evaluates a variety of regulatory restrictions that are typically imposed on investment. Points, as indicated below, are deducted from the ideal score of 100 for each of the restrictions found in a country's investment regime. It is not necessary for a government to impose all of the listed restrictions at the maximum level to effectively eliminate investment freedom. Those few governments that impose so many restrictions that they total more than 100 points in deductions have had their scores set at zero.

Investment restrictions:

National treatment of foreign investment

- No national treatment, prescreening — 25 points deducted
- Some national treatment, some prescreening — 15 points deducted
- Some national treatment or prescreening — 5 points deducted

Foreign investment code

- No transparency and burdensome bureaucracy — 20 points deducted
- Inefficient policy implementation and bureaucracy — 10 points deducted
- Some investment laws and practices non-transparent or inefficiently implemented — 5 points deducted

Restrictions on land ownership

- All real estate purchases restricted — 15 points deducted
- No foreign purchases of real estate — 10 points deducted
- Some restrictions on purchases of real estate — 5 points deducted

Sectoral investment restrictions

- Multiple sectors restricted — 20 points deducted
- Few sectors restricted — 10 points deducted
- One or two sectors restricted — 5 points deducted

Expropriation of investments without fair compensation

Common with no legal recourse	25 points deducted
Common with some legal recourse	15 points deducted
Uncommon but occurs	5 points deducted

Foreign exchange controls

• No access by foreigners or residents	25 points deducted
• Access available but heavily restricted	15 points deducted
• Access available with few restrictions	5 points deducted

Capital controls

• No repatriation of profits; all transactions require government approval	25 points deducted
• Inward and outward capital movements require approval and face some restrictions	15 points deducted
• Most transfers approved with some restrictions	5 points deducted

Up to an additional 20 points may be deducted for security problems, a lack of basic investment infrastructure, or other government policies that indirectly burden the investment process and limit investment freedom.

Sources. Unless otherwise noted, the *Index* relies on the following sources for data on capital flows and foreign investment, in order of priority: official government publications of each country; Economist Intelligence Unit, *Country Commerce*, 2010–2013; Office of the U.S. Trade Representative, *2013 National Trade Estimate Report on Foreign Trade Barriers*; and U.S. Department of Commerce, *Country Commercial Guide*, 2010–2013.

Financial Freedom

Financial freedom is an indicator of banking efficiency as well as a measure of independence from government control and interference in the financial sector. State ownership of banks and other financial institutions such as insurers and capital markets reduces competition and generally lowers the level of access to credit.

In an ideal banking and financing environment where a minimum level of government interference exists, independent central bank supervision and regulation of financial institutions are limited to enforcing contractual obligations and preventing fraud. Credit is allocated on market terms, and the government does not own financial institutions. Financial institutions provide various types of financial services to individuals and companies. Banks are free to extend credit, accept deposits, and conduct operations in foreign currencies. Foreign financial institutions operate freely and are treated the same as domestic institutions.

The *Index* scores an economy's financial freedom by looking into the following five broad areas:

- The extent of government regulation of financial services,
- The degree of state intervention in banks and other financial firms through direct and indirect ownership,
- The extent of financial and capital market development,
- Government influence on the allocation of credit, and
- Openness to foreign competition.

These five areas are considered to assess an economy's overall level of financial freedom that ensures easy and effective access to financing opportunities for people and businesses in the economy. An overall score on a scale of 0 to 100 is given to an economy's financial freedom through deductions from the ideal score of 100.

- **100—Negligible government interference.**
- **90—Minimal government interference.** Regulation of financial institutions is minimal but may extend beyond enforcing contractual obligations and preventing fraud.
- **80—Nominal government interference.** Government ownership of financial institutions is a small share of overall sector assets. Financial institutions face almost no restrictions on their ability to offer financial services.
- **70—Limited government interference.** Credit allocation is influenced by the government, and private allocation of credit faces almost no restrictions. Government ownership of financial institutions is sizeable. Foreign financial institutions are subject to few restrictions.
- **60—Significant government interference.** The central bank is not fully independent, and its supervision and regulation of financial institutions are somewhat burdensome. The government exercises active ownership and control of financial institutions with a significant share of overall sector assets. The ability of financial institutions to offer financial services is subject to some restrictions.
- **50—Considerable government interference.** Credit allocation is significantly influenced by the government, and private allocation of credit faces significant barriers. The ability of financial institutions to offer financial services is subject to significant restrictions. Foreign financial institutions are subject to some restrictions.
- **40—Strong government interference.** The central bank is subject to government influence, its supervision of financial institutions is heavy-handed, and its ability to enforce contracts and prevent fraud is weak. The government exercises active ownership and control of financial institutions with a large minority share of overall sector assets.
- **30—Extensive government interference.** Credit allocation is extensively influenced by the government. The government owns or controls a majority of financial institutions or is in a dominant position. Financial institutions are heavily restricted, and bank formation faces significant barriers. Foreign financial institutions are subject to significant restrictions.
- **20—Heavy government interference.** The central bank is not independent, and its supervision of financial institutions is repressive. Foreign financial institutions are discouraged or highly constrained.
- **10—Near repressive.** Credit allocation is controlled by the government. Bank formation is restricted. Foreign financial institutions are prohibited.
- **0—Repressive.** Supervision and regulation are designed to prevent private financial institutions. Private financial institutions are nonexistent.

Sources. Unless otherwise noted, the *Index* relies on the following sources for data on banking and finance, in order of priority: Economist Intelligence Unit, *Country Commerce* and *Industry Report Financial Services*, 2010–2013; International Monetary Fund, *Staff Country Report*, "Selected Issues," and *Staff Country Report*, "Article IV Consultation," 2010–2013; Organisation for Economic Co-operation and Development, *Economic Survey*; official government publications of each country; U.S. Department of Commerce, *Country Commercial Guide*, 2010–2013; Office of the U.S. Trade Representative, *2013 National Trade Estimate Report on Foreign Trade Barriers*; U.S. Department of State, *Investment Climate Statements*, 2010–2013; World Bank, *World Development Indicators 2013*; and various news and magazine articles on banking and finance.

GENERAL METHODOLOGICAL ISSUES

Period of Study. For the current *Index of Economic Freedom,* scores are generally based on data for the period covering the second half of 2012 through the first half of 2013. To the extent possible, the information considered for each variable was current as of June 30, 2013. It is important to understand, however, that some component scores are based on historical information. For example, the monetary freedom component uses a three-year weighted average rate of inflation from January 1, 2010, to December 31, 2012.

Equal Weight. In the *Index of Economic Freedom,* the 10 components of economic freedom are equally weighted so that the overall score will not be biased toward any one component or policy direction. It is clear that the 10 economic freedoms interact, but the exact mechanisms of this interaction are not clearly definable: Is a minimum threshold for each one essential? Is it possible for one to maximize if others are minimized? Are they dependent or exclusive, complements or supplements?

These are valid questions, but they are beyond the scope of our fundamental mission. The purpose of the *Index* is to reflect the economic and entrepreneurial environment in every country studied in as balanced a way as possible. The *Index* has never been designed specifically to explain economic growth or any other dependent variable; that is ably done by researchers elsewhere. The raw data for each component are provided so that others can study, weight, and integrate as they see fit.

Using the Most Currently Available Information. Analyzing economic freedom annually enables the *Index* to include the most recent information as it becomes available country by country. A data cutoff date is used so that all countries are treated fairly. As described above, the period of study for the current year's *Index* considers all information as of the last day of June of the previous year (in this case, June 30, 2013). Any new legislative changes or policy actions effective after that date have no positive or negative impact on scores or rankings.[9]

Endnotes

1. The following countries are not covered by the 2012 CPI: Belize, Fiji, Kiribati, Macau, Micronesia, Maldives, Samoa, Solomon Islands, Tonga, and Vanuatu.

2. Obtaining a license indicates necessary procedures, time, and cost in getting construction permits.

3. The recovery rate is a function of time and cost. However, the business freedom component uses all three sub-variables to emphasize closing a business, starting a business, and dealing with licenses equally.

4. The four countries that are not covered by the World Bank's *Doing Business* study are Cuba, North Korea, Macau, and Turkmenistan. The methodology for business freedom dates from the 2006 *Index* because of the limited availability of quantitative data before that date. For the 1995 through 2005 editions, we used a subjective assessment with a score of 1–5. Those earlier scores have been converted by means of a simple formula to make them comparable. Top scores were converted to 100, the next best to 85, and so on. This conversion formula is different from the one used for other subjective factors, but it is unique because those other factors are not bridging to a new, data-driven methodology.

5. The labor freedom assessment in the 2009 *Index* expanded its factors to six from the four used in previous editions. This refinement was applied equally to past editions' labor freedom scores to maintain consistency. The assessment of labor freedom dates from the 2005 *Index* because of the limited availability of quantitative data before that time.

6. For more detailed information on the data, see "Employing Workers" in World Bank, *Doing Business*, http://www.doingbusiness.org/MethodologySurveys/EmployingWorkers.aspx. Reporting only raw data, the *Doing Business 2011* study discontinued all of the sub-indices of Employing Workers: the difficulty of hiring index, the rigidity of hours index, and the difficulty of redundancy index. For the labor freedom component of the 2014 *Index*, the three indices were reconstructed by *Index* authors according to the methodology used previously by the *Doing Business* study.

7. See note 4.

8. MFN is now referred to as permanent normal trade relations (PNTR).

9. Occasionally, because the *Index* is published several months after the cutoff date for evaluation, more recent economic events cannot be factored into the scores. In the past, such occurrences have been uncommon and isolated to one region of the world. The Asian financial crisis, for example, erupted at the end of 1997 just as the 1998 *Index* was going to print. The policy changes in response to that crisis, therefore, were not considered in that year's scoring, but they were included in the next year's scores. Similarly, this year, the impact of government policies and more recently available macroeconomic statistics since the second half of 2013 have not affected the rankings for the 2014 *Index* but almost certainly will show up in scores for the next edition.

Major Works Cited

The 2014 *Index of Economic Freedom* relies on data from multiple sources to provide a picture of economic freedom in each country that is as comprehensive, impartial, and accurate as possible. The following sources provided the primary information for analyzing and scoring the 10 components of economic freedom. In addition, the authors and analysts used supporting documentation and information from various government agencies and sites on the Internet, news reports and journal articles, and official responses to inquiries. All statistical and other information received from government sources was verified with independent, internationally recognized sources.

African Development Bank, *Statistics Pocketbook 2013*; available at http://www.afdb.org/en/documents/publications/afdb-statistics-pocket-book/.

African Development Bank and Organisation for Economic Co-operation and Development, *African Economic Outlook 2013*; available at http://www.africaneconomicoutlook.org/en/.

Asian Development Bank, *Asian Development Outlook 2013: Asia's Energy Challenge*; available at http://www.adb.org/publications/asian-development-outlook-2013-asias-energy-challenge.

——, *Key Indicators for Asia and the Pacific 2013*; available at http://www.adb.org/publications/key-indicators-asia-and-pacific-2013.

Country statistical agencies, central banks, and ministries of finance, economy, and trade; available at http://unstats.un.org/unsd/methods/inter-natlinks/sd_natstat.asp; http://www.census.gov/aboutus/stat_int.html; and http://www.bis.org/cbanks.htm.

Deloitte, International Tax and Business Guides, *Country Highlights*; available at http://www.deloitte.com/view/en_PG/pg/insights-ideas/itbg/index.htm.

Economist Intelligence Unit, Ltd., *Country Commerce*, London, U.K., 2009–2013.

——, *Industry Report Financial Services*, London, U.K., 2009–2013.

——, *Country Report*, London, U.K., 2009–2013.

European Bank for Reconstruction and Development, *Country Strategies*, 2009–2013; available at http://www.ebrd.com/pages/country.shtml.

European Commission, Eurostat, *European Statistics*; available at http://epp.eurostat.ec.europa.eu/portal/page/portal/statistics/themes.

International Monetary Fund, *Article IV Consultation Staff Reports*, various countries, Washington, D.C., 2009–2013; available at http://www.imf.org/external/ns/cs.aspx?id=51.

——, *Country Information*; available at http://www.imf.org/external/country/index.htm.

——, *Selected Issues and Statistical Appendix*, various countries, Washington, D.C., 2009–2013.

——, World Economic Outlook Database, April 2013; available at http://www.imf.org/external/pubs/ft/weo/2013/01/weodata/index.aspx.

Low Tax Network, various countries; available at http://www.lowtax.net.

Organisation for Economic Co-operation and Development, *OECD Economic Outlook*, No. 93 (May 2013); available at http://www.keepeek.com/Digital-Asset-Management/oecd/economics/oecd-economic-outlook-volume-2013-issue-1_eco_outlook-v2013-1-en.

——, *OECD Factbook 2013*; available at http://www.oecd.org/publications/factbook/.

——, *OECD Statistics Portal*; available at http://stats.oecd.org/source/.

——, OECD Web site; available at www.oecd.org/home.

PricewaterhouseCoopers, *Worldwide Tax Summaries*; available with registration at http://www.pwc.com/gx/en/tax/corporate-tax/worldwide-tax-summaries/taxsummaries.jhtml.

Transparency International, *The Corruption Perceptions Index*, Berlin, Germany, 2000–2012; available at http://cpi.transparency.org/cpi2012/.

United Nations Conference on Trade and Development, *World Investment Report 2013: Global Value Chains: Investment and Trade for Development*; available at http://unctad.org/en/pages/PublicationWebflyer.aspx?publicationid=588.

United States Central Intelligence Agency, *The World Factbook 2013*; available at https://www.cia.gov/library/publications/the-world-factbook/index.html.

United States Department of Commerce, *Country Commercial Guides*, Washington, D.C., 2009–2013; available at http://www.buyusainfo.net/adsearch.cfm?search_type=int&loadnav=no.

United States Department of State, *Country Reports on Human Rights Practices for 2012*, released by the Bureau of Democracy, Human Rights, and Labor, April 2013; available at http://www.state.gov/j/drl/rls/hrrpt/humanrightsreport/index.htm#wrapper.

——, *Investment Climate Statements: 2009–2013*, released by the Bureau of Economic and Business Affairs; available at http://www.state.gov/e/eb/rls/othr/ics/.

United States Trade Representative, Office of the, *2013 National Trade Estimate Report on Foreign Trade Barriers*, Washington, D.C., 2013; available at http://www.ustr.gov/about-us/press-office/reports-and-publications/2013/NTE-FTB.

World Bank, *World Bank World Development Indicators Online*, Washington, D.C., 2013; available at http://data.worldbank.org/data-catalog/world-development-indicators.

——, *Country Briefs and Trade-at-a-Glance (TAAG) Tables*, Washington, D.C.; available at http://web.worldbank.org/WBSITE/EXTERNAL/TOPICS/TRADE/0,,contentMDK:22421950~pagePK:148956~piPK:216618~theSitePK:239071,00.html.

——, *Doing Business*, 2005–2014; available at www.doingbusiness.org.

World Trade Organization, *Trade Policy Reviews*, 1996–2013; available at http://www.wto.org/.

Our International Partners

Institute of Economic Affairs

2 Lord North Street,
Westminster
London, SW1P 3LB
United Kingdom

Phone: +44-20-7799-8900
Fax: +44-20-7799-2137
E-mail: iea@iea.org.uk
Website: www.iea.org.uk/

Adriatic Institute for Public Policy

Markovici 15, Srdoci
51000 Rijeka, Croatia

Phone: +385-51-626-582
E-mail:
AdriaticIPP@aol.com
Website:
www.adriaticinstitute.org

Istituto Bruno Leoni

via Bossi 1
10144 Torino
Italy

Phone: +39-011070-2087
Fax: +39-011437-1384
E-mail: info@brunoleoni.it
Website: www.brunoleoni.it/

Nadácia F. A. Hayeka Bratislava

Jašíkova 6
Bratislava
Slovakia
821 03

Phone: +421-2-48-291-585
Fax: +421-2-48-291-243
E-mail: hayek@hayek.sk
Website: www.hayek.sk

Institute for Market Economics

Bulgaria
1000 Sofia
22 Patriarh Evtimii Blvd., fl.3

Phone: +359-2-952-62-66
E-mail: mail@ime.bg
Website: http://ime.bg/en/

Lithuanian Free Market Institute

3A Šeimyniškių St.
LT-09312 Vilnius
Lithuania

Phone: +370-5-250 0280
E-mail: LFMI@freema.org
Website: www.lrinka.lt/

Fundación Libertad
Mitre 170
2000 Rosario Sta Fe Rep. Arg.

Teléfono: ++54 341 4105000
Email:
prensa@libertad.org.ar
Página Web:
http://www.libertad.org.ar

Fundación Libertad y Desarrollo
Pedro de Villagra 2265,
Vitacura

Teléfono: ++ (56-2) 377-4800
Email: lyd@lyd.com
Página Web:
http://www.lyd.com

Instituto de Ciencia Política (ICP)
Calle 70 No. 7A-29
Bogotá

Teléfono: ++54 317 7979
Email: info@icpcolombia.org
Página Web:
http://www.icpcolombia.org

Fundación para el Análisis y los Estudios Sociales (FAES)
C/ María de Molina 40 –
6ª planta
28006 – Madrid

Teléfono: +++34 91 576 6857
Email: fundacionfaes
@fundacionfaes.org
Página Web:
http://www.fundacionfaes.org

Centro de Investigaciones Sobre la Libre Empresa, A.C.
Camelia 329 Col. Florida C.P.
01030 México D.F.

Teléfono: +++56.62.42.50
Teléfono: +++ 56.62.45.00
Email: instituto@cisle.org.mx
Página Web:
http://www.cisle.org.mx/

Centro de Investigación y Estudios Legales (CITEL)
Coronel Portillo No 521
San Isidro, Lima 27

Teléfono: ++511-222-3286
Email: info@citel.org
Página Web: www.citel.org

Centro de Divulgación del Conocimiento Económico (CEDICE)
Av. Andrés Eloy Blanco (Este 2)
Edificio Cámara de comercio de Caracas, Nivel Auditorio Los Caobos, Caracas

Teléfono: ++58 212 571 3357
Página Web:
www.cedice.org.ve

Políticas Públicas para la Libertad (POPULI)
Calle Beni N° 678, Edificio Gabriela. 1° Piso. Santa Cruz - Bolivia.

Teléfono: +591 3 3216408
Email: populi@populi-bo.org
Página Web:
www.populi-bo.org

Moving Onward

This year marks the 20th anniversary of the *Index of Economic Freedom,* a data-driven research project that I have regarded as one of the "crown jewels" of The Heritage Foundation. Such an occasion gives us pause and allows us to step back and contemplate the progress the world has made toward freedom over the past two decades.

Since we began to measure and document countries' economic freedom 20 years ago—for many of those years in partnership with *The Wall Street Journal*—the world economy as a whole has become measurably more open and prosperous. Countries once riddled with violence and poverty have embraced the principles of economic freedom and consequently set themselves on a path toward long-term development and prosperity.

The past 20 years, however, have not been without challenges. In 1997, the Asian financial crisis tested the commitment of some of the world's most promising reformers to the advancement of economic freedom. The economic slowdown that followed the dot-com bubble in 2000 and the terrorist attacks of September 11, 2001, threw the United States into recession. And the world is still feeling the lingering effects of the recent global financial turmoil. Each of these crises has caused apprehension among policymakers, some of whom have even questioned whether the free-market system is still the best way to organize economic activity.

Fortunately, the world has experienced only temporary setbacks of economic freedom following such challenging times. As the 2014 *Index* documents, the advancement of economic freedom has, by and large, proceeded steadily. In fact, it is heartening to see just how unrelenting has been the march toward greater economic freedom.

The link between freedom and human progress has never been clearer. We know from history that the human spirit thrives on fairness, opportunity, transparency, and liberty. We have been vividly reminded of this truth by the downfall of the Soviet Union, the liberation of Eastern

Europe, the opening of China, and the ongoing "Arab Spring" today. The human spirit is the real engine of economic prosperity and development, and that spirit is at its most creative when it is unleashed from the chains in which it has been bound.

Even so, the fight for freedom is a never-ending struggle. There are those who persist in attacking individual freedom in the name of collectivism, solidarity, and social justice. These false idols of socialism may have emotional appeal for some, but the economic and social results when they become the touchstones of government policy are all too predictable: poverty, deprivation, oppression, and even the gradual erosion of the rule of law.

Economic freedom rests on the empowerment of the individual, nondiscrimination, and open competition. None of these requirements can exist in a society that lacks effective rule of law. The first and most important role of governments is to preserve the peace while simultaneously respecting human rights, dignity, and freedom. This balance enables peaceful resolution of conflict and ensures integrity in government's interactions with individuals.

As Friedrich A. Hayek, whose insightful guidance I cherished, foresaw decades ago, "The guiding principle in any attempt to create a world of free men must be this: a policy of freedom for the individual is the only truly progressive policy." Given what passes for progressivism in our public debates today, it is clear that the battle of ideas must be a battle even for the very meaning of the words with which we debate. How did the word "liberal" lose its identification with liberty? When did "progressive" become a synonym for statist? If we are going to continue to safeguard societies from errors that have brought nothing but misery throughout history, we may have to fight the battle of vocabulary in order to win the battle of ideas.

Perhaps the most critical lesson of the past two decades is that the proven superiority and value of economic liberty must be steadfastly reiterated. The data we collect in the *Index of Economic Freedom* are the foundation for that discussion.

Looking back on my two decades of involvement with the *Index of Economic Freedom*, I feel profoundly blessed to have played a role in the global fight for greater economic freedom. To those who join in that great struggle, I say "Onward!"

Edwin J. Feulner, PhD, Founder
The Heritage Foundation
November 2013